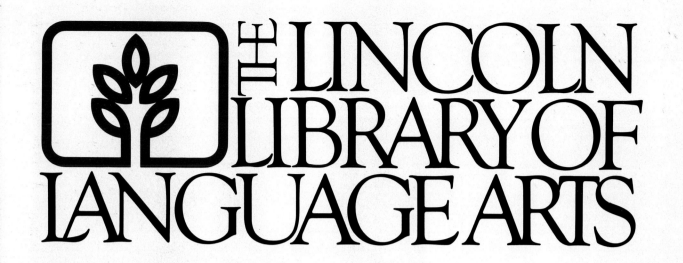

THE LINCOLN LIBRARY OF LANGUAGE ARTS

VOLUME 1

THE FRONTIER PRESS COMPANY, COLUMBUS, OHIO

PREFACE

THE LINCOLN LIBRARY OF LANGUAGE ARTS, performing the functions of both teaching aid and independent study guide, is based upon the latest edition of THE LINCOLN LIBRARY OF ESSENTIAL INFORMATION, the well-known compendium which has reliably served as an invaluable information source in homes and libraries across the nation since 1924. Today the language arts curriculum is complex and often difficult. New materials and ideas have emerged, and the older ones have been revised, to meet the demands of universities and colleges. The successful student needs not only information, carefully organized, but also intelligent understanding. This compact "library of language arts" will be helpful in both ways. Its three departments—Language, Literature, and Biography—present, in clearly written articles, a comprehensive treatment of major and minor topics in the language arts.

In the LANGUAGE department the thorough treatment of good usage, vocabulary-building, punctuation, speech and debate, synonyms and antonyms, abbreviations, and foreign terms provide crucial reference aids to the reader and writer. But it includes much more than this; one needs to understand the way his language works. Consequently this department provides detailed analyses of the English language from *both* the scholastic tradition of English grammar and the newer linguistic approach that is rapidly becoming an important part of the language arts curriculum in schools throughout the United States and Canada. For both teachers and students, the article on Linguistics will be illuminating because it is a clear and insightful presentation of the subject. Discussions of style, structure, meter, and literary forms rub shoulders with pronunciation, letter writing, and invaluable reading lists arranged according to grade.

The LITERATURE department is quite as rich. Not only are American and English literatures discussed in detail, but major world literatures and their histories are also recorded. The history of many national literatures is noted with detailed descriptions and easy-to-understand tables of authors and their major works from ancient epics to modern poetry. The reader seeking a general education, the student taking an English, an American, or a World Literature course, and the teacher requiring an accurate guide to literary movements and criticism, can all benefit from these articles and tables. They will also find useful the more than fifty pages on literary plots, characters, and allusions. These provide story outlines, explain allusions, identify characters, clarify terms drawing their meaning from other works and, in short, act as a guide through the complex world of literary study. Along with this, and serving the same end, is a guide to mythology containing both a table of Mythological Associations and a dictionary of Mythology.

The third department, BIOGRAPHY, contains some 4500 sketches of noteworthy people including such varied personalities as Vasco da Gama, the explorer; Albert Einstein, the Nobel physicist; Barry Goldwater and Franklin Delano Roosevelt, political leaders; and the writers T. S. Eliot, Geoffrey Chaucer, and James Gould Cozzens.

THE LINCOLN LIBRARY OF LANGUAGE ARTS combines the qualities of several powerful reference works with those of many good textbooks and study guides. The facts, ideas, and opinions provide a firm and broadly-based foundation for progress in language arts. As a further aid there are, at the end of two departments, questions testing the reader's grasp of what has been presented. A Master Index is included in each volume for added convenience.

The resourceful teacher will readily see how useful this work can be for individual study and research projects in literature, biography, and writing. Students reading a work of literature at home or in school can have by their sides a guide to those obscurities that blur and hinder individual understanding and class progress.

This work will be valuable in every school library and classroom where language and the literatures are taught. It will resolve queries unanswerable in textbooks. Moreover, the regular use of a work like this inculcates in the student respect for the language that he shares with great writers and thinkers, a healthy regard for accuracy and clarity, and a necessary self-reliance when his is the responsibility to inquire and to verify.

THE LINCOLN LIBRARY OF LANGUAGE ARTS, comprehensive as it is, is compact enough to be used as a supplemental text for students in the junior and senior high school grades. What is more, the teacher will appreciate not only this carefully-organized reference material, but also the purposefulness and clarity of explanation, much of it written by leading authorities in each field of knowledge.

 RODERICK A. JACOBS, B.A., Ed.M., Ed.D., Associate Professor of English, State University of N.Y. at Oneonta; Chairman, Committee on Teaching of Poetry, Nat'l Council of Teachers of English, 1968–70.

EDITORS AND CONTRIBUTORS

EDITOR-IN-CHIEF

WILLIAM J. REDDING, A.B., M.A., M.S. in L.S.

ASSISTANT EDITORS

DOROTHEA V. SCHNEIDER

DOROTHY G. SUDDUTH

MARCIA HILT

ART EDITORS

MARY ANNE LONERGAN

RICHARD SUMMERS

NORMAN R. WOLFE

SUBJECT EDITOR

JOHN H. LANCASTER, B.S. (L.S.), M.A., PH.D.

ADVISOR

RODERICK A. JACOBS, B.A., Ed.M., Ed.D.

PARTIAL LIST OF CONTRIBUTORS

ABBOTT, FRANK FROST, Ph. D.
Late Kennedy Professor of Latin Language and Literature, Princeton University.
Contributed the article on Latin Literature.

BOTHNE, GISLE C., M. A.
Professor of Scandinavian Languages and Literatures, and Head of the Department of Scandinavian Languages, University of Minnesota.
Contributed articles on Norwegian, Danish, Swedish, and Icelandic Literatures.

DEWING, HENRY BRONSON, Ph. D.
President of Athens College, Athens, Greece.
Contributed the article on Greek Literature.

FINEGAN, THOMAS EDWARD, M. A., Ph. D., LL. D., Litt. D.
Former Superintendent of Education for State of Pennsylvania.
Approved the sections on Introduction to the English Language, Word Building, and Forms of Literary Composition.

GAUSS, CHRISTIAN, A. M., Litt. D.
Former Dean of the College and Dean of the Alumni, Princeton University; Critic of Modern European History and Literature.
Contributed the Introduction to Literature and the table showing the Development of Modern Literature.

GIBBONS, OLIPHANT, A. B.
Supervisor of English, Secondary Schools, Buffalo, N.Y.; also lecturer in English, State University of New York at Buffalo.
Reviewed the section on Synonyms and Antonyms.

GORDON, ELIZABETH M., B. S. in Ed.
Deputy Supervisor, In Charge of Work With Children, Boston Public Library.
Revised Suggestions for The Family Library and The Children's Library.

HOEING, CHARLES, Ph. D.
Trevor Professor of Latin, and Dean of Graduate Studies, University of Rochester.
Reviewed the section on English Words Derived from the Latin; also the section on Latin Words and Phrases.

JOHNSON, ROSSITER, A. M., (Hon. Ph. D., LL. D.)
Author: *A History of the French War Ending in the Conquest of Canada.* Editor: *The Universal Cyclopædia; Cyclopædia of Notable Americans.*
Reviewed material on Biography.

LANCASTER, JOHN HERROLD, B. S., M. A., B. S. (L. S.), Ph. D.
Head Librarian, Baldwin-Wallace College, Berea, Ohio.
As Subject Editor, contributed the Bibliographies.

LEARY, DANIEL BELL, M. A., Ph. D.
Former Professor of Psychology and instructor in Russian, State University of New York at Buffalo. Author: *Education and Autocracy in Russia, from the Origins to the Bolsheviki.*
Reviewed and revised Russian Literature.

LEWIS, CALVIN LESLIE, A. B., A. M.
Former Upson Professor of Rhetoric and Oratory, Hamilton College, Clinton, New York. Author: *American Speech.*
Reviewed the section on Speaking and Writing.

LOPEZ, MANUEL LEON, A. B., A. M.
Department of Romance Languages, University of Oregon.
Reviewed Spanish Literature and Latin American Literature.

MacCRACKEN, HENRY NOBLE, Ph. D., LL. D., L. H. D.
Former President of Vassar College. Author: *First Year English; Manual of Good English* (part author).
Reviewed, with constructive suggestions, the manuscript on Sentence Building, Prepositions, and Conjunctions.

McLEOD, ALAN L., B. A., M. A., Dip. Ed., B. Ed., Ph. D.
Associate Professor of Speech and English, State University of New York at Fredonia.
Contributed article on Australian Literature.

MORGAN, BAYARD QUINCY, Ph. D.
Formerly Professor and Chairman of German Department, Stanford University.
Revised the article on German Literature.

MORGENSTERN, JULIAN, Ph. D.
President Emeritus of The Hebrew Union College, Cincinnati, Ohio. Author: *A Jewish Interpretation of the Book of Genesis.*
Contributed the articles on Hebrew, Syriac, Ethiopic, Arabic, and Assyro-Babylonian Literatures.

O'NEIL, WAYNE A., B. A., M. A., Ph. D.
Professor of Education and Linguistics, Harvard University. Author: *Kernels and Transformations;* numerous articles on modern linguistics; Co-author: *The Oregon Curriculum: Language.*

Contributed the article on Linguistics.

PARK, CLYDE W., A. M.
Formerly Professor and head of Department of English, College of Engineering, University of Cincinnati.

As former editor, contributed many biographies and other articles.

RHODENIZER, VERNON BLAIR, Ph. D.
Professor of English Language and Literature, Acadia University, Wolfville, N. S.

Contributed article on Canadian Literature.

SNOW, ROYALL H., S. B., B. A., B. Litt.
Professor of English, Ohio State University.

Reviewed American and English Literature and Literary Plots.

TAYLOR, JOHN W., M. A., Ph. D.

Contributed section on Mythology and numerous other articles, having been with The Frontier Press Co. as editor for many years.

VIZETELLY, FRANK HORACE, Litt. D., LL. D.
Late Managing Editor of New Standard Dictionary of the English Language. Author: *Essentials of English Speech and Literature; Words We Misspell in Business.*

Reviewed the section devoted to Good Usage.

WESTON, GEORGE BENSON, A. M.
Associate Professor of Romance Languages, Harvard University.

Contributed the article on Italian Literature and the section on Modern Phrases.

WILLIAMS, EDWARD THOMAS, M. A., LL. D.
Late Agassiz Professor of Oriental Languages and Literature, University of California.

Contributed the articles on Chinese Literature.

WOLFE, NORMAN R.
Art Director, University of Chicago.

Artwork and layout of illustrations.

CONTENTS

I. THE ENGLISH LANGUAGE

II. LITERATURE

III. BIOGRAPHY

INDEX

DICTIONARIES

TABULATIONS

KEY TO PRONUNCIATION

ā, as in farm, father; ȧ, as in ask, fast; ă, as in at, fat; ā, as in day, fate; â, as in care, fare. ĕ, as in met, set; ē, as in me, see; ẽ, as in her, perform. ĭ, as in pin, ill; ī, as in pine, ice. ŏ, as in hot, got; ō, as in note, old; ô, as in for, fought; ŏŏ, as in cook, look; ōō, as in moon, spoon. ŭ, as in cup, duck; ū, as in use, amuse; û, as in fur, urge. ou, as in out, about. oi, as in oil, boil.

å, ĕ, ô, û represent the sounds ā, ē, ō, ū; they are of shorter quantity but do not lose the quality of the "long" vowel, as in senåte, ĕvent, ôbey, lectûre.

TH indicates the sound of th in thee, though. In foreign words this symbol indicates a more distinct d sound than in English words, as in the Irish word

Dail. zh stands for the sound of z in azure.

ü cannot be exactly represented in English. The English sound of u as in *luke* and *duke* resembles the original sound of ü. ö cannot be exactly represented in English. The English sound of u in *burn* and *burnt* is perhaps the nearest equivalent to ö, or œ. κ represents ch in German *ich, ach.* N represents the nasal tone (as in French) of the preceding vowel, as in *encore* (äN'kōr'). н represents the guttural g or j in Spanish words, as in *jefe.*

The principal accent is indicated by a heavy mark,', and the secondary accent by a lighter mark,', placed at the end of the syllable.

SPECIAL MARKS AND THEIR USES

PUNCTUATION: For use see pages 69 and 70.

, Comma	" " Quotation Marks
; Semicolon	! Exclamation point
: Colon	( ) Parentheses
. Period	[ ] Brackets
— Dash	' Apostrophe
? Interrogation point, question mark	- Hyphen

FOOTNOTE INDICATORS: Used when number of footnotes is small, otherwise numbers or letters are employed, or special indicator marks may be used double.

* Asterisk	§ Also used to mean section or clause
† Dagger	‖ Also used to mean "is parallel to"
‡ Double Dagger	¶ or ℙ Also used to indicate paragraph

PRONUNCIATION INDICATORS: More common signs used, in English and some foreign languages, usually to show the value or quality of a vowel. Letters are supplied below to show how sign is applied.

ĕ Breve. Pronounce vowel short	ê or â Circumflex accent (French)
ā Macron. Pronounce vowel long	ä Umlaut (German). Alters quality of vowels a, o, or u
aë Diaeresis. Pronounce vowels as separate sounds	
é Acute accent (French)	ç Cedilla (French). Converts hard c to soft c
è Grave accent (French)	ñ Tilde (Spanish). Gives effect of a following y

WORD SUBSTITUTES: Many signs are used as a species of shorthand. Some of the more commonly used follow. Where the sign has a name, the name precedes the meaning.

Λ Caret. Insert	+ Plus. Add
{ or } Brace. Lines belong together	− Minus. Subtract
	× Multiply
= Is equal to	÷ Divide
☞ Index. See	> Is greater than
@ At or to	< Is less than
% Per cent	∴ Therefore
° Degree	∵ Since
' Minute (subdivision of degree) or foot (feet)	: Is to (term used in expressing proportion)
*** or . . . Ellipsis. Words are omitted.	:: As (term used in expressing proportion)
" Second or inch (inches)	√‾ Radical. Square root of
π Pi. The number 3.14159	℞ Take (used at beginning of prescriptions for drugs)

PROOFREADER'S MARKS: These are the more common signs used by publication and printing proofreaders,

ℐ Delete letters or words. Take ✗ out.	✗ Broken letter or poor type.
# Insert space where indicated.	stet Let it stand. Disregard marks made.
⑨ Turn inverted letter marked	Cap replace letter marked with a capital.
tr Transpose letters or words indicated.	lc Replace With a lower case (small) letter.
⊃ Close up letters or words	bf Reset words in bold face type.
= Straighten alignment of type.	ital Reset words in italic type.
[or] Move right or left to point indicated.	rom Reset words in roman (regular) type.
⊓ or ⊔ Raise or lower to point indicated.	⊙ Insert period where marked
eq # Equalize spacing ✓ of words.	Λ Insert comma where marked.
wf Wrong font. Incorrect size, weight or style of letter.	⋎ Insert apostrophe per proofreaders mark.

8

THE BUILDERS

This unique and comprehensive reference series owes its origin to the constructive foresight and untiring energy of Mr. M. J. Kinsella, founder and first president of The Frontier Press Company. Initially developed under his vigorous and able management, with the aid of a corps of workers who shared his vision, this organization has grown until it now stands in the foremost rank of American educational publishing houses. Beginning about the year 1908, with the publication of *The Standard Dictionary of Facts*, a compact digest of general information, this firm has concentrated during the following years upon the presentation of organized knowledge brought together in a series of reference works. The founder's aim of making a maximum quantity of useful knowledge readily available "under one roof," as a reviewer expressed it, led to the publication and later the continued improvement of the compact encyclopedia known everywhere as *The Lincoln Library of Essential Information.*

A Work for Desk Reference. Mr. Kinsella had completed a classical course at the Buffalo State Normal School and, in 1900, had received an A.B. degree from Cornell University. His experience as student, teacher, and businessman had impressed him with the need for having reference works on a desk at one's finger tips, not somewhere in a closet or on a shelf behind glass doors. While recognizing the importance of numerous volumes for leisurely reading and of specialized textbooks for formal study, he noted that busy people frequently have occasion to look for specific facts concerning an unlimited variety of subjects. To make it possible for them to obtain this information quickly, he conceived of a reference work in two or three volumes that should be developed according to certain ideas derived from his personal experience and also from consultation with others. Briefly summarized, these ideas were as follows: first, the typical "handy" reference work, usually containing 800 to 1000 pages, should be greatly expanded if it was to fulfill its mission; second, in its enlarged form, such a work could be made readable and interesting as well as informative and could be particularly helpful to the large percentage of the general public who could not afford to purchase the multi-volume A-to-Z encyclopedias; third, because of its convenience for quick reference, it could usefully supplement the larger reference works and other books found in well-stocked private libraries; and fourth, if presented in an organized way, the content of such a work could provide the means for a thorough review of anyone's knowledge or for an effective program of self-education.

According to Ward Lamon, one of his early biographers, Lincoln's formal education did not amount to more than one year of schooling. Not only his professional studies like law and surveying but also literature, geometry and other elementary subjects were mastered by a process of self-instruction. While profiting from the historical facts concerning Lincoln's study, the Builders recognized the present and future needs throughout America that are created by an ever-expanding program of adult education. Conse-

quently, *The Lincoln Library* series, because of the organization of knowledge, became not only enlarged "fact books" but also an educational media noted for effectiveness as a means of self-education.

CONTRIBUTORS AND EDITORS

The preliminary pages contain a list of men and women, occupying various positions of importance in the United States, Canada, and Australia, who have collaborated extensively in building The Lincoln Library series. After each name in this list is given the person's scholastic degree. Next is indicated the present or former position occupied by each collaborator, with a statement of the specific task performed.

In case a department, section, or article was prepared *in toto* by one of these collaborators, it is stated that he *contributed* it.

In case a section, prepared by the office editorial staff or by an outside contributor, was edited, revised, expanded, or approved by one of these collaborators, the exact service performed is specifically defined.

REVISIONS

One of the most serious problems facing the publishers of modern reference books is that of keeping abreast of the times. The policy adopted in that regard for The Lincoln Library series is in keeping with the high standards established when it was founded. At each new printing, those portions which are affected by the passage of events are thoroughly revised.

In some cases, the original contributor of a section or Department has made the necessary revisions. In other cases, the services of different outside editors have been secured, the list of editors being revised accordingly. A large part of this revision work, however, has necessarily been carried out by the editorial staff, which is engaged continually in surveying the progress of the world in order to select and report the most significant developments. In all such revisions, the original character of the articles has been left unaltered except insofar as necessary in order to present each topic in the perspective of the present time.

The policy of thorough revision at each new printing, inaugurated by M. J. Kinsella, has been carried on through a chain of leadership extending from his death in 1928 to the present. He was succeeded as president of The Frontier Press Company by his brother, Burt S. Kinsella, who served for nearly twenty years. Following his retirement the presidency was held from 1948 to 1958 by H. C. Goff, who was succeeded by Verne E. Seibert. On the latter's retirement in 1966, the reins were taken by his son William H. Seibert. Each of these men had worked closely with his predecessor, so that unbroken continuity of policy was assured. Even more important was the cumulative development of certain features of the encyclopedia series. Care in the selection of contributors, vigilance on the part of the editorial staff, and the maintenance of high standards of accuracy has given The Lincoln series a position of leadership in the field that has continued without serious challenge.

THE LINCOLN LIBRARY OF LANGUAGE ARTS has been so built that in some respects an index is superfluous. The material in the three departments has been arranged in such a manner that, with a brief period of intelligent use, the reader will be able to turn directly to a required fact without the initial step of consulting the master index.

This advantage is due to the arrangement of related material being grouped in sections, a large proportion of which takes the form of dictionaries and tables that have been carefully prepared.

Advantages of Arrangement. The intelligent user will take advantage of the general plan of these volumes by becoming so familiar with the location of the sections, dictionaries, and tables of the three departments that the mechanical consultation of the index will become less and less necessary. With practice, the driving of an automobile becomes one of the simplest of operations. Likewise, familiarity with the electric switches in a home makes the control of the lighting system easy even for a child. So in the use of this set, a little practice will insure a surprising mastery over its resources. When the reader has learned, for example, that the **English Language** department has several pages devoted to Public Speaking, he will go directly to that section and find not only suggestions for planning his speech, but also instructions in delivery, gestures, and voice management.

The extraordinary range of the facts in the text, dictionaries, and tables of this work makes it obviously inadvisable that every individual item should be entered in the master index, which would thereby become much too unwieldy for convenient and quick reference. Many words and their correct use, not in the master index, appear in the section **Good Usage** which may be found indexed in three places—1) Dictionaries, 2) Subject Guide page introducing the department of The English Language, and 3) the Master Index. After a brief period of use, however, the user will likely remember the exact location of this useful dictionary where the various words will be found arranged in alphabetical order. In the same way, he will soon be able, almost on opening the book, to find that, in the Dictionary of Synonyms and Antonyms, there are several hundred words given for careful examination. It will be noted that, while many words are similar, they differ slightly in their shades of meaning. Following the Dictionary of Synonyms and Antonyms is the "key" or "index" to the page where these words are discussed. For instance, if the reader wishes to use the word "achieve," he will find it in this "key" or "index" followed by the word "accomplish" in italics, which means "accomplish" is the key word to look for, and where "achieve" is discussed.

The **Literature** department contains a wealth of information on literatures of the world, as well as tables of leading authors of several countries indicating their more representative works. Also in this department, the dictionary of Mythology presents with brief but authoritative treatment a large number of the most important persons, places, and stories. Students of literature will find the indexing of mythological deities especially helpful. For example, not only do Venus, Aphrodite, and other love deities appear as separate index entries, but under "Love, Deities of" will be found a reference to the table giving all the chief deities of love. The same procedure is followed with practically all words having important mythological associations.

The **Biography** department consists of one big dictionary of more than 3600 separate biographical sketches of outstanding people from the dawn of history to the present time. As these are arranged in alphabetical order, it is hardly necessary to consult the master index.

Fullness and Simplicity of Index. Despite this surprising availability of material in a series embracing so much information, a master index has certain supplementary values which make its inclusion necessary in a work that is to give the greatest possible service. The Language Arts series has, therefore, been provided with a full, simple, systematic key to its contents.

Illustrations. The master index which follows is a guide, not only to the text, tabulations, and specialized dictionaries, but also to the illustrations throughout the set. When a page number in the master index is preceded by "op," the reference is to an illustration on the page opposite to the one whose number is given. For example, the entry "English Manuscript, Early . . . op 80" means that a picture of an early English manuscript will be found opposite page 80.

When four pages of pictures appear between two numbered pages, the two page numbers are given preceded by "bet." For instance, "Languages, Universal, Map of . . . bet 96–97" means that an interesting map of the world is shown indicating the predominating language in various countries.

Altogether, the master index contains several thousand entries, many of which include two or more page references. The following example will show with what ease a specific fact may be located by several different routes.

If the reader wishes to learn more about Letter Writing, he will probably turn first to "Letter Writing" in the index. He is there referred to page 104 where that section begins. Indented under "Letter Writing" is the word "Business" with reference to page 104, where the reader will find the principles of building a good business letter, such as *style of letterhead, form and appearance of letter, substance, clarity,* and *tone of message.* Should the user think first of the words "Business Letter," he will find under the B's "Business Letter . . . 104." Subindexed under that entry are given other references pertinent to making that type of letter attractive to the recipient. Since the art of good letter writing is so important in everyday life, several pages are devoted to different types of letters. Letter Writing is listed also on the Subject Guide page which introduces the English Language.

Suggestions. To get the greatest value from this index, it is well to keep in mind the following facts:

When a phrase appears in the index, its words are so arranged that the most important, usually a noun, occupies the first place.

In cases where an indexed item appears in the text as a heading, as the title of a separate article in a dictionary, or as an entry in a table, only the page number is given in the index. If, however, the item cannot so readily be located on its page, a letter is added, which indicates the particular quarter page in which the word or fact occurs. The letters **a** and **b** refer respectively to the upper and lower half of the first column, while **c** and **d** refer to the corresponding halves of the second column. Thus 204a means the upper left-hand quarter of page 204; 204d means the lower right-hand quarter of page 204.

Where two or more page references appear in one index entry, the most important reference is usually given first. Under all names of people in the Biography department, the first page reference is to the biographical article.

When an entry is followed by a second entry in italics, the latter is the title under which the first subject is treated.

The English Language

SUBJECT GUIDE

IN THE SHAKESPEARE COUNTRY

a.
  Anne Hathaway's cottage at Shottery, Warwickshire, where young Shakespeare and his wife Anne, lived from 1582 to about 1584.

Photos a, b, and c courtesy of British Travel Association

b.
  Shakespeare's birthplace in Stratford-on-Avon, Warwickshire, is located on Henley Street and annually attracts thousands of visitors.

  William Shakespeare. This portrait, supplied by the British Museum, is reproduced from a print in the first folio edition of his plays.

c.
  In this magnificent setting, the Royal Shakespeare Theatre at Stratford is a mecca for drama lovers of the world.

Shakespeare's church, Holy Trinity in Stratford-on-Avon, Warwickshire, England, was built during the 13th century. The spire was not added until 1763.

Historic England. *Above:* Stonehenge, on Salisbury Plain in Wiltshire, may date from as early as 1800 B.C. The monument's purpose is unknown, but one theory is that it was a temple or burial ground for ancient Britons. Excavations have yielded Stone Age relics and burial mounds of the Bronze Age. *Lower left:* **Big Ben,** the great clock-tower bell in the London Parliament, weighs 13 tons and was cast in 1856. It was named for Sir Benjamin Hall, London Commissioner of Works at the time. *Lower right:* **Windsor Castle,** residence of British monarchs, stands in Berkshire, 21 miles west of London. William the Conqueror first built a castle on the site. Rebuilt by later sovereigns, Windsor now covers some 24 acres. Queen Victoria and several English kings are buried here. (*Courtesy D. L. Sudduth*)

The English Language

INTRODUCTORY

LANGUAGE, spoken and written, is mankind's most valuable asset. How language first arose has long been a matter of debate, but it is certain that it was originally much simpler than at present and that it developed from a group of bodily movements and from sounds with which certain meanings were arbitrarily associated. As men's experience became more varied and complex, such gestures and sounds were elaborated and multiplied until there arose what might be called spoken language. Written language followed, when an ingenious man thought of making marks to represent spoken words. By writing a symbol for each sound, an alphabet was devised and written speech was simplified. Thus communications could be sent long distances and thoughts could be recorded and preserved for the use of later times. Each generation was thereby enabled to instruct the next, and rapid progress in knowledge and in skill became possible.

Our English Tongue. To no people has there fallen a richer inheritance of language or a more splendid opportunity to further enrich and perfect that heritage than belongs to the English-speaking nations. The English language has grown to its present excellence through the development of one of the world's great literatures. This fact means that the work of scholars, poets, story-tellers, orators, and scientists has been contributing, through a thousand years, to enlarge, strengthen, and refine the English vocabulary and grammar. Moreover, the nations that speak this tongue have been modern pioneers in free, democratic government, with all that this implies in popular education, in free discussion of political questions, and in wide circulation of books, magazines, and newspapers.

The English and the Americans have been adventurous, trading, and colonizing people, sailing all the seas, exploring every continent, trading with, civilizing, and governing, peoples of every race. Whenever, for unaccustomed things, strange ways, or novel ideas, new words have been needed, these men of English speech have unhesitatingly adopted foreign words that met the need, and have assimilated them to the forms of the English language. Thus English has gained an unparalleled variety of synonyms and turns of speech, and it is better fitted than any other to be the language of a nation derived, as are the Americans, from people of many races.

In the European theater of World War II, men from America, England, Canada, Australia, and South Africa met upon the ground of a common language. Allowing for minor differences of dialect, colloquialisms, and slang, they understood and misunderstood one another in the English tongue, and they read the same newspapers and books, whether published in London, New York, Melbourne, Montreal, or Cape Town. In the post-war period, through its use in international trade and in the Proceedings of the United Nations, English has become universally recognized as a world language.

English and Related Tongues. In connection with this world-wide use of the English language, it is important to observe its relationship to other tongues. A person of native English speech who begins the study of any western European language, such as French or German, finds at once certain striking resemblances to English in forms of words and in grammar. The student of Latin and Greek observes similar likenesses among their evident dissimilarities. If he pursues his studies into the Slavic languages of Eastern Europe, such as Russian and Polish, he finds that they also resemble English in notable particulars. Further, similar phenomena appear to the student of certain ancient Asiatic languages, notably Zend and Sanskrit, the former spoken by the ancient Iranians or Persians, and deciphered only in the 19th century through its resemblance to Sanskrit, once the language of the Hindus.

Careful study of such facts has led scholars to the conclusion that all these languages are to be regarded as belonging to a great family of languages, sprung from a single tongue spoken by an ancient people of central Asia, to whom the term Aryan is sometimes applied. Properly, Aryan designates this ancient language, but it is used also to include all the ancient and modern languages which developed from it. This family is also called Indo-European, because its members are the great languages of India and Europe.

The outstanding characteristics of these Indo-European languages, which mark their relationship to each other and distinguish them from all others, are three: (1) They possess in common a number of words not found in other languages. (2) They indicate grammatical relations by means of endings added to words. (3) They are similar in the sounds they employ and in the general laws of their syntax. Other characteristics, also, such as uniform consonant changes, serve to distinguish groups and branches of languages within the general family. In the course of centuries, among different groups of people, the original consonant sounds in words have passed into other closely related sounds.

The close resemblance between the languages of Europe and those of India and Persia is shown clearly in the following table:

English	German	Latin	Greek	Zend	Tokhar	Sanskrit
mother	mutter	mater	mētēr	matar	macar	mātā
father	vater	pater	patēr	pitar	pacar	pitā
brother	bruder	frater	phratēr	brata	pracar	bhrātā

The Story of Old English. The beginnings of the English language, spoken today by more people than speak any one other tongue, are to be found in the dialects of the Saxons, Angles, and Jutes. At the invitation of British chieftains, these tribes came to Britain in the early part of the 5th century from the low-lying shores and islands of what are now the Dutch, German, and Danish North Sea coasts, bringing with them other adventurers from the Scandinavian countries. Having aided the Britons to drive back their foes, the Picts. these settlers turned upon the Britons themselves. forcing them back to the west and to the north. The Jutes settled in Kent, in the Southeast of England; the Angles, in the North, the East, and the Midlands; and the Saxons, in the South and the Southwest. The language of these tribes belonged to the West Germanic group of the Teutonic languages, and was more closely related to the Dutch than to the modern German.

From the old tongue of the conquered Britons a few words, such as *druid, bannock, down* (hill), *dun* (color), and perhaps *lawn* (land), with a few place names, entered the new language. The mingling of the dialects of the conquerors produced Anglo-Saxon or English Saxon, virtually a new language, the speech of the English Kin. This language had in it very little foreign element; it was highly inflected, and it formed new words from its own resources. Our words of common life, such as *while, nevertheless, man, god, loaf,* and *town,* indicate that Anglo-Saxon is still the bone and sinew of the English language.

Probably the tribes brought a few words of Latin origin, such as *mint* (money), *pound, mile, street,* and *church* (of Greek derivation), from the continent; for Roman and Greek merchants as well as Roman armies had penetrated to the lands along the North Sea. However, though the Romans had ruled Britain for 400 years and Latin had been spoken in the towns, the new conquerors seem to have found but few words they wished to adopt. The Latin *castra* (camp) survives in the name *Chester* and in other place names ending in *caster* and *cester.* The name *London,* of British origin, remains from this early time. But, with the coming of Christianity in the 6th century, numerous Latin words, such as *creed, verse, clerk, rose, lily,* and *turtle* (dove), were introduced. This number increased to perhaps 300 by the end of the 10th century.

In the 9th century the Danish or Scandinavian pirates overran the northeast districts of England,—Northumbria and Anglia; in the 10th century there were in this territory probably as many Danes as there were English; a Danish king ruled England in the early part of the 11th century. The conquest by the Danes was marked by pillage and cruelty, so that culture and literature were practically destroyed in the territory they ruled. For this reason, they left little trace of their language in the Anglo-Saxon of the time, though many words were preserved in local dialects and appeared in written English 200 years later. Curiously enough, these people gave to the English the word *law,* perhaps by way of the Dane law, as the district was called to which the West Saxon king Alfred at one time confined them. We owe to the Danes also such words as *call, care, fellow, husband, sister, die, same, thrive, take,* such place name endings as *-by, -thorpe, -thwaite,* and many surnames ending in *-son.*

While the Danes were harrying England, another body of Scandinavian rovers had settled in northern France. Normandy perpetuates the memory of these Northmen. Like their fellows in England, they adopted the tongue of their subjects, so producing the Norman French. Between these Normans and the Englishmen, intercourse grew in the 11th century. Edward the Confessor was educated in Normandy and to his court brought Normans, who made Norman French the language of the court society.

The Middle English Period. When William the Norman won the battle of Hastings in 1066, Anglo-Saxon fell to the position of the tongue of a conquered race, a people excluded from the court and from public office by decrees of the conqueror as well as by their own pride. Yet, though shut out from literary, courtly, and school use, the vitality of the language remained unimpaired. Not only did it maintain itself, but, when the struggle against royal tyranny in the 12th and the 13th century had wrung from King John a great charter written in Latin, and had brought Norman nobles and Saxon commons together in a common cause, English emerged as the language of the English Kin and their conquerors. We are told that about 1350 John Cornwall, a "master of grammar," changed instruction in his grammar school from French into English. In 1368 English was declared the language of the law courts. The poetry of Chaucer and the prose of the Wiclif-Purvey Bible raised the Midland dialect to the level of a literary language.

The language of this period, now called by scholars Middle English, was, however, very different from the Anglo-Saxon of 300 years earlier. It had dropped inflectional endings and had changed many spellings; it had lost some words and had borrowed from the French and the Latin many more. The arrangement of the words in a sentence was uncertain, since endings had been dropped and writers had set the words in what seemed to them, at the time, the best order. It was not until the 16th century that rules for word order were again reasonably well settled. A most important fact, however, is that in the 13th and the 14th century, through borrowing and Anglicizing, there began that generous enrichment of the language which has ever since characterized English speech.

The Anglo-Saxon Chronicle, which closed in 1154, contained a very few French words, such as *rent, treasure, countess,* and *castle*; but the immediate predecessors of Chaucer in the 14th century drew lavishly upon the French for synonyms and for words having no equivalent in the English. Already many Latin words had come in through the language of religion and the law. The new learning brought more, and, since most of the borrowed French words were of Latin origin, the total Latin element in English became very large. In everyday speech, however, the French is now the most striking part of our borrowed vocabulary.

From the 14th century to the 16th, with the Midland dialect, or London English, as a nucleus, the processes of forming the language on its new scale of greatness went on. Inflections were dropped, word order was fixed, spellings were changed, and new words were borrowed—some to be retained and others to be finally rejected. Thus the beginnings of modern English were prepared in the 16th century.

Making the Modern English. The 16th century translations of the Bible and the writings of Shakespeare and of other great Elizabethans contain many old forms of words and of grammar unfamiliar to us. But these works mark the beginning of modern English. Their wide circulation by means of the printing press has helped to stabilize the language, and, during the last three centuries, to make slower its rate of change in respect to spelling and grammar. However, as long as the language is living, changes will occur; some words will be dropped, new ones will be made or borrowed, and new meanings will be given to old words. In this modern period, the extension of commerce and the development of science have brought about the introduction of thousands of new words, science especially drawing very largely from the Greek.

A comparison of English synonyms tells vividly the story of this borrowing. For example, the word *royal* is from the French, *regal* is directly from the Latin, while *kingly* is the Anglo-Saxon word. These words, side by side, have taken on important distinctions of meaning. *Acute* is Latin, *keen* is Anglo-Saxon, *shrewd* appears in Middle English and probably is Anglo-Saxon. Similarly, *admit* is Latin: *receive* comes from the Latin through the French.

Another group of words, applying to manners and conduct, is illustrated by *brave,* which comes from either French or Italian. *Gallant* is directly from the French or Italian, though perhaps it was originally a German word. *Business* is of Anglo-Saxon or Danish origin, *trade* is Anglo-Saxon, while *profession* and *art* come from the Latin through the French. *Copy* comes from the French, *model* from the French or Italian, *pattern* from the French, *specimen* from the Latin. The business terms, *cost, expense, price, charge,* were very early taken into the language from the Old French.

The sources of the following synonyms, relating either to law or to religion, are interesting: *crime* comes from the Latin through the French, *vice* is from the same source, and *sin* is from the Anglo-Saxon; *holiness* is Anglo-Saxon, while *sanctity* comes directly from the Latin. The common word *draw* is Anglo-Saxon; its synonym, *haul,* is of French origin, perhaps originally from the German or

Scandinavian; while *pull* is Anglo-Saxon and *tug* is probably Scandinavian.

The following list of words of French origin will show to what degree the French element has been worked into our language of daily use: *age, air, aunt, beauty, boil, boot, broil, cape, card, chair, cloak, coat, cousin, cry, dainty, debt, dine, ease, engine, face, fame, fork, grace, hasty, jolly, justice, napkin, nephew, niece, peace, plate, river, roast, soil, supper, table, uncle, virtue.*

Another group will illustrate well the picturesque interest that may be found in English synonyms: *breeze* is French or Spanish; *gale* may be Danish; *blast* and *storm* are certainly Anglo-Saxon; *gust* finds a likely source in Icelandic; *tempest*, so common a colloquial word in New England, is from the Old French; while *hurricane* is a Carib word which has entered the English through the Spanish.

The Dutch were the sailors and traders of the 17th century, and they gave us such terms as *boom, skipper, sloop*, besides some common words like *spool* and *wagon*. From the Portuguese come the words *binnacle, caste,* and *junta*. From the Arabic, we get the words *alkali, algebra,* and *tariff*. Hebrew contributions to English are chiefly religious words: *cherub, seraph, hallelujah, Messiah, Satan, Jehovah. Cabal* is of this origin as is also *cinnamon,* itself borrowed by the Hebrew from some other source. *Pilgrim,* the earliest Italian word in English, is recorded in the 12th century. This was in the time of the Crusades. Since the 14th century, we have taken from the Italian many musical and art terms, such as *opera, fresco, prima donna, sonnet, cartoon, cameo.* Other words of Italian origin, some borrowed through the French, are *fiasco, alarm, piazza, balcony, caprice.*

American Words. America has added to our stock of words in several interesting ways. Exploration in the 16th and the 17th century brought us, through the Spanish, such words as *potato, tobacco, cargo,* and *banana.* The contact of Americans and Spaniards in the West has given us such words as *pueblo, burro, broncho, coyote, loco, adobe, mesa, cinch, tornado, ranch, canyon, arroyo,* and *stampede,* besides some slang words like *vamoose,* and, in the Southwest, hundreds of plant and place names, such as *chaparral, mesquite, madroña, manzanita,* and *tule, Sierra, Santa Fe,* and *Colorado.* At the present time, because of increasingly close relations with the South American countries, we are constantly getting words of Spanish origin, such as *peon* and *hacienda.* From the French in America we have taken over *depot, levee* (dike), *bayou,* and *crevasse,* also place names like *Butte, Boise, Saint Louis,* and *Terre Haute.* The Dutch in New York are responsible for the words *patroon* and *stoop* (porch or steps).

Out of our political life in America have come the words *congressional, presidential, federalist, nullification, gerrymander.* We have coined the word *mileage,* the word *eagle* means a coin, *corduroy* is American English for a kind of road, and we speak of *locating* land. *Outsider* and *creek* (stream) are Americanisms, while several old or dialect English words, such as *fall* (autumn), *rare* (underdone), *slump, spry, lam,* have been preserved in America. At Baltimore the word *clipper* was first applied to sharp-prowed, fast-sailing ships; and at Gloucester the first *schooner* was christened.

No less interesting are the words taken from the American Indians: *squaw, wigwam, pemmican, tepee, papoose, cayuse, hominy, moccasin, chinquapin, opossum, skunk, succotash, toboggan,* and very many place names like *Canandaigua, Spokane, Chautauqua, Chattahoochee,* and *Willamette.* Some of these Indian words, such as *tepee,* and place names, like *Willamette,* have been affected in form by the analogy of French, others by the Spanish, as *potato, tobacco.* These illustrations will suggest that, in addition to the practical value to be realized from the study of words and the acquisition of skill in the use of them, there is the further worth of such study as an approach to the history of the race. Words are the symbols of ideas, and ideas have made history.

Word Building. Many words, as they were needed to express ideas, have been built from simple forms by the process called "composition." The simplest sounds or groups of sounds that had, in the beginnings of language, a separate existence and meaning are called roots. Examples are *duc,* meaning "lead," *ag,* meaning "drive," *ed,* meaning "eat," *cad,* meaning "fall." By the addition of other so-called nominal roots, as *i* which appears now in the pronoun "it," we reach the stage of stems. So from *agri,* meaning "of a field," and *colere,* meaning "to cultivate," the Latin formed the word *agricola,* meaning "a cultivator of a field," or "a farmer."

Some simple words have had very little change from the earliest stems, except alteration of the vowel sound. Frequently this change has resulted from altering the position of the accent. The following will illustrate this development:

The word *arm* is from a root *ar,* meaning a "joint." This word is to be distinguished from the word *arms* or *arm,* meaning "weapons," which comes from the Latin, although the Latin word may be from the same source. The word *book* comes from the stem *boc,* meaning "beech," probably because in early times, in northern Europe, letters were carved upon blocks of beechwood or upon beech trees themselves.

Birth was not used in Old English but probably was taken later from the Old Norse. It is derived from an ancient Aryan stem allied to the Sanskrit *bhrti,* which meant "bearing." Bread was in Anglo-Saxon *bréad* and in Old Saxon *brôd,* having the meaning originally of "piece" or "fragment." The Anglo-Saxon rarely used this word to mean *bread,* employing instead the word *hláf* in the sense both of "bread" and of "loaf." However, before the beginning of the 13th century, *bread* came to mean the substance, and *hláf* assumed the limited meaning it still retains in loaf. *Comb* is from an ancient Teutonic root, related apparently to the Sanskrit *gambha,* meaning "jaw" or "teeth." *Deep* is from a very ancient root *dhup,* meaning originally "hollow." *God* seems to come from a root *g'heu,* meaning "to invoke." *Hand,* a common Teutonic word, is thought by some to be derived from a Gothic word *hinthan,* meaning "catch" or "take."

Language and History. In the vocabulary of the English tongue we find embodied the power men possess of readily and happily imaging or ideally representing the mysterious world in which we live. In our words are recorded their inventions as well as their ideals and schemes for the establishment of religion, society, and education. Here are mirrored the growth and the decay of ideas and ideals, the rise of the new and the displacement of the old. The lofty and the low in human thought and imagination are reflected in our language.

Our word *guest,* for example, is from the same root as is the Latin word *hostis* meaning "enemy," the original meaning of the root being "stranger." *Cheat* is from the old word *escheator,* the name of an officer whose duty it was to look after estates which, on the death of the owner, reverted to the state, a sense still retained in the legal term *escheat.* The real or suspected corruption of the *escheators* in the 15th or 16th century probably brought about the degradation of the word.

History finds still further illustration in such words as *cabal,* which comes from the Hebrew through the Latin and the French and meant originally "tradition." In the middle ages it came to mean "secret scheming," and in English this meaning was re-enforced by the fact that the initials of the names of five members of the Foreign Affairs Council of Charles II spelled this word *cabal.* In similar fashion, the words *earl* and *alderman* in their changing meanings represent much of English and American local government history.

The word *cross* suggests Christianity; but we should see in it also the early faith and learning of the great Irish schools of the 5th and the 6th century, from which the Norsemen of Northumbria took the word and passed it on to the Anglo-Saxons. Our word *world* also carries in its form the thinking of our pagan ancestors, who made it from *wer* meaning "man" and *old* meaning "age." It thus carries the sense of the "age of man or mankind," hence the "dwelling place of man."

In the early 13th century the foreign words in common use in English made up probably 12 per cent of the entire vocabulary. In Shakespeare's works the foreign element is estimated at 40 per cent. Today in our writing it is probably 60 per cent. It is estimated that in the dictionaries of today about 20 per cent of the words are of Anglo-Saxon origin, about 35 per cent are from the French, about 15 per cent from the Latin directly, about 12 per cent from the Greek. But the proportion of Anglo-Saxon words in our everyday speech is much greater than these figures show, because our grammar is English and our connective words, such as *or*, *and*, *but*, are Anglo-Saxon. The English language has borrowed vocabulary, but not syntax, and it has Anglicized foreign words. Therefore, in spite of great differences of spelling, pronunciation, and accent, we may include in the term *English* the Anglo-Saxon of the 7th century, the Middle English of the 14th century, and the tongue of today.

The making of dictionaries has maintained a record of words and usage which presents a vivid picture of the growth of the language in the last 300 years. Samuel Johnson's dictionary of 1755 contained about 15,000 words. The latest dictionaries record more than 400,000. It is estimated that the average person without special education may know and use from 5000 to 10,000 words, while the educated man may use and be familiar with the meanings of from 20,000 to 50,000.

The Study of English. Language grows by adding new words, by giving new meanings to old words, and by developing the figurative or poetic senses of many words. All these processes depend upon increase of knowledge, upon invention and discovery, and upon the cultivation of art and poetry.

Words are, after all, only means to right understanding and true feeling; but many accurate, fine words are necessary to much good thinking. There is always a *best* word to express thought accurately and clearly. The student who would better his command of language will first direct his attention to those things which can be felt and seen, so that he may have something definite and concrete about which to talk or to write. He will next consult the dictionary for the meanings and the history of words; he will examine closely synonyms and antonyms for their accurate distinctions in meaning; nor will he fail to attend to the poetic suggestiveness of those words which give especial beauty both to the spoken and to the written phrase. He will, in a word, be always on his guard to avoid and to correct the errors and improprieties of usage which are likely to creep into his conversation.

Order of Study. English is treated in the following pages in a form to be referred to readily, to be used easily for help in speaking or writing, and to serve as a guide for systematic study. The various parts of the subject are arranged in the general order in which the boy or girl meets them in studying this most important of all school subjects. This arrangement would appear to be also the most convenient for older people.

Usage.—The correct and appropriate uses of words are given first place. During the early years of the child's life, before he knows much about sentences, he learns many words. Afterward, the value of his ability to use the correct and appropriate word, "to say the right thing in the right way," can never be overestimated. Therefore Usage, or approved uses of common words, is treated first.

Word Building and Spelling.—Again, the child's first words are naturally simple; most of them have but one syllable In the beginning these are all nouns, for he does not yet know the use of the pronoun. By degrees, as the infant mind develops, the child finds the need of other words to express his thoughts and ideas. Soon he discovers that, by adding little syllables to the words with which he is already familiar, he can make himself understood. Thus unknowingly does the child arrive at the art of word building.

It will at once be seen that a knowledge of word building is of great value to the student of English as an aid in enlarging his vocabulary. For this reason, the section on Word Building follows Usage. It precedes the important subject of Spelling, because a knowledge of the structure of many English words helps equally both in grasping their meanings and in learning their component parts.

Pronunciation.—The guide of everyday usefulness has directed the making of the spelling and pronunciation lists. These are arranged to help the child with troublesome school words and also to give ready aid in the use of common words in business, in the household, and in social life. Correct spelling and correct pronunciation are essential to a perfect command of the English language.

Sentence Building, Capitals, Punctuation and *Linguistics.*—Following Word Building or etymology comes syntax or Sentence Building, which is the next important stage in the study of language. The essential rules and principles of grammar are given in this section, including the use of capital letters and punctuation marks, and Linguistics, or the science of language.

Speaking and Writing.—The section which presents helps in writing papers and essays and in making talks and speeches appropriately follows the study of words and sentences. To the student who desires advanced work in oral and in written language, this section is invaluable.

Forms of Literary Composition.—Having made an exhaustive study of words, sentences, and practical composition, the student is next introduced to the various forms of literature. In this section the principal divisions and subdivisions of prose and poetry are described and illustrated.

Letter Writing.—Because of its importance, Letter Writing follows Speaking and Writing in a separate section. The writing of an interesting letter may be counted as one of the finest accomplishments. In writing letters, we must apply the principles given in all the preceding sections on words, sentences, and composition.

Reading.—The language a person uses is influenced largely by the kind of books and papers he reads. Therefore a condensed guide to the best types and examples of English reading is here given. The lists of books direct the reader to the masterpieces of English literature. They are arranged in groups suited to the various school grades. In each group are the books that teachers, librarians, and parents have found to interest most readily boys and girls of the corresponding grade or age. A lifetime might be spent in becoming acquainted with the books in these lists. Reading will reenforce all that can be learned from the preceding sections.

Synonyms and Antonyms.—The value of knowing the correct and appropriate word is pointed out above. We should now add to this the knowledge of how to choose with a nicety from among several appropriate words. It is this interest which leads to the study of the rich store of English Synonyms and Antonyms.

Foreign Words and Phrases and *Abbreviations.* Closing this department are two dictionaries— 1) Latin phrases frequently found in English books, and 2) phrases from Modern Languages, added to which are some examples of "tourist talk," consisting of current phrases useful to travelers; also a list of Abbreviations.

GOOD USAGE

A PERSON's language reflects his social background, his geographic origin, and, especially, the extent of his education. By its form, it makes a good impression or an unfavorable one. That is why the question of correctness arises even before one's language is tested for the important qualities of clearness and accuracy. Mispronounced words, colloquialisms, malapropisms, incorrect idioms, and grammatical errors are noticed at once and can place a speaker or writer at a serious disadvantage. *How* he says a thing will attract more attention than *what* he says. On the other hand, if one's language is easy, confident, and fluent because correct, his listener or reader will accept the form without question and will think only about the subject matter.

Whether it is gained through formal instruction or through self-education, the ability to use language well comes only by observation, study, and practice. Because English is a living language and is therefore subject to change, the question of good usage is one that calls for constant attention. Whether certain words or forms of expression are acceptable or not is determined, not by an edict of some individual or group in authority, but by the consensus of the best writers and speakers who are using the language at any particular time.

The average person's first problem is to rid his speech of certain forms of expression that attract undue or unfavorable attention. Many expressions condemned by standard usage have resulted from someone's lazy habit of taking over ready-made phrases without regard to their repute or their real meaning. An effort to vary the phrasing is likely to uncover a fresh, interesting expression that will say the thing more effectively as well as more correctly.

Slang is an inclusive term for words and phrases that come into the language on trial, sometimes with very questionable associations, sometimes on a more respectable basis. At the outset it should be noted that not all new words should be classed as "slang". As the language grows, new meanings call for special words, which may be either coined or imported. The word "camouflage," for example, is a French importation that was accepted readily as a part of everyday English speech.

Certain words which began as slang abbreviations for longer expressions were challenged at first, but later gained a place for themselves. Examples are "cab," short for "cabriolet," "mob," for *mobile vulgus,* and "hoax," for "hocus pocus," itself a slang contraction for a Latin phrase used by impostors. Current abbreviations such as "gym" for "gymnasium," "exam," for "examination," and "mike," for "microphone," will readily suggest themselves. Whether any of these newer contractions will be accepted as standard usage is still open to question.

Slang from various questionable sources may be made almost respectable by the fashion of the moment. From the all-too-numerous examples, a few typical cases may be cited. Who hasn't heard, and perhaps used, such expressions as "so what?," "screwball," "sourpuss," "behind the eight ball," "cock-eyed," and "ritzy"? It may be argued that many such phrases are expressive. So is profanity, for that matter, but that doesn't qualify it as an example of good usage. But in addition to being undignified, slang is short-lived. Expressions like "twenty-three" and "skiddoo" are as outmoded today as the bathing suits of a generation ago. So a language that was artificial and synthetic to begin with has the added disadvantage of rapid obsolescence. If the habit of depending upon slang has not dulled his perception, the average person will turn with satisfaction to the dignity, accuracy, and perennial timeliness of standard English.

CORRECT USE OF SOME COMMON WORDS AND PHRASES

A. General usage in America approves the use of the article *a* before consonants, before initial *h* when sounded, before long *u,* and before the words *one* and *once: a house, a hospital, a historical society; a university; such a one.*

Colloquially, when two objects are thought of as belonging together or as used together, *a* need not be repeated: *a coat and hat; a cup and saucer; a sword and belt.* But, "She bought *a coat and a hat,*" meaning two purchases, is correct.

The expression "*a black and white dress*" means but one, while "*a black and a white dress*" means two dresses—one black and one white. This second expression is awkward, and the form "*a black dress and a white one*" or "*a black dress and a white*" may be substituted. "They elected *a secretary and a treasurer*" implies two persons; but "*a secretary and treasurer*" implies one person.

Absolutely. This word, so frequently used instead of *indeed, assuredly, of course,* or *certainly,* should be discarded in favor of the accurate and appropriate word: "*Certainly* (not *absolutely*), I shall go." However, "It is *absolutely* certain that he will come" is correct when one intends to express positive assurance.

Accept, Except. *Accept* means "take when offered"; *except* means "leave out," "exclude": "I *accept* the gift." "We will *except* him from our requirements." Do not say "*accept of.*"

Acquire. This word should be distinguished from *obtain* and *procure.* We *acquire* that which we retain more or less permanently, but we *obtain* or *procure* anything which we enjoy temporarily. Thus, we *acquire* wealth, *obtain* a loan, *procure* supplies.

Across. "To get something *across,*" "to put a thing *across,*" "to come *across,*" are slang phrases. The first means usually "to make something understood," as an actor is said "to get it *across* (or *over*) to the audience." The second phrase implies *succeeding*; the third, *acceding,* as to a request or demand.

Adage. As this word describes a proverb, or old saying, one should never speak of an *old* adage.

Addict. This word, formed from the adjective *addicted,* has come into wide newspaper use. It means "one who has the habit of using" something generally harmful; as, "a drug *addict.*" It is widely used in medical works but has not yet come into general use. The term is a useful addition to our vocabulary. *Addicted* usually implies evil.

Addition. Number of verb. We say correctly, "Two and three *are* five," not "Two and three *is* five."

Administer. Do not say, "The man died from blows *administered* by the policeman." Oaths, medicine, affairs of state, are *administered.* Blows are *dealt.*

Admittance, Admission. In some uses these words are likely to be confused. *Admittance* refers to entrance to a place. "No *admittance*" means "entrance forbidden": "No *admittance* before 8 o'clock." *Admission* refers to entrance into a society or an audience, or into certain privileges: "*Admission* to the club depended upon scholarship." *Admission* may mean also the price or fee of entertainment: "*Admission* One Dollar."

Adore. This word means "worship," "venerate," or "hold in high respect or admiration." It is not appropriate to express a liking for chocolates.

Advert, Allude, Refer. The meanings of these words may be confused. We *advert* to that to which we turn the attention; we *allude* to a matter that we touch upon incidentally; we *refer* to a subject that we wish to bring back to notice.

Advise. In the jargon of business correspondence, "advise" is frequently misused to express some shading of "inform." Note the difference in the following example: "Our representative has informed (not 'advised') us of your application for additional credit. He advises us to grant the extension."

Advocate. Unlike propose, recommend, or urge, *advocate*, when used as a verb, is followed by a noun instead of a that-clause. We *recommend* that a measure be adopted; we *advocate* its adoption.

Aesthetic. This adjective preferably refers to abstract ideas, not to persons or objects. Do not speak of "an *aesthetic* person" or "an *aesthetic* decoration," but of "*aesthetic* standards" or "*aesthetic* considerations."

Affect. See *Effect*.

Affectation. Whether intentional or not, the use of "stylish" language arouses resentment in many people, who regard it as an assumption of superiority. The so-called "uppity" words may be clear and logically appropriate, but, because they are more bookish than conversational, they may produce an unfavorable reaction. Below are some typical pairs of what H. W. Fowler calls "working words" and "stylish words." Everyone can make up a similar list from his own experience.

WORKING WORDS	STYLISH WORDS
buy	purchase
class	category
drink	beverage
think	deem
wish	desire

Agendum, Agenda. The first (singular) indicates an item, as of business, to be considered; the second (plural), the list of all items for consideration or a program of business to be done.

Aggravate. Often inaccurately used when the speaker means *provoke, irritate,* or *anger.* The word means "increase" or "intensify." The following are correct uses: "His misery was *aggravated.*" "He is *irritated* by continually dealing with small matters." "She is easily *provoked* to jealousy."

Ago, Since. We say correctly, "a long time *ago*" and "some time *since*," or "many years *ago*" and "a few days *since*." *Ago* means before a certain time. If no point of time is specified, the word means before the present: "a year *ago* last Tuesday"; or, if we count back from the present, "a year *ago*." *Since* means after a certain time and up to the present: "We have not met *since* 1910."

Agree. Do not use *agree* for *admit.* We *admit* a fact but *agree* in doing or thinking something. We may *admit* that a wall is not attractive but we *agree* in refusing to spend any more money to improve its appearance.

Agriculturist. Prefer this form to *agriculturalist.*

Aim. The not infrequent colloquial use of this word as a verb instead of *intend* or *plan*, as, "I *aim* to treat all customers fairly," is not approved by careful speakers, though formerly it was good English. As a noun, meaning "purpose," it is an excellent figurative word: "Young man, have an *aim* in life."

Ain't. Formerly classed by high authority as belonging to "illiterate speech," the contraction "*ain't*" for "*am not*" is not in good standing, despite recent efforts by publicists to make it respectable. Use it at your own risk, if at all, and hope your listeners will credit you with knowing better.

Alibi (Latin *elsewhere*). This standard legal term signifying absence from the scene of a crime, is also a familiar sports slang expression used loosely as an equivalent for "*excuse,*" "*explanation,*" or even "*apology.*"

Alike. This word should not be preceded by *both*, nor by *both just*, as in "These hats are *both alike*" or "*both just alike.*" Say, "These hats are *alike* (or *just alike*)." *Both* is superfluous in these phrases. See *Both* and *Just.*

All, All of. In spite of critics, popular usage has sanctioned the employment of *all of it, all of them*, like *some of them.* The idioms may be regarded as established. One may say either, "I have *all of it*" or "I have *it all.*" From the viewpoint of economy, *it all* is preferable.

Similarly, the phrase *all over* has established itself, as in the sentence, "We have searched *all over* the place."

Do not say, "This is *all* the farther I have read." The use is vulgar. Say, "This is as far as I have read" or "I have read no farther." See *Farther, Further.*

Allege. Do not use this word as a synonym for *say* or *tell*, as in "He *alleges* that the engine ran sixty miles an hour." Instead, "He *says* or *tells* us that, etc." The word has a legal sense, and with this meaning it is used in news writing. To say "The reasons *alleged* for the nomination are, etc." is to imply doubt as to the truth of what is *alleged* or to disclaim responsibility for the statement. See *Assert.*

All—not, Not—all. A common mistake among usually careful speakers is the failure to distinguish between these two logically different negatives. To say, "All people are not allergic to dust" is really equivalent to saying that none are allergic. On the other hand, by saying, "Not all people are allergic to dust," we convey the intended meaning that some are and some are not.

All right. The phrase should never be written *alright*, though formerly this usage was correct.

All together, Altogether. *All together* means "all in the same place at the same time" or "all acting at once": "We are *all together* in the business" or "Let us pull *all together*" or "Now, *all together*, boys." *Altogether* means "entirely"; as, "The time was *altogether* too short."

Almost, Nearly. These two adverbs should not be used indiscriminately. *Almost* suggests the ending of an act; *nearly*, its beginning. A man who receives an injury so severe that he barely comes off with his life *almost* loses it; a man who just escapes what would have killed him is *nearly* killed, or, as we say, "comes very near to being killed." These words are correctly used in "I have *almost* finished my work" and "I *nearly* ran over the child."

Alone, Only. To avoid ambiguity, observe the following distinction between these words: That is *alone* which is unaccompanied; that is *only* of which there is no other. "*Only* virtue makes us happy" means that nothing else can do it. "Virtue *alone* makes us happy" means that virtue unaided makes us happy. "This means of locomotion is used by man *only.*" See *Only.*

Already, All ready. Discriminate carefully between these terms. *Already* means "beforehand" or "so soon"; *all ready*, "everything prepared" or "prepared in every way."

Also. Like *only*, this particle is often misplaced, as in "If he is satisfied, I am satisfied *also.*" Write instead, "If he is satisfied, I *also* am satisfied." Place the word as close as possible to and usually following the word to which it applies.

Alternative. Do not use this word when more than two things are referred to. You may have the choice of three courses, not of three *alternatives.*

Alumni, Alumnæ. An *alumnus* is a graduate of a college, a university, or a school. *Alumni* (pronounced *a-lŭm′nī*) is the masculine plural, but is used of men or women graduates. The feminine is *alumna*; plural, *alumnæ*, correctly pronounced *à-lŭm'nē*: "Association of Collegiate *Alumnæ*."

Amateur, Novice. *Amateur* means properly "one who pursues an art or plays a game *for the love of it*." The *amateur* may be highly skilled. The *novice* is a beginner; therefore, presumably unskilled.

Ambiguous. This word indicates uncertainty of meaning arising usually from lack of skill in the use of language. It is sometimes confused with "equivocal," which refers to intentional "double talk," in which more than one interpretation may best serve the speaker's purpose.

Ameliorated. This word means "bettered," "improved." "Her troubles are greatly *lessened* (not *ameliorated*)." We say correctly, "Conditions in the famine district have been *ameliorated*."

Amiable, Amicable. These two words of common origin appear so similar that important differences between them are sometimes overlooked. "Amiable" is a personal word, indicating a likeable or loveable disposition. "Amicable" is a more abstract term meaning friendly or agreeable, as in "an amicable settlement of a dispute."

Among. "He was there *among* the rest" should read "with the rest," because *rest* contradicts the idea of "mingling or including in a group" which is implied in *among*. "He was there *among* the first" is correct. *With* denotes simply accompaniment. Similarly, avoid such expressions as "*among one another, each other*." "*One another*" and "*each other*" imply individuals by themselves so that when they are used with *among* the resulting expression is self-contradictory. Say, "*among themselves*," "*with each other*," "*with one another*"; as "They exchanged hats *with each other*."

Amount. Used only of substances or material: "Only a small *amount* of grain could be purchased." Do not say, "a large *amount* of perfection" or "a large *amount* of people." *Degree of perfection* and *number of people* are correct.

Ample. This word should not be used, as it frequently is, to mean simply "sufficient." *Sufficient* means "enough to supply a need." *Ample* is a larger word and carries the sense of enough, as of space, time, supplies, with a wide margin for comfort or unforeseen demands.

An. Use this form of the article before words beginning with a vowel or a silent *h*; as, *an* inkpot, *an* oil well, *an* heir, *an* honor, *an* hour, *an* honest man.

And. See *Conjunctions*.

Answer, Reply. We *answer* a question, but we *reply* to a statement. *Reply* implies a more definitely planned expression than *answer*.

Ante-, Anti-. These prefixes are frequently confused. *Ante-* means "before"; *anti-* means "against" or "contrary to": "In *ante-*suffrage days the *anti-*suffragists were active." Pronounce the latter *ăn'tĭ*, not *ăn'tī*.

Antecedents. The use of this word to mean the ancestry and the past life of a person has good authority, though the use is of recent origin and the need for it infrequent. We may say of a person whose life history we wish to know, "What can you tell me of his *antecedents*?"

Anticipate. A stronger word than *expect* or *foresee*, and in some senses not synonymous with either. It means "take beforehand" (from Latin *ante*, "before," and *capere*, "to take"), "forestall," "get ahead of": "The committee was *anticipated* by the senator in introducing the water power bill."

The second meaning of the word is "look forward to," usually implying approval or enjoyment: "Only a few politicians *anticipated* his election" or "We *anticipated* a delightful vacation." One should say, "His death is daily *expected* (not *anticipated*)."

Antiquated, Ancient, Antique, Old. These words are frequently confused. *Old* is the opposite of *new, young, fresh; ancient* applies to what existed long ago, as *ancient states; antiquated* is a disparaging term for that which is old and in disuse or out of date, as "*antiquated* methods of business"; *antique* may be applied to something that has come down from olden times, as a vase or a piece of furniture, or to an imitation of the "real *antique*." See *Synonyms*.

Anxious. This word is often used loosely as a substitute for "eager" or some equally carefree expression. Note that in its original and correct sense, "anxious" conveys a suggestion of worry or concern.

Any. Sometimes used erroneously as an adverb to modify a verb; as, "Did you fish *any*?" Say rather, "Did you do *any* fishing?" *Any* should not be used for *all* in comparisons. Not, "That is the most beautiful car of *any* in the show," but "most beautiful car in the show." *Any* may modify adjectives; as, "*any* longer."

Anyhow, Anyway. Although sometimes disapproved as unscholarly, these are idiomatic expressions, meaning "in any event," "At any rate," or "be that as it may." Avoid *anyways* as vulgar.

Any place, Some place. These phrases should not be used for *anywhere* and *somewhere*. One should say, "I cannot find my umbrella *anywhere*," not "*any place*." One says properly, " I want to go *somewhere*"; but the expression "I want to go *some place*" is vulgar. The fault lies in needlessly using a noun in place of an adverb which accurately expresses the idea.

Anywheres. A vulgarism for *anywhere*. Similar vulgarisms are *somewheres* and *nowheres*.

A one. In such a sentence as "All who promised to come arrived, but not *a one* was on time," *a* is superfluous.

Apparently. This word stands midway between "seemingly," with its suggestion of deceptive outward appearances, and "evidently," with its convincing positiveness. "Apparantly" can be inflected in such a way as to indicate various shades of meaning, but its rightful use is to describe what is clear to the eye or the understanding, but is not necessarily untrue.

Appear, Seem. *Appear* refers usually to what is evident to the senses: "The fruit *appears* to be well ripened." Every object may *appear*, but nothing *seems* except that which the mind admits to *appear* in a given form. Thus, *seems* is used to imply a result of thought or reflection: "He *seems* to be an honorable man."

Appreciate. Along with its suggestion of enjoyment, as in reference to works of art, "appreciate" is a serviceable word in some other common meanings. To say "We appreciate the difficulty of your situation" means that we understand sympathetically, not that we relish or enjoy the other person's difficulty. In a very different sort of context, "appreciate" means to grow in value, as in the case of property or investments.

Apt. Often misused for *likely*, and sometimes for *liable*. The following are examples of correct usage: "What is he *likely* to be doing?" "Where shall I be *likely* to find him?" *Liable* properly introduces some unhappy or disagreeable possibility: "If you go there, you are *liable* to incur his displeasure." *Apt* implies natural *fitness* or *tendency*: "Experienced men are *apt* to give good advice."

Arise, Arouse. The first form belongs to archaic, literary contexts: "I will *arise* and go to my father." In everyday use, *rise* is preferred: "We *rise* at six o'clock." *Arouse* refers to feelings: "This act *aroused* our anger." *Rouse* is used, transitively, in a literal sense: "We *roused* him from his slumbers."

As—as, So—as. Either combination may be used in negative statements involving comparison, but care should be taken to apply them appropriately. "James is not *as* tall *as* Tom" is a direct statement concerning the height of the two *without* implication that the speaker considers either of the persons spoken of as *tall*. But, if *so* be used instead of the first *as*, then it is understood that the second person referred to is notably tall in comparison with the first. Likewise, when age is spoken of, if one says, "My daughter is not *as* young *as* yours," the idea conveyed is that they may be nearly of the same age; but, by substituting *so* for the first *as*, one changes the sense and emphasizes the youth of the younger child and a marked difference between the two ages: "My daughter is not *so* young *as* yours."

As—as, only, may be used in affirmative declarative statements; as, "He is *as* good a man *as* anyone can find." *So—as*, however, is appropriate in some affirmative interrogative sentences when comparison is involved: "Is his estate *so* large *as* that?" Here an estate of great size is implied.

As for *that* is a vulgarism in such a sentence as "I do not know *as* I like him." Say, "*that* I like him." In such an erroneous expression as "Not *as* I am aware of," substitute *that* for *as*.

As a matter of fact. Trite phrase, overused by many speakers and writers. If emphasis is wanted, use a phrase specifically suited, such as: "Scientists agree that . ." or "It is universally understood that . .".

Aspiration, Ambition. *Aspiration* is exalted desire and properly implies striving for something high and ennobling; as, "To the *aspiration* of the poet we owe Milton's *Paradise Regained*." *Ambition* may imply worthy eagerness to achieve some great purpose, but it also connotes persistent, often overweening or inordinate, desire for personal advancement: "An *ambitious* man may *aspire* to greatness"; but it is used in the bad sense by Shakespeare in "*Ambition* should be made of sterner stuff." It is not properly used for *energy* or *fitness* for work, as in "He shows no *ambition* since his illness"; but it is correctly employed in "Repeated reverses curbed his *ambition*."

Assert, Allege. Two words often erroneously applied. Properly, one *asserts* that which one is ready to prove if called upon to do so, as a claim to property; one *alleges* that which is open to doubt or to question, as the existence of a will or the commission of a crime. See *Allege*.

As though. Often used for *as if*. This use has been condemned; but it is accepted as idiomatic English, notwithstanding the claim that it expresses a condition of remoteness approaching to impossibility; "We were received *as though* (or *as if*) there had been no war between our countries." *As if* is generally followed by a clause containing (1) a past subjunctive or (2) an infinitive expressing purpose or destination: (1) "Treating history *as if* it were a panorama intended to please the eye." "*As if* the dead the living should exceed." (2) "Buying agate and aluminum ware *as if* to set up housekeeping."

At. Redundant in the expressions "Where are we *at*?" "Where does he live *at*?"

At, In. *At* is a less definite word than *in*. Distinctions between them are not clearly drawn. The following examples, however, represent authoritative usage. We may say, "*in* the South," "*in* Chicago," also "The meeting was held *at* (or *in*) Baltimore." Of small towns or villages we say correctly, "They live *at* Walden"; but of larger cities, "His home is *in* Boston." To distinguish between points in a journey and the final destination, it is correct to say, "The ship calls *at* Halifax but docks *in* New York." A similar distinction is appropriate with the verb *arrive*. Either "We arrived *at* Denver," in which case the city is considered as one of the points to be reached in the journey, or "We arrived *in* Denver," which then is considered as the final stopping place. But, if the final destination is a small place, *at* is the correct word.

At all. An intensive colloquial phrase condemned by some critics, but entitled to standing as emphatic idiomatic English. There is a difference of emphasis between "I do not know him" and "I do not know him *at all*"; for, while the former denies acquaintance, it does not dispose of the possibility of acquaintance as emphatically as does the latter and more decided statement.

At best, At worst, At last. These are well-established idioms and are preferable to *at the best*, etc. They arose from an early joining of the preposition and the article into the form *atte*, whence *at*. See *Prepositions*.

At fault, In fault. Both phrases are correctly used for *in the wrong, in error, blameworthy*. *At fault* is the more common American usage.

Athletics. The word, when restricted to mean a system of physical exercises and training, should take a verb in the singular. But, when it is understood to mean the games and sports of a school, a verb in the plural is frequently used and is not incorrect. Similar use is current for *gymnastics* and *tactics*. Avoid the common error of saying *atheletics*, for the word is one of three syllables, *ath-let'ics*.

At one fell swoop. A trite expression, unpleasant to those hearers who appreciate its literary power in Shakespeare's *Macbeth*.

At that. This colloquialism used as an intensified ending is usually redundant and as such is better omitted: "The new car has arrived, and is a beauty *at that*." This construction has been traced to the use of the phrase in matters in which the cost of an article is considered; as, "Here is a good umbrella for $8.00 and cheap *at that* (price, understood)."

Audience. Often inaccurately used in place of spectators: The *audience* hears; the *spectators* see. Say: "the *spectators* at the ball game," not "the *audience*"; "the *audience* at the concert," not "the *spectators*."

Aught, Naught, Ought. *Aught* means "anything"; *naught* means "not anything," "nothing," or "cipher, 0." *Ought* is a verb, implying duty: "I *ought* to go." *Aught* or *ought* should never be used in the sense of *nothing* or a *cipher*.

Auspicious, Propitious. The word *auspicious* is applied to an occasion, the beginning of an important undertaking, or the like, and indicates that such occasions are favored by the conditions and by the circumstances. *Propitious* is applied to the conditions themselves and indicates that they are favorable. The word was originally applicable to a person or to a god and was later transferred to the signs which showed favor. A picnic has an *auspicious* beginning when the weather is *propitious*.

Avenge, Revenge. To *avenge* is to punish on behalf of another; to *revenge* is to punish on one's own behalf. We *avenge* a wrong to satisfy justice; but we may take *revenge* merely to satisfy our own angry resentment.

Averse, Aversion. *Averse to* is the accepted usage instead of *averse from*: "He was not *averse to* discussing his failure." Also *aversion to*: "His *aversion to* hard work is well known."

Avoid. This word means "to free oneself from" or "keep away from," but is often inaccurately used for *prevent* or *hinder*; as, "Nothing shall be lost if I can *avoid* it." Here *prevent* is the correct word to use: "if I can *prevent* it." But, "I shall not go if I can *avoid* it" is correct, for *avoid* here means "to free oneself from."

Awful, Awfully. Too frequently used as intensives. Avoid such phrases as "an *awful* shame," "*awfully* glad to see you." *Awful* is correctly used of that which fills with dread or inspires fear: "an *awful* catastrophe." Both of these words are colloquialisms that border on vulgarity when they are used in the sense of *extraordinary, highly remarkable,* or *excessively.*

Bad. Such phrases as *bad* cold, *bad* break, *bad* case are in wide colloquial use. Careful speakers try to use a more accurate and appropriate word, such as *serious, severe, troublesome.*

Badly, Bad. Discriminating people will try to avoid too general use of these words. When *feel* is used intransitively, like *seem,* the adjective *bad* (a predicate adjective) is grammatically correct: "She feels *bad* about the failure." In such a sentence as "I shall miss you *badly,*" *very much* is to be preferred.

Balance. In bookkeeping, the sum to be added to the less or to be deducted from the greater of two amounts, as receipts and expenditures, so that the two "balance." It is incorrect to speak of the *balance* of a meal, the *balance* of an edition, etc. Here *rest* or *remainder* is correct. One may speak of the *balance* of an account.

Be back, Been to. Such expressions as "I will *be back* soon" and "I have *been to* town" are widely current. The first is approved, if *be back* signifies state or condition, not movement. For "I have *been to* town," one would better substitute "I have *been in* town." *In,* not *to,* is appropriate to the state or condition implied in *have been.*

Because. The word is a contraction of *by cause* and means "for the reason that." Therefore it is redundant in such constructions as "The reason we go is *because* we have been summoned." The correct form is "The *reason* we go is that we have been summoned" or, preferably, "We go *because* we have been summoned." The use of *why* after *because,* in "*because why,*" is a vulgarism in which *why* is redundant.

Begin, Commence. Although, historically, these words are precisely alike in meaning, *begin,* the Anglo-Saxon word, is preferred by careful speakers for general use. *Commence* has more formal associations and implies a beginning which involves a certain procedure and completion: One *begins* the practice of law, but one *commences* a lawsuit. We *begin* a day's work, but we *commence* a ceremony.

Behalf (on, in). A distinction worth noting is that *on behalf of* means "in the name of," while *in behalf of* means "in the interest of": "*On behalf of* the school, we thank you." "I make this appeal *in behalf of* the prisoner."

Beside, Besides. *Beside,* in present day usage, is a preposition and means "by the side of," as in "She stood *beside* the chair." *Besides* is either adverb or preposition and means "moreover," "beyond what has been said," or "in addition to": "*Besides,* they knew the road better"; "*Besides* wealth, he desired culture."

Better. This word is correctly used in the idiomatic form, *had better,* as in "We *had better* go."

Between. In its literal sense, this word applies to only two objects: "The candy was to be divided *between* the two boys, or *among* the four children."

When used of more than two objects, it brings them severally and individually into the relation expressed: "a treaty *between* three powers." One may say, "The steamers ply *between* San Francisco, Honolulu, and Yokohama."

"*Between* each desk there is a wide space." This is a frequent error. Say, "There is a wide space *between* each two desks" or "Wide spaces are left *between* desks."

Between may express contrast: "The two boys are brothers, but there is a great difference *between* them."

Biscuit. *Biscuits* is the correct plural. Although "Please pass the *biscuit*" is frequently heard, no one says, "Please pass the *cracker.*" There is a tendency to use *biscuit* as a collective singular by analogy with *bread,* but no one would say "Please pass the *roll*" of a number of rolls served at table.

Blame it on. A vulgarism used in place of *accuse* or *suspect*: "He *blames it on* his brother" should be "He *suspects* or *accuses* his brother" or "He *blames* his brother for it." In such an idiomatic phrase as "She is to *blame*" the passive meaning, "She is to be *blamed,*" is intended.

Both. Regarded as superfluous in the sentence "They are *both* alike." In "They *both* ran away from school," *both* has an intensive force. *Both,* as adjective or pronoun, may be applied to two objects or persons only. In "*Both* women spoke," *both* is an adjective; in "The general invited the colonel and the major and *both* went," *both* is a pronoun.

In the sentence, "They *both* met at the station," *both* is superfluous. "*Both* were alike good," meaning "*Both* were equally good," while approved usage, is not to be preferred to the latter sentence which is rhythmically perfect and linguistically sound.

As a conjunction, *both* may be used in connection with more than two things: "They lost all their property, *both* houses, barns, and crops."

Both of. Frequently condemned as colloquial; but the phrase has the support of literary usage, as in "*Both of* these arguments are sound."

Bother. Critics condemn this word when used as an imprecation or expression of impatience; as, "Oh, *bother* it all!" It is excellent English if used in the sense of *take trouble,* as in the sentence "You need not *bother* to return the paper."

Bound. In colloquial use to mean "determined" or "resolved," but challenged by the critics. *Bound* implies *compulsion* or *legal obligation*; as, "He is *bound* to pay it." "He is *bound* to do it" is correct if the person referred to is under obligation or promise, but not when the act depends on the resolution of the individual. Then say, "He is *certain, resolved,* or *determined* to do it." "He is *bound* to fail" should be "He is *sure* to fail." But we may say, "He is *bound* for destruction," meaning "He is *on the way* to destruction."

Brainy. A colloquialism meaning "mentally alert," "of quick understanding," or "of vigorous intellect"; as, a *brainy* man.

Broadcast. The past tense of this word is usually given as *broadcast.* In its new sense, however, of transmitting speech or programs by radio, the form *broadcasted* is so widely employed as to be regarded by many as standard usage.

Bunch. A word useful in describing bananas or grapes, but very objectionable slang when applied to people.

Bursted. A vulgarism sometimes rendered *busted.* Both are forms that cannot be too severely condemned, for the past participle and the past tense of the verb are the same as the infinitive, *burst.*

But. Frequently redundant before *that,* although sometimes required to make sense. When *but* is a preposition and *that* is a pronoun, there is no danger of error, for the meaning is "except that," as in "Nothing would please him *but that*." It is when both words are used as conjunctions that care must be exercised. In such a construction as "You need have no fear *that* she will go," the sense is clear that "she *will not* go"; but, in "You need have no fear *but that* she will go," the intention is clearly to express the feeling that "she is *sure* to go."

Best usage would eliminate *but* from "I have no doubt *but that* he will go," when the intention is to convey the feeling of certainty of his going. The form *but that* preceded by a negative becomes a positive—but it is more emphatic and less involved to say "I have no doubt *that* he will go."

"I cannot think (believe) *that* they will come" means that I believe strongly that they *will not* come; "I cannot think (believe) *but that* they will come" means that I must believe that they *will come*. "I can *but* believe him" means that, notwithstanding my own doubts, there is no other course open to me than to believe him; "I cannot *but* believe him" means that I am compelled to believe him—even against my will I am convinced. *But what* when used for *but that* is regarded as a vulgarism. These examples of the use of *but* illustrate what is meant by "English idiom."

By, With. *By* generally introduces the agent or doer; *with*, the instrument or means: "The window was broken *by* a boy *with* a ball." "The electricity is generated *by* water power." "The manager filled the theater *with* children." But, "The theater was crowded *by* the patrons of the opera."

By the name of. This phrase should not be confused with *of the name of*: "The business is owned by a man *of the name of* Brown." *Of the name* implies the real name; *by the name* suggests an assumed name; as, "Charles Farrar Browne was better known *by the name of* Artemus Ward than by his own name." It is well to substitute "a man *named* Brown" for "a man *of the name of* Brown."

By way of. We say correctly, "*by way of* illustration," meaning "*as* an illustration," or "*by way of* Cleveland" for "*through* Cleveland." In "He was *by way of* learning the country," *by way of* is an English colloquialism meaning "making progress in" or "occupied in."

Calamity. The word means, in an abstract sense, "source of misery or of loss," rather than the "loss" itself, for which it is often misused. *Calamities* are causes, of which *losses* may be the results. Any disaster produced by natural causes, as a hurricane, a cyclone, or a volcanic eruption, and attended by widespread destruction, is a *calamity* whether or not it be attended by loss of life.

Calculate. In the sense of *surmise, think, guess*, or *judge at random*, this word is a provincialism and is to be avoided: "I *think* (not *calculate*) tomorrow will be a fine day" but "His next move was *calculated* (that is, *designed*) to discourage his opponents."

Caliber. Often misused for *order*, as in "His work is of a higher *caliber* than hers." *Caliber* in its figurative sense applies to mental endowments. Thus, we may speak of a woman possessing great intellectual ability as being a person of *high caliber*, and of her work as being of high order, or excellent.

Can but, Cannot but. See *But*.

Can, May. Frequently confused. *Can* expresses power or ability; in most cases *may* expresses permission. Avoid "*Can* I speak to you a moment?" When you know that you *can speak* but wish merely for permission to do so, then substitute *may* for *can*. But, "*Can* you go?" is correct when the inquirer senses the possibility of obstacles that might prevent going; "*May* you go?" is also correct if permission to do so is involved.

Can not. Commonly and correctly written *cannot*. The origin of this form is in the shortened colloquial pronunciation of the two words.

Can't hardly. As *hardly* means "*not* easily" or "*not* quite," it must never be used with another negative as in this phrase. Substitute *can hardly*: "I *can hardly* believe the story."

Can't seem. Such an expression as "I *can't seem* to understand this problem" is to be avoided. Say, "I *seem unable* to understand." The inability is not in the *seeming* but in the *understanding*.

Capable, Susceptible. *Capable* is said of one's ability to do things, and in general it applies to the individual as having the capacity or intelligence to do; *susceptible* connotes action upon or sensitiveness to. Plans are *susceptible* of alteration; we are all *susceptible* to pain, that is, *capable* of being acted upon by it. One man may be *capable* of judging the fitness of another to fill a vacancy, yet he may not be *susceptible* to the blandishments of the applicant.

Capacity, Ability. These words are frequently confused. *Capacity* is the power of receiving or containing, and is used of the ability of the mind to accept ideas; it is the receptive mental faculty. *Ability* is power, either bodily or mental, and the word is sometimes used to describe mental endowments, or talents, of a superior kind. Some men possess the *ability* to help others although they have not the *capacity* to better their own conditions.

Carry. Provincial in the sense of *take, bring*, as in a carriage; as, "Father *carried* us all home with him." The word is archaic in the sense of *escort*: "He *carried* us to the party." Prefer "He *escorted (accompanied)* us."

Carry on. The phrase is in rather common colloquial use to mean "playing or behaving boisterously or indiscreetly." World War I gave us an intensified form of an old colloquial meaning, "maintain spirit and courage" or "keep work going in spite of difficulties."

Category. This formal word, preferably restricted to logical classification, should not be substituted indiscriminately for "class," "group," "rank," "species," and other more or less remotely associated synonyms.

Chairman. Correct usage sanctions *Mr. Chairman* and *Madam Chairman* as forms in which to address a presiding officer.

Cite, Quote. "Cite" means to refer definitely, as in footnotes listing sources and authorities. "Quote" is used only when the exact language of the source is given.

Claim. This word, as a verb, means "ask for" or "demand" by virtue of some authority or right, as in "We *claim* our share of the estate." It should not be used loosely for *say, assert, declare*, or *maintain*, as in "They *claim* that the water of the lake is warm."

Clever. As used in the sense of *good-natured* or *kindly*, this word is dialectal: "She is a *clever* woman." The commonly accepted sense today is *skillful, dexterous*, or *quick*. The word is used of mental alertness or mechanical ability. See *Synonyms*.

Clichés. The language is so full of ready-made phrases that it is easier to use them than to avoid them. Considered effective at first, these expressions have been worn threadbare by constant repetition. In the interest of freshness and originality, a different way of saying the thing should be attempted, at whatever cost in effort and initiative. It is really unnecessary to depend upon such stock phrases as "all nature seemed," "a bolt from the blue," "his better half," "the grim reaper," "the irony of fate," "wended our way," and "last but not least."

Clipped Endings. The practice of *"clipping"* the ending *-ing* is a vulgar error, as in *talkin', walkin', comin'.*

Coke Fiend. This is a vulgarism for an unfortunate individual addicted to cocaine or morphine. The term *addict* is the correct word to use. *Coke fiend* is in the same class as *rum hound* or *booze fighter.*

Commandeer. This word originated in South Africa during the Boer war. Its military meaning is "to compel to perform military service or to take for military purposes." As meaning "to take arbitrarily" it is in colloquial use only, the word *levy* or *requisition* being preferred by some as the literary term.

Company. The word is disapproved when used to mean "guests." Some writers look upon it as less formal, and therefore preferable, but no better word than *friends* need be used to express the intimacy of informal occasions. "The *company* has come" is decidedly provincial. "Our *friends* are here" and "The *guests* have arrived" serve to mark different degrees of formality.

Company, Corporation, Firm. With *company* or *firm*, either a singular or a plural verb is permissible; the word *corporation* takes a singular verb. A *corporation* is considered only as a unity, while one may think of a *company* or a *firm* either as a unit or as a number of partners.

Compared to, with. We may *compare* one thing *with* another in discussing the relative merits of both, but we *compare* one thing *to* another to point out some likeness: "*Compare* dead happiness *with* living woe." "*Compare* my life *with* his." "Life is *compared to* a voyage."

Comparison. In the *superlative degree*, comparison implies the inclusion of the things compared in a single group; in the *comparative degree* the things compared are thought of as in separate groups: *best of all; better than others.* See *Any, As, Else, Of.*

Complected. This is a dialectal word to be avoided. Say, "She is *dark-* (or *fair-*) *complexioned* (not *complected*)." Better still is the form, "She is of a dark (or fair) complexion." Frequently the simple "She is fair (or dark)" will serve.

Compliment, Complement. These words, so nearly alike and of the same origin, should not be confused. We say correctly, "They paid me the *compliment* of close attention" and "The ship had her *complement* (full number) of officers."

Comprised, Composed. These words are frequently confused. *Comprised* means "included"; *composed* means "made up" or "put together." We say correctly, "The ship's company *comprised* men of many nationalities," but "The bricks are *composed* of sand and clay."

Conclude, Decide. "Conclude" refers to the result of a reasoning process by which one reaches a point of mental certainty. "Decide" has to do with will and purpose. To decide is to resolve an issue or perhaps to settle upon a course of action.

Condone. The word should not be used for *compensate* or *atone*: "The abolition of the income tax would more than *compensate* (not *condone*) for the turmoil of an election." *Condone* means "forgive tacitly" or "overlook": "For the sake of tranquillity we *condone* many public faults."

Consequence. Etymologically, "a following together" and, from its original sense, "that which follows as a result of something that has preceded it." By an inversion, it has come to be used to signify importance or prominence acquired, as through the exercise of an office or through the ownership of land. Though some critics condemn this use of the word, it is authoritatively recognized and is logically sound: "He was a man of some *consequence* in his district."

Consider. The correct meaning of this word is "meditate," "deliberate," "reflect," "revolve in the mind." It should not be made to do service for *think, suppose,* and *believe*; as, "I *consider* that I have a bargain." This use, though frequent, is inappropriate.

Considerable. Frequently misused. Its association is with abstract rather than with concrete terms. A rich man may be one of *considerable* wealth, but we should not describe him as having *considerable* money. "We have had *considerable* rain" should be avoided. Prefer "an *abundance* of rain" or, more succinctly, "*plentiful* rain."

Contemptible, Contemptuous. Note the difference in point of view. A person who has done a wrong thing may be *contemptible*; that is, deserving of contempt. His attitude toward other people might be *contemptuous*; that is, he would show no regard for their judgments and opinions.

Continual, Continuous. The first of these words suggests recurring action, with intervals between; the second, unbroken occurrence, either in time or space: "Her *continual* nagging," "the *continuous* roar of the machinery."

Convince. This word, frequently misused in the sense of "persuade," means to gain mental assent, not to induce one to enter upon a course of action. "We persuaded (not convinced) him to go with us."

Correspond to, Correspond with. Things or people *correspond to* one another by agreeing or being parallel in certain respects; people *correspond with* one another by means of written communication.

Couple. The use of *couple* to mean merely "two" or "several" is vulgar or dialectal. The word correctly means "two like things or two persons acting in concert or so joined as to act together or to be considered together," as two mechanical parts or two partners in a dance.

Credible, Creditable. The latter word should not be used instead of *credible*, "believable." Say, "two *credible* (not *creditable*) witnesses." Say, "I am *credibly* (not *creditably*) informed." Formerly, *creditable* meant "credible," but this use is obsolete. It now means "commendable."

Curious. This word does not always mean "inquisitive," but frequently signifies "wrought with such care as to excite surprise" or "fashioned in such a way as to evoke surprise." The use of *curious* to mean "interesting," "unusual," or "novel" is sometimes condemned, but it is in good taste: "The museum possesses a collection of *curious* ornaments."

Data, Memoranda, Strata. These words are the plural forms of *datum, memorandum,* and *stratum,* but are sometimes construed erroneously as singulars: "The *datum* (singular) is here"; "The *data* (plural) are all here"; "This *memorandum* is clear"; "These *memoranda* are correct." To form the plural, an *s* has sometimes been added to the words *stratum, memorandum,* but never to *datum. Stratum,* being a technical word, should be more carefully used and its plural be written *strata.*

Deceiving. This should not be used in place of *trying to deceive.* When we suspect deception but are not *deceived,* we should say, not "He is *deceiving* me," but "He is *trying to deceive* me."

Defective, Deficient. "Defective" is used correctly to describe faultiness. "Deficient" refers to incompleteness in numbers or amount.

Delusion, Illusion. A "delusion" is an unsound idea arising within one's mind; an "illusion" is a false image from outside which deceives the senses, or sometimes an unreal concept that is more or less willingly accepted.

Demand. A transitive verb which always requires an object. We *demand* the payment of a debt. Do not say, "He *demanded* me to do it." Say, "He *demanded* that I should do it." "It" stands for the thing or act required. "They *demanded* their pay" is correct. The direct object of *demand* must be other than the person *of*, or *upon*, whom the demand is made.

Depot. See *Station*.

Deprecate, Depreciate. These words should not be confused. *Deprecate* means "regret," "express disapproval of": "His friends *deprecated* his hasty action." *Depreciate* means to "undervalue" or "decrease in value": "They *depreciated* the value of freedom"; "That stock has *depreciated* very greatly."

Desperately. The word should not be used to mean merely "seriously." It means "violently," "recklessly," "in a desperate manner." "He was *desperately* wounded" means wounded so seriously that he was beyond apparent hope of recovery.

Despite. This word may be preceded by *in* and followed by *of*, although *despite* has good standing as a preposition. Say, "*despite* all our efforts" or "*in spite* of all our efforts." *Notwithstanding* is a more dignified expression and has the same meaning.

Differ, Different. Persons or things *differ from* each other in appearance, size, etc. Persons may *differ with* each other in opinion. *Different from* is approved American usage, not *different to* or *different than*, both of which are accepted idioms in England, having substantial literary support, as of Goldsmith, John Henry Newman, and Thackeray. Shakespeare used *different from*.

Direct, Call. *To direct* some one's attention to a thing is more accurate and specific than *to call* his attention to a thing. Direct is the more formal.

Directly, Immediately. The use of *directly* as a synonym for *immediately* is sanctioned by good usage, though some critics pronounce it colloquial. One may say, "We will proceed *immediately* the train arrives" or "*immediately* after the train arrives." American usage prefers *immediately*. English usage favors *directly*.

Disapproval. Say, "He expressed *disapproval of* (not *with*) the dance."

Disinterested. Not lack of interest, but absence of partiality is indicated by this word. In the case of a controversy, for example, a disinterested third party is an unprejudiced observer.

Dissent. This word should be followed by *from*: "They *dissent from* our judgment." "They *dissent from* us." Compare *Differ*.

Do. Like other Anglo-Saxon verbs such as *make* or *put*, *do* has an almost unlimited variety of idiomatic uses. Examples are: "I *did* all the problems;" She *did* up the package;" "We could see that he was *done* for." Although many expressions containing *do* are informal, most of them are in good colloquial use and are popular because of their forcefulness. The various uses of *do* should be studied with the aid of a dictionary. Careful speakers will note the difference between acceptable and unauthorized forms. Thus they will say "I have *done* with the book," not "I am *done* (that is, *finished*,) with it."

Dock, Wharf. A *wharf* is a landing stage or pier; a *dock* is a body of water beside a *wharf* or between *wharves*. In American practice, *dock* is misused for *wharf*. Originally, *wharf* meant "bank" or "shore," and *dock* meant "ditch," "pit," or "pool." The distinction is more clearly apparent when one refers to the different forms of *dock* as *dry* or *graving dock*, *floating* and *wet dock*.

Don't, Doesn't. The first is a colloquial contraction for *do not*; the second, for *does not*. They should be used with care. Avoid "He *don't* want it." Say: "They *don't*," or "He *doesn't* want it."

Don't think. "I *don't think* it will rain" is an established idiom, as are other similar expressions in use.

Double Possessive. This construction is accepted as idiomatic English. Such phrases as "that house *of Brown's*" and "that car *of mine*" show the double possessive and may be used if required, but "*Brown's* house" and "*my* car" will usually express the thought more economically.

Doubtless. Because this word has become weakened through long use, it has given way in some cases to the stronger word "undoubtedly," or even to the intensive phrase, "beyond the shadow of a doubt." Other words denoting emphasis have fared similarly. Compare "soon" and "presently," which once meant "immediately."

Dozen, Dozens. After indications of price, *a dozen* or *the dozen* is correct. In American usage *a dozen* is preferred: "fifty cents *a dozen*." The phrases, "a pair," "a gross," "a tale," are used in like manner. Correctly we say, "several (or many) *dozens*"; but, when linked with definite numbers or used with *pairs*, *dozen* is the approved form, as, "four *dozen* pairs." See *Pair*.

Due to. That which may be attributed to a cause is *due to* it, but, to express cause or reason, *due to* is preferably used as a predicate complement: "His failure was *due to* unusual conditions." A sentence may begin with *because of* or *owing to*, but should not begin with *due to*. Example: *Because of* unusual conditions, he was unable to complete the work."

Each other. Properly applied to two only; *one another* must be used when the number referred to exceeds two. We say, "Great authors address themselves to *one another*," unless we refer to only two authors.

Eat, Ate, Eaten. These are the correct parts of the verb. Say, "He *ate* rapidly"; "I have *eaten* my dinner."

Effect, Affect. *Effect* means "bring about"; *affect* means "influence": "A man may *effect* a reform." "His ideas will *affect* the character of the reform." *Affect* may mean "pretend": "They *affect* an interest in the matter." *Effect* is sometimes used as a noun; *affect* is always a verb.

Effective. Associated with this word and related to it etymologically are several words that are usually differentiated from it in practice. Where "effective" means result-getting in a broad general sense, we speak of an "effectual" plea or prayer, an "efficacious" remedy, and an "efficient" machine or person.

Egoism, Egotism. One may be an *egoist*, that is, may habitually advocate the doctrine of *egoism*, or the pursuit of self-interest, as the supreme aim of human effort, and yet he may not be an *egotist*. *Egotism* is offensive conceit.

Either, Each, Both. Note the following correct expressions: "You may enter by *either* door (meaning *one* or the *other*)." "A bench is placed at *each* side of the doorway (that is, one on *one* side, one on the *other*)." "There were windows on *both* sides (or *each* side) of the doorway." Formerly, *either* was widely used in the sense of *each*, but this use is rare today.

Elemental, Elementary. "Elemental" refers to the basic forces or units of nature; "elementary" reduces anything to its simplest component parts for clear understanding.

Else, Else's. Such an expression as "Do not take *anyone else's* place" is good form and to be preferred to "Do not take *anyone's else* place," which has some defenders but is not accepted as sterling.

Else but. Avoid the use of *else* before *but* in the expression "I have no one *else but* you."

Emigrant, Immigrant. *Emigrants* are persons *going out* of a country, and *immigrants* are persons *coming into* it. *Emigrate* is derived from the Latin *e*, "out," and *migrare*, "to go from the land"; *immigrate*, from the Latin *im* for *in*, "into," and *migrare*.

Eminent, Imminent. Two words of similar sound but of widely different meanings. *Eminent* signifies "distinguished" or "well known": "He has become *eminent* in his profession." *Imminent* means "about to happen" or "threatening": "The defeat of the army was *imminent*."

Empty, Vacant. Anything that is "empty" is simply without contents or occupants. "Vacant" conveys the idea that it may have been occupied, or may be filled in the future.

Enclose, Inclose. The history of these words as well as general English usage favors *enclose* rather than *inclose*. But most recent dictionaries give *inclose* the preference. Either is correct.

Endorse, Indorse. Either form is correct, but, while *endorse* is used in literature, *indorse* finds favor in law and commerce. Do not say, "I *endorse* the movement." Say, "I *approve* it." Do not say, "*Indorse* the check *on the back*." Omit the last three words. *Indorse* means to write one's name *on the back* of commercial paper or documents.

Enjoyed the advantage. Trite phrase, elaborate and cumbersome substitute for "had."

Enthuse. It is better to speak of *being enthusiastic*. Typical of a large group of barbarisms known as "back-formations," *enthuse* is a coined verb suggested by the noun *enthusiasm*, but not derived from it by any proper linguistic procedure. Compare *burgle* (burglary), *laze* (lazy), and *orate* (oration). Although an occasional "back-formation" gains acceptance—for example, *diagnose*, *sidle*, *drowse*,—it is better as a rule to avoid such eccentric forms and to look for established synonyms.

Equally as well. An incorrect phrase. *As well* and *equally well* are correct forms.

Euphemisms. From an understandable wish to avoid offending sensitive ears, people tend to substitute long or abstract words for short plain ones. Thus, "imbibe" for "drink," "perspire" for "sweat," and "prevaricate" for "lie" stand for a long list of consciously watered-down synonyms. Not all of these substitute expressions are as ridiculous as "lady dog" and "gentleman cow," but euphemisms at best give an impression of linguistic timidity that is out of harmony with the times. People, especially moderns, are not so squeamish as these polite evasions would indicate. Within the bounds of decency, plain words are best.

Event, Eventuality. The first of these words indicates a definite happening; the second, an occurrence considered as a possibility.

Ever so, Never so. *Ever so* is correctly used to mean "exceedingly." Both phrases are used to mean "however" or "no matter how," as in "were he *ever so* (or *never so*) rich." Modern usage prefers *ever so* in all such cases.

Excuse, Pardon. While *pardon* is the more formal official word in respect to offenses, and *excuse* the more familiar in respect to minor matters, a further distinction is to be noted. For instance, when interrupting a conversation, one says, "*Pardon* the interruption," and, when leaving a guest, "*Excuse* me."

Exemption, Immunity. One claims *exemption* from taxes or from duty; one acquires *immunity* from disease, as by inoculation, or is granted *immunity* from punishment.

Expect. As this word means "look forward to as a contingency," it should never be used of any retrogression, for one cannot *expect* backwards. Not, "I *expect* you thought I would come yesterday," but "I *suppose*, etc." "I *expect* you know all about it" should be "*imagine*," "*think*," or "*suspect* you know." But "We *expect* that they will come" or "We *expect* them" is correct. Compare *Anticipate*.

Extempore, Impromptu. An *extempore* address is one delivered without manuscript and without memorization, though previous preparation may have been made by thought upon the subject treated. An *impromptu* speech is given on the moment, without previous preparation.

Farther, Further. Careful speakers and writers use *farther* for distances in space and *further* for continuity of other kinds: "We walked *farther* today than yesterday"; "The chairman said *further* (that is, *in addition*) that all dues must be paid promptly." *Further*, then, is used for expressions of continuity, as of thought or action: "I had no *further* dealings with him"; "a *further* rise in temperature."

Fascinating. As that which *fascinates* operates on its object as by some irresistible power, *fascinating* should not be used when *charming* or *attractive* is meant. Properly, that is *fascinating* or *bewitching* which possesses the art to please beyond the power of resistance; as, "Her *fascinating* manner and words disarmed suspicion."

Faulty Comparisons. Avoid double comparatives and superlatives. Say, "*worse*," not "*worser*"; "*abler*," not "*more abler*." Avoid impossible comparisons. Say, "*more nearly perpendicular, more nearly universal*," not "*more perpendicular, more universal*." Use the comparative degree for two objects, the superlative for more than two.

Fearful. A much overworked word. The meanings of the nouns from which such words as *dreadful*, *terrible*, and *fearful* are derived should always be borne in mind when the adjectives are used. The colloquial use of these words to express intense feeling or annoyance easily passes into extravagant hyperbole. Do not describe the falling off a horse as a *terrible* but rather as a *serious* accident. "He was *fearful* for our safety," that is, "He *feared* that we were in danger" is correct.

Female. In polite speech this word is restricted to sex or to animals. When applied to women, it is derogatory, and it should not be used in such expressions as "What is more delightful than the blush of a beautiful young *female*!"

Feminine words. Although the suffix "ess" is available for converting masculine nouns to feminine ones, usage rejects or questions some words formed in this way, while accepting others. Examples of well-established feminine words are "actress," "governess," "hostess," and "stewardess." Doubtful ones include "authoress," "doctress," "editress," "manageress," and "poetess." In such cases, the masculine word may be preferable for both men and women. It is the only one possible for words like "clerk," "lecturer," "singer," "teacher," and "typist."

Fewer, Less. *Fewer* refers to number; *less*, to quantity. Instead of "There were not *less* than ten chapters in the book," we should say, "There were not *fewer* than ten chapters in the book." But say, "The box weighed not *less* than ten pounds."

Fine. An adjective which should not be used as an adverb. Do not say, "She sang that *fine*," when you mean "well." "I like that *fine*" and "He is doing *fine*" are incorrect. Say, "I like that *very much*" and "He is doing *well* or *very well*."

First-rate. Do not use this adjective as an adverb. "She plays *first-rate*" is a vulgarism. *First-*

rate means "of the highest excellence or quality." "He is a man of *first-rate* ability" is correct.

Fix. Often misused colloquially for *arrange* or *repair*: "I must *fix* the books." "Who *fixed* the dishes on the shelves?" "He had the clock *fixed*." It is vulgarly used thus: "I will *fix* him"; "The jury was *fixed*"; "You must *fix* up, if you go"; "Your affairs are in a bad *fix*." *Fix* means "fasten," "make firm," or "settle": "The hooks are *fixed* in the wall." "Their income is a *fixed* amount."

Folk, Folks. Often incorrectly used interchangeably. Both words are construed as plurals, but the first refers to *people* or *peoples* generally, as "folk tales" or "fairy folk." In colloquial usage, *folks* has displaced *folk*. In "My *folks* have gone South," *folks* signifies "relatives." In "the *folks* next door," the word means "neighbors."

Forceful, Forcible. We speak of a "*forceful* style" or a "*forceful* personality," but of *forcible* ejection or *forcible* action of any kind. In usage, *forcible* is the more common word, and *forceful* the more special one.

Former—Latter. These words should be used only when they really economize space and save the reader's time. By repeating the antecedents (nouns or phrases), one avoids sending the reader back to see which is *former* and which is *latter*. Sometimes, however, a disagreeable repetition is avoided by using the *former*—the *latter*."

Fortuitous, Fortunate. "Fortuitous" refers to a chance happening that may be either favorable or unfavorable. "Fortunate" is restricted to favorable chance.

Funny. A word too frequently used when humor or amusement is not meant. Of something unusual, use *strange*, *odd*, *peculiar*, or a similar accurate word instead of *funny*: "It was a *peculiar* situation," not "*funny*" unless it is laughable.

Get, Got, Have. *Get*, like *do*, has many different meanings and is carelessly used. Avoid *get* for *be* and especially such expressions as "She will *get* laughed at for her pains." Say rather, "She will *be* laughed at," etc. If a man has inherited a fortune and has not dissipated it, we say correctly, "He *has* money"; if he obtains money through his own effort, we say correctly, "He *has gotten* money."

"*Get* a move on" is a forceful but inelegant Americanism for "Be quick about it."

Do not say, "*Get* up a show" when you mean plan or prepare. Colloquially, a *get-up* is an equipment consisting of dress and accessories and is very frequently correctly used, as in "a clever *get-up*" or "a stylish *get-up*." Avoid "Do you *get* me?" as the height of vulgarity.

"He *has got* to do it" is a common colloquialism. "He *has got* it to do" shows the wasteful character of the phrase. "He *has* it to do," "He *must* do it," or "He *has* to do it" is correct. We may, however, say correctly, "The cat *has got* the mouse," but "*caught* the mouse" is preferable.

Both *got* and *gotten* are correct forms of *get*, but careful writers tend to avoid *gotten*. As William Lyon Phelps said, "*Gotten* has *got* to go."

Get, meaning "become," is colloquial: "He will *get* well"; "as we *get* older."

Goes. In the phrase "anything *goes*" we have slang; in "the machine *goes*" we have idiomatic English. "That *goes* without saying" is a literal translation of a French idiom, in colloquial use.

Good. The use of the adjective *good* for the adverb *well* is vulgar. Avoid "I feel *good*" and "He is working *good*." Say rather: "I feel *well*"; "He is working *well*."

Grand. That which is *grand* is "magnificent," "noble," or "splendid," yet there is strong tendency to misapply the word. Today anything from a bit of chewing gum to Mt. Shasta is described as *grand*. The word should be used only of that which possesses grandeur.

Great. The indiscriminate use of this word is evidence of a poverty-stricken vocabulary: "We had a *great* time" is a colloquialism; "I like it *great*" is a vulgarism.

Had. "*Had* I thought of that, I should have come." This sentence is correct; but the common practice of inserting *have* after the pronoun is reprehensible. Shun "*Had* I have known," "*Had* I've known," "If I *had've*," "If I *had of* (*uv*)," if you wish to avoid being classed as illiterate.

Had better, as in "He *had better* look out," is excellent English idiom.

Had ought is a solecism for *should have*. *Ought* is not a participle. Say, "We *should have* or we *ought*," not "We *had ought*."

Hanged, Hung. Criminals are *hanged*, clothes are *hung*. This is an old distinction, still in force.

Hard, Hardly. The idiomatic adverb *hard* is in good use in such expressions as "He worked *hard*;" "Hit the line *hard*." *Hardly* cannot be used interchangeably with *hard*, because the two words differ in meaning. To say, "The battle was *hardly* won" may convey an idea opposite to the one intended. At best, the sentence is ambiguous. When a synonym for *scarcely* is needed, *hardly* is correctly used, as in the sentence "They will *hardly* succeed." In such cases the word is a useful negative of understatement. The adverb *hardly* is correctly followed by *when*, not *than*, as in "We had *hardly* taken our seats *when* the boat began to leak." The use of *hardly* with a negative added is a solecism, as in "I can't *hardly* tell." The correct form is "I can *hardly* tell."

Hate. A word that signifies "having a great aversion for," but used colloquially for *dislike* "I *hate* to do that kind of work." *Hate* is too strong a word for such use. Say, "I *dislike* to do that kind of work" or "I *detest* that kind of work."

Have to have. Avoid this useless repetition. Not, "I *have to have* my work done by three o'clock," but "I *must have* my work, etc." Do not say, "I *have got to get*" when "I *have to get*" is what you should say.

Healthful, Healthy. Note the distinction in meaning between these words. *Healthful* is applied to conditions or environments: "Children should be reared in *healthful* surroundings." *Healthy* describes a good physical condition, without disease. "A *healthy* mind in a *healthy* body is desirable."

Hear to it. We "*hear of*" an incident or "will not *hear of*" a course being pursued, but *hear to it* is archaic. *Hear* signifies "listen to"; formerly, "He will not *hear to* reason" was accepted as idiomatic, but it is now rendered "He will not *listen to* reason."

Hearty. "He ate a *hearty* breakfast" is good English idiom. *Hearty* means "strengthening" and "satisfying."

Hectic. A word which specifically means "habitual," "constitutional," being derived from the Greek *hexis*, "habit of body"; but it has come to mean "flushed" as with fever, or affected with such fever as accompanies tuberculosis. It is often misapplied, as in "*hectic* haste," in the sense of *feverish* or *excited*.

Hence, Thence, Whence. These words connote *removal from*; therefore, they should not be used with *from*. *Hence* is superfluous in such a sentence as "It will be many years *hence*, we apprehend, before he returns."

Historic, Historical. "Historic," a specialized word, means memorable; "historical," a more general term, means pertaining to history.

How. "I have heard *how*, in Italy, one is beset on all sides by beggars" should read "I have heard *that*, in Italy, etc." But "He told me *how* he worked his passage" is correct, since the reference is not to the fact, as in the first sentence, but to the manner of action.

How that and *as how*, as in "He told *how that* he would never return" or "He said *as how* he would go," are most objectionable colloquialisms.

However. Frequently misused for *how*, in such a sentence as "*However* could you tell such a story!" One should say, "*How* could you *ever* tell such a story!" *However* means "no matter what the extent of." "*However* careful you may be, you will make mistakes" is correct.

Hustle. Properly this word means "shove," "push," or "jostle roughly." Although frequently used colloquially for *hurry*, as in "*Hustle* that order along," it is not properly a synonym for *hurry*.

I, Me. These forms of the personal pronoun of the first person are frequently confused. *Me* is the form to use with a preposition. Say "between you and *me*," not "between you and *I*." Similarly, "with her (him) and *me*," not "with she (he) and *I*."

Idioms. Like every other living language, English is constantly forming idioms, that is, special combinations of words that do not follow the rules of either grammer or logic. Baffling to outsiders, these expressions are clear to the initiated and, despite their irregularity, are in good standing as language. Phrases like "by and large," "hold out," "make good," "pull through" and innumerable others illustrate this phase of English expression.

If. *Whether* in place of *if* is preferred by most authorities in sentences like these: "I do not know *if* (*whether*) the book will suit you"; "I wonder *if* (*whether*) he has come." The use of *if* for *whether* is colloquial or poetic. *Whether* is preferable to *if* especially where the additional idea of *or not* is implied. Compare "Let me know *if* you can go," and "Let me know *whether* you can go."

Ill, Sick. English usage confines the word *sick* chiefly to the meaning "nausea," as, *a sick headache;* but in America *ill* and *sick* are generally synonymous. However, we say: "He is a *sick* man," never "He is an *ill* man"; but, either "He is *ill*" or "He is *sick*."

In, Into. *In* is sometimes an adverb and sometimes a preposition, but its employment as an adverb is really an elliptical use of the preposition. As an adverb, *in* is correctly used in these sentences: "Come *in*," for here *in* means "into the house, room, etc."; and likewise, "Go *in*," meaning "Go into the room, house, etc." As a preposition, *in* may be used with verbs of rest or of motion and *into* with verbs of motion only: "He sat *in* his chair"; "The child runs *in* the yard"; "He walked *into* the house."

In back of. The expression "They sat *in back of* us," meaning "behind," though analogous to "They sat *in front of* us," is disapproved. *Behind* accurately expresses the thought. As to *in front of*, we have no corresponding preposition, since *before* may convey the idea of *facing* and thus may produce ambiguity.

Individual. The word is jocosely or contemptuously used for *person*. It is used correctly in "Changes both in *individuals* and in communities are often produced by trifles"; contemptuously in "That *individual* left here several hours ago."

Indulge. This word means "give oneself up to (something)"; "yield to one's longings or passions unrestrainedly"; "give free course to one's habits"; "humor to excess, as children." Thus, one *indulges* in idleness, or one *indulges* children's whims or wishes. While one may *indulge* a thirst for fame, one should avoid "I never *indulge*" as objectionable in declining an offer of refreshment.

Infer, Imply. These words are frequently confused. One *infers* or *reasons* or *draws a conclusion* from something heard or read. One may *imply* (*suggest*) in what one writes or says, for example "One *infers* from what Jefferson wrote that the Declaration of Independence *implies* belief in democracy."

Inferior to. Note that the correct form is *inferior to*, not *inferior than*. Example: "The substitute is nearly always *inferior to* the original product. *Superior to* is of course the corresponding idiom.

-ing. See *Clipped Endings*.

Ingenious, Ingenuous. *Ingenious* means "skillful," "inventive": "The boy is *ingenious* and loves machinery." *Ingenuous* means "candid," "frank," "open," "innocent," "guileless": "He made an *ingenuous* reply."

In our midst. Condemned by most critics as a substitute for *in the midst of* (*us*). The purist prefers *among us*.

In so far as. A phrase formed on the analogy of *in as much as*, but *so far as* expresses the thought and *far* is itself an adverb; therefore *in* is superfluous. "*In so far as* I know" should be "*so far as* I know." In "*in as much as*." *much* is a noun and requires a preposition to give the phrase adverbial force.

Intend. See *Mean*.

In or Under the circumstances. Both phrases are in good use. *Circumstances* may imply merely attendant conditions not thought of as seriously modifying action. *In* is then the proper preposition; as, "*In the circumstances* he hesitated." But when *action* is thought of as determined by the circumstances, as, "*Under the circumstances* prosecution of the case could not be avoided," *under* is the approved word.

Irrelevant. The word means "unconnected with" or "not related to": "His remarks were *irrelevant* to the discussion." Do not pronounce it *irrelevant*.

Is that so? Courtesy will prompt a thoughtful person to be careful *how* and *when* he uses this and the similar phrase, "You don't say so," for they imply doubt or disbelief as well as express surprise. As subject to equivocal interpretation they should be avoided. "I want to know," used in a similar sense, is vulgar.

Its, It's. Sheer carelessness causes many people to confuse the spelling of the possessive pronoun "its" ("A tree is known by its fruit") with the contraction of "it is" ("It's going to rain").

Junk. Colloquial or slang when used as a verb for *discard*, or "throw away as useless."

Just. This adverb is correctly used for *precisely, only, merely*, or *by a slight margin*; it is colloquial when the meaning is "quite," "very," "altogether," or "simply." Say, "I *just* missed the car," but not "The hostess was *just* lovely, but the food was *just* awful." Such a statement is ambiguous.

Kind. The word is singular. One should say, "this *kind*," not "these *kind*." But "those *kinds*," not "those *kind*." is correct.

Kind of. Avoid the use of *a* as a modifier before a noun when preceded by *kind of*. "What *kind of* man is he?" is correct. "What *kind of a* man is he?" is incorrect.

Kind of tired, amusing, etc., are slovenly speech. *Somewhat tired, rather amusing*, are preferred.

Lady. Address a woman who is a stranger to you as *Madam*, and not as *Lady*. Persons of culture do not say, "She is a fine *lady*," "a clever *lady*"; they use *woman* instead. Ladies say, "The *women* of America," "*women's* interests." In like manner use *man* or *men* instead of *gentleman* or *gentlemen*.

Last, Latest. We speak of an author's *latest* book, but hardly of his *last* book until he is dead. But we say properly, "Have you read the *last* number of this magazine?" Here *last* means "latest in a series."

Last two. This phrase is preferred by most authorities to *two last*: "They bought the *last two* copies."

Laundered. The clothes were *laundered*, not *laundried*.

Lay, Lie (verbs). *Lay* is transitive and denotes an *action* on an *object*; *lie* is intransitive and designates a *state* or a *condition*: "I *lay* the rug on the floor, and it *lies* there." "They *laid* him with his fathers." "He *lies* with his fathers." The following expressions are idiomatic: "A thing *lies* by us until we bring it into use"; "We *lay* it by for some future purpose."

The confusion arises probably from the fact that *lay* appears in both verbs. The words are correctly used in the following sentences:

I *lay* the book on the table today.
I *laid* it there yesterday.
I have *laid* it there every day.
I am *laying* it there now.
I *lie* on my bed today.
I *lay* there yesterday.
I have *lain* there every day.
I am *lying* there now.

Lay, Lie (nouns). Both of these words are in good use to signify the manner in which land *lies* in its relation to the surrounding country. "The *lay* of the land" is in popular favor; "the *lie* of the land" has the support of the scientists. The latter is the older English usage.

Learn, Teach. Formerly, *learn* and *teach* were used interchangeably, but now to confuse them is a mark of illiteracy. We *learn* things for ourselves; we try to *teach* others.

Leave, Let. One takes one's *leave*, after a call or visit. We ask *leave* or *permission*. One is *on leave*, that is, enjoying a permitted absence from his usual place of duty. Do not say "*Leave* him do it," but "*Let* him do it." Properly, one *leaves* (goes away from) a place, but he *lets* a person or thing alone, that is, does not meddle or interfere. Still, one correctly asks to be "*left* to himself," that is, asks others to "*leave*" or "go away from" him.

Legible, Readable. A "legible" piece of writing is clear to the eye, that is, easily deciphered. A "readable" book is one that invites reading because of its interesting style and content.

Lend, Loan. The verb *lend* is the general word to use when we supply something to another with the understanding that it is to be returned. Say, "*Lend* (not *loan*) me the books or money." The use of *loan* as a synonym for *lend*, although of English origin, has been condemned as an Americanism; but it has fallen into disuse except in financial circles. One says correctly, "He tried to get a *loan* from the bank," where *loan* is used as a noun. "The company *loans* money on good security"; here the word is used as a verb.

Less. See *Fewer*.

Let alone. A vulgarism when used to mean "excluding," "not to mention." Avoid such expressions as "The inconvenience was bad enough, *let alone* the expense."

Like, As. *Like* is not used for *as* in the New England States; the use is common in the South and the West. The phrase *like of that* should be avoided in "We spend our days fishing, canoeing, and the *like of that* (or *like that*)," for it is a vulgarism. Do not say: "Do *like* I do"; "I felt *like* I would faint"; "My feet were heavy *like*"; or "He had *liked* to have been killed," meaning "came near to being killed." Say: "Do *as* I do"; "I felt *as if*"; "My feet *seemed* heavy." But one may say, "She walks *like* a queen," meaning "in the manner of." To use the tautological phrase *like as if* is to display one's ignorance.

Like, Likely. The first is frequently erroneously used in conversation instead of the second. *Like* means "similar," "corresponding," "equal," and "resembling." *Likely*, as an adjective, means "probable," "suitable," "adaptable," or, adverbially, "to be reasonably expected." Avoid "He is *like* to call today" as illiterate. The following is correct: "In *like* circumstances, a repetition of the occurrence is *likely*."

Like, Love. See *Love*.

Literally. This word is often used for emphasis as a synonym for "actually," "positively" or some other intensive adverb. Its real meaning, "according to the letter," places it in direct opposition to "figuratively."

Loan. See *Lend*.

Locate. Colloquial for *settle* or *establish*. Prefer "He *settled* in Colorado"; "They *established* their business in Birmingham."

Lot, Lots. These words are in colloquial use for *much, many*; as, "a *lot* of money," "*lots* of people." Prefer "a *great deal* of money," "*much* money," "*many* people."

Love, Like. *Love* is a much abused English word. In modern practice *like* is used where taste is concerned and where no strong emotion is involved. One who delights in sweets is appropriately said to *like* candy. Of course one may *like* a person without *loving* him—that is, enjoy his companionship. We *love* wives, husbands, sweethearts, children, friends, truth, country.

Lunch, Luncheon. The second of these words is the more formal, or perhaps we should say, the more pretentious. Its use borders on verbal elegance. In general it will be avoided, except by people who *purchase* things instead of buying them, and who *reside*, not *live*, at a certain address.

Luxurious, Luxuriant. Do not confuse these words. The first describes that which is "gratifying to the senses"; the second means "growing in abundance." Correctly we speak of *luxurious* furnishings and of *luxuriant* foliage or vegetation.

-ly, adverbial suffix. Although "ly" is usually added to adjectives to form adverbs, only a misinformed purist would insist on using it in all cases. "Slow," for example, is a good adverb, with or without the "ly," and "fast" cannot use it. "Illy" and "thusly" are conspicuous examples of its mistaken application. Persons familiar with historical grammar will recall that adjectives ending in "ly" were once common. A few of them still persist, as "a comely lass," "a goodly number."

Mad. When used to signify "very angry," this word is a careless colloquialism. *Mad* properly means "crazy."

Manner, Manor. The correct phrase is *to the manner born*, not *to the manor born*. The phrase means "familiar with from birth."

Materialize. When used to mean "take shape" or "happen," the word is colloquial. Improperly used in the general sense of *appear*.

Mathematics. When considered as embracing the science of mathematics in its entirety as a concrete term, this word is construed with a verb in the singular; as, "*Mathematics is* the science that treats of quantities, their properties and relations, especially by the use of symbols"; "*Mathematics is* a subject in the course of study." But, when used distributively, to convey the idea of its different branches or divisions, the word is construed with a verb in the plural; as, "*Mathematics are* mere evolutions of necessary ideas." It should be borne in mind that mathematics are classified as *pure* or *abstract*, *applied* or *mixed*, and *qualitative*, as projective geometry.

Mean. Do not use *mean* as an adjective for *sick*, *unpleasant*, or *ashamed*. Say, "He felt *ashamed* of it," not "He felt *mean* about it."

Mean, Intend, Purpose. Best usage may be illustrated as follows: "By this statement I *mean*, etc."; "We *intend* to go"; "He *purposes* a thorough test of the machine." *Purpose* is a stronger word than *intend* and implies more careful thought.

Meanwhile. "Meanwhile" is an adverb of time equivalent to the phrase, "in the meantime." It is grammatically wrong, therefore, to say "in the meanwhile."

Meet. To say, "*Meet* Mr. A.," when introducing a friend, is bad form. But we say correctly, "Have you ever *met* Mrs. B.?" meaning "been introduced to." Prefer "I want you to *meet* Mrs. A." or "May I introduce Mr. A.?"

Middling. This word is an adjective, meaning "moderate," and should not be used as an adverb; therefore, we should not say that a thing is *middling* good, or that a thing is *middling* well done. "He resided in a town of *middling* size" is correct, but "of *moderate* size" is preferable.

Mighty. When used instead of *exceedingly very*, or *extremely*, this word is a colloquial intensive. Correctly used, *mighty* is a strong word indicating power of unusual force or quality; as, a *mighty* flood, a *mighty* monarch. It may connote uncommon size; as, *mighty* mountains.

Mistaken. The expression "If I am not *mistaken*," though sometimes condemned as incorrect, is idiomatic and has been in use for several centuries with the sense "If I am not making a *mistake*." "If I *mistake* not" is more formal, but it is thought by some to be stilted.

More than. Although its form implies plurality, this phrase is correctly construed as a singular: "*More than* one *is* there" or "There *is* more than one there."

Most. As a contraction of *almost*, this word is a provincialism: "The dress is *almost* (not *most*) finished." The use of *most* in the phrases *most perfect*, *most complete*, is sanctioned by good usage, on the ground that things are at best but relatively perfect or complete. Avoid the misuse of *most* in such colloquial forms as *most anybody* or *most anything*.

Muskrat. Do not say *mushrat*.

Mutual, Common. Recent writers do not insist so strongly upon the distinction between these two words. "We have *common* friends" or "We have *mutual* friends." *Mutual*, strictly, means "reciprocal," "existing between two parties"; but, because the meaning "ordinary" may be implied by the word *common*, many people prefer to say, "*mutual* friends," in spite of critics. There is, however, a clear and worth while distinction between the two words. *Common* means "belonging to all" as well as "ordinary." When we speak of a *mutual* friend we mean "one who reciprocates our friendship," and, when we refer to a *common* friend, we mean "one whose friendship we share in common with other friends of his." The sentence "We have many friends in *common*" illustrates the point clearly, and is a good substitute for "We have many *common* friends." Persons interested in the same things have *common* interests. When they are interested in each other, their interest is *mutual*.

Myself. This pronoun is an emphatic or reflexive form for the first person and should be used only where emphasis is required, as in "Who did it? I *myself*," that is, "I alone did it." It is incorrect to say, "Mary and *myself* were satisfied" or "Two friends and *myself* went." Say, "Two friends and I went" or "I went with two friends." Do not say, "*Myself*, I do not like it."

Named. See *By the name of*.

Neither, Neither nor. Because *neither*, like *either*, properly refers to one of two, it calls for a singular verb. Example: "Of the two leading candidates, *neither was* considered capable of filling the office." The singular is also used with *neither nor*, since the two persons or things mentioned are taken separately, and not together, as in "*Neither* John *nor* William is qualified."

New. Distinguish between *new* and *novel*. That which is *new* may be *novel*, but that which is *novel* need not be *new*. Anything striking or *different* from things with which we are familiar may be called *novel*. To say "*new* beginner" seems to argue utter indifference to the sense of words. To be a beginner is quite sufficient.

News. Notwithstanding its plural appearance, "news" is singular. Thus, we say "The news is good." Compare "acoustics," "politics" and other singular nouns ending in "s."

Nice. This word means "exact" or "discriminating," not "pleasant" or "good." A *nice* distinction is one resulting from discriminating reasoning; one who is *nice* in regard to matters of food is fastidious and hard to please; *nice* food is inviting, dainty food. Anything that is done or made with scrupulous exactness, precision, or accuracy is termed *nice*; as, a *nice* balance, that is, an exact balance; *nice* workmanship, that is, the result of skilled labor.

Nicely. This word is frequently misused in the attempt to make it do service for *well*, in this wise: "How will this pen do?" "*Nicely*." "How are you?" "*Nicely*." Use *well* or *very well*, for *nicely* means "accurately," "becomingly," "exactly."

None. A word that may be used with a verb in either the singular or the plural, depending on the intention of the person who uses it; as, "*None* of *these* things *move* me"; "*None* but the brave *deserves* the fair."

Nor, Not. Use *nor* and not *or* after *no* when the definite exclusion of two distinct persons or things is intended; as, "He has *no* father *nor* mother." But we use *or* when the following word merely explains the preceding: "The boy has *no* father *or* guardian." After *not*, when the single negation applies to both objects, use *or*: "They do *not* see *or* hear." But say, "They do *not* come, *nor* do they intend to come," where two separate negations are implied. Here *nor* is, logically, the equivalent of *and not*. For logic, watch the position of *not*. Do not say, for example, "All Democrats are *not* Free Traders," but "*Not* all Democrats are Free Traders."

No use. "It is *no use* to do that" should be "It is *of no use* to do that" or, preferably, "It is *useless* to do that."

Novice. See *Amateur*.

Nowhere. Do not say, "*nowhere* (or *nowheres*) near so much," because *nowhere* means "not in any place or anywhere" or, by extension, "at no time." "Not nearly so much" is correct.

Number. A word that can be correctly construed with a verb in the singular or the plural, depending on the idea to be expressed or the word on which emphasis is placed. We say correctly, when thinking of the individuals of a group, "A large *number were* (not *was*) there." Similarly, "There *are* a large *number* of people" or "There *are* many." But, if we intend to convey the idea of a unit, we say "The *number* of women present *was* small." When any phrase that has qualifying force seems to contradict in number the noun or verb with which it is used, an adjective should be substituted, so that the sentence shall correspond in form with the idea it is intended to convey. For example, "A *number* of changes *was* made," or "A *number* of changes *were* made." Better,—"*Numerous changes were* made."

Observance, Observation. *Observe* the following distinction: "Close *observation* of our customs shows too little *observance* of Sunday and of patriotic anniversaries." *Observation* means "the act of looking at or examining," or the result of such action. *Observance* implies recognition, as with service or ceremony.

Of, Off. See *Prepositions.* The two words are from the same source and are subject to confusion in common speech.

When *of* follows a superlative, the thing referred to as best, largest, etc., is to be thought of as included in a whole group; hence the rule requiring *of all* in the following: "She was the loveliest *of all* (not *any*)." "He was the least observed *of all* (not *all others*)." *Any* and *others* imply separation of groups for comparison, and are used appropriately only with the comparative degree: "He was less observed than *any* of the others (who were observed—understood)." *Any* requires *other*(*s*) or *one* else or a similar expression to follow it.

Off of, Off from. *Of* or *from*, in these phrases, should be omitted from such a sentence as the following: "The pears fell *off* (*of*) (*from*) the tree." *Off* expresses the idea of separation. *Of* and *from* are superfluous.

O. K. This commercial expression is used as noun, adjective, and verb: "Give this your *O. K.* (approval)"; "His work is *O. K.* (all right, correct)"; "He refused to *O. K.* (approve) the order." Since *O. K.* as an adjective means "all right," do not say "all O. K.": "The requisition is *O. K.* (not *all O. K.*)."

Old Adage. See *Adage.*

One—One's. While purists insist that *one*, as in the sentence "*One* meets *one's* friends in the city," should be followed by *one's* and never by *her* or *his*, usage sanctions either form where no ambiguity would result. But after *anyone, every one, no one*, etc., use *he* (*his*) or *she* (*hers*): "*No one* knows where *he* will meet an acquaintance." Never use *they* (*their*) with *one* in such a sentence as "*Every one* makes *his* own choice," for *one* is singular. Do not say, "When *one* travels, *you* want pleasant companions," for *one* is a pronoun of the third person, and any following pronoun used in its place should be of the same person. Generally, avoid the use of *one* when a repetition of the word would be required.

Ones. Instead of saying, "I do not like the other *ones*," say, "I do not like the *others*." *Ones* is in good use only in such phrases as "big *ones*" and "little *ones*": "Here are big stones and little *ones*."

One time, Then. Such expressions as her *one time* guardian and the *then* bishop of New York are convenient, clear, and economical, and they are approved by good authority.

Only. This word is probably more often misplaced than any other word in the language. "He *only* sang for us." "He sang *only* for us." The first sentence means that he *sang*, but did not *play* for us; the second means that he sang for *us* and not for *anyone else*. *Only* is regularly placed before the word it modifies: "*Only* he (or *only* John) sang for us. That is, no one else sang.

Onto, On to. The use of *onto* in such expressions as "He got *onto* the platform with difficulty" is justified by good authority. This use follows the analogy of *upon, into*, and others implying motion. Some authorities do not yet allow *onto*, although they approve *on to*, but the two forms have quite distinct uses. One should not say, "He walked *onto* the next town," but "He walked *on to* the next town."

Oral, Verbal. *Verbal* means "in words," either *spoken* or *written*; *oral* means "uttered by the mouth," "spoken."

Other. This word should not be omitted from sentences like the following: "He said that his wife was dressed better than any *other* woman there." The omission of *other* makes the statement include the person spoken of in the group with which she is compared. In stating a comparison avoid comparing a thing with itself.

Ought, Should. *Ought* is the stronger term. What we *ought* to do, we are morally bound to do: We *ought* to be truthful and honest, and we *should* be respectful to our elders.

Over, Across. There is a nice distinction between these words: A dog walks *across* the street, but he leaps *over* an obstruction. *Across* suggests merely passage from one limit to another; *over* also implies elevation. See *Prepositions.*

Overlook, Oversee. *Overlook* means, usually, "miss seeing," "not notice": "He *overlooked* the important point." *Oversee* means "supervise." *Look over* may mean "examine."

Own. The use of *own* to mean "admit to be true" or "concede" is supported by good usage; as, "He *owned* to his fault." Colloquially, *own* has come to mean "confess" or "clear one's mind of a matter," as in the sentence "He was accused and finally *owned* up."

Pair. With numbers, as "three *pairs*," best usage favors the plural, the use of the singular, as "three *pair*," being confined to trade cant. See *Dozen.*

Parcel post. This form is correct, not *parcels post.*

Partake. The word means, literally, "take part," "share." In this sense, several persons may *partake*, or one may *partake* with others. But the word is also in good use to mean "take" or "appropriate," without reference to sharing; as, "He *partook* of the food."

Party. The word should not be used generally for *person*. Not "the *party* that I saw," but "the *person* that I saw." We speak correctly, however, of the *parties* to a contract or an agreement.

Passive Progressive. Modern practice prefers "The church *is being built*" or "Cattle *are being sold* at fifty dollars a head" to the former usage "The church *is building*" or "Cattle *are selling*, etc. Say, "The boy *is being taught*," not "The boy *is teaching*," when the intention is to express the idea that the lad is receiving instruction.

Pep. Expressive slang for *energy, vigor*, but as yet it seems usually to need an apology.

Per. This preposition, originally taken from Latin phrases like *per diem* (by the day) and *per annum* (by the year), is often found in hybrid expressions such as "Ten dollars *per* day" or, worse still, in the clipped form, "Ten dollars *per*." It is much better to use consistent English, as in "Ten dollars *a* day."

Perform. Say, "She *plays* the piano beautifully," not "She *performs* beautifully on the piano." This sentence would be improved by using *well* or *admirably* in place of *beautifully*.

Place (verb). *Place* means "lay in position." Some authorities think one should say, "*place* a thing *into* a box"; but there is hardly enough of the idea of motion in the word *place* to justify *into*. *Place in* is more appropriate.

Plan on. "Do you *plan on* going?" A provincialism better expressed by "Do you *plan* going?"

Plebiscite. A word introduced into English from the French many years ago. Its recent revival is one of the results of World War I. The word means "a referendum, or vote of the people, in a district or state."

Plenty, Plentiful. One may say, "There will be *plenty* of fruit this fall"; but good usage calls for "Fruit will be *plentiful* (not *plenty*)." Used as an adverb, "plenty" has a colloquial crudity that is especially objectionable; for example, "plenty good" instead of "very good."

Plurality, Majority. "The president received a *plurality* of the votes cast for all candidates throughout the country" means that he received more than any other candidate. "The election of an officer requires a *majority*" means that election requires one vote or more in excess of half the total number of votes.

Point of view. Frequently expressed by *standpoint* or *viewpoint* in common usage. Most authorities frown upon *viewpoint* and prefer *point of view*. *Standpoint* is well established. Some would even use *angle* as a synonym. This last word is still colloquial, but there is a tendency to accept it.

Politics. American usage approves *politics is*; English usage approves *politics are*.

Ponderous phraseology. Either through deliberate affectation or through unconscious imitation of "fine" writing, people may fall into the habit of using showy or pedantic phraseology. For example, instead of being "thanked," a person may be "made the recipient of grateful acknowledgments." Charles Dickens depicted several characters whose linguistic finery emphasized the shabbiness of their personalities. Thus, instead of quoting the simple Anglo-Saxon saying that "a cat can look at a king," Mr. George, in *Martin Chuzzlewit*, translates: "I have heard it said that a cat is free to contemplate a monarch." On this subject, a word to the wise should be sufficient.

Possessive with Verbal Noun. "We did not know of *his* going." "The idea of *our* doing such a thing." "The fact of the *team's* playing at home interested him." These sentences represent approved usage. Occasionally, in the use of nouns, the possessive seems awkward or sounds harsh, and is omitted as unnecessary.

Post, Mail. The distinction in the use of these words is merely national. We *mail* letters in the United States and *post* them in Great Britain.

Posted. The use of this word for *informed*, in such expressions as "The man *posted* me" and "If I had been better *posted*," should be discouraged in favor of *informed*.

Practical, Practicable. *Practical* means "not theoretical" or "concerned with doing rather than with reasoning." *Practicable* means "capable of being done under given conditions": "A *practical* man will suggest *practicable* plans."

Practically, Virtually. These words are both used to mean "essentially" or "in reality": "The battle was *practically* over"; "He is *virtually* bankrupt." *Virtually* is preferred as expressing actuality in referring to conditions that exist but are not self-evident; for example, "Fighting continued *practically* all night, but the issue of the battle had already been *virtually* decided."

Prefer. "For making bread, do you *prefer* wheaten flour or corn flour?" "I *prefer* wheat *to* corn." Do not say, "I *prefer* wheat *rather than* corn." The *pre-* in *prefer* supplies the sense of *rather* or *before*.

Prejudice. This word connotes a bias or unfavorable attitude toward a person or thing and should not be used to indicate approbation, as in "The man is *prejudiced* in his favor." We should say, "He is *predisposed* (or *prepossessed*) in his favor."

Prepositions at Ends of Sentences. Sentences that end with prepositions are frequently more terse, always quite as idiomatic, and invariably simpler than they might be if differently constructed: "the man I gave it *to*" or "the man *to* whom I gave it"; "the verb it belongs *to*" or "the verb *to* which it belongs."

Pressure. This word in the sense of *influence* frequently carries a sinister meaning, but when it signifies *urgency* it is in good use; as, "the *pressure* of affairs or of business."

Pretty. Correctly used as an adverb, in such expressions as *pretty soon* or *pretty well*, meaning "rather," "somewhat." However, its repeated use tends to restrict one's vocabulary, to the exclusion of more appropriate words.

Preventive. Among careful speakers this word has never had any competition from the awkward and undesirable form *preventative*. Unless the long and the short form represent two different meanings, as in *visit* and *visitation*, the shorter one is always preferable. Compare the verbs *experiment* and *experimentalize*.

Previous to, Previously to. Both are in good use, but *previously* is necessary when the idea is adverbial: "*Previously to* our coming the affair had been settled." But we say correctly, "That event was *previous to* our coming." The same principle applies to *subsequent, relative*, etc.

Principal, Principle. *Principal*, usually an adjective ("The *principal* advantage"), is also used as a noun: "The *principal* of a school," "*principal* and interest." *Principle* is always a noun: "Both machines operate on this *principle*."

Proceeds. Use the plural verb with this word: "The *proceeds were* (not *was*) applied."

Procure. Usually, Anglo-Saxon *get* is preferable to Latin *procure*; e.g., "Where did you *get* it?", not "Where did you *procure* it?" *Procure* suggests provision for the future, as in the *procurement* of military supplies.

Promise. Often misused for *assure*, as in "I *promise* you I was agreeably surprised," which should be "I *assure* you, etc." The word *promise* refers to the future: "We *promise* to do our best."

Propose, Purpose. These words are not exact synonyms, as the following sentence shows: "I *propose* to build a house and *purpose* to live in it when it is ready." *Propose* implies a definite, specific plan; *purpose*, a more general intention.

Proposition. Commercial cant for *proposal, task*, or *undertaking*, all of which are preferable.

"Proud" words. At some time or other nearly everyone increases his working vocabulary by the addition of words that seem to lend distinction to his style. Through succeeding decades various words have served in this capacity. Once the favorite was "intriguing," then "devastating," then "priceless." As one man said when his attention was called to this matter, "Now that you have made me self-conscious, I believe that 'currently' is currently my favorite." Caution regarding these "vogue" words is advisable for two reasons. First, they are likely to be overused; secondly, they soon become vague and general in meaning.

Prove. In the past tense and the past participle, *proved*, not *proven*, is correct, except in legal papers.

Providing. This should not be used for *provided*: "He offered to furnish a car, *provided* (not *providing*) the company would pay for gasoline and repairs."

Punch. Slang for *energy, effectiveness*.

Put. Like *do*, *put* has many meanings that are not in good literary use: *put*, meaning "go" or "get out"; *put up with* (*endure*); *put out* (*displease*); *put past*, as in "I should not *put* it *past* him," meaning "I suspect him to be capable of it"; *put up*, as in "He *put up* at the hotel (*stayed at*)." A forceful idiomatic phrase is *stay put*.

Quite. The word means "entirely," "completely," "altogether": "The building is *quite* complete." It means, in addition, "to a considerable extent or degree," "noticeably"; as, "The water is *quite* cold"; "The day was *quite* warm." The word is not properly used to mean "very" or "rather," as in "The book is *quite* interesting" or "She is *quite* ill." Such a colloquial phrase as *quite a bit* is questionable. *Quite some* is vulgar.

Raise. This word is applied in America to the bringing up of children, although formerly its use was common in this sense in England also. Modern usage applies the word to the breeding and rearing of animals and to the propagation and nurture of plants. Thus one may raise children, animals, and plants. Children and animals may be reared.

Re, In re. A piece of old law Latin transferred to business letters and not an abbreviation of *regarding*, as it is frequently taken to be. It means "matter," "in the matter of," or "on the subject of." The English phrase *referring to* is preferable and is, in fact, very generally used.

Real. Avoid the misuse of this word as an adverb in the sense of *very*. Say, "The house is *very* (not *real*) pleasant." The adverb *really* means "actually," as in "The story is *really* true."

Recipe, Receipt. The confusion of these two words is very old. Both words formerly meant a "medical formula," for which today we use the word prescription. While both are still applied to *cookery directions* there is a strong tendency in the best modern usage to reserve this sense for the word *recipe*, *receipt* being employed for commercial and other use in the sense of *receiving* or in *acknowledgment of receiving*. Say, "He paid the bill and was given a *receipt*"; "She has an excellent *recipe* for making clam chowder."

Recollect, Remember. *Recollect* refers to the recalling of events or facts, while *remember* refers to what may be in the mind continually: "He *remembers* very well his early youth." "I *recollect* now my first visit to the circus."

Regard. The plural of this word is sometimes erroneously used in the phrase *in regards to*, meaning "relating to," "concerning," or "about." It is correctly used in "He spoke *in regard to* bonuses."

Regrettable, Regretful. Strange to say, these words are often confused, even by otherwise careful speakers. An act may be "regrettable," that is, something to be regretted. A person's attitude may be "regretful" as he contemplates the act and its consequences.

Relations, Relatives. The following sentence illustrates the preferred use of these words: "One's *relations* with one's *relatives* may be pleasant or unpleasant." *Kin* or *kinsfolk* implies blood relationship.

Respectively, Respectfully. Do not confuse these words: "They were called *respectively* (that is, *in the order named*) Jim, Sam, and Al"; but "They were *respectfully* called (that is, *in a respectful manner*) James, Samuel, and Albert."

Risqué. Sometimes written *risky*. The words are not properly used as synonyms. That which is *risqué* is broadly suggestive to the point of obscenity; it borders on the obscene or questionable in art or writing: "a *risqué* story." In English usage, *risky* means "bold," "audacious," "daring," but lacks the equivocal force of the French word.

Same. Disapproved as a substitute for *it*, *they*, etc.: "We have sent the goods by express, and we hope you will receive *them* (not *same*) promptly." Legal usage allows *the same* for *it*: "If said tenant defaces *the same*, etc."

"Says I." A vulgarism.

Scared. Do not use *scared of* when you mean *scared by*. Many people use this phrase carelessly. Prefer *afraid of* or *fearful of*.

Scrap. This is commercial cant, meaning, as a verb, "discard" as out-of-date or unprofitable: "The ships and the plant will be *scrapped*."

Secondhand. Say, "We bought the car *secondhand*, not *secondhanded*."

See. The frequent interrogatory "*See?*," with which some persons sprinkle their conversation in their anxiety to secure attention, is most objectionable from the point of view either of manners or of language.

Seen. Not to be used for *saw*, which is the correct past tense of *see*. Avoid "I *seen* him last week" or "He *seen* that," as the height of vulgarity.

Sell. Formerly, "to *sell* a person" meant "to play a joke upon him." Now the same phrase is commercial cant, meaning "to *sell* something to him." Colloquially, *sell* may mean to convince.

Sequel. *Sequel* means "something that follows," as a continuation or consequence. It is used frequently of events or stories related in books: "The *Gay-Dombeys* may be called a *sequel* to *Dombey and Son*"; "The *sequel* of their marriage was a divorce."

Set, Sit. These verbs, like *lay* and *lie*, have long been subject to confusion. In modern usage, *set* is transitive; *sit* is intransitive. I *set* the hen, but she *sits* on her eggs. Incorrectly we speak of a *setting* hen, instead of a *sitting* hen. In Matthew, it was prophesied that Christ should come "*sitting* upon an ass," and his disciples took a colt and "*set* him thereon." The verbs are correctly used in these sentences: "My coat *sits* well"; "We will *sit* up," that is, "will not go to bed"; "Congress *sits*." "We *set* down figures"; but "We *sit* down on the ground." But a very old intransitive use of *set* persists in the expressions, "the sun *sets*," "*sunset*," "*setting* sun," which are accepted as correct.

Sat.—This is both past tense and past participle of *sit*. I *have sat* is correct.

Sewage, Sewerage. *Sewerage* is the system of pipes and tunnels for carrying away the *sewage*, or waste matter, from buildings.

Shall, Will. These are auxiliary (helping) verbs, used to determine various modes and tenses of the action involved in a principal verb. In respect to these words, there are four important groups of idiomatic uses: (1) in declarative statements; (2) in questions; (3) in subordinate clauses; (4) in expressions of future requirement (veiled command).

1. *Declarative Statements.*—The following are the correct uses of *shall* and *will* with the personal pronouns, to express simple future action, declaratively and interrogatively:

DECLARATIVE	INTERROGATIVE
I shall	Shall I?
You will	Shall you?
He will	Will he?
We shall	Shall we?
You will	Shall you?
They will	Will they?

For the expression of the speaker's determination or command, *shall* and *will* exchange places in the foregoing table. For example: "I *shall*" becomes "I *will*"; "He *will*" becomes "He *shall*."

In the sense of *willing, determining, commanding,* or *requiring,* neither *shall* nor *will* has anything to do with "time," except as any command must be executed "after" it is given. This is clear in certain cases, where expression and action may well come together: "*Will* you sit here?" "Yes; I *will*," where the action is suited to the word, or, "*Wilt* thou have this woman to be thy wedded wife?" "I *will*."

2. *Questions.*—In questions, one uses the word expected in the answer: "*Shall* you speak?" expecting "I *shall* speak"; but "*Will* you speak?" expecting "I *will* speak."

But notice that "*Shall* you be glad to go?" is appropriate, while "*Will* you be glad to go?" is not, since gladness is not a matter of will. Only rarely may *will* be used interrogatively in the first person, because, as long as there is question in the mind, there is no will. Such a formal sentence as "We *will* ratify this treaty, *will* we not?" is approved· and we not infrequently exclaim, somewhat ironically, "Will I?" as if to say, "I *will* not" or "I certainly *will*."

3. *Subordinate Clauses.*—In subordinate clauses introduced by *that,* after such expressions as "It is said" or "Some one has said" or "It has been commanded," use the auxiliary that would be used in the original principal statement. For example: when the original statement or command was "He (or You) *shall* do the work," the clause of indirect quotation becomes "He has said that he (or you or I) *shall* do the work"; similarly, "He (or You) *will* do the work" becomes "He has said that he (or you or I) *will* do the work." In the former case *shall* retains its ancient force of obligation; in the latter, *will* retains its essential meaning of willingness or readiness. The following sentence further illustrates the use of *shall* to express determination: "We have decided that the contract *shall* be let to you, and that you *shall* follow specifications." If the subordinate clause follows such a verb as *suppose, think, believe,* or *know,* then the usage for *shall* and *will* in the subordinate clause is the same as for an independent declarative statement. Example: "I think that I *shall* never see a poem lovely as a tree."

In subordinate clauses introduced by such conjunctions as *if, when, whether,* or *although, shall* expresses simple future action in every person, while *will,* in every person, expresses willingness or determination. Examples: "If you *will* remember the rule, I *shall* be greatly obliged." "Although I *shall* see him, I *will* not speak." "If he *will* not meet me, I *will* not seek him."

Such use of *shall* is usually avoided by some other expression. Examples: "If I *see* him, I *will* speak"; "If he *does not meet* me, I *shall* not need to speak."

4. *Requirements and Commands.*—*Will* has a peculiar use to express a verbal command or a courteous request: "You *will* report back to headquarters on Sunday morning," that is, "You are required to report"; "You *will* please say no more about the matter" means that it is my wish, entreaty, or pleasure that you say no more about it.

Shape, Condition. A crude but common use of "shape" is to say that a person is "in bad shape" (ill), or that his affairs are "in good shape"(financially). The word "condition" is waiting to be used in such cases.

Should, Would. Although, in origin, these are past tenses of *shall* and *will,* they are now properly to be thought of as independent of the latter verbs. Their uses are highly idiomatic.

In affirmative principal clauses, *should* may express obligation in all persons: "I (You or He) *should* (*ought to*) attend the lecture." *Would,* in affirmative principal clauses and in all persons. may express willingness or determination dependent upon circumstances: "We (You, They) *would* come, if an invitation were given."

1. In the first person, *should,* and, in other persons, *would,* may express simply action dependent upon circumstances: "I *should* (They *would*) come, were it convenient."

2. In simple questions, the word expected in the answer is used: "*Should* he go?" "He *should*"; "*Would* you consider it?" "I *would*."

3. In *if* clauses, *should* expresses a condition involving action merely, *would* expresses a condition involving will: "If I *should* correct the error, the work would be approved"; "If you *would* permit me, I would correct the error."

4. *Would* may express intense desire: "I *would* that we might see them again." It expresses also, in reference to past time, habitual action: "He *would* walk up and down."

5. It should be observed that *would* is rarely used interrogatively in the first person except in such a half-ironical expression as "*Would* I?" implying "I certainly *would*" or "I certainly *would* not."

6. Many of the shades of meaning attached to *should* and *would* can be expressed only by changes in the tone of the voice. A fair-sized volume might be written about them.

Should seem, Would seem. These are useless locutions when plain *seem* or *seems* would express the meaning. They are appropriate, however, to suggest doubt, hesitation, or modesty in expressing a judgment.

Show me. Slang for *prove to me.*

Sick, Ill. See *Ill.*

Since when. This phrase, in which *when* is employed as a substantive, is used correctly in a relative clause: "We moved out West, *since when* (or *since which time*) we have not moved again." However, it is not approved in interrogative constructions: as, "*Since when* have you known that?" "How long have you known that?" is correct.

Sit up. We say to a child, "*Sit up*," meaning "sit erectly." We *sit up,* that is, *remain out of bed* until a late hour. Compare the expressive slang, "Make one *sit up* and take notice." These phrases are not in good literary use.

Size up. Slang for *estimate, judge, classify. Up* is very frequent in careless colloquial speech and slang; as, *eat up, all up* (*with*), *stay up,* etc.

Slow, Slowly. Many adjectives in English need no change of form for adverbial use. *Fast* and *slow* are examples of these. Space economy on signs probably helps to maintain this form *slow* in such expressions as "Go *slow,*" though it has a long history in the language.

Smart. One should carefully observe the various meanings of this word. It is in good use for *bright, intelligent, brisk,* and *lively.* But in "He is a *smart* boy," the word may have the sense commonly attributed to it formerly, "sharp and impertinent," or that implied by bright and intelligent. After the English manner, one hears of *smart* clothes. The phrase *right smart*, meaning "much," "a good deal of," is provincial.

Smell of. We *smell* the rose, not *smell of* it. But we say properly, "The jar *smells of* rose leaves." The verb is transitive and intransitive.

So. Avoid using *so* as a bridge between the parts of a loose sentence. Example: "We couldn't find the house, *so* we started to go home, but it began to rain, *so* we waited," et cetera. Colloquial use of the adverb *so* without a that-clause is undesirable. Example: "The game was *so* exciting." But it is proper to say, "The book is *so* interesting that you will want to finish it at one sitting."

Some, Somewhat. *Some*, properly an indefinite adjective denoting number or quantity, is often used erroneously for *somewhat*, an adverb of degree, even by educated men and women. Such use appears frequently in the newspapers; but it is condemned as dialectal or provincial by all authorities, and it has no support in literary usage. Say, "I am *somewhat* tired," never "I am *some* tired"; "His estimate is *somewhat* greater," not "*some* greater." The colloquial use of *some*, to suggest exceptional quality or importance, as in "He is *some* manager," is equally to be disapproved.

Somewhere. "I have seen him some place" is not an acceptable substitute for the correct form, "I have seen him somewhere." The same distinction should be observed in "any place" and "anywhere."

Sort of. See *Kind*.

Split infinitive. Since an infinitive consists of a verb plus the particle "to," the insertion of an adverbial modifier between them creates a "split infinitive," for example: "Be careful to thoroughly mix the ingredients." Unsplitting the infinitive may be done either (1) by placing the adverb after the verb ("Be careful to mix the ingredients thoroughly") or (2) by placing it just before the verb ("Be careful thoroughly to mix the ingredients"). The first of these two constructions is simple and natural, and is usually preferable. Although the second arrangement is technically correct, it is formal and rather consciously precise. Sometimes it is also obscure. In the example cited above, there is a suggestion that "thoroughly" applies to "be careful" instead of to "mix." Anyway, the normal order is for the adverb to follow the verb.

Stand. Colloquial for *endure* in such an expression as "They can't *stand* it."

Stand a chance. Colloquial for *be likely*. "Does he *stand a chance* of election?" means "*Is* he *likely* to be elected?"

Stand for. Colloquial for *endure* or *allow*; as, "We will not *stand for* such conduct."

Standpoint. See *Point of view*.

State. We may say, "He *stated* his reasons in writing." *State* is a formal word and should not be used, as it frequently is in newspapers, to mean simply "say" or "tell."

Station, Depot. A *depot* is properly a place where goods or stores of any kind are kept; the places at which the trains of a railroad stop for passengers and the points they start from or arrive at are properly the *stations*. But, as a *depot* is a place of storage, so a *terminal* of a railroad line, where the rolling stock is kept to make up trains, may be spoken of correctly as a *depot*.

Stimulant, Stimulus. A stimulant is an agent that produces a temporary increase of energy. More abstractly, a *stimulus* is an exciting motive or impulse.

Stop, Stay. The colloquial phrases, *stop off*, *stop in*, *stop over*, are frowned on by critics. The first means to "step off" or "alight and stay at" some place; the second means "step in and call" or merely "call"; the last has gained position in railway cant, as in "*stop-over* privileges."

To stop is to arrest motion; *to stay* is to remain where motion is arrested. We may *stop* at a hotel; but how long we *stay* depends upon circumstances.

Storm. A violent commotion of the atmosphere is a *storm*. Avoid the word when referring to *rains* or *snows*, unless *rainstorms* or *snowstorms* are involved.

Street. Many careful speakers regard the expression "They live *in* John *street*" as better and more accurate than "They live *on* John *street*." General American usage seems to approve *on the street*. Colloquially, we say, "play *in the street*," one's house being thought of as bordering *on* the real *street*. "He has offices *in* Wall *street*" is a form of speech frequently heard. This implies the idea of the *street* as a financial center, including the buildings on it. The whole question turns upon our idea of what the word *street* includes.

Stricken. This form of the past participle of *strike* is used when misfortune or disability is implied: "He was *stricken* with fever"; "They were panic-*stricken*." *Struck* is the usual form for other meanings: "He was *struck* by a stone."

Stylish words. See *Affectation*.

Such. "I have never seen *such a small* man" should be "I have never seen *so small a* man," as may be seen by transposing the words of the first sentence, which then becomes "I have never seen a man *such small*." Similarly, *such a pretty, lovely*, etc., should be *so pretty a, lovely a*. However, in the sentence "It was *such a large* package as could not be carried in the car," *such a* is regarded as correct, meaning "a *large package* like this one."

Suffixes. See *Word Building*. Several suffixes are sources of common error, because of indiscriminate use:

-ette. This syllable is a French feminine diminutive, the masculine being *-et*. A *kitchenette*, then, is a little kitchen, feminine because of associations, probably. But *leatherette* is imitation leather. So we pass to the half-humorous, half-contemptuous *farmerette* and *suffragette*.

-let. This is another French ending, meaning "little." One should not say, "little *booklet*," the *little* being superfluous.

Sure. "He will *surely* be here," not "He will be here *sure*." "*Sure*, I'll do it" is slang. *Surely* is the adverb; *sure*, the adjective.

Suspicion. *Suspicion* is not in good use as a verb; prefer *suspect*.

Take. A verb, either transitive or intransitive. Combined with various prepositions and adverbs, it forms many idiomatic phrases and also many colloquial and slang phrases: "One *takes* leave," that is, assumes or receives permission to leave a place or a company; "One *takes to* a person," that is, *likes him*. Some uses, however, are to be avoided as vulgarisms: "She *took on* (scolded, raged, cried) dreadfully"; "School *takes up* at 8:30." Compare "*lets out* at 4:00," which is school cant.

Tasty. This word is an objectionable colloquialism for *tasteful*, when applied to persons, dress, furniture, etc. It is allowable in application to food. The following distinction is correct: Pie may be *tasty*, but the decorations of a room should be *tasteful*.

Tautology. Through carelessness, repetitive or overlapping expressions find their way into the speech of many people. Note such common examples as "*old* veteran," "*ancient* adage," "widow *woman*," and, somewhat more subtly, "*consensus of opinion*." A different case is provided by intentional repetition for emphasis, as in "the same identical person," and the purposeful repetition in legal phrasing, as in "I hereby give, devise and bequeath," etc.

Teach. See *Learn*.

Tenses, Sequence of. The general rule to be observed regarding tenses is that the verb in a dependent clause takes its tense from the verb in the main clause. Thus: "I think (present) that he is (present) honest" becomes "I thought (past) that he was (past) honest" when the tense of the main verb is changed. Usually. we can depend upon our "feeling for language" to save us from such mixed forms as "Give that others *might* live" instead of the correct sequence "Give that others *may* live."

Terminal prepositions. Puristic people insist on following a rigid rule that a sentence should never end with a preposition. For a vigorous, if slightly colloquial, statement like, "This is something worth thinking about," they would substitute the formal and rather prissy phrasing, "This is something about which it is worth while to think." What they overlook is the close relationship that often exists between verb and preposition, making the two practically one word. "He is a man you can count on" is good idiomatic English. It is natural and conversational as contrasted with the bookish style that results from transposing the preposition. Of course, terminal prepositions that are used unnecessarily and carelessly are properly condemned. For example, to say, "what we end up with" instead of "what we have left" is inexcusable. At the same time, no one should hesitate to use a prepositional ending that is natural and forceful.

Terrible, Frightful. These belong to the class of extravagant adjectives. *Terribly* and *frightfully* are similarly misused for *very* or *very much* or *extraordinarily*, when "terror" and "fright" are not involved. Save strong words for occasions that demand them.

Than. See *Any, Else, Of*.

That, So. *That* is not in good use as an adverb in such phrases as the following: "*that* good," "*that* worthy." "She was *so* worthy that they could not turn her away" is correct. Do not say, "She was *that* worthy, etc." *That*, however, is approved as a demonstrative adverb with expressions of measure or degree: "We could not stay *that* long"; "You will be *that* much farther on your way."

The. As in the case of the indefinite article, the repetition of the definite article *the* in such a series as "*the* bear, *the* deer, and *the* panther" serves to emphasize the individual separateness of the things named. Such repetition is necessary in expressions like the following, to avoid ambiguity: "*the* secretary and *the* treasurer (two persons)," "*the* finished and *the* unfinished manuscript (two manuscripts)." "*The* secretary and treasurer" means one person only.

If used before the first adjective, *the* should be used before each of a series of adjectives applied to one substantive, but distinguishing different objects; as, "*the* expensive, *the* cheap, and *the* medium-priced goods." See *A, An*.

Them, Those. Do not confuse these words. *Them* is the objective case of the plural third personal pronoun; *those* is a plural demonstrative adjective. Say "*those* facts," never "*them* facts."

Then. Used in such a phrase as "the *then* Chief Justice," this word is approved. The use has a long and honorable history. The phrase *then some* for *some more* is slang.

Thence. The preposition *from* with *thence* is superfluous. "He came *thence*" is correct.

Therefor, Therefore. These two look-alike words may seem to be alternative spellings for the same word, but they have quite different meanings. "Therefor," accented on the second syllable, is equivalent to the phrase, "for that." "Therefore," an adverb, introduces a conclusion based on a reasoning process that has already been indicated. It is accented on the first syllable.

Think for. Such a word as *suppose* or *suspect* should be substituted for the phrase *think for* in a barbarous sentence like "He hears more than you *think for*."

Those kind. "*That kind* of shoe is good," not "*those kind*". *Those* is plural; *kind* is singular. Care should be taken to preserve the number in the sentence. See *Kind*.

Through. *To be through* is an American colloquialism, meaning "to have finished," "to have done": "How soon will you *be through* with the work?" The phrase is frequently used and may be classed among our idioms.

To. Never say, "She was *to* my house yesterday." Use *at* in place of *to*. We say, colloquially, "I have been *to* town," and some critics allow the phrase as idiomatic. See *Be back*.

Together. In *meet together* or *converse together*, *together* is superfluous.

Tomorrow. One may say, "*Tomorrow is* or *will be* Monday." But one should say, "*Tomorrow will be* a memorable day."

Transparent, Translucent. *Transparent* means "clear," allowing light to pass so that objects may be seen through the substance. *Translucent* means "partially transparent," allowing light to pass but not permitting vision.

Transpire. Do not use this word to mean *happen*.. We may say, "No information or news has *transpired*," meaning "None has become public."

Treat. A book *treats of* (not *treats on*) the subject of its contents.

Try. We *make* experiments, not *try* them, say some critics. Others point out that *try* experiments is laboratory usage; but *perform* is the more generally approved verb in this sense. "*Do* experiments" is school cant.

Try and. It is better to avoid the use of the phrase *try and do*. Use *try to do* instead. The use of this phrase is not quite like that of the phrase *come and see*, which is in good use.

Under the circumstances. See *In the circumstances*.

Unique. Since this word denotes one of a kind, it should not be used in the watered-down sense of unusual. Neither should it be accompanied by an adverb of degree, as in "very unique."

United States. Whether to use *is* or *are* after these words may be a political as well as a linguistic question. General usage approves *is*, though in government official usage there is warrant for *are*.

Universally, All. Do not say, "He was *universally* praised by *all* who heard him." The two words are so similar in meaning that the use of both is redundant. Say, "He was *universally* praised" or "He was praised by *all* who heard him."

Unkempt. Literally, the word means "uncombed," or, figuratively, "rough," "unpolished."

It is not to be used generally to mean "disordered," as in *unkempt* rooms. A person may be *unkempt*, a room never.

Up. Superfluously added to many verbs, as in *add up, open up,* etc. *Up* should be used with verbs only when it contributes definitely to the meaning or is in good colloquial use.

Use of Infinitive. The present infinitive is used after all tenses unless it refers to action occurring before the time implied in the assertion of the principal verb. Say, "He intended *to do* it," never "He intended *to have done* it." But "He is said *to have been* present" is correct, since his "being present" preceded the saying. *Ought,* being a defective verb, is followed by the present infinitive to express present or future duty, and by the perfect infinitive to express duty in past time: "They ought *to speak*"; "They ought *to have spoken.*"

Verbs, Agreement of. The verb in a sentence must agree with the substantive of the subject in person and number. But there are several puzzling cases which give rise to frequent error.

(1) The subject includes substantives of different numbers: Either the master or his servants *are* at fault. Usage approves a verb agreeing with the nearest substantive. Usually it is better to recast such a sentence and avoid this construction: "The fault lies either with the master or his servants."

(2) Subject collective or distributive: "There *are (is)* six dollars in the drawer." If the thought is of the total amount of money, use the singular verb; if the idea of several pieces of money is uppermost, use the plural verb.

Verdict. A word loosely used for *opinion.* *Verdict* should be reserved for official decisions, as of a jury, or for opinion publicly and formally expressed: "That he is unreliable is the *opinion* (not the *verdict*) of all who know him."

Very. Most critics insist that *very* should not immediately precede a past participle used as an adjective. Not, "He was *very* pleased," but "He was *very much* pleased." *Very* may directly precede an adjective: "That is a *very* good article." Where the participle has chiefly an adjective sense, *very* is authoritatively used: "She is a *very* charming person."

View of, to. "He worked with a *view to* the establishment of a business." "We talked with a *view of* discovering each other's opinions." These sentences represent approved usage.

Viewpoint. *Point of view* is preferable. It has more character when used in a sentence in written English and in spoken English.

Vocation, Avocation. A person's *vocation* is his profession, his calling, his business; his *avocations* are the things that occupy him incidentally; "Mr. Wharton's *vocation* is banking; his *avocation* is photography."

Want, Need. *Need* refers to the actual fact of lack; *want* implies a personal sense or view of the situation. A man may *want* an automobile, when he does not *need* it for his business. Avoid using *want* and *need* loosely in the sense of *lack.*

Was, Is. When, in a subordinate clause, an unchanging truth or a present fact is to be stated, use *is,* not *was,* no matter what the tense of the principal verb: "He knew that ice *is* formed at 32°." The same rule applies to the use of the present tense of any verb: "They should have realized that war *settles* no disputes."

Ways. Wrongly used for *way.* "The house is a long *ways* off" should be "The house is a long *way* off."

Well, Why. The use of these words as exclamations of surprise or dismay may be defended, but too frequently they are simply drawling noises at the beginning of a sentence.

Went, Gone. These forms of the verb *go* are frequently confused. *Went* is the past tense; *gone* is the past participle. Say, "They *have gone* (not *have went*)."

What. "He would not believe *but what* I said it" should be "He would not believe *but that* I said it." See *But.*

Whence. "*Whence* came ye?" not "*From whence* came ye?" *Whence* means "from what place, source, or cause."

Whereabouts. In "His *whereabouts* is unknown," observe the correct singular verb.

Who, Whom. Avoid the common error of misusing *who* for *whom.* Say, "*Whom* are you thinking of?" not "*Who* are you thinking of?" "*Whom* did they mention?" not "*Who* did they mention?" *Whom* is the form to use as the object of a verb or preposition.

Whoever. One should write, "I will give it to *whoever* can use it," but, "I will give it to *whomever* you designate." The syntax of the pronoun in the subordinate clause determines the case.

Whole lot. As a substitute for *much* or *a great deal, whole lot* is only in vulgar use; as, "I don't care a *whole lot* for the theater."

Whose, Of which. Some critics object to the use of *whose* in referring to things, but there is precedent for the usage. Sometimes *of which* would bring in an awkward manner of speech. In such cases *whose* should be used: "This is the latest of those political changes *whose* causes we can easily find."

Widow woman. The word *woman* is superfluous here.

Without. This word is a preposition and should not take the place of the conjunction *unless*: "I shall not go *without* my father consents" should read "*unless* my father consents," or the expression might be changed to "*without* my father's consent," where *without* is a preposition.

Worst kind. A vulgarism frequently used in the sense of *very much*; as, "I want to go the *worst kind.*"

Would have. Avoid the incorrect use of *would have* in conditional sentences. Not "If he *would have* come," but "If he *had* come." "*Would of*" is completely illiterate.

Yes. Avoid the various vulgar and provincial varieties of this important little word: *yeh, ya, yep, eh-uh.*

You-all. When used to mean simply "you," and applied to more than one person, this is a provincialism of the southern United States. It is not properly used to mean one person only.

Yours truly. This phrase used as a substitute for "I" or "me" is awkward and self-conscious. It arises from the same exaggerated modesty that prevents people from beginning a business letter with "I" and that causes essayists to introduce such circumlocutions as "from the standpoint of the present writer the conclusion seems evident" instead of saying "I think" or something equally natural and direct.

Z. The letter is *zee* or *zed,* the former being the common American name, the latter the British.

WORD BUILDING

To be skilled in language, one must know words and their right uses. The elements of spoken language are articulate sounds; those of written language are characters or letters which *represent* those sounds. From these elements, which are known as roots or stems, prefixes and suffixes, words are formed.

Roots. The *root* is the primitive form of any word and existed before the addition of prefix, suffix, or inflectional ending. The syllable preceding it is called the *prefix*; that which comes after it is named the *suffix*. For instance, the root of the word *prefix* is *fig* or *fix* from the Latin *figere*, "to attach"; the syllable *pre* signifies "before." Thus we get the meaning "to attach before." Similarly, the word *suffix*, from *sub* or *suf* meaning "under" or "after" and *figere* "to attach," means "to attach after." Since prefixes are attached before words or roots and suffixes are added at the end, prefixes or suffixes are called *affixes*, from *ad* or *af* meaning "to" and *figere* "to attach." Therefore, an *affix* is one or more letters or syllables added at the beginning or at the end of a word.

Stems. The *stem* is that part of a word to which the case endings or personal endings and tense signs are affixed; sometimes the *stem* is identical with the *root*, though generally it is derived from it with some formative suffix. Stems are so called because inflections were added to parts of words found in other languages, as branches are grafted to the stem or trunk of a tree. They have gradually been transplanted into the English language and may now be studied as constituent parts of our everyday speech. For example, in the Latin word *crucifigere*, "to crucify," we have the root *crux*, "a cross," changed into *cruci*, "to a cross," by the stem ending, *ci*; combining *cruci* and *figere*, which signifies "to attach," we get a word meaning "to attach to a cross."

By learning words from their etymology, we not only remember the meaning of the particular words thus studied, but we also immediately recognize all other words that are similarly formed.

Structure and Relations of Words. We know things best when we can relate them to other things and make comparisons. Besides, to understand a thing thoroughly we must know its parts; for instance, we know a house when we are familiar with its different rooms and the parts of its construction. Many words are built very much as houses are built; they have foundations, and to these are added various parts which are distinguished one from the other, thus making each word useful for definite purposes. We shall, therefore, learn words more intelligently if we are able to recognize the elements out of which they are built.

English has borrowed from Latin and Greek not only entire words, but also the elements of words; that is, stems, suffixes, and prefixes, out of which to make new combinations. By combining these elements, large groups of words have been built up, the words of each group being related through having the same stem.

An Aid to Memory. The meanings of words seldom used are easily forgotten. Recalling them is like groping in the dark. If, however, we know the elements of which these words are made, the difficulty largely disappears. Few people have time to learn Latin or Greek to get the meanings of these word elements; but the essential matters can be selected and grouped for ready reference and study. A little *grouping* of syllables will do away with much *groping* for word meanings. Learn the common meanings of the stems, prefixes, and suffixes given in this section. Master them, a few at a time. This study will largely increase your ability to remember and understand thousands of unfamiliar words.

It will also enable you to make much better use of the English dictionary.

Native and Foreign Words. The English language may be regarded as made up, for the most part, of the following groups of words:

1. Simple words retaining exactly or nearly their original Anglo-Saxon form and meaning; as, *man, will, and*.

2. Simple words borrowed from other languages, which words retain their original sense or become somewhat modified in meaning; as, *grand* (French), *pedal* (Latin).

3. Compound words made up of Anglo-Saxon, Latin, Greek, or other elements; as, *roadway* (Anglo-Saxon), *camshaft* (Dutch or French and Anglo-Saxon), *phonograph* (Greek).

4. Anglo-Saxon words formed of a stem and a prefix or suffix; as, *willful, undo, lengthen*.

5. Words made up of stems and prefixes or suffixes from other languages; as, *excise* (Latin), *engage* (French).

Short and Long Words. The English language, like every other cultivated tongue, comprises both short and long words, or, to express it better, "popular" and "learned" words. The former belong to the people in common—are limited to no particular class; the latter are words which may be used by educated speakers in ordinary conversation and are to be met with in general literature.

The short or popular words are those we have known from childhood—they are sufficient to express our immature thoughts and ideas. Later, the mind develops, and, through reading good literature, we become acquainted with a more formal and distinctive style of phraseology. It is thus unconsciously, yet naturally, that we pass from the use of simple words of Anglo-Saxon origin to those so-called learned words derived from the French, the Latin, or the Greek.

The following examples will illustrate methods of building up words to express more or less complicated ideas:

Cablegram, cable-gram (writing) means a writing or message sent by cable or wire.

Comprehensive, com (together) -prehens (grasping) -ive (adj.) means having the quality of seizing or grasping (much) together.

Cosmopolitan, cosmo (world) -polit (citizen) -an (adj.) means having the character or quality of a world citizen.

Impervious, im (not) -per (through) -vi (way) -ous (adj.) means having no way or passage through.

Periscope, peri (around) -scope (looker) means literally a looker around, or an instrument to look around with.

Prefixes and Suffixes. In the following lists are grouped the principal prefixes and suffixes and the most commonly used Latin stems of the English language. Their uses are illustrated by the analysis of about 350 common words. The principles illustrated in these lists may be applied generally, and the student will find his grasp of English meanings and spelling greatly improved by careful study of the significations, forms, and uses of the various word elements.

Prefixes commonly alter the meaning of the stem in some manner. Thus *hyper*tension adds the idea of excess; *un*wise contradicts the basic word. *Suffixes* may change only the meaning of a word, as in book*let*, but they frequently change its grammatical form also. For example, *ize* makes a verb out of an adjective (natural*ize*), and *ness* converts an adjective into an abstract noun (kind*ness*). It should be noted, however, that English often uses the same word for different parts of speech. Thus, without adding suffixes or otherwise changing its form, *iron* may be used as a noun ("The bridge is made of *iron*."), as a verb ("to *iron* a shirt"), or as an adjective ("He has an *iron* constitution.").

WORD FORMATIONS

Throughout the following lists of words compounded under *Prefixes*, the prefixes are printed in **boldface**, the rest of each word is printed in *italics*; thus, **ob-***stinate.* Similarly, under *Suffixes*, the suffixes are in **boldface**, other syllables in *italics*; as, *verd-***ant.** In the list of *Stems*, the stems are in **boldface**, other syllables in *italics*; as, *in-***clus-***ive.* Meanings of foreign language syllables not defined at the head of each group are given in parentheses; as, *pro* (forth) **-duce.** The word (noun), (adj.), (verb), (adv.), following a suffix, indicates that the suffix gives to the word of which it is a part the force of a noun, a verb, an adjective, or an adverb.

ANGLO-SAXON PREFIXES

A-, meaning *on* or *in.*
  A- *live* means *on* or *in* life.
  A- *board* means *on* board.
  A- *sleep* means *in* sleep.

Be-, meaning *affecting with* or *by,* or merely emphatic.
  Be- *witched* means *affected by* witchcraft.
  Be- *dewed* means wet as *with* dew.
  Be- *spattered* means spattered or spotted *all over,* as with mud.

For-, meaning *away* or *not.*
  For- *bid* means bid or command *not,* or refuse.
  For- *get* means *not* to hold, lose hold of.
  For- *give* means give or let go *away.*
  For- *bear* means keep *away* or *from.*

Fore-, meaning *in front, beforehand,* or *ahead of.*
  Fore- *arm* means the arm from elbow to hand.
  Fore- *tell* means tell *ahead of* time.
  Fore- *stall* means stop *beforehand.*
  Fore- *shadow* means to shadow or typify *beforehand.*

Half- and **No-,** as in half-done. nowhere.

Out-, meaning *excelling.*
  Out- *shine* means surpass (another) in brightness.
  Out- *play* means defeat at play.

To-, meaning *this* or *the.*
  To- *morrow* means *the* morrow or morning.
  To- *day* means *this* day.

Un-, a negative prefix.
  Un- *aware* means *not* heeding or noticing.
  Un- *kind* means *not* kind.
  Un- *fasten* means loosen bonds or fastenings.
  Un- *fair* means *not* fair.

LATIN PREFIXES

Ab-, meaning *from, not.*
  Ab- *duct* (lead) means lead *away.*
  Ab- *norm* (rule) *-al* (adj.) means *away* from the rule (norm).
  Ab- *sent* (being) means being *away* from, not present.
  Ab- *sorb* (suck in) means suck in *from,* as a blotter.

A-, Ad-, Ac-, Ag-, meaning *to.*
  A- *scribe* (write) means write *to* or give *to,* grant.
  Ad- *here* (stick) means stick *to.*
  Ac- *cede* (yield) means yield *to.*
  Ag- *gression* (stepping) means a stepping *to* or *forward,* crowding.
  Ag- *grav* (weight) *-ate* (verb) means add weight *to,* increase.

Ante-, meaning *before.*
  Ante- *cedent* (going) means going *before.*
  Ante- *date* means date *before* or *ahead of* time.

Bi-, Bis-, meaning *two.*
  Bi- *weekly* means every *two* weeks.
  Bis- *cuit* (cooked) means *twice* cooked (dry and hard).
  Bi- *sect* (cut) means cut in *two.*

Circum-, meaning *around.*
  Circum- *stance* (standing) means that which stands *around,* or accompanies.
  Circum- *scribe* (write) means write or draw *around.*
  Circum- *spect* (looking) means looking *around,* hence careful.

Com-, Con-, Co-, meaning *with, together,* or *completely.*
  Com- *pose* (place) means place *together,* to make.
  Con- *ceive* (take) means take to one's self *completely,* understand.
  Con- *dole* (sorrow) means sorrow *with.*
  Co- *oper* (work) *-ate* (verb) means work *together.*

Contra-, Contro-, meaning *against.*
  Contra- *dict* (speak) means speak *against.*
  Contro- *versy* (turning) means a turning *against.*

De-, meaning *down, out of, from, completely.*
  De- *scend* (climb) means climb *down.*
  De- *pend* (hang) means hang *down from.*
  De- *ment* (mind) *-ed* (adj.) means *out of* one's mind, insane.
  De- *port* (carry) means carry *from* or *away.*
  De- *nude* (bare) means make *completely* bare.

Dis-, Dif-, meaning *apart from, from.*
  Dis- *sect* (cut) means cut *apart.*
  Dis- *perse* (strew) means strew *apart,* scatter.
  Dis- *tend* (stretch) means stretch *apart.*
  Dis- *sent* (think) means think *apart* or *differently from.*
  Dif- *ferent* (bearing) means bearing *away from, not like.*

E-, Ef-, Ex-, meaning *from, out of.*
  E- *vade* (walk, go) means walk *away from.*
  Ef- *fect* (doing) means a doing *from,* something made *from* another.
  Ex- *claim* (cry) means cry *out.*
  Ex- *tort* (wrench) means wrench or force *from* or *out of.*
  Ex- *tradition* (giving over) means surrender *from,* as a prisoner is given over *from* one authority to another.

Extra-, meaning *outside.*
  Extra- *ordinary* (common) means *out of* the common.
  Extra- *territorial* means *out of* the territory.

In-, Il-, meaning *not* or *contrary.*
  In- *ept* (apt) means *not* apt or fit.
  In- *sensible* (feeling) means *not* feeling.
  In- *nocuous* (harmful) means *not* harmful.
  Il- *legal* (lawful) means *not* lawful.

In-, Im-, Il-, meaning *in, on,* or *upon.*
  In- *hale* (breathe) means breathe *in.*
  In- *voke* (call) means call *on* or *upon.*
  Im- *press* means press *upon.*
  Il- *lustr* (light) *-ate* (verb) means throw light *upon.*

Inter-, meaning *between.*
  Inter- *urban* (city) means *between* cities.
  Inter- *national* means *between* nations.

Intra-, Intro-, meaning *between, among,* or *within.*
  Intra- *mural* (wall) means *between* or *within* the walls.
  Intro- *duce* (lead) means lead *within* or *into* (knowledge).

Non-, meaning *not.*
  Non- *partisan* means *not* related to a party.
  Non- *entity* (something) means *not* anything.

Ob-, Op-, meaning *against, to, upon.*
  Ob- *stinate* (standing) means standing *against.*
  Ob- *ligate* (bind) means bind *to,* as *to* a promise.
  Op- *posite* (placed) means placed *against.*
  Op- *press* means press *upon,* crush; hence burden, tyrannize over.

Word Building

Word Building

Per-, meaning *through, completely, very.*
 Per- *ceive* (take) means take *through* (thoroughly) therefore, learn.
 Per- *manent* (staying) means staying *through,* continuing.
 Per- *forate* (bore) means bore *through.*
 Per- *verse* (turned) means turned *around.*

Post-, meaning *after.*
 Post- *pone* (place) means place *after,* put off, or defer.
 Post- *mortem* (death) means *after* death.
 Post- *lude* (play) means (music) played *after.*

Pre-, meaning *before* (in time, place, rank, or degree).
 Pre- *lude* (play) means play *before,* hence, music played *before.* Compare *Postlude.*
 Pre- *face* (say or speak) means something said or spoken *before.*
 Pre- *eminence* (elevation) means an elevation *before,* i.e., *above* others.
 Pre- *vail* (strength) means be strong *before* or *in excess of,* hence to be master of.

Pro-, meaning *forth, forward.*
 Pro- *pel* (drive) means drive *forward.*
 Pro- *ceed* (go) means go *forward* or *forth.*
 Pro- *ject* (throw) means throw or extend *forward.*
 Pro- *mote* (move) means move *forward.*

Re-, meaning *again* or *back.*
 Re- *form* (shape) means change *back,* or into a new shape or form.
 Re- *pel* (drive) means drive *back.*
 Re- *claim* (call) means call (for) *again,* hence get *back.*
 Re- *view* (look at) means look at *again.*

Retro-, meaning *backward.*
 Retro- *spect* (looking) means a looking *backward.*
 Retro- *gression* (going) means a going *backward.*

Se-, meaning *from, away.*
 Se- *cede* (go) means go *away* or *from,* withdraw.
 Se- *duce* (lead) means lead *away.*
 Se- *cure* (care) means *free from* care or anxiety.

Semi-, meaning *half.*
 Semi- *annual* (yearly) means every six months or *half-*yearly.

Sub-, Sup-, Sus-, meaning *under.*
 Sub- *marine* (sea) means *under* the sea.
 Sub- *soil* means the layer of material *under* or *below* the surface soil.
 Sup- *port* (carry) means carry *under,* that is, carry by being *under.*
 Sus- *pend* (hang) means hang *under.*

Super-, Sur-, meaning *above, upon.*
 Super- *structure* (building) means the building *above* the foundation.
 Sur- *pass* means pass *over* or *above,* hence excel.
 Sur- *tax* means a tax *above* another.

Trans-, Tra-, meaning *across.*
 Trans- *fer* (carry) means carry *across.*
 Tra- *verse* (turn, go) means turn or go *across.*

GREEK PREFIXES

A-, An-, meaning *without, not.*
 A- *byss* (bottom) means *without* bottom.
 A- *chromat* (color) *-ic* (adj.) means *not* colored.
 An- *archy* (government) means *no* government.

Amphi-, meaning *around.*
 Amphi- *theater,* means a theater *around* an open space.

Ana-, An-, meaning *up, according to, backward.*
 Ana- *tom* (cut) *-y* (noun) means cutting *up.*
 Ana- *gram* (writing) means a writing *backwards,* opposed to the usual order.
 Ana- *logy* (ratio or proportion) means *up* to the proportion; hence, a resemblance, a likeness.

Anti-, meaning *against.*
 Anti- *christian* means *opposed* to Christianity.
 Anti- *pathy* (suffering) means a suffering *against,* hence opposition of feeling.

Cata-, Cath-, meaning *down, according to, in respect to.*
 Cata- *lepsy* (falling) means a falling *down.*
 Cata- *log* (name) means *according to* the name, a list so arranged.
 Cath- *olic* (whole) means *in respect to* or *having to do with* the whole; hence, universal.

Dia-, meaning *through, across.*
 Dia- *meter* (measure) means a measure or distance *through.*
 Dia- *gonal* (angle) means *through* the angle or corner.
 Dia- *gram* (writing) means a writing *through,* a plan or drawing.
 Dia- *dem* (bind) means something that binds *across,* as a band or fillet across the head.

Hyper-, meaning *over, above.*
 Hyper- *critical* means *over*-critical.

Hypo-, meaning *below* or *under.*
 Hypo- *dermic* (skin) means *under* the skin.
 Hypo- *thesis* (placed) means something placed *under,* as a foundation for reasoning.

Meta-, most often denoting change.
 Meta- *phor* (carrying) means a carrying *over* (to another meaning).
 Meta- *morphosis* (form) means a *change of* form.

Syl-, Sym-, Syn-, meaning *with, together.*
 Syl- *lable* (taken) means taken *together.*
 Sym- *pathy* (suffering) means suffering *with.* Compare *Condole.*
 Syn- *opsis* (view) means a view *together,* hence a general view or exhibit.
 Syn- *thetic* (put) means put *together.*

ANGLO-SAXON SUFFIXES

The following are the principal Anglo-Saxon suffixes. Like the prefixes, these are used with either Anglo-Saxon or foreign stems in their appropriate meanings.

-dom, noun suffix, meaning state or authority of, as in *kingdom.*

-ed, or **-d,** suffix for the past tense and the past participle of verb, as in *load, loaded; hear, heard.*

-en, a verb suffix, meaning to make or cause, as in *deepen, lengthen.*

-er, noun suffix, meaning the agent, as in *leader* or *doer.*

-ful, noun or adjective suffix, meaning full or, sometimes, inclined to, as in *armful, handful, playful.*

-hood, noun suffix of state or quality, as in *manhood* or *hardihood.*

-ing, verbal noun or participial ending, conveying the idea of process, continuance, art, etc., as in *homing, speaking, painting.*

-ish, an adjective ending, with the meaning of resembling, somewhat like or inclined toward, as *bookish, childish.*

-le, a verb suffix often with frequentative and diminutive force, as in *handle, kindle, joggle, nestle, sprinkle.*

-less, adjective suffix, meaning lacking, deprived of, as in *armless, godless, homeless.*

-let, noun suffix, meaning little, as in *booklet, streamlet.*

-like, an adjective suffix, meaning resembling, as in *godlike.*

-ly, an adjective suffix, meaning resembling or having the quality of, as in *godly, homely;* also an adverbial suffix, as in *deeply, warmly.*

-ness, noun suffix, signifying quality, as in *lightness*.

-ship, noun suffix, signifying state, condition, office, or quality, as in *lordship, marksmanship*.

-some, an adjective suffix denoting considerable degree or quality, as in *handsome, wholesome, gladsome, winsome*.

-ty, meaning "ten times," as in *fifty*.

-wise, an adjective or adverbial suffix, signifying manner, as in *lengthwise, otherwise*.

-y, an adjective suffix, meaning like or pertaining to, as in *handy, windy*; or noun suffix, often equal to Latin *-ia* or French *-ie*, as in *history, villainy*.

SUFFIXES FROM THE LATIN, GREEK, AND FRENCH

-able, -ible, adjective suffix.
Vis (see) **-ible** means *possible to see*.
Sal (sell) **-able** means *possible to sell*.
Peace (peace) **-able** means *tending to peace*.
Terr (fright) **-ible** means *tending to create terror*.

-acious, -icious, adjective suffix.
Avar (greed) **-icious** means *given to greed, greedy*.
Aud (dare) **-acious** means *abounding in daring*.
Ten (hold) **-acious** means *given to holding*.

-acity, -icity, noun suffix, often equals *-ness*.
Cap (take) **-acity** means *power of holding or taking in*.
Authent (original) **-icity** means the *quality of genuineness*.
Loqu (talk) **-acity** means the *habit of excessive talking, talkativeness*.
Pugn (fight) **-acity** means *fighting quality*.

-acy, noun suffix.
Liter (letter) **-acy** means the *quality of knowing letters*.
Candid (white) **-acy** means *condition of whiteness* (Roman candidates for office were so called because clothed in white.).
Prim (first) **-acy** means the *state of being first or chief*.

-al, adjective or noun suffix.
Leg (law) **-al** means *according, or pertaining, to law*.
Plur (many) **-al** means *pertaining to more than one*.
Fin (end) **-al** means *pertaining to the end*.
Gener (class) **-al** means *pertaining to a whole class or body*.

-an, adjective suffix.
Hum (man) **-an** means *pertaining to mankind*.
Urb (city) **-an** means *pertaining to the city*.

-ant, -ent, adjective (-ing) or noun suffix.
Expect (await) **-ant** means *awaiting*.
Verd (green) **-ant** means *of green or like green*.
Ard (burn) **-ent** means *burning*.
Pot (power) **-ent** means *powerful*.
Visit **-ant** means *one who visits*.

-ary, adjective or noun suffix, signifying *like* or *connected with*.
Exempl (pattern) **-ary** means *fitted to be a model*.
Liter (letter) **-ary** means *having to do with letters*.
Plen (full) **-ary** means *having fullness* (as of power).

-ate, verb or adjective suffix.
Ex- (out) *cav* (hollow) **-ate** means *to make hollow, hollow out*.
Hibern (winter) **-ate** means *to winter, sleep through winter*.
Dis (out of) *-loc* (place) **-ate** means *to put out of place*.
Plac (please) **-ate** means *to please*.
Aspir (breath) **-ate** means *like breath, breathy*.
De (lacking) *-sper* (hope) **-ate** means *without hope*.

-ation, noun suffix.
Cre (make) **-ation** means *that which is made, or making*.
Ex (out of) *-clam* (cry) **-ation** means *that which is cried out, or a crying out*.
E (out of) *-limin* (bound) **-ation** means *putting out of bounds, getting rid of*.
Found (basis) **-ation** means *that on which anything stands or is founded*.

-ative, adjective suffix.
Authorit **-ative** means *serving for authority*.
Talk **-ative** means *inclined to talk*.
Tent (try) **-ative** means *serving for a trial or test*.

-fy, verb suffix.
Ampli (large) **-fy** means *make large*.
Veri (true) **-fy** means *make or establish as true*.
Testi (witness) **-fy** means *bear witness*.

-ic, adjective suffix.
Hero **-ic** means *like a hero*.
Poet **-ic** means *like poetry*.
Ascet (exercise, discipline) **-ic** means *pertaining to or characterized by self-denial*.

-ile, adjective suffix.
Ag (do, act) **-ile** means *capable of (easy) action*.
Fac (do) **-ile** means *fit for doing, easy*.
Duct (draw) **-ile** means *capable of being drawn, as metal into wire*.
Puer (child) **-ile** means *suited to, or like, a child*.

-ine (-in), adjective suffix.
Alkal (lye) **-ine** means *like an alkali or lye*.
Femin (woman) **-ine** means *pertaining to a woman*.
Sal (salt) **-ine** means *like salt*.

-ion, noun suffix, equals *-ing*.
Act (do) **-ion** means the *process of doing*.
Re (back) *-tent* (hold) **-ion** means the *act of holding back*.
Solut (loosen) **-ion** means the *process of loosening or clearing up*.

-ism, noun suffix.
American **-ism** means a *characteristic of, or the spirit of, America*.
Despot **-ism** means the *power of a despot*.
Buddh **-ism** means the *system of religion founded by Buddha*.

-ist, noun suffix.
Flor **-ist** means *seller of flowers*.
Pian **-ist** means *one who plays the piano*.

-ive, adjective suffix.
Primit (first) **-ive** means *like first things or beginnings*.
Ef (out) *-fus* (pour) **-ive** means *pouring out or like a pouring out*.

-ize, verb suffix.
Real **-ize** means *make real or think of as real*.
Civil **-ize** means *make civil or refined*.
Agon (struggle) **-ize** means *make, or go through, a struggle*.
Critic (judge) **-ize** means *judge or cause to pass under judgment*.

-or, noun suffix, equals *-er*.
Fact (do) **-or** means a *doer*, hence something that affects a result.
Con-duct (lead) **-or** means *one who leads (with)*.
In-struct (build) **-or** means *one who builds or prepares (teaches)*.

-ous, adjective suffix, often equals Anglo-Saxon *-y*.
Aque (water) **-ous** means *watery*.
Courage (boldness) **-ous** means *possessed of boldness*.
Lumin (light) **-ous** means *having or giving light*.
Por (hole) **-ous** means *full of minute holes or pores*.

-tude, noun suffix, often equals *-ness.*
Ampli (full) **-tude** means *fullness* or *large size.*
Soli (alone) **-tude** means *condition of being alone.*

-ure, noun suffix, often equals *-ing.*
Press **-ure** means a *pressing upon.*
En-clos (shut) **-ure** means a *shutting in.*

Latin Stems

Ag, Act, meaning *do.*
Act *-or* (noun) means *doer.*
Ag *-ent* (noun) means *doer,* especially for another, (derived through the French).
In (not) **-act** *-ive* (adj.) means not *doing* or *acting.*
Re (back) **-act** *-ion -ary* (adj.) means given to *acting back,* or acting according to former habits.

Anim, meaning *life.*
Anim *-al* (adj.) (having quality of) *-cule* (little) means a little thing *having life.*
Anim *-ated* (adj.) (having) means *lively.*
In (not) **-anim** *-ate* (adj.) means not *having life.*

Cap, Capt, Cept, Cip, meaning *take, get.*
Ac (to) **-cept** *-ance* (noun) (the act of) means the act of *taking* to one's self.
Cap *-able* (adj.) means able to *take.*
Cap *-acity* (noun) means power of *taking in* or *holding.*
Capt *-iv* (like) *-ate* (verb) means cause to be like one *taken.*
Con (together) **-cept** *-ion* (noun) (result) means the result of *taking* together or completely, e.g., an idea.
Per (through) **-cept** *-ion* (noun) means a *taking* thoroughly, seeing clearly.
Re (back) **-cept** *-ive* (adj.) (inclined to) means inclined to *take,* or *receive.*

Ced, Cess, meaning *move, go, yield.*
Ac (to) **-cede** means *yield* to.
Ac (to) **-cess** *-ible* (adj.) (possible) means possible to *go* to, or get at.
De (away) **-ced** *-ent* (noun) (one who) means one who *has gone* away, died.
Ex (from, beyond) **-ceed** means *go* beyond.
Pro (forward) **-ceed** means *go* forward.
Pro (forth) **-cess** *-ion -al* (noun) means something related to a *going* forth.
Re (back) **-cess** *-ion -al* (noun) means something related to a *going* back.
(These last two words are used of the music accompanying the entrance and the exit of a choir.)
Se (apart) **-cede** means *go* apart from.
Un (not) *-suc* (under) **-cess** *-ful -ly* (adverb) means not *going* or *following* under, that is, not attaining or succeeding.

Clud, Clus, meaning *close, shut.*
Con (completely) **-clude** means *shut* finally.
In (not) *-con* **-clus** *-ive* (adj.) *-ly* (adv.) means not *closing* completely.
In (in) **-clus** *-ive* (adj.) means *shutting* in or including.
Pre (before) **-clude** means *shut before,* hence put up a barrier against.
Se (away) **-clude** means *shut* away, withdraw.
Re (away) **-cluse** means one who is *shut away,* one who lives apart from society.

Dic, Dict, meaning *speak, tell, declare.*
Ab (away) **-dic** *-ate* (verb) means *speak* or *declare* away, as a position, a throne, give up.
De (apart) **-dic** *-ation* (noun) (an act) means an act of *speaking,* or *declaring* (a thing) apart; hence, setting apart, as a church.
Dict *-at* (the act) *-or* (noun) (agent) *-ial* (adj.) means characterized by the act or manner of a *speaker* or commander—like a dictator.
In (against) **-dict** *-ment* (noun) means a *declaration* against (a person), an accusation.

Domin, meaning *power* or *rule.*
Domin *-ant* (adj.) means *ruling, controlling,* or *principal.*
Domin *-ation* (noun) (state of) means the state or act of *ruling.*
Pre (above) **-domin** *-ate* (verb) means *rule* above or as superior to.

Duc, Duct, meaning *lead, draw, bring.*
Ad (to) **-duce** means *lead* or bring to, as proof to a statement.
Con (with) **-duc** *-ive* (adj.) (tending to) means tending to lead, or suitable to be led with, that is, helpful.
De (from) **-duce** means *draw* from, as a conclusion from a statement.
De (from) **-duct** *-ion* (noun) (act of) means a *taking* away from.
In (into) **-duct** *-ion* (noun) (act of) means a *leading* into, as an electric current is led into one coil from another.
Pro (forth) **-duce** means *bring* forth.
Pro (forth) **-duct** *-iv* (having power of) *-ity* (state of) means the state of having power of *bringing* forth.

Fac, Fact, Fect, Fict, meaning *make* or *do.*
Af (to) **-fect** means *do* to, as one thing does something to another.
Af (to) **-fect** *-ion* (noun) (-ing) means *making* toward, aspiring to, hence love.
Fac *-simile* (likeness) means a *made* likeness.
Fact *-ory* (noun) (place for) means a place for *making.*
Per (thoroughly) **-fect** means *made* completely.

Fer, Lat, meaning *bear, carry, move.*
Dif (apart) **-fer** *-ent* (adj.) means *bearing* apart.
E (from) **-lated** means *carried* from or out of, as out of one's usual self.
Ob (to) **-lat** *-ion* (noun) means something *borne* to or offered.
Re (back) **-late** means *bear* or *carry* back, that is, to some one or to something else, connect.
Super (above) **-lat** *-ive* (adj.) means *borne* over or above, the highest.
Un (not) *-trans* (across) **-lat** *-able* means not possible to *carry* across, as from one language to another.

Fid, meaning *belief, trust, faith.*
Con (with) **-fide** means share *trust* with.
Dif (apart) **-fid** *-ent* (adj.) means lacking *trust* or *faith,* especially in oneself.
In (not) **-fid** *-el* (noun) (one who) means one who lacks *faith,* unbeliever.

Fin, meaning *end* or *limit.*
De (from) **-fin** *-ition* (noun) (that which) means something that marks off or *limits* one thing from another.
In (not) **-fin** *-ite* (adj.) means not *limited.*
Un (not) *-con* (together) **-fin** *-ed* (Anglo-Saxon participle ending) means not *bounded* or shut in.
Fin *-ish* (verb) means make an *end.*

Flect, meaning *bend.*
De (from) **-flect** means *bend* from or aside.
Re (back) **-flect** *-ion* (-ing) means a *bending* back.

Flict, meaning *strike.*
Af (to, at) **-flict** means *strike* at.
In (on) **-flict** means *strike* on.

Frang, Frag, Fract, meaning *break.*
Frang *-ible* (adj.) means possible to *break.*
Frag *-ile* (adj.) means fitted, or likely, to *break.*
Frag *-ment* (noun) means that which is *broken.*
Fract *-ure* (noun) means a break or a result of *breaking.*

Grad, Gred, Gress, meaning *step, go.*
Con (together) **-gress** means that which *goes* together, hence, an official gathering or body.
De (down) **-grade** means cause to *step* down.

In (in) **-gred** *-i -ent* (noun) means that which *goes* into, as a part of a mixture.

Retro (backward) **-grade** (adj.) means *going* backward.

Un (not) *-pro* (forward) **-gress** *-ive* (adj.) means not *going* forward.

Leg, Lig, Lect, meaning *choose, pick, read.*

E (from) **-lect** *-or* (noun) means one who *chooses* from, as from a number of candidates.

In (not) *-e* (out) **-lig** *-ible* (adj.) means not possible to be *chosen.*

Intel (between) **-lig** *-ent* (adj.) means fitted to *select* between, or choose.

Leg *-ibil -ity* (noun) means *readableness.*

Se (from) **-lect** *-ive* (adj.) means fitted to *choose* from, or concerned with choosing.

Mand, Mend, probably from *manus* (hand) and *dare* (to give).

The stems imply authority.

Com (emphatic) **-mand** (verb) means exercise *authority.*

Com (emphatic) **-mend** *-at -ion* (noun) means an *authoritative* approval.

De (from) **-mand** (verb) means ask from with *authority.*

Mitt, Miss, meaning *send, let go.*

Ad (to) **-miss** *-ion* (noun) means a *sending* or letting in.

Com (with) **-mit** means *send* with.

Re (back) **-mit** means *send back,* hence *restore* or *forgive.*

Miss *-ive* (noun) means that which is *sent.*

Inter (between) **-miss** *-ion* (noun) means a *sending between,* hence an interruption or recess.

Per (through) **-miss** *-ion* (noun) means *letting go* altogether, allowing.

Mov, Mot, Mob, meaning *move.*

Auto (self) **-mob** *-ile* (adj.) means able to *move* itself. Used as noun.

Com (emphatic) **-mot** *-ion* (noun) means a disturbed, violent *moving.*

Mot *-or* (noun) means that which *moves.*

Pro (forward) **-mot** *-er* (noun) means one who *moves* (things) forward.

Re (back) **-move** means *move* back or away.

Pend, Pens, meaning *hang.*

Ap (to) **-pend** means *hang* to.

De (from) **-pend** *-ent* (noun) means one who *hangs* from.

Sus (under) **-pense** means a *hanging* under.

Pon, Pos, meaning *place, put.*

Com (together) **-pos** *-ite* (adj.) means *put* together.

Im (on) **-pos** *-it -ion* (noun) means something *put* upon, a burden.

Ex (forth, out) **-pon** *-ent* (noun) means *that which puts forth, sets out,* or *explains.*

Op (against) **-pon** *-ent* (noun) means one *placed* against.

Pro (forth) **-pose** means *put* forth or forward.

Port, meaning *carry.*

Ex (out) **-port** means *carry* out.

Im (in) **-port** means *carry* in.

Im (in) **-port** *-ant* (adj.) means *carrying* in, as if something weighty or of worth.

Re (back) **-port** means *carry* back.

Prob, meaning *proof, esteem.*

Prob *-at -ion* (noun) means a state or process of *proving.*

Re (back) **-prov** *-ing -ly* (adv.) means in a manner indicating withdrawal of *esteem.*

Reg, Rect, meaning *rule, lead, straight.*

Cor (with) **-rect** means *straight* with, as with some standard.

Di (apart, asunder, i.e., distinctly) **-rect** means distinctly *straight.*

E (out) **-rect** means *straight* out, or up, from.

Reg *-ul -ar* (adj.) means according to *rule.*

Reg *-ul -ate* (verb) means bring under *rule.*

Rupt, meaning *break, burst.*

Ab (off) **-rupt** means *broken off,* hence sudden or hasty.

Cor (together, altogether) **-rupt** means *break,* destroy completely.

Inter (between) **-rupt** means *break* in between.

Scrib, Script, meaning *write.*

De (down) **-scribe** means *write* down.

In (in or on) **-scribe** means *write* in or on.

Pre (before) **-script** *-ion* (noun) means something *written* before to be followed.

Sub (under) **-scribe** means *write* under, as one's name.

Sent, Sens, meaning *feel, think.*

Sense *-less* (adj.) means lacking *thought* or *feeling.*

Sent *-i -ment* (noun) means that which is *felt.*

Con (with) **-sent** means *feeling with,* hence agreement.

Sequ, Secut, meaning *follow.*

Con (with) **-sequ** *-ence* (noun) means that which *follows* with.

Per (through, thoroughly) **-secut** *-ion* (noun) means a *following* through to the end.

Sta, Sist, Stin, meaning *stand.*

As (to) **-sist** *-ance* (noun) means that which *stands* to or by.

Con (with) **-sist** *-ent* (adj.) means *standing,* or agreeing, with.

Per (through) **-sist** means *stand* through, hence remain unmoved, continue steadfastly.

De (apart) **-stine** means cause to *stand* apart, or to make fast for a particular end.

Un (not) **-sta** *-ble* (adj.) means not able to *stand.*

Tend, Tent, Tens, meaning *stretch.*

At (to) **-tend** means *stretch* to or toward.

Ex (out) **-tend** means *stretch* out.

Ex (out) **-tens** *-ive* (adj.) means *stretched* out.

In (to) **-tent** *-ion* (noun) means a *stretching* to or toward, as of the mind toward an object.

Tent, Tin, meaning *hold.*

Dis (apart) *-con* (together) **-tin** *-u -ous* (adj.) means not *holding* together, but apart.

Re (back) **-tent** *-ive* (adj.) means fitted with or able to *hold* back, or keep.

Tract, meaning *draw, lead.*

Con (together) **-tract** *-ion* (noun) means *drawing* together.

Re (back) **-tract** means *take* back.

Tract *-able* (adj.) means possible to be *led.*

Ven, meaning *come.*

Ad (to) **-vent** *-ure* (noun) means something that is *come* to or met, a happening.

Con (together) **-vent** *-ion* (noun) means a *coming* together.

Inter (between) **-vene** means *come* between.

Pre (before) **-vent** means *come* before.

Vert, Vers, meaning *turn.*

A (from) **-vert** means *turn* from.

Ir (not) *-re* (back) **-vers** *-ible* (adj.) means not possible to be *turned* back.

Sub (under) **-vert** means *turn* under or destroy.

Vid, Vis, meaning *see, look.*

In (not) **-vis** *-ible* (adj.) means not possible to be *seen.*

Pro (forward) **-vis** *-ion* (noun) means a *looking* forward, getting ready.

Re (again) **-vise** means *look at again,* hence examine again and alter.

Viv, Vit, meaning *live, life.*

Re (again) **-vive** means *live,* or cause to *live,* again

Vit *-al* (adj.) means like or connected with *life*

Viv *-ac -ious* (adj.), characterized by *life,* lively.

Voc, meaning *call.*

E (out) **-voke** means *call* out.

In (on) **-voc** *-ation* (noun) means a *calling* on.

Ir (not) *-re* (back) **-voc** *-able* (adj.) means not possible to be *called* back.

DERIVATION OF ENGLISH WORDS FROM THE LATIN

The foregoing list of prefixes, suffixes, and stems will aid in the study of the derivation of words. Moreover, it serves as a key to the means by which words are deduced from others known as primitives. Since more than half the words in the English language come directly or indirectly from the Latin, a study of the derivation of these words will be found of inestimable value.

While it is true that the study of one language may help one to learn another language, and that the study of Latin in particular makes one know English better, it does not follow that it is necessary to have studied Latin in order to understand words of Latin origin.

In the following groups of derivatives will be found first the Latin word with its English equivalent. That the structure of the English words built on the Latin may stand out as clearly as possible, the nominative and genitive (possessive) cases of the nouns have been given, while each verb is shown in the first person singular present indicative, together with the perfect participle.

No attempt has been made to give a list of all words derived from each root. With the aid of the dictionary, it will be found both interesting and instructive to see how many more words from the same root or stem may be added to the different groups. Always compare carefully each English word with the Latin word placed at the head of each group. Note how much or how little of the Latin word enters into the formation of the English word derived from it. The analysis of a few words taken from the list will serve as an excellent guide:

Capio is a Latin word meaning *I take*. It is formed from the verb stem *cap*. By attaching to the verb stem *cap* the Latin adjective suffix *a-ble* (able), meaning *tending* or *possible to*, we get the word *capable*, meaning *possible to take*, hence *having ability*.

The Latin word *duco, I lead*, is formed from the verb stem *duc*. The perfect participle of *duco* is *ductus*. The Latin stem, known as the supine stem, is *duct*. By affixing *intro*, a Latin prefix meaning *within* or *into*, and affixing the Latin noun suffix *ion*, meaning *the act of*, we get the word *intro-´ tion*, meaning the *act of leading into*.

Labor is a Latin word meaning *work*. The genitive singular, corresponding to the English possessive, is *laboris*. The stem is *labor*. By adding to the stem the Anglo-Saxon noun suffix *er*, meaning *one who does*, we get the word *laborer*, a workman.

Dens is a Latin word meaning *tooth*. The genitive singular is *dentis*. The stem is *dent*. By affixing to the stem the Greek noun suffix *ist*, meaning *one who is skilled in*, we get the word *dentist*, a tooth doctor. By adding to the stem *dent* the Latin prefix *tri*, meaning *three*, we get the word *trident*, meaning three toothed, hence a three-pronged fork or spear.

AL'TUS, high.

al'tar, a raised place for sacrifice.
al-tis'o-nant, high-sounding, lofty.
al'ti-tude, height, extent upward.

al'to, high, a term in music.
ex-alt', to raise, to extol, to elevate.
ex-al-ta'tion, a lifting up.

AN'GU-LUS, a corner. AN'GU-LI, of a corner.

an'gle, a corner.
an'gu-lar, having angles or corners.
e'qui-an-gu-lar, having equal angles.

quad'ran-gle, a figure having four angles, a square.
rec'tan-gle, a figure having right angles.
tri'an-gle, a three-angled figure.

AN'I-MA, life, breath. AN'I-MÆ, of life, breath.

an'i-mal, a living creature
an-i-mal'cule, a small animal.
an'i-mate, to impart life to.

an-i-ma'tion, state of possessing life.
in-an'i-mate, without life.
re-an'i-mate, to bring back to life.

AN'NUS, a year. AN'NI, of a year.

an-ni-ver'sa-ry, a yearly festival.
an'nu-al, yearly.
an-nu'i-tant, one who receives a yearly allowance.
an-nu'i-ty, an amount payable yearly.
bi-en'ni-al, occurring every two years.

cen-ten'ni-al, once in a hundred years.
per-en'ni-al, lasting for years.
su-per-an'nu-at-ed, disqualified by age.
su-per-an-nu-a'tion, a retiring allowance.
tri-en'ni-al, occurring every three years.

A'QUA, water A'QUÆ, of water.

a-qua-for'tis, (literally, powerful water) nitric acid.
a-qua'ri-um, an artificial pond for aquatic plants or animals.
a-qua'ri-us, the water bearer, a constellation.
a-quat'ic, adapted to water.

aq'ue-duct, a conduit for water.
a'que-ous, watery.
a'qui-form, in the form of water.
sub-a'que-ous, being under water.
ter-ra'que-ous, consisting of land and water.

AR'MA, arms, weapons AR-MO'RUM, of arms, weapons.

arm, a weapon, a limb.
ar'ma-ment, an armed force.
ar'mor-er, a maker of arms.
ar'mor-y, a place for arms, an arsenal.

ar'my, a body of soldiers.
dis-arm', to deprive of arms.
un-armed', without arms or weapons.

BE'NE, well, kindly.

ben-e-fac'tion, a doing good, a gift.
ben-e-fac'tor, one who benefits others.
ben-e-fi'cial, useful, advantageous.
ben'e-fit, aid, an act of kindness.

be-nev'o-lence, good will.
be-nev'o-lent, kind, charitable.
be-nign', gentle, mild.
be-nig'ni-ty, mildness, kindness.

CA'DO, I fall. CA'SUS, fallen.

ac'ci-dent, that which comes or falls by chance.
ca'dence, a fall of the voice.
case, condition, state.
cas'u-al, accidental, unexpected.

cas'u-al-ty, that which occurs by chance.
cas'u-ist, one who settles cases of conscience.
de-ca'dence, a falling away, a deterioration.
de-cay', to fall away, to decline.

CAL'CU-LUS, a pebble. CAL'CU-LI, of a pebble.

cal'cu-la-ble, that may be reckoned or depended on.
cal'cu-la-ry, pertaining to counting.
cal'cu-late, to count, to estimate, to plan.
cal-cu-la'tion, the process of counting.

cal'cu-la-tor, a ready reckoner, one who calculates.
cal'cu-li-form, shaped like a pebble.
cal'cu-lus, a stony concretion in the body, a disease; also a branch of mathematics.

CAP'I-O, I take. CAP'TUS, taken.

ac-cept', to take when offered.
ca'pa-ble, having ability, mental or physical.
ca-pa'cious, able to take on a large scale, spacious.
cap'tious, peevish, faultfinding.
cap'ti-vate, to capture, to take by charm.

cap'tive, one who is taken prisoner.
cap-tiv'i-ty, imprisonment, bondage.
cap'tor, one who takes or holds captive.
cap'ture, a seizure, a prize.

CA'PUT, the head. CAP'I-TIS, of the head.

cape, a headland.
cap'i-tal, standing at the head, chief.
cap-i-ta'tion, counting by heads.

pre-cip-i-ta'tion, headlong or rash haste.
re-ca-pit'u-late, to sum up or enumerate by heads.

CA'RO, flesh. CAR'NIS, of flesh.

car'nage, slain flesh, slaughter.
car'nal, fleshy, not spiritual.
car-na'tion, flesh color; a flower.

car-niv'o-rous, devouring flesh.
in-car'nate, clothed with flesh.
in-car-na'tion, state of being clothed with flesh.

CA'VE-O, I take care. CAU'TUS, avoided.

cau'tion, care, prudence.
cau'tion-a-ry, warning or caution.
cau'tious, careful, prudent.

ca've-at, a warning, a legal caution.
in-cau'tious, heedless, careless, rash.
pre-cau'tion, care beforehand.

CE'DO, I go, I yield, I give up. CES'SUS, given up.

cede, to give up, to grant, to surrender.
ces'sion, a yielding or a giving up.
con-cede', to yield, to grant, to admit to be true.
con-ces'sion, a conceding or yielding.
ex-ceed', to go beyond.
ex-cess', more than is necessary.

pre-cede', to go before.
pre-ced'ence, priority of place or rank.
pre-ced'ent, going before, previous.
prec'e-dent, an authoritative example.
pred-e-ces'sor, one who goes before.
pro-ceed', to go forward, to advance.

CEN'TRUM, the middle. CEN'TRI, of the middle.

cen'ter, the middle.
cen'tral, relating to the center.
cen-trif'u-gal, proceeding or flying away from the center.
cen-trip'e-tal, tending toward the center.

con'cen-trate, to bring to a common center.
con-cen'tric, having a common center.
ec-cen'tric, out of the center.
ec-cen-tric'i-ty, oddity.

CEN'TUM, a hundred.

cent, the hundredth part of a dollar.
cen'te-na-ry, a period of one hundred years.
cen-ten'ni-al, completing a hundred years.
cen'ti-pede, an insect with a hundred feet.

cen-tu'ri-on, the captain of a hundred soldiers.
cen'tu-ple, a hundredfold.
cen'tu-ry, one hundred consecutive years.

CIR'CU-LUS, dim. of CIR'CUS, a circle. CIR'CU-LI, of a circle.

cir'cle, a ring, a circumference.
cir'cled, surrounded.
cir'clet, a little circle.
cir'cuit, distance round any space or area.
cir-cu'i-tous, roundabout, indirect.

cir'cu-lar, in the form of a circle.
cir'cu-late, to move round.
cir'cus, an open space for sports.
en-cir'cle, to enclose in a circle, to surround.
sem-i-cir'cle, half of a circle.

CI'VIS, a citizen. CI'VIS, of a citizen.

civ'ic, pertaining to a city or a citizen.
civ'il, polite; pertaining to the rights of a citizen.
ci-vil'ian, a citizen, not a soldier.

ci-vil'i-ty, politeness; a state of civilization.
civ'i-lize, reclaim from savagery.
in-ci-vil'i-ty, neglect of courtesy.

CRE'DO, I believe. CRED'I-TUS, believed.

cre'dence, belief, credit.
cre-den'da, things to be believed.
cre-den'tial, that which gives a title to belief.
cred'i-ble, worthy of belief.
cred'it, belief, trust.
cred'i-ta-ble, worthy of belief.

cred'i-tor, one who believes, trusts, or credits.
cre-du'li-ty, belief, or readiness of belief
cred'u-lous, believing too readily.
creed, that which is believed, doctrine.
dis-cred'it, to disbelieve.
in-cre-du'li-ty, unbelief.

CRE'O, I create. CRE-A'TUS, created.

cre-ate', to make, to form.
cre-a'tion, the act of creating.
cre-a'tive, having the power to create.
cre-a'tor, one who creates.

crea'ture, that which has been created.
re-cre-a'tion, making or forming anew.
rec-re-a'tion, refreshment after toil.

DENS, a tooth. DEN'TIS, of a tooth.

dent, a slight depression.
den'tal, pertaining to the teeth.
den'ti-frice, tooth powder, paste, or wash.

den'tist, a tooth doctor.
in-dent', to make a toothlike cut into.
tri'dent, a three-pronged fork or spear.

DEX'TER, (on) the right hand (adj.).

am-bi-dex'trous, using both hands equally.

dex'ter, pertaining to the right hand (heraldry).

dex-ter'i-ty, skill in using the hands.

dex'ter-ous, clever, handy.

dex'ter-ous-ly, skillfully.

dex-tral'i-ty, state of being more efficient with the right hand.

DE'US, God. DE'I, of God. DI-VI'NUS, from DI'VUS, pertaining to God.

de'i-fy, to make a god of.

de'ist, one who believes in God, but denies supernatural revelation.

de'i-ty, divinity, godhead.

di-vine', holy, sacred.

div-i-na'tion, a foretelling of future events, the act of divining.

di-vin'i-ty, theology, the Deity.

DI'CO, I appoint, DI-CA'TUS, appointed.

ab'di-cate, to give up or relinquish.

ded'i-cate, to devote to a special use.

in'di-cate, to point out, to show.

in-di-ca'tion, a pointing out, a hint or suggestion.

in-dic'a-tive, pointing out.

pred'i-cate, to proclaim, declare, affirm.

DI'CO, I say. DIC'TUS, said.

ben-e-dic'tion, a blessing.

con-tra-dict', to say against.

dic'tate, to say to, to declare with authority.

dic-ta'tor, one who has power to command.

dic'tion, a mode of speech.

dic'tion-a-ry, a wordbook.

dic'tum, an authoritative statement.

in'ter-dict, to forbid, to prohibit.

mal-e-dic'tion, evil speaking.

pre-dict', to say beforehand.

val-e-dic'tion, a farewell.

ver'dict, opinion pronounced.

DI'ES, a day. DI-E'I, of a day.

an-te-me-rid'i-an, before noon.

di'al, a plate marked with the hours of the day.

di'a-ry, a daily record.

di-ur'nal, daily.

me-rid'i-an, mid-day, or noon.

post-me-rid'i-an, after noon.

quo-tid'i-an, recurring daily.

si'ne di'e, without day.

DI'GE-RO, I dissolve, separate. DI-GES'TUS, dissolved, separated.

di-gest' (verb), to dissolve (as of food).

di'gest (noun), a compilation, a compendium.

di-gest'i-ble, capable of being dissolved.

di-ges'tion, the process of dissolving food.

di-ges'tive, that which aids digestion.

in-di-gest'ed, not digested, without order.

in-di-gest'i-ble, not easily dissolved.

in-di-ges'tion, lack of digestion, dyspepsia.

DI'VI-DO, I divide. DI-VI'SUS, divided.

di-vide', to sever, to separate.

div'i-dend, the number to be divided.

di-vis'i-ble, capable of being divided.

di-vi'sion, the process of dividing.

di-vi'sor, the number that divides.

in-di-vis'i-ble, not separable into parts.

DOM'I-NUS, a lord or master. DOM'I-NI, of a lord or master.

dom'i-nant, ruling, governing, prevailing.

dom'i-nate, to exercise control over.

dom-in-eer', to rule with insolence.

do-min'i-cal, belonging to the Lord's day.

do-min'ion, supreme authority, the power of ruling.

don, a Spanish title.

pre-dom'i-nance, superiority, ascendancy

pre-dom'i-nate, to prevail, to rule.

DU'CO, I lead. DUC'TUS, led.

don-duct', to lead, to guide.

de-duc'tion, a withdrawing, an inference.

duc'at, a ducal coin.

duc'tile, capable of being drawn out.

duke, a leader, a chief.

ed'u-cate, to lead forth, to instruct.

in-duct', to lead in, to install.

in-tro-duc'tion, a leading into.

pro-duce', to bring forward, to lead forth.

pro-duc'tive, having the power to produce, fertile.

re-duc'tion, act of reducing, bringing down.

tra-duce', to slander, to defame.

DU'RUS, hard, solid, lasting.

du'ra-ble, able to endure, lasting.

dur'ance, personal restraint, imprisonment.

du-ra'tion, continuance in time.

dur'ing, throughout.

en-dur'ance, ability to bear, sufferance, patience.

en-dure', to last, to withstand, to suffer.

ER'RO, I wander. ER-RA'TUS, wandered.

err, to mistake, to wander from truth.

er'rant, roving, wandering.

er-rat'ic, wandering, moving.

er-ra'tum, an error or mistake in writing or printing.

er'ror, a wandering from the truth.

E-RUM'PO, I burst forth, break out. E-RUP'TUS, burst, broken out.

dis-rupt', to break asunder forcibly.

dis-rup'tion, bursting of rocks (in an earthquake).

e-rum'pent, bursting out (as of buds).

e-rupt', to burst forth (as a volcano).

e-rup'tion, a breaking out.

e-rup'tive, inclined to break out.

rup'ture, a breaking of tissues, or of a blood vessel.

rup'tured, having a hernia.

FAL'LO, I deceive FAL'SUS, deceived.

fal-la'cious, misleading, deceptive.

fal'la-cy, a deception.

fal'li-ble, liable to err.

false, not true.

fal-set'to, a feigned voice.

fal'si-fy, to make false

fal'si-ty, an untruth.

in-fal'li-ble, not liable to err.

FE'RO I carry, bring. **LA'TUS,** carried, brought.

con-fer', to consult together.
de-fer', to put off, to delay, to withhold.
fer'tile, capable of bearing, carrying.
pre-fer', to carry before or regard as better.
re-late', to bring into relation, to connect (as of facts).

rel'a-tive, that which can be brought close together, compared, connected.
trans-fer', to carry over.
trans-late', to carry across, to render into another language.

FI'DES, faith, trust. **FI-DE'I,** of faith, trust.

af-fi-da'vit, pledging one's faith, a declaration made on oath.
bo'na fi'de, in good faith.
con-fide', to trust in.
con'fi-dence, a firm trust.

dif'fi-dence, want of faith.
fi-del'i-ty, faithfulness.
fi-du'ci-a-ry, one who holds in trust.
in-fi-del'i-ty, unfaithfulness, unbelief.
per'fi-dy, a breach of faith.

FI-GU'RA, a shape. **FI-GU'RÆ,** of a shape.

con-fig'ure, to give form or shape to.
dis-fig'ure, to deform, to deface.
ef'fi-gy, an image, a likeness.

fig'ur-a-tive, not literal.
fig'ure, a shape, a digit.
pre-fig'ure, to shape beforehand, to foreshadow.

FI'NIS, the end or limit. **FI'NIS,** of the end or limit.

con-fine', to keep within limits.
con'fines, boundaries, limits.
de-fine', to mark limits.
def'i-nite, clearly defined.

fi'nal, at an end.
fin'ish, to bring to an end.
fi'nite, having an end.
in'fi-nite, without end.

FIR'MUS, strong, durable.

af-firm', to declare or assert positively.
con-firm', to make strong, to corroborate.
firm, fixed, strong, durable.

in-firm', weak, not strong.
in-fir'ma-ry, a place for the sick.
in-fir'mi-ty, weakness, feebleness.

FLAM'MA, a flame. **FLAM'MÆ,** of a flame.

flam'beau (*through Fr.*), a flaming torch.
flame, a stream of fire.
in-flame', to kindle, to excite.

in-flam'ma-ble, capable of being easily set on fire.
in-flam-ma'tion, a heated swelling, an excitement.
in-flam'ma-to-ry, tending to inflame, kindle.

FO'LI-UM, a leaf. **FO'LI-I,** of a leaf.

cinque'foil (*through Fr.*), a five-leaved clover.
foil, a leaf or thin sheet of metal.
fo-li-a'ceous, having the texture of leaves.
fo'li-age, a cluster of leaves, flowers, and branches.

fo'li-ate, to beat into leaves.
fo'li-o, a four-paged sheet.
port-fo'li-o, case for loose leaves.
tre'foil (*through Fr.*), a three-leaved clover.

FOR'MA, form, appearance. **FOR'MÆ,** of form, of appearance.

form, shape, figure.
for'mal, according to form.
for-mal'i-ty, state of being formal, ceremony.
for-ma'tion, the act of forming.
in-for'mal, without ceremony.

mul'ti-form, having many shapes.
ref-or-ma'tion, a reforming or changing for the better.
re-for-ma'tion, forming anew.
trans-form', to change form.
u'ni-form, alike in form.

FOR'TIS, strong, valiant.

com'fort, to give strength, to cheer.
ef'fort, to put forth strength.
en-force', to put in force.
fort, a stronghold.
for-ti-fi-ca'tion, a strong place.
for'ti-fy, to make strong.

for-tis'si-mo (*It.*), in music, a direction to sing with the utmost strength.
for'ti-tude, strength or firmness of mind.
for'tress, a fortified place.
re-en-force', to strengthen

FRA'TER, a brother. **FRA'TRIS,** of a brother.

con-fra-ter'ni-ty, a society, a brotherhood.
fra-ter'nal, brotherly.
fra-ter'ni-ty, brotherhood.

frat'er-nize, to join as brothers.
frat'ri-cide, killing a brother.
fri'ar (*through Fr.*), a monk.

FU'GI-O, I flee. **FU'GI-TUS,** fled.

cen-trif'u-gal, flying away from the center.
fu-ga'cious, fleeing away.
fu'gi-tive, a runaway.

ref'uge, a place of shelter.
ref-u-gee', one who flees for refuge.
sub'ter-fuge, a fleeing under, or an artful evasion.

GRA'DI-OR, I step. **GRES'SUS,** stepped.

deg-ra-da'tion, a lowering in degree.
di-gress', to step aside, to diverge.
e'gress, a stepping out of.
gra-da'tion, an advance step by step.
grade, step, rank, or degree.

grad'u-al, step by step.
grad'u-ate, to grade.
in'gress, a stepping into.
prog'ress, a stepping forward.
ret'ro-grade, stepping backward.

GRA'TUS, thankful, acceptable.

grate'ful, thankful, agreeable.
grat'i-fy, to delight, to please.
gra'tis, free, without recompense.

grat'i-tude, thankfulness.
gra-tu'i-tous, free, uncalled for.
gra-tu'i-ty, a free gift.

GREX, a flock. GRE'GIS, of a flock.

ag'gre-gate, to collect or unite into a mass.
con'gre-gate, to collect or assemble as a flock.
con-gre-ga'tion, a gathering, an assembly.

e-gre'gious, away from the flock, hence remarkably bad.
gre-ga'ri-ous, moving in flocks.
seg're-gate, to set apart, to separate.

HA'BE-O, I have. HAB'I-TUS, had, or held.

ex-hib'it, to hold forth to view.
hab'it, custom, use.
hab-i-ta'tion, a place held as an abode.

ha-bit'u-al, customary, commonly done.
in-hab'it, to dwell or live in.
pro-hib'it, to hold away, to prevent, to forbid.

HÆ'RE-O, I stick, or adhere. HÆ'SUS, adhered.

ad-here', to stick to.
ad-he'sion, a sticking to.
ad-he'sive, sticky.

co-her'ent, sticking together, cleaving.
in-co-her'ent, loose, unconnected.
in-her'ent, inseparable by nature.

HOS'PES, a host. HOS'PIT-IS, of a host (*through hostis*, a stranger, an enemy).

hos'pi-ta-ble, kind to guests.
hos'pi-tal, a place for the sick.
hos-pi-tal'i-ty, generosity, liberality toward guests.

host'ess, a female host, a landlady.
hos'tler, originally master of an inn, one who takes care of horses.

HU'MUS, the ground. HU'MI, of the ground.

ex-hu-ma'tion, the act of taking up from a grave.
ex-hume', to take up from the ground, to disinter.
hu-mil'i-ate, to reduce to a low condition.

hu-mil'i-ty, lowness of spirit (as on the ground).
in-hu-ma'tion, putting into the grave.
in-hume', to bury.

JU'DEX, a judge. JU'DI-CIS, of a judge.

ad-judge', to order or decree.
ad-ju'di-cate, to give sentence.
judge, one who decides.
judg'ment, decision, sentence.
ju-di'cial, pertaining to justice.

ju-di'cious, prudent, wise.
pre-judge', to decide before hearing.
prej'u-dice, judgment beforehand.
prej-u-di'cial, hurtful, injurious.
un-prej'u-diced, free from bias.

JUN'GO, I join. JUNC'TUS, joined.

ad'junct, something joined, but not essential.
con-join', to unite, to combine.
con-junc'tion, a connecting word.
en-join', to command, to order.

join, to unite.
junc'tion, a joining, a union.
junc'ture, a joint, or union.
sub-junc'tive, binding together, connecting.

JU'RO, I swear an oath. JU-RA'TUS, sworn on oath.

ab-ju-ra'tion, the act of forswearing.
ab-jure', to deny or renounce upon oath.
con-ju-ra'tion, solemn entreaty.
con-jure', to put under oath.

con'jure, to practice magic, to conspire.
con'jur-er, a juggler.
ju'ror, one of a jury.
ju'ry, a body of sworn men.

LA'BOR, work. LA-BO'RIS, of work.

e-lab'o-rate, to work out with care.
la'bor, hard work, toil.
lab'o-ra-to-ry, a scientist's workroom.

la'bor-er, a workman.
la-bo'ri-ous, toilsome, involving much labor.

LEV'O, I lift up. LE-VA'TUS, lifted up.

al-le'vi-ate, to lighten sorrow.
el'e-vate, to raise, to lift up.
el-e-va'tion, a lifting up.

le'ver, a bar for lifting.
lev'i-ty, lightness of manner.
lev'y, to raise money or soldiers.

LEX, a law. LE'GIS, of a law.

al-le'giance, loyalty
il-le'gal, unlawful.
le'gal, according to law.
le'gal-ize, to make lawful.

leg'is-late, to make laws.
leg'is-la-ture, the parliament or power that makes laws.
le-git'i-mate, lawful.

LO'CO, I place. LO-CA'TUS, placed.

a-lo-ca'tion, a placing for a set purpose.
dis'lo-cate, to displace, to disjoint.
lo'cal, belonging to a place.

lo-cal'i-ty, a place or situation.
lo'cate, to place.
lo-co-mo'tion, the act or power of changing place.

MAG'NUS, great. MA'JOR, greater.

mag-nif'i-cence, grandeur, spectacular beauty.
mag'ni-fy, to make great.
mag-nil'o-quence, pompous discourse.
mag'ni-tude, size, greatness.

ma'jor, greater, a military officer above a captain.
ma-jor'i-ty, the number greater than half; the age of 21 years.

MAN'DO, I command, MAN-DA'TUS, commanded.

com-mand', to give orders to.
com-mand'er, one who commands.
com-mand'ment, a precept.
coun-ter-mand', to revoke a command.

de-mand', to claim as a right.
man-da'mus, a legal order.
man'date, a command.
re-mand', to order or send back.

MA'NUS, a hand. MA'NUS, of a hand.

a-man-u-en'sis, one who writes what another dictates, a copyist.
e-man'ci-pate, to set free, to liberate.
man'a-cles, handcuffs
ma-nip'u-late, to handle.

man'u-al, done by hand, a handbook.
man-u-fac'ture, made by hand or by machinery.
man-u-mit', to release from slavery, to set free.
man'u-script, literally, written by hand.
quad-ru'ma-nous, having four hands.

MAR'E, the sea. MAR'IS, of the sea.

ma-rine', pertaining to the sea.
mar'i-ner, a seaman, a sailor.
mar'i-time, near the sea.
mer'maid (*through Fr.*), a sea monster.

sub-ma-rine', under the sea.
trans-ma-rine', across the sea.
ul-tra-ma-rine', a beautiful blue color (beyond the sea in color).

MI'GRO, I go from the land. MI-GRA'TUS, gone from the land.

em'i-grant, one who leaves his own country.
em'i-grate, to leave one's country.
im'mi-grate, to settle in another country.

mi'grate, to remove to another country.
mi'gra-to-ry, roving, wandering.
trans-mi-gra'tion, removal from one place to another.

MI'NOR, MI'NUS, less (comparative of PAR'VUS, small, little).

di-min'ish, to lessen.
dim-i-nu'tion, a reduction in size, a lessening.
di-min'u-tive, small in size.
min'i-a-ture, a small likeness.
min'i-mum, smallest amount.

mi'nor, less, inferior.
mi-nor'i-ty, the smaller of two numbers (or parties) making up a whole; the state of being under age.
min'ute, a brief time, a moment.
mi-nute', very small, little.

MORS, death. MOR'TIS, of death.

im-mor'tal, not subject to death.
im-mor'tal-ize, to cause to live forever.
mor'tal, subject to death.
mor-tal'i-ty, death.

mor-ti-fi-ca'tion, the death of a part of the body; vexation.
mor'ti-fy, to cause death: to humiliate.

MO'VE-O, I move. MO'TUS, moved.

com-mo'tion, excited movement.
e-mo'tion, a movement of the mind.
mo'tion, a movement.
mo'tive, the moving power.
move, to put in motion.

move'ment, change of place or position.
pro-mote', to advance, to forward.
pro-mo'tion, a moving forward.
re-mov'al, a change of place.
re-move', to move from its place.

MUL'TUS, much, or many.

mul-ti-fa'ri-ous, having much diversity.
mul'ti-form, of many forms
mul-ti-lat'er-al, having many sides.

mul'ti-plex, manifold.
mul'ti-ply, to increase in number.
mul'ti-tude, a great number.

NA'VIS, a ship. NA'VIS, of a ship. NAU'TA, a sailor. NAU'TÆ, of a sailor.

cir-cum-nav-i-ga'tion, sailing round the globe.
nau'ti-cal, seafaring.
nau'ti-lus, a shellfish that sails.
na'val, pertaining to ships.

nav-i-ga'tion, the art of sailing.
nav'i-ga-tor, a sailor.
na'vy, a fleet of ships.

NO'MEN, a name. NO'MIN-IS, of a name.

de-nom-i-na'tion, a distinguishing name.
mis-no'mer (*through Fr.*), a wrong name.
no'men-cla-ture, a list of names in any art or science.
nom'i-nal, in name only.

nom'i-nate, to name.
nom'i-na-tive, the case denoting the subject of a finite verb.
nom-i-nee', a person named.

NO'VUS, new.

in-no-va'tion, introduction of something new.
nov'el, new.
nov'el-ty, newness.

nov'ice, a beginner.
no-vi'ti-ate, state of being a novice.
ren'o-vate, to make new, to renew.

NU'TRI-O, I nourish. NU-TRI'TUS, nourished.

nour'ish (*through Fr.*), to cherish, to feed.
nour'ish-ing (*through Fr.*), promoting growth.
nour'ish-ment (*through Fr.*), act of nourishing.
nurse (*through Fr.*), one who nourishes.
nurs'er-y (*through Fr.*), apartment, in a house, appropriated to the care of children.

nur'ture (*through Fr.*), to feed, to foster.
nu'tri-ent, a nourishing substance.
nu'tri-ment, sustaining food.
nu-tri'tious, health giving.

OP'ER-A, work, labor. OP'ER-Æ, of work, labor.

co-op'er-ate, to work together.
in-op'er-a-tive, not at work.
op'er-a, a musical play.

op'er-ate, to work, to act.
op-er-a'tion, action.
op'er-a-tor, one who performs.

OS, a bone. OS'SIS, of a bone.

os'se-ous, bony.
os-sif'er-ous, containing or yielding bones.
os-si-fi-ca'tion, the process of changing into bone.

os'si-frage, the sea-eagle, or bone-breaker.
os'si-fy, to change into bone.
os-siv'o-rous, feeding on bones.

PA'TER, a father. PA'TRIS, of a father. PA'TRI-A, fatherland. PA'TRI-Æ, of the fatherland.

com-pa'tri-ot, a fellow countryman.
pa-ter'nal, fatherly.
pa-ter'ni-ty, fatherhood.

pa'tri-arch, a father and ruler.
pa'tri-ot, a lover of his country.
pa'tri-ot-ism, a love of country.

PEN'DE-O, I hang. PEN'SUS, hung. PEN'DO, I weigh, or value. PEN'SUS, weighed or valued.

de-pend', to hang from, to rely upon.
ex-pend', to lay out, to use up.
ex-pense', money, time, etc. laid out.
im-pend'ing, hanging over, threatening.

pend'ant, (n.) something hanging.
pend'ent, (a.) something hanging, awaiting decision.
sus-pend', to hang, to delay.
sus-pen'sion, a temporary withholding, a hanging up.

PES, a foot. PE'DIS, of a foot.

bi'ped, a two-footed animal.
cen'ti-pede, having a hundred feet.
ex-pe'di-ent, apt or suitable.
ex'pe-dite, to hasten, to facilitate.
ex-pe-di'tion, haste, speed.
im-ped'i-ment, something which impedes or hinders.

ped'al, pertaining to the foot.
ped'es-tal, the base or foot of a pillar, vase, or lamp, etc.
pe-des'tri-an, one who goes on foot.
ped'i-cle, a little foot, hence the stalk, or stem of a flower.
quad'ru-ped, having four feet.

PE'TO, I seek. PE-TI'TUS, sought.

ap'pe-tite, desire, longing.
cen-trip'e-tal, directed toward the center.
com-pete', to strive with another.
com-pe-ti'tion, common strife for the same object.

im'pe-tus, the force with which a body is driven forward.
pe-ti'tion, a request, a seeking after something.
re-peat', to say again, to recite.

PO'NO, I put, or place. POS'I-TUS, put, or placed.

com-pose', to put together.
com-pos'i-tor, one who sets up printing type.
dis-pose', to put in place, to arrange.
ex-pose', to place out, to lay open.
ex-pos'i-tor, one who explains.
op-pose', to set against.

op'po-site, placed against.
po-si'tion, place, situation.
post, a place or station.
pos'ture, the mode in which anything is placed, an attitude.
sup-pose', to put under, or imagine.

POR'TO, I carry. POR-TA'TUS, carried.

ex-port', to carry out.
im-port', to carry in.
port, carriage, bearing, demeanor.
port'a-ble, capable of being carried.

por'ter, a carrier.
port'ly, of noble carriage, stately.
re-port', to carry back or give an account of.
sup-port', to sustain, to carry, to hold up.

PRI'MUS, first.

pri'ma fa'ci-e, at first view.
pri'ma-ry, first in order of time.
pri'mate, an archbishop, ranking first among others.
prime, of the first rank.
prim'er, a first book.

pri-me'val, belonging to the first ages.
prim'i-tive, original, pertaining to early times.
pri-mo-gen'i-ture, the right which belongs to the first-born.
pri-mor'di-al, first in order.

QUÆ'RO, I seek, I inquire. QUÆ-SI'TUS, sought.

ex'qui-site, sought out with care, hence, matchless, perfect.
in'quest, an inquiry into the cause of death.
in-quire', to seek into.
in-qui-si'tion, a searching into.
in-quis'i-tive, prying, curious.

que'ry, a question.
quest, search, inquiry.
re-quest', to ask, to solicit.
re-quire', to demand, to ask.

RA'DO, I scrape, I shave. RA'SUS, scraped.

a-brade', to scrape off.
ab-ra'sion, a rubbing off.
e-rase', to scratch or rub out.

e-ra'sure, a scratching out.
raze, to level with the ground.
ra'zor, a shaving knife.

RID'E-O, I laugh at. RI'SUS, laughed at.

de-ride', to laugh at.
de-ri'sion, scorn, mockery.
rid'i-cule, to expose to laughter.

ri-dic'u-lous, laughable, silly.
ris-i-bil'i-ty, proneness to laugh.
ris'i-ble, exciting laughter.

RO'GO, I ask, I demand. RO-GA'TUS, asked, demanded.

ar'ro-gance, pride, making undue claims to self-importance.
in-ter'ro-gate, to ask questions
in-ter-ro-ga'tion, inquiry.

in-ter-rog'a-tive, a word used in asking questions; as, *Who? What?*
su-per-er-o-ga'tion, doing more than is asked

SANC'TUS, holy, sacred.

sanc'ti-fy, to make holy.
sanc-ti-mo'ni-ous, having the appearance of holiness.
sanc'ti-ty, holiness.

sanc'tu-a-ry, a consecrated place.
sanc'tum sanc-to'rum, the most holy place.

SA'NUS, sound, healthful.

in-sane', of unsound mind.
in-san'i-ty, madness, lunacy.
san'a-tive, curative, tending to heal.

sane, sound, healthy.
san'i-ta-ry, pertaining to health.
san'i-ty, soundness of mind.

SCI'O, I know. SCI'ENS (pres. part.), knowing.

con'science, inward conviction or acknowledgment.
con'scious, aware of, knowing.
om-nis'cience, knowing all things.
pre'sci-ence, foreknowledge.

sci'ence, precise knowledge.
sci-en-tif'ic, according to science.
sci'o-list, a pretender to science, one who knows little.

SE'CO, I cut. SEC'TUS, cut.

bi-sect', to cut in two.
dis-sect', to cut in pieces.
dis-sec'tion, the art of cutting up, anatomy.
in'sect, a small animal that appears to be cut into or divided.

in'ter-sect, to cut between.
sec-ta'ri-an, belonging to a sect.
sec'tion, a cutting, a division.
seg'ment. a piece cut off.
tri-sect', to cut in three.

SER'VO, I preserve, I keep. SER-VA'TUS, preserved.

con-serv'a-tive, wishing to preserve.
con-serv'a-to-ry, a place where choice plants are pre_served.
con-serve', to preserve from loss.

ob-serve', to notice, to keep in view.
res-er-va'tion, a keeping back.
re-serve', to keep back.
un-re-served', not kept back.

STRIN'GO, I bind, I hold fast. STRIC'TUS, bound or held.

as-trin'gent, binding, contracting.
con-strict', to draw together, to bind.
con-stric'tor, that which draws together; a class of ser_pents that crush their prey.

re-stric'tion, a holding back.
strict, held close, bound.
stric'ture, a contraction; a critical remark.
strin'gent, binding strongly.

TEN'DO, I stretch out. TEN'TUS or TEN'SUS, stretched out.

dis-ten'sion, a stretching asunder.
ex-tend', to spread out.
ex-ten'sion, a stretching out.
in-tense', strained, excessive.
pre-tend', to allege falsely.
pre-ten'sion, a claim, true or false.
su-per-in-tend', to overlook, to direct.

tend, to stretch towards.
tend'en-cy, direction, course.
ten'der, to offer, to stretch out the arm.
ten'don, a hard cord by which a muscle is attached to a bone.
tense, stretched to stiffness, rigid.
ten'sion, the state of being stretched.

TEN'E-O, I hold. TEN'TUS, held.

ab-stain', to hold back from.
ab'sti-nence, forbearance.
con-tain', to hold within limits.
con-tin'ue, to hold on.
de-tain', to hold from, to keep back.
de-ten'tion, a withholding.
main-tain', to uphold.

re-tain', to hold back, to keep.
ten'a-ble, capable of being held.
ten'ant, one who holds property of another.
ten'e-ment, that which is held by a tenant.
ten'et, a doctrine held.
ten'or, a state of holding on in a continuous course.
ten'ure, the manner of holding an estate.

TER'RA, the earth. TER'RÆ, of the earth.

dis-in-ter', to take out of the grave.
in-ter', to cover with earth, to bury.
in-ter'ment, burial, funeral.
sub-ter-ra'ne-an, underground.
ter'race, a raised level walk or platform of earth.

ter'ra cot'ta (*through It.*), cooked clay, potter's clay, of which statues and vases are made.
ter-ra'que-ous, consisting of land and water.
ter-res'tri-al, pertaining to the earth.

TEST'IS, a witness. TEST'IS, of a witness.

at-test', to bear witness.
pro-test', to declare, to witness against.
prot'es-tant, a Christian who rejects the tenets of the Roman Church.
test, a trial, a proof.

tes'ta-ment, a last will, a covenant.
tes'ti-fy, to bear witness to.
tes-ti-mo'ni-al, a writing which bears witness to one's character.

U'NUS, one. U-NI'US, of one.

u'ni-corn, a one-horned beast.
u'ni-form, of one appearance.
un'ion, concord, agreement.
u'ni-son, of one sound.

u'nit, a single thing.
u-nit'ed, joined, made one.
u'ni-ty, oneness, agreement.
u-niv'o-cal, of one meaning.

VE'RUS, true.

ve-ra'cious, observant of truth.
ve-rac'i-ty, truthfulness.
ver-i-fi-ca'tion, a proof of truth.

ver'i-fy, to prove true.
ver'i-ly, truly, indeed.
ver'i-ty, truth.

VI'A, a way, a road. VI'Æ, of a way, a road.

de'vi-ate, to go out of the way.
de-vi-a'tion, a wandering.
ob'vi-ate, to clear the way of
ob'vi-ous, easily discovered, plain, clear.

per'vi-ous, capable of being penetrated.
pre'vi-ous, going before.
vi'a, by the way of.
vi'a-duct, a large bridge built to carry a road.

VI'VO, I live. VIC'TUS, lived. VI'TA, life. VI'TÆ, of life.

re-vive', to live again, to arouse.
sur-vive', to live longer than, to outlive.
vi'tal, necessary to life.

vi-va'cious, full of life.
viv'id, lively, bright.
viv-i-sec'tion, anatomy practiced on living animals.

VO'LO, I wish, I am willing.

be-nev'o-lent, well-wishing, desirous of doing good.
in-vol'un-ta-ry, not having will or the power of choice.
ma-lev'o-lent, wishing evil.

vo-li'tion, the act of willing; the act of forming a purpose.
vol'un-ta-ry, of free will.
vol-un-teer', one who serves of free will.

CORRECT SPELLING

To be able to spell correctly is an accomplishment greatly to be desired. Two important elements enter into the habit of correct spelling: (1) to *observe* words correctly; (2) to *hear* words correctly. Errors often arise from a lack of *thoughtful attention* when studying spelling. In this way the impression made upon the mind by the word as a whole is *incorrect*, or the impression of the correct word has been so dimly made as to be easily forgotten. Difficult words are often more easily spelled because of the added attention they receive and, conversely, the short simple words are misspelled because attention is not directed to them.

It is well to be able to spell all words correctly, but especially should one be able to spell words in common use. Your stock of everyday words may number 2000 or 2500. These are the words of first importance in learning to spell.

The habit of consulting the dictionary is invaluable. The use of diacritical marks and the division of words into syllables are an aid to correct pronunciation; but it is only by practice and by a conscientious and frequent reference to the dictionary that proficiency in correct spelling can be acquired.

The meaning of words should be learned along with their spelling. This is particularly important in the case of homonyms, like *there* and *their*, which are pronounced the same but spelled differently. If the spelling and the meaning are learned together, no confusion arises in the use of these words.

How to Improve Your Spelling. With the hope of helping to overcome the poor spelling of the present day, the following suggestions are offered:

Pronounce words correctly and distinctly; clear enunciation is of great value.

Learn the analysis of words, that is, learn to recognize the syllables, prefixes, suffixes, and their values; for the analysis of words makes one's spelling more reliable.

With the analysis and meanings of words, associate their uses. This will lead to a mastery of words and tends to better power in spelling.

Make a special study of those words which by reason of a peculiar combination of letters present some difficulty; for example, *believe, receive, precede, proceed.*

Observe particularly silent letters, obscure vowels, or variations in vowel sounds which appear in certain words, as in *homage, heir, subtle, benefit, separate.*

A most troublesome factor in the spelling problem is the repetition of common errors. The habit of repeatedly misspelling the same words may be overcome by any method of study which directs special attention to them.

There is no better way to master the art of spelling than by repeated oral and written practice; for it is the *repetition* which forms the habit.

Because they lack special aptitude for spelling, or because of some difficulty not easily overcome, some persons believe they can never learn to spell. This is an error. Any person of average intelligence can learn to spell if he fully determines to do so, and then diligently strives toward the accomplishment of that end.

Spelling Lists. The following lists are prepared to give ever present help in spelling. They will be found useful for reference, for study, and for review. The first list contains one hundred "spelling demons" first published in *A Concrete Investigation of the Materials of English Spelling*, issued from the University of South Dakota. A comparison of these words with the spelling scale prepared by L. P. Ayres for the Russell Sage Foundation indicates that eighth grade pupils should earn marks of 90 to 100 on groups of 20 words each, selected from the list. However, a large number of these words are among those found to be most frequently misspelled in the College Entrance Board examinations. The other lists have been prepared after a careful study of frequent spelling errors and everyday vocabularies, such as *The Child and His Spelling* by W. A. Cook and M. V. O'Shea and *The Spelling Vocabularies of Personal and Business Letters* by L. P. Ayres.

Rules for Spelling

1. If a termination beginning with *e*, *i*, or *y* is added to a word ending in *c*, when *c* is not to be pronounced as *s*, *k* is inserted after *c*: *picnic, picnicking; traffic, trafficker.*

2. If a word of one syllable or a word accented on the last syllable ends in a single consonant preceded by a single vowel, the final consonant is doubled before a termination beginning with a vowel: *fit, fitting; clan, clannish; prefer, preferring; permit, permitted.*

3. When a digraph, that is, two coupled vowels, precedes the final consonant, or when the accent is not on the last syllable, or when it goes to a preceding syllable in the new word, the final consonant is not doubled before a termination beginning with a vowel: *sail, sailing; travel, traveler; benefit, benefited; prefer, preferable.* Exceptions are: *handicapped, humbugged.*

4. When a word ends in silent *e*, unless *e* is preceded by another vowel, the *e* is usually retained before a termination beginning with a consonant and omitted before a termination beginning with a vowel: *hide, hiding; come, coming; late, lateness; race, racial; provoke, provoking; fine, fineness; spite, spiteful, spiting; use, usable.* Exceptions: *judgment, acknowledgment, abridgment, duly, truly,* and *awful.*

5. Words ending in *ce* or *ge* do not drop the *e* before *able* or *ous.* Retaining *e* in this case preserves the soft sound of *g* and the *s* sound of *c*: *notice, noticeable; change, changeable.*

6. Words ending in *y* preceded by a consonant usually change *y* into *i* before an additional letter or syllable: *spy, spies; cry, crier; gratify, gratifies.* But *y* is not changed before *-ing*: *deny, denying; reply, replying.*

Words ending in *y* preceded by a vowel usually retain the *y* unchanged, as in *boy, boys, boyish, boyhood. Laid, paid, said,* are exceptions.

7. The spelling of many words in *ie* and *ei* may be determined by the following rule: If the coupled vowels follow *c*, the *e* comes first; if they follow *l* or *r*, the *i* comes first: *receive, believe, grief.* Some exceptions are: *financier, leisure, sleigh.*

8. In the singular number, the possessive of nouns is formed by adding to the noun an apostrophe and *s*: *Burns's, Jones's, St. James's, St. Giles's, Dickens's, Douglas's.*

The *s* is omitted in the singular when too many hissing sounds would come together: for *Jesus'* sake; for *conscience'* sake; for *goodness'* sake; *Damocles'* sword. When the word consists of more than two syllables, the apostrophe only is added: *Achilles'* sword; *Socrates'* wife; *Euripides'* dramas; *Demosthenes'* orations.

9. Derivatives formed from the Latin stem *ced* are usually spelled *cede*; the exceptions are *exceed, proceed, succeed.*

10. Generally spell in full rather than use abbreviations or numerals for the following: Titles of business, honor, or respect, preceding proper names; Christian names; numbers of fewer than three digits, unless the number is followed by a word of measure; all numbers beginning a sentence; the time of day, except when the number is used with A. M. or P. M.; numbers of centuries, sessions of congress, and the words "United States."

11. *Plurals.* Most nouns form the plural number by adding *s* or *es* to the singular: *state, states; inch, inches.*

The plural of numerals and of unusual or artificial word formations is formed by adding an apostrophe and *s*: *7's, 9's,* the *1900's, t's, y's.*

Plurals of proper names are generally formed by adding *s* or *es*: *Brown, Browns; James, Jameses.*

COMMON WORDS FREQUENTLY MISSPELLED

ONE HUNDRED SPELLING DEMONS

ache
again
always
among
answer
any
been
beginning
believe
blue
break
built
business
busy
buy
can't
choose
color
coming
cough
could
country
dear
doctor
does
done
don't
early
easy
enough
every
February
forty
friend

grammar
guess
half
having
hear
heard
here
hoarse
hour
instead
just
knew
laid
loose
lose
making
many
meant
minute
much
none
often
once
piece
quiet
raise
read
ready
said
says
seems
separate
shoes
since

some
straight
sugar
sure
tear
their
there
they
though
through
tired
tonight
too
trouble
truly
Tuesday
two
used
very
wear
Wednesday
week
where
whether
which
whole
women
won't
would
write
writing
wrote

SCHOOL WORDS

abbreviate
absence
absolutely
academy
accessory
accident
accidentally
accomplice
accomplish
accurate
accustom
acid
across
addition
adjoin
adjourn
affairs
affect
aggravate
algebraic
all right
almost
alphabet
already
ambition
ammonia
analogous
analysis
ancient
anecdote
angle
aniline (-in)
antarctic
antecedent
anthracite
Apollo
apostrophe
apparatus
apparent
appearance
appliance
appositive
architecture
arctic
argument
arithmetic
artificially
arouse
assembly
assignment
athletic
atmosphere
attempt

attendance
autobiography
auxiliary
avalanche
average
avoidance
awkward
barrier
battalion
benefit
biography
biology
blizzard
buoyant
cafeteria
candidate
canyon
caterpillar
chalk
changeable
chautauqua
chemistry
chosen
circuit
circumference
circumstance
citizenship
civilization
clever
climate
coherence
college
colloquial
combination
comedy
commencement
commission
communication
comparison
compulsory
concede
conceivable
conceive
conception
conscientious
consequence
conspicuous
contemplate
continent
continually
control
courageous
crater

criminally
criticism
crucifixion
crucify
curriculum
customary
cyclone
cylinder
daily
decide
decimal
declension
definitely
demonstrable
demonstrative
demonstrator
denominator
descend
description
descriptive
desirable
despair
desperately
develop
diagonal
dialogue (-log)
diameter
dictionary
difference
diligence
diphthong
disappear
discipline
disinfect
dismissal
dissatisfied
dissipated
distribute
division
dynasty
eclipse
e'er
effect
eighth
elegy
embarrass
emphasis
encouragement
encyclopedia
enemy
enmity
enthusiasm
envious

equation
equator
equipped
eraser
ere
erroneous
essential
exaggerate
examination
exceed
excel
excellent
exemption
exercise
exhibition
existence
expensive
explain
explanation
exposition
expression
extension
extremely
factoring
fascinate
felonious
figure
foreign
foresee
formally
formerly
frigid
gasoline
gauge (gage)
generally
genius
genuine
geology
geometry
glacier
granite
guard
gymnastics
happiness
height
hemisphere
hexagon
history
horizontal
humorous
hygiene
hypocrisy
hysterics
iambic
idiom
ignominious
ignominy
ignorance
illustrate
imagination
imperative
improvable
inborn
incident
incitement
incriminate
indefinitely
independence
independent
indictment
indispensable
infinite
infinitesimal
infinitive
influential
influentially
instigation
instigator
institute
intelligence
intelligible
intention
interrogative
intransitive
irregular
irresistible
island
isosceles
isthmus
its
it's
kindergarten
laboratory
later
latitude
latter

lead
lead pencil
learn
lecture
led
legend
lightning
literary
literature
livelihood
longitude
loyalty
Macaulay
machinist
malefactor
malign
malignant
malignity
maneuver
manual
marriage
martyr
martyrdom
mathematics
mechanic
mechanical
mechanism
mediocre
mediocrity
mercury
meridian
metaphor
metonymy
microscope
mirage
misspell
modifies
modifying
monosyllable
mountain
multiplication
municipal
muscular
naphtha
narration
nativity
neuter
nineteen
ninety
nominative
noticeable
numerator
obedience
occasion
occur
occurred
occurrence
o'clock
offense
omitted
opportunity
ostensible
ostentatious
oxygen
pageant
paragraph
parallel
paraphernalia
parliament
participial
participle
particularly
passed
passion
passionate
past
peaceful
peninsula
perfect
perfectly
perform
permanent
permission
perpendicular
perpetration
perpetrator
phenomenon
Philip
phrase
physics
physiology
picturesque
planet
plateau
poetry
polygon

polysyllable
positively
possess
possessive
possibility
practicable
practically
practice
prairie
precede
precinct
predicate
prejudice
preparation
principal
principle
prism
privilege
proceed
professor
progressive
pronounce
pronunciation
prophecy
prophesy
propitious
proportion
prove
psychology
punctuation
pyramid
quiet
quite
rabbit
rarefaction
rarefy
rareness
rarity
ravine
readiness
realize
reasonable
recess
recital
recognize
recollect
recommend
remember
remembrance
repellent
repetition
representative
review
rhetoric
rhythm
rhythmic
ridicule
rime (rhyme
sacrifice
sacrificial
sacrilege
sacrilegious
satire
satyr
saucy
scholarship
seize
semicircle
seminary
senate
sentence
separately
session
severely
shepherd
siege
signature
simile
socialist
soliloquies
soliloquy
solution
sometimes
sophomore
specific
specimen
speech
squirrel
statement
strait
strengthen
strenuous
studying
subordinate
subtraction
succeed

sufficiently
suit
suite
summary
superintendent
surely
susceptibility
susceptible
syllable
sympathize
synonym
syntax
synthesis
systematic
talented
tariff
technical
temperature
temptation
tendency
therefore
thermometer
tournament
tragedy
traveler
tropical
turpentine
twelfth
typical
unanimous
uncomfortable
undoubtedly
university
until
usually
vacation
valuable
vertical
villain
vocabulary
volume
wealthily
weird
whimper
wholly
zoology

assure
attorney
auction
auditor
balance
bankrupt
bankruptcy
bargain
bookkeeper
brief
calculation
calendar
capacity
capital
cashier
catalogue (-log)
certificate
check
clerical
collateral
collectable (-ible)
commercial
commodity
competent
competition
compromise
comptroller
confidential
consideration
consignment
convenient
conveyance
corporation
correspondent
counterfeit
credentials
credit
creditor
criminal
customer
debt
debtor
decision
defer
deficit
delivery
depositor
diary
difficulty
discount
discussion
dividends
draft
due
economical
efficient
elevator
embezzle
employee
enterprise
especially

estimate
evidence
expenditure
expense
experience
factory
finally
finance
financial
financier
fiscal
foreclosure
foreign
forfeit
forgery
franchise
fraudulent
freight
government
guarantee
heir
hundred
immediate
indorsement
information
insolvency
installment
insurance
interest
inventory
investment
invoice
issue
itemized
items
janitor
journal
judgment
judicial
lease
ledger
legacy
legislature
liability
license
lucrative
machinery
manager
manufacture
material
maturity
mercantile
merchandise
millionaire
mortgage
mortgagee
mortgagor
municipal
necessary
notary
oblige

operator
parcel
particular
position
preferred
preliminary
president
probably
proceeds
profitable
profits
promissory
proprietor
purchase
receipt
recommend
reference
referring
register
regular
remittance
renewal
request
requisite
resources
respectfully
responsible
résumé
retail
revenue
salary
salesman
schedule
secretary
securities
sincerely
situation
speculate
stationery
statistics
stenographer
stockholder
storage
substantial
success
suggest
surplus
syndicate
taxes
telegraph
telephone
testimony
treasurer
typewriter
unique
usury
value
warehouse
warrant
weight
wholesale

SOCIAL AND PERSONAL WORDS

accept
accompany
acquaintance
aeronaut
aeroplane
affectionately
afford
agreeable
airplane
aisle
almanac
altar
amateur
angel
angry
animal
anniversary
announcement
annual
anxiety
apartment
apologize
appetite
appreciate
appreciative
arrangement
arrival
assistance
association
asylum
audience
automobile
bachelor
baggage
banquet
baptize
baseball
bazaar
bicycle
billiards
borrow
breakfast
burglar
campaign
candidate
canoe
captain
career
carriage
catechism
cathedral
celebration
cemetery
ceremony
chapel
chaperon
character
chauffeur
chivalry
circus
citizen
cologne
colonel
committee
complement
complexion
compliment

conductor
congregation
contribution
convenient
coquette
cordially
cousin
croquet
crowd
daughter
delegate
delicate
dentist
dependent
dietitian
din
diner
dining
dinner
disappoint
economical
elaborate
embarrassment
emergency
engagement
environment
etiquette
euchre
excursion
fashionable
fatigue
fellowship
fiancé
fiancée
funeral
garage
golf
grief
guest
hammock
harassment
heathen
heavy
heresy
hospitable
hungry
icicle
idol
innuendo
invitation
kodak
laugh
league
liquor
luncheon
magazine
majority
matron
mischief
missionary
mosquitoes
motor
mucilage
neighbor
niece
nuisance
occupy

oculist
optician
orchestra
organization
pamphlet
parade
parasol
passenger
pennant
phonograph
photographer
pianist
picnic
picnicking
plaguy
playwright
pleasure
priest
prodigal
prohibition
promenade
protégé
providence
psalm
quarrel
quoits
rehearse
relative
religious
rendezvous
repentance
restaurant
revival
scene
sight-seeing
sincerely
sleigh
souvenir
spectacles
suffrage
surprise
synagogue
tabernacle
taxicab
temperance
tenant
tenement
testament
theater
thief
tobacco
tournament
umbrella
umpire
unfortunate
valise
vaudeville
vilify
village
waltz
wasteful
wealth
whistle
wholesome
yacht

HOUSEHOLD WORDS

abscess
ague
alcohol
almond
ambulance
anesthetic
anoint
antitoxine
appendix
apron
artery
asbestos
asparagus
asthma
automatic
banana
bandage
baste
bilious
biscuit
blouse
bread
breathe
bronchitis
bruise
buffet
bungalow
bureau
butcher
button
cabbage
calico

cambric
camphor
cancer
cantaloupe
capsule
caramel
carpenter
cashmere
casserole
cataract
catarrh
ceiling
celery
cellar
cereal
chamois
chandelier
chiffonier
chloroform
chocolate
cholera
cinder
cinnamon
cloth
clothes
coat
cocoa
coffee
collar
contagious
convalescent
corduroy

cough
cretonne
crochet
croquette
crystal
cucumber
culinary
currant
curtain
dairy
desiccate
dessert
diamond
diarrhea
diary
digestion
diphtheria
disease
doily
dye
electricity
embroidery
enamel
epidemic
ether
faucet
feather
flannel
flour
forehead
fragile
frieze

BUSINESS WORDS

acceptance
accommodate
accountant
accrued
acknowledge
acquire
acre

address
administration
advertise
affidavit
agency
agreement
allege

annuity
application
approximately
arbitration
article
assets
assignment

furnace
furniture
gasoline (-ene)
gelatine
gingham
glycerine
grease
grippe (grip)
groceries
handkerchief
hearth
hemorrhage
herbs
hoarse
homeopathic
hosiery
hospital
inoculate
invalid
iodine (-in)
ironing
jewelry
kernel
kerosene
khaki
kimono
knead
knee
knife
knob
knot
knuckle
larynx
lattice
lemon
lemonade
lettuce
library
licorice
ligament
liniment
macaroni
mackerel
mackintosh
mahogany
mantelpiece
mattress
measles
measure
medicine
melon
meringue
milliner

mirror
molasses
muscle
mustard
nainsook
nausea
nervous
neuralgia
odor
omelet
organdie (-y)
ostrich
oyster
palate
paneling
paraffine
paralysis
pattern
peach
pear
peritonitis
perspiration
physically
physician
picture
pillow
pitcher
plaid
plaited
plumber
pneumonia
poached
porcelain
porch
portière
portrait
potatoes
poultice
poultry
prescription
ptomaine (-in)
pumpkin
quinine
radiator
raisin
raspberry
recipe
refrigerator
relief
remedy
reservoir
rheumatism
rhubarb

roast
salad
sandwich
sanitary
sateen
satin
saucer
sausage
scissors
settee
sieve
sirloin
skein
sleeve
specialist
spigot
spinach
steak
stomach
sugar
sulphur (-fur)
surgeon
syringe
taffeta
tailor
threshold
tissue
tomato
tongue
trousers
trousseau
tuberculosis
turkeys
turnip
typhoid
unbleached
utensil
vaccinate
vacuum
vanilla
vaseline (-in)
vegetable
veil
ventilate
ventilation
veranda
vinegar
waist
woolen
worsted
yolk
zephyr

SINGULAR	PLURAL
trout	trout
swine	swine
attorney at law	attorneys at law
commander in chief	commanders in chief
court-martial	courts-martial
editor in chief	editors in chief
father-in-law	fathers-in-law
governor-general	governors-general
maid of honor	maids of honor
man-of-war	men-of-war
son-in-law	sons-in-law
knight templar	knights templars
man-child	men-children
manservant	menservants
woman servant	women servants
alumna (feminine)	alumnæ
alumnus (masculine)	alumni
analysis	analyses
animalcule	animalcules
antithesis	antitheses
apparatus	{ apparatuses / apparatus }
appendix	{ appendices / appendixes }
axis	axes
bacillus	bacilli
bacterium	bacteria
bandit	{ banditti / bandits }
basis	bases
beau	{ beaux / beaus }
brother	{ brothers (relatives) / brethren (of the same society) }
candelabrum	candelabra
cannon	{ cannons (individuals) / cannon (collectively) }
cherub	{ cherubim (collectively) / cherubs }
crisis	crises
cumulus	cumuli
curriculum	{ curricula / curriculums }
datum	data
die	{ dies (for stamping) / dice (for gaming) }
ellipsis	ellipses
erratum	errata
fish	{ fishes (individually) / fish (collectively) }
foot	{ feet (parts of the body) / foot (infantry) }
formula	{ formulæ / formulas }
genius	{ geniuses (men of genius) / genii (spirits) }
genus	genera
gymnasium	{ gymnasia / gymnasiums }
head	{ heads (parts of bodies) / head (of cattle) }
heathen	{ heathens (individuals) / heathen (collectively) }
hippopotamus	{ hippopotami / hippopotamuses }
horse	{ horses (animals) / horse (cavalry) }
hypothesis	hypotheses
index	{ indexes (tables of reference) / indices (signs in algebra) }
larva	larvæ
memorandum	{ memoranda / memorandums }
nebula	nebulæ
oasis	oases
parenthesis	parentheses
penny	{ pennies (single coins) / pence (quantity in value) }
phenomenon	phenomena
radius	radii
sail	{ sails (pieces of canvas) / sail (vessels) }
seraph	{ seraphim (collectively) / seraphs }
shot	{ shots (number of times fired) / shot (number of balls) }
stratum	strata
synopsis	synopses
tableau	tableaux
terminus	termini
thesis	theses
trousseau	trousseaux
vertebra	vertebræ

IRREGULAR PLURALS

SINGULAR	PLURAL
beef	beeves
calf	calves
elf	elves
half	halves
knife	knives
leaf	leaves
life	lives
loaf	loaves
self	selves
sheaf	sheaves
shelf	shelves
thief	thieves
wife	wives
wolf	wolves
ally	allies
city	cities
daisy	daisies
fairy	fairies
fancy	fancies
lady	ladies
lily	lilies
mystery	mysteries
gentleman	gentlemen
goose	geese
man	men
mouse	mice
tooth	teeth
woman	women
deer	deer
gross	gross
grouse	grouse
hose	hose
mackerel	mackerel
salmon	salmon
series	series
sheep	sheep
species	species

HOMONYMS

Words pronounced the same but differing in spelling and in meaning.

air, that which we breathe.
ere, before.
e'er, ever.
heir, one that is to inherit.

aloud, audibly.
allowed, permitted.

altar, a place for worship.
alter, to change.

arc, part of a circle.
ark, as Noah's ark; a chest.

ascent, going up; an upward slope.
assent, to agree to.

ate, past tense of eat.
eight, twice four.

aught, anything.
ought, is (are) bound in duty.

bad, ill or wicked.
bade, past tense of bid.

bale, a bundle.
bail, surety for some one; a handle.

ball, a sphere; a dance.
bawl, to shout; to cry out.

band, that which binds; a narrow strip.
banned, forbidden.

bard, a poet.
barred, hindered; shut out.

bare, naked.
bear, to carry; a wild beast.

base, the lowest part; mean.
bass, the lowest part in harmonized music.

beech, a kind of tree.
beach, shore.

beer, a drink.
bier, anything on which the dead are carried to burial.

beet, a vegetable.
beat, to strike.

bell, a hollow metal body that rings or tolls.
belle, a beautiful or admired young woman.

berry, a small fruit.
bury, to inter; to conceal.

birth, being born; descent.
berth, a sleeping place.

bold, daring; courageous.
bowled, rolled, as in a game of bowling.

bole, the trunk of a tree.
boll, seed vessel of cotton plant.
bowl, a circular vessel.

bow, a weapon for shooting arrows; a kind of knot.
beau, a man of dress; a lover.

brake, a thicket.
break, to split.

bred, reared.
bread, baked flour.

breech, the lower or hinder part of a thing.
breach, a gap or opening.

brews, ferments; plots.
bruise, to crush; a contusion.

broach, a spit; to pierce.
brooch, an ornament for the breast.

brows, plur., the forehead.
browse, to eat the tender leaves of shrubs, as "sheep browse."

burrow, hole in ground made by an animal.
borough, a corporate town.
burro, a donkey.

by, a preposition and a prefix.
buy, to purchase.
bye, as in good-bye; a goal.
bi-, two, as in biweekly.

call, cry out; a visit.
caul, a membrane.

canon, a law; a rule.
cannon, a large gun.

canvas, a coarse cloth.
canvass, to solicit.

cast, to throw; a form.
caste, a tribe; a class.

cede, to give up.
seed, the embryo of a future plant.

ceiling, cover of a room.
sealing, tight closing, as with wax.

cell, a small cavity; a room.
sell, to exchange for a price.

cellar, an excavation in the ground.
seller, one who sells.

cent, a hundred.
sent, past tense of send.
scent, perfume; to smell.

cereal, pertaining to grain; food made of grain.
serial, pertaining to successive parts, as in a series.

cession, a giving up.
session, a sitting; a meeting.

chews, grinds with the teeth.
choose, to select.

choir, a company of singers.
quire, a set of sheets of paper.

cite, to summon; to quote.
site, place; position.
sight, the power of seeing; a look.

clause, part of a sentence.
claws, sharp nails or toes of animal or bird.

clime, a region; a country.
climb, to mount; to ascend.

core, an innermost part; a center.
corps, an organized company, as of soldiers.

course, a place for running; career.
coarse, not fine.

coward, one wanting in courage.
cowered, crouched through fear.

creek, a small stream.
creak, to make a harsh, grating noise.

crews, bodies of seamen for ships.
cruise, to sail from place to place on the ocean.
cruse, a small cup; a small bottle.

currents, streams.
currants, small fruit.

dew, moisture condensed and deposited from the air.
due, owing.

discreet, prudent; cautious.
discrete, distinct; disjoined.

doe, female of deer.
do, a musical sound name.
dough, unbaked bread.

done, performed.
dun, a color; to demand payment of debt.

dying, ceasing to live.
dyeing, shading or coloring.

faint, very fatigued; to swoon.
feint, a pretense.

fane, a temple.
fain, anxious; desirous.
feign, to pretend.

fare, money paid for a journey; food.
fair, beautiful; right; a market.

faun, a sylvan deity.
fawn, a young deer; to flatter meanly.

find, to discover.
fined, subject to a money penalty.

flour, fine part of meal.
flower, blossom of a plant.

fore, in front.
four, a number.

forth, forward; out.
fourth, the ordinal of four.

freeze, to congeal.
frieze, a coarse woolen fabric; an ornamented band on a wall.

gate, entrance; a door.
gait, one's way of walking.

gild, to overlay and adorn with gold.
guild, a society or corporation.

gilt, overlaid with gold.
guilt, responsibility for crime.

great, large.
grate, a fireplace; to rub against.

groan, deep sound of pain or sorrow.
grown, mature, fully developed.

guessed, estimated at random.
guest, one who is entertained.

hair, as of the head.
hare, an animal.

HOMONYMS (cont'd)

hall, a large room.
haul, to drag; to pull.

heel, the hind part of the foot.
heal, to cure; to grow sound.
he'll, contraction for "he will."

herd, a collection of cattle.
heard, past tense of hear.

hoard, to lay up in secret.
horde, a wandering tribe; a savage band.

hoes, uses a hoe.
hose, stockings; socks.
hose, rubber pipe.

I, a pronoun.
aye or **ay,** yes.
eye, organ of sight.

indite, to compose and write.
indict, to charge or accuse formally.

isle, a contraction for island.
aisle, passage in an auditorium.
I'll, contraction for "I will."

kernel, the central part.
colonel, chief officer of a regiment.

lane, a narrow passage.
lain, past participle of lie, to rest lengthwise on or against.

leaf, as of a book, a tree, etc.
lief, willingly.

least, little; beyond all others.
leased, held on lease.

led, past tense and participle of lead.
lead, a metal.

liar, one who tells lies.
lyre, a musical instrument.

lone, solitary; alone.
loan, a temporary grant.

male, opposite of female.
mail, armor; letters.

mane, the long hair on the neck of an animal.
main, the sea; principal; chief.

manner, method or way.
manor, an estate; a domain.

mantle, a cloak; a cover.
mantel, the slab or shelf above a fireplace.

marshal, a military or police officer.
martial, warlike.

maze, an intricate place.
maize, Indian corn.

mean, shabby; low; to intend
mien, manner of look or appearance.

meet, fit; to assemble.
mete, to measure.
meat, food; flesh.

mind, the understanding.
mined, excavated.

miner, a worker in mines.
minor, one under age.

mite, something very small.
might, power; strength.

moan, to lament.
mown, cut down.

mussel, a shellfish.
muscle, the fleshy parts of an animal body.

mustard, a kind of plant.
mustered, assembled.

nave, hub of a wheel; main portion of a cathedral.
knave, a rogue.

nay, no.
neigh, cry of a horse.

need, want; poverty.
knead, to work the materials into dough.

new, not old.
knew, past tense of know.
gnu, a wild ox.

night, opposite of day.
knight, a title of honor.

no, opposite of yes.
know, to understand.

nose, the organ of smell.
noes, plural of no.
knows, has knowledge; understands

oar, implement for rowing a boat.
ore, metal as it comes from the earth.
o'er, contraction for over.

ode, a short poem.
owed, indebted to; past tense of owe.

our, a pronoun.
hour, sixty minutes.

pain, soreness.
pane, a piece of glass.

pair, two; a couple.
pare, to slice thinly.
pear, a kind of fruit.

passed, gone through; gone.
past, not present or future.

pause, a stop.
paws, feet of a beast.

peace, a state of quiet.
piece, a part.

pedal, a foot lever; to operate such a lever.
peddle, to sell from house to house.

peel, skin; outside.
peal, sound of bells.

peer, to look intently; an equal.
pier, a wharf.

plane, a perfectly flat or level surface; a kind of tree.
plain, level, flat country.

plate, a flat piece of metal; a shallow dish.
plait, to fold; to braid.

please, to delight or gratify.
pleas, pleadings in law; excuses.

plum, a fruit.
plumb, perpendicular; an instrument to determine whether a wall is perpendicular.

pray, to entreat.
prey, plunder.

prays, supplicates.
praise, approbation; to approve.
preys, attacks, as a wild beast.

principal, invested funds; chief.
principle, a fundamental rule or law.

quarts, measures of two pints each.
quartz, a variety of rock crystal.

rain, water from clouds.
rein, part of a harness; to check.
reign, to rule as a king.

rap, to strike sharply.
wrap, to wind or roll together; to fold.

rapped, struck.
rapt, transported; ravished.
wrapped, folded; enclosed.

rays, beams of light.
raise, to exalt; to lift up.
raze, to destroy utterly.

read, as a book; to study.
reed, a hollow cane.

red, a color.
read, past tense of read.

rest, peace; quiet.
wrest, to twist; to wrench.

right, just; correct.
rite, a ceremony.
write, to trace letters or characters.
wright, a workman.

road, a path; a way.
rode, past tense of ride.
rowed, propelled with oars.

rôle, a part in acting a play.
roll, a round thing; a register.

rood, fourth part of an acre.
rude, uncultivated; rough.
rued, grieved for.

root, as of a plant; origin.
route, direction; road.

ruff, an article of dress.
rough, unpolished; rugged.

rung, sounded, as a bell.
wrung, twisted.

rye, a sort of grain.
wry, crooked.

sac, a membranous receptacle.
sack, a large, strong bag.

sail, to navigate.
sale, act of selling.

HOMONYMS (cont'd)

sea, a wide expanse of water.
see, to perceive.

seam, a line of junction between pieces of cloth.
seem, to appear; to have a semblance.

sees, looks at.
seize, to take hold of.

skull, the whole bone of the head.
scull, a small boat; a light, short oar.

soared, mounted on the wing.
sword, a weapon of war.

sold, given for a price.
soled, furnished with a sole.

sore, painful.
soar, to mount by flight.

soul, the spirit.
sole, only; bottom of the foot; a fish

sow, to scatter seed.
sew, to fasten, as with a needle.
so, in this manner.

staid, steady; grave.
stayed, supported with ropes, as a mast.

stair, flight of steps.
stare, to look at.

stake, a pointed piece of wood.
steak, a slice of meat.

straight, direct; not curved.
strait, narrow; confined.

style, manner of dress or action.
stile, steps over a wall.

sucker, a young shoot of a tree.
succor, help; to relieve.

sum, the amount of anything; to add up.
some, more or less of a quantity.

sutler, one who follows a camp to sell provisions, etc.
subtler, more cunning; more acute.

sweet, pleasant; delightful.
suite, attendants; a set of rooms.

tale, a story.
tail, an appendage; hinder part.

taught, past tense and perfect participle of teach.
taut, stretched tight.

tear, water from the eye.
tier, a row; a series.

teem, to produce in abundance.
team, a pair of horses or oxen, working together.

their, possessive of they.
there, adv., in that place.

threw, past tense of throw.
through, from side to side, or from end to end.

throw, to cast; to fling.
throe, extreme pain.

time, fit season.
thyme, a garden plant.

told, expressed in words.
tolled, rung, as a bell.

tract, a quantity of land.
tracked, followed by the marks left.

two, a pair; twice one.
too, adv., also; excess, as too much.
to, preposition.

use, to apply or handle for some purpose.
ewes, female sheep.
yews, evergreen trees.

vale, a valley.
veil, a curtain, a covering.

vice, a fault.
vise, a tool.

wade, to walk through water.
weighed, past tense of weigh.

wait, to remain; to stay.
weight, heaviness; importance.

ware, sing. of wares; goods.
wear, to last; to endure.

waste, to squander.
waist, the middle part, as of the body.

wave, a moving ridge; to undulate.
waive, to defer; to abandon.

way, a road; manner.
weigh, to determine heaviness; to ponder.

wood, a forest; timber.
would, verb of wish or determination.

HETERONYMS

Words spelled the same but differing in sound and in meaning. Strictly, heteronyms, from the very etymology of the word, have no alliance between them except the accidental one of the same orthography. They are derived from different roots and their meanings are so distinct that their separate origin is at once indicated by such meanings. Mere change of accent, moreover, does not constitute a heteronym.

bass (*bās*), a term in music.
bass (*băs*), a fish.

bow (*bou*), the forward part of a vessel.
bow (*bō*), an archer's weapon; an implement for playing the violin; a knot.

chap (*chăp*), a fellow.
chap (*chŏp*), fleshy covering of a jaw.

dives (*dīvz*), goes under water.
Dives (*dī'vēz*), the rich man.

does (*dōz*), female deer.
does (*dŭz*), from the verb *do*.

gill (*jĭl*), quarter of a pint.
gill (*gĭl*), the organ of respiration of a fish.

glower (*glou'ĕr*), to stare.
glower (*glō'ĕr*), something that glows.

hinder (*hĭn'dĕr*), to prevent.
hinder (*hīn'dĕr*), back part.

job (*jŏb*), petty work.
Job (*jōb*), a man's name.

lead (*lĕd*), a metal.
lead (*lēd*), to conduct.

lower (*lō'ĕr*), to descend.
lower (*lou'ĕr*), to frown.

manes (*mānz*), the hair on the neck of animals.
manes (*mā'nēz*), departed spirits.

mate (*māt*), a companion.
mate (*mä'tā*), a beverage.

mow (*mō*), to cut down.
mow (*mou*), a heap of grain; a compartment for storing grain.

mowing (*mō'ĭng*), the act of cutting.
mowing (*mou'ĭng*), to store away.

polish (*pŏl'ĭsh*), to shine.
Polish (*pōl'ĭsh*), adjective derived from *Pole*—pertaining to Poland.

poll (*pōl*), a degree without honors.
poll (*pōl*), the head; a tax.

put (*pŏŏt*), to move; to push.
put (*pŭt*), a rustic; a clown.

repent (*rē'pĕnt*), creeping; prostrate; reptant.
repent (*rê-pĕnt'*), to feel penitence, contrition, or regret, for what one has done or has omitted to do.

row (*rō*), a rank or file; to propel with oars.
row (*rou*), a tumult.

sake (*sāk*), purpose, end, cause.
sake (*sä'kĕ*), liquor made from rice.

sewer (*sū'ĕr*), a ditch or a drain.
sewer (*sō'ĕr*), one who sews.

shower (*shō'ĕr*), one that exhibits.
shower (*shou'ĕr*), a light rain.

singer (*sĭn'jĕr*), one that singes.
singer (*sĭng'ᴜr*), one that sings.

slough (*slou, slōō*), a hole full of mire; a marshy place.
slough (*slŭf*), cast-off skin of a serpent.

sow (*sō*), to scatter seeds.
sow (*sou*), female pig.

stingy (*stĭn'jĭ*), penurious.
stingy (*stĭng'ĭ*), piercing.

swinger (*swĭng'ĕr*), one that swings.
swinger (*swĭn'jĕr*), one that beats or chastises.

tarry (*tär'ĭ*), covered with, or like, tar.
tarry (*tăr'ĭ*), to abide at or in a place; to stay; to loiter; to delay.

tear (*târ*), to divide or separate on being pulled.
tear (*tēr*), a drop of limpid saline fluid secreted by the lachrymal gland.

tower (*tou'ĕr*), a high edifice; a citadel.
tower (*tō'ĕr*), that which tows.

wind (*wĭnd*), air in motion.
wind (*wīnd*), to twist.

wound (*wŏŏnd*), an injury.
wound (*wound*), twisted.

SENTENCE BUILDING

ENGLISH GRAMMAR is both a science and an art. As a science, it investigates the principles in general on which the English language is based; as an art, it teaches the method of applying these principles in speaking and in writing the English language correctly.

In the whole range of school subjects there is none of greater importance than that of language. To facilitate the study of the English language, therefore, the true principles of grammar have been outlined in the following pages in a convenient form, expressed in a simple manner, and illustrated by appropriate examples.

THE ENGLISH SENTENCE

Word Groups. We express our thoughts in groups of words,—sentences, clauses, phrases.

A *sentence* is a group of words used to express a complete thought.

The complete sentence must always contain a subject and a predicate. The subject is the thing named; the predicate is the assertion about the thing named: "*Autumn* (subj.) *lingers* (pred.)."

In an imperative sentence, like "Go to him," the subject "you" is not usually expressed. This is an instance of *ellipsis*, or the omission of words otherwise necessary to grammatical completeness, when their meaning is well understood by the reader or hearer: "The knife belongs to Tom; the pencil (belongs) to William."

A *clause* is a group of words containing, like the sentence, a subject and a predicate, but used only as part of a complete sentence: "The motor, | which was new, | suddenly failed to work."

A clause may be either *independent* (principal) or *dependent* (subordinate): "He commanded, | who had never commanded before." The first words, *he commanded*, form an independent clause. The other words form a dependent clause; for, as they stand, they do not make a sentence. See *Complex Sentence.*

A *phrase* is a group of words so closely related as to express a single idea. The phrase is used as a part of speech: "*To become rich* (noun) was his ambition." "It was a matter *of importance* (adjective)." "Come *at your convenience* (adverb)."

Parts of Speech. In building sentences, we use name-words, action-words, modifiers, and connectives of various kinds. According to their use in sentences, these words are classified as *parts of speech*, of which there are eight:

1. A *noun* is a word used to name a person, a place, or a thing: *boy, city, foot, air, size.*

2. A *pronoun* is a word used in place of a noun: *it, her, none, who.*

Note.—Nouns, pronouns, and phrases or clauses used as nouns are called *substantives.*

3. A *verb* is a word used to say, or assert, something about a person, a place, or a thing: *walk, soften, drive, is.*

4. An *adjective* is a word used to modify, that is, describe or limit, a noun or pronoun: "*bright* sunshine," "*few* people," "I *alone.*"

5. An *adverb* is a word used to modify the meaning of a verb, an adjective, or another adverb: "speak *well*," "walk *swiftly*," "run *homeward*," "*very* pretty," "*so* quickly."

6. A *conjunction* is a word used to connect words, phrases, clauses, or sentences: *and, but, if, unless.*

7. A *preposition* is a word used to show the relation of some particular word, called its object, to another word: "flocks *of* birds (obj.)"; "strength *through* exercise (obj.)"; "peace *with* honor (obj.)."

8. An *interjection* is a word of exclamation used to express any emotion or feeling, as surprise, joy, grief, etc.: *ah! alas!*

Note.—Some words may be used as *several different parts of speech*:

Noun: "The *storm* was soon over."
Adjective: "The station displayed *storm* signals."
Verb: "The troops will *storm* the outworks."

Noun: "The *inside* of the house is pleasing."
Adjective: "He has *inside* information."
Adverb: "Will you step *inside?*"
Preposition: "*Inside* the door stood a clock."

Preposition: "I have been waiting *since* noon."
Conjunction: "*Since* I saw you, much has happened."

Adjective: "*Which* hat have you?"
Pronoun: "The hat *which* you see is mine."

Adjective: "*That* hat is mine."
Pronoun: "I want *that.*"
Conjunction: "He said *that* he would go."

PARTS OF THE SENTENCE

The Subject. The subject of a sentence is that about which the predicate asserts something: "*The weather* is cold." "*Health* counts for more than wealth."

Simple Subject.—The essential part of the *subject* is a substantive, that is, a noun, a pronoun, or a phrase or clause used as a noun. Noun means "name." The substantive is called the *essential*, or *simple, subject*, or the *subject substantive*: "A great *city* (noun substantive) is interesting"; "*She* (pro. substantive) is my friend"; "*To read well* (subst. phrase) requires much practice"; "*What he saw* (subst. clause) startled him."

Complete Subject.—The substantive with its modifiers is called the *complete subject*: "*His deposit* (subst.) *in the bank* (adj. phrase) | was large." The modifiers of the substantive may be adjectives, possessive nouns or pronouns, nouns in apposition, clauses or phrases used as adjectives or nouns.

The Predicate. The word *predicate* means "something said." The predicate of a sentence is that which is asserted about the subject: "Roses *were blooming.*"

The essential part of a predicate is a *verb*. We call the verb in the predicate the *essential*, or *simple, predicate*, or the *predicate verb*. "The car *ran* (pred. verb) *against the curb.*" *Ran* is the simple predicate; *ran against the curb* is the complete predicate.

The relation between subject and predicate may be shown graphically, as in the following diagram. Note that the simple elements appear on the main line and the complex or subordinate ones below this line. The practice of sentence diagramming is strongly recommended.

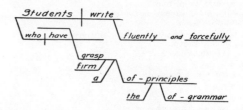

CLASSIFICATION OF SENTENCES

Kinds of Sentences. In respect to their *meaning*, sentences may be classified as declarative, interrogative, imperative, and exclamatory.

The *declarative sentence* makes a statement: "*John is not here.*"

The *interrogative sentence* asks a question: "*Where is my hat?*"

The *imperative sentence* gives a command; "*Answer his question.*"

The *exclamatory sentence* expresses a strong feeling, as of surprise, joy, etc.: "*How free are the pleasures of youth!*"

Note.—The foregoing is the common grouping of sentences. A more logical classification is the following: (1) *affirmative* and *negative*; (2) *declarative* and *interrogative*; (3) *exclamatory* and *nonexclamatory*.

Forms of Sentences. In respect to their *grammatical form*, sentences are simple, compound, or complex.

The *simple sentence* is a sentence of one clause, that is, a sentence having but one subject and one predicate. The simple sentence may be very short: "*Birds | sing.*" It may be longer, when the subject and the predicate are modified by several words and phrases: "*Those furs in the window | have been gathered from many different countries and climates.*"

A simple sentence may have a *compound subject*; as, "*The house and the grounds | are beautiful.*" It may have a *compound predicate*; as, "*They | sat and listened* to the music." Both subject and predicate may be compound; as, "*Mary and Elizabeth | lived and reigned* in England." These are important distinctions. Do not confuse the *long* sentence with the *complex* sentence.

The *compound sentence* is formed by two or more clauses of equal rank. These independent, or "coordinate," clauses may or may not be joined by coordinating conjunctions such as *and, but, for:* "*A man approaches. | and | we recognize him;*" "*Some men are born great; | others achieve greatness.*"

The *complex sentence* is formed of a principal, or independent, clause and of one or more subordinate, or dependent, clauses. These subordinate clauses are introduced by subordinate conjunctions, such as *if, unless, because,* by relative pronouns, *who, which, what, that,* and by conjunctive adverbs, such as *when, where, while:* "*I shall go if it stops raining*"; "*The child that is happy* makes friends"; "*Make hay while the sun shines.*"

The Parts of Speech

Grammatical Relations. The relations of a word, a phrase, or a clause to other words in a sentence are called its *syntax* or *construction.* Either of these words means "placing or bringing together."

Inflection, in grammar, is the changing of the forms of words to indicate grammatical relation and change of meaning. Inflection of verbs is called *conjugation.* Inflection of nouns and pronouns is called *declension.* Inflection of adjectives and adverbs is called *comparison.*

In the English sentence, the grammatical relations of words are indicated by their position and by the use of connectives. The English language has dropped so many of the endings formerly attached to nouns and verbs that inflection in English grammar is of slight importance. So-called declension becomes in English the systematic arrangement in tables of the various forms of nouns and pronouns used for different cases and numbers. Conjugation consists in arranging in tables the various verb forms and verb phrases used for different modes and tenses.

Kinds of Substantives: Nouns and Pronouns

A *substantive* is a word, phrase, or clause used as a noun.

KINDS OF NOUNS

Proper Nouns. A *proper noun* is the name of a particular person, place, or thing. It is always written with a capital letter; as, *John, Paris, England, Europe.*

Common Nouns. A *common noun* is the name of any one of a class of persons, places, or things; as, *table, book, rabbit, boy, weather.*

Abstract Nouns. An *abstract noun* is the name of an idea: as, *honesty, hope, truth, system.*

Collective Nouns. A *collective noun* is the name of a group or collection of single things, considered as one; as, *crowd, army, jury, family, committee.*

Verbal Nouns. A *verbal noun,* or *gerund,* is the name of an action; as, *walking, skating, working.*

An *appositive* is a noun used after another noun or pronoun to describe or explain the meaning of that noun or pronoun. An appositive is said to be *in apposition to* the noun or pronoun it defines or explains: "Milton, the *poet,* became blind."

A *predicate noun* or *pronoun* is a noun or a pronoun that completes the predicate verb and refers to the subject: "Lincoln was *president.*" "It is *I.*"

KINDS OF PRONOUNS

Pronouns are classified as *personal, interrogative, demonstrative, relative* or *conjunctive,* and *indefinite.*

Personal Pronouns. The following are the forms of personal pronouns:

SINGULAR

	First Person	Second Person	Third Person Mas. Fem. Neut.
Nominative	I	you	he she it
Possessive	{ my, { mine	{ your, { yours	his { her { hers } its
Objective	me	you	him her it

PLURAL

	First Person	Second Person	Third Person
Nominative	we	you	they
Possessive	{ our, { ours	{ your, { yours	{ their, { theirs
Objective	us	you	them

The possessive forms given in the table are sometimes called *possessive pronouns.* They are pronouns in origin, but in use they are *possessive adjectives.*

Special Uses. *Ye* and *thou, thy, thine, thee,* are old forms, now seldom used except in poetry or in the language of religion.

The masculine pronouns, *he, his,* and *him,* are used also as of common gender: "Let every child use *his* own book."

You, whether referring to one person or more, always takes the plural verb.

It often stands as the *impersonal subject* of a verb: "*It* rains"; "*It* is cold"; "*It* grew dark."

It may be used as the *impersonal object* of a verb: "He footed *it* all the way"; "They are roughing *it* in the woods."

It is sometimes used as an introductory word, the real subject following the verb: "*It* is well to think before you speak." See *There.*

Compound Personal Pronouns. The word *self* added to *my, thy, your, him, her, it,* and the plural *selves* to *our, your, them,* form *compound personal pronouns,* often called *reflexive pronouns.* They are used chiefly (1) to express emphasis, with or without the simple pronoun: "I *myself* am positive"; "She talks of no one but *herself.*" (2) as reflexive object of a verb, the object and the subject of the verb being the same person or thing: "He dressed *himself*"; "You will hurt *yourself.*"

These pronouns have the same form for *nominative* and *objective* cases. They are not used in the *possessive.*

The simple personal pronoun is sometimes used reflexively in poetry: "I lay *me* down."

Interrogative Pronouns. Pronouns used in asking questions are *interrogative pronouns: who, which, what.* "*Who* is here?" "*Which* do you like?" "*What* did you say?"

Singular and Plural
Nominative who
Possessive whose
Objective whom

The interrogatives *which* and *what* have no declension or change of form, however used. *Who* and *whom* refer to persons only; the other forms, to persons or things.

Which, *what*, and *whose* are used also as *interrogative adjectives*: "*Which* train did he take?" "*What* number is that?" "*Whose* book is this?"

Demonstrative Pronouns. *This*, *that*, and the plurals, *these* and *those*, are called *demonstratives*, because they point out definitely the persons or things to which they refer. Latin *demonstrare* means "to point out": "*That* is the question"; "*Those* are the bills"; "The reasons are *these*."

When used with nouns, like adjectives, the demonstratives are often called *demonstrative adjectives*: "*this* farm"; "*those* cattle."

Relative Pronouns. A relative pronoun is both pronoun and conjunction. As a *pronoun*, the word is used like a noun; as a *conjunction*, it joins clauses. Hence relative pronouns are sometimes called *conjunctive pronouns*. The relative pronouns are *who*, *which*, *what*, *that*. *As* and *but* may be used as relative pronouns.

Singular and Plural

Nominative	who	which
Possessive	whose	whose
Objective	whom	which

What and *that* have no change of form for the *nominative* and the *objective* and are not used in the *possessive*.

Who and *whom* refer to persons only.

Whose is used of both persons and things.

Which, as a relative, refers to things only.

That refers to both persons and things.

What may be called a *double relative*, being equivalent to *that which*, the demonstrative pronoun *that* and the relative pronoun *which*: "We know *what* (*that which*) he wants."

As is used as *relative pronoun*: "I want such *as* (*those which*) are desirable."

But is used as *relative pronoun*: "There is no fireside *but* (*that not*) has one vacant chair."

Which and *what* are used also as *relative adjectives*: "I know *which* (*that which*) book you mean"; "I see *what* (*that which*) reward she will receive."

Compound Relative Pronouns. *Who*, *which*, and *what* are combined with *ever* and *soever* to form *compound relative pronouns*: *whoever*. *whosoever*, *whichever*, *whichsoever*, *whatever*, *whatsoever*. The forms with *so* are rarely used.

Indefinite Pronouns. Indefinite pronouns do not point out definitely, but they refer in a general manner to persons or objects. Those commonly used are *each*, *every*, *either*, *neither*, *some*, *all*, *any*, *few*, *many*, *one*, *none*, *other*, *another*, *both*. Many of these words are used as indefinite adjectives:

(pro.) "*Some* dislike animals."

(adj.) "*Some* people dislike animals."

The only indefinite pronouns which have plural forms are *one* and *other*: "Give me a small *one* (sing.)"; "Give me small *ones* (plur.)"; "I want the *other* (sing.)"; "I want the *others* (plur.)."

Adjective Pronouns. The *demonstrative* and *indefinite pronouns* are also called *adjective pronouns*, because they are used both as adjectives and as nouns.

GRAMMATICAL RELATIONS OF NOUNS AND PRONOUNS

For nouns and pronouns, grammatical relations are said to be relations of *case*, *number*, *person*, and *gender*.

CASE

Nominative Case. The following are said to be in the *nominative* (naming) *case*:

1. A noun or pronoun used as subject: "The *boy* plays." "*He* came home."

2. A noun in apposition to a noun or pronoun in the nominative case: "John, my *brother*, is here." "She, the *woman* in black, wept bitterly."

3. A predicate noun or pronoun: "The man was *master*." "It is *he* whom you want."

4. A noun or pronoun used in direct address: "*Citizens*, remember your duties"; "O *thou* that rollest above! whence are thy beams?"

5. A noun or pronoun used absolutely with a participle: "The *storm* abating, the air grew colder."

6. A noun or pronoun used in exclamation: "A *horse*! A *horse*! My kingdom for a horse." "*He*, lost!"

Objective Case. The following are said to be in the *objective case* (*objective* meaning "thrown, or directed, toward," as the action of a verb is directed toward a noun):

1. A noun, a pronoun, a phrase or a clause used as the object of a transitive verb (*transitive* meaning "going across," as the action of a verb goes across to the object): "James studies *spelling*." "I like *her*." "I tried *to learn a foreign language*." "He said, '*I shall go*.'" "She knew *that all was well*."

2. Indirect object: "He wrote (to) his *brother* (indirect object) a *letter* (direct object)."

One may recognize the indirect object by the possibility of using *to* before it without changing the meaning of the sentence.

3. The object of a preposition: "He went into the *store*."

4. A word in apposition to a noun or pronoun in the objective case: "He found the house, a large stone *building*."

5. Objective of exclamation: "Oh, happy *me*!"

6. A noun of time, distance, or quantity used adverbially. This is called an *adverbial objective*: "I slept four *hours*"; "He walked three *miles*."

7. An objective complement (called also *predicate objective* and *adjunct accusative*): "They made him *chairman*"; "She called Mary *queen*."

8. The secondary object: "They allowed each speaker an *hour*." When such sentences are changed to the passive construction, the *secondary object* is retained as an object: "Each speaker was allowed an *hour*"

9. A subject of an infinitive: "I know *him* to be truthful."

10. A predicate of an infinitive: "I know it to be *her*."

Note.—Many recent authorities prefer the term *accusative case* for the foregoing constructions, except that of indirect object, for which they use the term *dative*.

Possessive Case. 1. A word expressing ownership or possession is in the *possessive case*: "*John's* books"; "*their* work."

2. When two nouns in the possessive case are in apposition, the second alone takes the possessive sign: "Webster the *statesman's* speeches"; "Jack the *giant-killer's* exploits."

3. The possessive form is used also to limit or define and does not necessarily indicate ownership: "six *days'* journey"; "*man's* duty"; "the *river's* brink."

Note.—Many authorities prefer the name *genitive* for the so-called possessive case.

Inflection.—English nouns have no inflection, or change of form, to denote cases, except the adding of the apostrophe and *s* for the possessive. See *Spelling*. Certain pronouns are inflected to denote cases. See *Kinds of Pronouns*.

Note.—Recent works on English grammar recommend the following classification of case forms and uses:

Forms,—*common* and *genitive*.

Uses,—*nominative*, *genitive*, *dative*, *accusative*.

SPECIAL USES

Compound names and groups of words add the possessive sign to the last word: "*William the Conqueror's* throne"; "the *king of England's* palace"; "my *father-in-law's* house."

Joint Possession. If two or more possessive nouns imply joint possession of the same thing, and are connected by *and*, the possessive sign is used with the last noun only:

"*Mary* and *John's* mother" implies common possession
—one mother.
"*Mason* and *Hamlin's* organs."
"*Wheeler* and *Wilson's* store."

Separate Possession. If separate possession is implied, or if the nouns are connected by *or* or *nor*, each one takes the possessive sign:

"*Mary's* and *John's* mother" implies separate possession
—two mothers.
"*Taft's* and *Wilson's* administration."
"Is that a *girl's* or a *boy's* voice?"
"He accepted neither the *skeptic's* nor the *clergyman's* view."

The possessive (genitive) case may be denoted by the objective case following the preposition *of*; "*Job's* patience," or "the patience *of Job*"; "*Somebody else's* work," or "the work *of somebody else*."

NUMBER

Nouns and pronouns denoting one person or thing are *singular*: *farm*, *wife*. Nouns and pronouns denoting more than one are *plural*: *farms*, *wives*. See *Spelling*.

Inflection.—English nouns regularly add *s* or *es* to form the plural. See *Spelling*. For pronoun plurals, see *Kinds of Pronouns*.

PERSON

The speaker or writer is the first person, *I*, *we*; the one addressed is the second person, *thou*, *you*; the person or thing spoken of is the third person, *he*, *it*, *they*.

Inflection.—English nouns are not inflected to distinguish person. See *Personal Pronouns*.

GENDER

In English, a noun or pronoun naming a male is *masculine*: *stag*. One naming a female, *feminine*: *girl*. One naming an object without sex, *neuter* (a Latin word, meaning "neither"): *tree*. Words which may be applied to either males or females are said to be of *common* gender: *animal*.

Inflection.—Nouns and pronouns are not inflected to distinguish gender. Personal pronouns have different forms to distinguish gender.

Antecedent. The substantive—word, phrase, or clause—for which a pronoun stands, and to which it refers, is called its *antecedent*, a Latin word, meaning "something going before":

"The man who planned the building made it his masterpiece." *Man* is the antecedent of *who* and of *his*.

"To sleep well, which is a blessing, is to repair and renew the body." *To sleep well* is a phrase, the antecedent of *which*.

Agreement. The pronoun is said to agree with its antecedent in *gender*, *person*, and *number*, but its *case* depends upon its use in the sentence:

"The book which you found is mine." The antecedent of *which* is *book*. *Book* is in the *nominative case*, the subject of *is*: *which* is in the *objective case*, the object of *found*.

"He is one of those who prefer winter." The antecedent of *who* is *those*, not *one*. Hence *who* is plural and requires a plural verb.

VERBS

KINDS OF VERBS

According to use, verbs are either *transitive* or *intransitive*.

Transitive Verbs. A transitive verb is one which requires an object to complete its meaning. The object, sometimes called *object complement*, names the receiver of the action of the verb: "The man *built* (verb) the *house* (object)."

Intransitive Verbs. An intransitive verb is one which does not require an object to complete its meaning. Some intransitives, however, need to be completed by a predicate noun or adjective, often

called *attribute complement*, which refers to or modifies the subject: "That village *is* (verb) *Millville* (attribute complement)"; "The action *seems* (verb) *right* (attribute complement)."

GRAMMATICAL RELATIONS OF VERBS

The syntax of verbs involves relations of *voice*, *mode*, *tense*, *person*, and *number*. For the forms to express these, see *Table of Specimen Verb Forms*.

VOICE

Meaning of the Voices. *Voice* is often defined as that property of verbs which indicates whether the subject acts or is acted upon.

Active Voice.—If the subject is acting, the verb is in the *active*, or "doing," voice: "The man *broke* his cane."

Passive Voice.—If the subject is being acted upon, or receiving an action, the verb is in the *passive*, or "suffering," voice: "The cane *was broken*."

Forms to Denote Voice. The terms "active voice" and "passive voice" are applied also to the forms of the verb.

That form of the verb which shows that the subject is acting is called *active voice*: "Mary *broke* the dish."

That form of the verb which shows that the subject is acted upon is called *passive voice*: "The dish *was broken* by Mary." Some part of the verb *be* is joined to the past participle of a transitive verb to make the *passive voice*: *is sold*, *were made*.

Any transitive verb may be used in the passive voice, its object in the active becoming its subject in the passive: "The boy *lights* (active) the lamps"; "The lamps *are lighted* (passive) by the boy."

Intransitive verbs ordinarily are active, but some verbs are used either as intransitive or transitive: "He *spoke* (intrans.) truthfully"; "He *spoke* (trans.) the truth." When used transitively, such verbs may become passive: "The truth *was spoken* by him."

Some intransitive verbs, used with a following preposition, have a transitive meaning; as, *laugh at*, *look over*, *wonder at*: "He *laughed at* me"; "She *looked over* the work"; "They *wondered at* his skill." Such phrases are transitive in the fullest sense as tested by the passive construction: "I *was laughed at* by him"; "The work *was looked over* by her"; "His skill *was wondered at* by them."

MODE

Meaning of the Modes. *Mode* (or *mood*) may be defined as that property of verbs which shows the manner in which the action or state is conceived.

If the action or state expressed is thought of simply as a fact, the mode is *indicative*; if it is regarded as doubtful or merely as desired, the mode is *subjunctive*; if it is viewed as a command, the mode is *imperative*.

Forms to Denote Modes. The term "modes" is applied also to the several series of verb forms. In this use, *mode* is the form of the verb which shows the manner of expressing an action or a state.

The indicative mode states a fact or asks a simple question; as, "The sun shines"; "Has the rain been heavy?"

The indicative forms, however, are commonly used to express subjunctive and imperative ideas: "The dam will break if the river *rises* (condition)"; "You *will report* at seven (command)."

The imperative mode expresses a command or an entreaty; as, "*Come* here"; "*Have* mercy upon me."

The subjunctive mode makes a doubtful or conditional assertion; as, "Though he *slay* me, yet will I trust him."

For the so-called *potential mode*, see *Modal Auxiliaries*.

TENSE

Meaning of Tenses. The *tense* of a verb indicates the time of the action or state.

As applied to verb forms, *tense* is the form the verb takes to indicate time.

According to the time expressed and the completeness or incompleteness of the action, state, or condition, the verb varies in tense.

Simple Tenses.—The simple (or incomplete) tenses, *present, past, future*, signify action or condition as continuing in present, past, or future time: "I *go*"; "I *went*"; "I *shall go*."

Perfect Tenses.—The perfect (or complete) tenses imply the completion of an act in present time (*present perfect*), in past time (*past perfect*), or in future time (*future perfect*): "I *hav gone*"; "I *had gone*"; "I *shall have gone*." See *Table of Specimen Verb Forms.*

Other Tenses.—Some authorities distinguish a *past future* tense, as, "We thought he *would go*," and a *past future perfect* tense, as, "We thought he *would have gone.*"

PERSON AND NUMBER

A verb must agree with its subject in person and in number: "I *do* not"; "He *does* not"; "You *do* not"; "They *do* not."

VERB FORMS

Inflection of Verbs, or Conjugation. In conjugation, English verbs change form to show voice, mode, tense, person, and number. The usually inflected forms are the third person singular of the present active indicative; the past active indicative; the present and past participles: *has, had, having, had.* For exceptions, see *Table of Specimen Verb Forms*: the verb *be*; *Subjunctive Mode.* See also *Thou Forms.*

Verb Phrases. All other mode, tense, and voice meanings are expressed by the simple verb or by verb phrases. A *verb phrase* is a group of verbs used as a single verb. A verb phrase is formed by prefixing an auxiliary (helping) verb to some infinitive or participle form of a principal verb: "Wars *shall cease*"; "It *may rain*"; "Fashions *have been changing.*"

Principal Parts. In order to conjugate any verb throughout its various modes and tenses, it is necessary to know only the *infinitive*, the *past tense*, and the *past participle.* These three, therefore, are called the *principal parts: find, found, found; go, went, gone.*

Regular Verbs. A regular (or weak) verb, in English, forms its past tense and past participle by adding *d* or *ed* to the present: *load, loaded; love, loved; wash, washed; persuade, persuaded.*

Irregular Verbs. An irregular (or strong) verb forms its past tense and past participle by a vowel change, frequently adding a change of ending: *hide, hid, hidden; drink, drank, drunk; eat, ate, eaten.*

A Defective Verb is one that lacks some of its principal parts; as, *ought, may, can.*

A Redundant Verb is one that has both a regular and an irregular form; as, *bereave, bereaved* or *bereft, bereaved* or *bereft.*

A Copulative Verb is an intransitive verb which connects the subject with a predicate noun or pronoun or with a predicate adjective. Such a verb is called a *linking* verb. Among intransitive verbs thus used are *be, become, seem, appear, feel, grow, remain, sit, stand*: "Mary *became* queen"; "He *grows* tall"; "She *feels* better."

A Reflexive Verb is a transitive verb, the subject and the object of which are the same individual: "I *wash* myself"; "He *contradicted* himself."

An Impersonal Verb is one used only in the third person singular with no definite personal subject: "It *rains*"; "It *snows.*"

Auxiliary Verbs. Auxiliary comes from the Latin *auxilium*, meaning "help"; hence, auxiliary verbs are verbs that help in the conjugation of other verbs. They are of two classes:

1. *Auxiliaries of tense and voice: will, shall, have, be, do, did.*

The forms of the auxiliary *be* used with a past participle make the passive voice; as, *are told, was told, shall have been told.*

Have and *had* are auxiliaries used with the past participle to form the present perfect and the past perfect tense, hence *have* and *had* are called "signs" of the perfect and past perfect tenses respectively:

Present Perfect.—I *have* told
Past Perfect.—I *had* told

Do and *did* are either emphatic or interrogative auxiliaries used with the present infinitive of another verb to form the present and past tenses respectively.

Present.—I *do* tell; *do* I tell?
Past.—I *did* tell; *did* I tell?

2. *Modal auxiliaries: may, might, can, could, would, should, must*, (in some cases *shall, will*, and *have*). For the uses of *shall, will, should, would*, see *Good Usage.*

The modal auxiliaries may be prefixed to the present infinitive or to the perfect infinitive of any verb in order to express various modes. They suggest doubt, permission, wish, ability, or duty: "I *may* tell, *may* have told"; "He *can* go"; "You *should* read."

May and *might* express permission, possibility, or doubt. *Might* was formerly used in the past tense, and it now expresses more doubt or dependence upon conditions than *may.* The time of the verb phrase formed with these auxiliaries is determined by the verb form following the auxiliary: "It *may* (*might*) have happened (past)."

Can and *could* express ability. *Can* signifies either present or future time: "We *can* go." *Could* may express past time: "Yesterday, I *could* do nothing." *Could* usually implies an uncertain condition: "They *could* have gone (if something had not interfered)."

Participles. Formed from a verb, usually by the addition of *ing* or *ed*, a participle retains the original verb meaning but is used in a subordinate or incidental way. Like the infinitive, the participle conveys in condensed form a verbal idea that might otherwise be expressed in a clause. Thus, instead of the sentence, "Because he walked rapidly, he soon reached the station," a parallel statement using a participle could be, "Walking rapidly, he soon reached the station." In the latter case, the word *walking* is a participle, which refers to "he." To avoid "dangling participles," every participial modifier should be placed next to its intended base.

In sentences like "Let *sleeping* dogs lie" and "A *burnt* child dreads the fire," the participle is used as an adjective. If it is not used in this way to modify a noun, it may be treated as a predicate adjective, as in the sentence "The visitor was *puzzled.*" In the opening sentence of a whimsical essay, Gilbert K. Chesterton illustrates the distinction between a true participle (action) and a participial adjective (condition): "Just now everybody is *revolting* in one sense of the word, except a few who are *revolting* in the other sense." The second *revolting* is really an adjective like "contemptible."

A verb has three participles:

Present participle—*speaking* (action is in progress): "He stood *speaking.*"

Past participle—*spoken* (action is completed): "A little word in kindness *spoken.*"

Perfect participle—*having spoken* (action is completed before the time implied in the principal verb): "*Having spoken* the word, he departed." See *Table of Specimen Verb Forms.*

Gerund or **Verbal Noun.** Verb forms ending in *-ing* are used also as nouns. They may be modified by adverbs, since they are verbal, or by adjectives, since they are used as nouns: "*Fishing constantly* (adv.) makes one taciturn"; "He found *good* (adj.) *fishing.*" A gerund may also take an object: "*Writing* the *letter* (obj.) was difficult."

When the gerund is preceded by an article, *a*, *an*, or *the*, or by an adjective, it requires a following phrase with *of*, signifying the *object* of its action: "The *building of* the ship took many days"; "Success depends upon careful *planning of* work."

The Subjunctive. With the exception of the forms given under the conjugation of *be*, English has no regularly inflected subjunctive forms. *Have* is used occasionally for *has* in the third person singular, and in other verbs the indicative singular third personal ending *s* is dropped, to make a subjunctive form: "If he *tell.*"

The ideas of *doubt, uncertainty, condition*, and *desire*, usually called *subjunctive*, are commonly expressed by the indicative or by various verb phrases. See *Good Usage: Should, Would.*

The past subjunctive *were* or *had* is often used in past conditional sentences when *if* is omitted. In such cases the verb precedes the subject: "*Were* I *going*, I should take supplies"; "*Had* we *thought* of it, we would have called on him."

The Infinitive. The *infinitive*, meaning "unlimited," is a form of the verb which partakes of the nature of a noun. It expresses action without person or number. The *present infinitive* represents incomplete action, *to go*; the *perfect infinitive* represents completed action. *to have gone.* Verb phrases are formed with the auxiliaries *be* and *have* to serve as present and perfect passive infinitives: *to be seen, to have been seen.* See *Table of Verb Forms.*

The English infinitive is usually preceded by the word *to*, which is a relic of an early stage of the language and no essential part of the infinitive. Most verbs, when they take a following infinitive, require the form with *to*: "I *want* him *to go.*" The following verbs generally take the infinitive without *to*: *bid, dare, feel, hear, let, make, need, see*, and all auxiliaries; as, "*See* him *go*," "They *may return.*"

The infinitive may be used as a *noun*, as an *adjective*, or as an *adverb*; but it takes only an adverbial modifier, and, if transitive, may take an object: "*To tell* the *facts* (obj.) *accurately* (adv.) is difficult."

In the sentence "I want you to buy some oranges," some authorities regard *you to buy some oranges* as an *infinitive clause*, the object of the verb *want*; *you* is the subject and *oranges* is the object of *to buy.* Others call the *infinitive phrase, to buy some oranges*, the objective complement, and *you* the object complement, of the verb *want.*

Thou Forms. An old form of the second person singular in present and past tenses, now found only in poetical or religious use, is made by adding *st* or *est* to the first person singular: "*Thou tellest*"; "*Thou toldst*"; "*Thou hast*"; "*Thou hadst*"; "*Thou lovest*"; "*Thou lovedst.*" The verb *be* has the following forms: "*Thou art*"; "*Thou wast.*"

ADJECTIVES

Kinds of Adjectives according to Meaning. Adjectives are classified, according to meaning, as *limiting* and *descriptive*. An adjective modifies a noun or pronoun either by *limiting*, that is, setting it apart definitely from others, or by *describing*, that is, naming a quality of the thing for which the noun or pronoun stands. To say "a *third* report" is merely to set apart, or limit, the report as belonging to one class; to say "a *complete* report" is to describe it by a certain quality.

Such words as *three, five, eleven, second*, are limiting adjectives. They are called *numerals.* Those which merely give a number, as *two, four*, are called *cardinals*; those which designate an order in a series, as *seventh*, are called *ordinals.*

The, a, an, are limiting adjectives. *The* is called the *definite article*; *a* and *an* are called *indefinite articles.* *A* is used before consonant sounds, *an* before vowels. See *Good Usage.*

Kinds of Adjectives according to Use. Adjectives are commonly classified, according to their use in the sentence, as *attributive* and *predicate.*

Attributive Adjectives.—An adjective used in close connection with a noun is called an *attributive adjective*, although some prefer the term *adherent adjective.* Regularly the attributive adjective precedes its noun: "*pretty* flowers." For emphasis, it may sometimes be placed after the noun: "the city *beautiful.*"

Predicate Adjectives.—An adjective which modifies the noun of the subject but is placed in the predicate, usually following the verb, is called a *predicate adjective*: "The book is *large.*" For *demonstrative, interrogative, relative*, and *indefinite* adjectives, see *Kinds of Pronouns.*

Appositive Adjectives.—Some authorities distinguish a third type of adjective, the *appositive*; as, "The boy, *careless* and *indifferent*, paid no attention." Such adjectives do not limit their nouns but describe them. They usually follow the nouns.

Other adjectives regularly follow their nouns, some of them only as predicate adjectives,—*alone, awake, aware, asleep, alive*: "Man *alive!*" "The child is *asleep*"; "One star *alone.*"

Grammatical Relations. The use of English adjectives is very simple, because, except *this* and *that*, they are not inflected to distinguish gender, person, number, or case. The only inflection used is that employed to distinguish the degrees of comparison.

Comparison.—Most English adjectives are compared by adding to the simple form, or positive degree, of the adjective, *r* or *er*, to form the comparative degree, and *st* or *est*, to form the superlative: *high, higher, highest; fine, finer, finest.* The comparative degree expresses a greater or lesser degree of the quality named by the adjective; the superlative expresses the greatest or least degree of that quality.

For spelling changes with added syllables, see *Spelling.*

Many adjectives, especially those of more than two syllables, are compared by prefixing *more* or *less* for the comparative, *most* or *least* for the superlative: "*more* merciful"; "*least* troublesome." Some adjectives admit of both forms of comparison: *able, abler (more able), ablest (most able).* A few adjectives are compared irregularly: *bad, worse, worst; good, better, best.*

ADVERBS

Meaning of Adverbs. Adverbs modify the meaning of verbs, adjectives, and other adverbs, in respect to some one of the following ideas:

1. Place,—there, nowhere, yonder.
2. Time,—now, afterwards, soon.
3. Manner,—well, badly, thoroughly.
4. Cause,—therefore, consequently.
5. Number,—first, secondly, rarely.
6. Degree,—somewhat, more, highly.

They are classified, therefore, as adverbs of *place, time, manner, cause, number*, and *degree.*

Interrogative Adverbs. The adverbs *how, whence, wherefore, why*, and a few others are used to introduce questions, either direct or indirect: "*How* shall you go?" "They wanted to know *why* he did that."

Relative Adverbs. *As, how, now, since, so, thence, when, whence, whenever, where, wherever, whither, why*, and a few others are used to introduce *subordinate clauses.*

Forms. Most English adverbs end in *-ly.* Many of these are formed from adjectives: *quick* (adj.), *quickly* (adv.); *easy* (adj.), *easily* (adv.). Some adverbs have the same form as the corresponding adjectives: *early, hard, long, loud, deep.*

Caution.—*Goodly, lovely, manly, lonely,* and *homely* are adjectives.

Comparison.—Most adverbs are compared by prefixing to the simple form or positive degree *more* or *less* to form the comparative and *most* or *least* to form the superlative: easily, *more* easily, *most* easily; truly, *more* truly, *most* truly, *less* truly, *least* truly.

Some adverbs having the same form as the corresponding adjectives are compared by adding *er* and *est* to the simple form: *early, earlier, earliest; deep, deeper, deepest.*

A few adverbs are compared irregularly: *well, better, best; badly, worse, worst; much, more, most.*

There.—The adverb *there* is sometimes used to introduce a sentence, with no idea of place. When so used, *there* is called an *expletive*, because it "fills up" and is unnecessary to the sense: "*There* are many ways of doing good." See *It* under *Pronouns: Special Uses.*

The.—The definite article *the* is sometimes used as an adverb before comparatives: "*the* more, *the* merrier; *the* sooner, *the* better."

First.—The word *first* may be an adjective or an adverb: "The *first* (adj.) boy is my brother"; "He came *first* (adv.)." See *Good Usage.*

Position of Adverbs. Because great liberty is allowed as to the position of English adverbs, care should be taken so to place an adverb that its grammatical relation shall be clear.

PREPOSITIONS

Position of Prepositions. The word preposition comes from the Latin *pre*, before, and *ponere*, to place. Hence prepositions commonly stand before the words they govern ("Give the pencil to *him.*"); but they may come after them. In English this inversion occurs most frequently when the preposition governs a *relative* or an *interrogative word*: "They are people *whom* we know nothing *about*"; "*What* are you looking *for?*" See *Good Usage.*

Prepositional Phrases. The preposition and its object, with the modifiers of the object, form a phrase, which may be used as an adjective or an adverb: "The picture *on the screen* (adj.)"; "He ran *at top speed* (adv.)"; "Home *at last* (adv.)." Some prepositions form such close combinations with certain verbs that these expressions have the force of single words: *look over, laugh at, carry off.* See *Verbs, Prepositions.*

SUBORDINATE CLAUSES

According to use, subordinate clauses are *substantive, adjective,* and *adverbial.*

A *substantive clause* is a clause that performs the function of a noun: "*That he came* (subj. of verb) is true"; "I know *that he came* (obj. of verb)"; "He was anxious for *what had been promised him* (obj. of prep.)"; "He is *what he seems* (attribute complement)"; "The fact *that he did it* (appositive) is wonderful."

An *adjective clause* is a clause that modifies a noun or a pronoun. It may be introduced by a relative pronoun: "He *whom thou lovest* is sick"; "This is the tree *that we planted.*" It may be introduced by a conjunctive adverb: "The town *where* (in which) *she lived*"; "The time *when* (at which) *Rome was built.*"

An adjective clause may be *restrictive*: "I took the peach *that was ripe.*" It was a particular peach. *That was ripe* restricts or limits *peach*, telling which one was taken.

An adjective clause may be *non-restrictive*: "I read 'Marmion,' *which was written by Scott.*" *Marmion* defines what book was read. *Which was written by Scott* is a *non-restrictive* clause, merely adding another thought to the one already expressed. A comma is used after *Marmion* to separate the non-restrictive clause from the rest of the sentence.

Relative Clause.—A clause introduced by a relative pronoun is sometimes called a *relative clause*: "This tree, *which has stood for years*, bears no fruit."

An *adverbial clause* is a clause that modifies the meaning of a verb, an adjective, or another adverb.

Adverbial clauses are introduced by subordinate conjunctions or by conjunctive adverbs:

Time—"*When duty calls*, I obey."
Place—"*Where I go*, ye cannot come."
Degree—"It is better *than I expected.*"
Manner—"The child does *as he pleases.*"
Purpose—"He came *that he might learn.*"
Result—"She was so weak *that she fainted.*"
Cause—"The snow melted *because it rained.*"
Condition—"*If you do right*, you will win."
Concession—"*Though I failed*, I shall try again."

Conjunctions. See special section devoted to this subject.

PARSING

To parse a word is to classify it as a part of speech, explain its form, and show its relation to other words in the sentence.

In the sentence "He bought a car," *car* is a common noun, of neuter gender, in the third person, singular number, and in the objective case because it is the object of the verb *bought.*

Bought is an irregular, transitive verb. The principal parts are *buy, bought, bought.* It is active voice, indicative mode, past tense; third person, singular number, to agree with its subject *he.*

He is a personal pronoun. Its declension is singular, nom. *he*, poss. *his*, obj. *him*; plural, nom. *they*, poss. *their* or *theirs*, obj. *them*. Third person, singular number; nominative case, the subject of the verb *bought.*

SENTENCE ANALYSIS

To analyze a sentence, first classify the sentence according to *form* and *use*. Then point out the simple subject; the complete subject. Classify the modifiers of the simple subject, analyzing phrases and clauses. Point out the simple predicate; the complete predicate. Classify the modifiers of the simple predicate, analyzing phrases and clauses. If the sentence is complex or compound, also name and classify the clauses and the connectives which join them.

Simple Sentence. "Truth, crushed to earth, shall rise again" is a *simple, declarative* sentence. *Truth* is the *simple* subject; *truth, crushed to earth* is the *complete* subject; *crushed* is a participle formed from the verb *crush* and modifies the noun *truth*; *to earth* is an adverbial phrase, modifying *crushed*; *shall rise* is the *simple* predicate; *shall rise again* is the *complete* predicate; *shall rise* is the predicate verb, which is modified by the adverb *again.*

Complex Sentence. "Blessed is he who has found his work" is a *complex, declarative* sentence, composed of one independent clause, *blessed is he*, and one dependent clause, *who has found his work.* The subject of the independent clause is *he*; the predicate is *is blessed.* The predicate consists of the copulative verb *is* and the predicate adjective *blessed*, which modifies the subject *he.* The dependent clause, *who has found his work*, is an adjective clause modifying the pronoun *he.* The subject of the clause is the relative pronoun *who*; the complete predicate is *has found his work*; *has found* is the predicate verb, the direct object of which is *work*; *his* is a possessive pronoun modifying *work.* The relative pronoun *who* joins the two clauses; its antecedent is *he.*

TABLE OF SPECIMEN VERB FORMS

The Verb, **tell.** Principal Parts: *tell, told, told*

INDICATIVE MODE

ACTIVE VOICE		PASSIVE VOICE	

Present Tense
Ordinary Form

SINGULAR	PLURAL	SINGULAR	PLURAL
I tell	We tell	I am told	We are told
You tell	You tell	You are told	You are told
He tells	They tell	He is told	They are told

Progressive Form

I am telling	We are telling	I am being told	We are being told
You are telling	You are telling	You are being told	You are being told
He is telling	They are telling	He is being told	They are being told

Emphatic Form — No corresponding forms in the passive voice.

I do tell	We do tell
You do tell	You do tell
He does tell	They do tell

Negative Form

I do not tell	We do not tell	I am not told	We are not told
You do not tell	You do not tell	You are not told	You are not told
He does not tell	They do not tell	He is not told	They are not told

Negative Progressive Form

I am not telling	We are not telling	I am not being told	We are not being told
You are not telling	You are not telling	You are not being told	You are not being told
He is not telling	They are not telling	He is not being told	They are not being told

Present Perfect Tense

I have told	We have told	I have been told	We have been told
You have told	You have told	You have been told	You have been told
He has told	They have told	He has been told	They have been told

Past Tense
Ordinary Form

I told	We told	I was told	We were told
You told	You told	You were told	You were told
He told	They told	He was told	They were told

Progressive Form

I was telling	We were telling	I was being told	We were being told
You were telling	You were telling	You were being told	You were being told
He was telling	They were telling	He was being told	They were being told

Emphatic Form — No corresponding forms in the passive voice.

I did tell	We did tell
You did tell	You did tell
He did tell	They did tell

Negative Form

I did not tell	We did not tell	I was not told	We were not told
You did not tell	You did not tell	You were not told	You were not told
He did not tell	They did not tell	He was not told	They were not told

Negative Progressive Form

I was not telling	We were not telling	I was not being told	We were not being told
You were not telling	You were not telling	You were not being told	You were not being told
He was not telling	They were not telling	He was not being told	They were not being told

Past Perfect, or Pluperfect, Tense

I had told	We had told	I had been told	We had been told
You had told	You had told	You had been told	You had been told
He had told	They had told	He had been told	They had been told

Future Tense

I shall tell	We shall tell	I shall be told	We shall be told
You will tell	You will tell	You will be told	You will be told
He will tell	They will tell	He will be told	They will be told

Future Perfect Tense

I shall have told	We shall have told	I shall have been told	We shall have been told
You will have told	You will have told	You will have been told	You will have been told
He will have told	They will have told	He will have been told	They will have been told

Infinitive Forms

| Present.—(to) tell | Present.—(to) be told |
| Perfect.—(to) have told | Perfect.—(to) have been told |

Participle Forms

Present.—telling	Present.—being told
Perfect.—having told	Past.—told
	Perfect.—having been told

Imperative Forms

Tell (Negative) Do not tell *or* Tell not   Be told (Negative) Do not be told *or* Be not told

The Verb **be.** Principal Parts: *am, was, been*

Present Tense		**Past Tense**	
SINGULAR	PLURAL	SINGULAR	PLURAL
I am	We are	I was	We were
You are	You are	You were	You were
He is	They are	He was	They were

The Verb **have.** Principal Parts: *have, had, had*

I have	We have	I had	We had
You have	You have	You had	You had
He has	They have	He had	They had

PREPOSITIONS

Through the study of prepositions, one gains a command of many idiomatic phrases found in every civilized language. Especially is this true of English, because English prepositions united with other words often take the place of corresponding inflected word forms in other languages.

From the following list of the more important English prepositions, the reader will learn the distinctive meanings attached to each according to the varied purposes for which it is used.

About. In its usual meanings of *around, close to, because of, concerning, not far from, over*, etc., this preposition is employed to express: (1) indefinite position, "The idlers hung *about* the saloon"; (2) in attendance on, "The king had his bodyguard *about* him"; (3) close at hand, on one's person, "He had no money *about* him"; (4) attention to, "We sent him *about* (*to attend to*) his business"; (5) abstract connection in the sense of concerning, "to see, ask, hear, write, think, dream *about* a thing." In expressing approximation, *about* has the force of an adverb of degree: "He is *about* my size."

Above. Commonly this word means *over, higher than, superior to*: "The colonel ranks *above* the major." "The airplane rose rapidly *above* the city." "Clouds seem to float just *above* the trees." "The man's record is *above* suspicion." "The president does not stand *above* the law." "Mr. Utterson could hear the footsteps *above* the hum of the city." "*Above* all, avoid the appearance of suspicion."

After. This word usually means *behind, following, as a result of, in spite of, for*, and *according to*. It may be used with the verb *be* and with any verb of motion, also after *seek, ask, hunt*, although, with these, modern usage generally prefers *for*. The following are examples of common usage: "The troops passed first and the supply train came *after* (*behind*) them." "It was *after* (*later than*) twelve when our friends left." "*After* (*as a result of*) careful examination the board approved the plans." "The picture is fashioned *after* (*according to*) an antique model." "Book *after* book was read." "Time *after* time Mr. Blank inquired *after* (*for*) you." "*After* (*in spite of*) all, they have failed." "*After* a while they grew tired."

Against. Common meanings: *opposite to* (in this sense expressed by *over against*), *opposed to, pressing upon, contrary, from*. Examples: "The mast stood out clearly *against* (*contrasting with*) the sky." "The governor had long held his ground *against* suffrage." "The machine was leaning *against* (*pressing upon*) the wall." "Such action seems *against* (*contrary to*) nature." "*Defend us against* (*from*) our enemies."

Along. Implies *motion* or *extension upon, at or near the side of*. In such connections it may mean *near, beside, following the line of*: "We wandered *along* (*beside*) the river bank." "Rare plants grow *along* (*by the side of*) that embankment." "Trees are planted *along* (*the whole length of*) the roadway." "The car proceeded *along* (*following the line of*) the Boston road."

Amid, Amidst. The two words do not differ essentially in meaning. Their first sense is that of *among, surrounded by*, used generally with plural substantives: "She dwelt *amid* (*surrounded by*) the ruins of her former glory." In an extended sense, the words apply to circumstances and conditions: "He was bewildered *amid* (*among*) the perplexities and temptations of his position." In poetry, *amid* is used with a singular noun to indicate *in the middle of*, or *surrounded by* some extended object: "She strayed *amid* the corn."

Among, Amongst. Like *amid* and *amidst*, these two words are interchangeable so far as meaning is concerned. Both words refer to several persons or things and convey the idea of dispersion or distribution. *Among* is the more common form: "We divided the profits *among* ourselves" (not *between*, unless only two persons are concerned). *Amongst* is the rarer, and perhaps more poetic, form.

Around, Round. Used interchangeably to signify motion or position *about, encircling, on all sides of, in all directions from, at random through*: "They made a journey *around* (*encircling*) the world." "*Around* (*on all sides of*) the mansion were gardens." "The beams of light radiate *around* (*in all directions from*) the central mass." "We spent the day riding *around* (*at random through*) the city." "They gathered *round* (*about*) the hearth."

At. This word primarily expresses the relation of *presence*, of *contact in place or time*, or of *direction towards*. (1) It designates more or less indefinitely the point or place where a thing is: "*at* the center," "*at* home," "*at* hand." (2) Sometimes it emphasizes contact with a place better than *in* or *by*: "*at* school," "*at* the helm." (3) It denotes presence at an event: "*at* the wedding," "*at* the ball"; also location of a feeling or quality: "sick *at* heart," "out *at* elbow." (4) It is likewise used to signify the end or object of directed effort: "look *at* it," "aim *at* the bull's eye"; similarly, with the verbs *strike, shout, wink, mock, laugh, be angry*, etc. (5) It implies action, occupation with, or employment: "*at* work," "*at* meals," "to pull *at* an oar."

Before. Usual meanings: *ahead of, preceding, face to face with, rather than, higher than*. Examples: "The visitors came *before* (*ahead of*) the appointed time." "The customer just *before* (*preceding*) you bought the last pound." "The culprit was brought *before* (*face to face with*) the judge." "The question is now *before* (*claiming the attention of*) (*subject to disposition by*) the house." "The ship drove *before* the wind." "Shakespeare comes *before* (*higher than*) Chaucer in rank though not in time."

Behind. Common meanings: *in the rear, at the back, toward the rear, not up with, supporting, backing*. Examples: "The garden was planted *behind* the house." "*Behind* (*in the rear of*) the army came the stragglers." "His shadow betrayed his presence *behind* (*at the back of*) the screen." "Many, worn out by the march, fell *behind* (*to the rear of*) their comrades." "His ideas are *behind* (*not up with*) the times." "The contractor did not have sufficient capital *behind* (*supporting*) him." "The train was *behind* time."

Below. Used literally of position or direction, signifying *lower than, under*: "The shot struck *below* (*lower than*) the water line." "The signature is placed on the line *below* (*under*) the complimentary close." "Three miles *below* (*farther down than*) the town, on the bank of the stream, stands the fort." Figuratively, *below* is used to express an inferior degree of rank, dignity, and excellence: "The corporal ranks *below* the sergeant." "They are as inferior as the fields are *below* the stars."

Beneath. This preposition is used generally of lower position. It suggests also influence or control and unworthiness. The following examples illustrate accurate uses of the word: "The plank roadway echoed *beneath* their tread." "Loch Katrine lay *beneath* him." "The trees were bent *beneath* their burden of fruit." "His knees shook *beneath* him." "The people were held *beneath* the yoke of the conqueror." "She thought her neighbors *beneath* her notice."

Beside. In its literal sense, used to mean *by the side of, near*: "The guard rode *beside* the carriage." Figuratively, *beside* is used to suggest comparison: "*Beside* (*in comparison with*) his son's achievement, his own seemed petty." *Beside* has the force of *outside of* in "*beside* himself" and "*beside* the question."

Besides. Formerly used interchangeably with *beside*, this word now signifies *over and above, in addition to, as well as*, and also *apart from*: "The house had many rooms *besides* (*in addition to*) those." "*Besides* (*as well as*) his income, he had other resources." "They are interested in nothing *besides* (*apart from*) their art."

Between. Used of position or movement in space separating two objects: "The courthouse was built *between* the rival towns." "He walks *between* his house and his office." *Between* is used also of intermediate qualities and conditions: "something intermediate *between* vice and virtue"; "a shade *between* orange and red." It may denote joint or reciprocal action either in agreement or opposition: "A struggle ensued *between* (*opposition*) the champions." "A compact was made *between* (*agreement*) the families." "*Between* them (*together*) they brought the game into camp." *Between* is likewise used to express confinement or restriction: "He took the bit *between* his teeth." It is employed particularly to signify privacy in conversation: "*between* ourselves," "*between* you and me."

Beyond. Used of an object in regard to both space and time, and signifying *farther on than, past, later than*: "They traveled *beyond* (*farther on than*) the mountains." "*Beyond* (*past*) the Alps lies Rome." "We were detained *beyond* (*past*) the usual hour of closing." Figuratively, the word is used in various senses of *exceeding* or *surpassing*: "The thing is *beyond* (*exceeds*) his power." "A scene lovely *beyond* (*surpassing*) expression was disclosed to view."

But. With the force of a preposition, *but* signifies *except, leaving out*: "The collector took all *but* (*except*) three." "There was no course open *but* (*except*) to submit." Some authorities treat these uses as conjunctive.

By. This word usually means *near, next to, in the course of, through the agency of, through the use of, according to* (*a specified unit of measure*). Examples: "The factory stands *by* (*near to*) the river." "Flight *by* (*in the course of the*) night was very dangerous." "No honest official is injured *by* (*through the agency of*) publicity." "*By* (*according to*) all physicians' rules he should have died." "More freight should be shipped *by* (*by way of*) water." "*By* whatever name it may be called, the tree is known *by* (*through the use of*) its fruit." "He works only *by* the day (work reckoned *according to* a day as a unit)." It may indicate a succession of units: "two *by* two"; "piece *by* piece"; "The timbers were dragged up the mountain one *by* one." The following are idiomatic expressions: "to take *by* and large" (to consider generally), "*by* seven o'clock," "to take *by* the hand," "two *by* the clock," "come *by*" (get), "do well *by* a person," "judge *by* appearance," "learn *by* experience," "take *by* surprise," "*by* the way," "*by* the pound," "*by* the book," "*by* hook and *by* crook," "*by* means of," "*by* dint of," "near *by*," "stand *by*" (help or support).

Down. Used literally of place and time and figuratively in various phrases, in the general sense of *descending direction*: "The machine sped easily *down* the incline." "A strange tradition comes *down* the years." The expression "*down* town" has the meaning of *into*, as denoting motion from a more elevated locality *down into* a lower one.

During. This word is used exclusively with reference to time, meaning *in the course of* or *throughout*: "We were repeatedly interrupted *during* (*in the course of*) the discussion." "*During* (*throughout*) this period a high temperature prevailed."

Except, Excepting. The two words are used interchangeably, in the sense of *exclusion* or *omission*: "Everybody was gay *except* the Major." "*Excepting* the last two articles, they adopted the agreement."

For. This preposition is a word of widely varied uses in reference to extent of space or of time, amounts of money, cause or occasion, purpose, seeking or reaching. It may mean *during, toward, in the interest of, in proportion to, in place of, in return, seeming, in relation to, in spite of*. Examples: "The road was torn up *for* (*throughout*) a distance of half a mile." "The firm's note is good *for* (*to the extent of*) that amount." "The mayor was censured *for* (*because of his*) permitting the meeting " "The farmers gave them ball *for* (*in return for*) ball." "*For* (*in proportion to*) one who sees anything, ten people look." "*For* (*in spite of*) all his bluster, the man was a coward." The following phrases are idiomatic: "leave *for* a destination," "atone *for*," "argue *for*," "account *for*," "allow *for*," "apologize *for*," "pay *for*," "call *for*," "care *for*," "go *for*," "write *for*," "look *for*," "name *for*" (*after*), "to be well *for*," "*for* thirty dollars," "*for* once," "*for* a while," "indebted *for*," "a time *for* anything," "a taste *for* luxuries," "a longing *for* home," "*for* the asking," "the train *for* (*going to*) Philadelphia."

From. This word denotes primarily separation in space; but it is used also of a starting point in time, and it may express distinction of ideas and the relation of cause or source. Examples: "The house was placed about three hundred feet *from* the barn." "*From* boyhood he was interested in flowers and trees." "Men pass quickly *from* youth to age." "Skill arises *from* constant practice." "Deliver us *from* (*out of the power of*) evil."

In. This word may mean "*within* a place, a group of people or a society, or a period of time." It may denote also the end of a period of time or the object of a motion or a feeling. It may further be used in respect to manner, method, material, cause or occasion, and of duty or measure. *In* should be carefully distinguished from *into*, which implies motion or change only. Examples: "The family lives *in* Jamestown." "*In* the 19th century there were many wars." "The note is due *in* three months." "*In* whom can one put confidence?" "He took great delight *in* his friends." "*In* my judgment, the man is guilty." "The picture was done *in* oils." "Undoubtedly you spoke *in* haste." We may say, "Come *in*"; but we must say, "Come *into* the house." The following are idiomatic expressions: "*in* the name of the law," "*in* time," "*in* wrath," "*in* health," "*in* doubt," "*in* error," "*in* scorn," "*in* fact," "*in* truth," "*in* love," "one *in* a thousand," "call *in* question," "hope *in*," "believe *in*," "trustworthy *in* word and deed," "originate *in*," "steeped *in*," "persist *in*."

Into. A preposition implying direction or motion, used regularly after the verbs *go, come, bring, put, send*, etc., also in referring to state or condition: "They went *into* the house." "He thrust the money *into* his purse." "The work extended well *into* the next month." "Their fathers had gone *into* business together." "The child burst *into* tears."

Notwithstanding. This word belongs to the class of participial prepositions. It means *in spite of* or *in the face of*: "The plan succeeded, *notwithstanding* strong opposition."

Of. This is the most commonly used English preposition. It may refer to position or location, distance, possession, extent of time, separation, source, material or character, relief. The following expressions will illustrate these meanings: "North *of* Boston," "the mountains *of* California," "a shore line *of* forty miles," "a creature *of* (*living only*) a day," "deprived *of* liberty," "the shadow *of* the glen," "a man *of* honor," "a form *of* great beauty," "cured *of* a cold," "a bridge *of* stone and iron." The following are idiomatic expressions: "fond *of*," "tired *of*," "best *of* all," "warned *of* danger," "hear *of*," "talk *of*," "beware *of*," "conscious *of*," "convicted *of*," "accounted *of*," "think well *of*," "afraid *of*," "big *of* heart," "*of* a cruel temper," "built *of*," "born *of*."

Off. This word means *from*, and is used chiefly to denote separation. It is employed idiomatically in various ways implying former dependence: "*off* one's hands," "*off* one's head." It sometimes indicates source or material with such verbs as *dine, eat*; as, "He dined *off* roast beef." It also signifies deduction or rebate; as, "They took it *off* the bill."

On, Upon. *On* and *upon* are nearly identical in meaning. *On* is used to indicate: (1) support or contact from elsewhere than beneath: "a fly *on* the wall"; (2) nearness: "a house situated *on* the river"; (3) employment or activity with or in respect to: "*on* the committee," "*on* duty," "*on* the run." It indicates the ground or basis of action: "stated *on* authority," "He bet *on* the red"; also position and boundary: "The town lay *on* the east." It likewise denotes state or condition: "*on* fire," "*on* sale," "*on* tap." Where simple contact or proximity to the surface is implied, *upon* is used interchangeably with *on*. The following are idiomatic uses: "The gifts arrived *on* time (*at the time set*)." "They bought the goods *on* time (*payment being deferred*)." "They lived *on* vegetables." To talk *on* or *upon* a subject implies more careful treatment of the theme than to talk *about* it.

Out. As a preposition, *out* is now obsolete or colloquial. *Out of* is used in its place. Examples: "He came *out of* (*from*) his retirement." "We frequently see things *out of* (*not according to*) their true proportion." "The bells were *out of* tune and harsh." The following are idiomatic phrases: "made *out of*," "*out of* order," "*out of* doors," "*out of* supplies," "*out of* season," "*out of* sight, *out of* mind."

Over. In the sense of *above*, this preposition is used to imply superiority, power, dignity, value, and preference; as, "to triumph *over* difficulties." It signifies *beyond*, in degree: "It cost *over* four dollars"; a whole surface: "to wander *over* the earth"; duration of time: "He let it soak *over* night." It has also the meanings of *across, from side to side*; as, "The dog leaped *over* the stream." *Over* is used idiomatically in such expressions as "*over* one's signature," "*over* head and ears in debt," etc.

Past*:* Used literally of space, time, and age signifying *beyond, farther on than, later than*: "He walked *past* (*farther on than*) the house." "They were just *past* (*beyond*) the boundary." "It is now ten minutes *past* (*later than*) twelve." "The old lady was *past* (*beyond the age of*) seventy." *Past* denotes also *beyond the power of*: "The man was troubled *past* endurance."

Round. See *Around*.

Save. Used in the sense of *except* or *excepting*: "There was no sign of human life *save* the chimney smoke."

Since. With the force of a preposition, this word is used altogether of time, signifying *from a time, within a following time*, and *duration*: "*Since* (*from*) that day we have not heard from him." "Where have you been *since* (*within the time after*) yesterday?" "It is a fortnight *since* he embarked."

Through. Used of space and time and in various other connections. It signifies *from one limit to another of, into every part of, passing within* in the sense of *penetrating* or *transmitting, during the period of, by means of, on account of*: "The hall runs *through* (*from end to end of*) the house." "The visitors were shown *through* (*into every part of*) the town." "A light shone *through* (*penetrating*) the woods." "The noise continued *through* (*during*) the night." "*Through* (*by means of*) his own perseverance, he held the position." "We were detained *through* (*on account of*) his blundering."

Throughout. The preposition *through*, reenforced by *out*, signifying *the whole of, every part of*, space, region, period of time, or course of action: "*throughout* the length and breadth of the land"; "*throughout* the night."

Till, Until. These words are used interchangeably in reference to time, signifying *to, up to*: "They can wait *till* (*up to*) next week." "He will not reply to the letter *until* (*up to*) the end of the month."

To. Used primarily to denote relation of approach and arrival. It indicates that toward which there is movement—a terminal point: "He went *to* law about it." "She stretched her arms *to* heaven." Idiomatic uses: "The remarks were addressed *to* the audience." "Let us keep this *to* ourselves." "It was sweet *to* the taste." "We were bored *to* death." "The hall rang *to* the tramp of armed men." "The drawing was made *to* scale." "It was John *to* the very life."

Touching. Used with the force of a preposition in the sense of *concerning, with regard to*: "*Touching* the life of the interior villages, we have no authentic information."

Toward, Towards. Used interchangeably in the sense of *facing* or *looking in the direction of, approaching, aiming at, in respect to*: "The door was open *toward* (*facing*) the east." "A procession came *toward* (*approaching*) the village." "*Toward* (*approaching*) night the sky became overcast." "A strong trend *toward* (*aiming at*) independence was evident." "She maintained a critical attitude *towards* (*in respect to*) her family."

Under. The primary meaning of this word is *below, lower than*; as, "*under* a tree," "a cellar *under* the house." Hence, analogously it may have the meaning of *being weighed upon, oppressed*, or *controlled by* affliction, subjection, government, authority, and the like: "to travel *under* a heavy burden"; "to be brave *under* trials"; "*Under* (*during the government of*) the Tudors, England made great political progress."

Underneath. Used in the sense of *directly below*: "*Underneath* the desk, papers were piled."

Up. With respect to motion or position, this word signifies *from a lower to a higher place on or along, at a higher place upon, toward, near, at the top of*: "The party tramped *up* (*from a lower place*) the slope." "His farm lies *up* (*at a higher point upon*) the river." It may also denote movement from the coast to the interior; as, "to journey *up* the country." It may indicate direction from the mouth to the source of the river; as, "He sailed *up* the Hudson."

With. Denotes relation of contact or association. After the verbs *fight, contend, vie*, and the like, it has the meaning of *against*; as, "The Greeks fought *with* the Persians." "They are *with* (*in the employ of*) the telephone company." It may signify association in the sense of attribute; as, "a man *with* (*characterized by*) a clean record"; also the instrument or means; as, "He slew him *with* a sword." It may denote an accessory, as of contents, material, etc.; as, "to fill the stable *with* straw," "to line the hat *with* silk." *With* is used idiomatically in such phrases as "*with* all one's heart," "*with* tooth and nail," "to bear *with*," "to put up *with*," and the like.

Within. Used of place, signifying *inside of*: "*Within* the building were many curious objects." Used of time, signifying *inside the limits of*: "The train will arrive *within* an hour." The word is used of various other relations: "It is not *within* (*in the limits of*) his power to forbid the transfer." "Such an act does not come *within* (*in the scope of*) the court's jurisdiction." *Within* also implies limitation as to quantity: "He lived *within* his income."

Without. This word in the sense of *outside of* or *excluded from* is now seldom used and may be regarded as almost obsolete: "The poor folk dwelt *without* the walls." "She was *without* the pale of society." Its present meaning denotes *lack of, absence of, deprivation*: "The association was *without* (*lacked*) funds." "He was buried *without* (*deprived of*) the usual rites."

SPECIAL PREPOSITIONS

The following is a list of certain nouns, adjectives, and verbs, which require *special prepositions*:

Abhorrence *of* evil.

Abhorrent *to* his strict principles.

Abide *in* a place, *for* a while, *with* a company, *by* a promise.

Abound *in* vigor and courage, *with* theaters and churches.

Absolve *from* debt or allegiance or a charge of guilt.

A plant **absorbs** moisture *from* the air; one becomes absorbed *in* thought; nutriment may be absorbed *into* the system *through* the skin.

An **accessory** *to* the crime, *before* or *after* the fact; the accessories *of* an automobile.

The **accident** *of* family; an accident *to* the car.

Accommodate *to* circumstances, *with* money, material, etc.

Accompanied *by* several friends, *with* a suggestion.

Accord *with* (agree) looks or profession.

Accuse *of* a crime or fault.

Acquaint *with* the facts.

Acquaintance *with* a subject, *of* one person *with* another, *between* persons.

Acquit a person *of* a charge.

Active *in* temperament, *in* business, *for* an object or purpose, *with* instruments, *about* something.

Adapted *to* a use or situation, *for* a purpose, *from* a source, as *from* Shakespeare.

Adequate *to* a demand, *for* a purpose.

Admit *to* membership, *into* a house, *of* exceptions.

Admonish *of* error or duty, *against* a proposed act.

Advantage *of* education, *of* some one as "to get the advantage *of* us," *over* an opponent.

Advocate *of* free speech, *for* another person.

Affinity *between* colors and sounds, *of* one chemical element *for* another.

We **agree** *in* opinion *with* the speaker, *to* a proposition; persons agree *on* or *upon* a statement of principles, a contract, etc.; men should agree *among* themselves.

Alarm was felt *in* the village, *among* the women, *at* the sound.

Aliens *to* our national customs and thought; aliens *in* a country, *among* a people.

Alive *in* every fiber; alive *to* every good suggestion; alive *with* fervor, hope, resolve.

Allegiance *of* the citizen *to* the government; the government has a right to allegiance *from* the citizen.

Alliance *with* a state or people, *against* the common enemy, *for* offense and defense; alliance *of*, *between*, or *among* nations.

Allied. Wit allied *to* madness, a state allied *with* another.

Alter *from* one form *to* another.

Amazement *at* such reckless driving.

Ambitious *of* power.

Amused *with* toys, *at* a remark or a situation.

The **analogy** *between* a society and the plant body; the analogy *of* sound *to* light.

Anger *at* the insult prompted a retort in kind; anger *toward* an offender exaggerates the offense; angry *with* a person.

An **answer** *to* the question, *in* writing, *by* post, or *by* word of mouth.

Antipathy *to* (sometimes *for* or *against*) a person or thing; antipathy *between* two persons.

Anxious *for* a decision, *about* or *concerning* a person's safety.

An **apology** *to* a person *for* an error is fitting.

Appeal *to* an authority, *from* a decision, *for* help.

Appear *at* the theater, *among* the first, *on* or *upon* the surface, *to* the eye, *in* evidence, *in* print, *from* reports, *near* the place, *before* the audience, *through* the mist; appear *for* in behalf *of*, or *against* one in court.

Apportion *to* each a fair share; apportion the property *among* the creditors, *between* two claimants; apportion *according to* rank, etc.

Apprehensive *of* danger, *for* one's safety.

Approximation *to* the correct solution.

Arraign *at* the bar, *before* the court, *of* or *for* a crime, *on* or *upon* an indictment.

Arrested *for* crime, *on* suspicion, *by* the officer, *on*, *upon*, or *by* virtue *of* a warrant.

Ask *for* a thing; ask a thing *of* or *from* a person; ask *after* or *about* one's health, welfare, friends, etc.

Astonished *at* a situation or a person's attitude, *by* an event.

Attend *to* (listen) instructions, *on* or *upon* (wait) an official or dignitary.

Attended *by* a train of servants, *with* difficulties, advantages, etc.

Behavior *of* a person *to* or *toward* people, *on* or *upon* the streets, *before* the multitude, or *in* a place, *with* companions.

Benevolence *of* or *from* a person, *to* or *toward* others.

Break *to* pieces or *in* pieces, *into* several pieces (when the object is thought of as divided rather than shattered), *with* a friend, *away from* a habit; break *into* a house, *out of* prison; break *across* one's knee; break *through* a barrier.

Burn *in* fire; burn *with* fire; burn *to* the ground; burn *to* ashes; burn *through* the skin or the roof; burn *into* the conscience, etc.

Call *on* or *upon* a person (to visit him), *after* (by the name of), *in* question, *at* a house.

Care *of* a property, *for* the future, *about* a matter.

Carry *to* a place; carry *from* or *out of* a place; carry qualities *into* conduct; carry *across* the street, *over* the bridge; carry a cable *under* the sea.

Catch *at* a straw; catch a person *by* the collar; catch a ball *with* the hand; catch a disease *from* a patient; catch one *in* the act, a bird *in* a snare.

Cause *of* disaster; cause *for* interference.

Change a house gown *for* a street dress; change *from* a caterpillar *to* or *into* a butterfly.

Cheat one *of* his desires, *out of* a right.

Choose *from* or *from among* a number; choose *out of* the army; choose *between* two, *among* many; choose *for* a purpose.

Commit *to* a person *for* safe-keeping; commit *to* prison *for* trial.

Complain *of* a thing *to* a person, *of* one person *to* another, *of* or *against* a person *for* an act, *to* an officer, *before* the court, *about* a thing.

Concerned *with* a person, *in* a result, *in* a proceeding, *about* a matter, *for* a person's health, etc.

Concur *with* a person, *in* an opinion.

Confirm *by* testimony; confirm *in* a belief.

Conformity *with* an opinion, *to* an order, custom, etc.

Considerate *of* a person's feelings.

Contend *with* a person, difficulties, trials, temptations, etc., *for* a principle, a truth, *against* an obstacle, *for* an object.

Contrast two things, one *with* another.

Controversy *with* a person, *between* two or more, *about* or *over* a subject.

Conversant *with* a subject or the facts in a case.

Conversation *with* people, *between* or *among* persons, *about* a matter.

Convey *to* a friend, a purchaser, etc.; convey *from* one place *to* another; convey *by* express, *by* hand, etc.

Copy *after* a person, a model, an example, *from* life, nature, *from* or *out of* a work.

Correspond *with* a person, *to* ideas, models, etc.

Deliver *from* temptation, *out of* difficulty, trouble, etc., *of* an opinion.

Die *of* fever, *by* violence; die *for* one's country; die *at* sea, *in* one's bed, *in* agony; die *to* the world.

Differ *among* themselves, *from* one another, *from* or *with* another in judgment, opinion, etc., *about*, *concerning* a question, subject, etc.

Discriminate *between* two or more things, one thing *from* another, *against* a person.

Disgusted *with* a person, *at*, *by*, *with* a thing.

Divide *between* two, *among* two or more, *in* or *into* parts, something *with* another person, a thing *from* another, *upon* a question.

Draw water *from* or *out of* a well; draw one *into* an argument; draw *with* cords or ropes; the truck is drawn *by* a tractor *along* the road, *across* the lots, *over* the bridge, *through* the streets, *to* the station.

Employ *in*, *on*, *upon*, or *about* a work, business, etc., *for* a purpose, *at* a certain rate of salary or wage.

Entrance *into* a place, *on* or *upon* a work or course of action, *into* or *upon* office, *into* a contest, *by* or *through* a door, *within* the gates, *into* or *among* the company.

Envious *of* (formerly *at* or *against*) a person; envious *of* another's wealth or power.

Faint *with* hunger; faint *in* color.

Fall *under* censure, observation, etc., *from* a high place, *into* water, a hole, bad habits, etc., *on* or *upon* a foe, *among* thieves, *to* or *on* the ground.

Friendship *of* one person *for* or *toward* another, or friendship *between* persons.

Good *at* a business or task, *for* some purpose, *to* another person.

Gratified *at* an action or course of conduct.

Grief *at* a loss, *for* a friend.

Hanker *after* or *for* amusement, dainties, luxury, etc.

A result **happy** *for* a person; happy *at* a reply; happy *in* his home, *with* his friends, *among* his children; happy *at* a discovery, *over* a success.

Help *in* business or emergency, *with* money; help *to* success, *against* opposition.

Impatient *with* a person, *at* conduct, delay, etc., *for* something expected, *under* grief, misfortune, etc.

Injury *of* a cause; injury *to* a structure; injury *by* fire, *by* or *from* collision, interference, etc.

Inquisitive *about*, *concerning*, *in regard to*, *regarding* matters.

Join *to* something more numerous or greater, *with* something equal.

A **journey** *from* Naples *to* Rome, *through* Mexico, *across* the continent, *over* the sea; a journey *into* Asia, *among* savages, *by* land, *by* rail, *for* health, *on* foot, *on* the cars, etc.

We **listen** *for* what we expect or desire to hear; we listen *to* what we actually do hear.

Love *of* country, *for* humanity; love *to* or *toward* God and man.

Made *of*, *out of* or *from* certain materials, *into* a certain form, *for* a certain purpose or person; made *with* hands, *by* hand.

Martyr *for* or *to* a cause, *to* disease, disappointment, sorrow, etc.

Mastery *of* a subject or a task, *over* an enemy or opponent.

Mourn *for* a loss, *over* misfortune or trouble.

Necessary *to* a purpose, *for* or *to* a result or a person. unity is necessary *to* completeness; decision is necessary *for* command, *for* or *in* a commander.

Offended *at* a remark or course of action, *by* a word or act, *with* a person.

Opinion *on* a question, *about* a subject or a person.

Opportunity *of* doing something, *for* service, thought, etc.

Pardon *for* the offenders. *for* all offenses; pardon *of* offenders or offenses.

Patient *of* toil, *with* a person, *toward* learners, *under* difficulty.

Plead *with* the tyrant, *for* the captive; plead *against* injustice; plead *to* the indictment, *at* the bar, *before* the court.

Pleasant *to*, *with* or *toward* persons, *about* a matter.

Present *to* a person, a person *with* something.

Prevail *on*, *upon*, or *with* (to persuade), *over* or *against* (to overcome).

Profit *of* labor, *on* capital, *in* business.

Provide *with* supplies, *for* the future, *against* misfortune.

Purchase *at* a price, *at* a public sale, *of* or *from* a person; *for* cash, *with* money, *on* time.

Rejoice *at* an occurrence or an event, *in* personal qualities or possessions.

Relieve *from* pain, trouble, *of* duty or responsibility.

Reproach a person *for* acts.

Rise *from* slumber; rise *to* an occasion or responsibility, *at* a summons; rise *with* the dawn.

Security *for* the payment *of* a debt; security *to* the state, *for* the prisoner, *in* a specified sum; security *from* attack, *against* loss.

Send *from* the hand *to* or *toward* a mark; send *to* a friend *by* a messenger or *by* mail; send a person *into* danger.

Shelter *under* a roof *from* a storm, *in* a stronghold, *behind* or *within* walls.

Skillful *at* or *in* a task, *with* tools.

Strive *with* or *against* a person opposed or a thing in opposition, *for* something to be obtained.

Suffer *from* a disease, *by* some one's act or conduct, *with* another (sympathy).

Taste *of* food, etc., *for* painting, music.

Versed *in* a subject.

CONJUNCTIONS

The correct use of conjunctions is necessary to well constructed, intelligible sentences. No matter how accurate a writer's use of other words may be, if he does not indicate appropriately the relations between words or clauses, his sentences cannot be clear.

Conjunctions are divided into two general classes, *co-ordinate* and *subordinate*.

A *co-ordinate* conjunction connects words, phrases, or clauses of the same rank; as, *and*, *but*, *or*, *nor*, *either*, *neither*: "Sun *and* moon are heavenly bodies." "To be *or* not to be, that is the question." "Be not overcome of evil, *but* overcome evil with good."

A *subordinate* conjunction connects clauses of different rank; as, *since*, *unless*, *because*, *for*, *if*, *though*, *although*: "*Unless* it rains, the crops will fail."

Conjunctions include adverbs used as conjunctions and known as *conjunctive adverbs*, such as *when*, *where*, *whence*, *whereby*, *while*, *why*: "*While* we sleep, the body is rebuilt."

Correlative conjunctions are those which are used in pairs; as, *both—and*, *either—or*, *neither—nor*, *whether—or*, *though—yet*: "He *neither* ate *nor* slept." "*Though* all men deny Thee, *yet* will I not."

The following list of the more important English conjunctions shows varied shades of meaning that these parts of speech may assume, according to the demands of the different sentences in which they are used.

Although and **Though.** These words do not differ in meaning. They introduce concessive ideas: "We must be content with this, *though* we had hoped for more." "*Although* clear writing is difficult to produce, it is worth earnest endeavor." Equivalent phrases are: *in spite of the fact that*; *granted that*; *albeit*. *Even though* is more emphatic, as *although* was formerly more emphatic than *though*.

And. The most nearly universal connective. It is the original Saxon word used to join sentence elements that are grammatically alike and is the typical copulative of narration. It has, besides, a variety of effective uses as follows: (1) to intensify a statement,—"He talked on for hours *and* hours"; "They worked, *and* worked hard, to get results"; (2) as almost equivalent to *but*,—"It is one thing to plan *and* quite another to carry out plans"; (3) in such expressions as "There are boys *and* boys," indicating differences of condition, class, or character; (4) to express result,—"After long search he found the lode *and* became very wealthy." *And* may be used to begin a sentence, especially where some feeling or thought of surprise or reproach is implied: "*And* did you once see Shelley plain?" "*And* do you mean to tell me such a story?"

As. Used where comparisons of quality, close likeness, or proportion are implied: "He was as happy *as* only a man with a clear conscience can be"; "*As* we approached the rapids, the roar became deafening." *As* may denote cause or reason: "*As* the ship was unseaworthy, it was abandoned."

Because. Originally a phrase consisting of preposition and substantive, *by cause*. The word signifies *for the reason that* or *in consequence of*. See *For*.

Both. This conjunction is used regularly to precede the first of two co-ordinate words or phrases, and is followed by *and* before the second. It signifies *alike*, *as well as*, *too*, *also*; "a masterpiece for *both* argument and style." It may follow the co-ordinate words; as, "Malice mars logic and charity *both* (alike, too, also)."

But. Used in a great variety of ways, the primary sense being that of contrast or opposition: "His progress was slow *but* sure"; "We cannot *but* believe." Sometimes *but* implies a concession:

"Lincoln is dead, *but* the government at Washington still lives." *But* may mean "that—not": "There is no rose *but* bears its thorn."

Either. A disjunctive connective used before two co-ordinated alternatives and followed by the correlative *or*: "*Either* the light is distant *or* it is dim." "We must *either* stay where we are *or* risk being carried away by the flood."

Ere. A conjunction used mostly in poetry, thus differing from its synonym, *before*: "We shall meet *ere* set of sun." *Ere* must be distinguished carefully from *e'er*, which is a poetic contraction of *ever*.

Except. The use of *unless* instead of *except* is preferred by modern writers: "I will not be satisfied *unless* (*except*) you come." After *except* or *unless*, the phrases *it be*, *it were*, etc. are frequently used instead of repeating the principal verb: "He never goes to church *except it be* (he goes) to hear the music." "He seldom laughed *except it were* (he laughed) at his own jokes."

For. As a conjunction, *for* introduces only clauses or sentences of cause or reason. It should be distinguished carefully from *as, since, because*. *Because* is now used to introduce a real cause; as, "The water boils *because* it is heated." But one may say, "The water must be hot, *for* I saw John light the gas." In the latter case, *for* introduces a reason for a belief. *As* and *since* introduce causes or reasons that may be taken for granted: "*Since* (*as*) the hat was mine, I took it."

If. Used to introduce a clause of condition with the *subjunctive* signifying *doubt*, and with the *indicative* implying *suspended opinion* in regard to a statement: "*If* that be true, this is false." "He shall not secure the property *if* we can prevent it." *If* also introduces a concession, as equivalent to *although*: "*If* (*although*) he is competent, he sometimes makes mistakes."

Lest. Used to introduce a negative intention or purpose, equivalent to *that—not* or *for fear that*: "We hastened to return *lest* our friends should be alarmed."

Neither. The negative of *either*, used to introduce the first of two or more co-ordinate words or clauses, and followed by *nor*: "They had *neither* food *nor* clothing." "Quarter was *neither* given *nor* asked."

Nevertheless. In meaning, this compound is equivalent to *yet, notwithstanding*, or *in spite of that*: "Although entrance is forbidden, *nevertheless* they will use the house."

Nor. See *Neither*.

Notwithstanding. Equivalent in meaning to *although* or *in spite of the fact that*: "John was a stranger to most of the villagers, *notwithstanding* he had lived in Oakfield for thirty years."

Or. See *Either*.

Save. Used with the force of a conjunction, this word is equivalent to *except* or *unless*: "The night was still, *save* that the distant cataract rumbled steadily." "'Tis said there were no thought of hell, *save* (*unless*) hell were taught."

Since. This word denotes either sequence or duration in time or a logical relation. As applied to time, it signifies *from* a time or *subsequent to* or *during* a time: "Many years have passed *since* they met." "It is a fortnight *since* he embarked." Logically, *since* means *because* or *inasmuch as*: "*Since* she has inquired, you may give her the facts."

So. In its conjunctive use, this particle has the sense of *provided that, on condition that*; as, "They will be satisfied, *so* their children receive an education." It is used also to introduce a clause of result; as, "The car had disappeared, *so* the entire party walked home."

Than. Formerly this word was thought of both as conjunction and as preposition, and such expressions as "older *than* me," "taller *than* him" were allowable. Now, however, *than* is recognized only as a conjunction; hence one must say "older *than* I," "taller *than* he." The expression *than whom* is an exception to the rule given; as, "Roosevelt, *than whom* no American has been better loved or more sincerely hated." This construction is now universally approved.

That. A few common uses of *that* should be noticed. Besides being generally used to introduce an objective or adjective clause, *that* is likewise employed to denote time, definitely or indefinitely: "It is time *that* we should be going home." "We left the day *that* he arrived." It may also denote the relation of purpose or result: "He was given leave *that* he might go to Paris." Both in speaking and in writing we often omit *that* when the connection may readily be supplied: "We believe (*that*) the work can be done in a week."

Therefore. A conjunction of formal sense, used to introduce a conclusion or consequence. Its meanings may be expressed by *in consequence, for this reason, on that ground, consequently*: "We have completed our examination of the case; *therefore* we should make our report."

Till, Until. These two words are used as conjunctions without any difference in meaning. Their general sense is that of expectancy or continuance, expressed by (*up*) *to the time when*: "They could not vote *until* the polls were opened." "It was his custom to remain in the house *till* darkness had fallen."

Unless. A word compounded of *on* and *less*, and meaning literally *in less* or *on less*, that is, *on any less grounds or condition than*, the conditions being stated in a following clause. Other equivalent phrases are *if—not, in the event that—not, supposing that—not*. The following are typical uses of the word: "How shall they learn *unless* they are willing to hear?" "*Unless* the government's plans miscarry, the ships will be built." "I cannot explain his conduct, *unless* he has not been warned."

Whereas. A conjunction of two principal uses: (1) In formal documents and arguments, expressing the idea of *since, considering*, it introduces a preamble or a reason upon which a conclusion or a resolution is based: "*Whereas*, The society has accepted the plan of the committee, therefore, be it Resolved, etc." (2) Like *although*, it may imply a contradiction between the clause it introduces and a preceding statement: "They claimed a victory, *whereas* they had really lost the contest."

Whether. As a conjunction, this word introduces an implied question. (1) It may introduce alternatives, followed by *or* before the second alternative: "He was uncertain *whether* he should reply *or* be silent." When the second alternative is a negative of the first, it is frequently expressed by *not* or *no* following *or*: "They will move, *whether* the order arrives *or not*." (2) It may introduce a single indirect question, with an alternative omitted but implied: "We do not know *whether* he has read that book (*or not*) (*or some other*)."

While. Used of time, in the sense of *as long as* or *during the time that*: "*While* I was musing, the fire burned." It may also have the sense of *although*, implying some contradiction: "*While* the cloth is very heavy, it is not firm in texture."

Yet. As a conjunction, meaning *however, nevertheless, yet* implies usually some opposition, or unlikeness: "The board approved the plan, *yet* was not ready to act." "The tools are similar in form, *yet* very different in use." It may be used in the sense of *although*, signifying a concession: "They were determined, *yet* courteous."

CAPITAL LETTERS

In early forms of writing, capital letters were exclusively employed. Gradually small letters appeared and initial letters were used at the beginnings of sections and paragraphs only. Later the first word of a sentence was capitalized to call attention to its importance. Finally words within the sentence were treated in the same manner. It became the custom to begin every noun with a capital. This custom however, conducing to no useful end, has long since been laid aside.

Modern capitalization is determined somewhat by the thought to be conveyed. The chief uses of capitals are (1) to show the beginning of a unit of thought; (2) to give particular prominence to certain words, as names of countries, cities, persons, etc.; (3) to relieve the uniformity of the page.

Certain rules for capitalization are fixed. However, a slight variation in some instances may result from the individual usage of competent writers.

In the sciences, such as botany and geology, as well as in other departments of knowledge, certain customs of capitalization have become well established. Many of these special rules are to be found in the "stylebooks" issued by various publishers.

The following list contains the most generally approved rules and customs of capitalization in present day writing:

Rules for Capitals

1. The first word of every sentence should begin with a capital.

We receive good by doing good.
Always speak the truth.

2. The first word of every line of poetry should begin with a capital.

Like to a coin, passing from hand to hand,
Are common memories, and day by day
The sharpness of their impress wears away.

3. The first word of every direct quotation should begin with a capital.

Coleridge said, "Friendship is a sheltering tree."

4. The first word of every direct question should begin with a capital.

Ask yourself this question: Are you making the best use of your time?

5. The pronoun I and the interjection O should be capitalized.

Guide me, O thou great Jehovah.

6. Every proper noun should begin with a capital letter.

Europe, America, Chicago, James.

7. Words derived from proper nouns should begin with capitals unless, by long usage, they have lost all association with the nouns from which they are derived.

American, Americanize, Christian, Christianize, Roman, Hebrew, Elizabethan, etc.
But china dishes, india ink, prussian blue, turkey red, majolica ware, delft, castile soap, oriental rugs, galvanize, pasteurize, romance.

Capitalize all abbreviations of proper names.

Eng. (England), Sun. (Sunday), N. J. (New Jersey)

8. Names of geographical sections of the world, when used as proper nouns, should be capitalized.

The Far North, the Orient, the Near East, the Riviera, in the West.

9. The words North, South, East, and West and their compounds should begin with capitals whenever they refer to parts of the country, and not simply to points of the compass.

I have a friend in the South.
The river flows southwest.
Gold is found in the great Northwest.

10. The names of the days of the week, of the months of the year, and of feasts, fasts, festivals, and holidays, both religious and civic, should begin with capitals.

Tuesday, June, Arbor Day, Easter.

The names of the seasons are not capitalized except when personified.

The New England autumn is a delightful season.
Thou breath of Autumn's being.

11. Names of personified objects should be capitalized.

O Death! where is thy sting?
Then Memory disclosed her face divine.

12. All names and expressions which may be regarded as titles of the Deity should be capitalized.

Lord, God, Father, Son, Son of Man, Heavenly Father. But write King of kings, Father of mercies, Prince of peace, where the phrase is merely descriptive and not an essential part of the name.

As a rule, a personal pronoun referring to Deity should be capitalized when the meaning might otherwise be mistaken.

Be true thyself, and follow Me!

In general, do not capitalize a relative pronoun referring to Deity, because its antecedent is usually given.

Follow Him, whose truth shall deliver you.

13. The names of versions and of books and divisions of the Bible, names of sacred books of all religions, and titles of psalms and of parables should be capitalized.

Exodus, Psalms, New Testament, Epistle to the Romans, Sermon on the Mount, the Pentateuch, the Koran, Parable of the Vineyard.

14. The words street, river, gulf, sea, canal, coast, etc., may begin with capital letters when they are used in connection with proper names.

Bryant Street, Hudson River, Persian Gulf, North Sea, Erie Canal, Pacific Coast.

15. Names of political parties and of religious organizations, and generally the first word and all other important words in the names of societies and corporations, should be capitalized.

Conservative, Liberal, Republican, Democrat, Presbyterians, The Society for the Prevention of Cruelty to Animals.

16. Capitalize the first word and all other words, except articles, prepositions, and conjunctions, in titles of books, poems, essays, periodicals, plays, and pictures.

Gray's Elegy in a Country Churchyard.
Hawthorne's The Great Stone Face.
The Inside of the Cup.

Some publishers and the American Library Association capitalize only the first word and proper nouns and proper adjectives in titles.

A history of English local government.

17. Titles of honor, of respect, and of relationship, when used before the names of persons, should be capitalized; but, when used after the name, such titles are not capitalized.

King George, President Truman, Sir James, Uncle John, Aunt Edith.
Harry S. Truman, president of the United States; Honorable Joseph W. Martin, Jr., representative from Massachusetts. George VI, king of Great Britain.

Abbreviated titles of honor or respect should be capitalized.

James Bryce, D.C.L.; Dr. S. Weir Mitchell; Henry Brown, D.D., LL.D.

18. Names of important historical events and movements are capitalized.

The Revolution, the Reformation, the Colonial Period, the Renaissance, the Space Age.

19. In formal resolutions, capitalize the words Whereas and Resolved and the word immediately following each.

Whereas, This society, etc.; therefore, be it Resolved, That the office of secretary, etc.

PUNCTUATION

Punctuation is the art of separating composition or discourse into sentences, and members of a sentence, by means of certain marks or points (1) to make clear the author's meaning and (2) to show grammatical relations between words.

In spoken language, these relations are indicated by the pauses and by the inflections of the voice; but in written language there are no such aids, and it is necessary to supply the deficiency with definite marks.

As a means of conveying thought, punctuation does not generally receive the attention its importance demands. An omission, an insertion, or a transposition of points may completely alter the meaning of a sentence. To illustrate: An English statesman, having charged a government officer with dishonesty, was required publicly to retract the accusation in the House of Commons. The statesman read the following recantation: "I said he was dishonest, it is true; and I am sorry for it." The following day the papers printed the retraction thus: "I said he was dishonest; it is true, and I am sorry for it." By a simple transposition of the comma and the semicolon, the printed statement not only failed to carry an apology, but it also reiterated the original charge of dishonesty.

To a limited extent it is true that usage varies. But it is equally true that, as an art, punctuation is founded upon certain definite principles; and, while some latitude is allowed in their application, whatever directly violates these principles is incorrect and inadmissible.

Punctuation is, therefore, an essential part of good writing. A clear idea of what one wishes to say, a knowledge of the structure of sentences, and intelligent care in the application of definite rules will do much to perfect one in the use of this important art.

The generally accepted rules for punctuation are as follows:

RULES FOR PUNCTUATION

The Period

1. A period should be placed at the close of every declarative or imperative sentence.

Washington is a beautiful city.
Think before you speak.

2. Place a period after all abbreviations, but not after chemical symbols, Roman numerals, per cent, or 8vo, 4to, 2d, 9th, etc. When an abbreviation ends a sentence, use only one period.

I know John Jones, M.D., LL.D.

When omission of letters is indicated by an apostrophe, a period is not used after the contraction: m'f'g for manufacturing; ass'n for association.

3. A period is not necessary after titles, headings, etc., on a page; but subheads and paragraph topics, not in separate lines, should be followed by a period.

The Exclamation Point

1. Place an exclamation point after every exclamatory sentence and after interjections and other expressions of emotion.

How welcome is the rain!
Alas! He died on the battlefield.
God forbid! May I never see it again!

In some cases, when an interjection is very closely connected with other words, the exclamation point is not placed between them, but is reserved for the close of the expression.

Oh, never may sun that morrow see!

2. The exclamation point is often used to express contempt or sarcasm.

And he is a writer!

The Interrogation Point

1. Place an interrogation point at the end of every direct question.

Is he telling the truth?
She asked, "When does school begin?"

The Colon

1. Place a colon between the great divisions of sentences, when minor subdivisions occur that are separated by semicolons.

We perceive the shadow to have moved along the dial, but did not see it moving; we observe that the grass has grown. though it was impossible to see it grow: so the advances we make in knowledge, consisting of minute and gradual steps, are perceivable only after intervals of time.

2. The colon separates a clause from the following clause or group of clauses illustrating or amplifying its meaning.

There is a singular and perpetual charm in a letter of yours: it never grows old; it never loses its novelty.

3. A colon precedes a formal enumeration of particulars.

Man consists of three parts: first, the body, with its sensual appetites; second, the mind, with its thirst for knowledge and other noble aspirations; third, the soul, with its undying principle.

4. A colon should be used before a long direct quotation.

Lord Bacon said: "Reading maketh a full man; conference, a ready man; writing, an exact man."

5. A colon follows *thus, as follows, this, these,* and similar expressions, introducing a statement or a series of clauses.

His credentials are as follows: he has studied economics; he has employed men; he has succeeded in business.

6 A colon usually follows the salutation in a letter.

My dear Mary: Sirs:

In short, informal letters, a comma may be used.

My dear Friend,

The Semicolon

1. A semicolon should be used to separate the parts of a compound sentence, when one or both members contain commas.

Mirth should be the embroidery of conversation, not the web; and wit the ornament of the mind, not the furniture.

2. When two clauses are joined by *for, but, and,* or an equivalent word, the one clause perfect in itself, and the other added as a matter of inference, contrast, or explanation, they are separated by a semicolon.

Economy is no disgrace; for it is better to live on a little than to outlive a great deal.

3. When the parts of a compound sentence, even though they are short, are not closely connected in thought, they should be separated by a semicolon.

Man proposes; God disposes.

4. If a series of expressions depends on a commencing or concluding portion of the sentence, the expressions should be separated by semicolons.

If we think of glory in the field; of wisdom in the cabinet; of the purest patriotism; of the highest integrity, public and private; of morals * * *,—the august figure of Washington presents itself as the personification of all these ideas.

5. A semicolon is commonly used before and a comma after *as, viz., to wit, namely, for example, i.e.,* or *that is,* when they precede examples or illustrations.

We have three great bulwarks of liberty; viz., schools, colleges, and universities.

The Comma

1. All nouns of direct address should be set off by commas.

Mary, shut the door.
I say, John, it is not true.

2. Parenthetical expressions or additional expressions that break the directness of the statement should be set off by commas.

Industry, as well as genius, is essential to the production of great works.
It is mind, after all, that does the work of the world.

3. Words or expressions used in apposition should be set off from the rest of the sentence by commas.

Milton, the blind poet, wrote *Paradise Lost.*
We, the people of the United States, do ordain and establish this constitution.

4. A comma is used to mark the omission of words grammatically essential.

To err is human; to forgive, divine.
Go today if you can; if not, tomorrow.

5. A comma is used before a short direct quotation or question.

He said, "Time will tell."
Jane shouted, "Are you going?"

6. A nominative absolute construction or an expression used independently should be separated from the rest of the sentence by a comma.

To tell the truth, I do not know.
Rome having fallen, the world relapsed into barbarism.

7. A series of words in the same construction should be separated by commas.

Ulysses was wise, eloquent, cautious, and intrepid.
Men, women, and children filled the building.

8. When the subject consists of a series of words not joined by a conjunction, use a comma before the predicate.

Men, women, children, filled the building.

9. As a rule, when a clause is used as the subject of a verb, it should not, even though long, be followed by a comma, unless it ends with a verb.

That he is a man well qualified to fill the position must be admitted.
Whatever is, is right.

A comma is sometimes needed to prevent ambiguity.

He who teaches, often learns himself.

10. Use a comma between words in the same construction when they are modified in different ways.

They saw fields, and hills covered with trees.

11. When the separation of sentence elements is desirable and is slightly marked, a comma is used between co-ordinate clauses.

I heard him speak, but I made no reply.
Jane frowned, and her friend turned away.

12. Words used in pairs take a comma after each pair.

The dying man cares not for pomp or luxury, palace or estate, silver or gold.

13. A phrase or a clause out of its natural order should be separated from the rest of the sentence by a comma. If the sentence is short, the comma may be omitted.

Of the five races, the Caucasian is the most enlightened.
To those who labor, sleep is doubly pleasant.
With this I am satisfied.

14. In a complex sentence, if the dependent clause comes first, it should be followed by a comma.

Where I go, ye cannot come.

15. When two or more antecedent portions of a sentence have a common connection with some succeeding clause or word, a comma should be placed after each.

She is as tall, though not as handsome, as her sister.

16. A comma should be placed before a relative clause, when it is explanatory of the antecedent, or presents an additional thought.

Why ask John, who knows nothing about it?

A comma should not be placed between a restrictive adjunct or clause and that which it restricts.

Bring me the book that lies on the table.
Who can respect a man that is not governed by good principles?

Quotation Marks

1. Every direct quotation should be enclosed in double quotation marks.

Franklin said, "One today is worth two tomorrows."

2. A quotation within a quotation should be enclosed in single quotation marks.

Said he, "I quoted Burns's line, 'A man's a man for a' that.'"

3. Words or phrases of unusual, technical, or ironical meaning, or to which particular attention is directed, may be enclosed in single or double quotation marks.

Ann was made "master of ceremonies."
The phrase "producer to consumer" is popular.
He always talks about 'contacts and aerials.'

4. When a quotation consists of more than one paragraph, quotation marks should be placed at the *beginning* of *each* paragraph, but at the *end* of the *last* paragraph only

The period and the comma are always placed inside the quotation marks. If at the close of a quotation any grammatical point other than the period or comma is required, it should be placed before the quotation marks if it is applicable to the quotation alone, but after them if it belongs to the sentence or member as a whole.

I read Tennyson's "In Memoriam."
He answered briefly, "Am I a knave that you should suspect me of this?"
Are our lots indeed cast "in the brazen age"?

The Parenthesis

1. Marks of parenthesis are used to enclose words loosely connected with the rest of the sentence in thought and structure.

Every star (and this great truth is inferred from indisputable facts) is the center of a planetary system.

Words within parenthesis should be punctuated as they would be in any other position, except before the last parenthetical mark. There, if the subject matter is complete in itself as regards both construction and sense, a period, an interrogation point, or an exclamation point should be used, according to the character of the sentence. If the parenthesis is incomplete in sense, there should be no point before the last mark.

Men are born equal (can you doubt it?); it is circumstances only that cast their lot in different stations.
Jane (such was her name) smiled sweetly.

The Dash

1. The dash is used to denote a sudden change in thought or in construction.

Closely following came—What do you suppose?

2. A dash is used after other points when a greater pause than they usually denote is required.

A traitor!—Yes.

3. A dash is used to set off parenthetical expressions which have a closer connection with the rest of the sentence than parenthesis marks would show.

You have a whole day—two days, if needful—to finish your work.

4. A dash is frequently used to set off an appositive or a supplementary word or phrase added for emphasis or for explanation.

He wrote an excellent article on chemistry—a subject to which he has devoted the greater part of his life.
Her features were plain but not repulsive—at least not so when you heard her speak.

The Hyphen

1. A hyphen should be used between syllables at the end of a line when a part of a word must be continued on the next line.

2. The hyphen is used in forming compound words which are not permanent compounds. Such words rightly united by a hyphen are of two kinds:

(1) Those used conventionally or for a certain occasion only.

A well-known man; fresh-water fish; open-hearth furnace.
After-deliberation showed they were wrong.

(2) Those which are attributively used as a phrase to transfer to an object a certain meaning that the literal sense of the words would not otherwise indicate.

A forget-me-not; Jack-in-the-pulpit; love-lies-bleeding.

LINGUISTICS

In the section *Sentence Building*, English grammar is defined as a science that investigates the principles in general on which the English language is based. This section will discuss some attempts to formulate these general principles more precisely. We must also note the relevance of these formulations to the study of the language and to what in language study is not reached through linguistics. These questions in turn will be embedded in some discussion of much larger and more general issues having to do with the goals of linguistic theory and with goals of education that can possibly be reached through linguistics.

FORMAL GRAMMAR

Three Linguistics Theories. The material in *Sentence Building* represents a distillation of grammatical knowledge that has accumulated for well over 2000 years. It is only because of certain developments in techniques of processing data and in modern mathematics that alternative ways of handling the "stuff" of language have become possible. We can now usefully distinguish between two general kinds of linguistic theories. One, a descriptive linguistic theory, has in general rejected the insights and conclusions of the ancients. The descriptivists ignore all but a narrowly defined set of data. Thus a descriptive grammar emerges as a statement of the patterns into which the sentences naturally fall.

The other theory, transformational grammar, has attempted to formulate the insights of traditional, classical grammar and thus to deepen our understanding of the insights, rejecting some and going beyond in others. For the *transformational* grammarian the data to be accounted for includes, not only the sentences of the language, but also the intuitions that speakers of a language have into their language about the relatedness of sounds in related words (div*i*ne, div*i*nity, etc.), the relatedness of structures in related sentences (John hit the ball, the ball was hit by John, etc.). The descriptivist considers nothing but the sentences themselves fair game for analysis and rejects mentalistic data.

Some examples will clearly distinguish among these three, including now the traditional, theories of grammar. We call them theories or, better, hypotheses, because they amount to claims only as to what is true of English sentences—claims that we have every reason to believe fall short of truth in one way or another. These and following examples are numbered for ease of reference:

1 John is difficult to please
2 John is anxious to please

A descriptive linguist, limiting himself to dealing with sentence structure facts, would also necessarily limit himself to considering the two to be sentences of the same type; that is, they exhibit a very general sentence pattern.

3 Noun *is* Adjective *to* Verb

He would have very little more to say, at the level of syntax.

The traditional grammarian responds to his intuitive sense that the relationship among "John", "is difficult", "to please" is quite different from that of "John", "is anxious", "to please". He thus rejects attending to the superficial similarities of the sentences for dealing with their important differences. His sentence diagrams capture these differences nicely:

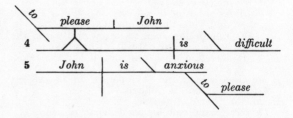

It really makes no difference to the traditional grammarian whether he is dealing with

1 John is difficult to please, *or*
6 to please John is difficult

That they differ in word order is trivial: what is important is that in both sentences "John" is the object of "please" and that in **2** "John" is the subject of "please". Thus the diagrams must reflect these crucial differences between **1** and **2** and the crucial relationship between **1** and **6**. The descriptive grammarian, ignoring the intuitions of relatedness and differences, thus salvages only a lower level fact of superficial sameness for **1** and **2**. He misses their important differences and is principally incapable of capturing the sameness of **1** and **6**. He is in fact forced to present **6** as manifesting a sentence pattern entirely different from that of **1**, namely

7 *to* Verb Noun *is* Adjective

The transformational grammarian is concerned to capture both the fact of the differences between **1** and **2**, between **1** and **6**, and of the sameness of **1** and **6**, and of **1** and **2**. All of these are facts; none is to be ignored though they must all be put in some proper order. The transformational grammarian's way of properly ordering facts such as these is to argue that sentences are characterized by having both an abstract, deep structure, captured somewhat and sometimes in traditional sentence diagramming, and a concrete surface structure. Many sentences can be related to a single deep structure. This relatedness is then accounted for, explained by operations known as transformations, thus the name of the theory.

To illustrate this discussion, let us enlarge the set of sentences **1** and **6** to include what seem to be further related sentences:

8 it is difficult to please John
9 it is difficult for someone to please John
10 for someone to please John is difficult
11 John is difficult for someone to please

The inclusion of **9**—**11** answers to our feeling that in **1**, **6**, and **8** there is an understood indefinite subject of "please". The deep structure of these sentences is captured in the following (tree) diagram:

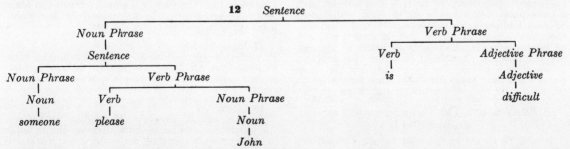

Depending on what set of transformations operates on some such structure as **12**, we get from it to one of the six sentences above. Note that **12** is in no sense a sentence so that *some* operations must necessarily operate on deep structures, relating them to surface structures. Informally presented, the necessary transformations are these:

13 (a) insertion of *to*, necessary for all six sentences
    (b) deletion of *someone*, optional
    (c) insertion of *for*, but only if *someone* is not deleted
    (d) re-ordering of the topmost Noun Phrase and Verb Phrase, optional
    (e) re-ordering *John* to initial position in the sentence, but only if (d) has taken place
    (f) insertion of *it*, but only if (d) has taken place and (e) has not.

If we then let (a) and (b) operate on **12,** we get
6 to please John is difficult
If (a), (c), (d), (e), then
11 John is difficult for someone to please
In this way the transformational grammarian, exploring the relationships among sentences, seeks to build up a consistent set of generalizations, a set of formally stated rules, that explains the sentences of English or of any language. The presentation of the theory here of course has been informal and vastly simplified. It is clear that the sentences handled above must be importantly related to, among others,
14 pleasing John is difficult
Also the formulations of transformations and deep structures have been too loose and imprecise. But enough has been presented to give an idea of the main outlines of the theory.

THE GOALS OF LINGUISTIC THEORY

The goals of linguistic theory are importantly: **(a)** to establish a set of generalizations or rules (a grammar) that explains consistently and adequately the sentences of English. This set of rules will then amount to a theory about the nature of the knowledge, subconscious to be sure, that speakers have of their language; **(b)** to learn how children internalize and acquire such a grammar, quickly and without much overt attention to learning the language of their environment; **(c)** to understand how speakers of a language bring their internalized grammar to bear in producing and receiving utterances; **(d)** to discover the universal properties of grammar and of language.

At present we know very little about **(b)** and **(c)**, but we are beginning to understand **(a)** somewhat. Our understanding of it is a necessary prerequisite to the study of **(b)** and **(c)**. Let us summarize what we have said of **(a)** so far. We understand a grammar of a language to be a set of rules in explanation of the sentences of the language. This set of rules must be finite in number, for the human mind in which the rules are neurally represented is of course of finite capacity. Language has, however, this peculiar property—the range of data, the possible data, is infinite, theoretically unlimited. Although all sentences are of a definite length, there is no sentence that can be said to be the longest. Thus the set of possible sentences in a language cannot itself be finite. A grammar must then explain infinity in a finite way. The ideas of deep and surface structures, of transformations, that allow, as in **12** above, certain structures such as Sentence to be embedded in other structures, are theoretically capable of handling this problem in a natural and adequate way. Furthermore, these notions are candidates for elaborating somewhat on **(d)** above, for universal properties of language.

PHONOLOGY: THE SOUND STRUCTURE OF LANGUAGE

It will be useful to examine in some detail another aspect of language structure, thus to see the operation of deep and surface notions, abstract and concrete, and transformational rule at work in a somewhat different context—sound structure or phonology. Traditionally, grammars have had little to say about phonology—at least school grammars. It is certainly of less interest, perhaps only less immediate interest, than the level of syntax, or sentence structure. This may be only because we attend to it less closely in using the language. As speakers and hearers, our purpose is to get quickly to meaning and to attend as little as possible to the actual sounds in the air.

However, the descriptive linguists made their most important contributions in the area of phonology. At this level of language structure they tried to establish the set of minimally distinct sounds for each language with which they worked. For example, since speakers could readily and consistently distinguish such pairs as *bat* and *pat*, it was clear that /b/ and /p/ were distinctive sound classes in English. (We shall follow the conventional practice of enclosing in virgules the symbol representing a distinctive sound class.) The differing /p/'s of *spat* (not followed by a puff of air—unaspirated), *pat* (aspirated), *tap* (often unexploded) do not constitute distinctive sound classes themselves—they are in fact members of the sound class /p/. Their differences are predictable on the basis of their positions with respect to the other sounds of the words.

The descriptive linguist thus worked to establish the set of distinctive sounds for each language and for each language to state the distribution of these classes and their members one to another. He also tried to describe the difference of stress or prominence of syllables in words and word groups. For example, in such pairs as *black bird* and *blackbird*, in the first case the vowel of *bird* is more prominent than *black*; in the second case the opposite is true.

But because these linguists operated without such notions as deep and surface, or at least with a very shallow conception of depth, and without a sense of complicated rules that lead from abstract representations to concrete, their discussions of phonology lacked insight and generality. Again, neglecting notions of relatedness and concentrating too much on superficial identity, they missed the obvious. They recognized, for example, that the antepenultimate sound of *rejection* (re-jek'**sh**un) was the same as the first sound of *ship* (**sh**ip). But they failed to relate the /sh/ of *rejection* to the *t* of *reject*, to free this /sh/ from any but a superficial relationship to the /sh/ of *ship*.

The descriptivists noted that there was a difference between *black bird* and *blackbird* without accounting for the general properties of that difference. Consider that, if we say *black* and *bird* separately, they will have equal prominence. (To mark prominence, the convention of placing 1 above a vowel that has primary stress, 2 above a vowel that has secondary stress, etc. has been adopted. We speak of weakening stress or prominence from 1 to 2, 2 to 3, etc.).

15 bl$\overset{1}{a}$ck

16 b$\overset{1}{i}$rd

If we combine the two in a noun phrase as in *black bird*, the prominence is maintained on the rightmost syllable, weakened on the left:

17 bl$\overset{2}{a}$ck b$\overset{1}{i}$rd

However, if we combine them into a noun—a compound noun, *blackbird*, the reverse is true—prominence is maintained on the left, weakened on the right:

18 bl$\overset{1}{a}$ckb$\overset{2}{i}$rd

This is a general property of English phonology. As words are combined into phrases, the syllabic prominences are adjusted, maintained and weakened as in *black bird*; as they are combined into compound words, the syllabic prominences are adjusted as in *blackbird*. Combine *saw* and *the black bird* into a verb phrase and we have

19 saw the black bird

Combine *John* and *saw the black bird* into a sentence and we have

20 John saw the black bird

In the discussion of phonology, generalizations of the power mentioned above are a goal, both in dealing with stress and with the relationships among individual sounds. In the latter, we must also speak of abstractions and rules that carry us from the abstract to the real. It is of little interest that the /sh/ of *rejection* is like or the same as the /sh/ of *ship*. But it is of considerable consequence that the /sh/ of *rejection* is related to the /t/ of *reject* (v.), and that there is a general /t/—/sh/ relationship in English, as in *detect, detection; delete, deletion; ignite, ignition;* etc. In fact, the relationship is even more general as these examples indicate: *divide, division;* etc. Once again, as in the *John is difficult/anxious to please* example, the obvious surface similarities are only of passing interest. They must of course be gotten to, but they must be reached from abstractions through rules.

Thus if we want to explain the very general relationship that exists among such items as *reject* (v.), *rejection* (n.), *reject* (n.); *abstract* (v.), *abstraction* (n.), *abstract* (n.), we need deep representations and rules to carry these into surface representations. Let us assume for the moment that English spellings are adequate representations of the abstract forms of words and that *reject, abstract,* etc. are basically verbs. If we then have a rule which assigns the stress prominence to the final syllable of verbs, but only if that syllable consists of a long vowel followed by any number of consonants or of a short vowel followed by two or more consonants, then *reject* (v.), *abstract* (v.), will be stressed

21 reject, abstract

but *edit*, though not *maintain* would be

22 edit

If we then derive an abstract noun from these verbs, the position of stress prominence remains unchanged, but the final consonant of the stem shifts from /t/ to /sh/ when followed by the ending *-ion*. This consonant shift, as mentioned earlier, is part of a more general phenomenon in English: *divide, division; logic, logician.*

Furthermore, if we derive concrete nouns from the same verbs, we must have a rule accounting for the attendant shift in syllabic prominence to the first syllable and the consequent weakening of stress in the last syllable. That is, *reject* (n.), *abstract* (n.), etc. will be stressed

23 reject, abstract, etc.

There are further facts to be accounted for. If a syllable is without any degree of prominence, as the /re/ of *reject* (v.), its vowel is reduced, or obscured, in quality. Thus the first vowel of *reject* (v.) differs from the first vowel of *reject* (n.) in a way that the first /a/ of *abstract* (v.) differs from that of *abstract* (n.); in fact in a way that generalizes to the difference between the final /a/'s of *algebra* and *algebraic*. Our decision above to assume that English spelling adequately captures abstract phonological representations was a sound one. English spelling obviously fails to represent in any simple way the superficial sound system of the language. But it is not clear that an orthography should seek the surface, neglecting the abstract relatedness.

THE GENERAL STRUCTURE OF GRAMMARS

In a very informal way we have seen that generalizations about syntax and phonology, about sentence structure and sound structure, have much in common. There are abstract representations and rules that mediate from these to concrete representations—the structures and sounds of real-life sentences. About another aspect of language, *meaning*, very little in the way of formal analysis can be given. We know that the relationship between sound and meaning is an arbitrary one. There is no way, for instance, in a language one knows nothing about, to get the meaning of a word or a sentence from its sound alone, though one may well get the emotional intention from the quality of the voice alone. From this, one can suggest that it is the syntactic component of a grammar that forms a bridge between sound and meaning. The following diagram captures the relationships among the parts of a grammar:

24

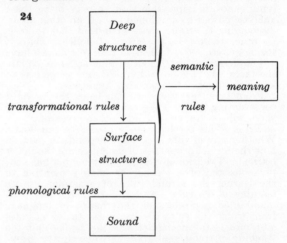

In receiving a sentence, one has somehow to construct from the sounds he hears a deep structure and its transformational relationship to a surface structure related to the sounds. From the deep structure and the transformations, meaning is somehow abstracted. Even more mysteriously, in uttering a sentence, a speaker must convert some intended meaning into sounds. Syntax in both these processes is the central component. This much seems certain. Exactly how it is that the mind attends to the finer details of the business of language, we have no idea. We are beginning to understand the nature of syntax and phonology and in that understanding lie the clues for understanding the nature of human intelligence itself.

THE USES OF LINGUISTICS

The uses of linguistics, real and imagined, are many. Here we shall deal only with the aims of formal grammar study. That is, why study the formal grammar of a language (English) of which you are a native speaker? And if it is studied, how should it be studied?

Goals of Grammar Study. Traditionally, the pedagogical aims of grammar study have been (a) to teach mental discipline, and (b) to improve verbal expression, both oral and written. What exactly *mental discipline* is to mean is not very clear, but we shall spend the greater part of this section trying to clarify what it *can* mean and *how* to accomplish it.

About (b), improving expression, we need say very little, though for decades, even centuries, students and teachers alike have believed that studying the formal properties of language would improve their writing, speaking, listening, and reading. There is no substance whatsoever to support that belief. In fact, there seems to be no relationship between a knowledge of formal grammar and the ability to express oneself well. Nor should we reasonably expect there to be. The results of educational research have thus far revealed no interesting relationships.

Mental Discipline. Some interesting substance can be given to the notion "mental discipline". It is clearly a goal of education to develop the intellect, to develop the rational powers of man so that he can introduce a sense of order into the chaos that surrounds him. In part, at least, this is what rational science is about—discovering the order underlying a seemingly confused and mad array of data. Insofar as grammar is a science, the goal of grammar is thus to discover a convincing order in the data of English. This point of view is exactly what we have presented in some detail above. If in the limited area of language that one is able to introduce to capture the order underlying chaos, it is possible that he may bring these analytic powers so developed to bear on other areas, discovering the order there or indeed that there is no order there. In the areas of politics, history, sociology, etc., it is foolish to believe that we have any understanding or theories that begin to explain the facts. It is good to hypothesize, as well as to know the limits of reasonable hypothesis.

From language study we can learn the ways of constructing theory. We can then hope that these ways will be transferred into other areas of study and life. This is what *mental discipline* can mean. Whether any of this is possible depends in part on how the formal properties of language are taught or learned. Traditionally, grammar teaching has simply consisted of a teacher or book presenting to the learner the formal rules of grammar. Rote learning is the rule. And this tradition has been maintained regardless of the theory of language from which the rules derive—presentation of rules and rote learning characterize the books and the teaching of traditional grammar, descriptive grammar, and transformational grammar.

If it is a goal of grammar study simply to learn a set of rules, then these books and the usual way of teaching from them will presumably reach that end. But, if the goal is for the individual or the class to reach towards an adequate and consistent theory of English sentences, then these materials and these ways of teaching are totally inadequate.

Learning Grammar. Granted that our goals are correct, we must consider other means of achieving them, for they will not be reached by rule-presentation and rote learning. Consider these alternatives:

25 (a) let the rules of a grammar book be taken as hypotheses, as terms in a theory of grammar, to be tested for their adequacy; (b) let the individual or class try to construct on the basis of their own sentences a set of rules, an hypothesis, about English sentences; then test the hypothesis against additional data and intuitions about English sentences.

Of course the notion of validating a grammar is quite far from what usually transpires in a grammar classroom, for grammar has come to be the Procrustean bed into which sentences must be crammed rather than a genuine scientific theory that must change, and be reformulated to accommodate the data. Grammar is truly a scientific endeavor only if it answers objections; if it ignores them, it is not.

Classroom grammar study can then be an attempt to construct a theory of what, as a speaker of the language, one already knows. Language, unlike history for example, is peculiarly adapted to this kind of study. For language is part of us all—it is ours by virtue of our humanness.

Some examples of how one might study language in this way are in order. It is a generalization of traditional grammar that all sentences contain a subject and a predicate or, in the terms presented above, a Verb Phrase and a Noun Phrase not contained in that Verb Phrase. There is, however, an important set of sentences that violates that generalization—imperative sentences that do not manifest a subject:

26 give him the money
27 tell her a story
28 eat the cake

Traditionally, grammars ignore the violation, save the generalization by asserting that these sentences have a subject, *you* being understood. They are then diagrammed in the following way:

29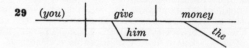

All of this seems right, as it answers our intuitions, but can it be *shown* to be right? It can, for consider the following facts:

If we add a tag question (one that questions the truth of the assertion) to a declarative sentence, as

30 he eats his food, doesn't he?
31 we gave our money to him, didn't we?
32 they are telling her a story, aren't they?

the pronoun of the tag question always repeats that of the sentence to which it is attached.

The following sentences are ungrammatical:

33 he eats his food, don't we/they/you?
34 we gave our money to him, didn't they/you/I?
35 they are telling her a story, aren't we/you?

33 through **35** are understood to be different from **30** through **32**. They are two quite separate entities—a declarative sentence followed by a separate question, not by a tag question.

What happens if we add a tag question to an imperative sentence?

36 give him the money, will/won't you?
37 tell her a story, will/won't you?
38 eat the cake, will/won't you?

Now if *he*, *we*, and *they* of the tags in **30** through **32** are right because they relate properly to the *he*, *we*, and *they* subjects of the declarative parts of **30** through **32**, then it would seem to follow that the *you's* of the tags for **36** through **38** are right because they relate properly to the *you* subjects of their imperative parts. *You* is right and anything else is wrong.

39 give him the money, won't I?
40 tell her a story, won't they?
41 eat the cake, won't we?

39 through **41** are clearly not English.

So there is a *you* in the imperative—the form of the tag question proves it. But there is other proof. And there is proof of other things. In English, the reflexive marker *-self* is added when the pronoun it attaches to has the same reference as and is identical to the subject of the sentence:

42 John gave himself the money
43 She told herself a story
44 I struck myself

When there is no identity, there is no reflexivization:

45 John gave him (i.e. somebody else) the money
46 She told them a story
47 I struck him

The following sentences then are not English:

48 John gave themselves the money
49 She told ourselves a story
50 I struck himself

Let us return now to the imperatives. Which of the following are grammatical sentences:

51 give himself the money
52 tell themselves a story
53 strike myself
54 give yourself the money
55 tell yourself a story
56 strike yourself

Clearly only **54** through **56** are well-formed. The

others do not follow a rule of English, as cited above: the reflexive marker -*self* is added when the pronoun it attaches to has the same reference as and is identical to the subject of the sentence. It follows that, if *strike yourself* is well-formed and *strike myself* is not, *you* must be the imperative subject. The generalization about subjects and predicates is saved and our intuition that the subjects of imperatives are *you's* is supported. In fact, we can suggest, employing the terminology developed above, that an imperative sentence has the following deep structure, using **26** as example:

57

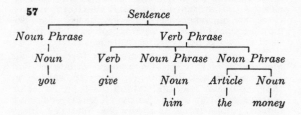

The *you* of this deep structure is then deleted by transformation, giving us: **26** give him the money

We now have supported a generalization of traditional grammar. Can we as suggested earlier go beyond it? Look back to the form of the tag questions in **36** through **38**, for there is more than *you* to meet the eye—a *will* (or *will + not = won't*) is also present in these tags. If we more thoughtfully examine the characteristics of the tag, what do we find?

58 he has given money in the past, hasn't he?
59 he is giving money this year, isn't he?
60 he can tell us a story, can't he?
61 he will be here tomorrow, won't he?
62 he should help eat the cake, shouldn't he?
63 he sees her every day, doesn't he?
64 he saw her yesterday, didn't he?

In **58** through **62** we note that the verbal of the tag is always the first piece (properly negated) of the main sentence verbal. If it is *has* in the main sentence it is *hasn't* in the tag, and vice versa; if it is *is* in the main sentence, then it is *isn't* in the tag. If the verbal is simple, that is, consists merely of a *see* or a *saw*, then a *do*, properly marked to agree in tense with the main sentence verb, is introduced, as in **63** and **64**.

What happens in the tags of imperatives? Which of the following are well-formed English sentences?

65 give him the money, don't you?
66 tell her a story, shouldn't you?
67 eat the cake, haven't you?
68 give him the money, won't you?
69 tell her a story, won't you?
70 eat the cake, won't you?

Clearly only **68** through **70** are properly formed. The others must violate a rule of English, specifically one that requires the verbal of the tag to repeat the first piece of the main sentence verbal. And just as clearly this must be *will* in the case of imperatives.

We must then revise our notion of the deep structure of imperatives **57** to account for this fact:

71

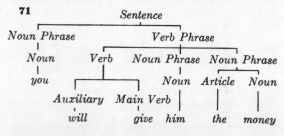

Transformations will then delete both *you* and *will*, giving us: **26** give him the money

Note though that, in very emphatic imperatives, these deletable elements are often retained:

72 you will give him the money!
73 you give him the money!

Working in ways sketched here, one can learn and teach grammar, seeking always better and more consistent generalizations that cover the data. Theories are constructed, destroyed, and modified as our perception of the data requires. But there are always, finally, questions hanging over. For example, as fully as we have looked into imperatives, we still haven't accounted for one apparent peculiarity. With regular declarative sentences, the verbal of the tag is negated if the main sentence verb is not; if the main sentence verb is negated, the tag verbal is not. Of the following sentences, **75** and **76** are properly formed:

74 he couldn't help us, couldn't he?
75 he couldn't help us, could he?
76 he could help us, couldn't he?

With imperatives, the negated *will* (*won't*) varies freely with the unnegated *will*:

36 give him the money, will/won't you?
37 tell her a story, will/won't you?
38 eat the cake, will/won't you?

There are always questions of formal grammar left unanswered. It makes constructing a theory of a language all the more exciting and all the more engaging as a classroom activity.

The formal study of grammar should be approached with a desire to seek the best answers, to seek truth, not fiction. This search can best go forward in the framework of theory and pedagogy sketched in above.

BEYOND GRAMMAR

There is, of course, much more than grammar to the study of language. Grammar is central, but there are other things of interest to deal with even though this must be done in quite informal ways. For example, what are we to say of meaning? of the structure of language units that go beyond the individual sentences? of the social and cultural connections of language, etc.? The present section concludes with some discussion of this last question.

It is clear that groups of men living in disparate regions of a country speak somewhat differently. In America, these differences are usually very slight, and are generally most noticeable in the phonology and vocabulary of the individual speakers. Little variation can be noticed in the deeper reaches of language—in the syntax and in the way the universe is atomized into units of meaning. These differences in pronunciation are simple distinctions in the grammars the separate groups or individuals control. Thus if,

for the word:	I say:	while you say:
tune	(a) toon	(a) tyoon
news	(b) nooz	(b) nyooz
duty	(c) dooty	(c) dyooty

for the same items, then it must be that I have a rule in my grammar that deletes /y/ when it follows a *dental* consonant (i.e., one made with the tongue placed against the back of the teeth or the ridge above the teeth) and precedes long *u*. For various reasons the rule must be so constrained.

In the formal structure of grammar, there are many slight differences among speakers of the same language. These *dialect* distinctions are attributable to nothing more than the natural separation of groups and individuals. Value judgments must be made carefully, since the differences are as natural as the geographical differences in similar plants and birds. It is often the case that the poor and the dispossessed speak a regional dialect different from that of the leaders of a community, and these differences are sometimes used to maintain the *status quo*. If society offers each person the same chances, then he will, up to his individual ability, develop ways of dealing with those chances in words and in actions.

WRITING AND SPEAKING

THE power to use effective language brings to its possessor ability to lead in social and civic affairs. Besides, more often than we commonly realize, personal success depends upon a command of good English.

Putting your thoughts together well in the sentences you speak or write is, therefore, always important. The social, professional, or business world measures you by the fitness of your language for the work you intend it to do. On the other hand, through persistent effort to adapt your language to your purposes, you gain a sense of self-command, an ease of manner, and a satisfying confidence in meeting people socially and in business.

Effective Language. Four requirements measure this fitness of language: *correctness, clearness, force, beauty*. Language is *correct* when it expresses thought in approved form. It is *clear* when those who hear or read it understand readily the thought of the speaker or writer. It is *forceful* when it interests those who hear or read it and impels them to respond according to the purposes of the speaker or writer. It is *beautiful* if it is correct, clear, and forceful, and also pleasing in sound or suggestion.

The art of expressing thought or feeling in effective language is called Rhetoric. The principles that govern the use of this effective language are rhetorical principles. One great principle underlies all others; namely, that true effectiveness of language depends upon the sincerity of the speaker or writer.

Semantics: Choosing and Arranging Words. Semantics is that branch of linguistics concerned with the meaning of words. Over and beyond the sincerity and enthusiasm of the speaker or writer is the choice of words to convey precise meaning, subtleties of connotation, avoidance of ambiguities, and to provide a climate of meaning by the use of well chosen words or signs. Language has no meaning apart from the thought it expresses.

You want to find pleasure in carrying on conversation with a friend or a stranger. You may have to make a report upon some work. You may want to sell a house or secure the interest and the support of voters in an election. You may want to persuade a friend to give up a harmful habit. You may have to convince a hostile audience of the truth of your opinions. In conversation you will be alert, interested, and responsive; in reporting, cool and accurate; in persuasion, positive, earnest, and impassioned. These are your personal problems. They will make you prize every help toward mastery of language.

Ordering of Thought. Both in speaking and in writing it is of the utmost importance to marshal the parts of a discourse into an effective order. This careful observance of arrangement should be followed both in regard to the discourse as a whole and in regard to each portion of it which deals with a single thought. The divisions into which a discourse falls when thus logically ordered are usually indicated by some more or less mechanical means. In speech, a judicious use of pauses and of vocal inflections serves the purpose, and in written compositions we employ the device of paragraphing.

The Paragraph. This term means a group of sentences in which a single subject is discussed, its beginning being marked usually by indention, or setting the first word a little to the right of the usual margin. This group of sentences may make a separate unit, as in the editorial columns of a newspaper, or it may serve as a division of a longer article. The structure and the length of the paragraph are matters of logic and convenience. Too long a paragraph, as well as a succession of very short ones, is to be avoided.

There are three important rhetorical requirements for a paragraph. The first requirement is *unity*, which means that there must be in the paragraph only one main thought. The second requirement is *coherence*, which implies that the sentences in the paragraph must be well connected and arranged so that each added thought helps to make the main idea clearer and more forceful. The third requirement is *emphasis*, which demands that the more important sentences shall be so placed in relation to the others as to draw immediate attention. Arranging sentences in contrasting pairs, or in order of climax, and alternating long and short sentences— these are means of securing emphasis. The beginning and the end of a paragraph are usually the most emphatic positions for sentences.

The purpose of the paragraph is to develop an idea, or, as often in stories, a single situation. Development means, literally, unfolding the subject so that the reader may understand the topic better or see the situation more clearly. To this end, give details, comparisons, and examples, or repeat ideas in slightly different words. Clearness is frequently effected by using vivid contrasts. The main idea should be stated in a single sentence, preferably either near the beginning or near the close of the paragraph. The following paragraph from *Ancient Times* by James H. Breasted illustrates well these methods of development:

"The Phœnicians learned the methods of manufacturing their goods, in almost all cases, from Egypt. There they learned to make glass and porcelain, to weave linen and dye it, to cast and hammer and engrave metal. On the other hand, we find that the *designs* employed in their art were international. Their metal platters they engraved with designs which they found in both Egypt and Asia. The art of Phœnicia was thus a kind of oriental composite or combination, drawn chiefly from the Nile and the Two Rivers. We remember that it was Phœnician workmen whom the Assyrian kings employed to make furniture and metal work for the royal palace. King Solomon likewise employed Phœnician workmen to build for him the Hebrew temple at Jerusalem (I Kings, V). After 1000 B. C. the Phœnicians were thus the artistic manufacturers of a great world extending from Nineveh on the east to Greece on the west."

GENERAL FORM OF DISCOURSE

Expression in language assumes, in relation to the purposes for which it is used, several well-recognized forms or types of discourse. We give talks or addresses, or we write papers or articles; we argue, explain, describe, or tell a story. Practical methods for everyday use of these various forms are given in the following paragraphs:

EXPLANATION

A pencil seems to be a simple, everyday thing, but you may sometime ask yourself: *How is this pencil made? What is it made of? Could it be made better?* You discover a problem that needs explanation or clearing up. This problem concerns the parts of the pencil and the relations between them. Other questions arise: *Why are these particular materials used in the pencil? What is the history of pencil making? Why is this thing called "pencil"?* Similarly, such subjects as *How is a gas engine made?* or *What is a bank?* call for explanation. *The clear, orderly answering of these questions is explanation.*

The first step in explanation is to divide the subject into topics to be discussed. The purpose of division is to give logical orderliness and simplicity, and consequently clearness, to your composition. The method to be followed is that of the outline, as illustrated in the following examples.

The headings in these specimen outlines are numbered in several different ways, any one of which may properly be used. In any outline, however, the numbering must be consistent throughout.

Subject. The Pencil.

Introduction.
1. The pencil is a thing of common use, but its nature, history, and manufacture are little understood.
2. The study of the pencil under these heads may be both interesting and suggestive.

Body.
1. Taking a common pencil apart.
   a. The case of wood, paper, or metal.
   b. The "lead."
2. The history of the pencil.
   a. Early forms.
   b. The word "pencil."
3. Process of manufacture.
   a. Preparation of materials.
   b. Construction.

Conclusion.
1. Skill with the pencil.
2. A stock of pencils in a store and the occupations it may suggest.

Such an outline may serve for a single treatment of the subject, or any one of the headings may be used as a separate topic. It should then be outlined in this same form. For example:

Subject.—A Stock of Pencils.
1. Pencils for drawing.
2. Pencils for various kinds of writing.
3. Pencils of different shapes and sizes.

The following is another common form of outline:

HOW TO USE CONCRETE

I. What is concrete?
   A. Elements.
   B. Mixtures.

II. Uses of concrete.
   A. Substitute for stone and wood.
   B. Unique uses.

III. Mixing concrete.
   A. Proportions.
   B. Method.

IV. Forms.
   A. Construction.
   B. Method of use.

The second step is to look up information. A common and practical method for preserving facts is to copy information on cards about 3 by 5 inches in size, one fact or topic to a card, with a reference to book and page where the facts were secured. The habit of thus looking up and noting facts will help to develop careful and trustworthy thinking.

The third step in planning explanation is the finding of apt comparisons; for we learn by observing likenesses and differences between things. The unknown or unfamiliar thing should be compared with something known or familiar. For example, to make dimensions clear, use comparisons in addition to figures. Compare a length of 15 or 20 feet to the length of a room, the extent of a small surface to a table top. Such expressions as *T-shape, S-shape, U-shape* are useful. More imaginative comparisons are suggested by figures of speech.

DESCRIPTION

Generally speaking, the purpose of description is to appeal so vividly to the senses through language that the reader or hearer feels as if he were actually in the presence of the object described. To produce good description: (1) Indicate clearly your point of view, that is, your position with reference to the thing described. A railroad wreck may be described by one who was a passenger on the wrecked train or by a reporter who was sent to the wreck. Their mental points of view will be different. A building or a mountain may be described as seen from a near-by or from a distant point. These different physical points of view determine the nature of the description. (2) Choose words to convey sense impressions, as of *sight, sound, smell, taste, touch.* (3) Select and use only such details as help to make the total impression clear and vivid. Notice the indications of the point of view and the appeals to the senses of sight, touch, and hearing in the italicized words of the following paragraphs:

"It was *close on noon*: there was no *breath* of wind, and the heat was scarce *bearable* when the two men came on deck, had the boat manned, and *passed down*, one after another, into the stern sheets. A *white* shirt at the end of an oar served as a flag of truce; and the men, by direction, and to give it the better chance to be observed, *pulled* with extreme slowness. The isle *shook* before them like a place *incandescent* on the face of the lagoon *blinding copper* suns, no bigger than *sixpences*, danced and *stabbed* them in the eyeball. There went up from sand and sea, and even from the boat, a *glare* of *scathing* brightness; and as they could only peer abroad from between closed lashes, the excess of light seemed to be changed into a *sinister* darkness, comparable to that of a *thundercloud* before it bursts."—Stevenson: *The Ebb Tide.*

"There could not be a more *somber* aspect of external nature than as then seen *from the windows of my study.* The great *willow tree* had caught and retained among its leaves a whole cataract of water, to be shaken down at intervals by the frequent *gusts* of wind. All day long, and for a week together, the rain was *drip-drip-dripping* and *splash-splash-splashing* from the eaves and *bubbling* and *foaming* into the tubs beneath the spouts. The old, *unpainted* shingles of the house and outbuildings were *black* with moisture, and the mosses of ancient growth upon the walls looked *green* and *fresh*, as if they were the newest things and afterthought of Time. The usually *mirrored* surface of the *river* was *blurred* by an infinity of raindrops. The whole landscape had a completely *water-soaked* appearance, conveying the impression that the earth was wet through *like a sponge*; while the summit of a *wooded hill*, about a *mile distant*, was enveloped in a dense mist, where the demon of the tempest seemed to have his abiding-place, and to be plotting still direr inclemencies."—Hawthorne: *Mosses from an Old Manse.*

NARRATION

This most interesting form of composition is simply the telling of stories.

Narration without Plot. This is telling about a series of actual events,—a day's travel, the course of an investigation, or a report of some piece of work. For telling such a story the most important directions are these: Select carefully the details to be told. Make a connected account that moves straight forward in the time order of events and is not lost in little, unimportant matters.

The carefully written news story furnishes a good example. It usually begins with a *lead*, that is, a first sentence that summarizes the most important features of the account. Then the connected story, consisting of several sentences or paragraphs, follows. See *The Book or Article Review.*

Description finds its chief use in helping to make narration or explanation vivid and interesting.

Narration with Plot. The telling of a story in such a way as to arouse interest and hold the hearer or reader in suspense and uncertainty as to the outcome of events. You can spoil an *anecdote* or a *story* by giving the "point" too soon. Even anecdotes have miniature plots. Give the setting or background and introduce the characters first, then bring in their action or conversation, and finally "come to the point or climax." This method secures suspense while your audience waits for the climax. A master of English fiction is credited with the following recipe for story-telling: "Make them laugh; make them cry; but make them wait."

For the composition of other story forms, see *Forms of Literary Composition; The Book or Article Review,—Plot; The Scenario.*

SPECIAL FORMS OF DISCOURSE

We find the General Forms of Composition most frequently useful in the immediate telling of a story or in the preparation of a talk, a paper, or an essay. These occasions usually call for combinations of argument, explanation, description, and narration. The following suggestions are helps in real problems. They serve to answer the questions: What shall I put into the toast, the talk, or the club paper? What shall I leave out? How shall I begin? Getting started is often the hardest problem. See *Public Speaking.*

THE CLUB PAPER

As a member of some organization, a club or society, you are often expected to read papers upon various subjects. The theme or subject is usually given in the program or course of reading. Frequently, however, your topic is too big or too general. When you come to the task of preparing the paper, you must narrow the theme to something that you can treat interestingly in fifteen to thirty minutes. Here are four important principles:

a. Two or three important points, not more, can be treated well in a brief time. The attention of an audience is easily exhausted by too many details.

b. Perfection in speaking and writing is achieved by leaving out superfluous matter.

c. Statements of principles, conditions, or definitions must be made plain by clear illustrations or examples.

d. A brief anecdote or story is often worth pages of laborious explanation.

Suggestion.—Suppose, then, that you have your subject. Whatever it may be, remember that many of the most interesting facts and illustrations for most subjects are things right around you, things that you can see and hear. Any given topic is related to many other themes and to many other fields of knowledge. To point out some of these relations is to enhance the clearness as well as the interest of your paper.

A topic in art, for example, as you begin to look it up, will suggest related topics in literature, in history, in geography, in biography. As you follow these suggestions you will find your paper growing, not as a task, but as a pleasant interest. Make notes of what you find in your reading. Follow each hint of a related topic. Make more notes.

The Working Plan

Always prepare an *outline*, or *working plan*. An outline shows a general sketch or an indication of a plan, a system, or a course of thought. See *Explanation for suggestions about reading and cards. For suggestions as to interesting order of topics, see The Advertisement. For suggestions as to presenting the paper, see Public Speaking.*

The following plans represent typical ways of dealing with various kinds of subjects:

Subjects which fall under the general theme, *Community Plans*, are very frequently used in club programs. They may be concerned with material improvements in streets or buildings, or with political or social plans and organizations. The following well-tested general order of discussion is appropriate and effective. Either a single paper or a whole program may be built upon this plan. In the latter case, the subordinate topics become the titles of separate papers.

a. The situation outlined,
1. By a summary of facts, or
2. By a story or description.

b. Analogies, or comparisons with
1. Other communities, or
2. Other local projects or plans.

c. Proposals for action,
1. Clearly stated, and
2. Urged persuasively by appeal to such motives as the following: (1) community pride; (2) rivalry; (3) self interest; (4) duty; (5) moral ideals involved in religion and education.

An interesting type of paper is one which discusses *new discoveries* or *inventions* or *new ideas* put into action in society. In such a paper, do at least these four things:

a. Give a clear, brief statement of the discovery or idea or plan.

b. Illustrate with examples the meaning of a discovery or an idea, to make the matter clear and interesting.

c. Give the circumstances of the discovery or statement of the idea as nearly as possible in story form.

d. Show plainly how the thing affects the everyday interests of your audience. See *Suggestions* in the following outlines. This last point should never be neglected. Anything worth writing or talking about has a bearing on everyday life.

Specimen Outlines

The following outlines illustrate the application of the general plan to the discussion of special themes:

I. Subject. Advertising.
Suggestion: This topic needs to be narrowed or divided as follows:

1. What Use Do I Make of Advertisements?
Suggestion.—An intimate chat with two or three friends on the subject of advertising and its uses will help you. You will get their points of view, which will suggest to you a greater variety of topics and a better balanced treatment of your theme.

2. Some Interesting Advertising Pages.
Suggestion.—You need not depend merely upon description. Have the actual pages to show to your audience. Then you can better explain why they are interesting.

3. Art in Advertising.
a. The Printer's Work.
b. Opportunities for Artists.

4. The Store Window.
Window Dressing.
Suggestion.—An interesting way to begin such a topic is to describe an actual window, especially if your audience may have seen it. If you have studied it carefully, you can surprise your audience and arouse interest by showing what they have failed to notice.

5. Advertising Associations and Ad Clubs.
Suggestion.—Any topic about organizations raises at least four questions: (1) How did they come to be formed? (2) What are their purposes? (3) What do they do? (4) Of what use are they to us?

6. The Responsible Advertiser.
Suggestion.—This kind of topic raises such questions as the following: (1) What gives the advertiser power? (2) For what is he responsible? (3) Do advertisers acknowledge this responsibility? (4) What are the reasons for your answer to (3)? (5) What personal experiences have you had with advertisers?

II. Subject. The Health of a Community.
The field of this theme is so large that a single paper should, as a rule, be restricted to one of the subordinate topics:

1. The Food Supply.
a. Sources.
Suggestion.—To make a paper on this topic interesting, you should get some first-hand facts from your local market. Such investigation will enable you to use more intelligently the material from magazines and books.
b. Markets.
(1) Prices.
(2) Handling the Food Supply.

2. Sanitation.
a. Housebuilding.
b. Water Supply.
c. Sewerage.
d. Waste and Garbage Removal.
e. Flies, Microbes, and Vermin.

3. Control of Diseases.
Public Health Service.
(1) School Inspection.
(2) Hospital Service.
(3) Quarantine Regulations.

4. Public Parks and Playgrounds.

THE BOOK OR ARTICLE REVIEW

Treatments of historical, scientific, or literary themes frequently involve the reviewing of books or articles from magazines. In writing a book or article review, try (1) to convey a truthful, distinct impression of the outline—the plot, if the original is a story, or the logical plan, if it is a discussion—(2) to give a more specific idea of some notable feature of the work, and (3) to interest and instruct your audience so thoroughly that they will know whether they want to read the book or article.

By way of preparation, *read the material you are to review*. Then make sure that you have some general *reaction*, that is, some opinion or feeling about the book. Stating your own opinion or feeling furnishes a personal element which adds much to the worth and to the interest of your work.

Plot Outline. Remember that the outline or plot of a short story or of a novel concerns itself with the answers to six questions: *Who? What? When? Where? Why? How?* Usually the answers to the first four may be found very readily in a first reading of a story; they form the obvious framework for any tale. The writer of stories exercises his skill in cleverly managing the "How" and the "Why" of events and actions. Sometimes the answers to these two questions are reserved to the very end of the story and there made clear; in other cases one must draw one's own conclusions from the course of the narrative.

In planning a story review, especially for a rather brief paper, take a lesson from the *lead* of the newspaper reporter. The *lead* is an opening sentence in a news story, which summarizes accurately and concisely the substance of the article. It answers the six questions mentioned above. Such an opening sentence places the whole story briefly and concisely before the audience. Practice in writing such *leads* is a most valuable means of improving one's style of speaking or writing. Follow the lead with a brief outline of the plot. Then comment upon some especially interesting or important part of the book.

Suggestive Outlines

St. Ives, a novel by Robert Louis Stevenson.
Lead.—Viscount Anne de St. Ives, a poor private soldier of Napoleon, escapes from the military prison in Edinburgh, becomes heir, through his uncle's will, to a great English estate which had been settled on the older line of his family, marries a Scotch girl who had visited the prison, and becomes an English country gentleman.

I. Beginning.
  1. *Setting.*—
    a. The French prisoners in Edinburgh Castle beguile their time by making souvenirs and toys to sell to the visitors from the city.
    b. One of the prisoners, St. Ives, is a gentleman of attractive manners, but a bungling craftsman.
  2. *Inciting moments.*—
    a. St. Ives, by his handiwork and his courtesy, attracts the attention of a girl, Flora, who, with certain relatives, visits the prison.
    b. A London lawyer appears, gives St. Ives news, leaves him money and the address of his wealthy uncle.
  3. *Complications.*—
    a. St. Ives fights a duel, killing his opponent, who had used vile language about Flora.
    b. The English lieutenant, in command of the prison, suspects St. Ives's part in the duel and threatens to become a rival for Flora.
    c. On the eve of escape through a tunnel, St. Ives incurs the hatred of a soldier who knows of the duel. A threat of trial for murder hangs over St. Ives.

II. The Story of a Fugitive.
  1. By the aid of Flora's aunt, St. Ives escapes to England in the company of two drovers.
    Complication.—In a fight he kills or severely injures a third, a rival drover.
  2. In England he is invested with his uncle's estate.
    Complication.—This brings on him the deadly hatred of his disinherited cousin.
  3. With a carriage and a valet he goes back to Scotland to find Flora and to save his drover friends from prosecution.
    Complication.—His cousin follows and they meet at a ball. But St. Ives escapes in a balloon.

III. The End.
  1. After sundry adventures St. Ives gets to Paris.
    Complication.—His cousin tries to trap him.
  2. The London lawyer, his uncle's solicitor, appears just in time to discomfit the spy and save the hero.
  3. Back to Scotland and Flora.

Any story may be reviewed in this manner, by answering the six questions in an outline of about three main divisions.

Abstract. Many books and articles upon scientific, historical, or social themes call for the writing of abstracts. These are connected condensed statements of the theme and contents of the book or essay. Four qualities must be aimed at: (1) *accuracy*, that is, truth to the ideas presented in the original work; (2) *completeness*, that is, treatment of all essential parts of the original; (3) *clearness*, which is a matter of especial difficulty, because, in the effort merely to condense the matter, one is tempted to leave out words essential to the meaning; (4) *brevity*, which is to be desired and yet may be sacrificed to the other three qualities.

Remember that people who have not seen the original writing must be able to understand your abstract. Observe the following directions for planning your work:

(1) Following the idea suggested in connection with the *lead*, select a title or a topic sentence which will summarize the entire article.
(2) Choose similar titles or topic sentences for each section of the article.
(3) Separate the essential points and necessary illustrations from the unessential and unnecessary. The abstract must omit most of the merely illustrative content of the original article.
(4) Write the new condensed version of the article.
(5) Review the new version in order to condense it further.
(6) Be careful to give the last part of the article as full treatment as you give the first part.

Paraphrase. This is a method of interpreting a writing by turning it into simpler or more common language. It is a much more widely used kind of writing than many people suppose. The preacher and the teacher use paraphrase constantly. Commentaries on the Scriptures and upon the writings of many great authors, Dante or Shakespeare for example, consist very largely of paraphrase.

Four kinds of writings usually call for paraphrase: the work of (1) old authors, such as Spenser or Chaucer, whose language has become unfamiliar; (2) such learned authors as Darwin or Emerson, whose expressions need simplifying; (3) writers like Francis Bacon, whose style is very condensed and therefore needs enlargement and illustration; (4) poets like Browning, whose language is obscure or figurative and therefore needs to be rendered into plain and literal expression.

The writer of paraphrase should first determine to which of these classes his author belongs; then he can suit his manner to the need. The preacher and the Sunday school teacher may find it necessary to render the language of the Bible in more familiar forms. They may wish to enlarge a parable or a proverb by some simple illustration or to turn the figurative language of a psalm into plain, everyday speech. Again, the teacher of science may be obliged to simplify certain paragraphs found in a very condensed textbook. He will develop single sentences into paragraphs and add illustrations. The general method of planning the *abstract* applies also to making the paraphrase.

THE ADVERTISEMENT

The purpose of an advertisement is persuasion. In general, the successful writer of advertising "copy" uses simple, direct language and keeps the reader and his interests most prominent in the advertisement. As a phase of selling, advertising gives the reader fresh information, or rather news, concerning products and services that will meet his needs.

RADIO WRITING

A demand for this form of writing appeared for the first time in the decade 1920-30, when the radio audience came into being. Radio writing differs from other forms of composition by reason of the following facts. The words are written not to be read but to be spoken. The listener hears the speaker but does not see him. The potential audience comprises people of all ages, conditions, beliefs, prejudices, and levels of intelligence.

Simplicity of Language. The mixed character and educational attainments of the radio audience necessitate the use of the simplest possible language. Long and unusual words should be avoided. Sentences should be short and contain vivid word pictures. Words of varied meanings are undesirable. In short, one who prepares script for radio broadcasting should write not merely so that he may be understood but so that he cannot be misunderstood.

Sentences which look well on paper may not be effective when spoken. Hence one who writes for the radio should be "ear minded." Sentences should have a pleasing rhythm. Moreover, certain sounds are apt to be distorted by the microphone and should be avoided as far as possible. Thus a succession of sibilants, "explosive" consonants, and words like "herd" with its obscure "r" sound are difficult to enunciate intelligibly over the radio. Other words which are often heard unsatisfactorily include apathetic, incessantly, statistics, inimitable, egregious, indubitably, perpendicular, and population.

THE EDITORIAL

This is a special form of writing used in newspapers and magazines to interpret items of news or to give opinion about subjects of current interest. The editorial may be a mere summary of information gathered from any source for the convenience of the reader. It may be an argument in support of some policy, or an informing essay on a political, social, moral, historical, literary, or scientific theme. The editorial should be timely. The judgments expressed should be based upon accurate knowledge of facts and upon sincere belief, and the style should be at once popular and dignified. The methods of writing given under *Argument*, *Exposition*, and *The Paragraph* apply to the composition of the editorial.

THE SCENARIO

This is a succinctly written sketch or outline of the scenes, situations, characters, and action of a story or play. Writers of fiction generally use it in planning their work. Producers of moving pictures, however, have developed a special form and technique of the scenario. Scenario making has come to be the business of specially trained writers employed by the producers.

Parts of the Scenario. An approved form of the scenario includes the following parts:

1. A summary or synopsis of the story.—This is the form in which producers require that stories be submitted. The synopsis should be written in ordinary direct narrative style. Each paragraph should present the essential characters of a scene in clear, vivid, descriptive language and tell the action in words that mean action. Thoughts and feelings should be conveyed through the suggested acts and movements of the characters. Each succeeding paragraph must carry the story straight toward its culmination. Action should, as far as possible, be written in the present tense. Titles and subtitles may be put in, preferably in capital letters, but all other technical directions should be omitted.

2. A list of characters, with the scenes in which each appears, thus: *Old Man, 3, 8, 15.*

3. A "scene plot," or schedule of the various stage settings, with the numbers of the scenes in which each setting is used, thus: *Hotel Entrance, 4, 10, 11, 18.*

A "scene," in moving picture studio language, is a part of the action that can be taken from one position of the camera. A move of the camera ushers in a new scene, except where the camera moves along with the actors or follows them, as in a race or some street scene.

4. A list of properties, or "props."

5. An outline of the scenes, numbered in order.—This is called the "continuity." The paragraph devoted to each scene gives (a) place or setting, (b) the characters, (c) the attitudes and actions of the characters (pantomime), (d) the thought or feeling these are intended to convey. The following is an approved short form of such a paragraph:

SCENE 5

Railroad Station. College boys and girls leaving after graduation. A send-off. Margaret and Winston meet. Realization of parting, long to speak; both too proud, part stiffly. Train pulls in. Boys and girls enter cars, waving good-byes. Margaret, assisted by Jim, enters end coach, her eyes following Winston, who enters adjoining car. Train pulls out. *Dissolve* into:

SCENE 6

Winston Library. Winston gazing at picture.—

Producers now employ professional continuity writers to work up synopses into the finished action plot, or continuity. The best authorities, however, advise writers to prepare their own continuities before writing synopses to submit to producers. This method gives clearer and firmer structure to the story, because the writer has followed his characters through all the details of the action that makes the story for the screen.

VERSE

For many people the writing of verse is an interesting and amusing pastime. It is also one of the best means of improving one's command of language: (1) It calls for condensed and vivid expression and for a selection of words to produce good measure and rime; (2) it gives one occasion for searching out figurative language that will give variety, point, and concreteness to expression; (3) it improves one's appreciation of verse, which today forms so large a part of our current literature.

There is a wide and pleasant field for agreeable, witty, humorous, and fanciful verse. You may use it for a short, pointed speech. Often an unexpected "hit" is made in this way. Many epigrams, proverbs, mottoes, and sentiments are more vivid and more easily memorized, if expressed in couplets or quatrains.

Observe the following suggestions: (1) Verse must have a rhythm more striking and regular than that of prose or spoken conversation. (2) In English verse this rhythm is marked by the succession of beats or strong accents. Each *line* in English verse is made up of a number of feet. A *foot* consists of an accented syllable with one or more unaccented syllables closely connected with it. Several kinds of verse are named from the kinds of feet used and the number of accents to the line. (3) Select a model that you wish to imitate; read it over, beating out the accents with a pencil, until you get the swing of the lines. Such attention to a model will cure many a set of limping feet.

Rhythms. Recent writers of verse employ a wide variety of rhythms. They also use great freedom in choosing different lengths of line within the same poems. The best popular verse, however, keeps close to the well-established rules. The most common feet in English verse are the following:

a. Iambic (ī-ăm'bĭk), composed of two syllables, an accented preceded by an unaccented syllable;

b. Trochaic (trô-kā'ĭk), which is an accented syllable followed by an unaccented.

Two other types of feet, sometimes used, are:

a. Dactylic (dăk-tĭl'ĭk), which is an accented syllable followed by two unaccented;

b. Anapæstic (ăn'ȧ-pĕs'tĭk), which is an accented syllable preceded by two unaccented.

A line of two accents is called a *dimeter* (dĭm'ê-tẽr); a line of three accents is called *trimeter* (trĭm'ê-tẽr); one of four accents, *tetrameter* (tĕt-răm'ê-tẽr); one of five accents, *pentameter* (pĕn-tăm'ê-tẽr).

SPECIMENS OF FEET AND METER

(Accented syllables are marked with ‾: unaccented, with ˘.)

Iambic.—
As flowers that bloom at morn, at eve decay.

Trochaic.—
Curls and ringlets of her tresses.

Dactylic.—
This is the story the sailorman told.

Anapæstic.—
Not a word, not a whisper, to soothe the sharp pain.

Mixed meter.—
Though it lashed the shallows that lined the beach.
Afar from the great sea deeps.

Dimeter.—
O'er folded blooms
On swirls of musk.

Trimeter.—
The lustrous blue of morn.
The night has a thousand eyes.

Tetrameter.—
They tempt the taste and charm the sight.
The crest and crowning of all good,
Life's final star, is Brotherhood.

Pentameter.—
Much have I traveled in the realms of gold,
And many goodly states and kingdoms seen.
Bowed by the weight of centuries he leans
Upon his hoe and gazes on the ground.

Rime. The agreement of syllables in sound. A syllable in the middle of a line may be rimed with one at the end: this is called *internal rime*. Usually, syllables are rimed at the ends of lines: this is called *end rime*. Lines of poetry are commonly written in groups of two or more, forming stanzas. The lines may rime in couplet or alternately or in some other of the patterns illustrated below. *Blank verse* is unrimed, usually iambic pentameter. *Free verse* is unrimed; and its rhythm is said to be a rhythm of thought rather than of accent. It is difficult to distinguish from rhythmical prose. At best, it is not a form for the amateur.

SPECIMENS OF RIME
Couplet.—
Why has not man a microscopic eye?
For this plain reason,—man is not a fly.
Bubble, Bubble, flows the stream,
Like an old tune through a dream.

Alternate rime.—
We, in some unknown power's employ,
Move on a rigorous line;
Can neither, when we will, enjoy
Nor, when we will, resign.

Quatrain with two rimed lines.—
I think that saving a child
And bringing him to his own
Is a derned sight better business
Than loafing round the throne.

Quatrain with two rimes.—
Why should I stay? Nor seed nor fruit have I
But, sprung at once to beauty's perfect round,
Nor loss nor gain nor change in me is found,—
A life—complete in death—complete to die.

Six-line stanza with two rimes.—
The hollow sea-shell, which for years hath stood
On dusty shelves, when held against the ear
Proclaims its stormy parent, and we hear
The faint, far murmur of the breaking flood.
We hear the sea. The Sea? It is the blood
In our own veins, impetuous and near.

Four lines with one rime.—
A little peach in an orchard grew,—
A little peach of emerald hue;
Warmed by the sun and wet by the dew
It grew.

Sonnet.—
What is a sonnet? 'Tis a pearly shell
That murmurs of the far-off murmuring sea,
A precious jewel carved most curiously;
It is a little picture painted well.
What is a sonnet? 'Tis the tear that fell
From the great poet's hidden ecstasy;
A two-edged sword, a star, a song—ah me!
Sometimes a heavy-tolling funeral bell.

This was the flame that shook with Dante's breath,
The solemn organ whereon Milton played,
And the clear glass where Shakespeare's shadow falls;
A sea this is—beware who ventureth!
For like a fiord the narrow floor is laid
Deep as mid-ocean to sheer mountain walls.
Richard Watson Gilder.

The *Limerick* is a form of nonsense stanza, made up of five lines with two rimes. The first, second, and fifth lines rime, and the third and fourth lines. The following specimen well represents the limerick:

Said the Snail to the Tortoise: "You may
Find it hard to believe what I say;
You will think it absurd,
But I give you my word,
They fined me for speeding today."
Oliver Herford.

The following school songs illustrate a method of adapting sentiment and words to a popular tune:

Tune: Come Back to Erin.
Come back to Normal, Good English, Good English
Back to the ones who have missed you so long.
Come back to Normal, Good English, Good English!
And all the building will ring with our song.

Tune: Row Your Boat.
Watch, watch, watch your speech,
Every word you say.
Carefully, carefully, carefully, carefully
Watch it every day.

PUBLIC SPEAKING

Public speaking, as commonly understood, though it does not lay claim to the more formal title of oratory, is nevertheless a term which includes that art. As oratory is the appeal of a high order of eloquence to the understanding and to the emotions, so, too, the province of public speaking is not only to entertain and inform, but also to convince and persuade.

Possibilities and Probabilities. Although it is not given to every one to become an orator, nevertheless, it is well within the scope and the power of the average intelligent person to become a good public speaker. Moreover, there never was a time when public speaking formed a more important factor in American life than it does today, nor was there ever a time when this talent brought to the individual more social and political influence.

Every citizen is likely at any time to be called upon to express his views on any topic which may be exercising the minds of the public. As an efficient member of the community, he should be ready to respond to the claim thus made upon him and be able to lay before his fellow-citizens or townsmen, in language at once clear and forceful, his opinions and his judgment on the question put before him for discussion.

Fundamentals. "What then," it will be asked, "is necessary in order to prepare one's self to become a successful public speaker?"

1. The first essential is a knowledge of one's fellow-men. By this is not meant that one must necessarily be a psychologist. He must, however, have an all-round knowledge of people in general, especially of the man in the street, with his prejudices to be overcome, his rights to be defended, and his wrongs to be rectified. Only in this way can a speaker get in touch with an audience. He must understand his audience before they will understand him.

2. In the second place, the speaker should have a knowledge of books. He should become acquainted with good literature. Not every intending speaker has had the advantages of a college training. He may not have enjoyed the privilege of extensive travel, and he may be wanting in that broader knowledge that comes only to those of wide and practical experience. But books are always open to him; they will furnish him with facts, ideas, and all that is needed for the illustration of his

subject. It was Bacon who said, "Reading maketh a full man." It is the man full of his subject, and thereby confident, who will interest and impress his audience.

3. As language is the chief means of conveying thought, it is a matter of the greatest importance to possess a ready command of words. To enlarge his vocabulary, the student of public speaking should make notes of all the new or strange words he meets in his general reading, or that he may hear in listening to lectures given by others. He should then make a point of using such words whenever opportunity offers; for it is by continuous use that they become his own.

The above three points sum up what may be regarded as the *remote preparation* for public speaking, in which lies in great measure the secret of success in this practical art. We now come to the *immediate preparation*, or the method to be followed in the actual planning and in the making of a speech.

Choice of Subject. Let the subject you choose be one of interest to yourself and one that is likely to be of interest to your audience. Remember you are to deliver a message. Unless you win the interest of your audience, your efforts to deliver a message will be in vain. Know beforehand the manner of audience you are about to address and adapt your subject to their capacity. In this way you will not be speaking "over their heads," and your purpose of convincing and persuading will be achieved.

The Plan. No matter how confident you may feel after you have gathered your material, always make in advance a plan or an outline of your intended talk or address. No builder undertakes the erection of a building until he has made a working plan of its different divisions, stories, and apartments. The same principle applies to an address. By making a plan you will put into your speech what you want to say, and will save time in saying it. Moreover, this much is due your audience. The habit of planning, if conscientiously cultivated, will enable you eventually to make a *mental* plan when opportunity will not allow of a penciled outline.

A speech to be convincing must be logical,— that is, it must be made up of an *introduction*, a *body*, and a *conclusion*. This rule is applicable to the formal address, to the simple talk at a club meeting, to an after-dinner speech, or to the toast at a wedding breakfast.

Introduction or Beginning. This should be a brief and clear forecasting of what the speaker proposes to discuss before or prove to his audience, and it should contain the logical scheme of his entire address. In plain words, he should let his hearers know how he intends to deal with his subject. In opening his speech his manner should be easy and natural. This end may be achieved in several ways; for instance, (1) by some happy compliment paid to the audience; (2) by reference to some interesting topic of the moment; (3) by an anecdote relating to some well-known character, or by a brief and apt quotation. In this simple manner a speaker may get in touch with his audience and at the same time may lead up to his subject.

Body of the Speech. This consists in the gradual and logical development of the proposition already set forth in your introduction. As you proceed in the unfolding of your main statements, make free use of illustration and comparison from other themes and topics familiar to your audience. This tends to greater clearness and insures interest. It is thus that you imperceptibly paint a background from which your word-picture will stand out in more sharply defined and vivid lines. As you pass from one point to another, revert occasionally to the argument already put forward, so that your audience may hold in mind the main divisions of your talk.

The Conclusion. The conclusion should be a careful summing up and welding together of the chief arguments developed in the body of the speech. They must be made to stand out lucidly and forcefully, and in such order that, by the presentation of their combined strength, conviction is driven home to the minds of those listening.

As has already been pointed out, public speaking may serve either to entertain, inform, convince, or persuade. The formal speech will always have dignity of form and of diction. So much will not be expected of the informal, short address, though the structure of each is essentially the same, both being built on the basis of logical thought. This being true, the informal speech is here dealt with, for practical purposes.

Informal Speeches. You may be called upon suddenly to say "a few words" in public, to propose a toast or to make an after-dinner speech, to take part in a discussion, or to talk as an executive to employees. A hundred different occasions may arise and demand from you some kind of address. You have to win the attention of your audience on the spur of the moment, and make your points as quickly. If you know the essentials that go to the making of a speech, as already stated above, a few hurried notes will be sufficient for the skeleton outline of what you intend to say.

A useful suggestive outline for the short talk or informal address is furnished by the following questions: 1—What is the fact or situation under discussion? 2—How has it come to be as it is? 3—How does it affect you? 4—What are you going to do about it?

Nucleus of an Informal Address. The nucleus, or concentrated matter, of a short talk may often be found (1) in the statement of some striking fact or incident, (2) in the presentation of clear and up-to-date statistics concerning a topic of real interest, (3) in the clever recital of a new story, or of an old one dressed in a new garb, and calculated to raise a laugh or a smile. The last method of beginning an address is perhaps the happiest of all, as by it the audience is warmed to sympathy with the speaker, the knowledge of which fact is no small aid to eloquence.

SOME STYLES OF SHORT TALKS

The occasions for the short talk are many, and there are almost as many styles as there are occasions. On the other hand, there are certain similarities to be noted in each, as the following examples will illustrate:

After-Dinner Speech. Usually, you have first to express some pointed sentiment in reference to the occasion, the host, or the guest of honor. A happy quotation or an adage which contains the gist of what you are about to say, will often serve as an appropriate *beginning*. Again, a half serious, half humorous comment will help in the development of the sentiment itself. Also, the flash light of a good crisp story will illumine your remarks so that your audience will see the point, and be won at once to your favor. As brevity is the soul of wit, so is it the essence of a good after-dinner speech.

Speech of Presentation or Award. Situations are constantly arising in which a gift or award is presented in token of friendship or in recognition of achievement. For example, a retiring employee receives a gift in recognition of his long service or an athlete is given a medal for outstanding proficiency. Whatever the occasion, the spokesman for the group making the award has an opportunity to show his best skill in paying tribute to the recipient. The theme of compliment and congratulation may be developed in various ways. It should always be handled with a light touch, but the degree and kind of humor depends, of course, on the persons present and the circumstances. How far whimsical humor may go, with entire appropriateness, is illustrated by

Sir James Barrie's famous compliment to Ellen Terry. He said, "The young men of my generation were madly, hopelessly in love with her. In fact, the standard formula for proposing marriage was for a young man to say to the woman of his second choice 'Since I can't have Miss Terry, may I please have you?'"

Impromptu Discussion. It may be that you are asked to take part in a running debate or discussion at which you happen to be present. In such a case you will have time to make a mental plan only. Nevertheless, you may adroitly begin your talk by referring to some salient fact or idea already mentioned in the debate, and thus gain time to put your thoughts in order. This is called a "point of contact" to which you may gradually attach your own trend of argument. Thus, often by an *impromptu* speech you can add to the interest of a debate by the orderly and well balanced presentment of your personal views. This happy facility comes from the persistent habit of making plans. To illustrate:

The debate is on the question of *safety*—an important topic to be discussed. Your opinion as an employer of labor, or as an employee, is sought on this subject. Possibly you will find a starting point for your talk by relating some accident which has taken place at the works or store in which you are employed. From this proceed to expand and make interesting your informal speech by putting forward your personal ideas on the best methods for preventing similar accidents in the future.

Again, the discussion may be on the question of *co-operation*. Once more you are asked to join in the debate. In such a case, a possible improvement in an industrial process, or a suggestion as to the better management of your business, may well supply you with a good opening and with excellent matter for an effective talk.

The examples given above illustrate some of the forms that a short address may take. It will be seen how some concrete and definite incidents, or accidents, may become the nucleus of your whole talk, and how, in time, you may find all the points you need to make a telling and striking address.

FORMS OF PUBLIC SPEAKING

The Expository Speech or Lecture. The aim of the expository speaker is to make something clear to his audience. It is usually the aim of the teacher. But there are many occasions outside of the school where a speaker has as his basic purpose the presentation of clarifying ideas. A new system of handling personnel may be set forth by a personnel director or a new plan for organized recreation may be presented by the chairman of the program committee. It is important for the speaker who is called upon to give clarifying information to keep his talk on an expository basis; that is, he must see to it that he does not bring in his own ax to grind and thus try to straddle exposition with persuasion. There are some six methods of exposition, any or all of which may be employed in a speech for clearness:

(1) *Comparison.* This is, perhaps, the most useful expository device. The audience is made to understand something new by having it compared with that which they already know. Analogy, which is a comparison of ratios, is a most useful form of comparison. When analogy is used the audience is enabled to understand a new relationship or process by seeing it compared to one with which they are familiar.

(2) *Analysis.* Through this device we come to understand something by having it taken apart for us. Thus we come to see the whole in terms of its parts. It is a good idea to remember that talks making use of analysis should end up with synthesis, so that the hearers see the relationship of the parts to the whole.

(3) *Definition.* Many effective speeches with clear-

ness as the end are based on the elaboration of a definition. We might, for instance, make an expository talk on Public Speaking by elaborating on the terms, and the relationship of the terms, in this definition: Public Speaking is the useful art of influencing human behavior through the medium of purposive speech.

(4) *Cause and Effect Relationship.* This method is often used where the material is of a historical character. A speaker might, for instance, explain Fascism by tracing its development in Germany.

(5) *Restatement.* When a speaker uses the expression, "in other words," and then goes on to give his audience another view of the same thing, he is using Restatement. It is different from *repetition* in that the same words are said over again in the latter.

(6) *Example.* The expository speaker uses *example* when he gives a demonstration, actually showing the thing he is explaining. The use of movies in teaching is an application of this method. It can also be said that illustrations by means of pictures or drawings on a blackboard are applications of the method. In the last few years, with the development of various techniques of visual education, expository presentations have been given added effectiveness by use of the example method.

Occasional and Commemorative Speeches. The purpose of the speaker in giving speeches at special occasions or in commemoration of some event or person is *Impressiveness*. The term Impressiveness is used to describe the purpose of those speeches in which the audience, already in agreement as to the concepts presented, is made to feel more deeply about them. Speeches of welcome, farewell speeches, speeches given when a gift is presented, and when one is accepted, have impressiveness as the purpose. Also those speeches given at dedication ceremonies and at anniversary gatherings have that purpose. Usually these speeches are eulogistic in character, that is, they are dominated by the mood of praise. Some of our finest oratory has been delivered at such occasions. The speakers have endeavored to catch the spirit of the hour, to voice the feelings of the listeners, to make the audience feel that their best thoughts and sentiments have been beautifully and effectively expressed.

It is in speeches of this kind that the expression comes close to the art of the poet. Metaphor, which is said to be the essence of poetry, is well employed in this form of speech composition. There also may be something of the rhythmic cadence of poetry. When the poetic element in such speech compositions springs from a genuine feeling of admiration of the subject being spoken of, there need be no fear of indulging in old-fashioned oratorical language. Love, affection, admiration, veneration, *when sincerely expressed*, is never out of date.

The Speech of Introduction. The function of the *speech of introduction* is to bring the speaker and the audience together in a proper spirit of acquaintanceship. It should meet this need and go no further. The listeners should be given that information about the speaker and his topic which will help them and the speaker. The introduction should be warm and friendly in spirit but should not embarrass the speaker by being eulogistic. It should be as short as possible and certainly should not encroach upon the speaker's topic. All too frequently the introducer is inclined to bask in the limelight of the main speaker, giving a speech of his own, indulging in oratorical flourishes, and generally stealing the main speaker's thunder.

DISCUSSION AND DEBATE

These two kinds of speaking are closely related in that they are a part of a general process, the process of arriving at a new point of view in regard to some public question. It can be said that *debate* picks up where discussion leaves off. Through the group discussion of a question or problem, a gathering of people may arrive at a point where it must decide whether or not to adopt a new policy in conducting its affairs. At this point debate begins: Should the new policy be adopted or not? For example, in group discussion the general question of obtaining proper medical care for the American people might be given consideration. At a certain point in the discussion the members of the group decide that the matter has reduced itself to the question: Should we or should we not adopt some form of nationalized health insurance? From that point on the gathering is on a debate basis. Following this line of thought, we shall give consideration first to the topic, group discussion.

Group Discussion. For hundreds of years the rhetoric of debating has been clearly set forth by textbook writers and followed by students in school debates and by lawyers and legislators. It is only in the last decade or so that the art of public discussion has been treated effectively in speech textbooks. However, public discussion of community and state problems has been effectively carried on in this country since the country's beginnings. The democratic method of open discussion of public questions was followed in New England Town Meetings in the 17th century. In the 18th century the same process of group thinking was to be observed in the Constitutional Convention. The delegates to the convention did not come to Philadelphia in 1787 to debate clearly defined issues nor to impress the gallery with persuasive oratory; they came to find a solution to a problem and to reach that solution by "negotiation and accommodation." We find the group discussion method manifested in the 19th century in the Lyceum and Chautauqua movements, the former being at its height in the middle of the century and the latter by the end of the century. The modern *open forum* movement had its beginnings in 1897 as a part of the adult education activities of Cooper Union in New York City. The movement was given fresh impetus in 1933 under the leadership of J. W. Studebaker, then superintendent of the Des Moines Public Schools. The Des Moines public Forums set the pattern for the discussion of public problems by citizens of a community. With the development of nationwide interest in this form of group thinking has come a substantial literature on the technique of discussion.

Today it is more important than ever that people be able to think through their problems in some co-operative fashion. We are no longer a world of isolated communities; the world itself is a community. This world community is endeavoring to find solutions to its problems in group discussions at the United Nations, in peace conferences, in industrial management-labor conferences, in organizations seeking racial harmony, and in international forums conducted by public spirited citizens.

The Process of Group Thinking. There are basically five steps in the process of thinking through to the solution of a problem. While it hardly can be said that any particular group discussion clearly follows the sequence, upon analysis it will be seen that the steps are involved. The steps are:

(1) Defining the problem.

(2) Analysis of the problem with the purpose of finding what values will be sought for in a solution.

(3) Suggestion of possible solutions or hypotheses.

(4) Consideration of relative merits of suggested solutions in the light of the values or criteria established in step two. Arrival at a tentative solution.

(5) Testing out the solution by visualizing it in operation.

A forum or discussion leader should keep these steps in mind in guiding a group in its problem solving efforts. He should have thought about the problem sufficiently beforehand and be sufficiently informed as to the basic aspects of the question so that he can detect tendencies to jump to conclusions, to reason in a circle, to generalize from insufficient evidence, to ignore minority interests, to fasten on trivial points, to indulge in personalities, and the many other all too human weaknesses to be found in our endeavors to be rational. When the leader sees that a member or members of the group are suggesting a solution before the problem has been adequately analyzed (step two) he should tactfully raise the question whether there are not values to be looked for in a solution which have not been considered and lead the members back to the second phase of the thought process. It will be found that this phase, the analysis step, is the one that is most difficult and which groups are prone to pass over too quickly. On the other hand, the leader must be on guard against having a preconceived solution to the problem and toward which he inflexibly directs the assembly. When that happens the discussion is no longer a co-operative, democratic process. The leader has become something of a dictator.

Types of Group Discussion. The type of group discussion taken up in the foregoing paragraphs is the type most commonly used. It is simple in its organization, there being only the chairman, or leader, and the gathering of people who sit before the leader, or with him around a table. This kind of discussion might be called the *conference* type. The unqualified word, *forum*, is also used as a term to describe this form of discussion.

Planning the Conference. The chairman or leader of the *conference* type of discussion must be imbued with the democratic principle of agreement in a group arrived at through full, free, and informed discussion. Collaboration for a common end should be the controlling objective. There are some things the leader can do to facilitate the attainment of that objective. He, himself, should command the respect of the group by being fair, tolerant, gracious, and firm, withal. He should be informed as regards the subject matter of the conference and as regards the process of democratic discussion. He should oversee the arrangements for the meeting, making sure that the room is a pleasant one, that the scheduled time for the meeting is a convenient one for the participants, that enough time is allotted for the meeting or meetings so that the group can arrive at a deliberative decision. When the discussion is going on he should carefully gauge the progress of the group, and if he sees that opposing interests are bringing about an impasse, he may well suggest a recess, in which heated tempers may cool off. Frequently, important concessions are made during recesses, especially if during the recess the members can get together on a good-fellowship basis.

Besides the conference type of discussion there are six others, each type having a distinguishing characteristic. They are similar to each other in one respect, all being more formal than the conference type of discussion. The six types are: the *Panel-Forum*, the *Symposium-Forum*, the *Lecture-Forum*, the *Colloquy* or *Dialogue*, the *Public Hearing*, and the *Debate-Forum*.

The Panel-Forum. In this type of discussion a panel of two to six speakers sit on the platform along with the chairman and converse on some chosen topic for the benefit of the audience facing the platform. This is a popular form of discussion especially in educational circles. Usually the group, the panel and chairman, have a meeting beforehand at which an outline covering the material for discussion is worked out and each member of the panel is assigned some part of the outline on which to talk. The chairman should keep these points in mind in directing the discussion: No member of the panel should talk for more than one minute at a time. All discussion should be directed toward the audience. The chairman and panel members should remain seated, for the sake of informality. Spontaneity should be encouraged in the panel members. If two speak up at the same time, the chairman designates who shall talk first.

After the panel members have finished their conversation and the chairman has made a summary of the discourse, the audience should be called upon to participate in an open-forum discussion. They may contribute ideas or ask questions of the panel members. It is a good idea to allow as much as half of the meeting time for audience participation and to inform the audience beforehand that they will have that time for discussion.

The panel-forum, as are the remaining types to be presented here, is better suited to the conveying of information than to problem solving. When a problem is to be solved, it is best to use the *conference* type of discussion.

The Symposium-Forum. This type is similar to the panel-forum in that it is made up of a panel of speakers, from two to four, and who have designated points upon which to speak. It differs from it in that each member of the panel gives a set speech, running from five to ten minutes in length. After the panel members have spoken and the chairman has summarized, the chairman invites the audience to participate as in the panel-forum.

The Lecture-Forum. Here one speaker takes the place of a panel of speakers. There may be a chairman, who opens the meeting, introduces the speaker, and conducts the open forum when the speaker finishes. However, the lecturer himself may act as chairman. This type is better suited to the conveying of information than to problem solving.

The Colloquy or Dialogue. Three units are found on the platform in this type of discussion, a panel of experts, an audience panel, and the chairman. The audience panel is usually chosen from the audience at the time of the meeting. The chairman and the panel representing the audience begin the discussion, after the manner of the ordinary panel-forum. The members of the expert panel are called upon to supply evidence when the need for it becomes apparent and to give opinions when they are desired. The *colloquy* is well suited for conventions where experts in a particular field are available and where the audience-members have a specialized interest in the subject-matter.

The Public Hearing. There are two types of public hearings, that which is held by legislative committees and that held by representatives of governmental agencies. In both types a legislative committee or government representatives seek information, evidence, and existing opinion from members of organizations, pressure groups, or individual citizens. At hearings the committee members and the audience face each other and the space between them is allotted to the particular speaker who happens to be speaking. He addresses the committee with his back to the audience. In the legislative hearing, members of the committee ask questions of the speaker. In the second type, audience and speakers usually ask questions of the governmental representatives. The chief problem for the speaker in hearings is to make himself heard by the audience at his back without shouting to the committee.

The Debate-Forum. This type is similar to the Symposium-Forum except for the fact that in the former the panel of speakers is broken up into two units each taking the affirmative or negative on some debatable question. When the two sides have presented their arguments, the chairman invites the audience to participate. After perhaps twenty minutes of open-forum discussion a final summary is made by the opponent of the proposed solution and by the advocate of the proposed solution. The debate-forum is best used when the audience is familar with the problem and almost ready to decide what to do about it.

ARGUMENT AND PERSUASION

An *argument* is a reason given in support of a proposition. As a form of composition, argument is also the logical arrangement of a proposition and the reasons urged in support of it. Sometimes we merely defend an opinion; sometimes we try to convince others that certain opinions are true or false. When we use arguments to make people believe or act as we want them to, we use *persuasion*. Persuasion is the means by which a speaker or writer tries to move his audience to belief or action.

We succeed in persuasion partly through logical argument and partly through personal appeal to the sympathies and interests of an audience. Both these elements are necessary. Sometimes one plays the larger part, sometimes the other. Sincere human interest, added to a logical argument, is as necessary to a salesman as to a lawyer before a jury or to a preacher in his pulpit.

Debate. The best way to learn to argue well is to practice in formal discussions or debates. Free discussion of public questions is necessary to the welfare of people in a democracy. Therefore, schools, clubs, and societies should encourage such discussion and give opportunity for debate. Any debate centers in a question about which two opposing propositions can be made and supported by arguments. We cannot debate words or phrases. We may speak of discussing "taxes" or "freedom of speech"; but the discussion cannot proceed until we have put together a sentence or proposition about the subject. Preparation for debate calls first for selecting a debatable question. This is a question (1) on which opinions may reasonably differ, (2) on which material for evidence and proof s available, (3) which is of real interest.

The steps in planning an argument or a debate are the following:

1. State the question clearly and definitely. Propositions should be stated affirmatively, and should be so worded as to throw the burden of proof upon the affirmative. For example:

"*Should the City of X purchase the local electric lighting plant?*" or "*Should James W. go to college?*" Sometimes the question is stated in the form of a resolution: "*Resolved, That the City of X should purchase the local electric lighting plant.*" The following form also is recommended by some teachers as a title for a debate: "*For and against the election of B. as mayor*"; "*For and against James W. going to college.*"

2. Define concisely the terms used in the question. For instance, the terms "purchase" and "plant," in the first question, and the term "college," in the second, need definition.

3. Find the main *issues*, or special subordinate questions, on which the decision may turn. This discovery of issues is really a most vital part of argument; for clear statement of main issues eliminates useless talk about unimportant details. The following is the best method of finding the issues: (1) set down a number of opposing statements upon the question; (2) analyze these to find what are the exact points on which they conflict; (3) state these points as questions. These questions are the issues. Such an analysis of arguments on the question as to the electric lighting plant would probably reveal the following issues:

Is the present electric service unsatisfactory? Is owning and operating public utilities a wise policy for this city? Is some other management to be preferred?

These issues appear in the form of questions, to which the affirmative answers *yes* and the negative, *no*. The skillful debater takes account of these questions and sifts them until he has found those which seem really essential. Then, by answering these essential questions, he answers the main question. Such an argument may be outlined as follows:

The body, or *brief*, for the affirmative or negative side of the argument should thus take up the issues in order and answer each question, with reasons and evidence. Then, on the basis of the reasoning given, the *conclusion*, or final answer to the main question should be stated.

In a debate on any question, certain of the apparent issues may be set aside, by mutual agreement, before opening the discussion. They are then called "admitted matter," and the discussion, for the sake of brevity and clearness, takes up only the issues on which there is clear difference of opinion.

Logic. "*Why?*" is the student's most troublesome question but no progress in argumentative thinking can be made without clear answers to questions beginning with *Why*. The corresponding word in answers is *because*. One thing is true because another thing is true.

All reasoning must be based on long and careful observation of facts. *Logic*, which is the science or art of exact reasoning, teaches us how to arrange and test our propositions so that our conclusions shall be warranted.

The *syllogism* is a common form of logical reasoning. It may be represented as follows:

Major premise (general statement): Wooden houses can be burned.

Minor premise (particular statement): Mr. A's house is wooden.

Conclusion: Therefore, Mr. A's house can be burned.

To make this reasoning true, a sufficient number of cases must have been observed to justify the general statement. It must be certain also that Mr. A's house belongs to the general class of wooden houses.

If we said, "*Plants are good for food; geraniums are plants; therefore, geraniums are good for food,*" our reasoning would be faulty, because not all plants are good for food. Our general statement is untrue though our particular statement is true. If we said, "*Lumber is expensive; houses are made of lumber; therefore, houses are expensive,*" our reasoning would be faulty because not all houses are made entirely or mainly of lumber. The particular statement is untrue though the general statement and the fact stated in the conclusion are true. Therefore, in the first example, we would *distinguish* or *question* the *major* premise, *grant* the *minor*, and *deny* the *conclusion*; in the second, we would *grant* the *major*, *distinguish* the *minor*, and *deny* the *conclusion*.

Evidence and Proof. Answering these *why* questions involves evidence and proof. *Evidence* is any fact, testimony, or accepted principle, which tends to bring about a belief in the proposition which is being urged. Evidence may be direct or circumstantial. Direct evidence is such as immediately supports the proposition. For instance, a theft may have been committed, the thief pursued and caught; his possession of the stolen property and the testimony of the person who saw him steal would be *direct evidence*. If, however, no such evidence as this were available, *circumstantial evidence* might be used. This would be made up of facts about the suspected person and his movements, which would tend to show that he probably committed the deed. *Proof* is convincing evidence.

Formal Debate: Rules. In a formal debate each side must know which are the most important of the issues raised, and the debaters must remember that the decision depends upon the balance of argument. Every argument advanced by one side must be answered by the other. Unanswered argument stands, no matter how weak the evidence presented by the side using it. *Refutation*, or the answering of opponents' arguments, is very important.

The debating leagues of colleges and high schools have developed certain customs and rules for the conducting of debates. The most important of these follow:

1. *Selection of the Question.*—Usually one team proposes a question and the other team is allowed to choose to support either the affirmative or the negative side.

2. *Teams.*—Each side of the argument is maintained by a team of two (or three) members. An additional member, or alternate, is sometimes chosen. He may take one of the regular places in an emergency. Otherwise, he helps in the preparation of the debate.

3. *Teamwork.*—All members of the team should work together in preparing the debate. They should confer upon the selection of the important issues and the arrangement of material. Before the debate, each member of the team should be familiar with the entire argument, but the actual presentation should be divided among the three debaters. Each one should have a definite part of the case to present.

4. *Division of Work.*—The first speaker on each side has to state the position of his side, make one strong point, and win the attention and the interest of his audience. The second speaker has to maintain interest, make at least one striking argument, and refute some of his opponents' arguments. The last speaker has to drive home the strongest argument of his side, answer some of his opponents' arguments, and sum up the case.

5. *Organization of a Debate.*—A formal debate is organized with a chairman, a timekeeper, and usually three judges. The chairman calls the meeting to order, announces the question and any special rules for the discussion, and introduces the speakers. The timekeeper gives each speaker a signal one minute or two before his speech is to close and another, if necessary, when his time has expired.

6. *Order of Speaking.*—The speakers on the two sides alternate, first an affirmative and then a negative speaker. Usually the debaters give two series of speeches. The first consists of direct argument; the second, entirely of refutation. This second series of speeches is called rebuttal. The order of speakers in rebuttal may be changed from that followed in the direct argument. The affirmative may elect either to open or to close the rebuttal.

7. *Time.*—Each speaker in direct argument is allowed a definite time—six, eight, or ten minutes—for his direct speech and a shorter time for rebuttal. The first direct speakers and the last rebuttal speakers are sometimes allowed two or three minutes more than the others.

8. *Intermission.*—At the close of the direct speeches the debaters are allowed a brief intermission for conference before beginning the rebuttal.

9. *Limitations of Rebuttal.*—In rebuttal a speaker must confine himself to refuting his opponents' arguments. He is not allowed to bring in new material.

10. *Decision of the Judges.*—At the close of the debate the judges render their decision, usually without conferring. The chairman announces the decision, which is accepted as final.

RADIO AND TELEVISION SPEAKING

Reversing the development from silent to spoken movies, radio broadcasting was soon followed by the combination of visual with sound communication that is universally familiar as television. Unlike the change in motion pictures, however, it was not a case of the earlier form being eclipsed by the later one, but of the survival of both kinds, each with its own special function and appeal. Because radio broadcasting continued undiminished in importance following the advent of television, the problems of speaking common to both remained. In some respects, of course, the radio announcer or actor standing before a microphone had the advantage of simpler requirements and an informal atmosphere. Relaxed in shirt-sleeve comfort, he could read from a typed script held in his hand. If his delivery was *natural and spontaneous enough to indicate speaking instead of reading*, his audience would be unaware of the manuscript unless the sheets were rustled, in which case the noise would be picked up and magnified into a loud crackling sound. By contrast, the speaker facing a television audience would have to rely on his memory or be content with quick side glances at a teleprompter to keep his lines straight. In using the air waves for either medium, radio or television, the speaker would have to recognize certain obligations owed to the public.

Requirements for Speaking. For his audience, whether only listening or both seeing and listening, the speaker must meet certain minimum requirements. These include particularly distinct utterance, correct pronunciation, and a manner and tone of voice suited to the situation. His speech is not formal oratory but person-to-person communication on the intimate level of the living room or the conference table. When Queen Victoria, exasperated by a prime minister's loud conversation, said: "He talks to me as if I were a public meeting!" she was making a criticism that might well apply to radio speakers who disregard the amplifying possibilities of their medium.

Distinct utterance, always an asset to any speaker, is vitally important in radio and television. To the millions of listeners, the experience of hearing words spoken clearly by someone who is both intelligent and intelligible is almost like taking a course of study in the art of speaking. Perhaps without suspecting the extent of his influence, the speaker is actually teaching by example, and his pupils, of all ages, are legion. Obviously, the educational opportunities involved impose a great responsibility, not only on the person before the microphone but also on the broadcasting industry as a whole and on the regulating authorities. It is not that a renewal of a license would necessarily depend upon anything so specific as the enunciation of particular words. It is rather that a general standard of excellence needs to be maintained in a medium of communication whose existence is justified only by its contribution to public service.

No Room for Errors. The microphone and the volume control dial are potent instruments for exposing carelessness or unsuspected mannerisms in speech. Anyone who says "watt" instead of "what" or pronounces "winter" like "winner" will be enlightened, and probably shocked, when listening to a play-back of his own words. If these sounds have occurred in an audition, his failure is likely, and the reason for it should be evident. To forestall such an unhappy outcome, he will do well to give special attention to stressed and unstressed syllables, to speech phrases" as units, and to word endings like *ing, ed*, and the plural *s*, along with inflections that are needed to bring out a particular shade of meaning. At the same time, however, he must see to it that his painstaking care is not noticeable to his audience: Art that conceals art, so important in many fields of endeavor, is nowhere more desirable than in speaking before a microphone. Deliberate striving for effect will get over to the listener and will cause amusement, annoyance, or possibly, that worst of all calamities, a twisting of the dial.

Your Pronunciation Is Showing. "What good," someone may ask, "is all this attention to distinct speaking if the wrong pronunciation is used in the first place?" A facetious answer might be that if a wrong sound is used it had better be slurred over rapidly in the hope that the speaker's mistake or uncertainty will not be too noticeable. An observation to be made here is that the speaker may not realize that he is wrong and may give the incorrect pronunciation with bold and positive distinctness. The member of a state legislature who accused his opponents of "chickenry" when he meant "chicanery" was doubtless an extreme case, but he could be a useful illustration of the principle

involved. His speech would be remembered, but for the wrong reason.

Indeed, one of the great educational services of radio and television is that they have encouraged the study of pronunciation. A large section of the public that was formerly "eye-minded," recognizing words by sight without being sure how they were pronounced, has lately become "sound-conscious." They have discovered a fact sometimes forgotten, that language is fundamentally a matter of sounds and pauses, and only secondarily a collection of written or printed characters on a page.

Questions of preferred usage in regard to disputed pronunciations call for careful study or perhaps, as in the case of the British Broadcasting Corporation (BBC), a committee of experts to rule upon difficult choices. Whether he is guided by the recommendations of a committee or by the authority of leading dictionaries, the radio or television speaker is expected to ascertain and follow the best current usage in his pronunciation. As a beginning he might profitably turn to the pages on Correct Pronunciation in this department, and pronounce aloud the words that are given there, with diacritical markings. Continuation of this study would of course include similar exercises in the pronunciation of proper names, biographical, geographical, historical, and otherwise. Names of musical composers form an interesting special group. Many lists of such words are available which can be helpful in clearing up doubts in the speaker's mind and giving trustworthy guidance to his listeners.

The Manuscript. Not only problems in pronunciation but also many difficulties of utterance may be avoided in the preparation of the script. Whether the words are written by the person who is to speak them or by someone preparing a manuscript for him, the question of delivery should always be uppermost in the writer's mind or, so to speak, in his inner ear. Long sentences, with clauses that leave the reader gasping for breath, are bad in any kind of writing, but they are especially objectionable in spoken discourse. Medium-long sentences alternating with shorter ones can provide a rhythm that will be comfortable for both speaker and listener. Short, Anglo-Saxon words, because of their familiar sound and meaning, are usually preferable to learned, bookish terms. The latter sometimes turn out to be rumbling polysyllables requiring vocal gymnastics of the speaker. Words like "concatenation," "supererogation," or "sesquipedalian" are not likely to be spoken naturally by the average person or understood readily by his listeners. Even if the individual words offer no difficulty they may be found in awkward combinations like the phrase "river improvement movement" that was edited out of one manuscript. Removal or avoidance of "built-in" difficulties for speakers is a matter that requires constant attention. A famous case of revision for this purpose was the first radio broadcasting of bridge games. Immediate difficulty was experienced by listeners in differentiating between "the eight of clubs" and "the ace of clubs" and similar expressions, no matter how carefully the words were spoken. A small change in editing substituted the words "eight spot" to designate the card of lower value, and the speaker's problem was solved.

The Speaker's Qualification. Anyone who wishes to engage in radio or television work can look forward to a period of training and experience. His chances for success will of course be better if he can build on a foundation of natural aptitude plus general education. The National Broadcasting Company, in a pamphlet entitled *The Selection and Training of Radio Announcers*, listed the principal attributes desirable in a candidate as follows:

A good voice, clear enunciation, and pronunciation free of dialect or local peculiarities; ability to read well; sufficient knowledge of foreign languages for the correct pronunciation of names, places, titles, etc.; some knowledge of musical history, composition and composers; ability to read and interpret poetry; facility in extempore speech; selling ability in the reading of commercial continuity; ability to master the technical details in operating the switchboard; a college education.

The foregoing list, although referring specifically to radio, will apply equally, and with very few changes, to persons planning to work in television. In addition, the announcer who faces a visible audience should have a good "stage presence." The qualities of poise, animation, and naturalness that are reflected in the voice of the radio speaker should extend to the manner and appearance, to the entire personality, of the announcer or performer on television. Even so comparatively simple an assignment as delivering a commercial message is a test of the television announcer's all-round adequacy.

Range of Communication. The potential reach of radio and television communication and, correspondingly, the opportunity and responsibility of speakers, actors, and producers, may be glimpsed in a few statistics for 1967. Data compiled by the Federal Communications Commission and published in *Statistical Abstract* give the number of broadcasting stations in the United States, including Puerto Rico and the Virgin Islands as follows:

	Authorized	On the Air
AM Radio	4185	4085
FM Radio	1854	1560
Television	758	608

Even more impressive are the totals in terms of radio and television households in the United States, published by Billboard Publishing Co. as of January 1, 1967:

Radio Households*, U.S. Total	58,600,000
Television Households, U.S. Total	57,600,000

* *A radio household is defined as an occupied dwelling unit having one or more radio sets.*

FORMS OF ORAL INTERPRETATION

In schools, in clubs, in social gatherings, and in the home, there are occasions when we desire to read, recite, act out, or tell about something from the printed page. Many of us hesitate to do so for fear of being elocutionary. It is true that the exhibitionary kind of recitation that flourished in the nineties and in the first decade of this century has gone out of style and is heard today only when it is being satirized. But there is no reason why one should be fearful of communicating to others what he has found worth-while in our literature. The sincere expression of fine literature is never out of date.

There are four forms of oral interpretation which are frequently used, the characteristics of which will be presented here. They are: *Interpretative Reading, Recitation, Impersonation,* and *Story Telling.* These forms might be called patterns of delivery. Each form is made up of certain factors of delivery which are so integrated that they make a characteristic pattern. It is well for the speech student to know these patterns. When he does he will be able to be judicious in his oral interpretations. He will know when to act out and when to recite. He will avoid the mistake frequently made of acting out in a literal fashion that which should be suggested. In other words, he can avoid being told he is "elocutionary."

Principles of Oral Reading. There are certain techniques in oral interpretation which are applicable to all the forms mentioned in the foregoing paragraph and which we take up here preliminary to our discussion of the four specific forms.

Phrasing. A speech phrase is different from a grammatical phrase. In the sentence, "While John was walking up the hill, he stopped and looked back at the sunset," there are two grammatical phrases, "up the hill" and "at the sunset." These grammatical phrases are only a part of the two speech phrases which go to make up the sentence. A speech phrase is a unit of speech expression which presents some element of experience for the audience to grasp. That element may be an idea, an image, an action, an emotion, an attitude. Thus, in the sentence about John we have two elements of experience, that of John walking up the hill, and John's turning to look at the sunset.

Characteristics of a Speech Phrase. The speech phrase is a *unit* in several respects. It is a unit in its separateness. Usually it is separated from other phrases by a pause. Sometimes, however, a change in pitch or volume or rate may indicate the end of one phrase and the beginning of another. It is a unit in its presenting one pattern of experience, something which can be grasped and reacted to by the listeners. It is a unit in its cohesiveness. The words in the phrase, "while John was walking up the hill," tie up with each other much in the same way as the syllables of a polysyllabic word are related. In fact, we can say one speaks a speech phrase just as he would pronounce a many-syllabled word, such as *unconstitutional.* Finally, it is a unit in that it has a beginning, a middle, and an end. Almost always it has a key word or combination of words which form the backbone of the phrase. The reader, both in voice and bodily movement, leads up to this key word, emphasizes it, and returns from it.

Phrasing in Oral Reading. Once a reader gets a command of phrasing, most of the battle for good reading is won. He will be reading ideas and images rather than words. His voice will have the spontaneous character of conversation, because he is really thinking and responding to the content of his phrase units. He must always remember to look ahead, grasp the meaning of the phrase he is to read, and speak that phrase, with the aim of stirring up the same meaning in his audience.

Emphasis. It would seem that if one had caught the meaning of a phrase he would give the proper emphasis to the words. But this does not always follow, since we are inclined, at least in reading aloud, unconsciously to give less emphasis to important words when we, the readers, are no longer reading the material for the first time. In other words, because the content is no longer fresh to us, the kind of emphasis which comes with the spontaneous realization of ideas and feelings is lost.

Three Kinds of Emphasis. The voice should give prominence, usually through raising the pitch of the voice, to that which is new or which advances the thought of the material; to that which involves contrast or comparison; and to that which is given emotional intensification because of its importance. The first two in the above have to do with new ideas; the third, intensifying emphasis, has to do with old ideas. Terms used to designate these three kinds of emphasis are (in the order given above): *Assertive, Antithetic,* and *Intensive.* In the sentence which follows, those words which require *assertive* emphasis will be italicized; those requiring ANTITHETIC will appear in lightface caps; and those requiring **intensive** will be in boldface:

There abides *faith, hope,* and *charity,* **these three;** but the *greatest* of these is CHARITY.

"Faith, hope, and charity" are *new* ideas; that is, it is the first time they have been spoken of by the reader, and consequently they get the downward stroke in the pitch of the voice that goes with *Assertive* emphasis. "These three" involves the giving of emotional significance to something already taken up and is consequently given *Intensive* emphasis. In the word "greatest" the thought is advanced with a new *assertion* and that kind of emphasis is given the word. When "charity" is repeated at the end of the sentence it is used in a comparative sense and consequently receives *Antithetic* emphasis. We have already pointed out that the voice takes a downward stroke in pitch for assertive emphasis. For antithetic emphasis it does likewise, but before starting down it takes a slight upward turn giving the voice what is called a *circumflex* inflection. For intensive emphasis the voice remains on a high level of pitch until the whole idea has been intensified. Thus, in "these three" the voice remains on the same high pitch for both words.

In applying these principles of emphasis the important thing to remember is that the reader must be constantly on the alert so that he distinguishes between that which is *new* or *important* and that which is *old*. On the new and important ideas his voice jumps to a high level and descends with a quick stroke; on that which is old, his voice remains on the neutral, "taken-for-granted" level. We mention again here that "new" and "old" are always used in terms of the audience. Good oral reading involves the constant fluctuation of the voice between the level of stress and the level of words which have been referred to before. If the reader effectively applies the two techniques taken up in the foregoing paragraphs, namely, *phrasing* and *emphasis*, he will have the necessary oral reading fundamentals for performing in the specialized forms to be taken up below.

Interpretative Reading. In the reading of literature from the printed page for the benefit of a listening audience, the reader acts as a mediator between his material and his audience. His aim is to recreate the material in the minds and imaginations of his listeners. Therefore, it is important that he subordinate himself as a personality and a performer to that end. If he calls too much attention to himself by displaying his elocutionary facility or by literally acting out the happenings of his material, his listeners will be distracted from their imaginative activity and pay attention to what is happening on the platform. If he concentrates on stirring up the imaginations of his listeners through the use of *suggestion* (as opposed to the literal portrayal of acting) he will be properly carrying out his function as an Interpretative Reader.

The following points should be kept in mind as important in the technique of Interpretative Reading:

1. The reader's relationship to the audience is a *mediate* one.

2. The reader's activities are on a *suggestive* basis, as opposed to the *literal*.

3. Because it is the literature being read which is the audience's chief concern, the manuscript or book *must* be used. It is best to have the book on a reading-stand, thus freeing the reader for suggestive activity.

4. What the reader does with his voice and body must always be *spontaneous* or *extemporaneous* in character. Conscious control of the voice and body to the extent that we in the audience listen to the reader's interesting inflections and notice his graceful gestures interferes with imaginative activity in the audience.

Interpretative Reading Today. This form of oral reading was developed at the end of the last century as a reaction to the elocutionary display of the *recitation* vogue, which had swept the country. It is a form of speech activity, which when understood and not confused with recitation or acting, has a real place in our everyday life. We can use it in our clubs and in church meetings and in library reading-hours. It is particularly adaptable to the reading of plays and novels.

Recitation. While it is true that Recitation easily turns into a display of the performer's elocutionary virtuosity, it need not be so, if the reciter appreciates the true character of the form. When one recites he is doing much the same thing as when one sings a song. The beauty and story of a poem is being conveyed to an audience through the reciter's body and personality. The more interesting the personality of the reciter, the more interesting will be the performance as a whole. As William Butler Yeats has said, the reciter is "an interesting and exciting messenger." It can be seen that the reciter's rôle is somewhat different from that of the interpretative reader's. Whatever the reciter can do to make more interesting what he has to report, he is at liberty to do. But he must make sure that what he does always pertains to what he is reporting. It was when the old "elocutionists" indulged in exaggerated graceful movements and poses and when they overused their vocal variations that the message was lost in the process.

Characteristics of Recitation.

1. The material is *memorized*.

2. Poetry of a musical nature and ballads are especially suited to recitation.

3. *Literal elements* are not out of place. What the performer does is not subordinated to the material as it is in Interpretative Reading.

4. *Formalized elements* in delivery are permissible. The reciter may consciously attend to the musical patterns of his material. He may also take on the formal movements of stylized behavior, when the material permits of it.

5. The reciter's relationship to his audience is *direct*. There may be an element of *display* in the relationship.

Choral Speaking as a Kind of Recitation. The speaking of a piece of literature by a group is a popular activity in our schools today. Usually the material used is strongly musical in character. The director of the choral speaking choir strives for a clear-cut unison in the voices and for interesting variations in the use of the bass and alto voices in the group. There are several good books to be found now which explain the technique of speech choir directing and which give suggested methods for handling poetry on a choir basis.

Impersonation. This form of speaking is closely related to *acting*. When a performer takes a dramatic monologue, such as Browning's *My Last Dutchess*, memorizes it, and acts out the character of the duke in that famous piece of literature, he is *impersonating*. Monologues, long speeches from plays, and short scenes from plays having few characters are best suited to impersonation.

Characteristics of Impersonation.

1. The material is *memorized*.

2. *Literal elements* predominate over *suggested elements*. What the audience sees before them is of primary importance; their own imaginative activity is subordinated.

3. The performer's personality is *submerged* in the character he is portraying. In Recitation the performer's personality is very much in evidence.

4. Impersonation differs from *acting* in that costumes, scenery, and make-up are seldom used and the activity on the platform is usually limited to an area about four feet in diameter.

5. The impersonator tries to create an *illusion*. Through literal activity and through suggestion he tries to give the audience a picture of life, sometimes realistic, sometimes idealized.

Story Telling. This form of oral interpretation is closest to public speaking in its character. In preparing to tell a story the performer should go about it much in the same way as he would prepare an extemporaneous speech. He should read the story carefully and set the gist of it down in outline form. Then he should rehearse the telling of the story just as he would rehearse an extemporaneous speech. In telling the story to his audience he should have the same spontaneous quality which is so desirable in speech-making.

Characteristics of Story Telling.

1. The story is *not memorized*. Only those parts of the story which the public have come to know and expect to hear should be spoken from memory. The dialogue in the story of *The Three Bears* would be well given as it is found on the printed page.

2. Story telling is *not reciting*. The story teller is conversing *with* an audience rather than performing *for* it. His relationship to his audience is that of social intercourse.

3. The *literal* and the *suggested* go hand in hand in this form. At times the speaker may appeal to the imaginations of his listeners and at times he may act out his characters quite completely.

4. The story teller's personality should play the same part it does in public speaking. It should enhance what he has to say.

DELIVERY

The following words of Quintilian, the famous Roman orator and teacher of rhetoric, contain advice for the speaker which is as appropriate now as when they were written:

"In all kinds of public speaking, but especially in popular assemblies, it is a capital rule to attend to all the decorum of time, place, and character. No warmth of eloquence can atone for the neglect of this. That vehemence which is becoming in a person of character and authority may be unsuitable to the modesty expected from a young speaker. That sportive and witty manner which may suit one assembly is altogether out of place in a grave cause and solemn meeting. No one should ever rise to speak in public without forming to himself a just and strict idea of what suits his own age and character; what suits the subject, the hearers, the place, the occasion; and adjusting the whole train and manner of his speaking to this idea."

There are, in general, four methods of delivering speeches. Each has its especial strength and its peculiar weakness. It is important that a speaker should adopt for his main dependence the method to which his abilities are best suited.

Speaking from Manuscript. The use of a carefully prepared manuscript is the most certain method of delivering a speaker's thought completely, logically, and economically. It is especially appropriate for formal occasions, such as lectures, when the speaker's chief purpose is to convey information to his hearers. The weakness of this method lies in the tendency of the speaker to keep his eyes too closely riveted to his manuscript and thus lose the attention of his audience. The speaker who uses manuscript usually sacrifices some of the directness of address which is so important a quality of oratory. For the speaker of small experience, however, the use of manuscript during delivery is to be recommended.

Speaking from Notes. The speaker who uses notes, that is, an outline of the previously prepared manuscript, has the advantage of possessing a ready guide through his argument, while at the same time he is freer to meet unexpected situations than is the man who must follow a complete manuscript. This is a weighty consideration in discussion or debate. All notes, however, should be clearly written. so that the speaker's eyes will not be taken from his audience for too long a time, while he attempts to decipher his outline.

Speaking from Memory. The memorized speech has the distinct advantage of permitting the speaker to look constantly at his audience. It does not, however, allow him to adapt himself readily to unforeseen circumstances, such as disturbances in an assembly or the necessity of answering unexpected arguments in debate. It is appropriate to formal occasions; for it permits the attainment of highly finished style both in composition and in delivery. The chief weakness of the method is that his effort to recall the memorized words may rob the speaker of directness and spontaneity. The ideal in the use of the memorized speech is to combine finished perfection of form with the appearance of that naturalness which marks the extemporaneous address.

Speaking Extemporaneously. Undoubtedly, the most effective form of public speaking is the extemporaneous address. This is to be defined as the presentation of thoroughly prepared thought in language which is the product of the occasion. As extemporaneous speaking is the most effective type of oratory, so it demands the most exacting and long-continued preparation and practice. However, the reward of the master of extemporaneous oratory is the consciousness of the most thorough command over his audiences. Extemporaneous speaking does not preclude the use of notes, and, for the short, informal address, the preparation of notes, outlining the thought to be clothed in extemporaneous language, is usually advisable.

Whichever of these general methods of speaking you choose to employ, you must observe certain well established principles pertaining to manner and to voice. The total effect of a speech is compounded of the words, the bodily attitudes, and the voice of the speaker. He must know how to adapt these elements to each other and to the spirit of his audience. It has well been said that the best oratorical style for a given individual is that of his best conversation.

The attainment of an effective manner before an audience is worthy of long and careful effort. Each speaker must study his own problems. However, there are two means which you will find to be fundamental:

1. Know your subject and your plan so well that you show *confidence* (a) by looking at your audience—letting them see your eyes, (b) by speaking directly to your audience—letting them see your lips move. The audience is entitled to this directness of address.

2. Be so thoroughly interested in your talk that you show ease (a) by standing so firmly *on both feet* that you can change your position without "teetering," (b) by such gestures with arms or body as are prompted by your thought and feeling *at the time*, (c) by directing your eyes and your voice at some time to every one in your audience, (d) by deep, steady breathing.

Gesture. The name for the bodily attitudes and movements and facial expressions by which a speaker supplements and emphasizes his words. Every speaker will use gesture in some way, because bodily movements are a fundamental mode of expressing ideas and feelings; and the more earnest and emphatic the speaker is, the more frequent and vigorous will be his gestures. Two rules you may well observe: (1) Do not try to repress all gesture. (2) Strive to make every gesture mean something definite. Superfluous gestures take the attention of your audience from what you are saying. Notice the gestures that you make spontaneously in conversation. Try to employ these and adapt them to the "enlarged conversation" of your public speech. We usually think of gestures as movements of the arms and hands. But remember that you can make many of your most effective gestures with your facial muscles, your head, or your whole body. This caution will help you to avoid the windmill method of gesture, or merely throwing your arms about. In gesture, as in every other phase of speaking, sincerity of thought and purpose is the best guard against meaningless expression.

Enunciation. For *good speech*, in uttering your own thoughts or reading orally the words of ano her, the first essential is this: *Carefully think* your words and phrases. Your voice will respond with wonderful accuracy to your understanding of the words you use. The second essential is this: Pronounce your words *distinctly and correctly*. This includes the true forming and arrangement of the sounds, faultless accent, and clear quality of voice. The list of words in the section entitled Correct Pronunciation will give you the precise sounds and accents for many words commonly used. For other words, consult unabridged dictionaries. Further, learn how to form these sounds exactly.

Voice Qualities. Pleasing and effective speech is very largely a result of the speaker's mastery of good voice qualities, the fundamental principle of which is proper breathing. Individual voices differ in quality because of the varied forms and conditions of the vocal cords and the resonance chambers of the mouth and nose. Each person has a normal quality of voice, which he uses in conversation, and by which it is possible to recognize him even when his features cannot be seen. But, by altering the shape of the mouth cavity or by opening or restricting the nasal and throat passages, each individual can produce several other qualities besides this normal one.

Eight qualities of the speaking voice are usually distinguished. Three of these the public speaker should cultivate: (1) *Normal*, which is a clear, resonant quality produced by the natural position of the vocal organs and the simple enunciation of vowels and consonants, the ordinary conversational voice. (2) *Orotund*, a fuller, clearer, and more resonant quality. It is appropriately used to express grandeur, sublimity, and similar thoughts and ideas of a lofty and impressive nature. The speaker should be careful not to use this quality too frequently, as it may easily pass into bombast and become unconvincing. (3) *Aspirate*, which is a breathy utterance either devoid of vocalization, as in a whisper, or partially vocalized, as in the so-called "stage whisper." The quality may suggest weakness or excessive emotion. It is sometimes used effectively in public speaking to give striking emphasis to an expression.

The remaining five qualities are generally undesirable and to be avoided in public speaking. They are confined to the art of the actor in portraying characters or in suggesting emotions with which they are associated. (4) *Guttural*, a throaty sound. (5) *Pectoral*, a hollow, breathy quality. (6) *Oral*, the result of a rather thin, mouth resonance. (7) *Nasal*, a quality characterized by a harsh twang. (8) *Falsetto*, a quality of tone above the speaker's natural range.

Cautions.—Three very common faults of American speech are *high pitch*, *nasality*, and *throatiness*. Too high a pitch of voice is due to nervousness and to lack of self-control. Nasality is not talking through the nose but failure to use the nasal cavity properly in speaking. It is frequently due to some obstruction of the nasal passages. Throatiness, or making sounds too low down in the throat, is usually caused by contraction of throat muscles.

Inflection. What punctuation is to written language, *inflection*, *change of pitch*, and *pauses* are to spoken language. The importance of changes of pitch in indicating emphasis was discussed under *emphasis* in the section on Oral Reading.

Change of Pitch. By pronouncing one of the words in a sentence with a decidedly high or low pitch as compared with the pitch of the others, you can give several additional meanings to the sentence. For instance: If *you* is given a higher pitch than *are going*, the sentence means that you are going and not some one else; pronouncing *are* with a higher pitch than *you* and *going* may indicate either surprise or decided determination. This abrupt shifting of the key, or tone, of speech *between* words, phrases, clauses, or sentences is called *change of pitch*.

Practice will show you the importance of this means of emphasis. It is, in fact, the natural method of marking off one idea from another in speech. If you think clearly, you can hardly keep such changes out of your voice.

Pauses. Plan your pauses as carefully as you arrange your words. Silences are the wells of thought. Definite pauses serve at least four main purposes: (1) They give your audience time to grasp important ideas. (2) They enable your audience to make the necessary transition from one thought to another and so to "follow" you. (3) They convey the impression that you are choosing your words carefully. (4) They impress your audience with a sense of your consideration for them. Thus, directly and indirectly, pauses serve to give emphasis to your speech.

Rate of Speaking. Just as the natural qualities of voice vary among individuals, so too their natural rates of speaking differ. Some people are naturally quick and nervous; others are slow and phlegmatic. It should be remembered, however, that the brain of the listener is capable of receiving and registering only a limited number of words in any given unit of time, and that a speaker should adjust his rate to the ability of the audience to take in what he says. Generally, it is unwise to exceed 125 words a minute in ordinary speaking. On the other hand, it is tiresome to listen to slow, drawling delivery. Hence, rate should be adapted (1) to the capability of the audience to grasp the speaker's meaning, as well as (2) to the nature of what is spoken.

It is important that, in the course of any speech or address, one should, from time to time, alter his rate of speaking. Change of rate (1) relieves monotony, (2) helps in emphasis, (3) suggests certain emotions or movements.

That which will quicken or retard a man's footsteps will also quicken or retard his rate of speaking. Narration, for example, is flowing, easy, and graceful; vehemence is firm and accelerated; anger and joy are sudden, sometimes hysterical. Again, dignity, authority, sublimity, and awe assume deeper tones and a slower movement. One may often hear a good speaker, at some sudden turn of thought or feeling, check himself in the full tide of utterance and give indescribable power to a passage by slackening his rate and by adopting a slow, deliberate enunciation.

Breathing. Breathe deeply and steadily, using the diaphragm and chest walls. Learn to feel your diaphragm, which is the flexible floor of your chest, expanding and moving downward as you "take in" breath. You can then control and steady its movement, keeping it expanded, and give *carrying power* to your voice. Practice this breathing. It will help you to avoid "stage fright." Take a "deep breath" before you begin to speak.

Correct Speech Sounds. These are secured by right breathing, proper shaping of the mouth, and correct placing of the various sounds. The voice is produced by vibrations, or waves, set up by the vocal cords in the column of air reaching from the lungs up into the mouth and the nose. The different shapes that the mouth cavity may take give special forms to these waves. The forms, thus produced, give rise to the *vowels*, or open voice sounds. Each vowel sound is made with the jaws and the flexible palate, lips, tongue, and cheeks in a definite position.

The cavities of the throat, nose, and mouth act as a *resonance chamber*, like an organ pipe or the body of a violin, to give volume and tone to the voice. Any obstruction, such as the mucus from a "cold," enlarged tonsils, or adenoids, interferes with the volume of the voice as well as with the purity and the clearness of its tone.

The *consonant* sounds we form by partially or entirely closing the mouth cavity with the teeth or tongue or lips. We thus, to some extent, shut off the vowel sound; at the same time, the friction or explosive force of the moving breath makes sounds which join or articulate with the vowels to form syllables.

CORRECT PRONUNCIATION

For key to pronunciation, see page 8.

A foreigner learning English pronounces a word like "concentrate" with the accent placed logically on the second, or "root" syllable. Then he learns that this word, like many others, has been affected by a recessive tendency which moved the accent to or toward the beginning, so that the correct pronunciation is *kŏn'sĕn-trāt*. However, as in spelling and other matters, the English language refuses to be consistent. The word *rê-mŏn'strāt* keeps the accent on the second syllable, while the comparable word *dĕm'ŏn-strāt* moves the accent back and changes both the syllabication and the vowel sounds. These are merely examples to indicate the need for careful examination of words in order to learn their present accepted pronunciation. At a time when many people are "eye-minded" and when reading aloud is almost a lost art, a study of diacritical marking for individual words is highly desirable. In this connection, a useful exercise for anyone would be the review and pronouncing aloud of the following list of more than 1600 words which have sometimes caused difficulty.

abbé, *à'bā'*
abdomen, *ăb-dō'mĕn*
abhor, *ăb-hôr'*
abhorrent, *ăb-hôr'ĕnt*
abject, *ăb-jĕkt'*
absent (adj.), *ăb'sĕnt*
absent (v.), *ăb-sĕnt'*
abstemious, *ăb-stē'mĭ-ŭs*
accent (n.), *ăk'sĕnt*
accent (v.), *ăk-sĕnt'*
accessory, *ăk-sĕs'ô-rĭ*
acclimate, *ă-klī'mĭt*
accompaniment, *ă-kŭm'pà-nĭ-mĕnt*
accuracy, *ăk'û-rà-sĭ*
acetylene, *à-sĕt'ĭ-lēn*
acorn, *ā'kôrn*
acoustic, *à-kōōs'tĭk*
acronym, *ăc'rō-nĭm*
actor, *ăk'tẽr*
acts, *ăkts*
acumen, *à-kū'mĕn*
adagio, *à-dä'jō*
address, *à-drĕs'*
adieu, *à-dū'*
adios, *ä'dyōs'*
adjourn, *à-jûrn'*
adobe, *à-dō'bĭ*
adult, *à-dŭlt'*
adventure, *ăd-vĕn'chûr*
adverse, *ăd-vûrs'*
advertisement, *ăd-vûr'tĭz-mĕnt*
advertiser, *ăd'vẽr-tīz'ẽr*
aerial, *â-ēr'ĭ-ăl*
a fortiori, *ā fôr'shĭ-ō'rī*
aft, *àft*
after, *àf'tẽr*
again, *à-gĕn'*
agile, *ăj'ĭl*
alas, *à-làs'*
albino, *ăl-bī'nō*
alder, *ôl'dẽr*
algebra, *ăl'jè-brà*
alias, *ā'lĭ-ăs*
alien, *āl'yĕn*
allegro, *ă-lā'grō*
allies, *ă-līz'*
alloy, *ă-loi'*
alma mater, *ăl'mà mā'tẽr*
almond, *ä'mŭnd*
alpaca, *ăl-păk'à*
alpine, *ăl'pīn*
alternate (v.), *ôl'tẽr-nāt*
alternate (adj.) (n.), *ăl'tẽr-nĭt*
alternately, *ôl-tẽr'nĭt-lĭ*
alternative, *ôl-tûr'nà-tĭv*
aluminum, *à-lū'mĭ-nŭm*
alumnæ, *à-lŭm'nē*
alumni, *à-lŭm'nī*
amateur, *ăm'à-tûr'*
ambivalent, *ăm-bĭv'à-lĕnt*
ambrosia, *ăm-brō'zhĭ-à*
ameliorate, *à-mēl'yô-rāt*
amenable, *à-mē'nà-b'l*
amenity, *à-mĕn'ĭ-tĭ*
ammonia, *ă-mō'nĭ-à*
amortization, *ăm-ôr'tĭ-zā'shŭn*
amortize, *à-môr'tīz*
ampere, *ăm'pēr*
ancestor, *ăn'sĕs-tẽr*

ancestral, *ăn-sĕs'trăl*
anchor, *ăng'kẽr*
anchovy, *ăn-chō'vĭ*
ancient, *ān'shĕnt*
and, *ănd*
anemone, *à-nĕm'ô-nê*
angina pectoris, *ăn-jī'nà pĕk'tô-rĭs*
aniline, *ăn'ĭ-lĭn*
annihilate, *à-nī'ĭ-lāt*
answer, *àn'sẽr*
antarctic, *ănt-ärk'tĭk*
anxiety, *ăng-zī'ĕ-tĭ*
anxious, *ăngk'shŭs*
aperient, *à-pēr'ĭ-ĕnt*
aperture, *ăp'ẽr-chûr*
aphelion, *à-fē'lĭ-ŏn*
apostle, *à-pŏs''l*
apotheosis, *à-pŏth'ê-ō'sĭs*
apparatus, *ăp'à-rā'tŭs*
appellate, *ă-pĕl'ăt*
appendicitis, *ă-pĕn'dĭ-sī'tĭs*
applicable, *ăp'lĭ-kà-b'l*
appreciation, *ă-prē'shĭ-ā'shŭn*
apricot, *ā'prĭ-kŏt*
apron, *ā'prŭn*
apropos, *ăp'rô-pō'*
aqua, *ăk'wà*
aquarium, *à-kwâr'ĭ-ŭm*
aqueduct, *ăk'wê-dŭkt*
arbutus, *är-bū'tŭs*
archangel, *ärk'ān'jĕl*
archbishop, *ärch'bĭsh'ŭp*
archetype, *är'kê-tīp*
archipelago, *är'kĭ-pĕl'à-gō*
architect, *är'kĭ-tĕkt*
archives, *är'kīvz*
archivist, *är'kê-vĭst*
arctic, *ärk'tĭk*
area, *ā'rê-à*
aria, *ä'rĭ-à*
arid, *ăr'ĭd*
armada, *är-mä'dà*
armistice, *är'mĭ-stĭs*
aroma, *à-rō'mà*
arras, *ăr'às*
arroyo, *ă-roi'ō*
artisan, *är'tĭ-zăn*
asafetida, *ăs'à-fĕt'ĭ-dà*
ascetic, *ă-sĕt'ĭk*
ask, *àsk*
askance, *à-skăns'*
asparagus, *ăs-păr'à-gŭs*
asphalt, *ăs'fôlt*
aspirant, *ăs-pīr'ănt*
assay, *ă-sā'*
associate (v.), *ă-sō'shĭ-āt*
associate (n.), *-ăt*
associate (adj.), *-ăt*
association, *ă-sō'sĭ-ā'shŭn*
assume, *ă-sūm'*
asthma, *ăz'mà*
atheneum, *ăth'ê-nē'ŭm*
athletics, *ăth-lĕt'ĭks*
attaché, *ăt'à-shā'*
attorney, *ă-tûr'nĭ*
audacious, *ô-dā'shŭs*
audience, *ô'dĭ-ĕns*
au gratin, *ō'grä'tăN'*

aunt, *ănt*
au revoir, *ō'rĕ-vwär'*
aurora borealis, *ô-rō'rà bô'rê-ā'lĭs*
authority, *ô-thŏr'ĭ-tĭ*
automobile, *ô'tô-mô-bēl'*
auxiliary, *ôg-zĭl'yà-rĭ*
avenue, *ăv'ê-nū*
aviator, *ā'vĭ-ā'tẽr*
avocado, *ăv'ô-kä'dō*
avoirdupois, *ăv'ẽr-dŭ-poiz'*
awry, *à-rī'*
axiom, *ăk'sĭ-ŭm*
aye, (yes) *ī*

bacilli, *bà-sĭl'ī*
bacillus, *bà-sĭl'ŭs*
bade, *băd*
badinage, *băd'ĭ-näzh'*
balcony, *băl'kô-nĭ*
ballad, *băl'ăd*
ballade, *bà-läd'*
ballet, *băl'à*
balm, *bäm*
banquet, *băng'kwĕt*
baptism, *băp'tĭz'm*
baptize, *băp-tīz'*
barbiturate, *bär-bĭt'û-rāt*
bargain, *bär'gĭn*
barrage, *bà-räzh'*
barrel, *băr'ĕl*
basin, *bā's'n*
basket, *bàs'kĕt*
bath, *bàth*
baton, *bà'tŏN'*
bayou, *bī'ōō*
because, *bê-kôz'*
bedstead, *bĕd'stĕd*
been, *bĭn*
begonia, *bê-gō'nĭ-à*
beige, *bāzh*
believe, *bê-lēv'*
belles-lettres, *bĕl'lĕt'r'*
belligerent, *bê-lĭj'ẽr-ĕnt*
bellows, *bĕl'ōz*
beloved (adj.), *bê-lŭv'ĕd*
beloved (part.), *bê-lŭvd'*
beneficent, *bê-nĕf'ĭ-sĕnt*
bequeath, *bê-kwēTH'*
bestial, *bĕst'yăl*
betrothal, *bê-trŏth'ăl*
bicycle, *bī'sĭk-'l*
biennial, *bī-ĕn'ĭ-ăl*
bijou, *bē'zhōō*
billet-doux, *bĭl'à-dōō'*
bindery, *bīn'dẽr-ĭ*
biography, *bī-ŏg'rà-fĭ*
biology, *bī-ŏl'ô-jĭ*
bipartite, *bī-pär'tīt*
bismuth, *bĭz'mŭth*
blackguard, *blăg'ärd*
blanch, *blànch*
blanc mange, *blà-mänzh'*
blasé, *blä'zā'*
blaspheme, *blăs-fēm'*
blasphemous, *blăs'fê-mŭs*
blast, *blàst*
blatant, *blā'tănt*
blessed (adj.), *blĕs'ĕd*
blessed (part.), *blĕst*

blouse, *blouz*
blue, *blōō*
boisterous, *bois'tĕr-ŭs*
bolero, *bô-lâr'ô*
boll weevil, *bōl wē'v'l*
bomb, *bŏm*
bona fide, *bō'nȧ fī'dê*
bon marché, *bôN'mȧr'shā'*
bonnet, *bŏn'ĕt*
borax, *bō'răks*
borrow, *bŏr'ō*
bosom, *bŏŏz'ŭm*
boudoir, *bōō' dwär*
bouquet, *bōō-kā'*
bourgeois, *bōōr' zhwä*
bourn (bound), *bōrn*
bourse, *bōōrs*
bovine, *bō'vĭn*
bowlegged, *bō'lĕg'ĕd*
brand-new, *brănd'nū'*
brassière, *brȧ-zēr'*
breviary, *brē'vĭ-ĕr'ĭ*
brigand, *brĭg'ănd*
bristle, *brĭs''l*
brochure, *brô-shōōr'*
brogan, *brō'găn*
bromide, *brō'mĭd*
bromine, *brō'mēn*
bronchitis, *brŏn-kī'tĭs*
brusque (brusk), *brŭsk*
buffet (sideboard), *bŏŏ-fā'*
bungalow, *bŭng'gȧ-lō*
buoy, *boi*
buoyant, *bōō'yȧnt*
bureaucracy, *bû-rŏk'rȧ-sĭ*
burlesque, *bûr-lĕsk'*
bursar, *bûr'sẽr*
business, *bĭz'nĕs*
butcher, *bŏŏch'ẽr*
butte, *būt*

cabal, *kȧ-băl'*
caballero, *kä'bäl-yā'rō*
cabaret, *kăb'ȧ-rā'*
cache, *kăsh*
cadaver, *kȧ-dăv'ẽr*
café, *kȧ'fā'*
cafeteria, *kăf'ê-tēr'ĭ-ȧ*
caisson, *kā'sŭn*
calf, *käf*
caliph, *kā'lĭf*
caliphate, *kăl'ĭ-fāt*
calk, *kôk*
calliope, *kă-lī'ô-pê*
calm, *käm*
caloric, *kȧ-lŏr'ĭk*
calorie, *kăl'ô-rĭ*
calve, *käv*
calyx, *kā'lĭks*
camembert, *kăm'ĕm-bâr'*
campanile, *kăm'pȧ-nē'lê*
cancel, *kăn'sĕl*
candelabra, *kăn'dê-lä'brȧ*
canine, *kā'nīn*
cañon, *kăn'yŭn*
cant, *kănt*
can't, *känt*
cantilever, *kăn'tĭ-lē'vẽr*
cantonment, *kăn-tŏn'mĕnt*
capitulate, *kȧ-pĭch'ů-lāt*
capon, *kā'pŏn*
caprice, *kȧ-prēs'*
carafe, *kȧ-răf'*
carburetor, *kär'bû-rā'tẽr*
caricature, *kăr'ĭ-kȧ-chûr*
carillon, *kăr'ĭ-lŏn*
carrousel, *kăr' ŏŏ-sĕl*
cartridge, *kär'trĭj*
cashmere, *kăsh'mẽr*
casino, *kȧ-sē'nō*

caste, *kȧst*
catalogue, *kăt'ȧ-lŏg*
catalpa, *kȧ-tăl'pȧ*
catch, *kăch*
catchup, *kăch'ŭp*
catechize, *kăt'ê-kīz*
catsup, *kăt'sŭp*
caveat, *kā'vê-ăt*
celestial, *sê-lĕs'chȧl*
celibacy, *sĕl'ĭ-bȧ-sĭ*
cello, *chĕl'ō*
celluloid, *sĕl'ů-loid*
cemetery, *sĕm'ê-tẽr-ĭ*
centenary, *sĕn'tê-nẽr'ĭ*
centennial, *sĕn-tĕn'ĭ-ȧl*
centime, *säN'tēm*
century, *sĕn'chů-rĭ*
ceramic, *sê-răm'ĭk*
cerebrum, *sĕr'ê-brŭm*
chagrin, *shȧ-grĭn'*
challis, *shăl'ĭ*
chamois, *shăm'ĭ*
champagne, *shăm-pān'*
chaos, *kā'ŏs*
chaperon, *shăp'ẽr-ōn*
character, *kăr'ăk-tẽr*
chargé d'affaires, *shär'zhā' dȧ'fâr'*
chartreuse, *shär-trûz'*
chassis, *shă'sĭ*
chasten, *chās''n*
chastise, *chăs-tīz'*
chastisement, *chăs'tĭz-mĕnt*
chatelaine, *shăt'ê-lān*
chauffeur, *shō'fûr*
chef, *shĕf*
chemise, *shê-mēz'*
chemisette, *shĕm'ĭ-zĕt*
chenille, *shê-nēl'*
chestnut, *chĕs'nŭt*
cheviot, *shĕv'ĭ-ŭt*
chew, *chōō*
chic, *shēk*
chicane, *shĭ-kān'*
chicken, *chĭk'ĕn; -ĭn*
chiffon, *shĭ-fŏn'*
chiffonier, *shĭf'ô-nẽr'*
children, *chĭl'drĕn*
chimera, *kĭ-mē'rȧ*
chirography, *kĭ-rŏg'rȧ-fĭ*
chiropodist, *kĭ-rŏp'ô-dĭst*
chisel, *chĭz''l*
chocolate, *chŏk'ô-lĭt*
choleric, *kŏl'ẽr-ĭk*
chorister, *kŏr'ĭs-tẽr*
chorus, *kō'rŭs*
christen, *krĭs''n*
chyle, *kīl*
chyme, *kĭm*
cinchona, *sĭn-kō'na*
cinematograph, *sĭn'ê-măt'ô-grȧf*
circuit, *sûr'kĭt*
circuitous, *sẽr-kū'ĭ-tŭs*
citadel, *sĭt'ȧ-dĕl*
civil, *sĭv'ĭl*
civilization, *sĭv'ĭ-lĭ-zā'shŭn*
clairvoyant, *klâr-voi'ănt*
clandestine, *klăn-dĕs'tĭn*
clapboard, *klăb'ẽrd*
clasp, *klȧsp*
class, *klȧs*
cleanly (adj.), *klĕn'lĭ*
cleanly (adv.), *klēn'lĭ*
clematis, *klĕm'ȧ-tĭs*
clew, *klōō*
clientele, *klī'ĕn-tĕl'*
clique, *klēk*
clothes, *klōᴛʜz*
coadjutor, *kō-ăd-jōō'tẽr*
coagulate, *kô-ăg'ů-lāt*
cocaine, *kô-kān'*
coccyx, *kŏk'sĭks*
codeine, *kō'dê-ēn*

coffee, *kŏf'ĭ*
cognac, *kō'nyȧk*
cognizance, *kŏg'nĭ-zȧns*
cognomen, *kŏg-nō'mĕn*
coiffure, *kwä-fūr'*
colander, *kŭl'ȧn-dẽr*
collation, *kŏ-lā'shŭn*
collect (n.), *kŏl'ĕkt*
collect (v.), *kŏ-lĕkt'*
colloquial, *kŏ-lō'kwĭ-ȧl*
colosseum, *kŏl'ŏ-sē'ŭm*
colporteur, *kŏl'pōr'tẽr*
column, *kŏl'ŭm*
columnist, *kŏl'ŭm-nĭst*
combatant, *kŏm'bȧ-tănt*
combine (v.), *kŏm-bīn'*
combine (n.), *kŏm'bĭn*
comeliness, *kŭm'lĭ-nĕs*
comely, *kŭm'lĭ*
comity, *kŏm'ĭ-tĭ*
commiserate, *kŏ-mĭz'ẽr-āt*
communal, *kŏm'ů-nȧl*
commune (v.), *kŏ-mūn'*
commune (n.), *kŏm'ūn*
comparable, *kŏm'pȧ-rȧ-b'l*
complex (n.), *kŏm'plĕks*
complex (adj.), *kŏm-plĕks'*
comport, *kŏm-pōrt'*
compromise, *kŏm'prô-mīz*
comptroller, *kŏn-trōl'ẽr*
concave, *kŏn'kāv*
concerto, *kŏn-chẽr'tō*
conclude, *kŏn-klōōd'*
conclusive, *kŏn-klōō'sĭv*
concourse, *kŏn'kōrs*
concrete (n. and adj.), *kŏn'krēt*
condolence, *kŏn-dō'lĕns*
conduit, *kŏn'dĭt*
confidant, *kŏn'fĭ-dănt'*
confiscate, *kŏn'fĭs-kāt*
congé, *kôN'zhā'*
congenial, *kŏn-jēn'yȧl*
congregate, *kŏng'grê-gȧt*
congress, *kŏng'grĕs*
congruous, *kŏng'grōō-ŭs*
conjure, *kŏn-jōōr'*
connoisseur, *kŏn'ĭ-sûr'*
conquest, *kŏng'kwĕst*
conscientious, *kŏn'shĭ-ĕn'shŭs*
considerable, *kŏn-sĭd'ẽr-ȧ-b'l*
consignee, *kŏn'sī-nē'*
conspiracy, *kŏn-spĭr'ȧ-sĭ*
constable, *kŭn'stȧ-b'l*
consul, *kŏn'sŭl*
consummate, (v.) *kŏn'sŭ-māt*
contemplate, *kŏn'tĕm-plāt*
contemplative, *kŏn-tĕm'plȧ-tĭv*
continuity, *kŏn'tĭ-nū'ĭ-tĭ*
contractor, *kŏn'trăk-tẽr*
contrary, *kŏn'trẽr-ĭ*
contumely, *kŏn'tû-mê-lĭ*
conversant, *kŏn'vẽr-sȧnt*
coquetry, *kō'kê-trĭ*
coral, *kŏr'ȧl*
cordial, *kôr'jȧl*
cornet, *kôr'nĕt*
corolla, *kô-rŏl'ȧ*
corps, *kōr*
corral, *kŏ-răl'*
corridor, *kŏr'ĭ-dôr*
corrugate, *kŏr'ŏŏ-gȧt*
cortege, *kôr-tĕzh'*
cosmetic, *kŏz-mĕt'ĭk*
costume (n.), *kŏs'tūm*
costumer, *kŏs-tūm'ẽr*
cotillion, *kô-tĭl'yŭn*
coup, *kōō*
coupé, *kōō'pā'*
coupon, *kōō'pŏn*
courier, *kŏŏr'ĭ-ẽr*
courteous, *kûr'tê-ŭs*
courtier, *kōr'tĭ-ẽr*

cousin, *kŭz″n*
couturier, *kōō'tü'ryā'*
covetous, *kŭv'ĕ-tŭs*
crabbed, *krăb'ĕd*
cranberry, *krăn'bĕr-ĭ*
crèche, *krāsh*
credence, *krē'dĕns*
credulous, *krĕd'ŭ-lŭs*
creek, *krēk*
crêpe de Chine, *krāp'dĕ-shēn'*
crescendo, *krĕ-shĕn'dō*
crew, *krōō*
crucial, *krōō'shăl*
cruel, *krōō'ĕl*
crux, *krŭks*
cuisine, *kwĕ-zēn'*
culinary, *kū'lĭ-nĕr'ĭ*
culture, *kŭl'chŭr*
cuneiform, *kû-nē'ĭ-fôrm*
cupboard, *kŭb'ĕrd*
cupola, *kū'pô-là*
curator, *kû-rā'tĕr*
cycle, *sī'k'l*
cynosure, *sī'nô-shōōr*

dachshund, *däks'hōōnt'*
daguerreotype, *dà-gĕr'ô-tīp*
dahlia, *dăl'yà*
damage, *dăm'ĭj*
dance, *dàns*
data, *dā'tà*
daub, *dôb*
deaf, *dĕf*
debacle, *dĕ-bä'k'l*
debauch, *dĕ-bôch'*
debenture, *dĕ-bĕn'chûr*
débris, *dĕ-brē'*
début, *dā'bū*
debutante, *dĕb'û-tänt'*
decade, *dĕk'ād*
decadence, *dĕ-kā'dĕns*
decent, *dē'sĕnt*
décolleté, *dā-kŏl'ĕ-tā; F. dà'kôl'tā'*
decorous, *dĕk'ô-rŭs*
dedicatory, *dĕd'ĭ-kà-tô'rĭ*
defalcate, *dĕ-făl'kāt*
defamation, *dĕf'à-mā'shŭn*
deficit, *dĕf'ĭ-sĭt*
deign, *dān*
delicatessen, *dĕl'ĭ-kà-tĕs'ĕn*
delirious, *dĕ-lĭr'ĭ-ŭs*
de luxe, *dĕ lōōks'*
demagogic, *dĕm'à-gŏj'ĭk*
demi-tasse, *dĕm'ĭ-tăs'*
democratize, *dĕ-mŏk'rà-tīz*
demon, *dē'mŭn*
demonetization,
   dĕ-mŏn'ĕ-tĭ-zā'shŭn
demurrage, *dĕ-mŭr'ĭj*
dénouement, *dà-nōō-mäN'*
depths, *dĕpths*
derisive, *dĕ-rī'sĭv*
deshabille, *dĕz'à-bēl'*
desist, *dĕ-zĭst'*
despicable, *dĕs'pĭ-kà-b'l*
dessert, *dĭ-zûrt'*
destine, *dĕs'tĭn*
detail, *dĕ-tāl'*
detonation, *dĕt'ô-nā'shŭn*
detour, *dĕ'tōōr*
devoir, *dĕ-vwär'*
devotee, *dĕv'ô-tē'*
dew, *dū*
dexterous, *dĕk'stĕr-ŭs*
diagnostician, *dī'ăg-nŏs-tĭsh'ăn*
diastole, *dī-ăs'tô-lē*
dictator, *dĭk-tā'tĕr*
dictionary, *dĭk'shŭn-ĕr'ĭ*
diesel, *dē'zĕl*
dietetics, *dī'ĕ-tĕt'ĭks*
dietitian, *dī'ĕ-tĭsh'ăn*

different, *dĭf'ĕr-ĕnt*
diffuse (adj.), *dĭ-fūs'*
diffuse (v.), *dĭ-fūz'*
digest (v.), *dĭ-jĕst'*
digest (n.), *dī'jĕst*
digestion, *dĭ-jĕs'chŭn*
digitalis, *dĭj'ĭ-tăl'ĭs*
digraph, *dī'gràf*
dilettante, *dĭl'ĕ-tăn'tĭ*
diocese, *dī'ô-sēs*
diphtheria, *dĭf-thĕr'ĭ-à*
diphthong, *dĭf'thŏng*
diploma, *dĭ-plō'mà*
direct, *dĭ-rĕkt'*
disaster, *dĭ-zàs'tĕr*
disburse, *dĭs-bûrs'*
discern, *dĭ-zûrn'*
discipline, *dĭs'ĭ-plĭn*
discourse, *dĭs-kōrs'*
discretion, *dĭs-krĕsh'ŭn*
disdain, *dĭs-dān'*
disease, *dĭ-zēz'*
dishabille, *dĭs'à-bēl'*
dishevel, *dĭ-shĕv'ĕl*
dispersion, *dĭs-pûr'shŭn*
disputant, *dĭs'pù-tănt*
district, *dĭs'trĭkt*
divan, *dī'văn*
diverge, *dĭ-vûrj'*
divulge, *dĭ-vŭlj'*
docile, *dŏs'ĭl*
domain, *dô-mān'*
domicile, *dŏm'ĭ-sĭl*
donkey, *dŏng'kĭ*
douche, *dōōsh*
drama, *drä'mà*
drawer, *drô'ĕr*
dromedary, *drŏm'ĕ-dĕr'ĭ*
drought, *drout*
drowned, *dround*
dubious, *dū'bĭ-ŭs*
due, *dū*
duty, *dū'tĭ*
dyspepsia, *dĭs-pĕp'shà*

eau de cologne, *ō dĕ kô-lōn'*
ebullition, *ĕb'ŭ-lĭsh'ŭn*
éclat, *ā'klä'*
economic, *ē-kō-nŏm'ĭk*
eczema, *ĕk'zĕ-mà*
edible, *ĕd'ĭ-b'l*
education, *ĕd'û-kā'shŭn*
effigy, *ĕf'ĭ-jĭ*
effort, *ĕf'ĕrt*
ego, *ē'gō*
egret, *ē'grĕt*
electoral, *ĕ-lĕk'tĕr-ăl*
electrometer, *ē-lĕk'trŏm'ĕ-tĕr*
elegiac, *ĕ-lē'jĭ-ăc*
eleven, *ĕ-lĕv'ĕn*
élite, *à'lēt'*
elm, *ĕlm;* not *ĕl'ŭm*
elongate, *ĕ-lŏng'găt*
embrasure, *ĕm-brā'zhĕr*
emeritus, *ĕ-mĕr'ĭ-tŭs*
emolument, *ĕ-mŏl'û-mĕnt*
employee, *ĕm-ploi'ē*
enchant, *ĕn-chànt'*
encore, *äng-kōr', äng'kôr*
encyclical, *ĕn-sī'klĭ-kăl;*
   ĕn-sĭk'lĭ-kăl
endive, *ĕn'dīv*
enema, *ĕn'ĕ-mà*
enfranchise, *ĕn-frăn'chīz*
engine, *ĕn'jĭn*
ennui, *än'wē*
en route, *än rōōt'*
ensemble, *än-sŏm'b'l*
ensign (n.), *ĕn'sīn*
entente, *äN'tänt'*
entree, *än'trā*
enunciate, *ĕ-nŭn'shĭ-āt*

envelope (n.), *ĕn'vĕ-lōp*
epaulet, *ĕp'ô-lĕt*
epistle, *ĕ-pĭs″l*
epitome, *ĕ-pĭt'ô-mĕ*
equine, *ē'kwīn*
equitable, *ĕk'wĭ-tà-b'l*
era, *ē'rà*
erasure, *ĕ-rā'zhûr*
erratum, *ĕ-rā'tŭm*
erudite, *ĕr'ōō-dīt*
erysipelas, *ĕr'ĭ-sĭp'ĕ-làs*
esquire, *ĕs-kwīr'*
etiquette, *ĕt'ĭ-kĕt*
etude, *ā'tūd*
euphemism, *ū'fĕ-mĭz'm*
euphonic, *ù-fŏn'ĭk*
evasive, *ĕ-vā'sĭv*
exaggeration, *ĕg-zăj'ĕr-ā'shŭn*
examine, *ĕg-zăm'ĭn*
example, *ĕg-zăm'p'l*
excise, *ĕk-sīz'*
exemplary, *ĕg-zĕm'plà-rĭ'*
exhalation, *ĕks'hà-lā'shŭn*
exist, *ĕg-zĭst'*
exit, *ĕk'sĭt*
exogenous, *ĕks-ŏj'ĕ-nŭs*
exorbitant, *ĕg-zôr'bĭ-tănt*
expedient, *ĕks-pē'dĭ-ĕnt*
exponent, *ĕks-pō'nĕnt*
exquisite, *ĕks'kwĭ-zĭt*
extant, *ĕks'tănt*
extempore, *ĕks-tĕm'pô-rĕ*
extraordinary, *ĕks-trôr'dĭ-nĕr'ĭ*

facet, *făs'ĕt*
facile, *făs'ĭl*
facsimile, *făk-sĭm'ĭ-lē*
factory, *făk'tŏ-rĭ*
falcon, *fôl'kŭn*
fallen, *fôl'ĕn*
falsetto, *fôl-sĕt'ō*
family, *făm'ĭ-lĭ*
fancy, *făn'sĭ*
far, *fär*
fast, *fàst*
faucet, *fô'sĕt*
favorite, *fā'vĕr-ĭt*
fecund, *fĕk'ŭnd*
fellow, *fĕl'ō*
feminine, *fĕm'ĭ-nĭn*
fête, *fāt*
fiancé, *fē'än-sā'*
fiancée, *fē'än-sā'*
fiasco, *fĕ-ăs'kō*
fichu, *fĭsh'ōō*
fidelity, *fī-dĕl'ĭ-tĭ*
figure, *fĭg'ûr*
fillet, *fĭl'ĕt*
film, *fĭlm*
finale, *fĕ-nä'lā*
finance, *fĭ-năns'*
financier, *fĭn'ăn-sēr'*
finis, *fī'nĭs*
fleur-de-lis, *flûr'dĕ-lē'*
flew, *flōō*
floral, *flō'răl*
florid, *flŏr'ĭd*
florin, *flŏr'ĭn*
flute, *flōōt*
food, *fōōd*
forbade, *fŏr-băd'*
forehead, *fŏr'ĕd*
forest, *fŏr'ĕst*
formidable, *fôr'mĭ-dà-b'l*
forum, *fō'rŭm*
fountain, *foun'tĭn*
foyer, *foi'à*
fragile, *frăj'ĭl*
frappé, *frà'pā'*
fraternize, *frăt'ĕr-nīz*
fricassee, *frĭk'à-sē'*
friendship, *frĕnd'shĭp*

frontier, *frŭn-tēr'*
fuel, *fū'ĕl*
fulminate, *fŭl'mĭ-nāt*
funereal, *fū-nēr'ê-ăl*
fungi, *fŭn'jī*
furniture, *fûr'nĭ-chûr*
fusillade, *fū'zĭ-lād'*

gala, *gā'là*
gallery, *găl'ēr-ĭ*
gangrene, *găng'grēn*
gape (v.), *gāp*
garage, *gà-räzh'*
garrulous, *găr'ū-lŭs*
gaseous, *găs'ê-ŭs*
gastritis, *găs-trī'tĭs*
gather, *găTH'ēr*
gazetteer, *găz'ĕ-tēr'*
geisha, *gā'shà*
genealogy, *jĕn'ê-ăl'ô-jĭ*
generally, *jĕn'ēr-ăl-ĭ*
genii, *jē'nĭ-ī*
genre, *zhäN'r'*
gentleman, *jĕn't'l-măn*
genuine, *jĕn'û-ĭn*
geography, *jê-ŏg'rà-fĭ*
geranium, *jê-rā'nĭ-ŭm*
gerrymander, *gĕr'ĭ-măn'dēr*
gerund, *jĕr'ŭnd*
gesture, *jĕs'chûr*
get, *gĕt*
ghastly, *gàst'lĭ*
ghoul, *gōōl*
gibber, *jĭb'ēr*
gibbet, *jĭb'ĕt*
gin, *jĭn*
giraffe, *jĭ-ráf'*
girl, *gûrl*
gist, *jĭst*
gladiolus, *glăd'ĭ-ō'lŭs*
glycerin, *glĭs'ēr-ĭn*
gneiss, *nīs*
golf, *gŏlf*
gondola, *gŏn'dô-là*
gone, *gŏn*
gospel, *gŏs'pĕl*
gourmet, *gōōr'mā*
government, *gŭv'ērn-mĕnt*
granary, *grăn'à-rĭ*
granddaughter, *grănd'dô'tēr*
grandeur, *grăn'dûr*
grasp, *gràsp*
grass, *gràs*
gratis, *grā'tĭs*
grimace, *grĭ-mās'*
grimy, *grīm'ĭ*
gripe, *grīp*
grisly, *grĭz'lĭ*
grotesque, *grô-tĕsk'*
grovel, *grŏv''l*
guardian, *gär'dĭ-ăn*
guillotine (n.), *gĭl'ô-tēn*
gymnasium, *jĭm-nā'zĭ-ŭm*
gyroscope, *jī'rô-skōp*

habitant, *hăb'ĭ-tănt*
habitué, *hà-bĭch'ŭ-ā'*
hacienda, *ä-syĕn'dä*
handbook, *hănd'bōōk'*
handkerchief, *hăng'kēr-chĭf*
hangar, *hăng'ēr*
harass, *hăr'ăs*
harbinger, *här'bĭn-jēr*
harem, *hā'rĕm*
hasten, *hās''n*
haunt, *hônt*
hearth, *härth*
heaven, *hĕv'ĕn*
hedonism, *hē'dŏn-ĭz'm*
hegemony, *hê-jĕm'ô-nĭ*
height, *hīt*
heinous, *hā'nŭs*

helm, *hĕlm*
hemoglobin, *hē'mô-glō'bĭn*
heroine, *hĕr'ô-ĭn*
hesitate, *hĕz'ĭ-tāt*
heteronym, *hĕt'ēr-ô-nĭm'*
hieroglyphic, *hī'ēr-ô-glĭf'ĭk*
highwayman, *hī'wā'măn*
hilarious, *hĭ-lâr'ĭ-ŭs*
hirsute, *hûr'sūt*
history, *hĭs'tô-rĭ*
hoist, *hoist*
holocaust, *hŏl'ô-kôst*
holograph, *hŏl'ô-gràf*
homage, *hŏm'ĭj*
homeopathic, *hō'mê-ô-păth'ĭk*
homestead, *hōm'stĕd*
homogeneous, *hō'mô-jē'nê-ŭs*
homonym, *hŏm'ô-nĭm*
honest, *ŏn'ĕst*
honorable, *ŏn'ēr-à-b'l*
honorarium, *ŏn'ô-râr'ĭ-ŭm*
hoof, *hōōf*
horrid, *hŏr'ĭd*
horse-radish, *hôrs'răd'ĭsh*
hospitable, *hŏs'pĭ-tà-b'l*
hovel, *hŭv'ĕl*
humble, *hŭm'b'l*
humor, *hū'mēr*
hundred, *hŭn'drĕd*
hydraulics, *hī-drô'lĭks*
hydrometer, *hī-drŏm'ê-tēr*
hygiene, *hī'jēn*
hygienic, *hī'jĭ-ĕn'ĭk*
hypocrisy, *hĭ-pŏk'rĭ-sĭ*
hypodermic, *hĭ-pô-dûr'mĭk*
hysteria, *hĭs-tēr'ĭ-à*
hysterical, *hĭs-tĕr'ĭ-kăl*

idea, *ī-dē'à*
ideal, *ī-dē'ăl*
ideology, *īd'ê-ŏl'ô-jĭ*
idiosyncrasy, *ĭd'ĭ-ô-sĭng'krà-sĭ*
ignoramus, *ĭg'nô-rā'mŭs*
illusory, *ĭ-lū'sô-rĭ*
illustrate, *ĭl'ŭs-trāt*
imbroglio, *ĭm-brōl'yō*
impious, *ĭm'pĭ-ŭs*
implacable, *ĭm-plā'kà-b'l*
importune, *ĭm'pôr-tūn'*
impotent, *ĭm'pô-tĕnt*
improvise, *ĭm'prō-vĭz*
inaugurate, *ĭn-ô'gù-rāt*
incise, *ĭn-sīz'*
incisive, *ĭn-sī'sĭv*
incognito, *ĭn-kŏg'nĭ-tō*
incomparable, *ĭn-kŏm'pà-rà-b'l*
incredulous, *ĭn-krĕj'û-lŭs*
incursion, *ĭn-kûr'zhŭn*
indisputable, *ĭn-dĭs'pù-tà-b'l*
industry, *ĭn'dŭs-trĭ*
inertia, *ĭn-ûr'shà*
inexplicable, *ĭn-ĕks'plĭ-kà-b'l*
inextricably, *ĭn-ĕks'.trĭ-kà-blĭ*
infamous, *ĭn'fà-mŭs*
infantile, *ĭn'făn-tīl*
influence, *ĭn'flōō-ĕns*
ingénue, *ăN'zhā'nū'*
initiative, *ĭ-nĭsh'ĭ-ā'tĭv*
innocent, *ĭn'ô-sĕnt*
inopportune, *ĭn-ŏp'ôr-tūn'*
inquiry, *ĭn-kwīr'ĭ*
insatiable, *ĭn-sā'shĭ-à-b'l*
insect, *ĭn'sĕkt*
insignia, *ĭn-sĭg'nĭ-à*
instead, *ĭn-stĕd'*
insulate, *ĭn'sù-lāt*
integer, *ĭn'tê-jēr*
interesting, *ĭn'tēr-ĕst-ĭng*
intermezzo, *ĭn'-tēr-mĕd'zō*
international, *ĭn'tēr-năsh'ŭn-ăl*
interpellate, *ĭn'tēr-pĕl'āt*
interpellation, *ĭn'tēr-pĕ-lā'shŭn*

interpolate, *ĭn-tûr'pô-lāt*
intricacy, *ĭn'trĭ-kà-sĭ*
intrigue, *ĭn-trēg'*
inundate, *ĭn'ŭn-dāt*
inveigle, *ĭn-vē'g'l*
iodine, *ī'ô-dīn*
irony, *ī'rô-nĭ*
irrefragable, *ĭ-rĕf'rà-gà-b'l*
irrefutable, *ĭ-rĕf'û-tà-b'l*
irremediable, *ĭr'rê-mē'dĭ-à-b'l*
irrevocable, *ĭ-rĕv'ô-kà-b'l*
isinglass, *ī'zĭng-glàs'*
isolate, *ī'sô-lāt*
italic, *ĭ-tăl'ĭk*
ivory, *ī'vô-rĭ*

jardiniére, *jär'dĭ-nēr'*
jocose, *jô-kōs'*
jostling, *jŏs'lĭng*
judgment, *jŭj'mĕnt*
jugular, *jŭg'ù-lēr*
jujitsu, *jōō-jĭt'sōō*
junta, *jŭn'tà*, pop. *hŭn'tà*
just, *jŭst*
jute, *jōōt*
juvenile, *jōō'vê-nĭl*

kaleidoscope. *kà-lī'dô-skōp*
kept, *kĕpt*
kettle, *kĕt''l*
khaki, *kăk'ĭ*
khedive, *kĕ-dēv'*
kiln, *kĭl*
kimono, *kĭ-mō'nō*
kindergarten, *kĭn'dēr-gär't'n*
kinetoscope, *kĭ-nē'tô-skōp*
kiosk, *kê-ŏsk'*
kismet, *kĭz'mĕt*
kitchen, *kĭch'ĕn*
knout, *nout*

laboratory, *lăb'ô-rà-tō'-rĭ*
laborer, *lā'bēr-ēr*
lamentable, *lăm'ĕn-tà-b'l*
language, *lăng'gwĭj*
largess, *lär'jĕs*
laryngitis, *lăr'ĭn-jī'tĭs*
larynx, *lăr'ĭngks*
laths, *làTHz*
lattice, *lăt'ĭs*
laudanum, *lô'dà-nŭm*
laugh, *läf*
lava, *lä'và*
lavaliere, *lăv'à-lēr'*
layette, *lā-ĕt'*
leaped, *lĕpt*
leapt, *lĕpt*
learned (adj.), *lûr'nĕd*
learned (v.), *lûrnd*
legate, *lĕg'ĭt*
legend, *lĕj'ĕnd*
legislature, *lĕj'ĭs-lā'chûr*
leisure, *lē'zhēr*
length, *lĕngth*
lenient, *lē'nĭ-ĕnt*
leper, *lĕp'ēr*
lese majesty, *lēz măj'ĕs-tĭ*
lethal, *lē'thăl*
lettuce, *lĕt'ĭs*
leverage, *lē'vēr-àj*
liaison, *lē'ā-zŏn'*
libel, *lī'bĕl*
libertine. *lĭb'ēr-tēn*
libido, *lĭ-bī'dō*, *lĭ-bē'dō*
librarian, *lī-brâr'ĭ-ăn*
library, *lī'brĕr'ĭ*
lichen, *lī'kĕn*
licorice, *lĭk'ô-rĭs*
lief, *lēf*
lilac, *lī'lăk*
limn, *lĭm*
lineament, *lĭn'ê-à-mĕnt*
lingerie, *lăN'zh'-rē'*

linoleum, lĭ-nō'lē-ŭm
linotype, līn'ô-tīp'
liqueur, lē'kûr'
liquor, lĭk'ẽr
literati, lĭt'ē-rā'tī
literature, lĭt'ẽr-à-chûr
lithographer, lĭ-thŏg'rà-fẽr
livelong, lĭv'lŏng'
loath, lōth
loathe, lōTH
loggia, lŏj'à
longevity, lŏn-jĕv'ĭ-tĭ
long-lived, lŏng'lĭvd'
lower (threaten), lou'ẽr
lure, lūr
lurid, lū'rĭd
lyceum, lī-sē'ŭm

machination, măk'ĭ-nā'shŭn
mackerel, măk'ẽr-ĕl
madras, mà-drás'
madre, mä'drà
maestro, mä-ĕ'strô
magazine, măg'à-zēn'
magna charta, măg'nà kär'tà
magnolia, măg-nō'lĭ-à
malaria, mà-lâr'ĭ-à
malefactor, măl'ē-făk'tẽr
malign, mà-līn'
mallow, măl'ō
malpractice, măl-prăk'tĭs
mama, mä'mà
mañana, mä-nyä'nä
mandamus, măn-dā'mŭs
mandatory, măn'dà-tō'-rĭ
mange, mānj
mania, mā'nĭ-à
maniacal, mà-nī'à-kăl
manor, măn'ẽr
manufactory, măn'û-făk'tô-rĭ
maraschino, măr'à-skē'nō
margarine, mär'jà-rēn
maritime, mär'ĭ-tīm
marquis, mär'kwĭs
marshmallow, märsh'măl'ō
masculine, măs'kû-lĭn
mask, màsk
massacred, măs'à-kẽrd
massage, mà-säzh'
masseur, mă-sûr'
masseuse, mă-sûz'
maté (drink), mä'tā
matinée, măt'ĭ-nā'
matron, mā'trŭn
mattress, măt'rĕs
mausoleum, mô'sô-lē'ŭm
mauve, mōv
mavournin, mà-vōōr'nēn
mayonnaise, mā'ô-nāz'
mayoralty, mā'ẽr-ăl-tĭ
measure, mĕzh'ẽr
mechanician, mĕk'à-nĭsh'ăn
medicament, mē-dĭk'à-mĕnt
medicinal, mē-dĭs'ĭ-năl
medieval, mē'dĭ-ē'văl
mediocre, mē'dĭ-ō'kẽr
megrim, mē'grĭm
melee mā'lā
memoir, mĕm'wär
memory, mĕm'ô-rĭ
ménage, mà-näzh'
meningitis, mĕn'ĭn-jī'tĭs
menu, mĕn'û
mercantile, mûr'kăn-tĭl
mere (lake), mēr
meringue, mē-răng'
mesa, mā'sä
mésalliance, mā'zàl'yàNs'
mesdames, mā'dàm'
mesmerism, mĕz'mẽr-ĭz'm
messieurs, mĕs'yẽrz
metallurgy, mĕt''l-ûr-jĭ

metric, mĕt'rĭk
mezzo, mĕd'zō
microscopic, mī'krô-skŏp'ĭk
microscopy, mī-krŏs'kô-pĭ
migraine, mī'grān
militia, mĭ-lĭsh'à
mime, mīm
mineralogy, mĭn'ẽr-ăl'ô-jĭ
mirage, mĭ-räzh'
misanthrope, ĭs'ăn-thrōp
miscellany, mĭs'ē-lā-nĭ
mischievous, mĭs'chĭ-vŭs
misconstrue, mĭs'kŏn-strōō'
miserable, mĭz'ẽr-à-b'l
misogynist, mĭ-sŏj'ĭ-nĭst
mitten, mĭt''n
mnemonics, nē-mŏn'ĭks
mock, mŏk
moderate (adj.), mŏd'ẽr-ĭt
modiste, mô'dēst'
modus vivendi, mō'dŭs vĭ-vĕn'dī
moiré, mwä'rā'
monetary, mŏn'ē-tẽr'ĭ
monogram, mŏn'ô-grăm
monologue, mŏn'ô-lŏg
monomania, mŏn'ô-mā'nĭ-à
monsieur, mē-syû'
monsignor, mŏn-sē'nyôr
morale, mô-rál'
mountain, moun'tĭn
mountainous, moun'tĭ-nŭs
municipal, mù-nĭs'ĭ-păl
museum, mù-zē'ŭm
mushroom, mŭsh'rōōm
musicale, mū'zĭ-kàl'
muskellunge, mŭs'kē-lŭnj
muskmelon, mŭsk'mĕl'ŭn
mustache, mŭs-tàsh'
mystery, mĭs'tẽr-ĭ
mythology, mĭ-thŏl'ô-jĭ

naïve, nä-ēv'
nape, năp
napery, nā'pẽr-ĭ
naphtha, năf'thà
nasal, nā'zăl
nascent, năs'ĕnt
natatorium, nā'tà-tō'rĭ-ŭm
natural, năch'û-răl
nature, nā'chûr
nausea, nô'sē-à
necessarily, nĕs'ē-sẽr'ĭ-lĭ
necrology, nē-krŏl'ô-jĭ
nee, nā
negligee, nĕg'lĭ-zhā'
nephritis, nē-frī'tĭs
nepotism, nĕp'ô-tĭz'm
nervine, nûr'vēn
neuralgia, nû-răl'jĭ-à
neuritis, nû-rī'tĭs
neurosis, nû-rō'sĭs
nicety, nī'sē-tĭ
niche, nĭch
nirvana, nĭr-vä'nà
nomad, nō'măd
nom de plume, nŏm'dē plōōm'
nominative, nŏm'ĭ-nà-tĭv
nonchalant, nŏn'shà-lănt
nonpareil, nŏn'pà-rĕl'
nostalgia, nŏs-tăl'jĭ-à
notice, nō'tĭs
novice, nŏv'ĭs
noxious, nŏk'shŭs
nuance, nü'äns'
nuisance, nū'sáns
nuncio, nŭn'shĭ-ô
nuptial, nŭp'shăl
nymph, nĭmf

oasis, ô-ā'sĭs
oaths, ōTHz
oatmeal, ōt'mēl'

obdurate, ŏb'dû-rât
obedient, ô-bē'dĭ-ĕnt
obeisance, ô-bā'sáns
obelisk, ŏb'ē-lĭsk
obesity, ô-bēs'ĭ-tĭ
obiter dicta, ŏb'ĭ-tẽr dĭk'tà
oblique, ŏb-lēk'; military, lĭk'
obscenity, ŏb-sĕn'ĭ-tĭ
occult, ŏ-kŭlt'
octave, ŏk'tāv
office, ŏf'ĭs
often, ŏf'ĕn
olden, ōl'dĕn
oleander, ō'lē-ăn'dẽr
oleomargarine, ō'lē-ô-mär'jà-rēn
olfactory, ŏl-făk'tô-rĭ
on, ŏn
onerous, ŏn'ẽr-ŭs
opponent, ŏ-pō'nĕnt
oral, ō'răl
orange, ŏr'ĕnj
orchestra, ôr'kĕs-trà
orchestral, ôr-kĕs'trăl
orchid, ôr'kĭd
ordeal, ôr-dēl'
ordinance, ôr'dĭ-năns
ordinarily, ôr'dĭ-nẽr'ĭ-lĭ
ordnance, ôrd'năns
orgy, ôr'jĭ
oriental, ō'rĭ-ĕn'tăl
orifice, ŏr'ĭ-fĭs
oriole, ō'rĭ-ōl
orthoepist, ôr'thô-ĕp'ĭst
orthopedic, ôr'thô-pē'dĭk
ostler, ŏs'lẽr
overalls, ō'vẽr-ôlz'

pacifist, păs'ĭ-fĭst
padre, pä'drĭ
padrone, pä-drō'nà
pageant, păj'ĕnt
pagination, păj'ĭ-nā'shŭn
pajama, pà-jä'mà
palatial, pà-lā'shăl
palette, păl'ĕt
palladium, pà-lā'dĭ-ŭm
palm, päm
palmistry, päm'ĭs-trĭ
paltry, pôl'trĭ
panacea, păn'à-sē'à
panegyric, păn'ē-jĭr'ĭk
panorama, păn'ô-rä'mà
papa, pä'pà
papier-mâché, pä'pẽr-mà-shā'
papyrus, pà-pī'rŭs
paraffin, păr'ă-fĭn
paramour, păr'à-mōōr
parasitic, păr'à-sĭt'ĭk
parasol, păr'à-sŏl
paresis, pà-rē'sĭs
parliament, pär'lĭ-mĕnt
parotid, pà-rŏt'ĭd
participle, pär'tĭ-sĭ-p'l
particularly, pẽr-tĭk'û-lär-lĭ
partner, pärt'nẽr
partridge, pär'trĭj
passé, pä-sā'
pasteurize, pàs'tẽr-īz
path, pàth
pathos, pā'thŏs
patience, pā'shĕns
patio, pä'tĭ-ō
patois, păt'wä
patriot, pā'trĭ-ŭt
patrol, pà-trōl'
patron, pā'trŭn
pecan, pē-kăn'
peculiar, pē-kūl'yẽr
peculiarity, pē-kū'lĭ-ăr'ĭ-tĭ
pedagogue, pĕd'à-gŏg
pedagogy, pĕd'à-gō'jĭ
pedal, pĕd'ăl

Correct Pronunciation

8]

pedometer, *pê-dŏm'ê-tēr*
penal, *pē'năl*
penchant, *pän'shäN'; pĕn'chănt*
penitentiary, *pĕn'ĭ-tĕn'shà-rĭ*
peon, *pē'ŏn*
peony, *pē'ô-nĭ*
peremptory, *pēr-ĕmp'tô-rĭ*
pergola, *pûr'gô-là*
perhaps, *pēr-hăps'*
peril, *pĕr'ĭl*
period, *pēr'ĭ-ŭd*
periodic, *pēr'ĭ-ŏd'ĭk*
peritoneum, *pĕr'ĭ-tô-nē'ŭm*
peritonitis, *pĕr'ĭ-tô-nī'tĭs*
perpetuity, *pûr'pê-tū'ĭ-tĭ*
persist, *pēr-sĭst'*
perspicuity, *pûr'spĭ-kū'ĭ-tĭ*
perspiration, *pûr'spĭ-rā'shŭn*
peso, *pā'sō*
petard, *pê-tärd'*
petite, *pĕ-tēt'*
petrel, *pĕt'rĕl*
pharmaceutic, *fär'mà-sū'tĭk*
pharyngitis, *făr'in-jī'tĭs*
phial, *fī'ăl*
philately, *fĭ-lăt'ê-lĭ*
philology, *fĭ-lŏl'ô-jĭ*
phlegmatic, *flĕg-măt'ĭk*
photogravure, *fō'tô-grà-vūr'*
phraseology, *frā'zê-ŏl'ô-jĭ*
physicist, *fĭz'ĭ-sĭst*
pianist, *pĭ-ăn'ĭst*
piano, *pĭ-än'ō*
picture, *pĭk'chŭr*
pillow, *pĭl'ō*
pincers, *pĭn'sērz*
piquant, *pē'kănt*
pique, *pēk*
piqué, *pê-kā'*
pistachio, *pĭs-tăsh'ĭ-ō*
pith, *pĭth*
placard, *plăk'ärd*
placer, *plăs'ēr*
plagiarist, *plā'jĭ-à-rĭst*
plague, *plāg*
plait, *plāt*
plant, *plànt*
plebiscite, *plĕb'ĭ-sĭt*
plenary, *plē'nà-rĭ*
plethora, *plĕth'ô-rà*
plural, *plŏŏr'ăl*
pneumonia, *nŭ-mō'nĭ-à*
poem, *pō'ĕm*
poignant, *poin'yănt*
poilu, *pwà'lü'*
poinsettia, *poin-sĕt'ĭ-à*
poll, *pōl*
polonaise, *pō'lô-nāz'*
pomegranate, *pŏm'grăn'ĭt*
poniard, *pŏn'yērd*
poor, *pŏŏr*
porcine, *pôr'sīn*
portiere, *pôr'tyär'*
posse, *pŏs'ê*
posterior, *pŏs-tēr'ĭ-ēr*
postern, *pōs'tērn*
posthumous, *pŏs'chŭ-mŭs*
potato, *pô-tā'tō*
potpourri, *pō-pŏŏ-rē'*
precedence, *prê-sēd'ĕns*
precedent (adj.), *prê-sēd'ĕnt*
precedent (n.), *prĕs'ê-dĕnt*
precise, *prê-sīs'*
predicament, *prê-dĭk'à-mĕnt*
preface, *prĕf'ĭs*
preferable, *prĕf'ēr-à-b'l*
prelate, *prĕl'ĭt*
prelude (n.), *prĕl'ūd*
premature, *prē'mà-tūr'*
premier, *prē'mĭ-ēr*
premise (n.), *prĕm'ĭs*
preparatory, *prê-păr'à-tō-rĭ*

presentation, *prĕz'ĕn-tā'shŭn*
president, *prĕz'ĭ-dĕnt*
presidio, *prê-sĭd'ĭ-ō*
presumptuous, *prê-zŭmp'chû-ŭs*
pretense, *prê-tĕns'*
pretext, *prē'tĕkst*
pretty, *prĭt'ĭ*
prima donna, *prē'mà dŏn'à*
prima facie, *prī'mà fā'shĭ-ē*
primates, *prī-mā'tēz*
pristine, *prĭs'tĭn*
prodigious, *prô-dĭj'ŭs*
produce (n.), *prŏd'ūs*
produce (v.), *prô-dūs'*
profile, *prō'fīl*
profuse, *prô-fūs'*
program, *prō'grăm*
progress (n.), *prŏg'rĕs*
projectile, *prô-jĕk'tĭl*
proletarian, *prō'lê-târ'ĭ-ăn*
promenade, *prŏm'ê-näd'*
pronunciation, *prô-nŭn'sĭ-ā'shŭn*
propinquity, *prô-pĭng'kwĭ-tĭ*
propitious, *prô-pĭsh'ŭs*
pro rata, *prō rā'tà*
prosperous, *prŏs'pēr-ŭs*
protean, *prō'tê-ăn*
protégé, *prō'tê-zhā*
protein, *prō'tê-ĭn*
protestant, *prŏt'ĕs-tănt*
protrude, *prô-trŏŏd'*
prussic, *prŭs'ĭk*
psalm, *säm*
pseudonym, *sū'dô-nĭm*
psychiatry, *sī-kī'à-trĭ*
psychic, *sī'kĭk*
psychosis, *sī-kō'sĭs*
ptomaine, *tō'mān*
publicist, *pŭb'lĭ-sĭst*
puerile, *pū'ēr-ĭl*
pumpkin, *pŭmp'kĭn*
punitive, *pū'nĭ-tĭv*
purée, *pû-rā'*
pursue, *pēr-sū'*
pyrites, *pĭ-rī'tēz*
pyrometer, *pĭ-rŏm'ê-tēr*

quaff, *kwàf*
quarrel, *kwŏr'ĕl*
quarter, *kwôr'tēr*
quatrain, *kwŏt'rān*
quay, *kē*
queue, *kū*
quietus, *kwĭ-e'tŭs*
quinine, *kwĭ'nīn; kwĭ-nēn'*
qui vive, *kê vēv'*
quixotic, *kwĭks'ŏt'ĭk*
quoit, *kwoit*
quorum, *kwō'rŭn*

rabies, *rā'bēz*
raceme, *rà-sēm'*
radish, *răd'ĭsh*
ragout, *rà-gŏŏ'*
raillery, *rāl'ēr-ĭ*
raja, *rä'jà*
rancor, *răng'kēr*
ransack, *răn'săk*
rapier, *rā'pĭ-ēr*
raspberry, *răz'bĕr-ĭ*
rather, *räTH'ēr*
ratio, *rā'shĭ-ō*
ration, *rā'shŭn*
rational, *răsh'ŭn-ăl*
rationale, *răsh'ŭn-ăl*
recipe, *rĕs'ĭ-pē*
recitative (n.), *rĕs'ĭ-tà-tēv'*
reclamation, *rĕk'là-mā'shŭn*
recluse, *rê-klŏŏs'*
recognizance, *rê-kŏg'nĭ-zăns*
recognize, *rĕk'ŏg-nīz*
reconnaissance, *rê-kŏn'à-săns*

reconnoiter, *rĕk'ô-noi'tēr*
referable, *rĕf'ēr-à-b'l*
referee, *rĕf'ēr-ē'*
regalia, *rê-gā'lĭ-à*
régime, *rā'zhēm*
regular, *rĕg'ù-lēr*
reiterate, *rê-ĭt'ēr-āt*
renaissance, *rĕn'ê-zäns'*
rendezvous, *rän'dê-vŏŏ*
reparable, *rĕp'à-rà-b'l*
repertoire, *rĕp'ēr-twär*
replica, *rĕp'lĭ-kà*
reputable, *rĕp'ù-tà-b'l*
requiem, *rē'kwĭ-ĕm (or rē')*
requital, *rê-kwīt'ăl*
research, *rê-sûrch'*
reservoir, *rĕz'ēr-vwôr*
residue, *rĕz'ĭ-dū*
resin, *rĕz'ĭn*
resolute, *rĕz'ô-lūt*
resonance, *rĕz'ô-năns*
resource, *rê-sōrs'*
respite, *rĕs'pĭt*
restaurant, *rĕs'tô-rănt*
restaurateur, *rĕs'tō'rä'tûr'*
résumé, *rā'zù-mā'*
reveille, *rĕv'ê-lĭ*
revenue, *rĕv'ê-nū*
reversion, *rê-vûr'shŭn*
revocable, *rĕv'ô-kà-b'l*
rheumatism, *rŏŏ'mà-tĭz'm*
rhythm, *rĭTH'm*
ribald, *rĭb'ăld*
ricochet, *rĭk'ô-shā'*
ridiculous, *rĭ-dĭk'ù-lŭs*
rind, *rīnd*
rinse, *rĭns*
ripeness, *rīp'nĕs*
rise (n.), *rīz*
risk, *rĭsk*
robust, *rô-bŭst'*
roil, *roil*
romance, *rô-măns'*
roof, *rŏŏf*
room, *rŏŏm*
root, *rŏŏt*
roquefort, *rōk'fērt*
roseate, *rō'zê-āt*
rostrum, *rŏs'trŭm*
route, *rŏŏt*
routine, *rŏŏ-tēn'*
rude, *rŏŏd*
rutabaga, *rŏŏ'tà-bā'gà*

sabot, *sà'bō'*
sabotage, *săb'ô-täzh'*
saccharin, *săk'à-rĭn*
sachem, *sā'chĕm*
sachet, *sà-shā'*
sacrament, *săk'rà-mĕnt*
sacrifice, *săk'rĭ-fīs*
sacrilegious, *săk'rĭ-lē'jŭs*
safari, *sà-fä'rĭ*
sagacious, *sà-gā'shŭs*
said, *sĕd*
salary, *săl'à-rĭ*
saline, *sā'lĭn*
salmon, *săm'ŭn*
salon, *sà'lôn'*
salve, *säv*
sanatorium, *săn'à-tō'rĭ-ŭm*
sanguine, *săng'gwĭn*
sarcasm, *sär'kăz'm*
sarcophagus, *sär-kŏf'à-gŭs*
sarsaparilla, *sär'sà-pà-rĭl'à*
satin, *săt'ĭn*
satire, *săt'īr*
satyr, *săt'ēr, sā'tēr*
savage, *săv'ĭj*
savant, *sà'vän'*
says, *sĕz*
scallop, *skŏl'ŭp*

scared, *skârd*
scenario, *sẻ-nä'rĭ-ō*
scenic, *sē'nĭk*
schism, *sĭz'm*
schizophrenia, *skĭz'ō-frē'nĭ-à*
scion, *sī'ŭn*
scrofula, *skrŏf'ů-là*
séance, *sī'äns'*
seckel, *sĕk''l*
secretary, *sĕk'rẻ-tĕr'ĭ*
sedative, *sĕd'à-tĭv*
seidlitz, *sĕd'lĭts*
seismic, *sīz'mĭk*
semiannual, *sĕm'ĭ-ăn'ů-ăl*
senile, *sē'nīl*
señora, *sā-nyō'rä*
separable, *sĕp'à-rà-b'l*
separate (v.), *sĕp'à-rāt*
separate (adj.), *sĕp'à-rĭt*
sesame, *sĕs'à-mẻ*
several, *sĕv'ẽr-ăl*
shampoo, *shăm-poō'*
shan't, *shänt*
sheik, *shēk, shāk*
shillelagh, *shĭ-lā'là*
shrill, *shrĭl*
shrine, *shrīn*
sibilant, *sĭb'ĭ-lănt*
sidereal, *sĭ-dēr'ẻ-ăl*
signora, *sẻ-nyō'rä*
silhouette, *sĭl'ōō-ĕt'*
simultaneous, *sī'mŭl-tā'nẻ-ŭs*
since, *sĭns*
sinecure, *sī'nẻ-kūr*
sirup; syrup, *sĭr'ŭp*
ski, *skē*
skiing, *skē'ĭng*
slake, *slāk*
sleek, *slēk*
slept, *slĕpt*
smorgasbord, *smûr'găs-bôrd'*
snout, *snout*
sofa, *sō'fà*
soften, *sôf'ĕn*
soirée, *swä-rā'*
solace, *sŏl'ĭs*
solarium, *sỏ-lâr'ĭ-ŭm*
solemn, *sŏl'ĕm*
sombrero, *sŏm-brâr'ō*
sonata, *sỏ-nä'tà*
soprano, *sỏ-prä'nō*
sotto voce, *sŏt'tỏ vō'chà*
souvenir, *soō'vẻ-nēr'*
specie (coin), *spē'shĭ*
species, *spē'shĭz*
spinach, *spĭn'ĭch*
spirit, *spĭr'ĭt*
splenetic, *splẻ-nĕt'ĭk*
spouse, *spouz*
stalactite, *stà-lăk'tīt*
stalagmite, *stà-lăg'mīt*
static, *stăt'ĭk*
status, *stā'tŭs*
steady, *stĕd'ĭ*
stipend, *stī'pĕnd*
stirrup, *stĭr'ŭp*
stoicism, *stō'ĭ-sĭz'm*
stomach, *stŭm'ăk*
strata, *strā'tà*
strategic, *strà-tē'jĭk*
stratosphere, *străt'ỏ-sfēr*
strew, *stroō*
strychnine, *strĭk'nĭn*
student, *stū'dĕnt*
suave, *swäv*
subdue, *sŭb-dū'*
submarine(n), *sŭb'mà-rēn'*
subpoena, *sŭb-pē'nà*
subtle, *sŭt''l*
suburb, *sŭb'ûrb*
succinct, *sŭk-sĭngkt'*
suède, *swād*

suggest, *sŭg-jĕst'*
suit, *sūt*
suite, *swēt*
sumac, *shoō'măk*
sumptuous, *sŭmp'chů-ŭs*
superfluous, *sủ-pûr'floō-ŭs*
supple, *sŭp''l*
suppose, *sŭ-pōz'*
surcease, *sûr-sēs'*
surprise, *sẽr-prīz'*
surveillance, *sûr-vāl'ăns*
swan, *swŏn*
swept, *swĕpt*
syndicate, *sĭn'dĭ-kāt*
synod, *sĭn'ŭd*
syringe, *sĭ-rĭnj'*

table d'hote, *tà'blĕ dōt'*
taciturn, *tăs'ĭ-tûrn*
tallyho, *tăl'ĭ-hō'*
tapestry, *tăp'ĕs-trĭ*
task, *tásk*
technique, *tĕk'nēk'*
tedious, *tē'dĭ-ŭs*
teething, *tēтн'ĭng*
telephonic, *tĕl'ẻ-fŏn'ĭk*
temperament, *tĕm'pẽr-à-mĕnt*
temperature, *tĕm'pẽr-à-chửr*
temporarily, *tĕm'pỏ-rẽr'ĭ-lĭ*
tenet, *tĕn'ĕt*
tepid, *tĕp'ĭd*
terrain, *tẻ-rān'*
tête-à-tête, *tāt'-à-tāt'*
textile, *tĕks'tĭl*
theater, *thē'à-tẽr*
thermostat, *thûr'mỏ-stăt*
thresh, *thrĕsh*
tiara, *tī-âr'à*
tincture, *tĭngk'chửr*
tolerable, *tŏl'ẽr-à-b'l*
tomato, *tỏ-mā'tō*
tongs, *tŏngz*
tonsorial, *tŏn-sō'rĭ-ăl*
tortoise, *tôr'tŭs*
toupee, *toō-pā'*
tournament, *toōr'nà-mĕnt*
tourniquet, *toōr'nĭ-kĕt*
toward, *tỏ'ẽrd*
transmigrate, *trăns-mī'grāt*
transparent, *trăns-pâr'ĕnt*
travail, *trăv'āl*
travel, *trăv'ĕl*
traveler, *trăv'ĕl-ẽr*
traverse (n. v. adj.), *trăv'ẽrs*
treacle, *trē'k'l*
tribune, *trĭb'ūn*
trichina, *trĭ-kī'nà*
triumph, *trī'ŭmf*
trough, *trŏf*
trousseau, *troō'sō'*
truculent, *trŭk'ů-lĕnt*
trustworthy, *trŭst'wûr'тнĭ*
tube, *tūb*
tulip, *tū'lĭp*
tune, *tūn*
turnip, *tûr'nĭp*
turquoise, *tûr'koiz*

ukulele, *ū'kủ-lā'lẻ*
ultimatum, *ŭl'tĭ-mā'tŭm*
umbrella, *ŭm-brĕl'à*
unaccented, *ŭn'ăk-sĕn'tĕd*
undersigned, *ŭn'dẽr-sīnd'*
unfrequented, *ŭn'frẻ-kwĕn'tĕd*
uninterested, *ŭn-ĭn'tẽr-ĕs-tĕd*
unprecedented, *ŭn-prĕs'ẻ-dĕn-tĕd*
untoward, *ŭn-tō'ẽrd*
usage, *ūs'ĭj*
used, *ūzd*
usually, *ū'zhoō-ăl-lĭ*
usurp, *ủ-zûrp'*
usury, *ū'zhoō-rĭ*

vagary, *và-gâr'ĭ*
vagrant, *vā'grănt*
valance, *văl'ăns*
valet, *văl'ĕt*
valuable, *văl'ủ-à-b'l*
vanquish, *văng'kwĭsh*
vase, *vās*
vast, *vást*
vaudeville, *vōd'vĭl*
vehement, *vē'ẻ-mĕnt*
velvet, *vĕl'vĕt*
venal, *vē'năl*
venison, *vĕn'ĭ-z'n*
venous, *vē'nŭs*
ventriloquist, *vĕn-trĭl'ỏ-kwĭst*
veracious, *vẻ-rā'shŭs*
verbatim, *vûr-bā'tĭm*
verdigris, *vûr'dĭ-grēs*
version, *vûr'shŭn*
veterinary, *vĕt'ẽr-ĭ-nẽr'ĭ*
via, *vī'à*
vicar, *vĭk'ẽr*
vice versa, *vī'sẻ vûr'sà*
victim, *vĭk'tĭm*
victual, *vĭt''l*
vicuña, *vĭ-koōn'yà*
vignette, *vĭn-yĕt'*
villain, *vĭl'ĭn*
vindictive, *vĭn-dĭk'tĭv*
vinous, *vī'nŭs*
virulent, *vĭr'ů-lĕnt*
virus, *vī'rŭs*
vis-à-vis, *vē'zà-vē'*
viscid, *vĭs'ĭd*
viscount, *vī'kount'*
visé, *vē'zā*
vitriol, *vĭt'rĭ-ŭl*
vituperation, *vĭ-tū'pẽr-ā'shŭn*
viva voce, *vī'và vō'sẻ*
viviparous, *vĭ-vĭp'à-rŭs*
volatile, *vŏl'à-tĭl*
volume, *vŏl'yŭm*
voluntarily, *vŏl'ŭn-tĕr'ĭ-lĭ*

waft, *wàft*
wainscot, *wān'skŭt*
warily, *wâr'ĭ-lĭ*
was, *wŏz*
wash, *wŏsh*
wasp, *wŏsp*
weird, *wērd*
well-bred, *wĕl'brĕd'*
when, *hwĕn*
where, *hwâr*
whisk, *hwĭsk*
whistler, *hwĭs'lẽr*
whole, *hōl*
whooping (cough), *hoōp'ĭng*
whortleberry, *hwûr't'l-bĕr'ĭ*
widow, *wĭd'ō*
window, *wĭn'dō*
wiseacre, *wĭz'ā'kẽr*
wistaria, *wĭs-tā'rĭ-à*
withes, *wĭтнs*
women, *wĭm'ĕn*
wondering, *wŭn'dẽr-ĭng*
wont (custom), *wŭnt*
wrath, *ráth*
wrestler, *rĕs'lẽr*

xenia, *zē'nĭ-à*
xylophone, *zī'lỏ-fōn*

yacht, *yŏt*
yolk, *yōk*

zealot, *zĕl'ŭt*
zenith, *zē'nĭth*
zodiacal, *zỏ-dī'à-kăl*
zoo, *zoō*
zoology, *zỏ-ŏl'ỏ-jĭ*

FORMS OF LITERARY COMPOSITION

Enjoyment in Reading. A good book is like an excellent dinner in good company, to which you bring a good digestion, a keen appetite, alert attention, and as ready a wit as you can muster. It is easy to indulge oneself in drifting idly through a maze of moving pictures. But some effort is necessary to keep the mind alert to the procession of thoughts on the printed page. If the author has written something worth while, he has taken much time to select the right words and set them in order. There is no higher pleasure than that of the reader who follows such an author through his pages and re-creates from the printed symbols his thought, his pictures, and his fancies. The book that you enjoy in this way becomes a part of your life.

Journals and Magazines. Business and professional people read the journals of their special interests. Members of churches, societies, and orders should read at least some of the papers and magazines published in their interest. Such reading is necessary to intelligent membership, as the reading of daily newspapers and weekly journals is necessary to efficient citizenship. But no one need read all of any paper or review. Let your special interest select and direct your attention. Reading the news that prompts to reflection upon the issues of the day is worth while; but trying to read the entire newspaper only produces a confused impression of many things, which serves to weaken the judgment. One should not, however, confine his reading to newspapers and magazines.

Books and Taste. The magazines offer, at small expense, acquaintance with the best literary work of the day. The novels of Charles Dickens were originally published in magazines. But the wise man will spend something for the sake of possessing at least a few good books. Even the public library cannot take the place of books on a shelf at home, whether home be a single room or a mansion. You may select your books according to your taste, but you should take pains to cultivate your taste.

A useful distinction has been drawn between the *literature of knowledge* and the *literature of power*. Keep this in mind in filling your bookshelf. Reliable volumes that contain the things one needs to know, or should be able to refer to on occasion, are of great importance; for exact information is indispensable. These make up the literature of knowledge. This class includes dictionaries, encyclopedias, histories, and books upon special sciences. Of even greater value are the books of power. These feed the imagination and inspire ideals. Such are the great biographies, classic stories, essays, and poetry. The wise man will value these, not for all they contain, but for what they actually bring to *him*. A single article in a work of reference, a single idea or fact in a history, one little poem out of a large volume, may be worth to you many times the cost of the book.

STORY OR NARRATIVE

Both of these words are derived from roots which mean simply *see* or *know*, but they have come to be applied to all accounts of events. The order of telling a story is either: (1) the time order in which things happen, as in history; or (2) an "arrangement" different from the time order. This "arrangement" may be made for the sake of (a) holding attention or (b) making clearer the relations of cause and effect among the events. Such an "arrangement" is called a plot, and stories so planned are fiction.

For plot outlines, refer to *The Book or Article Review* and *The Scenario* in the section Writing and Speaking.

Ancient Stories. Everybody likes a good story, and story-telling is very nearly, if not quite, the most ancient of the arts. The oldest discoverable collections of writing contain well-developed narratives in the form of myths and legends. A *myth* is an ancient tale which usually conveys some imaginative account of the origin of gods, various human arts, or natural phenomena. The *legend* is similar to the myth, but it is more directly concerned with the deeds of men. In the course of centuries, many of these tales were combined by master story-tellers into *epics*, which are stories of the lives and deeds of heroes, such as the *Iliad* and the *Odyssey*. The word epic comes from the Greek *epos*, meaning "speech" or "song," because these great stories were told or chanted for generations before the poems were actually written.

Medieval Romance: During the Middle Ages, long *romances* about the careers and conquests of Alexander and Charlemagne and their followers took shape from the tales and songs of minstrels who wandered from court to court and were welcomed in the castles for the entertainment they brought. The name *romance* was given to these stories because they were composed in the common Romance, or French, tongue rather than in the Latin of scholars. In similar manner, the romances of King Arthur and of the Holy Grail were built. Upon this fund of romance many modern writers have drawn. Tennyson embodied the Arthurian legends in the *Idylls of the King*.

In their early form, these stories were told in verse. Later they were recast in prose form by various writers. With these poems in prose there grew side by side the *prose tale*, which was a story of adventure, in which the events were strung together loosely and the interest depended on the strangeness of the events or the unforeseen outcome of the adventures. Several romantic prose tales were produced by Greek writers in the early Christian centuries. One of the most famous was *Apollonius of Tyre*. From this tale came Shakespeare's plot for *Pericles, Prince of Tyre*. To this general type of story belongs the series of tales known as the *Arabian Nights*. Washington Irving's *Tales of the Alhambra* furnish a more modern instance. Out of these loosely constructed legends there have developed in modern times the novel and the short story.

The Novel. Of the *novel* there are two general types. In the *romantic novel*, of which the stories of Sir Walter Scott are examples, the story is placed at a distance from the reader, in either time or space, and the strangeness of events and places contributes much to its interest. In romance our dreams come true. The *realistic novel* takes its subject matter from everyday affairs. The usual motives of people form the story, and the outcome must be made to seem reasonable and likely. William Dean Howells's work is among the best in the realistic style. The love motive is almost universal in the novel. The *psychological novel*, exemplified in Joyce's *Ulysses*, is primarily interested in recording the thoughts and feelings of the characters. The novel may vary in length from several thousand words to several hundred thousand.

The Short Story. The modern *short story* has been developed within the last hundred years. Its ancestors were many,—the Greek romances, the *fabliaux* in France, such tales as Boccaccio told in prose in Italy and Chaucer retold in verse in England; but it is a form clearly distinguished from all these. Edgar Allan Poe may be credited with the first characteristic work in the new form in America, and his stories are still reckoned among the best. The short story takes a small group of characters, carries them through a brief time, and, in rapid action, with a minimum of description, works out their fortunes and interactions. The story may vary in length from a few hundred to six or seven thousand words. The explanation of the plot must usually be cleverly concealed until the end of the story is reached, but it must then be made to seem reasonable and convincing. The works of Bret Harte, Francis R. Stockton, R. L. Stevenson, and Rudyard Kipling furnish examples of various types of the short story.

Special Forms of Prose Fiction. Both the novel and the short story appear in various special forms. The *mystery story*, for example, may be either long or short, but its plot turns upon some skillfully concealed relation between the events narrated. When this relation is revealed, in the end, as something very simple and commonplace, we have what is sometimes called a *surprise plot*. Or the mystery may be left as an unexplained something in the borderland of fancy or superstition, which human science has not yet mapped out. The mystery story is really a very primitive sort of tale, and many examples of it are to be found in early folk-lore. It carries all the thrills of unexpected and unexplained fortunes. Poe's *Gold Bug* and *Fall of the House of Usher* are classic examples of the modern mystery story.

The extraordinarily popular *detective story* is one sort of mystery tale, in which such a fascinatingly keen, questioning mind as that of Sir Arthur Conan Doyle's creation, Mr. Sherlock Holmes, is seen at work unraveling the tangled threads of the mystery. It is really a story built backward; for the real story is assumed to be already finished, and the detective is set to going over the obscure trail to discover the origin of the train of events. What we get is really two stories in one, the first being that of the original characters and events, the second, that of the detective and his discoveries. Such a story is *The Leavenworth Case*. The *adventure story* is more nearly like the old-fashioned tale. Its interest depends mostly upon the succession of unexpected and more or less complicated incidents calling for courage and address in the characters. *Robinson Crusoe, Treasure Island*, and *Kidnapped* are favorite examples of this kind.

Both the novel and the short story may be so written as to carry a special interest derived from the *location of the events*, from the *type of industry* in which the characters are engaged, or from the *class of society* in which they move. This last kind may involve only the people of one class of society. But more commonly it follows the ancient instinct of story-tellers for the effect of contrast. Then the clash of high and low, of rich and poor, which has interested mankind from the time of Aladdin and King Cophetua, furnishes the moving impulse.

The *historical novel* involves historical events as a necessary part of the story, and pictures some historical period. When it is based upon real scholarship and gives a trustworthy picture of the time in which its action is placed, it is not only interesting in itself but valuable as an aid to the study of history. *Hugh Wynne, The Crisis, The Cloister and the Hearth, Ivanhoe, Quentin Durward, The Last Days of Pompeii, The Conqueror, Quo Vadis*, and *Ben Hur* are excellent examples.

History. The almost universal desire for the true story finds satisfaction in *history*, the story of man's life from the beginning to the present time. Indeed, it is out of this material that most fiction and poetry are made. A knowledge of history is essential to a true education. An impartial and readable history, therefore, entitles its author to very high regard. The following works are masterpieces in this field: James F. Rhodes's *History of the United States*; Theodore Roosevelt's *Winning of the West*; Green's *History of England*; Ferrero's *Greatness and Decline of Rome*; Prescott's *Conquest of Mexico* and *Conquest of Peru*; Parkman's *France and England in the New World*; J. L. Motley's *Rise of the Dutch Republic*.

Biography. Second only to history in importance as a part of education, and in its masterpieces equally fascinating, is *biography*, or the life histories of important personages. To know the great thinkers and workers of the world through their biographies is not only interesting but of incalculable worth as an influence in developing character. The list of true and readable biographies is long. Many short lives have been written and published in such series as *American Statesmen* and *English Men of Letters*. The following are of high rank: Boswell's *Life of Johnson*, unique among biographies; Plutarch's *Parallel Lives of Illustrious Greeks and Romans*, an ancient work still full of interest; Morley's *Life of Gladstone*; Thayer's *Life of Cavour*; Carlyle's *Oliver Cromwell*; Palmer's *Life of Alice Freeman Palmer*; Booker Washington's *Up from Slavery*; Jacob Riis's *Making of an American*; Beveridge's *Life of John Marshall*. Letters and *journals* supplement biography.

Travel. Always and everywhere people are interested in *travelers' stories*, and many most entertaining books have been written to satisfy this appetite. A very large part of the *Odyssey* is made up of the wanderings of Odysseus, the Greek hero; the adventures of Sindbad the Sailor are proverbial; the book of the travels of Marco Polo through Asia is a classic. Among recent books, those of Harry Franck about his walking trips in various parts of the world are unique and interesting. The *Reminiscences of Rafael Pumpelly* contain some charming stories of travel in the 19th century. The stories of Arctic exploration by Peary and Stefansson, Roosevelt's travel and hunting narratives, the lives of Stanley and Livingstone, and Stevenson's chronicles of the South seas furnish mines of fascinating reading.

Folk Stories. The *folk tale*, or *folk story*, is what its name implies, a tale which has been told over and over again among the common people. This type of story is common to all peoples, and it is worthy of note that such stories circulated among widely separated peoples tell of similar adventures and teach similar truths. Many of these legends may be found in the collections made by Andrew Lang.

The *fairy tale* may be thought of as a type of folk story. Most fairy stories are of very ancient origin; some are modern. They are always concerned with a fanciful explanation of events and with the fate of people. The fairies are the little people of the air and the trees and the caves, who are either friendly or unfriendly to human folk. Some of these stories are very beautiful, while others are marred by the savage cruelty of barbarous times. Andersen's original tales and the *Märchen* gathered by the brothers Grimm offer excellent specimens of the fairy tale.

Stories That Teach. A very engaging type of story, of ancient origin, widely current in medieval times in Europe, and still to be found among remote and untutored peoples, is the *animal story*, in which the animals are personified, or endowed with human faculties. Frequently each sort of animal is supposed to embody a particular human trait, and the stories take on a moral flavor. In America, the finest examples of these tales are the Uncle Remus and Br'er Rabbit stories, retold in the negro dialect by Joel Chandler Harris.

Closely related to these animal stories are *fables*, pointed anecdotes in which animals are endowed with human qualities and are made to illustrate moral lessons. The fables of Æsop and of La Fontaine are universally popular.

The *parable* is a story of common events or happenings of every day, used to illustrate moral or religious truths. As the typical beginning of the old-fashioned story is "Once upon a time," so the typical beginning of the parable is "It is like." The New Testament affords us the best examples of the parable, though in one form or another a parable appears wherever any teaching of moral or social truth is to be done.

The *allegory* is a development of the story of common things which conveys moral and spiritual meanings. The allegory extends metaphor and personification into a story, in which the characters represent qualities, motives, or types of character. The morality plays of early English literature, such as *Everyman*, and many modern short, poetic plays are really allegories. Indeed, the short allegory may be found frequently in fiction.

In English, the great prose allegory is Bunyan's *Pilgrim's Progress*. Dante's *Divine Comedy* is perhaps the greatest of the world's allegories. There is also much allegory in Tennyson's *Idylls of the King*.

DESCRIPTIVE PROSE

This type of composition appears as an important part of books on travel, art, architecture, cities, and natural scenery. The books of travel referred to under *Travel* contain many fine examples of this graphic style of writing.

EXPOSITION AND ARGUMENT

The logical development of themes is to be found in the form of *essays* on literary, historical, and scientific subjects, and in *speeches* and *orations*. The *essay* presents, either in serious or in light style, a writer's thoughts upon a subject, to inform, convince, explain, or entertain. The essays of Bacon, Addison, and Macaulay are English classics. Huxley was the great scientific essayist of the 19th century. Lord Bryce's *American Commonwealth* is a long essay, combining exposition and argument. Current magazines contain many essays upon a wide variety of subjects, in the form of editorials, special articles, and studies. The *speech* or *oration* is usually a discussion of a theme of public human interest, argumentative and persuasive in character, and prepared for a particular public occasion. The works of Edmund Burke, William Pitt, Patrick Henry, Daniel Webster, Abraham Lincoln, Stephen A. Douglas, Henry W. Grady, and Rufus Choate furnish examples of English and American oratory.

POETRY

When emotion and the creative imagination rule expression in language, we have poetry. The province of poetry is to kindle the imagination and inspire fine sentiments and high enthusiasms through beautiful language. English literature is rich in poetry that does just these things.

The Lyric. This is the simplest and most familiar form of poetry. The word *lyric* implies singing, but the lyric poem need not be set to music. It is simply the poet's personal expression of feeling, and it may be written upon any theme that arouses in him an emotional response. This theme is usually suggested by some person, place, or natural object. Usually the lyric is short, not more than a few stanzas, so that it can be read easily in a short time and grasped as a whole.

The songs of Robert Burns are among the purest lyrics in the English language. Tennyson's work includes many separate lyrics of very great beauty as well as numerous short songs inset in some of his longer poems. Rudyard Kipling's poetry should be read for a more rugged and vigorous type. Sidney Lanier produced several very beautiful lyrics, among which are *The Woods and the Master* and *The Marshes of Glynn*. James Whitcomb Riley's verses, even when he is telling a story, often seem to sing themselves. Riley is the great American master of the lyric in popular language. Joaquin Miller, among American poets, is to be read for his *Songs of the Sierras*. Among present day poets, also, the works of Alfred Noyes and John Masefield, in England, and of Richard Le Gallienne and Bliss Carman, in America, should be read.

The Sonnet. A lyric poem of the fixed length of fourteen iambic pentameter lines. Usually it has a first section of eight lines and a second section of six, though the sonnets of Shakespeare do not conform to this rule. The sonnet was adopted into English from the Italian. It is a form that requires the finest mastery both of language and of thought. Every reader of literature should be acquainted with some of the greater sonnets of Shakespeare and Milton and also with sonnets by poets of the present

day. As fine examples of the English sonnet, one may read Wordsworth's *To Milton*, Keats's *On Chapman's Homer*, and Rupert Brooke's series of sonnets under the title "*1914.*"

The Ode. A lyric adopted from the Greek, but altered greatly in form by various English poets. Today it is simply a poem written in dignified and elevated style, often for some set occasion. It varies, in length and metrical form, from such poems as Wordsworth's *Ode to Duty* and Shelley's *Ode to a Skylark* to a poem of the length of Lowell's *Commemoration Ode* or Tennyson's *Ode on the Death of the Duke of Wellington*.

Hymns and Songs. Hymns are written in stanzas usually of four or six lines with three or four accents to the line, though there is no special rule for these. *Popular songs* have most frequently the trochaic meter because of its lightness and rapidity of movement.

Elegies. These are funeral laments, often of a reflective character. Gray's *Elegy Written in a Country Churchyard* is an English classic.

Narrative Poetry. Aside from the great epics—the *Iliad*, the *Odyssey*, the *Æneid*, and *Paradise Lost*—and the metrical romances, such as those about Charlemagne and King Arthur, the most interesting form of narrative poetry is the *ballad* This is really a folk story in lyric verse, though in modern use "ballad" means any short simple lyric. The manner of telling the story is frequently dramatic, that is, the characters are allowed to speak for themselves. The ballads of Robin Hood are perhaps the most familiar in English. These and many others may be found in such a collection as *English and Scottish Popular Ballads*, made by Francis J. Child.

Geoffrey Chaucer's *Canterbury Tales* mark the beginning of modern English narrative poetry. The stories of *Miles Standish* and *Evangeline*, as told by Longfellow, are familiar examples of the narrative poem of modern times. For many years the prose novel and the short story have crowded out the narrative poem, but it seems to be returning to favor in the work of several English and American poets. In America, Robert Frost was master of a type of short dramatic narrative, several examples of which are to be found in his volume *North of Boston*. John Masefield's *Dauber* and *Everlasting Mercy* and Alfred Noyes's *Drake* are excellent examples of poetic narratives.

Anthologies. The word means collections of flowers and was anciently used for compilations of short Greek poems and epigrams. Now it applies mostly to collections which represent the finest poetry of a given country, as an "American anthology," or poems about a certain class of subjects, as an "anthology of war poetry," or poems representing a certain type, as an "anthology of lyrics" or of hymns.

Vers libre, "Free Verse." This name is applied to a type of modern poetry in which the strict meters of the older verse do not appear and in which rime is rather deliberately rejected. Apart, therefore, from its arrangement in lines of irregular length, it is often difficult to distinguish this form of poetry from rhythmical prose. The writers of "free verse" attempt to make the rhythm of their poetry reflect truthfully the emotions that prompt them to write. Obviously, a poet must possess great skill to do this successfully. Hence very few pieces of good "free verse" have been written, the more successful being found in the works of Carl Sandburg, Amy Lowell, and Edgar Lee Masters.

DRAMA

A drama, or play, is essentially a story arranged to be told in action on the stage. This method of telling a story is very ancient, dating back to early festivals, when legends connected with the god or patron of a feast were represented with music, dancing, and recitation. The history of the stage and the drama in all countries shows more or less intimate connection with the service of religion as well as with the human love of entertainment.

English dramas are written either in verse or in prose. Sometimes the dramatists may use both forms in the same play, as Shakespeare did. At the present day, however, most plays that are to be both staged and printed are written in prose, for the modern public calls for a more "natural" mode of speech. The subject of the drama may be drawn from almost any source, according to the genius of the playwright, and, like the novel or short story, its manner may be romantic or realistic.

Tragedy and Comedy. Tragedy signifies a play of serious action and motive usually representing some human struggle having an adverse outcome. This struggle may be against the gods or fate, as in the ancient drama, against their own passions, as in the Shakespearean tragedies, or against their passions and social conditions, as in more modern plays. Comedy implies a lighter, more pleasant story, with a happy ending in place of the sad or disastrous close of tragedy. Few plays of the present day answer strictly to this classification, most of them exhibiting both tragedy and comedy.

Various Forms. We may have a *play of incident*, in which we are interested chiefly in what happens, or a *play of character*, in which we are interested chiefly in the people to whom things happen. The play may be said to belong either to *serious drama*, in the course of which some essential change or development in one or more characters is required, or to the *lighter drama*, in which there is frequently only change of situation or of relations among the characters. The *farce* is a light play of incident, carried to the extreme of artificial or ridiculous situations. The modern *melodrama* is characterized by exaggerated sensational features.

Goldsmith in the 18th century produced what is known as *comedy of manners*. He was followed by several playwrights in the same fashion. Plays in this class to be read are *The Good-Natured Man*, *She Stoops to Conquer*, *The Rivals*, and *The School for Scandal*.

A large number of English and American plays of recent years are to be classed as *social drama*. In these the method of the playwright is realistic, and his object is to portray the working of everyday human motives. Sometimes he rises to a discussion or criticism of modern social life and customs.

In America, William Vaughn Moody, Clyde Fitch, William Gillette, and Augustus Thomas produced plays suitable for reading and, among English playwrights, Sir Arthur W. Pinero, Henry Arthur Jones, and John Galsworthy did notable work.

There are in English several dramas which, while not successful on the stage, should be read by the student. Among these may be mentioned Tennyson's *Becket* and *Queen Mary*, and Browning's *The Falcon* and *Pippa Passes*.

During the 1920's there was marked interest in short plays of one or two acts, especially those of Lady Gregory, Lord Dunsany, and Sir James M. Barrie, but at the present time nothing important is being done in this field, and there is little interest in them. Dramas for television, however, have lately been receiving much attention. Some of the best writers for this medium are Norman Corwin, Paddy Chayefsky, and Horton Foote.

There is interest also in the *pageant*, which is simply an outdoor play with much action but with very little text. Its most frequent use is for portraying poetically the life and customs of past times, in celebrations of historical events.

For further references, see *Family Library*, *articles and tables on the various national literatures*, and the *Table of Modern World Literature*.

FIGURES OF SPEECH

Apt figures of speech are pictures of one's thoughts. A good comparison throws light on an idea, thereby helping people to understand it. For this reason, the language of the plain, matter-of-fact man is full of comparisons and figures, which he has inherited or unconsciously learned from those around him. He says, "plain as day," "heavy as lead," "level headed," as naturally as he says "see," "lift," or "think."

A *figure of speech* is a deviation from the usual application of words in order to impart clearness, force, and beauty to the composition. By saying "an army of ants" we give a vivid impression both of orderliness and of vastness in number. When David says "they were swifter than eagles" and "stronger than lions," we at once get a graphic description of the physical qualities of Saul and of Jonathan. Figures may be grouped in the four following classes:

I. Figures that picture a hidden resemblance or make use of a close association.

Simile (*sǐm'ǐ-lē*). In this figure, a likeness between things is expressed, usually by *like* or *as*, in the form of a comparison: "Sweet *as the morning air*." One may recount the kind words and acts and cheerfulness of a visitor and thus describe her prosaically very well, but if one says, "Her presence was *like a ray of sunshine* in a darkened room," the whole story is pictured in a single phrase. Other examples: "Quick *as lightning*"; "Abundant *as the light of the sun*"; "Deaf *as any tradesman's dummy*"; "A baby's feet, *like sea-shells pink*"; "Jolted *like a solitary penny* in an iron bank"; "White *as chalk*."

Metaphor (*mět'à-fŏr*). The word means "carrying over," "transfer." In this figure, the word *like* or *as*, used in *simile*, is omitted, and, by an implied comparison, a new meaning or picture is transferred directly to the word: "He was a *tower* of strength"; "*Seeds* of truth"; "Lowliness is young ambition's *ladder*"; "Sail on, O *Ship* of State"; "Hours and minutes are *dollars* and *cents*."

The next two figures, *synecdoche* and *metonymy*, are similar in that the things suggested for comparison are more closely associated than those used in *simile* or *metaphor*. They are not uncommon in everyday speech, and their skillful use is a secret of much that is fascinating in literature. It is often difficult to classify an expression definitely as one or other of these figures. The name "metonymy" is often used for both.

Synecdoche (*sǐ-něk'dô-kè*). A figure in which a striking part of the object is used to signify the whole, or sometimes the whole to signify the part: "A thousand *hands* waved farewell"; "This *roof* (house) protects you"; "Now the *year* (the summer) is beautiful"; "*Ten thousand swords* would have leaped from their scabbards"; "The *hearths* (homes) of the nation"; "The *city* welcomed him."

Metonymy (*mè-tŏn'ǐ-mǐ*). A figure by which we put the cause for the effect, or the effect for the cause, as when we say, "He reads Milton," i. e., Milton's works; "Gray hairs should be respected," meaning old age; "My son, give me thy *heart*" (affection); "He was the *sigh* of his mother's soul" (the boy she loved).

Personification. The figure by which inanimate things or ideas are endowed with the qualities of human beings: "*Wisdom crieth* in the streets"; "*Hope* hath never lost *her* youth"; "The little *Road says*, Go";

"The *Worm* aware of his intent
Harangued him thus, right eloquent";

"Hark! *Truth proclaims*, thy triumphs cease"; "The *Sea saw* it and *fled*."

Allusion. A figure in which reference, direct or indirect, is made to some personage, incident, expression, or custom, with which the reader is familiar, to convey a vivid picture of the subject in hand: "A *Daniel* come to judgment"; "A *Napoleon* of finance"; "*They shall not pass.*"

II. Figures that depend for their force partly upon the arrangement of words in the sentence and partly upon the mental attitude of the speaker or writer.

Interrogation. This figure consists in asking a question with an implied contrary answer. Its force amounts to a vigorous denial: "*Am I a dog?*" "Hath the Lord said it, *and shall He not do it?*" "Hath He spoken it, *and shall He not make it good?*" "He that planted the ear, *shall He not hear?*" "He that formed the eye, *shall He not see?*" The figure is appropriate in intense expression, especially in oratory.

Apostrophe (*à-pŏs'trô-fè*). Another figure which is appropriate in oratory or in exalted poetry. It consists in turning aside from the usual order of words and addressing an object, an absent person, or a personified idea, thus bringing the object or idea vividly to the reader or audience: "O *Duty*, if that name thou love!" "O *Death!* where is thy sting?" "O *Grave!* where is thy victory?"

Vision. A figure closely akin to apostrophe but less forceful. This figure consists in describing a scene, an object, or an event as if it were immediately in view: "*I see before me the gladiator lie.*" The value of the figure consists in its vividness. The use of the historical present is a form of vision: "*I remember well the day I entered the room, the familiar objects are all before me, but my mother is not there.*"

Irony (*ī'rô-nĭ*). This consists in saying the opposite of what is meant. A classical illustration of irony is to be found in the repeated phrase of Mark Antony in *Julius Cæsar*: "They are *honorable* men"; "We have, to be sure, great reason to believe the *modest* man would not ask him for a debt, when he pursues his life." Modern writing is characterized rather by touches of irony than by a full development of the figure. It is a dangerous tool to use even occasionally and not at all fit for habitual employment.

Litotes (*lĭ'tô-tēz*). A figure of speech by which a strong affirmative is expressed simply by the negative of the contrary: "a citizen of *no mean city*," i. e., "of an important city"; "A storm of *no small force* drove our vessel before it"; "To be polite in word and in deed is a matter of *no slight significance.*"

Hyperbole (*hī-pĕr'bô-lē*). An exaggeration for the purpose of compelling attention: "*Every word that Webster used weighed a pound*";

"The sky *shrunk upward with unusual dread* And trembling Tiber *div'd beneath his bed*";

"My song *shall blossom at your feet* My heart *your throne shall be.*"

Euphemism (*ū'fè-mĭz'm*). A mild or inoffensive expression used in place of what is regarded as an unpleasant statement. "*He was in the habit of removing people's goods out of their houses without previous arrangement with the owners*"; "*He passed away.*" These are euphemisms for stealing and for death. In everyday conversation this figure often takes the form of understatement: "His experiment was not too successful."

III. Figures that are simply arrangements of well-chosen words to produce packed and pointed expression.

Antithesis (*ăn-tĭth'ê-sĭs*). This figure depends for its force upon vivid contrast of opposite terms or ideas. It gains power through the balanced construction involved in the sentence: "If one would be rich, *should he labor to increase his possessions, or to diminish his desires?*" "The Puritans hated bear baiting, *not because it gave pain to the bear, but because it gave pleasure to the spectators.*" Many catch phrases are antitheses: "*rich and poor*"; "*capital and labor.*"

Climax. An arrangement of words or groups of words in ascending order of force or importance: "*I know it, I concede it, I confess it, I proclaim it.*" "*Force, force to the utmost; force without stint or limit; the righteous, triumphant force which shall make right the law of the world and cast every selfish dominion down in the dust.*" The strongest expression must be placed last in order.

Epigram. A short, forceful expression which depends for its value upon its brevity and upon some surprise involved in it. The best epigrams imply some antithesis: "*The silence was audible*"; "*So good that he is good for nothing*"; "*Some laborious orators mistake perspiration for inspiration.*"

Epithet (*ĕp'ĭ-thĕt*). A descriptive word or phrase into which has been packed an important meaning or a vivid picture. The epithet is an important element in poetry, and many epithets have become common words. There are two kinds of epithets:

1. *Essential Epithets*, or names of qualities always associated with the thing described: "*green* grass"; "*bright* sword."

2. *Conventional Epithets*, such as adjectives which become commonly associated with certain names: "*honest* Abe"; "*doubting* Thomas"; "*bright-eyed* Athena." The Greek poems, the *Iliad* and the *Odyssey*, are particularly rich in epithets: "the *wine-dark* sea"; "*hollow* ships"; "*rosy-fingered* dawn." Other examples: "our *honored* dead"; "*daisied* fields."

IV. The following names are given to certain uses of words for their sound values:

Euphony (*ū'fô-nĭ*). A name applied to the pleasing effects of sounds produced by the combination of words in sentences or of phonetic elements in spoken words. Euphony is a fundamental requirement of poetry: "The most sounding and euphonic surname that English history or topography affords";

"The bells of Shandon that sound so grand on The pleasant waters of the river Lee."

Onomatopœia (*ŏn'ô-măt'ô-pē'yà*). The word means name-making. Onomatopœia is the use of a word or phrase formed to imitate the sound of the thing signified. Many words in common use furnish examples: We say *rat tat tat* to denote a knocking at the door, *bow wow* to express the barking of a dog, or *buzz, buzz* to indicate the sound made by bees. Onomatopœia is frequently used in poetry where the sound of certain words is used to convey the sense; thus,

"When Ajax strives some rock's vast weight to throw *The line too labors, and the words move slow*";

"And the *light Latin tripped* along her tongue Amid the *roar of Irish gutturals.*"

Alliteration (*à-lĭt'ĕr-ā'shŭn*). The use of a succession of words having the same initial letter or sound. The chief value of alliteration is in challenging attention. Alliterative phrases, also, are easily memorized: "*babbling babes*"; "*feathered fowl.*" Early English poetry used alliteration in place of rime and meter. The device is frequently used in modern poetry; as, for example, "*Still stands* the forest primeval"; "*Lisp* of *leaves* and *ripple* of *rain.*"

Assonance (*ăs'ô-năns*). A name applied to the recurrence of the same vowel sound in a group of words. Assonance is likely to become monotonous and disagreeable in prose or even in poetry, though sometimes it is used with good effect: "*So all day long* the *noise* of battle *rolled*"; "*Hark! Hark! the lark.*"

LETTER WRITING

Among the arts of everyday life there is none more important than that of letter writing. Our business and social relations are so dependent upon our written communications that the ability to write a clear letter in correct form is regarded as an essential mark of an ordinary English education. No accomplishment is more highly prized than skill in writing tactful, effective business letters, unless it be the ability to write a graceful personal letter of friendship. The general principles that govern the writing of letters and many suggestions that will help the student of the art to perfect his work are given in the following pages. The very fact that a letter is taken as an index of the personal character of the writer should prompt us all to most careful study of this art which is at once so practical and so easy to master.

We all know the kind of letters we like to receive—social letters that are really sincere and hearty, like the personal talk of friends, business letters that are frank and clear and that bring the writers, as we say, face to face with us. The telephone conversation, instead of taking the place of the letter, has served to emphasize the importance of the personal, direct, well-planned letter, and to increase the demand for it. Telegrams often require "letters to follow," which state more completely the contents of the messages. Good business records demand letters to "confirm" important telephone conversations.

THE BUSINESS LETTER: PRINCIPLES

We judge people and business houses by the letters they write. First, the appearance of the letterhead, the quality of the paper, and the outward form or display of the letter attract or repel us; then the substance of the message and its style and its tone make their impression. All these elements contribute to the general effect of any letter and determine what the response to it shall be.

As we judge others, so we are judged. If our letters are to be worthy representatives of us and fulfill the missions on which they are sent, we must plan and construct them carefully and intelligently. No detail either of material or of dress can safely be neglected.

How do you plan your letters? Do you organize the ideas so that they can be quickly and easily understood? Do you present them with the ease of manner and with the touch of individuality that you would put into a personal interview? Do the sentences you write and the order in which you write them so clearly express what you wish to say that the reader will naturally make the response you want? Do you use the tone of courtesy and of respect that will leave in the reader's mind a pleasant impression and build his good will for you?

BUILDING YOUR LETTER

The object of practically every business letter is to secure action, either immediate or remote. But the reader is not likely to act as the writer wishes, unless it appears to his own advantage to do so. Hence, it is wise to study the merits of the proposed action from the reader's viewpoint, and to present them in such a light that he can see them plainly. In every legitimate transaction both sides profit, but it is necessary to lay greatest stress upon the reader's profit, since his self-interest is his most powerful incentive to action.

It is true that we all act upon suggestions, either in the form of commands or in the gentler forms of persuasion. First, however, our attention must be secured, our interest must be aroused, and we must have inducements to action. Hence, the following steps in the building of a business letter are well established and are of almost universal application: (1) Get the attention of the reader; (2) Give him

definite information; (3) Arouse his interest; (4) Offer him an inducement to act or to respond to you; (5) Give him a positive suggestion or direction; (6) Close your letter with a courteous expression that leaves a good feeling behind it.

The following example illustrates one way of building the letter. The headings in the left margin are, of course, not a part of the letter.

(LETTERHEAD)

FOREST PRODUCTS ASSOCIATION

LUMBERMAN'S EXCHANGE
LASALLE AND MADISON STS., CHICAGO, ILLINOIS 60602

HOMES BUILDING DEPARTMENT
WALTER C. HINES, *Manager*

June 17, 19—

Mr. Thomas C. Parsons   Subject: *Expert Service*
22 Elm Street
Utica, New York 13501

> *Dear Sir:*

ATTENTION AND INTEREST (the receiver's point of view)

> *As you say in your interesting reply to our advertisement, the time was, not so long ago, when a man built his house just as his neighbors built theirs. He used wood or brick or stone, because these were the only materials to be had. For the same reason, his roof was either shingle or slate.*

> *Nowadays, however, as you suggest, a man tries to express his taste in a home. He wants also to fit his house artistically to its location. In response to these demands, the variety of available materials and of plans for their combination has been increased beyond the range of any one man's knowledge.*

INFORMATION

> *Right here is where we can help you. Our business is to bring to the solution of your problem the best possible expert knowledge of materials and construction. This service we are able to supply economically through our large co-operative organization.*

INTEREST AND INDUCEMENT

> *We enable you to save money on the cost of building and to realize with greater satisfaction your ideals of convenience, quality, and beauty.*

> *Two booklets, "Some How's of Houses" and "Forest to Finish," which we are mailing to you today, will give you a suggestion as to our method of service. You will notice that we propose to furnish unbiased advice about ALL kinds of building materials.*

POSITIVE SUGGESTION AND COURTESY

> *When you have examined these booklets, just fill out and sign the enclosed card. It will bring our nearest expert representative for a personal conference at any time you suggest.*

> *Very truly yours,*

Enclosure   *Walter C. Hines*

This letter, to be sure, is a sales letter and therefore exemplifies more clearly the steps mentioned above than does a collection letter or letter of adjustment. All business letters, however, are in a sense sales letters, since all attempt at least to "sell" the writer's viewpoint and to secure the reader's favorable response.

Of course you can make these several steps in ways as varied as the kinds of people concerned and as the nature of the services involved. So, the particular contents of letters will vary with circumstances. Many very short notes, such as orders or brief acknowledgments, will not show all the steps. In general, however, the opening of the letter should recognize the reader's viewpoint. Beyond this very important approach to the recipient, the contents of the letter should further prepare him for the letter's real message by impressing upon him a sense of the writer's reliability, thus arousing his confidence. The next step is either direct statement or tactful suggestion of the writer's viewpoint. Persuasion of the reader to accept and to act according to that viewpoint is the final step.

The Letter as a Talk. You may think of the letter as a substitute for face to face talk. Hence, imagine as clearly as you can the characteristics of your reader, his immediate problems, and those features of his surroundings which you might see clearly in a personal interview. You will thus be able to put into your letter the welcome personal element. For instance, a letter planned to sell an article to a lawyer or to a doctor will be different in its appeal from letters designed to reach a farmer or a merchant. *Plan your letter for your reader.*

It should be noted that the letters quoted here are only illustrations of principles and methods and are not offered as models or guides. Since conditions vary greatly and every letter should be written with its particular reader definitely in mind, no set of letters, however extensive, could safely be copied or closely imitated. Imitation of models, moreover, destroys the element of personal character that is so important a part of the good business letter.

The Letter as a Record. The letter is a more permanent thing than the conversation. (1) It serves as a ready means of confirmation and of record. (2) In it matters may be elaborated, or treated more definitely and more connectedly than in a conversation. (3) Most people find it easier to understand an object or a statement if they can see it. They have more confidence in their eyes than in their ears. Besides, they can take more time to study the thing or the word that is before their eyes. Hence the letter frequently offers an occasion for clear, detailed explanation, which the reader may have before him for continuous study or for repeated examination.

In modern practice, clear explanation is recognized as the best means of persuasion through letters. Argument is generally regarded as out of place in a business letter, except as it appears in the form of a conclusion based upon clear explanation. This is a principle also of the best modern advertising; for an advertisement is really an "open letter" of business.

STYLE: QUALITIES

The preceding paragraph will suggest that the business letter is not necessarily brief. In practice, however, it is usually, if possible, limited to one page. But it must always be *clear, concise, positive,* and *courteous.*

I. Clearness. This is a quality to be secured through right order, simple, direct statements, and pleasing mechanical form. If you first arouse attention and interest, the way to understanding is open; clearness means ease of understanding for the reader, but nothing is clear to an inattentive mind. Clearness through style involves: (1) the use of accurate, definite, familiar words and phrases; (2) the use of well-made and well-punctuated sentences; (3) good paragraphing.

1. Words and Phrases. The words in your letter should be "loaded"—each one should carry a definite meaning. The habit of using a limited stock of words is easy to fall into, but it is fatal to clearness, except in the narrow circle of persons familiar with them. Every business has its peculiar set of *stock phrases,* its *cant* or *jargon,* which is unfamiliar to many people. For them, it must be translated into expressions they can understand readily. The letter writer should study *Usage* and *Synonyms.* If he rejects a stock phrase like *in re,* he will be obliged to choose a fresh one. Here are some outworn phrases that good writers are careful to avoid:

Advise, in the sense of *inform* or *tell.* The word is used too often. *Inform* or *notify,* except in formal writing, would be better.

Along these lines. A good phrase, but, when used too often, *lines* becomes indefinite. *In this way* or *following these plans* may be more definite.

And oblige, as in the phrase, "*and oblige* Yours truly." An obvious short-cut in courtesy, and therefore lacking in courtesy. Write "We (or I) shall be greatly obliged."

As per. Use *according to,* or some other phrase. See *Good Usage.*

At all times, At this time. The false formality in these phrases often repeated robs them of force. Prefer *always* and *now.*

At hand or **Has come to hand.** An obsolete phrase. Write "We have your letter—," or leave the fact to be understood.

Attached hereto. Appropriate only in the briefest, routine forms.

At the present writing. Prefer *now* or *at present.*

Beg, as in "We *beg* to state." An expression to be used only in the most formal correspondence. Otherwise it suggests a false humility.

Complaint. The word has been displaced in favor of *claim* and *adjustment.* The business advantage is obvious.

Contents carefully noted. A dead phrase. Use some words that will really convey the personal interest intended: "We have read with particular care, etc."

Enclosed herewith or **We enclose herewith.** *Herewith* is unnecessary.

Enclosed please find. *Please* is superfluous. Write "You will find enclosed" or "We enclose."

Earliest convenience. A faulty choice of words assumed to be courteous because of their indefiniteness. "As soon as possible" or "as soon as convenient for you" is the meaning usually intended.

Esteemed, as in "your *esteemed* favor." This and the following word are old forms of courtesy worn out by too frequent use. Say simply "your letter."

Favor, as in "*favor* us with a reply." Save the word for times when a reply is a real favor or courtesy.

Hand you herewith. Originally supposed to suggest personal presence in a letter, this phrase has lost its meaning through too frequent repetition. To say simply "inclose," or "enclose," is usually sufficient.

Inst., Ult., Prox. These are not now in good use to indicate present, last, or next month.

Kindly, as in "thanking you *kindly.*" Superfluous. Kindness is implied in thanks.

Our Mr......... No longer good form. Omit *our,* or say "our representative," or use his official title; as, "our manager."

Participial Construction, as in "*Hoping* for an early reply." In English, the present participle frequently gives a weak form of expression. Its use in the conclusion of letters is to be avoided. Write, "We hope for."

Party, meaning *person.* See *Good Usage.*

Passive Construction, as in "goods *were not able to be shipped.*" Use active form of expression: "It was not possible to ship" or "We could not ship."

Permit me to say. This phrase is too formal for ordinary use. It seems to imply some straining of relations.

Pronouns or Articles Omitted, as in "*Received yours and contents noted.*" The pronoun *I* or *we* is good form and should be used.

Proposition, meaning *affair.* See *Good Usage.*

Recent date, as in "yours *of recent date.*" Exactness is preferable. Give precise date.

Same, as in "the *same* shall receive prompt attention." The word is overworked. Use regular pronouns, except in formal papers.

State, meaning *say.* See *Good Usage.*

The writer. People are not so much afraid of the first personal pronoun as they used to be. Use *I* or *we,* instead of *the writer* or *the undersigned,* except in official letters, reports, and other formal documents.

Valued, as in "your *valued* communication." False formality, except on special occasions.

Would say or **Wish to say.** Too frequently these are mere wasteful, roundabout phrases. Omit them.

Your obedient servant. Another worn-out form. Many of these business forms are relics of the old servant attitude of the shopkeeper toward a patron. Let your phrases of courtesy express self-respect.

2. Sentences. The sentence is the common unit of thought expression. In some special types of letters the separate phrase may be used to challenge attention, but good sentence structure is necessary to the good letter. See *Sentence Building.*

Three rhetorical types of sentences are recognized.

(1) *The loose sentence* simply adds idea to idea; it can be closed at any one of several different points and still be a complete sentence. Example: "Students from Central and South America are already coming to our colleges and universities in considerable numbers—and nothing has done so much to make Latin America acquainted with the United States."

(2) *The periodic sentence* is more rarely used and must be definitely planned in advance. It piles up one subordinate idea after another, preparatory to the main statement. Its advantage is in its effect of climax. Example: "That there is a serious housing shortage today, not only in the United States but throughout the civilized world, is a generally known fact."

(3) *The balanced sentence* is so called because it is built of contrasting clauses of similar form, which seem to balance each other like a pair of scales. This sentence is much used in advertising and in business letters. Its value lies in the emphasis and clearness which come from the contrasts in the sentence. Example: "Not only is order Heaven's first law, but it is the first and last law of Earth."

The skillful writer will adapt his sentence form to the subject in hand and to the purpose in view. He will vary the forms of his sentences to avoid monotony, for monotony is the foe of attention and, therefore, of clearness.

See *Punctuation*.

3. Paragraphs. The paragraph is the common form for the relating and the developing of ideas. In its construction, we must consider logic, style, and form. For *Paragraph Development*, refer to *Speaking and Writing* and see below under *Form*. The skillful letter writer will study the psychology of the paragraph. Good paragraph arrangement enables the reader to see the relationship of sentences that belong together as parts of the treatment of a single topic. It enables him also to get the intended emphasis by observing the position of the various sentences in the paragraph. The beginning and the end of a paragraph, as of a sentence, are the emphatic points.

The following is an excellent example of a business paragraph:

"Saving should be more than the accumulation of money. It should include the use of money to add to the total; in other words, investment. Reckless investment is speculation, but careful investment is the best form of saving."

The first sentence states a topic clearly; the second enlarges on the topic; the third, a balanced sentence, develops the "investment" idea and repeats, for emphasis, the word "saving," which thus is kept the most emphatic word in the paragraph.

II. Conciseness. One attains conciseness through using the exact word, and by using no more words than necessary. The quality is the result of precision and of economy in diction. Skill in this matter is to be attained through study of *Synonyms* and of *Usage*. Conciseness is not improved by omitting the pronoun subject from a sentence; as, "Received yours of the 24th." Always put the subject into the sentence. (The imperative sentence is an exception.)

III. Positiveness. This is a matter of *contents* and of *style*. It means direct, definite, unmistakable meaning in directions and suggestions.

Strive for positiveness in the *contents* of a business letter. The reason for this rule is psychological. We know how the mind works. Desired action is best secured by positive suggestion; undesired action is best prevented, not by negative suggestion, but by positive suggestion of the opposite action. For example: instead of saying, "Do not delay writing us," say, "Write to us at once."

IV. Courtesy. The true quality of courtesy arises from the writer's consideration for the interests and feelings of his reader. It is usually manifested, however, in the choice and in the use of expressions of politeness that have been well established by convention. It is often made even more evident by what the letter leaves unsaid. Words and phrases that might wound or irritate or might suggest lack of respect for the reader should be scrupulously avoided. The quality of courtesy should pervade the whole letter, but it is especially vital at the beginning and at the end. Most of the specimen letters quoted here illustrate the value of courtesy.

FORM

Good psychology prompts attention to the *mechanical form* of the letter as a means of securing attention and favorable consideration. Not only must the letter be easy to read, but it must invite reading. No matter how important or interesting the contents of a letter may be, if its form is not attractive, it may be a failure.

Legibility and Neatness. If a manuscript has a clean-cut, finished look, anyone who sees it will be predisposed in favor of the writer and his work. Conversely, an illegible or untidy manuscript creates an unfavorable impression that can hardly be overcome by good style and content. Letters written by hand need not display artistic shading or Spencerian flourishes, but they should meet the minimum requirements for legibility. That is, they should identify the written characters by giving them proper slant, looping, and spacing—by rounding the "m's" and "n's" and by sharpening the "u's." Even more important is the distinct separation of words. A little practice in observing these simple requirements for legibility will make anyone's writing acceptable.

Quality and Form of Stationery. This is the first consideration. Select good stationery; then write letters of corresponding quality. Generally, commercial letter paper is about 8½ by 11 inches in size. A half sized sheet, 6 by 10 or 5½ by 8, is sometimes used, although the best form is the full sized sheet for all letters. For mailing, this full sized sheet should be folded from the bottom so as to bring the bottom edge within about a half inch of the top. This folding makes the opening of the letter easy. If a letterhead is used, this folding may be made so as to leave a part of the letterhead visible. The folded sheet is then again folded twice, the first fold beginning about one-third of the distance from the right, bringing the sheet to a convenient size for the ordinary business envelope.

For the long or legal envelope, fold the bottom third of the page upward, then the top third down. This folding allows the reader, on opening the letter, to see the heading at once. Folding the top third down first and the bottom third upward makes insertion in the envelope easier. Formal official letters are frequently written on stationery of the social form, that is, on a four-page, folded sheet adapted for folding once to fit either an envelope of commercial size or the square type of envelope. It may carry a short form of letterhead either printed or engraved.

The envelope should, of course, match the paper in color and in quality. A short form of letterhead or return address is printed in the upper left-hand corner of the envelope, or sometimes on the flap of the envelope, as on social stationery.

In general, white paper of the "bond" type is always good form. If tinted papers are used, the color should be such as will not interfere with ease of reading.

Placing the Letter Upon the Page. This is very important. For the positions of the various parts there are set rules. The reader habitually looks for the address of the writer in the upper right-hand part of the page, for his own address and the salutation at the upper left-hand part, on lines slightly below the writer's address, and for a formal conclusion at the bottom. Examples of these rules and of permissible variations are shown in the following specimens.

CORRECT BUSINESS LETTER FORMS

I. The Heading. This contains the address of the sender and the date of writing. It is the first item in the business letter. A printed or engraved letterhead should contain the address of the individual or firm. The address so given need not be repeated. The following forms are approved to be placed in the upper right-hand part of the page. Care should be taken that this heading is not too near the right-hand side. When the heading takes two lines or three, the second and third lines may be indented; as,—

> 810 Jefferson Avenue,
> Cleveland, Ohio 44113
> June 28, 19—.

or, in block,

> 810 Jefferson Avenue,
> Cleveland, Ohio 44113
> June 28, 19—.

or,

> 725 Tremont St., Boston 02118
> June 28, 19—.

To give a personal or social *tone* to the letter, numbers and dates may be written out. The following form for dates, in both heading and body of the letter, finds favor with some writers:

> 15 May, 19—.

II. The Introduction, or Address. This is the second item in the letter. It should be placed one or two lines below the heading and at the left of the page. The following forms are in good use:

1. Addressing a firm,—

> Messrs. Jones & Black
> 480 Main Street
> Buffalo, New York 14203

or, The Aetna Company
> 7 Archer Avenue
> Omaha, Nebraska 68107

or, Smith, Marks & Co.,
> P.O. Box 250,
> Boston, Mass. 02101

2. Addressing an individual, as a member of a firm,—

> Mr. James T. Girard'
> President Girard Steel Company
> Box 1768, Plaza Sta.,
> St. Louis, Missouri 63199

3. Addressing an individual,—

> Mr. Thomas Brown
> 513 Sacramento Street
> San Francisco, California 94111

Note.—These addresses may be written in block. Some writers prefer not to use commas at the ends of lines in the heading or address. This practice is permissible. Periods also, except after abbreviations, may be omitted from the ends of these lines. Omission of marks must, however, be consistent:

> 16 Park Ave., Denver 80218
> December 14, 19—

> Miss Jean Phillips
> 1014 Chamber of Commerce
> Columbus, Ohio 43215

The method of open punctuation, used in the above example, may be seen illustrated in the first sample letter under Letter Writing, by Walter C. Hines.

When the firm is addressed, but it is intended that the letter should go to some particular person, *Attention Mr. . . . . .* may be written at the right below the heading, or on a line with the salutation. Frequently, the *subject* of the letter is written at the right in line with the name of the firm or person addressed:

> The Aetna Company   Subject: Flour Shipment
> 7 Archer Avenue
> Omaha, Nebraska 68107
>
> Gentlemen: Attention Mr. Brown

4. Military Form,—

The following form is prescribed for U. S. Army correspondence:

> U. S. ARMY RECRUITING STATION,
> 5 EAST SWAN STREET, BUFFALO, N. Y. 14203
>
> 825   22 November, 19—.
> From: Recruiting Officer.
> To: The Adjutant General of the Army, Washington,
>   D. C. 20301
> Subject: Enlistments.

This is called the "brief." It occupies the upper third of the ordinary sheet and is folded back so as to be immediately visible in files or on opening the envelope. The usual *salutation* and the usual *complimentary close* are omitted. The number (825) refers to the office files.

Many business houses use a similar form, especially for routine letters between departments.

5. Addressing a firm of women,—

> Mesdames Trigg & New
> 5314 Michigan Avenue
> Chicago, Illinois 60615

Note.—Some authorities permit omission of the period after *Mr.* and *Messrs.*

III. The Salutation. This is the third item.

1. In addressing a firm, *Gentlemen* is preferred to *Dear Sirs* by most writers. This form is used also in addressing firms made up of men and women.

2. In addressing a firm made up of women, *Ladies* is the usual salutation.

3. For individuals, *Dear Sir* is the usual form. *My dear Sir* is regarded as rather more formal. A little more informal, according to occasion, is *Dear Mr. Girard* or *My dear Mr. Girard.*

4. *Dear Madam* or, more formal, *My dear Madam* is appropriate in addressing either a married or an unmarried woman. *Dear Mrs. Smith* or, more formal, *My dear Mrs. Smith* may be used if the degree of acquaintanceship permits.

5. In addressing an unmarried woman, use such a form as *Dear Miss Walker* or, more formal, *My dear Miss Walker.*

6. In addressing a letter to a man *and* a woman, use the form *Dear Sir and Madam.*

Note.—The husband's title, as, *Doctor, Professor,* or *Reverend,* should never be prefixed to the wife's name.

In a letter to a doctor or a professor, the address may be *Dr. James Martin* or *James Martin, M. D.* (or *D. D., Ph. D., D. O., D. D. S.*), or *Professor Wm. James.* If *Dr.* precedes the name, the abbreviation for the degree should not follow. In such cases, the salutation may be *Dear Sir* or, less formal, *Dear Doctor Martin* or *Dear Professor James.*

Note.—In general, good taste seems to approve, even in business letters, the spelling out of a title in the salutation, although the abbreviation may be used.

Note.—In the punctuation of the salutation, usage varies. The color is always correct. In short, informal letters, the comma may be used. The dash is superfluous. However, if the address takes more than three lines, the salutation may be made part of the first line of the letter and may be followed by colon and dash or by comma and dash:

> Gentlemen:—In your letter of June 26, etc.

IV. The Body of the Letter. This should be well centered on the page. The margins at top and bottom should be approximately equal, and the margins at the sides should be kept, as nearly as possible, equal. It is easy to keep the left-hand margin regular, but some care is necessary to get an even right-hand margin. Wide margins at right and left are advisable for two reasons: (1) Short lines are easier to read than long ones; (2) the contrast of blank and filled spaces makes reading easier.

The Paragraphing of a Business Letter. This is perhaps the most important feature of its form. First of all, the paragraphs should be reasonably short, for a well broken page is more inviting to the eye and easier to read than solid masses of type. Secondly, the paragraphs should not have too great a contrast in length. Absolute uniformity is, of course, impossible and undesirable as well. Variety in the matter of length, however, should be only great enough to avoid monotony. Generally speaking, the paragraphs at the beginning and at the end of the letter should be somewhat shorter than those in the middle.

The following paragraph forms are in use:

The indented paragraph, like this one. The first line is set in from the margin a number of spaces approximately equal to the margin allowed.

The hanging paragraph, like this. The first line begins at the margin, and all other lines are indented a number of spaces equal to the margin allowed for the first line.

The blocked paragraph, like this. No line is given extra indention. This last type of paragraph calls for very wide margins and for extra space between paragraphs. Examples of these various forms of paragraphing are given in the specimen letters on the following pages. Margins should be at least one inch wide, and two blank lines should be left between paragraphs.

V. The Complimentary Close. In business letters this should be *Yours truly*, or *Yours very truly*, or *Respectfully yours*, *Very respectfully yours*, except in cases where the writer, because of close acquaintance, may prefer a more informal phrase, such as *Sincerely yours*, *Faithfully yours*. Never write *respectively* for *respectfully*.

Such an expression as *With sincerest regards, I am* should begin a new, indented line, just above the complimentary close.

Envelope. *The address on the envelope* and that in the letter should correspond accurately, although some authorities permit the omission of the street address in the letter. On the envelope, the first line of the address should be placed approximately halfway between the top and the bottom of the envelope, beginning about one-fourth of the length of the envelope from the left-hand end.

Additional directions, such as *in care of*, *c/o*, or *introducing*, may be placed at the lower left-hand corner. A post-office box number is usually placed in this position, to avoid having more than three, or at most four, lines in the address. Neither the abbreviation *No.* nor the sign # should be placed before the street address, but the postal ZIP Code should always appear on the last line of both the address and the return address following the city and state. Punctuation may be used in the address or omitted entirely, except after abbreviations.

In *street numbers* involving *second* or *third*, it is sufficient to write *d* after the figures instead of *nd* or *rd*; as 32d, 23d. Many writers do not use *d* or *th*. To insure the return of a letter in case of failure of delivery, the writer's address, complete with ZIP Code, should be placed on the outside of the envelope, either in the upper left-hand corner on the front of the envelope or on the flap at the back of the envelope.

Cautions. Certain things the careful writer will always do: (1) He will use the *correct* address of the person to whom he is writing and will make the salutation *appropriate*; (2) he will have the complimentary close *appropriate* and his own signature *legible*. If the writer of the letter is a woman, she will add to her signature whatever may be necessary to indicate whether or not she is married, as in the following:

(*Mrs.*) or (*Miss*) *Anna M. Worden.*

or,

(*Mrs. J. C. Truman*)   *Mary V. Truman.*

If there are "enclosures" in the letter, such as stamps, money, or papers, these should always be mentioned; and it is customary to write in the lower left-hand corner either the word *Enclosure* or the abbreviation *Enc.*; similarly, *Inclosure* or *Inc.*

Letters sent in the name of a firm by an official or employee may be signed as follows:

Knight, Lymmes, and Co.
By (or *Per*) *L. R. Parsons.*

OFFICIALS AND DIGNITARIES

(*Your postmaster can furnish ZIP Code*)

The President of the United States.
Name and address,—The President, White House (or Executive Mansion), Washington, D. C.
Salutation,—*Mr. President:* or *Sir:*
Close,—*Respectfully yours*, or *Very truly yours*,

The Vice President of the United States.
Name and address,—The Honorable..........,Vice President of the United States, Washington, D. C. or, To the Vice President of the United States, Washington, D. C.
Salutation,—*Sir:* or *Dear Sir:*
Close,—*Very truly yours*, or *Respectfully yours*,

Member of Cabinet.
Name and address,—The Secretary of State, Washington, D. C.
Salutation,—*Dear Mr. Secretary:*
Close,—*Yours very truly*,
or,
Name and address,—The Honorable the Secretary of the Treasury, Washington, D. C. or, The Honorable A............ B............, Secretary of the Treasury, Washington, D. C.
Salutation,—*Sir:* or *Dear Sir:*
Close,—*Very respectfully yours*,

Members of Congress.
Name and address,—The Hon. Martin Warren, United States Senate, Washington, D. C.
or, The Hon. Martin Warren, House of Representatives, Washington, D. C.
Salutation,—*Sir:* or *Dear Sir:*
Close,—*Very truly yours*,

Foreign Ministers.
Name and address,—His Excellency,........, Ambassador to the Court of St. James, London, England.
Salutation,—*Your Excellency:* or *Sir:*
Close,—*Very truly yours*,

Governors.
Name and address,—His Excellency, the Governor of New York, Albany, N. Y.
or, His Excellency, the Governor, Albany, N. Y.
or, His Excellency, Governor S. M. Smith, Albany, N. Y.
Salutation,—*Your Excellency:* or *Sir:*
Close,—*Very truly yours*,

Mayors.
Name and address,—The Honorable ...., Mayor of New York City, New York City, N. Y.
Salutation,—*Sir:* or *Dear Sir:*
Close,—*Very truly yours*,

State Officers.
Name and address,—The Honorable Attorney-General of New York, Albany, N. Y.
or, The Honorable ...., Attorney-General of New York, Albany, N. Y.
Salutation,—*Sir:* or *Dear Sir:*
Close,—*Very truly yours*,

Judge of Supreme Court (or highest court of a State).
Name and address,—The Hon. William V. Hinton, State Capitol, Columbus, Ohio.
Salutation,—*Dear Mr. Justice:*
Close,—*Yours very truly*,

Judge (other than Supreme Court).
Name and address,—The Hon. Henry A. Freeman, State Circuit Court Building, Chicago, Ill.
Salutation,—*Dear Sir:* or (less formal) *Dear Judge Freeman:*
Close,—*Yours very truly*,

Minor Officials (City or County).
Name and address,—Mr. James Wingate, City Treasurer, City Hall, Des Moines, Iowa.
Salutation,—*Dear Sir:*
Close,—*Yours very truly*,

President of a University.
Name and address,—President Nathan M. Pusey, Harvard University, Cambridge, Mass.
Salutation,—*Dear Sir:* or (more formal) *My dear Sir:*
Close,—*Yours very truly*,

College or University Professor.
Name and address,—Professor Arthur K. Rimer, University of Denver, Denver, Colo. 80202 (Degree is usually omitted.)
Salutation,—*Sir:* or *Dear Sir:*
Close,—*Yours very truly,* or *Yours sincerely,*

Superintendent of Schools.
Name and address,—Superintendent Edward Jones, Department of Education, City Hall, Cleveland, Ohio 44114
Salutation,—*Sir:* or *Dear Sir:* or *My dear Sir:* or (very informally) *Dear Mr. Jones:*
Close,—*Yours very truly,* or *Yours sincerely,*

Protestant Clergyman.
Name and address,—The Reverend Thomas L. Warner, 1645 Earl Avenue, Harrisburg, Pa. 17109
Salutation,—*Sir:* or *Dear Sir:* or *My dear Sir:* or (very informally) *Dear Mr. Warner:*
Close,—*Yours very truly,* or *Yours sincerely,*

Parish Priest.
Name and address,—The Reverend Frederick E, Kane, 276 Francis Street, Detroit, Mich. 48217
Salutation,—*Reverend and dear Father:* or *Dear Reverend Father:*
Close,—*Yours sincerely,*

Jewish Rabbi.
Name and address,—Rabbi Stephen S. Wise, 340 W. 57th St., New York, N. Y. 10019
Salutation,—*Dear Sir:*
Close,—*Yours very truly,* or *Yours sincerely,*

Protestant Doctor of Divinity (or of Laws).
Name and address,—The Reverend Charles A. McArthur, D. D. (or LL. D.), 5927 Dorchester Avenue, Boston, Mass. 02224
Salutation,—*Sir:* or *Dear Sir:* or *My dear Sir:* or (very informally) *Dear Dr. McArthur:*
Close,—*Yours very truly,* or *Yours sincerely,*

The Pope.
Name and address,—His Holiness, Pope John XXIII The Vatican, Rome.
Salutation,—*Your Holiness:*
Close,—*Sincerely yours in Christ,*

Cardinal.
Name and address,—His Eminence, William Cardinal O'Connell, Archbishop of Boston, 25 Granby Street, Boston, Mass. 02215
Salutation,—*Your Eminence:*
Close,—*Faithfully your Eminence's servant,* or *Sincerely yours;* if the writer is a Catholic, the words "in Christ" are usually added.

Bishop.
Name and address,—The Most Reverend Moses E. Kiley, D. D., Bishop of Trenton, Trenton, N. J.
Salutation,—*Right Reverend and dear Bishop:* or *Right Reverend Bishop:* or, simply, and perhaps more commonly, *Sir:*
Close,—any of the ordinary forms, such as *Very truly yours,* or *Yours sincerely;* if the writer is a Catholic, the words "Sincerely yours in Christ" should be used.

Women in Religious Orders.
Name and address,—(1) The Reverend Mother Angela (in the case of the Mother Superior); (2) Sister Constance (in the case of a Sister); followed in each case by the address.
Salutation,—(1) *Reverend Mother:* (2) *Reverend Madam:* or *Dear Madam:*
Close,—*Yours sincerely,* or any of the more formal phrases.

Military Officer.
Name and address,—General Lyman L. Lemnitzer, Defense Department, Washington, D. C. 20301 or, The Commanding Officer, Niagara Falls Air Base, Niagara Falls, N. Y. 14306
Salutation,—*Sir:* or *Dear Sir:*
Close,—any of the ordinary forms.

Naval Officer.
Name and address,—Admiral Arleigh A. Burke, Naval Observatory, Washington, D. C. or, if at sea, U. S. S. *Pennsylvania,* c/o Postmaster, New York, N. Y. 10551
Salutation,—*Sir:* or *Dear Sir:*
Close,—any of the ordinary forms.

Note.—The salutation *Sir,* in nearly all cases, is used in formal official letters. This is also an approved salutation to use in addressing a letter to the editor of a newspaper or other journal. See *Official Letters.*

TYPES OF BUSINESS LETTERS

The following are the common types of letters. Each type has its own peculiar problems.

I. The Simple Order and **Reply.** This type, supplemented by the letter of inquiry and explanation, is the kind that most people have frequent occasion to use. Out of this simple exchange, however, may develop the elaborate system of *claim, adjustment,* and *follow-up* letters. Claim and adjustment letters, in particular, should be tactfully written. The wording should make plain the writer's intention to be accurate and fair.

1. Order for Goods.

> 572 East Avenue,
> Rochester, New York 14607
>
> April 3, 19—
>
> Messrs. Rowen, Winstead, & Company
> 437 State Street
> Chicago, Illinois 60605
> Gentlemen:
> Will you please send me by freight, addressed to James Wilson, Alton, N.Y., the following:
>
> 1 French row-motor;
> 1 set Franklin garage door tracks and hangers.
>
> I enclose check for $96.25, net price as listed in your special March bulletin.
>
> The building materials purchased from you last summer have proved so satisfactory that I am very glad to send you this further order. I hope that it can be shipped very promptly.
>
> Yours very truly,
>
> Enc.   Robert T. Vane.

2. Request for Adjustment.

> 572 East Avenue,
> Rochester, N. Y. 14607
>
> July 6, 19—
>
> Messrs. Rowen, Winstead, & Company
> 437 State Street
> Chicago, Illinois 60605
> Gentlemen:
> I have had shipped to you today from Cayuga, N. Y., by insured parcel post, the propeller and housing from the row-motor which I recently purchased from you.
>
> We have used this motor a very few times only. Yesterday, while we were on the river, the housing broke, and it was only by the merest accident that I was able to recover it at all. I do not know that the machine was subjected to any extraordinary strain, though, of course, it may have been. However, the metal looks to me as if it had been defective at the break. Will you please examine the housing and make such adjustment as you think is right.
>
> I shall be glad to have this matter attended to promptly in order that we may have the engine to use as soon as possible.
>
> Yours very truly,
> Robert T. Vane.

3. Reply to Adjustment Request.

> (LETTERHEAD)
>
> July 8, 19—
>
> Mr. Robert T. Vane
> 572 East Avenue
> Rochester, New York 14607
> Dear Sir:
> We are very sorry to learn from your letter of July 6 that you have had trouble with the row-motor. We have not yet received the broken parts, but we appreciate the fact that during vacation time you will want a motor to use. Accordingly, we will ship by today's parcel post a propeller and housing to replace the broken parts.
>
> When your shipment arrives, we will have an examination made and will make adjustment such as we think will thoroughly satisfy you. We appreciate your patronage and your good offices in our favor.
>
> Yours very truly,
> Rowen, Winstead, & Company
> By J. C. Marcus

4. Order for Magazine.

24 Winfield Street
Oswego, Illinois 60543
October 15, 19—

Time, the Weekly Newsmagazine
350 East 22nd Street
Chicago, Illinois 60616

Gentlemen:

I enclose money for $12.00 in payment for re-
newal of my subscription to Time, the Weekly Newsmagazine, for the year 196–.

Please note the change of address indicated at the head
of this letter.

Former address: 371 Otis Ave., Kenmore, Ohio 44314

Yours very truly,

Enc.   (Miss) Myra V. Killian.

5. Letter to College Officer.

622 Plymouth Avenue
Harrisburg, Pa. 17109
July 13, 19—

Mr. James Harvey, Registrar
University of Illinois
Urbana, Ill. 61801

Dear Sir:

Will you please send me a copy of your application
blank for entrance to the engineering school in Fairmount.
I completed my high school course in June, and I am
planning to enter college next fall. I should be glad to
receive also a copy of your catalogue and other information that would be useful.

Very respectfully yours,

William D. Brown.

II. Letters of Agreement. These usually supplement contracts of various sorts, and should be
worded as nearly as possible in the terms of the
accompanying contract

III. The Sales or Advertising Letter. This
has been very highly developed within the last few
years. It is really the standard or type of all business
letters. The psychological principles of the business
letter, as stated before, apply with special force to
this type, which has for its immediate purpose the
securing of business. In present day practice, sales
letters are frequently prepared in series, the whole
series being planned to cover the steps already given
for the typical business letter. The first letter is
designed, for instance, to get attention; the last in
the series is written as the "clincher," or final persuasive letter.

A short series of four or five letters may be used,
each one distinctly different in contents and purpose.
Again, a long series, sometimes called "continuous,"
may be employed, each letter differing only slightly
from the others in point of view, all aimed at persuading the "prospect."

These series are the common form of the follow-
up systems. The writer has a definite object in view,
usually to secure a new field of business or to maintain interest and good will among his present clients.
If his first letter fails to fulfil its purpose, he follows
it up with others in which the methods of approach
or inducements offered differ somewhat from those
of the first. For example, the letter of the Forest
Products Association (first sample under Letter
Writing), might be followed by one giving some
more definite, interesting details about the special
uses of woods to arouse the attention and the interest of Mr. Parsons, should he fail to return the
card. If he returns the card promptly, a second
letter should precede the representative's call, introducing him and encouraging the fullest use of his
services.

Such letters as the following (**6, 7**), when prepared
as circular or form letters, should be so printed that
the type style used in filling in the individual
addresses shall be like that in the body of the letter
The whole then will have the appearance of a
personal letter and will command attention.

6. Sales Letter.

(Letterhead)

April 6, 19—

Mrs. Marion T. Archer
1432 Delavan Avenue
Albion, Indiana 46701

Dear Madam:

ATTENTION — On that auto trip last summer, you enjoyed
tremendously the road and the ride
through beautiful scenery. But
when you came to the inn at the end
of the day, did you find your gowns
in the smooth, dainty condition you
could have wished for? Isn't it
annoying to find the only things you
have to "change to" all rumpled
and creased?

INTEREST — The answer, of course, is a wardrobe trunk.
It is a compact, dust-proof trunk in
your car, and a handy, complete
wardrobe in your hotel room.

INFORMATION / INDUCEMENT — Through an unusually large purchase of
the widely known Plico trunks, we
are able to offer, during the next
week, a full stock at prices that mean
to you a saving of more than one-
third the usual cost of these high-
grade trunks.

POSITIVE SUGGESTION — One look at the sturdy build of these trunks
and their complete and dainty ar-
rangement of trays and hangers for
every sort of hat and garment will
convince you that certainly, at these
prices, you cannot afford another
trip without such a convenience.

Members of our sales staff are enthusiastic
about these new Plico trunks, especially as regards the wide variety of
types, conveniences, and styles offered. They will do their best to show
you a wardrobe trunk which will best
meet your individual traveling needs
and your requirements in color and
decorative treatment.

Come in early and make your selection before the present full stock is picked
over by other buyers.

Very truly yours,

Eldridge, Warren and Company,
Per B. F. Warren,
Manager.

7. Sales Letter.

(Letterhead)

THE SECRETARY OF THE TREASURY
Washington

October 1946

To Newspaper Publishers,
Editors and Ad Managers:

The first lesson in a democracy is that the Government belongs to its millions of citizens. It belongs to you—all of us.
The Nation can be only as prosperous as are its cities, farms
and communities of the individual families which inhabit them.

When you help to promote the sale of U. S. Savings Bonds,
you help check inflation and subsequent depression. You help
to maintain stable economy.

Stability alone is not enough. The ownership of Savings
Bonds does more. It gives people an actual share in America.
It presents the possibility of providing the funds for homes
and higher education of your children, for old age security, and
for emergencies. In other words, your effort in securing bond
advertising provides for the security and prosperity of the
individual and his family. Prosperous families mean prosperous communities. Prosperous communities mean a prosperous Nation.

That is how you help your Government—that is how you
help yourself—when you assist in the U. S. Savings Bond
Program.

I urge you to be of all the help you can.

Sincerely,

John W. Snyder
Secretary of the Treasury.

IV. The Collection Letter. Collection letters are of two main types,—routine notifications of indebtedness and personal requests for payment. The first of these are standard, impersonal notices, and are therefore inoffensive. Usually, such reminders are all that is necessary. If personal requests are needed, they should be courteous and should avoid the use of threats or other offensive measures except as a last resort. In order to be courteous, however, a collection letter need not be apologetic. Firmness not only enhances the prestige of the creditor but also gains the debtor's respect. Collection letters are usually prepared as a series which begins with a mild suggestion that payment would be appreciated and ends with an insistent demand. The orderly and systematic mailing of such a series is often more important in making the work of collection letters effective than is the construction of any individual letter. Every letter, however, should have the double purpose of securing the money due and also of retaining the debtor's good will.

8. Collection Letter.

(LETTERHEAD)

June 20, 19—

Mr. M. C. Harris
12 Arthur Street
Conneaut, Ohio 44030
Dear Sir:
  We find on our books a charge against you of $15.87, under date of May 14. We wish to call your attention to the fact that this is past due.
  Your prompt remittance will be appreciated.
    Very truly yours,
    Owen, James, and Co.

9. Collection Letter (*a little more insistent*).

(LETTERHEAD)

June 1, 19—

Mr. L. R. Converse
356 Oliver Street
Baltimore, Maryland 21202
Dear Sir:
  According to our books, your account for invoice of April 7 amounting to $47.60 is unpaid and past due. We wrote you about this account on May 20, but we have had no reply. We wish again to call your attention to the need for payment.
  Please give this matter your immediate attention.
    Very truly yours,
    Owen, James, and Co.

V. The Letter of Application. The letter of application is in most respects similar to the sales letter. The writer is attempting to sell his own services. To be sure, he must be somewhat more modest and restrained in talking about himself than he is in talking about commodities and the services of others. He should not, however, run the risk of making his letter awkward as well as hypocritical by avoiding the use of the first personal pronoun *I* or by any other device that has its basis in false modesty. If the reader is to desire the writer's services, he must know enough about them to be able to judge their value to him in his business.

10. Direct Application for Commercial Position.

419 Marshall Street,
Syracuse, New York 13210
February 3, 19—

Messrs. G. A. Case & Son
193 Broad Street
Syracuse, New York 13210
Gentlemen:
  I wish to apply for the position in your engineering office which you mention in your advertisement in this morning's "Standard."
  I am nineteen years old, a graduate of the Technical High School in the class of 19—. I have also completed a course in drafting in the Mechanics' Institute of Rochester. At present I am employed in the shops of the J. W. Atkins Company, Machinists.
  I should be glad to be granted a personal interview at your convenience.
    Yours very truly,
    James Manson.

11. Application Letter, with Side Heads.

311 East Welker Street,
Buffalo, New York 14208
October 1, 19—

Box 176,
Buffalo Evening News.

Gentlemen:
Will you please consider me an applicant for the position mentioned in your advertisement in the Buffalo Evening News of October 1. My qualifications are as follows:
Education. I am a graduate of the Bennett High School of this city, in the class of 19—. My course included commercial work in bookkeeping, typewriting, and stenography. In all these subjects my standing was high.
Experience. During the last two years, I have been employed in the office of R. D. Ward & Son, Ellicott Square Building. My work has included stenography and general office assistance.
References. I can refer you, for information as to my ability and my character, to R. D. Ward & Son, and also to the following: Mr. J. W. Archer, head of Commercial Department, Bennett High School; Mr. Martin B. Allen, Supreme Court Judge.
    Very truly yours,
    Thomas R. Stafford.

VI. Letter of Resignation. The conclusion of an employee's services should be brought about in a courteous, businesslike manner, and this should be reflected in the correspondence. Although formal, in that it is a record of proceedings, the letter of resignation is usually somewhat personal in tone. Whereas the letter of application is nearly always directed to strangers, the letter terminating one's employment is addressed to persons with whom one has become acquainted. Also *consideration*, which is an important characteristic of "separation correspondence," can best be expressed in language that is more or less informal.

12.

Columbus, Ohio,
November 20, 19—

Mr. James B. Wilson, President
The Midwest Supply Company
Columbus, Ohio 43215

Dear Mr. Wilson:
Circumstances have arisen which make it necessary for me to be at home with my family in Cleveland. I am therefore submitting my resignation, effective January first, 196-. This will give you a month in which to find a successor for my position. Meanwhile, I will do everything I can to train the new person and otherwise insure the continuation of the work without loss of efficiency.
My stay with your firm has been very pleasant, and I regret the necessity of making a change. I am grateful to you and your associates for many courtesies that have been shown me. It is a privilege to have been a member of your organization.
    Yours sincerely,
    Susan T. Woodruff.

VII. Notes of Introduction. The writer should aim to make it easy for two of his friends to become acquainted with each other. The note may either be sent directly to the person whose good offices it bespeaks, or be given to the person introduced. In the latter case, the envelope is usually left unsealed. The wording should be frank and sincere and should suggest the opening for conversation.

13.

Tipton, Oklahoma 73570
May 7, 19—

Mr. Chas. R. Andrews, Trustee
School District No. 9
Tipton, Oklahoma 73570
My dear Mr. Andrews:
Miss Emily Smith desires to secure a position as assistant in your school. She holds a first grade certificate and has had three years of successful experience in our school. We regret to lose her, but she prefers your district because it is nearer to her home. I can recommend Miss Smith as a skillful teacher. She will exert an excellent influence in any school.
    Very truly yours,
    Charles J. Major,
    Trustee of School District No. 4.

14.

North Concord, Vermont 05858
July 6, 19—

Mr. Walter C. Strong
84 Arlington Avenue
Pittsburgh, Pa. 15203

My dear Mr. Strong:
    It gives me great pleasure to introduce to you my friend, Mr. Weston Beach, who is to become a resident in your city. You will find him an affable person. I shall greatly appreciate whatever courtesy you may show him in helping him to become acquainted.

    Cordially yours,
    Henry B. Johnson

VIII. Letters of Recommendation.

Recommendations are sometimes included in notes of introduction, but often they are written as separate letters. They may be written as general letters addressed "To whom it may concern," or as special letters to some definite person.

15. General Recommendation.

Wicomico, Virginia 23184
May 10, 19—

To Whom It May Concern:
    This is to certify that the bearer of this note, Miss Lillian Glades, was graduated from The Teachers' College, Cumberland University, and has since taught in the schools of this city. For the past three years she has taught in the Straymore School, and I have had opportunity to observe her work closely. I can recommend her as capable of filling any position in a city graded school.

    John W. Grove,
    Principal of Straymore School.

16. General Recommendation.

To Whom It May Concern:
    Mr. Henry Laird has been in our employ as bookkeeper the past six years. He is a skilled accountant and a loyal man; in every way he has served us well. We regret to part with him. He goes at his own request because he feels that he should receive a higher salary than we can afford to pay.

    We wish Mr. Laird every success.
    Jones, Martin and Co.
Birmingham, Alabama,
June 26, 19—

17. Special Recommendation.

Lehigh University,
Bethlehem, Pa. 18015
January 1, 19—

Mr. Harvey W. Jonson
Superintendent of Public Works
Topeka, Kansas 66603
My dear Mr. Jonson:
    We have in our junior class a young man, Mr. Thomas Redding, who has done excellent work in the engineering department. He is a fine, clean young man and has commanded the respect of instructors and students, alike. His home is in Nebraska, and he is anxious, on account of the illness of his father, to get employment for the next year or two near home.

    I shall greatly appreciate it if you will interest yourself in him and help him to get work.

    Very truly yours,
    Thomas Benedict.

IX. The Formal or Official Letter.

In formal or official letters, the heading is placed as in the business letter, but the best usage approves the spelling out of the date instead of the use of numerals.

In such letters, also, the address of the person to whom the letter is sent may be placed at the close of the letter, in the lower left-hand part of the sheet. The title of the person addressed, as *Reverend* or *Honorable*, should be spelled out and the initials or given name used. "The" is not necessary before these titles, although good formal usage approves such expressions as *The Reverend Mr. Thomas* in the body of the letter, and many good writers prefer this form for the address. The salutation in such a letter may be *Dear Sir* or simply *Sir*.

18. Note of Appreciation.

October eleventh,
Nineteen-sixty——

Dear Sir:
    By formal vote the Rivoli Club last night instructed me, as secretary of the club, to convey to you their very sincere appreciation of your courtesy and genuine service in the address which you delivered before the club members and their guests on Friday evening, October 10.

    I desire the privilege of adding also my own word of grateful acknowledgment.

    Very sincerely yours,
    James Wakefield.

The Honorable Thomas Downing,
    7 Harris Street,
        Denver, Colorado 80229

X. Excuse for Absence from School.

19.

    Will Miss Stringer please excuse Frances Prescott's absence from school, March 4 and 5, on account of illness in the family.
    Sarah C. Prescott.

(Mrs. J. W. Prescott),
    March 6, 19—

20.

Dear Miss Townsend,
    Please excuse James's absence from school, October tenth to fourteenth, on account of illness.
    Very truly yours,
    (Mrs.) James T. Orcutt.

Post Cards or **Postal Cards.** These are appropriate only for brief notices sent out by individuals or organizations, or for impersonal notes. They are not suitable for personal messages. Even the shortest note of any degree of intimacy should always be written as a letter and enclosed in an envelope. The *Picture Post Card* is no exception to this rule.

Telegrams. The rates for sending telegrams are based upon a message of twelve words, without punctuation. If punctuation is essential for clearness, the words *comma, period,* etc. may be inserted and paid for at regular word rates. No charge is made for the date, address, or signature. A message may be repeated back from the receiving office to the sender, for the sake of accuracy, at established rates.

Other classes of telegraphic service, known as night telegrams, night letters, and day letters, are also available. They offer the advantage either of lower rates or of greater length, but delivery is less prompt.

Cablegrams. Cablegrams, on account of higher cost, are more highly abbreviated than telegrams. The use of code words, that is, either ordinary words given unusual meanings by agreement of the sender and of the receiver, or artificial words whose meanings have been agreed upon, is common. Since the use of codes is governed by certain restrictions, however, the regulations of the cable companies should be consulted before writing a code message for transmission over their wires.

TAKING CARE OF THE DAILY MAIL

1. *Read carefully* letters received. Where the daily mail is heavy, have letters sorted into groups according to subject, as *orders, inquiries, adjustment,* etc. You can then deal with them more economically.

2. Keep incoming letters and envelopes together until you are certain that the writer's proper local address is *in the letter.* The omission of this item is a frequent offense.

3. Have your own local address on your letterhead. Omission of this often arouses in your correspondents the feeling that you are not a responsible business man.

4. *Reply promptly* to letters, usually within a day. If delay for full reply is necessary, acknowledge briefly the letter received, giving reasons for delay. Then, keep a reminder or "tickler file" to bring the matter again to your attention at the proper time.

5. *Plan your replies* to cover all points called for. Keep before you, while writing or dictating, the letter you are answering or a memorandum of its contents. An incomplete reply is annoying and unfair to your correspondent and to yourself.

6. *File together* in some orderly system the letters received and duplicates of your replies.

7. When replies are made by telegraph, *supplement and confirm* them by brief letters. These letters make useful records.

8. *Form letters*, printed on your regular stationery, to imitate typewriting, are convenient and economical when the same message is to go to a large number of people.

9. *Guide Forms.*—If your business does not call for much dictation of letters, you will find it worth while to prepare a few guide forms. These are letters prepared at leisure as carefully as possible, applying to various cases that arise frequently in your correspondence. Then, in the hurry of dictation, by making in the form letter only such changes as the particular case calls for, you can be certain of getting out a good letter.

10. *Filing.*—The purpose of filing correspondence is to keep an accurate, convenient record of past business and a guide for future correspondence. Any system used should be accurate, compact, readily accessible. There are in common use three systems:

a. *The Alphabetical System*, which is the simplest. In this system, letters are filed according to the names of the writers or the addressees; for example, letters received from and sent to *Williams* would be filed in a paper folder under *W*.

b. *The Subject System.*—The divisions of the file are made to correspond to the important items of the business: furnishings, clothing, etc. Usually an alphabetical order is kept within each subject.

c. *The Numerical System.*—In this system various subjects or correspondents are given numbers, and all papers connected with them are filed under the proper numbers in the file. The advantage of this is that it will take care of a file of any size and of any number of subjects. But a separate card index of names must be kept as a key. Each card carries the name of a subject or of a person and also the corresponding file number. The cards are arranged alphabetically.

Combination Systems are used also. Adapt your system to the requirements of your business, not your business to a system.

SOCIAL CORRESPONDENCE: FORMS

Stationery. Good usage approves a wide variety of forms and the indulgence of personal taste in the choice of stationery and in the writing of social letters and notes. The principles governing the form and appearance of business correspondence apply generally to social letters, but many informal variations from these rules are permitted.

White, unruled paper and envelopes to match are always in good taste, although pale-tinted papers which do not interfere with the clearness of the writing are permissible. Social note paper is usually a folded four-page sheet adapted to fold again once for the envelope. This paper, as well as the correspondence card, is prepared in various sizes and styles.

The Written Page. *The various parts of the letter*, as shown in the specimens, should be placed properly on the page, with due allowance for margins; no writing should be done in the margins. The heading should be placed as in the business letter, or, informally, the street address of the writer may be omitted, the date alone being written at the top of the sheet. An approved custom is to write out the date fully instead of using figures. The address of the recipient may be omitted in very familiar notes; that of the writer may be placed at the top of the paper or at the end of the letter in the lower left-hand part of the page.

Beginning and **End.** In the *salutation*, whatever form seems appropriate to the writer is permissible. except that certain abrupt and uncouth forms, such as *James* or *Friend John*, are ruled out, and the name of the person is preferred by many to the old form *Dear Friend*. *My dear Friend*, in this case, seems to be regarded as informal. *The complimentary close* may take any one of several forms, according to the degree of formality or familiarity in the letter. In such expressions as *Sincerely yours*, *Truly yours*, *Affectionately yours*, the first word only is capitalized.

TYPES OF SOCIAL NOTES AND LETTERS

The social note, written either upon the usual note-size paper or upon the commonly used correspondence card, is an important form of social writing. Such notes are brief, and the best taste dictates that the language should be as cordial and courteous as it can be made. The following specimens will suggest forms of expression appropriate for these notes. The heading is placed as in business or social letters, generally as follows:

439 East 23d Street,
June 7, 19—.

or,

Lyons Place,
November the Thirteenth.

The salutation may be as follows: *My dear Mr. Martin*, *My dear Mrs. Smith*, or *My dear Mary*. Best usage requires the addressing of a married woman by her husband's given name: *Mrs. Henry T. Myers*, not *Mrs. Laura Myers*. A widow may use her own given name or her husband's, as she pleases. The address of the recipient is placed at the lower left-hand corner of the sheet or card, or the date and the address of the writer may occupy this position. The complimentary close may be as for the social letter.

INFORMAL NOTES

1. Invitation.

515 Martin Place,
Thursday Evening.

Dear Frank,
   If you are free to accept an invitation for Saturday afternoon, Mrs. Archer and I shall be very glad to have you with us in a little auto party out at Fort Beach. We shall take luncheon with us, and I know you will enjoy the trip. We will call for you at two.

Very cordially yours,
William S. Archer.

2. Reply.

Friday Morning.

My dear Archer:
   I shall be more than glad to be one of your delightful party for tomorrow afternoon. and I shall be ready at two o'clock.

Sincerely yours,
Frank Adams Bates.

or,

3. Reply.

Friday Morning.

Dear Will,
   I am very sorry to miss the pleasant party I am sure you will have at the Fort, but, as I leave for Chicago at six this evening upon very important business, I shall not be able to be with you.

Very truly yours,
Frank Adams Bates.

4. Invitation.

Dear Mrs. Graham:

How about Thursday afternoon for a little theater party in honor of your guest, Miss Smith? If you and she are at liberty, I shall take pleasure in making the necessary arrangements for the play, and for tea at Huyler's later.

Sincerely yours,

Marie Langs.

909 Fountain Avenue
June the sixth

5. Reply.

Dear Miss Langs:

I thank you very much for your kind thoughtfulness for my guest. Miss Smith and I are delighted to set aside Thursday afternoon as you suggest.

Sincerely yours,

Julia Graham.

314 Kingsley Place
June the seventh

6. Note of Regret.

Dear Marie:

Such fascinating suggestions of "cake and tea and other things" you contrive to put into your note. I wonder if that same imagination of yours can help you to understand our disappointment at not being able to accept your invitation for Thursday afternoon. We have not words to express it. And all on account of an out-of-town appointment of such long standing that it must be kept on that particular afternoon.

Please try to imagine us just as "sorry as we can be."

Cordially yours,

Julia Graham.

7. Regrets.

Dear Miss Langs:

I regret that a previous engagement on the part of Miss Smith makes it impossible for us to accept your kind invitation for next Thursday afternoon.

Sincerely yours,

Julia Graham.

8. Invitation.

Sunnyslope Farm,
October 1, 19—

Dear Mrs. Walters,

My sister Margaret and I are inviting a few friends, quite informally, to meet our cousin, Mary Arthur, on Thursday afternoon. May we count on the pleasure of having you and your daughter, Miss Esther, with us?

Sincerely,

Sara Beeman.

9. Invitation.

The Poplars,
April 10, 19—

Dear Mrs. James:

Our Village Circle meets at our home on Monday evening next, April fifteenth. Mr. Williams and I shall be very glad to have you and Mr. James as our guests for the evening, that you may have an opportunity to meet some of your new neighbors.

Very cordially,
Harriet Williams.

10. Note with Birthday Gift.

Dear Miss Burns,

Please accept these flowers with my love and with the wish that you may enjoy many returns of this happy day.

Sincerely yours,

Helen Harvey.

73 Wellington Road
September tenth

11. Reply.

Thursday Morning.

Dear Miss Helen,

Your note and gift of beautiful flowers completed a day of perfect happiness. It is good to grow old when friends emphasize the years with increasing kindness. Thank you, dear friend, for the love which has never failed me.

Cordially yours,
Celia Burns.

The Bread-and-Butter Note. A short letter to some one whose informal hospitality one has enjoyed should never be neglected or postponed. Something like the following is appropriate, though the matter should vary according to the relations and hearts of people. The language of friendship and courtesy is none too familiar to our pens.

12.

Dear Mrs. Hartley,

Back at routine again, I catch myself fancying that I am yet in the little circle of your guests of last week.

That is the joy of such hospitality as yours,—that the memory of it lingers so long and happily.

Sincerely yours,

John W. Dare.

10 Martin Street
October 15, 19—

13.

Dear Alice:

I wish I could tell you how much I have benefited from the physical relaxation and mental stimulus of my week-end with you. I have come back to the good old grind with real enthusiasm, and it is all a result of your cleverly planned hospitality. Saturday's picnic alone put enough new life into me to last for some time. Thank you so much for all your thoughtfulness from beginning to end.

Cordially,
Marion.

35 Main Street, Overton
August 17, 19—

Letters of Condolence. Letters of condolence and sympathy are always difficult to write. Write only what is in your heart to say. In many instances the kindest thing is silence. The following letter of sympathy, now preserved in Oxford University, is a classic of this kind of expression, and appeals to us all.

14.

Executive Mansion,
Washington, November 21, 1864.

Dear Madam:

I have been shown in the files of the War Department a statement of the Adjutant General of Massachusetts, that you are the mother of five sons who have died gloriously on the field of battle. I feel how weak and fruitless must be any word of mine which should attempt to beguile you from the grief of a loss so overwhelming. But I cannot refrain from tendering to you the consolation that may be found in the thanks of the republic they died to save. I pray that our Heavenly Father may assuage the anguish of your bereavement, and leave you only the cherished memory of the loved and lost, and the solemn pride that must be yours to have laid so costly a sacrifice upon the altar of freedom.

Yours very sincerely and respectfully,

A. Lincoln.

To Mrs. Bixby,
Boston, Mass.

15.

December 7, 19—

Dear Margaret,

In the mail this morning came the sad news from Gertrude that your mother had passed away.

I wish I could be near you at this time to be of some comfort to you. But the greatest comfort you must have is the knowledge and feeling that your mother lived a full and happy life and left this world serene, largely because you and Emma and John did everything to make it so.

Affectionately,
Henry Jerome.

To Miss Margaret Jones.

16.

Dear Tom:

I am very sorry to hear that business affairs have been apparently "going into reverse" for you lately. Be sure that I believe your difficulties are only temporary. They can't be otherwise, with your ability and faithfulness. Here is my hand. If I can be of any help, call on me at once.

Sincerely yours,
Robert.

September 10, 19—

Letters of Congratulation. A letter of congratulation is easier to write.

17.

Dear Martin,

Heartiest congratulations on the good news. Of course I know you don't entirely deserve such good fortune as the promise of Frances to become your wife, but fortunately we are not always treated strictly according to our deserts. We shall all be happy in the happiness that is to be yours.

Sincerely your well-wisher,
Robert Howard.

April 8, 19—.

18.

384 Linden Avenue,
August 18, 19—.

Dear Louise,

We are all greatly delighted over the announcement in the newspaper that you have won a scholarship in the university. You have our heartiest congratulations on your success in this severe test, as well as our sincere good wishes for your enjoyment of college life and work.

Sincerely yours,
Arlene Benham.

FORMAL INVITATIONS AND REPLIES

Formal invitations are written in the third person and, for large affairs, are usually engraved or printed and mailed about two weeks in advance. An invitation sent out by a school, or a class in the school, a club, or any group of persons, is usually in the third person; and, if the invitation be to an entertainment, as at a church or a commencement program, no formal reply is needed. Formal replies, however, should always be sent where entertainment is to be provided for each individual, for the host or hostess will need to know how to provide.

The letters *R. S. V. P.* are sometimes put in the lower left-hand corner of an invitation. They stand for the French phrase, *Répondez s'il vous plaît,* meaning "Reply, if you please." The English words, *An answer will oblige* or *An answer is requested,* are now much used.

1. Invitation to Commencement Exercises.

The Senior Class of
Columbia Seminary
requests the pleasure of your presence at the
Commencement Exercises
June fifteenth to eighteenth

2. Invitation to Commencement Exercises.

The Faculty and Graduating Class
of the
Boston Teachers' Training School
invite you to attend the
Seventeenth Annual Commencement Exercises
Friday evening, April fifteenth, 19—
at half past eight o'clock
1124 Tremont Avenue

3. Formal Invitation to a Reception and Dance.

The Epsilon Mu Sorority
invites you to be present at a
reception and dance to be held at the

COLONIAL CLUB
Tuesday evening, April nineteenth
at half after eight o'clock

4. Wedding Invitation.

Mr. and Mrs. Joseph Suffolk
request the honor of your presence at the
marriage of their daughter
Mabel Grace
to
Mr. Andrew Jackman
Wednesday afternoon, June fifteenth
at three o'clock
Saint-Mary's-on-the-Hill Church

5. Acceptance of Wedding Invitation.

Mr. and Mrs. John T. Brown accept with pleasure the invitation of Mr. and Mrs. Joseph Suffolk to be present at the marriage of their daughter Mabel Grace on June fifteenth.

6. Announcement.

Mr. Andrew Jackman
Miss Mabel Grace Suffolk
Married
on Wednesday, June the fifteenth
Nineteen hundred and seventy—
Baltimore

Note.—At home cards are often inserted in the same envelope with the announcements.

7. For a Formal At Home.

Mrs. Jacques Randolph Stearns
At Home
on Wednesday, the seventh of December
from three until six o'clock
1106 Ballston Heights
to meet
Mrs. James Winchell Toynbee

8. Formal Note of Invitation.

Miss Belle Coe requests the pleasure of Miss Hinman's company on Thursday evening at eight o'clock.

128 Fremont St., January nine.

9. The Invitation Accepted.

Miss Hinman accepts with pleasure Miss Coe's invitation for Thursday evening at eight o'clock.

Wellington Place, January ten.

10. The Invitation Declined.

Miss Hinman sincerely regrets that she cannot accept Miss Coe's invitation for Thursday evening at eight o'clock.

Wellington Place, January ten.

11. A Less Formal Invitation.

Calling cards are often used for small informal gatherings of friends.

At Home
Mrs. James Winchell Toynbee
Wednesday, January 14, 3 to 4.
40 College St.

12. Dinner Invitation.

1432 Lincoln Avenue
Mr. and Mrs. Thomas Dowd
request the pleasure of
Mr. James Morley's
company at dinner
On Wednesday evening, March the fifth
at eight o'clock

February the twenty-fifth

13. Acceptance.

415 Martin St.

Mr. James Morley accepts with pleasure the invitation of Mr. and Mrs. Thomas Dowd for Wednesday evening, March the fifth, at eight o'clock.

February the twenty-seventh.

14. Regrets.

Mr. James Morley sincerely regrets that a professional engagement made several months since prevents his acceptance of Mr. and Mrs. Thomas Dowd's kind invitation for Wednesday evening, March the fifth

February the twenty-seventh.

SUGGESTIONS FOR A FAMILY LIBRARY

The collection of books that make up a family library represents the unity of the family's interests and needs, as well as the diversity of the approaches to reading and the use of books that individual members of the family make. When a portion of the collection is on view in the home, guests will often study it—not only to search for favorites of their own and to find new titles that may not be familiar to them, but also to get a sense of what the family enjoys. Thoughtfully selected and carefully maintained, the library may be an index to a family's characteristic personality, as well as a valuable aid to its pursuit of information and recreation.

Encyclopedias. Reference books of many kinds may be the cornerstone of the collection. There was a time when purchase of a single set of encyclopedias was considered the most important investment that a family could make in its book collection. Such a multivolume set is still a major investment and calls for care and consideration in selection. Examination of various sets in a library or other center where they may be available is an important part of the decision about purchase. Although reviews of encyclopedias are not frequent, the ones that appear should be read with care, and with special concern for the points they raise that are especially pertinent to family purchase.

When examining encyclopedias, a good technique is to select in advance several topics, including ones in several different subject areas and ones of varying timeliness, and to check several different encyclopedias, preferably ones of similar dates of publication, to see what differences there may be in treatment, accuracy, format, ease of locating information, and other important features of use.

Careful reading of the forewords of several sets is especially relevant in determining the audience to which the encyclopedia is primarily directed and in evaluating the internal aids, such as the index, maps, and the like, that will determine the set's usefulness.

Although the time and attention spent on the decision about purchase of an encyclopedia may be considerable, other additions to the family library should be made with the same concern. The tendency, even in today's mobile society, for families to retain their books and to move them frequently, should mean that the items finally selected are worth keeping. The aesthetic values of attractive bindings, clear print, illustrations that truly complement or enhance the text, and other characteristics should be considered as carefully as the titles themselves.

Nature of the Library. Since some of the books in a family library may come as gifts, and others selected by different members of the family at different times and for various purposes, there is likely to be variety in quality and appeal. Sentiment about the first book that prompted a child's interest in reading or the autographed copy presented by a new author may be responsible for a family's keeping some books long past the day when they are actively consulted or read. For other books, such as annuals or almanacs, there may be little reason to retain the books for any length of time. The library should be a constantly growing, changing collection, with some of the basic elements remaining, others changing as interests and attitudes change.

Many factors may determine what a family decides to keep in its library: the occupations of the parents, accessibility of materials in other libraries, the attitude of the children toward reading, the frequency of moves, and the size of the home.

Location. It is essential that there be at least one place where shelves in a convenient location allow for the collection and care of the family library. Ideally, there should be shelves or cupboards in several areas of the home where individual members of the family may keep their favorite books, or where ones currently being read can be kept within easy reach. Cookbooks in the kitchen, repair manuals in the workshop, nature guides in the car, are only a few examples.

Permanence of Appeal. The library should include books chosen for the permanence of their appeal, in addition to those that are useful or interesting only at a specific time in the family's life. Collections of prose and of poetry, for example, should be chosen with consideration for the range and quality of the selections. Their appeal to different members of the family may thus cause them to be kept in the library for many years.

Textbooks purchased during children's schooldays are too often kept as part of the library long after their value and accuracy have diminished. In such fields as science, it may be relatively easy to check for the current accuracy of materials. In the social sciences or in literature, such a check may be more difficult, but except in unusual instances, textbooks need not be kept beyond the period when the student consults them.

A family's shared interest in travel, hobbies, or other pastimes may be responsible for the development of an extensive segment of the library. Atlases, which are useful in the planning or the reminiscence of travels, may become outdated as new roads, buildings, or even new countries appear, and boundaries and natural features change. Atlases, however, provide an example of the exception that may warrant keeping material that is no longer currently accurate, but that is still desirable to have on hand to recall the experiences of a trip or to trace changes that have occurred in recent years. Travel guides tend to become dated quite rapidly, and the more specific and helpful they are at the time of purchase, the more rapid that dating may be. This is true in the case of prices quoted for fares, information about passports, prices for accommodations and meals, and even addresses for shops and other places to visit, which are subject to change. Again, the value of the book as an aid to planning may diminish, while an attachment to the places or events it helps to recall may be responsible for a family's choosing to keep the book on its shelves.

Such hobbies as stamp collecting, coin collecting, crafts, and various sports may cause the purchase of a large share of the family library. Especially when such titles are purchased as gifts for an individual of the family, his knowledge of the titles available in his field of interest should be considered, and the title chosen for him might best be selected with the understanding that he may exchange it.

A family's general reading for pleasure may span many subject areas and many kinds of books. The book that is to be read only once may be added to the library in paperback format, and kept only for a limited time. Readers of mysteries and science fiction frequently add books in these areas to their shelves, but except for those of a few favorite authors, they may not keep them as part of their permanent collection. Fiction of more lasting value may include literature and classics that have been tested by time, but the practice of purchasing sets of books by one author is less common than it once was. There are reprint editions of most major classics, and there are also special editions prepared for their aesthetic value. Both kinds may find a place in the library, and the choice may be chiefly a matter of taste. In some instances, however, where illustrations are an intrinsic part of the text, as in some of James Thurber's books, the careful selector of books will not be satisfied with editions in which the illustrations are omitted or are poorly reproduced.

Bookstores. The family engaged in developing its library may often have a problem in finding bookstores to serve its varied interests. Most of the all-purpose bookstores are in major metropolitan areas, and the problem of merchandising books of quality keeps their number low. Members of the family may thus find it helpful to keep lists of books they especially want when they have opportunities to shop. When it is possible to open an account or to order by mail, these sources may facilitate new purchases, and the catalogs or announcements that come to holders of accounts may help to keep them informed of what is new or available in bookstores. Shops that cater to special interests of readers, such as books on antiques, various periods of history, or children's literature, may offer more opportunities for the family to expand or compare its collection.

Personal and specialty bookshops have traditionally stressed their services in the selection of titles, and many are cooperative in suggesting titles and handling requests for books that are not currently in stock.

Care of Books. Caring for books is an important aspect of ownership of a home library. When dust jackets are available, they may help to enhance the appearance and prolong the life of the book if they are left in place. Transparent plastic jackets in adjustable sizes may be found in many book and stationery stores, and they may further preserve the jackets of the books themselves. When a book is added to the permanent collection, a bookplate showing family or individual ownership may be affixed to it. Just as the plastic jacket should be applied so that the endpapers, if decorated, are preserved as well as possible, the bookplate or some other simple statement of ownership should be placed near the front of the book on the endpapers or front pages before the text where it will be obvious to anyone examining the book, while it does not deface the book itself.

From the list given here it will be possible to form the nucleus of a private library which can serve for education and entertainment as well as for everyday use. A still wider range of selection may be had by consulting the bibliographies given in connection with different departments of these volumes.

REFERENCE WORKS

Title	Publisher
An Atlas: Readers Atlas	Rand McNally

English dictionaries: American Heritage or Webster's New International

Foreign Language dictionaries:
Cassell's New English-French French-English Dictionary
Pfeffer's Dictionary of Everyday Usage, German-English, English-German

Encyclopedias:
Junior emphasis A to Z: World Book, Compton's
Senior emphasis A to Z: Britannica, Americana, Colliers
Information departmentalized: The Lincoln Library of Essential Information
Webster's Biographical Dictionary

Other Sources:

Author	Title	Publisher
Bartlett, John—Familiar Quotations		Little Brown
Brewer, E. C.—Dictionary of Phrase and Fable		Lippincott
Cary, M. (Ed.)—The Oxford Classical Dictionary		Clarendon
Ellison, John W. (Ed.)—Complete Concordance of the Revised Standard Version of the Bible		Nelson
Dorland, W. A. and Miller, E. C. L.—American Illustrated Medical Dictionary		Saunders
Dyke, A. L.—Automobile and Gasoline Engine Encyclopedia (Latest Ed.)		Goodheart-Willcox
Keller, Helen R. (Ed.)—Reader's Digest of Books		Macmillan
Robert, Henry M.—Rules of Order (Rev. Ed.)		
Roget, Peter M.—Thesaurus (See *Synonyms*)		

GENERAL LITERATURE

Author	Title	Publisher
Æsop—Fables		
The Bible		
The Arabian Nights		
Bacon, Francis—Essays		
Botkin, Benj. A.—Treasury of American Folklore		Crown
Bunyan, John—Pilgrim's Progress		
Burke, Edmund—Reflections on the French Revolution		

Author	Title	Publisher
Cambridge History of American Literature		Macmillan
Cambridge History of English Literature		Macmillan
Cervantes, Miguel de—Don Quixote		
Chaucer, Goeffrey—The Canterbury Tales		
Chesterfield, Lord—Letters to his Son		Oxford
Cicero, Marcus Tullius—Essays		Dutton
Dante Alighieri—The Divine Comedy		Dutton
Demosthenes—Orations		Dutton
Emerson, R. W.—Essays (1st and 2d Series)		Macmillan
Galsworthy, John—Plays		Scribner
Garnett, R. and Gosse, E.—History of English Literature		
Homer—The Iliad and the Odyssey		Classics Club
Ibsen, Henrik—Selected Plays		Mod. Library
Lamb, Charles—Essays of Elia		Nelson
Legouis, Émile—History of English Literature		Macmillan
Machiavelli, Niccolo—The Prince		Oxford
Marcus Aurelius—Meditations		World Classics
Merejkowski, Dmitri—The Romance of Leonardo da Vinci		
Molière—Comedies		Mod. Library
Montaigne, Michel de—Essays		Dutton
Oates, W. J. and O'Neill, Eugene, Jr.—The Complete Greek Drama		Random House
Pepys, Samuel—Diary		Dutton
Plato—Dialogues and The Republic		Classics Club
Schuster, M. Lincoln—Treasury of the World's Great Letters		Simon & Schuster
Shakespeare—Plays (G. Lyman Kittredge, Ed.)		Ginn
Shaw, George Bernard—Nine Plays		Dodd Mead
Sheridan, Richard Brinsley—Plays		Oxford
Smith, Logan Pearsall—All Trivia		Harcourt Brace
Stevenson, R. L.—Virginibus Puerisque and Other Essays		
Thoreau, Henry D.—Walden		
Virgil—The Æneid		
Walton, Isaac—The Compleat Angler		

BIOGRAPHY

Adams, Henry—The Education of Henry Adams	
Adams, James T.—The Living Jefferson	Scribner
Boswell, James—Life of Johnson	Mod. Library
Bouyer, L. Newman: His Life and Spirituality	Kenedy
Canby, Henry S.—Thoreau	Peter Smith
Canning, John (Ed.)—100 Great Modern Lives	Hawthorn
Cellini, Benvenuto—Autobiography	Dutton
Eastman, Max—Einstein, Trotsky, Hemingway, Freud, and other great companions	Collier
Franklin, Benjamin—Autobiography	Macmillan
Freeman, Douglas Southall—Robert E. Lee	Scribner
Guedalla, Philip—Wellington	Harper
Holt, Rackham—George Washington Carver	Doubleday
Mersand, Jos. (Ed.)—Great American Short Biographies	
Phelps, William Lyon—Autobiography with Letters	Oxford
Plutarch—Lives	Mod. Library
Riis, Jacob—The Making of an American	Macmillan
Sandburg, Carl—Abraham Lincoln; The Prairie Years	
Sherwood, Robert—Roosevelt and Hopkins	Harper
Steffens, Lincoln—Autobiography	Harcourt Brace
Strachey, Lytton—Eminent Victorians	Harcourt Brace
Untermeyer, Louis—Makers of the Modern World	Sands
Van Doren, Carl—Benjamin Franklin	Viking
White, William A.—A Puritan in Babylon	Peter Smith

FICTION

Austen, Jane—Sense and Sensibility	Dutton
Balzac, Honore de—Old Goriot	Mod. Library
Bennett, Arnold—The Old Wives' Tale	Mod. Library
Bromfield, Louis—The Green Bay Tree	Stokes
Bronte, Emily—Wuthering Heights	Mod. Library
Buck, Pearl—The Good Earth	Grosset & Dunlap
Butler, Samuel—The Way of All Flesh	Dutton
Cather, Willa—Death Comes for the Archbishop	Knopf
Conrad, Joseph—Victory	Mod. Library
Cooper, James Fenimore—The Spy	Scribner
—The Last of the Mohicans	
Dickens, Charles—Pickwick Papers	Mod. Library
Dostoiévsky, F.—The Brothers Karamazov	Mod. Library
—Crime and Punishment	Mod. Library
Drury, Allen—Advise and Consent	Doubleday
Dumas, Alexandre—The Count of Monte Cristo	Nelson
Flaubert, Gustave—Madame Bovary	Dutton
Forster, E. M.—Howard's End	Knopf
France, Anatole—The Crime of Sylvestre Bonnard	
Galsworthy, John—The Forsyte Saga	Scribner
Glasgow, Ellen—Barren Ground	Peter Smith
Hamsun, Knut—Growth of the Soil	Mod. Library
Hardy, Thomas—The Return of the Native	Macmillan
—Tess of the D'Urbervilles	Mod. Library
Harte, Bret—The Luck of Roaring Camp	Houghton Mifflin
Hawthorne, Nathaniel—The Scarlet Letter	Mod. Library
—The House of the Seven Gables	
	Dutton

Author	Title	Publisher
Hemingway, Ernest—For Whom the Bell Tolls		Scribner
Henry, O.—Great Short Novels (ed. by Rahv)		Peter Smith
Hersey, John—A Bell for Adano		Mod. Library
Howells, William D.—The Rise of Silas Lapham		Houghton Mifflin
Hugo, Victor—The Hunchback of Notre Dame		Dodd
James, Henry—The American		Houghton Mifflin
Kafka, Franz—The Trial		Knopf
Kipling, Rudyard—Kim		Macmillan
Lardner, Ring—Collected Short Stories		Scribner
Lewis, Sinclair—Babbitt		Harcourt Brace
—Arrowsmith		Mod. Library
Lytton, E. Bulwer—The Last Days of Pompeii		Dutton
Mann, Thomas—The Magic Mountain		Knopf
Marquand, John P.—The Late George Apley		Grosset & Dunlap
Maugham, Somerset—Of Human Bondage		Mod. Library
Maupassant, Guy de—Short Stories		Dutton
Meredith, George—The Egoist		Oxford
Michener, Thomas—Tales of the South Pacific		Macmillan
Mitchell, Margaret—Gone With the Wind		Macmillan
Paton, Alan—Cry, the Beloved Country		Scribner
Poe, Edgar Allen—Tales		Mod. Library
Priestley, J. B.—The Good Companions		Harper
Reade, Charles—The Cloister and the Hearth		Dutton
Richardson, Samuel—Pamela		Dutton
Roberts, Kenneth—Northwest Passage		Doubleday
Rolland, Romain—Jean Christophe		Mod. Library
Scott, Sir Walter—The Heart of Midlothian		Nelson
—Waverly		Nelson
Sienkiewicz, H.—Quo Vadis?		Dutton
Steinbeck, John—Of Mice and Men		Viking
Stevenson, Robert Louis—The Strange Case of Dr. Jekyll and Mr. Hyde		Dutton
Tarkington, Booth—Alice Adams		Grosset & Dunlap
Thackeray, William M.—Vanity Fair		Mod. Library
Thirkell, Angela—Love at All Ages		Knopf
Tolstóy, Leo—War and Peace		Mod. Library
—Anna Karenina		Mod. Library
Trollope, Anthony—Barchester Towers		Dutton
Twain, Mark—The Gilded Age		Harper
Wells, H. G.—Tono-Bungay		Mod. Library
Wescott, Edward—David Harum		Peter Smith
Wharton, Edith—Ethan Frome		Scribner
—The Age of Innocence		Mod. Library
Wilder, Thornton—The Bridge of San Luis Rey		Grosset & Dunlap
Wolfe, Thomas—Of Time and the River		Scribner
—You Can't Go Home Again		Harper

POETRY

Author	Title	Publisher
Benét, Stephen Vincent—John Brown's Body		Rinehart
Browning, Robert—Selected Poems		Oxford
Burns, Robert—Poems		Dutton
Byron, George Gordon—Poems		Oxford
Dickinson, Emily—Bolts of Melody		Harper
Eliot, T. S.—Collected Poems		Harcourt Brace
Fitzgerald, Edward—Translation of the Rubaiyat of Omar Khayyam		Dutton
Frost, Robert—Complete Poems		Holt
Housman, A. E.—A Shropshire Lad		Holt
Hubbell, J. B and Beaty, J. O.—An Introduction to Poetry		Macmillan
Keats, John—Poems		Dutton
Longfellow, Henry W.—Poems		Mod. Library
Masefield, John—Selected Poems		Macmillan
Millay, Edna St. Vincent—Collected Sonnets		Harper
Palgrave, Francis—Golden Treasury		Dutton
Rodman, Selden—100 Modern Poets		New Amer. Library
Sandburg, Carl—Selected Poems		Harcourt Brace
Shelley, Percy Bysshe—Poems		Oxford
Tennyson, Alfred—Poems		Oxford
Whitman, Walt—Leaves of Grass		Mod. Library
Wordsworth, William—Poems		Oxford

HISTORY

Author	Title	Publisher
Adams, Henry—Degredation of Democratic Dogma		Smith
Adams, James T., ed.—Atlas of American History		Scribner
Adams, James T.—The Epic of America		Little Brown
Beard, Charles A. and Mary—The Rise of American Civilization		Macmillan
Carlyle, Thomas—The French Revolution		Mod. Library
Creasy, Edward S.—Fifteen Decisive Battles		Dutton
Creighton, Donald G.—Dominion of the North; A History of Canada		Houghton Mifflin
Green, John Richard—A Short History of the English People		Dutton
Hyma, A.—History of the Dutch in the Far East		Wahr
Johnson, Gerald W.—America is Born		Morrow
Langer, W. L.—An Encyclopedia of World History		Houghton Mifflin
Macaulay, T. B.—The History of England		Dutton
Motley, J. L.—The Rise of the Dutch Republic		Dutton
Parkman, Francis—The Oregon Trail		Mod. Library

Author	Title	Publisher
Seligman, E. R. H.—Economic Interpretation of History		Gordian
Toynbee, Arnold J.—A Study of History (Abridged ed.)		Oxford
Van Loon, H. W.—Story of Mankind		Tudor
Wells, H. G.—The Outline of History		Garden City
Whitehead, Alfred N.—Adventures in Ideas		Macmillan
Wilgus, A. Curtis—Argentina, Brazil, and Chili since Independence		Russell

HOME AND COMMUNITY

Author	Title	Publisher
Bromfield, Louis—Pleasant Valley		Harper
Crotty, William J. and Others—Political Parties and Political Behavior		Allyn & Bacon
Doob, Leonard W.— Political Opinion and Propaganda		Shoe String
Goldstein, Philip—Triumph of Biology		Doubleday
Hoyt, E. P.—Condition Critical: Our Hospital Crisis		Holt
Inkeles, Alex—What is Sociology		Prentice Hall
Kent, Robert W.—How to Choose Your House and Live in It Ever After		Lee Inst.
Lasswell, Harold D.—The Analysis of Political Behavior		Oxford
McDonald-Austin F.—American City Government and Administration		Crowell
McLaughlin, Andrew C.—A Constitutional History of the United States		Appleton-Century
Peach, W. N.—Principles of Economics, 3rd ed.		Irwin
Picton, Lionel J.—Nutrition and the Soil		Devin-Adair

HOME AND EDUCATION

Author	Title	Publisher
Anshen, Melvin—An Introduction to Business		Macmillan
Baebenroth, H. C. and Parkhurst, Charles C.—Modern Business English		Prentice-Hall
Britten, Jessie D.—Practical Notes on Nursing Procedure		Williams & Wilkins
Carlson, P. A., Forkner, H. L., and Prickett, A. L.—Twentieth Century Bookkeeping and Accounting		South-Western Pub. Co.
Craig, William—Care of Newly Born Infant, 3rd ed.		Williams & Wilkins
Crow, Lester D. and Alice—How to Study		Collier
Dacey, Norman F.—How to Avoid Probate		Crown
Davison, Eloise, Ed.—America's Housekeeping Book		Scribner
Durant, Will—The Story of Philosophy		Garden City
Farmer, Robert A.—How to Avoid Problems with your Will		Arco
Greenbie, Marjorie—The Arts of Leisure		Whittlesey
Hunter, Beatrice—Consumer Beware!		Devin-Adair
Hurlock, Elizabeth B.—Child Growth and Development		McGraw
James, William—Psychology		Harper
Kling, Samuel G.—Legal Encyclopedia for the Home and Business		Pocket Books
MacGibbon, Elizabeth G.—Fitting Yourself for Business		McGraw-Hill
Post, Emily—Etiquette		Funk & Wagnalls
Schifferes, Justus J.—How to Live Longer		Collier
Simpson, Jean I. and Taylor, Demetria—The Frozen Food Cook Book		Simon & Schuster

POPULAR SCIENCE

Author	Title	Publisher
Audubon, John J.—The Birds of America		Macmillan
Cox, Ian—Science Survey		S. Low Marston
Dampier, John B.—A History of Science		Macmillan
Ditmars, R. L.—Snakes of the World		Macmillan
Eddington, Sir Arthur—The Expanding Universe		Macmillan
Eiseley, Loren C.—Darwin's Century		Doubleday
Hecht, Selig—Explaining the Atom		Viking
Henney, Keith—Principles of Radio (5th ed.)		Wiley
Jaques, Harry E.—How to Know the Trees		Wm. C. Brown Co.
Jeans, Sir James—The Universe Around Us		Macmillan
Osborn, Fairfield—Our Plundered Planet		Little Brown
Peterson, Roger T.—A Field Guide to the Birds		Houghton Mifflin
Scheinfeld, Amram—Your Heredity and Environment		Stokes
Spencer, L. J.—A Key to Precious Stones		Emerson
Titiev, M.—Introduction to Cultural Anthropology		Holt
Whitehead, A. N.—Science and the Modern World		Macmillan

TRAVEL

Author	Title	Publisher
Barretto, Larry—Bright Mexico		Farrar
—Hawaiian Holiday		Dodd Mead
Bertram, Kate and Richard—Caribbean Cruise		Norton
Fleming, Peter—Brazilian Adventure		Scribner
Franck, H. A., with Lanks, H. C.—Pan American Highway		Appleton-Century
Hammond, C. S. and Co. World Travelog		Hammond
Hatcher, Harlan—The Great Lakes		Oxford
Look at America Series		Houghton Mifflin

Author	Title	Publisher

Look magazine—Guide books prepared by the magazine and the following editors:
- Allen, Frederick—New York City
- Bromfield, Louis—The Midwest
- Chase, Mary Ellen—New England
- Cohn, David I.—The South
- Jackson, Joseph H.—The Far West
- Johnson, Gerald W.—The Central Northeast
- Stegner, Wallace—The Central Northwest

The Reader's Digest Family Reference Series: These United States . . . . . . *The Reader's Digest Ass'n*
Rivers of America Series . . . . *Rinehart*
- Banta, R. E.—The Ohio
- Beston, Henry—The St. Lawrence
- Canby, H. S.—The Brandywine
- Carmer, Carl—The Hudson
- Dana, Julia—The Sacramento
- Davis, Julia—The Shenandoah
- Gutheim, F.—The Potomac
- Vestal, Stanley—The Missouri
- Waters, Frank—The Colorado
- Way, F., Jr.—The Allegheny

Stein, Howard and Adeline—Budget Guide to Europe *Van Nostrand*
Ullman, James R.—Kingdom of Adventure: Everest *Sloane*
Vestal, Stanley—The Old Sante Fe Trail *Houghton Mifflin*

THE CHILDREN'S LIBRARY

Every child should own some books. Every child should have access to the books that develop his sympathy, broaden his understanding, deepen his appreciation—of people and of the world about him. To become familiar with books, the child needs constant contact with more and more books. And, if children are to love books and reading, the books provided must satisfy their needs and interests and always they must give joy and pleasure.

The following list is arranged for convenience by grades from third through tenth. Because children within the same grade frequently differ in reading ability, no child should be restricted to books classified under his own particular grade level.

Although this list has been chosen by competent authorities, it should not be regarded as a complete selection of "the best" books for children. With almost a thousand new titles for children published each year, persons assisting in selection should be alert to the new, as well as to the older books that have stood the acid test of childhood choice.

READING REFERENCES FOR ADULTS

Title	Author	Publisher
Bequest of Wings—Duff		*Viking*
Books, Children and Men—Hazard		*Horn Book*
Parent's Guide to Children's Reading—Larrick		*Doubleday*
Reading with Children—Eaton		*Viking*
Way of the Storyteller—Sawyer		*Viking*

I. READ-ALOUD AGE

STORY COLLECTIONS

Here and Now Story Book—Mitchell . . . . *Dutton*
Little Bookroom—Farjeon . . . . *Walck*
Once the Hodja—Kelsey . . . . *McKay*
Once Upon a Time—Dobbs . . . . *Random*
Told Under the Green Umbrella—
Told Under the Christmas Tree—
Association for Childhood Education . . . . *Macmillan*

POETRY

Child's Garden of Verses—Stevenson . . . . *Scribner*
Come Hither—de la Mare . . . . *Knopf*
Favorite Poems, Old and New—Ferris . . . *Doubleday*
Gaily We Parade—Brewton . . . . *Macmillan*
Inheritance of Poetry—Adshead and Duff . . *Houghton*
Little Laughter—Love . . . . *Crowell*
Rainbow in the Sky—Untermeyer . . . . *Harcourt*
Rocket in My Pocket—Withers, comp. . . . . *Holt*
Silver Pennies—Thompson, comp. . . . . *Macmillan*
Sing-Song—Rossetti . . . . *Macmillan*
Sung Under the Silver Umbrella—
Association for Childhood Education International
This Way, Delight—Read . . . . *Pantheon*
Tirra Lirra—Richards . . . . *Little*
World of Christopher Robin—Milne . . . . *Dutton*

SONGS

American Folksongs for Children—Seeger . . *Doubleday*
Book of Favorite Hymns—Bertail . . . . *Garden City*
Cat Came Fiddling—Kapp . . . . *Harcourt*
Sing for Christmas—Wheeler . . . . . . *Dutton*
Singing Time—Coleman and Thorn . . . . . *Day*

Title	Author	Publisher

ABC AND MOTHER GOOSE BOOKS

ABC Book—Falls . . . . *Doubleday*
ABC Bunny—Gag . . . . *Coward*
Bible ABC—Hogarth . . . . *Lippincott*
Lavender's Blue—Lines . . . . *Watts*
Marguerite de Angeli's Book of Nursery and Mother Goose Rhymes . . . . *Doubleday*
Real Mother Goose—Wright . . . . . *Rand*
Ring o' Roses—Brooke . . . . *Warne*

PICTURE STORY BOOKS

Anatole and the Cat—Titus . . . . . . *McGraw*
And to think that I saw it on Mulberry Street—Seuss *Vanguard*
Angus and the Ducks—Flack . . . . . *Doubleday*
April's Kittens—Newberry . . . . . . *Harper*
Big Snow—Hader . . . . *Macmillan*
Blueberries for Sal—McCloskey . . . . *Viking*
Boats on the River—Flack . . . . . . *Viking*
Chanticleer and the Fox—Cooney . . . *Crowell*
Christ Child—Petersham . . . . . . *Doubleday*
Country Bunny—Heyward . . . . . . *Houghton*
Curious George—Rey . . . . *Houghton*
Golden Goose Book—Brooke . . . . . *Warne*
Happy Lion—Fatio . . . . *McGraw*
Hey Diddle, Diddle, Picture Book—Caldecott . *Warne*
In the Forest—Ets . . . . *Viking*
Jeanne-Marie Counts her Sheep—Françoise . *Scribner*
Johnny Crow's Garden—Brooke . . . . *Warne*
Little Auto—Lenski . . . . *Oxford*
Little Bear—Minarik . . . . *Harper*
Little House—Burton . . . . *Houghton*
Make Way for Ducklings—McCloskey . . *Viking*
Mike's House—Sauer . . . . *Viking*
Millions of Cats—Gag . . . . *Coward*
Over in the Meadow—Langstaff . . . . *Harcourt*
Poppy Seed Cake—Clark . . . . . . *Doubleday*
Prayer for a Child—Field . . . . . . *Macmillan*
Rooster Crows—Petersham . . . . . *Macmillan*
Rosa-too-little—Felt . . . . *Doubleday*
Snipp, Snapp, Snurr and the Red Shoes—Lindman *Whitman*
Story of Baber—Brunhoff . . . . . . *Random*
Story of Ferdinand—Leaf . . . . . . *Viking*
Tale of Peter Rabbit—Potter . . . . . *Warne*
Timothy Turtle—Graham . . . . . . *Viking*
A Tree is Nice—Udry . . . . *Harper*
Umbrella—Yashima . . . . *Viking*
White Snow, Bright Snow—Tresselt . . . *Lothrop*

II. GRADES THREE TO TEN

THIRD GRADE

Andy and the Lion—Daugherty . . . . . *Viking*
The Bears on Hemlock Mountain—Dalgliesh . *Scribner*
Billy and Blaze—Anderson . . . . . . *Macmillan*
Cowboy Tommy—Tousey . . . . *Hale*
Crow Boy—Yashima . . . . *Viking*
Dash and Dart—Buff . . . . *Viking*
Elf Owl—Buff . . . . *Viking*
Five Chinese Brothers—Bishop . . . . . *Coward*
500 Hats of Bartholomew Cubbins—Seuss . *Vanguard*
In My Mother's House—Clark . . . . . *Viking*
Katy and the Big Snow—Burton . . . . *Houghton*
Little Island—Macdonald . . . . . . *Doubleday*
Little Pear—Lattimore . . . . *Harcourt*
Little Toot—Gramatky . . . . *Putnam*
Madeline—Bemelmans . . . . *Viking*
My Father's Dragon—Gannett . . . . . *Random*
Ola—Aulaire . . . . *Doubleday*
Painted Pig—Morrow . . . . *Knopf*
Pedro, Angel of Olvera Street—Politi . . . *Scribner*
Pelle's New Suit—Beskow . . . . . . *Harper*
Riding the Rails—Olds . . . . *Houghton*
Roger and the Fox—Davis . . . . . . *Doubleday*
Story about Ping—Flack . . . . *Viking*
Swineherd—Andersen (tr. Blegvad) . . . *Harcourt*

FOURTH GRADE

Abraham Lincoln—Aulaire . . . . . . *Doubleday*
Appleseed Farm—Douglas . . . . . . *Abingdon*
Bed-knob and Broomstick—Norton . . . *Harcourt*
Betsy and Billy—Haywood . . . . . . *Harcourt*
Birds in Their Homes—Webb . . . . . *Doubleday*
Blue Fairy Book—Lang . . . . *Random*
Bright April—de Angeli . . . . *Doubleday*
Charlotte's Web—White . . . . *Harper*
Courage of Sarah Noble—Dalgliesh . . . *Scribner*
Dancing Cloud—Buff . . . . *Viking*
Down, Down the Mountain—Credle . . . *Nelson*
Fast Sooner Hound—Bontemps . . . . *Houghton*
First Bible, ill. by Sewell . . . . *Oxford*
King of the Golden River—Ruskin . . . . *World*
Little Boat Boy—Bothwell . . . . . . *Harcourt*
Many Moons—Thurber . . . . *Harcourt*
Melindy's Medal—Faulkner . . . . . . *Messner*

Title	Author	Publisher
On Indian Trails with Daniel Boone—Meadowcroft		*Crowell*
Peachtree Island—Lawrence		*Harcourt*
Pierre Pidgeon—Kingman		*Houghton*
Pollywiggle's Progress—Bronson		*Macmillan*
Who Goes There?—Lathrop		*Macmillan*
World of Pooh—Milne		*Dutton*

FIFTH GRADE

Title	Author	Publisher
Adventures of Pinocchio—Collodi		*Macmillan*
Æsop's Fables, ill. by Artzybasheff		*Viking*
Alice's Adventures in Wonderland—Carroll		*Macmillan*
At the Back of the North Wind—Macdonald		*Macmillan*
Away Goes Sally—Coatsworth		*Macmillan*
Bastable Children—		*Coward*
The Borrowers—Norton		*Harcourt*
Complete Nonsense Book—Lear		*Dodd*
Emil and the Detectives—Kastner		*Doubleday*
English Fairy Tales, ed. Jacobs		*Putnam*
Freddy, the Detective—Brooks		*Knopf*
Heidi—Spyri		*Lippincott*
Honk: The Moose—Stong		*Dodd*
Hundred Dresses—Estes		*Harcourt*
Just So Stories—Kipling		*Doubleday*
Little House in the Big Woods—Wilder		*Harper*
Little House on the Prairie—Wilder		*Harper*
Matchlock Gun—Edmonds		*Dodd*
Miss Hickory—Bailey		*Viking*
Misty of Chincoteague—Henry		*Rand*
The Moffats—Estes		*Harcourt*
Mr. Popper's Penguins—Atwater		*Little*
Paddle-to-the-Sea—Holling		*Houghton*
Peter and Wendy—Barrie		*Scribner*
Peterkin Papers—Hale		*Houghton*
Rabbit Hill—Lawson		*Viking*
The Rescuers—Sharp		*Little*
Ride on the Wind—Dalgliesh		*Scribner*
The Saturdays—Enright		*Rinehart*
Story of Dr. Dolittle—Lofting		*Lippincott*
Tales from Grimm—tr., Gag		*Coward*
Thee, Hannah!—de Angeli		*Doubleday*
This Boy Cody—Wilson		*Watts*
Wheel on the School—DeJong		*Harper*
Wind in the Willows—Grahame		*Scribner*
Wonder Clock—Pyle		*Harper*

SIXTH GRADE

Title	Author	Publisher
Adventures of Odysseus and the Tale of Troy—Colum		*Macmillan*
Arabian Nights—ed. Lang		*Longmans*
Call It Courage—Sperry		*Macmillan*
Cartier Sails the St. Lawrence—Averill		*Harper*
Daughter of the Mountains—Rankin		*Viking*
Fairy Tales—Andersen		*Macmillan*
Gift of the Forest—Singh and Lownsbery		*McKay*
Golden Nature Guides—Zim	*Simon (Golden Press)*	
Good Master—Seredy		*Viking*
Hans Brinker—Dodge		*Scribner*
Henry Reed—Robertson		*Viking*
Hitty: Her First 100 Years—Field		*Macmillan*
Homer Price—McCloskey		*Viking*
Jack Tales—Chase		*Houghton*
Judy's Journey—Lenski		*Lippincott*
Jungle Book—Kipling		*Doubleday*
Little Men—Alcott		*Grosset*
Little Vic—Gates		*Viking*
Little Women—Alcott		*Little*
Mary Poppins—Travers		*Harcourt*
Miracles on Maple Hill—Sorenson		*Harcourt*
Onion John—Krumgold		*Crowell*
Rebecca of Sunnybrook Farm—Wiggin		*Houghton*
Seabird—Holling		*Houghton*
Secret Garden—Burnett		*Lippincott*
Secret of the Andes—Clark		*Viking*
Shepherd's Nosegay—Fillmore		*Harcourt*
Strawberry Girl—Lenski		*Lippincott*
Swiss Family Robinson—Wyss		*Macmillan*
Thunder of the Gods—Hosford		*Holt*
Wonderful Adventures of Nils—Lagerlof		*Doubleday*

SEVENTH GRADE

Title	Author	Publisher
Adventures of Tom Sawyer—Clemens		*Harper*
The Ark—Benary-Isbert		*Harcourt*
Blue Willow—Gates		*Viking*
Caddie Woodlawn—Brink		*Macmillan*
Children of the Sea—Bronson		*Harcourt*
Favorite Uncle Remus—Harris		*Houghton*
Golden Fleece—Colum		*Macmillan*
Junior Book of Insects—Teale		*Dutton*
Kidnapped—Stevenson		*Scribner*
King of the Wind—Henry		*Rand*
Lassie Come-home—Knight		*Winston*
Li Lun, Lad of Courage—Treffinger		*Abingdon*
Pecos Bill—Bowman		*Whitman*
Robinson Crusoe—Defoe		*Lippincott*
Roller Skates—Sawyer		*Viking*
Shuttered Windows—Means		*Houghton*

Title	Author	Publisher
Silver Chief, Dog of the North—O'Brien		*Winston*
Stars for Sam—Reed		*Harcourt*
Story of King Arthur and His Knights—Pyle		*Scribner*
Swallows and Amazons—Ransome		*Lippincott*
Treasure Island—Stevenson		*Scribner*
Vulpes, the Red Fox—George		*Dutton*
Yankee Doodle's Cousins—Malcolmson		*Houghton*

EIGHTH GRADE

Title	Author	Publisher
Adventures of Huckleberry Finn—Clemens		*Harper*
Bambi—Salten		*Grosset*
Banner in the Sky—Ullman		*Lippincott*
Benjamin Franklin—Judson		*Follett*
Boys' Sherlock Holmes—Doyle		*Harper*
Boy with a Pack—Meader		*Harcourt*
Casting Away of Mrs. Lecks and Mrs. Aleshine—Stockton		*Meredith*
Chucklebait—Scoggins, ed.		*Knopf*
Daniel Boone—Daugherty		*Viking*
Fair Adventure—Gray		*Viking*
Harriet Tubman—Petry		*Crowell*
Lee of Virginia—Freeman		*Scribner*
Man Who Was Don Quixote—Busoni		*Prentice*
Mary McLeod Bethune—Sterne		*Knopf*
Men of Iron—Pyle		*Harper*
Merry Adventures of Robin Hood—Pyle		*Scribner*
Otto of the Silver Hand—Pyle		*Scribner*
Paul Bunyan—Shephard		*Harcourt*
Perilous Road—Steele		*Harcourt*
Peter the Great—Baker		*Vanguard*
Smoky—James		*Scribner*
Stories from Shakespeare—Chute		*World*
That Lively Man, Ben Franklin—Eaton		*Morrow*
These Happy Golden Years—Wilder		*Harper*
Trumpeter of Krakow—Kelly		*Macmillan*
Yankee Thunder—Shapiro		*Messner*
Young Fu—Lewis		*Winston*

NINTH GRADE

Title	Author	Publisher
Abe Lincoln Grows Up—Sandburg		*Harcourt*
Adam of the Road—Gray		*Viking*
All-American—Tunis		*Harcourt*
Bewitching Betsy Bonaparte—Desmond		*Dodd*
Big Doc's Girl—Medearis		*Lippincott*
Big Red—Knelgaard		*Holiday*
Boy on Horseback—Steffens		*Harcourt*
David Copperfield—Dickens		*Macmillan*
David Livingstone, Foe of Darkness—Eaton		*Morrow*
Florence Nightingale—Nolan		*Messner*
George Washington's World—Foster		*Scribner*
Great Heritage—Shippen		*Viking*
Invincible Louisa—Meigs		*Little*
Jim Davis—Masefield		*Macmillan*
Johnny Tremain—Forbes		*Houghton*
Lone Journey—Eaton		*Harcourt*
Lost World—White		*Random*
Martha, Daughter of Virginia—Vance		*Dutton*
My Friend Flicka—O'Hara		*Lippincott*
Narcissa Whitman—Eaton		*Harcourt*
National Velvet—Bagnold		*Morrow*
On Safari—Waldeck		*Viking*
Vast Horizons—Lucas		*Viking*
Watch for a Tall White Sail—Bell		*Morrow*
Witch of Blackbird Pond—Speare		*Houghton*

TENTH GRADE

Title	Author	Publisher
Book of Americans—Benét		*Rinehart*
Clouded Star—Parrish		*Harper*
Dark Frigate—Hawes		*Little*
Devil and Daniel Webster—Benét		*Rinehart*
Drums—Boyd		*Scribner*
Dune Boy—Teale		*Dodd*
Here I Stay—Coatsworth		*Coward*
Here is Alaska—Stefansson		*Scribner*
Ivanhoe—Scott		*Dodd*
Jane Eyre—Bronte		*Dodd*
Lad: A Dog—Terhune		*Dutton*
Lantern in Her Hand—Aldrich		*Meredith*
Les Miserables—Hugo		*Dodd*
Let the Hurricane Roar—Lane		*McKay*
Little Britches—Moody		*Norton*
Madame Curie—Sheean		*Garden City*
Moby Dick—Melville		*Winston*
Mrs. Mike—Freeman		*Coward*
My Antonia—Cather		*Houghton*
Old Man and the Sea—Hemingway		*Scribner*
Old Yeller—Gipson		*Harper*
Penn—Gray		*Viking*
Pride and Prejudice—Austen		*Dodd*
Red Chair Waits—Huggins		*Westminster*
The Sea Around Us—Carson		*Oxford*
Seventeenth Summer—Daly		*Dodd*
The Virginian—Wister		*Macmillan*
Wind, Sand and Stars—Saint Exupery		*Harcourt*
Winter Wheat—Walker		*Harcourt*
The Yearling—Rawlings		*Scribner*

The story of the Tower of Babel has not yet ended, for throughout the world men still speak a babble of over two thousand seven hundred various tongues and dialects that are a barrier between them.

It is difficult for men to "speak the same language" unless they all share the same language. The parochial prejudices and antipathies which have stood between them through the ages, have been caused, in part, by their fear, contempt or aversion of others who communicate among themselves in unintelligible sounds.

LANGUAGES

Under the demands of the modern world, speech barriers are breaking down to some extent. Many know or are learning one or more of our major languages and people of different lands have begun to converse more freely. But the concepts and nuances of one language . . . the essences . . . cannot always be translated literally into another, if at all.

Even within the confines of a single language, words sometimes fail us. As tools of communication, a number of them become dulled by overuse while others are burdened with a variety of meanings. The word "run," for example, has been defined in thirty-nine different ways as a verb, eighteen as a noun and four as an adjective. Of the more than one million words in the English vocabulary, whole segments comprise languages within the language . . . medical, technical, scientific and trade terminologies and jargons which, rather than informing the average person, often serve to exclude him.

While language is our most important means of communicating with one another, the number of languages, their elasticity and complexity, have served to divide us as well.

THE INDO-EUROPEAN LANGUAGE TREE
Dead branches denote dead languages.

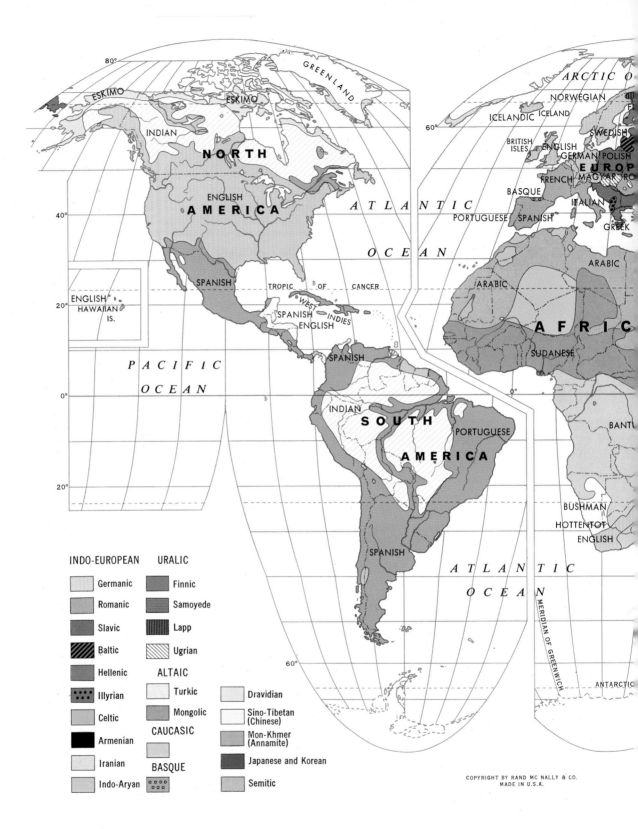

INDO-EUROPEAN

- Germanic
- Romanic
- Slavic
- Baltic
- Hellenic
- Illyrian
- Celtic
- Armenian
- Iranian
- Indo-Aryan

URALIC

- Finnic
- Samoyede
- Lapp
- Ugrian

ALTAIC

- Turkic
- Mongolic

CAUCASIC

BASQUE

- Dravidian
- Sino-Tibetan (Chinese)
- Mon-Khmer (Annamite)
- Japanese and Korean
- Semitic

Perennially fascinating is the study of languages—their possible origin, their various forms, their diffusion, and their differences or interrelationships as between main groups. An approach through the broader subject of communication deals with language for the eye, such as gestures or pictograph writing, and language for the ear, beginning with sounds to express simple physical needs and developing into words, which report past experience and convey ideas. This later stage implies cranial dimensions affording brain capacity for thinking.

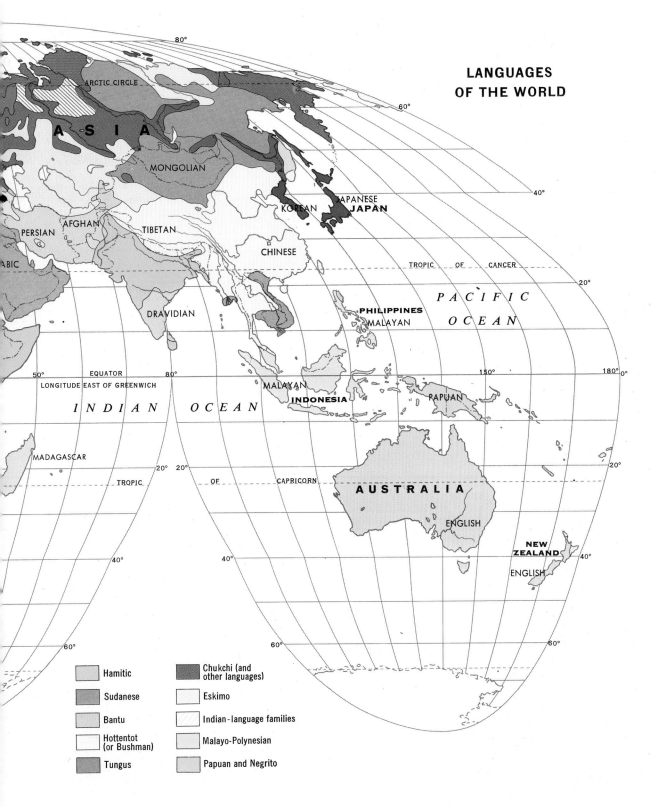

LANGUAGES
OF THE WORLD

ARCTIC CIRCLE

A S I A

MONGOLIAN

AFGHAN

PERSIAN   TIBETAN

ABIC

KOREAN   JAPANESE
               JAPAN

CHINESE

TROPIC   OF   CANCER

DRAVIDIAN

PHILIPPINES
MALAYAN   P A C I F I C

O C E A N

50°   EQUATOR   80°   150°   180° 0°
LONGITUDE EAST OF GREENWICH

MALAYAN

I N D I A N   O C E A N   **INDONESIA**   PAPUAN

MADAGASCAR

20°   20°

TROPIC   OF   CAPRICORN   20°

A U S T R A L I A

40°   40°   ENGLISH

NEW
ZEALAND   40°
ENGLISH

60°   60°   60°

▨ Hamitic	▨ Chukchi (and other languages)	
▨ Sudanese	▨ Eskimo	
▨ Bantu	▨ Indian-language families	
▨ Hottentot (or Bushman)	▨ Malayo-Polynesian	
▨ Tungus	▨ Papuan and Negrito	

   As Herskovits points out in his book "*Cultural Anthropology*," language
belongs with tool-using as one of the two criteria by which man is differentiated from other creatures. It is both an instrument of culture and a
means by which advancement in culture is measured. In the modern
world, close contact between peoples has necessitated a working knowledge of Swahili, Arabic, Russian, Japanese, and many other additions
to such long-established media as English for commerce, French for
diplomacy, and German for science.

THE GREAT LANGUAGES: NUMBER OF SPEAKERS

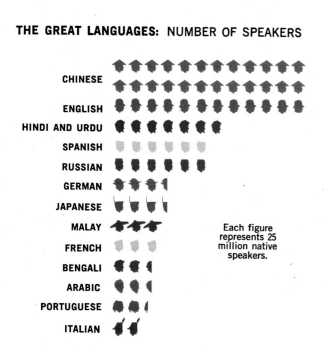

CHINESE
ENGLISH
HINDI AND URDU
SPANISH
RUSSIAN
GERMAN
JAPANESE
MALAY
FRENCH
BENGALI
ARABIC
PORTUGUESE
ITALIAN

Each figure represents 25 million native speakers.

THE ENGLISH LANGUAGE TIME-RIVER

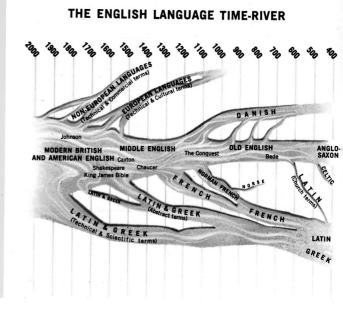

Mankind Divided

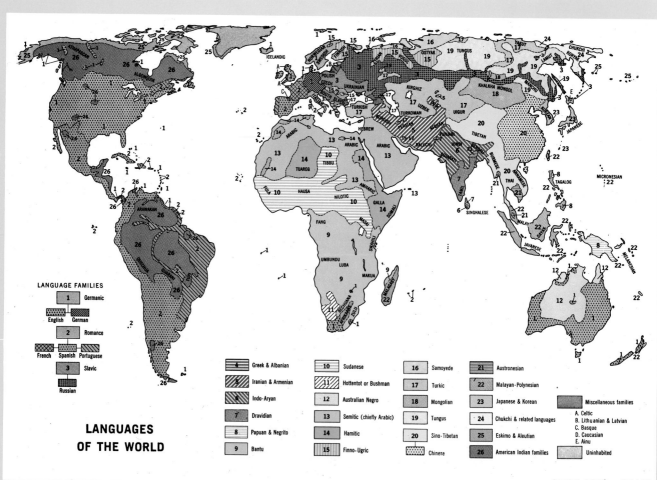

LANGUAGES OF THE WORLD

LANGUAGE FAMILIES

1 Germanic
English German
2 Romance
French Spanish Portuguese
3 Slavic
Russian

4 Greek & Albanian
Iranian & Armenian
Indo-Aryan
7 Dravidian
8 Papuan & Negrito
9 Bantu

10 Sudanese
11 Hottentot or Bushman
12 Australian Negro
13 Semitic (chiefly Arabic)
14 Hamitic
15 Finno-Ugric

16 Samoyede
17 Turkic
18 Mongolian
19 Tungus
20 Sino-Tibetan

21 Austronesian
22 Malayan-Polynesian
23 Japanese & Korean
24 Chukchi & related languages
25 Eskimo & Aleutian
26 American Indian families

Miscellaneous families
A. Celtic
B. Lithuanian & Latvian
C. Basque
D. Caucasian
E. Ainu

Uninhabited

SYNONYMS AND ANTONYMS

SYNONYMS are words that are grouped together because they express the same general idea, though they usually differ considerably from one another in shades of meaning. Examples are *custom, habit,* and *fashion.* Antonyms are words of opposite meaning, as *sharp, dull; long, short; weak, strong.*

The richness of a language in variety, flexibility, and precision may be measured by the number of synonyms it offers to writers and speakers. As English has grown from its Anglo-Saxon beginnings it has adopted and naturalized many words of foreign origin, which have become synonyms for native words. For example, the Latin word *transgression* is found side by side with the Anglo-Saxon word *sin.* Though seemingly equivalent in meaning, these words do not have the same effect upon the listener. Each word has its particular significance and its special overtones.

To cite a more elaborate example, a typical collection of synonyms can be gathered around the basic concept, *at the same time.* The group would include, among others, such words as *contemporary, synchronous, concurrent,* and *simultaneous.* From the standpoint of etymology, the first two words are exact equivalents. The Latin prefix *con* means with or together, the root form *temp* means time, and the word ends in a standard adjective suffix. A direct parallel for these word elements is seen in the Greek prefix *syn,* meaning with or together, the root form *chron,* meaning time, and the adjective suffix which ends the word. Having in mind only their literal meanings, one might suggest that either word would serve, and that two words for the same idea are superfluous. But these two words, although seemingly equivalent, are not interchangeable, and synonyms rarely are. We speak of contemporary writers, artists and other persons, but of synchronous motors. Taxes levied by the state and the nation may be concurrent, that is, running in parallel over the same period, and thus constituting double taxation. Explosions occurring at the same instant are said to be simultaneous. Each of the foregoing synonyms, though meaning essentially *at the same time,* has its own shade of meaning and its own set of associations.

Words with Overlapping Meanings. Occasionally situations arise in which a group of synonyms taken together can be more useful than any single example that might be chosen. To cite an illustration from everyday experience, take the phrasing of a statute requiring the purchase of a dog license, which begins with the words, "Any one who owns, keeps, or harbors . . . a dog," etc. Now here are three synonyms with related but different meanings. If you have a dog on your premises you may have acquired him by gift or purchase (owns), you may simply have him in your custody (keeps), or perhaps the dog has adopted you, as friendly mongrels have a way of doing, and you merely tolerate his presence as a permanent guest (harbors). The statute covers all three possibilities, and you must buy a license on the basis of whichever synonym applies to your particular case.

Choosing the Right Synonym. In contrast with the special case of legal phrasing, the usual problem is to choose just one word out of a group. A writer draws the various synonyms together and makes his selection, rejecting the unwanted words and keeping the one that fills the immediate need. For beginners, the process of selection may involve the consulting of reference sources and perhaps the compiling of written lists of words to be considered. More experienced writers and speakers can review the synonyms mentally, and of course very rapidly. Discrimination between words that goes on in this way is really an essential part of the thinking process. This fact is recognized in the popular short definition of thinking, "To think is to compare."

Precision is arrived at through a careful weighing of various possibilities.

In any given instance, the specific synonym chosen is valued, not only because it is precise in meaning, but also because it makes for economy of expression. The specific term is really the equivalent of a single base word plus a descriptive or explanatory phrase.

Antonyms. If an effect of clarification or emphasis can best be obtained by contrast, the choice will be among antonyms, or opposites, for the base word. To convey the positive idea of *able* by denying the contrary, it may be said of an applicant for a position that he is never *slipshod* or *slovenly* in his work. Such adjectives belong in a list of negative expressions contrasted with the base word, that is, in a list of antonyms. There are many cases in which the distinction between antonyms is more important than between the positive words from which they are derived or to which they correspond. For example, the positive forms *relevant* and *pertinent* are about as close to being interchangeable as any words that can be found. Their corresponding antonyms, *irrelevant* and *impertinent* show marked differences in shades of meaning.

Sometimes the antonyms are verbs, but more often they are adjectives or adverbs. In the latter case, a word of caution should be given. Laziness in word selection is encouraged by the fact that antonyms for adjectives and adverbs can be easily and cheaply formed. By prefixing *anti, dis, non, un,* or some other syllable of the kind, an antonym can be provided for almost any adjective or adverb. However, because the principle of variety is so important in every form of writing or speaking, only limited use should be made of the "prefix" type of antonym. To cite an extreme example, one would certainly not express the opposite of rich (wealthy) by coining a crude derivative word like *un-rich.* Instead, there could be a choice from a whole collection of words like *poor, indigent, penniless, poverty-stricken,* and other specific antonyms, ranging all the way to the possible but unlikely word *impecunious.*

How to Use. To get the greatest amount of value from the following dictionary of synonyms and antonyms, it is necessary that one should understand clearly the use of the index or key. Let us suppose, for example, that you are writing a letter in which you have used the word *trouble.* You may desire to repeat the idea of this word and yet you do not wish to employ the same word again. Perhaps you do not recall another word which will exactly express the thought you wish to convey.

Turn to the index or key beginning on page 156 and find the word *trouble* with a reference to page 154. You will also find *trouble* occurring twice followed by words in italics: once by *affliction* with a reference to page 123 and once by *difficulty* with a reference to page 135. First turn to page 154 and there you will find *disturb* and *molest* as variant words. It may be that one of these will suit your purpose. But, if both words fail, next refer to page 123 and look for *affliction.* Under it, in addition to *trouble,* are the words *distress, grief,* and *sorrow.* If up to this point you are not satisfied, you may turn to page 135 and look for *difficulty.* Under it you find the additional synonyms *obstacle, impediment,* and *embarrassment,* with an explanation of how each word is used. Among all these synonyms, you are almost certain to find a word to suit the need. But, in the very rare case that you do not find the precise word, you will have received many suggestions which will enable you to convey the desired idea in a different manner; for, by glancing at the antonyms under the three paragraphs you have read, you will have seen *soothe, quiet, compose, caress, happiness, comfort, satisfaction, cheer, aid, help, assistance, relief,* and *encouragement.*

DICTIONARY OF SYNONYMS AND ANTONYMS

Abandon, desert, forsake, relinquish, surrender. The general idea which these words have in common is that of giving up or leaving something or someone. Specific applications are represented by the various synonyms used in the following phrases: abandon a ship or an infant or a project, or abandon oneself to despair; desert one's wife, regiment or husband; forsake one's companions or a cause to which one has been committed; relinquish a hold or a possession; surrender one's freedom, a fortress or an army (implying formal capitulation). In everyday language, one may surrender an insurance policy.
Antonyms.—Keep, maintain, protect, support.

Abbreviate, abridge, condense. The common purpose of reducing or shortening indicated by these words is accomplished in three ways. Abbreviate deals in fragments, as when it makes initials stand for words. Abridge selects and combines portions of a book or article, but the parts retained are essentially the same as in the original version. Condense keeps the main ideas of the original but rephrases them in more concise language, as in the writing of a summary or abstract.
Antonyms.—Amplify, expand, elaborate.

Abeyance, postponement, suspense. Actions proposed or undertaken are kept waiting, that is, held in abeyance, pending some future development. Postponement implies delay with a more definite intention to resume action. Suspense keeps the idea of interruption and adds to it an element of uncertainty, or perhaps anxiety.
Antonyms.—Continuation, resumption.

Abhor, detest, loathe. These terms all denote aversion. We may abhor an act that is shocking to our moral sense; we may detest a person who is guilty of such an act. Using a still stronger word, we may loathe something that offends our taste, whether it be unacceptable conduct or unappealing food. In the case of both physical and moral repugnance, loathe carries with it a strong sense of physical revulsion.
Antonyms.—Admire, esteem, approve, desire.

Ability, capacity, faculty, talent, genius. In general, ability means the power of doing, without specifying the quality or degree. It may be either physical or mental. Capacity, when applied to persons, is mental only. It looks to the future and estimates the possibility of knowledge that can be absorbed and the productive brain activity that can be expected. The analogy here is obviously with such physical and mechanical concepts as the cubic contents of a container and the productive output of a machine. Ability may be the result of health, strength, and training. Faculty is a gift of nature to the species; for example, a sense of sight or hearing. Talent is a special aptitude born in the individual; genius is a phenomenal endowment by nature which enables an individual to do the highest form of creative work.
Antonyms.—Inability, incompetence, stupidity.

Abject, servile, slavish, cringing. Different kinds and degrees of self-depreciation are indicated by these words. An abject apology shows extreme humility as well as regret. A servile attitude toward one's superiors and a slavish devotion to routine tasks might lead to a cringing acceptance of degradation which is the antithesis of dignity.
Antonyms.—Proud, independent, overbearing.

Abolish, abrogate, repeal, revoke, annul. The word abolish, usually suggesting an act of power or authority, conveys the idea of putting a total end to a thing and is applied particularly to those things which have been long in existence and are firmly established. Laws are either repealed, as by a vote of public assemblies, or abrogated, as by the enactment of new laws which supersede the old ones. Revoking is an act of individual authority—edicts are revoked—while annulling is an act of discretion following sober second thought or a change in conditions. For example, contracts are annulled.
Antonyms.—Establish, institute, confirm.

Absolute, despotic, arbitrary, tyrannical. Absolute power is independent of and superior to all other power: an absolute monarch is uncontrolled, either by men or by things. Despotic power is power exercised as by a master or lord. Despotic power is, therefore, as complete as absolute power but carries the added idea that the ruler has the right to treat his subjects according to his will or pleasure. With arbitrariness are associated the ideas of caprice and selfishness. With tyranny are associated the ideas of oppression and injustice. In modern use, both arbitrariness and tyranny are associated with despotism.
Antonyms.—Limited, constitutional, accountable, mild, lenient, just.

Accomplish, effect, execute, achieve. To accomplish an object signifies more than simply to effect a purpose, both as to the thing aimed at and the means employed in bringing it about. Extraordinary means are requisite for accomplishing and ordinary means, for effecting. To accomplish is properly said of that which a person sets before himself; but to effect, execute, and achieve do not relate to the views of a person acting, but to the thing brought about. What is executed is complicated in its nature, as to execute a design or project; what is achieved is of greater and worthier conception, as to achieve success in a profession.
Antonyms.—Fail, come short, default, give up.

Accuse, charge, impeach, arraign. The idea of asserting something to the prejudice of another is common to these terms. But accuse is said of acts; charge, of moral qualities constituting the character. We accuse a person of murder; we charge him with dishonesty. High officials are impeached; criminals are arraigned.
Antonyms.—Clear, discharge, exonerate, acquit.

Act, do, make. We always act when we do, but we do not always do when we act. Act is applied to either persons or things, as a spring or a lock acts; do applies in this sense to persons only. Act is generally used intransitively, as to act well or ill in this or that manner; do is usually transitive, as to do right or wrong, to do one's duty. To make is to bring a thing to being or form as to make a pen.

Act, work, operate. A machine works, but each of its parts is said to act; so beer works, and bread works. Sometimes act as well as work is taken in the sense of exerting a power upon other bodies and producing changes, as the sun acts on the plants. Operate is applied to matters of a general nature in science or morals, as a measure operates, or words may operate on the mind, or reasons may operate on the understanding.

Action, gesture, gesticulation, posture, attitude. All these terms are applied to the state of the body; the first three indicate a state of motion, the last two a state of rest. Action respects the movements of the body in general; gesture is an action indicative of some particular state of mind; gesticulation is the act of making gestures. Raising the arm is an action; bowing is a gesture. Posture and attitude both imply a mode of placing the body, but the posture is either natural or assumed; the attitude is always assumed or represented. We assume a sitting posture or an attitude of prayer.

Active, diligent, industrious, assiduous, laborious, busy, officious. We are active if we are only ready to exert our powers, whether to any end or not; we are diligent when we are active for some specific end; we are industrious when no time is left unemployed in some serious pursuit; we are assiduous if we do not leave a thing until it is finished; we are laborious when the bodily or mental powers are regularly employed in some hard labor. Busy implies continuous occupation. Officious implies being busy without discretion, especially about other people's affairs.
Antonyms.—Inert, indolent, lazy, trifling, idle, shiftless.

Actual, real, positive, true. What is actual has proof of its existence within itself, and may be exposed to the eye; what is real may be satisfactorily proved to exist; and what is positive precludes the necessity of a proof. That is true which is genuine, in accord with evident facts or susceptible of proof.
Antonyms.—Supposititious, imaginary, doubtful, uncertain, false, artificial.

Actuate, impel, induce. One is actuated by motives, impelled by passions, and induced by reason or inclination. Whatever actuates is the result of reflection—it is a steady and fixed principle. Whatever impels is momentary and vehement, and often precludes reflection. Whatever induces is not vehement, though often momentary.
Antonyms.—Restrain, inhibit, impede, check.

Acute, keen, shrewd. An acute angle or a pointed instrument is sharp; the cutting edge of a knife is keen. In the mental sense, an argument may be acute, a reproach keen, and a judgment shrewd. Pain is sometimes acute, remorse keen, and suspicion shrewd.
Antonyms.—Dull, obtuse, stupid.

Adhere, stick, cohere. In the physical sense, an object attaches itself to another by adhering when their surfaces come in contact. If the objects are alike in composition they cohere, or unite on equal terms, and become unified. An object with a mucilaginous property or an animal with strong tentacles may stick to a surface. Figuratively, a man may adhere to a political party.
Antonyms.—Detach, disengage, separate.

Adjacent, abutting, juxtaposed. Two houses standing side by side are described as adjacent. If the lots which they occupy come together at a boundary line, the properties are said to be abutting. Objects or works of art placed side by side for comparison are said to be juxtaposed. *Antonyms.*—Distant, separated, disjoined.

Admit, allow, permit, suffer, tolerate. Admit in this sense is used mostly of ideas and propositions, usually used with *of*. Allow is of more general application, frequently implying only a tacit refraining from refusal. We admit that which concerns ourselves; we allow that which is for the convenience of others. What is suffered may be burdensome to the sufferer, if not morally wrong; what is tolerated is contrary to one's desires, and is suffered only because it cannot be prevented. Permit implies a positive grant of privilege. *Antonyms.*—Forbid, refuse, withstand, prevent, deny.

Admit, receive. Persons are admitted to the tables, and into the familiarity or confidence of others; they are hospitably received by those who wish to be their entertainers. We admit willingly or reluctantly; we receive politely or rudely. *Antonyms.*—Shut out, forbid, exclude.

Adoration, worship, reverence. Adoration is the service of the heart toward a superior being, in which we acknowledge our dependence and obedience by petition and thanksgiving; worship consists in the outward form of showing reverence to some supposed superior being. Reverence differs from adoration inasmuch as it has a mixture of awe, arising from consciousness of weakness and dependence, or of obligations for favors received. *Antonyms.*—Contempt, dishonor, impiety, sacrilege.

Advance, proceed. Advance implies movement forward; proceed, movement from one point to another, also resumption of movement after a pause. *Antonyms.*—Recede, retire, withdraw.

Advantage, benefit, utility. Advantage refers to external circumstances of profit, honor, and convenience; benefit, to the consequences of actions and events; utility respects the good which can be drawn from the use of any object. A large house or a particular situation may have its advantages; suitable exercise is attended with benefit; the utility of motor cars consists in their supplying means of rapid travel. *Antonyms.*—Disadvantage, futility, worthlessness.

Adverse, antagonistic, hostile. Adverse criticism is definitely unfavorable; an antagonistic attitude combines opposition with personal dislike. Nations at odds or individuals who are parties to a public conflict are said to be hostile toward one another. *Antonyms.*—Auspicious, favorable, friendly

Advice, counsel. Advice is given by physicians and other professional persons who have special knowledge in some technical field. We receive counsel in matters of conduct from wiser, and usually older, persons who have a superior acquaintance with moral principles. It is assumed that both advice and counsel are sought, and not proffered gratuitously.

Affect, assume, pretend. To affect is to use forced efforts to appear to have that which one has not; to assume is to appropriate to oneself that which one has no right to have. One affects to have fine feelings, and assumes great importance. We pretend by making a false declaration. One affects indifference to praise and pretends to have wealth.

Affect, influence, sway, concern. Things affect our well being when they cause some change in our outward circumstances; they concern us when they come closer and touch our personal interests. We are influenced by the example of someone and swayed, that is, impelled to action, by his persuasive arguments.

Affectionate, kind, fond. We are affectionate toward relatives and close friends. Kindness includes a wider circle of recipients and is expressed in considerate action. Fondness implies a tender, indulgent, and often unreasoning liking. Originally, kind suggested natural affection, as in Hamlet's words, "A little more than kin, and less than kind." *Antonyms.*—Indifferent, unfriendly, inconsiderate.

Affirm, assert. Affirm is said of facts; assert, of opinions. We affirm what we know; we assert what we believe. *Antonyms.*—Deny, retract, repudiate.

Affliction, distress, trouble, grief, sorrow. Affliction is applied both to severe misfortune and to the deep sorrow of heart that may come from it. Grief is keen, poignant sorrow springing from a definite cause. Distress implies severe, painful trouble from physical or mental causes. Trouble may imply merely confusion of mind, or it may signify deep-seated disturbance. *Antonyms.*—Happiness, comfort, satisfaction, cheer.

Affront, insult, outrage. To affront is to show reproach in the presence of others—it piques and mortifies; to insult is to attack with insolence—it irritates and provokes; to outrage is to combine all that is offensive, to add insult to injury. *Antonyms.*—Honor, gratify, please, benefit.

Afraid, fearful, timorous, timid. Afraid is the most general of these words, implying either a slight or a high degree of fear. Fearful is a stronger word than afraid: one may be fearful of defeat and yet not afraid in a discreditable sense. Timid and timorous imply constitutional liability to fear, even of slight matters. *Antonyms.*—Brave, bold, fearless, intrepid.

Agree, accede, consent, comply, acquiesce. Agree is the general term, meaning to fall in with. We accede by becoming a party to a thing; those who accede are on equal terms. We consent to a thing by authorizing it, we comply with a thing by allowing it; those who consent or comply are not on equal terms with those in whose favor the consent is given or compliance made. Consenting is an act of the will, complying an act of good nature or weakness. To acquiesce is quietly to accept; it is a passive act, dictated by prudence or duty. *Antonyms.*—Disagree, dissent, refuse, decline, oppose.

Agreeable, pleasant, pleasing. Agreeable expresses a less vivid feeling than pleasant; pleasing marks a sentiment less vivid and distinct than either. A pleasing countenance denotes tranquillity and contentment; a pleasant countenance bespeaks happiness. *Antonyms.*—Disagreeable, repulsive, irritating.

Aim, aspire. We aim at a certain proposed point by endeavoring to gain it; we aspire after that which we think ourselves entitled to, and which we flatter ourselves with gaining. Many men aim at riches and honor; it is the lot of but few to aspire to high office.

Aim, object, end. The aim is that which the person has in his own mind. The object lies in the thing. The end is that which follows or terminates any course or proceeding. It is the aim of the Christian to live peaceably; it is a mark of dullness or folly to act without an object; it is sophistry to suppose that the end will justify the means.

Air, manner, look, carriage, gait. Air lies in the whole person; manner refers to movement or action or expressive gesture. A man has the air of a common person; it discovers itself in all his manners. An air is noble or simple —it marks an elevation or simplicity of character; a manner is rude, rustic, or awkward, for want of culture, good society, and good example. We assume an air, and affect a manner. Look refers especially to the facial expression —an honest look. Carriage applies to the manner of holding or carrying the body. Gait is the manner of walking.

Alarm, terror, fright, consternation. Alarm is felt at the sudden approach of danger or signs of danger. Terror may arise from any appearance or event suggesting great harm or catastrophe; alarm prompts us to defense, and terror disarms us. Fright is a less vivid emotion than either, as it arises from the simple appearance or thought of danger. Consternation springs from the view of some very serious evil, and commonly affects many. Alarm affects the feelings, terror the understanding, and fright the senses; consternation seizes the whole mind and benumbs the faculties. *Antonyms.*—Calmness, repose, confidence, self-command.

Alertness, alacrity. Alertness signifies an attitude and manner of keen readiness, promising prompt, spirited action. Alacrity implies a quick, willing response to impulse or demand from without. *Antonyms.*—Inertness, sluggishness, languidness, apathy.

Allay, soothe, appease, mitigate, assuage. All these terms indicate a lessening of something painful. In a physical sense an irritating pain is allayed; a wounded part is soothed by affording ease and comfort. Extreme heat or thirst is allayed; extreme hunger is appeased; a punishment or suffering is mitigated. Temper or enthusiasm that is fervid and vehement is allayed; one soothes a mind that is distressed or irritated; one appeases what is tumultuous and boisterous; one mitigates the pains of others; one assuages grief or afflictions. *Antonyms.*—Arouse, irritate, intensify, kindle, excite.

Alleviate, relieve. A pain is alleviated by making it less burdensome; a necessity is relieved by supplying what is wanted. Alleviate refers to internal feelings only; relieve, to either internal feelings or external circumstances. That alleviates which affords ease and comfort; that relieves which removes the pain.
Antonyms.—Aggravate, intensify.

Alliance, league, coalition, confederacy. An alliance, as of families or states, is a joining of resources for mutual benefit. A league is a more formal organization designed to serve the common interests of its members. A coalition is usually a temporary union, as of states or political parties, to meet a particular situation. A confederation is a union of hitherto separate political units in which their previously distinct powers are delegated to a central authority.

Allot, appoint, destine. Allot is used only for things; appoint and destine for persons or things. A space of ground is allotted for cultivation; a person is appointed as steward or governor; a youth is destined for a particular profession. Allot and appoint imply immediate purposes; destine implies remote purposes.

Allow, grant, bestow. That is allowed which may be expected, if not directly required; that is granted which is desired, or directly asked for; that is bestowed which is wanted as a matter of necessity. A grant comprehends in it something more important than an allowance, and passes between persons in a higher station; what is bestowed is of less value than either. A boy is allowed money for expenses; a king grants pensions to his officers; relief is bestowed on the indigent.
Antonyms.—Refuse, withhold, disallow.

Allowance, wages, fee, salary, stipend, pay, honorarium. An allowance is a gratuitous payment of money —it ceases at the pleasure of the donor. Compensation for labor, particularly common labor, is called wages. A fee is a specific sum paid for professional services. Salary (in ancient times "salt money") means fixed compensation paid regularly over a long interval. Stipend, less permanent than salary, is a fixed income for teachers, clergymen, and others over a stated period. Pay is a general word covering reward for services, but it is used specifically for compensation received by soldiers. A small fee, as for lectures, may be made to seem more impressive by being called an "honorarium."

Allude, refer, hint, suggest. To allude is not so direct as to refer, but it is more clear and positive than either hint or suggest. We allude to a circumstance by introducing something collaterally allied to it; we refer to an event by expressly introducing it into our discourse; we hint at a person's intentions by insinuating what may possibly happen; we suggest an idea by some expressions relative to it.

Alone, solitary, lonely, desolate. Alone states the fact of being by oneself. Solitary is a more subjective word which carries a suggestion of isolation. One can be lonely in a crowd, that is, without acquaintances or understanding friends. Desolate, when applied to a person, indicates grief resulting from irreparable loss. A desolate landscape shows ruin and destruction.
Antonyms.—Accompanied, attended.

Ambiguous, equivocal, cryptic. Ambiguous language is obscure, capable of being interpreted in more than one way. Equivocal speech, or "double-talk," is intentionally left open to different and perhaps opposite meanings. The Frenchman's equivocal compliment on a young woman, "Her beauty is equaled only by her intelligence," could be taken in either of two ways. A cryptic remark is vague or puzzling because of its brevity.
Antonyms.—Clear, definite, plain.

Amend, correct, mend, repair. Amend and correct are applied to works of the understanding. Amend signifies to remove faults or defects, generally by adding or taking away or altering, as in amending a law. To correct is to remove faults by revising or reshaping, as to correct copy. Mend, often used in reference to mechanical or textile objects, means to replace or restore a defective part. Repair indicates a more thorough restoration of the object to its former state. One mends a garment and repairs a bridge.
Antonyms.—Damage, impair, destroy.

Amicable, friendly. Amicable implies a negative sentiment, a freedom from discordance; friendly implies a positive feeling of regard, the absence of indifference. We make an amicable settlement and have a friendly understanding.
Antonyms.—Ill-tempered, unfriendly, hostile.

Amuse, divert, entertain. Amusement kills time pleasantly during idle moments. Anything diverting pleases by drawing our attention away from work or serious thinking. Entertainment is planned to give active enjoyment. It makes a calculated appeal to the senses, the understanding, or the critical faculties—sometimes to all three.
Antonyms.—Bore, annoy, tire.

Anger, resentment, wrath, ire, indignation, rage, fury. Anger is a sudden sentiment of displeasure; resentment is a continued anger; wrath is a heightened sentiment of anger, which is poetically expressed by the word ire. Indignation is a sentiment awakened by the unworthy and atrocious conduct of others; as it is exempt from personality it is not irreconcilable with the temper of a Christian. Rage is a vehement show of anger, and fury is an excess of rage.
Antonyms.—Patience, acquiescence, gentleness, self-control, serenity, calmness.

Animate, enliven, exhilarate. To be animated is to have, or seem to have, the faculties of a living creature, as in the alertness of a person or the movements of an animated cartoon. Enliven refers to a raising of one's spirits and a quickening of one's impulses. Exhilarate (note the related word "hilarity") carries the idea of merrymaking as a phase of extreme liveliness.
Antonyms.—Deaden, dull, depress.

Announce, proclaim, publish. We announce an event that is expected or at hand; we proclaim an event that requires to be known by all the parties interested; we publish what is supposed likely to interest all who know it.
Antonyms.—Conceal, suppress, withhold.

Answer, reply, rejoinder, response. An answer is given to a question; a reply is made to an assertion or a letter; a rejoinder is made to a reply; a response is made in accordance with the words of another. We answer either for the purpose of affirmation, information, or contradiction; we always reply, or rejoin, in order to explain or confute; responses are made by way of assent or confirmation.
Antonyms.—Question, query, interrogation.

Answerable, responsible, accountable, amenable. Answerable and responsible convey the idea of a formal pledge or an implied obligation for the performance of some act or the fulfillment of some engagement. A person is accountable to his employer for the manner in which he has conducted business entrusted to him. Amenable refers more to one's disposition. A person is said to be amenable to reason, that is, open or susceptible.
Antonyms.—Independent, arbitrary, irresponsible.

Apologize, defend, justify, exculpate, excuse, plead. We apologize for an error by acknowledging ourselves guilty of it; we defend ourselves against a charge by proving its fallacy; we justify our conduct against any imputation by proving that it was blameless; we exculpate ourselves from all blame by proving that we took no part in the transaction. Excuse and plead are not grounded on any idea of innocence; a plea is frequently an idle or unfounded excuse, a frivolous attempt to lessen displeasure; we excuse ourselves for a neglect by alleging indisposition.

Apparent, visible, clear, plain, obvious, evident. That which is simply an object of sight is visible; that which presents itself to our view in any form, real or otherwise, is apparent. The stars themselves are visible to us; but their size is apparent. What is clear is to be seen in all its parts and in its proper colors; what is plain is seen by understanding; what is obvious presents itself readily to the mind of everyone; what is evident is unquestionably seen, and leaves no hesitation in the mind.
Antonyms.—Obscure, hidden, latent, doubtful.

Applause, acclamation, ovation. Applause is approval expressed by clapping of hands; acclamation calls for shouts and cries. Ovation represents still greater enthusiasm, in which an audience rises spontaneously and engages in prolonged cheering.
Antonyms.—Censure, hissing, booing.

Appoint, order, prescribe, ordain. To appoint is the act of either an equal or a superior; we appoint a meeting with any one at a given time and place; a king appoints his ministers. To order is the act of one invested with a partial authority; a master gives his orders to his servant. To prescribe is the act of one who is superior by virtue of his knowledge; a physician prescribes for his patient. To ordain is an act emanating from the highest authority; kings and councils ordain, but their ordinances must be conformable to what is ordained by the Divine Being.
Antonyms.—Forbid, prohibit, veto.

Apprehend, conceive, suppose, imagine. To apprehend is to become aware of something; to conceive is to create in the mind something that does not exist. One supposes, or conjectures, something that may be doubtful but seems probable and reasonable. One may imagine the most unreal creatures, objects or situations as well as realizable ones.

Approach, access, admittance. Approach signifies the coming near or toward an object, and consequently it is an unfinished act, but access and admittance are finished acts; access is coming to, or as close to, an object as is needful; admittance is coming into any place, or into the presence or society of any person.
Antonyms.—Recession, withdrawal, exclusion.

Approach, approximate. Approach means to draw or come nearer to, although the distance at any time may still be great. Approximate implies a very close approach—as close as conditions will permit.
Antonyms.—Avoid, miss, shun, evade.

Argue, evince, prove. To argue is to establish an indication amounting to probability; to evince denotes an indication so clear as to remove doubt; to prove marks an evidence so positive as to produce conviction.

Argument, reason, proof. An argument serves for defense; a reason, for justification; a proof, for conviction. Arguments are adduced in support of a hypothesis or a proposition; reasons are assigned in matters of belief and practice; proofs are collected to determine truth as to alleged facts.

Arise, rise, mount, ascend, climb, scale. Arise is used only in the sense of simply getting up, but rise is employed to express a continued motion upward. A person arises from his seat or his bed; a bird rises in the air; a person mounts a hill, and ascends a mountain. To climb is to rise step by step by clinging to a certain body; to scale is to rise as by an escalade, or species of ladder, employed in mounting the walls of fortified towns. Trees and mountains are climbed; walls are scaled.
Antonyms.—Settle, fall, descend, sink.

Arrogant, proud, presumptuous. The arrogant man seeks to impose his assumed superiority on others; he shows an aggressive self-assertion. A proud person is more quietly conscious of his own importance; he may stand aloof from people he considers inferior. A person is presumptuous who acts rashly in asserting claims for favors or attention; he lacks sufficient judgment for proper self-restraint.
Antonyms.—Modest, meek, humble, self-effacing.

Artist, artisan, mechanic, craftsman. The artist ranks higher than the artisan,—the former requires intellectual refinement, the latter nothing but to know the common, mechanical practice of an art or trade. The sculptor is an artist; the sign-painter is an artisan. Mechanic and artisan are used interchangeably. Craftsman implies technical skill and judgment; it is used of both artist and artisan. The mechanic is one whose work involves manual skill, or skill in the use of tools.

Ask, inquire, question, interrogate. We perform all these actions in order to get information; but we ask, for general purposes of convenience; we inquire from motives of curiosity; we question and interrogate from motives of discretion. Indifferent people ask of each other whatever they wish to know; learners inquire the reasons of things that are new to them; masters question their servants, or parents their children, when they wish to ascertain the real state of any case; magistrates interrogate criminals when they are brought before them.
Antonyms.—Answer, reply, respond.

Assemble, muster, collect. To assemble is to bring together by a call or invitation or, as machine parts, by mechanical process according to a plan; to muster is to bring together by an act of authority, or by a particular effort, into one point of view at one time, and from one quarter; to collect is to bring together at different times, and from different quarters.
Antonyms.—Adjourn, dismiss, scatter, disperse.

Assent, consent, approbation, concurrence. Assent concerns matters of judgment; consent, matters of conduct. We assent to what we admit to be true; we consent to what we allow to be done. Approbation is a species of assent, concurrence, of consent. To approve is not merely to assent to a thing as right, but to determine upon it positively; concurrence is properly the consent of many. Assent is given by equals or inferiors; consent, by superiors; approbation, by equals or superiors; concurrence, by equals.
Antonyms.—Dissent, refusal, disapproval, disagreement.

Association, society, company, partnership, corporation. Associations and societies are organizations for the promotion of literary, scientific, religious, or benevolent objects. Companies and partnerships are formed for business purposes. The partnership is the least stable of business organizations. A corporation is a more permanent organization, chartered by the state. It persists irrespective of the particular individuals owning or controlling its stock.

Asylum, refuge, shelter, retreat. Asylum is sought by a person who has no home; refuge by one who is apprehensive of danger; shelter by anyone who seeks protection from the elements. Retreat implies a wish for separation from the cares of life, an opportunity for meditation.

Attack, assail, assault. To attack is to make an approach in order to do some violence to the person; to assail or assault is to make a sudden and vehement attack. One assails by means of missiles, reproaches, or invective; one assaults by direct personal violence.
Antonyms.—Resist, withstand, sustain, defend.

Attempt, endeavor, effort, essay. An attempt is the act of setting about a thing with a view of effecting it; an endeavor is a continued attempt. An effort is to an attempt as a means is to an end; it is the act of calling forth those powers which are required in an attempt.

Attend, hear, listen. To attend is to have the mind intently engaged on what we hear; to listen is to strive to hear. People attend when they are addressed. Listen implies a lesser degree of heed than attend. To hear is merely to be conscious of sound.

Attentive, careful. We are attentive in order to understand and to improve; we are careful to avoid mistakes. Attentive refers to mental attitude; careful relates to mechanical action: we listen attentively; we read or write carefully.
Antonyms.—Inattentive, careless, heedless, indifferent.

Attract, allure, invite, engage. That is attractive which draws the attention toward itself; that is alluring which awakens desire; that is inviting which offers persuasion; that is engaging which takes possession of the mind.
Antonyms.—Repel, deter, estrange, disgust.

Austere, rigid, severe, rigorous, stern. The austere man is severe with himself; the rigid man binds himself to a rule. The manners of a man are austere when he refuses to take part in any social enjoyments. Severe is used with reference to conduct,—a man is severe in the restraints he imposes and the punishments he inflicts. Rigorous implies harshness. Sternness is a species of severity more in manner than in direct action; a commander may issue his commands sternly, or a despot may issue his stern decrees.
Antonyms.—Affable, gentle, indulgent, mild.

Avaricious, miserly, parsimonious, niggardly. An avaricious man shows his love of money in his ordinary dealings; but the miser lives for his money and suffers every privation rather than part with it. The avaricious man indulges his passion for money by parsimony, that is, by excessive personal saving, or by niggardly ways in his dealings with others.
Antonyms.—Unselfish, generous, lavish, free.

Awaken, excite, provoke, rouse, stir up. We awaken by a simple effort; we excite by repeated efforts or forcible means; we provoke by words, looks, or actions. The tender feelings are awakened; affections, or the passions in general, are excited; the angry passions are commonly provoked We are roused from an extraordinary state by extraordinary means; we are stirred up from an ordinary to an extraordinary state.
Antonyms.—Calm, quiet, pacify, restrain.

Awe, reverence, dread. Awe and reverence both denote a strong sentiment of respect, mingled to some extent with fear. Of the two, awe is the stronger, being inspired, for example, by the great forces of nature and the contemplation of their Divine origin. Reverence, also a religious sentiment, is associated with quieter and less disturbed feelings. Dread is a haunting fear of what is to come.
Antonyms.—Irreverence, familiarity, assurance.

Awkward, clumsy, bungling. Awkward applies to outward deportment; clumsy, to the shape and make of the object. A person has an awkward gait; he is clumsy in his whole person. Bungling applies to the result of awkwardness and clumsiness in performing work.
Antonyms.—Adroit, dexterous, neat, skillful.

Axiom, maxim, aphorism, saying, adage, proverb, byword. The axiom is a truth of the first value, a self-evident proposition which is the basis of other truths. A maxim is a truth of the first moral importance for all practical purposes; an aphorism is a truth set apart for its pointedness and excellence. Adage and proverb are common sayings, the former among the ancients, the latter among the moderns. The byword is a casual saying, originating in some local circumstance, frequently used in contempt.

Babble, chatter, chat, prattle. Babbling denotes rapidity of speech, which renders it unintelligible; chatter is an imitation of the noise of speech properly applied to magpies or parrots, and figuratively to a corresponding mode of speech in human beings. The winter's fireside invites neighbors to assemble and chat away many an hour which might otherwise hang heavy on hand, or be spent less inoffensively. The prattling of babes has an interest for every feeling mind, but for parents it is one of the highest enjoyments.

Band, company, crew, gang. All these terms denote a small association for a particular object. A band is an association in which men are bound together by some strong obligation, whether taken in a good or a bad sense, as a band of soldiers, a band of robbers; a company marks an association for convenience, without any particular obligation, as a company of travelers, a company of strolling players. A crew marks an association collected by some external power, or by coincidence of plan and motive; in the former case it is used for a ship's crew, in the latter and bad sense of the word it is employed for any number of evil-minded persons met together from different quarters and co-operating for some bad purpose. Gang and crew are applied to companies of workmen under one leader or on one job, or to bands brought together for boisterous or disorderly purposes. Gang is applied to groups of boys who play together under a leader.

Banishment, exile, expulsion. Banishment follows from a decree of justice; exile, either by the necessity of circumstances or by an order of authority; banishment is a disgraceful punishment inflicted by tribunals upon delinquents; exile is a disgrace incurred without dishonor; exile removes us from our country; banishment or expulsion drives us from it ignominiously.
Antonyms.—Recall, reinstatement, repatriation.

Be, become, grow. Be is positive; become is relative: a person is what he is without regard to what he was; he becomes that which he was not before. To grow is to become by a gradual process. A man may become a good man from a vicious one, in consequence of a sudden action of his mind; but he grows in wisdom and virtue by means of an increase in knowledge and experience.
Antonyms.—Die, stagnate, diminish.

Be, exist, subsist. We say of qualities, of forms, of actions, of arrangement, of movement, and of every different relation, whether real, ideal, or qualificative, that they are; we say of matter, of spirit, of body, and of substances, that they exist. Man is man, and will be man under all circumstances and changes of life; he exists under every known climate and variety of heat or cold in the atmosphere. Subsist implies generally dependence upon outside aid for existence. Cities subsist on the productivity of the country.

Bear, yield. Both words mean to produce: bear respects animals and plants, which bear young or fruit; yield respects plants or inanimate objects, which yield increase.

Beat, defeat, overpower, rout, overthrow. An army is beaten in important engagements; it is defeated and may be routed in partial attacks; it is overpowered by numbers, and overthrown in set engagements. These words are similarly applied to the fortunes of persons.
Antonyms.—Aid, help, succor, befriend.

Beautiful, fine, fair, handsome, pretty. Beautiful implies a certain perfection of form, correctness of proportion, unity of impression, harmony of details. Applied to human beings it connotes some spiritual excellence. Fine implies perfection of finish and design, both interior and exterior. Fair conveys the idea of external smoothness and freedom from blemish. Handsome implies superficial excellence, of proportion in particular. Pretty is confined to objects of refinement, especially those small and dainty, as a pretty fancy, a pretty child.
Antonyms.—Plain, uncouth, coarse, deformed, ugly.

Becoming, comely, graceful. Becoming applies to the decorations of the person and to the deportment; comely refers to natural embellishments; graceful, to natural or artificial accomplishments. Manner is becoming; figure is comely; air, figure, or attitude is graceful.
Antonyms.—Unsuitable, awkward, homely, uncouth.

Beg, beseech, solicit, entreat, supplicate, implore, crave. To beg denotes a state of want: to beseech, entreat,

and solicit, a state of urgent necessity; supplicate and implore, a state of abject distress; crave, the lowest state of physical want. One begs with importunity, beseeches with earnestness, entreats by the force of reasoning and strong representation; one solicits by virtue of one's interest, supplicates by a humble address, implores by every mark of dejection and humiliation.
Antonyms.—Command, demand, claim, extort, refuse.

Behavior, conduct. Behavior is more specific, and refers to acts, especially in the presence of or in reference to others. Conduct is more general and inclusive; it implies moral or ethical considerations governing behavior.

Belief, credit, trust, faith. Belief and credit are particular actions or sentiments; trust and faith are permanent dispositions of the mind. Things are entitled to our belief; persons are entitled to our credit; but people repose trust in others, or have faith in others. Belief is intellectual and may be quite impersonal. Faith and trust are personal and have immediate reference to conduct. Trust in God serves to dispel all anxious concern about the future.
Antonyms.—Doubt, denial, distrust, skepticism.

Benevolence, benignity, humanity, kindness, tenderness. Benevolence lies in the will; benignity, in the disposition or frame of mind. Humanity lies in the heart; kindness and tenderness, in the affections. Benevolence indicates a general good will to all mankind; benignity particular goodness or kindness of disposition. Humanity is a general tone of feeling; kindness and tenderness are particular modes of feeling.
Antonyms.—Malevolence, malignity, churlishness, harshness, brutality, ill will.

Bereave, deprive, strip. To bereave expresses more than deprive, but less than strip, which denotes a total and violent bereavement. One is bereaved of children, deprived of pleasures, and stripped of property. We are bereaved of that on which we set most value; the act of bereaving does violence to our inclination. We are deprived of the ordinary comforts and conveniences of life,—they cease to be ours. We are stripped of the things which we most want; we are thereby rendered, as it were, naked.
Antonyms.—Restore, supply, comfort, endow.

Blame, censure, condemn, reprove. To blame is simply to ascribe a fault to; to censure is to express disapprobation. The thing more than the person is blamed; the person more than the thing is censured. A person may be blamed for his good nature and censured for his negligence. That which is condemned is of a more serious nature, and it produces a stronger and more unfavorable expression of displeasure or disapprobation than that which is blamed; reprove is even more personal than censure. A reproof passes from one individual to another, or to a certain number of individuals.
Antonyms.—Praise, approve, applaud, countenance.

Blemish, stain, spot, speck, flaw, defect, fault. Whatever detracts from the seemliness of appearance is a blemish. In works of art the slightest dimness of color or want of proportion is a blemish. A stain or spot sufficiently characterizes itself as that which is superfluous and out of its place; a speck is a small spot; a flaw is a defect that prevents the substance from holding together properly, as a flaw in glazing on china, in a steel rail, in an argument. A blemish tarnishes; a stain spoils; a spot, speck, or flaw disfigures. Defect consists in the want of some specific essential in an object; fault conveys the idea not only of something wrong, but also of its relation to the author.

Blot out, expunge, erase, efface, cancel, obliterate. Letters are blotted out, so that they cannot be seen again; they are expunged, so as to signify that they cannot stand for anything; they are erased, so that the space may be used for other writing. Efface does not designate either the manner or the object; inscriptions on stone may be effaced, that is, rubbed off so as not to be visible. Cancel is principally confined to written or printed characters; they are canceled by striking through them with the pen. Letters are obliterated which are in any way made illegible.
Antonyms.—Write, record, confirm, perpetuate.

Bold, fearless, intrepid, undaunted. Boldness is a positive characteristic of the spirit; fearlessness is a negative state of the mind, that is, simply an absence of fear. A person may be bold through fearlessness, but he may be fearless without being bold; he may be fearless where there is no apprehension of danger or no cause for apprehension, but he is bold only when he is conscious or apprehensive of danger, and prepared to encounter it. A man is intrepid who has no fear where the most fearless might tremble; he is undaunted whose spirit is unabated by that which would make the stoutest heart yield.
Antonyms.—Afraid, fearful, cowardly, timid, fainthearted

Booty, spoil, prey. Booty and spoil are used as military terms in attacks on any enemy; prey, in cases of particular violence. The soldier gets his booty; the combatant, his spoils; the carnivorous animal, his prey. Booty implies something of personal service to the captor; spoils, whatever serves to designate his triumph; prey includes whatever gratifies the appetite and is to be consumed.

Bound, limit, confine, circumscribe, restrict, enclose. Bound applies to the natural or political divisions of the earth: countries are bounded by mountains and seas. Limit applies to any artificial boundary,—landmarks in fields serve to show the limits of one man's ground. To confine is to shut within limits,—in this manner we confine cattle in a yard by means of walls. To circumscribe is literally to write or draw around, as a circle around a square or limits about our desires. To restrict is to exercise a strong degree of control: a person is restricted in his movements by the narrowness of a room; laws often restrict privileges. To enclose is to bound or limit on all sides, as a garden is enclosed.

Boundless, unbounded, unlimited, infinite. Space is boundless so long as no bounds to it have been discovered; desires are often unbounded which ought always to be bounded; power is sometimes unlimited which would be better limited. That is infinite which is without bound or end, as: the power of God; the series of figures in the decimal expression of the fraction ⅓.
Antonyms.—Confined, restricted, circumscribed, finite.

Bravery, courage, valor, gallantry. Bravery lies in the blood; courage lies in the mind. The latter depends on the reason, the former on the physical temperament. The first is a species of instinct; the second is a virtue. A man is brave in proportion as he is without thought of danger; he has courage in proportion as he reasons or reflects. Valor is a higher quality than either bravery or courage—it combines the fire of bravery with the determination and firmness of courage. Gallantry is extraordinary bravery combined with high-spirited manner.
Antonyms.—Fear, cowardice, dismay, effeminacy.

Breach, break, gap, chasm. A breach and a gap are the consequence of a violent removal which destroys the connection; a break and a chasm may arise from the absence of that which would form a connection. A breach in a wall is made by means of cannon; gaps in fences are commonly the effect of some violent effort to pass through; a break is made in a page of printing by leaving off in the middle of a line; a chasm is left when an earthquake causes a gaping fissure.

Break, bruise, squeeze, pound, crush. Break always implies the separation of the component parts of a body; bruise denotes simply to injure without separation of parts. Hard, brittle substances, as glass, are broken; soft, pulpy substances, as flesh or fruits, are bruised. Squeeze is used for soft substances or for gentle compression. To pound is properly to crush in a mortar, so as to produce a separation of parts. To crush is the most violent and destructive of all operations, which amounts to destroying the structure of a body.

Break, burst, crack, split. To break does not specify any particular manner or form of action,—what is broken may be broken in two or more pieces, broken short or lengthwise, and the like; to burst is to break suddenly and with violence, frequently also with noise. To crack and to split are modes of breaking lengthwise: the former in application to hard or brittle objects, as clay, or the things made of clay; the latter in application to wood or substances like coal or rock that have seams or lines of cleavage.
Antonyms.—Join, attach, mend, unite, weld.

Breeze, gale, blast, gust, storm, tempest, hurricane. A breeze is gentle; a gale is brisk, but steady: we have breezes on a calm summer's day; the mariner has favorable gales, which keep the sails on the stretch. A blast is impetuous. The blare of a trumpet, the breath of bellows, are blasts. A gust is sudden and vehement; storm, tempest, and hurricane include other particulars besides wind. A storm throws the whole atmosphere into commotion; it is a war of the elements, in which wind, rain, hail, and the like conspire to disturb the heavens. Tempest is a violent storm. Hurricane is a species of storm which exceeds all the rest in violence, duration, and area.
Antonyms.—Lull, calm, stillness, fair weather.

Brightness, luster, splendor, brilliancy. Brightness and luster are applied properly to natural lights; splendor and brilliancy have been more commonly applied to that which is artificial or unusual. There is always more or less brightness in the sun or moon; there is an occasional luster in all the heavenly bodies when they shine in their unclouded brightness; there is splendor in the eruptions of flame from a volcano or from an immense conflagration; there is brilliancy in a collection of diamonds.
Antonyms.—Dullness, dimness, shadow, obscurity, gloom.

Bring, take, fetch, carry. Bring commonly means to transport something from a point more or less distant to the place occupied by the speaker. Take implies removal of something from the speaker's position to another location. To fetch is to go and get something, then bring it to the speaker's position. Carry simply means to transport or take along something without regard to destination or point of origin.

Bulky, massive. Whatever is bulky is large, unwieldy, often awkward to handle, whether heavy or not; what is massive is compact in substance and combines solidity with large size.
Antonyms.—Compact, small, slight, slender.

Burial, interment. We bury in order to conceal. Interment is accompanied with religious ceremonies. Burial is confined to no object or place; interment refers properly to burial in the earth.

Business, occupation, employment, avocation, vocation. Business occupies all a person's thoughts as well as his time and powers. Occupation and employment occupy only his time and strength; the first is mostly regular, the object of our choice; the second is casual, depending on the will of another. Vocation is applied to one's regular work; avocation, to the occupation with which one occupies his time outside the regular routine of work.
Antonyms.—Recreation, amusement, relaxation, pastime.

Business, trade, profession, art. Buying or selling of merchandise is inseparable from trade; but the exercise of one's knowledge and experience for purposes of gain constitutes a business. A profession implies scholarship and skill in application of principles. An art involves skill in the practice of accepted rules and methods of work to produce practical results with definite materials. We speak of the profession of letters, but of the art of writing. Trade is used also of mechanical occupation, as the carpenter's trade.

Bustle, tumult, uproar. Bustle has most of hurry in it; tumult, most of disorder and confusion; uproar, most of noise: the hurried movements of one, or many, cause a bustle; the disorderly struggles of many constitute a tumult. The loud elevation of many opposing voices produces an uproar; uproar is the consequence either of general anger or of mirth.
Antonyms.—Calm, quietness, order, tranquillity.

Calamity, disaster, misfortune, mischance, mishap. A calamity is a great disaster or misfortune; a misfortune is a great mischance or mishap. Whatever is attended with destruction is a calamity; whatever occasions mischief to the person, or defeats or interrupts plans, is a disaster; whatever is accompanied with a loss of property or the deprivation of health is a misfortune; whatever diminishes the beauty or utility of objects is a mischance or a mishap.
Antonyms.—Success, blessing, boon, achievement.

Calculate, reckon, compute, count. To calculate denotes any numerical operation in general, but is particularly applicable to the abstract science of figures. The astronomer calculates motions of the heavenly bodies; the mathematician makes arithmetical calculations. To reckon is to enumerate and set down things in detail. Reckoning is applicable to the ordinary business of life: tradesmen keep their accounts by reckoning; children learn to reckon by various simple processes. Calculation is therefore the science; reckoning, the practical art of enumerating. To compute is to come at the result by calculation. We count one by one,—we count the minutes.

Calendar, almanac. A calendar is a system of marking the divisions of time or, specifically, a chart showing the days, weeks, and months of the year. To this information an almanac adds such data as the changes of the moon, the times of sunset and sunrise, the signs of the zodiac, and so on.

Call, cry, exclaim. Call is used on all ordinary occasions in order to draw a person to a spot, or for any other purpose, when one wishes to be heard. To cry is to call loudly on particular occasions. A call draws attention; a cry awakens alarm. To exclaim implies the expression of some particular feeling.
Antonyms.—Hush, listen, be silent.

Call, invite, summon. In the act of calling, any sounds may be used; we may call by simply raising the voice. Inviting may be a direct or indirect act; we may invite by looks or signs as well as by words, by writing as well as by speaking. To summon is an act of authority, as to summon witnesses.
Antonyms.—Dismiss, disperse, send away.

Calm, placid, serene, composed, collected. Physically, calm means free from violent action; mentally, free from disturbing emotion or passion. Placid implies ease and contentment of mind. We speak also of a calm sea and a placid lake. Serene implies clearness and composure of mind. A sky is serene when free from clouds and clear. The mind is composed when excitement has been allayed; it is collected when all its powers are at command.
Antonyms.—Agitated, stormy, violent, passionate.

Candor, openness, sincerity. Candor obliges us to acknowledge even that which may make against ourselves; it is disinterested. Openness impels us to utter whatever passes in the mind—it is unguarded. Sincerity assures that our words and actions are true to our thoughts and feelings —it is positive.
Antonyms.—Cunning, deceit, craft, duplicity.

Captious, cross, peevish, petulant, fretful. Captious marks a readiness to find fault; cross indicates a readiness to offend or go contrary to the wishes of others; peevish expresses a strong degree of crossness; fretful, a complaining impatience. Captiousness is the consequence of ill will or pique; crossness, of ill humor; peevishness and fretfulness, of a painful irritability. Petulance is the result either of a hasty temper or a sudden irritability.
Antonyms.—Considerate, good-natured, appreciative, thoughtful, patient.

Capture, seizure, prize. A capture is made by force of arms; a seizure is made by direct and personal force. Prize relates only to the thing taken and its value to the captor.

Care, charge, management. Care includes both charge and management; but, in the strict sense, it comprehends personal labor. Charge involves responsibility; management includes regulation and order. A gardener has the care of a garden; a nurse has charge of children; a steward has the management of a farm.

Care, solicitude, anxiety. Care is the most indefinite of the three; it may be accompanied with pain or not, according to the nature of the object or the intensity of the application. Care may be exercised with or without feeling; solicitude has desire, mixed with fear; anxiety has distress for the present, mixed with fear for the future.
Antonyms.—Satisfaction, indifference, unconcern, trust.

Careful, provident. Careful, or full of care, that is, having care, is the general term. To be provident is to be careful in preventing straits and difficulties. The term careful is applied for the most part to present matters, but provident only to that which is future. One is careful of his money, but provident toward a time of need.
Antonyms.—Careless, neglectful, reckless, heedless, spendthrift.

Carnage, slaughter, massacre, butchery. Carnage pictures heaped corpses; slaughter, the wholesale taking of lives as in battle. Butchery is the brutal word for killing men and women as cattle are killed. Massacre implies the killing or butchery of many defenseless men, women, and children.

Case, cause. The case is matter of fact; the cause is matter of question. A case involves circumstances and consequences; a cause involves reasons and arguments. A case is something to be learned; a cause is something to be decided.

Cause, occasion, create. What is caused seems to follow naturally. What is occasioned follows incidentally, or what occasions may be incidental, but necessary. What is created receives its existence arbitrarily. A wound causes pain; accidents occasion delay; busybodies create mischief.

Cause, reason, motive. A cause is that which brings about any event, act, or fact. "The Creator is the first cause of all things." A reason is an explanation devised by the mind for a fact, an event, or an action. We give reasons also for our beliefs, that is, the grounds for them. A motive is an influence that determines choice or action. Effects follow causes, conclusions follow reasons, and actions spring from motives.

Cautious, wary, circumspect. We must be cautious on all occasions where there is danger, but we must be wary where there is great danger. A tradesman must be cautious in his dealings with all men, but he must be wary when he has to deal with designing men. Circumspect implies attention to all the conditions and probable consequences of action. A man must be circumspect when he transacts business of particular importance and delicacy.
Antonyms.—Rash, impulsive, audacious, precipitate.

Cease, discontinue. Cease is used for either particular actions or general habits; discontinue, for general habits. A restless, spoiled child never ceases crying until it has obtained what it wants; it is a mark of impatience not to cease lamenting when one is in pain. A sensitive person discontinues his visits when they are found not to be agreeable.
Antonyms.—Continue, persist, persevere.

Celebrate, commemorate. Everything is celebrated which is distinguished by any marks of attention, without regard to the time of the event, whether present or past; nothing is commemorated but what has already passed in point of time.
Antonyms.—Forget, ignore, disregard.

Celestial, heavenly. Celestial is applied mostly in the natural sense of the heavens; heavenly is employed more commonly in a spiritual sense. Hence, we speak of the celestial globe as distinguished from the terrestrial, and of the celestial bodies. But we speak of the heavenly habitation, of heavenly joys or bliss, of heavenly spirits and the like.
Antonyms.—Terrestrial, earthly, mundane.

Censure, carp, cavil. To censure respects positive errors; to carp and cavil have regard to what is trivial or imaginary. The former is employed for errors in persons; the latter, for supposed defects in things. Carping and caviling are resorted to only to indulge ill nature or self-conceit; party politicians carp at the measures of administration; infidels cavil at the evidences of Christianity, because they are determined to disbelieve.
Antonyms.—Praise, approve, sanction, uphold.

Cessation, stop, rest, intermission. Cessation refers to the course of things; whatever does not go on has ceased; things cease of themselves. Stop implies an abrupt cessation, as if due to an outside force. Rest is cessation from labor or exertion—whatever does not move or exert itself is at rest. Intermission is cessation only for a time or at certain intervals. That which ceases or stops is supposed to be at an end; rest or intermission supposes a renewal.
Antonyms.—Stir, work, persistence, continuance.

Chance, fortune, fate. Chance applies to all things personal or otherwise; fortune and fate are applied most often to that which is personal. Chance neither forms, orders, nor designs; neither knowledge nor intention is attributed to it; its events are uncertain and variable. Fortune forms plans and designs, but without choice; we attribute to it an intention without discernment; it is said to be blind. Fate forms plans and chains of causes; intention, knowledge, and power are attributed to it—its views are fixed; its results are decisive.
Antonyms.—Choice, free will, purpose.

Change, exchange, barter, substitute. To change in respect to persons is to take one for another, without regard to whether they are alike or different,—as a king changes his ministers, or any person may change his servants. To exchange is to take one person in return for another who is in like condition, as prisoners are exchanged in time of war. In respect to things, to change is to take anything new or fresh, whether alike or different; clothes may be changed. To exchange is to take one thing for another, that is, either of the same kind or equivalent in value, as to exchange one commodity for another. To change may often be the result of caprice, but to exchange is always an act of either discretion or necessity. To barter is to give any commodity for other commodities. To substitute is to put one person or thing in the place of another for the purpose of doing any service or filling any office, as to substitute one for another in military service, or to substitute wood for steel in building.
Antonyms.—Keep, hold, retain.

Change, alteration, variation, vicissitude. Change refers to any difference in persons, things or circumstances. Alteration is a minor change purposely made in details without affecting the identity of the whole, as in the alteration of a garment. Vicissitudes are the unpredictable but inevitable ups and downs of life for which every one is supposed to be prepared.
Antonyms.—Uniformity, consistency, monotony.

Character, reputation. Character lies in the man; it is the mark of what he is. A person's reputation depends upon others; it is what they think of him.

Chasten, chastise. Chasten is used only of spiritual correction, as the chastening of men by God. Chastise implies physical pain or punishment with a corrective purpose.

Cheat, defraud, trick. One cheats by direct and gross falsehood or artifice; one defrauds by a settled plan or contrivance; one tricks by a sudden invention.

Check, chide, reprimand, reprove, rebuke. A person is checked that he may not continue to do what is offensive; he is chidden for what he has done, that he may not repeat it. People are checked by actions and looks, as well as by words; they are chidden by words only. A person may chide or reprimand in anger; he reproves and rebukes with coolness. Omissions or mistakes occasion or require a reprimand; irregularities of conduct give rise to reproof; and improprieties of behavior demand rebuke.
Antonyms.—Allow, indulge, abet, approve, laud.

Cheer, encourage, comfort. To encourage is to give heart or courage for action, to strengthen resolution. To cheer and to comfort apply to the spirits or feelings; but to cheer expresses more than to comfort, the former signifying to produce a lively sentiment, the latter to lessen or remove a painful one. We are cheered in the moments of despondence, whether from real or imaginary causes; we are comforted in the hour of distress; we are encouraged in times of timidity and fear.
Antonyms.—Sadden, grieve, hurt, dishearten.

Chief, principal, main. Chief respects order and rank; principal has regard to importance and respectability; main, to degree or quantity. We speak of a chief clerk, of a commander in chief, of the chief person in a city, but of the principal people in a city, of the principal circumstances in a narrative, and of the main object.
Antonyms.—Subordinate, minor, inferior, attendant.

Choose, select, pick. Choose implies an act of judgment in which a decision is made in favor of one or more out of a number of things. Select emphasizes the exercise of taste in reaching a similar decision. Picking is usually done more hastily and somewhat at random.
Antonyms.—Reject, cull.

Circumstance, situation. Circumstance is to situation as a part is to a whole: many circumstances constitute a situation; a situation is an aggregate of circumstances. A person is said to be in circumstances of affluence who has an abundance of everything essential to his comfort; he is in an easy situation when nothing exists to create uneasiness.

Circumstantial, particular, minute. A circumstantial account contains all the leading events; a particular account includes many smaller details; a minute treatment of the subject goes beyond this and includes every incident and movement, however trivial. Circumstantial evidence consists of ascertained facts objectively discovered as against personal testimony.
Antonyms.—General, cursory, indefinite.

Cite, quote. We quote exact words or the substance of a passage. We cite an author or a passage in his work by giving the exact location or reference, as line and page, so that the words may be found readily.

Civil, polite, obliging. Polite expresses more than civil; it is possible to be civil without being polite. Politeness seeks the opportunity to please: it prevents the necessity of asking by anticipating the wishes; it is full of delicate attentions, and is an active benevolence in the minor concerns of life. Civil applies to words or manner as well as to the action; obliging, to the action only. Civil and obliging both imply a desire to do a kindness.
Antonyms.—Rude, discourteous, ill-mannered, churlish.

Clandestine, secret. To do a thing clandestinely is to elude observation; to do a thing secretly is to do it without the knowledge of anyone. What is clandestine is forbidden, which is not necessarily the case with what is secret.
Antonyms.—Authorized, public, open.

Clasp, hug, embrace. To clasp is to enclose another in one's arms. To hug is to press tightly to the bosom, whether it is done by a person or a bear. The more refined term embrace means to enfold in the arms in token of friendship or affection. It implies mutuality of sentiment between the persons concerned.

Classify, arrange. The general qualities and attributes of things are to be considered in classifying; their fitness to stand by each other must be considered in arranging. Classification serves the purposes of either public policy or science; arranging is a matter of convenience to the individual himself.
Antonyms.—Mix, disorder, jumble, confuse, scatter.

Clean, cleanly, pure. Clean expresses a freedom from dirt or soil; cleanly, the disposition or habit of being clean. Pure is used in a moral sense, as a pure heart; it is used also to mean free from other substances, as a solution is chemically pure.
Antonyms.—Soiled, dirty, foul, filthy.

Clearly, distinctly. That is seen clearly of which one has an unobstructed view. Distinctly, a stronger word, conveys the idea of things seen so clearly that they are distinguished from other objects. The same use of these terms applies to hearing and the other senses.
Antonyms.—Dimly, faintly, vaguely.

Clearness, lucidity, brightness, vividness. A mere freedom from stain or dullness constitutes clearness; a shining clearness, as of crystal, constitutes lucidity; brightness supposes a certain strength of light; vividness, a freshness combined with strength, and with a degree of brilliancy.
Antonyms.—Dimness, dullness, cloudiness, darkness.

Clearness, perspicuity. Clearness springs from right distinguishing of the ideas discussed. Perspicuity is a quality of the style in which thought is expressed. The argument is clear; the language, perspicuous.
Antonyms.—Obscurity, indefiniteness, ambiguity, vagueness.

Clever, skillful, expert, dexterous. Cleverness is mental power employed in the ordinary concerns of life—a person is clever in business. Skill implies both mental and physical ability, especially in mechanical operations and in science: a physician, a lawyer, or an artist is skillful; one may have a skill in divination or a skill in painting. Expertness and dexterity require more physical than mental power exerted in minor arts and amusements—one is expert at throwing quoits, dexterous in the management of horses.
Antonyms.—Awkward, bungling, stupid, slow.

Close, conclude, finish. We may close anything, as a discourse or a meeting, at any point by simply ceasing to have any more to do with it; but we conclude in a definite and positive manner. To conclude is to bring to an end by determination; to finish is to bring to an end by completion. What is settled by arrangement and deliberation is properly concluded; what is begun and ended on a certain plan is said to be finished.
Antonyms.—Begin, open, start, commence, initiate.

Close, near. Close is more definite than near; houses which are almost joined stand close to each other; men stand close when they touch each other. Objects are near which are within sight; persons are near each other when they can converse together.
Antonyms.—Distant, far, remote, removed.

Coarse, rough, rude. In the physical sense, coarse refers to the composition and materials of bodies, as coarse bread, coarse meat, coarse cloth; rough applies to the surface of bodies, as rough wood and rough skin; rude respects the make or fashion of things,—as a rude bark, a rude utensil. The application of these words to manners and conduct follows their physical sense. A person's language may be coarse, his appearance rough, and his manner rude.
Antonyms.—Fine, refined, smooth, pleasant, suave, polished, civil, polite.

Cogent, forcible, strong. Cogency applies to reasons individually considered; force and strength, to modes of reasoning or expression. Cogent reasons impel to decisive conduct; strong conviction is produced by forcible reasoning conveyed in strong language.
Antonyms.—Feeble, ineffectual, unconvincing, weak.

Colleague, partner, associate. Colleague is used properly of people associated in high office, as in court or in legislature. It is used popularly by debaters associated on teams. Associate is a more general term. Used officially, it implies subordination, as an associate professor. Partner is used popularly of men associated for business and sharing common risks, especially in some hazardous undertaking.
Antonyms.—Opponent, rival, foe, adversary, competitor.

Combat, oppose. A person's views or attitudes are combated; his interests or his measures are opposed.
Antonyms.—Advocate, aid, promote, support.

Come, arrive. To come specifies neither time nor manner; to arrive is employed with regard to some particular period or circumstances. Guests arrive; trains arrive; what is to come is uncertain.
Antonyms.—Go, leave, depart, set out, take leave.

Comfort, pleasure, happiness. Comfort implies a freedom of the whole person from annoyance or pain, a positive feeling of contentment. Pleasure lies in a vivid and intense experience and is fleeting in its nature. Happiness is an abiding state of agreeable feeling.
Antonyms.—Uneasiness, pain, heartache, sorrow.

Command, direction, order, injunction, precept. A command is an exercise of power or authority; it is im-

perative and must be obeyed. Direction contains the idea
of instruction; order, that of authority. Directions should
be followed; orders, obeyed. A superior issues commands.
Injunction imposes a duty by virtue of the authority which
enjoins. A precept lays down or teaches such duties as
already exist.
Antonyms.—Consent, leave, license, permission.

Commission, authorize, empower. We commission
in matters where our own will and convenience are concerned; we authorize in matters where our personal authority is requisite; we empower in matters where the
authority of the law is required.
Antonyms.—Refuse, prohibit, forbid, disallow, enjoin.

Commodious, convenient. Commodious is most often
applied to that which contributes to the bodily ease and
comfort; convenient, to whatever suits the purposes of men
in their various transactions.
Antonyms.—Narrow, restraining, ill-contrived, awkward.

Commonly, generally, frequently, usually. What is
commonly done is an action common to all; what is generally done is the action of the greatest part; what is frequently done is either the action of many, or an action many
times repeated by the same person; what is usually done is
done regularly by one or many.
Antonyms.—Rarely, occasionally, sometimes, seldom.

Communicate, impart. A thing may be communicated directly or indirectly, and to any number of persons,
as to communicate intelligence by signal or otherwise. Impart is a direct action that passes between individuals, as
to impart instruction.

Compatible, consistent. Compatibility has a reference
principally to plans and measures; consistency, to character,
conduct, and station. Everything which does not interrupt
its prosecution is compatible with a plan; everything by
which it is neither degraded nor elevated is consistent with
a person's station.
Antonyms.—Discordant, incongruous, contradictory,
inharmonious.

Compel, force, oblige, necessitate. To compel denotes
moral rather than physical force; but to force is properly
applied to the use of physical force or a violent degree of
moral force. A man may be compelled to walk if he has
no means of riding; he may be forced to go at the will of
another. Oblige expresses only an indirect influence, which
may be resisted or yielded to at discretion. We are compelled to do that which is repugnant to our will and our
feelings. That which one is obliged to do may have the
assent of the judgment, if not of the will. We are necessitated by circumstances, or by anything which puts it out
of our power to do otherwise.
Antonyms.—Induce, persuade, invite, tempt, lead.

**Compensation, amends, satisfaction, recompense,
remuneration, reward.** Compensation, whether in
money or otherwise, means a return for service given.
Amends attempts to repair damage done to someone's
interests or feelings. It is voluntarily offered. A person
who has a grievance may expect or demand, and possibly
receive, satisfaction. Recompense, literally a paying back,
carries the idea of reciprocal return, evening the score
of favors done. Remuneration means the discharge of
an obligation by payment of money. Reward is a token
of appreciation, usually a generous one, that is given
voluntarily.

Competent, fitted, qualified. Competent especially
regards the mental endowments and attainments; fitted,
the disposition and character; qualified, the artificial
acquirements or natural qualities.
Antonyms.—Unprepared, unsuitable, ill-adapted.

Complain, lament. Complaint implies dissatisfaction;
lamentation, grief. Complaint is expressed verbally; lamentation, either by words or signs. Complaint is made of
personal grievances; lamentation may be made on account
of others as well as of ourselves. We complain of our ill
health, of our inconveniences, or of troublesome circumstances; we lament our inability to serve another.
Antonyms.—Rejoice, welcome, hail, approve.

Complaint, accusation. A complaint is usually made
in matters that personally affect the complainant; an accusation is made of matters in general, but especially those
of a moral nature. A complaint is made for the sake of
obtaining redress; an accusation is made for the sake of as-
certaining a fact or for the sake of bringing to punishment.
Antonyms.—Defense, justification, exoneration, acquittal.

Complete, finish, terminate. The characteristic idea
of completing is that of making a thing altogether what it
ought to be; that of finishing, the doing all that is intended
to be done toward a thing; and that of terminating, simply
putting an end to a thing.
Antonyms.—Begin, commence, initiate.

Complete, perfect, finished. That is complete which
has no deficiency; that is perfect which has positive excellence; and that is finished which is at an end.
Antonyms.—Deficient, faulty, marred, unaccomplished.

Comply, conform, yield, submit. These words
represent various kinds and degrees of acquiescence. One
complies with requests or requirements, one conforms to
customs or standards of behavior, one yields to temptation
or to pressure of any sort, and one submits, usually with
reluctance, to the will of another.
Antonyms.—Rebel, disobey, resist.

Compose, settle. We compose that which has been
disjointed and separated, by bringing it together again; we
settle that which has been disturbed and put in motion, by
setting it at rest.
Antonyms.—Disturb, disarrange, confuse.

Composed, sedate. Composed implies a temporary
state of mental quiet and calm, arising from mastery of the
emotions. Sedate signifies a permanent habit of calm
steadiness of temper.
Antonyms.—Agitated, disturbed, flighty, frolicsome.

Compound, compose. Compound applies in a physical
sense only and refers especially to the mixing of substances
in fixed proportions. Compose, in a physical, social, or
moral sense, refers to the fact of a mixture of elements. The
chemist compounds medicines carefully; society is composed
of various classes. One composes music.
Antonyms.—Resolve, analyze, dissect, break up.

**Comprise, comprehend, embrace, contain, in-
clude.** A library comprises a variety of books; the whole
is comprised within a small compass. Laws comprehend a
number of cases. A discourse embraces a variety of topics.
A society contains very many individuals; it includes none
but those of a certain class, or it includes some of every class.
Antonyms.—Exclude, debar, except, omit.

Conceal, dissemble, disguise. To conceal is simply to
abstain from making known what we wish to keep secret;
to dissemble and disguise signify to conceal by assuming
some false appearance. We conceal facts; we dissemble
feelings; we disguise sentiments.
Antonyms.—Reveal, discover, divulge, show, unveil.

Conceal, hide, secrete. To conceal is to keep from observation; to hide is to put under cover; to secrete is to set
at a distance or in unfrequented places.
Antonyms.—Show, expose, exhibit, disclose.

Conceit, fancy. Conceit applies only to internal objects; it is mental in the operation and the result; it is a
species of invention. Fancy is applied to external objects,
or whatever acts on the senses. Nervous people are subject
to strange conceits; timid people fancy they hear sounds or
see objects in the dark which awaken terror.
Antonyms.—Actuality, reality, fact.

Conceive, understand, comprehend. Conception is
the simplest operation of the three: when we conceive we
may have but one idea; when we understand or comprehend
we have all the ideas which the subject is capable of presenting. The builder conceives plans; the scholar understands languages; the metaphysician attempts to explain
many things which are not to be comprehended.

Conception, notion, idea, image. Conception is the
general, scientific word for idea, the product of the mind's
relating and constructive work. Notion implies more direct
reference to the thing known. Idea is used popularly and
vaguely for conception, fancy, and image. An image is the
product of the picturing activity of the mind. We speak of
the conception of immortality, of the idea of God, of a
notion of proper conduct, of an image of a face.

Conciliate, reconcile. To conciliate is to get good will
and affection for oneself; to reconcile is to unite the affections of two persons to each other.
Antonyms.—Disaffect, estrange, alienate.

Conclusion, inference, deduction, induction. A
conclusion is a necessary consequence of certain admitted
facts or statements. An inference is a probable conclusion;
it may be hastily drawn from incomplete data. Induction
is a process of reasoning from particular facts toward a
general principle. Deduction is reasoning from a general

principle, from which conclusions are drawn regarding particular facts to which the principle applies. Scientific conclusions are reached through the alternate use of induction and deduction.

Conclusive, convincing. Conclusive applies either to practical or theoretical matters; convincing, to what is theoretical only. An argument is convincing, a chain of reasoning conclusive.
Antonyms.—Uncertain, dubious, questionable, hypothetical.

Condition, station. Condition commonly refers to circumstances, education, birth, and the like; station refers rather to rank, occupation, or fixed mode of life.

Conduce, contribute. To conduce signifies to serve the full purpose; to contribute signifies only to serve a secondary purpose. Exercise conduces to health; it contributes to give vigor to the frame.
Antonyms.—Counteract, contravene, hinder, defeat.

Conduct, manage, direct. Conducting requires most wisdom and knowledge; managing, most action; direction, most authority. A lawyer conducts the cause intrusted to him; an agent manages the mercantile concerns for his employer; a superintendent directs the movements of all the subordinate agents.

Confederate, accomplice. A confederate is a partner in a plot or a secret association; an accomplice is a partner in some active violation of the laws.
Antonyms.—Rival, adversary, betrayer.

Confidence, trust. Confidence is an extraordinary trust, but trust is always ordinary unless the term be otherwise qualified. Confidence involves communication of a man's mind to another, but trust is confined to matters of action.
Antonyms.—Doubt, mistrust, suspicion, misgiving.

Confident, assured, positive, sanguine. A person is confident who has faith in his ability or in the soundness of his position. Any one who has an assured manner is, or seems to be, certain of success. One who is positive has no doubt concerning the accuracy of his information or the rightness of his position. A calm form of optimism is indicated by sanguine, which connotes good health and normal cheerfulness.
Antonyms.—Apprehensive, diffident, doubtful, vacillating.

Confirm, corroborate. Confirm is the stronger word, implying support by established facts or assured knowledge. Corroborate implies support of a statement or belief by added statements or attendant circumstances.
Antonyms.—Refute, confute, invalidate, annul, weaken.

Conformable, agreeable, suitable. Conformable is employed for matters of obligation; agreeable, for matters of choice; suitable, for matters of propriety and discretion. What is conformable accords with some prescribed form or given rule of others; what is agreeable accords with the feelings, tempers, or judgments of ourselves or others; what is suitable accords with outward circumstances.
Antonyms.—Inconsistent, ill-adapted, unwelcome, unfitted.

Confound, confuse. A person confounds one thing with another; objects become confused, or a person confuses himself. It is a common error among ignorant people to confound names, and among children to have their ideas confused on commencing a new study.
Antonyms.—Distinguish, separate, discriminate.

Confront, face. Confront implies to set face to face, face signifies to set the face toward any object. Witnesses are confronted; a person faces danger.
Antonyms.—Avoid, evade, shun, dodge.

Confusion, disorder. Confusion supposes the absence of all order; disorder, the derangement of order where it exists or is supposed to exist.
Antonyms.—Method, regularity, orderliness.

Confute, refute, disprove. Confute applies to what is argumentative; refute, to what is practical and personal; disprove, to whatever is represented or related. An argument is confuted by proving its fallacy; a charge is refuted by proving the innocence of the party charged; an assertion is disproved by proving that it is incorrect.
Antonyms.—Prove, substantiate, support, uphold, defend.

Connect, combine, unite. Things connected and combined remain distinct, but things united lose all individuality. Things the most dissimilar may be connected or combined; things of the same kind only can be united. Houses are connected by means of a common passage; the armies of two nations are combined; two armies of the same nation are united.
Antonyms.—Separate, sever, disjoin, part.

Conqueror, victor. A conqueror is always supposed to add something to his possessions; a victor gains nothing but the superiority. Those who take possession of other men's lands by force of arms make a conquest; those who excel in any trial of skill are the victors.

Consent, permit, allow. As the act of an equal, we consent to that in which we have a common interest with others. We permit or allow what is for the accommodation of others: we allow by not opposing; we permit by a direct expression of our will. Contracts are formed by the consent of the parties who are interested. The proprietor of an estate permits his friends to sport on his grounds; he allows a passage through his premises.
Antonyms.—Refuse, forbid, prohibit, interdict.

Consequence, effect, result. A consequence follows of itself; an effect is brought about, or in other words, is produced directly by a cause. A result is the final outcome of a series of contributing causes.

Consider, reflect. To consider is employed for practical purposes; to reflect, for matters of speculation or moral improvement. Common objects call for consideration; the workings of the mind itself or objects purely spiritual occupy reflection.

Consonant, accordant, consistent. Consonant (with, to) implies such agreement as would avoid discord. Consistent (with) applies to agreement that avoids contradiction. Consonant and accordant are applied to matters of belief and sentiment; consistent, also to matters of conduct.
Antonyms.—Dissonant, discordant, incongruous, incompatible.

Constancy, stability, steadiness, firmness. Constancy involves the affections; stability, the opinions; steadiness, the action or the motives of action; firmness, the purpose or resolution.
Antonyms.—Variableness, fickleness, capriciousness.

Constitute, appoint, depute. To constitute is the act of a body or organization; to appoint and depute may be the act of either a body or an individual. The person who is deputed becomes the agent of the authority that appoints him; that is, he is a deputy.

Consult, deliberate. Consultations always require two persons at least; deliberations may be carried on either with a man's self or with others. An individual may consult with one or many; assemblies commonly deliberate

Consummate, complete. Consummate refers to desires or plans or movements brought to fulfillment. Complete is applied in the sense of finishing according to design.
Antonyms.—Fail, fall short.

Contagious, infectious, epidemic. The first two words, very closely related in meaning, differ chiefly in their reference to the manner in which disease may be transmitted. One may contract a contagious disease by receiving germs directly from a sick person or through contact with something he has touched. In current usage infectious refers especially to communicable disease that is transmitted through agents, such as rats and mosquitoes. Contagion may pervade the atmosphere. Epidemic indicates a wide and usually rapid spread of some specific form of communicable disease.
Antonyms.—Antiseptic, hygienic, sanitary.

Contaminate, defile, pollute, taint, corrupt. Whatever is impure contaminates; what is gross and vile, in the natural sense, defiles and, in the moral sense, pollutes; what is contagious or infectious corrupts; what is corrupted may taint other things.
Antonyms.—Wash, purify, cleanse, disinfect.

Contemplate, meditate, muse. Different species of reflection are marked by these terms. We contemplate what is present or before our eyes; we meditate on what is past or absent. The heavens and all the works of the Creator are objects of contemplation; the ways of Providence are fit subjects for meditation. One muses on events or circumstances which have recently passed.

Contend, contest, dispute. To contend is simply to exert a force against a force; to contest is to struggle with an opponent for an object; to dispute, according to its original meaning, applies to opinions only and is distinguished from contend in this,—that the latter signifies to maintain one's own opinion, the former to call in question the opinion of another.
Antonyms.—Yield, give up, surrender, acknowledge.

Contentment, satisfaction. Contentment lies in ourselves; satisfaction is derived from external objects. One is contented when one wishes for no more; one is satisfied when one has obtained all one wishes. Contentment is within the reach of the poor man, to whom it is a continual feast; but satisfaction has never been procured by wealth, however enormous, or by ambition, however boundless.
Antonyms.—Desire, distress, trouble, regret, mourning.

Continual, continuous, perpetual, constant, continued. Continual implies possible intermission but also regular beginning again. Continuous admits of no pause or interruption. What is perpetual admits of no termination. There may be an end to that which is continual, and there may be intervals in that which is perpetual. Constant, like continuous, admits of no interruption, and it also admits of no change. What is continual may not always continue in the same state; but what is constant remains in the same state; what is continued ceases for a time, only to be taken up again.
Antonyms.—Changing, intermittent, desultory, broken, concluded.

Continuance, continuation, continuity, duration. Continuance describes an action that is prolonged without interruption. Continuation suggests resumption after an interval, as in the parts of a serial story. Continuity, a term frequently used with reference to radio programs, means the linking of different parts to form an unbroken sequence. Duration refers only to the extent of time through which an action is continued.
Antonyms.—Cessation, interruption, termination.

Continue, persevere, persist. We continue from habit or circumstances; we persevere from reflection and the exercise of our judgment; we persist from attachment to a desire or purpose. A child perseveres in a new study until he has mastered it; he persists in making a request until he has obtained the object of his desire.
Antonyms.—Pause, stop, give up, desist, forbear.

Continue, remain. Continue is associated with a state of action; remain, with a state of rest. We are said to continue to speak or to do anything, to remain stationary or in a position.
Antonyms.—Cease, leave off, depart, remove.

Contradict, deny. One contradicts terms by asserting something directly opposite; one denies by advancing arguments or by suggesting doubts or difficulties. Both these terms may therefore be used in reference to disputations. We may deny the truth of a position by contradicting the assertions that are advanced in its support.
Antonyms.—Admit, assert, corroborate, support, maintain.

Controvert, dispute. To controvert has regard to speculative points; to dispute respects matters of fact: there is more of opposition in controversy, more of doubt in disputing. A sophist controverts; a skeptic disputes.
Antonyms.—Agree, accord, harmonize, concur, unite.

Contumacious, rebellious. The contumacious resist only occasionally; the rebellious resist systematically. The contumacious stand only on certain points and oppose the individual; the rebellious set themselves up against the authority itself. Contumacious implies a proud contemptuous air.
Antonyms.—Compliant, deferential, obedient.

Convenient, suitable, proper. Convenient circumstances or arrangements contribute to the ease or comfort of an individual. Anything that is suitable fits the ends or purposes one has in view. Proper relates to etiquette or to moral fitness, as judged by generally received opinion.
Antonyms.—Unsuitable, inconvenient, unseemly.

Conversant, familiar, versed. Conversant implies close acquaintance, the result of study or of frequent contact. Familiar refers to knowledge obtained in a more routine fashion, incidental perhaps to everyday experience. Versed carries with it the idea of proficiency or skill, as in an art or a profession. A person is familiar with his surroundings, conversant with a language, and versed in the law or in some other profession.
Antonyms.—Ignorant, unacquainted.

Conversation, dialogue, conference, colloquy. A conversation is actually held between two or more persons: a dialogue is usually fictitious and written as if spoken: any number of persons may take part in a conversation, but a dialogue always refers to the two persons who are expressly engaged. A conference is specifically appointed and is usually on public concerns. The colloquy has the same character as the dialogue but is not confined to two people.

Convert, proselyte. Convert is more extensive in its sense and application than proselyte,—in its full sense it includes every change of opinion, without respect to the subject. Proselyte, in its original application, denoted changes only from one religious belief to another; it now means a new convert to a religion, a religious sect, or to some particular system or party.

Convince, persuade. A person is convinced who is brought, intellectually, to accept the truth of a proposition or the accuracy of a statement of fact. He is persuaded by something that appeals to his judgment or inclinations and thus influences his will. Convince leads to mental assent; persuade leads to action. An unfortunately common error of usage is to interchange these two words, as in the sentence, "I convinced him to go," which should be, "I persuaded him to go."

Convivial, social. The prominent idea in convivial is that of sensual indulgence, which usually includes drinking; the prominent idea in social is that of enjoyment through intercourse with society. We speak of convivial meetings, convivial enjoyments, or the convivial board; but we say social intercourse, social pleasure, social amusements, and the like.
Antonyms.—Temperate, retiring, cold, solitary.

Copy, imitate, mimic, parody, burlesque. To copy is to duplicate an original. Imitate follows the plan or pattern of the original but allows some freedom in the handling of details. Mimic suggests the adoption of mannerisms closely resembling those of another person in order to produce a comic effect. Like mimic, burlesque and parody are imitations with humorous intent. To parody is to create a parallel closely resembling a poem or some other work but introducing clever and witty departures from it. To burlesque a piece of writing is to give an exaggerated imitation of it that is a travesty on the original.

Coquette, jilt. The coquette makes a traffic of her own charms by seeking a multitude of admirers; the jilt sports with the sacred passion of love, and lightly casts off those previously accepted as lovers.

Correct, accurate, exact, nice. Correctness meets a given standard, whether of information, taste, or something else. Accurate indicates care in the observation and reporting of details. Exact emphasizes complete agreement with requirements and suggests a rigorous application of standards. Nice, as in the expression "a nice distinction," indicates refined taste and acute perception.
Antonyms.—Faulty, careless, erroneous.

Correction, discipline, punishment. As correction and discipline have commonly required punishment to render them efficacious, custom has affixed to them a strong resemblance in their application, although they are distinguished from each other by obvious marks of difference. The prominent idea in correction is that of making right what has been wrong. In discipline, the leading idea is that of instructing or regulating. In punishment, the leading idea is that of inflicting pain. We remove an evil by correction; we prevent it by discipline.

Correspond, accord. To correspond is to answer or conform to the description of something else. Things that correspond must be alike in size, shape, color, and every minute particular. To accord is to agree or to be in harmony and without conflict. Things that accord must be suited to each other. His disposition accords with his looks.

Cost, price, charge, expense. The cost of an article is the amount of money that was paid for it. We may say also that the cost of producing the article (labor, materials, etc.) determines the price asked for it. In other words, the price is fixed by the seller and the cost is met by the buyer. A charge is an amount demanded for services. In a more general sense, charges (for example, fixed charges) are the items taken together which represent the cost of doing business. Expenses are miscellaneous disbursements incidental to the carrying on of business or the conducting of private affairs.

Courage, fortitude, resolution. Courage respects action; fortitude respects passion: a man has courage to meet danger, fortitude to endure pain. Resolution simply marks the will not to recede; we require resolution not to yield to the first difficulties that offer.
Antonyms.—Fear, timidity, pusillanimity.

Cover, hide. The ruling idea in the word cover is that of throwing or putting something over a body; in the word hide is that of keeping carefully to one's self, from the observation of others.
Antonyms.—Show, reveal, expose.

Covey, flock, bevy. Covey, usually applied to quail, is one of many special collective nouns referring to animals. Compare *school* of fish and *pride* of lions. Flock, a more general term, suggests birds but may also apply to sheep, while the verb *to flock* may describe the coming together of a crowd of people, drawn to some point by a common impulse. Bevy, though properly associated with quail, is sometimes used in a mildly complimentary way to identify a group of women.

Cozy(sy), comfortable, snug. Cozy contains essentially the same ideas as its less colorful synonyms, in that it describes a place or situation conducive to relaxation—perhaps an armchair before the fire on a cold, stormy night. Comfortable, in addition to denoting physical ease, may suggest freedom from worry, financial or otherwise. Snug, which also describes an agreeable situation, emphasizes small but well-arranged quarters.

Credit, favor, influence. These terms mark the state we stand in with regard to others as flowing out of their sentiments toward ourselves. Credit arises from esteem; favor from good will or affection; influence from credit or favor or external circumstances. Influence is employed in directing others; weak people easily give their credit or bestow their favor, by which an influence is gained over them to bend them to the will of others.

Crime, vice, sin. A crime is a social offense; a vice is a personal offense. Every action which does injury to others, either individually or collectively, is a crime; that which does injury to ourselves is a vice. Crime consists in a violation of human laws; vice, in a violation of moral law; sin, in a violation of the Divine law.

Criminal, culprit, malefactor, felon, convict. When we wish to speak in general of those who by offenses against the laws or regulations of society have exposed themselves to punishment, we denominate them criminals; when we consider them as already brought before a tribunal, we call them culprits; when we consider them in regard to the moral turpitude of their character, as the promoters of evil rather than of good, we entitle them malefactors; when we consider them as offending by the grosser violations of the law, they are termed felons; when we consider them as already under the sentence of the law, we call them convicts.

Criterion, standard. The criterion is employed only in matters of judgment; the standard is used in the ordinary concerns of life. The former serves for determining the characters and qualities of things; the latter, for defining quantity and measure.

Cruel, barbarous, sadistic, brutal, savage. A cruel person has no regard for the sufferings of others. One who is barbarous shows a primitive ferocity not controlled by the restraints of civilized society. Sadistic people, if they are true followers of the Marquis de Sade, delight in inflicting tortures ingeniously contrived for their victims. Brutal people use coarser methods in causing pain to others. A savage person gives full play to animal instincts of ferocity. *Antonyms.*—Kind, humane, gentle, refined, civilized.

Crying, weeping. Crying arises from an impatience in suffering bodily pains; weeping is occasioned by mental grief.

Cultivation, culture, civilization, refinement. Civilization implies for a people a high state of economic and social life. Cultivation primarily applies to the treatment of soil and plants to encourage growth. Applied to the human mind and character, it denotes the possession of training and refinement of which culture is the outcome. Culture comprehends the intellectual phases of civilization; in persons it implies a high mental, moral, and aesthetic development, with possession of graces and niceties of word and manner. Refinement connotes especially fineness and delicacy of feeling. *Antonyms.*—Rusticity, rudeness, coarseness, crudity, savagery.

Cure, heal, remedy. Diseases are cured, wounds are healed; the former is a complex process, the latter is simple. Whatever requires to be cured is wrong in the system; whatever requires to be healed is occasioned externally by violence, and requires external applications. To remedy has a moral application; an omission, a deficiency, or a mischief, requires to be remedied. *Antonyms.*—Injure, irritate, inflame, aggravate.

Curious, inquisitive, prying. Curious implies an interest in learning about things generally, especially matters not of immediate concern to the person. Inquisitive connotes a rather persistent and impertinent curiosity. Prying applies to an officious, unwelcome, disagreeable inquisitiveness. *Antonyms.*—Uninterested, indifferent, apathetic, nonchalant.

Cursory, hasty, slight, desultory. An author will take a cursory view of those points which are not necessarily connected with his subject; an author who takes a hasty view of a subject will mislead by his errors; he who takes a slight view will disappoint by the shallowness of his information. Between cursory and desultory there is the same difference as between running and leaping: we run in a line, but we leap from one part to another; so remarks that are cursory have more or less connection, but remarks that are desultory are without any coherence. *Antonyms.*—Detailed, careful, thorough, methodical, coherent.

Custom, habit, fashion, practice. Custom is the practice of doing a thing in like circumstances and in a uniform manner for definite reasons. Social customs regulate many important concerns of men. Habit is the series of acts, which, through practice, has become involuntary or reflex. Fashion is arbitrary and capricious, and is applied to matters of minor importance. Practice signifies actual doing or the thing done: it may be the practice of a person to do acts of charity, as the occasion requires; but, when he uniformly does a particular act of charity at any given period of the year, it is properly said to be his custom.

Danger, peril, hazard, risk. Danger is a general term for impending evil; peril suggests nearer and greater threat of harm, with the odds against the person threatened. Hazards are possibilities of danger that are latent in circumstances, as in road hazards for motorists. A risk is a chance of danger that is assumed voluntarily and with knowledge of a possible adverse outcome.

Daring, bold. He who is daring provokes resistance and courts danger; but the bold man is contented to overcome the resistance that is offered to him. A man may be bold in the use of words only; he must be daring in actions; he is bold in the defense of truth; he is daring in military enterprise. *Antonyms.*—Fearful, hesitating, timorous, faint-hearted.

Dark, obscure, dim, mysterious, abstruse. Dark is opposed to light; obscure, to bright. What is dark is altogether hidden; what is obscure is not to be seen distinctly, or without an effort. Dim expresses a degree of darkness, but it is employed more in relation to the person seeing than to the object seen. Any intricate affair, which involves the characters and conduct of men, may be mysterious. Obscure may be applied to things or ideas; abstruse to ideas only. *Antonyms.*—Light, bright, clear, distinct, plain.

Deadly, mortal, fatal, lethal. Deadly implies strong probability of death. Mortal, a more poetic word, indicates that death has already occurred or is in process of occurring. Thus we speak of deadly peril and of a mortal wound. Fatal suggests a chain of circumstances that inevitably cause death. Lethal describes an agency or a physical substance that produces death, as a lethal dose of poison. *Antonyms.*—Vital, life-giving, wholesome.

Debt, due. Debt, in its literal meaning, refers to an amount owed by some one in return for goods or services. The word may also express a moral obligation, as a debt of gratitude. Due is what is coming to someone, whether payable in money or in some other form of requital. According to the proverbial saying, we should even "give the Devil his due."

Deceit, deception, guile. Deceit is the habit of intentional falsehood. Deception, the act of misleading through false appearances, is not always blameworthy: a magician may practice deception. Guile implies crafty, insidious deceit. *Antonyms.*—Honesty, truth, candor, sincerity.

Deceiver, impostor. Deceiver is the general term for a person who practices deception, fraud, trickery or chicanery. An impostor is a person who passes himself off as someone else.

Decency, decorum. Decency respects a man's conduct; decorum, his behavior. *Antonyms.*—Unseemliness, impropriety, unfitness.

Decided, decisive. Decided marks that which is actually fixed and settled; decisive, that which appertains to decision. A person's aversion or attachment is decided; a sentence, a judgment, or a victory, is decisive. *Antonyms.*—Indecisive, unsettled, doubtful.

Decided, determined, resolute. A man who is decided remains in no doubt; he who is determined is un-

influenced by the doubts or questions of others; he who is resolute is uninfluenced by the consequences of his actions.
Antonyms.—Irresolute, doubting, wavering, uncertain.

Decision, judgment, sentence. A decision has no respect to the agent; it may be said of one or many; it may be the decision of the court, of the nation, of the public, of a particular body of men, or of a private individual. But a judgment is given in a public court or among private individuals. A sentence is passed in a court of law or at the bar of a public assembly.

Decree, edict. A decree is a more solemn and deliberative act than an edict; on the other hand, an edict is more authoritative than a decree. A decree is the decision of one or many; an edict speaks the will of an individual. Councils and courts, as well as princes, make decrees. An edict is peculiar to a despotic government.

Dedicate, devote, consecrate, hallow. There is something more solemn in the act of dedicating than in that of devoting, but less than in that of consecrating. To dedicate and devote may be employed in both temporal and spiritual matters; to consecrate and hallow, only in the spiritual sense. An author dedicates a book to a friend or patron by prefacing it with the name and the complimentary inscription. We dedicate a house to the service of God; we devote our time to the benefit of our friends or to the relief of the poor. To consecrate is to declare sacred by means of religious ceremony. The church is consecrated; particular days are hallowed.
Antonyms.—Desecrate, profane.

Deduction, abatement. Both these words imply a taking from something. A person may make a deduction in an account for various reasons, but he makes an abatement in a demand when it is objected to as excessive.
Antonyms.—Increase, addition, augmentation.

Deface, disfigure, deform. Deface implies marring of the surface, frequently by destroying some of it, as letters or inscriptions. Disfigure applies to the deeper injury which mars beauty of form or shape. Deform means so to alter the structure as to produce a misshapen thing.
Antonyms.—Amend, better, improve, rectify.

Defective, deficient. Defective implies the quality or characteristic of lacking something or of being incomplete. Deficient is used with regard to the measure or character of the defect. A book may be defective in consequence of lacking some leaves. A man may be deficient in courage.
Antonyms.—Perfect, complete, unimpaired, whole.

Defend, protect, vindicate. A person may be defended in any particular case of actual danger or difficulty; he is protected from what may happen as well as what does happen. Defense respects the evil that threatens; protection involves the supply of necessities and the affording of comforts. Vindicate implies successful defense against a charge or accusation.
Antonyms.—Endanger, imperil, expose, betray.

Defendant, defender. Technically, a defendant is an accused person against whom a case is brought in court. A defender is one who actively repels attacks upon a person or a cause. A king may be designated as a Defender of the Faith.
Antonyms.—Prosecutor, plaintiff, accuser, assailant.

Definite, definitive. Anything that is definite has its limits or boundaries clearly fixed. Definitive, especially in reference to biographies or histories, means final and decisive. A definitive statement settles an argument once and for all.
Antonyms.—Vague, ambiguous, doubtful.

Deity, divinity. Deity signifies a divine person; divinity signifies the divine essence or power.

Dejection, depression, melancholy. Depression is but a degree of dejection. Slight circumstances may occasion a depression; distressing events occasion dejection: the death of a near and dear relative may be expected to produce dejection in persons of the greatest self-possession. Melancholy is a severe form of depression which amounts to a mental disease.
Antonyms.—Rapture, happiness, elation, felicity, cheerfulness.

Delegate, deputy. A delegate is an authorized representative sent by an organization to a convention or some other gathering. A deputy is usually a person designated, or "deputized," to act in the place of another, for example, as assistant to a sheriff or to some other executive officer. In the expression Chamber of Deputies a representative has a status more permanent than that of delegate; he is the legislative equivalent of the executive deputy.

Deliver, rescue, save. One may be delivered from any evil, whether great or small, and in any manner. To rescue is to deliver from a great impending danger or immediate evil, as to rescue from the hands of robbers or from the jaws of a wild beast. To save signifies to keep from evil.
Antonyms.—Abandon, destroy, surrender, lose.

Demand, require. We demand that which is owing and ought to be given; we require that which we wish and expect to have done. The creditor makes a demand on the debtor; the master requires a certain portion of duty from his servant.
Antonyms.—Appeal (for), entreat, request, beg.

Demur, doubt, hesitation, objection. Demurs often occur in matters of deliberation; doubt, in regard to matters of fact; hesitation, in matters of ordinary conduct; and objections, in matters of common consideration. Artabanes made many demurs to the proposed invasion of Greece by Xerxes. Doubts have been suggested respecting the veracity of Herodotus as a historian. It is not proper to ask that which cannot be granted without hesitation. There are but few things which we either attempt to do or recommend to others that are not liable to some kind of an objection.
Antonyms.—Certainty, approval, promptness, consent.

Demur, hesitate. We demur from doubt or difficulty; we hesitate from an undecided state of mind. Demurring is a matter of prudence, it is always grounded on some reason—a lawyer for the defense demurs to evidence presented by the prosecution, in the hope of throwing doubt upon its contents. Hesitating is rather a matter of feeling. When a request of a dubious nature is made of us, we hesitate in complying with it; one hesitates to voice objection to a plan about the wisdom of which his friends have no doubts.
Antonyms.—Assent, acquiesce, decide, proceed.

Denote, signify. Denote is employed with regard to things and their characters; signify, with regard to the thoughts or movements. A letter or character may be made to denote any number, as words are made to signify the intentions and wishes of the person.

Deny, refuse. Deny applies both to matters of fact and to matters of wish or request; refuse, only to the latter. We deny a report or we deny or refuse a request.
Antonyms.—Grant, accede (to), allow.

Deplore, lament. Deplore indicates keen regret over something already done that is regarded as serious and irreparable. We deplore the action or the conduct of some one who has acted in a regrettable way. Lament conveys the idea of personal grief over something that has happened. Whereas deplore proceeds mainly from one's judgment, lament involves chiefly the emotions.
Antonyms.—Rejoice (at), exult or glory (in).

Deposit, pledge, security. Pledge is the general term applying to anything given as assurance of fulfillment of an agreement. It may be a deposit, a term now generally used of money as commonly paid "to bind a bargain," or security, now usually some form of commercial paper, such as bonds, notes, etc.

Depravity, contamination, corruption. Depravity implies a state of moral degradation, whether innate or acquired. Contamination refers to the process of bringing about a low state of morals through the introduction of external impurities, just as the word is used literally to describe the introduction of disease germs into drinking water. Corruption suggests a more thoroughgoing impairment of any one's moral nature through evil influences that work from within.
Antonyms.—Virtue, goodness, correction, purification.

Depth, profundity. Depth is indefinite in its signification; profundity is a positive and considerable degree of depth. Moreover, the word depth is applied to objects in general; profundity is confined in its application to matters of thought or feeling.
Antonyms.—Shallowness, superficiality.

Derive, trace, deduce. The act of deriving is immediate and direct; that of tracing, a gradual process; that of deducing, a reasoning process. We discover causes and sources by derivation; we discover the course, progress, and commencement of things by tracing; we discover the grounds and reasons of things by deduction.

Desert, merit, worth. Desert is taken for that which is good or bad; merit, for that which is good only. We deserve praise or blame; we merit a reward. Worth is that which is absolutely valuable—it must be sought for on its own account.
Antonyms.—Demerit, worthlessness.

Design, purpose, intend, mean. To design is to plan in a steady, methodical manner; to purpose is to propose to oneself, with some degree of determination; to intend is to have in mind to do something—a less definite expression than the others. Mean still has a colloquial flavor, signifying a vague intention.

Desire, wish, covet. To desire is imperious—it demands gratification; to wish is less vehement—it consists of a strong inclination. To covet is to desire that which belongs to another.
Antonyms.—Dislike, detest, be averse to, spurn.

Desist, leave off. To desist is voluntary or involuntary; to leave off is voluntary. We are frequently obliged to desist, but we leave off at our option. He who annoys another must be made to desist; he who does not wish to offend will leave off when requested.
Antonyms.—Persist, continue, keep on.

Despair, desperation, despondency. Despair is a state of mind produced by the view of external circumstances; desperation and despondency may be the fruit of the imagination. The former therefore always rests on some ground; the latter are sometimes ideal. Desperation marks a state of vehement and impatient feeling; despondency is hopelessness, and is often a disease of the mind.
Antonyms.—Assurance, hopefulness, confidence, courage.

Destiny, destination. Destiny is the point or line marked out in the walk of life; destination is the place fixed upon in particular: as every man has his peculiar destiny, so every traveler has his particular destination. Destiny is altogether set above human control; destination is, however, under the specific control of an individual, either for himself or for another.

Destiny, fate, lot, doom. Destiny is used in regard to one's station and walk in life; fate, in regard to what one suffers; lot, in regard to what one gets or possesses; doom is the final destiny which terminates unhappily and depends mostly upon the will of another. Destiny is marked out; fate is fixed; a lot is assigned; a doom is decreed.

Destroy, consume, waste. To destroy is to break or shatter or by other means put anything beyond hope of restoration. A house may be destroyed by fire or it may fall to ruin. To consume is to use up, as to consume food or merchandise; to waste is to expend unnecessarily, extravagantly, to spend to no purpose, as to waste time or property.
Antonyms.—Build, repair, restore, supply, preserve.

Destruction, ruin. Destruction is an act of immediate violence; ruin is a gradual process. A thing is destroyed by some external action upon it; a thing falls to ruin of itself. A reputation is destroyed; a character is ruined.
Antonyms.—Construction, upbuilding, preservation.

Determine, resolve. We determine how or what we shall do—this requires examination and choice. We resolve that we will do what we have determined upon—this requires a firm spirit.
Antonyms.—Hesitate, waver, question, vacillate.

Deviate, wander, swerve, stray. Deviate always supposes a direct path which is departed from; wander includes no such idea. The act of deviating is commonly faulty; that of wandering is indifferent. To swerve is to deviate from that which one holds right; to stray is to wander in the same bad sense. Men swerve from their duty to consult their interest; the young stray from the path of rectitude to seek that of pleasure.
Antonyms.—Continue, advance, progress.

Devise, bequeath. In the technical sense, to devise is to give lands by a will duly attested according to law; to bequeath is to give personalty for possession after one's death by a less formal instrument.

Dictate, suggestion. Dictate signifies the thing uttered, and has an imperative sense; the suggestion signifies the thing intimated, and conveys the idea of its being proposed secretly or in a gentle manner. These terms are both applied, with this distinction, to acts of the mind. When conscience, reason, or passion present anything forcibly to the mind, it is called a dictate; when anything enters the mind in a casual manner, it is called a suggestion.

Dictionary, encyclopedia. The definition of words, with their various changes, modifications, uses, acceptations, and applications, are the proper subjects of a dictionary; the nature and properties of things, with their construction, uses, powers, etc., are the proper subjects of an encyclopedia.

Dictionary, lexicon vocabulary, glossary. We speak of a lexicon of Greek or Latin, of a dictionary of a modern language. A vocabulary is a partial kind of dictionary, which may comprehend a simple list of words, with or without explanation, arranged in order or otherwise. A glossary is an explanatory vocabulary, which commonly serves to explain obsolete or technical terms.

Die, expire, perish. Die is the general word for cessation of life or extinction of being. Expire is a softened expression for die. Trees die and a flame expires; figuratively, a lease expires. Perish signifies utter decay and disappearance.
Antonyms.—Live, survive, persist, exist.

Difference, dispute, altercation, quarrel. A difference, as distinguished from the others, is generally of a less serious and personal kind; a dispute consists not only of angry words, but of much ill blood and unkind action; an altercation is a wordy dispute, in which difference of opinion is drawn out into a multitude of words; a quarrel is the most serious of all differences, which leads to every manner of violence.

Difference, distinction. Difference lies in the thing; distinction is the act of a person who recognizes differences. Those are equally bad logicians who make a distinction without a difference, or who make no distinction where there is a difference. A careful writer will make a distinction between synonyms.
Antonyms.—Similarity, likeness, agreement, identity.

Difference, variety, diversity, medley. Difference and variety seem to lie in the things themselves; diversity and medley are created either by accident or by design. A difference may lie in two objects only; a variety cannot exist without an assemblage. A difference is discovered by means of a comparison which the mind forms of objects to prevent confusion; variety strikes on the mind, and pleases the imagination with many agreeable images. Diversity arises from an assemblage of objects naturally contrasted; a medley is produced by a casual assemblage of objects often so illy suited as to produce a ludicrous effect.
Antonyms.—Likeness, sameness, correspondence.

Difficulty, obstacle, impediment, embarrassment, trouble. A difficulty is something or a circumstance that interferes with ease of action. Obstacle means anything directly opposed to one's effort toward an end. Impediment is like a clog or brake in hindering movement or progress. An embarrassment is any condition or circumstance that gives rise to confusion or perplexity, and so proves an obstacle or difficulty. Trouble is a general word applied to the circumstances or to feelings aroused by them.
Antonyms.—Aid, help, assistance, relief, encouragement.

Diffuse, prolix. Both words mark defects of style opposed to brevity. A diffuse writer is fond of amplification, the prolix writer is fond of circumlocution, minute details, and trifling particulars.
Antonyms.—Brief, concise, succinct, condensed.

Digress, deviate. Both in the original and the accepted sense, these words express going out of the ordinary course. We digress only in a narrative, whether written or spoken; we deviate in actions as well as in words, in our conduct as well as in writings.

Dilate, expand. Dilate implies enlargement, as a circular ripple on water widens; expand suggests enlargement in every direction, as a flower expands. A speaker dilates upon a theme, dwells upon it with many words; he expands his argument by discussing points in greater detail.
Antonyms.—Contract, condense, narrow, compress.

Diligent, expeditious, prompt. Diligent marks the interest one takes in doing something; he is diligent who loses no time, who keeps close to the work from inclination. Expeditious marks the desire one has to complete the thing begun. Prompt marks one's desire to get ready; he is prompt who sets about a thing without delay.
Antonyms.—Inattentive, neglectful, slow, hesitant, dilatory.

Disappear, vanish. A thing disappears either gradually or suddenly; it vanishes of a sudden: it disappears in the ordinary course of things; it vanishes by an unusual effort or as if by supernatural or magic power.
Antonyms.—Appear, arise, emerge.

Disapproval, dislike, disinclination. Disapproval is an act of the judgment; dislike, a matter of feeling and sentiments. Disinclination implies a mild or careless dislike, usually of something to be done.

Disapprove, dislike. Disapprove is an act of the judgment; dislike is an act of the will or of the affection. To approve or disapprove is peculiarly the part of a superior, or of one who determines the conduct of others; to dislike is altogether a personal act, in which the feelings of the individual are consulted.
Antonyms.—Approve, like, enjoy, delight in.

Disbelief, unbelief. Disbelief properly implies the believing that a thing is not, or refusing to believe that it is. Unbelief properly implies skepticism or a withholding of belief. As generally applied to religion, unbelief signifies disbelief of dogmas or doctrines, usually with the indication of willfulness. Disbelief is most properly applicable to the ordinary events of life; unbelief, to serious matters of opinion.

Disclaim, disown. One may disclaim responsibility for an act; he may disown his children.
Antonyms.—Claim, acknowledge, own, recognize.

Discord, strife, dissension, contention. Discord consists mostly in the feeling; strife consists mostly in the outward action. Discord evinces itself in various ways— by looks, words, or actions; strife displays itself in words or acts of violence. A collision of opinions produces dissension; a collision of interests produces contention; a collision of humors produces discord.
Antonyms.—Concord, peace, agreement.

Discover, reveal, betray, divulge. Discover suggests exposing to view something that has been hidden, or perhaps unknown. Reveal carries the idea of lifting a curtain or imparting information that has hitherto been kept secret. Betray indicates the violation of a confidence, or it might refer to evidence given involuntarily, as in the speech or action of an accused person. Divulge means giving up information with which one has been entrusted. There may be more reluctance than is associated with betray as a voluntary act, but in effect, divulge also suggests violation of a confidence.
Antonyms.—Conceal, hide, suppress.

Discredit, disgrace, reproach, scandal, dishonor, shame. Discredit interferes with a man's respectability; disgrace marks him out as an object of unfavorable distinction; reproach makes him a subject of adverse criticism; scandal makes him an object of offense or even of abhorrence. Dishonor connotes loss of dignity and favor; disgrace expresses positive reproach and fall from honorable regard; a consciousness of guilt and of the resulting disgrace will bring shame to a person. Shame, the consequence of open moral guilt, is the strongest of these words.
Antonyms.—Honor, favor, regard, respect, dignity.

Discuss, argue, debate. In discussing a question, one discourses upon it calmly and impartially, giving equal attention to pros and cons. Argue is a more personal word meaning to cite reasons and evidence, sometimes a bit heatedly, in support of one side. To debate is to present a formal, organized statement of the case for or against a proposition.

Disgust, loathing, nausea. Disgust is less than loathing, and loathing than nausea. When applied to sensible objects, we are disgusted with dirt; we loathe the smell of food if we have a sickly appetite; we nauseate medicine. When applied metaphorically, we are disgusted with affectation; we loathe the endearments of those who are offensive; we are nauseated by all the enjoyments of life, after having made an intemperate use of them and discovered their inanity.
Antonyms.—Desire, relish, craving.

Dishonest, knavish. What is dishonest violates the established laws of man; what is knavish supposes peculiar art and design in the accomplishment.
Antonyms.—Honorable, straightforward, upright.

Disjoint, dismember. Disjoint means to put out of joint, to dislocate, as a dislocated ankle, or to separate as the joints, as a tool or mechanism. Speech, when not well connected or when hesitating, may be called disjointed. Dismember implies mutilating or tearing apart of the animal or human body.
Antonyms.—Join, unite, assemble.

Dismay, daunt, appall. We are dismayed by alarming circumstances; we are daunted by terrifying circumstances; we are appalled by horrid circumstances.
Antonyms—Hearten, encourage, incite, rouse.

Disorder, disease, distemper, malady. Disease connotes any deviation from health, whether in plants or animals. Disorder implies usually a slight, temporary sickness. Distemper is now used only of animal diseases. Malady carries the sense of lingering, deep-seated diseases, often with the idea of a morbid state of mind or spirits.

Disparity, inequality. Disparity applies to two objects which should meet or stand in coalition with each other; inequality is applicable to those that are compared with each other. The disparity of age, situation, and circumstances is to be considered with regard to persons entering into a matrimonial connection; the inequality in the portion of labor which is to be performed by two persons is a ground for the inequality of their recompense.
Antonyms.—Parity, equality, equivalence.

Dispassionate, cool. A person who is dispassionate is characteristically temperate in his opinions and judgments. Coolness implies self-control in situations likely to cause excitement. We speak of considering a quarrel dispassionately and of being cool in moments of danger.
Antonyms.—Excitable, hasty, hot.

Dispel, disperse. Dispel means to drive away, as doubt or gloom. It applies only to intangible things. Disperse means to drive apart, to scatter, as a crowd.
Antonyms.—Collect, gather, accumulate.

Dispense, distribute. Dispense is an indiscriminate action; distribute is a particularizing action: we dispense to all; we distribute to each individually. One dispenses charity, but he distributes gifts.
Antonyms.—Hold, keep, retain, withhold.

Displeasure, anger, disapprobation. Displeasure is a softened and gentle feeling. Anger is the intense feeling of dissatisfaction and resentment, rising often to vehement expression. Displeasure may be slight or intense, but it lacks the element of resentment and may not reveal its true intensity in words. Disapprobation is a definite sentiment of censure or of disapproval.
Antonyms.—Satisfaction, pleasure, approval.

Disposal, disposition. Disposal implies merely the removal of things; disposition implies their orderly or appropriate placing or arrangement.

Disposition, inclination. We may always expect a man to do that which he is disposed to do; but we cannot always calculate upon his executing that to which he is merely inclined. We indulge a disposition; we yield to an inclination. Disposition comprehends the whole state of the mind; inclination refers always to a particular object.

Disposition, temper. Disposition is permanent and settled; temper may be transitory and fluctuating. The disposition comprehends the springs and motives of actions; the temper influences the action of the moment. It is possible and not unusual to have a good disposition with a bad temper, and vice versa.

Disregard, neglect, slight. We disregard the warnings, the words, or opinions of others; we neglect their injunctions or their precepts. To disregard results from the settled purpose of the mind; to neglect, from a temporary forgetfulness or oversight. Slight is altogether an intentional act toward an individual.
Antonyms.—Attend to, regard, observe, respect.

Distant, far, remote. Distant is' used to designate great space; far, only that which is ordinary. Astronomers estimate that the sun is nearly 93 million miles distant from the earth; a person lives not very far off, or a person is far from the spot. Remote expresses the relative idea of having disappeared from sight.
Antonyms.—Near, close, neighboring, contiguous.

Distinguish, discriminate. To distinguish, whether by the senses or the understanding, is to recognize differences between objects and ideas. Discriminate (literally, to divide) means to separate and select according to certain standards of judgment or taste. We may speak of a distinction as true, but of discrimination as nice, that is, exact.
Antonyms.—Confuse, overlook, confound.

Distinguished, conspicuous, noted, eminent, illustrious. A thing is distinguished in proportion as it is distinct or separate from others; it is conspicuous in proportion as it is easily seen; it is noted in proportion as it is widely known. Eminent applies to those things which set a man high in the circle of his acquaintances; illustrious applies to that which makes him shine before the world.
Antonyms.—Ordinary, common, unknown, humble.

Distress, anxiety, anguish, agony. Distress is the pain felt when in a strait from which we see no means of extricating ourselves; anxiety is that pain which one feels on the prospect of an evil. Distress always depends upon some outward cause; anxiety often lies in the imagination; anguish arises from the reflection on the evil that is past; agony springs from witnessing or suffering intense mental or bodily pain.
Antonyms.—Comfort, calm, apathy, tranquillity.

Distress, harass, perplex. A person is distressed either in his outward circumstances or in his feelings; he is harassed in mind or body; he is perplexed in his understanding more than in his feelings. A deprivation distresses; provocations and hostile measures harass; stratagems and ambiguous measures perplex.
Antonyms.—Soothe, console, comfort, compose.

Distrust, suspicion, diffidence. Distrust is said either of ourselves or of others; suspicion is said only of others; diffidence, only of ourselves. To be distrustful of a person is to impute no good of him; to be suspicious of a person is to impute positive evil to him. As regards oneself, a person may distrust his own powers for the execution of a particular office, or have a distrust of himself in company; he has a general diffidence, or he is naturally diffident.
Antonyms.—Trust, confidence, faith, self-confidence.

Disturb, interrupt. Disturb implies more or less constant breaking up or unsettling as regards one's attitude, activities or affairs. Interrupt connotes a sharp, sudden break in continuity. One's mind may be disturbed from within, but one's thinking is interrupted from without.
Antonyms.—Quiet, tranquilize, pacify.

Divide, distribute, share. We divide the thing; we distribute to the person. To share is to make into parts, the same as divide, and it is to give those parts to some persons, the same as distribute. The person who shares takes a part himself; he who distributes gives it all to others.
Antonyms.—Keep, reserve, withhold, retain.

Divide, separate. That is divided which has been or has been conceived to be a whole; that is separated which might be joined. An army may be divided into two or three divisions or portions; the divisions are frequently separated in their march.
Antonyms.—Join, connect, unite, unify, coalesce, fuse.

Doctrine, dogma, tenet. Although doctrine is historically understood to mean a body of principles taught by theologians and philosophers, the word is now used more generally to identify any formulated statement of theory or of principles governing action. Thus, we speak of the Monroe Doctrine or of Einstein's doctrine (theory) of relativity. Dogma refers to principles positively asserted and definitely laid down by some authority, for example, the leader or governing body of a church. A tenet is a belief that is commonly held, even though not formally taught or officially promulgated.

Doubt, question. Doubt lies altogether in the mind; it is a less active feeling than question: by the former we merely suspend decision; by the latter we actually demand proofs in order to assist us in deciding. We may doubt in silence; we cannot question without expressing doubt, directly or indirectly. We doubt the truth of a position; we question the veracity of an author.
Antonyms.—Accept, believe, assume.

Doubt, suspense. Doubt respects that which we should believe; suspense, that which we wish to know or ascertain. We are in doubt for lack of decisive, positive evidence; in suspense for lack of certainty about the future. Doubt interrupts our progress in the attainment of truth; suspense impedes us in the attainment of our objects.
Antonyms.—Confidence, certainty, assurance.

Draw, drag, haul, pull. Draw expresses here the idea common to the first three terms, namely, that of putting a body in motion from behind oneself or toward oneself. To drag is to draw a thing with violence, or to draw that which makes resistance; to haul is to drag it with still greater violence. To pull signifies only an effort to draw without the idea of motion; horses pull very long sometimes before they can draw a heavily laden cart uphill.

Dream, vision, reverie (revery). Primarily, dreams are visions, thoughts, or images passing in the mind during sleep. One's imagined ideals in life when far from realization are called dreams. A vision may come to one during waking hours. A reverie is a loose train of thought or imagery, running through the mind when one is awake but given over to musing—a waking dream or daydream.

Dull, gloomy, sad, dismal. When applied to natural objects, dull and gloomy denote the want of necessary light or life; in this sense metals are more or less dull according as they are stained with dirt. The weather is dull when the sun is obscured by clouds, and gloomy when the atmosphere is darkened by fogs or thick clouds. Dismal denotes not merely the want of that which is necessary, but also the presence of that which is repugnant to the senses. Dismal carries the sense of evil omen or unlucky foreboding. Sad implies a gloomy or downcast countenance and suggests grief.
Antonyms.—Bright, happy, joyous, merry, cheerful.

Durable, lasting, permanent. Durable is naturally said of material substances; lasting, of those which are spiritual, although in ordinary discourse sometimes they exchange offices. Permanent connotes fitness to endure or remain. We make permanent improvements of lasting or durable materials. That which perishes quickly is not durable; that which ceases quickly is not lasting; that which is only for a time is not permanent.
Antonyms.—Perishable, flimsy, unstable, temporary.

Duty, obligation. Duty has to do with the conscience, and arises from the natural relations of society; an obligation arises from circumstances and is a species of duty. He who guarantees to pay a sum of money contracts an obligation. He who marries contracts new duties.

Ease, quiet, rest. Ease implies absence of anything causing strain on mind or body. Quiet is freedom from external disturbance, such as noise or violence. Repose carries with it the idea of refreshing rest, especially sound sleep.
Antonyms.—Disturbance, toil, strain.

Ease, dexterity, facility. In reference to action, ease denotes such positive qualities as gracefulness and directness. Dexterity connotes a high degree of proficiency or skill. Facility adds the idea of lightness and speed in the performance of tasks.
Antonyms.—Difficulty, awkwardness, constraint.

Eclipse, obscure. Heavenly bodies are eclipsed by the passing of other bodies between them and the beholder; things are in general obscured which are in any way rendered less striking or visible. So, figuratively, real merit is eclipsed by the intervention of superior merit; it is often obscured by an ungracious exterior in the possessor or by his unfortunate circumstances.
Antonyms.—Reveal, show, illuminate.

Education, instruction, breeding. Instruction and breeding are to education as parts to a whole. Instruction implies the communication of knowledge, and breeding connotes the manners or outward conduct. Education comprehends the formation of the mind, the regulation of the heart, and the establishment of the principles. Good instruction makes one wiser; good breeding makes one more polished and agreeable.

Effect, produce, perform. To produce signifies to bring something forth or into existence; to perform, to do something completely. To effect is to produce a result by performing. Whatever is effected is the consequence of a specific design; it always requires, therefore, a rational agent. What is produced may follow incidentally, or arise from the action of an irrational agent or an inanimate object; what is performed is done by specific efforts.

Elderly, aged, old, senile. An elderly person has passed the meridian of life; an old man is approaching the normal maximum allotment of years; an aged person has reached this maximum or exceeded it. A senile person, whether old by the calendar or not, exhibits the characteristics commonly associated with older people, such as forgetfulness and childishness.
Antonyms.—Young, youthful.

Embarrassed, abashed, perplexed. A person is embarrassed by actions or circumstances that impede his freedom of movement or his ease in social contacts. He is abashed by something that shakes his self-confidence. Extensive dealings with others often cause him to be perplexed and thus to be both puzzled and confused.
Antonyms.—Self-possessed, confident, composed.

Emissary, spy. Both these words designate a person sent out by a body on some public concern among their enemies; but they differ in their office according to the etymology of the words. The emissary is sent so as to mix with the people to whom he goes, to be in all places, and to associate with every one individually, as may serve his purpose. The spy takes his station wherever he can best perceive what is passing; he keeps himself at a distance from all but such as may particularly aid him in the object of his search. The emissary is generally employed by those who have some illegitimate object to pursue; spies, on the other hand, are employed by all regular governments in a time of warfare.

Employ, use. We employ either persons or things; we use only things, unless, in an evil sense, we use persons. One may be employed in his own or another's affairs.
Antonyms.—Reject, discharge, overlook.

Encouraged, emboldened. One is encouraged (literally, heartened) toward a course of action by cheering words

from others or by circumstances that seem favorable. Emboldened refers chiefly to the strengthening of resolution within oneself, preparatory to doing something audacious.
Antonyms.—Discouraged, frightened, intimidated.

End, terminate, close. End is a general term; an end may come by chance or intention. A discussion may end without being finished, closed, or properly terminated. Close implies a preceding opening in the sense of beginning, as we open and close meetings. Terminate implies usually a purposed end or definite means of ending. His visit was terminated by an abrupt departure. The lane terminated in a high wall.
Antonyms.—Begin, open, commence, initiate.

Endeavor, aim, strive, struggle. An endeavor springs from a sense of duty; we endeavor to do that which is right and avoid that which is wrong. Aiming is the fruit of an aspiring temper—the object aimed at is always something superior either in reality or imagination. Striving is the consequence of an ardent desire—the thing striven for is always conceived to be of importance. Struggling is the effect of necessity—it is proportioned to the difficulty of attainment; the thing struggled for is indispensably necessary.

Endeavor, attempt, effort. Endeavor indicates sustained exertion in the pursuit of an important objective; attempt carries the idea of an experimental undertaking in which one is prepared for failure. Effort is a more general word denoting the exertion of one's will and ability toward the accomplishing of some purpose.
Antonyms.—Rest, slackness, negligence.

Energy, force, vigor, power. Energy is power, thought of or expressed in terms of actual or possible work,—as electrical energy, the energy of his words. Force implies resistance to be overcome. Vigor connotes physical or mental power in daily use, as vigorous growth of a plant. Power is the most general term for ability to do,—as a powerful engine, a speaker of great power.
Antonyms.—Weakness, inefficiency, impotence, incapacity.

Enlarge, increase, extend. Enlarge is applied to dimension and extent; increase is applicable to quantity, signifying to become greater in size by the junction of other matter; extend signifies to make greater in space. We speak of enlarging a house, a room, premises, or boundaries; of increasing an army, or property, capital, expense; of extending the boundaries of an empire.
Antonyms.—Lessen, decrease, contract.

Enmity, animosity, hostility. Enmity lies in the heart; it is deep and malignant. Animosity, from *animus*, a spirit, lies in the passions—it is fierce and vindictive. Hostility, from *hostis*, a political enemy, lies in the action—it is mischievous and destructive. Enmity is altogether personal; hostility respects public or private measures; enmity often lies concealed in the heart and does not betray itself by any open act of hostility.
Antonyms.—Friendliness, love, affection, amity.

Enormous, prodigious, monstrous. The enormous goes beyond our rules of estimating and calculating; the prodigious raises our minds beyond their ordinary standard of thinking; the monstrous contradicts nature and the course of things, frequently with implications of evil.
Antonyms.—Small, minute, usual, natural, reasonable.

Enough, sufficient. Sufficient sometimes implies, more distinctly than enough, the idea of an end or purpose, but in general the words are used without distinction of meanings. Sufficient may be thought more genteel than enough.
Antonyms.—Scanty, sparing, meager.

Enterprising, adventurous. The enterprising character conceives great projects and pursues objects that are difficult to obtain. The adventurous character is contented with seeking that which is new and with placing himself in dangerous and unusual situations.
Antonyms.—Shrinking, contented.

Epithet, adjective. Epithet is the technical term of the rhetorician; adjective, that of the grammarian. The same word is an epithet as it qualifies the sense; it is an adjective as it is a part of speech. Thus, in the phrase, "Alexander the Great," great is an epithet, inasmuch as it designates Alexander in distinction from all other persons; it is an adjective as it expresses a quality in distinction from the noun, Alexander, which denotes a thing. In current usage, epithet may signify abuse or, at least, an unfavorable opinion.

Equal, even, equable, like, alike, uniform. Equal is said of degree, quantity, number, and dimensions, as equal in years; even is said of the surface and position of bodies—a board is made even with another board. Like is said of accidental qualities in things, as alike in color or in feature; uniform is said of things only as to their fitness to correspond; those which are unlike in color, shape, or make, are not uniform, and cannot be made to match as pairs. Equable signifies free from sudden or violent changes,—as an equable climate, equable temper.
Antonyms.—Variable, irregular, unlike, different.

Error, mistake, blunder, fault. Error is the general term, applied to the judgment or to conduct. Mistake is an error of choice; blunder, an awkward error of action. Fault is more serious error, implying frequently a flaw in character or habits.

Eruption, explosion. Eruption is the sudden, and perhaps later continuous, coming into view of something that has been confined, as the eruption of a volcano. Explosion signifies bursting with a noise, with violence, and, characteristically, with the disintegration of a substance.

Estimate, compute, rate. To estimate is to obtain the aggregate sum in one's mind either by an immediate or a progressive act; estimate allows for some inaccuracy in results. To compute is to obtain the sum by the gradual process of putting together items; to rate is to fix the relative value in one's mind by deduction and comparison. A builder estimates the expense of building a house on a given plan; a proprietor of houses computes the probable diminution in the value of his property in consequence of wear and tear; the surveyor rates the present value of lands or houses.

Eternal, endless, everlasting. The eternal is set above time; the endless lies within time. That is properly eternal which has neither beginning nor end; that is endless which has a beginning but no end; that which is everlasting has neither interruption nor cessation.
Antonyms.—Finite, temporary, transitory, passing.

Evade, equivocate. Evade means to turn away from a subject by calling attention to something else. To equivocate is to avoid a positive commitment by using ambiguous language.
Antonyms.—Confront, face.

Event, incident, episode. Event denotes an occurrence of major importance. An incident is a subordinate happening, usually attendant upon an event. An episode is an occurrence somewhat apart from the usual chain of happenings. Although of relatively minor importance, the episode is a self-contained narrative unit and deserves attention for its own sake.

Exact, extort. To exact is to demand peremptorily—it is commonly an act of injustice. To extort is to get with violence—it is an act of tyranny.

Exact, nice, particular. Exact indicates precision that meets objective standards of measurement. Nice refers to refined differentiation with regard to matters of taste; it represents a subjective form of precision. Particular suggests a conscientious attitude and close attention to minute details.
Antonyms.—Careless, crude, slipshod.

Example, instance, illustration. An example is a typical case used to explain a general principle or a classification. An instance is a concrete "case in point" offered in support of an assertion. Whereas instance is associated chiefly with evidence used in an argument, example and illustration are concerned primarily with instruction. Illustration, whether in words or pictures, gives a more complete, and usually a more interesting, view of the subject under consideration.

Example, pattern. The example must be followed generally; the pattern must be followed particularly, not only as to what but how a thing is to be done. The former serves as a guide to the judgment; the latter, to the actions.

Excite, incite, provoke. To excite is said more particularly of the inward feelings; incite is said of the external actions; provoke is said of both. A person's passions are excited; he is incited by any particular passion to a course of conduct; he is provoked to a particular step by some feeling.
Antonyms.—Calm, inhibit, deter, restrain.

Excursion, ramble, tour, trip, jaunt. Excursion is properly a journey out of one's usual range of travel. It may be long or short. A tour is usually a more carefully planned "round trip" of some length, as a tour of the lakes. Trip, formerly a short journey on foot, is now applied generally. Ramble is a purposeless, pleasant walk. Jaunt is a short ramble or journey.

Excuse, pardon. We excuse a person by exempting him from blame; we pardon by giving up the punishment of the offense one has committed. We excuse a small fault; we pardon a great fault; we excuse that which personally affects ourselves; we pardon that which offends against morals. Pardon is also conventionally used as a courteous term in place of excuse, as in "pardon the suggestion."
Antonyms.—Blame, condemn, convict, punish.

Execute, fulfill, perform. To execute is to bring about an end; it involves active measures and is peculiarly applicable to that which is extraordinary, or to that which requires particular spirit and talents. Schemes of ambition are executed. To fulfill is to satisfy a moral obligation. We fulfill the duties of citizens. To perform is to carry through by simple action or labor; it is more particularly applicable to the ordinary and regular business of life. We perform a work or a task.

Exercise, practice. Exercise is action for the purpose of stimulating or developing power; practice is regular exercise for the purpose of acquiring or increasing skill and ease of action.

Exigency, emergency. The exigency is more common but less pressing; the emergency is imperious when it comes, but it comes less frequently. A prudent traveler will never carry more money with him than will supply the exigencies of his journey; in case of an emergency he will borrow of his friends rather than risk his property.

Exonerate, exculpate, acquit. To exonerate is to relieve some one from suspicion or charge of moral guilt. Exculpate commonly refers to removal of blame in small matters, as when we exculpate (excuse) ourselves. Acquit carries the idea of a decision which frees one officially from a charge of misdoing.
Antonyms.—Accuse, blame, indict, convict.

Expediency, fitness. The expediency of a thing depends altogether upon the outward circumstances; the fitness is determined by a moral rule.

Expedient, resource. The expedient is an artificial means; the resource is a natural means. A cunning man is fruitful in expedients; a fortunate man abounds in resources.

Explain, expound, interpret. Single words or sentences are explained; a whole work, or a considerable part of it, is expounded; the sense of any writing or symbolical sign is interpreted.

Explain, illustrate, elucidate. To explain is simply to render intelligible; to illustrate and elucidate are to give additional clearness. Everything requires to be explained to one who is ignorant of it; but the best informed will require to have abstruse subjects illustrated and obscure subjects elucidated; that is, made light.

Expostulate, remonstrate. We expostulate in a tone of authority; we remonstrate in a tone of complaint. He who expostulates passes a censure and claims to be heard; he who remonstrates presents his case and requests to be heard.
Antonyms.—Abet, countenance, urge (on).

Extraneous, extrinsic, foreign. The extraneous is that which forms no necessary or natural part of anything. The extrinsic is that which forms a part or has a connection with a thing, but only in an indirect form; it is not an inherent or component part. The foreign is that which forms no part whatever, and has no kind of connection with an object or an incident.
Antonyms.—Essential, intrinsic, native.

Extraordinary, remarkable, phenomenal. All of these words represent a departure in some degree from common experience. Extraordinary (literally, beyond the ordinary) describes something so unusual as to attract attention. Remarkable, a word often applied to persons as well as to incidents and achievements, means deserving of special notice. Phenomenal describes unique occurrences or unexplainable facts observed by the senses.
Antonyms.—Common, ordinary, usual.

Extravagant, prodigal, lavish, profuse. The extravagant man spends his money without reason; the prodigal man spends it in excesses. One may be extravagant with a small sum where it exceeds one's means; one can be prodigal only with large sums. Lavish and profuse are properly applied to particular actions,—the former to denote an expenditure more or less wasteful or superfluous, the latter to denote a full supply without any sort of scant.
Antonyms.—Careful, thrifty, provident, sparing.

Exuberant, luxuriant. These terms are both applied to any flourishing growth or abundance: exuberance expresses the excess; luxuriance, the profusion. Luxuriant is the more usual and of wider application,—as luxuriant foliage, hair, fancy. Exuberant is applied specifically to the feelings,—as exuberant spirits, fancy, joy.
Antonyms.—Impoverished, scanty, poor, deficient, short.

Facetious, jocular, jocose. Facetious refers to comments that are intended to be taken lightly and to be appreciated for their wit. Jocular describes a jesting manner in action or conversation. A jocose person is one who is naturally inclined to be merry or sportively humorous.
Antonyms.—Serious, solemn, crabbed, lugubrious.

Factious, seditious. Factious is an epithet to characterize the tempers of men; seditious characterizes their conduct. The factious man attempts to raise himself into importance; he aims at authority, and seeks to interfere in the measures of government. The seditious man attempts to excite others and to provoke their resistance to established authority. The first wants to be a lawgiver; the second does not hesitate to be a lawbreaker.
Antonyms.—Loyal, complaisant, governable.

Fair, clear. Fair is used in a positive sense; clear, in a negative sense. There must be some brightness in what is fair; there must be no spots in what is clear. The weather is said to be fair, which is not only free from what is disagreeable, but somewhat enlivened by the sun; it is clear when it is free from clouds or mists.
Antonyms.—Dark, cloudy, murky, dull, stormy.

Faith, creed. These words are synonymous when taken for the thing trusted in or believed; but they differ in this; faith has always a reference to the principle in the mind; creed respects a formulated doctrine which is the object of belief.

Faith, fidelity. Faith here denotes a mode of action, namely, in acting true to the faith which others repose in us; fidelity, a disposition of the mind to adhere to that faith which others repose in us. We keep our faith; we show our fidelity.
Antonyms.—Untruth, faithlessness, treachery.

Faithless, perfidious, treacherous. A faithless man is faithless only for his own interest; a perfidious man is expressly so to the injury of another. Perfidy may lie in the will to do; treachery lies altogether in the thing done.
Antonyms.—Faithful, true, trustworthy, dependable.

Fall, downfall, ruin. Fall applies generally to decline from erectness or to descent from high position or state—it applies to things, institutions, and persons. Downfall now generally applies to descent from rank, place, or position—it implies destruction and ruin. The fall of Sedan brought the downfall of Napoleon and the ruin of French hopes.
Antonyms.—Elevation, ascent, rise.

Fallacious, deceitful, fraudulent. Fallacious applies to falsehood in opinion; deceitful, to that which is externally false: our logic is often fallacious; the appearances of things are often deceitful. Fallacious, as characteristic of the mind, excludes the idea of design; deceitful excludes the idea of mistake; fraudulent describes a gross species of the deceitful.
Antonyms.—Logical, true, real, genuine.

Fame, report, rumor, hearsay. Fame serves to form or establish a reputation either of a person or of a thing; it will be good or bad, according to circumstances,—the fame of our Savior's miracles went abroad through the land. A report serves to communicate information of events; it may be more or less correct according to the veracity or authenticity of the reporter. A rumor serves the purposes of fiction; it is more or less vague according to the temper of the times and the nature of the events. The hearsay is an indefinite report, passed from mouth to mouth, its origin quickly lost.

Famous, celebrated, renowned, illustrious. Famous signifies being of conspicuous note. It is applicable to that which causes a noise or sensation, to that which is talked of, written upon, discussed, and thought of, or to that which is circulated among all ranks and orders of men. Celebrated signifies kept in the memory by a celebration or memorial and is applicable to that which is praised and honored with solemnity. Renown means named again or repeatedly and signifies wide and exalted fame. Illustrious implies conspicuous nobility or worth.
Antonyms.—Unknown, obscure, commonplace, humble.

Fanciful, whimsical, capricious, fantastic. A fanciful tale, although a product of the imagination, may have consistency and may give a momentary impression of plausi-

bility. A fantastic account of something is so exaggerated or so far from reality as to be beyond belief. Whimsical implies quaint turns of fancy or imagination indulged in by a person who is recognized as eccentric. A capricious person displays sudden, unreasonable changes of mind or temper.
Antonyms.—Logical, realistic, serious, regular.

Fancy, imagination. The fancy forms combinations, either real or unreal, as chance may direct; but the imagination is less often led astray. The fancy is busy in dreams, or when the mind is in a disordered state; but the imagination is supposed to act when the intellectual powers are in full play.

Fatigue, weariness, lassitude. Fatigue is an exhaustion of the animal or mental powers; weariness is a wearing out of the strength, or a breaking of the spirits; lassitude is a general relaxation of the animal frame.
Antonyms.—Freshness, strength, endurance, elasticity.

Fearful, dreadful, frightful, tremendous, terrible, terrific, horrible, horrid. A contest is fearful when the issue is important, but the event doubtful; the thought of death is dreadful to one who feels himself unprepared. The frightful is less than the tremendous; the tremendous, less than the terrible; the terrible, less than the horrible. Shrieks may be frightful; thunder and lightning may be tremendous; the roaring of a lion is terrible; the glare of his eye terrific; the actual spectacle of killing is horrible or horrid. We may speak of a frightful, dreadful, terrible, or horrid dream, or of dreadful or terrible consequences.
Antonyms.—Pleasant, agreeable, inspiriting, encouraging.

Feel, be sensible, conscious. Feel is generally an indefinite word for a function of the senses and the emotions. Sensible has a more definite use in both cases, always with reference to some object, as to be sensible of light or of error, or of a friend's sympathy. One is aware of external things; conscious refers to the working of the mind in respect to either inner or outer purposes. The expression "conscious of a fault" may refer to the intellectual grasp of it; "sensible of a fault," to the emotion aroused by it.
Antonyms.—(Be) apathetic, indifferent, insensible.

Feign, pretend, simulate. Pretend, or pretend to, is the general word for assuming a false appearance or character. Feign implies more careful invention; simulate, more specific representation of resemblance. One pretends to be occupied; he feigns illness; but he simulates the action of a lunatic. Feign and simulate are very close synonyms.
Antonyms.—(Be) frank, sincere, open, ingenuous.

Felicitate, congratulate. Felicitate is the more formal term; congratulate, the more hearty word. Properly, we congratulate others only; we may felicitate others or ourselves.

Female, feminine, effeminate. Female applies to animal and human species. Feminine connotes the qualities and characteristics peculiar to woman. Effeminate implies reproach for men marked by weak or womanish qualities.
Antonyms.—Male, masculine, mannish, manly.

Ferocious, fierce, savage. All these imply predominance of brute passion. Ferocious signifies a settled, bloodthirsty cruelty or the appearance of it. Fierce connotes blazing, angry temper or sometimes simply an intense purpose or determination. Savage, whether applied to nature, animals, or men, signifies a disposition or character untamed, heartless, of a natural cruelty.
Antonyms.—Gentle, mild, tame, civilized.

Fervent, ardent. Fervent implies warmth of feeling, earnestness. Ardent connotes keen passion, burning enthusiasm in a cause or in pursuit of a purpose. We may speak of fervent prayers and ardent lovers.
Antonyms.—Cold, dispassionate, sluggish, phlegmatic.

Final, conclusive. Final designates simply the circumstance of being the last. Conclusive implies fitness to be final because of being convincing. Final proof may be the last introduced in a discussion; conclusive proof shuts off further argument. If the reasoning is conclusive the conclusion will be final.
Antonyms.—Temporary, tentative, partial, inconclusive.

Find, discover, invent. Find is the general word for coming to know or bringing to knowledge what was not known before. We discover the things not before known to exist; we invent combinations or processes. Iron was discovered; processes for making steel were invented. The principles of flying were discovered; the airplane was invented.
Antonyms.—Imitate, copy, reproduce.

Fine, delicate, nice. Fine, in the natural sense, denotes smallness in general. Delicate denotes a degree of fineness that is agreeable to the taste. Thread is said to be fine; silk is said to be delicate, when to fineness of texture it adds softness. Nice is said of what is agreeable to a discriminating taste and judgment.
Antonyms.—Coarse, crude, uncouth, unrefined.

Finite, limited. Finite is the natural property of things; limited is the artificial property. The former is opposite only to the infinite; but the latter, which lies within the finite, is opposed to the unlimited or the infinite. This world is finite and space infinite; one's powers or resources are limited.
Antonyms.—Infinite, illimitable, boundless.

Firm, fixed, solid, stable. Firm implies steadiness. Fixed denotes the state of being secure; solid implies power of resisting deforming forces; stable implies ability to maintain a constant position. That is firm which is not easily shaken; that is fixed which is fastened to something else, and not easily torn away; that is solid which is able to bear and does not easily give way; that is stable which is able to make a stand against resistance or the effects of time.
Antonyms.—Insecure, unstable, shaky, loose.

Fit, apt. A house is fit for the accommodation of the family, according to the plan of the builder; the young mind is apt to receive either good or bad impressions.
Antonyms.—Ill-adapted, inappropriate, unsuitable.

Flattery, compliment, praise. Flattery refers to insincere praise which plays upon a person's vanity, usually with an ulterior motive on the part of the flatterer. Compliment may be either sincere or insincere praise, but in any case it arises from some specific occasion and does not suggest deliberate, far-reaching design. Praise is a natural and usually disinterested expression of appreciation. It rests on proven merit.
Antonyms.—Detraction, censure, disparagement.

Flexible, pliable, pliant, supple, limber. Flexible implies ease of bending or of being changed in shape—figuratively, susceptible to external impression. Pliable suggests ease of bending, folding, or working (as with the hands). Pliant implies more distinctly an inherent quality of easy bending to meet resistance. Figuratively, pliable suggests readiness for control (especially by evil influence); pliant suggests a temper of easy complaisance or accommodation. Supple implies freedom of easy movement. Limber applies to flexible material objects.
Antonyms.—Rigid, stiff, cross-grained, unyielding, stubborn, unbending, intractable.

Fluctuate, waver. To fluctuate conveys the idea of alternate movement; to waver, that of constant motion backward and forward. When applied in the moral sense, to fluctuate designates the action of the spirits or the opinions; to waver is said of the will or purpose.
Antonyms.—Stand, (be) firm, determined, resolute.

Follow, pursue. The idea of going after any object in order to reach or obtain it is common to these terms, but under different circumstances: to follow a person implies usually a friendly intention; to pursue, a hostile intention.
Antonyms.—Lead, go ahead of, flee from.

Follow, succeed, ensue. Follow and succeed are used of persons and things; ensue, of things only. Follow, in respect of persons, denotes going in order; succeed denotes going or being in the same place immediately after another. Many persons may follow one another at the same time, but only one individual properly succeeds another. Ensue is used in specific cases,—quarrels too often ensue from the conversations of violent men who differ either in religion or politics.
Antonyms.—Lead, precede, occasion.

Folly, foolery. Folly is the general word for inconsiderate, foolish conduct, especially when leading to easily foreseen disaster. Foolery implies absurd, nonsensical, though frequently amusing, performances.
Antonyms.—Sense, sobriety, prudence, judgment.

Fool, idiot, buffoon. Fool, as commonly used, signifies one who acts or talks senselessly, or one who uses no judgment. Buffoon—a word, like fool, connected in origin with wind, windbag—signifies a state fool or clown. Idiot implies lack of reasoning powers; imbecile, meaning weak-minded, is the proper synonym for this word.

Foolhardy, adventurous, rash. The foolhardy man ventures in defiance of consequences; the adventurous man ventures from a love of the arduous and the bold; the rash man ventures for want of thought.
Antonyms.—Calculating, hesitating, cautious, careful.

Force, violence. The arm of justice must exercise force in order to bring offenders to a proper account; one nation exercises violence against another in the act of carrying on war. Force is mostly conformable to reason and equity; violence is always resorted to for the attainment of that which is unattainable by law. Force is often something desirable; violence is always something hurtful. We ought to listen to arguments which have force in them; we endeavor to correct the violence of all angry passions.
Antonyms.—Indulgence, clemency, gentleness, kindness.

Foretell, predict, prophesy, prognosticate. Foretell frequently implies some occult powers; predict generally implies reasonable inference from facts, though the words are used loosely to mean merely "tell before." Prophesy implies inspiration or great assurance on the part of the speaker that his predictions are true. Prognosticate means to predict from observation of symptoms, as a physician prognosticates. The word is sometimes used humorously for predict.

Forgetfulness, oblivion. Forgetfulness characterizes the person or that which is personal; oblivion, the state of the thing. The former refers to him who forgets; the latter to that which is forgotten.
Antonyms.—Remembrance, memory, recollection.

Forgive, pardon, absolve, remit. Individuals forgive each other personal offenses; they pardon offenses against law and morals. The former is an act of Christian charity; the latter, an act of clemency. To remit is to refrain from inflicting—it has more particular regard to the punishment. Remission is granted by an authority—it arrests the execution of justice. To absolve is to free from penalty either by the civil judge or the ecclesiastical minister—it re-establishes the accused in the rights of innocence.
Antonyms.—Condemn, convict, punish, inflict.

Form, ceremony, rite, observance. Form respects all determinate modes of acting and speaking, adopted by society at large, in every transaction of life; ceremony respects those forms of outward behavior which are made the expressions of respect and deference; rite and observance are applied to ceremonies, especially those of religion.

Form, fashion, mold, shape. Form conveys the idea of producing. When we wish to represent a thing as formed in any distinct or remarkable way, we may speak of it as fashioned. God formed man out of the dust of the ground; he fashioned him after his own image. When we wish to represent a thing as formed according to a precise rule, we should say it is molded. Thus the habits of a man are molded at the will of a superior. When we wish to represent a thing as receiving the qualities which distinguish it from others, we talk of shaping it.
Antonyms.—Break, destroy, demolish, mutilate.

Formidable, dreadful, terrible, shocking. The formidable acts neither suddenly nor violently; the dreadful may act violently but not suddenly. Thus the appearance of an army may be formidable, but that of a field of battle is dreadful. The terrible and the shocking act both suddenly and violently, but the former acts both on the senses and the imagination, the latter on the moral feelings. Thus the glare of the tiger's eye is terrible; the unexpected news of a friend's death is shocking.
Antonyms.—Weak, trivial, commonplace, insignificant.

Forsaken, forlorn, destitute. To be forsaken is to be deprived of the company and the assistance of those we have looked to; to be forlorn is to be lost—to be without a guide in an unknown road; to be destitute is to be deprived of the first necessaries of life.
Antonyms.—Protected, cherished, cared for, supported, supplied.

Forswear, perjure, suborn. To forswear is applied to all kinds of oaths; to perjure is employed only for such oaths as have been administered by the civil magistrate. A soldier forswears himself who breaks his oath of allegiance by desertion; a man perjures himself in a court of law who swears to the truth of that which he knows to be false. Suborn signifies to make to forswear. A perjured man has all the guilt upon himself; but he who is suborned shares his guilt with the suborner.

Foster, cherish, harbor, indulge. These terms are all employed here in the moral acceptation, to express the idea of giving nourishment to an object. To foster in the mind is to keep with care and positive endeavors, as when one fosters prejudices by encouraging everything which favors them; to cherish in the mind is to hold dear or set a value upon, as when one cherishes good sentiments by dwelling upon them with inward satisfaction. To harbor is to allow room in the mind, and it is generally taken in the worst sense of giving admission to that which ought to be excluded, as when one harbors resentment by permitting it to have a resting place in the heart. To indulge in the mind is to give the whole mind to it, to make it the chief source of pleasure, as when one indulges an affection by making the will and the outward conduct bend to its gratifications.
Antonyms.—Cast off, reject, refrain from, abjure, forswear.

Foundation, ground, basis. A report is said to be without any foundation when it has taken its rise in mere conjecture or in some arbitrary cause independent of all fact. A man's suspicion is said to be without ground when not supported by external evidence. Foundation and base are the lowest parts of a structure; but the former lies underground, the latter stands above. Basis is used now only in the figurative sense. Rumor which has no basis in fact may be called baseless fabrication.

Fragile, frail, brittle. That is fragile which, like a flower or a vase, is easily broken or destroyed; brittle implies liability to crack or shatter, as an eggshell. Frail is close to fragile in meaning, but it is applied to weak physical or mental natures. The human body is frail or a person's virtue shows frailty.
Antonyms.—Tough, strong, firm, unbreakable.

Frank, candid, ingenuous, free, open, plain. The frank man is under no constraint; his thoughts and feelings are both set at ease, and his lips are ever ready to give utterance to the dictates of his heart. The candid man has nothing to conceal; he speaks without regard to self-interest or to any like consideration—he speaks only the truth. The ingenuous man throws off all disguise; he scorns all artifice and brings everything to light—he speaks the whole truth. Free, open, and plain have not so high an office as the first three. Frank, free, and open men all speak without constraint, but the frank man is not impertinent nor indiscreet. The plain man speaks plainly but truly—he gives no false coloring to his speech.
Antonyms.—Insincere, disingenuous, close, reserved, shuffling.

Free, exempt, immune. Free describes the negative condition of absence from restraint or obligation. One who is exempt is relieved from the necessity of meeting common legal requirements, such as taxes or jury duty or military service. Immunity indicates a privileged situation with regard to small obligations, or it may mean a condition in which one is no longer susceptible to disease.
Antonyms.—Bound, restricted, liable.

Free, familiar. To be free is to be disengaged from the constraints which the ceremonies of social intercourse impose; to be familiar is to be upon the footing of a friend or a relative or of one of the same family.
Antonyms.—Restrained, reserved, distant.

Free, liberal. To be free signifies to act or think at will; to be liberal is to act according to the dictates of a large heart and an enlightened mind.
Antonyms.—Narrow, constrained, conservative.

Frequent, resort to, haunt. Frequent is generally used only of resorting often or repeatedly to a place and applies either to one person or to several together. Resort implies the gathering of a number of people in a place. Haunt implies frequenting continually or pertinaciously when unwelcome. He haunted the neighborhood or the memory haunts him.

Frighten, intimidate. Danger immediately present or evident to the senses frightens; danger distant but apprehended intimidates.
Antonyms.—Attract, encourage, stimulate.

Gape, stare, gaze. Gape and stare are taken in an ill sense. The former indicates the astonishment of gross ignorance; the latter, not only ignorance but impertinence. Gaze is taken in a good sense, as indicating a feeling of astonishment, pleasure, or curiosity.

Gather, collect. To gather signifies to bring things of a kind together; to collect annexes also the idea of binding or forming into a whole. We gather that which is scattered in different parts, as stones are gathered into a heap; vessels are collected so as to form a fleet.
Antonyms.—Scatter, disperse, separate.

General, universal, common. General refers to characteristics, actions or practices associated with all members of a group. Universal goes farther and admits of no exceptions. Common is a milder word describing shared characteristics or usual actions.
Antonyms.—Particular, specific, individual.

Genteel, polite. Gentility respects rank in life; politeness, the refinement of the mind and outward behavior. Genteel indicates now a pretension of superiority. All decent, intelligent people are polite; a decayed gentleman may be genteel.
Antonyms.—Common, uncouth, unpolished.

Gentle, tame. Gentle implies quietness, kindness; tame implies obedience and willingness, often with some lack of spirit.
Antonyms.—Fierce, wild, spirited.

Gift, present, donation. The gift is an act of generosity or condescension—it contributes to the benefit of the receiver. The present is an act of kindness, courtesy, or respect—it contributes to the pleasure of the receiver. The gift is private and benefits the individual; the donation is public and serves some general purpose. What is given to relieve the necessities of any poor person is a gift; what is given to support an institution is a donation.

Give, grant, bestow, present, award. To give is to transmit something one has to someone else. The gift, or thing transmitted, is for the benefit or use of the recipient. One grants a favor or a pardon or a sum of money intended for a specific use. A grant may be made by a person to a subordinate or by an organization to an individual. Bestow suggests the settling of something having considerable value upon a designated recipient. To present something is to transmit it usually as a token of esteem or good wishes. Presents pass between individuals. An award is made to a person or group by judges or some other authority in recognition of merit.
Antonyms.—Withhold, refuse, deny.

Give up, abandon, resign, forego. To give up is applied to familiar cases; abandon, to matters of importance. One gives up an idea, an intention, a plan, and the like; one abandons a project, a scheme, a measure of government. A man gives up his situation by a positive act of his choice; he resigns his office when he feels it inconvenient to hold it. So, likewise, we give up expectations and resign hopes; we resign that which we have, and we forego that which we might have.
Antonyms.—Hold fast, guard, retain, enjoy, seize

Glaring, barefaced. Glaring designates the thing; barefaced characterizes the person. A glaring falsehood is that which strikes the observer in an instant as a falsehood; a barefaced lie or falsehood betrays the effrontery of him who utters it.

Glimpse, glance. Glimpse is a casual or fleeting view determined by the position or movement of the object or the observer; a glance is a hasty look, determined by the eye alone. From a moving car one, glancing at the landscape, catches glimpses of trees.

Glory, boast, vaunt. To glory is to exult or to rejoice; to boast is to set forth to one's advantage; to vaunt is to set oneself up before others. To glory is more particularly the act of the mind, the indulgence of the internal sentiment; to boast denotes rather the expression of the sentiment; to vaunt is properly to proclaim praises aloud and is taken either in an indifferent or in a bad sense.

Glory, honor. Glory is something dazzling and widely diffused; honor is something less splendid but more solid. Glory impels to extraordinary efforts and to great undertakings; honor induces to a discharge of one's duty.
Antonyms.—Shame, discredit, disgrace.

Godlike, divine, heavenly. Godlike is a more expressive but less common term than divine. The former is used only as an epithet of peculiar praise for an individual; divine is generally employed for that which appertains to a superior being, in distinction from that which is human. A heavenly being denotes an angel or inhabitant of heaven, in distinction from earthly beings.
Antonyms.—Human, earthly.

Good nature, good humor. Good nature and good humor both imply the disposition to please and be pleased, but the former is habitual and permanent while the latter is temporary and partial. The former lies in the nature and frame of the mind, the latter in the state of the spirits.
Antonyms.—Ill nature, ill humor, sullenness, petulance.

Govern, rule, regulate. The exercise of authority enters more or less into the signification of these terms, but to govern implies the exercise likewise of judgment and knowledge. To rule implies rather the unqualified exercise of power, the making the will the rule. A king governs his people by means of wise laws and an upright administration; a despot rules over a nation according to his arbitrary decision. To regulate is to govern or control simply by judgment; the word is applicable to things of minor moment, where the force of authority is not so requisite. One governs the affairs of a nation or a large body where great interests are involved; one regulates the concerns of an individual.

Government, administration. Both these terms may be employed to designate either the act of governing and administering or the persons governing and administering. In both cases government has a more extensive meaning than administration. The former includes every exercise of authority; administration implies only that exercise of authority which consists in putting the laws or the will of another in force. When we speak of the government, as it respects the persons, it implies the whole body of constituted authorities; but the administration implies only that part which puts in execution the intentions of the whole.

Grace, charm, elegance. Grace is altogether physical; charm is either physical or mental. Grace qualifies the action of the body; charm is an inherent quality in the person. A lady moves, dances, and walks with grace; the charms of her person are equal to those of her mind. A graceful figure is rendered so by the deportment of the body. A comely figure has that in itself which pleases the eye. Grace is a quality pleasing to the eye, but elegance is a quality of a higher nature and inspires admiration. Elegance implies niceties and polish of manner. All these words are extended in meaning, figuratively, to language and dress.

Gratify, indulge, humor. To gratify is a positive act of the choice; to indulge is a negative act of the will, a yielding of the mind to circumstances. One gratifies his desires or appetites; he indulges his humors or indulges in pleasures. We gratify and indulge others as well as ourselves, and mostly in the good sense. To gratify, when directed toward others, is an act of generosity. To indulge is to yield to the wishes or to be lenient to the infirmities of others—it is an act of kindness or good nature. To humor is taken mostly in an unfavorable sense, bordering on placate or appease.
Antonyms.—Restrict, mortify, discipline, restrain.

Gratuitous, voluntary. Gratuitous implies a giving or conferring beyond what is required; voluntary connotes free, willing, uncompelled action.
Antonyms.—Obligatory, compulsory, necessary, demanded.

Grave, serious, solemn. Grave expresses more than serious. It bespeaks not merely the absence of mirth, but that heaviness of mind which is displayed in all the movements of the body. Serious, on the other hand, bespeaks no depression but simply steadiness of action and a refraining from all that is jocular. A judge pronounces the solemn sentence of condemnation in a solemn manner; a preacher delivers many solemn warnings to his hearers.
Antonyms.—Light, cheery, frivolous, gay.

Great, grand, sublime. These terms are synonymous only in their moral application. Great simply designates extent; grand includes likewise the idea of excellence and superiority. A great undertaking characterizes only the extent of the undertaking; a grand undertaking bespeaks its superior excellence. A scene may be either grand or sublime. It is grand as it fills the imagination with its immensity; it is sublime as it elevates the imagination beyond the surrounding and less important objects.
Antonyms.—Mean, petty, unimpressive, ordinary.

Great, large, big. Great applies to all sorts of dimensions by which things are measured; large usually refers to magnitude, bulk, or scope. Big denotes great as to expansion or capacity. Great suggests the impression on the speaker, and is used more often of abstract ideas. Large suggests absolute size, and is used mostly of things. Big is in loose colloquial use for all these meanings of great and large.
Antonyms.—Little, small, diminutive, inconsiderable.

Groan, moan. Groan is a deep sound produced by hard breathing; moan is a plaintive, long-drawn sound produced by the organs of utterance. The groan proceeds involuntarily as an expression of severe pain, either of body or mind; the moan proceeds often from the desire of awakening attention or exciting compassion.

Gross, coarse. These terms are synonymous in their moral application. A person becomes gross by an unrestrained indulgence of his sensual appetites, particularly in eating and drinking; he is coarse from the want of polish either as to his mind or manners.
Antonyms.—Refined, polished, delicate, elegant.

Guard, defend, watch. To guard, in its largest sense, comprehends both watching and defending, that is, both preventing the attack and resisting it when it is made. In the restricted sense, to guard is properly to keep off an enemy; to defend is to drive him away when he makes the attack. Watch, like guard, consists in looking to the danger, but it does not necessarily imply the use of any means to prevent the danger—he who watches gives an alarm.

Guess, conjecture, surmise. We guess when we have no means or facts from which to reason. Conjecture is to conclude upon incomplete evidence. Surmise implies still slighter foundation for opinion.
Antonyms.—Reason, calculate, compute, conclude.

Guest, visitor, or visitant. Guest signifies one who is entertained; visitor or visitant is the one who pays the visit. The visitor simply comes to see the person, but the guest partakes also of hospitality. Visitant implies a visitor from outside one's sphere or usual environment, as a supernatural visitant.

Guise, habit. The guise is that which is unusual and often only occasional; the habit is that which is usual among particular classes. A person sometimes assumes the guise of a peasant, in order the better to conceal himself; he who devotes himself to the clerical profession puts on the habit of a clergyman.

Habitation, home, house, residence. Habitation implies merely a dwelling place; house refers to a building constructed purposely for dwelling. Home is usually restricted to mean a dwelling endeared as the scene of domestic ties and family life. Residence is a more formal term than house, though less exact.

Happen, chance. Happen applies to all events, without including any collateral idea; chance comprehends likewise the idea of lack of causation in events. Whatever comes to pass happens, whether regularly in the course of things or particularly and out of the order; whatever chances happens altogether without concert or intention and often without apparent relation to any other thing.

Happy, fortunate. Both words are applied to the external circumstances of a man. The former conveys the idea of that which is abstractly good; the latter implies rather what is agreeable to one's wishes. A man is happy in his marriage; he is fortunate in his trading concerns. Happy excludes the idea of chance; fortunate excludes the idea of personal effort.
Antonyms.—Unlucky, unsuccessful, infelicitous.

Harbor, haven, port. The idea of a resting place for vessels is common to these terms. Harbor carries with it little more than the common idea of affording a resting or anchoring place; haven conveys the idea of security; port conveys the idea of an enclosure. A haven is a natural harbor; a port is an artificial harbor.

Hard, firm, solid. That is hard which will not yield to a closer compression; that is firm which will not yield so as to produce a separation. Ice is hard, so far as respects itself, when it resists every pressure; it is firm, with regard to the water which it covers, when it is so closely bound as to resist every weight without breaking. Hard and solid respect the internal constitution of bodies and the adherence of the component parts, but hard denotes a much closer degree of adherence than solid.
Antonyms.—Soft, yielding, fluid.

Hasten, hurry, speed, expedite, dispatch. To hasten expresses little more than the general idea of quickness in moving toward a point; he hastens who runs to get to the end of his journey. Hurry implies planless and restless or perturbed haste. The word speed includes not only quick but forward movement. He who speeds goes effectually forward and comes to his journey's end the soonest. This idea is excluded from the term haste, which may often be a planless, unsuitable quickness. Hence the proverb, "The more haste, the worse speed." Expedite and dispatch are terms of higher import, in application to the most serious concerns in life. Expedite expresses a process, a bringing forward toward an end; dispatch implies a putting an end to, making a clearance. We do everything in our power to expedite a business; we dispatch a great deal of business within a given time.
Antonyms.—Impede, retard, clog, check.

Hateful, odious. Hateful is properly applied to whatever violates general principles of morality: lying and swearing are hateful vices. Odious is more commonly applied to such things or persons as excite especial repugnance by their nature or conduct.
Antonyms.—Pleasing, attractive, desirable.

Hatred, enmity, antipathy. Hatred refers to intense personal dislike; it is therefore stronger than the abstract term hate. Enmity is a strong feeling of ill will. Antipathy is aversion on a temperamental basis; it is felt, rather than explained.
Antonyms.—Love, amity, friendship, attraction.

Haughtiness, disdain, arrogance. Haughtiness is founded on the high opinion we entertain of ourselves; disdain, on the low opinion we have of others; arrogance is the result of both, but, if anything, more of the former than of the latter. Haughtiness and disdain are properly sentiments of the mind; arrogance, a mode of acting resulting from a state of mind.
Antonyms.—Modesty, respectfulness, consideration, courtesy.

Have, possess. One may be said to have what is in one's hand or within one's reach, but to possess is to have as one's own. A clerk has the money which he has fetched for his employer; the latter possesses the money which he has the power of turning to his use.

Healthful, wholesome, salubrious, salutary. Healthful is applied to exercise, to air, situation, climate, and most other things except food, to which wholesome is commonly applied. The life of a farmer is reckoned the most healthful; the simplest diet is the most wholesome. Healthful and wholesome are rather negative in their sense; salubrious and salutary are positive. That is healthful and wholesome which does no injury to the health; that is salubrious which serves to improve the health; that is salutary which serves to remove a disorder.
Antonyms.—Hurtful, deleterious, unwholesome.

Heap, pile, accumulate. To heap is to bring together numerous objects, placing them loosely in a moundlike mass. Pile suggests a more careful placing of the objects gathered, with one unit laid on top of another. Accumulate is a more general word used to describe the collecting of things and the gradual growth of their number.

Hearty, warm, sincere, cordial. There are cases in which it may be peculiarly proper to be hearty, as when we are supporting the cause of religion and of virtue; there are other cases in which it is peculiarly proper to be warm, as when our affections ought to be roused in favor of our friends. In all cases we ought to be sincere when we express either a sentiment or a feeling; it is peculiarly happy to be on terms of cordial regard with those who stand in any close relation to us. The man himself should be hearty; his heart should be warm; professions should be sincere; a reception, cordial.
Antonyms.—Formal, cold, insincere, indifferent.

Heed, care, attention. Heed applies to matters of importance to one's moral conduct; care, to matters of minor import. A man is required to take heed; a child is required to take care. The former exercises his understanding in taking heed; the latter exercises his thoughts and his senses in taking care. We speak of giving heed and paying attention. Heed is applied only to that which is conveyed to us by another, in the shape of a direction, a caution, or an instruction; the latter is said of everything which we keep within our notice.
Antonyms.—Heedlessness, carelessness, oversight, neglect, rashness.

Help, aid, assist. In everyday usage, help is the common word and assist is a genteelism which says the same thing. In natural, informal style we ask, "May I help you?" instead of using the more formal expression, "May I assist you?" However, in its more legitimate use, assist adds the idea of standing by, recalling something of its original French meaning of being present. Aid suggests response to a need; in this way it is specialized within the general meaning of the inclusive word help.
Antonyms.—Oppose, hinder, obstruct.

Hesitate, falter, stammer, stutter. A person who is not in the habit of public speaking or of collecting his thoughts into a set form will be apt to hesitate even in familiar conversation; he who first addresses a public assembly will be apt to falter. Children who first begin to read will stammer at hard words; one who has an impediment in his speech will stutter when he attempts to speak in a hurry.

Heterodoxy, heresy. Heterodoxy means a belief different from an accepted doctrine; heresy usually implies pernicious erroneous doctrine. But one who has heterodox opinions is a heretic.
Antonyms.—Orthodoxy, conformity.

High, tall, lofty. High is the general word meaning elevated above some point of reference; for example, a high mountain towers above a plain. Tall, the opposite of short, suggests the unusual height of something as compared with others of its class; for example, a tall tree or a tall man. Lofty is a more poetic term implying elevated in sentiment or in a moral sense.

Antonyms.—Low, short, base.

Hinder, stop. To hinder is to interfere with the progress of a person or a thing; to stop implies entire, and usually sudden, cessation of motion.

Antonyms.—Further, promote, advance.

Hold, keep, detain, retain. To hold is a physical act and requires a degree of bodily strength, or at least the use of the limbs; to keep is simply to have by one at one's pleasure. Detain and retain are modes of keeping. The former signifies keeping back what belongs to another; the latter signifies keeping a long time for one's own purpose.

Antonyms.—Give up, surrender, return, restore.

Hold, occupy, possess. We hold a thing for a long or a short time; we occupy it permanently; we hold it for ourselves or others; we occupy it only for ourselves. We hold it for various purposes; we occupy only for the purpose of converting it to our private use. To occupy is to hold only under a certain compact; to possess is to hold as one's own.

Holiness, sanctity. Holiness implies inherent qualities of piety and godliness; sanctity is a character given or conferred upon persons or places because of relation to holy men or things. A priest should be holy; there is an air of sanctity about a church.

Antonyms.—Profaneness, impiety.

Hollow, empty. That is hollow which has an empty space, or cavity, as a hollow tree. That which has nothing in it is empty, as an empty chair.

Antonyms.—Solid, full.

Holy, sacred, divine. Whatever is most intimately connected with religion and with religious worship, in its purest state, is holy, uncontaminated by any worldly thought, and elevated in the greatest possible degree, so as to suit the nature of an infinitely perfect and exalted Being. The sacred derives its sanction from human institutions, and is connected rather with our moral than our religious duties. What is holy is altogether spiritual and abstracted from the earthly. The divine is often contrasted with the human, but there are many human things that are denominated divine. What is divine, therefore, may be so superlatively excellent as to be conceived of as having the stamp of inspiration from the Deity.

Antonyms.—Human, profane, secular.

Honor, reverence, respect. To honor is only an outward act; to reverence either is an act of the mind or is the outward expression of a sentiment; to respect is mostly an act of the mind, though it may admit of being expressed by some outward act. We honor God by adoration and worship; we honor our parents by obeying them and giving them our personal service; we reverence our Maker by cherishing in our minds a dread of offending him; we respect a person or a thing that is lofty, worthy, or honorable.

Antonyms.—Scorn, contemn, despise, disdain.

Hot, fiery, burning, ardent. In the figurative application, a temper is said to be hot or fiery; rage is burning; the mind is ardent in pursuit of an object. Zeal may be hot, fiery, burning, or ardent; but in the first three cases it denotes the intemperance of the mind when heated by religion or politics. Ardent is admissible so long as it is confined to a good object.

Antonyms.—Cool, calm, stolid, dispassionate.

Human, humane. The human race or human beings are opposed to the irrational part of the creation; a humane race or a humane individual is opposed to one that is cruel and fond of inflicting pain.

Antonyms.—Animal, divine, beastly, inhuman, cruel.

Humble, modest, submissive. A man is humble from a sense of his comparative inferiority to others in point of station and outward circumstances; he is humble from a sense of his imperfections, and a consciousness of not being what he ought to be. He is modest, inasmuch as he sets but little value on his qualifications, acquirements, and endowments. Between humble and submissive there is this prominent feature of distinction,—that the former marks a temper of mind, the latter a mode of action. We may be submissive because we are humble; but we may likewise be submissive from fear, from interested motives.

Antonyms.—Haughty, arrogant, vain, conceited, obstinate.

Humor, temper, mood. Humor is fluctuating, so that it varies continually in the same mind; temper is a more permanent quality, showing itself to be the same whenever it appears at all. Humor makes a man appear different at different times; temper makes him different from others.

Hence we speak of the humor of the moment, the temper of youth or old age. Humor and mood denote temporary states of feeling, but mood is of a rather more pervasive, controlling nature than humor, which seems more capricious. There is no calculating on the humor of the man; it depends upon his mood whether he does work ill or well.

Hurtful, pernicious, noxious, noisome. Between hurtful and pernicious there is the same distinction as between hurting and destroying: that which is hurtful may hurt in various ways; but that which is pernicious necessarily tends to destruction. Confinement is hurtful to the health; bad company is pernicious to the morals. Noxious and noisome are forms of the hurtful. That which is noxious inflicts a direct injury; that which is noisome inflicts it indirectly. Noxious insects are such as wound; noisome vapors are such as tend to create disorders.

Antonyms.—Healthful, wholesome, salutary, salubrious.

Ideal, imaginary. The ideal improves upon the real by selecting merits and eliminating defects; hence, the definition, "Art is idealized imitation of nature." The imaginary departs freely from reality. An ideal commonwealth, or Utopia, is developed from known principles of government and thus bears a certain relationship to actual states, however much it may improve upon them. The fanciful description of a country governed wisely by horses, in *Gulliver's Travels*, is created by the imagination working with complete abandon. Invention, whether mechanical or literary, can utilize imaginary concepts to excellent advantage.

Antonyms.—Real, actual, practical.

Idle, lazy, indolent. One is termed idle who will do nothing useful; one is lazy who will do nothing at all without great reluctance; one is indolent who does not care to do anything or undertake anything.

Antonyms.—Busy, industrious, energetic, active.

Illuminate, illumine, enlighten. We illuminate by means of artificial lights; the sun illuminates the world by its own light. Preaching and instruction enlighten the minds of men. Illumine is but a poetic variation of illuminate. Figuratively, we speak of an illuminating remark. Illuminating examples are an aid to understanding principles.

Antonyms.—Darken, shadow, obscure, cloud.

Imminent, impending. Both terms are used in regard to some evil that is exceedingly near. Imminent conveys no idea of duration; impending excludes the idea of what is momentary. A person may be in imminent danger of losing his life in one instant, and the danger may be over the next instant; but an impending danger is that which has been long in existence and gradually approaching.

Antonyms.—Doubtful, unexpected, improbable, unheralded, unlikely.

Impair, injure. To impair is a progressive mode of injuring; to injure is to do harm either by degrees or by an instantaneous act. Straining of the eyes impairs the sight, but a blow injures rather than impairs the eye.

Antonyms.—Benefit, help, remedy, repair.

Imperious, lordly, domineering, overbearing. A person's temper and his tone is said to be imperious; his air or deportment is lordly; his tone is domineering. Overbearing is employed for men in the general relations of society, whether superiors or equals. A man of an imperious temper and some talent will frequently be so overbearing in the assemblies of his equals as to awe the rest into silence.

Antonyms.—Servile, submissive, humble, pliant.

Implicate, involve. Implicate denotes folding into a thing; involve, rolling into a thing. To implicate therefore marks something less entangled than to involve; for that which is folded may be folded only once, but that which is rolled is turned many times. In application to human affairs, therefore, people are said to be implicated who have taken ever so small a share in a transaction; they are involved only when they are deeply concerned. Implicate is now always used in an unfavorable sense. Involve may have this sense also, but is of more general use.

Antonyms.—Extricate, disentangle.

Impugn, attack. He who impugns may sometimes proceed insidiously to undermine the faith of others; he who attacks always proceeds directly with more or less violence.

Antonyms.—Defend, uphold, vindicate.

Inability, disability. Inability refers to weakness or powerlessness that is inherent and always has been present. Disability indicates that power formerly possessed has been lost, either temporarily or permanently.

Antonyms.—Ability, competence.

Inadvertency, inattention, oversight. Anyone may be guilty of inadvertency, since the mind that is occupied by several subjects may be concentrated so closely on one that another may escape notice. Inattention denotes a willful lack of attention. It is always a fault, or at least a discourtesy. Oversight, a species of inadvertency, is perhaps a more pardonable fault, since it suggests passing by something in haste, and usually in spite of good intentions.
Antonyms.—Attention, care, scrutiny.

Inclination, tendency, propensity, proneness. Inclination denotes a leaning in the direction of something or a first movement toward it. Tendency is a more settled and persistent form of inclination. It provides a more reliable basis for the prediction of someone's conduct. Propensity, which in its milder form may be no more than a flair or a predilection, is often an inherent tendency such as an appetite for drink or some other kind of craving. Proneness is something outside the will and is the result of circumstances difficult to explain, as when we say that a particular individual is "accident-prone."
Antonyms.—Aversion, repugnance.

Inconvenience, annoy, molest. To inconvenience anyone is to interfere with his plans, his movements, or his comfort. To annoy him is to impose a strain on his patience or equanimity. Molest indicates a serious and often malicious invasion of a person's rights or security.
Antonyms.—Accommodate, appease, gratify.

Increase, grow. Things that increase become larger or more numerous, either gradually or quickly. Grow implies a gradual increase brought about by an organic cause. A tree grows; the profit from a business increases.
Antonyms.—Decrease, diminish, shrink.

Indebted, obliged. Indebted is more binding and positive than obliged. We are indebted to whoever confers an essential service; we are obliged to him who does us any service. A man is indebted to another for the preservation of his life; he is obliged to him for an ordinary act of civility.

Indifferent, unconcerned, regardless. Indifferent applies only to the will; unconcerned, to either the will or the understanding; regardless, to the understanding only. We are indifferent about matters of minor consideration; we are unconcerned about, or regardless of, serious matters that have remote consequences. An author will seldom be indifferent about the success of his work; he ought not to be unconcerned about the influence which his writings may have on the public, or regardless of the estimation in which his own character as a man may be held.
Antonyms.—Heedful, anxious, careful, mindful, observant.

Indubitable, unquestionable, indisputable, undeniable, incontrovertible, irrefragable. When a fact is supported by such evidence as admits of no kind of doubt, it is termed indubitable; the authority of a man whose character for integrity stands unimpeached, is termed unquestionable authority; when a thing is believed to exist on the evidence of every man's senses, it is termed undeniable; when a sentiment has always been held as either true or false, without dispute, it is termed indisputable; when arguments have never been refuted in any degree, they are termed incontrovertible; when arguments have never been satisfactorily answered, they are termed irrefragable.
Antonyms.—Doubtful, questionable, uncertain, dubious.

Indulgent, fond. Indulgence lies more in forbearing from the exercise of authority; fondness, in the outward behavior and endearments. They may both arise from an excess of kindness or love. An indulgent parent is seldom a prudent parent; a fond parent is foolishly tender and loving.
Antonyms.—Strict, stern, exacting.

Infamous, scandalous. Infamous and scandalous are both said of that which is liable to excite great displeasure in the minds of all who hear it, and to degrade the offenders in the general estimation. But the infamous seems to be that which produces greater publicity and more general reprehension than the scandalous, consequently it is more serious in its nature and a greater violation of good morals.
Antonyms.—Honorable, respectable, creditable.

Inform, instruct, teach. To inform is the act of persons in all conditions; to instruct and teach are the acts of superiors, either on one ground or another. One informs by virtue of an accidental superiority or priority of knowledge; one instructs by virtue of superior knowledge or superior station; one teaches by virtue of superior knowledge rather than of station.
Antonyms.—Misinform, delude, mislead.

Ingenuity, wit. Ingenuity comprehends invention; wit in this sense implies only quickness of apprehension. He had the ingenuity to make good use of the opportunity if he had had the wit to see it.
Antonyms.—Dullness, slowness, stupidity.

Injustice, injury, wrong. Injustice is unfairness toward someone, as in an action or a judgment which violates his rights. Injury refers to more tangible damage, causing loss or pain to the victim. The word wrong reflects upon the doer and denotes a flagrant kind of injustice.
Antonyms.—Justice, right, benefit.

Inside, interior. The term inside may be applied to bodies of any magnitude, small or large; interior is peculiarly appropriate to bodies of great magnitude. We may speak of the inside of a nutshell but not of its interior. The interior of the church was beautifully decorated.
Antonyms.—Outside, exterior.

Insinuation, reflection. An insinuation always deals in half words; a reflection is commonly open. They are both leveled at the individual with no good intent. The insinuation is general and may be employed to convey any unfavorable sentiment; the reflection is particular and commonly passes between persons in close connection.

Insist, persist. Both these terms express the idea of resting or keeping to a thing; but insist signifies to rest on a point, and persist signifies to keep on with a thing, to carry it through. We insist on a matter by maintaining it; we persist in a thing by continuing to do it.
Antonyms.—Desist, yield, abandon, forego, cease.

Insolvency, failure, bankruptcy. Insolvency is a state; failure, an act flowing out of that state; bankruptcy, an effect of that act. Insolvency is a condition of not being able to pay one's debts; failure is a cessation of business, from the want of means to carry it on; bankruptcy is a legal surrender of all one's remaining goods into the hands of one's creditors, in consequence of a real or supposed insolvency.
Antonyms.—Solvency, soundness.

Instant, moment. A dutiful child comes the instant he is called; a prudent person embraces the favorable moment. When both words have respect to the present time, instant expresses a much shorter space than moment.

Insurrection, sedition, rebellion, revolt. There may be an insurrection against usurped power, which is always justifiable; but sedition and rebellion are leveled against power universally acknowledged to be legitimate. Insurrection is always open,—it is a rising up of many in a mass, but it does not imply any concerted, or any specifically active, measure. Rebellion is the consummation of sedition; the scheme of opposition which has been digested in secrecy breaks out into open hostilities and becomes rebellion. Revolt is mostly taken either in an indifferent or a good sense for resisting a foreign dominion which has been imposed by force of arms.
Antonyms.—Subjection, obedience, submission, acquiescence, allegiance.

Intellect, genius, talent. Intellect is the power or faculty of knowing, improved by cultivation and exercise,—in this sense we speak of a man of intellect, or of a work that displays great intellect. Genius is the particular bent of the intellect which is born with a man, as a genius for poetry, painting, or music. Talent is a particular mode of intellect which qualifies its possessor to do some things better than others, as a talent for learning languages, a talent for the stage, etc.

Interchange, reciprocity. Interchange is an act; reciprocity is an attitude as well as an act. By an interchange of sentiment, friendships are engendered; the reciprocity of good services is what renders them doubly acceptable to those who do them and to those who receive them.

Interest, concern. We have an interest in whatever touches or comes near to our feelings or our external circumstances; we have a concern in that which demands our attention. Interest may be slight or intense; concern implies a serious care about something.
Antonyms.—Indifference, apathy, unconcern, insensibility.

Interval, respite. The term interval respects time only; respite includes the idea of ceasing from action for a time. Intervals of ease are a respite to one who is oppressed with labor.

Intervention, interposition. The light of the moon is obstructed by the intervention of the clouds; the life of an individual is preserved by the interposition of a superior.

Intrude, obtrude. To intrude is to go into any society unasked and undesired; to obtrude is to put oneself in the way of another by joining the company and taking a part in the conversation without invitation or consent.
Antonyms.—Recede, withdraw, remove.

Invalid, patient. An invalid is so called because he lacks his ordinary share of health and strength; the patient is one who is laboring under some bodily suffering for which he is receiving care and treatment.

Invest, endue, or **endow.** One is invested with that which is external; one is endued with that which is internal. We invest a person with an office or a dignity; a person is endued with good qualities. Endow carries the sense of bestowing upon, supplying, or equipping. One may endow a college; a man is richly endowed with intellect or ability; but he is endued with piety or virtue.
Antonyms.—Divest, deprive, strip, dispossess.

Irrational, foolish, absurd, preposterous. Irrational is applicable more frequently to the thing than to the person, to the principle than to the practice. Foolish, on the contrary, is commonly applicable to the person as well as to the thing, to the practice rather than to the principle; absurd is applied to anything, however trivial, which in the smallest degree offends our understanding. The conduct of children is therefore often foolish, but not absurd and preposterous. It is absurd for a man to persuade another to do that which he in like circumstances would object to do himself; it is preposterous for a man to expose himself to the ridicule of others, and then be angry with those who will not treat him respectfully.
Antonyms.—Reasonable, rational, sensible, consistent.

Irreligious, profane, impious. All men who are not positively actuated by principles of religion are irreligious. Profanity and impiety are, however, of a heinous nature; they consist not in the mere absence of regard for religion, but in a positive contempt for it and open outrage against its laws. The profane man treats what is sacred as if it were profane. The impious man is directly opposed to the pious man. The former is filled with defiance and rebellion against his Maker; the latter is filled with love and fear.
Antonyms.—Religious, pious, God-fearing, reverent.

Jealousy, envy. We are jealous of what is our own; we are envious of what is another's. Jealousy fears to lose what it has; envy is pained at seeing others have that which it wants for itself.
Antonyms.—Friendliness, magnanimity, generosity, trust.

Journey, travel, voyage. Journey signifies the course that is taken in the space of a day or, in general, any comparatively short passage from one place to another. Travel signifies such a course or passage as requires labor and causes fatigue; in general, any long course. Voyage is now confined to passages by sea.

Joy, gladness, mirth. What creates joy and gladness is of a permanent nature; that which creates mirth is temporary. Joy is the most vivid sensation in the soul; gladness is the same in quality but inferior in degree. Joy is awakened in the mind by the most important events in life.
Antonyms.—Sorrow, sadness, distress, mourning.

Judgment, discretion, prudence. Judgment is conclusive,—it decides by positive inference, and it enables a person to discover the truth. Discretion is intuitive,—it discerns or perceives what is in all probability right. A person who exercises prudence does not inconsiderately expose himself to danger; a measure is prudent that guards against the chances of evil; the impetuosity of youth naturally impels to imprudence.
Antonyms.—Foolishness, recklessness, injudiciousness.

Justness, correctness. We estimate the value of remarks by their justness, that is, by their accordance with certain admitted principles. Correctness of outline is of the first importance in drawing; correctness of dates enhances the value of a history.
Antonyms.—Looseness, inexactness, inaccuracy, partiality.

Keep, preserve, save. The idea of having in one's possession is common to all these terms, which is, however, the simple meaning of keep. To preserve signifies to keep with care and free from all injury; to save is to keep laid up in a safe place and free from destruction.
Antonyms.—Lose, neglect, waste.

Keeping, custody. Keeping amounts to little more than having purposely in one's possession; but custody is a particular kind of keeping, for the purpose of preventing an escape. Inanimate objects may be in one's keeping; but a prisoner or that which is in danger of getting away is placed in custody.

Know, be acquainted with. We may know things or persons in various ways; we may know them by name only, or we may know their internal properties or characters. One is acquainted with either a person or a thing only in a direct manner, and by an immediate intercourse in one's own person.

Knowledge, science, learning, erudition. Knowledge is a general term which simply implies the thing known; science is the department of systematized knowledge; learning is that kind of knowledge which one derives from schools or through the medium of personal instruction; erudition is scholastic knowledge obtained by profound research.
Antonyms.—Illiteracy, ignorance, smattering.

Land, country. The term land, in its proper sense, excludes the idea of habitation; the term country excludes that of the earth or the parts of which it is composed. Hence we speak of the land as rich or poor according to what it yields; of a country as rich or poor according to what its inhabitants possess.

Large, big, great. Large refers to magnitude—to above-average size, capacity or number. Big implies particularly bulk. Great, formerly a close synonym with large, is now used more to signify importance and other abstract ideas.
Antonyms.—Small, diminutive, trivial.

Laudable, praiseworthy, commendable. Things are laudable in themselves; they are praiseworthy or commendable in this or that person. That which is laudable is entitled to encouragement and general approbation. An honest endeavor to be useful to one's family or oneself is at all times laudable. What is praiseworthy obtains the respect of all men.
Antonyms.—Censurable, reprehensible, blameworthy.

Lay or **take hold of, catch, seize, snatch.** To lay or take hold of is here the generic expression; it denotes simply getting into one's possession, which is the common idea in the signification of all these terms, which differ in regard to the motion in which the action is performed. To catch is to lay hold of with an effort; to seize is to lay hold of with violence; to snatch is to lay hold of by a sudden effort.
Antonyms.—Let go, let slip, miss, lose.

Lead, conduct, guide. One leads by helping a person onward in any manner, as to lead a child by the hand; conduct and guide are different modes of leading,—the former by virtue of one's office or authority, the latter by one's knowledge or power, as to conduct an army, to guide a traveler in an unknown country.

Lean, incline, bend. In the proper sense, lean and incline are both said of the position of bodies; bend is said of the shape of bodies. That which leans, rests on one side or in a sideward direction; that which inclines, turns only in a slight degree; that which bends, forms a curvature.
Antonyms.—Rise, be erect, straighten.

Leave, quit, relinquish. We leave that to which we may intend to return; we quit that to which we return no more; we relinquish something unwillingly. We leave persons or things; we quit and relinquish things only.
Antonyms.—Stay by, retain, keep, hold.

Lethargy, lassitude, languor, stupor. Lethargy, a general term for sluggishness, describes a state of inactivity that is usually temporary, the result of overeating or perhaps physical exertion. Lassitude, suggesting weariness caused by worry or strain, emphasizes listlessness, inertia of the mind or spirit. Languor indicates the sort of faintness that is associated with a delicate constitution or with soft living. Stupor suggests a condition approaching insensibility, the result of fatigue or possibly of narcotic poisoning. None of the foregoing synonyms would apply to a phlegmatic person, whose slowness of reaction is constitutional, characteristic, and entirely comfortable.
Antonyms.—Alertness, vigor, energy, sprightliness.

Liberal, generous, bountiful, munificent. A liberal person is open-handed in spending his money; a liberal offer goes beyond what might be expected. Anyone who is generous is warm-hearted and unselfish; he gives cheerfully to needy people and worthy causes. Bountiful implies lavish giving by a wealthy person. Munificent goes beyond bountiful and indicates a truly princely largess.
Antonyms.—Stingy, close-fisted, niggardly.

Liberal, progressive, radical. Like many other words that express shades of political opinion, liberal is a term of either praise or reproach, according to one's point of view.

In the sense of a disposition to accept new ideas and put them into practice, liberal, referring to attitude, is closely related to progressive, which refers chiefly to policies and actions. Both liberal and progressive are words likely to be used by people who wish to speak well of themselves. These are almost fighting words to their conservative opponents, whose favorite term of denunciation is the still stronger word radical. Having a literal meaning connected with root, radical suggests an extreme departure from accepted ideas, leading to a "root-and-branch" destruction of the present system.

Antonyms.—Conservative, moderate, tory.

Lift, heave, hoist. We lift with or without an effort; we heave and hoist always with an effort. We lift a child up to let him see anything more distinctly; workmen heave the stones or beams which are used in a building; they hoist materials to the upper parts of the structure.

Antonyms.—Drop, lower, let fall.

Likeness, resemblance, similarity. Likeness refers to either external or internal properties; resemblance, only to the external properties; similarity applies to the circumstances or properties. We speak of a likeness between two persons, of a resemblance in the cast of the eye, of a similarity in age and disposition.

Antonyms.—Unlikeness, dissimilarity, contrast, difference.

Linger, tarry, loiter, lag, saunter. To linger is to stop altogether, or to move but slowly forward; to tarry is properly to suspend one's movements: the former proceeds from reluctance to leave the spot on which we stand; the latter, from motives of discretion. To loiter is to move slowly and reluctantly. To lag is to move more slowly than others. To saunter is altogether the act of an idler; those who have no object in moving either backward or forward will saunter if they move at all.

Antonyms.—Hasten, hurry, press forward, rush, march.

Literate, educated, learned. Although the word literate could formerly be applied to a learned or literary person, its present meaning is generally restricted to the mere ability to read and write, at the lowest level of schooling. In Fourteenth Century England, literate presupposed a knowledge of Latin, the universal language of scholarship, as is shown by the following quotation from official instructions for administering the Coronation oath: "If the King is illiterate, let him swear in French." Educated goes considerably beyond literate as a description of one's schooling, while learned goes still farther and indicates the accomplishments of a scholar.

Antonyms.—Illiterate, ignorant, unlettered.

Little, small, diminutive. What is little is so in the ordinary sense in respect to size; it is properly opposed to great. The small is that which is less than others in point of bulk; it is opposed to the large. The diminutive is that which is less than it ought to be, as a person who is below the ordinary stature is said to be diminutive in stature.

Antonyms.—Large, great, big, huge, immense.

Look, appearance. Look or looks refers to an impression a person or thing makes; appearance implies outward characteristics. He presented a travel-stained appearance, but he had the look of a gentleman.

Lose, miss. What is lost is supposed to be entirely and irrecoverably gone; what is missed may be only out of sight or not at hand at the time when it is wanted.

Antonyms.—Find, hold, have.

Madness, frenzy, rage, fury. Madness is a confirmed derangement in the organ of thought; frenzy is only a temporary derangement from the violence of any disease or from any other cause. Rage refers more immediately to the agitation that exists within the mind; fury refers to that which shows itself outwardly. A person contains or stifles his rage, but his fury breaks out into some external mark of violence.

Antonyms.—Sanity, calmness, patience, self-control.

Magnificence, splendor, pomp. Magnificence lies not only in the number and the extent of the objects presented, but in the degree of richness as to their coloring and quality. Splendor is but a characteristic of magnificence, attached to such objects as dazzle the eye by the quantity of light or by the beauty and strength of coloring. Pomp signifies, in general, formality and ceremony.

Antonyms.—Plainness, meanness, simplicity, somberness.

Make, form, produce, create. To make is the most general and unqualified term; to form signifies to make after a given shape or pattern; to produce is to bring forth into the light, to call into existence; to create is to bring into existence by an absolute exercise of power.

Malevolence, maliciousness, malignity. Malevolence has a deep root in the heart and is a settled part of the character; we denominate the person malevolent, to designate the ruling temper of his mind. Maliciousness may be applied as an epithet to particular parts of a man's character or conduct; one may have a malicious joy or pleasure in seeing the distresses of another. Malignity is not so often employed to characterize the person as to describe the thing; the malignity of a design is estimated by the degree of mischief which was intended.

Antonyms.—Good will, kindness, good nature, benevolence.

Manly, masculine, virile. Manly refers to behavior and indicates possession or manifestation of qualities considered most admirable in a man. Masculine denotes physical attributes such as size, strength, and vigor, or it may suggest courage and other characteristics associated with adult male human beings. Virility emphasizes vigor and robust physical health.

Antonyms.—Boyish, effeminate, weak.

Manners, morals. Manners applies to the minor forms of acting with others and toward others; morals includes the important duties of life. By an attention to good manners we render ourselves good companions; by an observance of good morals we become good members of society.

Mark, trace, vestige. Mark implies a fresh and uninterrupted line; trace a more or less temporary mark left by something or someone passing. Originally meaning footstep, vestige now means a faint remaining sign of something that has been lost or has disappeared. In physiology vestigial organs are parts of the body which are now imperfectly developed but were formerly more important, such as the vermiform appendix.

Martial, warlike, military. We speak of martial array, martial preparations, martial law, a court-martial, but of a warlike nation, meaning a nation which is fond of war, of a warlike spirit or temper, or a warlike appearance. We speak of military in distinction from naval, as military expeditions, military movements, and the like.

Antonyms.—Peaceful, unwarlike, civilian, unsoldierly.

Memory, remembrance, recollection, reminiscence. Memory is the power to recall experiences; remembrance is the act of recalling. Recollection, frequently used for both the power and the act, implies a conscious effort to bring back details from past experience. Reminiscence, a sort of autobiographical musing, seeks to recapture images and happenings stored long ago in the mind.

Antonyms.—Forgetfulness, oblivion.

Mercantile, commercial. Mercantile applies to the actual transaction of business or to a transfer of merchandise by sale or by purchase. Commercial comprehends the theory and practice of exchange; hence we speak in a peculiar manner of a mercantile house, a mercantile situation, and the like, but of a commercial education, a commercial people, and the like.

Mitigate, alleviate, assuage. Mitigate, meaning literally to soften, describes the process of lessening harshness, suffering, or anything else that is unpleasant. Alleviate, used mainly with reference to physical suffering, provides, not a cure, but a temporary remedy to relieve distress. Assuage deals with the emotions, particularly grief or sorrow, and seeks to make one's mental suffering more endurable.

Antonyms.—Aggravate, intensify.

Mix, mingle, blend. Mix is here a general and indefinite term, signifying simply to put together, but we may mix two or several things. We mingle several objects; things are mixed so as to lose all distinction, but they may be mingled and yet retain a distinction. To blend is only partially to mix, as colors blend which shade into each other.

Antonyms.—Distinguish, separate, segregate, sort.

Modesty, bashfulness, diffidence. Modesty refrains from boasting and preserves a wholesome awareness of its own limitations. Bashfulness is shy because of youth or inexperience and hence is the cause of hesitation and awkwardness in dealing with others. Diffidence is distrust of one's powers, though it need imply no more than hesitation about beginning an undertaking. Because diffidence is a useful corrective for overconfidence, the diffident person may do very well, once he has started.

Antonyms.—Boldness, forwardness, egotism.

Moisture, humidity, dampness. Moisture is used in general to express any small degree of infusion of a liquid into a body; humidity is employed scientifically to describe the state of holding any portion of such liquid. Hence we speak of moisture on a table, moisture on paper, but of the

humidity of the air. Dampness is the popular term for the condition resulting from a permeating of a substance by moisture, as a wall or the earth may be damp.
Antonyms.—Aridity, drought, dryness.

Money, cash. Money is applied to everything which serves as a circulating medium; cash is, in ordinary use, coin or paper, legal tender, actually in hand for use.

Motion, movement. We speak of a state of motion as opposed to a state of rest, of perpetual motion, the laws of motion, and the like. On the other hand, we use movement generally in speaking of change of position, as an upward movement, a person's movements. As applied to a person, motion implies gesture.
Antonyms.—Rest, quiet, pause.

Moving, affecting, pathetic The good or bad feelings may be moved; the tender feelings only are affected. A field of battle is a moving spectacle; the death of a friend is an affecting spectacle. The pathetic applies only to what is addressed to the heart; hence an address is pathetic.

Mutual, reciprocal, common. Mutual describes a shared feeling between two persons in which the sentiment of each toward the other is similar in kind and equal in intensity. The word could refer to hostility on this basis, but is more often associated with respect or affection. Reciprocal, indicating an exchange on equal terms, is not restricted to feelings, but could also apply to favors or actions. It frequently suggests a response in kind by one party after the other has taken the initiative, or in other words, a return exchange. Common, a more general term, relates to shared experiences that do not involve an interchange between the persons concerned. Even people who have no direct relationship with one another may have ideas, friends, or property in common. Incidentally, the phrase "in common" provides a way of correcting without ambiguity such faulty expressions as "mutual friend," made popular by the title of a Dickens novel.
Antonyms.—Individual, separate.

Naïve, ingenuous, unsophisticated. A naïve person is free from artificiality or guile. Formerly used in a favorable sense, to denote naturalness with fresh and charming simplicity, the word more recently has come to suggest amusing gullibility. Ingenuous connotes a sort of childish innocence, or perhaps a disconcerting frankness in contrast with the evasiveness of designing people. Unsophisticated implies lack of experience and want of worldly wisdom.
Antonyms.—Urbane, artful, worldly-wise.

Name, nickname, pseudonym, acronym. Name is a general word used to identify persons, objects, and, in fact, almost anything. A nickname, which may be either an abbreviation of a person's real name or a substitute for it, is usually applied in affection or derision by the person's associates. A pseudonym is a fictitious name, for example, a pen name adopted by an author. Acronym, a word of comparatively recent origin, means a synthetic word formed by a series of initial letters, as CARE, WAVE, NATO. An extreme example of this popular word coinage is MOUSE, which stands for Medium Orbital Unmanned Satellite of the Earth.

Native, natural. Of a person we may say that his worth is native, to indicate that it is some valuable property which is born with him; we may say that it is natural, as opposed to that which is acquired.
Antonyms.—Acquired, adventitious, affected.

Neglect, omit. To neglect is to disregard, to treat with little or no attention or respect; to omit is to leave out, to leave unnoticed or undone. We neglect an opportunity, we neglect the means, the time, the use, and the like; we omit a word, a sentence, or a figure, and we may omit an item from the day's work. To omit does not always involve the censure that attends neglect.
Antonyms.—Attend to, notice, grasp, insert.

Neighborhood, locality, vicinity. Neighborhood refers to a community, with emphasis on the comparative nearness of the inhabitants to one another. Locality is more of a geographical and impersonal term fixing the area within which something is situated. Vicinity implies nearness to a point or place of reference, for example, the vicinity of Washington.

New, novel, modern, fresh, recent. All these epithets are applied to what has not long existed. New expresses this idea simply without any qualifications; novel is something strange or unexpected; the modern is the thing of today, as distinguished from that which existed in former times; the fresh is that which is so new as not to be the worse for use, or that which has not been before used or employed; the recent is that which is so new as to appear as if it were just made or done.
Antonyms.—Old, familiar, accustomed, ancient, stale.

News, tidings, information, intelligence, notice. News is the general term for communicated knowledge of happenings. Tidings is used poetically in the same sense. Information implies knowledge of some particular thing or event. Intelligence implies that the knowledge has been gained systematically or through organized agencies. Notice involves announcement, especially of a formal nature.

Notice, remark, observe. To notice is a more cursory action than to remark; we may notice a thing by a single glance, or on merely turning the head. To remark supposes a reaction of the mind on an object. We observe things in order to judge of, or draw conclusions from, them, as to observe the condition of the weather. We remark things as matters of fact, as to remark the manner of a speaker.
Antonyms.—Overlook, pass over, disregard, slight.

Noticeable, conspicuous, prominent, remarkable, striking. All of these synonyms describe persons or things that attract attention in varying degrees and with different effects on the observer. Noticeable, the most general term, is neutral and carries rather mild emphasis. In fact, hairsplitting critics have argued with some justification that the word noticeable is superfluous, since anything that was not perceptible would not be mentioned in the first place. Nevertheless, the word is useful in many contexts, and particularly where a certain degree of understatement is desirable. Conspicuous, often used with deprecatory overtones, may suggest that a person or thing commands more attention than is warranted. However, the word may also be used in a favorable sense, as in the phrase "conspicuous for bravery." Although neutral in a phrase like "prominent features of the landscape," the word prominent in reference to persons connotes favorable distinction. Remarkable suggests attributes or qualities, usually of a commendable sort, that are encountered unexpectedly and with some degree of pleasure. Striking applies to something that makes a strong bid for the observer's attention and creates a lasting impression.
Antonyms.—Obscure, hidden, inconspicuous.

Numeral, numerical. Numeral, or belonging to number, is applied to a class of words in grammar, as a numeral adjective or a numeral noun. Numerical, or containing number, is applied to whatever involves number or calculation of numbers, as a numerical difference, where there is a difference between any two numbers or a difference expressed by numbers.

Obedient, submissive, obsequious. One is obedient to command, submissive to power or the will, obsequious to persons. Obedient is always taken in a good sense; submissive, in a humble sense; obsequious, in a mean sense.
Antonyms.—Rebellious, stubborn, recalcitrant, self-respecting.

Object, oppose. To object to a thing is to propose or start something against it; but to oppose it is to set oneself up steadily against it.
Antonyms.—Support, maintain, promote, encourage.

Obnoxious, offensive. In the sense of giving offense, obnoxious implies as much as hateful, offensive little more than displeasing. A man is obnoxious to a party, whose interest or principles he is opposed to; he may be offensive to an individual merely on account of his manners or on account of any particular actions.
Antonyms.—Acceptable, agreeable, pleasing, attractive.

Occasion, opportunity. The occasion is that which offers us the possibility of doing an act or the chance of giving rise to a result. The opportunity is that which invites to action—it tempts us to embrace the moment for taking the step.

Occasional, casual. Occasional carries with it the idea of infrequency; casual, that of unfixedness or the absence of all design. Our acts of charity may be occasional, but they ought not to be casual.
Antonyms.—Regular, systematic, frequent, periodic.

Offender, delinquent. Those who do forbidden or prohibited acts are offenders; those who fail in required or prescribed conduct are delinquents.

Offspring, progeny, issue. Offspring is a familiar term applicable to one or many children; progeny is employed only as a collective noun for a number; issue is used in an indefinite manner without particular regard to number. When we speak of the children themselves we call them the offspring; when we speak of the parents we call the children their progeny. Issue is used only in regard to a man that is deceased.
Antonyms.—Parents, parentage, stock.

Ominous, fateful, portentous. These three words are closely related in their ancient origin and are fairly similar in their present use. Ominous, once associated superstitiously with evil omens, is now used more broadly to describe anything that bodes ill or seems threatening. Fateful, a stronger term, suggests a happening or turn of events pointing definitely toward a disastrous outcome. Portentous is a somewhat more poetic word hinting darkly of calamity in prospect.
Antonyms.—Favorable, auspicious.

Opinionated, conceited, egotistical. An opinionated man is not only fond of his own opinion but full of his own opinion; he has an opinion on everything, which is the best possible opinion. A conceited man has an inordinately high opinion of his own talent,—it is not only high in competition with others, but it is so high as to be set above others. The egotistical man makes himself the darling object of his own contemplation; he admires and loves himself to such a degree that he can talk and think of nothing else.
Antonyms.—Modest, generous, simple, unassuming.

Option, choice. The option or the power of choosing is given; the choice itself is made. Hence we say a thing is at a person's option, or it is his own option, or the option is left to him, in order to designate his freedom of choice more strongly than the word choice itself expresses it.
Antonyms.—Necessity, compulsion.

Outward, external, exterior. Outward signifies tending out from or appearing on the outside. Exterior applies to the outer side or face, as the exterior of a building. External adds to the idea of exterior the notion of whatever is outside and separate from a thing.
Antonyms.—Inward, internal, interior.

Paint, depict. To paint is employed either literally to represent figures on paper, or figuratively to represent circumstances and events by means of words; to depict is used mostly in this latter sense, but paint expresses a greater exercise of the imagination than the latter. It is the art of the poet to paint nature in lively colors; it is the art of the historian or the narrator to depict in strong colors a real scene of misery.

Palatable, appetizing, tasty. Palatable food is acceptable to the palate, but the word arouses little enthusiasm, even though it adds something to edible. Figuratively, we speak of advice or criticism as being palatable or the reverse, and in this connection the word seems a bit more expressive than when used in its literal sense. Appetizing has a kind of lip-smacking suggestion that makes the food it describes appealing. Tasty is a word for epicurean diners, or possibly gourmets. Many other synonyms can be assembled which awaken anticipation of savory puddings, piquant relishes and toothsome desserts. Writing in this vein offers unlimited opportunity for a display of verbal gusto that may or may not be justified by the actual foods recommended.
Antonyms.—Distasteful, insipid, offensive, nauseous.

Part, piece, patch. Things may be divided into parts without any express separation; but when divided into pieces they are actually cut asunder. Hence we may speak of a loaf as divided into twelve parts when it is only conceived to be so, and divided into twelve pieces when it is really so. The patch is that which is always broken and disjointed, a something imperfect; many things may be formed out of a piece, but the patch serves only to fill up a rent or break.

Particular, individual. Particular is much more specific than individual. The particular confines us to one object only of many; the individual may be any one object among many.
Antonyms.—General, collective, common.

Peace, quiet, calm, tranquillity. Peace implies an exemption from public or private broils; quiet implies a freedom from noise or interruption. Calm is a form of quiet which applies to objects in the natural or the moral world; it indicates the absence of violent motion as well as violent noise. Tranquillity expresses the situation as it exists in the present moment, independently of what goes before or after; it is sometimes applicable to society, sometimes to natural objects, and sometimes to the mind.
Antonyms.—War, disturbance, noise, commotion, storm, violence.

Pedantic, academic, bookish. An exhibition of learning which appears to be valued chiefly for learning's sake shows a person to be pedantic. This is particularly true when the exhibitionist displays the technical vocabulary of scholarly research. Academic refers not so much to personal characteristics of scholars as to dryness and abstractness of subject matter. The word also suggests a theoretical rather than a practical approach to subjects and issues. When we say, "That question is purely academic," we mean that it is too remote from present reality to be tested in practice. Bookish describes a person who has learned more from reading than from living.
Antonyms.—Natural, realistic, practical.

Penurious, economical, saving, sparing, thrifty, niggardly. To be economical is a virtue in those who have but narrow means. Saving implies care in the use of money. To be sparing is to use frugally or stintingly; thrifty suggests careful management; penurious means miserly or sparing in regard to the use of money; niggardly implies spending grudgingly or letting go in the smallest possible quantities.
Antonyms.—Generous, lavish, extravagant, unthrifty, wasteful.

Perpetrate, commit. One may commit offenses of various degrees and magnitude; but one perpetrates crimes only, and those of the more heinous kind.

Pillar, column. A pillar is an upright supporting part of a structure. Figuratively, a pillar of a church or of society is a person who plays an essential part in supporting the organization. Columns—for example, columns in the Grecian orders—are more for ornament than for support.

Piteous, doleful, woeful, rueful. Piteous is applicable to one's external expression of bodily or mental pain; a child makes piteous lamentations when it suffers from hunger or has lost its way. Doleful applies to those sounds which awaken a feeling of pain; there is something doleful in the tolling of a funeral bell or in the sound of a muffled drum. Woeful applies to the circumstances and situations of men; a scene is woeful in which we witness a large family of young children suffering under the complicated horrors of sickness and want. Rueful applies to the outward indications of inward sorrow depicted in looks or countenance.
Antonyms.—Happy, joyous, merry, cheerful.

Pity, compassion. Pity is excited principally by the weakness or degraded condition of the subject; compassion, by his uncontrollable and inevitable misfortunes.
Antonyms.—Pitilessness, hardness, antipathy.

Playful, gamesome, sportive. Playful is applicable to youth or childhood, when there is the greatest disposition to play. Gamesome and sportive are applied to persons of maturer years, the former in the bad sense, and the latter in the good sense. A person may be said to be gamesome who gives in to idle jests, or sportive who indulges in harmless sport.
Antonyms.—Sober, dull, serious, gloomy.

Poise, balance. To poise is properly to keep the weight from pressing on either side; to balance is to adjust or equalize two forces. The idea of bringing into an equilibrium is common to both terms. A thing is poised as respects itself; it is balanced as respects other things.
Antonyms.—Mispoise, unbalance, tilt, upset.

Poison, venom. Poison is the general word for substances deadly when introduced into the human system. Venom now means the particular poison of serpents, etc. It applies figuratively to hatred or malignity as blighting to life.

Politeness, polish, refinement. Politeness and polish do not extend to anything but externals; refinement applies as much to the mind as to the body. Rules of conduct and contact with good society will make a man polite; lessons in dancing will serve to give a polish; refined manners or principles will naturally arise out of refinement in mind.
Antonyms.—Impoliteness, rudeness, crudity, boorishness.

Pour, spill. We pour with design; we spill by accident. We pour water over a plant or a garden; we spill it on the ground.

Powerful, potent, mighty. Powerful is applicable to strength as well as to power: a powerful man is one who by size and make can easily overpower another; a powerful person is one who has much in his power. Potent is used only in this latter sense, in which it expresses a larger extent of power; a potent monarch is much more than a powerful prince. Mighty expresses a still higher degree of power; might is power unlimited by any consideration or circumstance. A giant is called mighty in the physical sense; genius which takes everything within its grasp is said to be mighty.
Antonyms.—Weak, impotent, powerless, feeble.

Predicament, dilemma, quandary, plight. A predicament is an uncomfortable situation from which one cannot easily be extricated, either by his own efforts or by the help of others. A dilemma, literally a two-horned situation, is a condition in which two ways of escape are offered, both of which are unacceptable. Historically, dilemma was generally understood to mean a trap set by an opponent in debate, but the word now has much wider application, as for example in describing a choice between two evils or, in fact, between equally undesirable alternatives of any kind. A quandary is a state of perplexity that paralyzes effort and leaves one helpless. Robert Benchley's book, *My Ten Years in a Quandary*, brings out the humorous implications of the word. Plight indicates a sorry situation in which the victim becomes an object of pity or, at least, of sympathy. Whereas one who is in a predicament may experience nothing worse than embarrassment or mild discomfort, the person who is in a plight suffers real distress.

Preliminary, preparatory, introductory. Preliminary indicates a kind of getting ready or warming up in advance of an undertaking. Preparatory refers to still earlier activity, as in collecting needed materials or obtaining instruction required for a task. Introductory leads directly into a job or a piece of writing and may thus be considered a part of the main action.
Antonyms.—Following, concluding, final.

Press, squeeze, pinch, grip. The forcible action of one body on another is included in all these terms. In the word press this is the only idea; the rest differ in the circumstances. We may press with the foot, the hand, or any particular limb. One squeezes commonly with the hand. One pinches either with the fingers or with an instrument constructed in a similar form; one grips with teeth, hands, or any instrument that can gain hold of the object.
Antonyms.—Ease, let go, relieve, relax.

Presumptive, presumptuous, presuming. A presumptive heir is one presumed or expected to be heir; presumptive evidence is evidence founded on some supposition; so likewise presumptive reasoning. But a presumptuous man, a presumptuous thought, a presumptuous behavior, all indicate an overconfidence in regard to one's own powers.

Privacy, retirement, seclusion. Privacy is opposed to publicity; he who lives in privacy is one who follows no public line, who lives so as to be little known. Retirement is opposed to openness or freedom of access: he who lives in retirement withdraws from the society of others. Seclusion is excess of retirement: he who lives in seclusion bars all access to himself and shuts himself from the world.
Antonyms.—Publicity, prominence, notoriety.

Proceeding, transaction. Proceeding signifies literally going forward; transaction, the thing carried through. We are witnesses to the whole proceeding; we inquire into the whole transaction.

Production, performance, work. The term production cannot be employed without specifying or referring to the source from which it is brought forth or the means by which it is brought forth, as the production of art, the production of the inventive faculty. A performance cannot be spoken of without referring to the individual by whom it has been executed; hence we speak of this or that person's performance. When we wish to specify anything that results from labor, it is termed a work; in this manner we speak either of the work of one's hands, or of a work of the imagination.

Profligate, abandoned, reprobate. A profligate man has lost all by his vices. An abandoned man gives way to his passions, which, having the entire sway over him, naturally impel him to every excess. The reprobate man is one who has been reproved until he becomes insensible to reproof, and becomes a prey to the malignity of his own vices.
Antonyms.—Virtuous, high-principled, self-controlled, conscientious.

Prominent, conspicuous, noticeable. Prominent carries the idea of extending or projecting beyond some point of reference: a prominent nose stands out from the face; a prominent man stands out from the crowd. Conspicuous persons or things attract attention so singularly that the eye cannot miss them. Noticeable is a milder and sometimes less offensive term for the idea in conspicuous.
Antonyms.—Obscure, retiring, inconspicuous.

Promise, engagement. In promises the faith of an individual is admitted upon his word, and built upon as if it were a deed; in engagements the intentions of an individual for the future are all that are either implied or understood.

Proportionate, commensurate, adequate. Proportionate implies an adaptation to some assumed standard, as a reward may be proportionate to an act. Commensurate connotes greater accuracy of measurement, as a man's powers may be commensurate with his task. Adequate signifies sufficient, without the implications of the other words.
Antonyms.—Disproportionate, incommensurate, unequal, inadequate.

Provide, procure, furnish, supply. Provide and procure are both actions that have a special reference to the future; furnish and supply are employed for that which is of immediate concern. One provides a dinner in the contemplation that some persons are coming to partake of it; one procures help in the contemplation that it may be wanted. We furnish materials for a building as they are needed. One supplies a family with any article of domestic use.
Antonyms.—Miss, fail of, withhold, deprive of.

Publish, promulgate, divulge, reveal, disclose. To publish is the most general of these terms, conveying in its extended sense the idea of making known; it is in many respects indefinite,—we may publish to many or few. To promulgate is always to make known to many. We may publish that which is a domestic or a national concern; we promulgate properly only that which is of general interest; we divulge things intended to be kept secret; we commonly divulge the secrets or the crimes of another; we reveal the secret or the mystery of a transaction; we disclose from beginning to end an affair which has never before been known or accounted for.
Antonyms.—Hide, conceal, suppress, hush up.

Put, place, lay, set. To put is a general term meaning to bring to a position,—we may put a thing into one's room, one's desk, one's pocket, and the like. To place is to put in a specific manner, and for a specific purpose, as one places a book on a shelf. To lay and to set are still more specific than place, the former being applied only to such things as can be made to lie, and set only to such as can be made to stand. A book may be said to be laid on the table when placed in a downward position, and set when placed on one end.
Antonyms.—Take up, move, remove, disturb.

Qualification, accomplishment. The qualification serves the purpose of utility; the accomplishment serves to adorn. By the first we are enabled to make ourselves useful; by the second we are enabled to make ourselves agreeable.

Quarrel, broil, feud. Quarrel is the general and ordinary term; broil and feud, including active hostility, are particular terms. The idea of a variance between two or more persons is common to these terms; but the first involves the complaints and charges which are reciprocally made. Broil implies the confusion and the entanglement which arise from a contention and a collision of interests; feud, the mutual hostilities which arise out of the variance.

Question, query, questionnaire, quiz. Questions and queries are both put for the sake of obtaining an answer. Question, the more general term, may apply to either reasonable or unreasonable inquiries. It may even be used at times to entrap the person asked, as in the case of so-called loaded or leading questions. A query is usually a rational inquiry and may be addressed to a scholar or some other authority. A questionnaire is an organized group of questions designed to aid someone in making an investigation. A quiz is a brief off-hand test of a person's information.
Antonyms.—Answer, reply, report.

Radiance, brilliancy. Radiance denotes the emission of rays and is therefore peculiarly applicable to bodies naturally luminous, like the heavenly bodies; brilliancy denotes the whole body of light emitted, and it may therefore be applied equally to natural and artificial light. Radiance implies the activity of the shining source of light; figuratively we speak of a radiant face or personality. Brilliancy applies specifically to the appearance; figuratively we speak of a brilliant wit.
Antonyms.—Dullness, murkiness, darkness, dimness.

Rapacious, ravenous, voracious. Rapacious is the quality peculiar to beasts of prey, or to what is like beasts of prey. A lion is rapacious when it seizes on its prey; it is ravenous in the act of consuming it. The word ravenous respects the haste with which one eats; the word voracious respects the quantity which one consumes. A ravenous person is loath to wait for the dressing of his food; he consumes it without any preparation. A voracious person not only eats in haste, but he consumes great quantities, and continues to do so for a long time.
Antonyms.—Frugal, fastidious, dainty.

Rashness, temerity, haste, precipitancy. Rashness is a general and indefinite term, in the signification of which an improper celerity is the leading idea; in temerity the leading idea is want of consideration, springing mostly from an overweening confidence, or from a presumption of character. Haste and precipitancy are but modes or characteristics of rashness and are consequently employed only in particular cases, as haste in regard to our movements and precipitancy in regard to our measures.
Antonyms.—Prudence, deliberation, caution, circumspection.

Ready, prompt, apt. Ready is in general applied to that which has been intentionally prepared for a given purpose; prompt is applied to that which is at hand so as to answer the immediate purpose; apt is applied to that which is fit, or from its nature has a tendency to produce effects.
Antonyms.—Unprepared, unfit, dilatory, unavailable.

Reclaim, reform. Reclaim signifies to call back to its right place that which has gone astray; reform signifies to form anew that which has changed its form; the words are allied only in their application to the moral character. A man is reclaimed from his vicious courses by the force of advice or exhortation; he may be reformed by various means, external or internal.
Antonyms.—Corrupt, degrade, impair, vitiate, confirm.

Recover, retrieve, repair, recruit, restore. We repair that which has been injured; we recruit that which has been diminished; we recover that which has been taken away; we retrieve our misfortunes or our lost reputation; we restore that which has been lost or misplaced, as health or money.
Antonyms.—Lose, lessen, wreck, diminish, injure.

Redundant, wordy, prolix, tautological. These synonyms all refer to the use of unnecessary words. A redundant style of expression substitutes phrases for single words and circumlocutions for direct statements. A person given to wordiness shows delight in using words for their own sake. He is inclined to pile up synonyms instead of choosing the particular one that fits. Prolix suggests a drawing out of subject matter, with resulting bulkiness of expression. Tautological describes the common fault of repetition, as in a phrase like "old veteran," where the idea of old is already present in veteran.
Antonyms.—Concise, succinct, terse, pithy.

Reform, reformation. Whatever undergoes such a change as to give a new form to an object occasions a reform; when such a change is produced in the moral character, it is termed a reformation. The concerns of a state require occasional reform; those of an individual require reformation.

Refuse, decline, reject, repel, rebuff. We refuse what is asked of us, for want of inclination to comply; we decline what is proposed, from motives of discretion; we reject what is offered to us, because it does not fall in with our views. To repel is to reject with violence; to rebuff is to refuse with contempt or with what may be considered as such.
Antonyms.—Accept, receive, acquiesce, comply, welcome.

Relevant, pertinent, apposite. In logic, an idea is considered to be relevant if it belongs clearly to a given subject and helps to explain it. Anything that is pertinent, for example, "a pertinent observation," goes to the heart of a discussion or presents an important phrase of a subject. Something apposite, as "an apposite remark," illuminates a discussion with striking effect. It may even be considered a flash of inspiration. Like wit, it combines appropriateness with unexpectedness.
Antonyms.—Irrelevant, foreign, extraneous.

Repeat, recite, rehearse, recapitulate. To repeat is to say or utter again; to recite is to repeat in a formal manner; to rehearse is to repeat or recite by way of preparation; to recapitulate is to repeat the chapters or principal heads of any discourse, or to summarize the main points.

Repress, restrain, restrict, suppress. Repress implies usually a temporary holding back of something from action; restrain is a stronger word, frequently implying physical force and more permanent holding back. Restrict adds to restrain the idea of bounds within which the restricted activity is free. Suppress implies permanent repression or stifling of activity.
Antonyms.—Release, loose, arouse, set free, incite.

Reproach, rebuke, reprimand. Reproach is a general term for an expression of disapproval with regard to someone's character or conduct. Rebuke implies an immediate reaction in criticism of someone's wrong conduct. Specifi-

cally, it suggests a form of justified scolding. A reprimand is a considered rebuke administered formally by a superior.
Antonyms.—Praise, commendation.

Reputation, fame, renown. Reputation is the estimate formed by others. It may be good or bad. Fame often means widespread reputation. Renown is both widespread and favorable.
Antonyms.—Ignominy, infamy.

Restore, return, repay. We restore upon a principle of equity; we return upon a principle of justice and honor; we repay upon a principle of undeniable right. We cannot always claim that which ought to be restored; we not only claim but enforce the claim in regard to what is to be returned or repaid.
Antonyms.—Withhold, retain, default.

Retard, hinder, thwart. We retard, or slow down, the progress of an action. We hinder people who are doing something by interfering with their freedom of action. We thwart unworthy plans and purposes, and in so doing frustrate the activities of their originators.
Antonyms.—Accelerate, further, help.

Right, claim, privilege. Right, in its full sense, is altogether an abstract thing which is independent of human laws and regulations; claims and privileges are altogether connected with the establishments of civil society. We have often a claim to a thing which is not in our power to substantiate; and, on the other hand, claims are set up in cases which are totally unfounded on any right. Privileges are rights granted to individuals, depending either on the will of the grantor, on the circumstances of the receiver, or on both; privileges are, therefore, partial rights transferable at the discretion of persons individually or collectively.
Antonyms.—Duty, obligation, responsibility.

Royal, regal, kingly. Royal signifies belonging to a king, in its most general sense; regal signifies appertaining to a king, in its particular application. A royal carriage, a royal residence, royal authority—all designate the general and ordinary appurtenances of a king. Regal government, regal state, regal power, denote the peculiar properties of a king; kingly always implies what is becoming a king, or after the manner of a king—a kingly crown is such as a king ought to wear.

Rural, rustic. Rural applies to all country objects except man; it is, therefore, often connected with the charms of nature. Rustic, as here compared, applies only to persons or to what is personal, with reference to the country—it is generally associated with the want of culture.
Antonyms.—Urban, refined, cultured, urbane.

Safe, secure. We may be safe without using any particular measures; but none can reckon on any degree of security without great precaution. A person may be safe on the top of a coach; but, if he wish to be secure from falling off, he must be fastened.
Antonyms.—Unsafe, insecure, endangered.

Salute, salutation. A salute may consist of either a word or an action; salutations pass from one friend to another. The salute may be either direct or indirect; the salutation is always direct and personal. Guns are fired by way of a salute. Bows are given in the way of a salutation.

Satisfy, please, gratify. What satisfies is not always adapted to please; nor is that which pleases that which will always satisfy: plain food satisfies a hungry person; it does not please him when he is not hungry. To gratify is to please in a high degree, to produce a vivid pleasure; we may be pleased with trifles; but we are commonly gratified with such things as act strongly either on the senses or the affections.
Antonyms.—Displease, offend, disgust, anger.

Seaman, sailor, mariner. All these words denote persons occupied in navigation. The seaman, as the word implies, follows his business on the sea. The sailor and the mariner are both specific terms to designate the seaman; every sailor and every mariner is a seaman, although not every seaman is a sailor or a mariner. The former is one who is employed about the work of the vessel; the latter is one who traverses the ocean to and fro, and passes his life upon it.

Secret, hidden, latent, occult, mysterious. What is secret is known to some one; what is hidden may be known to no one. It rests in the breast of an individual to keep a thing secret; it depends on the course of things if anything remains hidden. The latent is the secret or the concealed, especially forces which give no hint of their presence by external appearances; a latent fury may exist in an apparently gentle tiger. An occult science is one that is hidden from the view of persons in general, and is attainable by but few; occult causes or qualities are those which lie too remote to be discovered by the inquirer. The operations of Providence are said to be mysterious, as they are altogether past our finding out.

Antonyms.—Open, revealed, evident, plain, understandable.

See, perceive, observe. The eye sees when the mind is absent; the mind and the eye or other senses perceive in conjunction. Hence, we may say that a person sees, but does not perceive. We observe not by a mere simple act of the mind, but by its positive and fixed exertion.

Seem, appear. Seem is said of that which is dubious, contingent, or future; appear, of that which is actual, positive, and past. A thing seems strange which we are led to conclude is strange from what we see of it; a thing appears clear when we have a clear conception of it.

Sensualist, voluptuary, epicure. The sensualist lives for the indulgence of his senses; the voluptuary is devoted to his pleasures, and, as far as these pleasures are the pleasures of sense, the voluptuary is a sensualist. The epicure as one who makes the pleasures of sense his god, and in this sense he is a sensualist and a voluptuary. In the application of these terms, however, the sensualist is one who is a slave to the grossest appetites; the voluptuary is one who studies his pleasures so as to make them the most valuable to himself; the epicure is a kind of voluptuary who practices more than ordinary refinement in the choice of his pleasures, especially of food.

Antonyms.—Stoic, ascetic, hermit.

Servant, domestic, menial, drudge. In the term servant is included the idea of service performed; in the term domestic, the idea of one belonging to the house or family; in the word menial is included the idea of servile labor; and in the term drudge, that of wearisome labor.

Antonyms.—Master, mistress, employer, boss.

Shade, shadow. Both these terms express that darkness which is occasioned by the sun's rays being intercepted by any body; shade simply expresses the absence of light; hadow signifies also the figure of the body which intercepts he light.

Antonyms.—Light, brightness, sunshine.

Sharp, acute, keen. The general property expressed by these epithets is that of ability to cut. The term sharp is generic and indefinite; the two others are modes of sharpness differing in circumstance or in degree. Acute is not only more than sharp in the common sense, but signifies also sharp-pointed; a knife may be sharp, but a needle is properly acute. Things are sharp that have either a long or a pointed edge; but keen is applicable only to the long edge, and that in the highest degree of sharpness. A common knife may be sharp; a razor or a lancet is properly said to be keen. All these words are applied figuratively to mental ability, their meanings corresponding to their literal senses.

Antonyms.—Dull, blunt, obtuse.

Short, concise, terse, succinct. To the general word short, in reference to brevity in writing or speaking, concise adds the idea of compactness. Terse combines brevity with wit and polish, as in a proverb or an epigram. Succinct compresses a great deal into a small space.

Antonyms.—Bulky, redundant, diffuse, wordy.

Show, exhibition, representation, sight, spectacle. A show consists of that which merely pleases the eye—it is not a matter either of taste or art, but merely of curiosity. An exhibition, on the contrary, presents some effort of talent or some work of genius; a representation sets forth the image or imitation of something by the power of art. Hence we speak of a show of wild beasts, an exhibition of paintings, and a theatrical representation; sights and spectacles present themselves to view. Whatever excites notice is a sight; a spectacle, on the contrary, is that kind of sight which has something in it to interest either the heart or the head of the observer. Processions are sights; battles or bullfights are spectacles.

Showy, pretentious, ostentatious, pompous. These words, all connoting fundamental insincerity, have in common the idea of vainglorious display. Showy refers chiefly to the spectacle itself, though the vanity of the person responsible for the exhibition is clearly implied. Pretentious seeks to make much out of little, while ostentatious presents a person's wealth, generosity or other possession or quality with elaborate flourishes. Pompous describes the self-important manner of the person concerned. All the synonyms listed picture the person or display in an unfavorable or perhaps a humorous light.

Antonyms.—Modest, reserved, sincere, self-effacing.

Sick, sickly, diseased, morbid. Sick denotes a partial state of illness; sickly, a permanent state of the body, a proneness to be sick. He who is sick may be made well; but he who is sickly is seldom really well. Sickly expresses a permanent state of indisposition unless otherwise qualified; but diseased expresses a violent state of derangement without specifying its duration. Sickly and morbid are applied to the habitual state of the feelings or character: a sickly sentimentality; a morbid sensibility.

Antonyms.—Well, healthy, whole, cheerful.

Sign, signal. The sign enables us to recognize an object; it is, therefore, sometimes natural. Signal serves to give warning; it is always arbitrary.

Simple, single, singular. We may speak of a simple matter as something easily grasped or understood. A single instance or circumstance is unaccompanied by any other; a singular instance is one that rarely has its like.

Antonyms.—Complex, complicated, accompanied, common

Simulation, dissimulation. Simulation is making oneself like what one is not; dissimulation is making oneself appear unlike what one really is. The hypocrite puts on the semblance of virtue to recommend himself to the virtuous; the dissembler conceals his vices when he wants to gain the simple or the ignorant to his side.

Antonyms.—Truth, frankness, sincerity, ingenuousness.

Slack, loose. Slack is said only of that which is tied, or of that with which anything is tied; loose is said of any substances, the parts of which do not adhere closely.

Antonyms.—Taut, tight, stretched, compact.

Slant, slope. Slant is said of small bodies only; slope is said indifferently of all bodies, large and small. A book may be made to slant by lying in part on another book on a desk or a table; but a piece of ground is said to slope.

Antonyms.—Be perpendicular, erect, level.

Slip, slide, glide. Slip is an involuntary, and slide a voluntary, motion. Those who go on the ice in fear will slip; boys slide on the ice by way of amusement. To slip and slide are lateral movements of the feet; but to glide is the movement of the whole body, and just that easy motion which is made by slipping, sliding, flying, or swimming. A person glides along the surface of the ice when he slides; a vessel glides along through the water.

Soak, drench, steep. A person's clothes are soaked in rain when the water has penetrated every thread; he himself is drenched in the rain when it has penetrated, as it were, his very body. Steep respects a manner of soaking employed as an artificial process. Soak is, however, a permanent action by which hard things are rendered soft; steep is a temporary action by which soft bodies become penetrated with a liquid. Dried fruits are prepared for eating by soaking; herbs are steeped to extract their essences or flavors.

Antonyms.—Dry, dehydrate, desiccate, evaporate.

Social, sociable. Social people seek others; sociable people are sought for by others.

Antonyms.—Solitary, retiring, uncompanionable.

Solicitation, importunity. Solicitation is general; importunity is particular. Solicitation itself may give trouble to a certain extent, but it is not always unreasonable; importunity is troublesome, insistent solicitation.

Solitary, desert, desolate. Solitary simply denotes the absence of all beings of the same kind—a place is solitary to a man where there is no human being but himself. Desert conveys the idea of a place made solitary by being shunned, because of its unfitness as a place of residence. Desolate conveys the idea of a place made solitary or bare of inhabitants and of all traces of habitation by violent means.

Antonyms.—Populous, peopled, cultivated, inhabited, fruitful.

Sound, sane, healthy. Sound is extended in its application to all things that are in the state in which they ought to be to preserve their vitality. A horse is said to be sound in mind and limb; a tree is sound when not decayed in any part. Healthy expresses more than either sound or sane; we are healthy in every part, but we are sound in that which is essential to life. He who is sound may live, but he who is healthy enjoys life. Sane is applicable to human beings, in the same sense, but with reference to the mind; a sane person is one of sound mind.

Antonyms.—Decayed, diseased, flawed, corrupt.

Speak, say, tell. To speak may simply consist in uttering an articulate sound; but to say is to communicate some idea by means of words. A child begins to speak the moment it opens its lips to utter any acknowledged sound; but it will be some time before it can say anything. To say is to communicate that which passes in our own minds, to express our ideas and feelings as they rise. To tell is to communicate events or circumstances respecting ourselves or others.

Specious, plausible, colorable. These words represent different kinds and degrees of acceptableness in a claim or an argument. A specious argument is fraudulent even though it may seem outwardly and momentarily convincing. Plausible explanations commend themselves to one's reason, though they are admittedly subject to further consideration, and perhaps revision or rejection. Colorable evidence is that which seems valid on the face of it. Circumstances point in its favor. Specious is the only word in the group that suggests intentional deception.
Antonyms.—Sound, valid, convincing.

Spread, expand, diffuse. To spread may be said of anything which comes to occupy more space than it has done, whether by a direct separation of its parts or by an accession to the substance; but to expand is to spread by means of extending or unfolding the parts. A mist spreads over the earth; a flower expands its leaves. To diffuse is to scatter, to cause to spread, as to diffuse information.
Antonyms.—Contract, condense, restrict, close, draw in.

Staff, stay, prop, support. Anything may be called a staff which holds up after the manner of a staff, particularly as it relates to persons, as bread is said to be the staff of life. The stay makes a thing secure for the time being—it keeps it in its place. A prop is usually of a temporary nature; a support is more permanent. Every pillar on which a building rests is a support; the timbers which keep a damaged structure from falling are props.

Stain, soil, sully, tarnish. All these terms imply the act of diminishing the brightness of an object, but the term stain denotes something grosser than the other terms, and is applied to inferior objects. Things which are not remarkable for purity or brightness may be stained, as hands when stained with blood. Nothing is sullied or tarnished but what has some intrinsic value. A fine picture or piece of writing may be easily soiled by a touch of the finger. The finest silver is the soonest tarnished; a man's life may be stained by the commission of some gross immorality; his honor may be sullied, or his glory tarnished.
Antonyms.—Cleanse, clean, brighten, polish, clear.

Stalwart, strong, brawny, sturdy. From its original Anglo-Saxon meaning of serviceable, stalwart has usually emphasized the idea of physical strength, by which one is fitted for service. Hence its association with strong and brawny in their reference to muscular development. A related meaning of stalwart which has partially displaced the notion of muscularity is that of fortitude, strength of purpose, dependability. Here the word comes closer to sturdy and shares with it a connotation of resoluteness.

Starry, stellar, astral. Although closely related in origin, these words, all pertaining to star, have rather widely different associations. Starry is the poetic, or at least non-technical, term for celestial bodies, or perhaps for a person's contemplation of them. Thus the current adjective *starry-eyed* indicates someone's preoccupation with things beyond the range of earthly practicalities. Starry is descriptive, suggesting brilliance and remoteness n the celestial object, while stellar is a working word used technically to convey an astronomical concept. We may speak of a stellar eclipse, but not of a starry one. Astral takes us out of astronomy into the field of occult influences, manifestations or ideas that are assumed to be associated with the stars.

Stately, majestic, grand, grandiose. These synonyms are representative of a large group of words, including magnificent, splendid, princely, august, noble, regal, and sumptuous. All of these related terms are used to describe a display, an official ceremony, or something else that is impressive for its size, richness, beauty, or other distinguished qualities. Stately connotes dignity, gracefulness, and restraint, as in the bearing of a person or the measured tread of a band marching to music. Majestic refers to something that is not only imposing because of its size and beauty but also inspiring by reason of its solemnity.

Grand, if not misapplied, conveys the ideas of size and beauty in the works of man and of sublimity in the works of nature. Grandiose suggests pretentiousness, a kind of sham grandeur that is too exaggerated to be taken seriously.

Steal, pilfer, purloin. Steal, whose everyday meaning is all-too familiar, has accumulated a large collection of synonyms, most of which are euphemisms for the plain word denoting a crime of property. If, instead of steal, the word for appropriating someone else's possessions is pilfer, there seems to be a partial scaling down of guilt, as in the removal of small sums from a petty cash drawer or the depredations of children with "sticky fingers." Purloin, being a literary word and therefore seldom used in common parlance, may be considered almost complimentary in its glossing over of guilt. Whether the act is denoted by steal, pilfer, purloin or some other expression, the illegal transfer of property remains the same so far as its rightful owner is concerned.

Steep, abrupt, precipitous, sheer. When the angle of ascent or descent approaches the perpendicular, an incline is said to be steep. If its departure from a given plane of reference is sudden, the slope may be described as abrupt. If a descent is not only sudden but also headlong, it is called precipitous. Sheer describes a drop straight down, or perhaps a cliff that towers directly above a point of observation. The words precipitous and sheer deal not only with the angle of the incline but also with the feelings of the person who is present at the scene.

Stereotyped, trite, hackneyed, bromidic, platitudinous. There is great need for words to describe lack of originality in people's writing or speaking. Stereotyped is particularly useful for this purpose because it indicates the mechanical following of a fixed pattern, as if the language it describes had been previously cast in a mold. A trite expression probably had merit when it was fresh and has been repeated for that reason. Having been handed down through decades or perhaps even centuries, it has become as flat as a wornout proverb. "Ignorance is bliss," "sadder but wiser," and countless other phrases bear witness to this observation. In hackneyed, the "wornout" suggestion is pictorially conveyed by the image of a horse that has been overworked beyond the point of response. Bromidic came into use after the appearance of a small volume, *Are You a Bromide?*, by Gelett Burgess. People whose conversation offered nothing more original than such comments as "Better late than never" were enabled to classify themselves, or others might do it for them. Platitudinous language is used by orators who utter commonplaces volubly and sonorously.

Sterile, aseptic, antiseptic. Sterile describes a condition of freedom from bacteria or any kind of living organisms. Surgical instruments, for example, are rendered sterile by heating. Aseptic refers to preventive measures which avoid contact between a person and any source of infection. Antiseptic indicates the destruction of microorganisms that are already present. Commonly used as a noun, the word means any substance capable of destroying germs.

Stigma, brand, blot. Originally meaning a mark burned or made by a pointed instrument, a stigma was the visible sign that a person was a criminal or a slave. In this sense the word was almost an exact equivalent for brand, which denotes a mark made by a hot iron on animals, and formerly on human beings. Gradually, stigma has come to mean not so much an actual mark as a reproach, an unfavorable association that has not resulted from the fault of the one who carries it but has been applied from the outside as a means of discrediting him. Name-calling and the attribution of guilt by association are well-known devices for detraction. Guedalla's famous pun on "Any stick to beat a dog" "Any stigma to beat a dogma," contains a wise observation on the modern stigma technique. In contrast with a reproach gratuitously offered by outsiders, a blot—for example, "a blot in the scutcheon"—arises from some fault within the person who bears it, or within his family. He may live it down eventually, but in the meantime he must assume responsibility for it.

Stir, move. We may move in any manner, but to stir is to move so as to disturb the rest and composure of either the body or the mind.

Story, tale. Story is either a narrative of fictitious happenings or an account of actual events, as in a news story. Tale implies a longer, more wandering narrative or sometimes a made-up report of events intended for deceptive purposes.

Stream, current, tide. All rivers are streams, more or less gentle according to the nature of the ground through which they pass. The force of the current is very much increased by the confinement of any water between rocks, or between artificial embankments. The tide is high or low, strong or weak, at different hours of the day; when the tide is high, the current is strongest. Stream is the general term implying flow; current implies a more or less definite direction and rate of flow; tide applies to a regular flow, alternating in direction. In these senses the words are applied figuratively to human affairs.

Successive, alternate. The successive may be accidental or intentional; the alternate is always intentional. It may rain for three successive days, or a fair may be held for three successive days. Trees are placed sometimes in alternate order, when every other tree is of the same size and kind.

Surround, encompass, environ, encircle. We may surround an object by stationing people at certain distances all round it; in this manner a person may be surrounded by other persons; a garden is surrounded by a wall. Encompass applies to objects of a great or indefinite extent, as the earth is encompassed by the air. To surround is to extend around an object of any form; but to environ and to encircle carry with them the idea of forming a circle round an object. Thus a town or a valley may be environed by hills, a basin of water may be encircled by trees, or the head may be encircled by a wreath of flowers.

Sympathy, compassion, commiseration, condolence. Sympathy has the literal meaning of fellow feeling, that is, a kindred or like feeling, or feeling in company with another. Compassion, commiseration, and condolence signify a like suffering, or a suffering in company. Sympathy preserves its original meaning in its application, for we laugh or cry because of sympathy. Compassion is altogether a moral feeling, which makes us enter into the distresses of others. We may sympathize with others without essentially serving them; but, if we feel compassion, we naturally turn our thoughts toward relieving them. Commiseration is awakened toward those who are in an abject state of misery. Condolence is expressed sympathy.
Antonyms.—Antipathy, harshness, mercilessness, unkindliness, inhumanity.

Tease, vex, taunt, tantalize, torment. To tease is applied to that which is most trifling; torment, to that which is most serious. We are teased by a fly that buzzes in our ears; we are vexed by the carelessness and stupidity of our servants; we are taunted by the sarcasms of others; we are tantalized by the fair prospects which present themselves only to disappear again; we are tormented by the importunities of troublesome beggars or by the pain of anxious fears.
Antonyms.—Calm, comfort, gratify, satisfy, console, relieve.

Thick, dense. We speak of thick in regard to hard or soft bodies, as a thick board or thick cotton; we speak of thick in regard to solid or liquid bodies, as a thick cheese or thick milk. Dense specifically adds the idea of great closeness of parts and consequent weight and solidity. Applied to mind, dense is a stronger term than thick.
Antonyms.—Thin, tenuous, rarefied, quick, clever.

Think, suppose, imagine, believe, deem. We think a thing right or wrong; we suppose it to be true or false; we imagine it to be real or unreal. In regard to moral points, in which case the word deem may be compared with the others, to think is to draw a conclusion from certain premises. I think that a man has acted wrongly. To suppose is to take up an idea arbitrarily or at pleasure; to imagine is to take up an idea by accident, or without any connection with the truth or reality. To deem is to form a conclusion; things are deemed hurtful or otherwise in consequence of observation. We think as the thing strikes us at the time; we believe as the result of a course of thought.
Antonyms.—Know, prove, demonstrate.

Threat, menace. We may be threatened with either small or great evils; but we are menaced only with great evils.
Antonyms.—Attraction, allurement, enticement.

Timely, seasonable, opportune. Anything that is timely comes just when it is of greatest interest or value. Seasonable refers to occurrences, or perhaps articles of merchandise, which come at appropriate periods of the year. Opportune suggests a sort of accidental fitness, as in the case of help which arrives "in the nick of time."
Antonyms.—Ill-timed, inopportune, unseasonable.

Torment, torture. Torture is an excess of torment. We may be tormented by a variety of indirect means; but we are mostly said to be tortured by the direct means that may be compared to the rack or a similar instrument.
Antonyms.—Comfort, ease, solace.

Trembling, tremor, trepidation. Trembling expresses any degree of involuntary shaking of the frame, from the affection of either the body or the mind; cold, nervous affections, fear, and the like are the ordinary causes of trembling. Tremor is a slight degree of trembling, which arises mostly from a mental affection; when the spirits are agitated, the mind is thrown into a tremor by any trifling incident. Trepidation is more violent and springs from fear or alarm; it shows itself in the action, or the different movements of the body, rather than in the body.
Antonyms.—Firmness, immobility, steadiness, self-command.

Trouble, disturb, molest. Trouble is the most general in its application; we may be troubled by the want of a thing, or troubled by what is unsuitable; we are disturbed and molested only by that which actively troubles. Trouble may be permanent; disturbance and molestation are temporary, and both refer to the peace which is destroyed. A disturbance ruffles or throws out of a tranquil state; a molestation burdens or bears hard on either the body or the mind.
Antonyms.—Soothe, quiet, compose, caress.

Truth, veracity. Truth belongs to the thing; veracity to the person. The truth of a story is admitted upon the veracity of the narrator.
Antonyms.—Deception, falsehood, falsity.

Turn, bend, twist, distort, wring, wrest, wrench. We turn a thing by moving it about a fixed point; thus we turn the earth over. To bend is simply to change direction; thus a stick is bent, or a body may bend its direction to a certain point. To twist is to bend many times, to make many turns. To distort is to turn or twist out of the right form; thus the face is distorted in convulsions. To wring is to twist with violence; thus linen that has been wetted is wrung. To wrest or wrench is to separate from a body by means of twisting; thus a stick may be wrested out of the hand, or a hinge wrenched off the door.

Turn, wind, whirl, twirl, writhe. To turn is to cause to rotate; wind is to turn a thing around in a regular manner; whirl, to turn it around in a violent manner; twirl, to turn it around in an irregular and unmeaning way. Writhe implies a twisting about within the thing itself, a contortion, as writhing in pain.

Unbelief, infidelity, incredulity. Unbelief implies a settled doubting state of mind; infidelity carries the idea of unfaithfulness to vows or responsibilities; incredulity is a doubting attitude toward tales more or less strange. In religion both unbelief and infidelity convey a sense of failure in duty, the latter being the stronger word.
Antonyms.—Belief, faith, faithfulness, credulity.

Understanding, intellect, intelligence. Understanding is employed to describe a familiar and easy power or operation of the mind in forming distinct ideas of things. Intellect is employed to mark the same operation in regard to higher and more abstruse objects. Understanding applies to the first exercise of the rational powers; it is therefore aptly said of children and savages that they employ their understandings on the simple objects of perception. Intellect, being a matured state of the understanding, is most properly applied to the efforts of those who have their powers in full vigor. Intelligence is less abstract, and is used of a particular person, often to denote large understanding or capacity for understanding.

Unspeakable, ineffable, unutterable, inexpressible. Unspeakable is sometimes used in religion to refer to those objects which are above human conception and surpass the power of language to describe, as the unspeakable goodness of God. Ineffable is said of such objects as cannot be painted in words with adequate force, as the ineffable sweetness of a person's look. Unspeakable is now applied especially to things too evil for utterance; ineffable is used of things too high or good for utterance. Unutterable and inexpressible are extended in their signification to that which is incommunicable by signs from one being to another. Grief is unutterable which it is not in the power of the sufferer by any sounds to bring home to the feelings of another; grief is inexpressible that is not to be expressed by looks, or words, or any sign.
Antonyms.—Common, commonplace, obvious, trivial.

Unworthy, worthless. Unworthy is a term of less reproach than worthless: the former signifies not to be worthy of praise or honor; the latter signifies to be without all worth, and consequently in the fullest sense bad. There are many unworthy members in every religious community; but every society that is conducted upon proper principles will take care to exclude worthless members.
Antonyms.—Worthy, estimable, admirable, noble.

Usage, custom. Usage is what one has been long accustomed to do; custom is what one generally does. The usage acquires force and sanction by dint of time; the custom acquires sanction by the frequency of its appearance or by the numbers following it.
Antonyms.—Innovation, novelty, fancy.

Utter, speak, articulate, pronounce. Utter signifies to put out; that is, to send forth a sound. This, therefore, is a more general term than speak, which is to utter an intelligible sound. We may utter a groan; we speak words only, or that which is intended to serve as words. Speak, therefore, is only a form of utterance—a dumb man has utterance, but not speech. Articulate and pronounce are modes of speaking. To articulate, from *articulum*, "a joint," is to pronounce distinctly the letters or syllables of words; this is the first effort of a child beginning to speak. To pronounce is to speak words intelligibly.
Antonyms.—Mutter, mumble.

Value, prize, esteem. To value is to estimate the worth, real or supposed, relative or absolute, of a thing; in this sense men value gold above silver, or an appraiser values goods. Prize and esteem are taken only as mental actions; the former is taken in reference to sensible and moral objects, the latter, only to moral objects. We may value books according to their market price, or we may value them according to their contents; we prize books only for their contents; in this sense prize is a much stronger term than value.
Antonyms.—Contemn, disregard, depreciate, disprize, despise.

Vex, annoy, bother, irk. Any of the various kinds of disturbance which these words imply is a sufficient tax on our endurance, though some are perhaps more serious than others. Vex, a rather strong word, suggests worry added to perplexity. Annoy refers to a comparatively mild attack upon our comfort, such as the buzzing of a fly, but its persistence makes it unwelcome. Bother is objectionable because it suggests a needless invasion of our quiet or comfort. Irk connotes a rather severe trial of our patience, with sometimes a violation of our sense of justice or fairness.
Antonyms.—Comfort, soothe, please, gratify.

View, survey, prospect. We take a view or survey; the prospect presents itself. The view is of an indefinite extent; the survey is always comprehensive in its nature. Ignorant people take but narrow views of things; the capacious mind of a genius takes a survey of all nature. Prospect, used literally, signifies an outlook as from a window; figuratively, it implies a person's outlook or view toward the future.

Violent, furious, boisterous, vehement, impetuous. A man is violent in his opinions, violent in his measures, violent in his resentments; he is furious in his anger, or has a furious temper; he is vehement in his affections or passions, vehement in love, vehement in zeal, vehement in pursuing an object. Violence transfers itself to some external object on which it acts with force; but vehemence respects that manner of violence which is confined to the person himself; we may dread violence, because it is always liable to do mischief. Impetuosity is rather the extreme of violence or vehemence. An impetuous attack is an excessively violent attack; an impetuous character is an excessively vehement character. Boisterous is said of the manner and of the behavior rather than of the mind.
Antonyms.—Mild, quiet, gentle, cool, collected, self-restrained.

Wakefulness, watchfulness, vigilance. Wakefulness is an affair of the body and depends upon the temperament; watchfulness is an affair of the will and depends upon the determination. Some persons are more wakeful than they wish to be; few are as watchful as they ought to be. Vigilance expresses a high degree of watchfulness. A sentinel is watchful who on ordinary occasions keeps good watch; but it is necessary for him, on extraordinary occasions, to be vigilant in order to detect whatever may pass.
Antonyms.—Drowsiness, heedlessness, inattention, negligence.

Want, need, lack. To want is to be without that which contributes to our comfort or is an object of our desires; to need is to be without that which is essential to our existence or our purposes. To lack expresses little more than the general idea of being without. It is usual to consider what we want as artificial, and what we need as natural and indispensable. What one man wants is a superfluity to another; but that which is needed by one is in like circumstances needed by all.
Antonyms.—Have, share, possess.

Wave, billow, surge, breaker. Waves which swell more than ordinarily are termed billows; waves which rise higher than usual are termed surges; waves which dash against the shore, or against vessels, with more than ordinary force, are termed breakers.

Weak, feeble, infirm. We may be weak in body or in mind; we are feeble and infirm only in the body; we may be weak from disease, or weak by nature—both words convey the gross idea of a defect. But the terms feeble and infirm are qualified expressions for weakness. An old man is feeble from age; he may likewise be infirm in consequence of sickness.
Antonyms.—Strong, sound, healthy, well.

Weight, burden, load. A person may sink under the weight that rests upon him; a platform may break down from the weight upon it; a person sinks under his burden or load; a cart breaks down from the load.

Whole, entire, complete, total, integral. Whole excludes subtraction; entire excludes division; complete excludes deficiency. A whole orange has had nothing taken from it; an entire orange is not yet cut; a complete orange is grown to its full size. Total is the opposite of partial. Integral is applied now to parts or to numbers not broken.

Will, wish. We can will nothing but what we can effect; we may wish for many things which lie above our reach.

Wisdom, prudence. Wisdom directs all matters present or to come; prudence, which acts by foresight, directs what is to come. Rules of conduct are framed by wisdom, and it is the part of prudence to apply these rules to the business life.
Antonyms.—Unwisdom, imprudence, indiscretion, folly.

Wonder, miracle, marvel, prodigy, monster. Wonders are natural; miracles are supernatural. The whole creation is full of wonders; the Bible contains accounts of miracles. Wonders are real; marvels are often fictitious; prodigies are extravagant and imaginary; monsters are violations of the laws of nature. The production of a tree from a grain of seed is a wonder; but a calf with two heads is a monster.

Wonder, surprise, astonishment, amazement. Wonder is the feeling induced by something strange or unusual. Surprise has the idea of sudden wonder. Astonishment is stronger, and includes failure to understand. Amazement adds the idea of bewilderment at something strange or unexpected.
Antonyms.—Comprehension, coolness, composure.

Work, labor, toil, drudgery, task. Every member of society must work for his support, if he is not in independent circumstances. The poor are obliged to labor for their daily subsistence; some are compelled to toil incessantly for the pittance which they earn. Drudgery falls to the lot of those who are the lowest in society. A man wishes to complete his work; he is desirous of resting from his labor; he seeks for a respite from his toil; he submits to drudgery. Task is a work imposed by others, and it is, consequently, more or less burdensome.
Antonyms.—Play, ease, relaxation, recreation, amusement.

Writer, author. Writer refers us to the act of writing; author, to the act of inventing. There are, therefore, many writers who are not authors; but there is no author of books who may not be termed a writer. Compilers and contributors to periodical works are properly writers, though not always entitled to the name of authors. Poets and historians are properly termed authors rather than writers.

Youthful, juvenile, puerile. Of these three words, youthful is the one most often used in a favorable sense, referring to a natural and usually admirable kind of youngness. Even an older person may be credited with youthful traits, or at least with a youthful spirit. Juvenile and puerile, the Latin words for youthful and boyish, respectively, are frequently used in a deprecatory way to describe immature conduct in adults. Of the two, puerile is the stronger term of disparagement.
Antonyms.—Mature, adult, grown-up.

KEY TO THE DICTIONARY OF SYNONYMS

The following is an index to the synonyms which occur in the preceding section. Combined in a single alphabetical list are the key words, in italics, and the other words, printed in Roman type, which appear as synonyms in connection with the various key words. In the index, each of these secondary words is followed by the italicized key word under which its meaning is discussed in the text. Sometimes the same key word, used in a different sense or having a different grammatical classification, heads more than one group of synonyms. This is shown in the index below by numerals in parentheses placed in line with the key word. Similarly, the same secondary words, having different shades of meaning, may be listed under more than one key word. In every instance, the page reference at the right of the column is to the key word concerned.

References for Further Study

No process of self-education is more rewarding than the cultivation of a good working vocabulary. The importance of such study is universally recognized. A popular magazine of large circulation has consistently devoted space to a department called "Increasing Your Word Power," and many newspapers regularly publish articles dealing with the same subject. Such instruction for the public, supplementing the work of schools and textbooks, clearly indicates both the need and the widespread demand for a better understanding of words and their uses.

It will be noted that in all such discussions the main emphasis is not merely on the expansion of one's vocabulary—for example, the learning of three new words a day. The measure of anyone's progress is qualitative, not quantitative. Each word has overtones derived from its origin, background and associations, and whenever ideas of importance are to be expressed, the search is for the one particular word that best conveys the intended meaning. Moreover, each word has a precise definition that sets it apart from other words, even from some that are closely associated with it. A careful study of the words discussed on pages 122–155 will point the way toward the development of greater effectiveness in the use of words. Additional suggestions will be found in the works cited below.

Evans, Bergen and Cornelia—A Dictionary of Contemporary American Usage. *Random House*

Fernald, James C.—Standard Handbook of Synonyms, Antonyms and Prepositions.
 Funk & Wagnalls

Hogan, Homer—Dictionary of American Synonyms. *Philosophical Library*

Laird, Charlton G.—Promptory. *Holt*

Nicholson, Margaret—A Dictionary of American English Usage. *Oxford University Press*

Reifer, Mary—Dictionary of New Words.
 Philosophical Library

Roget, P. M.—Thesaurus. *Crowell*

Webster—Dictionary of Synonyms. *Merriam*

DICTIONARY OF LATIN WORDS AND PHRASES

A considerable number of Latin words and phrases have found their way into English. Some of these are familiar legal terms; some are church terms; some are quotations from poets; and some are merely convenient expressions without an exact English equivalent. Often they cannot be understood without some information in regard to the manner in which they were used in the past. It is frequently necessary to know the meaning which was attached to such phrases by those who spoke Latin and also to know the precise sense in which they have come to be employed in English. Such information is seldom given in the ordinary Latin dictionaries and yet it is necessary for an adequate understanding of the terms. The following is a list of Latin words and phrases which are frequently met with; it is particularly valuable in that it contains the pronunciation and the meaning of all terms used.

Roman Pronunciation. The Roman method of pronunciation is an approximation to the ancient pronunciation of the Latin language, or to that used by the Romans themselves in the days of Cicero and Augustus. It is the system now used almost exclusively in the public schools, and is the one employed in the preparation of the following list.

But many Latin words and phrases have become so thoroughly anglicized that it would be pedantic to disregard their customary English pronunciation. Therefore, the English pronunciation of an anglicized word or phrase is given in parentheses immediately after the Roman.

The key to the English pronunciation will be found on page 8.

The key to the Roman method is as follows:

Vowels and Diphthongs

Long vowels (marked ‾) are supposed to take twice as long to utter as short vowels (marked ˘). All diphthongs are long. The following table shows the *approximate* sound of the Latin vowels and diphthongs:—

ā is pronounced like *a* in *father*
ă is pronounced like *a* in *what*
ē is pronounced like *e* in *prey*
ĕ is pronounced like *e* in *met*
ī is pronounced like *i* in *machine*
ĭ is pronounced like *i* in *pin*
ō is pronounced like *o* in *note* (close o)
ŏ is pronounced like *aw* in *law* (open o—uttered very rapidly)
ū is pronounced like *u* in *rude*
ŭ is pronounced like *u* in *pull*
ȳ is pronounced like *French u* or *German ü*
y̆ is pronounced like *French u* or *German ü* (but uttered very rapidly)
ae is pronounced like *ai* in *aisle*
au is pronounced like *ow* in *how*
eu is pronounced like *eh-oo* (run rapidly together)
oi is pronounced like *oi* in *boil*

Consonants

The consonants have *approximately* the same sounds as in English, with the following exceptions:—

c is pronounced like *k* (never like *s*)
g is pronounced like *g* in *get* (never like English *j*)
j is pronounced like *y* in *yet* (never like English *j*)
s is pronounced like *s* in *sin* (never like *z*)
t is pronounced like *t* in *tin* (never like *sh*)
v is pronounced like *w* in *win* (never like *v* in *very*)
ch* is pronounced like *k-h* (in *back home*)
ph* is pronounced like *p-h* (in *up hill*)
th* is pronounced like *t-h* (in *at home*)

* But these three aspirates are commonly, if improperly, pronounced as *k*, *f*, and *th* (in *thin*) respectively.

AB INITIO, *ăb ĭn-ĭ′tĭ-ō (ăb ĭn-ĭsh′ĭ-ô).* From the beginning.

AB OVO AD MALA, *ăb ō′vō ăd mā′lă.* From the eggs to the apples; from beginning to end. The Roman dinner began with eggs and ended with apples.

ABSIT OMEN, *ăb′sĭt ō′mĕn.* May no harm come from it, that is, from a word just used.

AD ASTRA PER A PERA, *ăd ăs′tră pĕr ăs′pĕ-ră.* To the stars through difficulties. Motto of Kansas.

AD CAPTANDUM VULGUS, *ăd căp-tăn′dŭm vŭl′gŭs.* To attract the rabble, like "playing to the gallery."

AD INFINITUM, *ăd ĭn′fĭ-nī′tŭm (ăd ĭn′fĭn-ī′tŭm).* To infinity without end.

AD LIBITUM, *ăd lĭb′ĭ-tŭm.* At one's pleasure.

AD NAUSEAM, *ăd nau′sĕ-ăm (ăd nô′sĕ-ăm).* To the point of disgusting or nauseating.

AD REM, *ăd rĕm.* To the purpose; to the point.

AD VALOREM, *ăd vă-lō′rĕm (ăd văl-ō′rĕm).* According to value.

ÆQUO ANIMO, *æ′quō ăn′ĭ-mô.* With a calm mind; with equanimity.

ÆTATIS SUÆ, *æ-tā′tĭs sū′æ.* Aged; in the year of his or her age.

ÆTERNUM VALE! *æ-tĕr′nŭm vă′lē.* Farewell forever!

A FORTIORI, *ā fōr′tĭ-ō′rī (ā fōr′shĭ-ō′rī).* For the stronger reason; all the more.

ALIAS, *ā′lĭ-ăs (ā′lĭ-ăs).* Otherwise; generally indicating the variant of a name.

ALMA MATER, *ăl′mă mā′tĕr (ăl′mă mā′tĕr).* Beloved or foster mother; one's college or university.

ALTER EGO, *ăl′tĕr ĕ′gō (ăl′tĕr ē′gô).* Another or second self.

ANNO DOMINI, *ăn′nō dŏ′mĭ-nī (ăn′ō dŏm′ĭ-nī).* In the year of our Lord. *A. D.*

ANNO URBIS CONDITÆ, *ăn′nō ŭr′bĭs cŏn′dĭ-tæ.* In the year of the founding of the city (Rome, 753 B. C.). A Roman method of dating. *A.U.C.*

ANTE BELLUM, *ăn′tĕ bĕl′ŭm (ăn′tĕ bĕl′ŭm).* Before the war.

A POSSE AD ESSE, *ā pŏs′sĕ ăd ĕs′sĕ.* From possibility to actuality.

A POSTERIORI, *ā pŏs′tĕ-rĭ-ō′rī (ā pŏs′tĕ-rĭ-ō′rī).* By induction; an *a posteriori* argument,—inferring causes from effects.

A PRIORI, *ā prī-ō′rī (ā prī-ō′rī).* Deductively; an *a priori* argument,—one which infers effects from known causes.

ARS ARTIUM OMNIUM CONSERVATRIX, *ărs ār′tĭ-ŭm ŏm′nĭ-ŭm cōn′sĕr-vā′trĭx.* The art preservative of all arts,—printing.

ARS EST CELARE ARTEM, *ărs ĕst cē-lā′rĕ ăr′tĕm.* Art is to conceal art.

ARS LONGA, VITA BREVIS, *ărs lŏn′gă vī′tă brĕ′vĭs.* Art is long, life is short. A Latin translation from Hippocrates.

ARTIUM MAGISTER, *ăr′tĭ-ŭm mă-gĭs′tĕr (ăr′shĭ-ŭm mă-jĭs′tĕr).* Master of arts.

ASINUS AD LYRAM, *ăs′ĭ-nŭs ăd lў′răm.* An ass at the harp; an awkward fellow.

AUDACES FORTUNA JUVAT, *au-dā′cēs fōr-tū′nă jŭ′văt.* Fortune favors the bold. A paraphrase from Virgil.

AUT CÆSAR AUT NIHIL, *aut cæ′săr aut nĭ′hĭl.* Either Cæsar or nothing. A saying attributed to Cæsar Borgia and applicable to those unduly ambitious.

AUT VINCERE AUT MORI, *aut vĭn′cĕ-rĕ aut mŏ′rī.* To conquer or die.

AVE, IMPERATOR! MORITURI TE SALUTANT, *ă′vē ĭm′pĕ-rā′tŏr mŏ′rĭ-tū′rī tē să-lū′tănt.* Hail, Emperor! Those about to die salute thee.—Suetonius. Cry of the Roman gladiators on entering the arena.

BEATÆ MEMORIÆ, *bĕ-ā′tæ mĕ-mō′rĭ-æ.* Of blessed or happy memory.

BIS PUERI SENES, *bĭs pŭ′ĕ-rī sĕ′nēs.* Old men are in second childhood.

BONAFIDE, *bō′nă fī′dē (bō′nă fī′dĕ).* In good faith.

BONAFIDES, *bō′nă fī′dēs (bō′nă fī′dēz).* Good faith; word of honor.

BONUM VINUM LÆTIFICAT COR HOMINIS, *bŏ′nŭm vī′nŭm æ-tĭ′flĭ-căt cŏr hŏm′ĭ-nĭs.* Good wine gladdens man's heart.

CACOETHES SCRIBENDI, *că′cŏ-ē′thĕs scrī-bĕn′dī.* The incurable passion for scribbling.—Juvenal.

CARCERE DURO, *căr′cĕ-rĕ dū′rō.* In durance vile; at hard labor.

CARPE DIEM, *căr′pĕ dī′ĕm.* Seize the day, enjoy life. —Horace.

CASUS BELLI, *cā′sŭs bĕl′lī (kă′sŭs bĕl′ī).* The cause that brings about war.

CAVEAT EMPTOR, *kā′vĕ-ăt ĕmp′tŏr.* Let the buyer beware. An old maxim of the common law, which still applies to titles of real estate transferred.

CEDANT ARMA TOGÆ, *cē′dănt ăr′mă tŏ′gæ.* Let arms give place to the toga.—Cicero. Let the statesman's glory outshine the soldier's.

CETERIS PARIBUS, *cē′tĕ-rĭs păr′ĭ-bŭs.* Other things being equal,—expressing a condition.

CIVIS ROMANUS SUM, *cĭ′vĭs rō-mā′nŭs sŭm.* I am a Roman citizen.

COGITO, ERGO SUM, *cō′gĭ-tō ĕr′gō sŭm.* I think, therefore I exist. The basis of Descartes's philosophy.

CONSENSUS OMNIUM, *cŏn-sĕn′sŭs ŏm′nĭ-ŭm.* Universal agreement

CONSUETUDO PRO LEGE SERVATUR, *cŏn′suĕ-tū′dō prō lē′gĕ sĕr-vā′tŭr.* Custom is held as law. The basis of English common law.

CORPUS DELICTI, *cŏr′pŭs dē-lĭc′tī.* The body of a crime; anything which serves to prove its commission; essential proof in a case.

CREDO QUIA ABSURDUM, *crē′dō quĭ′ă ăb-sŭr′dŭm.* I believe because it is absurd; the conquest of reason by faith.

CRUX, *crŭx.* A cross, a difficulty; as, the crux of the matter.

CUI BONO? *cŭ′ĭ bŏ′nō (ki bō′nō).* To whose advantage? The criminal may possibly be traced by the answer to the question.

CUI FORTUNA IPSA CEDIT, *cŭ′ĭ fŏr-tū′nă ĭp′să cē′dĭt.* To whom Fortune herself yields; that is, a lucky person.

CUIQUE SUUM, *cŭ′ĭ quē sū′ŭm.* Let each one have his own.

CUM GRANO SALIS, *cŭm grā′nō să′lĭs.* With a pinch of salt; not to be taken seriously.

DA LOCUM MELIORIBUS, *dā lŏ cŭm mĕ′lĭ-ō′rĭ-bŭs.* Give place to your betters.

DE FACTO, *dē făc′tō.* Actually; as a matter of fact.

DE GUSTIBUS NON EST DISPUTANDUM, *dē gŭs′tĭ-bŭs nŏn ĕst dĭs′pŭ-tăn′dŭm.* There's no use disputing about tastes,— an old scholastic proverb.

DEI GRATIA, *dē′ĭ grā′tĭ-ā (dē′ĭ grā′shĭ-à).* By the grace or favor of God. Part of the inscription on British coinage.

DE JURE, *dē jū′rĕ (dē jū′rê).* Lawfully, by right.

DELENDA EST CARTHAGO, *dē-lĕn′dă ĕst căr-thā′gō.* Carthage must be destroyed. Applicable to the intention of overcoming a difficulty.

DE MORTUIS NIL NISI BONUM, *dē mŏr′tŭ-ĭs nil nĭ′sĭ bŏ′nŭm.* Say nothing but good of the dead.

De novo *dē nō′-vō.* From the beginning; anew.

DEO GRATIAS, *dē′ō grā′tĭ-ās (dē′ô grā′shĭ-ăs).* Thanks be to God. Used in the liturgy of the Mass.

DEO VOLENTE, *dē′ō vŏ-lĕn′tĕ.* God willing. *D. V.*

DE PROFUNDIS, *dē prŏ-fŭn′dĭs.* Out of the depths. An appeal made *de profundis*, that is, in dire distress.

DEUS EX MACHINA, *dē′ŭs ĕx măch′ĭn-ā.* A god from a machine; an artificial solution of a problem, from the practice in the Greek drama of introducing a god by stage machinery to bring an otherwise insoluble plot to a satisfactory end.

DIES IRÆ, *dĭ′ēs ī′ræ.* The day of wrath; the judgment day. The title of a celebrated Latin hymn.

DIVIDE ET IMPERA, *dī′vĭ-dĕ ĕt ĭm′pĕ-rā.* Divide and rule. A motto of Roman imperialism.

DOCTUS CUM LIBRO, *dŏc′tŭs cŭm lĭ′brō.* Learned with the aid of a book.

DOMINUS VOBISCUM, *dŏm′ĭ-nŭs vō-bĭs′cŭm.* The Lord be with you,—words used frequently in the Roman liturgy.

DONEC ERIS FELIX MULTOS NUMERABIS AMICOS, *dō′nĕc ĕ′rĭs fē′lĭx mŭl′tōs nŭ′mĕ-rā′bĭs ă-mī′cōs.* While you are happy, you will count many friends.—Ovid.

DULCE ET DECORUM EST PRO PATRIA MORI, *dŭl′cĕ ĕt dĕ-cō′rŭm ĕst prō pă′trĭ-ā mŏ′rī.* It is sweet and glorious to die for one's country.—Horace.

DUX FEMINA FACTI, *dŭx fē′mĭ-nă făc′tī.* A woman was the leader in the adventure.—Virgil.

ECCE HOMO! *ĕc′cĕ hō′mō (ĕk′sĕ hō′mô).* Behold the man! Applied specifically to any picture of Christ wearing the crown of thorns.

EDITIO PRINCEPS, *ē-dĭ′tĭ-ō prin′cĕps (ē-dĭsh′ĭ-ô prin′sĕps).* A first edition of a printed work.

EGO SUM QUI SUM, *ĕ′gō sŭm qui sŭm.* I am who I am.— Exodus III:14. The answer of the Supreme Being to Moses.

EHEU! FUGACES LABUNTUR ANNI, *ē′heu fŭ-gā′cēs lā-bŭn′tŭr ăn′nĭ.* Alas! how the years slip by.—Horace.

E PLURIBUS UNUM, *ē plū′rĭ-bŭs ū′nŭm* From many, one. Motto of the United States of America.

ERRARE EST HUMANUM, *ĕr-rā′rĕ ĕst hŭ-mā′nŭm.* To err is human.

ESSE QUAM VIDERI, *ĕs′sĕ quăm vĭ-dē′rī.* To be, rather than to seem.

ESTO QUOD ESSE VIDERIS, *ĕs′tō quŏd ĕs′sĕ vĭ-dē′rĭs.* Be what you seem to be.

ET CETERA, *ĕt cē′tĕ-ră (ĕt sĕt′ĕ-rà).* And the rest; *etc., &c.*

ET IN ARCADIA EGO! *ĕt ĭn ăr-cā′dĭ-ā ē′gô.* I, too, once lived in Arcadia! An exclamation of regret for happiness no longer possessed.

ET SEQUENTIA, *ĕt sĕ-quĕn′tĭ-ă.* And what follows; *et seq.*

ET TU, BRUTE! *ĕt tū brū′tĕ.* And thou also, Brutus! Usually given as the last words of Julius Cæsar, when he saw Brutus among his murderers.

EX CATHEDRA, *ĕx că′thĕ-drā (ĕks kă′thē-drà).* "From the chair." A statement bearing unquestionable authority.

EX DONO, *ĕx dō′nō.* As a gift. Used preceding the name of a public benefactor on what he has presented.

EXEMPLI GRATIA, *ĕx-ĕm′plī grā′tĭ-ā (ĕg-zĕm′plī grā′shĭ-à).* By way of example,—written *e.g.*

EXEUNT OMNES; EXIT, *ĕks′ē-ŭnt ŏm′nēs ĕx′ĭt (ĕks′ē-ŭnt ŏm′nēz ĕk′sĭt).* All go out; he or she goes out.

EX NIHILO NIHIL FIT, *ĕx nĭ′hĭ-lō nĭ′hĭl fĭt.* From nothing, nothing comes.

Ex parte, *ĕx pär'tĕ*. On one side only. An *ex parte* argument.

Experto crede, *ĕx-pĕr'tō crē'dĕ*. Believe one who has tried it.—Virgil.

Ex tempore, *ĕx tĕm'pŏ-rĕ (ĕks tĕm'pŏ-rē)*. Offhand; without preparation.

Facile princeps, *fă'cĭ-lĕ prĭn'cĕps (făs'ĭ-lê prĭn'sĕps)*. The acknowledged chief; one who stands indisputably first.—Cicero.

Facilis descensus Averni, *fă'cĭ-lĭs dē-scĕn'sŭs ă-vĕr'nĭ*. The descent to hell is easy.—Virgil. It is easy enough to get into trouble.

Fama volat, *fā'mă vŏ'lăt*. Fame flies,—expressing the rapidity with which news is spread.

Felix culpa, *fē'lĭx cŭl'pă*. Happy fault.—St. Augustine. Applicable when a mistake turns out to be a benefit.

Feræ naturæ, *fĕ'rœ nā-tū'rœ*. Of a wild nature. Applied to wild beasts.

Festina lente, *fĕs-tī'nā lĕn'tĕ*. Make haste slowly; don't rush serious work.

Fiat justitia ruat cælum, *fī'ăt jŭs-tĭ'tĭ-ă rŭ'ăt cœ'lŭm*. Let justice be done though the heavens should fall.

Fiat lux, *fī'ăt lŭx*. Let there be light.

Fidei defensor, *fī'dĕ-ī dē-fĕn'sŏr*. Defender of the faith.

Fidus Achates, *fī'dŭs ă-chā'tēs (fī'dŭs â-kā'tēz)*. Faithful Achates.—Virgil. A trusty friend.

Flagrante delicto, *flă-grăn'tĕ lē-lĭc'tō*. The crime blazing; red-handed; in the very act.

Fortiter, fideliter, feliciter, *fŏr'tĭ-tĕr fĭ-dĕl'ĭ-tĕr fē-lĭc'ĭ-tĕr*. Boldly, faithfully, successfully.

Fortiter in re, *fŏr'tĭ-tĕr ĭn rē*. With firmness in action.

Fugit irreparabile tempus, *fū'gĭt ĭr'rĕ-pă-rā'bĭ-lĕ tĕm'pŭs*. Time flies, never to be recalled.—Virgil.

Gaudeamus igitur, *gaud-ĕ-ā'mŭs ĭ'gĭ-tŭr*. Therefore, let us rejoice,—the burden of a macaronic song.

Gloria in excelsis Deo, *glō'rĭ-ă ĭn ĕx-cĕl'sĭs dĕ'ō (glō'rĭ-à ĭn ĕk-sĕl'sĭs dē'ô)*. Glory to God in the highest.

Gradus ad Parnassum, *grā'dŭs ăd pär-năs'sŭm*. A step to Parnassus; aid in writing Latin poetry; a work on Latin verse-making containing rules and examples.

Græcum est, non legitur, *grœ'cŭm ĕst nŏn lĕ'gĭ-tŭr*. It is Greek, so skip it; don't meddle with what you know nothing about.

Gratis pro Deo, *grā'tĭs prō dĕ'ō*. Freely for God,—the manner in which charity should be bestowed.

Habeas corpus, *hă'bĕ-ās cŏr'pŭs (hā'bê-ăs cŏr'pŭs)*. Have the body. A writ issued for the purpose of bringing a person before a court or a judge, usually to determine whether he should be retained in custody or given his freedom.

Hic et nunc, *hĭc ĕt nŭnc*. Here and now.

Hic jacet, *hĭc jă'cĕt (hĭk jā'sĕt)*. Here lies. Inscribed on tombstones.

Hinc illæ lacrimæ, *hĭnc ĭl'lœ lă'crĭ-mœ*. Hence these tears.—Terence. This is the cause of the trouble.

Homo sum; humani nihil a me alienum puto, *hŏ'mō sŭm hū-mā'nī nĭ'hĭl ā mē ā'lĭ-ē'nŭm pū'tō*. I am a man; there is naught which touches man that is not my concern.—Terence.

Hortus siccus, *hŏr'tŭs sĭc'cŭs*. A dry garden; a collection of dried plants; a herbarium.

Imperium in imperio, *ĭm-pĕ'rĭ-ŭm ĭn ĭm-pĕ'rĭ-ô*. A government existing within another. Said of a power set up against constituted authority.

Imprimatur, *ĭm'prĭ-mā'tŭr*. It may be published. A censor's permission at the beginning of certain Catholic works.

In esse, *ĭn ĕs'sĕ*. In being.

In extenso, *ĭn ĕx-tĕn'sō (ĭn ĕks-tĕn'sô)*. Entirely, at full length; as, to treat a subject *in extenso*.

In extremis, *ĭn ĕx-trē'mĭs (ĭn ĕks-trē'mĭs)*. In very bad circumstances; at the point of death.

Infra dignitatem, *ĭn'frā dĭg'nĭ-tā'tĕm*. Beneath one's dignity, *infra dig.*

In hoc signo vinces, *ĭn hōc sĭg'nō vĭn'cēs (ĭn hŏk sĭg'nô vĭn'sēz)*. In this sign thou shalt conquer. The motto is said to have been adopted by Constantine after his vision of a cross in the heavens just before his decisive battle with Maxentius, 312 A. D.

Initium sapientiæ timor Domini, *ĭ-nĭ'tĭ-ŭm să'pĭ-ĕn'tĭ-œ tĭm'ŏr dŏm'ĭ-nī*. The fear of the Lord is the beginning of wisdom.

In loco parentis, *ĭn lŏ'cō pă-rĕn'tĭs (ĭn lō'kô pâ-rĕn'tĭs)*. In the place of a parent.

In medias res, *ĭn mĕ'dĭ-ās rēs*. Into the middle of the subject; without wasting words.

In memoriam, *ĭn mĕ-mŏ'rĭ-ăm (ĭn mĕ-mō'rĭ-ăm)*. In memory of.

In perpetuam rei memoriam, *ĭn pĕr-pĕt'ŭ-ăm rĕ'ī mĕ-mŏ'rĭ-ăm*. In everlasting remembrance of the event.

In posse, *ĭn pŏs'sĕ*. In possible existence.

In propria persona, *ĭn prŏ'prĭ-ă pĕr-sō'nă*. In one's own person.

(In) re, *ĭn rē (ĭn rē)*. In the matter of, concerning; as, *(in) re* the election.

In situ, *ĭn sĭ'tū (ĭn sĭ'tû)*. In position; the actual spot. A phrase especially employed in mineralogy.

In statu quo, *ĭn stă'tū quō (ĭn stā'tû kwō)*. In its former state.

Integer vitæ scelerisque purus, *ĭn'tĕ-gĕr vī'tœ scĕ'lĕ-rĭs'quĕ pū'rŭs*. A man upright in life and free from blame.—Horace.

Intelligenti pauca, *ĭn-tĕl'lĭ-gĕn'tī pau'că*. But few words necessary for one who is intelligent (also *verbum sapienti, verb. sap.*).

Inter alia, *ĭn'tĕr ā'lĭ-ă (ĭn' tĕr ā'lĭ-à)*. Among other things.

Inter nos, *ĭn'tĕr nōs (ĭn'tĕr nōs)*. Between, among ourselves.

In toto, *ĭn tŏ'tō*. In the whole; entirely.

In vacuo, *ĭn vă'cŭ-ō (ĭn văk'û-ô)*. In a vacuum.

In vino veritas, *ĭn vī'nō vēr'ĭ-tās*. In wine there's truth; a man becomes more confidential when he drinks.

Ipse dixit, *ĭp'sĕ dĭx'ĭt (ĭp'sĕ dĭk'sĭt)*. He himself has said it; a mere assertion.

Ipsissima verba, *ĭp-sĭs'sĭ-mă vĕr'bă*. The identical words.

Ipso facto, *ĭp'sō făc'tō (ĭp'sô făk'tô)*. By the very fact; actually.

Ita est, *ī'tă ĕst*. It is so.

Jacta alea esto, *jăc'tă ā'lĕ-ă ĕs'tō*. Let the die be cast.—Julius Cæsar. It is probable that the exact words uttered by Julius Cæsar on crossing the Rubicon were from a Greek play of Menander, the Latin being a translation.

Jus civile, *jŭs cĭ-vī'lĕ (jŭs sĭ-vĭ'lĕ)*. The law of citizens. The Roman law applied to citizens. See *Jus gentium.*

Jus est ars boni et justi, *jŭs ĕst ärs bŏ'nī ĕt jŭs'tī*. Right is the art of the good and of the just.

Jus gentium, *jŭs gĕn'tĭ-ŭm (jŭs jĕn'shĭ-ŭm)*. The law of nations. The Roman law applied to foreigners, or between foreigners and citizens. See *Jus civile.*

Labor omnia vincit improbus, *lă'bŏr ŏm'nĭ-ă vĭn'cĭt ĭm'prŏ-bŭs*. Stubborn labor overcomes all things.—Virgil.

Lapsus calami, *lăp'sŭs că'lă-mī (lăp'sŭs kăl'â-mĭ)*. A slip of the pen.

Lapsus linguæ, *lăp'sŭs lĭn'guœ (lăp'sŭs lĭng'gwê)*. A slip of the tongue.

Lares et penates, *lā'rēs ĕt pĕ-nā'tēs (lā'rêz ĕt pê-nā'tēz)*. Household gods.

Latet anguis in herba, *lă'tĕt ăn'guĭs ĭn hĕr'bă*. A snake lies hid in the grass.—Virgil. Said by way of warning.

Lato sensu, *lā'tō sĕn'sū*. In a broad sense; with a wide meaning.

Laudator temporis acti, *lau-dā'tŏr tĕm'pŏ-rĭs āc'tī*. One who praises the good old days,—generally to the disparagement of the present.—Horace.

Laus Deo, *laus dĕ'ō*. Praise to God.

Levius fit patientia quidquid corrigere est nefas, *lĕ'vĭ-ŭs fĭt pă'tĭ-ĕn'tĭ-ă quĭd'quĭd cŏr-rĭ'gĕ-rĕ ĕst nĕ'făs*. What cannot be cured may be lightened by patience.—Horace.

Lex talionis, *lĕx tăl'ĭ-ō'nĭs*. The law of retaliation.

Loco citato, *lŏ'cō cĭ-tā'tō (lō'kô sĭ-tā'tô)*. In the place quoted. *(loc. cit.)*

Magister dixit, *mă-gĭs'tĕr dĭx'ĭt (mâ-jĭs'tĕr dĭks'ĭt)*. The master has said it,—hence no more argument.

Magna cum laude, *māg'nă cŭm lau'dĕ*. With high honors.

Magnum opus, *māg'nŭm ŏ'pŭs (măg'nŭm ō'pŭs)*. A great undertaking; the great work of a man's life.

Mater familias, *mā'tĕr fă-mĭ'lĭ-ās (mā'tĕr fâ-mĭl'ĭ-ăs)*. The mother of the family.

Materiam superabat opus, *mā-tĕ'rĭ-ăm sŭ'pĕ-rā'băt ŏ'pŭs*. The workmanship surpassed the materials.—Ovid.

Mea culpa, *mĕ'ā cŭl'pā (mĕ'à kŭl'pă)*. Through my fault.

Medice cura teipsum, *mĕd'ĭ-cĕ cū'rā tē-ĭp'sŭm*. Doctor, cure yourself; practice what you preach.

Memento homo quia pulvis es, *mĕ-mĕn'tō hŏ'mō quĭ'ă pŭl'vĭs ĕs*. Remember, man, thou art but dust.

Mens sana in corpore sano, *mĕns sā-'nă ĭn cŏr'pŏ-rĕ sā-nô*. A sound mind in a sound body.—Juvenal. Often wrongly interpreted to mean that the one depends on the other.

Minima de malis, *mĭn'ĭ-mă dē mă'lĭs*. Of evils, choose the least.

Mirabile dictu, *mĭ-rā'bĭ-lĕ dĭc'tū*. Wonderful to relate.

Mirabile visu, *mĭ-rā'bĭ-lĕ vĭ'sū*. A wonderful sight.

Modus operandi, *mŏ'dŭs ŏ'pĕ-răn'dī (mō'dŭs ŏp-ĕr-ăn'dĭ)*. Mode, or manner, of working.

Modus vivendi, *mŏ'dŭs vĭ-vĕn'dī (mō'dŭs vĭ-vĕn'dĭ)*. Mode, or manner, of living.

Multi sunt vocati, pauci vero electi, *mŭl'tī sŭnt vŏ-cā'tī pau'cĭ vĕ'rō ē-lĕc'tī*. Many are called, but few are chosen.

Multum in parvo, *mŭl'tŭm ĭn păr'vô*. Much in little.

Mutato nomine, *mū-tā'tō nōm'ĭ-nĕ*. The name being changed; the story fits you.

NECESSITAS NON HABET LEGEM, *ně-cěs'sǐ-tās nōn hǎ'bět lē'gěm.* Necessity knows no law.

NE PLUS ULTRA, *ně plŭs ŭl'trā (ně plŭs ŭl'trà).* Nothing beyond. The *ne plus ultra* of elegance; also *nec* or *non plus ultra.* Hercules engraved these words on the summits of Abyla and Calpe, the modern Iebel Musa and Gibraltar, the "Pillars of Hercules."

NE QUID NIMIS, *ně quǐd nǐ'mǐs.* Let there be nothing too much; excess is a fault.

NESCIT VOX MISSA REVERTI, *ně'scǐt vŏx mǐs'sǎ rě-věr'tǐ.* A word uttered cannot be recalled.

NIHIL OBSTAT, *nǐ'hǐl ŏb'stǎt.* Nothing prevents; there is no objection. A phrase sometimes placed at the beginning of books. See *Imprimatur.*

NIL ADMIRARI, *nǐl ǎd'mǐ-rā'rǐ.* To be astonished at nothing. —Horace. A *nil admirari* state of mind.

NIL NOVI SUB SOLE, *nǐl nǒ'vǐ sŭb sō'lě.* Nothing new under the sun.

NOLENS VOLENS, *nō'lěns vŏ'lěns (nō'lěnz vō'lěnz).* Whether one will or not.

NOLI ME TANGERE, *nō'lǐ mē tǎn-gě,ěr.* Touch me not.

NOLLE PROSEQUI, *nŏl'lě prō'sě-qui (nŏl'ê prŏs'ê-kwi).* To be unwilling to proceed. A legal phrase to indicate the abandonment of a suit.

NON EST, *nŏn ěst (nŏn ěst).* It is not; wanting; minus.

NON MULTA, SED MULTUM, *nŏn mŭl'tǎ sěd mŭl'tǔm* Not many things, but much; quality, not quantity.

NON NOVA SED NOVE, *nŏn nǒ'vǎ sěd nǒ'vě.* Not new things, but old things in a new manner.

NON OMNIA POSSUMUS OMNES, *nŏn ŏm'nǐ-ǎ pŏs'sǔ-mǔs ŏm'něs.* We cannot all of us do everything.—Virgil.

NON POSSUMUS, *nŏn pǒs'sǔ-mǔs (nǒn pǒs'ǔ-mǔs).* We cannot,—an irrevocable refusal; as, to utter a *non possumus.*

NON SEQUITUR, *nŏn sě'qui-tǔr (nǒn sěk'wǐ-tǔr).* It does not follow; an unwarranted conclusion.

NOSCE TEIPSUM, *nōs'cě tē-ǐp'sǔm.* Know thyself. From the Greek inscription written over the entrance to the Delphian temple.

NOTA BENE, *nō'tǎ bě'ně (nō'tà bē'ně).* Mark well; give good heed. *N. B.*

NUNC EST BIBENDUM, *nǔnc ěst bǐ-běn'dǔm.* It is time for a drink.—Horace.

OBIIT, *ŏb'ǐ-ǐt.* He (or she) died.

OBITER DICTA, *ŏb'ǐ-těr dǐc'tǎ.* Things said incidentally; an unofficial expression or opinion.

OCULOS HABENT ET NON VIDEBUNT, *ŏc'ǔ-lōs hǎ'běnt ět nōn vǐ-dē'bǔnt.* They have eyes but will not see. Said of those who are obstinate.

ODI PROFANUM VULGUS, *ō'dǐ prō-fā'nǔm vǔl'gǔs.* I hate the vulgar crowd.—Horace.

ODIUM THEOLOGICUM, *ŏ'dǐ-ǔm thě'ŏ-lŏ'gǐ-cǔm (ō'dǐ-ǔm thě'ŏ-lŏ'jǐ-cǔm).* The hatred of theologians.

OMNE IGNOTUM PRO MAGNIFICO EST, *ŏm'ně ǐg-nō'tǔm prō māg-nǐ'fǐ-cō ěst.* Everything unknown is magnified; distance lends enchantment.—Tacitus.

OMNIA VINCIT AMOR, *ŏm'nǐ-ǎ vǐn'cǐt ǎ'mŏr.* Love conquers all things.—Virgil.

ORA PRO NOBIS, *ō'rǎ prō nō'bǐs.* Pray for us.

O SANCTA SIMPLICITAS! *ō sānc'tǎ sǐm-plǐ'cǐ-tās.* O blessed simplicity!—said ironically.

O TEMPORA! O MORES! *ō těm'pŏ-rǎ ō mō'rěs.* Alas, for the age we live in and its manners!—Cicero.

O TERQUE QUATERQUE BEATI! *ō těr'quě quǎ-těr'quě bě-ā'tǐ.* O thrice and again happy!—Virgil. Meaning,—those who die for their country.

OTIUM CUM DIGNITATE, *ō'tǐ-ǔm cǔm dǐg'nǐ-tā'tě.* Ease with dignity.—Cicero. A phrase applied humorously to stout people.

PANEM ET CIRCENSES, *pā'něm ět cǐr-cěn'sěs.* Bread and the games.—Juvenal. Words applied contemptuously to those who think only of pleasure.

PARTICEPS CRIMINIS, *pǎr'tǐ-cěps crǐ'mǐ-nǐs (pǎr'tǐ-sěps crǐ'-mǐ-nǐs).* An accomplice.

PARTURIUNT MONTES, NASCETUR RIDICULUS MUS, *pǎr-tǔ'rǐ-ǔnt mŏn'těs nās-cē'tǔr rǐ-dǐ'cǔ-lǔs mǔs.* The mountains labor, a ridiculous mouse will be born; big boasting results in nothing.—Horace.

PATER FAMILIAS, *pǎ'těr fǎ-mǐl'ǐ-ǎs (pā'těr fà-mǐl'ǐ-ǎs).* The father of the family.

PATER NOSTER, *pǎ'těr nǒs'těr (pā'těr nǒs'těr).* Our father.

PATER PATRIÆ, *pǎ'těr pǎ'trǐ-æ.* The father of his country.

PATRES CONSCRIPTI, *pǎ'trēs cǒn-scrǐp'tǐ (pā'trēz kǒn-skrǐp'tǐ).* The conscript fathers; the Roman senate. The words are often jocularly applied to the members of a town council.

PAUCA SED BONA, *pau'cǎ sěd bǒ'nǎ.* A few things, but good things.

PAX VOBISCUM! *pǎx vō-bǐs cǔm.* Peace be with you!

PECCAVI, *pěc-cā'vǐ.* I have sinned. Used to acknowledge one's mistake.

PER JOCUM, *pěr jŏ'cǔm.* For fun.

PER JOVEM! *pěr jŏ'věm.* By Jove! By Jupiter!

PER SALTUM, *pěr sǎl'tǔm.* By a jump.

PER SE, *pěr sě.* Of itself; without other support.

PERSONA GRATA, *pěr-sō'nǎ grā'tǎ.* A favored person; one always welcome. In diplomacy, a *persona non grata* is an unacceptable ambassador or other official representative from a foreign country.

POETA NASCITUR, ORATOR FIT, *pǒ-ē'tǎ nās'cǐ-tǔr ō-rā'tŏr fǐt.* The poet is born, the orator made. The French say: "You can learn to cook but not to grill."

PONS ASINORUM, *pŏns ǎ'sǐ-nō'rǔm (pŏnz ǎs'ǐ-nō'rǔm).* The bridge of asses. Applied to first difficult proposition in Euclid's textbook of geometry.

POST HOC ERGO PROPTER HOC, *pōst hŏc ěr'gō prŏp'těr hŏc.* After that, therefore, on account of that; bad logic, taking an antecedent as a cause.

POTIUS MORI QUAM FŒDARI, *pǒ'tǐ-ǔs mǒ'rǐ quǎm fœ-dā'rǐ.* Death before dishonor.

PRIMA FACIE, *prǐ'mǎ fǎ'cǐ-ē (prǐ'mà fā'shǐ-ê).* At the first glance; as, *prima facie* evidence.

PRIMO MIHI, *prǐ'mō mǐ'hǐ.* First of all myself. Motto of the egotist.

PRIMUM VIVERE DEINDE PHILOSOPHARI, *prǐ'mǔm vǐv'ě-rě dě-ǐn'dě phǐ-lǒ'sǒ-phā'rǐ.* Earn your living first, then you may talk.

PRIMUS INTER PARES, *prǐ'mǔs ǐn'těr pǎ'rēs.* First among equals; for example, the president of a republic.

PRINCIPIA, NON HOMINES, *prǐn-cǐ'pǐ-ǎ nŏn hŏ'mǐ-nēs.* Principles, not men.

PRO ARIS ET FOCIS, *prō ā'rǐs ět fō'cǐs.* For altars and hearths; for faith and fatherland.

PRO BONO PUBLICO, *prō bǒ'nō pǔb'lǐ-cō (prō bǒ'nò pǔb'lǐ-kô).* For the public good.

PRO FORMA, *prō fŏr'mǎ.* As a matter of form.

PROH PUDOR! *prōh pǔ'dŏr.* For shame!

PROPAGANDA FIDE, *prō'pā-gǎn'dǎ fǐ'dě (prō'pà-gǎn'dà fǐ dě).* For extending the faith.

PRO TEMPORE, *prō těm'pŏ-rě (prō těm'pò-rê).* For the time being. *Pro tem.*

QUALIS PATER TALIS FILIUS, *quǎ'lǐs pǎ'těr tā'lǐs fǐ'lǐ-ǔs.* Like father, like son; a chip of the old block.

QUANDOQUE BONUS DORMITAT HOMERUS, *quǎn-dō'quě bǒ'nǔs dǒr-mǐ'tǎt hǒ-mē'rǔs.* Even the good Homer sometimes nods.—Horace. Not even the greatest always excel.

QUID NUNC? *quǐd nǔnc (quǐd nǔnc).* What now? A newsmonger or gossip.

QUOD ERAT DEMONSTRANDUM, *quǒd ě'rǎt dē'mǒn-strǎn'dǔm (kwǒd ěr'ǎt dē'mǒn-strǎn'dǔm).* Which was to be proved. *Q.E.D.*

QUOD ERAT FACIENDUM, *quǒd ě'rǎt fǎ'cǐ-ěn'dǔm.* Which was to be done. *Q.E.F.*

QUOD SCRIPSI SCRIPSI, *quǒd scrǐp'sǐ scrǐp'sǐ.* What I have written, I have written. To express an unalterable decision. Words attributed to Pontius Pilate.

QUOMODO VALES? *quō'mŏ-dŏ vǎ'lēs.* How are you?

QUOT HOMINES, TOT SENTENTIÆ, *quǒt hŏ'mǐ-nēs tǒt sěn-těn'-tǐ-æ.* As many opinions as there are persons.—Terence. Too many cooks spoil the broth.

RARA AVIS IN TERRIS, *rā'rǎ ǎ'vǐs ǐn těr'rǐs.* A rare bird on earth.—Juvenal. Sometimes used of a sly or knowing person.

REDUCTIO AD ABSURDUM, *rě-dǔc'tǐ-ō ǎd ǎb-sǔr'dǔm (rě-dǔk-shǐ-ô ǎd ǎb-sǔr'dǔm).* A reducing to an absurdity.

RELIGIO LAICI, *rě-lǐ'gǐ-ō lā'ǐ-cǐ (rě-lǐj'ǐ-ô lā'ǐ-sǐ).* The religion of a layman.

RELIGIO MEDICI, *rě-lǐ'gǐ-ō mě'dǐ-cǐ (rě-lǐj'ǐ-ô měd'ǐ-sǐ).* The religion of a physician.

REQUIESCAT IN PACE, *rě'qui-ēs'cǎt ǐn pā'cě (rěk'wǐ-ěs'kǎt ǐn pā'sě).* May he rest in peace. *R.I.P.*

RES JUDICATA, *rēs jū'dǐ-cā'tǎ.* A matter decided; a case already settled. The French phrase is *chose jugée.*

RES, NON VERBA, *rēs nŏn věr'bǎ.* Deeds not words. The secret of success.

RUS IN URBE, *rǔs ǐn ǔr'bě (rǔs ǐn ǔr'bê).* A residence in or near town, with many of the advantages of the country.

SALUS POPULI SUPREMA LEX, *sǎ'lǔs pǒ'pǔ-lǐ sǔ-prē'mǎ lěx.* The welfare of the people is the first law.—From the Laws of the XII Tables.

SANCTUM SANCTORUM, *sānc'tǔm sānc-tō'rǔm (sǎnk'tǔm sǎnk-tō'rǔm).* The holy of holies.

SAPIENS NIHIL AFFIRMAT QUOD NON PROBET, *sǎ'pǐ-ēns nǐ'hǐl ǎf-fǐr'mǎt quǒd nōn prǒ'bět.* A wise man says nothing he cannot prove.

SEMPER FIDELIS, *sěm'pěr fǐ-dē'lǐs.* Always faithful.

SERVUS SERVORUM DEI, *sěr-vǔs sěr-vō'rǔm dě'ǐ.* Servant of the servants of God. A title used by the pope.

SESQUIPEDALIA VERBA, *sěs'qui-pě-dā'lǐ-ǎ věr'bǎ.* Words a foot and a half long.—Horace. Pompous twaddle with little meaning.

SIC SEMPER TYRANNIS, *sǐc sěm'pěr tў-rǎn'nǐs (sǐk sěm'pěr tǐ-rǎn'ǐs).* Thus ever to tyrants. The motto of Virginia.

SIC TRANSIT GLORIA MUNDI, *sǐc trǎn'sǐt glō'rǐ-ǎ mǔn'dǐ.* Thus passes the glory of the world. Words addressed to the pope on his election,—accompanied by the burning of flax.

SILENT LEGES INTER ARMA, *sǐ'lěnt lě'gēs ǐn'těr ǎr'mǎ.* The laws are silent in the midst of arms.—Cicero.

SIMILIA SIMILIBUS CURANTUR, *sǐ-mǐl'ǐ-à sǐ-mǐl'ǐ-bǔs cū-răn'-tǔr.* Like things are cured by like. The principle of homeopathy.

SI MONUMENTUM REQUIRIS, CIRCUMSPICE, *sǐ mǒn'ǔ-měn'-tǔm rě-qui'ris cir-cǔm'spǐ-cě.* If you seek my monument, look around. The epitaph of Sir Christopher Wren in St. Paul's Cathedral, of which he was the architect.

SINE DIE, *sǐ'ně dǐ'ē (si'ně dǐ'ě).* Without a day; finally. E.g., an adjournment *sine die.*

SINE QUA NON, *sǐ'ně quā nǒn (si'ně kwā nǒn).* Without which, not; essential; as, a *sine qua non* condition.

SI VIS PACEM PARA BELLUM, *sǐ vǐs pā'cěm pär'ā běl'lǔm.* If you wish peace, prepare for war. A specious maxim.

SOLITUDINEM FACIUNT, PACEM APPELLANT, *sǒ'lǐ-tū'dǐ-něm fǎ'cǐ-ǔnt pā'cěm ǎp-pěl'lǎnt.* They make a wilderness and call it peace.—Tacitus.

SOL LUCET OMNIBUS, *sǒl lū'cět ǒm'nǐ-bǔs.* The sun shines for all; even the poorest have certain natural rights.

SPIRITUS PROMPTUS EST, CARO AUTEM INFIRMA, *spǐr'ǐ-tǔs prǒmp'tǔs ěst cǎ'rō au'těm ǐn-fǐr'mà.* The spirit is willing, but the flesh is weak; good-natured but indolent.

STATU QUO ANTE BELLUM, *stǎ'tū quǒ ǎn'tě běl'lǔm (stǎ'tù kwō ǎn'tě běl'ǔm).* As things were before the war, or in *statu quo.* Used to express the unchanged state of things in general.

SUB LEGE LIBERTAS, *sǔb lē'gě lǐ-běr'tàs.* Liberty under the law; the only freedom compatible with order.

SUB POENA, *sǔb pœ'nà (sǔb pē'nà).* Under a penalty. A judicial writ requiring attendance at a certain time and place under penalty.

SUB ROSA, *sǔb rǒ'sā (sǔb rō'zà).* Under the rose; secretly.

SUB SPECIE, *sǔb spě'cǐ-ē.* Under the appearance of.

SUFFICIT DIEI MALITIA SUA, *sǔf'fǐ-cǐt dǐ-ē'ǐ mà-lǐ'tǐ-à sǔ'à.* Sufficient for the day is the evil thereof; don't meet trouble halfway.

SUI GENERIS, *sū'ǐ gě'ně-rǐs (sū'ǐ jěn'ěr-ǐs).* Of its own kind; unlike any other.

SUMMA CUM LAUDE, *sǔm'mā cǔm lau'dě.* With highest honors.

SUNT LACRIMÆ RERUM, *sǔnt lǎ'crǐ-mœ rē'rǔm.* There are tears for suffering.—Virgil.

SURSUM CORDA, *sǔr'sǔm cǒr'dǎ.* Lift up your hearts; take courage.

TÆDIUM VITÆ, *tœ'dǐ-ǔm vǐ'tœ (tē'dǐ-ǔm vǐ'tě).* The weariness of life, which comes from doing nothing.

TE DEUM LAUDAMUS, *tē dě'ǔm lau-dā'mǔs (tē dē'ǔm lô-dā'mǔs).* We praise thee, O God.

TEMPUS EDAX RERUM, *těm'pǔs ě'dāx rē'rǔm.* Time is the devourer of all things.—Ovid.

TEMPUS FUGIT, *těm'pǔs fū'gǐt (těm'pǔs fū'jǐt).* Time flies.

TEMPUS OMNIA REVELAT, *těm'pǔs ǒm'nǐ-à rě-vē'lǎt.* Time reveals all things.

TERMINUS AD QUEM, *těr'mǐ-nǔs ǎd quěm.* The limit to which; the goal.

TERMINUS A QUO, *těr'mǐ-nǔs ā quǒ.* The limit from which; the starting point.

TERRA FIRMA, *těr'rǎ fǐr'mǎ (těr'à fěr'mà).* The firm land; the continent.

TERRA INCOGNITA, *těr'rǎ ǐn-cǒg'nǐ-tǎ (těr'à ǐn-kǒg'nǐ-tà).* An unknown land.

TERTIUM QUID, *těr'tǐ-ǔm quid (těr'shǐ-ǔm kwǐd).* A third something, produced by the union of two different things or the collision of two opposing forces.

TIBI GRATIAS, *tǐb'ǐ grā'tǐ-ās.* Thank you.

TIMEO DANAOS ET DONA FERENTES, *tǐm'ě-ǒ dǎ'nà-ōs ět dō'nǎ fě-rěn'tēs.* I fear the Greeks even when they bring gifts. The guileful should never be trusted.—Virgil.

TIMEO HOMINEM UNIUS LIBRI, *tǐm'ě-ō hǒm'ǐněm ū-nǐ'ǔs lǐ'brǐ.* I fear the man of one book; he who possesses thorough knowledge of a book is a redoubtable adversary. —St. Thomas Aquinas.

TU QUOQUE, *tū quǒ'quě (tū kwō'kwě).* Thou also; a *tu quoque* argument, that is, a weak and worthless one.

UBI BENE IBI PATRIA, *ū'bǐ bě'ně ǐ'bǐ pǎ'trǐ-à.* Where one is well off, there is his country. A paraphrase of Pacuvius.

ULTIMA RATIO REGUM, *ǔl'tǐ-mǎ rā'tǐ-ō rē'gǔm.* The last argument of kings,—engraved on French cannon by order of Louis XIV.

ULTRA VIRES, *ǔl'trā vǐ'rēs (ǔl'trà vǐ'rēz).* Beyond power; transcending authority. A phrase used frequently in relation to acts by corporations in excess of their legal rights.

UT INFRA; UT SUPRA, *ǔt ǐn'frà ǔt sǔ'prà.* As below; as above (quoted). Direction notes in books.

VADE MECUM, *vā'dě mē'cǔm (vā'dě' mē'cǔm).* Go with me; a constant companion.

VÆ VICTIS, *vœ vǐc'tǐs.* Woe to the conquered. Said to have been the exclamation of Brennus, when he threatened to exterminate the Romans.

VARIORUM, *vā'rǐ-ō'rǔm.* Of various things. With the comments of various critics; as, a *variorum* edition of Shakespeare.

VENI, VIDI, VICI, *vē'nǐ vǐ'dǐ vǐ'cǐ (vē'nǐ vǐ'dǐ vǐ'sǐ).* I came, I saw, I conquered. The laconic dispatch in which Julius Cæsar announced to the Senate his victory in Asia Minor.

VERBUM SAPIENTI (see INTELLIGENTI PAUCA).

VIA MEDIA, *vǐ'ǎ mě'dǐ-à (vǐ'à mě'dǐ-à).* A middle course.

VICE VERSA, *vǐ'cě věr'sā (vǐ'sě věr'sà).* The terms being interchanged.

VI ET ARMIS, *vǐ ět är'mǐs.* By main force.

VIR BONUS DICENDI PERITUS, *vǐr bǒ'nǔs dǐ-cěn'dǐ pě-rǐ'tǔs.* A good man skilled in the art of speaking. The Roman definition of an orator.

VIS COMICA, *vǐs cǒm'ǐ-cà.* The comic element or power; the gift of causing laughter.—Julius Cæsar.

VIS INERTIÆ, *vǐs ǐn-ěr'tǐ-œ (vǐs ǐn-ěr'shǐ-ě).* The power of inertia.

VIVA VOCE, *vǐ'vā vō'cě (vǐ'và vō'sě).* With the living voice; by word of mouth.

VIVE VALEQUE! *vǐ'vě vǎl-ē'quě.* Long life and prosperity!— Horace. Used at the end of letters.

VOX CLAMANTIS IN DESERTO, *vǒx clā-mǎn'tǐs ǐn dē-sěr'tō.* A voice crying in the wilderness. Said of one whose advice is not heeded.

VOX ET PRÆTEREA NIHIL, *vǒx ět prœ-tě'rě-ā nǐ'hǐl.* A voice and nothing more; sound without sense.

VOX POPULI VOX DEI, *vǒx pǒ'pǔ-lǐ vǒx dě'ǐ (vǒks pǒp'ǔ-lǐ vǒks dě'ǐ).* The voice of the people, God's voice.

VULNERANT OMNES, ULTIMA NECAT, *vǔl'ně-rǎnt ǒm'nēs ǔl'tǐ-mǎ ně'cǎt.* They all wound, the last kills. An inscription found on old clocks referring to the hours.

WORDS AND PHRASES FROM MODERN LANGUAGES

All phrases from the Italian are marked (It.); those from the Spanish, (Sp.); and those from the German, (Ger.). The unmarked phrases are from the French.

The key to pronunciation of the following list of words and phrases will be found in the introductory pages of this volume.

ABANDON, *a'bän'dôn'.* Unconstraint; an amiable negligence in speech or manner.

A BAS, *à bä'.* Down with (disapproving).

À BAS L'INJUSTICE, *à bä' län'zhüs'tēs'.* Down with injustice.

ABSENCE D'ESPRIT, *àp'säns' děs'prě'.* Absence of mind.

À CHEVAL, *à shě-väl'.* On horseback.

A CHICO PAJARILLO CHICO NIDILLO (Sp.), *ä chě'kō pä-Hä-rēl'yō chě'kō nē-THěl'yō.* Little bird, little nest; adapt your manners to your company.

À COMPTE, *à kôNt'.* On account.

À CORPS PERDU, *à kôr' pěr'dü'.* Headlong; desperately.

À COUVERT, *à kōō'věr'.* Under cover; protected; sheltered.

À DEUX MAINS, *à dü' mäN'.* With or for both hands; having a double office or employment.

À DISCRÉTION, *à děs'krä'syôN'.* At discretion; unrestrictedly.

A DONDE FUERES HAZ LO QUE VIERES (Sp.), *ä dôn'dä fwä'rěs äth lō kä vyä'rěs.* Where you are, do what you see; when in Rome, do as Rome does.

À DROI TE, *à druät'.* To the right.

AFFAIRE D'AMOUR, *a'fär' dä'mōōr'.* A love affair.

AFFAIRE D'HONNEUR, *a'fär' dô'nûr'.* An affair of honor; a duel.

AFFAIRE DE CŒUR, *a'fär' dě kûr'.* An affair of the heart; a love affair.

À FIN, *à fäN'.* To the end or object.

À FOND, *à fôN'.* To the bottom; thoroughly.

À GAUCHE, *à gôsh'.* To the left.

À GENOUX, *à zhě-nōō'.* On one's knees; kneeling.

À GRANDS FRAIS, *à gräN' frě'.* At great expense.

À HAUTE VOIX, *à ōt' vwä'.* Aloud.

À HUIS CLOS, *à üě' klō'.* With closed doors; secretly.

À L'ABANDON, *à lä'bän'dôn'.* In confusion; uncared for.

À LA BELLE ÉTOILE, *à lä běl' ä'twäl'.* Under the canopy of heaven; in the open air at night.

A LA BONNE HEURE, *à lä bǒ'nûr'.* Well done! That's something like!

A L'ABRI, *à lä'brě'.* Under shelter.

À LA CAMPAGNE, *à lä kän'pàn'y'.* In the country.

À LA CARTE, *à lä kärt'.* By the bill of fare; to dine *a la carte.*

À LA CRÉOLE, *à lä krä'ōl'.* With tomatoes.

À LA DÉROBÉE, *à lä dä'rô'bä'.* Stealthily.

À LA FRANÇAISE, *à lä fräN'säz'.* In the French fashion.

À LA GRECQUE, *à lä grěk'.* After the Greek fashion.

A LA MODE, *à lä mōd'.* In the fashion; according to the custom or fashion.

A LA TEMPESTAD SIGUE LA CALMA (Sp.), *ä lä těm-pěs-täTH' sě'gä lä käl'mä.* After the storm comes the calm.

AL BUON VINO NON BISOGNA FRASCA (It.), äl bwŏn vē'nŏ nŏn bē-zŏn'yä fräs'kä. Good wine needs no bush.

AL CONTADO (Sp.), äl kŏn-tä'THŏ. For cash; ready money.

A L'ENVI, á län'vē'. In emulation of one another.

AL FRESCO (It.), äl fräs'kō. In the open air.

A L'IMPROVISTE, á län'prō'vēst'. Unawares; on a sudden.

ALLA VOSTRA SALUTE (It.), äl'lä vŏs'trä sä-lōō'tĕ. To your good health.

ALLEZ-VOUS-EN, ä'lä'vōō'zän'. Away with you; be off.

ALLONS, ä'lŏn'. Come; now then!

AL PIÙ (It.), äl pyōō'. At most.

A MAIN ARMÉE, á män'när'mā'. By force of arms.

AM ANFANG (Ger.), äm än'fäng. In the beginning.

AMAR Y SABER NO PUEDE SER (Sp.), ä-mär' ē sä-bĕr' nŏ pwä'THä sĕr. No one can love and be wise at the same time.

AMENDE HONORABLE, á'män'dŏ'nŏ'rä'bl'. Fit reparation; a satisfactory apology.

À MERVEILLE, á mĕr'vā'y'. Marvelously; to perfection.

AMI DE COUR, ä'mē' dĕ kōōr'. A friend of the court; a false friend; one who is not to be depended on.

AMI DU PEUPLE, ä'mē' dü pû'pl'. Friend of the people.

AMI EN VOIE, ä'mē' än vwä. A friend at court; one who has influence.

AMOR CON AMOR SE PAGA (Sp.), ä-mŏr' kŏn ä-mŏr' sä pä'gä. Love is paid with love; one good turn deserves another.

AMOUR PROPRE, ä'mōōr' prŏ'pr'. Vanity; self-respect.

ANCIEN RÉGIME, än'syän' rä'zhēm'. The former condition of things; of French government before 1789.

À OUTRANCE, á ōō'träns'. To the death; to the last extremity.

À PAS DE GÉANT, á pä' dĕ zhä'än'. With a giant's stride.

À PAS DE LOUP, á pä' dĕ lōō'. With stealthy steps.

À PERTE DE VUE, á pĕrt' dĕ vü'. Till out of sight.

À PEU PRÈS, á pû' prä'. Nearly.

À PIED, á pyä'. On foot.

À POINT, á pwän'. Just in time; to a turn; exactly right.

APRÈS NOUS LE DÉLUGE, áp'rä' nōō' lĕ dä'lüzh'. After us, the deluge.

À PRIMA VISTA (It.), ä prē'mä vĭs'tä. At the first glance.

À PROPOS, á prŏ'pŏ'. To the point; pertinently.

À PROPOS DE RIEN, á prŏ'pŏ' dĕ ryän'. Apropos to nothing; motiveless; for nothing at all.

AQUÍ SE HABLA ESPAÑOL (Sp.), ä-kē' sä ä'blä ĕs-pä-nyŏl'. Spanish is spoken here.

ARGENT COMPTANT, är'zhän' kŏn'tän'. Ready money.

ARMUTH IST KEINE SCHANDE (Ger.), är'mōōt ĭst kī'nĕ shän'dĕ. Poverty is no disgrace.

ARRIÈRE PENSÉE, ä'ryär' pän'sä'. Mental reservation; unavowed purpose.

À TORT ET À TRAVERS, á tŏr'tä ä trä'vär'. At random.

AU BOUT DE SON LATIN, ō bōō' dĕ sŏn' lä'tän'. At the end of his Latin; at one's wit's end; in a fix.

AU CONTRAIRE, ō kŏn'trär'. On the contrary.

AU COURANT, ō kōō'rän'. Well acquainted with; well informed.

AU DÉSESPOIR, ō dä'zĕs'pwär'. In despair.

AU FAIT, ō fĕ'. Expert; up-to-date.

AU FOND, ō fŏn'. At bottom; at heart; really.

AU GRATIN, ō grä'tän'. With cheese or bread raspings to form a crust.

AU JUS, ō zhü'. With the natural juice.

AU PAS DE CHARGE, ō pä dĕ shärzh'. Double quick time.

AU PIS ALLER, ō pē' zä'lä'. At the very worst; let the worst come to the worst. Un pis aller means a last resource, a makeshift.

AU RESTE, ō rĕst'. As for the rest.

AU REVOIR, ō rĕ-vwär'. Till we meet again.

AUSSITÔT DIT, AUSSITÔT FAIT, ō'sē'tō' dĕ' ō'sē'tō' fĕ'. No sooner said than done.

AUTANT D'HOMMES, AUTANT D'AVIS, ō'tän' dŏm' ō'tän' dä've'. Many men, many minds.

AUTRE FOIS, ō'tr' fwä'. Another time.

AUX ARMES, ō zärm'. To arms.

À VOLONTÉ, á vŏ'lŏn'tä'. At pleasure.

À VOTRE SANTÉ, á vŏ'tr' sän'tä'. To your health.

Á VUESTRA SALUD (Sp.), ä vwäs'trä sä-lōōTH'. To your health; good health.

BALLON D'ESSAI, bá'lŏn' dĕs'sĕ'. A balloon sent up to test the direction of air currents,—hence, anything said or done to gauge public feeling on any question.

BAS BLEU, bä' blû'. A bluestocking; a woman who seeks a reputation for learning.

BEAUX YEUX, bō' zyû'. Handsome eyes, a fair face.

BEL ESPRIT, bĕl' ĕs'prē'. A wit; a genius.

BEN TROVATO (It.), bĕn trō-vä'tō. Well invented.

BÊTE NOIRE, bât' nwär'. A black beast; a bore; a nuisance.

BILLET DOUX, or BILLET D'AMOUR, bē'yĕ' dōō' or bē'yĕ' dä'mōōr'. A love letter.

BIZARRE, bē'zär'. Odd; fantastic.

BLASÉ, blä'zä'. Surfeited; term applied to a pose of indifference.

BON AMI, bŏn'nä'mē'. Good friend.

BON GRÉ, MAL GRÉ, bŏn' grä' mäl' grä'. With good or bad grace; willing or unwilling.

BONHOMIE, bŏn'nŏ'mē'. Good nature; simplicity.

BON JOUR, bŏn' zhōōr'. Good day; good morning.

BON MOT, bŏn' mŏ'. A witticism.

BONNE ET BELLE, bŏn' nä-bĕl'. Good and handsome,— said of a woman.

BONNE FOI, bŏn' fwä'. Good faith.

BON SOIR, bŏn' swär'. Good evening.

BON TON, bŏn' tŏn'. Good breeding; the style and manner of gentlefolk.

BOUTE-EN-TRAIN, bōō' tän trän'. Mirth inspirer, merry companion.

BREVETÉ, brĕv'-tä'. Patented.

BUENAS NOCHES (Sp.), bwä'näs nŏ'chĕs. Good evening.

BUENAS TARDES (Sp.), bwä'näs tär'dĕs. Good afternoon.

BUENO (Sp.), bwä'nŏ. Good; all right.

BUENOS DIAS (Sp.), bwä'nŏs dē'äs. Good morning.

CADA ONEJA CON SU PAREJA (Sp.), kä'THä ō-nä'Hä kŏn sōō pä-rä'Hä. Every sheep with its like; birds of a feather flock together.

CADA UNO SABE DONDE LE APRIETA EL ZAPATO (Sp.), kä'THä ōō'nŏ sä'bĕ dŏn'dä lä ä-pryä'tä ĕl thä-pä'tŏ. Each one knows where his own shoe pinches.

CARTE BLANCHE, kärt' blänsh'. Full power; full permission.

CASTELLO CHE DÀ ORECCHIA SI VUOL RENDERE (It.), käs-tĕl'lō kä dä ō-räk'kyä sē vwŏl rĕn'dĕ-rĕ. The fortress that parleys soon surrenders.

CELA VA SANS DIRE, sĕ-lä' vä' sän' dēr'. That goes without saying; that is understood.

CE N'EST QUE LE PREMIER PAS QUI COÛTE, sĕ nĕ' kĕ lĕ prĕ-myä' pä' kĕ' kōōt'. It is only the first step that is difficult.

C'EST À DIRE, sĕ' tä' dēr'. That is to say.

C'EST UNE AUTRE CHOSE, sĕ'tün' ō'tr' shōz'. That is quite another thing.

CHACUN À SON GOÛT, shä'kûn' nä sŏn' gōō'. Every one to his taste.

CHACUN TIRE DE SON CÔTÉ, shä'kûn' tēr' dĕ sŏn' kō-tä'. Every one inclines to his own side or party.

CHANSON DE GESTE, shän'sŏn' dĕ zhĕst'. A song of heroic deeds; medieval French epic poem.

CHAPEAU DE BRAS, shä'pō' dĕ brä'. A military cocked hat.

CHAPELLE ARDENTE, shä'pĕl' är'dänt'. The chamber where a dead body lies in state.

CHÂTEAU, shä'tō'. A castle.

CHAUVINISTE, shō'vē'nēst'. Over-aggressive patriot; "jingo."

CHEF-D'ŒUVRE, shĕ'dû'vr'. A masterpiece; a crowning piece of work.

CHEMIN DE FER, shĕ-män' dĕ fär'. Iron road; a railway.

CHERCHEZ LA FEMME shĕr'shä' lä fäm'. Find the woman. Compare the Latin, Dux femina facti.

CHÈRE AMIE, shär' ä'mē'. A dear (female) friend.

CHE SARÀ, SARÀ (It.), kä sä-rä' sä-rä'. What will be, will be.

CHEVAL DE BATAILLE, shĕ-väl' dĕ bä'tä'y'. A war horse; chief dependence or support; one's strong point.

CHI LO SA? (It.), kē lō sä. Who knows?

CHI TACE CONFESSA (It.), kē tä'chĕ kŏn-fĕs'sä. He who keeps silent admits his guilt

CHI VA PIANO VA SANO (It.), kē vä pyä'nŏ vä sä'nŏ. Who goes slowly goes surely.

CI GÎT, sē zhē'. Here lies. (A common inscription on tombstones.)

COMME IL FAUT, kŏ mēl fō'. Proper; as it should be.

COMMENT VOUS PORTEZ VOUS? kŏ'män' vōō' pŏr'tä' vōō'. How are you?

¿COMO SE DICE EN INGLES—? (Sp.), kō'mŏ sä dē'thä ĕn ēn'glĕs. How do you say in English—?

¿COMO SE ESCRIBE EN ESPAÑOL? (Sp.), kō'mŏ sä ĕs-krē'bä ĕn ĕs'pä-nyŏl'. How is it written in Spanish?

¿COMO SE PRONÚNCIA ESA PALABRA? (Sp.), kō'mŏ sä prō-nōōn'thyä ä'sä pä-lä'brä. How is this word pronounced?

¿COMO VA? (colloq. Sp.), kō'mŏ vä. How are you?

COMPAGNON DE VOYAGE, kŏn'pä'nyŏn' dĕ vwä'yäzh'. A traveling companion.

COMPTE RENDU, kŏnt' rän'dü'. An account rendered; a report.

CONCIERGE, kŏn'syärzh. A portress, hall porter, lodge keeper.

CONCOURS, kŏn'kōōr'. Competition (as for a prize); contest.

CON DILIGENZA (It.), kŏn dē-lē-jĕn'tsä. With diligence.

CON DOLORE (It.), kŏn dō-lō'rĕ. With grief; sadly.

CON MUCHO GUSTO (Sp.), kŏn mōō'chŏ gōō'stŏ. With great pleasure.

CONSEIL D'ÉTAT, kŏn'sĕ'y' dä'tä'. A council of state; a privy council.

CONSOMMÉ, kŏn'sŏ'mä'. A clear soup.

CON TRABAJAR ADELANTAMOS (Sp.), kŏn trä-bä-Här' ä' THĕl-än-tä'mŏs. By working we progress.

CONTRETEMPS, kŏn'tr'-tän'. An awkward mishap.

CORDON SANITAIRE, kŏr'dŏn' sä'nē'tär'. A line of sentries to prevent, as far as possible, the spread of contagion or pestilence. (Used also of other precautionary measures.)

COULEUR DE ROSE, kōō'lûr' dĕ rōz'. Rose color.

Coup, *kōō*. A stroke; a blow; a thrust; a dig.

Coup de grace, *kōō' dĕ gräs'*. A finishing-stroke. (Formerly applied to the fatal blow by which the executioner put an end to the torments of a culprit broken on the wheel.)

Coup de main, *kōō' dĕ măn'*. A sudden attack; an enterprise (military); an undertaking; a helping hand.

Coup de maître, *kōō' dĕ mâ'tr'*. A master stroke.

Coup d'essai, *kōō' dä'sĕ'*. A first attempt; an experiment.

Coup d'état, *kōō' dä'tä'*. A stroke of policy, bringing about a sudden change of government (usually by unconstitutional means).

Coup d'œil, *kōō' dü'y'*. A rapid glance; a view.

Coup de pied, *kōō dĕ pyä'*. A kick.

Coup de poing, *kōō dĕ pwăn'*. A blow of the fist; a punch.

Courage sans peur, *kōō'räzh' săn pûr'*. Fearless courage.

Courant d'air, *kōō'răn' dâr'*. A draft.

Course de chevaux, *kōōrs' dĕ shĕ-vō'*. A horse race.

Coûte que coûte, *kōōt' kĕ' kōōt'*. Cost what it may; at any price.

Cuisine, *küē'zĕn'*. A kitchen; cookery.

Dame d'honneur, *dăm' dŏ'nûr'*. A maid of honor.

Dar la mano a (Sp. and It.), *där lä mä'nō ä*. To give the hand to; to shake hands with.

Dar un paseo (Sp.), *där ōōn pä-sä'ō*. To take a walk.

Das geht Sie nichts an (Ger.), *däs gāt zē nĭkts än*. That does not concern you.

De bonne grâce, *dĕ bŏn' gräs'*. With good will; willingly.

Début, *dā'bü'*. First appearance.

Débutante, *dā'bü'tänt'*. A young lady just entering society.

De but en blanc, *dĕ bü' !än blän'*. Bluntly; right off.

Décolleté, *dā'kŏ'l'-tā'*. Wearing a low-necked dress.

Dégagé, *dā'gä'zhä'*. Free; easy; without constraint.

De gaieté de cœur, *dĕ gâ'tä' dĕ kûr'*. In sport; sportively.

De la fama el atajo se entra por el trabajo (Sp.), *dä lä fä'mä ĕl ä-tä'hō sä ĕn'trä pōr ĕl trä-bä'hō*. The path of fame begins by work.

De mal en pis, *dĕ mäl' än pē'*. From bad to worse.

Déme la mano (Sp.), *dā'mä lä mä'nō*. Give me your hand; shake hands.

De moda (Sp.), *dä mō'thä*. Fashionable.

Dénouement, *dā'nōō'män'*. An unraveling or disclosure, as of a plot in a play; a wind-up; a catastrophe.

Dernier ressort, *dĕr'nyä' rē-sôr'*. The last resource.

Désagrément, *dā'zä'grā'män'*. Something disagreeable or unpleasant.

De sol á sol (Sp.), *dä sŏl ä sŏl*. From morning till night.

Dieu est toujours pour les plus gros bataillons, *dyü'ĕ' tōō'zhōōr' pōōr lä plü' grō' bä'tä'yŏn'*. God is always on the side of the largest battalions; the largest army has the best chance.

Dieu et mon droit, *dyü' ā mŏn' drwä'*. God and my right. Motto on the British royal coat of arms.

Dieu vous garde, *dyü' vōō' gärd'*. God protect you.

Di grado in grado (It.), *dē grä'dō ĭn grä'dō*. Step by step; gradually.

Dios me libre de hombre de un libro (Sp.), *dē'ôs mä lē'brä dä ôm'brä dä ōōn lē'brō*. God deliver me from a man of one book.

Di salto (It.), *dē säl'tō*. By leaps.

Dispénseme usted (Sp.), *dēs-pĕn'sä-mä ōōs-tĕth'*. I beg your pardon; allow me.

Di tutti novello par bello (It.), *dē tōōt'tē nō-vĕl'lō pär bĕl'lō*. Everything new seems beautiful.

Dolce far niente (It.), *dōl'chĕ fär nyĕn'tĕ*. The sweet do-nothing; sweet idleness.

Donnant donnant, *dŏn'nän' dŏn'nän'*. Give and take.

Dorer la pilule, *dŏ'rā' lä pē'lül'*. To gild the pill.

Double entente, *dōōb'län'tänt'*. Double meaning.

Durante vita (It.), *dōō-rän'tä vē'tä*. During life.

Eau de cologne, *ō' dĕ kô-lôny''*. Cologne water.

Eau de vie, *ō' dĕ vē'*. Water of life—applied usually to brandy.

Éclat, *ā'klä'*. Splendor, brilliancy.

Édition de luxe, *ā'dē'syôn' dĕ lüks'*. A costly edition of a book, handsomely bound, and usually well illustrated.

Ehrlich währt am längsten (Ger.), *âr'lĭk vârt äm lĕngs'tĕn*. Honesty is the best policy.

Eile mit Weile (Ger.), *i'lĕ mĭt vi'lĕ*. Make haste slowly.

Eine Schwalbe macht keinen Sommer (Ger.), *i'nĕ shväl'bĕ mäkt ki'nĕn zō'mer*. One swallow does not make a summer.

Ein gebranntes Kind scheut das Feuer (Ger.), *īn gä-brän'tĕs kĭnt shoit däs foi'ĕr*. A burnt child dreads the fire.

Élan, *ā'län'*. Military dash; quick, sudden movement.

El árbol se conoce por su fruto (Sp.), *ĕl är'bŏl sä kō-nō'thä pōr sōō frōō'tō*. The tree is known by its fruit.

El ejercicio hace maestro (Sp.), *ĕl ĕh-ĕr-thē'thyō ä'thä mä-ĕs'trō*. Exercise makes the master; practice makes perfect.

Élite, *ā'lēt'*. A select body of persons; society.

El trabajo hace la vida agradable (Sp.), *ĕl trä-bä'hō ä'thä lä vē'thä ä-grä-thä'blä*. Work makes life worth living. (cf. Ger. *Arbeit macht das Leben susz*.)

Embarras des richesses, *än'bä'rä' dä rē'shĕs'*. The plague of riches; difficulty of choice.

Embonpoint, *än'bôn'pwän'*. Roundness; corpulence; mostly used in humorous reference.

En ami, *än nä'mē'*. As a friend.

En arrière, *än nä'ryâr'*. In the rear; behind.

En attendant, *än nä'tän'dän'*. In the meantime.

En avant, *än nä'vän'*. Forward.

En badinant, *än bä'dē'nän'*. In sport; jestingly.

En casa (Sp.), *ĕn kä'sä*. At home.

En cueros, en cueros vivos (Sp.), *ĕn kwä'rōs vē'vōs*. Naked; without clothing.

Ende gut, Alles gut (Ger.), *ĕn'dĕ gōōt ä'lĕs gōōt*. All's well that ends well.

En déshabillé, *än dä'zä'bē'yä'*. Carelessly dressed as at early morning; unprepared.

En Dieu est tout, *än dyü' ĕ tōō'*. In God are all things.

En effet, *än nĕ'fĕ'*. Indeed; really; in effect.

En famille, *än fä'mē'y'*. With one's family; at home.

Enfant gâté, *än'fän' gä'tä'*. A spoiled child.

Enfants perdus, *än'fän' pĕr'dü'*. Lost children; a forlorn hope.

Enfant terrible, *än'fän' tĕ'rē'bl'*. A child or person whose acts or remarks are embarrassing.

Enfant trouvé, *än'fän' trōō'vä'*. A foundling.

Enfin, *än'fän'*. In short; finally; at last.

En grande tenue or toilette, *än' gränd' tĕ-nü' or twä'lĕt'*. In full official, or evening, dress.

En masse, *än' mäs'*. In a body or mass.

Ennui, *än'nwē'*. Weariness; boredom.

En passant, *än' pä'sän'*. In passing; by the way.

En plein jour, *än' plän' zhōōr'*. In broad daylight.

En queue, *än' kü'*. Immediately after; in the rear. Used especially of persons waiting in line, as at the door of a theater or at the ticket office of a railway station.

En rapport, *än' rä'pôr'*. In harmony, relation, or agreement.

En règle, *än' rĕg'l'*. Regular; in order.

En route, *än' rōōt'*. On the way.

Ensemble, *än'sän'bl'*. The whole; together.

En suite, *än' süēt'*. In company; in a set.

Entente cordiale, *än'tänt' kôr'dyäl'*. A good understanding, especially between two states.

Entêté, *än'tĕ'tä'*. Headstrong.

Entourage, *än'tōō'räzh'*. Surroundings; associates.

Entre deux feux, *än'tr' dü' fü'*. Between two fires.

Entre deux vins, *än'tr' dü' vän'*. Between two wines; half drunk.

Entrée, *än'trä'*. Entry; first course.

Entre nous, *än'tr' nōō'*. Between ourselves; in confidence.

En venir aux coups, *än' vĕ-nēr' ō kōō'*. To come to blows.

En verité, *än' vä'rē'tä'*. In truth; really.

En vez de oro es dorado (Sp.), *ĕn väth dä ō'rō ĕs dō-rä'thō*. In place of gold 'tis only gilt; a false friend.

En voiture! *än' vwä'tür'*. All aboard!

E pur si muove! (It.), *ā pōōr sĕ mwô'vĕ*. Nevertheless it moves! (Supposed words of Galileo after his condemnation; referring to the motion of the earth.)

Es freut mich sehr (Ger.), *ĕs froit mĭk zär*. I am very glad.

Est ist nicht Alles Gold, was glänzt (Ger.), *ĕs ĭst nĭkt ä'lĕs gôlt väs glĕntst*. All is not gold that glitters.

Esprit de corps, *ĕs'prē' dĕ kôr'*. The animating spirit of a collective body of persons, as of a regiment, the bar, the clergy, a school.

Esprit des lois, *ĕs'prē' dä lwä'*. Spirit of the laws.

Es thut mir leid (Ger.), *ĕs tōōt mĕr līt*. I am sorry.

Ewigkeit (Ger.), *ā'vĭk-kīt*. Eternity.

Façon de parler, *fä'sôn' dĕ pär'lä'*. Manner of speaking; phrase; locution.

Faire bonne mine, *fâr' bôn' mēn'*. To look pleasant.

Faire les cent coups, *fâr' lä sän' kōō'*. To play all sorts of tricks.

Faire sans dire, *fâr' sän' dēr'*. To act without ostentation.

Faire son devoir, *fâr' sôn' dĕ-vwär'*. To do one's duty.

Fait accompli, *fĕ'tä'kôn'plē'*. An accomplished fact.

Faux pas, *fō' pä'*. A false step; an act of indiscretion.

Femme de chambre, *fäm' dĕ shän'br'*. A chambermaid.

Femme de charge, *fäm' dĕ shärzh'*. A housekeeper.

Fête, *fât*. A feast; festival; holiday.

Fête champêtre, *fât' shän'pâ'tr'*. A rural out-of-door feast; a festival in the fields.

Feu de joie, *fü' dĕ zhwä'*. A bonfire or discharge of firearms as a sign of rejoicing.

Fille de chambre, *fē'y' dĕ shän'br'*. A chambermaid.

Fille d'honneur, *fē'y' dŏ'nûr'*. A maid of honor; a lady in waiting.

Fleur-de-lis, *flûr'dĕ-lē'*. The flower of the lily. The coat of arms of France (a heraldic iris).

FRISCH BEGONNEN, HALB GEWONNEN (Ger.), *frĭsh bĕ-gŏn'nĕn hälp gĕ-vŏn'nĕn.* Well begun is half done.
FROIDES MAINS, CHAUDE AMOUR, *frwäd' măn' shō'dä'mōōr'.* Cold hands, warm heart.
FRONT À FRONT, *frŏn'tä frŏn'.* Face to face.
FUYEZ LES DANGERS DU LOISIR, *füĕ'yä' lä dän'zhä' dü lwä'zēr'.* Fly from the dangers of leisure.

GAIETÉ DE CŒUR, *gâ'tā' dĕ kûr'.* Gaiety of heart.
GARÇON, *gàr'sŏn'.* A lad; a waiter.
GARDE À CHEVAL, *gàr'dä shĕ-väl'.* A mounted guard.
GARDE DU CORPS, *gàrd' dü kŏr'.* A bodyguard.
GARDEZ LA FOI, *gàr'dā' lä fwä'.* Keep the faith.
GARDEZ-VOUS-EN BIEN, *gàr'dā' vōō' zän' byăn'.* Don't you do it; do nothing of the kind.
GENDARME, *zhän'därm'.* Policeman; a turbulent woman; a flaw (as in a diamond).
GENS DE CONDITION, *zhän' dĕ kŏn'dē'syŏn'.* People of rank.
GENS DE MÊME FAMILLE, *zhän' dĕ mâm' fà'mē'y.* People of the same family; birds of a feather.
GENTILHOMME, *zhän'tē'yŏm'.* A gentleman; a nobleman.
GIOVINE SANTO, DIAVOLO VECCHIO (It.), *jō'vē-nĕ sän'tō dyä'vō-lō vĕk'kyō.* A young saint, an old devil.
GLEICH UND GLEICH GESELLT SICH GERN (Ger.), *glīk ōōnt glīk gĕ-zĕlt' zĭk gârn.* Birds of a feather flock together.
GLI ASSENTI HANNO TORTO (It.), *lyē äs-sĕn'tē än'nō tŏr'tō.* The absent are in the wrong.
GOUTTE À GOUTTE, *gōō'tä-gōōt'.* Drop by drop.
GOUVERNANTE, *gōō'vēr'nänt'.* A governess; housekeeper.
GRÂCE À DIEU, *grä'sà dyŭ'.* Thanks be to God.
GRANDE CHÈRE ET BEAU FEU, *gränd' shâr' ā bō' fŭ'.* Good fare and a good fire; comfortable quarters.
GRAND MERCI, *grän' mēr'sē'.* Many thanks.
GROSSE TÊTE ET PEU DE SENS, *grŏs' tât' ā pŭ' dĕ sän'.* A big head and little sense.
GUERRA Á CUCHILLO (Sp.), *gär'rä ä kōō-chēl'yō.* War to the knife.
GUERRE À MORT, *gâr à mŏr'.* War to the death.
GUTEN MORGEN (Ger.), *gōōt'ĕn mŏr'gĕn.* Good morning.

HACE BUEN TIEMPO (Sp.), *ä'thä bwän tyĕm'pō.* It is fine weather.
HASTA LUEGO (Sp.), *äs'tä lwä'gō.* Until by and by; I'll see you later.
HASTA OTRA VEZ (Sp.), *äs'tä ō'trä vāth.* Until another time; till we meet again.
HASTA MAÑANA (Sp.), *äs'tä män-yä'nä.* Good-by; until tomorrow.
HAUT GOÛT, *ō' gōō'.* High flavor; elegant taste.
HAUT TON, *ō' tŏn'.* Highest fashion.
HOMME D'AFFAIRES, *ôm' dà'fâr'.* A man of business; an agent.
HOMME DE ROBE, *ôm' dĕ rôb'.* A person in a civil office.
HOMME D'ESPRIT, *ôm' dĕs'prē'.* A wit; a genius.
HOMME D'ÉTAT, *ôm' dä'tä'.* A statesman.
HONI SOIT QUI MAL Y PENSE, *ô'nē' swä' kē' màl' ē päns'.* Evil to him who evil thinks. (The motto of the Order of the Garter.)
HORS DE COMBAT, *ôr' dĕ kŏn'bà'.* Out of the fight; disabled; unfit to continue a contest.
HORS DE LA LOI, *ôr' dĕ là lwä'.* Outlawed.
HORS DE PROPOS, *ôr' dĕ prō'pō'.* Wide of the point; inapplicable.
HORS DE SAISON, *ôr' dĕ sĕ'zŏn'.* Out of season; unseasonable.
HORS D'ŒUVRE, *ôr' dûv'r'.* Out of course; a side dish; a digression.
HÔTEL DE VILLE, *ō'tĕl' dĕ vēl'.* A town hall.
HÔTEL DIEU, *ō'tĕl' dyŭ'.* The chief hospital of a town.
HÔTEL GARNI, *ō'tĕl' gär'nē'.* Furnished lodgings.

ICH DIEN (Ger.), *ĭk dēn.* I serve.
IDÉE FIXE, *ē'dā' fēks'.* A fixed idea; a mental conviction or attitude.
IGNORANCE CRASSE, *ēn'yŏ'räns' kräs'.* Gross ignorance.
I GRAN DOLORI SONO MUTI (It.), *ē grän dō-lō'rē sō'nō mōō'tē.* Great griefs are silent.
IL FAUT DE L'ARGENT, *ēl fō' dĕ làr'zhän'.* Money is needed.
IL N'A NI BOUCHE NI ÉPERON, *ēl nä' nē bōōsh' nē äp'-rŏn'.* He has neither mouth nor spur; he has neither wit nor courage.
IL NE FAUT JAMAIS DÉFIER UN FOU, *ēl nĕ fō' zhà'mĕ' dä'fyä' ŭn fōō'.* One should never provoke a fool.
IL NE FAUT POINT DISPUTER DES GOÛTS, *ēl nĕ fō' pwän' dĕs'pü'tä' dä gōō'.* There is no accounting for tastes.
IL N'EST SAUCE QUE D'APPÉTIT, *ēl nĕ' sōs' kĕ dä'pä'tē'* Hunger is the best sauce.
IL SOUFFLE LE CHAUD ET LE FROID, *ēl sōōf'l' lĕ shō ā lĕ frwä'.* He blows hot and cold; he's a timeserver.
IMPOLI, *än'pō'lē'.* Unpolished; rude.
IN UN GIORNO NON SI FE' ROMA (It.), *ēn ōōn jōr'nō nōn sē fä rō'mä.* Rome was not built in a day.

JAMAIS BON COUREUR NE FUT PRIS, *zhà'mĕ' bŏn kōō'rûr' nĕ fü' prē'.* A good runner is not to be taken; old birds are not to be caught with chaff.

JE NE SAIS QUOI, *zhĕ nĕ sä' kwä'.* I know not what; hard to describe; used humorously, as a "je ne sais quoi."
JE N'OUBLIERAI JAMAIS, *zhĕ nōō'blyä'rä' zhà'mĕ'.* I will never forget.
JE SUIS PRÊT, *zhĕ süĕ' prĕ'.* I am ready.
JET D'EAU, *zhĕ' dō'.* A fountain; a jet of water.
JEU DE MOTS, *zhŭ' dĕ mō'.* A play upon words; a pun.
JEU D'ESPRIT, *zhŭ' dĕs'prē'.* A witticism.
JEU DE THÉÂTRE, *zhŭ dĕ tä'ät'r'.* A stage trick; claptrap.
JEUNESSE DORÉE, *zhŭ'nĕs' dô'rä'.* Gilded youth.
JOUER DE BONHEUR, *zhwä' dĕ bô'nûr'.* To be in luck.

L'ADDITION, *là'dē'syŏn'.* The bill.
L'ADDITION S'IL VOUS PLAÎT, *là'dē'syŏn' sē vōō' plĕ'.* Give me my bill please.
LA CARIDAD BIEN ORDENADA EMPIEZA POR UNO MISMO (Sp.), *lä kä-rē-THäd' byän ôr-dä-nä'THä ĕm-pyä'thä pôr ōō'nō mēs'mō.* Charity well directed begins with oneself; charity begins at home.
LA COSTUMBRE ES OTRA NATURALEZA (Sp.), *lä kôs-tōōm'brä ĕs ō'trä nä'tōō-rä-lä'thä.* Custom is second nature.
LA CRITIQUE EST AISÉE, L'ART EST DIFFICILE, *lä krē'tēk' ĕ'tä'zä' lärt' dē'fē'sēl'.* Criticism is easy enough, but art is difficult.
LADE NICHT ALLES IN EIN SCHIFF (Ger.), *lä'dĕ nĭkt ä'lĕs ĭn īn shĭf.* Do not load all in one ship; do not put all your eggs into one basket.
L'ADVERSITÉ FAIT LES HOMMES, ET LE BONHEUR LES MONSTRES, *lä'dvĕr'sē'tä' fĕ' lä'zôm' ā lĕ bô'nûr' lä môn'str'.* Adversity makes men, and prosperity, monsters.
LA FORTUNA AIUTA I PAZZI (It.), *lä fôr-tōō'nä ä-yōō'tä ē pät'sē.* Fortune helps fools.
LA FORTUNE PASSE PARTOUT, *là fôr'tün' päs' pàr'tōō'.* Fortune passes everywhere; all men are subject to the vicissitudes of fortune.
LAISSEZ FAIRE, *lĕ'sä' fâr'.* Let it alone.—A *laissez faire* (careless) attitude.
LOYAUTÉ M'OBLIGE, *lwä'yō'tä' mô'blēzh'.* Loyalty binds me
L'AMOUR ET LA FUMÉE NE PEUVENT SE CACHER, *là'mōōr' ā là fü'mä' nĕ pŭv' sĕ kà'shä'.* Love and smoke cannot be hidden.
LA PATIENCE EST AMÈRE, MAIS SON FRUIT EST DOUX, *là pà'syän' sĕ'tà'mâr' mĕ sŏn' früĕ' tĕ' dōō'.* Patience is bitter, but its reward is sweet.
LA PLUMA ES LENGUA DEL ALMA (Sp.), *lä plōō'mä ĕs lĕn'gwä dĕl äl'mä.* The pen is the tongue of the mind.
LA POINTE DU JOUR, *là pwänt' dü zhōōr'.* Daybreak.
LA POVERTÀ È LA MADRE DI TUTTE LE ARTI (It.), *lä pō-vĕr-tä' ĕ lä mä'drĕ dē tōōt'tä lä är'tē.* Poverty is the mother of all the arts.
L'ARGENT, *làr'zhän'.* Silver; money.
L'ART POUR L'ART, *làr' pōōr làr'.* Art for art's sake.
LASCIATE OGNI SPERANZA, VOI CH'ENTRATE (It.), *lä-shä'tĕ ōn'yē spĕr-än'tsä vō'ē kän-trä'tĕ.* All hope abandon, ye who enter here. The inscription over the gates of hell in Dante's "Inferno" (III.9).
L'AVENIR, *làv''nēr'.* The future.
LA VERDAD ES AMARGA (Sp.), *lä vĕr-däTH' ĕs ä-mär'gä.* Truth is bitter.
LA VERTU EST LA SEULE NOBLESSE, *là vĕr'tü' ĕ là sŭl' nô'blĕs'.* Virtue is the sole nobility.
LE BEAU MONDE, *lĕ bō' môND'.* The world of fashion; society.
LE BON TEMPS VIENDRA, *lĕ bŏn' tän' vyän'drä'.* There's a good time coming.
LE COÛT EN ÔTE LE GOÛT, *lĕ kōō'tän' ōt' lĕ gōō'.* The expense takes away the pleasure.
LE DEMI-MONDE, *lĕ dĕ-mē'môND'.* The half-world, that is, of women of equivocal reputation, demimondaines.
LE JEU N'EN VAUT PAS LA CHANDELLE, *lĕ zhŭ'nän' vō' pà' là shän'dĕl'.* The game is not worth the candle; the object is not worth the trouble.
LE MALHEUR NE VIENT JAMAIS SEUL, *lĕ màl'ûr' nĕ vyän' zhà'mĕ' sŭl'.* Misfortune never comes alone.
LE MONDE EST LE LIVRE DES FEMMES, *lĕ môn'dĕ' lĕ lēv'r' dä fàm'.* The world is woman's book.
L'EMPIRE DES LETTRES, *län'pēr' dä lĕt'r'.* The empire of letters.
LE PAROLE SON FEMMINE, E I FATTI SON MASCHI (It.), *lä pà-rō'lĕ sŏn fäm'mē-nĕ ĕ ē fät'tē sŏn mäs'kē.* Words are feminine, and deeds are masculine.
LES CONVENANCES, *lä kŏn'v'-näns'.* The proprieties; the rules of politeness.
LÈSE MAJESTÉ, *lĕz' mà'zhĕs'tä'.* High treason.
LES MURAILLES ONT DES OREILLES, *lä mü'rä'y'-zŏn' dä' zō'rä'y'.* Walls have ears.
LES PLUS SAGES NE LE SONT PAS TOUJOURS, *lä plü' säzh' nĕ lĕ sŏn' pàs tōō'zhōōr'.* The wisest are not always wise.
LE TOUT ENSEMBLE, *lĕ tōō'tän'sän'bl'.* The whole taken together.
LETTRE DE CACHET, *lĕt'r' dĕ kà'shä'.* A sealed letter containing orders; a royal warrant, usually authorizing the imprisonment, without trial, of a person named therein.
LE VRAI N'EST PAS TOUJOURS VRAISEMBLABLE, *lĕ vrĕ' nĕ' pàs' tōō'zhōōr' vrĕ'sän'blà'bl'* Truth is not always probable.

L'HOMME PROPOSE, ET DIEU DISPOSE, *lôm' prô'pōz' ā dyû' dĕs'pōz'*. Man proposes and God disposes.

L'INCONNU, *lăn'kō'nü'*. The unknown.

L'INCROYABLE, *lăn'krwä'yȧ'bl'*. The incredible; the marvelous. (The word incroyable was applied substantively to the fops of the Directory period in the great French Revolution.)

LINGERIE, *lăn'zh'-rē'*. Linen goods; also, collectively, all the linen, cotton, and lace articles of a woman's wardrobe.

LITTÉRATEUR, *lē'tä'rȧ'tûr'*. A literary man.

LO BARATO ES CARO (Sp.), *lō bä-rä'tō ĕs kä'rō*. A bargain is dear.

LO MÁS PRONTO POSIBLE (Sp.), *lō mäs prōn'tō pō-sē'blä*. As soon as possible.

LO QUE NO SE PUEDE REMEDIAR SE HA DE AGUANTAR (Sp.), *lō kä nō sä pwä'THä rä-mä'THē-är' sä ä' THä ä-gwän-tär'* What cannot be cured must be endured.

LOYAUTE' M'OBLIGE, *lwä' yō' tä' mô' blēzh'*. Loyalty binds me.

MA CHÈRE, *mä' shȧr'*. My dear (fem.).

MADEMOISELLE, *mȧd'mwä'zĕl'*. Miss.

MAESTRO DI COLOR CHE SANNO (It.), *mä-ĕs'trō dē kō-lōr' kä sän'nō*. Master of those that know. (Applied by Dante to Aristotle.)

MA FOI, *mä' fwä'*. Upon my faith; upon my word.

MAINTIENS LE DROIT, *măn'tyȧn' lĕ drwä'*. Maintain the right.

MAISON DE CAMPAGNE, *mä'zōn' dĕ kän'pän'y'*. A country house.

MAISON DE SANTÉ, *mä'zōn' dĕ sän'tä'*. A private asylum or hospital.

MAISON DE VILLE, *mä'zōn' dĕ vēl'*. A town hall.

MAÎTRE D'HÔTEL, *mâ'tr' dō'tĕl'*. A house steward.

MALADIE DU PAYS, *mä'lä'dē' dü pĕ'ē'*. Homesickness.

MAL À PROPOS, *mȧl' ȧ' prô'pō'*. Out of place; ill suited.

MAL DE MER, *mȧl' dĕ mȧr'*. Seasickness.

MALENTENDU, *mȧl'än'tän'dü'*. A misunderstanding; a mistake.

MALGRÉ NOUS, *mȧl'grä' nōō'*. In spite of us.

MALHEUR NE VIENT JAMAIS SEUL, *mä'lûr' nĕ vyȧn' zhä'mĕ' sŭl'*. Misfortunes never come singly.

MARDI GRAS, *mär'dē' grä'*. Shrove Tuesday.

MARIAGE DE CONSCIENCE, *mä'ryäzh' dĕ kôn'syȧns'*. A private marriage.

MARIAGE DE CONVENANCE, *mä'ryäzh' dĕ kôn'v'-näns'*. A marriage of convenience, or from interested motives.

MARQUER LE PAS, *mär'kä' lĕ pä'*. To mark time.

MARZO VENTOSO Y ABRIL LLUVIOSO SACAN Á MAYO HERMOSO (Sp.), *mär'thō vĕn-tō'sō ē ä-brēl' lyōō'vyō'sō sä'kän ä mī'ō ĕr-mō'sō*. Windy March and showery April bring flowery May.

MÁS QUIERO ASNO QUE ME LLEVE QUE CABALLO QUE ME DERRUEQUE (Sp.), *mäs kyä'rō äs'nō kä mä lyä'vä kä kä-bäl'yō kä mä dĕr-rwä'kä*. I prefer the ass that carries me to the horse that throws me.

MÁS SABE UN NECIO PREGUNTAR QUE PUEDEN CIEN SABIOS CONTESTAR (Sp.), *mäs sä'bä ōōn nĕ'thyō prä-gōōn'tär kä pwä'THĕn thyĕn sä'byōs kōn-tĕs-tär'*. One fool can ask more questions than a hundred learned men can answer.

MÁS VALE PÁJARO EN MANO QUE CIENTO VOLANDO (Sp.), *mäs vä'lä pä'Hä-rō ĕn mä'nō kä thyĕn'tō vō-län'dō*. A bird in the hand is worth two in the bush (a hundred flying).

MÁS VALE TARDE QUE NUNCA (Sp.), *mäs vä'lä tär'dä kä nōōn'kä*. Better late than never.

MÁS VALE UN TOMA QUE DOS TE DARÉ (Sp.), *mäs vä'lä ōōn tō'mä kä dōs tĕ dä-rä'*. One "take" is better than two "I'll give."

MAUVAISE HONTE, *mō'vä' zōnt'*. False modesty.

MAUVAIS GOÛT, *mō'vĕ' gōō'*. False taste.

MI CARO AMIGO (Sp.), *mē kä'rō ä-mē'gō*. My dear friend.

MIR IST ALLES EINERLEI (Ger.), *mēr ist ä'lĕs ī'nĕr-lī*. It's all the same to me.

MISE-EN-SCÈNE, *mē'zän'sän'*. The staging of a play.

MON AMI, *môn' nä'mē'*. My friend.

MON CHER, *môn' shȧr'*. My dear (fellow).

MONSIEUR, *mĕ-syü'*. Sir; Mr.; gentleman.

MOT DU GUET, *mō' dü gĕ'*. A watchword.

MOTS D'USAGE, *mō' dü'zäzh'*. Words in common use.

MUCHOS POCOS HACEN UN MUCHO (Sp.), *mōō'chōs pō'kōs ä'thĕn ōōn mōō'chō*. Many littles make much; many a mickle makes a muckle.

MURAGLIA BIANCA, CARTA DI MATTO (It.), *mōō-räl'yä byän'kä, kär'tä dē mät'tō*. A white wall is the fool's paper.

NAÏVE, *nä'ēv'*. Having unaffected simplicity.

NAÏVETÉ, *nä'ēv''tä'*. Native simplicity.

NÉE, *nā*. Born; maiden name.

NÉGLIGÉ, *nā'glē'zhä'*. A morning dress.

NESSUN MAGGIOR DOLORE CHE RICORDARSI DEL TEMPO FELICE NELLA MISERIA (It.), *nĕs-sōōn' mä-jōr' dō-lō'rĕ kä rē-kôr-där'sē dĕl tĕm'pō fĕ-lē'chĕ näl'lä mē-zä'rē-ä*. No greater sorrow than to remember happy days when in misery.—Dante.

NEUE BESEN KEHREN GUT (Ger.), *noi'ĕ bä'zĕn kä'rĕn gōōt; A new broom sweeps clean.

NI FIRMES CARTAS QUE NO LEAS, NI BEBAS AGUA QUE NO VEAS (Sp.), *nē fēr'mĕs kär'täs kä nō lä'äs nē bä'bäs ä'gwä kä nō vä'äs*. Sign no letter you have not read, nor drink water you cannot see; be very cautious.

NI L'UN NI L'AUTRE, *nē lûn' nē lō'tr'*. Neither the one nor the other.

N'IMPORTE, *năn'pôrt'*. It is of no consequence.

NOBLESSE OBLIGE, *nô'blĕs' ô'blēzh'*. Nobility imposes obligations; much is expected from persons of good position.

NO ES ORO TODO QUE RELUCE (Sp.), *nō ĕs ō'rō tō'THō kä rä-lōō'thä*. All is not gold that glitters.

NO HAY BIEN NI MAL QUE CIEN AÑOS DURE (Sp.), *nō ī byän nē mäl kä thyän än'yōs dōō'rä*. No good or evil lasts a hundred years.

NO HAY DE QUE (Sp.), *nō ī dä kä*. You are welcome; don't mention it.

NO IMPORTA (Sp.), *nō ēm-pōr'tä*. No matter; 'tis all the same.

NO LAS MERECE (Sp.), *nō läs mä-rä'thä*. It is not worth it (in answer to *Gracias*).

NOM DE GUERRE, *nôn' dĕ gȧr'*. A war-name; an assumed name in controversy.

NOM DE PLUME, *nôn dĕ plüm'*. An assumed title; a pen name.

NON MI RICORDO (It.), *nôn mē rē-kôr'dō*. I do not remember.

NON OGNI FIORE FA BUON ODORE (It.), *nôn ōn'yē fyō'rĕ fä bwôn ō-dō'rĕ*. It is not every flower that smells sweet.

NON VENDER LA PELLE DELL' ORSO PRIMA DI PIGLIARLO (It.), *nôn vän'dĕr lä pĕl'lĕ däll ōr'sō prē'mä dē pēl-yär'lō*. Don't sell the bearskin before you have caught the bear.

NO SE GANÓ ZAMORA EN UNA HORA (Sp.), *nō sä gä-nō' thä-mō'rä ĕn ōō'nä ō'rä*. (Zamora was not won in an hour), Rome was not built in a day.

NO SE PERMITE HURTAR PARA DAR POR DIOS (Sp.), *nō sä pĕr-mē'tä ōōr-tär' pä'rä där pôr dē'ōs*. It is not lawful to steal in order to give to God.

NOT KENNT KEIN GEBOT (Ger.), *nōt kĕnt kīn gä-bōt'*. Necessity knows no law.

NOTRE DAME, *nô'tr' dȧm'*. Our Lady; the Virgin Mary; the great cathedral of Paris.

NOUS AVONS CHANGÉ TOUT CELA, *nōō'zä'vōn' shän'zhä' tōō' sĕ-lä'*. We have changed all that.

NOUS VERRONS, *nōō' vĕ'rôn'*. We shall see.

NOUVELLES, *nōō'vĕl'*. News.

NO VALE LA PENA (Sp.), *nō vä'lä lä pä'nä*. It is not worth the trouble.

NO VALE NADA (Sp.), *nō vä'lä nä'THä*. It is worthless; no use; no matter.

NUL BIEN SANS PEINE, *nül' byän' sän pân'*. No pains, no gains

NULLA NUOVA, BUONA NUOVA (It.), *nōōl'lä nwô'vä, bwô'nä nwô'vä*. No news is good news.

OGNI BOTTEGA HA LA SUA MALIZIA (It.), *ōn'yē bôt-tä'gä ä lä sōō'ä mä-lē'tsyä*. Every shop has its trick; there are tricks in all trades.

OJOS QUE NO VEN, CORAZÓN QUE NO SIENTE (Sp.), *ō'Hōs kä nō vĕn' kō-rä-thōn' kä nō syĕn'tä*. Eyes that see not, heart that feels not; out of sight, out of mind.

OLLA PODRIDA (Sp.), *ôl'yä pō-THrē'THä*. A heterogeneous mixture; a stew of meat and vegetables.

ON CONNAÎT L'AMI AU BESOIN, *ôn kô'nä' lä'mē' ō bĕ-zwȧn'*. A friend is known in time of need; a friend in need is a friend indeed.

ON DIT, *ôn' dē'*. They say; a rumor.

ORO È CHE ORO VALE (It.), *ō'rō ĕ kä ō'rō vä'lĕ*. That is gold which is worth gold.

OUBLIER JE NE PUIS, *ōō'blyä' zhĕ nĕ püĕ'*. I can never forget.

OUÏ-DIRE, *ōō-ē' dēr'*. Hearsay.

OUVRAGE DE LONGUE HALEINE, *ōō'vräzh' dĕ lôn'gȧ'lȧn'*. A work of time.

PARA TRABAJAR HACEN FALTA LOS BURROS (Sp.), *pä'rä trä-bä-Här' ä'thĕn fäl'tä lōs bōōr'rōs*. For work you must have the donkeys; let others do the work while you pocket the results.

PAR CI, PAR LÀ, *pȧr sē' pȧr lä'*. Here and there.

PAR EXCELLENCE, *pȧr ĕk'sĕ'läns'*. Pre-eminently.

PAR EXEMPLE, *pȧr ĕg'zän'pl'*. For instance.

PAROLE D'HONNEUR, *pä'rôl' dô'nŭr'*. Word of honor.

PARTOUT, *pȧr'tōō'*. Everywhere.

PARVENU, *pȧr'vē-nü'*. An upstart.

PAS À PAS, *pä'zä'pä'*. Step by step.

PASSÉE, *pä'sä'*. Worn; faded, said of a woman no longer young.

PÂTÉ DE FOIE GRAS, *pä'tä' dĕ fwä' grä'*. A pie made from the livers of geese.

PEINE FORTE ET DURE, *pân' fôr'tä dür'*. Very severe punishment; a kind of judicial torture.

PENSÉE, *pän'sä'*. A thought expressed in terse, vigorous language.

PÈRE DE FAMILLE, *pȧr dĕ fä'mē'y'*. The father of the family.

PERDU, *pĕr'dü'*. Lost.

PER PIÙ STRADE SI VA A ROMA (It.), *pär pyōō' strä'dĕ sē vä ä rō'mä.* There are many roads to Rome.

PERRO QUE LADRA NO MUERDE (Sp.), *pĕr'rō kä lä'THrä nō mwĕr'dä.* His bark is worse than his bite.

PETIT, *pē-tē'.* Small.

PETIT À PETIT L'OISEAU FAIT SON NID, *pē-tē' tä pē-tē' lwä'zō' fä sôn nē.* Little by little the bird builds its nest.

PETIT COUP, *pē-tē' kōō'.* A small mask; a domino.

PETIT-MAÎTRE, *pē-tē' mä'tr'.* A little master; a fop.

PEU À PEU, *pû'ä pû'.* Little by little; by degrees.

PEU S'EN FAUT, *pû' sän fō'.* Nearly so; very near.

PIED À TERRE, *pyä' tä târ'.* A resting place; a temporary lodging.

PIGLIAR DUE COLOMBI A UNA FAVA (It.), *pēl-yär' dōō'ĕ kō-lōm'bē ä ōō'nä fä'vä.* To catch two pigeons with one bean; to kill two birds with one stone.

PIS ALLER, *pē' zä'lā'.* The worst or last shift.

POCO A POCO (It.), *pô'kō ä pô'kō.* Little by little; by degrees.

POINT D'APPUI, *pwän' dä'püĕ'.* Prop; point of support.

POMMES DE TERRE, *pôm' dĕ târ'.* Potatoes (apples of the earth).

POR DONDE MENOS SE PIENSA SALTA EL LIEBRE, *pôr dôn'dä mä'nôs sä pyĕn'sä säl'tä ĕl lyä'brä.* The hare leaps whence you least expect; never be surprised.

PORTER UN COUP FUNESTE, *pôr'tā' ûn kōō' fü-nĕst'.* To deal a fatal blow.

POT-POURRI, *pô'pōō'rē'.* A medley.

POUR ACQUIT, *pōōr ä'kē'.* Paid; settled. (The usual form of receipt.)

POUR FAIRE RIRE, *pōōr fâr' rēr'.* For fun; for a joke.

POUR FAIRE VISITE, *pōōr fâr' vē'zēt'.* To pay a visit,—written in the corner of a visiting card to notify of a formal call.

POUR PASSER LE TEMPS, *pōōr pä'sā' lĕ tän'.* To while away the time.

POUR PRENDRE CONGÉ, *pōōr prän'dr' kôn'zhā'.* To take leave. Usually abbreviated to P.P.C. on a visiting card.

PRENDRE LA LUNE AVEC LES DENTS, *prän'dr' lä lün' ä'vĕk' lä dän'.* To seize the moon in one's teeth; to aim at impossibilities.

PRESTO MATURO, PRESTO MARCIO (It.), *prĕs'tō mä-tōō'rō prĕs'tō mär'chō.* Soon ripe, soon rotten.

PRÊT D'ACCOMPLIR, *prĕ' dä'kôn'plēr'.* Ready to accomplish.

PRÊT POUR MON PAYS, *prĕ' pōōr' môn' pĕ'ē'.* Ready for my country.

PREUX CHEVALIER, *prû' shĕ-vä'lyā'.* A brave knight.

PROTÉGÉ, *prō'tä'zhā'.* One protected by another; one to whom patronage is given.

PURÉE, *pü'rā'.* A thick soup, or mashed potatoes.

PURÉE AUX CROUTONS, *pü'rā' ō krōō'tôn'.* A thick soup with small cubes of toasted bread.

QUELQUE CHOSE, *kĕl'k' shōz'.* Something; a trifle.

¿QUE QUIERE DECIR ESO? (Sp.) *kä kyä'rä dä-thēr' ä'sō.* What does that mean?

QUERIDO AMIGO MIO (Sp.), *kä-rē'THō ä-mē'gō mē'ō.* My dear friend.

QUI A BU BOIRA, *kĕ' ä' bü' bwä'rä'.* The tippler will go on tippling; it is hard to break off bad habits.

QUIEN ABROJOS SIEMBRA, ESPINAS COGE (Sp.), *kyän ä-brō'Hōs syäm'brä ĕs-pē'näs kō'Hä.* He who sows brambles reaps thorns.

QUIEN CALLA OTORGA (Sp.), *kyän käl'yä ō-tôr'gä.* Silence gives consent.

QUIEN MÁS TIENE MÁS QUIERE (Sp.), *kyän mäs tyä'nä mäs kyä'rä.* The more one has, the more one wants.

QUIEN MUCHO DUERME, POCO APRENDE (Sp.), *kyän mōō'chō dwĕr'mä pō'kō ä-prĕn'dä.* He who sleeps much learns little; the indolent make little headway.

QUIEN POCO SABE, PRESTO LO REZA (Sp.), *kyän pō'kō sä'bä prĕs'tō lō rä'thä.* He who knows little soon tells it.

QUIEN QUITA LA OCASIÒN, QUITA EL PECADO (Sp.), *kyän kē'tä lä ō-kä-syôn' kē'tä ĕl pä-kä'THō.* He who avoids the occasion avoids sin.

¿QUIÉN SABE? (Sp.), *kyän sa-bä.* Who knows?

QUIEN TODO LO QUIERE TODO LO PIERDE (Sp.), *kyän tō'THō lō kyä'rä tō'THō lō pyĕr'dä.* He who wants all loses all.

QU'IL SOIT COMME IL EST DÉSIRÉ, *kēl' swä' kô'mē' lĕ' dä'zē'rä'.* Let it be as desired.

QUI AIME BERTRAND AIME SON CHIEN, *kĕ'âm' bĕr'trän' âm' sôn' shyän'.* Love me, love my dog.

QUI N'A SANTÉ, N'A RIEN, *kĕ' nä' sän'tä' nä' ryän'.* He who has not health, has nothing.

QUI PRÊT À L'AMI PERD AU DOUBLE, *kĕ' prät' ä lä'mē' pĕr' tō' dōō'bl'.* Loan oft loses both itself and friend.

QUI VA LÀ? *kĕ' vä' lä'.* Who goes there?

QUI VIVE? *kĕ' vēv'.* Who goes there? On the "qui vive," adroit, watchful.

RAISON D'ÉTAT, *rĕ'zôn' dä'tä'.* Interest of the state.

RAISON D'ÊTRE, *rĕ'zôn' dä'tr'.* The reason for a thing's existence.

RÉGIME, *rä'zhēm'.* Mode or style of rule or management.

RENDEZVOUS, *rän'dä'vōō'.* A place of meeting.

RENDEZ MES DEVOIRS, *rän'dä' mä' dĕ-vwär'.* Pay my respects.

RENTRER EN GRÂCE, *rän'trä' än gräs'.* To be restored to favor.

RÉPONDEZ S'IL VOUS PLAÎT (R.S.V.P.), *rä'pôn'dä' sēl vōō' plĕ'.* Reply if you please, written on invitation cards.

RÉPONDRE EN NORMAND, *rä'pôn'dr' än nôr'män'.* To answer in Norman; to speak evasively.

RÉSUMÉ, *rä'zü'mä'.* A summing up.

RETE NUOVA NON PIGLIA UCCELLO VECCHIO (It.), *rä'tĕ nwô'vä nōn pēl'yä ōōt-shĕl'lō vĕk'kyō.* A new net won't catch an old bird.

REVENONS À NOS MOUTONS, *rē-vnôn' à nô' mōō'tôn'.* Let us return to our sheep; let us come back to our subject.

RIEN N'EST BEAU QUE LE VRAI, *ryän' nĕ' bō' kĕ lĕ vrä'.* There is nothing beautiful but truth.

RIRA BIEN QUI RIRA LE DERNIER, *rē'rä' byän' kĕ' rē'rä' lĕ dĕr'nyä'.* He laughs best who laughs last.

RIRE ENTRE CUIR ET CHAIR; RIRE SOUS CAPE, *rēr' än'tr-küĕr' ä shär'; rēr' sōō' käp'.* To laugh in one's sleeve.

ROBE DE CHAMBRE, *rôb' dĕ shän'br'.* A dressing gown; a morning gown.

ROBE DE NUIT, *rôb' dĕ nüĕ'.* A nightdress.

RÔLE, *rōl.* A part in a performance.

RUSE DE GUERRE, *rüz' dĕ gâr'.* A military stratagem.

SALUD Y PESETAS! (Sp.), *sä-lōōTH' ē pä-sä'täs.* Health and money (a toast).

SANAN CUCHILLADAS, MÁS NO MALAS PALABRAS (Sp.), *sä'nän kōō'chĕl-yä'THäs mäs nō mä'läs pä-lä'bräs.* Wounds from a knife will heal, but not those from the tongue.

SANS CÉRÉMONIE, *sän sä'rä'mô'nē'.* Without ceremony.

SANS PEUR ET SANS REPROCHE, *sän pûr' ä sän rē-prōsh'.* Fearless and stainless.

SANS RIME ET SANS RAISON, *sän rēm'ä sän rĕ'zôn'.* Without rime or reason.

SANS SOUCI, *sän sōō'sē'.* Free from care.

SAUVE QUI PEUT, *sōv' kĕ' pû'.* Save yourselves; let each one look out for himself; headlong flight.

SAVOIR FAIRE, *sä'vwär' fâr'.* Tact.

SAVOIR VIVRE, *sä'vwär' vē'vr'.* Good breeding.

SDEGNO D'AMANTE POCO DURA (It.), *zdän'yō dä-män'tĕ pô'kō dōō'rä.* A lover's anger is short-lived.

SÉANCE, *sä'äns'.* A sitting given for a painting; an assembly gathered for some set purpose.

SE FAIRE JOUR, *sĕ fâr' zhōōr'.* To force one's way.

SELON LES RÈGLES, *sĕ-lôn' lä rĕg'l'.* According to rule.

SEMPRE IL MAL NON VIEN PER NUOCERE (It.), *sĕm'prĕ ĕl mäl nōn vyĕn pär nwôt'shä-rĕ.* Misfortune is not always an evil.

SE NON È VERO, È BEN TROVATO (It.), *sĕ nōn ĕ vä'rō ĕ bĕn trō-vä'tō.* If it is not true, it is cleverly invented.

SÍ GRACIAS (Sp.), *sē grä'thyäs.* Yes, thank you.

SI JEUNESSE SAVAIT, SI VIEILLESSE POUVAIT, *sē zhû'nĕs' sä'vä' sē vyä'yĕs' pōō'vä'.* If youth but knew, if age but had strength.

SI JUVENTUD SUPIERA Y SI VEJEZ PUDIERA (Sp.), *sē Hōō-vĕn-tōōTH' sōō-pyä'rä ē sē vä-häth' pōō-THyä'rä.* If youth but knew, if age but had strength; lost chances.

SOIRÉE, *swä'rä'.* An evening party.

SOUFFLER LE CHAUD ET LE FROID, *sōō'flä' lĕ shō' ä lĕ frwä'.* To blow hot and cold.

SOUS UN FAUX JOUR, *sōō' zûn fō' zhōōr'.* In a bad light.

SO VIEL ICH WEISS (Ger.), *zō fēl ĭk vis.* As far as I know.

STURM UND DRANG (Ger.), *shtōōrm ōōnt dräng.* Storm and stress.

TABLE D'HÔTE, *tä'bl' dōt'.* Table of the host; a meal served entire, not from separate orders.

TÂCHE SANS TACHE, *täsh' sän täsh'.* A work without a stain.

TANT MIEUX, *tän' myû'.* So much the better.

TANT PIS, *tän' pē'.* So much the worse.

TEL MAÎTRE, TEL VALET, *tĕl mä'tr' tĕl vä'lä'.* Like master, like man.

TÊTE-À-TÊTE, *tä'tä-tät'.* A conversation between two parties.

TOUJOURS PERDRIX, *tōō'zhōōr' pĕr'drē'.* Always partridges; the same thing over and over again; too much of a good thing.

TOUJOURS PRÊT, *tōō'zhōōr' prĕ'.* Always ready.

TOUR DE FORCE, *tōōr' dĕ fôrs'.* A feat of strength or skill.

TOUT À FAIT, *tōō'tä-fĕ'.* Wholly; entirely.

TOUT À L'HEURE, *tōō'tä-lûr'.* Presently; just now.

TOUT AU CONTRAIRE, *tōō'tō-kôn'trâr'.* Quite the contrary.

TOUT À VOUS, *tōō'tä-vōō'.* Entirely yours.

TOUT BIEN OU RIEN, *tōō' byän'nōō ryän'.* All well or nothing.

TOUT DE SUITE, *tōō'dĕ-süĕt'.* Immediately.

TOUT ENSEMBLE, *tōō'tän'sän'bl'.* All together, entire effect (of a work of art).

TOUT LE MONDE EST SAGE APRÈS COUP, *tōō' lĕ môn'dĕ'sazh' ä'prĕ' kōō'.* Everybody is wise after the event,—when it's too late.

TRADUTTORI, TRADITORI (It.), *trä-dōōt-tō'rē trä-dē-tō'rē.* Translators are traitors,—they often give a wrong meaning to an author.

TRAVAUX FORCÉS, *trä'vō' fôr'sä'.* Hard labor (legal sentence).

TUTTE LE STRADE CONDUCONO A ROMA (It.), *tōōt'tĕ lĕ strä'dĕ kōn-dōō'kō-nō ä rō'mä.* All roads lead to Rome.

UEBUNG MACHT DEN MEISTER (Ger.), *ü'bōōng mäkt dĕn mĭs'tēr.* Practice makes perfect.

UN BIENFAIT N'EST JAMAIS PERDU, *ŭn byăn'fĕ' nĕ' zhă'mĕ' pĕr'dü.* A kindness is never lost.

UN SOT À TRIPLE ÉTAGE, *ŭn sō'ä trē'pl' ā'tàzh'.* A consummate fool.

UN "TIENS" VAUT MIEUX QUE DEUX "TU L'AURAS," *ŭn tyăn' vō' myŭ' kĕ dû tü lō'rä'.* One "take it" is worth two "you shall have it"; a bird in the hand is worth two in the bush.

VALET DE CHAMBRE, *và'lā' dĕ shäN'br'.* An attendant.

VAMOS (Sp.), *vä'mŏs.* Let us go; now, then!

VAYA USTED CON DIOS (Sp.), *vä'yä ōōs-tĕтн' kŏn dē'ŏs.* Go with God; good-by and good luck!

VEDI NAPOLI E POI MORI (It.), *vä'dē nä'pō-lē ĕ pō'ē mō'rē.* See Naples and then die.

VERDADES Y ROSAS TIENEN ESPINAS (Sp.), *vĕr-dä'тнĕs ē rō'säs tyä'nĕn ĕs-pē'näs.* Truth and roses have their thorns.

VÉRITÉ SANS PEUR, *vä'rē'tä' sän pŭr'.* Truth without fear.

VIELE HÄND' MACHEN BALD EIN END' (Ger.), *fē'lĕ hĕnt' mäk'ĕn bält in ĕnt'.* Many hands make quick work.

VIGUEUR DE DESSUS, *vē'gŭr' dĕ dĕ-sü'.* Strength from on high.

VINO DENTRO, SENNO FUORI (It.), *vē'nō dän'trō sän'nō fwō'rē.* When the wine is in, the wit is out.

VIS-À-VIS, *vē'zà vē'.* Face to face.

VIVE LA BAGATELLE, *vēv' là bä'gà'tĕl'.* Success to trifles! Said on hearing something ridiculous related.

VIVE LE ROI, *vēv' lĕ rwä'.* Long live the king.

VOILÀ, *vwà'lä'.* See there; there is; there!

VOILÀ TOUT, *vwà'lä' tōō'.* That's all; there you are!

VOILÀ UNE AUTRE CHOSE, *vwà'lä' ü'nō'tr' shōz'.* That's quite another thing.

VOIR LE DESSOUS DES CARTES, *vwàr lĕ dĕ-sōō' dä kärt'.* To see the face of the cards; to be in the secret.

VOUS Y PERDREZ VOS PAS, *vōō'zē pĕr'drä' vō' pä'.* You will have your walk for nothing; you will lose your labor over it.

WAS FEHLT IHNEN? (Ger.), *väs fält ē'nĕn.* What ails you? What is the matter with you?

WIE DIE ARBEIT, SO DER LOHN (Ger.), *vē dē är'bĭt zō där lōn.* As the labor, so the reward.

ZEITGEIST (Ger.), *tsīt'gīst.* The spirit of the age.

HAWAIIAN PHRASES

Noted for its prominent vowel sounds, the language originally spoken by natives of Hawaii (*ha wy'ee*) has a musical quality and an exotic charm. Although English is the standard medium of communication, many visitors to the fiftieth state will pick up some phrases as linguistic souvenirs. Here are a few examples:

ALOHA AHIAHI (*ä lō'hä ä hē ä'hē*)—Good evening.

ALOHA AU IA OE (*ä lō'hä ou ē'ä ō'ä*)—I love you.

ALOHA KAKAHIAKA (*ä lō'hä kä kä hē ä'kä*)—Good morning.

ALOHA NUI LOA (*ä lō'hä nōō'ē lō'ä*)—Much love.

HAUOLI LA HANAU (*hou ō' lē lä hä nä'oo*)—Happy birthday.

HAUOLI MAKAHIKI HOU (*hou ō'lē mä kä hē'kĕ hō'oo*)—Happy New Year.

MAHALO NUI LOA (*mä hä'lō nōō'ē lō'ä*)—Many thanks.

MAIKAI (*mī'kī*)—I am fine.

MELE KALIKIMAKA (*mä'lä kä lē kē mä'kä*)—Merry Christmas.

PEHEA OE? (*pä hä ä ō ä*)—How are you?

TOURIST TALK—EXCERPTS FROM A FOREIGN PHRASE BOOK

As George Bernard Shaw once pointed out, a traveler attempting to use the language of a foreign country will get all the more attention if his speech is halting and fractured, and is therefore barely understandable. The natives are suspicious of a stranger whose accent and idiom are faultless, but they find linguistic clumsiness amusing, and they are pleased at their own cleverness in grasping a foreigner's partly hidden meaning. Since pronunciation is usually the chief obstacle, the prospective tourist will do well to take instruction in this, supplemented perhaps by drill with phonograph records, in order to be sure of pronouncing approximately the sounds that will make his phrases intelligible.

The examples of tourist phrases given in the following collection are typical, but of course are merely illustrative. Because each traveler has his own individual needs based on particular situations, his phrase book collection will naturally be a highly personalized one. In case of emergencies he can probably fall back on English, but meanwhile a good part of his enjoyment will come from attempting, more or less successfully, to speak like a native.

ENGLISH	FRENCH	GERMAN	SPANISH	ITALIAN
Where does this train go to?	Où va ce train?	Wohin fährt dieser Zug?	¿Adónde va este tren?	Dove va questo treno?
When does the train for . . . . start?	À quelle heure le train pour . . . . part-il?	Wann geht der Zug nach . . . . fort?	¿A qué hora sale el tren para . . . .?	A che ora parte il treno par . . . .?
Is there a dining car on this train?	Ya-t-il un wagon-restaurant à ce train?	Hat der Zug einen Speisewagon?	¿Hay (Wagón) comedor (o restaurante) en este tren?	C'e un vagone ristorante in questo treno?
How long does the boat stop at . . . .?	Combien de temps le bateau s'arrête-il à . . . .?	Wie lange legt das Boot in . . . . an?	¿Cuanto tiempo para el buque en . . . .?	Che fermata fa il battello a . . . .?
Please take me to the . . . . airport.	Veuillez me conduire a l'aéroport de	Fahren Sie mich bitte zum Flugplatz in	Haga el favor de conducir me a la estación . . . . de aviación.	Per favore, portate mi all' aeroporto di . . . .
Is smoking allowed?	Peut-on fumer?	Ist Rauchen gestattet?	¿Se permite fumar?	È permess d fumare?
I have nothing to declare.	Je n'ai rien à déclarer.	Ich habe nichts zu verzollen.	No tengo nada que declarar.	Non ho nulla da dichiarare.
Please give me back my passport.	Veuillez me rendre mon passeport.	Kann ich meinen Pass zuruckhaben?	Haga el favor de devolver me mi passaporte.	Prego di restituir mi il passaporto.
Which is the way to the station?	Quel est le chemin qui conduit à la gare?	Welches ist der Weg nach dem Bahnhof?	¿Cuál es el camino de la estación?	Qual' è la strada per la stazione?

English	French	German	Spanish	Italian
Where does this road lead to?	Où conduit cette route?	Wohin führt diese Strasse?	¿Adonde conduce este camino?	Dove porta questa estrada?
Cabby! Are you disengaged?	Cocher! Êtes-vous libre?	Kutscher! Sind Sie frei?	!Cochero! Está usted libre?	Cocchiere! Siete libero?
Where can I get a bus to . . . .?	Où puis-je prendre un omnibus pour . . . .?	Wo kann ich einen Bus nach . . . . Bekommen?	¿En dónde puedo tomar el ómnibus para . . . .?	Dove posso prendere un omnibus per . . . .?
Which is the best hotel at . . . .?	Quel est le meilleur hôtel de . . . .?	Welches ist das beste Hotel in . . . .?	¿Cuál es el mejor hotel en . . . .?	Qual' e il migliore albergo a . . . .?
Kindly post this letter.	Veuillez mettre cette lettre à la poste.	Würden Sie bitte diesen Brief einwerfen.	Haga el favor de echarme esta carta al correo.	Favorisca impostarmi questa lettera.
At what time is the set meal?	À quelle heure est la table d'hôte?	Um wieviel Uhr ist die Table d'hôte?	¿A qué hora sirven la comida?	A che ora è la tavola rotonda?
Give me the bill of fare, please.	Donnez-moi la carte, s'il vous plait.	Geben Sie mir bitte die Speisekarte.	Haga el favor de darme la lista de platos.	Datemi il menu, per favore.
I will take the set dinner.	Je dinerai à la table d'hôte.	Ich nehme das Menu.	Comeré a la table d'hôte.	Io mangerò alla tavola rotonda.
Some more bread, if you please.	Encore du pain, s'il vous plait.	Noch etwas Brot, bitte.	Haga el favor de darme más pan.	Un altro poco di pane, per placere.
Thank you, I have enough.	Merci, j'en ai assez.	Danke, ich habe genug.	Gracias, hasta ya o con eso basta.	Grazie, ne ho abbastanza.
Waiter! another cup of coffee.	Garçon! Encore une tasse de café.	Ober! Noch eine Tasse Kaffee, bitte.	!Camarero! Otra taza de cafe.	Cameriere! Un' altra tazzina di caffe.
Can I borrow a book?	Puis-je emprunter un livre?	Kann ich ein Buch asuborgen?	¿Puedo tomar un libro prestado?	Posso avere in prestito un libro?
Please make up this prescription.	Veuillez préparer cette ordonnance.	Können Sie mir bitte diesen Rezept herstellen.	Haga el favor de preparme esta receta.	Per favore, preparatemi questa ricetta.
I want a lounge suit.	Il me faut un complet veston.	Ich möchte einen Strassenanzug.	Necessito un traje de americana.	Io desidero un vestito completo da mattina.
I wish to cash this traveller's check.	Je désire encassier ce cheque de voyage.	Ich mochte diesen traveller's cheque einlösen.	Deseo cobrar este traveller's cheque.	Desidero incassare questo traveller's cheque.

From TRAVELLERS' FOREIGN PHRASE BOOK by J. O. Kettridge
Quoted by permission of the Publishers,
Routledge & Kegan Paul, Ltd.

SOME FAMOUS FIRST LINES

Many of the "poems every one should know" are recognized better by their opening lines than by their titles. In some cases, a poem worth remembering may not even have a title. For example, a great sonnet by Shakespeare may be designated only by the Roman numeral XXXIII, which is no more revealing than the label "Opus 33" for a piece of music. However, for those who know and appreciate Shakespeare's poem, its opening words, "Full many a glorious morning have I seen," will immediately identify it. In many cases, the first line contains the key to the thought and acquaints the reader at once with the concept of the poem as a whole. From another point of view, it may be said that, originally, the first line gave the poet a running start into the process of composition. Until he had a good first line to give him impetus, he was not ready to write the poem.

Those who recognize poems by their first lines may or may not remember the lines that come next. People differ greatly in their ability to memorize long passages of poetry, but they can usually remember the opening words from their favorites, in the same way that they recall the opening bars of a well-liked symphony or overture. The famous first lines quoted below may lead either to the renewing of old acquaintance or, in some cases, to the addition of hitherto unknown works of poetry.

Afoot and light-hearted, I take the open road
  WALT WHITMAN—*Song of the Open Road*
A garden is a lovesome thing, God wot!
  THOMAS EDWARD BROWN—*My Garden*
A gentle Knight was pricking on the plaine
  EDMUND SPENSER—*The Faerie Queene*
A late lark twitters from the quiet skies
  WILLIAM E. HENLEY—*Margaritae Sorori*
All I could see from where I stood
  EDNA ST. VINCENT MILLAY—*Renascence*

All thoughts, all passions, all delights
  SAMUEL TAYLOR COLERIDGE—*Love*
And did those feet in ancient time
  WILLIAM BLAKE—From *Milton*
April is the cruellest month, breeding
  T. S. ELIOT—*The Waste Land*
Ask me no more where Jove bestows
  THOMAS CAREW—*Ask Me no More*
A thing of beauty is a joy forever
  JOHN KEATS—*Endymion*

A sweet disorder in the dress
  ROBERT HERRICK—*Delight in Disorder*
Ay, tear her tatterèd ensign down!
  OLIVER WENDELL HOLMES—*Old Ironsides*
Bards of passion and of mirth
  JOHN KEATS—*Bards of Passion*
Behind him lay the great Azores
  JOAQUIN MILLER—*Columbus*
Bowed by the weight of centuries, he leans
  EDWIN MARKHAM—*The Man with the Hoe*
Breathes there a man with soul so dead
  SIR WALTER SCOTT—*Patriotism*
Bright Star! would I were steadfast as thou art
  JOHN KEATS—*Sonnet*
By the rude bridge that arched the flood
  RALPH WALDO EMERSON—*Concord Hymn*
Come live with me and be my love
  CHRISTOPHER MARLOWE—*The Passionate Shepherd*
Come Sleep, O Sleep! the certain knot of peace
  SIR PHILIP SIDNEY—*Sleep*
Crabbed Age and Youth
  WILLIAM SHAKESPEARE—*The Passionate Pilgrim*
Death, be not proud, though some have called thee
  JOHN DONNE—*Sonnet, Death*
Drink to me only with thine eyes
  BEN JONSON—*To Celia*
Ethereal minstrel! pilgrim of the sky!
  WILLIAM WORDSWORTH—*To the Skylark*
Fair stood the wind for France
  MICHAEL DRAYTON—*Agincourt*
Fear death? To feel the fog in my throat
  ROBERT BROWNING—*Prospice*
Gather ye rosebuds while ye may
  ROBERT HERRICK—*To the Virgins*
Give a man a horse he can ride
  JAMES THOMSON—*Gifts*
God of our fathers, known of old
  RUDYARD KIPLING—*Recessional*
Had we but world enough, and time
  ANDREW MARVEL—*To His Coy Mistress*
Hail to thee, blithe spirit!
  PERCY BYSSHE SHELLEY—*To a Skylark*
Happy those early days when I
  HENRY VAUGHAN—*The Retreat*
Harp of the North, farewell! the hills grow dark
  SIR WALTER SCOTT—*Lay of the Last Minstrel*
Helen, thy beauty is to me
  EDGAR ALLAN POE—*To Helen*
Hence, loathed Melancholy
  JOHN MILTON—*L'Allegro*
Here's to the maiden of bashful fifteen
  RICHARD BRINSLEY SHERIDAN—*Drinking Song*
How do I love thee? Let me count the ways
  ELIZABETH BARRETT BROWNING—*Sonnet*
How happy is he born and taught
  SIR H. WOTTON—*The Character of a Happy Life*
How sleep the brave who sink to rest
  WILLIAM COLLINS—*How Sleep the Brave*
I bargained with Life for a penny
  JESSIE B. RITTENHOUSE—*My Wage*
I come from nothing, but from where
  ALICE MEYNELL—*A Song of Derivations*
If I should die, think only this of me
  RUPERT BROOKE—*The Soldier*
If I were Lord of Tartary
  WALTER DE LA MARE—*Tartary*
I fled him, down the nights and down the days
  FRANCIS THOMPSON—*The Hound of Heaven*
I must go down to the seas again
  JOHN MASEFIELD—*Sea-fever*
In after days when grasses high
  AUSTIN DOBSON—*In After Days*
In the grey wastes of dread,
  ROY CAMPBELL—*Horses on the Camargue*
In Xanadu did Kubla Khan
  SAMUEL TAYLOR COLERIDGE—*Kubla Khan*
I saw Eternity the other night
  HENRY VAUGHAN—*A Vision*
It is portentous, and a thing of state
  V. LINDSAY—*Abraham Lincoln Walks at Midnight*
I wandered lonely as a cloud
  WILLIAM WORDSWORTH—*Daffodils*
Jenny kiss'd me when we met
  LEIGH HUNT—*Jenny Kiss'd Me*
Let me live out my years in heat of blood
  J. G. NEIHARDT—*Let Me Live Out My Years*
Much have I traveled in the realms of gold
  JOHN KEATS—*Sonnet, Chapman's Homer*
My days among the dead are past
  ROBERT SOUTHEY—*The Scholar*

My hair is gray, but not with years
  LORD BYRON—*The Prisoner of Chillon*
My heart aches, and a drowsy numbness pains
  JOHN KEATS—*Ode to a Nightingale*
No coward soul is mine
  EMILY BRONTE—*Last Lines*
Of Man's first disobedience and the first
  JOHN MILTON—*Paradise Lost*
Others abide our question, thou art free
  MATTHEW ARNOLD—Sonnet, *Shakespeare*
Out of the night that covers me
  W. E. HENLEY—*Invictus*
Over his keys the musing organist
  J. RUSSELL LOWELL—*The Vision of Sir Launfal*
O Wild West Wind, thou breath of Autumn's being
  PERCY BYSSHE SHELLEY—*Ode to the West Wind*
Say not the struggle nought availeth
  ARTHUR HUGH CLOUGH—*Say Not the Struggle*
Serene, I fold my hands and wait
  JOHN BURROUGHS—*Waiting*
Shall I compare thee to a summer's day?
  WILLIAM SHAKESPEARE—*Sonnet XVIII*
She walks in beauty like the night
  LORD BYRON—*She Walks in Beauty*
Slowly, silently, now the moon
  WALTER DE LA MARE—*Silver*
Speak! speak! thou fearful guest
  H. W. LONGFELLOW—*The Skeleton in Armor*
Sweet Auburn! Loveliest village of the plain
  OLIVER GOLDSMITH—*The Deserted Village*
Swiftly walk over the western wave,
  PERCY BYSSHE SHELLEY—*To the Night*
Tears, idle tears, I know not what they mean
  ALFRED LORD TENNYSON—*Tears*, from *The Princess*
Tell me not, sweet, I am unkind
  RICHARD LOVELACE—*To Lucasta*
The Assyrian came down like a wolf on the fold
  LORD BYRON—*The Destruction of Sennacherib*
The blessed Damozel lean'd out
  DANTE GABRIEL ROSSETTI—*The Blessed Damozel*
The glories of our blood and state
  JAMES SHIRLEY—*Dirge*
The red rose whispers of passion
  JOHN BOYLE O'REILLEY—*A White Rose*
There was a time when meadow, grove, and stream
  W. WORDSWORTH—Ode, *Intimations of Immortality*
The splendor falls on castle walls
  ALFRED LORD TENNYSON—*Bugle Song*
The sun that brief December day
  JOHN GREENLEAF WHITTIER—*Snowbound*
The time you won your town the race
  A. E. HOUSMAN—*To an Athlete Dying Young*
The wind was a torrent of darkness
  ALFRED NOYES—*The Highwayman*
The world is too much with us; late and soon
  WILLIAM WORDSWORTH—*Sonnet*
The year's at the spring
  ROBERT BROWNING—*Pippa Passes*
Thou still unravished bride of quietness
  JOHN KEATS—*Ode On a Grecian Urn*
'Twas at the royal feast for Persia won
  JOHN DRYDEN—*Alexander's Feast*
Two roads diverged in a yellow wood
  ROBERT FROST—*The Road Not Taken*
Under the wide and starry sky
  ROBERT LOUIS STEVENSON—*Requiem*
Wake! For the Sun, who scattered into flight
  EDWARD FITZGERALD—Trans., *The Rubaiyat*
We are the music-makers
  ARTHUR O'SHAUGHNESSY—*Ode*
What dire offence from amorous causes springs
  ALEXANDER POPE—*The Rape of the Lock*
What is this life if, full of care,
  W. H. DAVIES—*Leisure*
When all the world is young, lad
  CHARLES KINGSLEY—"*The Old, Old Song*"
When I consider how my light is spent
  JOHN MILTON—*Sonnet on his Blindness*
When I consider Life, and its few years,
  LIZETTE WOODWORTH REESE—Sonnet, *Tears*
When the hounds of Spring are on Winter's traces
  A. C. SWINBURNE—Chorus from *Atalanta*
When you are old and gray and full of sleep
  WILLIAM BUTLER YEATS—*When You Are Old*
Whither, O splendid ship, thy white sails crowding
  ROBERT BRIDGES—*A Passer-by*
Why so pale and wan, fond lover?
  SIR J. SUCKLING—*Encouragements to a Lover*
Ye distant spires, ye antique towers
  THOMAS GRAY—Ode, *Eton College*
Yet once more, O ye laurels, and once more
  JOHN MILTON—*Lycidas*

DICTIONARY OF ABBREVIATIONS

Note:—In some abbreviations, particularly those used for government agencies, the periods after the initials are customarily omitted. In fact, many such combinations of initials are treated as actual words. (See *Acronyms*.)

A. Alto.
A1. First class.
A., a., adj. Adjective.
A., ans. Answer.
a., @. (Lat. *ad*), To; At.
A. A. Alcoholics Anonymous.
AAA. Agricultural Adjustment Agency; American Automobile Association.
A. A. A. & L. American Academy of Arts and Letters.
A. A. A. S. American Association for the Advancement of Science.
AAF. Army Air Forces.
A. A. O. N. M. S. Ancient Arabic Order of the Nobles of the Mystic Shrine.
a. a. r. Against all risks.
A. & A. S. R. Ancient and Accepted Scottish Rite.
AASA. American Ass'n of School Administrators.
A. A. S. S. (Lat. *Academiæ Antiquarinæ Societatis Socius*), Member of the American Antiquarian Society.
A. A. U. P. American Association of University Professors.
A. A. U. W. American Association of University Women.
A. B. (Lat. *artium baccalaureus*), Bachelor of Arts.
Abbr., Abbrev. Abbreviated, abbreviation.
ABC. American Broadcasting Corp.
Abp. Archbishop.
A. B. S. American Bible Society.
A. C. (Lat. *ante Christum*), Before Christ; Analytical Chemist; Alternating Current; Air Corps; Athletic Club.
Acc., Acct. Account.
A. D. (Lat. *anno Domini*), In the year of our Lord.
Ad., advt. Advertisement. Plur. *ads.*
A. D. C. Aide-de-camp.
Ad. inf. To infinity.
Adjt. Adjutant.
Adjt. Gen. Adjutant General.
Ad lib., Ad libit. (Lat. *ad libitum*), At pleasure.
Adm. Admiral.
Admr. Administrator.
Admx. Administratrix.
Adv. Advertising; Advocate; Adverb.
Æ., Æt. (Lat. *ætatis*), Of age, aged.
AEC. Atomic Energy Commission.
A.E.F. American Expeditionary Force.
AFL-CIO. American Federation of Labor and Congress of Industrial Organizations.
Agr., Agric. Agriculture, agricultural.
Agt. Agent.
A. H. (Lat. *anno Hegiræ*), In the year of the Hegira, or flight of Mohammed.
A. H. C. American Hospital Corps.
A. H. M. S. American Home Missionary Society.
A. H. S. (Lat. *anno humanæ salutis*), In the year of human salvation.
A. I. D. American Institute of Decorators; Agency for International Development.
AKC. American Kennel Club.
A. L. American Legion.
ALA. American Library Ass'n.
Ala., Al. Alabama.
Alas., Ak. Alaska.
Ald. Alderman.
A. L. of H. American Legion of Honor.
Alta. Alberta.
A. M. (Lat. *anno mundi*), In the year of the world.
A. M. (Lat. *ante meridiem*), Before noon.
A. M. (Lat. *artium magister*), Master of Arts.
Am., Amer. America, American.
AMA. American Medical Association.
A. M. D. Army Medical Department.

Amp. Ampere; amperage.
Amt. Amount.
AMVETS. American Veterans (World War II).
A. N. Anglo-Norman.
an. (Lat. *anno*), In the year.
Anat. Anatomy, anatomical.
Anc. Ancient.
Anon. Anonymous.
A. N. S. Army Nursing Service.
Ant., Antiq. Antiquities, antiquarian.
ANZAC. Australian and New Zealand Army Corps.
A. O. H. Ancient Order of Hibernians.
A. O. U. American Ornithologists' Union.
A. O. U. W. Ancient Order of United Workmen.
AP. Associated Press.
Ap., App. Apostle, apostles; Appendix.
Apl., Apr. April.
APO. Army Post Office.
Apoc. Apocalypse; Apocrypha.
Apog. Apogee.
approx. Approximate, -ly.
A. P. S. Associate of the Pharmaceutical Society.
Aq. (Lat. *aqua*), Water.
Ar., Arab. Arabic, Arabian.
Ar., Arr. Arrives, arrived, arrival.
A. R. A. Associate of the Royal Academy.
Aram. Aramaic.
ARC. American Red Cross.
Arch. Architecture.
Archæol. Archæology.
Archd. Archdeacon; Archduke.
Ariz., Az. Arizona.
Ark., Ar. Arkansas.
Arm. Armorican; Armenian.
ARP. Air-raid precautions.
Art. Article; Artificial; Artillery.
A. S., A.-S. Anglo-Saxon.
ASCAP. American Society of Composers, Authors, and Publishers.
ASEE. American Society for Engineering Education.
ASPCA. American Society for Prevention of Cruelty to Animals.
Assoc., Assn. Association.
Asst. Assistant.
A. S. S. U. American Sunday School Union.
Astrol. Astrology.
Astron. Astronomy, astronomical.
ATC. Air Transport Command.
A. T. S. American Tract Society; Army Transport Service.
Atty. Attorney.
A. U. A. American Unitarian Ass'n
Aug. Augustus; August.
A. V. Authorized Version.
Avoir. Avoirdupois.
Awol. Absent without leave.

B. Bass; Book.
b. Born.
B., Brit. British.
B. A. Bachelor of Arts.
Bal. Balance.
Balt., Balto. Baltimore.
Bap., Bapt. Baptist.
Bar. Barometer.
Bart., Bt. Baronet.
Bat., Batt. Battalion, battery.
B. B. C. British Broadcasting Corp.
bbl. Barrel. Plur. *bbls.*
B. C. Before Christ; British Columbia.
B. Ch. (Lat. *baccalaureus chirurgiæ*), Bachelor of Surgery.
B. C. L. (Lat. *baccalaureus civilis legis*), Bachelor of Civil Law.
B. C. S. Bachelor of Commercial Science.
B. D. (Lat. *baccalaureus divinitatis*), Bachelor of Divinity.
Bd. Bound; Bond; Board; Band.
Bdls. Bundles.
Bds. Bound in boards.

B. E. Bachelor of Engineering; Bachelor of Elocution.
b. e. Bill of exchange.
Belg. Belgic, Belgian.
Ben., Benj. Benjamin.
Berks. Berkshire (England).
Bib. Bible, biblical.
Biog. Biography, biographical.
Biol. Biology, biological.
B/L. Bill of lading.
B. L., B.LL. (Lat. *baccalaureus legum*), Bachelor of Laws.
bldg. Building.
B. M. (Lat. *baccalaureus medicinæ*), Bachelor of Medicine.
B. M., B. Mus. (Lat. *baccalaureus musicæ*), Bachelor of Music.
BMEWS. Ballistic Missile. Early Warning System.
Bot. Botany, botanical.
Bp. Bishop.
B. P. O. E. Benevolent and Protective Order of Elks.
Br., Bro. Brother.
Brig. Brigade, brigadier.
Brig. Gen. Brigadier General.
B. S. Bachelor of Surgery; Bachelor of Science.
B. S. A. Boy Scouts of America.
B. Sc. (Lat. *baccalaureus scientiæ*), Bachelor of Science.
bu., bush. Bushel.
B. V. Blessed Virgin.
B. V. M. Blessed Virgin Mary.
B. W. I. British West Indies.

c. About (for approximate dates).
C. Cent, cents; Centigrade; Consul; Centime, centimes; Hundred.
C., Cap. (Lat. *caput*), Chapter.
C. A. Chartered Accountant.
CAA. Civil Aeronautics Administration.
CAB. Civil Aeronautics Board.
Cal. Calendar.
Cal., Calif. California.
Cam., Camb. Cambridge.
Cant. Canticle; Canterbury.
Cantab. (Lat. *Cantabrigiensis*), Of Cambridge.
CAP. Civil Air Patrol.
Caps. Capitals.
Capt. Captain.
car., k. Carat.
Card. Cardinal.
CARE. Co-operative for American Relief Everywhere.
Cath. Catharine; Catholic; Cathedral.
C. B. Companion of the Bath.
CBC. Canadian Broadcasting Corp.
CBS. Columbia Broadcasting System.
C. C. Catholic Clergyman, Catholic Curate.
CCC. Civilian Conservation Corps.
C. D. S. Companion of the Distinguished Service Order.
C. D. V. or *c. d. v.* Carte-de-Visite.
C. E. Civil Engineer.
Celt. Celtic.
Cent. (Lat. *centum*), Hundred; Centigrade.
Cert., Certif. Certify, certificate.
Cf. (Lat. *confer*), Compare.
c. f. i. Cost, freight, and insurance.
c. ft. Cubic feet.
C. G. Coast guard; Commissary General; Consul General.
C. G. S. Centimeter-Gram-Second.
Ch. Church; Chapter.
Chal., Chald. Chaldee.
Chanc. Chancellor, chancery.
Chap. Chapter; Chaplain.
Chas. Charles.
Chem. Chemistry, chemical.
Chin. Chinese.
Chr. Christ; Christian.
Chron. Chronology, chronological.
C. I. Order of the Crown of India.
CIA. Central Intelligence Agency.
C.I.F. Cost, Insurance, freight.

Cit. Citation; Citizen.
Civ. Civil.
C. J. Chief Justice.
Cl. Clergyman.
Clk. Clerk.
cm. Centimeter.
C. M. Common meter.
C. M. (Lat. *chirurgiæ magister*), Master in Surgery.
CO. Commanding Officer.
Co. Company; County.
C. O. D. Cash on Delivery; Collect (payment) on delivery.
   of C. Chamber of Commerce.
Col. Colonel; Colossians: Column.
Coll. College; Collection.
Colloq. Colloquial, colloquialism.
Colo., Co. Colorado.
Com. Commander; Commerce; Commissioner; Committee; Commodore.
Comm. Commentary; Commerce.
Comp. Compare, comparative; Compound, compounded.
Compar. Comparative.
Com. Ver. Common Version.
Con. (Lat. *contra*), Against.
Conelrad. Control of Electronic Radiation.
Cong. Congregation, Congregational, Congregationalist; Congress.
Conj. Conjunction.
Conn., Ct. Connecticut.
Cont. Contents; Continued.
Co-op. Co-operative.
Cop., Copt. Coptic.
Cor. Corinthians.
Corrup. Corruption, corrupted.
Cor. Sec. Corresponding Secretary.
C. P. Clerk of the Peace; Common Pleas.
c. p. Chemically pure.
C. P. A. Certified Public Accountant; Civilian Production Administration.
C. Q. D. Come quick—danger.
Cr. Credit, creditor.
Cres. Crescendo.
Crim. con. Criminal conversation, or adultery.
cryst., crystal. Crystallography.
C. S. Christian Science.
C. S. A. Confederate States of America.
Csks. Casks.
Ct. (Lat. *centum*), A hundred.
Ct. Court.
C. T. A. U. Catholic Total Abstinence Union.
ctge. Cartage.
Cu., Cub. Cubic.
Cu. ft. Cubic foot.
Cur., Curt. Current—this month.
CVA. Columbia Valley Authority.
Cwt. Hundredweight(s).
C. Y. M. A. Catholic Young Men's Association.
C. Z. Canal Zone.

D. Deputy; Democrat; Dutch.
d. (Lat. *denarius, denarii*), Penny, pence.
d. Died; Daughter.
D. A. District Attorney.
Dan. Daniel; Danish.
D. A. R. Daughter(s) of the American Revolution.
Dat. Dative.
D. C. Doctor of Chiropractic.
D. C. (Ital. *da capo*), From the beginning; Direct Current.
D. C., Dist. Col. District of Columbia.
D. C. L. Doctor of Civil (or Canon) Law.
D. D. (Lat. *divinitatis doctor*), Doctor of Divinity.
D-Day. Day designated for military operation against enemy.
D. D. S. Doctor of Dental Surgery.
D E. Dynamic Engineer.
Dec. December.
decim. Decimeter.
Def. Definition; Defendant.
Deg. Degree, degrees.
Del., De. Delaware.
Del. (Lat. *delineavit*), He (or she) drew.
D. Eng. Doctor of Engineering.

Dep., Dept. Department; Deputy; Deposit.
Der. Derived, derivation.
Deut. Deuteronomy.
DEW. Distant Early Warning.
dft. Draft; Defendant.
D. G. (Lat. *Dei gratia*), By the grace of God.
Dict. Dictionary.
Dim., Dimin. Diminutive.
Dis., Disct. Discount.
Dist. District.
Div. Divide, dividend, division, divisor.
D. Lit., D. Litt. Doctor of Literature.
D. M., D. Mus. Doctor of Music.
D. M. D. Doctor of Dental Medicine.
DNA. Deoxyribonucleic Acid.
D. O. Doctor of Osteopathy; Doctor of Oratory.
Do. (Ital. *ditto*), The same.
Dols. Dollars.
Doz. Dozen.
D.P. Displaced Person.
Dpt. Deponent; Department.
Dr. Debtor; Doctor; Dram, drams.
D. S. (Ital. *dal segno*), From the sign.
D. S., D. Sc. Doctor of Science.
D. S. C. Distinguished Service Cross.
D. S. M. Distinguished Service Medal.
D. S. O. Distinguished Service Order.
DST. Daylight Saving Time.
D. T. (Lat. *doctor theologiæ*), Doctor of Theology.
Du. Dutch; Duke.
Duo., 12mo. Duodecimo (twelve folds).
D. V. (Lat. *Deo volente*), God willing.
D. V. M. Doctor of Veterinary Medicine.
D. V. S. Doctor of Veterinary Surgery.
dwt. (Lat. *denarius,* and English *weight*), Pennyweight, pennyweights.
Dyn., Dynam. Dynamics.

E. East, Eastern; English.
Ea. Each.
Eben. Ebenezer.
Eccl., Eccles. Ecclesiastical.
Econ. Economy, economics.
Ed. Editor; Edition; Edinburgh.
Ed., Edm. Edmund.
Ed.D. Doctor of Education.
Edin. Edinburgh.
Edw. Edward.
E. E. Errors excepted; Electrical Engineer.
EEC. European Economic Community (Common Market).
e. g. (Lat. *exempli gratia*), For example.
Elec., Elect. Electric, electricity.
Eliz. Elizabeth, Elizabethan.
e. m. f. Electromotive force.
Emp. Emperor, empress.
Enc., Encl. Enclosure.
Ency., Encyc. Encyclopedia.
E. N. E. East northeast.
Eng. England, English.
Eng., Engin. Engineer, engineering.
Ent., Entom. Entomology.
Eph. Ephesians; Ephraim.
Epiph. Epiphany.
Epis., Episc. Episcopal.
Epis., Epist. Epistle, epistolary.
ER. Endoplasmic Reticulum.
ERP. European Recovery Program.
E. S. E. East southeast.
ESP. Extra-sensory perception.
EST. Eastern Standard Time.
Esq., Esqr. Esquire.
et al. (Lat. *et alibi*), And elsewhere.
et al. (Lat. *et alii, aliæ,* or *alia*), And others.
etc., &c. (Lat. *et cetæri, cæteræ,* or *cætera*), And the others, and so forth.
Ethnol. Ethnology, ethnological.
Etym. Etymology.
Ex. Example; Examined; Exception; Exodus; Export; Executive.
Exch. Exchange; Exchequer.
Exd. Examined.
Exec., Exr. Executor.
Execx., Exrx. Executrix.
Ex. Gr. (Lat. *exempli gratia*), For example.
Exod. Exodus.
Exon. (Lat. *Exonia*), Exeter.
exp. Express; Export; Expense.

Ezek. Ezekiel.
F. Fellow; Fahrenheit; France.
f. Farthing, farthings; Folio; Feminine.
f. Franc, francs.
Fahr. Fahrenheit.
F. & A. M. Free and Accepted Masons.
f. a. s. Free alongside ship.
FBI. Federal Bureau of Investigation.
FCA. Farm Credit Association.
FCC. Federal Communications Commission.
Fcp. Foolscap.
F. D., Fid. Def. (Lat. *fidei defensor*), Defender of the Faith.
FDIC. Federal Deposit Insurance Corp.
Feb. February.
Fec. (Lat. *fecit*), He (or she) did it.
Fem. Feminine.
FEPC. Fair Employment Practice Committee.
F. F. V. First Families of Virginia.
F. G. S. Fellow of the Geological Society.
FHA. Federal Housing Administration.
F. I. A. Fellow of the Institute of Actuaries.
F. I. C. Fellow of the Chemical Institute.
Fig. Figure, figurative, figuratively.
Finn. Finnish.
Fl. Flemish; Florin, florins; Flourished.
Fla., Fl. Florida.
FLA. Federal Loan Administration.
F. M. Field Marshal; Frequency Modulation.
fo., fol. Folio.
f. o. b. Free on board.
fol. Folio; Following.
For. Foreign.
for'd., fwd. Forward, forwarded.
FPC. Federal Power Commission.
Fr. France, French; Francis; Francs.
F. R. A. S. Fellow of the Royal Astronomical Society.
Fred. Frederick.
F. R. G. S. Fellow of the Royal Geographical Society.
Fri. Friday.
FRS. Federal Reserve System.
F. R. S. Fellow of the Royal Society.
F. R. S. L. Fellow of the Royal Society of Literature.
frt. Freight.
FSA. Federal Security Administration.
ft. Foot, feet.
FTC. Federal Trade Commission.
Fth. Fathom.
Fur. Furlong.

G. Genitive; Guinea, guineas; Gulf.
Ga. Georgia.
Gael. Gaelic.
Gal. Galatians.
Gal., Gall. Gallon.
G. A. R. Grand Army of the Republic.
GATT. General Agreement on Tariffs and Trade.
G. B. Great Britain.
G. C. B. Grand Cross of the Bath.
G. C. L. H. Grand Cross of the Legion of Honor.
G. C. S. I. Grand Commander of the Star of India.
G. C. V. O. Grand Cross of the Royal Victorian Order.
G. D. Grand Duke, Grand Duchess.
Gen., Genl. General.
Gen. Genesis; Genitive.
Gend. Gender.
Geo. George.
Geog. Geography, geographical.
Geol. Geology, geological.
Geom. Geometry, geometrical.
Ger., Germ. German, Germany.
G. H. Q. General Headquarters.
Gi. Gill, gills.
G. I. Government Issue.
G. L. Grand Lodge.
G. M. Grand Master.
Gm. Gram.
GMT. Greenwich Mean Time.
Go., Goth. Gothic.
G. O. P. Grand Old Party (applied to Republican party).
Gov. Governor, government.

Gov.-Gen. Governor-General.
Govt. Government.
Gr. Grain(s); Great; Greek; Gross.
gr. gram(s).
Gram. Grammar, grammatical.
Gro. Gross.
G. T. Good Templars; Grand Tyler.
Gtt. (Lat. *guttæ*), Drops.

H., hr. Hour, hours.
Hag. Haggai.
Hamps. Hampshire.
Haw., Hi. Hawaii.
H. C. House of Commons.
h. e. (Lat. *hoc est*), That is or this is; (*hic est*), Here is.
Heb., Hebr. Hebrew, Hebrews.
HEW. Department of Health, Education and Welfare.
H. H. His (or Her) Highness; His Holiness (the Pope).
Hhd. Hogshead, hogsheads.
H.I.H. His (or Her) Imperial Highness.
Hind. Hindu, Hindustan, Hindustani.
Hist. History, historical.
H. J. (Lat. *hic jacet*), Here lies.
H. J. S. (Lat. *hic jacet sepultus*), Here lies buried.
H. M. His (or Her) Majesty.
H. M. S. His (or Her) Majesty's service, ship, or steamer.
Hon., Honble. Honorable.
Hor., Horol. Horology, horological.
Hort., Hortic. Horticulture, horticultural.
H. P. Half pay; High priest; Horse power.
H. R. House of Representatives.
H. R. H. His (or Her) Royal Highness.
Hun., Hung. Hungary, Hungarian.
Hyd., Hydros. Hydrostatics.
Hydraul. Hydraulics.
Hypoth. Hypothesis, hypothetical.

I., Isl. Island.
Ia. Iowa.
Ib., Ibid. (Lat. *ibidem*), In the same place.
ICBM. Intercontinental ballistic missile.
ICC. Interstate Commerce Com's'n; Indian Claims Com's'n.
Ice., Icel. Iceland, Icelandic.
Ich., Ichth. Ichthyology.
Ida., Id. Idaho.
IDA. International Development Ass'n.
i. e. (Lat. *id est*), That is.
I. H. S. Greek contraction for Jesus, —used as abbrev. for Lat. *Jesus Hominum Salvator*, "Jesus, the Savior of Men," and *In hoc signo*, "In this sign (cross)."
Ill. Illinois.
ILO. International Labor Organization.
Imp. (Lat. *imperator*), Emperor; Imperial; Impersonal.
In. Inch, inches.
Incog. (Ital. *incognito*), Unknown.
Ind. India, Indian; Indiana.
In lim. (Lat. *in limine*), At the outset.
In loc. (Lat. *in loco*), In its place.
in re. In regard to.
I. N. R. I. (Lat. *Jesus Nazarenus Rex Iudæorum*), Jesus of Nazareth, King of the Jews.
Ins. Insurance.
Inst. Instant; The present month; Institute, institution.
Int. Interest.
Int. Dept. Department of the Interior.
Intrans. Intransitive.
Int. Rev. Internal Revenue.
Intro., Introd. Introduction.
I. O. O. F. Independent Order of Odd Fellows.
I. O. R. M. Improved Order of Red Men.
I. O. U. I owe you.
I. Q. Intelligence Quotient.
i. q. (Lat. *idem quod*), The same as.
Ir. Ireland, Irish.

IRBM. Intermediate range ballistic missile.
IRS. Internal Revenue Service.
Is., Isa. Isaiah.
I. S. Irish Society.
I. S. M. (Lat. *Jesus Salvator Mundi*), Jesus, Savior of the World.
It., Ital. Italy, Italian; Italic.
Itin. Itinerary.

J. Judge; Justice.
Jac. Jacob, Jacobus (— James).
JAG. Judge Advocate General.
Jan. January.
Jav. Javanese.
J. C. Jesus Christ.
J. C. D. (Lat. *juris civilis doctor*), Doctor of Civil Law.
J. D. (Lat. *jurum doctor*), Doctor of Laws.
Jer. Jeremiah.
J. H. S. See *I. H. S.*
Jno. John.
Jon., Jona. Jonathan.
Jos. Joseph.
Josh. Joshua.
Jour. Journal; Journey.
J. P. Justice of the Peace.
Jr. Juror; Junior.
J. R. Joint Resolution.
J. U. D. (Lat. *Juris utriusque doctor*), Doctor of both laws (of civil and canon law).
Jud. Judith; Judicial.
Judg. Judges.
Jul. July; Julius, Julian.
Jun., Je. June.

K. King; Knight.
k. Karat.
Kans., Kan., Ks. Kansas.
K. B. Knight of the Bath; King's Bench.
K. C. King's Counsel; Knights of Columbus; Kansas City.
kg. Kilogram.
Ki. Kings.
Kingd. Kingdom.
K. L. H. Knight of the Legion of Honor.
K. M. Knight of Malta.
km. Kilometer.
K. P. Knight of St. Patrick.
K. of P. Knights of Pythias.
Kt. Knight.
K. T. Knight Templar.
Kw. Kilowatt.
Kwh. Kilowatt hour.
Ky. Kentucky.

L. Latin; Lake; Lord; Lady.
L., l., £. (Lat. *libra*), Pound, pounds (sterling).
L., lb., ℔. (Lat. *libra*), Pound, pounds (weight).
La., Lou. Louisiana.
Lat. Latin; Latitude.
LC. Landing Craft.
l. c. Lower case (in printing).
L. c., loc. cit. (Lat. *loco citato*), In the passage cited.
l/c. Letter of credit.
L. D. S. Licentiate of Dental Surgery; Latter Day Saints.
Leg., Legis. Legislature, legislative.
Lev., Levit. Leviticus.
Lex. Lexicon.
Lexicog. Lexicography, lexicographer, lexicographical.
L. H. D. (Lat. *Litterarum Humanarum Doctor*), Doctor of Humanities.
L. I. Light Infantry; Long Island.
Lib. (Lat. *liber*), Book; Library, librarian.
Lieut., Lt. Lieutenant.
Lieut. Col. Lieutenant Colonel.
Lieut. Gen. Lieutenant General.
Lieut. Gov. Lieutenant Governor.
Linn. Linnæus, Linnæan.
Liq. Liquor, liquid.
Lit. Literally, literature, literary.
Lit. D., Litt. D. (Lat. *literarum doctor*), Doctor of Literature.
LL. B. (Lat. *legum baccalaureus*), Bachelor of Laws.

LL. D. (Lat. *legum doctor*), Doctor of Laws.
LL. M. Master of Laws.
L. M. Long meter.
loc. cit. In the place quoted.
Lon., Lond. London.
Lon., Long. Longitude.
Log. (Lat. *loquitur*), He (or she) speaks.
LP. Long play (phonograph record).
LSD. Lysergic acid diethylamide.
L. s. d. (Lat. *libræ, solidi, denarii*), Pounds, shillings, pence.
Lt. Lieutenant.
Ltd. Limited.
Lt. Inf. Light Infantry.
LTL. Less than truckload.
Luth. Lutheran.

m. Married; Masculine; Meter, meters; Mile, miles; Minute, minutes.
M. Marquis; Middle; Monday; Morning; Monsieur.
M. (Lat. *mille*), Thousand.
M. (Lat. *meridies*), Meridian; Noon.
MA. Master of Arts.
Mac., Macc. Maccabees.
MAD. Magnetic airborne detector.
Maj. Major.
Maj. Gen. Major General.
Mal. Malachi; Malay, Malayan.
Man. Manitoba.
Manuf. Manufactures, manufacturing.
Mar. March; Maritime.
Marq. Marquis.
Mas., Masc. Masculine.
Mass., Ma. Massachusetts.
M. Ast. S. Member of the Astronomical Society.
Math. Mathematics, mathematical.
Matt. Matthew.
M. B. (Lat. *medicinæ baccalaureus*), Bachelor of Medicine.
M. B. (Lat. *musicæ baccalaureus*), Bachelor of Music.
MC. Member of Congress; Master of Ceremonies.
MD. Muscular dystrophy.
M. D. (Lat. *medicinæ doctor*), Doctor of Medicine.
Md. Maryland.
Mdlle., Mlle. (Fr. *mademoiselle*), Miss.
Mdse. Merchandise.
M. E. Most Excellent; Military Engineer; Mining Engineer; Mechanical Engineer; Methodist Episcopal.
Me. Maine.
Meas. Measure.
Mech. Mechanics, mechanical.
Med. Medicine, medical; Medieval.
Med. Lat. Medieval Latin.
Mem. Memorandum, memoranda.
Messrs., MM. (Fr. *messieurs*), Gentlemen.
Met. Metaphysics, metaphysical.
Metal., Metall. Metallurgy.
Metaph. Metaphysics; Metaphorically.
Meteor. Meteorology, meteorological.
Meth. Methodist.
Mex. Mexico, Mexican.
MFH. Master of Fox Hounds.
Mfr. Manufacturer; manufacture.
mg. Milligram.
Mi. Michigan.
M. I. C. E. Member of the Institute of Civil Engineers.
Mich. Michaelmas; Michigan.
Mid. Middle; Midshipman.
Mil., Milit. Military.
M. I. M. E. Member of the Institute of Mining Engineers.
Min. Mineralogy, mineralogical; Minute, minutes.
Minn., Mn. Minnesota.
Min. Plen. Minister Plenipotentiary.
Miss., Ms. Mississippi.
ML. Master of Laws; Multiple listing (real estate).
mm. Millimeters.
Mme. Madame.
M. O. Money order.
Mo. Missouri; Month.
Mod. Modern.
Mon. Monday.

Mons. (Fr. *monsieur*), Sir; Mr.
Mont. Montana.
M. P. Member of Parliament; Military Police.
M. P. P. Member of Provincial Parliament.
Mr. Master, Mister.
M. R. G. S. Member of the Royal Geographical Society.
M. R. I. Member of the Royal Institute.
Mrs. Mistress.
M. S. Master of Surgery; Master of Science.
Ms. Manuscript; *Mss.* Manuscripts.
MS. Multiple sclerosis.
MSG. Monosodium glutamate.
MST. Mountain Standard Time.
Mt. Montana, Mount; *Mts.* mountains.
mth., mo. Month.
Mus. Museum; Music, musical.
Mus. B. (Lat. *musicæ baccalaureus*), Bachelor of Music.
Mus. D., Mus. Doc., Mus. Doct. (Lat. *musicæ doctor*), Doctor of Music.
MVA. Missouri Valley Authority.
M. V. O. Member of the Royal Victorian Order.
M. W. A. Modern Woodmen of America.
Myth. Mythology, mythological.
N. Noon; North; Noun; Number; New; Neuter.
N. A. North America, North American.
NAA. National Aeronautic Ass'n.
NAACP. National Association for the Advancement of Colored People.
Nah. Nahum.
NAM. Nat'l Ass'n of Manufacturers.
NAS. National Academy of Sciences.
NASA. National Aeronautics and Space Administration.
Nat. Natural; National.
Nat. Hist. Natural History.
NATO. North Atlantic Treaty Organization.
Naut. Nautical.
Nb. Nebraska.
N. B. New Brunswick.
N. B. (Lat. *nota bene*), Note well; Take notice.
NBC. National Broadcasting Company.
N. C. North Carolina.
N. Dak., N. D. North Dakota.
N. E. New England, Northeast.
N. E. A. National Education Ass'n.
Nebr., Neb. Nebraska.
Neg. Negative, negatively.
Neh. Nehemiah.
Nem. con. (Lat. *nemine contradicente*), No one contradicting, unanimously.
Nem. diss. (Lat. *nemine dissentiente*), No one dissenting, unanimously.
Neth. Netherlands.
Neut. Neuter.
Nev. Nevada.
New Test., N. T. New Testament.
N. F. Newfoundland.
N. H. New Hampshire.
N. J. New Jersey.
N. L., N. Lat. North Latitude.
NLRB. Nat'l Labor Relations Board.
NMB. National Mediation Board.
N. Mex., N. M. New Mexico.
NNE. North northeast.
No., Nos. Number, numbers.
nol. pros. (Lat. *nolle prosequi*), To be unwilling to prosecute.
Nom., Nomin. Nominative.
non-com. Non-commissioned officer.
Non con. Non-content, dissentient. (The formula in which Members of the House of Lords vote.)
Non obst. (Lat. *non obstante*), Notwithstanding.
Non pros. (Lat. *non prosequitur*), He does not prosecute.
Non seq. (Lat. *non sequitur*), It does not follow (as a consequence).
Nor., Norm. Norman.
Nor. Fr., Norm. Fr. Norman French.
Norw. Norway, Norwegian, Norse.
Nov. November.

N. P. Notary Public.
NROTC. Naval Reserve Officers' Training Corps.
N. S. New style; Nova Scotia.
NSF. Nat'l Science Foundation.
N. S. J. C. (Fr. *Notre Seigneur Jesus Christ*), Our Lord Jesus Christ.
N. S. W. New South Wales.
Num., Numb. Numbers.
N. V. M. Nativity of the Virgin Mary.
N. W. Northwest, northwestern.
N. Y. New York.
N. Z., N. Zeal. New Zealand.
O. (unofficial) Ohio; Old.
OAS. Organization of American States.
OAU. Organization of African Unity.
ob. (Lat. *obiit*), He (or she) died.
Obj. Objective.
Obs. Obsolete.
Oct. October.
Oct., 8vo. Octavo.
Oh. Ohio.
O. K. "All correct."
Okla. Oklahoma.
Old Test., O. T. Old Testament.
Olym. Olympiad.
O. M. Order of Merit.
O. M. I. Order of Mary Immaculate.
Ont. Ontario
Op. Opposite, opposition.
Opt. Optative; Optics, optical.
Ord., Ordn. Ordnance.
Oreg., Ore. Oregon.
Orig. Original, originally.
Ornith. Ornithology, ornithological.
O. S. Old Style; Old Saxon.
O. S. A. Order of St. Augustine.
O. S. B. Order of St. Benedict.
O. S. F. Order of St. Francis.
Oxf. Oxford.
Oxon. (Lat. *Oxonia, Oxoniensis*), Oxford, of Oxford.
Oz. Ounce. (The *z* in this contraction and in *viz.* represents an old symbol (ʒ), used to mark a terminal contraction.)
P. Page; Participle; Past; Pole; Port.
Pa. Pennsylvania.
Pal., Palæont. Palæontology, palæontological.
Par. Paragraph.
Parl. Parliament, parliamentary.
Part. Participle.
Payt. Payment.
Pd. Paid.
Pd. D. Doctor of Pedagogy.
P. E. Protestant Episcopal.
P. E. I. Prince Edward Island.
P. E. N. Poets, Playwrights, Editors, Essayists, and Novelists (International).
Pent. Pentecost.
Per., Pers. Persian; Person, personal.
Per. an. (Lat. *per annum*), Yearly.
Per cent., per ct. (Lat. *per centum*), By the hundred.
Peruv. Peruvian.
pfd. Preferred.
Phar., Pharm. Pharmacy.
Ph. B. (Lat. *philosophiæ baccalaureus*), Bachelor of Philosophy.
Ph. D. (Lat. *philosophiæ doctor*), Doctor of Philosophy.
Phil. Philip; Philippians; Philosophy, philosophical.
Phil., Phila. Philadelphia.
Philol. Philology.
Philos. Philosophy, philosophical.
Ph. M. Master of Philosophy.
PHS. Public Health Service.
Phys. Physics, physical.
Physiol. Physiology, physiological.
Pinx., Pxt. (Lat. *pinxit*), He (or she) painted it.
Pk. Peck.
Pl. Place; Plate; Plural.
Plf., Plff., Pltff. Plaintiff.
Plur. Plural.
P. M. (Lat. *post meridiem*), Afternoon.
P. M. Past Master; Peculiar meter; Postmaster.

P. O. Post Office.
Pol. Polish, Poland.
Polit. Econ. Political Economy.
Pop. Population.
Port. Portugal, Portuguese.
POW. Prisoner of War.
Pp. Pages.
P. P. Parish Priest.
P. P. C. (Fr. *pour prendre congé*), To take leave. See *T. T. L.*
Pph. Pamphlet.
Pr. Present; Priest; Prince.
Pr. par. Present participle.
P. R. (Lat. *Populus Romanus*), The Roman People; Puerto Rico.
P. R. C. (Lat. *post Roman conditam*), After the building of Rome.
Pref. Prefix; Preface.
Pres. President; Present.
Prim. Primary.
Prin. Principal.
Prob. Problem; Probable, probably.
Prof. Professor.
Pron. Pronoun; Pronounced, pronunciation.
Pro tem. (Lat. *pro tempore*), For the time being.
Prov. Proverbs, proverbial, proverbially; Provincial; Provost.
Prox. (Lat. *proximo*), Next; Of the next month.
Prus. Prussia, Prussian.
P. S. (Lat. *post scriptum*), Postscript.
Ps., Psa. Psalm, psalms.
pseud. Pseudonym.
pt. Part; Payment; Point; Port.
PTA. Parent-Teacher Association.
Pub. Public; Published, publisher.
Pvt., pte. Private.
Pwt. Pennyweight.
Q., Qu. Query; Question.
q. e. (Lat. *quod est*), Which is.
Q. E. D. (Lat. *quod erat demonstrandum*), Which was to be proved.
Q. M. Quartermaster.
Qr. Quarterly; Quire.
Qt. Quart.
Quar., quart. Quarterly.
Quar., 4to. Quarto.
Que. Quebec.
q. v. (Lat. *quod vide*), Which see.
R. Réaumur; River.
R. (Lat. *rex*), King; (Lat. *regina*), Queen.
R. A. Royal Academy, Royal Academician; Rear Admiral; Royal Arch; Royal Artillery; Royal Art.
Rad. (Lat. *radix*), Root.
RAF. Royal Air Force.
R. C. Roman Catholic; Red Cross.
R. E. Reformed Episcopal.
REA. Rural Electrification Administration.
Rec. Recipe; Receipt.
Recd. Received.
Recpt. Receipt.
Ref. Reference; Referee.
Ref. Ch. Reformed Church.
Reg. Regular; Registered.
Reg., Regr. Registrar.
Reg., Regt. Regiment.
Rel. Religion, religious.
Rel. Pron. Relative Pronoun.
Rem. Remark, remarks.
Rep. Report; Representative.
Rep., Repub. Republic; Republican.
Res. Reserve; Residence.
Rev. Revelation; Revenue; Reverend; Review; Revise.
Rev. Stat. Revised Statutes.
RFC. Reconstruction Finance Corp.
R. F. D. Rural Free Delivery.
Rhet. Rhetoric, rhetorical.
R. I. Rhode Island.
R. I. P. (Lat. *requiescat in pace*), May he (or she) rest in peace.
Riv. River.
R. N. Registered Nurse; Royal Navy.
RNA. Ribonucleic Acid.
Rom. Roman, Romans.
Rom. Cath. Roman Catholic.
ROTC. Reserve Officers' Training Corps.

R. R. Railroad.
R. S. V. P. (Fr. *Répondez s'il vous plaît*), Please reply.
Rt. Right.
Rt. Hon. Right Honorable.
Rt. Rev. Right Reverend.
Russ. Russia, Russian.
R. V. Revised Version.
Ry. Railway.

S. Saint; Saturday; Section; Shilling; Sign; Signor; Solo; Soprano; South; Sun; Sunday; Sabbath.
s. Second, seconds; See; Singular; Son; Succeeded.
S. A. South Africa; South America; Salvation Army.
Sab. Sabbath.
SAC. Strategic Air Command.
Sam. Samuel.
Sans., Sansc., Sansk., Skr. Sanscrit, Sanskrit.
Sask. Saskatchewan.
Sat. Saturday.
Sax. Saxon, Saxony.
SBA. Small Business Administration.
S. C. South Carolina.
S. caps., Sm. caps. Small capitals (in printing).
Sc. B. (Lat. *scientiæ baccalaureus*), Bachelor of Science.
Sc. D. (Lat. *scientiæ doctor*), Doctor of Science.
Sch. (Lat. *scholium*), A note.
Sci. Science.
Scot., Sc. Scotland, Scotch, Scottish.
Scrip., Script. Scripture, scriptural.
Sculp. Sculpture.
Sculp., Sculpt., Sc. (Lat. *sculpsit*), He (or she) engraved it.
S. D. Doctor of Science.
S. Dak., S. D. South Dakota.
SE. Southeast.
SEATO. Southeast Asia Treaty Organization.
SEC. Securities and Exchange Commission.
Sec. Second.
Sec., Sect. Section.
Sec., Secy. Secretary.
Sen. Senate, senator.
Sen. Doc. Senate Document.
Sep., Sept. September.
Seq. (Lat. *sequentes, sequentia*), The following, or the next.
Serg., Sergt. Sergeant.
Sess. Session.
SHAPE. Supreme Headquarters Allied Powers in Europe.
sic. As in the original (mistake uncorrected).
S. J. Society of Jesus.
Slav. Slavonic.
Snafu. Situation normal, all fouled up.
SNAP. Systems of Nuclear Auxiliary Power.
Soc., Socy. Society.
Sol. Gen. Solicitor-General.
S. O. S. Wireless distress signal at sea.
Sp. Spain, Spanish; Spirit.
s. p (Lat. *sine prole*), Without issue.
SPARS. (Lat. *Semper parati* [æ]), Always ready; Coast Guard motto and translation, initials being used as designation for Women's Coast Guard Reserves.
SPCA. Society for the Prevention of Cruelty to Animals.
SPCC. Society for the Prevention of Cruelty to Children.
Spec. Special, specially.
sp. gr , s. g. Specific gravity.
S. P. Q. R. (Lat. *Senatus Populusque Romanus*), The Senate and the People of Rome.
sq. Square; *sq. ft.* Square foot, feet; *sq. in.* Square inch(es); *sq. m.* Square mile(s); *sq. yd.* Square yard(s); *sq. rd.* Square rod(s).
Sr. Senior.
S. R. Senate Resolution.
SRO. Standing room only.
SS. Sunday School; Steamship.
SSA. Social Security Administration.

SSE. South-southeast.
SSW. South-southwest.
St. Saint; Stone; Street.
st. (Lat. *stet*), Let it stand (in printing).
Stat. Statute, statutes; Statuary.
STD. (Lat. *sacræ theologiæ doctor*), Doctor of Sacred Theology.
ster., stg. Sterling.
Str. Steamer; Strait.
Subst. Substantive; Substitute.
Sun., Sund. Sunday.
Sup. Superior; Superlative; Supplement; Supine.
Sup. Ct. Supreme Court.
Supt. Superintendent.
Surg. Surgeon, surgery.
Surg.-Gen. Surgeon-General.
Surv Surveying, surveyor.
Surv.-Gen. Surveyor-General.
SW. Southwest.
Sw. Sweden, Swedish.
Swit., Switz. Switzerland.
Syn. Synonym, synonymous.
Syr. Syria, Syriac.

T. Tenor; Ton; Tun; Tuesday.
Tab. Table; Tabular statement.
Tass. The Soviet News Agency.
Tcs. Tierces.
Tech. Technical, technically.
Tenn., Tn. Tennessee.
Term. Termination.
Teut. Teutonic.
Tex., Tx. Texas.
Text. rec. (Lat. *textus receptus*), The received text.
Th. Thomas; Thursday.
Theo. Theodore.
Theol. Theology.
Tho., Thos. Thomas.
Thu., Thur., Thurs. Thursday.
Tim. Timothy.
Tit. Title; Titus.
TNT. Trinitrotoluene, an explosive.
Tob. Tobit.
Tom. Tome, volume.
Tonn. Tonnage.
Topog. Topography, topographical.
Tr. Translation, translator, translated; Transpose; Treasurer; Trustee.
Trans. Transaction; Translation, translator, translated.
Treas. Treasurer.
Trig., Trigon. Trigonometry, trigonometrical.
Trin. Trinity.
T. T. L. To take leave. See *P. P. C.*
Tu., Tues. Tuesday.
Turk. Turkey, Turkish.
TVA. Tennessee Valley Authority.
twp. Township.
Typ. Typographer.
Typog. Typography, typographical.

UAR. United Arab Republic.
u.c. Upper Case (Capital letters in printing).
UFO. Unidentified flying object.
U. J. D. See *J. U. D.*
UK. United Kingdom.
Ult. (Lat. *ultimo*), Last; Of the last month.
UN. United Nations.
UNESCO. United Nations Educational, Scientific, and Cultural Organization.
UNICEF. United Nations Internat'l Children's Emergency Funds.
Unit. Unitarian.
Univ. University.
UPI. United Press International.
U. S. United States.
USA. United States of America; United States Army.
USAF. United States Air Force.
USCG. United States Coast Guard.
USES. United States Employment Service.
USIA. United States Information Agency.
U. S. L. United States Legation.
U. S. M. United States mail; United States marine.
U. S. M. A. United States Military Academy.
U. S. N. United States Navy.

U. S. N. A. United States Naval Academy.
USO. United Service Organizations.
U. S. S. United States Senate; United States ship or steamer.
U. S. S. Ct. United States Supreme Court.
USSR. Union of Soviet Socialist Republics (Russia).
V. Verb; Verse; Victoria; Violin.
V. (Lat. *vide*), See.
V. A. Vicar Apostolic; Vice Admiral; Veterans Administration.
Va. Virginia.
Val. Valve; Value.
Vat. Vatican.
V. C. Victoria Cross.
V-E Day. Official date of Germany's surrender in World War II.
V. F. W. Veterans of Foreign Wars.
V. G. Vicar General.
V.I. Virgin Islands.
Vice pres. Vice President.
Vid. (Lat. *vide*), See.
VIP. Very important person.
Vis., Visc. Viscount.
VISTA. Volunteers in Service to America.
Viz. (Lat. *videlicet*), Namely; To wit. See *Oz.*
V-J Day. Official date of Japan's surrender in World War II.
Voc. Vocative.
Vol., Vols. Volume, Volumes.
V. P. Vice President.
V. Rev. Very Reverend.
V. S. Veterinary surgeon.
vs., v. (Lat. *versus*), Against.
Vt. Vermont.
Vul., Vulg. Vulgate.

W. Wednesday; Week; Welsh; West, western.
WAC. Women's Army Corps.
WAF. Women in the Air Force.
Wash., Wa. Washington.
WAVES. Women Appointed for Volunteer Emergency Service (Women's naval reserve).
W. C. A. Women's Christian Ass'n.
W. C. T. U. Women's Christian Temperance Union.
Wed. Wednesday.
Wel. Welsh.
w. f. Wrong font (in printing).
WHO. World Health Organization.
W. I. West Indies, West Indian.
Wis., Wisc., Wi. Wisconsin.
Wk. Week.
W. Long. West Longitude.
Wm. William.
WNW. West northwest.
W. R. C. Women's Relief Corps.
WSW. West southwest.
Wt. Weight.
W. Va., W.V. West Virginia.
Wyo., Wy. Wyoming.

X., Xt. Christ.
Xm., Xmas. Christmas.
Xn., Xtian. Christian.
Xnty. Christianity.
Xper., Xr. Christopher.

Y. Year.
Yd. Yard; *Yds.* Yards.
YMCA. Young Men's Christian Ass'n.
Y. M. Cath. A. Young Men's Catholic Association.
YMHA. Young Men's Hebrew Ass'n.
Y. P. S. C. E. Young People's Society of Christian Endeavor.
Yr. Year; Younger; Your.
Yrs. Years; Yours.
YWCA. Young Women's Christian Ass'n.

Zach. Zachary.
Zech. Zechariah.
Zeph. Zephaniah.
Z. G. Zoological Gardens.
ZIP. Zone Improvement Program.
Zool. Zoology, zoological.

TEST QUESTIONS

THE following list of *test* questions has been prepared to serve as a *review* of the preceding subject matter on the English language. As the questions have been arranged in logical order for the proper development of each subject, they should serve also to suggest a thorough and systematic *course of study* for those who desire to improve their everyday English.

Although the list contains several hundred questions, it includes but a small fraction of the thousands of questions which the English department will answer. A similar list will be found at the end of each of the other departments of the book.

HISTORY AND DEVELOPMENT OF THE ENGLISH LANGUAGE

180

What is the meaning of *majority?* of *plurality?*. 27
Distinguish between *practical* and *practicable* . 27
What are "proud" words? Illustrate their use 27
Distinguish between *recipe* and *receipt* 28
Illustrate the proper use of the words *regrettable* and *regretful* 28
Explain and illustrate the correct use of *respectively* and *respectfully* 28
Explain clearly the use of the words *set* and *sit*. 28
Distinguish between *sewage* and *sewerage* . . . 28
Mention two adjectives which have the same form when used as adverbs. 29
What is meant by the *split infinitive?* When is it permissible? 30
Is there any difference between *station* and *depot?* 30
Point out the error in this sentence: "I have never seen such a pretty car." 30
Is it correct to say, "the finished and unfinished manuscript"? Give a reason for your answer 31
Is it ever permittible to use the word *whose* in referring to things? 32

WORD BUILDING

From what elements are words formed? . . . 33
What is meant by the *root* of a word? 33
What is meant by the *stem* of a word? 33
How does the *root* of a word differ from the *stem?* 33
Of what advantage is a knowledge of *roots* and *stems?* 33
What is a *prefix?* a *suffix?* 33
Explain the meaning of *affixes* 33
Show how the following words are built: *cablegram, periscope* 33
Name three Anglo-Saxon prefixes 34
What is the meaning of each of the following prefixes: *dis, contra, circum, non?* 34
Show the formation of the following words: *descent, illegal, exclaim, unkind, forgive.* 34
Mention three Anglo-Saxon suffixes 35
What is the meaning of each of the following prefixes: *semi, re, hypo, sub, trans, pre, per, pro?* 35
What is the meaning of each of the following suffixes: *like, er, ful, ly?* 35
Name a suffix which may be adjective or verbal 36
What Latin suffix corresponds to the Anglo-Saxon suffix *er?* Illustrate 36
Show how the following words are built: *factor, florist, legal, creation, peaceable, feminine* . 36
Name two suffixes which may be adjective or noun and give words showing both uses . . 36
Name an adjective built upon each of the following stems: *cap, fin, clus, duc* 37
Give two words built upon the stem *dict*, each having a prefix and a suffix 37
Explain the meaning of the following words by showing how they are built: *dependent, unstable, senseless* 38
Show how the word *automobile* is built 38
Point out the stems, prefixes, and suffixes in the following words: *irrevocable, convention, vital*. 38
Show how adjectives are formed from verb stems 38

DERIVATION OF ENGLISH WORDS FROM THE LATIN

Explain in what way the study of English words from the Latin is of use to you 39
Mention three nouns from the Latin word *bene*. 39
What Latin word means "I believe"? From the stem of this word, build two English nouns. 40
Explain the derivation of the following: *dictionary, indigestible, division* 41
From the supine stem of *duco* form three English nouns 41
What Latin verb is the source of the word *relative?* 42
What is the meaning of *gratus?* Name three words derived from *gratus* 42
From what Latin word is each of the following words derived. *illegal, allegiance, legitimate?* 43

By pointing out the stems, prefixes, and suffixes, explain how these words are built: *interrogative, competition, portable* 45
Explain the derivation of *reservation, bisect, tenant* 46
What Latin word means "I live"? Name a noun, an adjective, and a verb derived from it 46

SPELLING

Mention some aids in mastering the art of spelling 47
How is the possessive case of nouns formed? . 47
Show the possessive of the following words: *Achilles, Dickens, conscience*. 47
What is the plural of each of the following words: *thief, goose, ally, mouse?* 50
Why are the following words called homonyms: *wait, weight; time, thyme?* 53
What are heteronyms? 53
Mention two words which are heteronyms . . 53

SENTENCE BUILDING

What is a sentence? What two parts are essential to the building of a sentence? Illustrate. 54
How does a clause differ from a sentence? . . 54
What is meant by a *part of speech?* 54
Name the different parts of speech and define and illustrate each. 54
What is a substantive? 54
Illustrate a simple sentence having a compound subject and a compound predicate 55
How does a complex sentence differ from a compound sentence? 55
What is meant by *inflection* of words? 55
What is an *appositive?* a *predicate noun?* . . . 55
Name five kinds of pronouns 55
What are interrogative pronouns? 55
Show the difference between an interrogative pronoun and an interrogative adjective . . 56
Give a sentence containing a demonstrative pronoun; a demonstrative adjective 56
Give a sentence containing a relative pronoun; an adjective pronoun; an indefinite pronoun. 56
By means of a sentence, show the use of the *direct* and the *indirect* object 56
What change in English nouns is made to show the possessive case? 56
By what other name is the possessive case known? 56
Write a sentence which shows the possessive case of two nouns implying separate possession 57
Explain and illustrate the meaning of the singular and the plural number 57
Define antecedent 57
Explain and illustrate the meaning of a *transitive* verb; an *intransitive* verb 57
As applied to verbs, what does *mode* show? . . 57
Explain the mode of each verb in the following sentence: "If thine enemy hunger, feed him." 57
What do we call the form the verb takes to show *time?* 58
Explain what is meant by a *copulative* verb. . 58
Define and illustrate an *impersonal* verb. Why are such verbs called impersonal? 58
What is an *auxiliary* verb? Why is it so called? 58
What auxiliary verb is a "sign" of the present perfect tense? of the past perfect tense? . . 58
Give a sentence containing an irregular, transitive verb in the active voice, indicative mode, past perfect tense, first person, plural number 57-58
What is a *participle?* 58
What is a *gerund?* How does a *gerund* differ from a *participle?* 59
What word usually precedes the English infinitive? 59
Classify the following adjectives as *limiting* or *descriptive: large, those, green, five, troublesome* 59
Give a sentence containing an *appositive* adjective 59

BIBLIOGRAPHY

HISTORY OF THE ENGLISH LANGUAGE

Baugh, A. C.—A History of the English Language *Appleton*
Bloomfield, L.—Language . . . . *Holt*
Brin, Joseph G.—Applied Semantics . *Humphries*
Graff, W. L.—Language and Languages . *Russell*
Greenough, J. B. and Kittredge, G. L.—Words and Their Ways of Speech . . . . . *Macmillan*
Nelson, Francis—History of English . *Macmillan*
Robertson, S.—The Development of Modern English . . . . *Prentice-Hall*

GOOD USAGE

Dean, Leonard F.—Essays on Language and Usage. *Oxford*
Evans, Bergen and Cornelia—A Dictionary of Contemporary American Usage . . . . *Random*
Fowler, H. W.—A Dictionary of Modern English Usage . . . . *Oxford*
Glover, D. M.—Daily Guide to Correct English. *Christopher*
Ives, Sumner—A New Handbook for Writers. *Knopf*
Partridge, Eric—The Concise Usage and Abusage. *Citadel*
Taintor, Sarah A.—The Secretary's Handbook. *Macmillan*

WORD BUILDING

Brown, Ivor J.—A Word in Your Ear . . *Dutton*
Ernst, Margaret S.—More About Words . *Knopf*
Garrison, Webb—What's In a Word . *Abingdon*
MacDonald, A. M., ed.—Chambers Etymological Dictionary . . . . *Littlefield*

SPELLING AND PRONUNCIATION

Allen, Robert L., and Others—English Sounds and Their Spelling . . . . *Crowell*
Colby, Frank—University Pronouncing Dictionary of Troublesome Words . . . . . *Apollo*
Crowell, Thomas L., Jr.—NBC Handbook of Pronunciation, 3rd Ed. . . . . . . *Crowell*
Gleeson, Ruth and Colvin, James—Words Most Often Misspelled and Mispronounced *Pocket Books*
Thomas, Charles K.—An Introduction to the Phonetics of American English . . . . . *Ronald*

DICTIONARIES

New Standard Dictionary . . *Funk and Wagnalls*
Webster's New International Dictionary . *Merriam*
Oxford English Dictionary . . . . . *Oxford*
Craigie, Sir Wm. A.—A Dictionary of American English . . . . *Univ. of Chicago Press*
Desk Dictionaries for Ready Reference:
 American College Dictionary . . . . . *Harper*
 College Standard Dictionary *Funk and Wagnalls*
 Webster's Collegiate Dictionary . . . *Merriam*
 The Winston Dictionary . . . . . . *Winston*

SENTENCE BUILDING

Bryant, M. M.—Functional English Grammar *Heath*
Curme, G. O.—Parts of Speech and Accidence *Heath*
Faulkner, Claude W.—Writing Good Sentences *Scribner*
Fernald, J. C.—English Grammar Simplified *Funk and Wagnalls*
Fries, Charles C.—The Structure of English *Harcourt*
Gleason, H. A., Jr.—Linguistics and English Grammar . . . . *Holt*
Romine, Jack S.—Sentence Mastery *Prentice-Hall*

PUNCTUATION AND CAPITALIZATION

Collins, F. W.—Authors' and Printers' Dictionary *Oxford*
Hutchinson, Lois D.—Standard Handbook for Secretaries, 7th ed. . . . . . . *McGraw-Hill*
Prentice-Hall Editorial Staff—Punctuation Made Easy . . . . *Prentice-Hall*
West, L.—300 Commas . . . . . . *McGraw-Hill*

LINGUISTICS

Chomsky, N.—Syntactic Structures . . . *Mouton*
Chomsky, N. and Halle, Morris—The Sound Pattern of English . . . . *Harper*
Gleason, H. A.—Linguistics and English Grammar. *Holt*
Hymes, D.—Language in Culture and Society. *Harper*

WRITING AND SPEAKING

Archer, Wm.—Playmaking .*Small, Maynard & Co.*
Cypreansen, Lucille—Speech Development, Improvement and Correction . . . . . *Ronald*
Ferguson, Charles W.—Say It with Words . *Knopf*
Fields, Victor A.—Voice and Diction . *Macmillan*
Flesch, R.—The Art of Plain Talk . . *Harper*
Ford, N. A. and Waters, Turpin—Basic Skills for Better Writing, Vols. A & B, paper . . *Putnam*
Guth, Hans P.—Words and Ideas . . . *Wadsworth*
Hodges, John C. and Laws, S. Y.—Harbrace Writing Counsel . . . . *Harcourt*
Hook, Julius N.—Guide to Good Writing: Grammar, Style and Usage . . . . *Ronald*
Ives, Sumner—New Handbook for Writers . *Knopf*
Loren, B. B.—English Essentials . . . *Macmillan*
Nelson, Herbert B.—English Essentials. *Littlefield*
Quiller-Couch, Sir Arthur—On the Art of Writing. *Putnam*
Shaw, Harry—Errors in English and Ways to Correct Them . . . . *Barnes & Noble*
Wallace, Karl R.—A History of Speech Education in America . . . . *Appleton*

FORMS OF SPEAKING

Baird, Albert C.—American Public Addresses. *McGraw-Hill*
Culp, Ralph B.—Basic Types of Speech. *Brown Co., W. C.*
Machelin, E.—Speech for the Stage . *Theatre Arts*
Monroe, A. H.—Principles and Types of Speech. *Scott-Foresman*
Sanford, Wm. P. and Yeager, W. H.—Effective Business Speech . . . . *McGraw-Hill*
Sarett, Lew and Others—Basic Principles of Speech, 4th ed. . . . . *Houghton*
Simmons, Harry—How to Talk your Way to Success . . . . *Prentice-Hall*
Zemlin, W.—Speech and Hearing Science. *Prentice-Hall*

LETTER WRITING

Aurner, Robert R.—Effective Business English. *South-Western*
Prentice-Hall Editorial Staff—How to Write a Good Letter . . . . *Prentice-Hall*
Shidle, N. C.—Art of Successful Communication. *McGraw-Hill*

SYNONYMS AND ANTONYMS

Allen, F. S.—Synonyms and Antonyms . *Harper*
Basescu, Sophie—Know the Word . . . *Helios*
Fernald, J. C.—Standard Handbook of English Synonyms, Antonyms, and Prepositions. *Funk and Wagnalls*
Roget, Peter—Thesaurus of English Words and Phrases (3rd ed.) . . . . *Grossett and Dunlap*
Soule, R. and Howsam, G.—Dictionary of English Synonyms, Antonyms, and Parallel Exp. *Shalom*
Synonyms, Antonyms, and Homonyms *Hawthorne*
Trench, R. C.—On the Study of Words *Dutton*

Literature

HOME OF
EMILY DICKINSON
1830-1886

HOMES OF NOTED AMERICAN WRITERS

Located in Tarrytown, New York and called "Sunnyside," this beautifully maintained home of Washington Irving looks as if it, too, was once a part of "Sleepy Hollow."

photo courtesy of Sleepy Hollow Restorations, Tarrytown, New York

Emily Dickinson's home at Amherst, Massachusetts, is now under the supervision of Amherst College and visitors are welcome by appointment.

The home of Mark Twain (Samuel L. Clemens) sits serenely near the banks of the Mississippi at Hannibal, Missouri.

Home of James Russell Lowell, American author and critic, in Cambridge, Massachusetts.

Literature

INTRODUCTORY

THE meaning of the term literature has been so widely extended during the past century that careless writers have sometimes used it to cover in rough-and-ready fashion all that has been written or printed. Thus we sometimes hear men in highly specialized professions speak of the "literature" of their subjects, and officers of corporations will speak of distributing their "literature." Such uses of the word are not only extreme, they are certainly incorrect. A chronological list of the presidents of the United States would contain many facts and would constitute a valuable historical record, but it would not be literature. On the other hand, the brief address which President Lincoln delivered at the dedication of the Gettysburg battlefield is imperishable literature. It differs from the historical list in both purpose and form.

Literature an Art. In order to be properly designated as literature, subject matter must be so arranged and ordered that it will appeal to the heart and mind of man, or, as we sometimes say, to the imagination. When any work, whether a musical score or a book, a painting, a statue, or a monument, succeeds in making this appeal, we say that it has the qualities of art. This, then, is the first requisite of literature. The appeal of art can be made only by works that have form. For a literary work to have form it is necessary that its creator shall be a master of language and construction. The author must have "style." He must be able to express or communicate effectively the emotion or idea that possesses him, and in ranking works of literature this must be one of our criteria. We shall give them a higher or a lower ranking in proportion as they have greater or less perfection of form. A work of art, like a story of the Greek gods, like a fable or a fairy tale, or a play or novel about an imagined character, may dispense with facts and still be great; but it cannot dispense with form.

Literature an Interpretation of Life. In addition to form, literature must have significant content. A statement of the rules of Latin grammar in perfect verse will not be great poetry. Without form, a work is not literature at all; without significance, it cannot be great literature. If, then, we assume that the form is adequate, a work of literature will be entitled to a higher ranking in proportion as the truths with which it deals are of greater significance to humanity.

Literature "Truer than History." Literature which meets these demands upon form and content constitutes our most valuable record of the inner life of man. Nowhere is the life of humanity, that is, the history of man's spiritual existence as distinguished from his mere animal existence, so thoroughly and fundamentally presented to us as in the world's great masterpieces; for, though literature is not valuable in proportion to the number of isolated facts presented, it is valuable because of the truths of life which it sets before us. It deals, not with what may once have chanced to happen, but with man's most vital, permanent, and significant relationships. It studies society and evaluates all those allegiances which man has found most fitting and necessary, the ties that bind him to his fellows, to his country, to nature. It provides, therefore, a standard of values for our human activities. It gives us, not the facts primarily, but, what is much more important, it gives us in beautiful form the meaning of human history and what may be called the logic of life. For this reason, Aristotle said that "poetry is truer than history." Literature may be studied with the greatest profit, therefore, not only by those who are interested in art, but also by those who wish to understand humanity's progress.

Three Types of Literary Excellence. Because of this dual appeal of literature we find that there are three types of literary excellence.

1. Judged from the point of view of construction and style, a certain work may stand in its formal perfection as a representative of one of the art forms—the epic, the elegy, or the short story, for instance. Such is the case with Milton's *Paradise Lost*, Gray's *Elegy Written in a Country Churchyard*, or a tale of De Maupassant's.

2. On the other hand, we may have other works not so perfect in form, which nevertheless give us profound insight into the life of men at certain periods of history. Such poems are the German *Nibelungenlied*, the French *Chanson de Roland*, and the Spanish *Poem of the Cid*.

3. In rare cases both of these elements—the artistic form and the historic or spiritual significance—will be present in the highest degree. This is true of the *Iliad* and the *Odyssey* of Homer, the *Divine Comedy* of Dante, and the *Hamlet* or *Macbeth* of Shakespeare. Such works will naturally constitute the world's greatest masterpieces.

Modern Literature largely Western European. When we speak of "the world's" greatest literature, it should be remembered that we generally include in our survey only the literature and literary tradition which, first developed in Europe by the Greeks, has been passed down through the Romans to the modern European nations, from whom it has spread to the colonies which these nations founded. This literature, to be sure, includes the Bible, which comes to us from farther East, and there have been thin streams of influence from Persia and India. As a matter of fact, however, the literary traditions of the Hindus, of the Persians, or of the Chinese, for instance, have remained largely alien to us and are therefore not considered as constituting a part of our literary heritage.

The Test of Greatness. It is, of course, extremely difficult to give final rank to all the great works which have been passed down to us, and many works which enjoyed a great vogue in their day, like *Ossian* for instance, have been found subsequently to contain but little that is permanently valuable either as art or as a criticism of human ideals. Occasionally, a work like *Uncle Tom's Cabin*, appearing at a particular juncture, has exercised great immediate influence on history but is of relatively little permanent value as art. Insofar as the critic himself applies principles, they should be the principles which we have stated: the degree of perfection exemplified in the construction of the work, and the significance of its content. The safest test, however,—and this should always be used as a corrective of personal judgment—is the sifting of time. Humanity has naturally taken to itself those works which it has found to express the great lessons of life.

MODERN LITERATURE IN THE WESTERN NATIONS FROM ABOUT 500 A. D. TO ABOUT 1900 A. D.

The table given below aims to present summarily the following points: (1) The general inheritance of the modern from the ancient world; (2) Important influences at work in each period; (3) The most important general types of literature developed in each period or century; (4) The characteristic contributions of each country to general world literature in each period; (5) The origin and flourishing of the chief types of literature; (6) The names of the greatest and most characteristic authors in each period. Necessarily many worthy names are omitted, and it is very difficult, especially in ages of great literary activity, to tell just where the line of exclusion should be drawn. Authors who belong only to their particular national literature will be found in the separate tables and sketches of the literatures of the world. A relative ranking of authors and books in point of greatness and world influence is indicated by different styles of type, as: (1) *PSALMS*, (2) CICERO, (3) *Juvenal*, (4) Pliny.

EUROPE'S COMMON INHERITANCE: WORKS MORE GENERALLY KNOWN OR WHOSE INFLUENCE IS STILL FELT AT THE BEGINNING OF THE SIXTH CENTURY

POETRY	SOURCES	PROSE

PSALMS, also in Latin and Greek.
 	
Epic: *HOMER'S ILIAD* and *ODYSSEY*.
    Known through references in Latin literature, by reputation as the work of the greatest of the poets, but in original unknown even to Petrarch.
Tragedy: ÆSCHYLUS, SOPHOCLES, and EURIPIDES, the great Greek dramatists, will remain unknown until the Renaissance, except insofar as they influence Seneca.
Comedy: *Menander*, through Latin adaptations and influence on Latin comedy.
    ARISTOPHANES, seemingly unknown until time of Renaissance.
Lyrics: Lyric poets SAPPHO and ANACREON, and particularly the anthologies, known through their influence on Latin poetry and verse forms and through translations or imitations by Latin poets.
    PINDAR becomes an important influence only in the Renaissance and later period.
Pastoral: *Theocritus* and Bion, known through Latin imitations but will become models in Renaissance.
	From the Hebrew
	
	From the Greek
	    At the beginning of the so-called dark ages, Greek culture, and knowledge of and interest in Greek literature, become virtually extinct. Greek is known and sometimes used in commerce in southern Gaul during the 6th century, and later many Greek monks driven out by the Eastern Church take refuge in Italy. Charlemagne is supposed to have known it, and there are sporadic centers, especially monasteries, where Greek is taught as far west as Ireland up to the period of the Renaissance. But it may be safely said that the spirit of Greek literature is unknown, and Greek literature as such has little direct influence until after Petrarch.
		OLD TESTAMENT, also in Latin and Greek.
		
		Religion: *NEW TESTAMENT*, in Latin translations. *The Church Fathers*, known through influence on Latin Church fathers.
		Philosophy: *ARISTOTLE*. Known only in part, through fragmentary Latin translations, and, during Mohammedan occupation of Spain, through influence of Arabian schools and teachers. After 1000 A. D. the most important influence on medieval philosophy.
		    PLATO. Known through Boethius and Latin translation of the *Timæus*. His influence early enters the Church through the Greek fathers, from whom it passes to the Latin fathers. His is the strongest philosophical influence on the early Church, and tends to give literature first its allegorical turn and later its idealistic tendency.
		Biography and morals: PLUTARCH. Though not read in Greek, subject matter known in Latin. Will become one of most popular works of the Renaissance period because of subject matter and conception of the heroes of antiquity.
		Late Greek romances: Greek romances and tales of Greek mythology and Greek life pass into tradition, and at a later period Greek materials will enter through trade with Byzantium and through contacts during time of the Crusades.
		History and oratory: Historians like *Herodotus*, *Xenophon*, and *Thucydides*, and orators like DEMOSTHENES will become known as such and enter literary tradition in period of Renaissance.
		Fables: *Æsop*. Well known in popular tradition and in Latin versions used in medieval schools.

POETRY	SOURCES	PROSE

Epic: *VIRGIL'S ÆNEID*; Statius.
Pastoral: VIRGIL: ECLOGUES and BUCOLICS.
Lyric: HORACE; *Catullus* (almost unknown).
Elegiac: Tibullus; Propertius; OVID.
Narrative: Lucan; OVID.
Philosophical: *Lucretius*.
Didactic: HORACE.
Tragedy: *Seneca*.
Comedy: Plautus; *Terence*.
Satire: HORACE; *Juvenal*; *Martial*.
Fables: Phædrus.
	From the Latin
	    The Latin authors fare much better than the Greek. Many of them are available, and some of them, like Ovid, Horace, and Virgil, have their readers, even during the dark ages. Latin itself continues to be the language of the Church. It is the failure to comprehend the spirit and the form of Latin literature, and occasionally the hostility of the Church, that leads to the disappearance of ancient culture in its Latin form. Knowledge of the language and the letter will remain, but the spirit of Latin culture will become moribund for some centuries. It will not, however, be so nearly extinguished as the Greek; consequently Latin culture will be the first to revive. Most of the great Latin poets, and particularly Virgil, will be known to Dante (1265–1321). He will take Virgil as his master and will know him by heart.
	
	From the East
	    Persian ideas and faint Persian influence are apparent in later books of the Old Testament and in later Greek philosophy. During the middle ages there will be some contact with the East, especially during the Crusades; the Hindu story of Buddha, for instance, will be found in the old French *Barlaam and Josaphat*.
	
	From the North
	    During the invasion of the barbarians, folklore and folk tales and possibly unwritten songs are brought by the Germanic tribes into southern Europe.
		Oratory: CICERO, great master of style for Renaissance.
		Philosophy: Cicero; *Boethius, Consolations of Philosophy*.
		History: *Cæsar*; *Livy*; Sallust; *Tacitus* (little known).
		Natural history: Pliny the Elder.
		Religion: Church Fathers: Tertullian; *St. Augustine,— Confessions, City of God*.

THE MEDIEVAL PERIOD

6th TO 12th CENTURY—The Disappearance of Classical Culture

COUNTRY	POETRY	PROSE	IMPORTANT MOVEMENTS AND INFLUENCES
Europe	Latin hymns.	Sermons, Latin chronicles.	The "dark ages," particularly the 7th to the 10th century.
France	Saints' lives. Beginnings of liturgical drama, about 10th century. Epic: Chansons de Gestes,—CHANSON DE ROLAND.	The Oaths of Strasbourg, 842, first document written in Old French.	Disappearance of urban and development of feudal civilization. Romance languages supersede vulgar Latin as spoken language. Continuance of Latin tradition. Dominance of Church.
Germany	Nibelungen sagas, unwritten.		
Scandinavia and Iceland	"*Elder Edda*" and *sagas* in oral tradition, written in 12th and 13th centuries.		Development of monasteries as centers of learning, 9th to 12th century. Charlemagne crowned, 800.
Ireland	Growth of tale and folklore.		Development of schools.
England	Epic: *Beowulf*, 7th century(?). Religious poems. Songs of sea and travel: The Wanderer; The Seafarer.	Bede's Ecclesiastical History, 731, in Latin. Translations: King Alfred. Chronicles: Anglo-Saxon Chronicle.	Norman conquest, 1066. The introduction of Nordic element into literary tradition from Scandinavia, Germany, and Britain. First Crusade, 1095.

12th CENTURY—The Great Age of Medieval Romance

COUNTRY	POETRY	PROSE	IMPORTANT MOVEMENTS AND INFLUENCES
France	Religious poetry: Bernard of Cluny, in Latin; Bernard of Clairvaux, in Latin; medieval hymns, in Latin. Drama: Early miracle plays in Latin and French. Lyric: Provençal poetry; songs of troubadours and trouvères. Epic: Later Chansons de Gestes celebrating Charlemagne and French heroes. Romances of chivalry and adventure, dealing with "matter of Britain," King Arthur, etc. *Christian of Troy.* Beast epic: *Reynard the Fox.*	Romance, in prose and verse: *Aucassin and Nicolette.*	Founding of universities of Paris and Oxford. The development of modern lyric verse forms in Provence. Woman comes to occupy a more important place in courtly life, and love becomes the theme of poets. Development of Arabic civilization, particularly in Spain, through which knowledge of Aristotle is spread.
England		Chronicles and legendary history: Geoffrey of Monmouth,—History of the Kings of Britain, including stories of King Arthur and King Lear.	
Germany	Epic: NIBELUNGENLIED, written; *Gudrun.*		
Scandinavia		History: Saxo Grammaticus, includes story of Hamlet.	

13th CENTURY—High Point of Medieval Civilization

COUNTRY	POETRY	PROSE	IMPORTANT MOVEMENTS AND INFLUENCES
France	Folk song and satire: *The Fabliaux.* Allegory: *The Romance of the Rose.* Religious poetry: Saints' lives; Gautier de Coincy,—The Miracles of Our Lady. Drama: Beginnings of secular drama and farce.	Chronicles: Joinville.	Gothic art reaches its point of perfection. Epics gradually succeeded by romances in verse. Popularity of stories of King Arthur, Lancelot, and the Grail. Beginnings of romance in prose.
Italy	Poems of courtly love: The Sicilian School. Lyrics: *Dante.* Hymns: THOMAS OF CELANO,—DIES IRÆ, Latin.	Biography: *Dante,—The New Life.* Travel: *Marco Polo.* Theology: *Thomas Aquinas*, in Latin. Saints' lives: JACOPO DA VORAGINE,—THE GOLDEN LEGEND, in Latin.	Struggle for supremacy between popes and emperors. Growth of cities and development of guilds and municipal government.
Spain	Epic: THE CID.		
Germany	Romances: *Wolfram von Eschenbach,—Parzival*; Hartmann von Auc; Gottfried von Strassburg. Lyrics: *Walther von der Vogelweide.*	Encyclopedia: Albertus Magnus, in Latin.	
England	Romances: Imitations of Norman-French romances. Layamon's Brut. Songs and ballads.		The rise of parliaments. Magna Charta. Fusion of Saxon and Norman peoples and of English and Norman-French speech.

14th CENTURY—End of the Literature of Feudalism

COUNTRY	POETRY	PROSE	IMPORTANT MOVEMENTS AND INFLUENCES
France	Drama: Miracle plays,—The Miracles of Notre Dame. Mystery plays.	Chronicles: Froissart.	Societies for the production of plays become more numerous. Froissart shows the decay of feudalism and the end of chivalry. He marks the end of knighthood. Civilization will soon become urban.
Italy	Epic: *DANTE,—DIVINE COMEDY.* Love sonnets: PETRARCH.	Prose tales: BOCCACCIO,— THE DECAMERON. Politics: Dante,—On Monarchy, in Latin.	Petrarch introduces that enthusiasm for the study of the classical authors and intimate acquaintance with them which marks the beginning of the Revival of Learning. His interests and curiosities have earned him the title of "the first modern man." His younger admirer, Boccaccio, is the first modern man really to learn Greek.
England	Miracle plays. Allegory: Langland,—Piers Plowman. Narratives: CHAUCER,— CANTERBURY TALES. Romances: Sir Gawain and the Green Knight.	Religion: Wiclif,—Translation of Bible. Travels: Sir John Mandeville, originally in French (?).	Chaucer visits Italy and meets Petrarch.

THE RENAISSANCE
15th CENTURY—The Period of Transition

France	Poems in the medieval forms: Ballades. Charles of Orleans. VILLON. Religious drama: Mysteries,— The Mystery of the Passion. Farce: *Master Pathelin.*	Memoirs: Commines.	The Renaissance is sometimes taken to begin with the discovery of America, though the movement is under way before this time. Beginnings of modern personal poetry.
Italy	Romantic and burlesque epic: Pulci; Boiardo. Sonnets and songs: Lorenzo the Magnificent.	Translations: Boiardo's translation of Apuleius and Lucian; Bruni's renderings of Demosthenes, Æschines, Plutarch, Xenophon, Plato, Aristotle; Valla's Iliad, Thucydides, Herodotus, Æsop. Pastoral romance: Sannazzaro.	Early in century Greek masterpieces are brought to Italy, and the literature of the ancient Greek world begins strongly to influence modern literary tradition. Enthusiasm for art, literature, and science for their own sakes and not as subsidiary to theology. Struggle for dominance in literature between writing in Latin and Greek and writing in the modern languages.
Germany	Satire and allegory: Brant,— The Ship of Fools.	Popular romance: Till Eulenspiegel.	Gutenberg's invention of printing.
England	Morality plays.	Religion: *Thomas à Kempis,— Imitation of Christ.* Tales of chivalry: *Malory's Morte D'Arthur.*	Caxton prints first book in England, 1477. Fall of Constantinople, 1453.

16th CENTURY—The Reformation

France	Lyric: The Old School: Marot. The New School: *Ronsard;* Du Bellay.	Humor: RABELAIS. Essays: MONTAIGNE. Theology: *Calvin.* Translation: *Amyot's Plutarch.*	Enthusiasm for study and worship of ancients. Reform in religion, and wars of religion.
Italy	Epic: *Ariosto; Tasso.* Lyric and sonnet: *Michelangelo.*	Politics: *Machiavelli.* Biography: *Cellini;* Vasari.	The influences of classical drama,—of Plautus and Terence in comedy and of Seneca in tragedy,—as well as of the theories of critics like Aristotle and Horace, make themselves felt in modern drama.
Germany	Meistersinger: Hans Sachs. Hymns: *Luther.*	Translation: LUTHER'S BIBLE.	The end of Humanism.
Holland		Letters and colloquies: *Erasmus,* in Latin.	The Renaissance passes from Italy to France and England.
Spain	Drama: *Lope de Vega.* Ballads: The *Romancero General.*	Romances of chivalry: Montalvo's Amadis de Gaula.	
Portugal	Epic: *Camoëns,—The Lusiad.*		
England	Allegory: *Spenser's Faery Queen.* Sonnets: Sidney; SHAKESPEARE. Drama: *Marlowe;* SHAKESPEARE'S EARLY PLAYS.	*Romances of Roguery.* Politics: More's Utopia. Defense of Poesy: Sidney. Voyages: Hakluyt. Romance: Lyly's Euphues.	Age of adventure and discovery.

THE MODERN ERA
17th CENTURY—The Great Age of Drama

COUNTRY	POETRY	PROSE	IMPORTANT MOVEMENTS AND INFLUENCES
France	Poets of the French Classical Period: Tragedy: *Corneille*; RACINE. Comedy: *MOLIÈRE.* Fables: LA FONTAINE. Criticism: *Boileau.*	Drama, comedy: *MOLIÈRE.* Philosophy: *Descartes; Pascal.* Religion: *Pascal;* Bossuet. Letters: *Mme. de Sévigné.* Critics and moralists: *La Rochefoucauld;* La Bruyère.	Golden age of French literature; Richelieu, Louis XIV, and the "century of authority." French Academy founded and strict standards established.
Germany		Picaresque novel: Grimmelshausen's Simplicissimus. Religion: Jacob Böhme.	
Holland		Philosophy: *Spinoza*, in Latin. Law: Grotius, in Latin.	
Spain	Drama: *Lope de Vega*; CALDERÓN.	Novel: *CERVANTES' DON QUIXOTE.*	
England	Drama: *SHAKESPEARE,—THE GREAT TRAGEDIES; Jonson;* Webster; Otway; Beaumont and Fletcher. Lyric: *Donne;* Herrick. Cavalier poets: Lovelace. Epic: MILTON. Satire: *Dryden.*	Translation: *KING JAMES VERSION OF THE BIBLE;* Chapman's Homer. Essays: *Bacon.* Religion: Jeremy Taylor. Politics: *Milton.* Walton's Compleat Angler. Diary: Pepys Philosophy: *Locke.* Science and philosophy: Bacon's Novum Organum, in Latin, and The Advancement of Knowledge.	End of the Age of Elizabeth and rise of the Puritans. Settlement of America. The Commonwealth and the Restoration. Growth of political liberalism.

18th CENTURY, FIRST HALF—The Age of Reason

COUNTRY	POETRY	PROSE	IMPORTANT MOVEMENTS AND INFLUENCES
France	Drama: Voltaire.	Politics: *Montesquieu,—Spirit of Laws.* Novel: *Lesage,—Gil Blas; Abbé Prévost,—Manon Lescaut.* Drama: Marivaux. Translation: Abbé Galland's translation of the Arabian Nights. Morals: Fénelon.	Beginnings of cosmopolitan attitude. Rise of public opinion as a force in social and political affairs. English influence strong in France.
Italy		Philosophy: Vico.	
England	Poet of Classicism: POPE. Nature poetry: Thomson.	Translation: Sale's Koran. Novel: DEFOE; *Richardson;* Fielding. Essay: *Addison.* Satire: SWIFT. Philosophy: Hume; Berkeley.	Increasing importance of novel. Great advances in science by Newton and others.

18th CENTURY, SECOND HALF—Development of the Idea of Progress

COUNTRY	POETRY	PROSE	IMPORTANT MOVEMENTS AND INFLUENCES
France	The end of Classicism. Lyric, satire: Voltaire; Chénier.	The Encyclopedia: *Diderot.* Return to nature; Beginnings of Romanticism: ROUSSEAU. Novel: *Rousseau;* Saint-Pierre. Critic and satirist: VOLTAIRE. Natural history: Buffon. Drama: *Beaumarchais.*	Age of criticism and unrest preparing for overthrow of the existing order in the French Revolution. Beginnings of Romanticism, and return to nature. Increasing interest in human history, political and social problems. The French Revolution.
Italy	Drama: Alfieri.	Drama: *Goldoni.*	Growth of individualism and lyricism.
Germany	Lyric and ballad: GOETHE; *Schiller;* Bürger. Drama: *Goethe; Schiller;* Lessing.	Novel: *Goethe.* Criticism: *Lessing.* History: Herder. Philosophy: *Kant.*	Great age of German literature.
England	Narrative poetry: Goldsmith. Romantic songs and folk poetry: Percy's Reliques; BURNS; "Ossian"; Blake. Elegy: *Gray.*	History: Gibbon. Criticism: *Samuel Johnson.* Politics: Burke. Novel: *Goldsmith;* Sterne. Drama: Goldsmith; Sheridan. Biography: *Boswell.*	Beginnings of English Romanticism.
America		Autobiography: Franklin. Politics: Jefferson; Hamilton.	The American Revolution.

19th CENTURY, FIRST HALF—Romanticism and Beginnings of Realism

COUNTRY	POETRY	PROSE	IMPORTANT MOVEMENTS AND INFLUENCES
France	Romantic School: *Lamartine*; *De Vigny*; HUGO; *De Musset*. Drama: Hugo.	Religion: Chateaubriand. Criticism: Mme. de Staël; *Sainte-Beuve.* Romantic novel and novel with social thesis: *Hugo*; George Sand. Psychological novel: Stendhal. Realistic novel: BALZAC. Drama: Dumas the Elder; Scribe; De Musset. History: Michelet; Guizot.	Era of social and political reconstruction, following French Revolution. Development of nationalism and the spirit of nationalism in literature. Glorification of individualism. Increasing liberalism in politics, soon turning to humanitarianism.
Italy	Poetry of pessimism: Leopardi.	Historical novel: Manzoni.	The romanticists turn to the "rich and strange," and present with enthusiasm pictures of the middle ages, using "local color." With this comes the development of the historical novel and of history. Under the influence of science there develops an increased respect for the facts, even the brutal facts of life, and many novelists turn more and more toward realism. Invention of steamboat and railroad, and application of steam to industry.
Germany	Lyric poetry: *GOETHE*; Heine; Uhland. Poetry of Romantic School: Novalis. Drama: *GOETHE'S FAUST*; *Schiller.*	Novel: *Goethe.* Tale: Hoffmann. Philosophy: *Hegel*; Schelling; *Schopenhauer.* Criticism: A. W. von Schlegel.	
England	Poets of liberty: BYRON; *Shelley.* Poets of beauty and romance: *Keats*; Coleridge; Scott. Nature poetry: WORDSWORTH.	Essay: *Lamb* Historical novel: *Scott*; *Thackeray.* Novel of contemporary life: *Dickens*; *Thackeray;* Austen. History and criticism: *Carlyle.*	
America	Lyrics: Poe.	Philosophy: Emerson. Essay and tale: Irving. Frontier and sea stories: Cooper. Romance and psychological tales: Hawthorne. Short story: *Poe.*	
Poland	Poet of liberty: Mickiewicz.		
Russia	National poet: Púshkin.	Novel: Gógol.	
Hungary	Lyric poetry: Petöfi.		

19th CENTURY, SECOND HALF—The Age of Science and Evolution

COUNTRY	POETRY	PROSE	IMPORTANT MOVEMENTS AND INFLUENCES
France	*Later work of Victor Hugo.* The Parnassian School: Leconte de Lisle. Art for art's sake: Gautier and Baudelaire. The Symbolists: Paul Verlaine. Drama: Rostand.	Novel: *Hugo's Les Misérables*; *Flaubert*; Anatole France; Bourget. Naturalistic novel: Zola. Short story: *Maupassant*; Daudet. History: Renan; *Taine.* Criticism: Brunetière; Anatole France; *Taine.* Drama: Dumas the Younger; Maeterlinck.	The development, formulation, and spread of evolution, and its application, not only to the study of biology, but also to that of the social sciences and even to literature, constitute the most striking phenomenon of this time. There arises a bitter quarrel between the older theology and the newer science. For this reason two opposed tendencies appear in literature. One, the idealistic, emphasizes the life of the spirit; the other, the materialistic, attempts to explain everything in terms of matter and scientific laws. Widespread application to industry of new discoveries in electrical and other sciences. The basis of wealth and society becomes more and more industrial. Profound unrest and beginnings of strife between capital and labor. As America extends itself to the West, with Whitman and Mark Twain a newer and more characteristically American note appears. Unification of Germany and Italy. The further development of the idea of nationality.
Italy	Lyric poetry: Carducci; D'Annunzio. Drama: D'Annunzio.	Novel and drama: D'Annunzio.	
Spain		Drama: Echegaray. Novel: Galdós; Pereda; Valera.	
Germany	Drama: Hauptmann.	Novel, short story: Heyse. Drama: Hauptmann; Sudermann. Philosophy: *Nietzsche.* National history: Treitschke. History: Mommsen.	
England	Poets of the Victorian age: *Tennyson*; *Browning*; Swinburne. Love sonnets: Elizabeth Barrett Browning. The Pre-Raphaelites: William Morris; Christina Rossetti; D. G. Rossetti.	Science: DARWIN'S ORIGIN OF SPECIES; Huxley. Novel: George Eliot; *George Meredith*; *Thomas Hardy.* Religion: Newman. Romance and short story: Stevenson; Kipling. Scholarship and criticism: Ruskin; *Matthew Arnold*; Pater.	
America	Poet of democracy: Whitman. New England poets: Longfellow; Lowell; Whittier; Holmes.	Novel: *Mark Twain*; Henry James; W. D. Howells. State papers: Lincoln.	
Poland		Historical novel: Sienkiewicz.	
Russia	Realistic poet: Nekrásov.	Novel: *Tolstóy*; *Turgéniev*; Dostoiévsky. Short story and drama: Chékov.	
Norway		Drama: Ibsen. Novel: Björnson.	
Sweden		Prose tale: Selma Lagerlöf.	
Denmark		Fairy tales: *Hans Christian Andersen.* Criticism: Georg Brandes.	

20TH CENTURY—Europe to World War II and Its Aftermath

COUNTRY	POETRY AND DRAMA	PROSE WORKS	MOVEMENTS AND INFLUENCES
France	Dadaist and Surrealist Poets: Breton, Apollinaire, Aragon, Eluard, Soupault, Char. Drama: Maeterlinck (Belgian). A major Symbolist, he rejected Naturalism. Maeterlinck also wrote essays, and on philosophy and nature. His Blue Bird was a children's classic. Major Poets: Claudel, Valery, St. John Perse. Later Dramatists: Anouilh, Giraudoux, Sartre, Cocteau. Theater of the Absurd: Samuel Beckett (Irish), Eugene Ionesco (Rumanian).	Henri Bergson: Creative Evolution, a major philosophical work, profoundly influenced literature, psychology, and social thought. Marcel Proust: Novel, Remembrance of Things Past. Proust's analytical style cast a wide influence. Andre Gide: His psychological plays, novels, and journals influenced both literature and philosophy. Theology: Maritain, Teilhard de Chardin. Novelists: Rolland, Romains, Martin du Gard, De Montherlant, Malraux, Colette, Sagan, Sarraute, Le Clézio. Catholic Novelists: Mauriac, Bernanos, Bloy, Julian Green (American). Existentialist Writers: Sartre, De Beauvoir, Camus.	Commercial expansion extended ties between Europe, America, and the world. Literacy expanded and the power of the press developed. Naturalism in literature continued as a force. Stemming from 19th-century thinkers, with its conformity to nature, realistic representation, and exploration of all aspects of life, it dominated fiction and the drama. Symbolism, also a 19th-century movement, continued to represent events and states of mind through symbols. Stream of Consciousness. A new technique of fiction began to record in first-person narration a character's mind processes at key turns of plot. Through Proust, Joyce, and Svevo, it became a widespread device, dominating fiction and deeply affecting both poetry and drama.
Italy	Poets: Ungaretti, Montale, Quasimodo. Drama: Pirandello, Betti.	Philosophy, Criticism, History: Croce, Papini, Gentile, Ferrero, Borgese. Novelists: Deledda, Silone, Lampedusa, Svevo. Postwar Fiction: Malaparte, Levi, Vittorini, Pratolini, Moravia.	Marxism brought the social and economic thought of Marx and Engels into the political arena, causing polarity and revolution in the world.
Spain	Poets: Machado, Jimínez, Garcia Lorca, Dario (Nicaraguan), Mistral (Chilean), Guillen, Alberti, Cernuda.	Philosophy, Criticism, History: Unamuno, Benavente, Ortega y Gasset, Madariaga, Pelayo. Novelists: Galdos, Ayala, Miro, Ibanez, Gironella, Barea, Baroja, Valle-Inclan.	
Germany	Poets: Stefan George, Rilke, Benn, Borchardt, Hofmansthal. Drama: Hauptmann, Schnitzler, Wedekind, Zuckmayer, Duerrenmatt, Brecht, Hochuth.	Philosophy, Science, History, Politics: Marx, Freud, Jung, Spengler, Heidegger, Jaspers. Novelists: Mann, Wassermann, Kafka, Hesse, Werfel, Zweig, Remarque, Junger, Johnson, Grass.	World War I. The great powers became embroiled in large-scale conflict. The automobile and airplane were developed at rapid pace, mobilizing warfare and drastically changing transport and communication.
Norway	Poets: Obstfelder, Vogt, Bull. Drama: Krog, Grieg, Heiberg.	Fiction: Knut Hamsun, Bojer, Falkberget, Dunn, Sigrid Undset, Hoel.	Realism continued Naturalistic traditions to the extreme. Describing all aspects of life and states of mind, it moved to drop all barriers from expression.
Sweden	Poets: Froding, Karlfeldt, Lagerkvist. Drama: Strindberg—A major voice.	Fiction: Selma Lagerlof, Von Heidenstam, Johnson, Moberg.	Dadaism and Surrealism, on the other hand, moved forms of expression in poetry and drama to nonlogical ends, exerting wide influence in sculpture and painting.
Denmark	Poets: Drachmann, Jorgensen, Holstein.	Criticism: Georg Brandes. Fiction: Jacobsen, Pontoppidan, Gjellerup, Knudsen, Jensen.	Developing technology brought an era of major scientific advance. Medicine changed birth and death rates throughout the world.
Greece	Major Poets: Seferis, Cavafy, Kazantzakis.	Fiction: Melas, Kazantzakis.	Democratic institutions began to lose ground as Communist, Socialist, and Fascist states controlled expanding areas. The Spanish Civil War became the testing ground for growing militarism.
Russia	Drama: Chekhov. Poets: Blok, Mayakovsky, Mandelstam, Pasternak, Akhmatova, Yevtushenko, Yesenin.	Fiction: Bunin, Andreev, Gorki, Chekhov, Kuprin, Babel, Sholokov, Ostrovsky, Simonov, Ehrenburg, Dudintsev, Nekrasov, Pilnak, Zhdanov, Gondharov, Korolenko, Solzhenitsyn.	World War II. The Axis Powers and Japan aligned against the Allies, the Soviet Union, and most nations of the world.

20TH CENTURY—U.S., Canada, Britain, to the Present

COUNTRY	POETRY AND DRAMA	PROSE WORKS	MOVEMENTS AND INFLUENCES
United States	Traditionalist Poets: Markham, Masters, Robinson, Jeffers. The New Poetry: Lindsay, Sandburg, Aiken, MacLeish, Hart Crane, Wallace Stevens, Marianne Moore, E. E. Cummings. Imagists: Amy Lowell, H. D. (Hilda Doolittle). Fugitive Poets: Southern Agrarian Movement—Ransom, Warren, Tate. Major Voices: T. S. Eliot, Ezra Pound. World War II Poets: Karl Shapiro, Randall Jarrell. Postwar Voices: Robert Lowell, John Berryman, Delmore Schwartz, Theodore Roethke, Richard Wilbur, W. S. Merwin, Robert Bly, James Dickey. Black Poets: Paul Laurence Dunbar, Langston Hughes, Countee Cullen, Owen Dodson, Leroi Jones. Drama: Eugene O'Neill, Maxwell Anderson, Elmer Rice, Macleish, Paul Green, Philip Barry, Robert Sherwood, Thornton Wilder, Lillian Hellman, Clifford Odets, Tennessee Williams, Arthur Miller, Edward Albee.	Philosophy, History, Politics, Science: William James, Henry Adams, John Dewey, Thorstein Veblen, George Santayana, H. L. Mencken, Edmund-Wilson, Samuel E. Morison, Henry Steele Commager. Novel: Major Voices—Henry James, Theodore Dreiser, Gertrude Stein, Thomas Wolfe, Ernest Hemingway, F. Scott Fitzgerald, Vladimir Nabokov. Black Writers: Richard Wright, Ralph Ellison, James Baldwin. Other Novelists: Edith Wharton, Willa Cather, Frank Norris, Sherwood Anderson, Sinclair Lewis, John Dos Passos, John O'Hara, John Steinbeck, James T. Farrell. Jewish Life Novelists: Saul Bellow, Herbert Gold, Philip Roth. Younger Novelists: J. D. Salinger, J. F. Powers, Flannery O'Connor, Norman Mailer, Truman Capote, Gore Vidal, William Styron.	From 1900, the US expanded Westward: Railroads crossed the nation and new sources of wealth brought great business development. Advances in science and inventions changed the US from an agrarian society to an urbanized industrial power. World-wide education and social philanthropy developed. Labor unions formed and grew rapidly, changing work conditions. World War I. US involvement brought the US into the arena of world politics. Freudianism became the leading force in treatment of the mentally ill in postwar years. It also acted as a strong influence on theme and expression in art and literature. European states suffered war and threats of war during the 1920's and 1930's.
Canada	French-Canadian Poets: Nerée Beauchemin, Emile Nelligan, Pierre Trottier, Alain Grandbois, Anne Hébert, Rina Lasnier, Francois, Hertel, Gatien Lapointe. Poets Writing in English: G. D. Roberts, Bliss Carman, D. C. Scott, Pauline Johnson, Robert Service, A. J. M. Smith, A. M. Klein, E. J. Pratt, F. R. Scott, Dorothy Livesay, Earle Birney, Robert Finch, W. E. Ross, Irving Layton, Jay Macpherson, James Reaney, Douglas Le Pan, Patrick Anderson, Margaret Avison.	French-Canadian Historians: Sir James MacPherson, Joseph Edmond Roy. French-Canadian Fiction: Lionel Groulx, Robert Elie, Yves Thereault, André Giroux, Germaine Guévremont, André Langevin, Roger Lemelin, Gabrielle Roy. Writers in English: Natural History—Ernest Thompson Seton. Humor and Essays: Stephen Leacock. Fiction: F. P. Grove, Morley Callaghan, Philip Child, Hugh MacClennan, Mazo de la Roche, Ethel Wilson, Adele Wiseman, Nicholas Monsarrat, Brian Moore.	World War II. US participation in the second major war was marked by the creation of vast armed forces, battles on many fronts, and development of the strongest industrial resources in US history. Scientific advance brought the emergence of the US as the first nuclear power. Combined Allied forces defeated the Axis bloc in 1945. The atom bomb was developed, ending the Pacific war. The United Nations organization was then founded in an effort to avert future war and to limit atomic power to peaceful uses. Existentialist thought—Centering on the uniqueness and isolation of individual human existence and experience, the growing body of existentialist writers described human life as unexplainable, yet stressed man's freedom of choice and man's responsibility for the consequences of his actions.
Britain	Poets: Kipling, Yeats, Masefield, Rupert Brooke, Hugh MacDiarmid (Scottish), Wilfred Owen, Robert Graves, Day-Lewis, Louis MacNeice, Stephen Spender, Dylan Thomas (Welsh), W. S. Graham (Scottish), Thom Gunn, Ted Hughes. Drama: George Bernard Shaw, J. M. Barrie, T. S. Eliot, Christopher Fry, J. M. Synge (Irish), Sean O'Casey (Irish), Brendan Behan (Irish).	Fiction: Arnold Bennett, John Galsworthy, Norman Douglas, Ford Madox Ford, W. Somerset Maugham, John Buchan, E. M. Forster, James Joyce (Irish), Virginia Woolf, D. H. Lawrence, Joyce Cary, Rebecca West, J. R. R. Tolkien, J. B. Priestley, Aldous Huxley, C. S. Lewis, Frank O'Connor (Irish), George Orwell, Evelyn Waugh, Alan Paton (South African), Graham Greene, C. P. Snow, Samuel Beckett (Irish), William Golding, Lawrence Durrell, Muriel Spark.	The Cold War developed, pitting Communist nations against the free world. Communism engulfed mainland China. United Nations forces won in the Korean conflict. Yet the arms race continued throughout the world. France was defeated in Indochina. The US then became involved and in the 1970's, the war issue divided the US. Space travel became an area of competition for the US and USSR, with the US landing the first man on the Moon in 1968. Colonialism declined across the world. Nations of Africa, Asia, and the Americas emerged as new states. Revolution and insurrection also occurred in nations of Africa, Asia, and the Americas. Separation along racial, ethnic, and social lines marked many nations of both East and West. Civil rights became a major issue in the US, while widespread pollution threatened the ecology of the entire world.

AMERICAN LITERATURE

AMERICAN literature, like the literatures of all peoples who have emigrated from lands already in an advanced stage of culture, is not an original native growth. On the contrary, from the very first, American writers began with a long tradition behind them. They brought with them an intimate familiarity with a rich literature and a deep interest in certain burning problems of religion and conduct. Faced with a new and stubborn land to conquer, they had at first little leisure to write, and, even when the leisure was available, it was long before they wrote with the consciousness that they belonged to a people having an individuality and a life of its own.

Colonial Period (1608–1775). Literary history in America begins with such accounts of life, travels, and adventures as appear in the simple, direct narrative of John Smith's *True Relation of Virginia* (1608). Smith followed this with a more pretentious work, *A Map of Virginia, with a Description of the Country* (1612). Of all the early accounts of explorers, this *Description* has made the greatest appeal to the popular imagination. It is fairly representative of many English pamphlets, written to draw attention to America and other distant parts of the world, and published in London during the 17th century. In New England, also, there were some who wrote narratives similar to John Smith's *True Relation.* One of these was Edward Winslow, whose *Good News from New England* was published in 1624.

Colonial Journals and Diaries.—To these published works there must be added numerous diaries and journals which long remained unpublished. The most important of these in New England were written by William Bradford and Edward Winslow of Plymouth and John Winthrop of Massachusetts Bay. The *Journal of Bradford and Winslow* is vivid and full of interesting incidents. Bradford's *History of Plymouth Plantation,* bringing the story of that colony down to the year 1646, is a book of dignity, reflecting the best qualities of early Puritanism. Less interesting but no less valuable is the journal of John Winthrop. This diary was faithfully kept by the first governor of Massachusetts Bay from 1630 until a few months before his death in 1649. Although it bears the title *A History of New England,* it is concerned with little outside the author's own colony.

In the 18th century, the greater degree of leisure and comfort attained in the older settlements gave opportunity for journeys, of which several accounts have survived. These are frequently illuminated with comment upon the life of the times that gives them literary flavor. One of the most interesting of these narratives is the journal kept by a New England woman, Mrs. Sarah Knight, on a trip from Boston to New York in 1704-05. The *History of the Dividing Line* (between Virginia and North Carolina) by William Byrd of Westover in Virginia, which recounts his experiences and observations on a surveying expedition in the region of the Great Dismal Swamp in 1729, is of great value. Not only does it supply information, but, like other journals of this Virginia gentleman, it bears the impress of a genial and humane personality. Byrd was, in his European education, in his knowledge of the ancient and modern classics, and in his interest in public affairs, a typical Virginia aristocrat, while in his vivacious style and quaint humor he was one of the best colonial writers.

Of the more ambitious attempts to write colonial history, the most notable are the unfinished *Chronological History of New England,* by the Reverend Thomas Prince, of Boston, and the *History of the Colony of Massachusetts Bay,* likewise incomplete, by Thomas Hutchinson.

Religion.—In connection with the religious writing which was so important in colonial New England, the names of Roger Williams, Thomas Hooker, and John Wise should be mentioned as defenders of democratic church polity and of freedom of thought. These men stood in clear opposition to the powerful family of the Mathers,—Richard, Increase, and Cotton, father, son, and grandson. Of all the voluminous works published by this extraordinary family succession, only the *Magnalia Christi Americana* (1702), by Cotton Mather, retains today any real interest. It is a useful collection of material for the study of early New England, which reflects the curious compound of power, scientific spirit, and superstition that marked the character of its author.

Philosophers.—The 18th century produced, apart from the group of political thinkers and writers of the Revolutionary period, two outstanding figures, Jonathan Edwards and Benjamin Franklin. Edwards, descended from families of high standing and culture in New England, was educated at Yale college. After a stormy period as minister of the church at Northampton, Mass., he was sent as a missionary to the Indians at Stockbridge. Here he wrote his famous treatise upon the *Freedom of the Will,* which is widely known as one of the greatest of American contributions to philosophical thought. Edwards was also one of the leaders in the religious movement in New England, known as the Great Awakening.

Franklin, the son of a tallow chandler in Boston, inherited a sound taste for life and letters, was largely self-educated, and became the best exponent of the average American's practical philosophy of life. He wrote on many themes, political, scientific, and commercial, but his literary fame rests now upon his *Autobiography* and upon the proverbial sentences of *Poor Richard's Almanac.*

Two other names should be noted in this time. Samuel Johnson, an Episcopal clergyman of Connecticut and a friend of Franklin, is reckoned one of the clearest of American thinkers in religion and philosophy. John Woolman, a Quaker, who lived at Mt. Holly, New Jersey, where he was a tailor "by the choice of providence," left a *Journal* which is remarkably attractive in its sincerity.

Newspapers.—During the first half of the 18th century, newspapers and magazines multiplied in America. These publications encouraged discussion of public questions and contributed largely to that growth of public opinion which resulted in the Revolution. The first newspaper published in the colonies was *Public Occurrences* (Boston, 1690). The *Boston News Letter* was first issued in 1704, and the *Boston Gazette* was founded in 1719 by James Franklin, an older brother of Benjamin Franklin. He also started the *New England Courant* in 1721. Benjamin was employed upon both papers as a printer.

Colonial Verse.—What has been called the "one really American poem" of the 17th century is an epitaph of 44 lines on Nathaniel Bacon, the insurrectionary leader in Virginia. This poem belongs to the class of elegies, of which a large number were produced in the colonies, especially by the New England clergy. The best one credited to New England is a "Funeral Song" by the Reverend Samuel Wigglesworth. His father, Michael Wigglesworth, was the author of the most widely read poem of colonial times, "The Day of Doom," a vivid résumé of the main tenets of Calvinism.

An attractive figure in this period is Anne Bradstreet. Amid her family of eight children on a frontier farm in the town of Andover, she found time to write many verses. These were published in London in 1650, by her brother, in a volume entitled *The Tenth Muse, Lately Sprung Up in America.*

Revolutionary Period (1775–1800). Ballads and satirical verses mark the next notable stage in American poetry. Among all the patriotic ballads of the Revolution, one on the death of Nathan Hale is notable for its real poetic quality. Francis Hopkinson's "Battle of the Kegs" is the best-known of the purely humorous ballads of the time. Joel Barlow's mock-heroic "Hasty Pudding" is one of the best longer pieces of humorous verse in early American literature. The same author's *Columbiad* is an attempt to write an American epic, but it fails to reach the level of poetry. John Trumbull's "McFingal" is the most effective of the many political satires of the period.

The Hartford Wits.—From about 1780 to 1800 a group of talented and versatile men, known as the "Hartford Wits," formed a literary center at New Haven and Hartford. The chief of these were Timothy Dwight, John Trumbull, Joel Barlow, David Humphreys, Richard Alsop, Lemuel Hopkins, and Theodore Dwight. Timothy Dwight, afterward president of Yale, wrote a long poem, *Greenfield Hill*, in which he imitated the English poets from Milton to Goldsmith. His *Conquest of Canaan* represents a type of biblical epic which was popular at this time.

Freneau.—In quality and range of subject and style, Philip Freneau is equaled by none in the Revolutionary period, and is in fact the first of American poets. He first acquired reputation by his satirical verse, but his fame now rests upon his romantic lyrics, especially of the sea and of nature. In such poems as "The Indian Burying Ground," "Eutaw Springs," and "The Wild Honeysuckle," he anticipates the spirit of the English romantic poets.

Politics.—The political literature of the Revolutionary period includes the speeches of James Otis, Samuel Adams, Patrick Henry, and others, as well as many pamphlets and letters which appeared during the period of controversy ushered in by the opposition to the Writs of Assistance in 1761. These publications discussed trenchantly, from both sides, the pressing problems of the times. The passage of the Townshend acts brought forth John Dickinson's *Letters from a Farmer in Pennsylvania to the Inhabitants of the British Colonies*, which were widely copied and translated. In his earlier days Franklin did much to bring about the union of the colonies, and the letters and published papers of his later life helped to interpret his country to Europe. From the loyalist point of view, the best statements came from Myles Cooper, president of King's college, and from Jonathan Boucher, at one time a clergyman in Maryland and Virginia, who wrote *A View of the Causes and Consequences of the American Revolution* (1797). Thomas Paine's pamphlet entitled *Common Sense* probably contributed more powerfully than any other single utterance to bring about the final break between the colonies and England. Paine wrote also the most effective of the war time pamphlets, *The Crisis* (1776–83), a series of stirring appeals, the first of which was published just after Washington's disastrous retreat across New Jersey. Jefferson gave classic form to the statement of the case for the colonies in the *Declaration of Independence*.

Of all the writings of this period, however, the most important are the 85 essays included in the collection known as *The Federalist*. These papers, written by Alexander Hamilton, James Madison, and John Jay, were first published in the *Independent Journal* of New York in 1787-88. They did more than any other one thing to bring about the adoption of the Constitution, and they remain of the highest value in American political history and literature.

Early American Drama.—The first American drama was *The Prince of Parthia*, a romantic tragedy by Thomas Godfrey, first acted at the Southwark theater in Philadelphia, 1767. The first American comedy to be presented by a professional company was *The Contrast* by Royall Tyler. It was produced in New York, 1787. Tyler was the author of more than 50 plays, most of which were successful. His immediate successors were James N. Barker and John Howard Payne. Barker used American Material in *The Indian Princess* (1808) and *Superstition* (1824). During the next 25 years, many national themes were used by playwrights, of which R. P. Smith's *William Penn* is a good example. In 1855 George H. Boker's *Francesca da Rimini*, notable for literary and acting quality, was first presented. In *The Forest Rose* (1825) by Samuel Woodworth, the first permanent Yankee character, "Jonathan Plowboy," was developed.

First National Period (1800-1840). Two centuries of American writing had prepared the way for rapid development in the first decades of the 19th century. After Philip Freneau, the next American poet is William Cullen Bryant, lawyer, successful journalist, and publicist. His literary career extended over almost 70 years,—from "Thanatopsis," which he produced when he was but 18 years of age, to his translation of Homer, the work of his old age. Like Freneau, Bryant hewed his own paths and produced distinctively American work. Minor poets of Bryant's early years were Samuel Woodworth, author of "The Old Oaken Bucket," Joseph Rodman Drake, who wrote "The Culprit Fay," the first fairy story in American verse, and Fitz-Greene Halleck, whose "Marco Bozzaris" is still popular.

The Knickerbocker Group.—In the first two decades of the 19th century, when the tempest of harsh criticism of American writers was at its height, a group of young men in New York were cultivating the informal, humorous, and half-satiric essay. The leaders were James K. Paulding and Washington Irving. They, with William Irving, published the *Salmagundi* papers. Washington Irving's literary career, however, really began with the *History of New York* (1809). This work attracted the attention of Walter Scott and afterward helped to secure for the author much-needed assistance in England. *The Sketch Book* was issued in New York and London (1819-20). Irving's writings established the prestige of American letters in Europe and at the same time interpreted the charm of Europe, especially of England, to the new nation. He was recognized as continuing in America the fine tradition of Addison. His early successes were followed by a long series of works in biography and travel.

First American Novelists.—American fiction in the longer novel form began with the work of Charles Brockden Brown, who was deeply influenced by the English writer, Godwin. He was a romancer. His first work was *Wieland* (1798); *Edgar Huntley*, his best. He anticipated Cooper in adventure and Poe in his use of mystery and horror.

James Fenimore Cooper made his reputation with *The Spy* (1821), a romance of the Revolution. *The Pilot* is a sea story. His greatest work is a series of five novels published between 1823 and 1841 called "The Leatherstocking Tales," of which *The Last of the Mohicans* is the most gripping. The series deals in a romantic fashion with frontier life and centers around a great trapper and his Indian friends. The books won wide European approval. Less significant romantic novelists were Daniel Pierce Thompson (*The Green Mountain Boys*) and John Pendleton Kennedy of Baltimore, author of *Swallow Barn*. William Gilmore Simms of South Carolina wrote *The Yemasee* (1835) dealing with Colonial Indian warfare. *The Partisan* is the best of his revolutionary tales.

Transcendentalism.—In New England, during the third and the fourth decade of the 19th century, interest centers in the group of literary and religious leaders who reacted from rigid Puritanism toward Unitarianism and Transcendentalism. W. E. Channing, the leader of the Unitarians, was the greatest figure in the religious thought of the time. About 1836 the Transcendental Club, an informal group, was founded. It included Bronson Alcott, Margaret Fuller, Theodore Parker, and Ralph Waldo Emerson.

Second National Period (1840-1870). *Prose.*—
Emerson became the prophet of the idealism which
ruled the literature of the three decades just before
the Civil War. His essays, poems, and addresses assert
the importance of the individual as a spirit. His Phi
Beta Kappa address, *The American Scholar*, has been
called our "literary declaration of independence."
Many of Emerson's essays were given as lectures,
the vigor and sincerity of his personality adding
to their effect. Henry David Thoreau's *Walden*,
which tells of his effort to withdraw to a simple
life, is rich with reflection. Thoreau was one of the
most sturdily individualistic of the "Concord
Group." Hawthorne and Melville are the two great
novelists of the period. Hawthorne is haunted by
his puritan background with its sense of sin and
retribution. His ethical import is conveyed through
symbolic devices. Chief volumes are *The Scarlet
Letter* (1850), *The House of Seven Gables* (1851).
Herman Melville, after youthful years as a seaman,
published *Typee* (1846), the record of four months
in the Marquesas. His *Moby Dick* (1851) with its
philosophic sweep is open to rich interpretation.
Against a universe inscrutable and unfathomable
is hurled a tremendous human defiance symbolized
in the pursuit of the white whale. Only recently has
Melville been truly appreciated.

Poetry.—Henry W. Longfellow and John G.
Whittier belong to New England. Longfellow's narratives and simple didactic poems have made him a
household poet. As a translator, teacher, and diligent
gatherer of material from the literatures of the
world, he had a profound influence on this culture
of his time. Whittier, with a scanty formal education
was more limited. Poems such as "Snowbound,"
focussed upon New England life, give him a permanent place in American literature. He was also
active in liberal movements, notably anti-slavery.
James Russell Lowell, ambassador to England, was
our second literary ambassador to Europe (Irving
having gone to Spain). He was a distinguished
essayist and critic. His poetry includes *The Bigelow
Papers*, dialect satire and his famous "Commemoration Ode," though some prefer his less formal
lyrics to the "Ode." Oliver Wendell Holmes maintained through many years his hold upon a
wide public with his polished verse of humor and
sentiment, as well as by his witty essays published
as *The Autocrat of The Breakfast Table.*

But of all the poets to emerge in mid-century, Edgar Allan Poe and Walt Whitman are by far the greatest. Poe's poems such as "The Raven," "Israfel,"
"Ulalume," "The City of the Sea," achieve their
effects by a haunting music and an eerie power of
suggestion which evoke an atmosphere quite irrespective of the intellectual content. Whitman (*Leaves
of Grass*, 1855) was more robust and created a sensation. He is the first of the free verse poets and his
long crashing lines disturbed many. His frankness of
expression disturbed more. He aspired to be the poet
of democratic America— a dynamic land full of
healthy men and women. He came into poetry like
a great wind and now his genius is fully recognized.

Oratory and History.—Among the orators and
statesmen of this period are Daniel Webster,
Edward Everett, Rufus Choate, Wendell Phillips,
and Charles Sumner. Contemporary with these
were the great orators of the South,—Henry Clay,
Robert Y. Hayne, and John C. Calhoun. To these
must be added the name of Abraham Lincoln, not
the least of whose titles to immortality is his
Gettysburg Speech. The writing of history has
employed the pens of many Americans whose work
rises to the plane of literature. Most notable among
these are George Bancroft, Francis Parkman, John
Lothrop Motley, William Hickling Prescott, and
John Fiske.

Humor.—The humorous writing of the 19th
century began with Seba Smith's *Letters of Major
Jack Downing* (1830). Benjamin P. Shillaber created
the character of "Mrs. Partington." George Horatio
Derby (1823-61) is credited with originating the
type of humor that ruled in the works of Henry W.
Shaw ("Josh Billings"), David Ross Locke ("Pe-
troleum V. Nasby"), and Charles Farrar Browne
("Artemus Ward"). Chief among American humorists was Samuel L. Clemens ("Mark Twain")
with such works as *Innocents Abroad.* *Huckleberry
Finn*, in its vivid sense of the American scene and
its natural expression, puts him in the front rank
of novelists.

Later Poetry—The Civil War period was productive of many lyrics from minor poets. The
most noted is "Battle Hymn of the Republic" by
Julia Ward Howe. To the South in this period belong Paul Hamilton Hayne, Henry Timrod, and
Sidney Lanier, who achieved a rare music in "The
Marshes of Glynn."

Paul Laurence Dunbar, a black poet, produced
many lyrics of merit. Other poets of the time include John Bannister Tabb, the popular poets
James Whitcomb Riley and Eugene Field, and
Cincinnatus Heine ("Joaquin") Miller.

Turn of the Century to the Present. *The
Novel.*—There is always a taste for the novel of
action in far times or places. Lew Wallace's *Ben
Hur* (1880) was widely read for years. Jack London's stories were of primitive life and action and
were written with literary quality.

At the turn of the century there were many romantic novels, usually of the Revolution or the
Civil War. Paul Leicester Ford, Winston Churchill, and Mary Johnston wrote in this pattern,
and Nelson Page sensitively depicted the South.

The period also brought Henry James, one of the
great American novelists. James explored a subtle
realism of the mind, showing different national cultures in interaction. Among his important works
are *The American*, *Portrait of a Lady*, and *The
Golden Bowl.* Edith Wharton (*The Age of Innocence*)
followed his manner.

In later years a more forthright realism developed,
closer to the common life and of a style that became
increasingly more explicit. Hamlin Garland (1860–
1940) wrote true accounts of post-pioneer days on
the plains. Frank Norris (1870–1902) died young,
but in *The Octopus* and *The Pit* he had written two
powerful novels dealing with the railroad trust and
the wheat market of Chicago. Upton Sinclair is
considered responsible for reform in the meatpack-
ing industry through his novel *The Jungle* (1906).
William Dean Howells (1837–1920) was a realist
who told well-plotted stories. Theodore Dreiser
also stands high in rank among American writers.
Despite his uneven style, *Sister Carrie* (1900) and
An American Tragedy (1925) are eminent works of
fiction. By his initial daring, Dreiser made later
degrees of realism possible. Sinclair Lewis made
his reputation with satires of business and small-
town life—notably in *Main Street* (1920) and *Babbitt* (1922). F. Scott Fitzgerald spoke for the
younger generation in the 1920's with *The Great
Gatsby* (1925) and *Tender Is the Night* (1934). Gertrude Stein emigrated to Paris and established a
literary salon. Beginning in the 1920's she influenced many writers as she developed a new style of
writing, attempting to reproduce primitive states
of consciousness. Ernest Hemingway was a novelist of range and seriousness. In *A Farewell to Arms*
(1929), he vividly describes the World War I retreat from Caporetto. Later novels, especially *For
Whom the Bell Tolls* (1940), more than fulfilled his
earlier promise. James T. Farrell completed his
trilogy *Studs Lonigan* in 1935; John Dos Passos
published *U.S.A.*, also a three-part work, in 1937.
Dos Passos described poverty and migrant workers,
while experimenting with the forms of fiction. Also
concerned with workers and the poor were John
Steinbeck—notably in *Grapes of Wrath* (1939)—and
Erskine Caldwell, with *Tobacco Road* (1933).

Willa Cather wrote in a lyric style of the different
regions of America. Mississippi provides the setting for many of Eudora Welty's sensitive charac-
terizations (*Delta Wedding*, 1946).

Among novelists achieving critical recognition in their time were Thomas Wolfe and William Faulkner. Wolfe, in his gigantic novels *Look Homeward, Angel* (1929) and *Of Time and the River* (1935), gives a realistic view of life that also conveys romantic idealism. An outstanding artist with a complex style, Faulkner was largely preoccupied with basic aspects of life among Southern whites and Negroes. *The Sound and the Fury* (1929) and *Intruder in the Dust* (1948) illustrate his range.

John O'Hara portrayed the middle class with realism in *Appointment in Samarra* (1934), but turned to more popular and larger-scale novels. Carson McCullers and J. D. Salinger expressed serious themes through adolescent eyes in *The Member of the Wedding* (1946) and *Catcher in the Rye* (1951).

Divergent themes are expressed through middle-class Jewish figures in the works of Saul Bellow (*The Adventures of Augie March*, 1953; *Mr. Sammler's Planet*, 1970), Bernard Malamud (*The Fixer*, 1966), and Philip Roth (*Goodbye, Columbus*, 1959).

Racial problems in U. S. society have emerged in many forms in literature. Among Negro writers, Richard Wright developed a kind of black documentary in *Uncle Tom's Children* (1938). His best work, *Native Son* (1940), is often called the Negro American tragedy. James Baldwin followed Wright as spokesman for the Negro, with works that are violent in their impact (*Go Tell it on the Mountain*, 1953; *Nobody Knows My Name*, 1960). Ralph Ellison's psychological study, *The Invisible Man* (1952), is considered a classic of black writing.

Born in Russia, Vladimir Nabokov came to the U. S. in 1940. He gained notoriety with *Lolita* (1958), an ironic and explicit novel, combining humor with horror. Truman Capote produced a genre, described as the "nonfiction novel," combining fact and conjecture (*In Cold Blood*, 1965). Other recent novelists are Gore Vidal (*The Judgment of Paris*, 1952) and John Cheever (*The Wapshot Chronicle*, 1957). The works of John Barth (*The Sotweed Factor*, 1960; *Giles Goat-Boy*, 1966) and Thomas Pynchon (*V*, 1963) are inventive grotesqueries. Of an earlier generation, both James Agee (*A Death in the Family*, 1957) and Mary McCarthy (*The Group*, 1963) have established critical recognition.

Short Story—Beginning with Washington Irving's narratives in *The Sketch Book*, the type gained popularity through the tales of Edgar Allan Poe and the character studies of Nathaniel Hawthorne. Poe established the pattern for the detective story.

Many novelists, from Henry James to Hemingway and John Updike, have written memorable short works. A few, including Bret Harte, Mary Wilkins Freeman, and Katherine Anne Porter, have built reputations on short stories alone. The tales of O. Henry (William Sidney Porter), with their surprise endings, were highly popular early in the century. More recent story writers included Sherwood Anderson, Stephen Vincent Benet, Dorothy Canfield Fisher, Jesse Stuart, J. F. Powers, and Flannery O'Connor.

Drama—America's theater lacked greatness until the triumph of Eugene O'Neill. His chief plays include *Strange Interlude* (1928), *Mourning Becomes Electra* (1931), *The Iceman Cometh* (1946), and *Long Day's Journey into Night* (1957), now considered his masterpiece. Maxwell Anderson (*Mary of Scotland*, 1934; *Both Your Houses*, 1933) was a prolific writer whose dialogue was often poetic. Lillian Hellman produced psychological dramas, including *The Children's Hour* (1934). Thornton Wilder's influence has been felt in both Europe and America. He used a minimum of stage props in *Our Town* (1938) and *The Skin of Our Teeth* (1942). Robert Sherwood's *Idiot's Delight* and *There Shall Be No Night* express his opposition to war. Basic instincts often mark the work of Tennessee Williams —yet his work is evocative of poetic sentiment. His best plays are considered *The Glass Menagerie* (1945)

and *A Streetcar Named Desire* (1947). Arthur Miller became known for tragedies of the common man, including *All My Sons* (1947) and *Death of a Salesman* (1949). Of recent writers, Edward Albee (*Who's Afraid of Virginia Woolf*, 1962), Neil Simon (*Barefoot in the Park*, 1963), and Lorraine Hansberry (*A Raisin in the Sun*, 1959) have been well received.

Modern Poetry—With the publication in 1912 of *Poetry* magazine in Chicago—followed by other small magazines—came a revival of interest in poetry. From the Middle West, Carl Sandburg, Edgar Lee Masters, and Vachel Lindsay became popular. Freedom in choice of subject and form increased. In the East, Amy Lowell took the lead of a free-verse group called the Imagists. Hilda Doolittle (H. D.) was one of the most original of this group. Elinor Wylie wrote finely tuned lyrics and poetic prose. Perhaps most popular in her day was Edna St. Vincent Millay, writing largely in the sonnet form. Edwin Arlington Robinson, with his psychological studies, and Robert Frost, with his thoughtful poems, preferred traditional forms.

In 1917 T. S. Eliot published his first volume— his poetry, drama, and criticism were to place him among the preeminent forces in letters. Close to Eliot for some years in England was Ezra Pound, a brilliant shaper of the directions of modern writing. Another original voice, purely in the American pattern, was William Carlos Williams. Hart Crane, an experimenter as well, made powerful and imaginative achievements. Marianne Moore, who followed Eliot as editor of the *Dial*, was also a strong influence. In poetry and fiction, Conrad Aiken worked experimentally through a long career. Robinson Jeffers created an intense view of man and nature. In the South, the Fugitives, an agrarian group of writers, included John Crowe Ransom, Robert Penn Warren, and Allen Tate. Active in public life, Archibald MacLeish also wrote poetry and drama. Wallace Stevens, with his richly imaginative verse, emerged from the obscurity of an insurance career. Most original in virtuosity in these years was E. E. Cummings.

Among poets of the 1940's and later years to use classic forms and models and write translations and adaptations from other literatures were Louise Bogan, Horace Gregory, Richmond Lattimore, Dudley Fitts, Rolfe Humphries, and Leonie Adams, and later Ben Belitt and W. S. Merwin.

During the 1940's and later, a strong influence in poetry was clearly felt in the vision and metric range of the English poet W. H. Auden, who had settled in the U. S. and whose "Age of Anxiety" branded the era.

World War II and its aftermath brought younger poets into the mainstream, some attaining major reputations. Robert Lowell is widely placed in the first rank, and probably the most lyric and individual was Theodore Roethke. Randall Jarrell was noted for his criticism and the philosophic sophistication of his work. Poetry of serious depth was also produced by Delmore Schwartz and John Berryman. Other wartime and postwar poets include Richard Eberhart, Karl Shapiro, who became editor of *Poetry*, and John Ciardi.

Moving from traditional forms, toward oral unstructured forms, the "Beat" movement produced few notables. The most enduring is Allen Ginsberg.

Following the earlier Negro poets Paul Laurence Dunbar and James Weldon Johnson were Countee Cullen, Langston Hughes, and Owen Dodson. Perhaps most widely known for his bitter verse and drama is Leroi Jones.

Other important postwar poets, of a later generation, include Richard Wilbur, Robert Bly, Sylvia Plath, Robert Creeley, and Carolyn Kizer.

TABLE OF AMERICAN LITERATURE

Time	Author	Prose	Poetry and Drama
1588–1649	John Winthrop	History of New England	
1590–1657	William Bradford	History of Plymouth	
1612–1672	Anne Bradstreet		Poems (Contemplations).
1631–1705	Michael Wigglesworth		Poems (The Day of Doom).
1663–1728	Cotton Mather	New England Church History	
1674–1744	William Byrd	History of the Dividing Line	
1687–1758	Thomas Prince	History of New England	
1696–1772	Samuel Johnson	Philosophy	
1703–1758	Jonathan Edwards	Freedom of the Will	
1706–1790	Benjamin Franklin	Poor Richard's Almanac	
1711–1780	Thomas Hutchinson	History of Massachusetts	
1720–1772	John Woolman	Journal	
1737–1791	Francis Hopkinson		Battle of the Kegs.
1737–1809	Thomas Paine	Common Sense, The Crisis	
1750–1831	John Trumbull		Satire (McFingal).
1752–1817	Timothy Dwight		Conquest of Canaan.
1752–1832	Philip Freneau		Lyrics (Eutaw Springs).
1754–1812	Joel Barlow		The Columbiad, Hasty Pudding.
1771–1810	Charles B. Brown	Novels (Wieland, Clara Howard).	
1780–1842	William E. Channing	Essays, Addresses	
1783–1859	Washington Irving	History of New York, Sketch Book	
1789–1851	James F. Cooper	The Pilot, Leatherstocking Tales.	
1790–1867	Fitz-Greene Halleck		Poems (Marco Bozzaris).
1791–1852	John Howard Payne		Home, Sweet Home, Plays.
1793–1868	Daniel P. Thompson	Novels (Green Mountain Boys)	
1794–1878	William C. Bryant		Poems (Thanatopsis).
1795–1820	Joseph R. Drake		Poems (The Culprit Fay).
1795–1856	James G. Percival	History	Prometheus.
1795–1870	John P. Kennedy	Novels (Horse-Shoe Robinson).	
1796–1859	William H. Prescott	History (Ferdinand and Isabella, Conquest of Mexico)	
1799–1888	Amos Bronson Alcott	Philosophy	
1800–1891	George Bancroft	History of the United States	
1803–1882	Ralph W. Emerson	Philosophy, Conduct of Life	
1804–1864	Nathaniel Hawthorne	Novels (Scarlet Letter), Tales	
1806–1867	Nathaniel P. Willis	Sketches of Travel and Biography	Scriptural Poems.
1806–1870	William G. Simms	Novels (The Scout), Biography	Poems (Atalantis).
1807–1882	H. W. Longfellow	Outre-Mer	Poems (Hiawatha).
1807–1892	John G. Whittier		Poems (Maud Muller, Snowbound)
1808–1895	Samuel F. Smith	Biographies, Sketches	Poems (America).
1809–1849	Edgar Allan Poe	Tales (The Gold Bug)	Poems (The Raven).
1809–1865	Abraham Lincoln	Addresses (Gettysburg Speech)	
1809–1894	Oliver W. Holmes	Autocrat of the Breakfast Table	Poems (Chambered Nautilus).
1810–1860	Theodore Parker	Essays, Sermons	
1811–1896	Harriet B. Stowe	Novels (Uncle Tom's Cabin)	
1814–1877	John L. Motley	History (Rise of the Dutch Rep.)	
1815–1882	Richard H. Dana, Jr.	Two Years before the Mast	
1817–1862	Henry D. Thoreau	Essays (Walden)	Poems.
1818–1885	Henry Wheeler Shaw, "Josh Billings"	Humor	
1819–1881	J. G. Holland	Novels (Sevenoaks), Essays	Poems (Kathrina).
1819–1891	James R. Lowell	Essays (Among My Books)	Poems (Commemoration Ode).
1819–1891	Herman Melville	Typee, Moby Dick	Poems.
1819–1892	Walt Whitman		Poems (Leaves of Grass).
1819–1910	Julia Ward Howe	Essays	Battle Hymn of the Republic.
1822–1909	Edward E. Hale	The Man without a Country	
1823–1893	Francis Parkman	History (Conspiracy of Pontiac).	
1823–1911	Thomas W. Higginson	Essays (Outdoor Papers)	
1824–1892	George W. Curtis	Essays, Biography	
1824–1906	Adeline D. Whitney	Novels (The Gayworthys)	Poems.
1825–1878	Bayard Taylor	Travel, Novels (Hannah Thurston)	Poems, Translation (Faust).
1825–1903	Richard H. Stoddard	Criticism	Poems (Songs of Summer).
1827–1905	Lew Wallace	Novels (The Fair God, Ben Hur)	
1829–1867	Henry Timrod		The Cotton Boll.
1829–1900	Charles D. Warner	Essays (Backlog Studies)	
1829–1914	Silas Weir Mitchell	Essays, Novels (Hugh Wynne)	
1830–1886	Emily Dickinson		Lyrics.
1830–1896	Mary A. Dodge	Novels, Biography	
1830–1886	Paul H. Hayne		Poems (Legends and Lyrics).
1831–1885	Helen Hunt Jackson	Novels (Ramona)	Poems.
1831–1922	Mary V. Terhune	Novels (Alone, Hidden Path)	
1832–1888	Louisa May Alcott	Stories (Little Women)	
1833–1888	David Ross Locke, "Petroleum V. Nasby"	Humor, Satire	
1833–1908	Edmund C. Stedman	Criticism	Poems (Alice of Monmouth).
1834–1867	Charles Farrar Browne, "Artemus Ward"	Humor	
1834–1902	Francis R. Stockton	Stories (The Lady or the Tiger)	
1835–1910	Samuel L. Clemens, "Mark Twain"	Humor (Huckleberry Finn)	
1836–1907	Thomas B. Aldrich	Stories (Marjorie Daw)	Songs, Sonnets.
1836–1902	Francis Bret Harte	Stories (Luck of Roaring Camp)	Poems (The Heathen Chinee).
1837–1902	Edward Eggleston	Novels (Hoosier Schoolmaster)	
1837–1920	William D. Howells	Novels (The Rise of Silas Lapham)	
1837–1921	John Burroughs	Essays (Wake Robin, Signs and Seasons)	
1838–1905	Mary Mapes Dodge	Stories (Hans Brinker)	
1838–1914	John Muir	Story of My Boyhood and Youth	
1838–1915	F. Hopkinson Smith	Stories	
1838–1918	Henry Adams	The Education of Henry Adams	
1839–1886	Abram Joseph Ryan		Civil War Poems.

TABLE OF AMERICAN LITERATURE—Con.

Time	Author	Prose	Poetry and Drama
1839–1908	James Ryder Randall		Maryland, My Maryland.
1841–1913	Joaquin Miller		Songs of the Sierras.
1842–1881	Sidney Lanier	Essays, Criticism	Poems (The Marshes of Glynn).
1842–1901	John Fiske	Histories, Essays	
1842–1908	Bronson Howard		Plays (The Henrietta, Shenandoah).
1843–1916	Henry James	Novels (Daisy Miller, Portrait of a Lady)	
1844–1925	George W. Cable	Novels (Old Creole Days)	
1848–1908	Joel Chandler Harris	Uncle Remus Tales, The Tar Baby	
1848–1927	James Ford Rhodes	Histories, Essays	
1849–1887	Emma Lazarus		Songs of a Semite.
1849–1916	James W. Riley		Poems (Pipes o' Pan).
1849–1925	James Lane Allen	Novels (The Choir Invisible)	
1849–1924	Frances H. Burnett	Little Lord Fauntleroy	Plays.
1850–1895	Eugene Field		Poems (With Trumpet and Drum).
1852–1930	Mary E. W. Freeman	Stories, Novels	Poems.
1852–1932	John B. McMaster	Histories, Biographies	
1852–1940	Edwin Markham		Poems (Lincoln).
1852–1929	Brander Matthews	Essays, Criticism	
1852–1933	Henry van Dyke	Essays, Stories (The Blue Flower)	Poems.
1853–1922	Thomas Nelson Page	Novels (In Ole Virginia)	
1854–1909	F. Marion Crawford	Novels (Saracinesca)	Ballads.
1854–1931	David Belasco		Plays (The Return of Peter Grimm).
1855–1950	Agnes Repplier	Essays (Points of View)	
1855–1930	George E. Woodberry	Essays, Criticism	Poems.
1856–1924	Woodrow Wilson	History, Essays	
1856–1923	Kate Douglas Wiggin	Rebecca of Sunnybrook Farm	
1857–1948	Gertrude Atherton	Novels (Ancestors)	
1858–1919	Theodore Roosevelt	History, Travel, Politics	
1859–1929	Katharine L. Bates	Essays, Criticism	Poems (America the Beautiful).
1859–1923	William R. Thayer	History, Biography	Poems.
1860–1940	Hamlin Garland	Stories (Main-traveled Roads)	
1860–1954	Bliss Perry	Novels, Stories, Essays	
1860–1932	Clinton Scollard		Pictures in Song, Lyrics.
1860–1938	Owen Wister	Novels (The Virginian)	Poems.
1860–1946	Ernest Thompson Seton	Wild Animals I Have Known	
1862–1910	William S. Porter "O. Henry"	Short Stories (The Four Million)	
1862–1937	Edith Wharton	Novels (Ethan Frome)	Poems.
1863–1932	Gamaliel Bradford	Biographical Essays	
1863–1952	George Santayana	Essays (The Life of Reason)	Poems (The Hermit of Carmel).
1864–1937	Paul Elmer More	Shelburne Essays	
1865–1902	Paul Leicester Ford	Novels (Janice Meredith)	
1865–1909	William Clyde Fitch		Plays (Beau Brummell, The Truth).
1865–1943	William Lyon Phelps	Criticism, Autobiography	
1865–1946	Logan Pearsall Smith	Essays (Trivia, More Trivia)	
1866–1944	George Ade	Humor (Fables in Slang)	Plays (The College Widow).
1867–1936	Finley Peter Dunne	Humor (Mr. Dooley's Philosophy)	
1868–1938	Robert Herrick	Novels (The Common Lot)	
1868–1924	Gene Stratton Porter	Stories (Freckles)	
1868–1944	William A. White	Novels (A Certain Rich Man)	
1869–1910	William V. Moody		Poems, Dramas (The Great Divide).
1869–1935	Edwin A. Robinson		Poems (Merlin), Dramas (Van Zorn).
1869–1946	Booth Tarkington	Novels (The Plutocrat)	Plays (The Intimate Strangers).
1869–1950	Edgar Lee Masters	Novels (Mitch Miller)	Poems (Spoon River Anthology).
1870–1902	Frank Norris	Novels (The Octopus)	
1871–1900	Stephen Crane	Novels (Red Badge of Courage)	Poems (Black Riders).
1871–1945	Theodore Dreiser	Novels (American Tragedy)	
1872–1906	Paul Laurence Dunbar	Stories	Dialect Poems.
1873–1947	Willa Sibert Cather	Novels (My Antonia), Stories	
1874–1946	Gertrude Stein	Novels (The Making of Americans)	Poems (Tender Buttons).
1874–1922	Josephine P. Peabody	Folk Stories	Poetic Dramas (The Piper).
1874–1945	Ellen Glasgow	Novels (The Sheltered Life)	
1874–1925	Amy Lowell	Criticism	Poems (What's O'clock).
1874–1963	Robert Frost		Poems (North of Boston).
1875–1939	Zane Grey	Novels (Riders of the Purple Sage)	
1875–1956	Percy Mackaye	Essays	Poetic Dramas (The Scarecrow).
1876–1916	Jack London	Novels (The Sea Wolf)	
1876–1941	Sherwood Anderson	Stories, Novels (Marching Men)	
1876–1958	Mary Roberts Rinehart	Stories (The Circular Staircase)	
1877–1962	William Beebe	Nature Essays (Jungle Peace)	Plays (Double Life).
1878–1927	James Oliver Curwood	Novels	
1878–1937	Donald Marquis	Humor (The Old Soak)	
1878–1949	James Truslow Adams	The History of New England	
1878–1967	Carl Sandburg	Biography (Abraham Lincoln)	Poems (Smoke and Steel).
1878–1961	Henry Seidel Canby	Criticism, Biography (Thoreau)	
1878–1968	Upton Sinclair	Novels (The Jungle)	
1879–1958	James Branch Cabell	Novels (Jurgen)	
1879–1958	Dorothy Canfield Fisher	Novels (The Brimming Cup)	
1879–1931	N. Vachel Lindsay	The Golden Book of Springfield	Poems (The Congo).
1879–1951	John Erskine	Essays, Novels	
1879–1948	Simeon Strunsky	Essays (Sinbad and His Friends)	
1879–1955	Wallace Stevens		Poems.
1880–1930	Henry Sydnor Harrison	Novels (Queed; St. Teresa)	
1880–1954	Joseph Hergesheimer	Novels (Java Head)	
1880–1966	Kathleen Norris	Novels (Lucretia Lombard)	
1880–1950	Ernest Poole	Novels (The Harbor)	
1880–1956	Henry L. Mencken	Essays, Social Criticism	
1881–1968	Witter Bynner		Poems (Songs for Celia).
1882–1948	Susan Glaspell	Novels (Brook Evans)	Plays (Alison's House).
1882–1932	James Oppenheim	Novels and Short Stories	Poems (Songs for the New Age).
1882–1944	Hendrik Willem Van Loon	History (Story of Mankind)	

American Literature

TABLE OF AMERICAN LITERATURE—Con.

Time	Author	Prose	Poetry and Drama
1883—1959	Coningsby Dawson	Novels (Garden without Walls)	The Worker, and Other Poems.
1883—1963	William Carlos Williams	Essays, stories	Poems (Pictures from Breughel).
1884—1933	Sara Teasdale		Helen of Troy, and Other Poems.
1885—1928	Elinor Wylie	Novels (Jennifer Lorn)	Poems (Nets to Catch the Wind).
1885—1951	Sinclair Lewis	Novels (Main Street; Babbitt)	
1885—1977	Louis Untermeyer	Criticism	The Younger Quire.
1885—	Will Durant	Essays (Story of Philosophy)	
1885—1950	Carl Van Doren	Biography (Benjamin Franklin)	
1885—1965	Thomas B. Costain	Novels (Below the Salt)	
1886—1918	Joyce Kilmer		Rouge Bouquet, and Other Poems.
1886—1941	Elizabeth Madox Roberts	Novels (Great Meadow)	Poems (Under the Tree).
1886—1950	John Gould Fletcher		Goblins and Pagodas.
1886—1946	Edward B. Sheldon		Dramas (Romance).
1886—1970	Wilbur Daniel Steele	Novels, Stories (Land's End)	
1886—1963	Van Wyck Brooks	The Flowering of New England	
1886—1953	Douglas Southall Freeman	Biography (Lee, Washington)	
1887—1973	Mary Ellen Chase	Novels (A Goodly Heritage)	
1887—1962	Robinson Jeffers		Poems (Thurso's Landing).
1887—1972	Marianne Moore		Poems (Selected Poems).
1888—1953	Eugene G. O'Neill		Plays (Mourning Becomes Electra).
1888—1959	Maxwell Anderson		Plays (High Tor, Winterset).
1888—1974	John Crowe Ransom	Criticism (The World's Body)	Selected Poems (1945).
1888—1965	Thomas Stearns Eliot	Criticism (The Sacred Wood)	Poems (The Wasteland), Plays.
1889—1949	Hervey Allen	Novels (Anthony Adverse)	Poems (New Legends).
1889—1973	Conrad Aiken	Short Stories, Novels	Poems (Brownstone Eclogues).
1889—1945	Robert Benchley	Humor (Inside Benchley)	
1890—1957	Christopher Morley	Essays, Novels (Thorofare)	Poems (Song for a Little House).
1892—	Archibald MacLeish	Essays (A Time to Speak)	Poems (Conquistador).
1892—1950	Edna St. Vincent Millay		Poems (Renascence), Plays.
1892—1973	Pearl Buck	Novels (The Good Earth)	
1893—1970	Joseph Wood Krutch	Criticism (The Modern Temper)	
1893—1960	John P. Marquand	Novels (The Late George Apley)	
1894—1962	E. E. Cummings		Poems.
1894—1961	Dashiell Hammett	Detective stories	
1894—1972	Katherine Anne Porter	Stories, novel (Ship of Fools)	
1894—1961	James Thurber	Humor, cartoons	Plays (The Male Animal).
1894—1972	Mark Van Doren	Short Stories (Home with Hazel)	Poems (A Winter Diary).
1896—1970	John Dos Passos	Novels (U.S.A.)	
1896—1956	Louis Bromfield	Novels (The Rains Came)	
1896—1955	Robert Sherwood		Plays (Abe Lincoln in Illinois)
1896—1940	F. Scott Fitzgerald	Novels (The Great Gatsby)	
1897—1962	William Faulkner	Novels, Stories (Go Down Moses)	
1897—1975	Thornton Wilder	Novels (Bridge of San Luis Rey)	Plays (Our Town).
1897—1973	Catherine D. Bowen	Biography (Yankee from Olympus)	
1898—1943	Stephen V. Benét	Stories	Poems (John Brown's Body).
1899—1978	Bruce Catton	History (This Hallowed Ground)	
1899—1961	Ernest Hemingway	Novels (Farewell to Arms)	
1899—	Allen Tate		Poems (The Winter Sea).
1899—	E. B. White	Essays (One Man's Meat)	
1899—1932	Hart Crane		Poems (The Bridge).
1900—1949	Margaret Mitchell	Novel (Gone with the Wind)	
1900—1969	John Mason Brown	Dramatic criticism	
1900—1938	Thomas Wolfe	Novels (Of Time and the River)	
1902—1968	John Steinbeck	Novels (The Grapes of Wrath)	
1902—1971	Ogden Nash		Humorous Verse.
1903—1978	James Gould Cozzens	Novels (By Love Possessed)	
1905—	Robert Penn Warren	Novels, essays	Poems.
1907—	Leon Edel	Criticism and biography (Henry James, four volumes)	
1908—	William Saroyan	Stories (My Name Is Aram)	
1908—1960	Richard Wright	Novels (Native Son)	
1910—	Norman Corwin		Plays, Radio Plays
1914—	John Hersey	Novels (A Bell for Adano)	
1914—	Ralph Ellison	Essays, novels	
1914—	Bernard Malamud	Stories, novels (The Fixer)	
1914—	Tennessee Williams		Plays (The Glass Menagerie).
1915—	Arthur Miller		Plays (The Crucible).
1915—	Saul Bellow	Novels (The Victim; Herzog)	
1917—1978	Robert Lowell		Poems.
1919—	J. D. Salinger	Stories, novels	
1923—	Norman Mailer	Essays, novels	
1924—	Truman Capote	Stories, Novels (In Cold Blood)	
1924—	James Baldwin	Novels (Another Country)	
1925—	William Styron	Novels	
1928—	Edward Albee		Plays (A Delicate Balance).
1932—	John Updike	Novels (The Centaur)	
1933—	Philip Roth	Novels, Stories	

ENGLISH LITERATURE

WHEN the Angles and Saxons went from the continent to Britain in the 5th and the 6th century, they had no written language, but they carried with them the love of song. Bards and gleemen accompanied them and sang the tales of the Northland. The oldest of the ancient songs which have been preserved for us is *The Far-Traveler*. *Beowulf* is their epic song. At the time of their invasion of Britain, these Anglo-Saxons were heathen, but when, after two long centuries of struggle, they had become possessed of the land, they came under the softening influence of Christianity. Monasteries were built, and in these safe shelters literature had a beginning. The glory of this beginning belongs to Northumbria in the 7th century. For nearly two centuries, this was the seat of learning.

Old English Period. The poem *Beowulf* is Anglo-Saxon, but it is not native to English soil. Cædmon's *Paraphrase of the Scriptures* is the first great native British poem. With Christianity a new spirit entered into English poetry.

Old English prose also began in the monastery of Northumbria with Bede. His learning was famed throughout Europe. How industrious he was is indicated by the tradition that he wrote no less than 45 works in Latin. His last work was a translation of the Gospel of St. John into English.

During the 9th century the greater part of England was laid waste by the Danes, and literature was almost extinguished. The long battle against these invaders was lost in Northumbria, but was gained for a time by Alfred the Great in Wessex. The center of learning was transferred from the North to the South, and as Whitby was the cradle of English poetry in the North, so Winchester became the seat of English prose in the South. Alfred gathered scholars about him, who translated the Latin works of Bede and the *Chronicles* of Orosius, adding an account of the voyages of Othere and Wulfstan. Many other works were rendered into the vernacular in Alfred's time. "At Winchester the king took the English tongue and made it the tongue in which history, philosophy, law, and religion spoke to the English people." He also established schools and wrote textbooks for these schools, so that every free-born youth might attend to his books till he "could read English writing perfectly."

The next great name in literature after King Alfred is Ælfric. He wrote numerous ecclesiastical works and was the first translator of any considerable portion of the Bible. His translations of the Pentateuch, Joshua, Judges, and part of Job are the best examples we possess of the language at the beginning of the 11th century. Indeed, our greatest Old English prose is perhaps to be found in the sermons and saints' lives by Ælfric. The *Old English Chronicle* records the most significant happenings of history, chiefly English history, and was continued in Peterborough Abbey down to the death of King Stephen in 1154.

Middle English Period. The overthrow of Saxon rule in England by William the Conqueror is an event of vast importance in literature as well as in history. For a hundred years after the conquest, literature was inert. A foreign king and an aristocracy of a foreign people ruled the land; an alien language had been introduced. However, after a few generations of such domination there were signs of returning life. The language could not die while the bulk of the people remained Saxon, but it underwent a great change. England was still to remain the land of the Saxon tongue, but the language was to be greatly modified by its contact with the Latin of the clergy and with the French of the Norman conquerors. For 300 years after the conquest these languages contended with the Saxon English for supremacy in England. In the reign of Edward

III it had been fully demonstrated that the English were to be the ruling people, and Parliament enacted important laws making English the official language of law courts and schools.

But the English of King Edward's time was quite unlike the rude Saxon speech of *Beowulf* and Cædmon's *Paraphrase* or the later chronicles. Pure Anglo-Saxon was an energetic language, able to express with vigor the practical common thoughts of every day, but it lacked delicacy and flexibility of expression. The Saxon mind, too, was lacking in quickness of thought and in the creative play of the imagination. It has been well said that in this blending of languages the Saxon furnished the dough and the Norman French the yeast. Out of the combined product we get a strength and flexibility of language that belonged to neither element alone.

Chronicles and Romances.—The literature of England during the 12th century was almost entirely Latin and French, but we reckon it as a rich source of our story-telling. Geoffrey of Monmouth wrote twelve short books in Latin, which he called *History of the Kings of Britain.* It is a clever compilation of Welsh legends, a source to which we go for some of our King Arthur stories. These stories were afterward translated into French and were later brought back into English verse by Layamon in his *Brut d'Angleterre.* Later many other stories were added, and other cycles of romance were introduced into English literature. There were four of these great romantic cycles: (1) the King Arthur legends, to which later stories were added, such as *Quest of the Grail, Le Morte D'Arthur, Romance of Sir Tristram;* (2) Charlemagne and his Twelve Peers, containing the stories of Roland, Charlemagne, Roland and Otuel, the *Siege of Milan,* and others; (3) the *Life of Alexander,* romantic wonder stories from the East; (4) the *Siege of Troy,* derived from Latin sources. Popular ballads, such as "Robin Hood," Robert of Gloucester's *Rhyming Chronicles,* and lyrics sung among the people, kept the love of poetry alive until the greater burst of song in the 14th century.

Mandeville and Wiclif.—In the three centuries following the conquest there was very little prose writing done in England, but in the 14th century there appeared a book of stories entitled *The Voiage and Travaile of Sir John Mandeville.* We do not know who is the author of this book. Many of the stories seem to be translations. The exaggerations in the book make it valueless as a record of travel, but it did establish the love of story-telling. It is the first example of a definitely achieved prose style, and after the invention of printing it long remained one of the most popular books. John Wiclif, next to Chaucer, is the greatest literary name of the century. He and his friend, John Purvey, were the first to give a complete version of the Scriptures to the English people in their own tongue. The influence of such a translation read by all the people was to raise a dialect to the dignity of a national language. Besides this great work, Wiclif is the author of a large number of sermons and polemical writings. Contemporary with these religious tracts which Wiclif distributed so freely was *Piers Plowman,* by William Langland. It was a satire in verse upon certain ecclesiastical corruptions of the period and remained the greatest allegory in the language until the publication of Bunyan's *Pilgrim's Progress.*

Chaucer.—The most distinguished name in the literature of the 14th century is that of Geoffrey Chaucer. Some critics maintain that before him there was no permanent English verse. He is therefore often called the "Father of English Poetry." Chaucer's earlier poems are "Romaunt of the Rose," "The Book of the Duchess," and "Parlement of Foules." His greatest work is *Canterbury Tales,* the plan of which was suggested by Boccaccio's *Decameron.* The Prologue to the *Canterbury Tales* is one of the finest pieces of descriptive poetry in our language. Before Chaucer's time English was a language of dialects. He wrote in the Midland dialect and made that the language of the nation. Chaucer died in 1400, just 334 years after the Norman Conquest. To sum up the most important literary events of these years, we note the development of the English language, the translation of the Bible, and the creation in English of one of the world's supreme masterpieces, *Canterbury Tales*.

There was but little progress in the development of literary art in the century following Chaucer. Social conditions were changing, and there was intellectual and political unrest. The struggle between the houses of York and Lancaster absorbed men's minds. These are the reasons assigned for the dearth of literature. To the genius of Chaucer there arose no successor.

Printing and the Bible.—The greatest prose work of the 15th century is Sir Thomas Malory's *Morte D'Arthur*. This is a prose epic of the deeds of King Arthur and his knights of the Round Table. In 1476 Caxton established his printing press and, in 1477, issued the first printed book in England,— the *Dictes and Sayings of the Philosophers*. He had already printed in English on the continent his *Recuyell of the Histories of Troy* and the *Game and Playe of the Chesse*. The 16th century was a period of Bible translation. Wiclif had made his rendering from the Latin, but, in the early years of the 16th century, Greek was being taught in the English universities, and William Tyndale made the first translation of the New Testament directly from the Greek text. He later translated the Pentateuch from the Hebrew, and in 1535 Miles Coverdale published the first printed copy of the whole Bible. In 1560 a new translation, called the Genevan Bible, was issued from Geneva in Switzerland. This was long the popular Bible among Protestants, even after the publication of the King James Version. In 1582, scholars in the Catholic college at Reims in France issued a translation of the New Testament.

The Elizabethans. The Elizabethan age is marked by features so distinct and so superior that it has been called the "Golden Age in English literature." Two mighty forces, the Renaissance and the Reformation, combined to make this a great intellectual age. Men's minds were stimulated, and a language completely formed was ready at their hand. There was freedom for thought to express itself, and there was variety in life and freshness of experience to nourish the mind. The printing press, travel, and social intercourse all stimulated intellectual activity. The great period began with Spenser and Marlowe, reached its climax in Shakespeare, but was still capable of producing Donne and Webster.

Spenser.—Spenser had a rich, dreamy music and a skill in poetic form which has caused him to be called "the poet's poet." Later such poets as Byron, Shelley, and Keats used the "Spenserian Stanza." His first great work, *The Shepherd's Calender*, was an exercise in which he tried out and stabilized certain metrical forms. *The Faery Queen*, although incomplete, is one of the longest poems in the language. It is a combination of Reformation moral thinking, of the Renaissance sense of luxury, of Aristotle's ethics, and of Spenser's own great musical genius. To some modern readers, however, his style is cloying.

The Drama.—The beginnings of the drama in England may be traced to the *miracle plays* and *mysteries* which were introduced soon after the Norman Conquest. Following these were the later dramatic recitals, the *moralities, interludes, masks,* and *pageants*.

As early as the 11th century, *miracle plays* were performed in the monasteries by monks and choristers. Later, companies of professional players traveled about the country and enacted their plays

in the yards of inns. In 1575 the Puritans expelled the players from the city, and theaters were built outside the limits. Shakespeare was born in 1564. Twenty-two or twenty-three years later he made his way to London, where he was attracted by one of these forbidden theaters. Already English drama had attained classical utterance in the great plays of Christopher Marlowe, *Tamburlaine the Great, Faustus, The Jew of Malta*. The greatest of these plays is *Faustus*. Marlowe established the use of blank verse in the English drama, a form of verse which Shakespeare adopted and brought to technical perfection.

Shakespeare.—That Shakespeare quickly rose to prominence in his art, we may judge from the fact that in 1592, when he had been in London not more than five or six years, he was already writing plays and was the object of a jealous attack by a rival playwright. At the age of 49 he was able to leave London with a competence and to return to his home at Stratford-on-Avon. This also argues for his success as a dramatist. In 1598 Francis Mere writes of the growing fame of Shakespeare and prints the titles of a number of his plays. Ben Jonson, the second dramatist of the age, was his intimate friend. These are facts worth knowing about the personality of the man who is the greatest figure in English literature, perhaps in all literature.

Attributed to Shakespeare are 34 plays, counting as single plays those written in several parts. His dramatic work may be divided into three classes: comedies, histories, tragedies. The following are a few of the best in each class. Every reader should be familiar with them:

Comedies: *Midsummer Night's Dream, As You Like It, Merchant of Venice, Winter's Tale, Twelfth Night, The Tempest*.

Histories: *Richard III, Henry IV, Henry V, Henry VIII, King John, Julius Cæsar*.

Tragedies: *Hamlet, Macbeth, King Lear, Othello, Romeo and Juliet, Antony and Cleopatra*.

In addition to his dramas, Shakespeare wrote two long narrative poems and 154 sonnets. It is said that the measure of Shakespeare's greatness is his universality; he was "not of an age, but for all time." Other writers have equaled Shakespeare in some one quality, but he excels them all in the combination of these diverse qualities.

Even without Shakespeare, the age of Elizabeth and James I would be considered a great dramatic period. Beaumont and Fletcher with a long series of tragedies and romantic comedies, among which *The Maid's Tragedy* and *Philastor* are notable, rivalled Shakespeare in popularity. They had a genuine dramatic sense and wrote beautiful blank verse but their sense of character was inferior and their morals dubious. Ben Jonson, writing according to the classical "three unities," scored successes with comedies such as *Volpone, The Alchemist,* and *Every Man in His Humor*. Jonson's figures are exaggerated, each being dominated by a special bias, or "humor" of the mind, a device which enabled Jonson to satirize the foibles of human nature. John Webster's few plays are somber and haunted by death and disaster. He is notable for the creation of two great heroines, The Duchess of Malfi and The White Devil, in plays of those names. The one is a gentle and generous woman, the other all that the title implies.

Elizabethan Prose.—One of the most remarkable of the men who adorned the court of Queen Elizabeth was Sir Francis Bacon, the greatest prose writer of the age. As courtier and scholar he adorned both this and the succeeding reign of Jamrs I. His political success and his political disgrace are familiar stories in history. His enduring works in literature. He was both poet and philosopher. His great work in philosophy is magnificent in scope, as may be inferred from the title *Instauratio Magna*, or "The Great Institution of True Philosophy." This monumental work was designed to be written in six parts, but it was never finished.

The second part, *Novum Organum*, or the "New Instrument," is described as "the science of a better and more perfect use of reason in the investigation of things, and of the true aids of the understanding." It sets forth the methods to be adopted in searching after truth, points out sources of error, and suggests the means of avoiding errors in the future. His entire philosophy is built upon the idea of inductive investigation. Bacon had so little respect for the English language that he wrote his great philosophy in Latin. His *New Atlantis*, like Sir Thomas More's *Utopia*, pictures in romance an ideal commonwealth. The most important among his English works is his volume of essays, clear, concise, practical in observation, and of profound wisdom. Sir Walter Raleigh contributed to prose his ambitious *History of the World*, and to poetry a few beautiful lyrics.

Transition.—With the death of Bacon in 1626, we pass from the glory of the Elizabethan age into the Puritan age. There are some characteristics which sharply separate this age from the preceding. Intense patriotism, peace within the realm, general prosperity, and much worldliness characterized the reign of Elizabeth. The Stuart reign was characterized by controversy in religion and politics; the open rupture between the king and Parliament was protracted into the great Civil War. Puritan standards became triumphant during this period. Literature, which always reflects life, presented the somber tone of the age and was in large part religious. In 1609 the Roman Catholic English version of the Bible, the *Douai Bible*, was issued from Douai, France. The *King James Version of the Bible* was printed in 1611. It is impossible to overestimate the influence of both translations upon the lives of the people and upon the language of the day. The study of the Bible became more universal, so much so that it colored the imagination and the speech of the common people. Even those who were irreligious in their lives spoke in the language of the Scriptures.

The Puritan Age. The great literature of the Elizabethan age was in poetry. With one exception, John Milton, the main achievement of the Puritan age was in prose. But the prose writers of the Puritan age were not without imagination and delicacy of humor. Bunyan's *Pilgrim's Progress*, thought by some to be the crowning work of the Puritan imagination, is a product of this age. During the same period, Thomas Fuller brightens his *History of the Worthies of England* by irresistible touches of humor, and Izaak Walton gives expression to delight in nature and rustic pastimes in his *Compleat Angler*; but for the most part the world was looked upon seriously.

Milton.—John Milton is usually regarded as the second greatest name in English literature. He was born eight years before the death of Shakespeare. It may be that Shakespeare saw the boy Milton,—perhaps on Bread street as the great dramatist strolled past Milton's doorstep on his way to the Mermaid Tavern. One likes to think so. Milton's childhood was very happy. He had every advantage of a liberal education and of long quiet years of study at his father's country home in Horton. Here he stored up strength of mind and soul for the years of struggle that followed. Milton's literary career may be divided into three periods: his youth, his manhood, and his old age. It has been called "a drama in three acts." The first may be stated in years as extending from 1623 to 1640; the second, from 1640 to 1660; and the third, from 1660 to 1674.

The first period, that of his youth, was spent at school and with his family at Horton. During this period he wrote the "Hymn on the Morning of Christ's Nativity," the *Masque of Comus*, "Lycidas," "L'Allegro," "Il Penseroso," and a number of his sonnets. Some critics consider *Comus* Milton's finest poem. It is perfect in lyric qualities and, as an apotheosis of virtue, is lofty in conception. "If virtue feeble were, Heaven itself would stoop to her."

"Lycidas," an elegy on Milton's classmate, Edward King, ranks as one of the great elegies in our language. "L'Allegro" and "Il Penseroso" are companion poems; one describes the delights of social life, the other the deep enjoyment of the scholar in seclusion. These poems will always remain favorites for their beautiful imagery and for their truthful study of the emotions. Milton's sonnets have for their theme such subjects as religion, patriotism, domestic affection; whereas the older poets, Shakespeare, Spenser, Wyatt, Surrey, and their imitators, preferred to write sonnets on love.

The second period of Milton's life may be called the time of "storm and stress." For 20 years, from 1640 to 1660, his life was filled with religious and political controversy. He was forced to turn from poetry to prose, and lamenting it he says: "I have the use, as I may account it, but of my left hand." His prose works are voluminous. They are upon varied subjects but upon one theme, liberty. He struck heavy blows for liberty in church and state and in all the relations of life. He pleaded for more freedom of speech and for more liberal ideas in education. His greatest prose work is the *Areopagitica: A Speech for the Liberty of the Press*. In 1652, at the age of 43, Milton became totally blind; but, even in his blindness, he served the Commonwealth as secretary for foreign tongues under Oliver Cromwell, the lord protector, and continued to write his burning pamphlets against the royalists, who were struggling to regain power.

The third period is that which succeeds the Restoration, in 1660. With the return of Charles II, the leaders of the Commonwealth had to flee for their lives. Milton's life was at first endangered, and he was concealed by friends. Later, he preferred retirement where he might have leisure to do the great work of his life, the writing of *Paradise Lost*, *Paradise Regained*, and *Samson Agonistes*.

The beauty of *Paradise Lost* has been compared to that of a stately temple; its style is the loftiest in the whole range of English poetry. Its scenes are laid in heaven and earth and hell, its characters are God and the holy angels, Satan and his legions, and the newly created race of man. In *Paradise Regained* Christ is tempted in the wilderness and resists Satan. In *Samson Agonistes* we have a choral drama modeled upon the form of a Greek tragedy. In the noble grandeur of his work, Milton can be compared only to the great classic writers, Homer and Virgil.

Bunyan.—The second notable name in the Puritan age is that of John Bunyan, the prince of prose writers for his time. *Pilgrim's Progress* has been pronounced the greatest of all allegories. Bunyan's pre-eminence is undoubted. It is no exaggeration to approve this estimate of him: "What Shakespeare is to English dramatists, what Milton is to English epic poets, that John Bunyan is to writers of English allegory." From extreme poverty and ignorance and years of imprisonment in Bedford jail, he rose to the respected position of pastor over a large church. His biographer says of him, "The fame of his sufferings, his genius as a writer, his power as a speaker, gave him unbounded influence among the Baptists; while the beauty of his character and the catholic liberality of his views secured him universal esteem. His ministrations extended over the whole region between Bedford and London."

Pepys and Hyde.—One of the most interesting prose works of the century is Samuel Pepys's *Diary*. It is a gossipy record of nine years and gives a lifelike picture of the gay and profligate portion of society, engaged in vigorous and not always edifying reaction against Puritanism, which fell under the diarist's observation. The chief historical work of the age is the *History of the Great Rebellion* by Edward Hyde, Earl of Clarendon. A curious coincidence marks the life and the death of Clarendon. His life (1609–74) is virtually coextensive with that of John Milton, his principal opponent in the great civil strife. Clarendon has been called the "Cavalier-prince of historic portrait painters," and Milton the "Puritan-prince of epic poets."

Poetic Transition. *Dryden.*—Milton, whose life overlapped Shakespeare's, belongs because of his splendor of style to the Renaissance; Dryden (d. 1700), whose life overlapped Milton's, is the precursor of a new period, a somewhat cynical period which prided itself on its "commonsense" and its epigrammatic wit. Dryden's greatest works are his satires, *MacFlecknoe*, directed against a personal literary enemy, and especially his *Absalom and Achitophel*, a political satire on the Whigs which he wrote in support of the court party of Charles II. Both poems were deadly in effectiveness. English satire to Dryden's time had been rough-and-tumble but he "substituted the rapier for the bludgeon" and his crisp, biting couplets prepared the style that Pope, his successor, was to use. Dryden also wrote rather dull didactic poems such as *The Hind and the Panther* and *Religio Laici*, in which he argued religious questions with himself. As a critic, he ranks very highly but his criticism is scattered through many prefaces and essays. *The Essay on Dramatic Poetry* is most quoted. Also, he wrote many successful plays in a fashion which is now outmoded. One play, *All for Love*, just misses true greatness.

The English revolution of 1688 secured peace for the realm and an opportunity for the development of arts and sciences. The investigations of Newton and the development of philosophy under Locke mark this period.

The Eighteenth Century. Alexander Pope is the literary successor of John Dryden and the representative poet of his time. He was a precocious boy whose life was "one long disease," and as an adult, he was so frail that he had literally to be laced into a canvas corset in order to sit erect. To understand Pope, one must remember his deformity and the spirit of the time in which he lived. The first half of the 18th century is marked by a low standard of morals. Political unrest and political double-dealing, coarse social life,—dull, unimaginative, brutal,—these are the common characteristics ascribed to it. Drunkenness was common and morality was laughed at. Out of such conditions, Pope, Swift, and Steele gathered the material for their satires. Of this distinguished group of writers, Addison and Steele, although very serious, kept a genial and gentle tone.

Pope.—As a boy, Pope heard that there had been many poets but no "perfect poet" and he set out to be one, driving his sickly body and brain to the effort. He became the literary dictator of his age. Dryden's sharpness in the couplet Pope improved upon so well that he is one of the most quoted authors of the language. Scholars dispute whether the Bible, Shakespeare, or Pope is most frequently quoted. Pope was treacherous personally and his intelligence was limited, but he had an uncanny skill in saying the obvious, such as "A little learning is a dangerous thing." As the "perfect poet" he wrote "What's oft been thought but ne'er so well expressed."

Gray's "Elegy," Collins's *Odes*, and Cowper's hymns belong in date to the 18th century, as do the works of Burns and Blake, but their spirit is more that of the following Romantic Period.

Steele and Addison.—The first half of the 18th century is far more remarkable for its prose than for its poetry. A new and excellent field for essayists was found in the *Tatler*, planned by Richard Steele. Periodical papers containing news had existed in England from the time of the Commonwealth, but this was the first periodical designed to have literary merit, to discuss questions of common, everyday interest, and to include lively sketches, anecdotes, and humorous discussions. It was succeeded by the *Spectator*, which appeared every week day morning in the shape of a single leaf, from March 1, 1711 to December 1712; after a suspension it reappeared three times a week in 1714 and extended to 635 numbers. The *Guardian* was begun in 1713 but ceased after the 176th number. Steele was the principal contributor to the *Tatler* and to the *Guardian*, and Addison to the *Spectator*, but papers were also furnished by Swift, Pope, Berkeley, and Hughes. The essays, especially those of Addison, were often models of grace and delicacy and were highly influential in correcting and refining the tone of society.

The Novel.—Prose fiction is another development of the 18th century. Daniel Defoe (c. 1660–1731) first gave to English fiction a simple, direct, matter-of-fact human interest, and the narrative of *Robinson Crusoe* has never been excelled. The *Tale of a Tub* and *Gulliver's Travels*, by Swift, and *The History of John Bull*, by Arbuthnot, are satires in the form of fictitious narratives. Swift's style is famous for its ease and clarity. One of the ironies of history is that *Gulliver's Travels*, the bitterest and most comprehensive satire in the language, has become a favorite children's book. The novel proper became more complex, showing greater diversity in the handling of plot and character, and giving realistic pictures of the social life of the time. *Joseph Andrews*, *Tom Jones*, and *Amelia*, by Fielding, and *Pamela*, *Clarissa Harlowe*, and *Sir Charles Grandison*, by Richardson, were published near the middle of the century. *Peregrine Pickle*, *Humphrey Clinker*, and other novels by Smollett are distinguished for coarse, comic incidents and broad humor. *Tristram Shandy* and *Sentimental Journey* by Sterne, contain passages sparkling with wit and humor and full of rare tenderness of sentiment. The *Vicar of Wakefield*, by Oliver Goldsmith, is a most delightful romantic novel. It is not a book without artistic faults, but it combines delicate humor with sweet human emotion. Goldsmith was a writer in every field of invention, but he will be remembered chiefly because of the Vicar and his family. His "Deserted Village" and his "Traveler" contain passages that cannot be forgotten.

History and Oratory.—The 18th century, which gave us the modern essay and the novel, also produced writers of carefully elaborated and finished history: *History of England* by David Hume; *History of the Decline and Fall of the Roman Empire* by Gibbon; and Robertson's histories of Scotland, Germany, and America. This century produced great orators, like Burke, Fox, and Pitt, and great philosophers, like Berkeley, Paley, and Hume, besides the economist, Adam Smith, and the great lawyer, William Blackstone.

Samuel Johnson.—In striking personality and in power to make others think, Doctor Samuel Johnson was, without doubt, the foremost man of later 18th century literary London. He was the central figure around whom all the literary men and women gathered, the Nestor of his age. Doctor Johnson founded and carried on as sole editor two periodicals, the *Rambler* and the *Idler*, in the style of the *Spectator*, which Addison had made so popular. His most famous work was a *Dictionary of the English Language*. His critical estimates of poetry must be read with caution, and his criticisms are often stilted and overstrained in language. His best prose is his romance, *Rasselas, the Prince of Abyssinia*. Johnson is better known because of the intimate record of his life, written by his biographer, Boswell, than for what he wrote.

Romanticism. At the turn of the century a new spirit which might be called the quality of wonder—a sense of the richness and mystery of life—in contrast to the skeptical temper of the 18th century became dominant. There had been gropings toward this new spirit in such men as Gray, Collins, and Blake. Robert Burns, probably the greatest writer of song lyrics, had written in Scottish dialect. He was thoroughly familiar with the tunes of the countryside and he put into his lyrics the natural things— girls and love and laughter, mice and men.

In 1798 Wordsworth and Coleridge published *Lyrical Ballads*—a dramatic announcement of a new era. Like Burns, Wordsworth drew on the simple things of life for materials but added a philosophic comprehension of little things. Wordsworth is known as a "nature poet" because of his sense of communion with the physical world. Wordsworth also insisted on honest language, and he killed once and for all the idea that there is such a thing as "poetic diction"—a language for poetry distinct from the speech of men. Among his representative poems are "Tintern Abbey," "Ode on Intimations of Immortality," "Expostulation and Reply," and "Resolution and Independence." *The Prelude*, in fourteen books, describes the development of a poetic personality.

Coleridge had only a brief period of poetic production but for magic and flair of imagination he is unequalled. Unlike Wordsworth, in his best work such as "The Ancient Mariner," "Kubla Khan," and "Christabel," he took for his subject matter the far away in time and space. He also was a great critic, in his lectures and *Biographia Literaria*. These two poets with their friend Southey are called *The Lake Poets* because of their residence in the Lake district.

Often called *The Revolutionary Poets* are Byron and Shelley. Wordsworth and Coleridge had in their youth been in sympathy with the French Revolution but later turned reactionary. Byron in the later cantos of *Childe Harold*, with smashing rhetoric expresses the individual's defiance of the world in which he finds himself. In the great and rollicking satire *Don Juan*, he makes fun of that world Byron's earlier cantos of *Childe Harold* so completely eclipsed Scott's poetry (*Lady of the Lake, Marmion*) that Scott turned to the novel. Another popular poet was Thomas Moore whose oriental romance *Lalla Rookh* is not read today although his song lyrics retain a well deserved popularity. Shelley equalled Byron in revolutionary ardor. His personal lyrics are intense and beautiful. Politically, he believed in the possibility of a perfect world. The world he desired and its way of attainment he pictures in *Prometheus Unbound*. His magnificent "Ode to the West Wind," builds up in the last stanza to a burst of symphonic music and triumphant hope.

Keats, another great poet of the period, was not indifferent to political ideas but his greatest quality is amazing responsiveness to the beauty of the physical world in which we live and his skill in making his reader also respond. "The Eve of St. Agnes," "Ode to a Nightingale," and "Ode on A Grecian Urn" all show his richness of appreciation.

The Victorian Age. The prose of this first half of the 19th century also takes high rank. Scott will always be remembered as the creator of the historical novel; Charles Lamb, for his rare humor and delicate use of language. His *Essays of Elia* have been called the best representative of the personal, chatty essay in English. De Quincey's *Opium Eater* and his *English Mail Coach* are also brilliant specimens of English. Mill, Bentham, and Malthus are the chief contributors to philosophical prose.

In 1837 Queen Victoria ascended the throne. The rest of the century is usually called the Victorian age. This age is remarkable, not for the development of any new type of literature, but for the quantity and general excellence of literature in every department. Representative names of the Victorian age are Browning, Tennyson, Matthew Arnold, the Rossettis, in poetry; Thackeray, Dickens, George Eliot, Trollope, in prose fiction; Carlyle, Macaulay, Ruskin, Matthew Arnold, Leslie Stephen, in essay writing; Spencer, Newman, Hamilton, Darwin, Tyndall, Huxley, Faraday, Mill, in philosophy and science; Milman, Grote, Froude, Freeman, Buckle, Green, and Lecky, in history.

Novelists.—Problems of life occupy the minds of the Victorian writers. It is an age of scientific thought and of practical reform. There is an upward struggle of the masses, a striving for better government, for higher moral ideals. Prose and poetry alike are imbued with an ethical purpose. Dickens desired to bring out what he called "the romantic aspect of familiar things," and he began with the study of "vicious poverty." Most of Dickens's novels were inspired by a firm purpose to accomplish some reform. While Dickens with inimitable humor and exuberant optimism was presenting the cause of the submerged poor, Thackeray wrote of the follies of the upper classes of society, and George Eliot pictured the English middle class. These great novelists pictured the interdependence of human beings, the relation that every man bears to his surroundings. Thus fiction kept in close touch with the social ideas of the time. Later in the century, Meredith wrote brilliantly in a mannered style not much approved today, and Stevenson wrote romantic yarns, of which *Treasure Island* is one of his best.

Poets and Critics.—Alfred Tennyson carried on the richness of Keats allied to the moral seriousness of his own age. It has been said that all of his Knights of King Arthur (*Idylls of the King*) are Victorian gentlemen on the way to church. Nevertheless he did retell the old stories effectively, and his *In Memoriam*, with its expression of grief and ultimate faith, is one of the great English elegies. His best lyrics, although sometimes thin in emotional content, are technically nearly perfect. Robert Browning was more robust in style and adventurous of mind. His greatest contribution is his effort to understand human motive, which he attempted through his "dramatic monologues," a literary form which he perfected. *The Ring and the Book* (1868), which is an extreme elaboration of the form, is unquestionably one of the great books of the century. Matthew Arnold as a poet published little, but that of such high quality that it places him as one of the great poets. His critical and controversial works are numerous. *The Essays in Criticism* which came out over a series of years and *Culture and Anarchy* (1869) are his most important prose works. Thomas Carlyle was crusty and dyspeptic of temper, but he believed in personal integrity, the essential spirituality of the world and, above all, in the destruction of shams. *Sartor Resartus* and *Past and Present* are his great works. Ruskin saw a relationship between economics, art, and daily life. His art criticism is not now highly esteemed but his basic idea of good workmanship under good conditions has never been challenged.

In 1847, still in his teens, Dante Gabriel Rossetti wrote the first version of *The Blessed Damozel* but he matured and revised his work and published his *Poems* in 1870. His younger sister Christina wrote lyrics of great delicacy. In 1886, Algernon Charles Swinburne scandalized Victorian England with his *Poems and Ballads*. He is famous for his skillful control of every device known to English prosody.

Transition. According to modern standards, the "naughty nineties" were neither so naughty nor so gay as they were supposed to be, but there was a revolt from Victorian formalism and a great deal of talk about "Aestheticism" and "beautiful sins." As early as the seventies Gilbert and Sullivan with their operettas had begun making fun of almost everything. Less healthy was the brilliant conversationalist Oscar Wilde, who put his wit to advantage in such plays as *Lady Windermere's Fan* (1892) and his drollery in *The Importance of Being Earnest* (1895), one of the best farces in English. His *Salome*, written in French, was illustrated in black and white by the brilliant but sinister artist Aubrey Beardsley. Arthur Symons wrote poetry; as an editor of *The Savoy* he encouraged artistic adventure. John Davidson, Ernest Dowson, and Lionel Johnson were writing skillful verse, and Francis Thompson wrote "The Hound of Heaven," a great religious poem. In the nineties there existed in London The Rhymer's Club, whose membership is not perfectly clear. Somewhere in the late seventies or eighties Gerard Manley Hopkins was writing, but he received no recognition until the publication of his poems in 1918. Most significant in the late 1800's was the sense of stir and the beginning of recognition of such diverse figures as Kipling, Hardy, and Yeats.

Twentieth Century. *Prose and Drama.*— Thomas Hardy must be considered a remarkable man. He began publishing novels in 1873 and through the beginning of the next century they were treated with increasing respect. From 1904 to 1908 he published *The Dynasts*, a poetic drama in 19 acts and 130 scenes plus prologues and epilogues, dealing with the Napoleonic Wars, and in 1909, when over 70, he began publishing poetry. His most significant novels are *The Return of the Native* (1878), *Tess of the D'Urbervilles* (1891), and *Jude the Obscure* (1895). He is unsparing in his realism; he has been called a "philosophic realist." Kipling was a young newspaper correspondent in India selling his books cheaply on newspaper stalls in the late eighties. The news of him spread and he became a sensation. His stories are adroit; his vocabulary, no matter what subject he deals with, is accurate. *Kim* is his best book. *The Jungle Books* have been loved by generations of children. His poetry varies. Everyone knows "Mandalay." His "Tommy Atkins" poems have endeared him to the British army all around the world. Kipling also wrote deeper poetry as in "Recessional," where he asks "Lord God of Hosts, be with us yet!"

Joseph Conrad, Polish by birth, learned English "the language of his secret choice" only after he was 21 but became one of the most remarkable stylists in the language. His novels frequently have far Eastern or shipboard settings which reflect his long experience in the merchant marine. They are, however, predominantly psychological, involving very subtle analysis of human motive. *Lord Jim* (1900) is his greatest, but *Youth*, *Chance*, and *Victory* also display his genius admirably.

John Galsworthy had published a series of distinguished novels before he developed the theme upon which his fame must really rest. In 1906 he published *The Man of Property*; in 1920 he returned to the Forsyte family, adding in subsequent years two more novels which were combined into the trilogy *The Forsyte Saga*. Later he wrote six more novels ending with *One More River* (1933) and a volume of short stories dealing with the Forsytes. In addition to being first class novels, the Forsyte series is a remarkable social document. He also wrote more than 25 plays. *Old English* exhibits the same sense of character he showed in *The Forsyte Saga*. As a dramatist he mainly is concerned with social questions: the true nature of justice in *Justice*, personal obligations in *Loyalties*.

Arnold Bennett wrote much. His best work is *The Old Wives' Tale*, although a series of novels dealing with the industrial cities (*Clayhanger*, etc.) is preferred by some critics. H. G. Wells also was a prolific writer. He made his reputation with pseudoscientific romances such as *The Time Machine* but at the time of his death in 1946 he himself felt them outmoded, as science had gone beyond him. Some novels such as *Tono Bungay* retain their freshness. There was an energy and comprehensiveness to Wells's mind which influenced his age. To his *The Outline of History* scholars object on details but admire the large plan.

William DeMorgan (1839–1917) wrote his first and best novel *Joseph Vance* when he was 66 and then wrote eight more. His books have considerable charm. W. H. Hudson (1841–1922) had a great vogue in the 1920's. His appreciation of nature and the grace of his writing in *Green Mansions* was recognized, but he is a naturalist rather than a novelist. C. M. Doughty (1843–1926), in his *Travels in Arabia Deserta*, wrote one of the great travel books. After World War I, H. M. Tomlinson wrote another, *The Sea and the Jungle*, spicy with

humanity and gifted phrase. T. E. Lawrence (Lawrence of Arabia), who had been the leading British agent in the Near East, re-enlisted as a private because he wanted to be "anonymous" and wrote *The Seven Pillars of Wisdom*. D. H. Lawrence (1885–1930) is marked by power and ruthlessness in his stories and novels. *Lady Chatterley's Lover* is his most sensational novel; *Women in Love*, his best.

Somerset Maugham was versatile. His comedies, such as *The Circle*, are sophisticated and sparkling; the dramatization of his story *Rain* is stark and dreadful. *Of Human Bondage* is one of the best examples of the autobiographical novel in English. The half century has produced many other novelists of ability. Notable are E. M. Forster (*Passage to India*); J. B. Priestly (*The Good Companion*); C. S. Forester, whose *Captain Horatio Hornblower* is an excellent historical novel. P. G. Wodehouse is a master of English foolery, and Dorothy S. Sayers was a modern master of detective fiction. Lytton Strachey with his *Eminent Victorians* set a fashion in "debunking" biography. G. K. Chesterton, a master of paradox, and Hilaire Belloc were important essayists and critics. Max Beerbohm was a cartoonist and writer, and his caustic wit, always fair, was notable.

Bertrand Russell and Sir Winston Churchill received Nobel prizes in literature in 1950 and 1953 respectively for works of nonfiction. Russell was noted as a mathematician and philosopher; Churchill published monumental historical works.

A number of important novelists emerged in the middle 20th century. Among notable women writers, Dorothy Richardson (*Pilgrimage*, 1915–38) was one of the first to use the stream-of-consciousness technique. Virginia Woolf adapted this technique to her own intellectual and expressionistic style (*To the Lighthouse*, 1927), and she in turn had a strong impact on writers and thinkers. Anglo-Irish Elizabeth Bowen told her stories with a distinctly feminine touch. Dame Rebecca West published an excellent travel diary, *Black Lamb and Grey Falcon*, in 1941. Others include philosopher-novelist Iris Murdoch and Ivy Compton-Burnett.

Many writers made a commentary on their times through their fiction. Outstanding of these is William Golding, whose *Lord of the Flies*, 1955, was a delayed success. Gabriel Fielding in *The Birthday King*, 1963, examined Hitler's Germany. Also important are C. P. Snow and Angus Wilson.

Satirists abound in 20th-century British literature. The most gifted include Wyndham Lewis (*Self Condemned*, 1955), George Orwell (*Animal Farm*, 1945), Evelyn Waugh (*Brideshead Revisited*, 1945), and Kingsley Amis (*Lucky Jim*, 1954).

Graham Greene gained a wide popular audience with his novels; *The Power and the Glory*, 1940, is concerned with good and evil. L. P. Hartley is highly rated for his trilogy *Eustace and Hilda*, 1944–47. Anthony Powell, with his projected sequence of novels called *The Music of Time* (1951–) has been likened to Marcel Proust. A master of fantasy, J. R. R. Tolkien published *The Lord of the Rings* trilogy in 1954–56. Lawrence Durrell dealt with love and art in the *Alexandria Quartet* (1956–60). Allan Sillitoe portrayed the English working class in *Saturday Night and Sunday Morning* (1959) and received critical praise for his imaginative short-story collection, *The Loneliness of the Long-Distance Runner* (1960). P. H. Newby is a prolific writer of sophisticated humor.

Drama. The English stage early in the century was dominated by George Bernard Shaw, an Irishman, and James Barrie, a Scotsman. Shaw began to attain prominence in the nineties but with the appearance of *Man and Superman* (1901–03) his position was established. He is sharp of tongue, paradoxical of thought, and has a real genius for stage surprises. Among other plays of his are *Arms and the Man*, and *Caesar and Cleopatra*. Barrie, in contrast, is tender and sentimental. *Peter Pan* really established his reputation. *What Every Woman Knows* is a favorite. Maugham, Milne, and Galsworthy brought out distinguished plays between the two wars. John Van Druten, a naturalized American, produced *The Young Woodley*, a play dealing with English public school life. The thirties saw the emergence of the brilliant Noel Coward. His wit is his best asset, but he is not afraid of seriousness. His best plays are *Bittersweet*, *Private Lives*, and *Tonight at Eight-thirty*. Terence Rattigan (*O Mistress Mine*, 1945) and Christopher Fry (*The Lady's Not for Burning*, 1949) have been prominent playwrights in their time. J. B. Priestley's plays, particularly the humorous ones, achieved notable success (*The Good Companions* and *When We Are Married*). John Whiting skillfully adapted Aldous Huxley's *The Devils of Loudun* into a play. Harold Pinter's plays (*The Collection*, 1961) are straightforward, with a minimum of symbolism. Other significant playwrights include Arnold Wesker, Peter Shaffer, James Bridie, Peter Ustinov, Shelagh Delaney, and Anne Jellicoe.

Poetry. The skill of Tennyson and the frail and beautiful lyrics of the 1890's stifled poetry at the turn of the century, but there was a change coming. Masefield published his *Everlasting Mercy* (1911) in which a drunkard gains grace in some very intentionally crude verses and some beautiful pages. In 1918 the poet laureate Robert Bridges published the poems of Gerard Manley Hopkins (d. 1889). Also in operation were the Imagists, and the old traditional formality was shaken. Masefield wrote some exquisite sonnets in traditional form, notably "On Growing Old" and vigorous narratives such as *Dauber*. Masefield succeeded Bridges as poet laureate. Bridges' *The Testament of Beauty* will probably stand as his greatest work but his publication in 1918 of his old classmate's poems (Hopkins and Bridges were together at Oxford in 1863) had a profound influence on the course of modern poetry. Hopkins ad-

vanced a technique called "sprung rhythm" and insisted on intensity of phrase. A. E. Housman (*A Shropshire Lad*, 1896, and *Last Poems*, 1922), with his perfectly written lyrics of great charm in spite of their pervading melancholy, was a distinguished figure. In the years prior to World War I, the series of *Georgian Anthologies* printed such poets as Walter de la Mare, a master of music, Wilfred Gibson, William H. Davies, Ralph Hodgson, and Rupert Brooke, all of whom went on to distinction. Brooke, killed in the war, is justly famous for his sonnets. His war poetry may be contrasted with the bitter poems of Gibson and Siegfried Sassoon. Hardy's reputation as a poet continued to increase.

In the late 1930's, the most striking poets to emerge were W. H. Auden, Stephen Spender, C. Day-Lewis, and Louis MacNeice. Of these Auden and Spender are most influential. Welsh-born Dylan Thomas established himself as a major poet of the century before his early death. Some of his best work appears in *Deaths and Entrances* (1946).

Some 20th-century poets resisted modern trends. Dame Edith Sitwell was particularly hostile to the moderns. John Heath-Stubbs used classical forms, often translating or adapting Greek and Latin verse. The poetry of Blake strongly influenced Vernon Watkins, and John Betjeman revived the Victorian style of poetry.

Also known as a novelist, Lawrence Durrell has published lyrical and meditative verse. Robert Graves has crafted highly original poems, in addition to his novels and other works.

A separatist Scottish literary movement surged in the 20th century. At the fore is Hugh MacDiarmid, who writes vigorously in a Scots dialect of his own. A younger poet, W. H. Graham, is also well known beyond Scotland.

TABLE OF ENGLISH LITERATURE

Time	Author	Prose Works	Poetry and Drama
?	Unknown		The Far-Traveler.
?	Unknown		Beowulf.
665 (about)	Cædmon		Paraphrase of the Scriptures.
673–735	Bede	Ecclesiastical History	Poems.
750 (about)	Cynewulf		Christ, Elene, Andreas.
849–901	Alfred the Great	Translations	
1095–1143	William of Malmesbury	History of Kings of England	
1100–1154	Geoffrey of Monmouth	History of English Kings	
1200 (about)	Layamon		Chronicles of Britain, Brut.
1324–1384	John Wiclif	Translation of Bible, Sermons	
1325–1408	John Gower		Ballads, Lover's Confession.
1332–1400	William Langland		Piers Plowman.
1340–1400	Geoffrey Chaucer		Canterbury Tales, Short Poems.
1422–1491	William Caxton	Translation (History of Troy)	
1430–?	Thomas Malory	Le Morte D'Arthur	
1478–1535	Sir Thomas More	Utopia	
1484–1536	William Tyndale	Translation of New Testament	
1488–1568	Miles Coverdale	Translation of Bible	
1503–1542	Sir Thomas Wyatt		Sonnets, Lyrics.
1536–1608	Thomas Sackville		Mirror for Magistrates.
1552–1599	Edmund Spenser		Faery Queen, Shepheardes Calender.
1554–1586	Sir Philip Sidney	Arcadia	Sonnets.
1559–1634	George Chapman		Translation of Homer, Dramas.
1561–1626	Francis Bacon	Essays, Philosophy	
1564–1593	Christopher Marlowe		Dramas (Faustus), Poems.
1564–1616	William Shakespeare		Dramas, Poems, Sonnets.
1573–1631	John Donne	Sermons	Lyrics, Sacred Sonnets.
1573–1637	Ben Jonson		Dramas (The Alchemist, Volpone).
1577–1640	Robert Burton	Anatomy of Melancholy	
1579–1625	John Fletcher		Dramas (Philaster, Maid's Tragedy).
1584–1616	Francis Beaumont		
?1580–?1625	John Webster		Dramas (The Duchess of Malfi).
1591–1674	Robert Herrick		Poems.
1593–1633	George Herbert		Poems (The Temple).
1593–1683	Izaak Walton	The Compleat Angler	
1608–1674	John Milton	Areopagitica	L'Allegro, Comus, Paradise Lost.
1609–1674	Edward Hyde	History of the Great Rebellion	
1612–1680	Samuel Butler		Hudibras.
1613–1667	Jeremy Taylor	Holy Living	
1628–1688	John Bunyan	Pilgrim's Progress, Holy War	
1631–1700	John Dryden	Essays, Prefaces	Absalom and Achitophel.
1632–1704	John Locke	Philosophy	
1633–1703	Samuel Pepys	Diary	
1661–1731	Daniel Defoe	Robinson Crusoe	
1667–1745	Jonathan Swift	Gulliver's Travels, Tale of a Tub.	
1672–1719	Joseph Addison	Essays (The Spectator)	Dramas, Poems.

TABLE OF ENGLISH LITERATURE—Con.

Time	Name	Prose	Poetry and Drama
	AUTHORS		**REPRESENTATIVE WORKS**
1672–1729	Sir Richard Steele	Essays (The Tatler)	
1685–1753	Bishop Berkeley	Philosophy	
1688–1744	Alexander Pope		Poems (Essay on Man).
1689–1761	Samuel Richardson	Novels (Clarissa Harlowe, Pamela)	
1700–1748	James Thomson		The Seasons.
1707–1754	Henry Fielding	Novels (Tom Jones, Amelia)	
1709–1784	Samuel Johnson	Dictionary, Rasselas, Essays	
1711–1776	David Hume	History of England	
1713–1768	Laurence Sterne	Novels (Tristram Shandy)	
1716–1771	Thomas Gray	Criticism	Poems.
1721–1759	William Collins		Odes.
1721–1771	T. George Smollett	Novels (Humphrey Clinker)	
1728–1774	Oliver Goldsmith	Vicar of Wakefield, Essays	Plays (She Stoops to Conquer), Poems.
1729–1797	Edmund Burke	Essays, Speeches (On Conciliation)	
1731–1800	William Cowper		Poems (The Task, John Gilpin).
1737–1794	Edward Gibbon	Decline and Fall of the Roman Empire.	
1740–1795	James Boswell	Life of Samuel Johnson.	
1745–1833	Hannah More	Cœlebs in Search of a Wife	Sacred Dramas.
1748–1832	Jeremy Bentham	Political Essays	
1749–1806	Charles James Fox	Orations	
1751–1816	Richard B. Sheridan	Speeches	Plays (The Rivals).
1757–1827	William Blake		Songs of Innocence and Experience.
1759–1796	Robert Burns		Lyrics.
1759–1806	William Pitt	Orations	
1767–1849	Maria Edgeworth	Novels (Castle Rackrent)	
1770–1835	James Hogg	Shepherd's Calendar	Pastorals.
1770–1850	William Wordsworth		Poems (Tintern Abbey).
1771–1832	Sir Walter Scott	Waverley Novels	Lady of the Lake.
1771–1845	Sydney Smith	Sermons, Essays	
1772–1834	S. T. Coleridge	Essays	Poems (The Ancient Mariner).
1774–1843	Robert Southey	Biographies of Nelson and Wesley	Poems (Madoc).
1775–1817	Jane Austen	Pride and Prejudice, Emma	
1775–1834	Charles Lamb	Essays of Elia	
1775–1864	Walter S. Landor	Imaginary Conversations	Count Julian, Heroic Idyls.
1776–1850	Jane Porter	Scottish Chiefs	
1777–1844	Thomas Campbell		Pleasures of Hope, Lyrics.
1777–1859	Henry Hallam	History	
1778–1830	William Hazlitt	Table Talk, English Poets	
1779–1852	Thomas Moore	Biographies	Lalla Rookh, Irish Melodies.
1784–1859	Leigh Hunt	Essays, Sketches, Memoirs	Poems.
1785–1854	John Wilson	Noctes Ambrosianæ	Poems.
1785–1859	Thomas De Quincey	An English Opium Eater	
1788–1824	Lord Byron	Letters	Poems (Childe Harold).
1792–1822	Percy B. Shelley	Essay on Poetry	Poems (Prometheus Unbound).
1792–1848	Frederick Marryat	Mr. Midshipman Easy	
1793–1835	Felicia Hemans		Lyrics.
1795–1821	John Keats	Letters	Poems and Odes.
1795–1881	Thomas Carlyle	French Revolution, Cromwell	
1797–1868	Samuel Lover	Handy Andy, Rory O'More	Songs, Ballads.
1799–1845	Thomas Hood		Poems.
1800–1859	Thomas B. Macaulay	Essays, History of England	Lays of Ancient Rome.
1801–1890	John H. Newman	Essays (The Idea of a University)	Poems, Hymns.
1803–1873	Edward Bulwer-Lytton	Last Days of Pompeii	
1804–1881	Benjamin Disraeli	Novels (Lothair, Vivian Grey)	
1806–1861	E. B. Browning		Poems (Aurora Leigh).
1806–1872	Charles Lever	Novels (Charles O'Malley)	
1809–1892	Alfred Tennyson		In Memoriam, Idylls of the King.
1811–1863	William M. Thackeray	Novels (Vanity Fair, The Newcomes)	
1812–1870	Charles Dickens	David Copperfield, Oliver Twist	
1812–1889	Robert Browning		Poems (The Ring and the Book).
1814–1884	Charles Reade	The Cloister and the Hearth	Plays (Peg Woffington).
1815–1882	Anthony Trollope	Novels (Barchester Towers)	
1816–1855	Charlotte Brontë	Novels (Jane Eyre, The Professor)	
1818–1894	James A. Froude	Essays, History of England	
1819–1875	Charles Kingsley	Novels (Hypatia)	Poems.
1819–1880	George Eliot	Novels (Silas Marner)	Poems (Spanish Gypsy).
1819–1900	John Ruskin	Essays (Modern Painters)	
1820–1897	Jean Ingelow		Poems.
1821–1862	Henry T. Buckle	History of Civilization in England.	
1822–1888	Matthew Arnold	Essays, Criticism	Poems (Sohrab and Rustum).
1822–1896	Thomas Hughes	Tom Brown at Oxford	
1824–1889	Wilkie Collins	Novels (Woman in White)	
1825–1895	Thomas H. Huxley	Essays (Man's Place in Nature)	
1825–1900	R. D. Blackmore	Novels (Lorna Doone)	
1826–1887	Dinah Maria Mulock	Novels (John Halifax, Gentleman)	Poems.
1828–1882	Dante G. Rossetti		Poems (The Blessed Damozel).
1828–1909	George Meredith	Novels (Diana of the Crossways)	Poems (Modern Love).
1834–1896	William Morris	Essays (Mural Painting)	Poems (Earthly Paradise).
1835–1902	Samuel Butler	Novel (The Way of all Flesh)	
1837–1909	A. C. Swinburne	Essays (Study of Shakespeare)	Poems, Ballads.
1838–1922	James Bryce	American Commonwealth	
1838–1923	John Morley	Essays, Biography	
1839–1917	Wm. F. De Morgan	Novels (Joseph Vance)	
1840–1928	Thomas Hardy	Novels (Wessex Tales)	Poems, Drama (The Dynasts).
1844–1889	Gerard Manley Hopkins		Poems.
1844–1930	Robert Bridges		Poems, Shorter Poems, Plays (Ulysses)

TABLE OF ENGLISH LITERATURE—Con.

Time	Author	Prose Works	Poetry and Drama
1850—1894	Robert L. Stevenson . . .	Essays, Romances	Child's Garden of Verses.
1855—1934	Arthur W. Pinero		Plays (The Second Mrs. Tanqueray).
1856—1950	George B. Shaw	Essays	Plays (Man and Superman).
1857—1924	Joseph Conrad	Novels (Lord Jim, Victory) . .	
1859—1930	Sir A. Conan Doyle . . .	Novels (Sherlock Holmes) . . .	
1859—1936	A. E. Housman		Poems (A Shropshire Lad).
1860—1937	Sir James Barrie	Novels (The Little Minister) . .	Plays (Peter Pan).
1861—1941	Sir Rabindranath Tagore .	Essays, Stories (Gitanjali) . . .	Poems.
1865—1936	Rudyard Kipling	Tales (Jungle Book, Kim) . . .	Barrack-room Ballads, Poems.
1866—1946	Herbert G. Wells	Novels, History	
1867—1931	Arnold Bennett	Novels (The Old Wives' Tale) .	Plays.
1867—1933	John Galsworthy	Novels, Stories, Essays	Plays (Loyalties).
1868—1915	Stephen Phillips		Poems, Dramas (Herod).
1870—1953	Hilaire Belloc	Essays, Stories	Poems.
1872—1970	Bertrand Russell	Philosophy	
1873—1956	Walter de la Mare	Novels (Memoirs of a Midget) .	Poems (Peacock Pie).
1874—1936	G. K. Chesterton	Essays, Fiction	Poems.
1874—1965	Sir Winston Churchill . .	History, biography, oratory . .	
1874—1965	W. Somerset Maugham . .	Novels	Plays (Rain).
1878—1967	John Masefield	Novels, Stories	Poems, Plays.
1879—1970	Edward Morgan Forster .	Novels (Passage to India) . . .	
1880—1932	Lytton Strachey	Biography (Eminent Victorians)	
1880—1958	Alfred Noyes	Essays, Criticism	Poems (The Loom of Years).
1882—1937	John Drinkwater	Essays	Poems, Plays (Lincoln).
1882—1941	Virginia Woolf	Novels (Mrs. Dalloway).	
1882—1956	A. A. Milne	Novels, Essays	Poems, Plays (The Dover Road).
1885—1930	David H. Lawrence . . .	Novels (Women In Love) . . .	Poems, Plays.
1887—1964	Dame Edith Sitwell . . .	Novels (Fanfare for Elizabeth) .	Poems.
1888—1923	Katherine Mansfield . . .	Stories (The Garden Party) . .	
1888—1935	Thomas E. Lawrence . . .	Memoirs(Seven Pillars of Wisdom)	
1889—1975	Arnold Toynbee	History	
1892—1962	Richaid Aldington	Novels (All Men Are Enemies) .	Poems (Images of Desire).
1892—1962	Victora Sackville-West . .	Novels (The Edwardians) . . .	
1894—	J. B. Priestley	Novels (The Good Companions)	Plays.
1894—1963	Aldous Huxley	Novels (Eyeless In Gaza) . . .	Poems.
1895—	Robert Graves	Novels (I, Claudius)	Poems.
1896—1974	Edmund Blunden	Criticism	Poems (Poems of Many Years).
1898—1963	C. S. Lewis	Essays (Screwtape Letters) . .	
1899—1973	Noel Coward		Plays (Hay Fever, Cavalcade).
1899—1966	Cecil Scott Forester . . .	Novels (Captain Hornblower) . .	
1903—1950	George Orwell	Novels, (Animal Farm)	
1903—	A. L. Rowse	History, Biography	
1903—1966	Evelyn Waugh	Novels (Brideshead Revisited) .	
1904—	Graham Greene	Novels, stories	
1904—	Christopher Isherwood . .	Novels	Plays (with W. H. Auden)
1904—1972	C. Day-Lewis*	Criticism (The Poetic Image) . .	Poems (An Italian Visit).
1905—	Anthony Powell	Novels (Music of Time) . . .	
1905—	C. P. Snow	Novels (The Search)	
1907—1973	Wystan Hugh Auden . . .		Poems (Collected Poems).
1909—	Stephen Harold Spender .		Ruins and Visions (Poems 1934-42).
1911—	William Golding	Novels (Lord of the Flies) . .	
1912—	Lawrence Durrell	Novels (Alexandria Quartet) . .	Poems.
1914—1953	Dylan Thomas		Poems.
1919—	Iris Murdoch	Novels (The Sandcastle) . . .	
1922—	Kingsley Amis	Novels (Lucky Jim)	

*Chosen poet laureate, 1968.

CANADIAN LITERATURE

French Canadian Literature. The most important French Canadian prose writings are *Les relations des Jesuits; Les anciens canadiens,* by Philippe Aubert de Gaspé, a mine of information about life under the old Régime, translated into English by Charles G. D. Roberts; *Histoire du Canada,* by François Xavier Garneau, which started the first school of French Canadian literature; *Un pèlerinage au pays d'Evangeline,* by Abbé Casgrain. The first school of French Canadian poetry developed in Quebec between 1860 and 1870. Gérin-Lajoie wrote a truly national poem, *Un canadien errant,* voicing the homesickness of a French Canadian exiled on account of the rebellion of 1837. Octave Crémazie, regarded as the father of French Canadian poetry, wrote verse of distinct merit, including colorful, sentimental descriptions of the Canadian scene. Pamphile Le May translated Longfellow's *Evangeline* into French. Louis Fréchette, who married a sister of William Dean Howells and who is regarded as the greatest French Canadian poet, approached epic grandeur in his chief poem, *La légende d'un peuple.* The second school of French Canadian poetry began in Montreal in 1895. To it belong in fact Emile Nelligan and Albert Lozeau, and in spirit Paul Morin.

English Canadian Literature. The Hon. Joseph Howe, of the Loyalist tradition, whose published speeches are the best political literature in Canada, powerfully influenced Canadian prose by publishing in his paper, the *Novascotian,* his own sketches, the papers of the *Club,* of which he and Haliburton were members, and the series of sketches by Haliburton that constitute *The Clockmaker.*

Thomas Chandler Haliburton, a native of Nova Scotia, after a long career in that province as lawyer and judge, removed to England in 1856, where he was elected to the British House of Commons. *The Clockmaker, or The Sayings and Doings of Sam Slick of Slickville,* the first edition of the first series of which appeared in book form at Halifax in 1836, was the first Canadian work to achieve widespread fame and translation.

The greatest Canadian humorists in nonfictional prose since Haliburton are Peter McArthur and Stephen Leacock.

As to history and biography, the older Canadian historians, whether writing voluminously like William Kingsford or on a smaller scale like James Hannay, tended to lack style when they were accurate or to fall short of fairness and proportion when they wrote with imaginative power. In recent years, Canadian scholars have done much diligent and careful work in organizing and writing the history of their country. Of those who have written somewhat extensively and have combined good material and style, William Wood is one of the best. There have been at least a dozen good biographers, but none of high distinction.

As literary essayists may be mentioned Sir William Osler, Sir Andrew MacPhail, and Professor Archibald M. MacMechan.

Canada has a good literature of voyages, travels, and color writing. This includes Alexander Mackenzie's *Voyages from Montreal through the Continent of North America* (1801); Alexander Henry's *Travels and Adventures in Canada and the Indian Territories* (1807); Mrs. Jameson's *Winter Studies and Summer Rambles in Canada* (1838); Mrs. Moodie's *Roughing It in the Bush* (1852); Lady Edgar's *Ten Years of Peace and War in Upper Canada* (1890); L. J. Burpee's *Search for the Western Sea* (1907); and the recent color writing of Arthur Heming, W. H. Blake, "Katherine Hale" (Mrs. J. W. Garvin), and F. P. Grove.

Fiction. What is regarded as the first Canadian novel, Mrs. Frances Brooke's *Emily Montague*, a story of frontier life, was published in 1769. In 1832, John Richardson published *Wacousta*, the earliest Canadian novel that has secured and held a place in Canadian fiction. To the middle of the 19th century belong several stories of pioneer life by Catherine Parr Traill and her sister, Susanna Moodie. James De Mille wrote voluminously,—humorous, romantic, and juvenile fiction. William Kirby was the first Canadian novelist to use with great power the romantic material in early Canadian history. His *Golden Dog* (1877), an excellent novel of 18th century life in Quebec, has been widely read in English and in translation into French.

Edward William Thompson did good work in short juvenile fiction. William McLennan wrote habitant tales in prose that correspond somewhat to Drummond's poetic stories, and essayed longer fiction. "Ralph Connor" (Rev. Charles William Gordon) has written novels of the West that have been widely read throughout the English-speaking world. Sara Jeanette Duncan (Mrs. Everard Cotes) wrote clever, humorous novels of travel and of life in India. Sir Gilbert Parker, most popular and productive of Canadian novelists, has set his novels and short stories in every part of the British Empire, but his Canadian fiction is probably his best.

Norman Duncan wrote successful travel sketches, atmosphere stories of land and sea, and juvenile fiction. Margaret Marshall Saunders and Grace Dean McLeod Rogers have attracted attention to Nova Scotia by their fiction. Lucy Maud Montgomery has done a similar work for Prince Edward Island. Gordon Hill Grahame has written fiction set in early French Canada. Robert Stead and Arthur J. Stringer interpret understandingly the Canadian West. William Alexander Fraser, Ernest Thompson Seton, and Charles G. D. Roberts have given Canada great animal fiction. A new school of realism of great promise is represented by Laura Goodman Salverson, Frederick Phillip Grove, and Martha Ostenso writing of the West.

Writing of the East, Mazo de la Roche produced a cycle of novels centering around an imaginary ancestral estate, Jalna, and around the characters who lived there. The popularity of these novels bore witness to the power of her inventive imagination and to its rise above regional limitations. Morley Callaghan belongs likewise to the school of realistic observers, his *Strange Fugitive* and *They Shall Inherit the Earth* being characterized by an incisive directness rare among Canadian authors.

Poetry. The first English Canadian verse of note is credited to Nova Scotia. Joseph Howe wrote some good poems. Oliver Goldsmith, a kinsman of the English Oliver, published *The Rising Village* at London in 1825. Charles Heavysege, an emigrant from England to Montreal, wrote several volumes of verse. His dramatic poem *Saul* was highly praised by Bayard Taylor and Longfellow in the United States and by Coventry Patmore in England. Alexander McLachlan, a disciple of Burns, was widely read in pre-Confederation Canada. Canadian natural scenery appears as poetic subject matter in Charles Sangster's *The St. Lawrence and the Saguenay, and Other Poems* (1856); in Charles Mair's *Dreamland and Other Poems* (1868) and collected poems (1901) (containing his poetic drama *Tecumseh*); and in Isabella Valancy Crawford's *Old Spookses' Pass, Malcolm's Katie, and Other Poems* (1884) and collected poems (1905). Miss Crawford, compared in intensity to Emily Brontë, was an artist in dialect narrative and in original handling and delicate workmanship in lyric.

Charles G. D. Roberts, most versatile of Canadian writers, was the leader of the greatest school of Canadian poetry, the first post-Confederation school. In his poetry he is an exquisite painter of Canadian scenes, a singer of ideals learned from nature, and a lyrist of love. Archibald Lampman, a great admirer of the poetic gift of George Frederick Cameron (most like Shelley of all Canadian poets), throughout his career wrote poetic descriptions of nature that in appreciation of beauty and felicity of diction rival the best work of Keats. Duncan Campbell Scott, who prefixed an excellent memoir to the 1900 edition of Lampman's poems, is one of Canada's greatest poets. Since his first volume in 1893, he has published several volumes of poetry of versatility and range. He images every aspect of the Canadian year, and expresses in apt meters the thoughts, sentiments, or emotional experiences of vastly different characters. William Wilfred Campbell, of the same stock as the poet Thomas Campbell and the novelist Henry Fielding, was chiefly interested in human life, but wrote some good nature poems in addition to his poetry of man. He wrote poetic dramas as well as lyrics and narratives, and essays and novels. Bliss Carman was a worshiper of beauty, especially in nature, and a master of melodious verse. Beginning with *Low Tide on Grand Pré* (1893), he wrote a large amount of excellent poetry and several volumes of prose. Some critics rank him as Canada's major poet. Frederick George Scott published several volumes of poetry, the first in 1888. As a nature poet, he is especially associated with the Laurentians. His broad human sympathy manifests itself in poems on old literary themes, on the subject of empire, and on love and brotherhood. Pauline Johnson, the Indian poetess whose mother belonged to the Howells family, in striking verse interpreted the spirit of Indian life. Ethelwyn Wetherald wrote charming nature poetry.

Somewhat apart are two poets of Irish birth. Thomas D'Arcy McGee, enamored of the cause of freedom, at length came to think that it could not be realized in Ireland, but saw for it a future in Canada. William Henry Drummond in a unique form of dialect monologue has most sympathetically interpreted the French Canadian *habitant* and *voyageur*. E. J. Pratt wrote movingly on heroic themes, such as men against the sea.

Of many later women poets, such as Jean Blewett, Helena Coleman, Virna Sheard, "Katherine Hale," Jean Graham, Louise Morey Bowman, Norah M. Holland, Marjorie Pickthall, the greatest artist is the last. Among the later men to attract considerable attention by their verse are Tom MacInnes, Robert W. Service, Robert Norwood, John McCrae, and Bernard Freeman Trotter.

TABLE OF CANADIAN LITERATURE

AUTHORS		REPRESENTATIVE WORKS	
Time	Name	Prose	Poetry and Drama
1739–1824	Alexander Henry	Travels	
1745–1789	Frances Brooke	Emily Montague	
1763–1820	Alexander Mackenzie	Travels	
1781–1861	Oliver Goldsmith		The Rising Village
1786–1871	Philippe A. de Gaspé	Les Anciens Canadiens	
1796–1852	John Richardson	Fiction, History	
1796–1865	Thomas C. Haliburton	Satiric Humor, History	
1802–1899	Catherine P. Traill	Stories	
1803–1885	Susanna Moodie	Stories, Color Writing	Poems
1804–1873	Joseph Howe	Essays, Orations	Poems
1809–1866	François X. Garneau	History of Canada	
1816–1876	Charles Heavysege		Saul
1817–1906	William Kirby	The Golden Dog	Poems
1818–1896	Alexander McLachlan		Poems
1819–1898	William Kingsford	History of Canada	
1822–1893	Charles Sangster		Poems
1824–1882	Gérin-Lajoie		Poems (French)
1825–1868	Thomas D'A. McGee	History, Oratory	Poems
1827–1879	Octave Crémazie		Poems (French)
1833–1880	James de Mille	Fiction	
1837–1918	Pamphile Le May		Poems (French)
1838–1927	Charles Mair		Poems, Poetic Drama
1839–1908	Louis Fréchette		Poems (French)
1842–1910	James Hannay	History of Acadia	
1844–1910	Lady Edgar	History, Biography	
1849–1919	Sir William Osler	Essays, Orations	
1850–1887	Isabella V. Crawford		Poems
1854–1907	William H. Drummond		Habitant Poems
1856–1904	William McLennan	Habitant Tales	
1860–1937	"Ralph Connor" (C. W. Gordon)	Novels	
1860–1943	Sir Charles G. D. Roberts	Fiction, Animal Tales	Poems
1861–1918	W. Wilfred Campbell	Essays, Novels	Poems, Poetic Dramas
1861–1947	M. Marshall Saunders	Fiction	
1861–1929	Bliss Carman	Essays	Poems
1861–1944	Frederick G. Scott		Poems
1861–1924	W. H. Blake	Color Writing	
1862?–1922	Sara J. Duncan (Mrs. E. Cotes)	Novels	
1862–1932	Sir Gilbert Parker	Fiction	Poems
1862–1947	Duncan C. Scott	Stories	Poems
1866–1924	Peter McArthur	Humor	Poems
1869–1944	Stephen Leacock	Essays, Stories, Humor	
1871–1916	Norman Duncan	Fiction	
1872–1918	John McCrae		Poems
1873–1946	L. J. Burpee	Search for the Western Sea	
1874–1942	Lucy M Montgomery	Novels (Anne of Green Gables)	
1874–1958	Robert W. Service		Rhymes of a Rolling Stone
1875–1924	Albert Lozeau		Poems (French)
1880–1913	Louis Hemon	Novels (Maria Chapdelaine)	
1883–1922	Marjorie L. C. Pickthall	Stories, Novels	Poems, Poetic Drama
1883–1964	Edwin J. Pratt		Poems (Titans, Behind the Log).
1885–1961	Mazo de la Roche	Novels (Jalna)	
1903–	Morley Callaghan	Novels (Strange Fugitive)	Poems
1907–	Hugh MacLennan	Novels (Two Solitudes)	
1910–	Nicholas Monsarrat	Novels (The Cruel Sea; The White Rajah.)	
1912–	Irving Layton		Poems (Balls for a One-armed Juggler; The Improved Binoculars.)
1913–1965	Gwethalyn Graham	Novels (Earth and High Heaven)	
1920–	Arthur Hailey	Novels (The Final Diagnosis; In High Places.)	

AUSTRALIAN LITERATURE

In the last thirty years Australian literature has become recognized as a discrete branch of English literature, and has therefore received special critical and scholarly attention. The principal reasons for this new status are an increased output by writers of distinct merit, a noticeably Australian character of atmosphere, location, plot, and language, and the publication or republication of Australian writers' work in Britain and the United States.

Within Australia there is a great awareness of the growth of a distinctly national literature: the Federal Government has established a Commonwealth Literary Fund which, upon the recommendation of an Advisory Board, awards Fellowships to approved writers, subsidizes the publication of works of literary merit, and provides pensions to older writers who have made significant contributions to the nation's literature. In addition, the Fund supports a series of lectures, delivered annually, in each of the Australian universities and colleges, on the subject of Australian literature. Canberra University College now gives a course in Australian Literature and the University of Sydney is about to appoint a professor of the subject. Courses in Commonwealth Literature, including Australian and New Zealand writing, are now being offered in some American universities. All these developments indicate the growing interest in the creative writing produced in Australia.

Colonial Period. The first creative writing produced in Australia was poetry, and that form of literature has been the most common ever since. Michael Massey Robinson (1744–1826), poet laureate to Governor Lachlan Macquarie, composed commemorative birthday odes for George III and Queen Charlotte from 1810 to 1820 and for George IV's birthday in 1821. These odes, printed in the *Sydney Gazette*, the government journal, provide the starting point of Australian literature. Barron Field (1786–1846), a Judge of the Supreme Court of New South Wales, was one of Lamb's "distant correspondents" and his *First Fruits of Australian Poetry* (1819) was the first book of verse published in Australia. In a much quoted letter to the Judge, Lamb refers delicately to the prevalence of hanging at that time.

CANADIAN WRITERS

Mazo de la Roche wrote the world famous "Jalna" novels. The first book won the $10,000 Atlantic Monthly prize, and in 1936 actress Ethel Barrymore appeared in a play based on the Whiteoaks saga.

Gabrielle Roy is a recently successful novelist. She writes about industrialism in a realistic style. In polished, finished prose, Mlle. Roy sees the industrial world as sordid, soul-destroying slavery.

Madame Germaine Guèvremont laid the background for her novel "The Outlander" in familiar eastern Canada. This novel was written in French.

Thomas Raddall is one of the most successful of contemporary short story writers and historical novelists. He wrote "The Nymph and the Lamp" and several excellent sea stories.

For the style, range, and spirit of his verse, Edwin J. Pratt was recognized as a leading poet of his time.
National Film Board

Stephen Leacock wrote some of Canada's best humorous essays, as well as a number of serious works in economics and political science.

Duncan Campbell Scott was one of Canada's foremost poets. He also was a high government official. He showed great range and versatility.

WORLD WRITERS

Noel Coward

Maurice Maeterlinck

Thomas Mann

Albert Camus
United Press International

Salvador de Madariaga

T. S. Eliot

Boris Pasternak
Intercontinentale

Recalling that some early colonists were convicts, he asks, "Do they grow their own hemp?" The first Australian-born poet was Charles Tompson (1806–1883), whose *Wild Notes from the Lyre of a Native Minstrel* (1826) showed but slight influence of the locality. Sir Henry Parkes (1815–1896), the "Father of Federation," wrote verse of slight merit, but encouraged others by publishing their poetry in his newspaper, *Empire*.

Beginnings of a National Literature. Charles Harpur (1813–1868) was the first important Australian poet. He was a frequent contributor to Parkes' *Empire* and to the *Australian Chronicle*, and published six volumes of poetry, much of which is influenced by Wordsworth. He was the first to use local subject matter extensively, and he employed the ballad form with great effect. His "Midsummer Noon in the Australian Forest" is still popular. His claim to be poetry's "first high priest in this bright southern clime" can be allowed.

Henry Kendall (1839–1882), who took Harpur as his model, was also a contributor to the *Empire*. His *Poems and Songs* (1862) and *Leaves From an Australian Forest* (1869) gained him widespread popularity. He left Sydney and went to Melbourne where he joined a literary circle associated with *The Australasian*, a journal which for a time was a literary arbiter. Intemperance brought on poverty and he returned to Sydney to publish his *Songs from the Mountains* (1880). He received a minor government appointment from Parkes. While Kendall had more vivid imagery than Harpur, he was too bound by traditional English diction to make his poems of Australian rivers, forests, and mountains truly original. His work was nonetheless praised by the London *Athenaeum*.

Adam Lindsay Gordon (1830–1870) was born in the Azores and was educated in England. He settled in South Australia and became a mounted policeman, horse trainer, steeplechase rider, and his own publisher. *Sea Spray and Smoke Drift* (1867) was lauded by both Kendall and Parkes, but the subsequent *Bush Ballads and Galloping Rhymes* (1870) was not immediately successful. When unable to pay the printer's bill, Gordon took his own life. Gordon's output was small but his importance is great: he popularized the outback as a subject for poetry, and established the fashion of writing about horses, cattle, droughts, and the like, that lasted for almost fifty years. Influenced by Byron and Swinburne, his verse is frequently pessimistic, reflective, and marked by frustration.

Later Nineteenth Century. With establishment of the weekly *Bulletin* in Sydney in 1880, the literary center of Australia shifted from Melbourne. Its literary editor, A. G. Stephens (1865–1933), was a poet, dramatist, anthologist, and editor of great merit. He encouraged most of the modern poets and short story writers by publishing their best work in the *Bulletin*. Victor Daley (1858–1905), whose verse is of a Celtic lyric quality and epigrammatic, and E. J. Brady (1869–1952), who wrote numerous poems in the tradition of the bush ballad, as well as many worthwhile poems marked by nostalgia for the sea, were two of the principal poets of the *Bulletin* school. Others were Dowell O'Reilly and Edward Dyson.

Two late nineteenth century poets who stand apart from the above the others are Andrew ("The Banjo") Barton Paterson (1864–1941) and Henry Lawson (1867–1922). Paterson's father was a minor contributor to the *Bulletin*. The son became a newspaper correspondent in China, South Africa, and London. His *The Man From Snowy River* (1895), *Rio Grande's Last Race* (1902) and *Saltbush Bill* (1917), popularized the bush ballad and made Paterson the most popular writer in Australia. His "Waltzing Matilda" is known throughout the world. Paterson avoided the harshness of life in the outback, which Lawson dwelled on, and had both an ever-present sense of humor and a sentimentality for his country. He was awarded the Order of the British Empire for his service to Literature in 1939.

Henry Lawson's mother was editor of the women's page in a newspaper and the author of two volumes of verse. His father was a Norwegian seaman who became a gold-digger. "Faces in the Street," a picture of wretchedness and poverty, appeared in the *Bulletin* in 1888, and thereafter his poems and short stories were published regularly in that journal. Lawson's reputation was firmly established by *While the Billy Boils* (1896) and *On the Track and Over the Sliprails* (1900). He is today regarded as Australia's foremost short story writer and one of its great bush balladists. Lawson rejected Paterson's "inexperienced idealization" of the outback and showed the bush in all its unpleasantness. His stories lacked action and his total output lacked a single piece of sustained composition; yet when he died, he was given a State funeral.

C. J. Dennis (1876–1938) achieved a short-lived yet very widespread fame with the publication of his *Songs of a Sentimental Bloke* (1915) and *Moods of Ginger Mick* (1917). Written in outback and soldier argot, these entertaining verses sold over 140,000 copies in three years.

Contemporary Poetry. The poetry of Dame Mary Gilmore (1865–1962), of which she published over seven volumes, deals mainly with nature, Australia, aborigines, the less fortunate, and democratic themes. She was widely respected. Undoubtedly the most important modern Australian poet is C. J. Brennan (1870–1932). A brilliant scholar, Brennan taught philosophy, Greek, Latin, German, French, and English in the University of Sydney. Intemperance and an unsavory court case, which resulted in a legal separation, caused his dismissal from the university in 1925. Brennan's poems reflect the techniques of Mallarmé, Baudelaire, and the symbolist poets. His "The Wanderer" sequence is a remarkably polished piece of poetry. In the past twenty years Kenneth Slessor, R. G. Howarth, A. D. Hope, Judith Wright, Hugh McCrae, and Roland Robinson have dominated the field of poetry in Australia. Howarth with his lyrics, Hope with his satires, and Robinson with his "Jindyworobak" verse have been especially noteworthy.

Prose and Drama. In Australia the drama has languished. Only Louis Esson (1879–1943) and Douglas Stewart (1913–   ) deserve mention. While Esson is no longer staged, Stewart is very often produced, both on legitimate stage and for radio. His *Ned Kelly* (1943) and *Fire on the Snow* (1948) are excellent verse dramas of a remarkable degree of competence.

Short story writers have not established a firm reputation in Australia since Lawson's time, though E. O. Schlunke, Ken Levis, Gavin Casey, Dal Stivens, and Judith Wright all produce stories of literary interest. *Coast to Coast*, which appears each two years, is an anthology of the best Australian short stories.

Literary criticism in Australia is of a high order. Professor Walter Murdoch of the University of Western Australia, Vance Palmer, R. G. Howarth, S. J. Baker, and Brian Elliott, writing in the Melbourne *Age*, the *Sydney Morning Herald*, *Meanjin* or *Southerly* are competent and influential critics.

The nineteenth century produced three "masterpieces" in the Australian novel: *Such is Life*, by Joseph Furphy ("Tom Collins") (1843–1912), *For the Term of His Natural Life*, by Marcus Clarke (1846–1881), and *The Fortunes of Richard Mahoney*, by (Mrs.) Henry Handel Richardson (1870–1946). All three books display fine narrative skill, careful character delineation, and detailed description of the Australian countryside.

Katherine Susannah Prichard, Marjorie Barnard, Flora Eldershaw, Eleanor Dark, Mrs. Aeneas Gunn, Margaret Trist, Charmian Clift and, Ruth Park have, in recent years, all produced praiseworthy novels.

IRISH LITERATURE

Since the disappearance of Gallic, the ancient language of Gaul, the Celtic, or westernmost group of the Indo-European family of languages, has been represented by: (1) the Goidelic, or Gaelic, which includes the Irish, the Scotch Gaelic, and the Manx; (2) the Brythonic, which includes the Welsh or Cymric, the Cornish, and the Celtic dialects of Brittany, these last being the language of refugees from Britain at the time of the Anglo-Saxon invasion.

In the Scotch Gaelic there is a very rich store of ballads, folklore, and proverbs, besides versions of the Ossianic cycle of Ireland. The two most famous monuments of earlier Scotch Gaelic are (1) *The Book of the Dean of Lismore*, compiled by James and Duncan Macgregor, and (2) *The Book of Femaig*, compiled by Duncan Macrae. The Cymric of Wales is the language of large collections of poetry, dating from the poets Aneurin of the 12th and Taliessin of the 13th century. The *Mabinogion* are poetic tales which were told by men during their training for admission to the guilds or societies of bards. The Eisteddfod, or annual poetry and music contest, is still maintained in Wales, and today more printing is done in this language than in all other Celtic languages combined.

In ancient Irish literature, the attention of almost all the leading modern scholars of the subject has hitherto been given mainly to the epic tales. In style these tales are forcible and abrupt, but they are shot through with gleams of strange, fierce tenderness, and are relieved, at unexpected moments, by the emergence of the unique humor of the Celt. Hardly less attractive is the early Christian poetry of the Irish, which is full of a beautiful awareness of all the natural loveliness of sea wave and cloud and tree and star. Such sensitive response to the changing moods of nature is unique in the earliest European poetry. "The bardic order," in W. B. Yeats's words, " . . . .had gone down in the wars of the 17th century, and poetry had found shelter amid the turf smoke of the cabins."

Poetry and prose in Irish never quite ceased to be written. The 18th century produced the poems of Red O'Sullivan, blind O'Heffernan, John Mac-Donnell of Claragh, Turlough O'Carolan, who has been called "the last of the bards," and Anthony Raftery, of whom Lady Gregory writes fully in her *Poets and Dreamers*. The distinct success, in our own day, of the Gaelic League (an Irish organization having for object the restoration of Gaelic as the spoken language of the people) has greatly increased the number of speakers and writers of Irish in Ireland. Among significant modern Gaelic writers are Canon O'Leary, Reverend P. S. Dinneen, Thomas Hayes, P. J. O'Shea (Conán Máol), and the late Padraic Pearse.

Irish Writers in English; Prose. The achievement of Irish writers in English is by no means the least glory of English literature. Richard Steele (1672–1729), Jonathan Swift (1667–1745), Oliver Goldsmith (1728–74), Edmund Burke (1729–97), and Richard Brinsley Sheridan (1751–1816) are the most famous names of an earlier day. But there was little in the writings of these men from which their nationality might be deduced. An indubitable entrance of Irish national sentiment into the work of Irish men of letters, a movement toward the restoration of a national literature, is hardly noticeable until after the passing of the act of Union (1801).

But the externals of Irish life are described with vigor and skill by Maria Edgeworth (1767–1849), whose best-known novels are *Castle Rackrent* and *The Absentee*, and whose work influenced Scott not a little. The name of Samuel Lover (1797–1868) will always be kept alive by the boisterous verve of his *Handy Andy*, and Charles James Lever (1806–72) is still read for his rollicking records of soldier and squireen life. His masterpiece is *Charles O'Malley*. Gerald Griffin (1803–40) has written, in *The Collegians*, one of the tenderest and most delightful of Irish novels. The Banim brothers, Michael (1796–1876) and John (1798–1844), wrote in conjunction a powerful series of *Tales by the O'Hara Family* which do not deserve the oblivion into which they seem to have fallen. Charles J. Kickham (1830–82) displayed a subtle understanding of the Irish peasant in *Knocknagow, or the Homes of Tipperary*. William Carleton (1798–1869) is, however, generally esteemed the greatest of all Irish novelists and has been called "the prose Burns of Ireland." His *Traits and Stories of the Irish Peasantry*, a series of tales of which the finest is *The Poor Scholar*, is his best-known contribution to fiction, but *The Black Prophet*, a novel of the great famine of '49, is harrowing in its tragic intensity, and *Fardorougha the Miser* is reminiscent of the genius of Balzac at its greatest.

More recent novelists who have achieved fame are Canon P. A. Sheehan (1852-1913), (author of *My New Curate, The Triumph of Failure*, and *The Blindness of Dr. Gray*), the finest interpreter in fiction of the Irish priest; James Stephens (1882-1950), who has displayed his mastery of realistic fantasy in *The Charwoman's Daughter* (American title *Mary, Mary*), in his volume of sketches, *Here are Ladies*, and in his best and most characteristic work, *The Crock of Gold;* and George Moore (1852–1933), who in *The Lake* evokes delicately and beautifully the spirit of the Western Irish countryside, and in the three volumes (*Ave, Salve*, and *Vale*) of his trilogy *Hail and Farewell* has recorded his participation in the Irish Literary Revival. Most of George Moore's major works (*Esther Waters, Evelyn Innes, A Mummer's Wife*, etc.) belong, however, to English rather than to Irish literature.

James Joyce (1882-1941) became internationally famous by his autobiographical novel, *A Portrait of the Artist as a Young Man* (1916), a merciless and morbid study in self-analysis set forth in prose of rare beauty; also by *Ulysses* (1922) which has been severely criticized for its unprecedented liberation of suppressions. St. John Ervine (1883-1971) is most widely known for his *Changing Winds*, a "war novel" which includes a description of the Irish insurrection of 1916. Seumas O'Kelly (1881-1918) won well-deserved recognition by his *Waysiders* (1917), a volume of sketches of Connaught life, and by two posthumously published tales, *The Golden Barque* and *The Weaver's Grave* (1919), which contain some of the best writing that has been done in Ireland. Daniel Corkery, (1878-1964), author of *A Munster Twilight* (1916), a collection of sketches of Munster life, and of *The Threshold of Quiet* (1917), a long novel, has written in his *Hounds of Banba* (1920) a series of remarkable studies of life in Ireland during the months of conflict between the Irish Republican forces and the Black and Tans. This writer is hardly less distinguished as poet and as dramatist. Sean O'Faolain (b. 1900) has won distinction as a biographer. Joyce Cary (1888-1957), whose themes often dealt with the creative imagination, was successful with *The Horse's Mouth*. Elizabeth Bowen (1899-   ), although she later lived in England, spent part of her life in Ireland, recounting her experiences in *Seven Winters and Afterthoughts* (1962).

Irish Writers in English; Poetry. Irish poetry written in English may be divided into four somewhat overlapping classes:

First, the work of such poets as Goldsmith, Oscar Wilde (1856–1900), and Edward Dowden (1843–1913), which is distinctly English in matter and manner.

The second class embraces that poetry of the closing 18th and the opening 19th century which was Irish in sentiment. Examples of this are the patriotic songs of Thomas Moore (1779–1852), author of the famous *Irish Melodies*, the poems of Wm. Drennan (1802–73), of Gerald Griffin, of James Joseph Callanan (1795–1829). The work of

South African Literature

215

all these men is characterized by grace and tenderness, while the songs of Charles Lever, Samuel Lover, and "Father Prout" (Francis Sylvester Mahony, 1804–66) exhibit the gaiety and exuberance which is so marked an element in the Irish temperament.

To the third division belong the poets of *The Nation*, the organ of the Young Ireland party, founded in 1842 by Sir Charles Gavan Duffy. Irish patriotism is almost exclusively their theme, and to inspire a love of country or a hatred of foreign domination, their object. Chief among these poets were Thomas Davis (1814–45) and Richard Dalton Williams (1822–62).

To the fourth division belong the poets of the modern Irish Literary Revival, who are essentially and pervasively Irish, but whose concern is with poetry primarily as a fine art. The great precursor of this movement was James Clarence Mangan (1803–49), author of *My Dark Rosaleen*. The initiator of it was Sir Samuel Ferguson (1810–86), who wrote *Lays of the Western Gael*. The chief figure in the movement was William Butler Yeats (1865-1939), whose place is conceded to be the highest among Irish artists in verse who have used English as their medium.

Among the other Irish poets, especial mention must be made of Padraic Cclum (b. 1881), whose *Wild Earth* is one of the best books of Irish poetry dealing with peasant types; "Seumas O'Sullivan" (James Starkey, 1879–1958), author of *The Twilight People*; "A. E." (George W. Russell, 1867–1935), mystical poet and painter; James Stephens (1882–1950), who strikes out a sturdy full-bodied music in his *Insurrections;* Joseph Campbell (1879–1944), a poet of mystic and brooding intensity, at his best in *The Mountainy Singer;* Winifred Letts, who sings simple and delightful *Songs from Leinster*; and "Moira O'Neill" (Nesta Higginson, Mrs. John Skrine) whose voice rises no less clearly and sweetly in *Songs from the Glens of Antrim*.

Irish Drama. There is no drama of literary significance to be found in modern Irish literature before the Irish Literary Theatre was established in 1899 by William Butler Yeats, Augusta Lady Gregory, and Edward Martyn (1859-1923). The most interesting plays produced by these pioneers were Yeats's *Cathleen Ni Houlihan Deirdre* by "Æ" (George Russell, 1867-1935), and *The Heather Field* by Edward Martyn. The story of the foundation and early struggles of the modern Irish movement in the theater has been told finally by Lady Gregory in *Our Irish Theatre*. The latent powers of John Millington Synge (1871–1909), the most vivid and powerful genius of the new drama, were evoked by W. B. Yeats. Synge then left Paris to live in loneliness upon the Aran Islands. While his greatest single work, *Riders to the Sea*, is the expression of a tragedy of frequent occurrence in those bleak coasts, his fantastic comedy, *The Playboy of the Western World*, gave rise to the most violent controversy in America no less than in Ireland.

The prevailing theme of Padraic Colum's plays is "the land" and the influence exercised by it. His dramatic characterization is consistently fine and searching, and in his three most important dramas, *The Land, The Fiddler's House*, and *Thomas Muskerry*, he displays an Ireland which one may take to be Ireland "on the average, as one cannot take it that what we have in the plays of Synge or Lady Gregory is Ireland on the average" (Professor Weygandt in *Irish Plays and Playwrights*). The best plays of Augusta Lady Gregory (1852–1932) are probably *The Rising of the Moon* and *Spreading the News*. W. B. Yeats's *The Countess Cathleen* perhaps best represents the essentially lyrical quality of his dramatic energy. Samuel Beckett, an Irish playwright who writes primarily in French, is noted for his pessimistic plays in which little happens on stage (*Waiting for Godot*, 1953). Other Irish dramatists are Baron Dunsany, St. John Ervine, William Boyle, Sean O'Casey and Brendan Behan.

SOUTH AFRICAN LITERATURE

Like Canadian, Australian and other literatures written in the English language but reflecting a regional background that is distinctly foreign, the division known as "South African Literature" has both British and colonial characteristics. In a cultural sense, the writers are transplanted Englishmen, and their products could be listed under the broad classification of English Literature. The people and situations in their fiction, like the themes of their poetry, are of local derivation, but the works themselves sometimes have sufficiently broad interest and sufficiently permanent interest to warrant their classification as literature.

Despite communication in Bantu and Afrikaans that is common throughout South Africa, a considerable English-writing section of the population has described the life and interpreted the spirit of a strangely mixed people whose contrasting and conflicting qualities impinge upon one another to create an uneasy truce. In the midst of old tribal customs and persistent Dutch colonial traditions, the articulate minority who express themselves in English poetry and prose occupy a somewhat anomalous position. However, their intermediate status qualifies them as reliable interpreters of the "wind of change" that is now sweeping through South Africa as well as the rest of the continent.

Because they are settled residents, and are thus closely identified with the economic and cultural life of the region, the South African writers mentioned below are in a position to give a trustworthy account of the people and events around them. Although they show understanding and sympathy, and nearly always careful impartiality, as between the Boer colonists and native tribesmen who are their neighbors, it is understandable that, in referring to political and social issues, they should sometimes encounter hostility from one side or the other. In fact, some of the best writers have found voluntary exile advisable because of intense feeling regarding the *apartheid* issue. This is a natural result of the modern realistic approach in literature dealing with Africa, as contrasted with the treatment by H. Rider Haggard and others who depicted a romantic never-never land for readers of escape literature in an earlier era. In the poetry and fiction of modern South African writers there is neither sentimental romanticism nor imperialistic condescension toward the native population. Today's approach is more nearly that of the late Roy Campbell's poem, *The Zulu Girl*, as reflected in the lines:

"The tamed ferocity of beaten tribes,
The sullen dignity of their defeat."

In addition to several works of fiction, of which the outstanding example is Alan Paton's powerful novel, *Cry, the Beloved Country*, contemporary South African writers have produced a wide variety and a high quality of poetry. Typical examples of their poems are the following:

Butler, Guy (1918-   )—*Cape Coloured Batman; Home Thoughts*.
Campbell, Roy (1901–1957)—*The Serf; The Zulu Girl; Rounding the Cape*.
Cripps, A. S. (1896–1952)—*Lazarus; A Pagan's Baptism*.
Currey, R. N. (1907-   )—*Durban Revisited; In Memoriam Roy Campbell*.
Delius, Anthony (1916-   )—*The Explorer; The Great Divide*.
Fuller, Roy (1912-   )—*The Plains; The Tribes; The Green Hills of Africa*.
Macnab, Roy (1923-   )—*The Settler; The Man of Grass*.
Miller, Ruth (1919-   )—*The Floating Island*.
Plomer, William (1903-   )—*The Pioneers; The Devil-Dancers; The Scorpion*.
Wright, David (1920-   )—*Seven South African Poems*.

FRENCH LITERATURE

The colloquial speech of Rome was the Latin that Cæsar's legions and their following of colonists and traders carried into Gaul. Absorbing possibly forty Celtic words there and, later, several hundred Germanic, this speech developed, clipping its unaccented syllables and changing vowel sounds, until by the 8th century the average Gallo-Roman could not understand the church offices, and preachers were ordered to preach in the "rustic, Roman tongue." In 842 it was used for the oath of an armistice; by 900, for the translation of a Latin hymn. In the 11th century it was called "French" from the kingdom of "France," around Paris and Orleans.

Medieval Verse and Story. The 11th century saw hymns to saints, secular lyrics, and war songs against the Moors who were barring the way to St. James's tomb at Santiago in Galicia, which French pilgrims were seeking. Minstrels (*jongleurs*) may have begun these songs, but they were soon aided by the monks, who found in Latin chronicles of Charlemagne's day the record of invasions of Spain, and of that emperor's wars against the infidels. So racial pride was added to religious zeal, and, these factors being given the environment of the newly formed feudal system, the national French epic was created. It grew until no less than eighty specimens of it (*chansons de gestes*—"songs of deeds") were known. Its masterpiece, in style and plot, was the *Song of Roland*, that told (about 1106) of the destruction of Charlemagne's rear guard and his Peers, by treason and overwhelming numbers, in a pass of the Pyrenees.

The 12th century witnessed the bloom of medieval French literature. There were didactic and narrative poems, often from the Latin, like *Saint Brendan's Voyage*. There were poems praising Alexander, the longest being in lines of twelve syllables that were henceforth known as "alexandrines." And there were romances of love and war, based on Virgil's *Æneid* and other epics of antiquity. The folklore and legends of the Celts, often called the "matter of Britain," also went into French poetry. Marie de France rimed short *lais* in octosyllabic couplets, on the loves of fairies for mortals; the story of Tristan and Isolt was expanded into long poems; and Chrétien de Troyes, choosing for his heroes the knights of Arthur's Round Table, emphasized knightly gallantry in his *Lancelot* and *Story of the Grail*. At the same time, following the example of the troubadours of southern France and profiting by the development of the art of music, lyric poetry claimed many writers.

Fables and Plays.—Animal fables, generally about the quarrels of the fox and the wolf, were rimed into the long *Romance of Reynard*. Jocose and coarse stories, often of wanton wives tricking their dull husbands, were made into poems called *fabliaux*. Good comedy in verse appeared at Arras after 1200. But the main effort of the playwrights was spent on the liturgical drama, which had begun centuries before in the churches, by interpolations of Scripture into the liturgy of Easter and Christmas. These interpolations had grown. They had become real scenes, too long for church services; they had been translated from Latin into French; and their stage had been removed from the choir to the front of the church. Continuing to expand, they presented to admiring crowds many of the leading events of the Old and New Testaments.

Prose.—In the early 12th century the Psalter had been translated into French prose. By 1200, Latin lives of saints and didactic and dogmatic treatises had followed in its train. History also was being written in French prose, notably Villehardouin's picturesque account of the Fourth Crusade with its capture of Constantinople. Huge prose romances on Lancelot's guilty love and the quest for the Grail were written, while in the quaint *chantefable* of *Aucassin and Nicolette* only the chapter headings were in verse.

Devout poetry and allegory developed in the 13th century. Guillaume de Lorris's *Romance of the Rose* (about 1235) told how the lover, aided by Friendly Greeting, would pluck the bud that Resistance defended. It also laid down Love's commands. The Parisian poet, Rutebeuf, composed saints' lives and saints' plays for pious patrons, and tried realistic, personal verse also. Jean de Meung, continuing the *Romance of the Rose*, made almost an encyclopedia of it, criticizing abuses and enjoining naturalness. Adam de la Halle, of Arras, produced in Italy the operetta "Robin and Marion" (1285). A farce written about the tricks played on a blind beggar by his boy guide was acted, while all kinds of learned and moral works went into prose.

The early 14th century saw Joinville's sympathetic memoirs of Louis IX, besides various short stories. Later, lyric poetry, which had survived the Hundred Years' War under the lead of the musician, Guillaume de Machaut, produced Deschamps, Froissart, Christine de Pisan, and Chartier, author of *La Belle Dame sans Merci*. Plays on Christ's Passion and dramatized *miracles* of the Virgin, together with a play on Griselda, represent the stage. Then came Froissart's dazzling chronicles of court and camp life, written by a gifted author from personal observation of events and intimate association with warring princes in the long 14th century struggle between France and England.

The old epic went into storybooks in the 15th century, short tales abounded, and the *Cent Nouvelles Nouvelles*, salacious anecdotes from the Italian and from native wit, offered models of clarity and conciseness. La Salle may have written them, as he did that amusing novel of manners, *Little John of Saintré*. Sermons, often abusive of the higher classes, moral treatises, and chronicles were numerous. And Commines compiled his philosophical memoirs of Louis XI.

Drama.—The liturgical drama had now grown into enormous plays called "mysteries," as the *Mystery of the Old Testament*. Paid for from the public purse and requiring crowds of actors, these plays would entertain entire populations with their mixture of Scriptural scenes and rough horseplay. In Paris they were performed by the Fraternity of the Passion, chartered in 1402. Associations of amateurs, as the *Basoche*, formed of law clerks, or the *Sots*, "Fools," improved the *farces*, invented diverting or instructive *monologues*, and played allegorical *moralities* in which personified vices and virtues edifyingly dealt with themes of daily existence. But the best medieval play was the farce of *Pathelin* (about 1470), where a seedy lawyer, who had wheedled a cloth merchant and then confused him by appearing in court as attorney for the merchant's thievish shepherd, was cheated of his fee through the very trick he had taught his client.

The larger part of the century's poetry is too rhetorical, too extravagant in its rimes. But Charles d'Orléans wrote pleasing society verse, and there was François Villon, the penniless, dissipated student, the best poet, the most human writer of them all. Having nothing in the world of his own, he amused himself and delighted posterity with a series of pretended legacies, written in separate stanzas that were formed into the *Little* and *Great Testaments*. To his ill-wishers he left his worthless garments or whatever else they could get; to his friends, his gratitude and his pity; to his mother, a *ballade* in honor of the Virgin. Of his other poetry, the "Ballade of the Hung," on the Montfaucon gibbet at Paris, and the "Ballade of the Ladies of Olden Time," with its haunting refrain, "Where are the snows of yesteryear?" would alone make him famous.

The Renaissance. Printing, the immigration of Greek scholars, the French invasion of Italy, and Luther's schism, all contributed to the intellectual and spiritual upsetting of the 16th century. Rabelais' *Gargantua and Pantagruel*, a romance of giants, father and son, of a lively, gluttonous monk and the tricky Panurge, told in ludicrous language, with much coarseness, erudition, and mother wit, well illustrated the prevailing confusion of thought, impatience of dogma, and desire for new standards of living. A reformer also, yet rigidly logical, was Calvin, who translated his *Institutes of the Christian Religion* (1541) from its original Latin into French, in order to reach the laity. Lighter prose came with Marguerite of Navarre's *Heptameron* and the romance, *Amadis of Gaul*, which Francis I brought back from Spain.

The liturgical drama, attacked by both the Reformers and the lovers of good literature, was killed in 1548 by an edict of the Paris parliament. That year also saw Ronsard and Du Bellay form a group of seven writers, the "Pléiade," for the purpose of renewing poetry and the theater after classical and Italian models. Marot had already written sonnets. Now odes and elegies were composed, while five-act tragedies in twelve-syllable lines, with an action which did not last over 24 hours, replaced the forbidden *mysteries*. The public taste was improved also by Bishop Amyot's translations of Greek novels and Plutarch's *Lives*. Then Montaigne summed up the efforts of the age in his rambling, piquant *Essays*, replete with human experience, fortified by copious quotations from the ancients, yet constantly postulating the skeptical query "What do I know?"

The Seventeenth Century. To reduce the confusion of the Renaissance to reason and order was the first task of the 17th century. Malherbe, arguing that poetry should express universal ideas in general terms and harmonious phrases, and that the rime should always emphasize the sense, was supported by Madame de Rambouillet's *salon* and by the French Academy, founded by Richelieu in 1634. Malherbe's views were also adopted by Corneille in his comedies and tragedies. Corneille's *Cid* (1636), with its theme of love struggling with honor and duty, was rhythmically perfect.

The Great Dramatists.—Molière, the greatest of French dramatists, learned his art from Corneille and the Italian farces. In 1658 he established himself at Paris with a satire, *The Affected Misses*, on women of the trades class who tried to copy the refinements in language practiced at the *salon* of Madame de Rambouillet. The success won with this comedy was increased by plays that ranged from amusing skits to studies of character, like *The Misanthrope* and *Tartufe*, on hypocrisy, and studies of manners, like *The Learned Ladies*. He preached the favorite doctrines of the French people,—moderation, common sense, avoidance of extremes.

Racine, Molière's contemporary, wrote tragedies which dealt especially with woman. In *Andromache* he showed the heroine divided between maternal love and respect for her husband's memory. In *Phædra* he pictured the result of unrestrained jealousy. In *Athaliah*, he painted an ambitious woman vanquished by a more determined man.

Writers of Prose.—Descartes had affirmed the dominance of reason in his *Discourse on Method* (1637) which, with its dictum, "I think, therefore I exist," introduced philosophy to the public. Pascal's biting *Provincial Letters*, against hypocrisy, and his unfinished *Thoughts*, on man's need of God, offered genuinely classical prose. La Rochefoucauld's *Maxims*, on human selfishness, were most cutting, while La Bruyère tellingly painted man's foibles in his *Characters*. Madame de Sévigné's sprightly *Letters* chronicled court doings, as did Saint-Simon's *Memoirs* later. Pulpit oratory reached its height with Bossuet's sermons and funeral orations, on the vanity of the world.

Fiction had developed many long romances, with portraits of society folk in disguise as a leading feature. But Madame de La Fayette's *Princess of Cleves* is modern in its theme of self-renunciation. Perrault, who preferred modern writers to ancient, wrote down the *Tales of Mother Goose* (1697).

Poetry, outside the drama, was found mainly in society verse. But the critic, Boileau, used it for his attacks on other poets and for his defense of Malherbe's ideas. La Fontaine, advocating naturalness, like Boileau, Molière, and Racine, chose poetry for his famous *Fables*.

The Eighteenth Century. Newtonian science and increasing humanitarianism characterized the 18th century. Bayle's *Dictionary*, partly encyclopedic, foreshadowed the one. The other appeared in Fénelon's *Telemachus*, a romance of adventure, filled with wise counsels for his pupil, the Dauphin. Voltaire, skeptical and argumentative, preached religious tolerance and the equality of man in his plays, studied national movements in his *Essay on Manners*, and attacked abuses in tales and pamphlets. Brilliant, clever, daring, he advanced both scientific thought and political freedom. His correspondence remains a model of epistolary style.

Montesquieu was more philosophical, discussing social changes in his *Causes of the Greatness and Decline of the Romans*, and arguing in his *Spirit of Laws* (1748) for a division of governmental authority into the executive, the legislative, and the judicial—a plan adopted later in the Constitution of the United States. The *Encyclopedia*, edited mainly by Diderot and D'Alembert, was the mouthpiece of scientific criticism. It exerted an enormous influence. Buffon's *Natural History* (1748) gave to zoology the charm of literature.

Molière and Racine were followed by many playwrights. Marivaux created light comedies of intrigue. Destouches, La Chaussée, and Diderot undertook the problems of the family. But Beaumarchais, master of stage effects and witty dialogue, excelled all, making his valet, Figaro, who was a most merry jester in the *Barber of Seville*, a defender of the rights of man in *Figaro's Marriage*, a play which anticipated some of the ideas of the French Revolution.

Rousseau.—Fiction was much cultivated in short stories and novels. Lesage's *Gil Blas* and Marivaux's *Life of Marian* studied manners. Prévost's *Manon Lescaut* is a faithful history of love's errors. Rousseau's *New Heloïse* (1760) is as much a thesis as a romance. Hating social restraints and hostile to science and civilization, Rousseau had appealed in essays for a return to the primitive state of man. His *Social Contract* was communistic, anarchical. His *New Heloïse* carried on the same warfare, with much praise of nature and the simple life. His *Emile* advocated education through nature and experience, before books are studied. Rousseau had most intense convictions. He expressed them in burning language. Pleading for justice, he inaugurated the present social unrest. Egotistical, a lover of nature, he was the father of French Romanticism. Saint-Pierre's delightful idyl, *Paul and Virginia*, is an illustration of his theories.

Throughout this century, poetry was neglected, its best specimens being Chénier's odes and elegies and Rouget de Lisle's "Marseillaise" (1792).

19th Century. Chateaubriand described Mississippi as seen by the sorrowful eyes of his characters, Atala and René, in his *Genius of Christianity*, a book which attacked modern science and eulogized medieval and Christian art. Madame de Staël, in her novels, *Delphine* and *Corinne*, pleaded for woman's freedom, while her *Germany* introduced German thought and literature to France and England. George Sand sided with Madame de Staël in various novels.

Romanticism.—Romantic fiction as a whole, however, imitated Scott. De Vigny's *Cinq-Mars*, Hugo's *Notre Dame de Paris*, Dumas's *Three*

Musketeers are instances. Hugo's *Les Misérables* described man's futile efforts against society and nature. Romanticism, with its insistence on what is individual and peculiar in races and epochs, transformed historical studies. Thierry was picturesque and dramatic in his essays on history, and Michelet eloquent and democratic in his *History of France.* Guizot, who discussed national development in his *Courses on Modern History,* was more philosophical, as was De Tocqueville in *Democracy in America* (1835). Renan's works on religious history were more critical and scientific.

Romanticism was at its best in lyric poetry. Lamartine, De Vigny, Hugo, and De Musset have few equals. Admirers of form, such as Gautier and Baudelaire, followed them. Then came the Parnassians (1866) with Leconte de Lisle, Mallarmé, and Coppée. Later still were Verlaine and the Symbolists, with Arthur Rimbaud. Paul Claudel produced symbolic plays that showed a Catholic influence, and Maurice Maeterlinck combined naturalism with symbolism.

Romantic drama, taking Shakespeare for its guide, discarded the unities of time and place and mingled the comic with the tragic. But it produced few good plays, the elder Dumas's historical tragedies, Hugo's *Hernani* and *Ruy Blas,* and De Musset's comedies being the best. It was soon supplanted by the broader theater of Scribe, whose ideas were carried on by the next generation. Dumas *fils* and Augier found their subjects in contemporary life. Sardou, who began with the comedy of manners, continued with tragedies. But Rostand, with *Cyrano* and *Chantecler,* went back to the praise of the homely virtues.

The Realists. Stendhal's *Red and Black* and Balzac's *Human Comedy* showed men fighting for wealth and power, while Mérimée's *Colomba* and *Carmen* described the influence of race and environment. More positive and agnostic after 1850, realism produced Flaubert, an exceptional stylist who traced human decadence in *Madame Bovary.* Zola, choosing his characters from a lower class, emphasized heredity in *Rougon-Macquart,* while Maupassant excelled in exactness of description. Less extreme, Daudet wrote of the trades class, the politician, and the adventurer.

Modern Period. Realism still holds in fiction. Anatole France protested against injustice. Rolland's *Jean Christophe* is the careful biography of a talented musician. Loti, seeing death at the end of everything, imbued his descriptions of customs and peoples with melancholy. Jules Romains's *Men of Good Will* depicts French life at every level. In André Malraux appears the revolutionist as writer, whose tales evoke the tragedy of class warfare. The psychological novels of Marcel Proust (*Remembrance of Things Past*), carrying introspection to the extreme, enlarged the scope of the novel. Others who produced valued multiple-volume narratives, as did Proust, were Georges Duhamel and Roger Martin du Gard. Nobel Prize winner François Mauriac was a leading novelist in the Catholic revival. Independent of thought, André Gide wrote brilliant psychological novels, and Antoine de Saint-Exupéry's poetic prose was popular. After World War II, the most powerful literary force in France, extending to other literatures, was Existentialism, led by Jean Paul Sartre, Simone de Beauvoir, and Albert Camus. Another recent trend is the avant-garde "new novel" group. Its controversial forerunners are Alain Robbe-Grillet and Nathalie Sarraute. This group rejects the philosophy of the absurd in an attempt to present bare experience. In a lighter vein, the narratives of Colette held greater durability than the popular novels of Françoise Sagan.

The drama, under Ibsen's influence, continued the study of manners with Hervieu and Brieux. Eugène Ionesco and Samuel Beckett have become internationally known as proponents of the theater of the absurd with their bizarre plays. Henry de Montherlant is an outstanding dramatist writing in the classical tradition about human problems. Widely acclaimed are Jean Anouilh (France's most successful playwright), Jean Giraudoux (an optimistic realist), and Jean Cocteau (a surrealist).

Poetry developed free verse and offers in the rhythms of Paul Fort lyric pages, while the Comtesse de Noailles returned to traditional forms. St.-John Perse added distinguished verse to the school of symbolism, and Paul Valéry was admired for his skeptical philosophical works. Guillaume Apollinaire mastered the trends of his time and was influential. Important surrealists are André Breton and René Char.

TABLE OF FRENCH LITERATURE

Time	Author	Prose Works	Poetry and Drama
1140–?	Chrétien de Troyes		Arthurian Romances.
1150–?	Marie de France		Lais.
1160–1213	Villehardouin	Conquest of Constantinople	
1210–1235	Guillaume de Lorris		Romance of the Rose.
1224–1317	Joinville	Chronicles	
1240–1287	Adam de la Halle		Robin and Marion.
1240–1305	Jean de Meung		Romance of the Rose.
1336–1406	Eustache Deschamps		Poems.
1338–1410	Jean Froissart	Chronicles	
1364–1430?	Christine de Pisan		Poems.
1387–1460	Antoine de la Salle	Stories	
1394–1465	Charles d'Orléans		Poems.
1431–1465	François Villon		Ballads.
1445–1511	Philippe de Commines	Memoirs	
1492–1549	Marguerite of Navarre	Heptameron	
1495–1553	François Rabelais	Lives of Gargantua and Pantagruel	
1497?–1544	Clément Marot		Sonnets.
1509–1564	John Calvin	Institutes of the Christian Religion	
1513–1593	Jacques Amyot	Translation of Plutarch's Lives	
1524?–1560	Joachim du Bellay		Poems.
1524–1585	Pierre de Ronsard		Sonnets, Odes.
1533–1592	Michel de Montaigne	Essays	
1555–1628	François de Malherbe		Poems.
1596–1650	René Descartes	Philosophy	
1606–1684	Pierre Corneille		Plays (The Cid, Le Menteur).
1613–1680	Duke de La Rochefoucauld	Maxims, Memoirs	
1621–1695	Jean de la Fontaine		Fables, Contes.
1622–1673	Molière		Comedies (The Misanthrope, Tartufe).
1623–1662	Blaise Pascal	Mathematics, Thoughts	
1626–1696	Mme. de Sévigné	Letters	
1627–1704	Jacques Bossuet	Sermons, Funeral Orations	
1628–1703	Charles Perrault	Tales of Mother Goose	
1634–1693	Mme. de La Fayette	Princess of Cleves	
1636–1711	Nicolas Boileau-Despréaux		Poems, Art Poétique.

TABLE OF FRENCH LITERATURE—Con.

Time	Author	Prose Works	Poetry and Drama
1639—1699	Jean Racine		Tragedy (Andromache, Athaliah)
1645—1696	Jean de la Bruyère	Characters	
1651—1715	François de Fénelon	Telemachus	
1657—1757	Bernard Fontenelle	Dialogues of the Dead	Tragedies.
1668—1747	Alain René Lesage	Gil Blas, Translations	
1675—1755	Saint-Simon	Memoirs	
1688—1763	Marivaux	Novels	Comedy.
1689—1755	Montesquieu	Spirit of Laws	
1692—1754	P. C. Nivelle de La Chaussée		Plays.
1694—1778	Voltaire	Critical Essays, Satires, Letters	Poems, Dramas.
1697—1763	Abbé Prévost	Manon Lescaut	
1707—1788	Buffon	Science	
1712—1778	Rousseau	The New Heloïse, Confessions	
1713—1784	Denis Diderot	Fiction, Encyclopedia	Plays.
1717—1783	D'Alembert	Essays, Encyclopedia	
1732—1799	Pierre de Beaumarchais		Comedies (The Marriage of Figaro).
1737—1814	Bernardin de Saint-Pierre	Paul and Virginia	
1760—1836	Rouget de Lisle		Marseillaise.
1762—1794	André Chénier		Odes, Elegies.
1766—1817	Mme. de Staël	Delphine, Corinne, Germany	
1768—1848	Chateaubriand	René, Genius of Christianity	
1783—1842	Stendhal	Novels	
1787—1874	François P. G. Guizot	Courses on Modern History	
1790—1869	Alphonse de Lamartine	History of the Girondists	
1791—1861	Eugène Scribe		Poems.
1795—1856	Augustin Thierry	History of France	Comedy (Bataille de Dames).
1797—1863	Alfred de Vigny	Novels (Cinq-Mars)	
1798—1857	Auguste Comte	Philosophy	"Poèmes Antiques et Modernes."
1799—1850	Honoré de Balzac	Novels ("Comédie Humaine")	
1802—1870	Dumas the Elder	Novels (Three Musketeers)	
1802—1885	Victor Hugo	Novels (Les Misérables)	Dramas.
1803—1870	Prosper Mérimée	Novels (Colomba), Letters	Lyrics, Dramas (Hernani).
1804—1857	Eugène Sue	Wandering Jew, Mysteries of Paris	
1804—1869	C. A. Sainte-Beuve	Criticisms	
1804—1876	George Sand	Novels (Indiana), Peasant Tales	
1805—1859	Alexis de Tocqueville	Democracy in America	
1810—1857	Alfred de Musset	Short Stories	
1811—1872	Théophile Gautier	Criticisms, Novels	Poems, Comedies.
1811—1883	Jules Sandeau	Novels (Marianna)	Poems.
1821—1867	Charles Baudelaire		Plays.
1821—1880	Gustave Flaubert	Novels (Madame Bovary)	Poems.
1821—1890	Octave Feuillet	Novels, "Feuilletons"	
1822—1899	Emile Erckmann	Novels, with Chatrian	Dramas.
1823—1892	Ernest Renan	Life of Jesus	
1824—1895	Dumas the Younger	Novels	
1826—1890	Alexandre Chatrian	Novels, with Erckmann	Dramas.
1828—1893	Hippolyte Taine	Criticism	
1828—1905	Jules Verne	Novels	
1830—1914	Frédéric Mistral		Provençal Poetry (Mireille).
1831—1908	Victorien Sardou		Dramas (Patrie).
1839—1907	Sully-Prudhomme	Criticism	Poems (Les Solitudes).
1840—1897	Alphonse Daudet	Novels, Short Stories	
1840—1902	Emile Zola	Novels (La Débâcle)	
1844—1896	Paul Verlaine		Poems.
1844—1924	Anatole France	Novels, Essays	Poems.
1850—1893	Guy de Maupassant	Short Stories (The Necklace)	
1850—1923	Pierre Loti	Novels, Travel	
1852—1935	Paul Bourget	Novels (La Terre Promise)	
1853—1932	René Bazin	Novels	
1854—1891	Arthur Rimbaud		Poems.
1857—1915	Paul Hervieu	Novels	Dramas (The Labyrinth).
1858—1932	Eugène Brieux	Essays	Dramas (The Red Robe).
1859—1941	Henri Bergson	Creative Evolution	
1859—1940	Henri Lavedan	Novels	Dramas.
1862—1923	Maurice Barrès	Novels (Le Voyage de Sparte)	
1862—1949	Maurice Maeterlinck	Essays (Life of the Bee)	Poems, Dramas.
1866—1944	Romain Rolland	Novels (Jean Christophe), Essays	Plays.
1868—1955	Paul Claudel	Essays	Poems, plays (Partage de Midi)
1968—1918	Edmond Rostand		Dramas (Cyrano de Bergerac).
1869—1951	André Gide	Novels, Travel Books	
1871—1945	Paul Valery	Essays (Varietés)	Poems (Charmes).
1871—1922	Marcel Proust	Psychological Novels	
1873—1954	Sidonie Gabrielle Colette	Novelist	Gigi
1876—1933	Comtesse M. de Noailles	Novels	Poems (The Quick and the Dead).
1881—1958	Roger Martin du Gard	Novels (Les Thibault)	Plays.
1882—1973	Jacques Maritain	Essays (True Humanism)	
1885—1970	François Mauriac	Novels (Genitrix)	Plays, poems.
1885—1967	André Maurois	Biographical Novels	
1885—1972	Jules Romains	Novels (Men of Good Will)	
1887—1975	Alexis Leger, (St.-John Perse)		Poems
1896—1966	André Breton	Novel (Nadja)	Poems (surrealistic).
1896—1972	Henry de Montherlant	Novels (The Bachelors)	Plays, poetry.
1900—1944	Antoine de Saint-Exupéry	Novels (Night Flight)	
1901—1976	André Malraux	Novels (Man's Fate)	
1905—	Raymond Aron	History	
1905—	Jean Paul Sartre	Essays (Existentialism)	Plays.
1908—	Simone de Beauvoir	Novels (The Mandarins)	Plays.
1910—	Jean Anouilh		Plays (Antigone).
1912—	Eugène Ionesco		Plays (The Bald Soprano).
1912—	Henri Thomas	Novel (Le Promontaire.)	
1913—1960	Albert Camus	Essays (La chute), Novels	Plays (Caligula).

ITALIAN LITERATURE

For convenience, the history of Italian literature may be divided into five periods: (1) beginning about 1230 with the Sicilian poets gathered at the court of the emperor Frederick II and including the three writers of cardinal importance, Dante, Petrarch, and Boccaccio (d. 1375); (2) the Revival of Learning, initiated by Petrarch and extending through the age of Lorenzo de' Medici (1449–92); (3) the mature Renaissance, to the death of Tasso (1595); (4) a period of decline extending to the middle of the 18th century; (5) the period of the regeneration of Italy, extending to the present.

The Early Period. The poetry of the Sicilians is mainly amatory as to subject, but the individualities of the poets are not strongly marked. The writer of courtly lyrics celebrates the perfections of his lady in an emphatic but somewhat conventional manner that does not often convince us of the sincerity of his emotions. However, it should be borne in mind that this poetry depended for no small part of its effect upon the music to which it was set. Nor is it by any means all artificial; a number of poems have survived, which bear a partially popular stamp, and which charm through their evident genuineness of feeling. Such poems are a girl's lament for her lover who has gone on a crusade overseas; and a dialogue between a lover and his beloved—the so-called *Contrasto* (debate), attributed to an otherwise unknown Cielo d'Alcamo—famous enough to have been quoted by Dante. A notable achievement as to form was the invention of the sonnet by Giacomo da Lentino, a member of this group.

Among poets of continental Italy, who continued the work of the Sicilians but broadened their range of subjects, was Guittone d'Arezzo, who was regarded as a leader by a considerable group of minor writers in central Italy, and who is noteworthy besides for a collection of letters written about 1260 as models for prose writing. Italian prose was then in its infancy, but it developed speedily, largely through translations, from Latin and French, of lives of saints, religious treatises, romances of chivalry, and Latin classics, but also through original works, such as chronicles and collections of short stories.

The wave of intense religious emotion which swept over Italy in the 13th century, in the wake of the Franciscan movement, found expression in religious poetry of deep sincerity, such as the *laudi* (hymns) of Jacopone da Todi. These, being sometimes written in the form of dialogues, became the starting-point of the religious drama which reached the climax of its development in the Florentine religious plays of the 15th century.

Outside of the more or less faithful followers of the Sicilian poets in central Italy, there arose, in opposition to them, two groups of writers that were powerful forces in advancing the rapid development of Italian poetry.

The earlier group was composed mainly of Florentine poets of the middle class, in whom the courtly, artificial idealism of the Sicilians and their adherents provoked a reaction, out of which came a quantity of realistic and often broadly humorous verse. The second group includes a number of Florentine poets whose work began around 1280. To them came a new lyric impulse from an ode by a distinguished poet of Bologna, Guido Guinizelli, beginning "Love e'er betakes him to the gentle heart." Guinizelli's theory of the source of love differed from that of his predecessors in declaring that love, instead of being merely communicated from the eyes to the heart—as had been held by the earlier poets—has its natural home in the "gentle heart," and that none but gentle hearts can know true love. Such a conception of a company of elect souls, to whom alone true love can be known, was bound to prove a kindling spark to this young and enthusiastic group,

who are referred to in the *Divine Comedy* as the writers of the "sweet new style."

Their leader was for a time the noble and scholarly Guido Cavalcanti, a member of one of the most powerful Florentine families, to whom Dante dedicated his first great work, the *Vita Nuova*, "New Life." On the appearance of this little book, however, its young author speedily took the first rank.

Dante.—The *Vita Nuova* is at once a selection from the lyric poetry of the writer's youth and early maturity (interspersed with explanatory and narrative prose passages), the story of his spiritual awakening through the love of a gentle lady, Beatrice, and the forerunner of his greatest work, the *Divine Comedy*.

The ten years between 1292, when the *Vita Nuova* was probably completed, and 1302, when Dante was forced into exile, were the period of the poet's preparatory studies for his masterpiece; likewise, of his political career, that ended in disaster. In spite of the handicap of lifelong banishment, he not only wrote some lesser though highly important works, but planned and brought to a triumphant conclusion the *Divine Comedy*, one of the most monumental achievements of the poetic imagination in the world's literature. See *Divine Comedy*.

The purpose of helping his fellow men, by diffusing among them useful knowledge which might otherwise have remained inaccessible to them, is revealed in several of the poet's minor works, particularly the *Convivio*, "Banquet," a philosophical commentary, preceded by an introduction, on three of the poet's own odes. The *Monarchia* is a treatise in Latin, setting forth the necessity of a universal temporal monarchy coexistent with the spiritual sovereignty of the pope. *De Vulgari Eloquentia* is another Latin treatise on Italian language and poetry, of great value though unfinished. The most important of Dante's Latin letters defines the structure and purpose of the *Divine Comedy*.

Petrarch.—Francesco Petrarca, the second of Italy's great writers, came into prominence about a dozen years after the death of Dante, and was for more than forty years the undisputed leader in Italian poetry and scholarship. The main inspiration of his lyric poetry was his love for Laura, a French lady of Avignon; but patriotic and religious sentiments find noble expression in his work. His shorter Italian poems number well over 300, the majority of which are sonnets.

Petrarch wrote many treatises, poems, and letters in Latin. An enthusiastic student of the Latin classics, he broke away from the medieval method of seeking in them allegorical meanings wholly foreign to their spirit, and tried to understand them by striving to put himself back in the times in which they were written. He thus probably unconsciously initiated a new era in the study of the classics, and is rightly regarded as the pioneer of the movement known as the Revival of Learning. He has been styled, on the whole justly, the "first modern man." His discovery, in a northern Italian library, of some letters of Cicero, hitherto believed lost, started the search for vanished literary treasures, and, from his time on, the monastery libraries of Europe were ransacked with diligence and notable success by generations of scholars, mostly Italians.

Petrarch, after an honored and varied career, died peacefully (1374) in his little country home in the Euganean hills in northern Italy.

Boccaccio.—The third great figure of this period is Giovanni Boccaccio, to whom the Italians owe their first masterpiece of prose,—the collection of 100 stories known as the *Decameron*. The materials for this famous collection were derived from a variety of sources, European and Oriental. The tales are as varied in character as in origin, ranging from gay anecdote to tragic story, and reveal the author's great gift of lifelike portrayal of human types from every class of society. Whatever the alleged scenes of their action, it was the life of his country and time that Boccaccio put into his tales, in such profusion and variety as to suggest to some its characterization as the "Human Comedy," in contrast to the *Divine Comedy* of Dante.

A devoted admirer of Dante, Boccaccio made with his own hand a copy of the *Divine Comedy*, and wrote a life of the poet. Later, he publicly read and expounded Dante's great work, appointed to the task by the government of Florence, which thus strove to make amends for its injustice to its greatest citizen. Like his friend Petrarch, Boccaccio was an eager student of the Latin classics, and wrote in Latin numerous treatises that were useful to generations of scholars.

As a result of the work of Dante, Petrarch, and Boccaccio, the prestige acquired by Tuscan Italian established it definitely as the literary language of Italy.

The Revival of Learning. The second period of Italian literature, extending until nearly the end of the 15th century, is more remarkable for the vigorous development of classical studies, fostered by the fresh impulse given them by Petrarch, Boccaccio, and their followers, than for the production of great works in Italian; although such were by no means lacking, especially toward the close of the period. In this age the field of studies was immeasurably extended by the revival of the knowledge of Greek. Even Petrarch and Boccaccio had been able to acquire but the merest smattering of this language, owing to the lack of competent teachers. In 1397, however, Coluccio Salutati (1331–1406), a friend and the worthiest successor of Petrarch in the domain of scholarship, who had risen to be chancellor of the Republic of Florence, extended, in the name of the government, an invitation to a Greek scholar in Constantinople—then still in Greek hands—to come to Florence as official instructor in Greek. This scholar, Manuel Chrysoloras (1350?–1415), was the first of a notable line of Greek men of learning who, after the break of nearly seven centuries between the Greek and the Roman world, brought back to western Europe the language, literature, and philosophy of ancient Greece.

Enthusiasm for these studies was not confined to scholars alone, but spread rapidly and widely. The rulers of many Italian states—including the popes, several of whom were famous scholars—invited humanists, as these men of learning came to be called, to grace their courts; wealthy merchants fitted out ships to sail for Constantinople and to return with cargoes of precious manuscripts. The collections made in this age formed the nuclei of many famous libraries, such as those of Venice, Florence, and Rome.

It was natural that during this intensive revival of classical studies the cultivation of Italian should have been relatively neglected. In the end, however, Italian literature, far from losing, was incalculably benefited by the widening of the intellectual horizon achieved through the scholarship of this time. Indeed, the masterpieces of the ensuing age, in both poetry and prose, could never have been written without the background of classical culture derived from the humanistic period.

The neglect of Italian was also, as has been said, only relative. From about 1465, we come upon a generation of admirable poets, some of whom, like Pulci, Boiardo, Poliziano, and the great Lorenzo de' Medici, were themselves classical scholars of high attainments. Of these writers, Pulci and Boiardo wrote mainly narrative poetry; the others, chiefly lyric and dramatic.

The Renaissance. In the third period of Italian literature, the elements of classical culture, blended with those of the brilliant life of the epoch, combined to produce the ripest fruits of the age of the Renaissance, a term broader than humanism, as it is not, like the latter, applied exclusively to literary activities, but to those in all the arts—painting, sculpture, architecture, and music—which flourished with incomparable splendor at this time in Italy. A further aid to men of letters of this time was the art of printing, which, invented during the preceding age, incalculably multiplied the resources and opportunities of literary production.

Ariosto.—Among the remarkable number of distinguished writers brought forth by this age, the greatest are the following: (1) Ludovico Ariosto, author of the *Orlando Furioso*, "Orlando in Madness," a romance of chivalry in verse (46 cantos) continuing the *Orlando Innamorato*, "Orlando in Love," of his predecessor Boiardo. The hero is the medieval Roland, whom legend made into a nephew of Charlemagne. Vividness of imagination, fertility of invention, skill in character drawing, and a rich, mellow style, through which the attractive personality of the author is pleasantly revealed, have combined to insure the permanent vitality of the work, in which the life of Renaissance Italy is mirrored as faithfully as is that of the end of the middle ages in the tales of Boccaccio's *Decameron*. Ariosto wrote, besides, five comedies—mostly free adaptations of the Latin plays of Plautus and Terence—and seven partly autobiographical satires, as well as some lyric poetry in Italian and in Latin.

Machiavelli.—(2) Niccolo Machiavelli, the first great modern writer on statecraft and the art of war. His treatise entitled *The Prince*—an examination of the methods of acquiring and maintaining sovereign power—has been discussed more than any other single work of this period. Written for its time, when might usually made right, and intended as a practical guide for the ruler, its advocacy of expediency and ruthlessness over justice and good faith naturally laid it open to the harsh criticism of later ages that have witnessed vast improvements in methods of government. Machiavelli's *History of Florence* shows his characteristic political and historical insight, as do his *Discourses on Livy*, which deal with popular forms of government. Besides minor works, he wrote, in a lighter vein, several comedies, a fantastic, satirical short story, and some poetry.

Castiglione.—(3) Baldesar Castiglione, the author of the *Cortegiano*, "Courtier," the best treatise in dialogue form since those of Plato and Cicero. The discussions of the qualifications of the courtier are represented as having taken place during four successive evenings in 1506 at the court of Urbino, the capital of a diminutive duchy in central Italy. The artistic handling of one of the most difficult literary forms, and the realistic and pleasing picture of Italian society of the Renaissance at its best, unite to make the *Cortegiano* perhaps the most delightful prose work of 16th century European literature.

Tasso.—(4) Torquato Tasso, the last great figure of this age. The son of a minor but not negligible poet and scholar, Bernardo Tasso (1493–1569), he achieved fame at eighteen with *Rinaldo*, a romance of chivalry in verse. In 1573 he obtained another great success with *Aminta*, a pastoral drama, a form to which the popularity of this work gave a great vogue. His highest achievement, however, was in the field of epic poetry. His *Gerusalemme Liberata*, "Jerusalem Delivered," first published complete in 1581 (20 cantos), is the last truly great work of Italian poetry until the middle of the 18th century. Tasso chose for his subject the stirring story of the First Crusade (1095–99), handling it imaginatively, but still preserving the dignity of the theme.

Minor Writers.—Besides these four principal writers, there are many others of distinction and influence: Bembo, scholar, poet, and historian; Vasari, the biographer of painters, sculptors, and architects; Guicciardini, the historian; Bandello and Giraldi Cinthio, authors of voluminous collections of tales, drawn upon for plots by many dramatists of the 16th and 17th centuries, including Shakspere. The "Othello" story was derived from Cinthio, who himself wrote tragedies, but never rose above mediocrity in this form. Among the most picturesque figures of the time was the Florentine sculptor and goldsmith, Benvenuto Cellini, whose autobiography, one of the most original works of its kind, is of inestimable value to the student of the life of the Renaissance. This work is likewise accessible in English, having been finely translated by John Addington Symonds, an authority on the Renaissance.

The Period of Decline. In the interval between 1595, the year of Tasso's death, and the middle of the 18th century, there are no writers of enduring significance in the purely literary field. National life was at a low ebb, and the official censorship of books, which had been established about the middle of the 16th century, increasingly hampered free expression of thought. Poetry declined notably, not in quantity of production, but in quality. In this era of Italy's political weakness and dependence, her writers could derive no inspiration from the life of the nation. Literature, as a consequence, lost contact with life; its subjects, especially in poetry, became artificial and futile; taste and style deteriorated in a welter of exaggeration, sensationalism, and affectation. Toward the end of the century a reaction led to an attempt at reform; but this ended in puerile artificialities of pseudo-Arcadian simplicity. The Muse of Poetry was all powder and rouge.

Until a regeneration of the national life could set in, and contact between writing and reality could be restored, nothing great in literary production was to be expected.

Even during this time, however, the Italian genius was by no means dormant in all fields. The 17th century is the period of the development of a hybrid but still vital compound of poetry and music, the opera—originally planned as a revival of the Greek tragedy; and it was likewise in this time that the spirit of scientific investigation was nobly embodied in the imposing figure of Galileo. The early part of the age, moreover, produced one historical masterpiece, the *History of the Council of Trent* (1619), by the brilliant and fearless Venetian ecclesiastic, Fra Paolo Sarpi.

The Regeneration. About the middle of the 18th century, signs of a change appear. The Treaty of Aix-la-Chapelle (1748) brought relief from protracted wars and inaugurated a long era of peace for Italy, during which the currents of liberal ideas and the spirit of investigation characteristic of the 18th century manifested their quickening influence there as elsewhere. Aspirations toward the moral progress of the individual and toward the social betterment of the people as a whole began to find expression in writings of enduring value.

One of the most striking literary reforms belonging to the middle of the 18th century is that which was effected in comedy, through the efforts of Carlo Goldoni, who became the founder of modern Italian comedy. His great achievement was to substitute written-out comedy, as we know it, for the unwritten improvisations based upon stock scenarios and characters—the so-called *commedia dell' arte* (professional comedy)— which had monopolized the Italian comic stage for 200 years.

Parini.—In lyric poetry, amid the long-cultivated futilities of unreal Arcadianism, the note of moral earnestness and sincerity finally makes itself heard in the work of Giuseppe Parini, who, more than any other Italian writer, joined again the broken links between literature and life. A man of humble origin but of genuine nobility of soul, he felt keenly the moral laxity and social injustices of his age, and, throughout his life, he devoted himself to combating these with the powerful weapon of satire. Some of the contemporary abuses he attacked in powerful odes; in a longer poem, *Il Giorno*, "The Day," he treats, in a mock-heroic vein, of a day in the life of a young Italian nobleman, a representative of the prevailingly corrupt privileged class of his time. The whole constitutes one of the most

effective and cleverly handled pieces of satire in all literature.

Alfieri.—Parini's endeavors toward the moral reform of his contemporaries were extended to the political field by the dramatic poet, Vittorio Alfieri. Nobody felt more deeply than he the degradation of the national life of his country. The task he set before himself was the reawakening of the national consciousness, deadened in the majority of his countrymen by ages of foreign domination. This he strove to achieve through a series of tragedies glorifying champions of liberty against oppression. He tells us himself that, unable to fight alone, in the literal sense, against tyranny in rulers and apathy in the ruled, he is forced to content himself with the "mimic warfare of the stage." He chose the drama as the most appropriate vehicle for his propaganda, in order to reach the Italians through their passion for the theater, and for the purpose of reforming their taste in the drama by substituting the spoken tragedy for the song of the long popular opera, which he considered effeminate and demoralizing. The poet at whom he particularly struck was the popular Pietro Metastasio, whose sentimental tragedies, set to music by two generations of Italian composers, were sung all over Europe.

Alfieri was not so richly endowed with poetic gift as with energy and determination, and his tragedies are not dramatic masterpieces—with the possible exception of the biblical tragedy *Saul*, which is still occasionally revived in Italy. Nor was he able to wean his countrymen from their love of opera. His tragedies were widely read, however, and his principal aim was attained. Furthermore, he inspired greater poets, who followed him, with his passion for the national regeneration of Italy, to which they were able to give higher artistic expression than he could attain.

The Nineteenth Century. Among the successors of Alfieri were Ugo Foscolo, Giacomo Leopardi, and Alessandro Manzoni.

Foscolo.—In a much read epistolary novel, *The Last Letters of Jacopo Ortis* (1802), Foscolo eloquently voiced his sorrow over the fate of the ancient republic of Venice, which had been traded to Austria by Napoleon in 1797. His best lyric poem is *I Sepolcri*, "The Graves," in which he feelingly expresses his reverence for Parini, Alfieri, and other great Italians. His odes and sonnets, while not numerous, are of a very high poetic quality. His collected correspondence gives interesting pictures of himself and of his time. Unwilling to take the oath of allegiance to Austria in 1815, he went into exile, first to Switzerland and then, in 1817, to England, where he died in 1827.

Leopardi.—Leopardi, the greatest of modern Italian poets, achieved renown at twenty with two remarkable odes. The first of these, beginning "O Italy, I see thy walls, arches, columns, statues and solitary towers, but thy glory I do not see," contains the keynote of his patriotic poetry, which echoed widely among his contemporaries and maintains its appeal to this day. After three or four further odes, he discarded the patriotic strain and devoted what little strength remained to him during a long period of distressing invalidism to the expression of his personal disillusionments with life, which he came to consider not worth living.

In spite of the sterile pessimism of the poet's thought, the later odes live through their unsurpassed beauty of style. Among miscellaneous prose works, he wrote a series of essays—some in dialogue form—which display the learning for which he was as famous as for his poetry, and in which the pessimistic theme reappears in many variations. Leopardi's personality, as revealed in his poems, essays, and correspondence, has the quality of haunting the imagination of his reader as does that of his contemporary, Keats, different as were their natures.

Manzoni.—In proportion to the length of his life, the amount of Manzoni's literary output is small.

He belongs among those writers whose vein of inspiration is not copious but is intense while it lasts. He wrote when deeply stirred, with a resultant sincerity which his readers cannot help but feel. His conversion from a skeptical attitude in religion to an abiding faith he voiced in hymns (*inni sacri*) of deep feeling. In the discouraging, reactionary period of the so-called restoration which followed Napoleon's fall and the Congress of Vienna, he contributed two plays and a historical novel to the national and patriotic literature of his country.

In both novel and plays the background is historical. In the first of the latter, the *Conte di Carmagnola* (1820), Manzoni pictures the disastrous policy of the Italian states of the 15th century, whose internecine strife only prepared the way for foreign domination. The scene of the other play, the *Adelchi* (1822), is laid in northern Italy of the 8th century, during the struggle for supremacy between the Lombards and the Franks. The moral of the play is that an oppressed people can hope for no improvement of its lot from a mere change of masters, but solely from its own efforts. In the *Promessi Sposi*, "The Betrothed," the application of the rule of force in government and the petty tyranny of the nobles over the weak are exhibited in a series of vivid pictures from 17th-century life in the Milanese district. The story is unified by the adventures of three or four humble characters, victims of the forces of injustice. Manzoni's insight into human nature, his power to create living characters, his descriptive force, and his sustained excellence of style make of this work perhaps the greatest historical novel of the 19th century.

Manzoni's life was prolonged until well into the period when the aspirations of his predecessors and contemporaries with respect to Italy's unity and independence were happily fulfilled. The stirring years leading up to the great campaign of 1859, when, with French help, the Austrian grip on the country was loosened, and that of 1866, when it was finally broken—except in limited areas recovered by Italy after the World War—produced numerous writers whose work, while valuable and effective at the time, is hardly of permanent vital quality. There are, however, five outstanding figures in this period who should be mentioned. Giuseppe Giusti, Giuseppe Mazzini, Francesco de Sanctis, Pasquale Villari, and Giosuè Carducci.

Giusti's field was political satire. A number of his poems possessed intrinsic value sufficient to preserve their vitality long after the causes they advocated or condemned had passed into history.

Mazzini's power and versatility as a writer on political and miscellaneous subjects ensure him a place in the literary as well as in the political history of his time. De Sanctis is the greatest literary critic yet produced in Italy. His numerous essays on various literary subjects, as well as his *History of Italian Literature*, have attained the rank of classics.

Carducci.—Carducci became the leading poet of Italy from about 1870 until his death in 1907. As was natural in one who had lived through one of his country's greatest crises, his inspiration was largely derived from history. His great historical odes, some of them in meters adapted from Greek and Latin lyric poetry, are the finest in Italian literature since Leopardi. He excels also in the smaller forms, such as the sonnet. He was professor of Italian literature at the University of Bologna, and in this period he published many volumes of critical essays. His style is characterized by nervous vigor.

Villari.—Like Carducci, Villari, whose literary career covered nearly 70 years, was a link between the Italy of the old order and that of the new. An admirable historian, he treated early Florentine history, the life and times of the reformer Savonarola (1452–98), and the life and times of Machiavelli, in highly readable and accurate books.

Recent Literature. Among men of letters whose work was done chiefly or wholly after the establishing of Rome as the capital of the Kingdom of Italy (1870), the most notable are Giovanni Verga, Antonio Fogazzaro, Renato Fucini, Edmondo de Amicis, Giuseppe Giacosa, and Giovanni Pascoli.

Verga, a powerful realist, excels in depicting in a peculiarly intense but restrained manner. the peasant and middle-class life of his native Sicily. His best work is in the short story or sketch, in which he has achieved highly original and artistic effects.

As both poet and prose-writer, Fogazzaro reveals a noble, sympathetic nature, endowed with keen psychological insight and ability to create a great variety of characters. His *Piccolo Mondo Antico*—translated into English under the title of "The Patriot"—is the best Italian historical novel since Manzoni's *Promessi Sposi*. It vividly portrays life in northern Italy during the period culminating in 1859.

Fucini, blending humor and pathos, wrote delightful and penetrating sketches of Tuscan peasant life, that are likely to stand the test of time. He produced also a set of sonnets, mostly in dialect.

De Amicis was a versatile and popular writer, mainly of short stories and books of travel. His clever and kindly personality has endeared him to a host of readers.

Giacosa was the author of a number of successful plays that, in an effective, if not always original, way, usually deal with modern social life. His best work is *Come le Foglie*, "Like Falling Leaves."

Pascoli was looked upon as the legitimate successor to Carducci in poetry, but survived him only a few years. He was a poet of great delicacy of feeling, a lover of nature and of country life.

Several 20th-century Italian writers have become established names. Gabriele d' Annunzio was a poet, novelist, and playwright whose main asset was a colorful style, used with strong effect in descriptive passages. Benedetto Croce, a Neapolitan critic and philosopher, was prolific and influential. A follower of De Sanctis, he headed the younger school of aesthetic criticism, which arose in Italy in opposition to the historical method of criticism. Luigi Pirandello, a profound pessimist, was a novelist and dramatist whose theme is the necessity and vanity of illusion. Giovanni Papini, a brilliant and versatile writer, became widely known as an iconoclast. He subsequently evolved into a mystic with his famous *Life of Christ*. Because of extended political exile and Fascist censorship of his works, Ignazio Silone had many of his novels published in other languages. Salvatore Quasimodo was little known before he won a Nobel prize in 1959 for his lyric poetry; a founder and leading representative of the "hermetic" school of Italian literature, he was influenced by the symbolists of France. Widely translated, Alberto Moravia's works, including *The Woman of Rome* (1949) and *Two Women* (1958), have become popular as well as critical successes.

In recent Italian literature, Guiseppe Ungaretti contributed lyric and sensitive poems with a minimum of ornament. Cesare Pavese, besides writing distinguished novels and poems, popularized American works in Italy by translating such writers as Melville and Dos Passos. Roberto Bracco was a playwright of considerable power, but used themes of rarely relieved gloom. Ugo Betti cast off the excessive pessimism of Pirandello and produced notable plays.

Several Italian women have attained distinction as writers. Matilde Serao successfully portrayed Neapolitan life and character, and Grazia Deledda, recipient of a Nobel prize, described the people of her native Sardinia.

In modern Italian literature, it is necessary to mention the literary and critical periodicals *La Critica*, *La Voce*, and *La Ronda*. They have influenced and promoted Italian letters, classical and modern.

TABLE OF ITALIAN LITERATURE

Time	Author	Prose Works	Poetry and Drama
1230?—1276	Guido Guinizelli		Sonnets, Canzoni (odes).
1230?—1294	Guittone d'Arezzo	Letters	Sonnets, Canzoni.
1230—1306	Jacopone da Todi		Hymns.
1250?—1300	Guido Cavalcanti		Sonnets, Canzoni.
1255?—1336	Cino da Pistoia		Sonnets, Canzoni.
1265—1321	Dante Alighieri	Monarchia (Latin), De Vulgari Eloquentia (Latin), Letters (Latin)	Divina Commedia, Vita Nuova (poetry and prose), The Banquet (poetry and prose), Various Lyric Poems.
1304—1374	Francesco Petrarca (Petrarch)	Letters (Latin), De Viris Illustribus (Biographies in Latin), De Vita Solitaria (Latin), De Contemptu Mundi (Latin), Epistola ad Posteros (Autobiographical Letter to Posterity, Latin)	Sonnets, Canzoni, Madrigals, Sestinas, Ballads, Triumphs, Latin Epic Poem (Africa).
1313—1375	Giovanni Boccaccio	Decameron, Filocolo, Fiammetta, Corbaccio	Narrative Poems (Teseide, Filostrato), Ameto (Pastoral, poetry and prose).
1432—1484	Luigi Pulci		Romance of Chivalry (partly burlesque), Il Morgante.
1440—1494	Matteo Maria Boiardo	Translation of Herodotus	Romance of Chivalry (Orlando Innamorato), Lyric Poems.
1449—1492	Lorenzo de' Medici		Sonnets, Canzoni, Ballads, Carnival Songs, Pastoral Poems, a Sacred Drama.
1454—1494	Angelo Poliziano	Letters, Critical Works (Latin)	Lyric Poetry, Drama (Orfeo), Stanze per la Giostra.
1458—1530	Jacopo Sannazzaro		Arcadia (Pastoral, poetry and prose), Sonnets, Canzoni, Latin Poetry.
1469—1527	Niccolo Machiavelli	The Prince, The Discourses on Livy, The Art of War, History of Florence	Comedies (La Mandragola, La Clizia).
1470—1547	Pietro Bembo	History of Venice, Asolani	Poems (Sonnets, Canzoni).
1474—1533	Ludovico Ariosto		Romance of Chivalry (Orlando Furioso, continuation of Boiardo's work), Lyric Poems.
1478—1529	Baldesar Castiglione	Il Cortegiano (The Courtier)	
1490—1547	Vittoria Colonna		Sonnets and Canzoni, commemorating her husband, and on religious subjects.
1500—1571	Benvenuto Cellini	Autobiography	
1504—1573	Giraldi Cinthio	Tales	
1512—1574	Giorgio Vasari	Lives of Celebrated Artists	
1544—1595	Torquato Tasso	Treatises, Dialogues, Letters	Romance of Chivalry (Rinaldo), Pastoral Play (Aminta), Epic on First Crusade (Jerusalem Delivered).
1548—1600	Giordano Bruno	Scientific Treatises	Comedy (Il Candelaio).
1552—1623	Fra Paolo Sarpi	History of the Council of Trent	
1564—1642	Galileo Galilei	Scientific Treatises	
1568—1639	Tommaso Campanella	Philosophical Treatises, The City of the Sun (System of Ideal Government)	
1672—1750	L. A. Muratori	Annals of Italy, Italian Antiquities, Publication of Medieval Chronicles	
1698—1782	Pietro Metastasio		Dramas (used as opera librettos).
1707—1793	Carlo Goldoni		Comedies.
1729—1799	Giuseppe Parini		Odes, Il Giorno (satirical mock-heroic).
1731—1794	Girolamo Tiraboschi	Literary History	
1749—1803	Vittorio Alfieri	Autobiography	Lyric Poetry, Tragedies (Saul).
1754—1828	Vincenzo Monti		Poems, Tragedies, Epic (Mascheroniana).
1766—1837	Carlo Botta	History of Italy (continuation of Guicciardini)	
1778—1827	Ugo Foscolo	The Last Letters of Jacopo Ortis	Odes, I Sepolcri.
1785—1873	Alessandro Manzoni	I Promessi Sposi	Dramas, Odes, Hymns.
1788—1854	Silvio Pellico	My Prisons	Tragedies (Francesca da Rimini).
1789—1853	Cesare Balbo	History, Politics	
1798—1837	Giacomo Leopardi	Moral Essays	Odes.
1804—1895	Cesare Cantù	History, Novels	
1805—1872	Giuseppe Mazzini	Essays (Political and Literary)	
1817—1883	Francesco de Sanctis	History of Italian Lit., Essays	
1827—1917	Pasquale Villari	History, Biography, Essays	
1835—1907	Giosuè Carducci	Essays	Poems.
1840—1922	Giovanni Verga	Short Stories, Novels	
1842—1911	Antonio Fogazzaro	Novels (The Patriot)	Poems, Dramas.
1843—1921	Renato Fucini	Short Stories	Sonnets.
1846—1908	Edmondo de Amicis	Novels, Travel	
1847—1906	Giuseppe Giacosa		Dramas (Triumph of Love).
1856—1927	Matilde Serao	Novels, Short Stories	
1863—1938	Gabriele d'Annunzio	Novels (Il Piacere)	Poems, Dramas (Francesca da Rimini).
1866—1952	Benedetto Croce	Criticism, Philosophy, Æsthetics	
1867—1936	Luigi Pirandello	Short Stories	Dramas.
1875—1936	Grazia Deledda	Novels, Short Stories	
1881—1956	Giovanni Papini	Criticism, Autobiography	Poems.
1888—1970	Guiseppe Ungaretti		Poems.
1892—1953	Ugo Betti		Plays (La Padrona).
1900—1978	Ignazio Silone	Novels (Bread and Wine)	
1901—1968	Salvatore Quasimodo		Poems (The Promised Land).
1907—	Alberto Moravia	Novels (Two Adolescents)	
1910—	Mario Tobino	Novels (Il Clandestino.)	
1916—	Giorgio Bassani	Novels	

SPANISH LITERATURE

The Spanish language, like the French, is a descendant of the popular Latin spoken by soldiers and colonists brought into Spain by the Roman conquest. This conquest, completed by Augustus, changed the language of the country as thoroughly as it changed the customs. During the period of the Empire, Spain gave to Rome not a few Latin writers, the greatest of whom were Martial, Quintilian, Lucan, and the Elder and the Younger Seneca. The languages of Germanic origin, introduced into Spain by the barbarian invasions of the 5th century, gradually changed the character of the Latin spoken in the peninsula. The Arabian occupation of the country, begun in the 8th century and continued for seven centuries, also left important traces in the language of the population.

Early Writers. The oldest manuscript in Spanish is a fragment of a mystery play of the Magi, written for the Church of Toledo about the middle of the 12th century. Allusions in later literature suggest that the early heroic poetry of Spain may have been quite rich, and from prose passages in the *Crónica General*, or "Universal Chronicle," begun by Alfonso X, scholars have been able to reconstruct parts of several early poems. But the only work of any length from this period is the *Poema del Cid*, which was composed probably about the middle of the 12th century, though our earliest manuscript copy is of the 14th. A later manuscript, *Crónica rimada del Cid*, or "The Rimed Chronicle of the Cid," supplements the poem with a story of the youth of this hero, who was a certain Rodrigo Díaz de Bivar of the 11th century, called "El Cid" or "Lord" by the Moors.

Many ballads of later centuries also give clear evidence that early minstrels sang of Roderick the Goth and several other popular heroes.

Side by side with the school of heroic poetry, whose subjects were chosen from history and legends, there grew up in the 13th century one of religious and narrative verse written mostly by monks and of much greater bulk than was that of the romantic school. Among these monastic writers was Gonzalo de Berceo, who wrote poetical lives of the saints, devotional poems, and religious hymns. To this century belong the *Book of Apollonius*, from a Latin version, and a *Life of St. Mary of Egypt*, translated from the French. The miracle play, *El Auto de los Reyes Magos*, or "The Drama of the Three Kings," said to have appeared as early as 1120, is regarded as the oldest drama extant in any modern literature.

King Alfonso X (1221–84), better known to history as Alfonso the Wise, was author of that admirable compilation of laws known as the *Siete Partidas*, from which is derived all subsequent Spanish legislation, and of which traces are found in the state laws of Florida and Louisiana. Under his patronage many scientific compilations were made, and he is honored as the founder of history written in Spanish. The *Crónica General*, begun under his direction, tells of universal history from the creation of the world. The parts of it devoted to Spanish history, called *Historia de España*, form a veritable treasure house of Spanish tradition.

King Alfonso's example encouraged the production of various prose works, chronicles, biographies, romances, and translations of many foreign works, particularly proverbs and sayings from the Arabic. To the beginning of the 15th century belongs the most famous of the tales of chivalry, the *Amadis de Gaula*, translated from the Portuguese by Montalvo. There is also evidence that the principal themes of French romance were familiar to the Spanish writers of this time.

Don Juan Manuel, a nephew of Alfonso X, is one of the foremost prose writers of the 14th century. Both soldier and statesman, he found time to write didactic and historical treatises, but his most famous work is the *Conde Lucanor*, a collection of 51 tales drawn from various Spanish and foreign sources, each one intended to illustrate some principle of conduct or to point a moral. Juan Manuel's style is simple, dignified, and unpretentious.

Development of Poetry and Fiction. In the 14th century appeared the first of the genuine Spanish poets, Juan Ruiz, a wayward priest, who called his work *The Book of Good Love*. The genius and the skill of this Spanish poet, though lacking the dignity and tenderness of Chaucer, have nevertheless won for him a comparison to the great English master. Pedro López de Ayala, who lived in the 14th century, is the author of the didactic poem, *Rimado de Palacio*, "Court Rimes," which is a grim satire on the society of the period. He wrote also the *Chronicles of the Kings of Castile*, a narrative of great vividness and historic accuracy.

It was the 15th century which saw a full development of poetry. In the reign of John II of Castile (1406–54) there appeared a court poetry, written in short fragments and in complicated verse form. It was made up of love ditties, debates, repartees, burlesques, and satirical songs. To understand or appreciate these poems, one must read them in connection with the history of the time. Mendoza, marquis of Santillana, stands first among these courtiers and poets, and some of his lighter poems are very graceful and full of melody. Not less fascinating are those of Enrique de Villena, a scion of the royal houses of both Castile and Aragon, who is justly celebrated as being the chief propagator of the Provençal style of verse. He was, moreover, the forerunner of the Spanish humanists. Juan de Mena belongs to a succeeding phase of this period, when the influence of Italy, and especially that of Dante, began to dominate lyrical writing in general and such allegorical poems as *The Labyrinth*, from the pen of De Mena.

The 16th century produced a long line of artificial and religious epics, numerous novels of the pastoral and chivalric type, and also the first of the realistic picaresque (roguery) tales. Such tales as *El Lazarillo de Tormes*, *Guzmán de Alfarache*, *La Pícara Justina*, and *Marcos de Obregón* set the pace for all nations in the novel of adventure and intrigue. At the beginning of the 17th century, Miguel de Cervantes Saavedra produced in *Don Quixote* the supreme example in this kind of literature and put an end to the vogue of the exaggerated romance of chivalry. *Don Quixote* is Spain's greatest contribution to universal literature and remains one of the world's indestructible treasures.

The Drama. As the beginning of Spanish drama during these centuries, liturgical representations, or miracle plays, had been given at church festivals, with the object of explaining the ritual to the lay folk. Gradually, dialogue was added and plays were enacted in the public squares. Near the close of the 15th century appeared *La Celestina*, a book written by Fernando de Rojas, a most astonishing work, exhibiting for the first time persons of all classes, particularly the lowest, talking in harmony with their natural surroundings. This work, consisting of 21 acts or parts, could not have been represented on the stage, but nevertheless it left its mark on the later drama and romance of Spain.

Cervantes wrote in the great period of the Spanish drama, and he had some degree of success with play-writing, as well as with the short story. But the two great names of this period are Lope de Vega and Calderón.

The life of Lope de Vega (1562-1635) is profoundly interesting. He was a prodigy of learning and imagination. Besides tales, poems, and dramatic sketches, he produced about 1500 regular dramas, with a very large proportion of real masterpieces among them. His themes ranged from history to everyday life, the latter to be found in his comedies of character and manners. Calderón de la Barca (1600–81) succeeded Lope de Vega as head of the Spanish drama. His plays are of four kinds: sacred dramas from Scriptural sources, historical dramas, classic dramas, and pictures of society and manners. The most celebrated are *La vida es sueño*, "Life Is a Dream," and *El Mágico Prodigioso*. Calderón was attached to the court for the purpose of furnishing dramas for the royal theater. But it is as a writer of the Sacramental drama, *auto sacramental*, that his fame as a Spanish playwright stands imperishable.

The work of Lope de Vega, Calderón, Tirso de Molina, Moreto, Rojas, and others produced for Spain one of the three great dramatic literatures of the world, destined to exercise a considerable influence on other literatures.

History. With the celebrated Jesuit Juan de Mariana (1536–1623), a new manner of writing history appeared. In place of merely recording one fact after another, with no apparent connection, he wrote a general survey of the history of Spain, *Historia de España*. Garcilaso de la Vega, a descendant of the Incas, wrote a history of Florida, based upon the adventures of De Soto. To the historian, Antonio de Solís y Ribadeneira belongs a *Conquest of Mexico*, a flattering picture. López de Gomara, Oviedo y Valdéz, and Bartolomé de las Casas left records of adventures in the New World, and on these records all history of early Spanish settlements in America is founded. Among numerous writers of letters and memoirs, none surpasses Antonio Pérez (1539–1611) in style and interest. Pérez was minister to Charles V and secretary to Philip II. His *Relaciones* give a most vivid picture of the intrigues, policies, and vices of the court of Philip.

Lyric Poetry. Juan Boscán (1493?–1542?) and Garcilaso de la Vega, born in 1503, were the leaders in Spain of the Italian school of lyric poetry, led by Petrarch. Other lyric poets of great merit are Fray Luis Ponce de León and Fernando de Herrera. De León, recognized as the prince of all Spanish lyrists, is the first to have freed himself from Italian influence. Much of their verse shows a mystical inspiration drawn from the Hebrew Scriptures. To the category of mystic writers must also be added such brilliant masters of style as Fray Luis de Granada, St. John of the Cross, and St. Theresa, whose prose and verse rank them among the shining lights of Spanish literature. Nor are the popular ballads (*romances*) of this period to be overlooked. No poetry of modern times has so thoroughly influenced national life. The earliest collections of ballads, in praise of the valorous deeds of national heroes, date from the 15th century.

The Eighteenth Century. With the coming of the Bourbons to the throne of Spain in 1700, France gained a large place in Spanish thought; French customs crept into use, and French became the language of the court.

Native Spanish literature had, in the 17th century, followed in the path of the poet Luis de Góngora y Argote (1561–1627), who had introduced freaks of style and meaningless obscurity into his work. The result was a decay which left the first three decades of the 18th century practically barren, but for the establishment of the Royal Academy (1713) and the publication of its dictionary, which had no equal in any other European language. Ignacio de Luzán attempted to reform the Spanish theater upon French principles, and his *Poética* (1737), a work dealing with the French system of dramatic unities, marks the beginning of this renovation, which was assiduously promulgated by his followers, Nasarre, Montiano, and Luis Velásquez. Ramón de la Cruz delighted the Spanish public at this time with witty *sainetes*, short dramatic pieces imitated or freely translated from the French.

Leandro Fernández de Moratín, an enthusiastic disciple of Molière and a son of Nicolás de Moratín, himself a writer of some repute, produced *El Sí de las Niñas*, a still popular masterpiece of comedy.

José Francisco de Isla, a Jesuit, in his novel *Fray Gerundio*, ridiculed the extravagant pedantry of the pulpit of his day, and succeeded in bringing about some wholesome reform. Tomás Iriarte, a contemporary of De Isla, evoked the spirit of La Fontaine in fabled verse of poetic excellence.

The Nineteenth Century. Imitation of the French Classicists still persisted in the opening decades of the 19th century. Two poets, Manuel José Quintana and Juan Nicasio Gallego, acknowledge French models, even while, as patriotic Spaniards, in their heroic odes they assail the Napoleonic invaders. The highly gifted Mariano Jose de Larra (1809–37), famous as a political writer and satirist under the pseudonym "Fígaro," shows in some of his novels and plays a tendency toward Romanticism, as may be seen in his *Macías*.

The romantic movement reached Spain in the 1820's through a group of patriotic writers. These men looked to the middle ages for inspiration, and in their writings voiced the enthusiasm for social and political freedom which marked this movement in other countries. Angel de Saavedra, author of *Don Alvaro*, the most celebrated of the romantic plays, José Zorrilla, author of the popular *Don Juan Tenorio*, and Antonio García-Gutiérrez, upon whose play *El Trovador* Verdi's opera "Il Trovatore" is founded, are notable writers of this period. In 1850 the romantic movement gave way to realism.

Contemporary Writers. Spain experienced a literary revival at the end of the 19th century, and the writers initially involved are often styled the "generation of 1898." As the Spanish-American war drew to an end, artists became concerned with the "problem of Spain." They strove to upgrade their country intellectually and sociologically, deriving much of their literary inspiration from other European countries with more advanced literatures. The foremost of these writers was Miguel de Unamuno, who sought to draw the modern world into a deeper and more sympathetic understanding of Spain. Unamuno's masterpiece is generally conceded to be *Del Sentimiento Tragico de la Vida* (The Tragic Sense of Life). As Spain's foremost literary critic, Azorín (pseudonym of José Martínez Ruiz) wrote numerous essays that were responsible for renovating some of Spain's literary values. Ramón del Valle Inclán and Pio Baroja were gifted prose writers, and Antonio Machado excelled as an existentialist and mystic poet-philosopher. Successful dramatists were José Echegaray, whose sensational plays often dealt with moral problems, and the brothers Álvarez Quintero.

Because other groupings, such as the "generation of 1927," are more elusive than the "generation of 1898," it is perhaps better to speak of other writers individually. Spain's literary prowess has been seen to advantage in the novel. Two of the greatest novelists were Benito Pérez Galdós (whose monumental *Episodios nacionales* rivals Balzac's *Comédie Humaine*) and Vicente Blasco Ibáñez (*The Four Horsemen of the Apocalypse*). Outstanding essayists, vital to the development of Spanish literature, were Ramón Pérez de Ayala, Salvador de Madariaga, Ramón Menendez Pidal, and José Ortega. The brilliant dramatist Jacinto Benavente, winner of a Nobel prize in 1922, translated Shakespeare and Molière into Spanish. Gregorio Martínez Sierra, gifted as a dramatist (*The Cradle Song*), was also a novelist of merit.

Poetry flourished during the literary reawakening. In 1892, Nicaraguan poet Rubén Darió introduced modernism in Spain. This movement, rebelling against naturalism and influenced by French symbolism, principally affected the Spanish poets. Juan Ramón Jiménez won a Nobel prize in 1956 for his lyric poetry. He and others, including Pedro Salinas, Jorge Guillén, and Rafael Alberti, went into exile after the Spanish Civil War. Federico García Lorca expressed the spirit of Spain in his poems and dramas, and Blas de Otero is an outstanding poet of a younger generation.

TABLE OF SPANISH LITERATURE

Time	Authors	Prose Works	Poetry and Drama
1176—1250	Juan Lorenzo de Segura . .	. . . .	Poem on Alexander the Great.
1198—1268	Gonzalo de Berceo		Religious Poems.
1226—1284	Alfonso X	Works on Laws, Astronomy, Hist.	Canticles of the Virgin.
1282—1349	Don Juan Manuel	Tales (Conde Lucanor)	Poems.
1300—1360	Juan Ruiz de Hita		Poems (The Book of Good Love).
15th Cent.	Fernando de Rojas	La Celestina	
1411—1456	Juan de Mena		The Labyrinth.
1474—1566	Las Casas	History of the Indies	
1478—1557	Oviedo y Valdéz	History of the Indies	
1493?—1542?	Juan Boscán		Poems.
1503—1536	Garcilaso de la Vega . .		Poems, Pastorals, Sonnets.
1503—1575	Diego de Mendoza . . .	History, Fiction	
1512—1581	Jerónimo de Zurita . . .	Annals of Aragon	
1527—1591	Fray Luis de León . . .		Religious Lyrics.
1533—1595	Alonso de Ercilla		La Araucana.
1534—1597	Fernando de Herrera . .		Lyrics.
1535—1616	Garcilaso de la Vega, Inca .	History of Florida	
1536—1623	Juan de Mariana	History of Spain	
1539—1611	Antonio Pérez	Letters, Memoirs, Revelations . .	
1547—1616	Cervantes	Novels (Don Quixote, Galatea)	Short Dramatic Pieces.
1561—1627	De Góngora y Argote . .		Sonnets, Odes, Ballads, Songs.
1562—1635	Lope de Vega	Tales	Dramas (La Moza de Cántaro).
1569—1631	Guillén de Castro . . .		Dramas.
1580—1645	Gómez de Quevedo	Theology, Satires	Poems.
1590—1639	Ruiz de Alarcón y Mendoza		Dramas (Truth Suspected).
1600—1681	Calderón		Dramas (Life Is a Dream).
1610—1686	Antonio de Solís	Conquest of Mexico	
1676—1764	Benito Jerónimo Feijóo . .	Essays	
1702—1754	Don Ignacio Luzán . . .	Art of Poetry (Poética)	Poems.
1703—1781	José Francisco de Isla . .	Fray Gerundio, Translations . .	
1731—1799	Ramón de la Cruz		Dramas.
1750—1791	Tomás de Iriarte	Proverbs	
1760—1828	Leandro F. Moratín . . .		Dramas (El Sí de las Niñas), Poems.
1772—1857	Manuel José Quintana . .		Poems.
1791—1865	Angel de Saavedra . . .		Dramas, Poems (Don Alvaro).
1796—1877	Fernán Caballero . . .	Novels (La Gaviota)	
1796—1873	M. Bretón de los Herreros .		Comedy of manners.
1799—1867	S. Estébanez Calderón . .		Sketches of manners.
1803—1882	R. de Mesonero Romanos .		Sketches of manners.
1808—1842	Jose de Espronceda . . .		Poems (Canto a Teresa).
1809—1837	Mariano José de Larra . .	Political Satires, Novels . . .	Plays.
1817—1893	José Zorrilla y Moral . . .		Poems (Don Juan Tenorio).
1824—1905	Juan Valera y Alcalá . . .	Stories (Pepita Jiménez) . . .	Poems.
1829—1898	Manuel Tamayo y Baus . .		Dramas (Un drama neuvo)
1832—1916	José Echegaray		Plays (The Great Galeoto).
1833—1891	Antonio de Alarcon . . .	Novels (The Three-Cornered Hat)	Poems.
1833—1906	José M. de Pereda . . .	Novels (Sotileza)	
1836—1870	Gustavo Bécquer		Poems
1843—1920	Benito Pérez Galdós . . .	Novels (Doña Perfecta)	Dramas
1853—1938	Armando Palacio Valdés . .	Novels (Marta y María)	
1856—1912	Marcelino Menendez y Pelayo	Criticism, history	Poems, plays
1864—1936	Miguel de Unamuno . . .	Novels, Essays	Poems (El Cristo de Velazquez).
1866—1954	Jacinto Benavente		Dramas (Los Intereses Creados).
1866—1936	Ramón del Valle Inclán . .	Novels	Poems, plays
1867—1928	Blasco Ibáñez	Novels (The Four Horsemen) .	
1869—1968	Ramón Menéndez Pidal . .	Literary history	
1872—1956	Pío Baroja	Novels	
1873—1967	Azorín (José Martínez Ruiz)	Essays, novels	Plays
1875—1939	Antonio Machado		Poems, plays
1881—1947	G. Martínez Sierra . . .	Novels	Dramas (The Cradle Song).
1881—1958	Juan Ramón Jiménez . . .		Poems (Silver and I)
1883—1956	José Ortega	Essays, philosophy	
1886—1962	Ramon Perez de Ayala . .	Essays, novels	Poems
1886—1978	Don Salvador de Madariaga .	Essays (The Genius of Spain) . .	
1898—1936	Federico García Lorca . .		Poems, plays

LATIN AMERICAN LITERATURE

Latin American literature of the colonial period represents the life of the colonies. It interprets also the life of the native Indians. Long before the arrival of the Spanish conquerors, we find from fragments still preserved that the Aztecs, Mayas, and other tribes possessed literatures of oratory and storytelling in which are disclosed both grandeur of conception and transcendent power of imagery.

Mexico. After the conquest, numbers of native Indians acquired proficiency in the Spanish tongue, but, under the fierce oppression of their new masters, this activity was ruthlessly checked. Yet, in the latter part of the 16th century, native-born Mexicans manifested an extraordinary enthusiasm for literature, and we are told of literary contests taking place in which as many as 300 competitors strove for the laurels of poetry alone.

One of the most popular writers of this period was Fernán González de Eslava, whose *autos sacramentales*, or "sacred dramas," continued to be performed for over a hundred years. Francisco Terrazas, a contemporary of De Eslava's, was another poet of prominence, whose polished style won for him the praise of the great Cervantes.

A poet of rare excellence among those of the 17th century, whose name is well worthy of recording, was Sister Juana Inés de la Cruz, a nun of the Convent of St. Jerónimo. She was known in her time as "The Tenth Muse." Her writings are full of exquisite tenderness, spiritual beauty, and grace. Indeed, it may be remarked that most of the Mexican poetry of this and the following century was imbued with the deep religious feeling of the age.

José Fernandez de Lizardi (1771–1817) belongs to the transition period which marks the passing of Mexico from beneath the sway of the Spanish crown. He was the fiery evangelist, who evoked in his writings the spirit of Mexican independence. He is known as "The Mexican Thinker," and his

El Periquillo Sarniento is regarded as a classic wherever the Spanish language is spoken.

Manuel de Gorostiza (1789–1851) wrote mainly for the Spanish public, although he adapted some of his comedies to please the Mexican public. It was Ignacio Rodríguez Galván (1816–42) who first drew on national themes for his dramas. Fernando Calderón and Manuel Carpio were other contemporary writers who attained distinction, the former as a playwright and the latter as an epic poet.

The latter half of the 19th century in Mexico is remarkably prolific of literary genius. Undoubtedly, the most striking figure among the many brilliant writers of this period is Guillermo Prieto (1818–97). He was the leading spirit of republicanism. In his lyrics and novels, as well as in his political and historical works, he wrote with a flaming pen and did much to reform the abuses of his time. His style is seen to best advantage in his work *El Romancero Nacional*.

In the field of the drama, it will be noted, Mexico has ever been exceedingly rich and fertile. Nor in recent times has this fecundity shown any signs of weakening. So true is this that today Mexico City is the stronghold of a dramatic talent surpassing, it is said, that which produced the *autos sacramentales* of former times.

Among present day writers, Juan Tablada ranks high as a lyrist of tender melodies. In much of his poetry is to be found a wealth of imagery and oriental coloring strongly reminiscent of Moore's *Lalla Rookh*. Both Francisco Bulnes and Luis Obregón won distinction as historical writers. The genius of Antonio Plaza, realist and anticlerical in tendency, brought him into conflict with conservative circles. Octavio Paz has recently come to the fore as a surrealist poet with lyric skill.

Argentina. As in other colonies, the early literature of the Argentine Republic is full of that revolutionary spirit that gave birth to the nation. Pre-eminent among these early Argentine poets was Estéban Echeverría (1805–51). A cultured linguist, he wrote profusely, and in "La Cautiva" established new literary ideals which in great measure influenced the later writers of Latin America.

Ricardo Gutiérrez (1836–96) is the best interpreter of *criollo* life in Argentina. He possesses an intimate knowledge of the lower classes on the plains and has portrayed these people with vividness and imagination. Among contemporary writers are Carlos María Ocantos, whose novels are read throughout Spain as well as Latin America, and Emma de la Barra, who draws her characters from society life in Buenos Aires. Leopoldo Lugones stands out as the greatest of recent poets, his writings being a manifesto for social and political reform. Jorge Luis Borges, who became internationally known in the 1950's, excels as poet, short-story writer, and critic.

Chile. The Spaniard José Joaquín de Mora (1783–1864) and the Venezuelan Andrés Bello (1780–1865) first gave impetus to Chilean literature, which had languished since the early days of independence. Due to the sturdy homogeneity of their race and to their comparative geographical isolation, Chilean writers have excelled particularly in the more objective type of literature, such as history, the chronicle, the general essay, and historical fiction. In history and the general essay, such writers as José Victorino Lastarria (1817–88), the brothers Amunátegui, Benjamin Vicuña Mackenna (1831–86), and Diego Barros Arana (1830–1907), author of the monumental *Historia general de Chile*, have imparted to Chilean letters a note of seriousness and scholarship which richly compensates for the more brilliant but uneven literature of most of the other Spanish American countries. In the field of fiction, Alberto Blest Gana (1830-1920) is undoubtedly the greatest novelist Chile has yet produced, and perhaps the greatest in Spanish America. His realistic manner betrays keen powers of observation and bold characterization. His best work is *Martín*

Rivas. Among his followers may be mentioned Martín Palma (1821–84), Vicente Grez (1843–1909), and, more recently, Luis Orrego Luco (b. 1866), all well known for their keen studies of Chilean life.

Although poetry has had many clever devotees, it has flourished more as a cultivated plant than as one of spontaneous growth. The grandiloquent patriotic note and the narrative form set in classic molds have been especially dominant in Chilean poetry. Of late, however, romantic and *modernista* influences have inspired the verse of such writers as Eduardo de la Barra, Pedro Antonio González, Diego Dublé Urrutia, Miguel Luis Rocuant, and others. In 1945, the Chilean poetess Gabriela Mistral (Lucila Godoy Alcayaga) was awarded the Nobel Prize for Literature, the first such honor to come to a Latin American.

Uruguay. The literatures of Uruguay and Argentina have always been intimately related because of the geographical propinquity of the two countries. Each country has given refuge to literary men exiled from the other. The most brilliant name in the literature of Uruguay is unquestionably that of Alejandro Magariños (1825–93), who was at once diplomat, dramatist, poet, and novelist. Not only in his native Uruguay, but throughout Latin America and Spain, was he the object of unstinted and enthusiastic admiration. *Caramarú*, a novel of great constructive power, is looked upon as his finest work. Juan Zorilla de San Martín (1857–1931) is admitted to be the leading figure among romantic poets, as Eduardo Ocevedo Díaz (1851–1921) is the chief of story-writers, while with pungent realism Carlos Reyles depicts ranch life in the interior of the country.

Peru. For a considerable period the disturbed conditions in Peru and Bolivia retarded an otherwise natural development of native literature. Yet despite this fact the land of the Incas has shown signs of rejuvenation throughout the years of the 19th century and onward. Peru claims Carlos Agusto Salaverry (1831–90) as essentially a lyric poet with depth of feeling and great attractiveness. Manuel González Prada (1848–1918), albeit displaying a wayward and turbulent fanaticism, shows himself a past master in beauty of style. Clorinda Matto de Turner, the Peruvian wife of an Englishman, has written much patriotic poetry besides several stories and novels. Her *Aves sin Nido*, "Birds without a Nest," in which she portrays the distress of the native Indians, has been compared to *Uncle Tom's Cabin*.

Colombia. Colombia has, in the short span of its national life, produced a goodly number of literary men. The figure which looms largest among those of the 19th century is that of José María Samper (1828–98), a dramatist and novelist of rare versatility and of a high order. Rafael Núñez (1825–94), president of Colombia for many years, was a writer of polished verse as well as of political prose at once dignified and trenchant. Jorge Isaacs (1837–1895) is the author of *María*, one of the best novels in Spanish American literature.

Venezuela. In Venezuela, as in Argentina, we find literature in its earlier stages chiefly political and revolutionary. Of distinctively literary fame, however, Rafael María Baralt (1810–60), historian, poet, and scholar, is known to every student of literature in Venezuela as well as in Spain, where his talents received the recognition of membership in the Spanish Academy. Cecilio Acosta, orator and poet, is justly famous as a prose writer of great dignity and power, no less than as a master of verse full of simple grace and beauty, recalling at times the quaint and fascinating rhythm of the native Indian writers. Julio Calcana, essayist and novelist, whose work *The Castilian Language in Venezuela* has done much to inspire literary progress among his countrymen, was well known in both Europe and America. As a delineator of Venezuelan life with all its local details, Manuel Romero

García became the model for later writers. The modernist verse and political tracts of Rufino Blanco and the colorful, dramatic novels of Romulo Gallegos made them outstanding figures in recent Venezuelan literature.

Brazil. The freedom of the press and the abolition of the censorship in Brazil (1821) opened up a new era for the literature of the country. Previously, literature had been gagged and bound by political partisans, and at best there existed but a desultory spirit of dilettantism among those who were educated. Once the shackles were removed, the real soul of the Portuguese awoke and began to express itself in prose and verse. Intellectual activity was aroused, and a band of brilliant journalists and polemic writers proceeded to exert a wholesome influence on a hitherto intractable government. Tavares Bastas by his forceful *Cartas do Solitario*, "Letters of a Solitary," brought about the abolition of slavery and forced the hands of those in power to throw open the Amazon to the world's commerce. Francisco Adolpho Varnhagen is a historian of eminence, whose *Historia do Brazil* ranks high as a standard work. José de Alencar holds first place among writers of romance, to which list may be added the names of Escragnolle Taunay and Machado de Assis. The most popular of the poets are Bernardo Guimarães, Thomaz Gonzaga, Antônio Dias, and Olovo Bilac. João Guimãraes Rosa, probably Brazil's most prominent contemporary writer, produced a multi-faceted image of Brazil in *The Devil To Pay in the Backlands*.

Cuba. Cuba has contributed to literature mainly through her verse. "Every one in Cuba," writes a celebrated critic, "makes verses." The first of the great Cuban poets in the order of time is Manuel de Zequeira (1760–1846), whose patriotic odes breathe the intensive fervor of the Spaniards, Quintana and Gallego. Next, but greater than De Zequeira, comes José María de Heredia (1803–39), noted not only for his political poems, but for his descriptive verse such as "Niágara" and "Tempestad," full of glowing imagery shot with a dark and fateful melancholy.

Gabriel de la Concepción Valdés (1809–44), if a lesser light, was a poet of true worth. A mulatto foundling, his lyrics will live as long as the Spanish tongue is spoken. Of Gertrudis Gómez de Avellaneda (1814–73), it is said she has no rival of her sex as a lyric poet in any literature, unless we go back to Sappho and Corinna or to the Italian Renaissance and Vittoria Colonna.

Cuba shows a lamentable dearth of prose writers, and the work of the few that can be mentioned ranks much inferior to that of her poets. In the list of historians, the names of Arrati and Urrutia in the 18th century and those of Valdés and Arrango y Castillo in the 19th are perhaps the most prominent and noteworthy. Outstanding among Cuban novelists is Cirilo Villaverde, known especially for his *Cecilia Valdez*. Carlos de la Torre's *Historia Natural de Cuba* is well and favorably known.

An interesting essay by Menéndez y Pelayo on the lyric poets of Cuba forms the preface to the *Antología de poetas hispano-americanos*, in which may be found an excellent selection of the works of the more important.

No literary sketch of Latin America as a whole would be complete without touching upon the *modernista* movement, which has not only transcended the several Spanish American nationalities, but has extended also to the mother country. The *modernistas*, finding their source of inspiration in the French Parnassians, decadents, and symbolists, and in Poe and Walt Whitman, have enriched the Spanish language and made it more lucid and vigorous. The leader of this important movement is the Nicaraguan Rubén Darío, whose *Azul*, published in 1888, set the pace for a brilliant galaxy of poets and essayists, of whom the Peruvian José Santos Chocano and the Uruguayan José Enrique Rodó are perhaps the best-known representatives.

GERMAN LITERATURE

The origins of German literature are shrouded in obscurity, but it is certain that the Germans were the last important people of western Europe to achieve international literary repute. This was due partly to their geographical isolation from Roman and Gallic culture (the Alps, the Rhine), partly to the great migrations which swept across the German lands again and again (Visigoths, Vandals, Huns) and which diverted the minds of the people from literary pursuits.

Early Medieval Epics. The bases of their literary beginnings were the same as in other Western lands: songs and epic lays celebrating their military triumphs, written in rugged alliterative verse, such as that of *Beowulf*, and sung in the halls of the chiefs by professional bards. These were orally transmitted, and are largely lost to us, for the great collection which Charlemagne caused to be made was subsequently destroyed by pious zealots. Only a fragment is preserved for us in very nearly its original form: a bit of the *Hildebrandslied* (about 800), which relates in crude but powerful alliterative verse the widely popular story of a father who is forced to do battle with a knight and slay him, knowing it is his own unsuspecting son.

Ancient saga material, though in a modernized form, comes to us in the *Nibelungenlied*, the greatest national epic of Germany, and one of the great epics of the world. Crude in form, it tells a story which for primitive dramatic power can hardly be surpassed. It is the story of Siegfried, who wins Brunhild for his master Gunther; of his death at the hands of Gunther's henchman Hagen because Siegfried's wife, Kriemhild, boasts of his triumph over Brunhild; and of Kriemhild's vengeance on her kinsmen, Gunther and the Burgundians.

From the monasteries, which alone kept literature alive in the 9th and the 10th century, we have two interesting literary figures. One is Otfried von Weissenburg, who (about 868), using rime for the first time in Germany, wrote a Gospel harmony to show his disapproval of "the obscene songs of the laymen." The other was the nun Hroswitha of Gandersheim (10th century), who wrote Latin plays dealing with the struggle between the virtues and the vices. *Dulcitius* is a typical example of her art, which derives from the Latin poet Terence.

The Crusades, that ushered in the age of chivalry (11th to 13th century), fostered a new narrative literature that grew out of the old epics and sagas, but was adapted to a courtly audience and a modern taste. Among the many writers of the so-called court epic, the three outstanding figures are Hartmann von Aue, Wolfram von Eschenbach, and Gottfried von Strassburg. Hartmann (d. 1220?) takes his *Erec* and *Iwein* from the French romances of the Arthurian cycle, and tells in *Der Arme Heinrich* (see Hauptmann's drama) one of the most affecting tales of medieval literature: a peasant girl offers her lifeblood to cure her master's leprosy; his refusal of her sacrifice purifies his soul and his body.

Gottfried (1165?–1215?) writes in *Tristan und Isolde* a story of forbidden love, with a tragic outcome, which Wagner's opera has made famous. Nowhere else in medieval German literature do we find so convincing a study of the love-passion.

Wolfram (d. 1225) is the greatest thinker and philosopher of the three. He gets the theme of *Parzival* from the French, but deepens and broadens it until it becomes the epitome of the development of the human soul. The raw youth Parzival sins and errs, is purified by suffering, and finally becomes worthy to be lord of the castle of the Holy Grail.

Minnesinger and Meistersinger. With the Crusades and chivalry came the development of the feudal system, one of whose happier by-products was the so-called *minnesong*, in which poets embodied in lyric verse a chivalric conception of love. Scores of noble knights turned to song in praise of their ladyloves, until such lyrics became almost a standard product. One poet, however, Walther von der Vogelweide (d. 1230), succeeded in making the conventional love song the vehicle for some of the most charming lyrics in the German language. Nor did Walther confine himself to songs of courtly *minne* or "love"; he also wrote lines glowing with religious fervor, and some of the earliest patriotic verses in German come from his pen. He was also a master of humor, as are all who come close to life.

The rapid bloom of this great epoch faded as rapidly, and German literature entered upon a long decline (1350–1650). The minnesong grew more and more conventional and empty, and in its place rose the *Meistergesang*, or "mastersong," so deliciously satirized in Wagner's "Meistersinger." Poetry and song were to be produced by rule of thumb, like shoes or bricks, and judged by pedantic criteria. Yet there were powerful forces at work; only they found no master minds to bring them to full fruition. The natural fondness of the common people for songs of love and war and history, of religious fervor and the joys of wine, burst forth in the artless but vigorous folk song, in which Germany still stands pre-eminent. The religious spirit of the time and of the German people found expression in the mysticism of Meister Eckhart (about 1260–1328), and in the only less powerful Heinrich Suso (1295–1366) and Johannes Tauler (1290–1361). Aside from their own writings, their importance lies in the fact that their individualistic trend was preparing for the struggle in which the Protestants battled for the rights of the individual conscience; and their early translation of the Bible paved the way for Martin Luther.

At this period the drama begins to emerge as a special literary category, growing out of the so-called mystery plays, which were at first given in the churches as genuine religious performances, then gradually became secularized. The influence of Latin comedy, brought in by the humanists, was especially marked in the form of the German plays. One of the most productive writers of short comedies was Hans Sachs (1494–1576), the famous cobbler of Nuremberg, who deserves more notice, however, as singer and story-teller.

Mention might be made, too, of Sebastian Brant (1458–1521) and his *Ship of Fools*, a bitter and widely influential satire on the gross ignorance of the common people. Grotesque and often coarse practical jokes were collected as the pranks of *Till Eulenspiegel*, and the animal fables of the middle ages developed into the fascinating epic of *Reynard the Fox* (printed 1498).

The Reformation. Great importance in the history of German literature must be accorded to Philipp Melanchthon (1497–1560), Ulrich von Hutten (1488–1523), and Martin Luther (1483–1546). Hutten and Melanchthon were reformers of the intellect, Luther a reformer of the spirit. The labors of the former, who were leaders in the humanistic movement in Germany, sharpened men's wits and polished their speech through the study of the classics; the labors of the latter came to work a profound change in the relations of men to God. Luther's prime literary service, however, apart from his stirring and devout hymns, was the great translation of the Bible into the language of the Saxon chancelleries, whereby he created a classic that set the standard for the literary speech of his country.

On the other hand, Luther's work brought upon the literature of Germany the most disastrous blight it had ever known, when the deluge of the Thirty Years' War (1618–48) left Germany at a lower stage of political and moral degradation than that reached by any European people since the middle ages. The crushing of the middle classes destroyed all political and religious liberty; the country was inpoverished; its population was reduced by three-fourths; the best energies of its citizens were needed in the indispensable work of restoration.

For nearly one hundred years German literature sank into utter insignificance. One great novel did indeed result from the turmoil: Grimmelshausen (1625–76) bequeathed to us in his *Simplicissimus*, a story of life in Germany during the Thirty Years' War, that is worthy of its place among the great books of the world. But otherwise we have mediocrities: Opitz (1597–1639) with his unsuccessful efforts to reform German poetry; Gryphius (1616–64) with his two farce-comedies, of which *Peter Squentz* alone has any vitality; and other lesser lights, such as Gellert, writer of fables and odes, Haller, author of the didactic poem *The Alps*, Gessner, whose pastoral idyls were widely read in his day, and Gottsched (1700–66), the advocate of French classicism on the German stage.

The German Revival. By an odd paradox, it is with the reign of Frederick the Great of Prussia (1740–86), who himself spoke and wrote only French and had nothing but contempt for the best German writers of his day, that we associate the renaissance of German letters. The German people were recovering from the effects of the Thirty Years' War; conditions had become more settled, and were more favorable to the leisure that literary production requires. The stage was set for the most dramatic literary development that any European literature has witnessed. Three men stand out as leaders of the German people toward the brilliance of its classical period in letters. Klopstock (1724–1803), in his *Messiah*, was the first German poet to attempt the sublime, and he succeeded in voicing the religious idealism of the German people of his time; in his *Odes* he sounds the note of cosmopolitanism coupled with genuine patriotism. Wieland (1733–1813) attempted, in his *Agathon*, to exemplify by an object lesson the true way toward individual perfection, and gave expression in it to the same spirit that was to underlie Goethe's *Faust*—faith in the innate goodness and the unwearied aspiration of the human soul. His graceful, charming style and manner cultivated German taste as Klopstock's work had promoted German idealism and moral sentiment. Greater than either is Lessing (1729–81), whose versatility and keenness of intellect hardly yield the palm to Goethe's own. He it was whose fierce polemic freed German letters from the fallacies that hemmed its growth, and who set up the new canons of theory and technique that the literary world has subsequently justified. But not only was he a critic; he could produce. *Minna von Barnhelm* is the first great play of German life, the first German comedy to outlive its author, and the first German work to voice the plea for national unity. *Emilia Galotti* is a bitter indictment of the evils of monarchic absolutism. *Nathan the Wise* champions, in the very teeth of intolerance, the now universally accepted principle of free inquiry in religious as in other matters.

The seeds of the doctrine of individualism which the Mystics had preached and the Protestants had died to defend, which Lessing had championed and Rousseau had made into a passionate slogan, became as grains of dynamite in France, whereas in Germany they flowered out in a golden age of literature. The frenzy of "Storm and Stress"—the term is the title of a play by Maximilian Klinger—soon gave place to the restrained symmetry of the classic writers.

The Classic Period. There are four men that guide the peaceful triumph of this German revolution. Herder (1744–1803) defended individualism, but viewed it as an element in national character, thus enforcing the patriotic lesson of *Minna von Barnhelm*. He drove home the theory of the embodiment of national traits in all significant literature, and made the first studies in what we now call comparative literature. As Herder showed history to blend individual and collective forces, Kant (1724–1804) revealed a similar ideal in the mental and moral life of man. First proving that all human knowledge is subjective, in his *Critique of Pure Reason*, he proceeded to formulate, in his *Critique of Practical Reason*, religious and ethical principles which still sway the civilized world. Our individual freedom, Kant says, lies in obedience to the moral law that speaks within us.

What Kant and Herder taught, one as critic, the other as philosopher, was creatively embodied in the works of the two great poets of the age. Goethe (1749–1832) saw life as an organic whole, like Herder; Schiller (1759–1805) saw it as a continual struggle for perfection. Goethe strove for æsthetic universality; Schiller, for moral freedom. Both began as poets of "Storm and Stress": Goethe's *Götz von Berlichingen*, *Werther*, and *Faust*, Schiller's *Robbers*, *Love and Intrigue*, and *Fiesco*—all deal with excessively emotional and impulsive natures, and all are more or less tragically conceived. Their influence and their appeal to contemporaries were unexampled: utter strangers embraced and wept on each other's necks at the first performance of *The Robbers*.

But this early individualism was soon transmuted into a classic collectivism, partly under Italian influence. Goethe produced *Iphigenia*, *Wilhelm Meister*, and *Hermann und Dorothea*; Schiller, his great dramas,—*Wallenstein*, *Mary Stuart*, *William Tell*. Still later, at the very close of his life, Goethe embodied in the second part of *Faust* a supreme utterance of one of the fundamental tendencies of all modern life.

Romanticism. The individualistic note of the closing 18th century rings through the discordant harmonies of the Romantic school, in the unrestrained imaginings and fantastic self-assertiveness of Tieck (*William Lovell*), F. Schlegel (*Lucinde*), Novalis (*Henry of Ofterdingen*), and J. P. Richter (*Quintus Fixlein*, *Siebenkäs*).

On the other hand, the collectivistic humanism of Goethe and Schiller was held fast by Kleist (*Prinz von Homburg*) and by Uhland, author of many of the best-known lyrics and ballads in the language; while the speculative genius of Kant found worthy successors in Fichte, Schelling, Hegel, and Schleiermacher.

The reaction from the liberalizing tendencies of the late 18th century was fateful for German literature, and a fresh decline set in, which reached almost as low a level between 1850 and 1870 as it had a hundred years before. The Austrian censorship stunted the growth of Grillparzer (*Sappho*, *The Golden Fleece*); political pressure forced Rückert, a patriotic lyric poet, into retirement; Schopenhauer, the pessimistic thinker, Lenau, the morbid poet, and Platen, the morose one, are characteristic results of this discordance. Gravest harm was done to Heine (1797–1856), one of the most original lyric poets Germany has had, who, despite his patriotic fervor, was virtually driven into exile, a humiliated, embittered, disappointed man.

Recent and Contemporary Writing. With the turn of the mid-century, however, there began a steady rise of German letters. Friedrich Hebbel (*Agnes Bernauer*, *Herodes und Mariamne*) writes some of the most powerful dramas of the 19th century; Richard Wagner combines drama and music with surpassing genius in creations of overwhelming power. There is a new school of novelists: Freytag (*Debit and Credit*), Ludwig (*Between Heaven and Earth*), K. F. Meyer (*The Saint*), Spielhagen (*Storm and Flood*), Anzengruber (*Meteor Farm*), Sudermann (*Dame Care*), Frenssen (*Jörn Uhl*), Thomas Mann (*Buddenbrooks*), including the women writers Böhlau (*The Switching-Station*), Ebner-Eschenbach (*The Child of the Parish*), and Viebig (*Our Daily Bread*). And of short story writers several are notable—Gottfried Keller (*Seldwyla Folk*), Heyse (*The Fury*), Storm (*Immensee*), Rosegger, and others. Foremost in the field of biography is Emil Ludwig.

Lyric poetry remains at a high level throughout. One might mention, as outstanding figures of recent years, Liliencron, Dehmel, Hofmannsthal, and some of the above-mentioned novelists, notably Keller, Meyer, and Storm.

With the eighteen-nineties, German drama entered into a new period of success and eminence, under the influence of Zola, Ibsen, Tolstóy, and other naturalistic writers. Chief among the dramatists are Gerhart Hauptmann (*The Weavers*, *Lonely Lives*, *Rose Bernd*, *Henry the Wretched*, *The Sunken Bell*), who cultivates both a romantic and a realistic vein, and Sudermann (*Heimat*, *Sodom's End*), a playwright rather than a dramatist. Mention might also be made of Hofmannsthal (*The Adventurer and the Singer*), Schnitzler (*Light o' Love*), and Wedekind (*Spring's Awakening*).

In the early 20th century the Austrian-born Kafka confused, depressed, and fascinated with his insidiously horrible tales—a representative of the age of anxiety. His influence spread throughout most of the world. Then came the Nazi holocaust and a dispersion of the best German writers to the United States and other countries. Prime among them was the novelist Thomas Mann (*Glass Mountain*, *Buddenbrooks*). Others included Feuchtwanger (*Power*), Zweig (*Education before Verdun*), and Remarque (*All Quiet on the Western Front*).

TABLE OF GERMAN LITERATURE

Time	Name	Prose	Poetry and Drama
About 865	Otfried		Rimed Gospel Harmony.
About 967	Hroswitha		Latin Comedies (Dulcitius).
?–1225	Wolfram von Eschenbach		Court Epics (Parzival).
?–1230	Walther von der Vogelweide		Love Songs, Hymns, Patriotic Poems
1165?–1215?	Gottfried von Strassburg		Epic (Tristan).
1170–1220?	Hartmann von Aue		Epics (Der Arme Heinrich).
1458–1521	Sebastian Brant		Satiric Poem (Ship of Fools).
1483–1546	Martin Luther	Bible Translation	Hymns (Ein Feste Burg).
1494–1576	Hans Sachs		Verse Tales, Plays (The Hot Iron).
1597–1639	Martin Opitz	Literary Theory	Songs, Odes, Sonnets.
1607–1676	Paul Gerhardt		Hymns (O Haupt voll Blut und Wunden).
1625–1676	H. J. K. von Grimmelshausen	Novel (Simplicissimus)	
1700–1766	J. C. Gottsched	Criticism (Versuche einer Kritischen Dichtkunst)	
1708–1777	A. von Haller		Odes, Didactic Poems (The Alps).
1724–1803	F. G. Klopstock		Messiah, Odes.
1724–1804	Immanuel Kant	Philosophy (Critique of Pure Reason)	
1729–1781	G. E. Lessing	Criticism (Laokoön)	Dramas (Minna von Barnhelm).

TABLE OF GERMAN LITERATURE—Con.

Time	Author	Prose Works	Poetry and Drama
1730–1788	S. Gessner	Idyls.	
1733–1813	C. M. Wieland	Novels (Agathon)	Epic (Oberon).
1744–1803	Johann G. von Herder	Criticism	Translations (Cid, Folk Songs).
1747–1794	G. A. Bürger		Ballads (Lenore), Lyrics.
1749–1832	Wolfgang von Goethe	Novel (Wilhelm Meister)	Dramas (Faust), Lyrics, Epic.
1751–1826	Johann H. Voss		Translation (Iliad), Idyl (Luise).
1759–1805	J. C. F. von Schiller	History of Thirty Years' War	Dramas (William Tell), Ballads.
1762–1814	Johann G. Fichte	Philosophy (System of Ethics).	
1763–1825	Jean P. Richter	Humorous Novels (Awkward Age)	
1767–1845	A. W. von Schlegel	Criticism	Translations (Shakspere, Calderón).
1768–1834	F. E. D. Schleiermacher	Philosophy of Religion.	
1770–1831	Georg W. F. Hegel	Philosophy	
1772–1801	Novalis	Novels (Henry of Ofterdingen)	Lyrics (Hymns to Night).
1772–1829	F. von Schlegel	Criticism, Novel (Lucinde)	
1773–1853	Ludwig Tieck	Satire, Fancy (Puss in Boots)	Dramas (Genoveva).
1775–1854	F. von Schelling	Philosophy	
1777–1811	H. von Kleist	Tales (Michael Kohlhaas)	Dramas (Prinz von Homburg).
1781–1838	A. von Chamisso	Tales (Peter Schlemihl)	Ballads.
1785–1863	Jakob Grimm	Fairy Tales	
1786–1859	Wilhelm Grimm	Fairy Tales	
1787–1862	Ludwig Uhland		Ballads, Lyrics.
1788–1860	Arthur Schopenhauer	Pessimistic Philosophy	
1791–1813	Karl Theodor Körner		War Lyrics (Lyre and Sword).
1791–1872	Franz Grillparzer	Tale (The Poor Fiddler)	Dramas (Sappho).
1797–1856	Heinrich Heine	Pictures of Travel (Harz Journey)	Love Songs, Ballads (Lorelei).
1812–1882	Berthold Auerbach	Novels (Black Forest Stories)	
1813–1863	Friedrich Hebbel		Dramas (Maria Magdalena).
1813–1865	Otto Ludwig	Novel	Dramas (Der Erbförster).
1816–1895	Gustav Freytag	Novels (Debit and Credit)	Plays (Journalists).
1817–1888	Theodor Storm	Stories (Immensee)	Lyrics.
1817–1903	Theodor Mommsen	History (Roman History).	
1819–1890	Gottfried Keller	Novels (Der Grüne Heinrich)	Poems.
1819–1898	Theodor Fontane	Novels (Effi Briest)	
1825–1898	K. F. Meyer	Novels (The Saint)	Poems.
1829–1911	F. Spielhagen	Novels (Storm and Flood).	
1830–1914	Paul Heyse	Stories (The Fury).	
1830–1916	Marie von Ebner-Eschenbach	Novel (Child of the Parish).	
1839–1889	Ludwig Anzengruber	Novel (Meteor Farm).	
1843–1918	Peter Rosegger	Stories of Peasant Life	
1844–1900	F. Nietzsche	Philosophy	
1844–1909	D. von Liliencron	Stories (Kriegsnovellen)	Lyrics.
1857–1928	Hermann Sudermann	Novels (Dame Care)	Dramas (Heimat).
1860–1952	Clara Viebig	Novels (Our Daily Bread).	
1862–1946	Gerhart Hauptmann	Novels (Emanuel Quint)	Dramas (Sunken Bell).
1862–1931	Arthur Schnitzler	Stories (Sterben)	Dramas (Liebelei).
1863–1920	Richard Dehmel		Poems (Zwei Menschen), Lyrics.
1863–1945	Gustav Frenssen	Novels (Jörn Uhl)	
1864–1918	Frank Wedekind		Dramas (Spring's Awakening).
1864–1947	Ricarda Huch	Novels (Ludolf Ursleu).	
1874–1929	H. von Hofmannsthal		Lyrics, Dramas (Death and the Fool).
1875–1955	Thomas Mann	Novels (Buddenbrooks)	
1875–1926	Rainer M. Rilke		Poems (Life and Songs).
1877–1962	Hermann Hesse	Novels (Steppenwolf)	
1880–1936	Oswald Spengler	Philosophy (Decline of the West)	
1881–1948	Emil Ludwig	Biography (Napoleon)	
1884–1958	Lion Feuchtwanger	Novels (Power, Success)	
1886–1956	Gottfried Benn		Poems
1887–1914	Georg Trakl		Poems
1887–1968	Arnold Zweig	Novels (Education before Verdun)	
1890–1945	Franz Werfel	Novels (The Song of Bernadette)	
1891–1970	Nelly Sachs		Poems, plays
1897–	Karl H. Waggerl (Austrian)	Novels (Das Jahr des Herra)	
1898–1970	Erich Remarque	Novels	
1898–1956	Bertolt Brecht		Plays (The Trial of Lucullus).
1911–	Max Frisch (Swiss)	Novels	Plays (Andorra)
1911–	Fritz Höchwalder		Plays (The Holy Experiment)
1916–	Peter Weiss		Plays (The Investigation)
1917–	Heinrich Böll	Novels (Tomorrow and Yesterday)	
1920–1970	Paul Celan		Poems
1921–	Friedrich Dürrenmatt		Plays (The Visit)
1927–	Günter Grass	Novels	
1934–	Uwe Johnson	Novels	

DUTCH LITERATURE

Dutch literature, including Flemish, begins with the rise of the Low Frankish dialect, or *Niederdeutsch*, about the middle of the 13th century. The first writing of literary rank is said to be a version of the French romance of Floris and Blanchefleur. Very soon several Dutch authors gave their countrymen tales from the romances of Charlemagne and Arthur. In the latter part of the 13th century, the language was used with such skill and vigor by Jakob van Maerlant that to him has been assigned the title "Father of Dutch Poetry."

Popular Drama. Like that of England and France, the drama of the Netherlands began in the medieval mystery and miracle plays. In the 14th and 15th centuries, burgher literary guilds or clubs arose in the towns from the organizations that produced these sacred dramas. Poetic and dramatic contests, held by these clubs on popular festivals, served to popularize literature among the people. However, virtually no important original work came out of this period of comparative barrenness, which corresponds to the Burgundian and Spanish supremacy in the Netherlands. The publication of the *Staatenbijbel*, the Dutch authorized version of the Scriptures, in the 16th century, exerted a powerful influence in stabilizing the language. One cultured writer, Dirk Potter (d. 1428), who had traveled to Italy, wrote a long poem, *Der Minnen Loep*, "Course of Love," after the manner of Boccaccio.

Renaissance and Reformation. The 16th century saw, along with the Reformation, a revival of classical learning. Three names in this century are notable. Anna Bijns (1494–1575) is said to have been the "first writer to use the Dutch tongue with grace and precision of style." Dirk Volkertszoon Coornhert (1522–90), a man of philosophic bent, wrote poetry, drama, and prose, all of considerable merit. Philip van Marnix (1538–98) produced a famous folk song, "William of Nassau," and satirized the Roman Church. To this period belongs the famous Dutch scholar, Erasmus (1466?–1536); and in the following century the works of Spinoza, the philosopher (1632–77), and those of Grotius, the great jurist and theologian (1583–1645), imparted luster to Dutch scholarship. But these authors wrote mostly in Latin.

Amsterdam, with its freedom of thought, was the center of Dutch literary activity in its Augustan age, the 17th century. Pieter Corneliszoon Hooft (1581–1647), author of a valuable history of the Netherlands, is regarded as the prose master of this period, as Joost van den Vondel, his contemporary (1587–1679), is the greatest of all Dutch dramatists. His powers were well adapted to the treatment of sublime conceptions. Of 32 tragedies that he wrote, half are founded upon biblical subjects. The influence of his drama *Lucifer* is discoverable in Milton's *Paradise Lost*. Two other great lyric poets worthy of mention are Dirk Camphuizen (1586–1627) and Constantine Huygens (1596–1687). Other dramatists of the century were Geeraerdt Brandt (1626–85) and Antonides van der Goes (d. 1684), the latter noted for a beautiful descriptive poem called *De Ystroom*. The popular poet of the time was Jakob (Father) Cats (1577–1660). He took his themes from everyday life, and through his verse there runs a vein of homely wit mingled with shrewd common sense that appealed to the people.

Decadence and Revival. After the close of the wars in the late 17th century, there began a period of literary decadence. For nearly a century, Dutch writers were, for the most part, mere imitators under French influence. The literary society "Nil volentibus arduum," established by Andries Pel, followed strictly the French school of drama, while Johann Oudaen (d. 1692), Van Focquenbrock, and Rotgans held to traditions of a more native cast. Voltaire's *Henriade* was translated with elaborate detail by Sybrand Feitama (1694–1758); Hoogvliet produced the remarkably fine epic, *Abraham* (1763); and Van Waagenaar, his great history of Holland. In the last quarter of the 18th century, however, the influence of the great literary awakening in Germany touched the Dutch genius. A fresh stream of romantic and patriotic poetry flowed in the verse of Jan Helmers (1767–1813) and Hendrik Tollens (1780–1856). Willem Bilderdijk (1756–1831),—after Vondel the most powerful among Dutch writers,—and likewise his successor, Isaac da Costa (1798–1860), showed themselves in brilliant opposition to the classic spirit.

The Nineteenth Century. After the resplendency of Bilderdijk, a new period of Dutch literature begins with the 19th century. Jakob van Lennep (1802–68), poet, dramatist, and romancer, has been called the "Dutch Sir Walter Scott." He was followed by Mrs. Bosboom-Toussaint, Schimmel, and a host of other excellent writers. In the work of Nikolaas Beets (1814–1903), who is reckoned the greatest Dutch humorist, the influence both of Scott and of Dickens may be seen. Edward Dekker (1820–87), known by his pen name

of "Multatuli," is celebrated outside of the Netherlands for his romance, *Max Havelaar*, in which he attacked Dutch rule in Java.

The novel is still the most representative phase of Dutch literature. Adèle Opzoomer (A. S. C. Wallis) and Louis Couperus are both well-known authors of popular stories. Among several poets who have attained distinction since 1880 are the lyrist Hélène Lapidoth-Swarth, M. Emants, and F. Van Eeden, the last a writer of both lyrics and drama. The feminist writer and novelist, Jo van Ammers-Küller, wrote many novels, short stories, and plays. Anne Frank (1929–1945) is known for her revealing diary written while in hiding during Nazi occupation of Holland.

DANISH LITERATURE

Outside of the runic inscriptions, no literary monument from pagan times (before 1000) has been preserved in Denmark. The first half of the middle age (1000–1500) was a period of growing power and influence culminating in the age of the Waldemars, while the second half shows decline. The earliest written literature is in Latin, the most famous Latin work being *Gesta Danorum*, the early history of Denmark, written by Saxo. The provincial laws of Scania and Zealand and the later law of Jutland (1241) were in Danish. The famous Danish ballads had their beginning in the 12th century. This popular literature reached its highest development in the 14th century but continued for many generations after that.

At the time of the Reformation (1530), the most important name is that of Kristiern Pedersen, who contributed an important part to the first complete Danish translation of the Bible (1550). The early leaders of the Lutheran Reformation tried to reach the common people by publishing, in the mother tongue, polemical writings, songs, and satires. The first Danish hymn book was printed in 1528. In the Age of Learning, following the Reformation, Latin was again used by the learned. The sciences have brilliant representatives in this age: Tyge (Tycho) Brahe, Thomas Bartholin, Steno, Ole Römer. A. S. Vedel, who translated Saxo's work, and A. Huitfeldt were historians. To the 17th century belongs the famous hymn writer, Thomas Kingo. Toward the close of the century there was a revival of interest in the Danish language.

The greatest name of the 18th century is that of the Norwegian Ludvig Holberg, the real father of modern Dano-Norwegian literature. He towers far above his contemporaries. Yet, in his age lived the great hymn writer, A. Brorson, and Ambrosius Stub shows his love of nature in poems that still are popular. The latter half of the century is the Age of Enlightenment. The Norwegian Tullin wrote his highly admired *May Day*, the Norwegian Brun wrote *Zarine* in imitation of the French classical drama, the Norwegian Wessel wrote his immortal parody *Love without Stockings*, which cleared the atmosphere of bombast and artificiality. The outstanding Danish genius of the time is Johannes Ewald, author of the Danish national hymn "King Christian."

With the 19th century came the Age of Romanticism, beginning the golden age of Danish literature. A. G. Oehlenschläger is the greatest name of the period. His *Poems* of 1803 were epoch making, and after that he published one successful work after another, among them *Hakon Jarl* and *Aladdin*. Contemporary with him was N. F. S. Grundtvig, one of the most powerful men Denmark has produced, exerting great and lasting influence. Ingemann is Denmark's Walter Scott, Blicher portrays life in Jutland in masterly fashion, Hauch is a prominent writer, Winther a great lyric poet. J. L. Heiberg created the popular form of comedy, technically called "vaudeville," and was an eminent literary critic. *The Soul after Death* is his best-known work. Henrik Hertz was a versatile dramatist and a master of style. H. C. Andersen won world fame through his fairy tales, and Paludan-Müller was an author of great power and depth. Ploug became the poet of the historical movement called Scandinavianism; Goldschmidt, the great prose writer, attacked absolutism in politics unsparingly, till Denmark adopted her constitution in 1849. The most generally popular author in this period is Hostrup, whose comedies are most entertaining, rivaling the works of Heiberg and Hertz. In the period of 1850–70, several new men of talent appear, winning much popularity, but there is no outstanding genius.

With the famous lectures of 1871 by Georg Brandes, for over fifty years Europe's best-known literary critic, begins the Age of Realism. Of the new men, the best-known are Drachmann, who was Denmark's greatest lyric poet, Schandorph, and J. P. Jacobsen, two of whose novels have recently been translated into excellent English. Somewhat later appear K. Gjellerup, H. Pontoppidan—these two are the Danish writers who have won the Nobel prize—H. Bang, G. Wied, Karl Larsen. Of other recent writers, the best-known are K. Michaelis, J Jörgensen, V. Rördam, L. C. Nielsen, J. Aakjær, J. V. Jensen. The last mentioned is a master of style and is endowed with a superior creative imagination. Andersen-Nexö has powerfully depicted the life of the proletariat.

TABLE OF DANISH LITERATURE

Time	Name	Prose	Poetry and Drama
1200–?	Saxo Grammaticus	History of Denmark	
1480–1554	Kristiern Pedersen	Tales, Translation of Bible	
1494–1561	Hans Tausen	Religion	
1495–?	Broder Niels		Rimed Chronicle.
1587–1637	Anders Arrebo		World's First Week, Poetic Version of David's Psalms, Hexameron.
1634–1703	Thomas Kingo		Psalms, Hymns, Winter Psalter.
1684–1754	Ludvig Holberg	History of the World, Philosophy	Comedies, Comic Poetry.
1694–1764	Hans A. Brorson		Hymns.
1743–1781	Johannes Ewald		King Christian, Lyrics, Tragedies.
1744–1812	Werner Abrahamson	Criticism	
1760–1830	Knud Lyne Rahbek	Novels, Essays	Dramas, Songs.
1764–1826	Jens Baggesen	Novels, Essays, Travels	Humorous Poems, Lyrics, Rimed Letters.
1769–1826	Adolph Schack-Staffeld		Lyrics.
1773–1856	Baroness Gyllembourg	Novels	
1775–1854	Bishop Mynster	Theology	
1777–1817	Peter T. Foersom		Translation of Shakspere.
1779–1850	A. G. Oehlenschläger	Romances	Tragedies, Poems (Hakon Jarl, Aladdin).
1783–1872	N. F. S. Grundtvig	Theology, Politics	Poems, Hymns.
1789–1862	Bernhard S. Ingemann	Historical Novels	Lyrics, Epics.
1791–1860	Johan L. Heiberg		Lyrics, Dramas.
1791–1862	Niels M. Petersen	History, Mythology	
1793–1877	H. N. Clausen	Criticism	
1794–1838	Poul Möller	Novels	Poems, Student Songs.
1796–1876	Christian Winther	Tales	Poems.
1798–1865	A. N. de Saint-Aubain	Romances	
1798–1870	Henrik Hertz		Lyrics, Satire, Dramas, Epics.
1805–1875	Hans C. Andersen	Fairy Tales, Novels (Only a Fiddler)	Dramas, Poems.
1809–1876	Frederik Paludan-Müller		Dramas, Poems.
1813–1855	Sören A. Kierkegaard	Philosophy	
1819–1887	Meir Goldschmidt	Journalism, Novels, Short Stories.	
1840–1921	T. F. Troels-Lund	History, Biography, 16th Century	
1842–1927	Georg Brandes	Criticism (Main Currents in 19th Century Literature)	
1846–1908	Holger Drachmann	Novels	Lyrics, Dramas.
1857–1919	Karl Gjellerup	Novels	
1857–1943	Henrik Pontoppidan	Novels	Plays.
1869–1954	Martin Andersen-Nexö	Novels (Pelle the Conqueror)	
1872–1950	Karin Michaelis	Novels (The Dangerous Age)	
1895–1962	Isak Dinesen	Autobiography (Out of Africa)	(Pen name of Karen Blixen).

NORWEGIAN LITERATURE

The earliest Norwegian literary monuments are the runic inscriptions, of which the oldest are from about 400. At the beginning of the 9th century, the viking age brought the Norwegians into contact with western Europe. Their religious views had by this time found their final form in all essentials, but influence from Christian Britain and Ireland may also be traced in the Elder Edda, a collection of poems dealing with gods and heroes. While the manuscript was preserved in Iceland, the greater number of the poems are of Norwegian origin. These poems are all anonymous. Also the oldest lays of known scalds, or poets, are Norwegian. The greatest of Norwegian scalds was Eyvind Skaldaspillir, whose mighty Hakonarmal, "Poem about Hakon," was composed in memory of Hakon the Good (961). In 874 the first settler came to Iceland from Norway, and in the following centuries this island became the center of Norwegian-Icelandic literature. While the Icelandic sagas to a great extent treat of persons and happenings in the mother country, Norway herself contributed only a smaller part of the Norwegian-Icelandic literature.

Among Norwegian works may be mentioned an excellent translation of (a part of) the Bible, a translation of a collection of sermons, and The King's Mirror (13th century), the remarkable handbook of court customs, which has since become a gold mine of knowledge concerning the highly developed culture of that period. During the reign of Hakon IV and his successors (13th century), numerous French poems and stories were translated in Norway into old Norwegian (Icelandic). Other Norwegian works of importance to be mentioned are the provincial laws and King Magnus's law for the whole country (1274). The most important work in Latin produced in Norway was About the Old Norwegian Kings by Theodoricus Monachus.

When the old royal house became extinct in the 14th century, and Norway later was united with Denmark, the fellowship in culture between Norway and her colony Iceland ceased, and the upper classes gradually acquired a Danish and North German stamp of culture. In this period, preceding the Lutheran Reformation of the 16th century, the old literary language of Norway was broken up into dialects; the ballads, folk stories, and fairy tales produced were not reduced to writing, but were handed down from generation to generation until they were printed in the 19th century.

After the Reformation the writers of Norway used the Danish language. This Dano-Norwegian period lasted until the two countries separated in 1814. The most prominent name in this period is that of the Norwegian Ludvig Holberg (1684–1754). He produced excellent historical works and his comedies are immortal. He is a representative of the farseeing and liberal men of his times.

After the separation from Denmark, Norway declared her independence and adopted a constitution, May 17, 1814. In a general way, it may be said that the great literary men Norway has produced in the 19th century have served the historical mission of making the two fundamental principles of the constitution a reality: national independence and democracy.

Henrik Wergeland (1808–45), the most beloved and honored of all Norwegian writers, was the very embodiment of the aspirations of the rejuvenated nation. No Scandinavian has written more beautiful, more strongly felt, more powerfully conceived, or more luxuriously formed, lyrics. But, because so much of his verse is well-nigh untranslatable, his fame has not spread as that of some other writers of his country. The poetry of his contemporary, Welhaven, is harmonious and perfect in form and shows the reflection of a more critical nature. The central figure in the succeeding period is the historian, P. A. Munch, whose monumental work is *The History of the Norwegian People.* Around him are arrayed many talented men who brought into the light of day the hidden treasures of national poetry, music, and dialects. Most important were the fairy tales, edited by Asbjörnsen and Moe, fresh and full of humor, truly reflecting the national

character, creating a new style and infusing new life into the language. Out of the dialects, descendants of the old Norwegian language, Aasen created the idiom called *Landsmaal,* which he himself used for literary work, and in which he was later succeeded by such masters as Vinje, Garborg, and others. At this period appeared Wergeland's famous sister, Camilla Collett, whose *The Governor's Daughters* made her the leader of the woman's emancipation movement.

With the appearance of Björnson (1832–1910) and Ibsen (1828–1906), comes the great era of Norwegian literature. From Björnson's *Synnöve Solbakken* (1857) until the end of the century, the Norwegians took the lead in Scandinavian literature, and many of their works, through translations, became known throughout the world. Björnson, winner of the Nobel prize in 1903, excelled as poet, story-teller, and dramatist. As an orator he was without a peer in his age. Ibsen became the leading dramatist of the 19th century, and his dramatic technique has been imitated by authors of many lands. Contemporary with these giants of the North were Jonas Lie, whose stories of sea life, of the Northland, and of family life made him very popular; and Alexander Kielland, whose charm and wit at once won the reading public. Of recent authors, the best-known outside of Norway are Knut Hamsun, whose *Growth of the Soil* won the Nobel prize in 1920, and Johan Bojer, the author of *The Great Hunger* and *The Last Viking.* Sigrid Undset, winner of the Nobel prize for 1928, shows remarkable insight into feminine psychology and into the medieval mind.

Other writers include Gunnar Heiberg, Hans Kinck, Nils Kjær, Peter Egge, Olav Duun, Sigurd W. Christiansen; among women writers, Barbra Ring and Nini R. Anker; and the poets Th. Caspari, N. C. Vogt, Olaf Bull, H. Wildenwey.

TABLE OF NORWEGIAN LITERATURE

	AUTHORS		REPRESENTATIVE WORKS	
Time	Name		Prose	Poetry and Drama
800?–?	Bragi Boddason			Poem on Ragnar's Shield.
850–933	Harold Haarfagre			Poem on Snefrid.
9th Century	Thorbjörn Hornklovi			Poem on King Harold.
9th Century	Thjodolf of Hvin			Ynglingatal, Genealogy of Royal Family.
910–995	Eyvind Finnson Skaldaspillir			Poem on Hakon the Good.
1200–?	Anonymous		King's Mirror	
1545–1623	Peder Clausen (Friis)		Description of Norway	
1647–1708	Petter Dass			Poems (Northland's Trumpet).
1684–1754	Ludvig Holberg		History, Philosophy	Comedies, Comic Poetry.
1722–1780	Gerhard Schöning		History of Norway	
1728–1780	C. B. Tullin			Poems.
1742–1785	J. H. Wessel			Lyrics, Play (Love without Stockings).
1746–1791	Claus Fasting			Poems.
1749–1794	Edv. Storm			Poems.
1751–1833	Niels Treschow		Philosophy	
1792–1842	H. A. Bjerregaard			Dramas, Poems (Sons of Norway).
1794–1842	M. C. Hansen		Novels	
1802–1880	M. B. Landstad			Hymn Book, Ballads.
1803–1864	R. Keyser		History	
1807–1873	J. S. C. Welhaven			Poems (The Dawn of Norway).
1808–1845	H. A. Wergeland			Patriotic Poems, Dramas.
1810–1863	P. A. Munch		History (Scandinavian)	
1811–1884	A. Munch			Lyrics, Translations, Dramas.
1812–1885	Peter Asbjörnsen		Folk Tales	
1813–1882	J. I. Moe		Folk Tales	Poems, Lyrics.
1813–1895	Camilla Collett		Novels, Essays	
1813–1896	Ivar Aasen		Philology	Dramas, Poems
1818–1870	A. O. Vinje		Journalism	Lyrics.
1828–1906	Henrik Ibsen			Dramas (A Doll's House), Poems.
1832–1910	B. Björnson		Novels	Dramas (Sigurd Slembe), Lyrics.
1833–1908	Jonas Lie		Novels	
1835–1917	J. E. Sars		History, Essays	
1849–1906	Alexander Kielland		Novels	
1851–1924	Arne Garborg		Novels	Lyrics.
1856–1925	Gerhart Gran		Literary Criticism, Essays	
1859–1952	Knut Hamsun		Novels (Growth of the Soil)	
1869–1959	Peter Egge		Novels (Hansine Solstad)	
1872–1959	Johan Bojer		Novels (The Great Hunger)	
1876–1939	Olav Duun		Novels (The People of Juvik)	
1882–1949	Sigrid Undset		Novels (Kristin Lavransdatter)	
1891–1947	Sigurd W. Christiansen		Novels (Two Living and one Dead)	

SWEDISH LITERATURE

Traces of ancient Swedish literature are very rare and consist principally of inscriptions on the rune stones. There are about 2000 of these in Sweden, the oldest from the 6th century, the majority belonging to the period of transition from paganism to Christianity. Some of the inscriptions are in alliterative versification, the most famous being *Rökstenen*, the longest known in the world, consisting of 750 runes.

The oldest of the written provincial laws is the *Västgöta Law*, "Westgothian Law," from the beginning of the 13th century. St. Bridget (1302–73) is the most eminent Swedish author of the middle ages; her *Revelations*, first written in Swedish, then translated into Latin, are distinguished by glowing fancy and imagery. The purest national poetry of medieval times consists of what we call national ballads, which have survived on the lips of the people to the present day.

The greatest name of the time of the Reformation is that of Olaus Petri (1497–1552), a personal disciple of Luther. All his writings are marked by a powerful genius, and his style bears the stamp of simplicity coupled with erudition and an exceptionally keen insight. After the Thirty Years' War, poetry for the first time became an art with patriotic aims, and not merely a handmaid of religion. Stiernhielm (1598–1672) is the most prominent author of the 17th century. Efforts were made to prove that the ancient history of Sweden could be traced as far back as that of any other nation, or still further. O. Rudbeck (1630–1702) has given a good expression of these ideas in his brilliant and learned though fantastic *Atland*.

In the Period of Liberty, after the fall of Charles XII, scientific interests were uppermost. It is the age of Linnæus and Scheele. In literature the principal name is O. von Dalin (1708–63), pre-eminent because of his prose style and because he opened the way for the ideas of the Age of Enlightenment.

K. M. Bellman (1740–95) is the most original and perhaps the greatest of Sweden's poets and is entirely national. He has especially an eye for the beauties of nature, and he has depicted the scenery around Stockholm as no other poet has. French influence reached its climax during the reign of Gustavus III (1771–92). With the French Academy as a model, the king founded the Swedish Academy, now awarding the Nobel literary prize. Gustavus himself took a great interest in the drama. Kellgren is, side by side with the king, the most typical representative of the period. His contemporaries were K. G. Leopold and Anna M. Lenngren.

T. Thorild (1759–1808) was a follower of Rousseau and advocated the rights of feeling and of nature. J. O. Wallin (1779–1839) is the greatest hymnologist of the country.

After the revolution of 1809 and the loss of Finland, the Romantic school appears. Atterbom's

The Island of Felicity is one of the most beautiful works created by Romanticism. Other writers are Stagnelius and Sjöberg. The men through whom Swedish literature attained almost classical perfection were Esaias Tegnér (1782–1846) and E. G. Geijer (1783–1847). Geijer's poems are not numerous, but possess a manly and national ring. He was also a philosopher and composer and is above all the greatest historian of Sweden. The best-known of Tegnér's works is his lyrical epic *Frithjof's Saga*, which has been translated by some fifty different hands into eleven foreign languages. Almqvist (1793–1866) is an exponent of Romanticism in a state of dissolution. His chief literary works are the two collections called *The Book of the Thorn Rose*.

In the following age of Liberalism, several noted names appear in literature: Sturzen-Becker is the finest and most brilliant Swedish publicist; Blanche is known by his comedies and novels; Strandberg was a great lyric poet and a distinguished translator; Malmström produced poems born of patriotism and ancient classical studies; Witterbergh wrote short, highly appreciated sketches.

The realistic tendencies of the age found expression in the ever-increasing predominance of prose in literature. Fredrika Bremer (1801–65) wrote many novels, advanced the emancipation of women, and gained fame outside of Sweden. A very popular novelist was Emilie Flygare-Carlén (1807–92). Living in Finland but of Swedish descent was the great writer, J. L. Runeberg (1804–77). His most famous work is *The Tales of Ensign Stål*. Another Finnish writer using the Swedish language was Topelius (1818–98), whose *The Surgeon's Tales* is extremely popular.

In the middle of the 19th century, Viktor Rydberg (1829–95) gradually obtained the position of intellectual leader in modern Swedish literature. His contemporaries were the lyrical poets, Count Snoilsky and C. D. af Wirsén. The greatest name afterward is that of August Strindberg (1849–1912), a genius of extraordinary dimensions and overwhelming production. He is Sweden's greatest dramatist, but he produced great works in many other fields. Geijerstam (1858–1909) portrayed the life of the peasantry and the middle classes in a fresh and good-natured style and also wrote comedies. Heidenstam produced *Karolinerna*, "The Heroes of Charles XII," inspired by love of nation and the history of Sweden. G. Fröding (1860–1911) showed a masterly handling of rimes and meters and was as great a poet as was Bellman. The foremost of all recent Swedish authors is Selma Lagerlöf (1858–1940), who won the Nobel prize in 1909. Ellen Key (1849–1926) aroused attention by her treatment of social problems. Others are Gellerstedt, Österling, Karlfeld, F. Hedberg, T. Hedberg, Ossiannilsson. Very popular in most recent times is the dialect literature. Among authors cultivating this style are Dahlgren and Bondeson.

TABLE OF SWEDISH LITERATURE

	AUTHORS		REPRESENTATIVE WORKS	
Time	Name		Prose	Poetry and Drama
1302–1373	St. Bridget (Birgitta) . . .		"Revelations"	
–1484	Johannes Budde.		Translation of Bible	
1497–1552	Olaus Petri		Chronicle of Swedish History, Religious Works, History . .	Hymns.
1499–1573	Laurentius Petri			Psalms.
1579–1636	Johannes Messenius . . .		History of Sweden	Poems, Lyrics.
1594–1632	Gustavus Adolphus . . .		Speeches, History	Hymns.
1598–1672	Georg Stiernhielm		Works on Language and Mathematics	Masques, Poems.
1605–1669	Lars Wivallius			Lyrics.
1688–1772	Emanuel Swedenborg . . .		Philosophy	
1707–1778	Karl von Linné (Linnæus) .		Botany, Travels	
1707–1787	Sven Lagerbring		History of Sweden	
1708–1763	Olof (von) Dalin		History of Sweden, Journalism, Swedish Freedom	Poems, Dramas.
1714–1763	Jakob Henrik Mörk . . .		Novels	

TABLE OF SWEDISH LITERATURE—Con.

| AUTHORS | | REPRESENTATIVE WORKS | |
Time	Name	Prose	Poetry and Drama
1718–1763	Charlotta Nordenflycht . .	. . . .	Lyrics.
1731–1785	Gustav Filip Creutz . . .		Poems.
1731–1808	G. F. Gyllenborg		Poems.
1740–1795	Karl M. Bellman		Odes, Lyrics, Songs.
1751–1795	J. H. Kellgren	Journalism	Poems.
1754–1817	Anna Maria Lenngren . .		Household Poems.
1759–1808	Thomas Thorild	Criticism	
1772–1847	Frans Franzén		Lyrics, Hymns.
1779–1839	Johan Olof Wallin . . .		Hymns.
1782–1846	Esaias Tegnér	Speeches	Poems (Frithjof's Saga).
1783–1847	Erik Gustaf Geijer . . .	History, Philology . .	Poems.
1789–1877	Gustav W. Gumaelius . .	Historical Novels . .	
1791–1844	K. F. Dahlgren	Novels, Short Stories.	Poems.
1793–1823	E. J. Stagnelius		Dramas, Lyrics, Sonnets.
1793–1866	K. J. L. Almqvist . . .	Novels (Thorn Rose), Essays . .	Poems.
1795–1881	Anders Fryxell	History	
1800–1877	Per Wieselgren	History of Swedish Literature . .	
1801–1865	Fredrika Bremer	Novels	
1804–1877	J. L. Runeberg.		Poems, Dramas.
1811–1868	August Blanche	Novels, Short Stories, Sketches .	Comedy.
1818–1898	Zakarias Topelius . . .	Historical Novels . .	
1829–1895	Viktor Rydberg	Historical Novels, Philosophy, Mythology, History	Poems.
1829–1907	King Oscar II	Criticism	Poems.
1841–1903	Karl Snoilsky		Poems.
1849–1912	August Strindberg . . .	Novels, Short Stories.	Dramas (The Father), Lyrics.
1858–1940	Selma Lagerlöf	Novels, Tales (Wonderful Adventures of Nils)	
1859–1940	V. von Heidenstam . . .	Novels, Essays, Short Stories . .	Poems.
1860–1911	Gustav Fröding		Lyrics.
1862–1906	Oskar Levertin.	Short Stories, Essays.	Poems.
1866–1960	Per Hallstrom	Novels, Short Stories	Lyrics, Dramas.

ICELANDIC LITERATURE

The Icelandic literature is a continuation of the Old Norwegian literature. Most of the poems of the *Edda* were composed in Norway, but they were preserved in Iceland, where the art of poetry flourished after it had all but disappeared from Norway. The Icelandic scalds, or poets, were welcomed at the courts of the British Isles and in the Scandinavian countries. In honor of the princes and chieftains, they composed poems and songs, which are now of historic as well as of poetic value. The first great Icelandic poet is Egil Skallagrimson (about 900). He was both poet and warrior. Glum Geirason was the first poet at the court of the Norwegian king (10th century), and from that time on practically all of the poets at the royal court are Icelanders. Many of them are prominent. Most famous is Sigvat Tordson, a friend of St. Olaf and his son Magnus the Good.

The first historical saga is Are Frode's *Islendingabok* (beginning of 12th century). Soon after follows *Landnamabok*, which tells about the settlement of Iceland. This is succeeded by a long series of family sagas. These, for the most part, tell of persons and events in the period from the first settlement of the island until about the year 1030. The most important are *Egil's Saga*, *Gunlaug's Saga*, *Laxdölasaga*, *Vatsdölasaga*, *Njal's Saga*. The series ends with the very comprehensive *Sturlungasaga*. Another series deals with the history of Norway: *Morkinskinna*, "Rotten-skin" (so called from the appearance of the manuscripts), *Fagrskinna*, "Fairskin" (the Icelandic authors of which are unknown), and Snorre's famous *Sagas of the Kings of Norway* (to 1177), often called "Heimskringla" from the first words in the original text. Snorre is the greatest writer among the Icelanders. Abbot Jonson wrote *Sverri's Saga*; Sturla Tordson, *Hakonarsaga*. In connection with these there are historical descriptions of the Faroe islands, the Orkney islands, Greenland—all old Norwegian settlements—and Denmark. In addition to these, sagas which were mostly fiction were written. Best-known among these are *Frithjof's Saga* and the *Volsung Saga*. From this period (1100–1300) is also Snorre's *Edda*— the *Younger* or *Prose Edda*—dealing with mythology and the art of poetry.

In the following period (1300–1550), the day of the old scald, or bard, is passed. A new form of narratives in verse form, called *rimur*, arises, taking its material from the earlier sagas and the *Eddas*. Religious poetry has several notable representatives, the most important of whom are Eysteinn Asgrimson, the author of *Lilja*, and Jon Arason, the last Catholic bishop, who was executed in 1550.

With the introduction of the Lutheran Reformation, the last remnants of political independence in Iceland are lost, and, as far as literature is concerned, the following period (1550–1780) is one of even greater decline than the preceding period. Of outstanding writers there are only few. Reverend Hallgrimur Pjetursson has become famous because of his hymns. After 1600 there is a revival of interest in the early history and literature of Iceland, and a number of learned works in Latin, dealing with these subjects, were produced. Best known among the men of this period is Professor Arni Magnusson, who made a large collection of manuscripts, which he presented to the University of Copenhagen.

It is only from about 1830 that one can speak of a real revival of Icelandic literature. The famous Dane, Rasmus Rask, one of the world's greatest philologists, had been a great influence in awakening the new interest. Four prominent Icelanders started a new periodical whose object was to purify the language, elevate the literature, and arouse the national sentiment. Hallgrimsson's beautiful poem *Island*, "Iceland," may be said to contain the program of the new movement. A number of poets produced lyric poetry, some have excelled as writers of novels, and in most recent times powerful dramas have been produced by Icelanders. Of poets who made their home in America, the best-known name is that of Stephan G. Stephansson. Jon Sigurdsson, most beloved of Icelanders in recent times and the champion of Icelandic independence, which was finally won in 1918, has written much on politics and history. Björn Olsen became the first president of the Icelandic university at Reykjavik (established 1911); Gudbrandur Vigfusson has done much to acquaint the English-speaking world with Iceland; Professor Finnur Jonsson of the University of Copenhagen, besides being a very learned philologist, has written the most important works on Icelandic literature.

RUSSIAN LITERATURE

Russia, the vague territory known to the ancients as the land of wandering Scythian tribes and the Hyperboreans, enters the pale of history in the 9th century. Rurik, a Norse chieftain, came to Novgorod. At the invitation of the people, who were beset by neighboring enemy tribes, he established himself as prince. Out of this dim period of tribal warfare, there has come down to us only oral tradition in the form of *skazki* (prose folk tales) and *byliny* (tales of old time).

Early Folk Tales. There was no writing in the Russian language before the time of Peter the Great. A few of the byliny, which are rude, epic songs depending for rhythm upon a certain cadence and the endless repetition of stock figurative phrases, were first written down by an Oxford scholar in the early 17th century. A Cossack writer made another collection early in the 18th century. These songs reflect native Russian history and beliefs as well as some foreign elements. They cover in all a long period, some of the latest dealing with Napoleon.

Differences of subject matter and locality, as well as of time, mark off several distinct groups of stories. (1) The earliest of them, belonging to the period before 1000 A. D., represent a nature mythology, the characters depicted being monstrous creatures, such as the Giant of the Mountain. Other more human characters are Pagan Idol, a glutton, and Nightingale, the robber. (2) Kiev, one of the most famous and beautiful of medieval cities, and her great prince, Vladimir, of the 10th century, are the center of a large group of these byliny. (3) A third group of stories arose around the northern merchant republic of Novgorod. In these, the adventures of Sadko, a rich merchant, figure largely. (4) Another group of tales reflects the Tatar conquest and the transfer of the government to Moscow. (5) The Cossack group pictures with vigorous realism the life of the times and the surrender of the Cossack republic to the czars, and tales about the exploits of Peter the Great are numerous. The beliefs and religious customs of the middle ages in Russia are reflected in a large number of religious poems.

Slavic Writings. With the introduction of the Greek Church into Russia through the conversion of Vladimir of Kiev in the 10th century, the old church Slavic (a Bulgarian language) came into use for the liturgy. Very soon this imported language was used for all official and literary purposes. From this period and from the following centuries, we have numerous sermons, lives of the saints, accounts of pilgrimages, some real and some imagined, and a great variety of books of instruction, as well as some romances and chronicles, such as the *Chronicle of Kiev*. An edition of the Slavonic Gospels dates from the years 1056-57. Hilarion's discourse concerning the Old and New Testaments is a famous piece of medieval writing. The most interesting of these productions, however, is the story of the Raid of Igor, a 12th century epic, which recounts the expedition of Prince Igor of Novgorod against his troublesome neighbors, the Polovtzes.

The period from the 13th century to the middle of the 17th is the time of Tatar supremacy. Under a pernicious Oriental tyranny in Moscow, literature and learning as well as piety and morality disappeared. During this time, Kiev was united with the kingdom of Lithuania and became a center of learning from which scholars and teachers afterward went into Russia. Reform began in the middle of the 17th century with Simeon Pólotsky of Kiev, the pioneer of modern culture and the first Russian versifier. His writings include secular as well as religious subjects, with several religious plays which he composed in his attempt to introduce Western culture as he knew it. The first Russian theater was opened in 1674, and the first newspaper was issued in manuscript shortly after this date.

Royal Patronage of Letters. Peter the Great, who came to the throne in 1689, undertook, in connection with all his other radical reforms, to modernize and purify the Russian language. In this task he had the assistance of Bishop Prokopovitch, a very learned and politic scholar. The most important work in this reform of the language was done by Lomonósov in the early 18th century. He wrote extensively upon grammar, rhetoric, and versification, besides producing some original verse and prose. A remarkable work was produced in this time by a peasant, Pososhkóv, entitled *Poverty and Riches*.

The latter part of the 18th century in Russia was a period of French influence, especially during the reign of Catherine II (1762-96), who herself wrote much. Catherine gathered around her a group of poets, mediocre for the most part, whom she exhorted to imitation of the classics, especially Ovid and Virgil, but whose real models were the French pseudo-classicists. To her court she invited many French scholars and writers who, because of their liberal ideas, were threatened in their own country. This classical influence, however, soon passed away.

Sumarókov deserves an important place in the early history of literature in Russia. His writings were of various kinds, but he was most successful in the drama, both prose and verse. He was made director of the first theater opened in Petrograd in the year 1766, just a year after the founding of the University of Moscow. Before this time only religious plays had been permitted, but Sumarókov both wrote and produced in the theater work after the style of Racine, Corneille, and Voltaire. Other members of Catherine's court circle were Denis Fonvizin, who produced a real national comedy keenly satirizing Russian life, and Gabriel Derzhávin, who has been called Catherine's poet laureate, and whose poems, "Ode to God," "The Nobleman," and "The Taking of Warsaw," are well known.

Catherine held a tight rein upon real literary development, fearing the spread of modern ideas among the people. In a small book entitled *A Journey to St. Petersburg and Moscow*, Radístchev criticized severely the treatment of the serfs. So he was banished to Siberia. Nicholas Nóvikov was a hard-working journalist who did much for education in Russia, but he too overstepped the bounds that Catherine thought proper, and she put him in prison.

Karamzín, under the reign of Alexander I (1801-25), refined the Russian language and developed a reading public in Russia through his writings on history and travel, and by his fiction and translations.

Translation from Western languages was in this time an important contribution to Russia. Vasilii Zhukóvsky translated numerous works from the English, including poems by Gray and Byron. Out of the German he translated selections from Goethe and Schiller, and he also rendered into Russian some German translations from the Indian *Mahabharata* and the Persian *Shah Nameh*. Through these translations the Romantic movement, which was dominant elsewhere in Europe in the early years of the 19th century, came into Russia, but, like the classical influence, it soon disappeared before the rise of the peculiarly Russian realistic style. Alexander Púshkin (1799-1837) in his short life became the father of Russian literature. He first truly expressed the Russian spirit, drawing upon Russian antiquity and legends for subject matter, as in his verse novel *Eugene Onegin*, probably his greatest work. Ivan Kozlóv translated Burns's "Cotter's Saturday Night." He expressed the peasant life of Russia in his poetry.

The Novel and the Drama. The greatest work of Russian writers has been in the field of the novel. Russia may be said to have contributed to the world's literature the realistic method in prose fiction, and it is notable that this development took place within a very few years after 1840. There is in Russian prose literature no such long development as is to be seen in the history of either English or French prose. The first of the Russian novelists is Nikolai Gógol. His *Taras Bulba* is a story of the Cossack and Polish wars; his other masterpiece, *Dead Souls*, which he did not live to finish, is a vivid realistic picture of the peasant life of Russia and a bitter satire upon the official class.

Some critics give the highest place in Russian literature to Ivan Turgéniev. His work, which began with a volume of short stories, entitled *A Sportsman's Sketches*, furnishes an unsurpassed record of the Russian life of his time, and his prose in style and structure is unequaled among Russian writers. Dosteovsky is the greatest psychological novelist of Russia. His masterpiece is *Crime and Punishment*, a work which grew out of his experiences during his period of imprisonment and exile in Siberia. His analysis of character is very skillful. Count Leo Tolstóy is recognized as a great genius in various fields. He became famous in the last two decades of the 19th century for his social and religious opinions, which led him to adopt a life of asceticism. His *Anna Karenina* and *War and Peace* rank among the world's masterpieces of fiction. In recent years the folk life of the lower classes in Russia has been portrayed in a masterly fashion in the stories of Grigórvitch and Maxim Gorky (Alexei Pyeshkov), Leonid Andreev, and Anton Chékhov have notably developed the short story and have influenced this genre in the Western world in both form and matter.

The Russian drama, although not so important as the novel, has had a remarkable development since the work of Sumarókov in the 18th century. *The Woes of Wit* by Griboedov and *The Inspector General* by Gógol are still reckoned as the greatest Russian comedies, though the greatest dramatist is Alexander Ostróvsky. His masterpieces are *Poverty Is No Vice* and *The Thunderstorm*. Anton Chékhov is famous as a writer of both comedies and short stories. *The Cherry Orchard* probably represents his best work in the drama. His numerous stories are crowded with brilliantly drawn characters from humble life. In Russian literature, as in no other, there is a deep sense of seriousness and social purpose.

War and revolution have pervaded the literature to date. In 1942, Alexander Korneichuk produced a widely acclaimed war play, *The Front*. S. N. Sergeyev-Tsensky glorified Russia's military past in *The Ordeal of Sevastopol*. In the late 1960's, several new war memoirs were published.

With the 20th century came significant changes in Russian letters. Immediately after the Bolshevist revolution in 1918, when there was yet no policy of political censorship, Valentin Katayev satirized abuses of the new regime, as did Mikhail Zoshchenko, Russia's greatest humorist. Leonid Leonov carried the influence of the old 19th-century realism into psychological realms (*The Badgers*). Isaac Babel gave a subjective account of the Civil War with the old style of realism. In 1928, with the full arrival of the Communist Party, came regimentation of literature. In 1932, writers were required to produce only "socialist realism." This brought several reactions, varying as censorship slackened or tightened. Some writers dissented, some fell silent or were silenced, some fell into step with the new order, others simply endured the censorship. Fydor Gladkov anticipated the effects of this new regime in *Cement*. Some older Russian writers, like Nobel prize-winner Ivan Bunin went into exile. One of the latest to defect was Anatoli Kuznetsov (*Babi Yar*) in 1969.

Purges eliminated some artists and cowed others. Alexei N. Tolstoy produced some popular novels, including *The Road to Calvary*, in which intellectuals accept the Revolution. Leonov, distinguished by two war plays, grew dull when he adopted socialist realism. Mikhail Sholokhov's *Virgin Soil Upturned* was praised by the Communist Party, and his *The Quiet Don*, set in war and revolution, seemed to combine the old and new realism. He was awarded the Nobel Prize in 1965. Vladimir Mayakovsky experimented with verse, using a new language and new subject matter—that of the common people. He was lauded by the party and the public, and yet committed suicide. Boris Pasternak wrote many fine lyrics; those not in the prescribed vein were severely criticized. Such a furor arose when he was selected for the Nobel Prize (1958) for the novel *Doctor Zhivago*, published abroad, that he did not accept it. Ilya Ehrenburg vacillated between supporting Stalin and complaining of the uninteresting quality of his native literature. His novel *The Thaw* labeled the period after Stalin. Boris Pilnyak, author of the novel *Bare Year*, and Anna Akhmatova, who wrote highly subjective verse, fell silent during the Stalin years, but resumed publishing after his death.

The best strictly propagandistic novel to turn up was Nikolai Ostrovsky's *How the Steel Was Tempered*, and Nikolai Pogodin was a successful dramatist of socialist realism. Konstantin Fedin was strongly influenced by the regime, showed dislike for elements of it, altered his talent for it, was criticized for the pessimism in his work, and somehow survived all the purges. Others were not as fortunate. In 1966, despite vociferous protest from fellow writers, Andrei Sinyavsky and Yuli Daniel were imprisoned for publishing works abroad that allegedly damaged the Soviet regime. For some time the liberal poet Alexander Tvardovsky, honored by the state in 1970, seemed permitted to voice dissent relatively unfettered, but he was forced to resign as editor of the foremost Soviet literary magazine, *Novy Mir*, in the same year. The poets Yevgeny Yevtushenko, who clearly loves his country, and Andrei Voznesensky, the more imaginative, have made outspoken demands for more freedom of the arts, as has Nobel Prize-winner Alexander Solzhenitsyn (*One Day in the Life of Ivan Denisovich*), whose works are banned in the Soviet Union.

TABLE OF RUSSIAN LITERATURE

Time	Author	Prose Works	Poetry and Drama
About 1200	Unknown		Lay of Igor's Raid.
1629–1680	Simeon Polotsky		Mystery Drama.
1712–1765	Mikhail Lomonosov	Science, Philosophy, History	Odes.
1743–1816	Gavril Derzhavin		Poems.
1744–1818	Nikolai Novikov	Essays, Philosophy	
1744–1792	Denis Fonvizin		Comedies (The Brigadier General).
1766–1826	Nikolai Karamzin	Historical Novels	
1768–1844	Ivan Krylov		Poems, fables.
1779–1840	Ivan Kozlov		Poems, Translations.
1795–1829	Alexander Griboedov		Drama.
1799–1837	Alexander Pushkin	Novels	Odes, Lyrics, Drama.
1809–1852	Nikolai Gogol	Novels, Satire	Comedies.
1814–1841	Mikhail Lermontov	Novels, History	Nature Poetry, Odes, Drama.
1817–1875	A. K. Tolstoy		Poems, Drama.
1818–1883	Ivan Turgeniev	Novels, Sketches	Comedies.
1821–1881	Fyodor Dostoevsky	Novels, Essays	
1823–1886	Alexander Ostrovsky		Comedies, Tragedy.
1828–1910	Leo N. Tolstoy	Novels, Tales, Essays, Criticism	Poems, Drama.
1860–1904	Anton Chekhov	Short Stories, Sketches, Novels	Plays.

TABLE OF RUSSIAN LITERATURE—Con.

Time	Author	Prose Works	Poetry and Drama
1865—1941	Dmitry Merezhkovsky	Criticism, Novels, Essays	Poems.
1868—1936	Maxim Gorky	Tales, Short Stories	Poems, Plays.
1870—1953	Ivan Bunin	Novels (The Grammar of Love)	Poems.
1871—1919	Leonid Andreev	Short Stories, Tales	Plays.
1880—1921	Alexander Blok		Poems.
1882—1945	Alexei N. Tolstoy	Novels (Road to Calvary)	
1883—1958	Fyodor Gladkov	Novels (Cement)	
1888—1966	Anna Ahkmatova		Poems.
1890—1960	Boris Pasternak	Novels (Doctor Zhivago)	Poems.
1891—1967	Ilya Ehrenburg	Novels (The Storm, The Thaw), Essays	
1892—	Konstantin Fedin	Novels (Cities and Years)	
1893—1930	Vladimir Mayakovsky		Poems.
1894—1941	Isaac Babel	Stories (Red Cavalry)	
1894—1937	Boris Pilnyak	Novels (The Naked Year)	
1895—1958	Mikhail Zoshchenko	Humorous stories	
1897—	Valentin Katayev	Novels (The Embezzlers)	
1899—	Leonid Leonov	Novels (The Badgers)	Plays.
1900—1971	Alexander Tvardovsky		Poems.
1905—	Mikhail Sholokhov	Novels (And Quiet Flows the Don)	
1915—	Konstantin Simonov	Novels (Days and Nights)	
1918—	Vladimir Dudintsev	Novels (Not By Bread Alone)	
1918—	Alexander Solzhenitsyn	Novels (Cancer Ward)	
1933—	Yevgeny Yevtushenko		Poems.

POLISH LITERATURE

Of Polish literature before the advent of Christianity (965), but few fragments have been left to us. Chroniclers, such as Gallus, Kadlubek, and Boguchwal, appearing between the 12th and 13th centuries, wrote in Latin. However, we have a version of the Psalms in Polish dating from 1292 and also a manuscript copy of the Psalter, known as that of Queen Margaret, belonging to the 14th century.

The Renaissance. The University of Cracow, which had its origin in the famous academy founded by Casimir the Great in the year 1400, attracted many students within its walls. A great number of young Poles also went abroad to foreign universities.

As a consequence of this development of national intellectual life, the Polish language superseded the Latin tongue in literary usage. A printing press was established at Cracow in 1474, and the first book printed in Polish was *The Sayings of the Wise King Solomon*. Other books—translations, paraphrases, versions of the Bible—now followed in rapid succession.

Poland's Golden Age. The period between 1548 and 1600 is known as the golden age of Polish literature. Jan Kochanowski (1530–84), called the prince of Polish poets, in 1557 wrote the first of his poems. Especially notable are his *Lamentations* on the death of his daughter Ursula. Two other writers, Rey and Bielski, wrote didactic poems and satires of considerable merit. Peter Skarga, a Jesuit (1536-1612), did much to enhance the literature of his country.

Decadence. After the beginning of the 17th century, a decadence in Polish literature became evident. The period between 1606 and 1764 has been styled *macaronic*, owing to the fashion, in vogue among writers, of introducing Latin words into their compositions. At best, it was a period of imitation when poets who affected the style of Jan Kochanowski mistook imitation for inspiration.

Polish literature may now be said to have reached its lowest ebb, and, between the years 1696 and 1763, but few writers can lay claim to any distinction. Among the few may be mentioned Druzbacka (1695–1760), the first Polish authoress, who wrote many poems showing both grace and depth of feeling. With her name may be coupled those of Krasicki (1735-1801) and Trembecki (1722-1812).

The Nineteenth Century. The period of the last division of Poland (1796–1822) saw a vigorous revival of the native literature. The first promulgator of the Romantic movement was Kasimir Brodzinski (1791–1835), author of the idyl *Wieslaw*.

Following him came Adam Mickiewicz (1798–1855), the sublimest of all Polish poets.

With Mickiewicz, Slowacki (1809–49) and Krasiński (1812–59) form a transcendent trio of lyric and idyllic writers. Alexandro Fredo (1793–1876) appeared as a writer of successful comedies.

Among numerous poets writing since the middle of the 19th century, Adam Asnyk (1838–97) and Marya Konopnicka are two of the most notable. The outstanding master of prose fiction of recent times was Henryk Sienkiewicz (1846–1916), famous for his *Quo Vadis* and for his great trilogy of Polish history, *With Fire and Sword*. Glowacki (1847–1912), under the pen name of "Boleslaw Prus," was a writer of romances, notably *The Outpost* and *The Doll*. Wladislaw Reymont (1868–1925), a writer of the realistic school, is known especially as the author of *The Peasants*.

CZECH LITERATURE

The Czech language was the first of the Slavonic tongues to be developed scientifically. The earliest literary impulse came with the introduction of Christianity into Moravia and Bohemia by Cyril and Methodius in 863. With the exception of the Bulgarian, Czech is the oldest among all Slav literatures and, until the 17th century, was the richest and most copious. Cyril adapted the characters of the Greek alphabet to the demands of the Czech speech and originated what is known as the Cyrillic alphabet. For a long period, however, the influence of the Latin churchmen gave Latin precedence over the native language. Literary remains from the period before the 14th century include various chronicles and a few national songs. The famous Reims Gospel is said to date from the 11th or 12th century; what is known as the newer part of it, however, was written in 1395 and is the only remnant of Old Slavonic extant. The church song *Hospodine pomiluj ny*, "Lord, have mercy," belongs to the 11th century and is the most precious relic of this period.

The Awakening. About the year 1250, through the crusaders and wandering minstrels from the Western lands, Bohemia came into touch with the manners and customs of the world outside her boundaries. Crusaders' tales of the East and troubadours' songs of chivalry and knightly adventure profoundly influenced the Bohemian spirit and imagination. The *Book of Marco Polo* and the *Travels of John Mandeville* were translated, and an adaptation of the *Alexandreis* of Walter de Chatillon testifies to the eager rendering of episodes from the Alexandrian and Arthurian cycles of romance. The University of Prague became one of the most noted establishments of learning and culture in the whole continent.

The Reformation Period. The period from 1410 to 1620 is looked upon as the greatest age of Czech literature. The era opened with religious discussion which gave rise to sermons and controversial prose, as well as to translations of the Bible. John Huss (1370?–1415), a thorough Latin scholar, used the Bohemian language for writings designed to reach the people. He employed the dialect of Prague and its surrounding territory. In addition to his sermons, addresses, and letters, Huss composed and translated many beautiful hymns. To his genius and scholarship is due also the present system of accents used with the Czech vowels and consonants.

The schools of learning were at this period thrown open to all classes in Bohemia, as was the case in but few other countries. A group of brilliant writers belonging to the Bohemian Brethren appeared (about 1457) and added a new luster to the native literature. Printing was introduced in 1468, the *Trojan Chronicle* being the first book printed. In the 15th and 16th centuries many translations were made from Latin and Greek. The first printed Bible appeared in 1488. The Kralická Bible, translated from the original Hebrew and Greek languages, under the supervision of Jan Blahoslav, and published 1579–93, took in Bohemia a place similar to that held in England by the King James Version. In the 17th century, Bishop Jan Komenský, better known as Comenius (1592–1670), attracted international attention by his writings on education. His masterpiece, *The Labyrinth of the World and the Paradise of the Heart*, was a forerunner of *Pilgrim's Progress*. He prepared also the *World in Pictures*, probably the first illustrated textbook ever published for children.

Decline and Revival. The year 1620, notable in Bohemian history for the battle of the White Mountain, saw the end of this glorious development in Czech literature. A period of decadence, occasioned by the desolation of Bohemia in the Thirty Years' War, continued until about 1774. The German language came to be in the ascendant for official and school use. Not a single literary work of any particular merit appeared in Bohemia during the 17th century. However, near the close of the reign of the emperor Joseph II, Bohemian writers were again encouraged. The Bohemian Society of Sciences was established, and the emperor founded professorships of the Czech language in the universities of Vienna and Prague. Joseph Jungmann, leader of a group of national poets, translated *Paradise Lost*, in addition to his renderings of Goldsmith, Pope, Goethe, and many other Western writers.

The Nineteenth Century. The years from 1820 to 1848 form a period of brilliant activity. In poetry, the two greatest names are Kollar, author of *The Daughter of Slava*, a collection of poems in praise of Slavic life and speech, and Čelakovský (1799–1852), a diligent collector of folk songs and a popular writer of lyric and epic verse.

After 1848 a rich revival of Czech literature took place. The impulse of this movement has been continued to the present day in the production of a strong and varied literature. Karel Havlichek, in journalism, and Ján Néruda and Vitezslav Hálek (1835–74), in poetry, were leaders in the first enthusiastic years of the new era. In the field of the drama, Joseph Jiri Kolar was the first Czech to translate and stage Shakespeare's plays. He followed this work with popular original dramas.

Jaroslav Vrchlický (1853–1912) is recognized as the most versatile and prolific of modern Czech writers, having to his credit no less than 67 volumes of original verse, and a vast number of translations from almost every language in Europe. Eliska Krasnohorska has long been a leader in the modern women's educational movements, and is a skillful writer of verse and stories. The foremost historical novelist is Alois Jirasek (1851–1930), who draws his inspiration from the hopes and struggles of his native land.

Among other prominent writers of recent years should be mentioned Karel Rais (1859-1926); Brodsky (b. 1862); Jan Havlasa (b. 1883); and the Bohemian American poet Jan Vránek, of Omaha, Nebraska.

It is a matter of no small interest to note how, in the short space of little more than a century, Czech literature has grown to such dignity of stature, grace, and beauty, that it can today take its place worthily among the literatures of civilized countries. The native of Czechoslovakia certainly owes a debt of lasting gratitude to that small group of patriotic priests and teachers who, in its darkest hour, saved their language from threatened dissolution and became the heralds of its glorious resurrection.

HUNGARIAN (MAGYAR) LITERATURE

The Hungarian language, spoken at the present day by nearly twelve millions of people, is terse, cogent, and full of rich vowel sounds, lending itself readily both to oratory and to serious poetry. Differing essentially from the majority of literary tongues, it belongs to the Ural-Altaic group of languages, in which are included the Lapp, the Finnish, and the Turkish.

Its literary development was long retarded, owing chiefly to the fact that Latin was, up to comparatively recent times, the official language of Hungary. Not until 1840, after a struggle dating from a literary movement begun in 1780 against the Germanizing efforts of Austria, did Hungarian receive official recognition as the dominant language of the country.

Reformation and Counter-Reformation. Before the year 1450, there is little to record of vernacular literature, save a few scanty remnants of the elusive songs of the bards and gypsies who sang in praise of Attila and the Arpáds. Scattered legends of the saints are here and there also to be found. Two of the oldest literary monuments of this era are *Halotti Beszéd*—a funeral oration (1230)—and a hymn to the Virgin dating from 1300. Literary productions during the period between 1570 and 1711 are notably influenced by the spirit both of the Renaissance and of the Reformation as well as imbued with the fiery enthusiasm called forth by Matthew Hunyadi. Impetus too was given to the vernacular literature of this age by the establishment of a printing press at Buda (1473) and the founding of the Pozsony university with the Corvina library. Many controversial writings, spiritual books, and volumes of sermons were the natural outcome of the Reformation. A complete translation, for the first time, of the Protestant Bible by Karolyi appeared in 1589, as did one of the Catholic Bible by Kaldi, a Jesuit, in 1626.

Profane literature in the 16th and 17th centuries is represented by the following writers: Michael Sztarai, who produced the first Hungarian drama, *The Marriage of Priests* (1550); the epic poet and wandering minstrel Tinodi (d. 1557); Balassi, the author of many beautiful lyrics, including the notable *Flower Songs* (1551–94); and Albert Gergei, who wrote the well-known and still popular *Argivius Kiralyfi*. Hungarian literature throughout the 17th century was considerably hampered, owing to the preference affected by Latin Schoolmen and by the upper classes for Italian and French productions. The two outstanding figures in the prose of this epoch are Cardinal Pazmany (1570–1637) and Molnar de Szenick (1574–1634). The publication of an encyclopedia (1655) and that of a dictionary (1708) mark the close of what may be called the Reformation and Counter-Reformation period.

The Modern Revival. After the Peace of Szatmar, 1711, began an age of peaceful development for Hungary. But not until the third quarter of the 18th century is there anything of notable interest in the native literature to be chronicled. In 1772 a revival set in, fostered by the influence of the French Revolution. Journals and periodicals of great repute were founded, and notable establishments arose, such as the Magyar and Classical schools and that known as the Hungarian Guard, which produced many brilliant writers, among others, Kazinczy (1759–1831), Alexander Kisfaludy (1772–1844), and Daniel Berzsenyi (1776–1826)—three poets of the foremost rank.

Modern Hungarian literature owes much in particular to Count Stephen Széchenyi, through whose efforts and inspiration it may be said to have reached its acme of perfection. Through his instrumentality, also, the Academy was founded in 1830 and the National Theater at Pest in 1837. It was the eloquence of Count Széchenyi in Parliament which finally succeeded in banishing Latin from the Hungarian Diet in 1844.

Among a galaxy of brilliant writers, may be mentioned, in particular, Charles Kisfaludy (1788–1830), regarded as founder of the modern Hungarian drama; Vörösmarty, composer of the national hymn, *Szózat*; Petöfi (1823-49), author of *Rise O Magyar*; and John Arany (1817–82), who wrote the *Toldi Trilogy, Flower Fables,* and the humorous poem, *The Lost Constitution.* A few of the more notable novelists are Nicolas Jósika (1796–1865), author of *The Bohemians in Hungary*; Joseph Eötvös (1813-71), who wrote *The Carthusian* and *The Village Notary*; and Mór Jókai (1825–1904), writer of no less than 250 novels, the best of which are *A Hungarian Nabob, Black Diamonds,* and *Love's Fools.*

Katona comes first in order among the dramatists, followed by Szigligeti (1814–78), a writer of folk-plays, Charles Bernstein (1817–77), author of *Banker and Baron,* and Gregory Gsiky (1842–90). The name of Joseph Bajza (1804–58), director of the National Theater, ranks high as that of poet, historian, and critic.

In the 20th century, Hungarian writers were divided into two groups. Of these the so-called traditionalists drew their inspiration from the East, the early home of the Magyar race. The other group, led chiefly by Endré Ady (1877-1919), comprised the moderns, who accepted gladly the industrial, cosmopolitan world of today.

Native periodical literature is fully represented in the United States, where between twenty and thirty periodicals are published in Hungarian. In Canada likewise are published several Hungarian periodicals.

CHINESE LITERATURE

Four important and clearly distinguished epochs should be noticed in the history of Chinese literature. The first is the classical period, distinguished by the work of Confucius (551–478 B. C.) and Mencius (372–289 B. C.) and by that of Lao Tzu (604 B. C.) and Chuang Tzu (330 B. C.).

The Classical Period. Confucius modestly declared that he was merely a lover of the ancients, a transmitter and not a creator, but he was really an original thinker and he did an important work. He gathered together the fragmentary records of antiquity and edited them: (1) the Book of History; (2) the Book of Changes, used in divination; (3) a selection from the ancient odes, including those few of religious character, used in sacrifices; and (4) perhaps a collection of the Rites,—a sort of Leviticus which prescribed the ceremonies to be used in private and public worship, in marriages, in funerals, and upon all other important occasions in life. His collection, if made, was not identical with the extant Book of Rites. In addition (5) he wrote the Spring

and Autumn Annals, drawn from the official records of his native state, which, with the commentary by Tso, forms a continuation in brief outline of the chronicles of the Book of History.

Mencius, although a devoted disciple of Confucius, surpassed his master in his comprehension of the principles of government. In his teaching he emphasized the rights of the people. "The people," he said, "are the foundation of the state; the national altars are second in importance, and the sovereign is the least important of all."

Some deny to Lao Tzu the authorship of the *Tao Te King,* but the greatness of Lao Tzu is evidenced by the teachings of his disciple, Chuang Tzu, the idealist. The *Tao Te King,* no matter who wrote it, is one of the most remarkable books of this period. It preserves many striking sayings ascribed to Lao Tzu, rejoices in paradox, declaims against war, preaches the simple life, and urges us to "recompense evil with kindness."

The Reconstructive Period. The second period begins with the overthrow of the Chou dynasty (249 B. C.). The greatest monarch of the new dynasty called himself the "First Emperor." He tried to destroy all Confucian literature and was guilty of the murder of many scholars because their bigoted conservatism hindered the reforms he sought to introduce.

The Han dynasty which followed restored Confucius to honor, but the period was one given very generally to the things which Confucius contemned, —tales of the marvelous. The philosopher's stone, the elixir of immortality, and the isles of the blessed, where the elixir was to be found, were the objects of search. It was probably at this time that the *Shan Hai King,* or "Classic of Mountains and Seas," was written. Although its tales are ridiculous to us, it undoubtedly has a certain value as preserving much of the folklore and many of the traditions of the Chinese.

The time was one, too, during which foreign influences crept in. Alexander's conquests in central Asia and Chinese exploration of adjoining lands created a channel of communication between the East and the West. Buddhism spread into Turkestan in the 3d century B. C. In the early years of the Christian era it received imperial recognition in China. In the following centuries, a great volume of Hindu literature was translated into Chinese by Buddhist missionaries,—not only Buddhist religious works, but Hindu mathematical, astronomical, and philosophical treatises. Chinese thought was profoundly affected.

This age may very properly be called the reconstructive period. In striking contrast to the credulity of the masses of the people were the works of two men: Ssu-ma Ch'ien (163–85 B. C.), the Herodotus of Chinese history, whose careful method and love of accuracy have become the model of later historians; and Wang Ch'ung (19–90 A. D.), whose originality and boldness won praise in spite of his heretical attacks upon the sages of antiquity and in spite of his denial of the immortality of the soul.

The Golden Age. This period of reconstruction prepared the way for what has sometimes been called the "golden age" of Chinese literature, which may be said to begin with the T'ang dynasty (618 A. D.) and include the Sung (960–1278). For our purposes it will cover also the period of the Mongol rule (to 1368). The T'ang period was noted for its poets, conspicuous among whom were Li Po, also called "Li T'ai Po" (699–762), whose verses in form and sentiment remind one of Omar the "tentmaker." Scarcely second to him was Tu Fu (712–770).

The Sung dynasty was adorned by its love of philosophy. The speculations of Buddhists and Taoists had produced a reaction. Confucianism separated itself entirely from their metaphysical theorizing. Chou Tun-i (1017–1073), the brothers Ch'eng (1032–1107), and, greatest of all, Chu Hsi (1130–

1200), although calling themselves Confucianists, departed far from the cautious views of the master. Their philosophy, which has generally been regarded as materialistic but has also been interpreted otherwise, has dominated Confucian thought from that day to this. The Sung period also had its poets, among whom Su Tung-po (1036–1101) may be mentioned as justly celebrated.

The Mongol dynasty, glorified by the praise given to it by Marco Polo, was distinguished in its literature chiefly for its attention to the drama and the novel. Because the drama and the novel use the spoken rather than the written style of language, the Confucianist of the old school was disposed to regard these forms of literature as beneath his notice. Yet the Chinese are among the most confirmed playgoers in the world. The most popular plays are representations of historical incidents, and this is true also of many of the novels.

Period of Western Influence. The fourth period in the history of Chinese literature, the period of Western influence, may be said to begin with the close of the 15th century, after the discovery by the Portuguese of the sea route to the Far East around the Cape of Good Hope. From that date, European intercourse with China increased rapidly.

Foreign missionaries aided both the Mings and the Manchus by preparing mathematical and scientific works, and since the beginning of the 19th century they have published an enormous mass of literature, both religious and secular. Chinese, educated abroad or in mission schools, have added greatly to the volume of translations. Original works by native authors have not been lacking. Poetry and fiction flourished both under the Mings and during the Manchu dynasty. One of the most celebrated novels, the *Hung Lou Meng*, commonly translated "The Dream of the Red Chamber," was written about the beginning of the Manchu period. The *Liao Chai*, by P'u Sung-ling, is a collection of stories that dates from about the same time. The K'anghsi Dictionary belongs to this period, which is distinguished also for its topographical histories, in which China excels, and for its voluminous encyclopedias.

The influence of Western thought increased greatly after China's defeat by Japan in 1894-95. China saw her former pupil transformed by the new learning. The old viceroy, Chang Chih-tung, in a small volume appealed to his countrymen to take up the study of the sciences. The advice was not taken by the Manchu government until after further humiliation through the suppression of the Boxer rising. Chang Chih-tung was called to assist in creating a new system of public education. This caused a demand for translations of Western literature, particularly treatises on political science, economics, engineering, and medicine. A new impetus was given to literary effort. The stilted style, once so popular, with its penchant for literary allusion and empty verbiage, is giving way to a simple, direct expression. The invention and adoption of a syllabary is supplementing, but not supplanting, the use of ideograms and thus is popularizing learning. Polite literature is not neglected, but urgent need prompts discussion of political and economic problems. Newspapers and magazines abound; the periodical press is a powerful engine of reform.

JAPANESE LITERATURE

There is some reason to believe that the Japanese in the island of Kyushu had come into possession of the Chinese written characters some centuries before the time of Christ, yet the oldest Japanese literary works extant today are the *Kempo*, a constitution of 17 articles (604 A. D.); the *Kojiki*, a record of ancient events (612); the *Rokkokushi*, which consists of six works on national history, including the famous *Nihongi* or *Nihon Shoki* (620–901); and the *Manyoshu*, a collection of renowned ancient poets and poetesses (756). All these works were written in the Chinese characters. The *Kempo* and the *Rokkokushi* were written in pure Chinese classical style. The *Kojiki* and the *Manyoshu* used the Chinese characters as phonetics.

Early Poetry. Japanese poetry, which has neither meter nor rime, is peculiarly a native product. Its form is the same as in ancient times. The essential feature of a popular poem is that it consists of 5 successive lines of 5, 7, 5, 7, and 7 syllables respectively, that is, a total of 31 syllables. Longer poems are sometimes written, but the present tendency is toward shorter ones. Near the close of the 17th century, *Hokku* (*haiku*) poems, which consisted of 3 lines of 5, 7, and 5 syllables respectively, a total of 17 syllables, became very popular. The poets Basho and Kikaku are rightly regarded as originators of this style. The poetry of Japan, like her pictorial art, gives strong impression and suggestion.

Many Japanese believe that poetry has declined since the *Heian* era (9th and 10th centuries). Yet the poets Tsurayuki and Katei and the poetess Murasaki-Shikibu rank as high as do Hitomaru and Akahito of the golden age of Japanese poetry, during which period many poetic works were compiled in accordance with imperial decree.

The Drama. The period from the 13th to the 17th century is known as the dark ages of Japanese literature. Because most men were engaged in warfare, literature was neglected. Only one or two schools in the entire empire remained open. Yet, even under such conditions, many famous works were produced, such as the *Hojoki*, a journal of important events, and the *Tsurezuregusa*, a collection of essays and anecdotes. In this period appeared also the splendid type of classical drama known as the *Nō* which somewhat resembles the drama of ancient Greece. Singers, dancers, and musicians plied their arts both at Shinto shrines and at imperial and shogunate courts. In the *Nō* drama, Chinese and Japanese historical narrations are frequently delivered in conversational tone. The singing part of the *Nō*, which is often performed by itself, is called *Yokyoku* or *Utai*. In the same period, the *Kyogen*, a sort of farce or comedy, had its beginning. Most of the *Nō* and the *Kyogen* were composed by Buddhist priests along the lines of the drama of the Yuan dynasty of China (12th century). They were both enacted and patronized chiefly by the nobility. Even at the present time, these types are very popular with the higher classes. In presentation, magnificent costumes are worn.

Toward the end of the 16th century, the *Kabuki*, a type of popular drama, was introduced. Notwithstanding that the *Kabuki* was originated by a woman, and was for some time enacted only by women of the courtesan class, yet from the early 18th to the latter part of the 19th century, because actors and actresses were strictly forbidden by law to play on the same stage, the higher type of *Kabuki* productions came to be presented entirely by men, who took the part of both sexes. The *Kabuki* has recently been subjected to critical reform and has become a popular amusement with all classes. Amateurs and professionals both play the *Kabuki*, and men and women appear together now on the same stage. This has led to the translation and presentation of many Western plays.

Another popular drama is the marionette play, accompanied by songs which are called *joruri*. Such songs also form an essential part of the *Kabuki*, taking the place of the orchestra in Western plays. The marionette plays originated in a chant (*Gidayu*) telling a love story, to which the marionettes were added. The development of this since the 17th century has produced most skillful performers. The chanters sit in one corner of the stage, while the marionettes are worked by players in harmony with the chant. These plays always aim at the encouragement of good and at the condemnation of evil.

Modern Fiction. Since the beginning of the 18th century, Japan has produced a large body of fiction. Children's stories, in particular, have been very popular and have frequently been translated. Many novels and romances have been produced.

In all periods of Japanese literature the work of women has been notable. It is said that the *Kojiki* and *Nihongi* were produced under the patronage of empresses. During the 10th and the 11th century, feminine authorship was at its best. Shikubu Murasaki (c. 978–1025) produced (*The Tale of Genji*, a masterpiece in world literature, which is often considered to be the first novel. To the same century belong the *Makura no Zoshi*, "Pillow Sketches," a realistic picture of social life in Kyoto written by Sei Shonagon.

The distinction attained by women in Japanese literature may be ascribed to the fact that in the 8th and 9th centuries the two forms of the Japanese syllabary, the Katakana and the Hiragana, were brought to perfection. This enabled the women to write without having to learn the Chinese ideograms, and they were quick to seize upon the new style of writing, while the men still clung to the Chinese classical models.

Western Influence. With the Meiji Period (1868–1912) came important changes. Japanese life, government, and literature were profoundly influenced by Western culture. Writers began to experiment with new styles and genres, but few, if any, strayed entirely from their rich and powerful literary heritage. Much translation from English and other European languages has been done, and at first the translations were widely, and most often poorly, imitated. Kakuzo Okakura (1862–1913) published his works in many languages and was instrumental in promoting Western understanding of Japanese culture. The first important Meiji novelist was Shimei Futabatei, an admirer of Turgenev. A prominent novelist, poet, and dramatist, Ogai Mori (1861–1922) derived his influence from German literature. Kafu Nagai (1879–1959), influenced by Maupassant, wrote his first novels in a naturalistic vein. Akiko Yosano, a gifted woman poet, produced verse that was romantic in style, and Shiki Masaoka modernized the *haiku* and *tanka* verse forms.

Although it is seldom mentioned in writing, World War II administered a shock to Japanese literature from which its recovery was slow. Western and native ideas clashed. Among the earliest postwar figures to emerge was Junichiro Tanizaki (1886–1965), whose *The Thin Snow* (1948) and other popular works bespeak a fondness for diabolical or scandalous themes, as does much of Japanese literature. Yasunari Kawabata (1899–   ), winner of a Nobel prize in 1968, early leaned toward Western fiction, but later turned to his own literary tradition. His *Snow Country* contains striking imagery. Natsume Soseki (1867–1922), one of the greatest 20th-century novelists, was influenced by English literature, and his prose often reflects his interest in *haiku*. Successful as dramatist (*Death in Midsummer*) and novelist (*The Temple of the Golden Pavilion*), Yukio Mishima (1925–1970) employed a variety of techniques. Tsuneari Fukada (1912–   ), has been successful as a dramatist, although Japanese drama has been largely without distinction in recent years. The Japanese film industry, however, with its excellent directors, has given to the drama new quality and freshness.

ASSYRO-BABYLONIAN LITERATURE

The literature of Babylonia and Assyria has for us a threefold interest, because of (1) the romantic progress of discovery in the last century, (2) the revelations of a rich and ancient civilization given us by the excavations in the Tigris and Euphrates valley, and (3) the light these discoveries have thrown on the Old Testament.

In 1835 Henry C. Rawlinson, an English officer, found at Behistun, in Persia, a long inscription on the smoothed face of a high rock. The writing was in three languages, old Persian, Elamite, and Babylonian. Although these tongues belong to different families of languages, the cuneiform characters were used for all. Rawlinson succeeded first in deciphering the old Persian, and during the next twenty years he, with other scholars, particularly a German named Grotefend, penetrated the secrets of the other two languages of the inscription. Thus we were given the means of studying the culture and the literature of Babylonia in its records on rocks, walls, and vast collections of clay tablets.

Early Sumerians and Babylonians. The cuneiform writing, which consists of wedge-shaped characters placed at various angles and in groups of from two to thirty, probably originated among the Sumerians at a quite remote date. The Sumerians were a non-Semitic people who migrated into the fertile Mesopotamian valley, probably from the northeast, before 4000 B. C. They early developed a high civilization, a complex nature religion, and an elaborate system of writing. Most of the inscriptions found in the temple libraries at Telloh and Nippur are in Sumerian. The oldest Sumerian inscriptions are short, historical in character, and were probably composed shortly after 4000 B. C.

Commencing apparently about 4000 B. C., Semites from the southwest also settled in Mesopotamia. Gradually they conquered and absorbed their Sumerian neighbors. But, although the Babylonian people resulting from this fusion was predominantly Semitic, and the Babylonian language was Semitic, nevertheless the superior Sumerian civilization prevailed. The Babylonian religion contains many elements of Sumerian origin. Sumerian survived for over thirty centuries as the language of religious documents, while the Semitic Babylonian, or Akkadian as it is commonly called, became the language of daily intercourse and profane literature. And Sumerian cuneiform writing was employed in all Babylonian documents.

Babylonian and Assyrian Libraries. The libraries, like the very ancient one in the temple of En-Lil, the Sumerian god, at Nippur, provided a record department and an educational department, equipped with grammars, dictionaries, commentaries, and interlinear translations. The great Babylonian period lasted from about the 22d to the 13th century B. C. After this time the Assyrians, a kindred people, succeeded to power. Among them, warfare and conquest were held in honor, and the works of culture were but little regarded. In consequence, their literary work shows little originality. They copied the Babylonian writings and preserved them in libraries, notably that of Assurbanipal (668–626 B. C.)—better known perhaps by the Greek version of his name, Sardanapalus—at Nineveh, which contained about 30,000 clay tablets. This library, explored by Layard and George Smith, was our first great source of information about Babylonian literature. It contained histories, grammars, lexicons, law books, works on astrology and astronomy, mathematics, epic poems, books of magic and incantations, omens, liturgies, psalms, and prayers. With the fall of Nineveh (607 B. C.), the library was buried in the ruins of the palace.

The Gilgamesh Epic. But, while these libraries are rich in all manner of writings, their principal treasures are the great mythological epics of the Babylonians. Chief of these is the Gilgamesh epic. It is the story of Gilgamesh, semimythical king of the ancient city, Erech. Ishtar, the Babylonian Venus, tries to win his love. But he rejects her advances and, instead, with his faithful companion En-Gidu, goes forth to seek immortal life. After many adventures, during which En-Gidu is killed, Gilgamesh finds his ancestors, Ut-Napishtim and his wife, enjoying immortality upon the Isle of the Blessed far to the west across the waters of death. Ut-Napishtim tells Gilgamesh the story of the great flood brought by the gods, from which only he and his companions in the ship escaped, while all the rest of mankind perished. This Babylonian flood story parallels the biblical flood story so exactly that it is probable that the biblical story was borrowed from the Babylonian. Ut-Napishtim tells Gilgamesh that at the bottom of the sea grows a magic plant which will restore his youth. But, just as he is about to possess it, a serpent steals it, and thus gains immortality for serpents, while Gilgamesh and all mankind forfeit it. The epic concludes with the account of the bringing up of the ghost of En-Gidu, who describes for Gilgamesh the abodes of death and the nature of life after death and informs him that his search is vain, that for mankind there is no escape from death. This Gilgamesh epic has a peculiar literary significance. It is written in twelve books or tablets, corresponding seemingly to the twelve months of the year, and must have initiated the custom of composing epic poems in twelve books or multiples thereof.

Epic of Creation. Another epic of almost equal interest tells the story of Creation. Marduk, the great god, slays Tiamat, the dragon of Chaos. Out of one half of her body he forms the heaven, out of the other half the earth. He then creates plants, animals, and man on earth. This story is strikingly similar to the biblical Creation story, and again it is likely that borrowing has taken place. This epic is arranged in seven tablets, corresponding probably to the seven days of the week, or else to the seven days of creation.

Other poems of epic character exist, chief among them being the legend of Adapa and the South Wind, the descent of Ishtar into Hell, the legend of Etana and the Eagle, the legend of the Zu-bird and the tablets of destiny, and the myth of Ura, the plague god.

Code of Hammurabi. Of equal literary and historical significance is the Law Code of Hammurabi, king of Babylon about 2100 B. C. It is engraved upon a large diorite column which was found at Susa in 1898. It contains almost 300 laws dealing with all manner of subjects, and is probably the oldest law code in the world's history.

Up to the present time, about 150,000 tablets and inscriptions have been discovered in Babylonia. Comparatively few of these have been deciphered, but scholars are continually at work, and each year adds to our knowledge and understanding of this great ancient literature.

The principal collections of tablets are in the British Museum at London, in the Louvre at Paris, in the Royal Museum at Berlin, in the National Museum at Istanbul, and in America in the museums of the universities of Pennsylvania, Chicago, and Yale.

HEBREW LITERATURE

The people of Israel form a part of the Semitic branch of the Caucasian race. Their language, Hebrew, belongs to the Western group of Semitic languages. Cradled in the great Arabian desert, they migrated to Palestine about 1400–1200 B. C. and established a nation which endured until overthrown by the Romans in 70 A. D. Since then, Israel has been scattered throughout the world.

In the solitudes of the Arabian desert the Israelite mind pondered over the deep mysteries of life. Gradually there was revealed to it through the long course of its history the knowledge of one, only God, sole Creator of the universe, who has fashioned all things in infinite wisdom, goodness, and love, and has ordained laws of justice and righteousness for human guidance. This ethical monotheism is the foundation principle of Judaism. It became the eternal and unquenchable passion of the Jewish people and the keynote of Hebrew literature.

Early Songs and Legends. Hebrew literature began, like almost every other ancient literature, in folk songs and legends probably recited in camp and village gatherings by tribal bards. As civilization developed, some of these poems were written down. The Bible mentions two collections of ancient Hebrew songs, *The Book of Yashar* and *The Book of the Wars of Yahwe.* Unfortunately, both books have been lost, and only a few fragments of these ancient poems, such as the "Song of Lamech" (Genesis IV: 23-24), the "Song of the Well" (Numbers XXI: 17), and the "Song of Deborah" (Judges V) survive.

By the time of David (1000 B. C.), Israelite culture had advanced materially. One of David's court officials was the scribe, who recorded the important events of Israelite history. This marks the definite beginning of literary activity in Israel.

The history of Hebrew literature may be divided into four periods: (1) the Biblical (from the earliest times to 70 A. D.); (2) the Rabbinic (70 to about 1000); (3) the Medieval (1000 to about 1800); and (4) the Modern.

The Bible. This constitutes the sacred book of Christian peoples. To the Jews, however, only the Old Testament is so regarded. It is far from being the whole of Hebrew literature. Unlike the Koran, the sacred book of the Mohammedans, the Bible was not composed at any one period. It is, rather, a collection of books, a small library, a national literature—all that survives of the quite considerable mass of writings composed during the national period of Israel's history. Therefore, it naturally contains many kinds of writing, including historical sketches and unhistorical or semihistorical legends, religious and social laws, the inspired utterances and visions of the prophets, liturgical and lyric poems (the Psalms), didactic poetry (Proverbs and Ecclesiastes), pragmatic fiction (Ruth), and even a pure love poem (Song of Songs) and two dramas (Job and Esther).

Pentateuch and Hexateuch. After the ancient poems referred to above, the oldest biblical writings are found in the Pentateuch and in Judges and Samuel. They were composed during the 10th and 9th centuries B. C. Science has established that, contrary to tradition, the Pentateuch is not the work of Moses, nor of any one man, but was composed by different groups of writers between 900 B. C. and 400 B. C., or even somewhat later. It has proved also that the book of Joshua was composed by these same writers; therefore, science speaks of the *Hexateuch,* "the six books," rather than of the *Pentateuch,* "the five books."

The oldest document of the Hexateuch, composed probably in 899 B. C. in the Southern Kingdom, is found in Exodus XXXIII: 12–XXXIV: 28. It contains an interesting and historically important tradition about Moses and also a little code of laws, which Exodus XXXIV: 28 calls explicitly the "Ten Commandments." These are by no means identical with the Ten Commandments of Exodus XX, which were composed much later, probably in the 8th century B. C.

About a half century after this first document, a similar work was composed in the Northern Kingdom. It is found in Exodus XX: 23–XXIV: 8, and is generally designated by the name applied to it in Exodus XXIV: 7, "The Book of the Covenant." It contains a code of laws, of greater extent than the code in the older document. In fact, several of the laws of the Book of the Covenant were borrowed from this older book, with minor changes to meet conditions obtaining in the Northern Kingdom.

Following these two oldest writings came the so-called Yahwist and Elohist documents, composed in the Southern and the Northern Kingdom respectively. The former, the product of the 8th and 7th centuries B. C., is so called by scholars because it uses only the name Yahwe (usually, but mistakenly, pronounced Jehovah) for the Deity. The Elohist Document, written during the 8th century B. C., is likewise so designated because it employs the word Elohim for God. The vast majority of the narratives of Genesis, Exodus, Numbers, and Joshua belong to the Yahwist and Elohist documents.

The Book of Deuteronomy. II Kings XXII and XXIII tell of the finding of a book in the Temple at Jerusalem in the eighteenth year of Josiah. This pious king, persuaded that this was the law of Moses, made it the basis of a far-reaching religious, social, and economic reformation. Scholars have established conclusively that this book was the book of Deuteronomy, or rather the greater part thereof. But, instead of having been written by Moses, then lost for centuries, and suddenly found again, it was composed by prophetic writers at this very time, 621 B. C., and the story of its discovery was merely a pious fiction designed to induce the devout and credulous king to institute the legal provisions of Deuteronomy as the law of the land. The plan succeeded, and the ensuing reformation brought about a greatly needed, thoroughgoing purification of the Israelite religion, and an abolition of the idolatrous rites. The book of Deuteronomy is animated by the fine religious spirit of the prophets. It adapts many of the laws of the Book of the Covenant to the conditions of the end of the 7th century B. C., and reveals a deep humanitarian spirit and a marked progress in civilization.

The Priestly Code. One unforeseen result of this Deuteronomic reformation was the centralization of the worship in the Temple. Gradually the priestly influence overshadowed that of the prophets, and the religion of Israel became steadily more ritualistic. This tendency grew during the Babylonian Exile (586–536 B. C.). This spirit of ritualism and formal religion characterizes the last main stratum of the Hexateuch, which is known, therefore, as the Priestly Code. This was composed, partly in Babylonia and partly in Palestine, between 570 and 400 B. C. or somewhat later. The main body of the Priestly Code is found in Exodus XXV–XXXI and XXXV–XL, the whole of Leviticus, and Numbers I–X:28, while other portions are scattered through Genesis, the early chapters of Exodus, and the latter chapters of Numbers and Joshua.

Sometime after 400 B. C., these various documents were woven together into a kind of running narrative that purported to recount the history of Israel in the period preceding its entrance into Palestine. In this way the Pentateuch, or better, the Hexateuch, came into being.

The Prophets. The prophetic writings, in the main, come from the same period as the Hexateuch. Amos, oldest of the literary prophets, lived about 760 B. C. A generation later came Hosea, Isaiah, and Micah. Nahum wrote about the middle of the 7th century B. C.; Zephaniah, Habakkuk, and Jeremiah, in the last quarter of the same century. Both Jeremiah's style and the content of his prophecy show a marked affinity to the book of Deuteronomy. Ezekiel wrote in Babylon at the very beginning of the Exile. His writings, in turn, exhibit a significant relationship to the Priestly Code. The great anonymous prophet, called Deutero-Isaiah because his supremely rhapsodic utterances are found in Isaiah XL–LVI, lived at the end of the Exile.

The Hagiographa. To the postexilic period belong the books of Zechariah, Haggai, Obadiah, Malachi, Jonah, and Joel. All the books of the Hagiographa, the third division of the Old Testament, were composed during the Exile or in the postexilic period, with the possible exception of a few pre-exilic psalms. Many of the Psalms, however, and also the book of Daniel, were written as late as the 2d century B. C. The book of Job, written about 400 B. C., is generally regarded as one of the masterpieces of the world's literature.

Apocryphal Writings. The Old Testament, in its present arrangement, came into being in the 2d century A. D. through a clear-cut distinction made by the rabbis between those books that were pronounced sacred and those that were declared profane. The latter were forbidden to be read, and gradually disappeared from use in Palestine. Many, however, continued to be regarded as sacred by the Greek-speaking Jews of Alexandria, and have been preserved in Greek translations in two collections known as the Apocrypha and the Pseudepigrapha. The books of the Apocrypha are included in Catholic editions of the Bible. Of the Apocryphal writings, the three books of Maccabees, Esdras, Judith, Tobit, Ben Sirach, and the Wisdom of Solomon are the most important. Recently a large portion of the Hebrew original of Ben Sirach was discovered in Egypt. Of the Pseudepigrapha, Enoch, Jubilees, The Testaments of the Twelve Patriarchs, the Sibylline Oracles, and the Psalms of Solomon are best known. All these works were composed between 200 B. C. and 200 A. D.

The Mishna. With the destruction of the Temple at Jerusalem by the Romans in 70 A. D., the religious life of Israel underwent a complete transformation. Without altar and priesthood. sacrifice and elaborate ritual were impossible, Prayer, reading of the Scriptures, and ceremonies in synagogue and home became the main elements of religious practice. The biblical laws were carefully studied, commented upon, and amplified by the rabbis in the great schools of the land. New laws that regulated all the activities of daily life were devised. Eventually they became so numerous that codification was necessary. This work was successfully accomplished by the great teacher and leader, Rabbi Judah the Prince, about 200 A. D. His work, called the *Mishna*, or "Teaching," is a systematic compilation in six books of all the laws evolved by the rabbis up to that time.

The *Mishna* almost immediately came to be regarded as second in authority only to the Bible. Along with the Bible it became the chief object of discussion by the rabbis in the schools of Palestine and Babylonia. Constantine the Great closed the schools in Palestine in 327, but not until the discussions of the laws of the Bible and *Mishna* had been compiled into a large work known as the *Palestinian* or *Jerusalem Talmud*.

The Talmuds. About the middle of the 6th century, a similar compilation of the rabbinical discussions of the laws of the Bible and *Mishna* in the Babylonian schools was made. This is known as the *Babylonian Talmud*. Hence there are, actually, two *Talmuds*. But, since the *Babylonian Talmud* was compiled two centuries after the *Palestinian*, it is naturally a far larger work, and contains practically everything found in the latter, with much new material. When the *Talmud* is referred to, the *Babylonian Talmud* is usually meant.

But it must not be imagined that these *Talmuds* are purely legalistic works. They abound in information about diverse matters,—folklore, medicine, history, geography, religion and ethics, legends, stories, wise maxims, and the like. This material constitutes a good half of the content of the *Talmud* and is known as *Haggada*, or "Narrative," in contrast to the legalistic matter, called *Halacha*, "Rule." Moreover, a vast store of additional Haggadic material is contained in various collections known as *Midrashim*, or "Expositions" (of biblical texts). Of these, the *Midrash Rabba* is the largest and most popular. The many well-known stories and sayings of the rabbis are taken from the *Haggadic* portions of the *Talmud* and the *Midrashim*.

Medieval Hebrew Literature. After the year 1000 A. D., the center of Jewish life shifted from Babylonia to southwestern Europe. During this period the Jews transmitted much of Arabic science and culture to the European nations and thus contributed mightily to the Renaissance. Hebrew literature during the medieval period dealt with a wide range of subjects,—philosophy, ethics, biblical commentaries, history, mathematics, astronomy, geography, travel, Hebrew grammar, poetry, and the like. The leading Jewish philosopher, Moses Maimonides, exerted a strong influence upon medieval scholasticism. The best-known medieval Hebrew poets were Judah Halevi and Solomon ibn Gabirol.

The Modern Period. During the 16th, 17th, and 18th centuries, Hebrew literature declined noticeably both in extent and in the value of its content. The last century, however, has witnessed a remarkable revival of Hebrew literature, due chiefly to the Zionist movement, which has sought, with some success, to revive Hebrew as a spoken language. This modern Hebrew literature deals with the same wide range of themes as do other modern literatures. Of the present day Hebrew dramatists, David Pinski is perhaps the foremost. The most gifted modern Hebrew poet is H. N. Bialik, while Asher Ginzberg, better known by his pseudonym, *Achad Haam*, "One of the People," is recognized as the leading essayist.

SYRIAC LITERATURE

The Syriac language belongs to the Aramaic group of Semitic languages, and is, therefore, akin to Hebrew. Syriac was the vernacular of Syria and Iraq until after the Arab conquest (7th century), when Arabic gradually superseded it. Today, Syriac survives as a spoken language only in a few isolated communities in Iraq.

Syriac literature had its beginnings early in the Christian era, and reached its zenith between the 4th and the 7th century. Thereafter it gradually declined and eventually ceased about 1300. It is largely a church literature, and was cultivated chiefly in the Jacobite and Nestorian ecclesiastical schools, particularly those of Edessa and Nisibis. It is rich in hymns, homilies, martyrologies, church histories, and the like.

Of especial interest are the early Syriac versions of the Bible. At least three such are known, composed probably between the 2d and the 5th century. Most important is the version known as the *Peshitta* (the "simple" text). Of some biblical books it is a literal translation, of others a free translation, and of still others merely a paraphrase. In those books of which it is a literal translation, its text frequently varies materially from the Hebrew. It is therefore much used by biblical scholars in determining the original and correct text of the Bible.

Besides church writings, Syriac literature contains many important scientific works, such as treatises on the Syriac grammar and language, histories, and translations, chiefly from the Greek. Some of the works in Aristotle's *Organon* were known to Europe, prior to the Revival of Learning, only by translation from Syriac versions.

Among the leading Syriac writers may be mentioned Bardesanes (b. 154), seemingly the father of Syriac literature, author of an interesting account of the heathen religions of the Orient; Ephraem Syrus (d. 373), the homilist and hymnologist; and Gregory Abulfarag bar Hebræus (1226–86), one of the last and probably the greatest Syriac writer. His extant works are exceedingly numerous and treat a great variety of subjects, mostly scientific. Of particular value is his *Chronikon*, one of the earliest attempts at a universal history in the world's literature.

ARABIC LITERATURE

The Arabic language commands the attention of students of the history of civilization because (1) with the exception of English it is spoken by more people than is any other language; (2) it is the language of the *Koran*, and therefore the sacred tongue of one of the world's great religions; (3) it is the instrument of expression of a vast and varied literature, through which the elements of science and philosophy were communicated to European scholars during the middle ages, thus, in large part, giving rise to the Renaissance; and (4) through it many familiar stories, such as those of the *Thousand and One Nights*, were brought to the Western world.

Arabic is a Semitic language, with a vocabulary far larger probably than that of any other language, and possessing a flexibility that permits the utmost delicacy and imagery of expression. It is primarily the language of the nomad tribes of the Arabian desert, but through the rapid development and spread of Mohammedanism it became the language of a very large part of the Orient.

Pre-Islamic Poetry. Arabic literature began, as might be expected, in the songs of tribal bards extolling the glories of their respective tribes. At the great gatherings of the tribes, and notably at the annual fair at Ukaz, when the tribes came together each year in peaceful intercourse, contests of skill were regularly held between the poets of the various tribes. Poems were first committed to writing in the 6th century A. D., shortly before the birth of Mohammed and the rise of Islam. The greatest of pre-Islamic poets was Imru-'l-Qais, though others, notably Labid and Amr-ibn-Kultum, rank with him. Antar, another famous poet of this time, was the hero of a very long, romantic poem that goes by his name.

The Koran. The *Koran*, the Bible of Islam, contains the inspired utterances of Mohammed, the supposed revelations of God through the prophet to his people. It is written in rimed prose, which produces a rhythmic, dignified, and impressive effect. It is divided into 114 sections or *suras*. For a time after Mohammed's death (632) various versions of the *Koran* were current, but under Caliph Uthman (644–656) these were collected into the present official text. Since then the *Koran* has served as the chief model and inspiration of all Arabic literature. It has been widely studied and commented upon by Mohammedan scholars, and commentaries upon it form an extensive branch of Arabic literature. Baidawi (d. 1282) is the best-known and most authoritative commentator of the *Koran*.

Forms of Arabic Poetry. Pre-Islamic poetry likewise exerted an important and lasting influence upon subsequent Arabic literature, particularly upon its poetry. The poems of the five greatest pre-Islamic poets were collected and hung up, as the lasting glories of the Arab tribes, in the Kaaba, the great temple at Mecca. Hence they were known as the *muallakat*, "the suspended ones." They served as the models of later Arabic poetry. Therefore it happens that the Arabic *qasida*, or long poem, usually begins with a description of a camping ground and with a lamentation for the fallen or absent companions of the poet. After this introduction the poet takes up the story of his love, his sufferings, and his journey, and adds many details in praise of his horse, his arms, and the like. And then he usually concludes, in typical Oriental manner, with fulsome praise of some influential man, from whom a substantial reward is expected in return.

After the time of Mohammed, when cities and courts developed, these early literary forms, which had sprung out of wandering tribal life, were retained for a time. But in the atmosphere of the cities they became so artificial that, about the 8th century, poets began to employ new forms and treat new subjects. In this century, Abu Nuwas is the most distinguished name in Arabic poetry.

A closely related type of Arabic literature is the *maqama* (assembly), consisting of stately rimed prose interspersed with metrical passages. It therefore exhibits the influence of both pre-Islamic poetry and the *Koran*. It is a combination of legend and story, in which the writer tells how in various places he meets a wandering scholar who puts all his rivals to shame. This type of writing was practiced as late as the 19th century. Hamadhani in the 10th century was the originator, and Hariri in the 11th century is regarded as the most brilliant writer, of the *maqama*.

Arabic Fables and Stories. From the 8th through the 15th century, and particularly during the brilliant reign of the caliph Haroun-al-Raschid (786–809), Arabic literature reached the height of its development. Arabic writers drew largely upon outside sources. Thus the fables of Bidpai were borrowed from the Persian, and the story of Kalilah and Dimnah, from Indian literature. Best-known of this class of writing is the widely read collection of stories known as the *Thousand and One Nights*, or, less correctly, the *Arabian Nights*. These have been translated into almost every European language.

History and Science. Historical composition has been diligently cultivated by Arabic writers. Their method is peculiar. The historian follows the principle that, if a thing has once been told well, the words of this account can be used again; therefore he keeps as close as possible to his sources. Moreover, if two or more accounts of an incident are current, instead of attempting to determine which is the correct, or at least the most probable, account, he usually cites all the accounts, scrupulously stating his sources for each, and leaves it to his readers to choose whichever tradition pleases him best. In this way thirty or more accounts of a single incident are frequently recorded by Arabic historians.

Other sciences besides history were diligently cultivated by Arabic sages, and the literature is extremely rich in important works on mathematics, astronomy, chemistry, grammar, and philosophy

Recent Literary Revival. With the advent of the Turks into western Asia and Europe and the conquest of the Moors in Spain in the 15th century, Arabic literature began to decline. The 19th century, however, saw numerous attempts to revive and modernize Arabic literature, due to the increasing contact between Arabic and Western writers and thinkers. Large printing presses have been set up and numerous works of poetry and history as well as historical novels by both Mohammedan and Christian writers have been published. The Latin alphabet has been officially adopted by order of the Turkish government.

ETHIOPIC LITERATURE

Ethiopic is a Semitic language, closely related to Arabic. The Ethiopians were Semites who, about the beginning of the Christian era, were driven from their home in Sheba in southern Arabia by kindred tribes pushing in from the Arabian desert. They crossed over the narrow strait of Bab el Mandeb at the southern end of the Red Sea and settled in Abyssinia, where they established a powerful kingdom. Today Ethiopic has resolved itself into several dialects spoken by the Abyssinians, the modern descendants of the Ethiopians.

The introduction of Christianity into Ethiopia in the 4th century marks the systematic beginning of Ethiopic literature. The Bible and other writings of the ancient Church were early translated from Greek, Coptic, and Syriac into Ethiopic. Although quite extensive, Ethiopic literature is almost entirely religious in character, occasionally varied by some work of historic or semihistoric nature. Ethiopic writers have been, almost without exception, devoid of distinctive individual merit.

None the less, the literature is important because it contains several important Jewish and early Christian pseudepigraphic writings which have survived only in Ethiopic. Chief of these are the books of Enoch (one version) and Jubilees, the Apocalypse of Ezra, the Ascension of Isaiah, and the Life of Adam and Eve.

There are a few modern works of secular character in the Amhari and Geez dialects.

EGYPTIAN LITERATURE

Egyptian literature presents to modern readers several unusual features: (1) the long history of the Egyptian language, from 4000 B. C. to 1500 or 1600 A. D. (including the Coptic period); (2) the very slight connection of ancient Egyptian literature with that of neighboring countries; (3) an almost total lack of progress in style or subject matter; (4) the fragmentary and inaccurate manuscripts in which the large mass of writings have come down to us.

Three forms of writing were used in ancient Egypt: (1) the hieroglyphic (priestly writing), consisting of pictures to represent ideas, a system in use for inscriptions down to the 2d or 3d century B. C.; (2) the so-called hieratic, an abbreviated form of the hieroglyphic, used by the priests for writing manuscripts; (3) the demotic (popular) script, which came into use very late. The key to these forms of writing was found on the famous Rosetta Stone, discovered in 1798-99 in Fort St. Julien de Rosetta near the Rosetta mouth of the Nile. Knowledge of writing, however, was apparently never widely distributed in Egypt, and the numerous errors and corruptions in the most beautiful of existing papyri show that the copyists were more interested in making accurate characters to be placed with the dead in tombs than in reproducing the thought for living readers.

The remains of Egyptian literature include inscriptions upon monuments and in tombs and a vast mass of papyri which, well preserved in the dry Egyptian climate, have been gathered into the various museums of the world. Most of this literature was produced during the period of the Middle Kingdom (3000 to 1600 B. C.), and the papyri were copied in later times. In general, although the records reveal an ancient, busy, and religious civilization, they are devoid of significance as literature.

Herodotus remarked the devotion of the Egyptians to their gods, and modern scholars find that much of the literature that has survived is concerned with the religious beliefs of the people and with accounts of ceremonies and magical charms and incantations. These are gathered into collections, such as the *Book of the Dead*, portions of which are found on tombs and sarcophagi.

The mythology of the Egyptians seems to have been very rich. It is said that every sanctuary had local legends of the gods, which the priests presented in dramatic form at the local festivals. But very little of such material has survived.

In philosophy, nothing has been found except a few collections of proverbs, sayings such as those ascribed to Ptah Hotep. One such collection, known as the *Papyrus Prisse*, is assigned to the 12th dynasty (about 2500 B. C.) and is called the oldest book in the world.

In poetry a few hymns and some graceful love songs have survived; and one epic poem, celebrating the victory of Rameses II over the Hittites in the battle of Kadesh, is well known. But the Egyptian verse, while it sometimes resembles Hebrew poetry, has very little of real poetic quality and was never highly developed.

The largest body of literary remains, other than the religious works, consists of tales and stories, such as are found in the *Arabian Nights*. These bear evidence of having been passed down through many generations. Some of them are in the form of fables, such as the story of *The Lion and the Mouse*; among fairy tales a Cinderella story appears. For the most part these are written in a simple and unaffected style. Fairly representative of these collections is the story of King Cheops of the Middle Kingdom, who, to relieve his insomnia, called upon his sons for entertainment. They, in obedience, narrated in turn tales of wonders wrought by famous magicians.

In the time of the Middle Kingdom another more

artificial or rhetorical type of story developed, in which the interest centers rather in the semipoetical passages than in the plot. The most famous of such stories have been called *The Fated Prince*, *The Tale of Two Brothers*, and *The Eloquent Peasant*. In the last of these the peasant has been robbed of his ass and applies to an official of his district for redress. The official is so charmed by the peasant's speech that he makes report to the king, and the case is carried on from term to term to give occasion for the peasant to make more of his eloquent speeches. This rhetorical narrative gave place under the New Kingdom to a simpler style of tales of magic and adventure.

After the Greek conquest (about 300 B. C.) Egyptian literature ceased. Its place was taken by the work of Greek authors, and Alexandria became a center of Greek learning. From the 3d to the 16th century A. D., Coptic, a descendant of the ancient Egyptian language, was the tongue of Christian Egypt, but it gave way to Arabic, which is now the popular language of the country. Except for a few unimportant fragments, the only Coptic literary remains are religious,—stories of saints and martyrs, and translations of parts of the Bible. The Gospels and Epistles are still taught to children in Coptic Christian schools in both the Coptic and the Arabic language.

PERSIAN LITERATURE

Persian literature has for Western readers three chief points of interest: (1) its long history and great works; (2) its influence on the later Greek and Hebrew writers; (3) its transmission of Hindu thought and story to the West.

Zoroaster, living probably in the 11th century B. C., did so thoroughly his work of religious teaching and reform, that but scant traces of earlier Persian religion and customs survive. But he and his followers left the world one of its noblest bodies of religious writing, the *Avesta*, which is our earliest example of Persian literature. The language of the *Avesta* is called *Zend*, a word which means literally "interpretation," *Zend-Avesta* meaning "commentary and text." This language and the Vedic Sanskrit were dialects of an earlier Aryan or Indo-European language spoken on the highlands of Iran. Both very early passed out of general use and knowledge.

With the conquest of Persia by the Greeks under Alexander in the 4th century B. C., the "middle" period of Persian literature begins. The *Avesta* was translated into Pehlevi, the language of this period, a mixture of Persian and Arabic. Other literary remains of the time are very scanty.

The successive waves of conquest and tyranny which passed over Persia during the next few centuries, as well as the introduction of Mohammedanism, severely restricted the variety of themes for Persian writers, but these very influences enriched their stock of materials through contact with Greece, Arabia, and especially India, where for several centuries Persian was the official language. From the winning of a partial independence from the caliphs in the 9th century A. D. dates modern Persian literature, written in an Aryan language mixed with many Arabic words.

The 10th century brought the first high tide of Persian literature. Chief among a multitude of writers stands the name of Firdousi, whose greatest work, the *Shah Nameh* or "Book of Kings," is ranked as one of the world's great epics. This poem is a source from which Persian and Western poets and story-tellers have drawn much material. Matthew Arnold made Rustan or Rustum, Firdousi's greatest hero, familiar to English readers in his narrative poem *Sohrab and Rustum*. Firdousi also produced the earliest poetic treatment of the biblical story of Joseph, which has been retold by many of his followers.

Firdousi is counted the originator of romantic, didactic, and mystic Persian poetry. A contemporary of his, a mystic poet, originated the form of the *ruba'i* or "quatrain," peculiarly adapted for the writing of moral and ethical reflections in the skeptical strain characteristic of Persian poetry. It is familiar to Western readers through Fitzgerald's translation of the *Rubaiyat* (Quatrains) of Omar Khayyam, the fascinating freethinker and ironist of the 11th century.

Rather strangely, the next great period of Persian literature falls in the fearful time of conquest and devastation under the Mongolian conqueror, Jenghis Khan. In the 14th century, Hafiz wrote what are called the most perfect of Persian lyrics. The last of the great Persian poets is Djami, who wrote epic, lyric, and mystic verse. These poets, perhaps because of the tyranny of government, did not attempt new themes but gave themselves to treating old themes in new ways; hence their elaborate system of figures, synonyms, and rimes, which in translation often produce an effect monotonous to Western taste. It should be noted that romantic passion, as known among Western nations, does not appear in Persian poetry.

The three centuries after 1500 produced a great wealth of prose in the form of fables, fairy tales and myths, novels and short stories, as well as folklore and history. This Persian telling of many of these stories is the first stage of their journey from India toward the West. Many of them find a place in the collection known as the *Arabian Nights*.

The 19th century in Persia was marked by the late beginnings of the drama. As in other countries, this found its origin in religious ceremonies. The range of themes is very small, although some biblical stories and Christian legends have been used upon the stage. Although much restricted as compared with earlier periods, there is today in Persia literary activity which produces both prose and poetry.

INDIAN LITERATURE

The literature of India (Sanskrit and Hindustani) claims our interest for three reasons: (1) its antiquity; (2) its peculiarly rich development; (3) its vast contributions to Western literature, especially in the form of proverbs, fairy stories, and fables.

This ancient literature, so amazingly vigorous and luxuriant, was opened up to the Western world by the discovery of the Sanskrit language in the 18th century. The discovery revealed the *Vedas*, the most ancient sacred books of the Brahman religion. The contents of these four *Vedas* or "Books of Knowledge," an elaborate body of religious ritual and legend, had been handed down by tradition through many centuries before they were committed to writing perhaps ten centuries before the Christian era. The language in which they are written is called Vedic (knowledge) or Vedic Sanskrit, and it is the ancestor of the Classic Sanskrit. The name Sanskrit (formed, refined) was given to this "older sister" of the western Aryan tongues by grammarians about the 4th century B. C. Since that time, at least, it has been the special language of the high literary and priestly classes, distinguished from the Prakrit (common) dialects of medieval India and from the modern Hindi and Urdu.

The immense literature of this Classic Sanskrit is very rich in epic, didactic, lyric, and dramatic poetry, as well as in prose fables, fairy tales, and romances.

There are two classes of Sanskrit epics. Of the *puranas* (ancient tales) the greatest are the *Mahabharata* (great poem or tale of the Bharatas) and the later and more artistic *Ramayana* (poem concerning Rama). These are partly legendary histories and partly mythical accounts of the universe, all with a religious motive. The greater ones antedate the Christian era, but lesser puranas were written in the first and following centuries A. D. to promote special Brahman beliefs. The *kavyas* (court epics) are artificial epics, most of which belong to the period between 500 and 1300 A. D. Of these the two best-known are *The Family of Rama* and *The Birth of the War God.* These epics mingle many grotesque fancies with passages of high poetic grace and power. Their delineation of the sentiments of love and forgiveness make an appeal to Western readers that is not always found in the Greek epic.

All forms of Sanskrit literature are strongly lyric, but long lyric poems are rare, their place being taken by series of little poetic pictures. Many poets are known only through some of these detached stanzas, which are commonly intensely sensuous in feeling and full of elaborate figures drawn from natural scenery. A very famous long lyric is *The Cloud Messenger* of Kalidasa. Bhartrhari in the 7th century was a much admired writer of both long and short lyrics.

In didactic and proverb verse, the Sanskrit literature is very prolific. It is said that practically all the proverbs and sayings to be found in other languages can be matched in the Sanskrit. One collection of about eight thousand of these didactic stanzas, representing all periods of the Sanskrit, has been made.

In the 5th or 6th century A. D., the Sanskrit drama began to develop from the pantomime dances connected with religious service. Although rather meager in extent, it is very noteworthy in theme and style. In several points it is similar to the romantic Shakespearean drama; the jester is there, and both comic and serious actions are included in the same play. Its themes are taken from heroic legend or contemporary court life, and its action always ends happily. The most famous of the dramatists, as he was the most illustrious poet of his time, is Kalidasa, whose best-known play is the *Sakuntala.*

The 4th century B. C. saw the earliest collection of fables, made for the purpose of instruction. Assigning of manlike parts to animals and mingling of prose and poetry are characteristic of these stories. We may trace the beast fable, so popular in medieval Europe, to the *jatakas* or Buddhist birth stories, in which the chief character is identified with some previous existence of Buddha. The most famous collection of fairy tales was put together in verse by Somadeva in the 11th century A. D. The titles of three story collections of this period are interesting: *Seventy Stories Told by the Parrot, The Great Cluster of Stories,* and the *Ocean of the Streams of Story.*

The 6th or 7th century A. D. may mark the beginnings of prose romances somewhat like the earlier English novels. One of the best-known is *The Adventures of the Ten Princes.* These romances are sometimes classed with the *kavyas.*

In modern times, two principal dialects, Hindi and Urdu, both of which contain a large Persian element, have achieved the standing of literary languages. The literature in Hindi is said to permeate all classes of the people more thoroughly than is the case with any literature of Europe. Its great poetic period was the 16th century, the Elizabethan period of English. Both Hindi and Urdu have been encouraged by the schools established in India during the 19th century, and they are adapting themselves in style and vocabulary to the expression of modern native and foreign thought. Native presses issue large numbers of books and periodicals. The newspapers of India are of unusual literary importance, because through them rather than through books, modern thought is disseminated among the people.

Extended instruction in English in the schools of India has been accompanied by the rise of numerous Hindu writers of English, several of whom have attained very high rank. The best-known to Western readers is Rabindranath Tagore, teacher and author, to whom the Nobel prize for literature was awarded in 1913.

GREEK LITERATURE

Greek literature is the living record of a great people, comprising works in many fields, which have served as models for all succeeding ages. This remarkable contribution was made possible by the sheer force and originality of the Greek genius, which displayed extraordinary creative power. For the literature of Greece is in the truest sense original; it is the unhampered expression of her great men in a language unsurpassed in grace and dignity.

Epic Poetry. The literature of Greece, as we know it, begins with epic poetry which is plainly the finished product of a society long familiar with this form of literary expression. When these poems were written, the Greeks already possessed, besides the myths of the gods, a large body of so-called historical myths,—of Thebes, of Troy, of the Argonauts, of Theseus, and of Heracles, or Hercules. These myths had long been the subject of the songs of the bards, or wandering minstrels, before Homer composed the two greatest of the world's epic poems. The *Iliad* tells the story of the incidents in the tenth year of the Trojan War; the *Odyssey* recounts the adventures of the return of Odysseus, one of the Trojan heroes, to his home in Ithaca after ten years' wandering. From both their matter and their style, most scholars conclude that a great master poet, Homer, living probably in the neighborhood of Smyrna in Asia Minor, in the 9th century B. C., gave final form in these poems to the stories and songs of a long line of earlier poets. The degree of originality shown by Homer in composing the *Iliad* and the *Odyssey* can only be estimated, and will probably never be known with certainty.

In the two centuries following Homer's time, there flourished a number of writers, known as the cyclic poets, who told and retold in the language of Homer many early legends and hero stories from the well-known "cycles," or groups of myths. During this epic age the Greeks created a larger body of literature of myth and legend than has been developed by any other people, but the most of this literature has not been preserved.

About 100 years after Homer, Hesiod, who wrote the *Works and Days,* a sort of farmer's almanac, wrote also a *Theogony,* an account of old beliefs about the gods and the origin of the world; in the former work he set forth an account of the five ages, beginning with the age of gold and passing through the ages of silver, of bronze, and of heroes, coming finally to the present wicked age of iron.

Reflective and Lyric Poetry. In the next period of Greek literature (about 700–475 B. C.) the turbulent growth of democracy seems to have encouraged reflective and lyric verse, though we know the early writers of this poetry only in tantalizing fragments of their work; these, however, are sufficient to prove its exquisite beauty. Pure lyric poetry was written early in the Æolian island of Lesbos, and the local dialect was one of the first used for lyric expression. This poetry was always sung to the accompaniment of the harp, just as the songs of the epic writers had been sung. At about the same time, lyrics were produced in the Dorian city of Sparta, where life was still free and natural, and not yet hardened into the rigid artificiality which was the blight of Sparta in the 5th century. Sappho and Alcæus, both of Lesbos, are the greatest of the Æolian school of lyric poetry. Toward the end of the period under consideration, a Dorian poet, Pindar, born in the Æolian city of Thebes, rose to the distinction of a national lyric poet of all Greece, and his works are for the most part preserved.

Reflective poetry, with its calmer mood, adopted the elegiac couplet for the treatment of a great variety of subjects. This measure, derived from the Homeric hexameter, was accompanied by a strain of flute music, the "elegy," which had been heard by the Greeks in Asia in songs of mourning. Simonides employed this measure in epitaphs honoring the Greek heroes who fell in the Persian wars. Solon, the lawgiver, used the elegy to publish his political precepts.

The Drama; *Origin.*—After the Persian wars in the beginning of the 5th century, Athens became one of the chief political centers of Greece, and she maintained a position of intellectual and literary leadership in the Mediterranean world for over 200 years. The drama is the most important literary development of this period, and it belongs peculiarly to Athens. It had its origin in very ancient religious observances, and its performance always remained essentially an act of worship of the god Dionysus. It grew out of a dance-song performed annually in honor of the god; this simple dance-song, rendered by a large group of men, came to be called a *dithyramb*, and at Corinth it became dignified into a literary form. Arion is said to have been the first to introduce this improvement, limiting the number of dancers to fifty and dressing them in goatskins as satyrs. At first they sang only of Dionysus and his adventures as he first journeyed into Greece, but later the theme was taken at will from any of the stories of the heroic *saga*.

Tragedy.—The beginning of the tragic drama, as distinguished from the dithyramb, is ascribed to Thespis of Icaria, a village near Athens, in the 6th century; he introduced an actor or speaker distinct from the chorus of singers, so that a legendary story might be enacted by the single actor and the chorus leader, supported by the chorus. Because of the satyrlike dress of the chorus (goatskins) the performance came to be called *tragœdia* or "goat-song"—hence *tragedy*. Æschylus, the first great tragic poet, added a second actor to the one used before his time. Of the eighty or more tragedies which he wrote, only seven remain. He took all his stories from the Homeric and cyclic poems, except that of the *Persians*, in which he celebrated the victory of the Greeks over Xerxes. His greatest work is the *Agamemnon*, which tells the story of the return of Agamemnon from Troy and of his treacherous murder. Sophocles we know through eight plays, the greatest of which is the *Œdipus Tyrannus*, a story taken from the epic cycle of Thebes. Sophocles is held to be the greatest of the Greek writers of tragedy in portrayal of character, and his work holds an unchallenged position among the world's greatest masterpieces. Euripides closely followed Æschylus and Sophocles, but, while the work of his predecessors was marked by profound religious feeling, that of Euripides was characterized by a rationalizing or "modern" spirit. He was regarded with suspicion during his lifetime, but after his death he became the most popular of the three tragedians, so that more tragedies of Euripides have been preserved than of Æschylus and Sophocles together. His is a realistic art, and it was well said by an ancient that, while Sophocles represents men as they should be, Euripides represents them as they are. His songs are particularly admired for their beautiful lyric quality.

Comedy.—Soon after tragedy had been molded by Æschylus into a noble literary form, another kind of dramatic performance came to the front, inspired by the same god. This grew out of the boisterous revels which took place during the festivals in honor of Dionysus—hence the name, *comœdia*, or "revel-song." The earliest comedy is known as the "old comedy"; in this, Aristophanes was the master; he used it as a vehicle of satire, both personal and political. The "middle comedy," which succeeded this Aristophanic comedy, became an instrument of social satire. The "new comedy," beginning about the end of the 4th century, was a light comedy of manners. The greatest writer of this type of comedy was Menander, of whose plays large fragments have recently been discovered in Egypt. This was the comedy which was adopted and imitated in Rome by Plautus and Terence.

Prose Literature; *History.*—The story of Greek prose begins after many centuries during which poetry was the only form of literary expression. The earliest prose, in the 6th century, recorded the speculations of philosophers or the monotonous records of chroniclers; the first prose of lasting importance is the history written by Herodotus in the 5th century, telling the story of the wars between Persia and Greece. Thucydides later wrote a history of the Peloponnesian war, in which he showed the critical insight of a philosophic historian. Xenophon, master of a simple, delightful style, wrote a continuation of Thucydides' history and also the *Anabasis*, an account of the expedition of the Greeks under Cyrus; besides recollections of Socrates and minor essays.

Oratory.—The free Athenian democracy of the 5th century was bound to encourage the art of public speaking and the study of rhetoric. Pericles himself was an orator of pre-eminent ability, and by this gift he maintained his leadership. The art of writing speeches for delivery by clients in the Athenian courts was perfected by Lysias, the master of the plain style, and he was himself an orator of no mean ability. In the following century, the greatest Athenian orators, Isocrates and Demosthenes, pleaded eloquently, but vainly, for a Greece united against the barbarian.

Philosophy.—The profound speculations of mature Greek philosophy are recorded in the writings of Plato, who stands pre-eminent among the writers of Greek prose. Socrates, the teacher of Plato, left no writings; and Aristotle's work, though characterized by the acute penetration of one of the greatest minds of all time, lacks the imaginative quality and the literary value of Plato's writings.

The Alexandrian Age. The productive period of Greek literature ends with the Alexandrian age. The center of intellectual life had shifted from Athens to Alexandria, and great scholarly industry took the place of creative work. Theocritus was the one outstanding exception. He, as the first writer of pastoral poetry, has furnished models and inspiration to many poets of succeeding ages, beginning with the Roman, Virgil. In this period the Hebrew Scriptures were translated into Greek in the version known as the Septuagint.

The Roman Period. In the Roman period, which extends from the middle of the 2d century B. C. to the beginning of the 6th century A. D., among a host of writers we find one of conspicuous ability, Lucian, who wrote in a clear and sparkling style a number of works on a variety of subjects, always handled in a light or playful manner. His *Veracious History* is a story of adventure such as Swift later produced in his *Gulliver's Travels*. His work often assumed a satiric tone, as in his *Dialogues of the Dead*. Plutarch, the father of biography, placed all succeeding centuries in his debt with his *Parallel Lives of the Illustrious Greeks and Romans*, while Strabo wrote on geography, and Josephus produced his *History of the Jews*. It was in this period that the modern novel had its beginning in such writings as the romance of *Daphnis and Chloe*, ascribed to Longus.

The Byzantine Period. From the 6th to the 15th century, the time of the fall of Constantinople, Greek, in the form of a stereotyped literary dialect imitating the Attic, continued to be the language of the culture which centered at Byzantium (Constantinople), as Latin was the language of Rome and the West. Apart from the work of a few able historians, such as Procopius of Cæsarea, most of the writings produced are of theological interest only, being the work of the Church fathers, such as Eusebius and Chrysostom. But it was during this period that the collection of short poems known as the *Greek Anthology* was completed. This collection includes thousands of poems, some of universal interest, and others inspired by some particular occasion, ranging in date from the 5th century B. C. to the 6th century A. D.

MODERN GREEK LITERATURE

Greek literature in the modern period, beginning about 1453, has been written partly in classical Greek, partly in the vernacular, but mainly in a literary language based on the classical tongue but modified by the vernacular and given definiteness through the work of the philologian Cortaës (1748–1833). The literary language was not spoken, but until the early years of the 20th century it was employed generally in prose writing. The use of the vernacular, or Romaic, language spread from poetry to all other types and had virtually completed its conquest of the literary tongue by 1925.

Before the national revival in the 18th century, few modern works were produced in Greek. A number of philosophical tracts in the classical tongue appeared during the 15th century, and an anonymous ballad poetry expressed in the vernacular

arose in the mountainous districts of Greece. Crete too was represented by a number of poems in the local dialect, of which the *Eratocritus* by Cornaro (16th century) was the most noted. Several chronicles appeared in the literary tongue.

The period of the revolution in the 18th century is represented by many writers, among whom the more noted were Rhigas (1760–89), who wrote stirring patriotic odes, and Trikoupis (1788–1873), the author of *History of the Revolution*.

Best known of modern Greek poets is Kostes Palamas (1859–1943), whose *Immutable Life* won him international recognition. Towering above all others, however, as novelist, thinker, and poet is Nikos Kazantzakis (1883–1957), whose crowning work was *Odysseus: A Modern Sequel*. In the form of a continuation of Homer's poem, it manages within the narrative to encompass a modern-day view of history and human destiny.

TABLE OF ANCIENT GREEK LITERATURE

AUTHORS		REPRESENTATIVE WORKS	
Time	Name	Prose	Poetry and Drama
B. C.			
About 900	Homer		Iliad, Odyssey.
About 800	Hesiod		Works and Days, Theogony.
About 700	Tyrtæus		Elegies.
About 600	Sappho		Lyrics.
About 600	Alcæus		Lyrics.
639–559	Solon		Elegies.
6th Cent.	Thespis		Tragedy.
About 563	Anacreon		Lyrics.
556–468	Simonides		Choral Lyrics, Elegies.
525–456	Æschylus		Tragedy (Prometheus Bound, Agamemnon).
522–443	Pindar		Choral Poetry.
500–428	Anaxagoras	Natural Philosophy	
495–406	Sophocles		Tragedy (Antigone, Œdipus Tyrannus).
484–424	Herodotus	History (Persian Wars)	
480–406	Euripides		Tragedy (Medea, The Bacchæ).
454–399	Thucydides	History (Peloponnesian War)	
445–385	Aristophanes		Comedy (The Birds, The Frogs)
445–378	Lysias	Oratory (Eratosthenes)	
436–338	Isocrates	Oratory (Panegyricus)	
434–355	Xenophon	History (Hellenica, Anabasis)	
429–347	Plato	Philosophy (Republic, Phædo)	
389–314	Æschines	Oratory (Against Ctesiphon)	
385–322	Demosthenes	Oratory (Philippics, On the Crown)	
384–322	Aristotle	Philosophy (Organon)	
372–287	Theophrastus	Philosophy (Characters)	
342–291	Menander		Comedy.
342–270	Epicurus	Philosophy	
About 300	Euclid	Geometry	
About 300	Theocritus		Pastoral Lyrics (Idyls).
287–212	Archimedes	Mechanics	
276–196	Eratosthenes	Astronomical Geography	
205?–122?	Polybius	History of world, 264–146 B. C.	
B. C. A. D.			
64– 21	Strabo	Geography	
A. D.			
37–100	Josephus	History (Jewish War)	
46–125	Plutarch	Biography (Parallel Lives of the Illustrious Greeks and Romans).	
125–192	Lucian	Dialogues of the Dead, Veracious History.	
264–340	Eusebius	Church History (Chronicle).	
347–407	Chrysostom	Sermons.	
5th Cent.	Longus	Pastoral Romance (Daphnis and Chloe)	

LATIN LITERATURE

Latin literature is to be prized because it contains such masterpieces as the poems of Lucretius, Virgil, and Horace, and the prose writings of Cicero and Livy. It has also transmitted to the Western world and adapted for it much of Greek thought and culture. Thus it has had an abiding influence on the form and content of the literatures of Europe and America. It deserves careful study also because the Latin language is one of the most perfect vehicles of literary expression that man has ever perfected, and because Latin is not only the predominant element in French, Spanish, and Italian, but also a very powerful factor even in the English language.

Early Epic and Drama. The early development of pure literature among the Romans is closely related to their political and military history. Southern Italy and Sicily were Greek. The war which the Romans carried on in the South against Pyrrhus and later in Sicily against the Carthaginians gave them a better acquaintance with the Greek people, Greek literature, and the Greek theater than they had had before. It was a Greek teacher, Livius Andronicus, brought to Rome as a captive from Tarentum in southern Italy in 272 B. C., who composed the first piece of formal Latin literature. It was a translation of the *Odyssey*. Later, in 241 B. C., to celebrate the successful conclusion of the long war with Carthage, a festival was held, and for this festival Andronicus adapted a Greek tragedy and a comedy. Nævius, the successor of Andronicus, and a native Italian, broke away in part from the Greek tradition by writing in verse the story of the first Punic war, and by basing some of his plays on Roman subjects.

Ennius also chose a Roman theme for his great epic, the *Annals*, which Virgil has followed here and there in the *Æneid*. Ennius used the hexameter verse too for the first time in Roman epic poetry. Greek tragedy in a Roman dress flourished in the early period, but it never attained great popularity with the Romans, and the writing of it for the stage ceased before the time of Cicero. The drama was best represented by the comedies of Plautus and Terence, in the latter part of the 3d and the early part of the 2d century B. C. Twenty of the plays of Plautus and six plays of Terence have come down to us. These two writers contented themselves with adapting Greek plays to their Roman audiences, but, in the century after them, plays based on Italian life made their appearance and won a place on the stage.

Oratory and History. While some native themes appeared in comedy and satiric verse, the practical Latin genius found best expression in this period in the prose of history and oratory. Cato the Censor is called the first of the orators, as he was the first historian in Latin. One hundred and fifty of his speeches are said to have been extant in the time of Cicero. He wrote also on agriculture and country life, and his *Origines* furnished Virgil with much material on the local history of Italian towns.

The following century (about 150–50 B. C.) witnessed the development of a Latin prose which combined the earnestness of the Roman temperament with something of the Greek artistic skill. The republican form of government was friendly to political discussion and furnished the motive for reflective political and historical prose. Sallust wrote history of the philosophic type found in the Greek historian, Thucydides. Cæsar, in his *Commentaries on the Gallic War*, created a model of direct, simple prose narrative.

Cicero. But the greatest figure of this time is Cicero, whose career falls in the first half of the 1st century B. C. Cicero was the greatest orator of his time, both in training and in performance. He developed a temperate style of oratory in contrast to the more florid Asiatic style then in vogue, and set a high standard for all orators of later centuries. His best-known speeches are those delivered against the conspirator Catiline. But, besides being a master of oratory, Cicero was a practical interpreter of the Greek philosophers. He was a finished critic and a graceful writer of letters which, in historical interest and personal charm, have perhaps never been surpassed. Among his famous books on criticism and philosophy are those *On the Orator*, *On Old Age*, and *On Friendship*.

The Augustan Age. To this "age of Cicero" belong two poets,—Lucretius, who wrote what has been called the world's greatest didactic poem, *De Rerum Natura*, an exposition of the atomic theory of Epicurus, and Catullus, the first great lyric poet of Rome. But the half century immediately following Cicero, called the Augustan age, saw the great outburst of Roman poetry. Loss of political freedom brought about the decline of oratory and political writing. Livy is the only great historian of the time, and he devoted his attention to giving the world splendid pictures, especially of the earlier periods of Roman history. Horace, for whom Catullus had prepared the way, wrote satires, epistles in verse, and odes, producing the finest Latin lyric verse. Ovid is best known through his *Metamorphoses*, in which he retold many Greek myths.

Virgil. The work of these men, as well as that of their greater contemporary, is still a living influence. The greatest of Roman poets is Virgil, whose earlier work, prompted by his own love of country life and perhaps by a suggestion of Augustus that he might

kindle a like enthusiasm among the people, consisted of *Eclogues*, that is, shepherd or pastoral poems, and *Georgics*, or poems of farming, which have inspired many later poets. But Virgil's greatest theme was the glorification of Rome and through Rome the praise of the empire and Augustus. In his crowning work, the *Æneid*, which he modeled upon the Greek *Iliad* and *Odyssey*, he gave deathless form to the story, first attempted by Nævius and Ennius 200 years before, of the adventures of Æneas and his companions from the fall of Troy to the founding of Rome.

The Period of Decline. After the Augustan age, Latin literature begins to decline. In the years following the death of Virgil, we have in the drama only Seneca, whose artificial, closet-tragedies were taken as models by early French and English dramatists. Pliny the elder left a great name as an encyclopedist. Martial, who was the court poet of Domitian, is known as the creator of the epigram. Juvenal is the great satirist of the period. By an age that had lost creative power much attention was given to rhetoric, in which Quintilian was, for many centuries, the highest authority. In the reigns of Nerva and Trajan, Tacitus, embittered by the persecutions of the reign of Domitian, wrote independently and with some republican bias upon the early empire. He is the last of the great historians of antiquity.

Up to the time of Tacitus, Rome had been the center of literary activity. All the great writers had been born there or had come there to live. In the later period, Rome and Italy lose their primacy in the literary as well as in the political world. Their vitality is gone. But literature springs up afresh in the new soil of the Western provinces, especially in Africa and in Gaul, and flourishes there from the 2d to the 6th century. In this latter century we find the last piece of pure literature which seems to belong to the old civilization, the *Consolations of Philosophy* of Boethius. It is to the 6th century also that we owe the *Code* of Justinian, which has served as a basis for all later jurisprudence. It does not fall within the field of pure literature, but it is the most characteristic product of the Roman genius. It summarizes in its *Institutes* the great principles of law which the Romans had developed through the generations; in the *Digests* it sets forth the opinions of distinguished jurists on important points of law; while in the *Code* proper and in the *Novels* edicts and decrees of the emperors are grouped together.

It is quite impossible to fix any point as marking the end of Latin literature, but, by the 7th century, French, Italian, and Spanish were beginning to develop, and it is convenient to take Isidore, the bishop of Seville, who died in the year 636, as marking the end of the long line of Latin authors. As if conscious of the fact that he closed the series of writers in Latin, he tried to sum up in his great work on *Etymologies* all the learning of past generations of Romans.

Medieval Latin. Even after French, Italian, and Spanish came into use in everyday life, Latin continued to be the language employed by the scholar, by the diplomat, and especially by the churchman, even in the services of the Church and in the sermons of the clergy. The rapid spread of Christianity from the 3d century on made radical changes in both the form and the content of Latin literature, and to the scholars of the Church and to her institutions we owe such learning as the middle ages had and the transmission of the masterpieces of Latin literature to us. So far as literary form was concerned, Christian writers brought in accentual, rimed poetry in place of the quantitative blank verse of pagan literature. This new form of verse was used especially in their hymns, which St. Hilary of Poitiers introduced into the Latin Church in the 4th century.

Shortly afterward, in 405 A. D., St. Jerome completed his translation of the Bible into Latin, the Vulgate so called, perhaps the most widely used book that the world has ever known. A contemporary of his, St. Augustine, wrote his great treatise on the *City of God*, the first philosophic interpretation of history from the Christian point of view. As we come into the later period, we find in the 6th century the valuable *History of the Franks* by Gregory, bishop of Tours, and, corresponding to this work, the *Ecclesiastical History of the English People* by Bede, the monk of Jarrow. The classical tradition is kept alive in the Latin plays of the German nun, Hroswitha, in the 10th century, and in the works of John of Salisbury, the great English scholar of the 12th century.

Manuscripts in Monasteries. The preservation of the classics also is due primarily to the Church. In 540 Cassiodorus established a monastery in southern Italy, in which he employed the monks in copying Latin authors. When the rest of Europe was sunk in ignorance and poverty, the Irish monks kept up this practice, until order was restored on the continent by Charlemagne, and the copying of manuscripts was again taken up there, in the great monastery and school of Tours. When, in the time of the Renaissance, the works of Cicero, Virgil, and the other great writers of the early period were found in the monasteries and carefully studied, their Latin appeared so much finer than that in current use, that the latter fell into disrepute, and consequently the humanists may be said to have put an end to Latin as the accepted vehicle of literary expression.

Roman literature as we have it owed much to the Greeks, but it may well have been a misfortune to it that in the very beginning it was brought under the influence of so highly perfected a literature as was that of the Greeks. As a consequence, it never had an opportunity to develop along the lines of the Roman national genius. In the writing of satire, in letter writing, and in the realistic romance, the Romans found fields essentially new and especially adapted to their talent; but all the other literary *genres*—the epic, the lyric, the pastoral, the drama, oratory, history, biography, and the essay,—they found represented by finished Greek productions. That their prose literature in the last century B. C. and their verse in the Augustan age did attain such a high degree of excellence, is an indication that the Romans had a marked strain of originality and made themselves masters of literary technique.

TABLE OF LATIN LITERATURE

AUTHORS		REPRESENTATIVE WORKS	
Time	Name	Prose	Poetry and Drama
B. C.			
3d Cent.	Livius Andronicus		Translation of the Odyssey, Tragedy.
269?–199	Nævius		Comedy, Tragedy, Epic (The Punic War).
254–184	Plautus		Comedy, (Aulularia, Captivi, Pseudolus).
239–169	Ennius		Epic (The Annals), Tragedy, Miscellanies.
234–149	Cato the Censor	De Re Rustica, Origines	
220–130	Pacuvius		Tragedy.
190?–159	Terence		Comedy (Andria, Phormio, Adelphi).
180–103	Lucilius		Satires.
170– 90?	Accius		Tragedy.
116– 27	Varro	On Agriculture, Antiquities	
106– 43	Cicero	Orations, Letters, Essays	
100– 44	Julius Cæsar	Commentaries on the Gallic War and the Civil War	
99?– 55	Lucretius		De Rerum Natura.
87– 54	Catullus		Lyrics.
86– 34	Sallust	History (Conspiracy of Catiline, War with Jugurtha)	
70– 19	Virgil		Eclogues, Georgics, Æneid.
65– 8	Horace		Odes, Satires, Epistles, Epodes.
1st Cent.	Nepos	Biographies	
B. C. A. D.			
59 – 17	Livy	History of Rome	
54?– 19?	Tibullus		Elegies.
50?– 15?	Propertius		Elegies.
43 – 18	Ovid		Heroides, Metamorphoses, etc.
4?– 65	Seneca	Investigations, Moralistic Essays.	Dramas.
A. D.			
23– 79	Pliny the Elder	Natural History	
35– 95?	Quintilian	Rhetoric	
39– 65	Lucan		Pharsalia.
40?–104?	Martial		Court Poetry, Epigrams.
55?–120?	Tacitus	Germany, History, Annals	
60?–140?	Juvenal		Satire.
61–113?	Pliny the Younger	Letters	
70?–150?	Suetonius	Lives of the Cæsars	
125?–200?	Apuleius	Romance	
?–366	Hilary		Hymns.
340–420	St. Jerome	The Vulgate	
354–430	St. Augustine	Confessions, City of God	
480?–524	Boethius	De Consolatione Philosophiæ, Translations	
490?–580?	Cassiodorus	History, Rhetoric	
538–593	Gregory of Tours	History (of the Franks).	
540?–604	Gregory the Great	Commentaries, Letters	
560?–636	Isidore of Seville	Theology, Encyclopedia	
673–735	The Venerable Bede	Ecclesiastical History	
About 967	Hroswitha	Legends	Epics, Plays.
1100–1156	Bernard of Cluny		Hymns (Jerusalem the Golden; For Thee, O Dear, Dear Country; The World Is Very Evil).
1118–1180	John of Salisbury	Encyclopedia, Letters	Elegies.
?–1192	Adam of St. Victor		Hymns.

LITERARY PLOTS, CHARACTERS, AND ALLUSIONS

No one can hope to be conversant with all the stories that have been told and with all the characters that have been depicted in literature.

Not even the more famous books can be familiar to those who have limited time to devote to reading. Nevertheless, one cannot go far in reading, or even in conversation, without being confronted with some allusion or some reference to a great literary work or to a story or a character drawn from such a book.

The following dictionary is intended to make such allusions more intelligible: to *outline* the stories in a few words; to *place* the characters; to *explain* terms that get their meaning from their connection with celebrated works; and, in general, to be a *guide* through that complex, imaginary world built up by the literatures of all lands.

Abbot, The. Sir Walter Scott. A story of thrilling adventures and vivid historic scenes around Lochleven Castle, north of Edinburgh, where Mary Queen of Scots was imprisoned. The story centers about the fortunes of Mary. A famous scene in the book is Mary's signing of her abdication, at the insistence of Lindsay and Ruthven, the royal commissioners.

Abdallah. Life of Mohammed, Washington Irving. A hero in Mohammedan legend. It is said that Abdallah, the father of Mohammed, was so beautiful that, when he married Amina, 200 virgins died of broken hearts.

Abdiel (ăb′dĭ-ĕl). **Paradise Lost, Milton.** The name, meaning "servant of God," of the seraph, who, when Satan stirred up a revolt, boldly withstood him.

Abou ben Adhem (ä′bōō bĕn ä′dĕm). Title and hero of a short poem by Leigh Hunt. An angel appearing to him, inscribes his name first among those "whom love of God hath blessed," since he loved, not God, but his fellow men.

Abou Hassan (ä′bōō häs′än). **Arabian Nights.** According to *Arabian Nights*, a merchant of Bagdad who was carried in his sleep to the bed of Caliph Haroun-al-Raschid and on waking was made to believe himself the caliph, a deception which occurred twice. He afterward became in reality the caliph's favorite and companion.

Abracadabra (ăb′rȧ-kȧ-dăb′rȧ). A mystical work to be repeated in conjurations or to be worn as a charm for warding off evil spirits.

Abraxas. In Persian literature a word denoting a supreme being. In Greek notation it stands for the number 365. In old tales or romances Abraxas presides over 365 impersonated virtues, one of which is supposed to prevail on each day of the year. In the 2d century the word was employed by the Basilidians for the deity; it was also the principle of the Gnostic hierarchy, and that from which sprang their numerous Æons. The word is found on stones used as talismans in the middle ages, called abraxas stones.

Absalom. Absalom and Achitophel, Dryden. A name given by Dryden, in his satirical poem "Absalom and Achitophel," to the duke of Monmouth, a natural son of Charles II. Like Absalom, the son of David, Monmouth was remarkable for his personal beauty, his popularity, and his undutifulness to his father.

Absolute, Captain. The Rivals, Sheridan. The hero in Sheridan's comedy *The Rivals*. He is distinguished for his gallant, determined spirit, his quickness of speech, and his dry humor.

Absolute, Sir Anthony. The father of the hero in Sheridan's *Rivals*. He is represented as testy, positive, impatient, and overbearing, but yet of a warm and generous disposition.

Abudah (ȧ-bōō′dä). A merchant of Bagdad. He finds the only way to rid himself of the torment of an old hag by whom he is haunted is "to fear God and keep his commandments." In James Ridley's *Tales of the Genii* (1764).

Acadia. The original, now the poetic, name of Nova Scotia. The name is derived from the Micmac Indian word *akade*, meaning plenty; in old documents the territory was called L'Acadie or La Cadie. It was granted by Henry IV of France, November 8, 1603, to De Monts, a Frenchman, and a company of Jesuits. They were finally expelled from the country by the English governor and colonists of Virginia, who claimed all that coast by virtue of its prior discovery by the Cabots in 1497. In 1621, Sir William Alexander, a Scotsman, applied to and obtained of James I a grant of the whole peninsula, which he renamed Nova Scotia, in honor of his native land. In 1755, the French inhabitants were seized, forcibly removed, and dispersed among the English colonists on the Atlantic coast. Longfellow has made this event the subject of his poem "Evangeline."

Achitophel (ȧ-kĭt′ô-fĕl). **Absalom and Achitophel, Dryden.** Achitophel, a nickname given to the first earl of Shaftesbury by his contemporaries, and made use of by Dryden in his poem "Absalom and Achitophel," a satire designed as a defense of Charles II against the Whig party. There is said to be a striking resemblance between the character and career of Shaftesbury and that of Achitophel, or Ahithophel, the treacherous friend and counselor of David, and the fellow conspirator of Absalom.

Acrasia (ȧ-krā′zhĭ-ȧ). **Faery Queen, Spenser.** A witch represented as a lovely and charming woman, whose dwelling is the Bower of Bliss, situated on an island floating in a lake or a gulf, and adorned with everything in nature that can delight the senses. The word signifies intemperance. She is the personification of sensuous indulgence and intoxication. Sir Guyon, who represents the opposite virtue, is commissioned by the faery queen to bring her into subjection and to destroy her residence.

Acres, Bob. The Rivals, Sheridan. A character in *The Rivals*, celebrated for his cowardice and his peculiar method of allegorical swearing.

Acrostic (ȧ-krŏs′tĭk). A form of verse in which the first letters of the lines form a word, usually a name. The Hebrews wrote a form of acrostic poetry in which the initial letters made their alphabet in regular order. Some of the psalms of the Old Testament are on this plan, especially the 119th Psalm.

Adam. Meaning "the made one." (1) A character frequently alluded to in the *Talmud*. Many strange legends are related of him. He was buried, so Arabian tradition says, on Aboncais, a mountain of Arabia. (2) In Shakespeare's *As You Like It*. An aged servant to Orlando, who offers to accompany Orlando in his flight and to share with him his carefully-hoarded savings of 500 crowns. (3) In Shakespeare's *Comedy of Errors*. An officer known by his dress, a skin-coat.

Adams, Alice. The tragic heroine of Booth Tarkington's novel of that name, whose social ambitions are thwarted by the shortcomings of her family.

Adams, Parson. Joseph Andrews, Fielding. A character in Fielding's story *Joseph Andrews*. He is distinguished for his goodness of heart, poverty, learning, and ignorance of the world, combined with courage, modesty, and a thousand oddities.

Adelphi (ȧ-dĕl′fī), "The Brothers." A play by Terence. Two brothers are brought up, one under stern parental discipline, the other under a scheme of indulgence. The play shows neither plan by itself to be successful. A golden mean between the extremes is suggested as the right method of education.

Adonais (ăd′ô-nā′ĭs). A poetical name given by Shelley to the poet Keats, on whose untimely death he wrote an elegy bearing this name for its title. The name was coined by Shelley probably to hint an analogy between Keats's fate and that of Adonis.

Adrastus. (1) *Jerusalem Delivered*, Tasso. An Indian prince from the banks of the Ganges, who aided the king of Egypt against the crusaders.

Æneas (ê-nē′ȧs). A Trojan prince, son of Anchises and the goddess Venus. When Troy fell, he quitted the city with his followers, accompanied by his father and son, visited various countries, settled in Latium, and married Lavinia, the daughter of Latinus. To him tradition ascribes the founding of the Roman state. Virgil tells his story in the *Æneid*.

Æneid. An epic of Latin national life. Virgil introduces into his poem the outlines of the Roman history and a number of interesting episodes. The first three books are not arranged in the order of time. The second book, which relates the downfall of Troy, and is the basis of the poem, is the first in time. The third, which relates the voyage of Æneas until after his departure from Sicily for Italy, follows. The first, which relates the dispersion of his fleet and his arrival in Africa, with his kind reception by Dido, succeeds the third. By this change the hero relates the downfall of his country, and the fortunes of his long and eventful voyage. The idea which underlies the whole action of the poem is the great part played by Rome in the history of the world.

Æsop's Fables. In the 5th century B. C., fables were in circulation in Athens, which were attributed to a certain Æsopus. Nothing is known for certain of his career. Probably he did not write the stories, but merely told them. The common collections bearing the name "Æsop" are versions of a book made by Phalereus in Athens about 320 B. C. and translated into Latin by Phædrus in the 1st century A. D.

Agamemnon. A Tragedy by Æschylus. The first of a trilogy consisting of *Agamemnon*, *Choëphori*, and *Eumenides*. In the play, Clytemnestra, wife of Agamemnon, aided by Ægisthus, kills him, ostensibly to avenge their daughter Iphigenia, whom he had sacrificed.

Agib. Arabian Nights. The third Calendar in the story of "The Three Calendars," in the *Arabian Nights*. Also, in "The Story of Noureddin Ali and Bedreddin Hassan," the son of the latter.

Agnes. (1) A young girl in Molière's *L'Ecole des Femmes*, who affects to be remarkably simple and ingenuous. The name has passed into popular use, and is applied to any young woman unsophisticated in affairs. (2) A strong, womanly character in *David Copperfield*, who proves a true friend to David's "childwife," Dora, and to David himself. Later, Dora dies and David marries Agnes.

Agramante (ä'grä-män'tä) or **Agramant** (ăg'rà-mănt). King of the Moors in Ariosto's poem *Orlando Furioso*.

Aguecheek (ā'gū-chēk'), **Sir Andrew. Twelfth Night, Shakespeare.** A simpleton to whom life consists only of eating and drinking. He is stupid even to silliness, but so devoid of self-love or self-conceit that he is delightful in his simplicity.

Ahmed, Prince. Arabian Nights. A hero who possessed a magic tent which would cover a whole army but might be carried in the pocket. He also possessed a magic apple which would cure all diseases.

Al Aaraaf (ăl ä-räf'). The Mohammedan limbo, or abode of souls who have been about equally good and bad. The subject of an uncompleted poem by Edgar Allan Poe.

Aladdin. One of the best-known characters in the *Arabian Nights*. Aladdin becomes possessed of a wonderful lamp and ring. On rubbing them, two genii appear, who are the slaves of anyone who possesses the lamp and ring. They obey Aladdin and perform incredible deeds by their magic.

Alasnam. The hero of a story in the *Arabian Nights* entitled "The History of Prince Zeyn Alasnam and the Sultan of the Genii." Alasnam had eight diamond statues, but had to go in quest of a ninth more precious still, to fill the vacant pedestal. The prize was found in the lady who became his wife, at once the most beautiful and the most perfect of her race.

Alastor, the Spirit of Solitude, Shelley. A poem in which he pictures an uncorrupted youth who, in seeking sympathy in the world, finds only the solitude of the crowd. In Greek story, Alastor is the avenger who follows the guilty man.

Albany, Albainn. A name given to Scotland or the Scottish Highlands in old romances and early histories. The title "Duke of Albany" has been frequently conferred since the 14th century. The "Duke of Albany" is the husband of Goneril in Shakespeare's *King Lear*.

Alberich, Dwarf. In the *Nibelungenlied* the dwarf "Alberich" is the guardian of the famous "hoard" won by Siegfried from the Nibelungs. The dwarf is twice vanquished by the hero, who gets possession of his "Tarnhelm," or cap of invisibility.

Albion. An ancient name of Britain, now used only in poetic allusion. Some say the name is derived from the lofty white cliffs on the south coast. Others derive it from the name of a fabulous giant, Albion, son of Neptune, who called the island after his own name and ruled it 44 years.

Albracca (ăl-bräk'kä). **Orlando Innamorato, Boiardo.** A castle of Cathay to which Angelica retires in grief at being scorned and shunned by Rinaldo, with whom she is deeply in love. Here she is besieged by Agricane, king of Tartary, who resolves to win her, notwithstanding her indifference to his suit.

Alceste (ăl-sĕst'). **Le Misanthrope, Molière.** A noble but misanthropic man, the hero of Molière's comedy.

Alchemist, The, Ben Jonson. A comedy. The alchemist is Subtle, a quack, who makes dupes of Sir Epicure Mammon and others. He leads them to believe that he has discovered the philosopher's stone. The best of Jonson's dramas.

Alcina. Orlando Innamorato, Boiardo. A fairy represented as carrying off Astolfo. She reappears in great splendor in Ariosto's *Orlando Furioso*.

Aldiborontiphoscophornio. A character in Henry Carey's burlesque tragedy *Chrononhotonthologos*.

Aldine (ăl'dĭn) **Edition.** This name is now applied to some editions of English works. The original Aldine editions were books from the press of Aldus Manutius, printed in the years 1490–1597 in Venice. These books have been highly prized for both their literary value and

their handsome exterior. The distinguishing mark of the Aldine books is an anchor entwined with a dolphin. Collections of these books have been made. Many of the works are now very rare and are highly prized.

Aldingar (ăl'dĭn-gär), **Sir.** A character in an ancient legend, and the title of a celebrated ballad, preserved in Percy's *Reliques*. This ballad relates how the honor of Queen Eleanor, wife of Henry Plantagenet, impeached by Sir Aldingar, her steward, was submitted to the hazard of a duel, and how an angel, in the form of a little child, appeared as her champion and established her innocence.

Alexandrian Codex (kō'dĕks). A manuscript of the Scriptures in Greek, which belonged to the library of the patriarchs of Alexandria, in Africa, A. D. 1098. In 1628 it was sent as a present to Charles I and was placed in the British Museum. It is on parchment, in uncial letters, and contains the Septuagint version (except the Psalms), a part of the New Testament, and the Epistles of Clemens Romanus. It is much consulted by biblical scholars, especially in the critical study of the epistles.

Alhambra (ăl-hăm'brà), **The, Washington Irving.** A series of legends of this famous Moorish fortress and palace near Granada, Spain. The book contains the finest descriptions of the palace. The name means "Red Castle."

Alice Brand. Lady of the Lake, Scott. Alice signed Urgan the dwarf thrice with the sign of the cross, and he became "the fairest knight in all Scotland." Then Alice recognized in him her own brother.

Alice's Adventures in Wonderland. A popular children's story by Lewis Carroll (C. L. Dodgson). In the story Alice, in a dream, in which she follows a rabbit into his burrow, comes out in a marvelous land underground where the animals act and talk like human beings. Her later adventures are given in *Through the Looking-Glass*.

Allan-a-Dale. A friend of Robin Hood's in the ballad. He is introduced into Sir Walter Scott's *Ivanhoe* as Robin Hood's minstrel.

All's Well that Ends Well. A comedy by Shakespeare. The hero and heroine are Bertram, count of Rousillon, and Helena, a physician's daughter, who are married by the command of the king of France, but separate because Bertram thinks the lady not sufficiently well born for him. Ultimately, however, all ends well.

Allworthy. Tom Jones, Fielding. Tom's foster father. He is distinguished for his benevolence. This character is said to be drawn from Fielding's friend, Ralph Allen.

Almighty Dollar, The. A phrase credited to Washington Irving. Its first recorded appearance in print was in Irving's "Woolfert's Roost."

Alph. Kubla Khan, Coleridge. A name invented by Coleridge and applied to a river mentioned in this poem.

Alquife (ăl-kē'fā). A personage that figures in all the books of the lineage of Amadis as a powerful wizard.

Al Rakim (ăl rà-kēm'). A fabulous dog connected with the legend of the "Seven Sleepers." The Mohammedans have given him a place in paradise.

Al Sirat (ăl sê-rät'). A bridge from this world to the next, extending over the abyss of hell. This narrow bridge, less than the thread of a famished spider, must be passed over by every one who would enter the Mohammedan paradise.

Amadis (ăm'à-dĭs) **of Gaul.** The hero of a celebrated medieval romance. The first part of the story is said to have been written by Lobeira of Portugal in the 14th century. Other portions were added later in Spain and France. Amadis, the hero, is a prince of Gaula, or Wales. He is exposed to the sea in his cradle, is rescued, brought up in Scotland, and, finally, after numerous adventures, marries the princess Oriana, in some versions daughter of a king of England, in others, of a king of Denmark.

Amaimon or **Amaymon.** An imaginary king of the East, one of the principal devils who might be bound or restrained from doing hurt from the third hour till noon, and from the ninth hour till evening. He is alluded to in Shakespeare's *Merry Wives of Windsor*.

Amanda. A young woman who impersonates spring in Thomson's "Seasons."

Amaurot. Utopia, Sir Thomas More. Amaurot was the chief city in Utopia.

Amaurote. A bridge in Utopia. The word means "faintly seen."

Amelia. The title of one of Fielding's novels, and the name of its heroine, who is distinguished for her tenderness and affection. The character of Amelia is said to have been drawn from Fielding's wife.

Amine (ăm'ĭ-nē). In *Arabian Nights* a female character who leads her three sisters by her side as a leash of hounds.

Amlet, Richard. The name of a gamester in Vanbrugh's *Confederacy*.

Amoret. (1) The name of a lady married to Sir Scudamore, in Spenser's *Faery Queen*. She is the type of a devoted, loving wife. (2) The heroine of Fletcher's pastoral drama, *The Faithful Shepherdess*.

Amys and Amylion. Two faithful friends. The Pylades and Orestes of the feudal ages. Their adventures are the subjects of ancient romances. An abstract of this early romance is found in Ellis's *Specimens of Early English Metrical Romances*.

Anabasis (á-năb'á-sĭs). A Greek work by Xenophon, which describes the expedition of the 10,000 Greeks, allies of Cyrus, particularly their retreat after the defeat and the death of Cyrus in 401 B. C.

Anacreontic (á-năk'rê-ŏn'tĭk) **Verse.** Commonly of the jovial or Bacchanalian strain, named after Anacreon of Teos, the Greek lyric poet, born at Teos, an Ionian city in Asia Minor. He died at the age of 85, probably about the year 550 B. C. In his poems Anacreon sang chiefly the praises of love and wine, to the enjoyment of which his life appears to have been dedicated. Many fragments of his songs are preserved, which are models of delicate grace, simplicity, and ease.

Anagram. A transposition of the letters of a name or sentence, the change of one word or phrase into another, by reading the letters backward or by transposing them

Anastasius (ăn'ăs-tā'shĭ-ŭs). **Anastasius, Thomas Hope.** The hero of this novel purports to be a Greek, who, to escape the consequences of his own crimes and villainies, becomes a renegade, and passes through a long series of the most extraordinary vicissitudes.

Ancient Man. Idylls of the King, Tennyson. Merlin, the old magician, King Arthur's protector and teacher.

Ancient Mariner. Rime of the Ancient Mariner, Coleridge. The ancient mariner, for the crime of having shot an albatross, a bird of good omen to voyagers, is doomed to undergo terrible suffering. Dreadful penalties are visited upon his companions, who have made themselves accomplices in his crime. The penalties are at last remitted in consequence of his repentance. When pity enters his heart he can pray, and the dead albatross, bound about his neck, falls off. The ship moves on, and he returns to his home port. There he encounters a hermit to whom he relates his story. At certain times the agony of remorse returns and drives him on, like the Wandering Jew, from land to land, compelled to relate the tale of his suffering and crime as a warning to others, and as a lesson of love and charity toward all God's creatures.

Andrews, Joseph. The hero in a novel of the same name, written by Fielding, to ridicule Richardson's *Pamela*. Fielding presents Joseph as a brother to the modest and prudish Pamela, and pictures him as a model young man.

Androclus or **Androcles** (ăn'drô-klēz) **and the Lion.** A story of a runaway slave who extracted a thorn from the paw of a lion. Later the slave, Androclus, was condemned to fight with a lion in the arena at Rome. The lion let out against him, turning out to be the animal he had befriended, expressed affection for him. G. B. Shaw wrote a satirical play on the subject.

Angel of the Schools, Angelic Doctor. Epithets applied to the medieval philosopher, Thomas Aquinas.

Angelica (ăn-jĕl'ĭ-ká). An infidel princess of exquisite beauty in Boiardo's *Orlando Innamorato* and Ariosto's *Orlando Furioso*. A beautiful heiress in Congreve's *Love for Love*.

Anna Karenina (kä-rä'nē-ná), **Count Tolstóy.** One of Tolstóy's most powerful books. The story of an attractive and, in many points, admirable woman, who forsakes her husband for a lover. The end, for her, is tragic suicide.

Antipholus of Ephesus, Antipholus of Syracuse. Twin brothers, sons of Egeon and Emilia, in Shakespeare's *Comedy of Errors*.

Antiquary, The, Scott. One of the Waverley novels. The Antiquary is Sir Jonathan Oldbuck, who has William Lovel as his guest at Monkbarns. Lovel there meets the daughter of Sir Arthur Wardour. He reveals himself as the earl of Glenallan and marries her.

Antonio. A frequent name in Shakespeare's plays. (1) In *The Merchant of Venice*, the friend to Bassanio, and the object of Shylock's hatred. (2) The usurping duke of Milan, and brother to Prospero, in *The Tempest*. (3) The father of Proteus, in *Two Gentlemen of Verona*. (4) A minor character, in *Much Ado about Nothing*. (5) A sea captain, friend to Sebastian, in *Twelfth Night*.

Antony and Cleopatra (klē'ô-pā'trá). Historical tragedy by Shakespeare, which may be considered as a continuation of *Julius Cæsar*. In the opening scene of *Julius Cæsar* absolute power is lodged in one man. In the conclusion of *Antony and Cleopatra* a second Cæsar is again in possession of absolute power, and the entire Roman world is limited under one imperial ruler. There are four prominent characters in this play: Cleopatra, voluptuous, fascinating, gross in her faults, but great in the power of her affections; Octavius Cæsar, cool, prudent, calculating, avaricious; Antony, quick, brave, reckless, prodigal; Enobarbus, a friend of Antony, at first jocular and blunt, but transformed by penitence into a grief stricken man who dies in the bitterness of despair.

Aonian Mount. Milton says his muse is to soar above "the Aonian Mount," i. e., above the flight of fable and classic themes, because his subject was "Jehovah, lord of all " Mount Helicon, home of the Muses, was in Aonia in Greece.

Apemantus (ăp'ê-măn'tŭs). A churlish philosopher in Shakespeare's play *Timon of Athens*.

Apocalypse (á-pŏk'á-lĭps). The Greek name of the last book of the New Testament, termed in English "Revelation." It has been generally attributed to the apostle St. John, but some wholly reject it as spurious. In the first centuries many churches disowned it, and in the 4th century it was excluded from the sacred canon by the council of Laodicea, but was again received by other councils, and confirmed by that of Trent, held in the year 1545. Most commentators suppose it to have been written after the destruction of Jerusalem, about A. D. 96, while others assign it an earlier date.

Apocrypha (á-pŏk'rĭ-fá). The word originally meant secret or hidden. The books of the Apocrypha are not found in either the Aramaic or the Hebrew language. The Old Testament apocryphal writings are fourteen in number: Baruch, Ecclesiasticus, Wisdom of Solomon, Tobit, Judith, two books of the Maccabees, Song of the Three Children, Susannah, Bel and the Dragon, The Prayer of Manasses, Esdras 1 and 2, parts of Esther found only in Greek. Their style proves that they were a part of the Jewish-Greek literature of Alexandria, within 300 years before Christ; as the Septuagint Greek version of the Hebrew Bible came from the same quarter, it was often accompanied by these Greek writings, and they gained a general circulation. No trace of them is found in the *Talmud*; they are mostly of legendary character, but some of them are of value for historical information, for their moral and maxims, and for the illustrations they give of ancient life. Several of these books were received as canonical by the Roman Catholic Church, at the Council of Trent. Protestant churches differ in the use of them. New Testament Apocrypha are certain letters and gospels, mostly of the 2d century, written to supplement the canonical books.

Apollyon. An evil spirit introduced by Bunyan in his allegorical romance *Pilgrim's Progress*.

Arabian Nights Entertainments. A series of one thousand and one stories, told by the sultana of the Indies to divert the sultan from the execution of a bloody vow which he had made to marry a lady every day and have her head cut off next morning, to avenge himself for the disloyalty of the first sultana. The story on which all the others hang is familiar. Scheherazade, the generous, beautiful young daughter of the vizier, like another Esther, resolves to risk her life in order to save the poor maidens of her city whom the sultan is marrying and beheading at the rate of one a day. She plans to tell an interesting story each night to the sultan, breaking off in a very exciting place in order that the sultan may be tempted to spare her life so that he may hear the sequel.

Arcadia, Sir Philip Sidney. Familiar in the title of Sir Philip Sidney's novel, "The Countess of Pembroke's Arcadia," the word is of ancient origin. The phrase, "I too have been in Arcadia," calls up the picture of a pastoral scene with shepherds and nymphs in the foreground, but a skull is also visible, showing that Death has invaded even this idyllic setting. Thus a similar fate is suggested for those who are now enjoying life. Variations on this theme are found in the writings of Ovid and Virgil. Earlier versions trace back to Polybius and Theocritus.

Archer. The Beaux' Stratagem, Farquhar. A servant to Aimwell and an amusing fellow.

Archimago (är'kĭ-mä'gō) or **Archimage. Faery Queen, Spenser.** The name implies a hypocrite or deceiver. He is an enchanter in the *Faery Queen*, opposed to holiness embodied in the Red Cross Knight. In the disguise of a reverend hermit, he wins the confidence of the knight, and, by the help of Duessa, or Deceit, separates him from Una, or Truth.

Arcite (*är′sĭt*). **Palamon and Arcite, Chaucer.** "Palamon and Arcite" is the first story told by Chaucer in his *Canterbury Tales*. Chaucer borrowed this story from Boccaccio, who, in his turn, borrowed it from a more ancient medieval tale. Dryden later put the same story into verse. Dryden pronounced the word Ar′cite′ or Ar-ci-te′. Arcite, a young Theban knight, made prisoner by Duke Theseus, is shut up in a prison in Athens with Palamon. Both the captives fall in love with Emily, the duke's sister-in-law. Both gain their liberty, and Emily is promised by the duke to the one who wins in a tournament. Arcite wins but is killed by a fall from a horse, and Emily marries Palamon.

Arden, Enoch. The hero of Tennyson's poem of the same name, a seaman who is wrecked on an uninhabited, tropical island, where he spends many years. He returns home at last only to find that his wife, believing him to be dead, has married his old playfellow and rival, and is prosperous and happy. In a spirit of heroic self-sacrifice, he determines not to undeceive her, and soon dies of a broken heart.

Arethusa. The name of a sylph in Pope's "Rape of the Lock." A reference to the Greek story of the love of Alpheus for Arethusa.

Argalus. An unhappy lover in Sir Philip Sidney's *Arcadia*.

Argan. The hero of Molière's comedy *Le Malade Imaginaire*.

Argonauts of '49. A literary name applied to the gold seekers who made the long overland trip or the longer sea journey to California in 1849 in search of gold. A reminiscence of the ancient Greek search for the golden fleece.

Ariel. (1) In the demonology of the cabala, a water spirit. (2) In the fables of the middle ages, a spirit of the air, the guardian angel of innocence. (3) In Shakespeare's *Tempest*, a bright, airy spirit whom Prospero had released from a tree to do his bidding and work his magical spells. By obedience Ariel is to win freedom when Prospero leaves the island.

Ariodantes (*är′ĭ-ô-dăn′tēz*). A lover in Ariosto's *Orlando Furioso*.

Armageddon. The name of the field in the plain of Esdraelon where the Israelites fought many battles with their enemies. Now applied to any great, decisive conflict.

Armida (*är-mē′dä*). **Jerusalem Delivered, Tasso.** A beautiful sorceress whom Rinaldo loved. By a talisman he is disenchanted. Not being able to allure him back, Armida rushes into the midst of a combat, is defeated, and, after conversion to Christianity, regains his love.

Arnolphe (*är′nôlf′*). **L'Ecole des Femmes, Molière.** A selfish and morose cynic.

Aroundight (*är′ŭn-dīt*). The sword of Lancelot of the Lake.

Arrow-Maker, The, Mary Austin. A drama of Indian life. The story is that of Chisera, a Piute medicine woman. Wearying of the loveless rôle she is compelled to play, she gives her love to Simwa, the "arrow-maker." He deserts her for the chief's daughter. Chisera ceases to serve as intermediary between the gods and the Indians. Disaster for the tribe follows. Chisera dies by one of her own magic arrows.

Arsinoe (*är-sĭn′ô-ē*). **Le Misanthrope, Molière.** A prudish character in this comedy.

Artegal. Also written Artegall, Arthegal, and Artegale. (1) A legendary king of Britain mentioned by Geoffrey of Monmouth in his chronicles and by Milton in his *History of Britain*. (2) A character in Spenser's *Faery Queen*, representing justice. (3) The hero in a poem by William Wordsworth, entitled "Artegal and Elidure."

Art for Art's Sake. Usually associated with Theophile Gautier's *L'Art pour l'Art*, this phrase conveys the idea that art should not be didactic or have any other purpose than to create beauty. It assumes that the artist, like an engraver of gems, is concerned solely with using his best skill to produce something fine.

Artful Dodger. See *Dawkins*.

Arthur, King. A poetical character, based on historical traditions. The Arthur of the old Welsh bards was a warrior chieftain ruling over fierce and warlike tribes. Every generation of poets has added something to this picture, until the Arthur of modern romance is the Christian gentleman as Tennyson pictures him in his *Idylls of the King* surrounded by his chivalrous knights, all bound together in one quest for the Holy Grail.

Arthurian Romances. These may be divided into six parts: (1) The romance of the "San Graal." (2) "Merlin," which celebrates the birth and exploits of King Arthur. (3) "Lancelot." (4) The search or "Quest of the San Graal." (5) "Le Morte D'Arthur," or death of Arthur. (6) "Sundry Tales."

Arthur's Drinking-Horn. No one could drink from this horn who was either unchaste or unfaithful.

Arthur's Round Table. It contained seats for 150 knights. Three were reserved,—two for honor, and one, called the "siege perilous," for Sir Galahad, destined to achieve the quest of the Holy Grail.

Arthur's Sword. Excalibur or Excaliber. Geoffrey of Monmouth calls it Caliburn and says it was made in the isle of Avalon, by Merlin.

Ascapart. The name of a giant whom Bevis of Southampton conquered. This is a favorite story of the old British romancers.

Ashton, Sir William. The lord keeper of Scotland; a prominent character in Scott's *Bride of Lammermoor*.

Asmodeus (*ăz′mô-dē′ŭs*). (1) In the Jewish demonology, an evil spirit, sometimes the demon of vanity, or dress. One legend makes him the destroyer of seven husbands of Sara, daughter of Roguel, on their bridal nights. In modern times he has been spoken of as the destroying demon of matrimonial happiness. (2) The demon hero of *Le Diable Boiteux* by Lesage, from which Foote took his play *The Devil on Two Sticks*.

Aspasia (*ăs-pā′shĭ-à*). A woman of ancient Athens, celebrated, in the age of Pericles, for wit, beauty, and influence.

Aspatia (*ăs-pā′shĭ-à*). The unfortunate heroine of Beaumont and Fletcher's play *The Maid's Tragedy*.

Astolat. The home of Elaine, "the lily maid of Astolat," in Tennyson's *Idylls of the King*.

Astolfo or **Astolpho.** A boastful and generous English knight in the tales of the adventures of Charlemagne and his Paladins. He was the possessor of a magic horn and book.

Astoria, Irving. A book of rambling sketches of Western trading and exploration, centering about the founding of Astoria, at the mouth of the Columbia, by John Jacob Astor in 1811. Still interesting and valuable.

As You Like It. A comedy by Shakespeare. A French duke, driven from his dukedom by his brother, sought a refuge in the forest of Arden with a few of his followers. Here they lived a free and easy life. Rosalind, the daughter of the banished duke, remained at court with her cousin Celia. At a wrestling match Rosalind fell in love with Orlando, who threw his antagonist, a giant and professional athlete. The usurping duke, Frederick, now banished her from the court, but her cousin Celia resolved to go to Arden with her; so Rosalind in boy's clothes, and Celia, as a rustic maiden, started to find the deposed duke. Orlando, being driven from home by his elder brother, also went to the forest of Arden, and was taken under the duke's protection. Here he met the ladies, and a double marriage was the result—Orlando married Rosalind, and his elder brother Oliver married Celia. The usurper retired to a religious house, and the deposed duke was restored to his dominions.

Athalie (*ăt′à-lē*). **Athalie** (Anglicized, **Athaliah**), **Racine.** Daughter of Ahab and Jezebel, and usurping queen in Jerusalem; in Racine's famous tragedy by this name.

Athos, Porthos, and Aramis. The inseparable comrades in Dumas' "The Three Musketeers" and in some of his other romances.

Attic Salt. The phrase is used to mean a certain wit or vigor of style in writing, in reference to the superior quality anciently attributed to Athenian works. The Roman style was heavier, less spirited.

Auburn. The name of a village immortalized by Oliver Goldsmith in his "Deserted Village." Some critics are disposed to connect it with Lissoy near Athlone in Ireland; but Goldsmith's "Auburn" is purely poetical.

Aucassin and Nicolette (*ō′kä′săN′*) (*nē′kô′lĕt′*). The delicate and vivid love story of Aucassin, son of the French count of Beaucaire, and Nicolette, a captive daughter of a king of Carthage. A product of the 12th century, it is the best of early French tales. Translated into English by Andrew Lang.

Audrey. A country wench, in Shakespeare's *As You Like It*.

Aulularia (*ô-lōō-lā′rĭ-à*). A comedy by Plautus, in which a miser, Euclion, is the central character. The name comes from *aulula*, meaning "a pot." This play has influenced several modern "miser" plays.

Autolycus. The craftiest of thieves. He stole the flocks of his neighbors and changed their marks. Sisyphus outwitted him by marking his sheep under their feet. Shakespeare introduces him in *The Winter's Tale* as a peddler, and says he was called the son of Mercury.

Plots, Characters, and Allusions 259

Avalon or **Avilion.** The earthly paradise of the Britons. In medieval romance the name of an ocean island and of a castle. It is represented as the abode of Arthur and Oberon and Morgan le Fay. It is most fully described in the old French romance of *Ogier le Danois.* It is the island kingdom to which King Arthur is finally borne by the mysterious barge in Tennyson's "Passing of Arthur." Some identify Avalon with the modern Glastonbury.

Avare, L' (*là'vàr'*). A comedy by Molière. The old miser, Harpagon, who has planned to marry a young girl, Marianne, finds his son, Cléante, a rival for her affection. Cléante obtains possession of Harpagon's gold and gives his father a choice of girl or gold. He chooses the gold.

Aymer (*ā'mēr*), **Prior.** A Benedictine monk, prior of Jorvaulx Abbey, in Sir Walter Scott's *Ivanhoe.*

Aymon (*ā'mŏn*). The family name of four brothers who lived in France in the 8th century. Their exploits are celebrated in many chivalric tales of the middle ages.

Azazel (*à-zā'zĕl*). **Paradise Lost, Milton.** Represented in this poem as Satan's standard bearer. According to the *Koran,* when God commanded the angels to worship Adam, Azazel replied, "Why should the son of fire fall down before a son of clay?" and God cast him out of heaven

Azo. The name given by Byron to the prince of Este, in his poem "Parisina."

Bab Ballads, The. A collection of light satiric and comic verses by W. S. Gilbert which appeared as occasional poems in "Fun" (1866–71), and were published in volumes as "The Bab Ballads" (1869) and "More Bab Ballads" (1873). They have been issued later in several editions. The "Yarn of the Nancy Bell" and "Bob Polter" are famous examples of these pieces.

Babbitt. The central character in Sinclair Lewis's novel of the same name. Babbitt is a type of the successful business man whose viewpoint and sympathies are determined solely by his business interests and personal pride and comfort. Lewis depicted this type so convincingly that the term Babbitt has passed into popular use to designate a person of this character.

Babes in the Wood. See *Children in the Wood.*

Baboon, Lewis. History of John Bull, Arbuthnot. A name given to Louis XIV of France. The name Philip Baboon was given in the same writing to Philip Bourbon, duke of Anjou.

Babu or **Baboo** (*bä'bōō*). A Hindu title equivalent to "Mr." Often used of a native official or clerk who writes English.

Backbite, Sir Benjamin. School for Scandal, Sheridan. A vacantly busy man who peddled scandal.

Bagstock, Joe. Dombey and Son, Dickens. The insistent and selfish "J. B.," "old J. B.," and "Joey B." of the story.

Baillie, Harry. Canterbury Tales, Chaucer. The jolly landlord at Tabard Inn, where the Canterbury Pilgrims gathered in making ready for their journey.

Balafré, Le (*lĕ bä'là'frā'*). **Quentin Durward, Scott.** Nickname given to an old archer belonging to the Scottish guards. The name means "the man with a scar."

Balderstone, Caleb. Bride of Lammermoor, Scott. The butler of the Ravenswoods, who tries to conceal the poverty of the family. A type of faithful servant. His pretentions have often been laughingly quoted.

Baldwin. Jerusalem Delivered, Tasso. The brother of Godfrey of Bouillon. In the tale of *Reynard the Fox* the name Baldwin is given to one of the beasts.

Balmawhapple (*bäl'mà-hwäp''l*). **Waverley, Scott.** An obstinate, stupid-faced, blundering Scotch laird.

Balthazar (*bäl-thā'zàr*). (1) In Shakespeare's *Comedy of Errors,* a merchant, ordered to furnish impossible merchandise. (2) In *Much Ado about Nothing,* Balthazar appears as servant to Don Pedro. (3) Portia takes the name in the *Merchant of Venice.* (4) Chaucer, in "The Monk's Tale," gives this name to Belshazzar. (5) Balthazar is also the traditional name of one of the wise men who followed the star to Bethlehem.

Balwhidder (*bäl'hwĭTH-ēr*). **Annals of the Parish, Galt.** A sincere, kind, talkative Scotch Presbyterian clergyman. With natural prejudices and old-fashioned ways he is too "easy" to carry on his parish work with zeal. His friends enjoy Balwhidder's jokes.

Banquo. Macbeth, Shakespeare. A thane of Scotland, said to belong to the 11th century and to be ancestor of the Stuarts. In fiction, made immortal as the innocent laird murdered by Macbeth. Banquo's ghost is more famous than Banquo himself.

Barabas (*băr'à-bàs*). **The Jew of Malta, Marlowe.** A monster, the hero of the tragedy, who wears a big nose and invents infernal machines.

Barbara Frietchie, Whittier. A poem based on an alleged incident at Frederick, Md., in the Civil War. It exhibits the patriotism of the aged Barbara Frietchie, who dared to fly the Union flag in the presence of Confederate troops, and the chivalry of Stonewall Jackson, who forbade punitive measures against her.

Barber of Seville, Beaumarchais. A witty comedy. The plot, in which Bartolo, who wants to marry his ward Rosina, is duped and outwitted by her lover, Almaviva, and the ex-valet and barber, Figaro, serves to carry brilliant dialogue and satire. First presented in 1775.

Bardell, Mrs. Pickwick Papers, Dickens. The landlady, a widow, who sues Mr. Pickwick for breach of promise to marry her.

Bard of Avon. Name given to Shakespeare, who was born and buried in Stratford-on-Avon.

Bard of Ayrshire. A name often given to Robert Burns, the great poet of Scotland, who was a native of the county of Ayr.

Bard of Rydal Mount. An epithet sometimes applied to the poet Wordsworth, who resided at Rydal Grasmere, in the county of Westmoreland from 1813 to 1850. His dwelling overlooked a beautiful view of the lake.

Bardolph, Merry Wives of Windsor, Shakespeare. A follower of Falstaff, known as the "knight of the burning lamp," from his red nose.

Barkis. David Copperfield, Dickens. Remembered by the much-quoted "Barkis is willing," his form of proposing marriage to his beloved Clara Peggotty.

Barleycorn, Sir John. Tam O'Shanter, Burns. Name given to the personification of a malt liquor made from barley. Sir Barleycorn has also been noticed by Scott and Hawthorne. The name comes down to us from an old English pamphlet in which Sir John Barleycorn is arraigned in court, tried by jury, and acquitted.

Barmecide (*bär'mê-sĭd*) **Feast.** The phrase, which means a feast with little or nothing to eat, refers to a Persian story. One of the Barmecide family invited a poor man to dine, but, while the host called for the most delicious dishes and urged his guest to eat, there was nothing to eat. The poor man played the game, even feigning to get drunk on the make-believe wine and knocking his host down. This so pleased the Barmecide that he provided a real banquet and took the poor man into his household.

Barnaby Rudge. Barnaby Rudge, Dickens. A half-witted lad who wanders about with a pet raven. They experience together many adventures, including a no-popery riot.

Barry Lyndon, The Memoirs of, W. M. Thackeray. A famous story of the picaresque, or roguery, type. The hero, Barry Lyndon, is represented as telling his own story of scoundrelly adventure. Throughout his revelations of rascality and villainy in gaming and in illtreatment of his wife, he maintains a confident air of gentility. His life ends in imprisonment and a sordid death. Thackeray wrote the story in a vein of sustained irony.

Basilisco (*bàs'ĭ-lĭs'kō*). **Soliman and Persida, Old Play.** A boasting knight who became so popular with his foolish bragging that his name grew into a proverb.

Bassanio (*bà-sä'nĭ-ō*). **Merchant of Venice, Shakespeare.** The lover of Portia, who won her when he chose a leaden casket in which her portrait was hidden.

Bath, Major. Amelia, Henry Fielding. A noble-minded gentleman, pompous in spite of poverty, and striving to live according to the "dignity and honor of man." He tries to hide his poverty under bold speech even when found doing menial service.

Battle, Sarah. Essays of Elia, Lamb. Sarah considered whist the business of life, and literature one of the relaxations. When a young gentleman, of a literary turn, told her he had no objection to unbending his mind for a little time by taking a hand with her, Sarah declared "Whist was her life business, her duty, the thing she came into the world to do. She unbent her mind afterwards over a book."

Battle of the Books, The, Jonathan Swift. A famous satire, in which Swift discusses the endless controversy over the comparative merits of ancient and modern writers.

Battle of the Kegs, Francis Hopkinson. A humorous poem. It ridiculed the British, who are represented as firing at all the kegs floating in the river at Philadelphia, because some explosive machines had been sent among their ships. The ballad was one of the greatest sources of inspiration to the colonists in the trying revolutionary crises.

Bayard (bā'ärd). **Old Poems and Romances.** Bayard was a famous horse belonging to the four sons of Amyon, a semimythical character. He seemed but an ordinary horse when one person rode, but, if the four mounted, the horse accommodatingly grew in length. Among wonderful things related of him is that his hoofprints have been found on rocks and in deep forests. Bayard is also known as the property of Amadis of Gaul in an old Portuguese romance. He was found under the watch of a dragon whom a wizard knight charmed in order to rescue the horse. In French tales Bayard is represented to be yet living in some of the forests of France but disappearing when disturbed. Bayard is also the name of the horse belonging to Fitz-James in Scott's poem "Lady of the Lake." He appears as Bayardo in *Orlando Furioso* and other poems. It is said that Rinaldo was riding on his favorite steed, when a demon sprang behind him, but the animal in terror took three tremendous leaps and unhorsed the fiend.

Bayes. The Rehearsal, George Villiers, second duke of Buckingham. This farce, or satire, was brought out in 1671, and its wit has been much quoted. In its present form the hero, Bayes, is intended to represent Dryden as at the head of heroic rimes. He is shown as greedy for applause, impatient of censure or criticism, inordinately vain, yet obsequious to those who, he hopes, will gratify him by returning his flattery, and, finally, as anxiously mindful of the minute parts of what, even as a whole, is scarce worthy of attention.

Bay Psalm Book, The. The first book printed in the British American colonies (1640). A metrical version of the psalms, prepared by Richard Mather, Thomas Wilde, and John Eliot.

Beatrice. (1) Daughter of an illustrious family of Florence, for whom Dante had a great love. In the *Divine Comedy* she is represented as being his guide through paradise. (2) Beatrice is also the name of the heroine of Shakespeare's *Much Ado about Nothing.* Of her Mrs. Jameson says: "The extraordinary success of this play in Shakespeare's own day, and ever since, in England, is to be ascribed more particularly to the parts of Benedick and Beatrice, two humorsome beings, who incessantly attack each other with all the resources of raillery. In Beatrice, high intellect and high animal spirits meet, and excite each other like fire and air. But Beatrice, though willful, is not wayward; she is volatile, not unfeeling."

Beau Brummell. This was the nickname of George Bryan Brummell, a dandy and "glass of fashion" of the time of George IV. He finally fell from royal favor and lived in exile in Calais. His life was made the subject of a play by William Blanchard Jerrold (1859) and the subject of another by Clyde Fitch (1891).

Beauty and the Beast. Fairy Tale, Mme. Villeneuve. Often repeated in stories for children. "Beauty and the Beast" is known in many forms and in many languages. In the tale referred to, young and lovely Beauty saved the life of her father by putting herself in the power of a frightful, but kind-hearted, monster, whose respectful affection and deep melancholy finally overcame her aversion to his hideousness, and induced her to consent to marry him. By her love, Beast was set free from enchantment and allowed to assume his own form, that of a handsome and graceful young prince.

Bede, Adam. Adam Bede, George Eliot. An ideal workman, hero of the novel.

Bedivere (bĕd'ĭ-vēr). **Tales of the Round Table.** Bedivere was the last knight of King Arthur's Round Table. He had served as a butler, was of much importance, and was sent by the dying king to throw his sword, Excalibur, into the lake. A hand and an arm rose from the lake, caught the sword, flourished it three times, and sank. Bedivere watched King Arthur's departure for Avalon, the "Isle of the Blest." This knight is noticed, under the name Bedver, in Geoffrey's British History.

Beggar's Daughter. Reliques, Percy. First known as the Beggar's Daughter of Bethnal Green, a beautiful girl named Bessie, who is wooed by a knight, and whose father turns out to be a son of Simon de Montfort, living in disguise as a blind beggar. The story was dramatized by James Sheridan Knowles.

Beggar's Opera, The. This work, by John Gay, with music by Dr. Pepusch, was given in London in 1728. It satirized the polite society and the opera of the day. The characters are mostly thieves and highwaymen, among them Captain Macheath and his wife, Polly Peachum. It is said that three actresses who played the part of Polly won marriages into the English nobility. The play with the original music was reproduced in England and in the United States and Canada with the greatest success in 1919-20.

Bel and the Dragon. (1) Two stories, apocryphal additions to the book of Daniel, telling how Daniel convinced Cyrus of the fraud imposed upon him and his people in the worship of the god, Bel, and the Dragon. (2) A story found in the Babylonian cuneiform tablets, which is thought to resemble closely the account of the struggle of Michael and the Dragon in the Book of Revelation.

Belch, Sir Toby. Twelfth Night, Shakespeare. Uncle to Olivia, a jolly care-free fellow, type of the roisterers of Queen Elizabeth's days.

Belinda. Rape of the Lock, Pope. Poetical name of the heroine whose real name was said to be Arabella Fermor. In a frolic Lord Petre cut a lock from the lady's hair. This was so much resented that it broke the great friendship between the two families. The poem, "Rape of the Lock," was written to bring them into a better temper and lead to reconciliation. Belinda is also the name of the heroine in a novel written by Maria Edgeworth.

Bell, Adam. Old Ballad. A famous wild outlaw belonging to the north country and celebrated for his skill as an archer.

Bell, Laura. Pendennis, Thackeray. One of the sweetest heroines in English literature.

Bell, Peter. Peter Bell, a Tale in Verse, Wordsworth. A wandering tinker, subject of Wordsworth's poem, whose hard heart was touched by the fidelity of an ass to its dead master. Shelley wrote a burlesque of this poem, entitled "Peter Bell the Third," intended to ridicule the ludicrous puerility of language and sentiment which Wordsworth often affected. This burlesque was given the name of the Third because it followed a parody, already published as "Peter the Second."

Bellman. L'Allegro, Milton. The watchman who patrolled the streets and called out the hour of night. Sometimes he repeated scraps of pious poetry in order to charm away danger.

Bell-the-Cat. Name given to a nobleman at Lauder, Scotland, early in the 16th century. King James II called an assembly of Scottish barons to resist a threatened invasion of his realm by Edward IV of England. After long discussion one of the barons related the nursery tale of a convention of mice in which it was proposed to hang a bell on the cat's neck, to give warning of her presence. No one would serve on the mouse committee. To the story Archibald Douglas responded by saying, "I will bell the cat" and was afterwards known by the name, Bell-the-cat.

Beloved Physician. Bible. Name given to St. Luke and first used in the Apostle Paul's epistle to the Colossians.

Belphœbe (bĕl-fē'bē). **Faery Queen, Spenser.** A delicate and graceful flattery offered to Queen Elizabeth through the huntress, Belphœbe, intended to represent the queen. The name is taken from *belle,* meaning beautiful, and *Phœbe,* a name sometimes bestowed on Diana.

Belvawney, Miss. Nicholas Nickleby, Dickens. She belonged to the wonderful Portsmouth theater, always took the part of a page, and gloried in silk stockings.

Belvidera (bĕl'vĭ-dē'rà). **Venice Preserved, Otway.** The beautiful heroine of this almost forgotten tragedy. Sir Walter Scott said, "More tears have been shed, probably, for the sorrows of Belvidera and Monimia than for those of Juliet and Desdemona."

Benedick. Much Ado about Nothing, Shakespeare. A young lord of Padua who is gentleman, wit, and soldier. He was a pronounced bachelor, but after a courtship full of witty sayings and coquetry he marries the lovely Beatrice. From this gentleman comes the name Benedick or Benedict, applied to married men who had thought they never were going to marry. See *Beatrice.*

Benengeli, Cid Hamet (sĭd hăm'ĕt bĕn'ĕn-gē'lĭ). **Don Quixote, Cervantes.** Supposed to be a writer of chronicles among the Moors and claimed as authority for the tales of adventure recorded by Cervantes. The name, Cid Hamet, has been often quoted by writers.

Ben Hur, General Lew Wallace. Messala, the Roman playmate and young friend of Ben Hur, afterward became his remorseless enemy. Ambitious, hard, and cruel, when he came into power he made Ben Hur a galley slave, confiscated his property, and imprisoned his mother and sister. Ben Hur escaped, returned later as a wealthy Roman, and entered in the famous chariot race against Messala who had put up enormous sums in wagers. Messala recognized Ben Hur and hoped to win the race and bring him to final ruin; but Messala himself was thrown and seriously injured. His cruelties were made known, and he was at last slain by his wife, Isas, the daughter of Balthasar.

Benvolio (bĕn-vō'lĭ-ō). **Romeo and Juliet, Shakespeare.** One of Romeo's friends who would "quarrel with a man that had a hair more or a hair less in his beard than he had." Mercutio says to him, "Thou hast quarreled with a man for coughing in the street."

Beowulf (*bā'ô-wōōlf*). **Anglo-Saxon Poem.** He was a Gothic warrior who slew the monster Grendel, which infested the great hall of Hrothgar, king of the West Danes. This great poem of over 6000 lines is divided into two parts. The first part describes the beautiful palace of King Hrothgar, the ravages wrought by the fiend Grendel and his mother, and the deliverance wrought by the hero Beowulf. The second part describes the combat between the aged king Beowulf and the dragon which was wasting the land of the Goths. The Beowulf who took part in Hygelac's historical expedition against the Hetware is probably historical, but the Beowulf of the four great exploits of the poem, the swimming match with Breca, and the contests with Grendel, with his dam, and with the dragon, is more probably a character allied to the Norse divinities.

Bergerac, Cyrano de (*sē'rä'nô' dě běr'zhě-räk'*). In history, he was a French poet, a contemporary of Molière. Edmond Rostand makes him the exaggerated hero of the play named for him. The hero is violently in love with Roxane, but aids Christian de Neuvillette to win her, writing letters for the rather dull gallant. After the death of Christian, Cyrano plays the part of platonic friend to the widow, revealing the truth of his feelings only in the immediate prospect of death.

Bertram. Guy Mannering, Scott. The character was suggested by James Annesley, rightful heir of the earldom of Anglesey, of which he was dispossessed by his uncle Richard. He died in 1743. Bertram was also the name of a haughty and dissolute count, the husband of Helena in Shakespeare's comedy *All's Well that Ends Well*.

Bianca (*bĭ-äng'kà*). **Othello, Shakespeare.** Cassio's sweetheart.

Bibliomania. A passion for rare and curious books The word means book madness, and is usually applied by people unsympathetic toward those who collect books for their rarity rather than for their value in use. The term bibliophile, "lover of books," is the more complimentary word for amateur or professional book collectors.

Big-endians (*bĭg'ěn'dĭ-ănz*). **Gulliver's Travels, Swift.** The name of a religious party in the imaginary empire of Lilliput who made it a matter of duty and conscience to break their eggs at the large end. They were regarded as heretics by the law, which required all persons to break the smaller end of their eggs, under pain of heavy penalties in case of disobedience.

Birch, Harvey. The Spy, Cooper. The chief character of the novel.

Black Beauty, Anna Sewell. Full title, "Black Beauty, His Grooms and Companions." The story of a horse. Written in the form of a horse's autobiography, it is a strong plea for kind treatment of animals.

Black-eyed Susan. Ballad, John Gay. The heroine of the popular sea song.

Blatant Beast. Faery Queen, Spenser. A bellowing monster typical of slander; or, an impersonation of what we now call *vox populi*, or the "voice of the people."

Blifil (*blī'fĭl*). **Tom Jones, Fielding.** Allworthy's nephew, a talebearer and consummate hypocrite.

Blimber, Miss Cornelia. Dombey and Son, Dickens. The daughter of Dr. Blimber, the head of a first-class educational establishment conducted on the forcing or cramming principle. She is a very learned, grave, and precise young lady, "no light nonsense about her," who has become "dry and sandy with working in the graves of deceased languages."

Bluebeard. A fairy tale by Perrault (1697). The ugly, blue-bearded rich man has for his seventh wife Fatima. One day, when he is away, she finds in a closet the bodies of the former wives. Bluebeard discovers her disobedience of his command, and is about to kill her, when her brothers rescue her. Earlier Italian and Arabian stories resemble this tale.

Bluebird, The. (1) A fairy tale by Countess d'Aulnoy. A prince, refusing to marry the ugly one of two sisters, is changed into a bluebird. Finally, a friendly fairy restores him to his former shape and to his sweetheart. (2) A fairy play by Maurice Maeterlinck, in which two children, Mityl and Tyltyl, set out to seek for happiness, the bluebird. They wander in a dream through the lands of Memory, Night, and the Future. At last, when Tyltyl gives up his dove to a neighbor's sick child, they find happiness for a moment. The bird turns blue and then flies away.

Bob, Son of Battle, Alfred Ollivant. The hero and title of a popular dog story. Bob is the last of a famous breed of shepherd dog; his adventures are most realistic.

Bobadil (*bŏb'à-dĭl*), **Captain. Every Man in His Humor, Jonson.** A boasting coward, who passes himself off with young and simple people for a Hector.

Bois Guilbert, Brian de (*brê-äN' dě bwä gēl'běr'*). **Ivanhoe, Scott.** A brave but cruel, crafty, and dissolute commander of the Knights Templars.

Boniface (*bŏn'ĭ-fās*). **The Beaux' Stratagem, Farquhar.** A fine representation of an English landlord. Hence, the name is applied to landlords generally.

Bontemps, Roger (*rô'zhä' bôN'täN'*). **Song, Béranger.** Known in France as the personification of care-free leisure. The equivalent, among the French peasantry, for the English proverb, "There's a good time coming," is "Roger Bontemps," one of Beranger's most celebrated songs (1814).

Bottom, Nick. A Midsummer Night's Dream, Shakespeare. A man who fancies he can do everything, and do it better than anyone else. Shakespeare has drawn him as profoundly ignorant, and with an overflow of self-conceit. Oberon, the fairy king, desiring to punish Titania, his queen, commissioned Puck to watch her till she fell asleep, and then to anoint her eyelids with the juice of a plant called "love-in-idleness," the effect of which, when she awoke, was to make her dote upon Bottom, upon whom Puck had fixed an ass's head.

Bowdlerize. In 1818 Thomas Bowdler published an expurgated edition of Shakespeare; whence the term to bowdlerize, meaning to expurgate, especially a book.

Bowling, Tom. Roderick Random, Smollett. A name made almost famous as hero of the novel. Critics have said, "The character of Tom Bowling, in *Roderick Random*, will be regarded in all ages as a happy exhibition of those naval heroes to whom Britain is indebted for so much of her happiness and glory." The Tom Bowling referred to in Charles Dibdin's famous sea song was his brother, Captain Thomas Dibdin.

Box and Cox. Farce, Morton. Principal characters in the farce known as a "dramatic romance of real life." The two men, Box and Cox, rent the same room from a Mrs. Bouncer. One works in the daytime, the other at night, so they do not meet until a holiday reveals the situation. The conflict, however, is adjusted amicably.

Bramble, Matthew. Humphrey Clinker, Smollett. Noted character in the novel, described as "an odd kind of humorist," afflicted with the gout, and "always on the fret," but full of generosity and benevolence.

Brass, Sally and Sampson. Old Curiosity Shop, Dickens. Brother and sister, well mated, he a "shystering" lawyer and she outreaching him in villainy. Sampson was dishonest, sentimental, and affected in manner.

Brave New World. This phrase, the title of a prophetic book by Aldous Huxley, comes from Shakespeare's "The Tempest." When Miranda, who has lived in seclusion on an island, discovers that other human beings exist, she exclaims, "Oh brave new world that has such people in it!"

Brentford, The Two Kings of. The Rehearsal, Villiers. Much question has been raised as to who was to be ridiculed under these characters. The royal brothers, Charles II and James II, have been suggested; others say the fighting kings of Granada. In the farce the two kings are represented as walking hand in hand, as dancing together, as singing in concert, and, generally, as living on terms of the greatest intimacy and affection.

Br'er Rabbit. In the plantation stories of Uncle Remus, he is the personification of mental agility and craft, by which he vanquishes Br'er Fox.

Bretêche, La Grande. One of Balzac's most famous short stories, in which the lover of a faithless wife is walled up in a closet by her husband after the wife has sworn that there was no one there.

Brick, Mr. Jefferson. Martin Chuzzlewit, Dickens. A ranting American politician who makes a ridiculous figure as editor.

Britomart. Faery Queen, Spenser. The embodiment of chastity. Having seen in a magic mirror the face of Sir Artegal, who embodies justice, she falls in love with him. After a long search and many adventures, she at last finds him and they are united.

Brook Farm. The full name was "Brook Farm Institute of Agriculture and Education," a stock company of nearly 70 members, located on a farm of 200 acres at West Roxbury, Mass. Among the members were George Ripley, Charles A. Dana, George William Curtis, Margaret Fuller, and Nathaniel Hawthorne. Among their frequent visitors were Ralph Waldo Emerson, Theodore Parker, Bronson Alcott. This idyllic life lasted about five years, from 1841 to 1846. Brook Farm was a financial failure, but it was important in intellectual results. Hawthorne took from it some suggestions for his *Blithedale Romance*.

Brown, Tom. Tom Brown's School Days and **Tom Brown at Oxford, Thomas Hughes.** The hero of these stories of school days, a typical English schoolboy and undergraduate.

Brunhild (*brŏŏn'hĭlt*). **Nibelungenlied.** The story of Brunhild figures largely in ancient German romance. She was, herself, a warrior, proud and skillful, and she promised to be the bride of the man who could conquer her in three trials: in hurling the lance, in throwing the stone, and in leaping after the stone when thrown. By the arts and bravery of Siegfried, she was deluded into marrying Gunther, king of Burgundy; but, discovering the trick, she planned and accomplished the destruction of Siegfried and the humiliation of Kriemhild, his wife.

Bumble, Mr. Oliver Twist, Dickens. A pompous, disagreeable beadle who figures largely in the beginning of the story. The name Bumble has since attached itself to the office.

Bunsby, Jack. Dombey and Son, Dickens. A commander of a ship, looked up to as an oracle by his friend, Captain Cuttle. He is described as wearing a "rapt and imperturbable manner" and seeming to be "always on the lookout for something in the extremest distance."

Bunthorne. Patience, Sullivan. A gloomy poet shown most distinctly in his gloom when surrounded by the characters of a comic opera. He was inserted as a satire on the æsthetic cult affected at the time by Oscar Wilde and his imitators.

Bunyan, Paul. A legendary figure of American folklore, the hero of many tall tales told in the lumber camps of the Northwest. Among the remarkable feats invented and ascribed to Paul Bunyan by the lumberjacks, was his creation of the Grand Canyon of the Colorado river by dragging his pick behind him.

Burchell, Mr. Vicar of Wakefield, Goldsmith. A prominent character who passes himself off as a poor man, but is really a baronet in disguise. He is noted for his habit of crying out "Fudge!" by way of expressing his strong contempt for the opinions of others.

Burd, Helen. Scotch Ballad. A traditional name standing for constancy. She was carried to England by fairies and imprisoned in a castle. The youngest brother of the fair Helen was guided by the enchanter Merlin and accomplished the perilous task of rescuing his sister. This is recited in the line "Childe Roland to the dark tower came," quoted by Shakespeare. Only a fragment of the old ballad has been preserved.

Buskin. A name used to mean "tragedy." Known in English since the 16th century. The word means "boot." It early took on the sense given here. The Greek tragic actors used to wear a sandal some two or three inches thick, to elevate their stature. To this sole was attached a very elegant boot top. The whole boot was called *cothurnus*. Milton uses the phrase "buskined stage" in *Il Penseroso*

Buzfuz, Serjeant. Pickwick Papers, Dickens. A pompous, chaffing lawyer, who bullies Mr. Pickwick and the witnesses in the famous breach of promise suit, Bardell *v.* Pickwick.

Byfield. A New England parish, the scene of a historical novel by John Lewis Ewell. Here lived the ancestor of Longfellow, to whom the poet dedicated "The Village Blacksmith," himself a blacksmith, keeping his accounts in peculiar orthography.

Cabala (*kăb'ȧ-lȧ*). The oral law of the Jews handed down from father to son by word of mouth. It is the usual belief that God instructed Moses, and Moses his brother Aaron, and so on from age to age. The cabalists developed an elaborate system of mystic symbolism, in which combinations of letters and numbers are important.

Cadmean (*kăd-mē'ăn*) **Victory.** A victory purchased at great expense of life. The allusion is to the armed men who sprang out of the ground from the teeth of the dragon sown by Cadmus. These men fell foul of each other, and only five of them escaped death.

Caius (*kā'yŭs*), **Doctor. Merry Wives of Windsor, Shakespeare.** A physician in the comedy, who adds a touch of humor. He is conspicuous as the lover of Anne Page.

Calandrino (*kä-län-drē'nō*). A simpleton frequently introduced in Boccaccio's *Decameron*; expressly made to be befooled and played upon.

Caleb. (1) The enchantress who carried off St. George in infancy. (2) A character in Dryden's satire of "Absalom and Achitophel," meant for Lord Grey, one of the adherents of the duke of Monmouth

Caleb Quotem. A parish clerk or jack-of-all-trades, in Colman's play *The Review*, or *Wags of Windsor.* Col-

man borrowed the character from *Throw Physic to the Dogs*, an old farce.

Caliban. (1) A savage and deformed slave of Prospero in Shakespeare's *Tempest*. He is represented as being the "freckled whelp" of Sycorax, a foul hag, who was banished from Argier, or Algiers, to the desert island afterward inhabited by Prospero. From his rude, uncouth language we get the phrase "Caliban style," "Caliban speech," meaning the coarsest possible use of words. (2) A character in Browning's *Caliban on Setebos*.

Calidore. A knight in Spenser's *Faery Queen*, typical of courtesy, and said to be intended for a portrait of Sir Philip Sidney.

Calipolis. Battle of Alcazar, George Peele. A character in the *Battle of Alcazar*, used by Sir Walter Scott and others as a synonym for ladylove, sweetheart, charmer. Sir Walter always spells the word Callipolis.

Calydon. A forest celebrated in the romances relating to King Arthur and Merlin. Also an ancient city of Ætolia, in Greece, celebrated in the stories of the Calydonian Hunt.

Camacho (*kä-mä'chō*). **Don Quixote, Cervantes.** A character in an episode in *Don Quixote*, who gets cheated out of his bride after having made great preparations for their wedding.

Camaralzaman (*kăm'ȧ-răl'zȧ-măn*), **Prince. Arabian Nights.** One of the stories of the *Arabian Nights* and the name of a prince who fell in love with Badoura, princess of China, the moment he saw her.

Cambalo or **Cambel. Faery Queen, Spenser.** A brother of Canace. He challenged every suitor to his sister's hand, and overthrew all except Triamond, who married the lady.

Cambalu (*kăm'bȧ-lōō*). In the *Voyages* of Marco Polo, the chief city of the province of Cathay.

Cambuscan (*kăm-bŭs'kăn*). A Tatar king identical with Jenghis Khan. The king of the Far East sent Cambuscan a "steed of brass, which, between sunrise and sunset, would carry its rider to any spot on the earth." All that was required was to whisper the name of the place in the horse's ear, mount upon his back, and turn a pin set in his ear. When the rider had arrived at his destination, he had to turn another pin and the horse instantly descended, and, with another screw of the pin, vanished till it was again required. This story was begun by Chaucer in the *Squire's Tale* but was never finished. Milton refers to Chaucer as the poet who "left half told" this story (*Il Penseroso*).

Camelot. A parish in Somersetshire, England, now called Queen's Camel, where King Arthur is said to have held his court. In this place there are still to be seen vast intrenchments of an ancient town or station—called by the inhabitants "King Arthur's Palace." Several other localities dispute the tradition, notably Winchester.

Camille (*kȧ-mēl'*). English adaptation of *La Dame aux Camélias*, a play by Dumas the younger. Also known in America as *The Lady of the Camellias*. The story is that of Marguerite Gautier, a courtesan, whose genuine love for Armand Duval prompts her to live only for him. But his father persuades Marguerite that such a union would wreck Armand's career. Therefore she deliberately estranges him, and really sacrifices her life for him. The meaning of her acts Armand learns too late.

Canace (*kăn'ȧ-sē*). **Faery Queen, Spenser.** A paragon among women, the daughter of King Cambuscan, to whom the king of the East sent as a present a mirror and a ring. The mirror would tell the lady if any man on whom she set her heart would prove true or false, and the ring, which was to be worn on her thumb, would enable her to understand the language of birds and to converse with them. Canace was courted by a crowd of suitors, but her brother announced that anyone who aspired to her hand must encounter him in single combat and overthrow him. She ultimately married Triamond, son of the fairy Agape.

Candide (*kăɴ'dēd'*). The hero of Voltaire's work of the same name. All sorts of misfortunes are heaped upon him, and he bears them all with philosophical indifference.

Candour, Mrs. A most energetic slanderer in Sheridan's *School for Scandal*.

Canidia. A sorceress, alluded to by Horace, who could bring the moon from heaven.

Canterbury Tales, Chaucer. The Prologue to the "tales" introduces the reader to "full nine and twenty" pilgrims, each of whom, on the way to and from Canterbury, is to tell two stories, the one telling the best tale to be treated to a dinner on their return to the Tabard Inn in Southwark, whence they start. Only 24 of the 58 tales called for in the scheme have come down to us. These are:

"The Knight's Tale," "The Miller's Tale," "The Reeve's Tale," "The Cook's Tale," "The Man of Law's Tale," "The Wife of Bath's Tale," "The Friar's Tale," "The Summoner's Tale," "The Clerk's Tale," "The Merchant's Tale," "The Squire's Tale," "The Franklin's Tale," "The Doctor's Tale," "The Pardoner's Tale," "The Shipman's Tale," "The Prioress's Tale," "Chaucer's Tale of Sir Thopas," "Chaucer's Tale of Melibœus," "The Monk's Tale," "The Nun's Priest's Tale," "The Second Nun's Tale," "The Canon's Yeoman's Tale," "The Manciple's Tale," "The Parson's Tale." The plan of the work affords artistic scope for introducing a company of pilgrims on their way to the shrine of Thomas Becket. It represents all classes of society and presents a series of tales of great interest set in the midst of beautiful descriptions of nature. Perhaps the most interesting tales by which to gain introduction to Chaucer are: "The Clerk's Tale" (Griseldis); "The Knight's Tale" (Palamon and Arcite); "The Man of Law's Tale" (Constance); "The Prioress's Tale" (Hugh of Lincoln); "The Nun's Priest's Tale" (Chanticleer and Pertelote).

Caora. Description of Guiana, Raleigh. A river, on the banks of which are a people whose heads grow beneath their shoulders. Their eyes are in their shoulders, and their mouths in the middle of their breasts. The original picture is found in Hakluyt's *Voyages* 1598.

Cape Cod Folks. The group of characters drawn from Cape Cod life in the stories of Joseph C. Lincoln.

Captains Courageous, Kipling. One of the best stories for boys. The young son of a wealthy American family is lost overboard from an Atlantic liner. He is picked up by a fishing boat off Newfoundland. The captain sets him to work. He learns much of fishing and fishermen. When the boat returns to Gloucester, his parents come, and the family are reunited.

Capulet (kăp'ū-lĕt). The head of a noble Veronese house in Shakespeare's tragedy *Romeo and Juliet*—hostile to the house of Montague. He is at times self-willed and tyrannical, but a jovial and testy old man.

Capulet, Lady. The proud and stately wife of Capulet and mother of Juliet.

Carabas, Marquis of. (1) The master of the cat in the nursery tale of *Puss in Boots*. (2) In a lyric by Béranger, Carabas is an emigré who comes back after the battle of Waterloo to reclaim his property. (3) In Disraeli's *Vivian Gray*, a servile and pompous character, the Marquess of Carabas.

Carker. A scoundrel clerk in Dickens's *Dombey and Son*

Carpetbaggers. Name applied to Northerners who, after the enfranchisement of the negroes, went into the South for the purpose of representing the negroes in state and national offices. Since most of these men held no property in the South, their possessions were all supposed to be in their "carpetbags" or grips. Hence the name. *A Fool's Errand* by A. W. Tourgee is a story of the period.

Carrasco, Sanson (sän-sŏn' kär-räs'kō). A waggish bachelor of Salamanca, in Cervantes' *Don Quixote*.

Carton, Sidney. A hero transformed by unselfish love in Dickens's *Tale of Two Cities*. He voluntarily goes to the guillotine to save his successful rival in love.

Casca. Julius Cæsar, Shakespeare. A blunt-witted Roman, one of the conspirators against Julius Cæsar.

Casella. The name of a musician and old friend of Dante, immortalized by him in his *Divine Comedy*.

Cassandra. A daughter of Priam, king of Troy, gifted with the power of prophecy; but Apollo, whom she had offended, brought it to pass that no one believed her predictions, consequently now a name applied to one who makes gloomy forecasts. Shakespeare makes use of this character in *Troilus and Cressida*.

Cassibelan. Great-uncle to Cymbeline, in Shakespeare's play by that name.

Cassio (kăsh'ĭ-ō). A Florentine lieutenant of Othello and a tool of Iago, in Shakespeare's tragedy *Othello*. Iago made Cassio drunk, and then urged on Roderigo to quarrel with him. Cassio wounded Roderigo. Othello suspended Cassio, but Iago induced Desdemona to plead for his restoration. This interest in Cassio aroused the jealous rage of Othello and moved him to murder Desdemona and to kill himself. After the death of Othello, Cassio was appointed governor of Cyprus.

Castle Dangerous. A keep belonging to the Douglas family, which gives its name to one of Sir Walter Scott's *Tales of My Landlord*. It was so called by the English because it was always retaken from them by the Douglas.

Castle of Indolence. The title of a poem by Thomson, and the name of a castle described in it as situated in a pleasing land of drowsiness, where every sense was steeped in the most luxurious and enervating delights.

Castlewood, Beatrix. The heroine of Thackeray's novel *Henry Esmond*, a picture of splendid, lustrous, physical beauty.

Cathay. A mysterious country of eastern Asia reportedly visited by Marco Polo. As a poetic allusion it is best known in Tennyson's line, "Better fifty years of Europe than a cycle of Cathay."

Cattle Raid of Cooley. An early Irish story. Queen Maeve of Connaught, to make her herd equal to that of her husband Ailill, asked Daré Mac Fiachne, of Ulster, for the loan of his wonderful "Brown Bull of Cooley." He at first granted the request, but later, in anger, refused. Upon this, the queen invaded Ulster, to take the bull by force. It happened that a disease unfitted the Ulstermen for battle during the winter. A youth of 17, Cuchulain, exempt from the disease, faced the foe alone. Agreement was made that each day a Connaught warrior should fight with him, and that when he had killed this opponent Queen Maeve's forces should halt and camp for the night. Day after day Cuchulain was victorious, until, when the queen impatiently broke her agreement, the Ulstermen were able to do battle. They drove the invaders out, but not until Queen Maeve had captured and carried off the "Brown Bull."

Caudle, Mrs. Margaret. The feigned author of a series of curtain lectures delivered to her husband, Job Caudle, who was a patient sufferer under this form of persistent nagging by his wife. The real author of these humorous lectures was Douglas Jerrold.

Cauline, Sir. The hero of an ancient English ballad preserved in Percy's *Reliques*.

Cave of Mammon. The abode of the god of riches, described in the second book of Spenser's *Faery Queen*.

Caxton, Pisistratus (pĭ-sĭs'trā-tŭs). The hero of Bulwer-Lytton's novel *The Caxtons*, and of its sequel *My Novel*.

Cecilia (sê-sĭl'ĭ-à), **St.** A patron saint of the blind, also patroness of musicians, and "inventor of the organ." According to tradition, an angel fell in love with her for her musical skill, and used nightly to visit her. A crown of martyrdom was bestowed upon both her and her husband. Dryden and Pope have written odes in her honor, and both speak of her charming an angel by her musical powers.

Cedric (sĕd'rĭk). A Saxon thane in Scott's *Ivanhoe*. Father of Ivanhoe and uncle of Rowena.

Celia. (1) In Spenser's *Faery Queen*, the mother of Faith, Hope, and Charity. She was herself known as Heavenliness and lived in the hospice Holiness. (2) Celia, cousin to Rosalind, in Shakespeare's comedy *As You Like It*. Celia is a common poetical name for a lady or a ladylove.

Cephalus (sĕf'à-lŭs) **and Procris** (prŏk'rĭs). Cephalus was the husband of Procris, who, out of jealousy, deserted him. Cephalus went in search of her, and rested awhile under a tree. Procris discovered him, and crept through some bushes to ascertain if a rival was with him. Cephalus heard the noise and, thinking it to be made by some wild beast, hurled his javelin into the bushes and slew Procris. When the unhappy man discovered what he had done, he slew himself in anguish of spirit with the same javelin. This story is alluded to in "Pyramus and Thisbe," in Shakespeare's *Midsummer Night's Dream*, where they are humorously miscalled "Shafalus and Procus"

Chadband, The Rev. A clerical character in Dickens's *Bleak House*. He will always stand as a type of hypocritical piety.

Chanticleer. The cock, in the tale of "Reynard the Fox" and in Chaucer's "Nun's Priest's Tale."

Characters, "Caractères." A work by Jean de la Bruyère, in which he sketches with great skill the men and women and manners of the 17th century in France. The work is based in part upon the "Characters" of Theophrastus, which La Bruyère had translated. John Earle wrote similar studies in English.

Charge of the Light Brigade, The, Tennyson. A famous descriptive lyric celebrating the tragic charge of the brigade of light cavalry at Balaklava in the Crimean war.

Charlemagne (shär'lê-mān). The romance of Charlemagne and his Paladins is of French origin, as the romances of King Arthur and the Knights of the Round Table are of Celtic or Welsh origin. According to one tradition, Charlemagne is not dead, but waits, crowned and armed, in Odenberg, near Salzburg, till the time of antichrist, when he will wake up and deliver Christendom. According to another tradition, Charlemagne appears in seasons of plenty. He crosses the Rhine on a golden bridge and blesses both cornfields and vineyards.

Charmian. A kind-hearted but simple-minded female attendant on Cleopatra in Shakespeare's play *Antony and Cleopatra.*

Chauvinism (*shō'vĭn-ĭz'm*). An attitude of exaggerated, unreasoning patriotism. The word is said to be derived from the name of Nicolas Chauvin, a soldier in the army of Napoleon and a person in Cogniard's *Cocarde Tricolore* (1831). The equivalent English word is "jingoism," derived from a jocular oath, "By Jingo," which came into vogue through a popular patriotic song.

Cheeryble Brothers, The. A firm of benevolent London merchants in Dickens's *Nicholas Nickleby.*

Cherry Orchard, The, Chékov. A play of Russian life, portraying the reversal of relations between the old landed families and the freed serfs. Through the futile wastefulness of Madame Ranévsky and her brother Leonid Gayef, their estate, on which is a cherry orchard, has become hopelessly involved in debt. Their sentimental love for the place blinds them to practical matters. Lopákhin, son of a former serf on the estate, suggests that the orchard be cut up into building lots, since it is near the city, but his suggestion is ignored. Finally, he buys the place at auction, and the family, including Anya, Madame Ranévsky's daughter, and her adopted daughter Barbara, are scattered. The tragic element is heightened by the presence of Firs, an old servant, who, forgotten by all, lies down to die in the abandoned house.

Chery and Fair-Star. Countess d'Aulnoy's Fairy Tales. Two children of royal birth, whom their father's brothers and their mother's sisters cast out to sea. They are found and brought up by a corsair and his wife. Ultimately they are told of their birth by a green bird and marry each other. A similar tale is found in the *Arabian Nights.*

Chevy Chase. The subject and the title of a famous old English ballad. Percy Hotspur entered the domain of Douglas, in Scotland, slew 100 deer, and was attacked by Douglas. The ensuing combat resulted in the slaughter of both leaders and many of their bravest followers. The ballad is apparently intended to commemorate the battle of Otterburn in 1388, but it is impossible to reconcile the incidents of the poem with history.

Childe. A title of honor often used in old English ballads, as "Childe Harold," "Childe of Ellechilde Waters," "Childe Roland," "Childe Tristram," "Childe Arthur." Use is made of the term in Byron's poem entitled *Childe Harold's Pilgrimage.* See *Harold, Childe.*

Children in the Wood. Two characters in an ancient and well-known ballad entitled "The Children in the Wood, or The Norfolk Gent's Last Will and Testament," which is said to be a disguised recital of the alleged murder of his nephews by Richard III. This is the story as related in Percy's *Reliques.* The master of Wayland Hall, Norfolk, on his deathbed left a little son, three years old, and a still younger daughter, named Jane, to the care of his wife's brother If the children died before they came to their majority, their uncle was to inherit their estate. After twelve months had elapsed, the uncle hired two ruffians to murder the two babes. As they went along, one of the ruffians relented and killed his fellow; then putting down the children in a wood, left them. The poor babes gathered blackberries to allay their hunger, but died during the night, and "Robin Redbreast" covered them over with strawberry leaves. Addison says of the ballad referred to, that it is "one of the darling songs of the common people."

Children of the Abbey, The, Regina Maria Roche. A famous novel (1798). The heroine, Amanda, daughter of the earl of Dunreath by his first wife, is cast out through the influence of her stepmother. After rather more than her share of misfortune and slander, she triumphs over her enemies and lives happily.

Chillingly, Kenelm. The hero in a novel of this name by Bulwer-Lytton.

Chillon (*shĭl'ŏn*; Fr., *shē'yôN'*). A castle in Vaud, Switzerland, at the eastern end of Lake Geneva. It covers an isolated rock on the edge of the lake, and is a very picturesque combination of semicircular and square towers and machicolated curtains grouped about a higher central tower. It is famous in literature and song, especially as the prison of Bonnivard, a defender of Swiss liberties against the duke of Savoy in the 16th century. This is the theme of Byron's "Prisoner of Chillon."

Chimmie Fadden. The hero of a series of stories by E. M. Townsend. The character is drawn from that of Patrick O'Connell, or "Chuck Conners," known as "The White Mayor of Chinatown" in New York. Chimmie Fadden's career has been dramatized.

Chingachgook. A sagamore of the Mohicans, and father of Uncas, in Cooper's *Leatherstocking Tales.*

Chloe. (1) In *Daphnis and Chloe*, by Longus, the shepherdess loved by Daphne. (2) *Paul and Virginia* by St. Pierre is founded on this romance. (3) Chloe is also a shepherdess in Shakespeare's *As You Like It.* (4) The heroine in George Meredith's *Tale of Chloe.*

Chœreas. The lover of Callirrhoë, in Chariton's Greek romance.

Choir Invisible, The, James Lane Allen. A story of the pure love of a man and a woman who were separated by marriage. The scene is Kentucky in the period following the Revolution. A story of the inner life, with little action.

Chouans, Les (*lā shōō'äN'*), **Balzac.** This romance is a story of the Chouans, or bands of Vendean peasants, who maintained a guerrilla warfare against the French Republican forces from 1792 to 1800. Their leader, Cottereau, a salt-smuggler, had acquired the title "Chouan" from the screech owl cry he used as a signal.

Christabel. (1) The subject and heroine of an old romance by Sir Eglamour of Artois. (2) The heroine of an ancient ballad "Sir Cauline." (3) The lady in Coleridge's poem "Christabel."

Christian. The hero of John Bunyan's allegory *Pilgrim's Progress.* He flees from the City of Destruction and journeys to the Celestial City. He starts with a heavy burden on his back, but it falls off when he stands at the foot of the cross. All his trials on the way are depicted.

Christiana. The wife of Christian, who started with her children and Mercy from the City of Destruction, forms the subject of Bunyan's *Pilgrim's Progress*, part II. She was placed under the guidance of Mr. Greatheart, and met her husband at the Celestial City.

Christmas Carol. See *Scrooge, Ebenezer.*

Christopher, St. The giant that carried a child over a brook and said, "Chylde, thou hast put me in grete peryll. I might bere no greater burden." The Chylde was the Christ and the burden was the "sin of the world." This has been a favorite theme for painters.

Christus, a Mystery. A dramatic trilogy by Henry W. Longfellow: Part I, "Divine Tragedy"; Part II, "The Golden Legend"; Part III, "New England Tragedies."

Chrysalde (*krē-säld'*). A character in Molière's *L'Ecole des Femmes*; a friend of Arnolphe.

Chrysale (*krē'zäl'*). An honest, simple-minded, henpecked tradesman, in Molière's *Les Femmes Savantes.*

Chuzzlewit, Jonas. A miser and murderer, the opposite type of character from Martin.

Chuzzlewit, Martin. The hero of Dickens's novel of the same name.

Cid, The, Corneille. This play established Corneille's fame, although it was bitterly criticized. He borrowed material from many Spanish sources. The play tells the story of the love of Rodrigue, "the Cid," and Chimène. Rodrigue, to defend his father's honor, kills Chimène's father. She demands his life, though not concealing her love. Meanwhile, Rodrigue has defeated the Moors. Chimène accepts Don Sanche as her champion, but when he returns from the duel with a bloodstained sword, she scorns him and plans to enter a convent. It then appears that Rodrigue has merely disarmed Don Sanche, refusing, because of his love, to injure a champion of Chimène. After this proof of loyalty the lovers are wedded.

Cid Campeador (*thēTH käm'pā-ä-THōr'*). The name given in histories, traditions, and songs to the epic hero of Spain. So greatly was he honored that he was called *Mio Cid el Campeador*, "my lord the champion." Relics of the "Blessed Cid," as he is still called in Spain, such as his sword, shield, banner, and drinking-cup, are still held in great reverence by the populace. The numerous "Cid romances" that were first published in the 16th century contain the most romantic improbabilities concerning the life and deeds of the Cid. The most interesting chronicle of the Cid for English readers was written by Robert Southey.

Cinderella. Heroine of a fairy tale. She is the drudge of the house, while her elder sisters go to fine balls. At length a fairy enables her to go to the prince's ball; the prince falls in love with her, and she is discovered by means of a glass slipper which she drops. This will fit no foot but her own. She is represented as returning good for evil and heaping upon her half sisters every kindness a princess can show.

Cipango (*sĭ-păng'gō*). A marvelous island, described in the *Voyages* of Marco Polo, the Venetian traveler. It is represented as lying in the Eastern seas, some 1500 miles from land, and of its beauty and wealth many stories are related. Columbus and early navigators made a diligent search for this island.

Clare, Ada. The wife of Carstone, and one of the most important characters in Dickens's *Bleak House.*

Clayhanger, Arnold Bennett. The hero of the novel *Clayhanger* is a shy, average young man of the Five Towns in the Potteries district of England, in which Bennett places his stories of common life. He marries Hilda Lessways.

Clementina, The Lady. An accomplished woman who appears in Richardson's novel, *Sir Charles Grandison.*

Clifford, Paul. An attractive highwayman and an interesting hero in Bulwer's novel of the same name. He is familiar with the haunts of low vice and dissipation but afterward is reformed and elevated by the power of love.

Clinker, Humphrey. The hero of Smollett's novel entitled *The Expedition of Humphrey Clinker,* a philosophic youth who meets with many adventures. Brought up in the workhouse, put out by the parish as apprentice to a blacksmith, he was afterward employed as a hostler's assistant. Having been dismissed from the stable, and reduced to great want, he at length attracts the notice of Mr. Bramble, who takes him into his family as a servant. He becomes the accepted lover of Winifred Jenkins, and at length turns out to be a natural son of Mr. Bramble.

Cloister and the Hearth, The, Charles Reade. The great historical novel of the Renaissance. The time is the close of the 15th century. Gerard Eliassoen, a humble Dutch boy, is betrothed to Margaret, daughter of a wealthy alchemist-physician. But their marriage is prevented and Gerard flees to Rome. There he hears that Margaret is dead. Hopeless of love, he becomes a monk. Returning to Holland, he finds Margaret alive and the mother of a boy. But Gerard, devoted to the Church, cannot return to Margaret. The son grew up to be the great scholar Erasmus.

Clorinda. Jerusalem Delivered, Tasso. Clorinda, the heroine of this poem, is represented as an Amazon inspiring the most tender affection in others, especially in the Christian chief Tancred; yet she is herself susceptible of no passion but the love of military fame.

Cloten. A rejected lover of Imogen, in Shakespeare's play *Cymbeline.*

Clout, Colin. A name that Spenser applies to himself in the *Faery Queen* and "Shepherd's Calendar." Colin Clout also is introduced into Gay's pastorals.

Cœlebs (sē′lĕbz). The hero of a novel by Hannah More, *Cœlebs in Search of a Wife.*

Collean, May. The heroine of a Scottish ballad.

Cologne, The Three Kings of. A name given to the three Magi who visited the infant Savior, and whose bodies are said to have been brought by the empress Helena from the East to Constantinople, whence they were transferred to Milan. Afterward, they were removed to Cologne and placed in the principal church of the city, where, says Cressy, "they are to this day celebrated with great veneration." Their names are commonly said to be Gaspar, Melchior, and Balthazar.

Colonel Carter of Cartersville, F. Hopkinson Smith. A story of an old Virginia gentleman set down among New York financiers, and involved in railroad building schemes.

Comédie Humaine (kô′mä′dē′ ü′mân′). The uncompleted series of nearly a hundred novels by Balzac, designed to give a panoramic picture of the manners and morals of his time. He began the work in 1829, adopting the general title in 1842. The appearance of the same characters in various stories binds them into a single series.

Comedy of Errors. Shakespeare. Twin brothers of exact likeness, named Antipholus, are served by attendant slaves named Dromio, also of striking resemblance. The humor of the play lies in the complications that arise. The two brothers are lost at sea with their servants and are picked up by different vessels. After long separation they all reappear in Ephesus. There is great entanglement of plot until both brothers face each other in a trial before the duke and all is explained.

Common Sense, Thomas Paine. The title of a famous pamphlet published by Paine in Philadelphia in 1776, in which he urged separation of the colonies from England. The work helped to crystallize American sentiment for independence.

Compleat Angler, The. A famous book by Izaak Walton. It was first published in 1653, and it is said to have been issued in a new edition, on the average, every two and a half years since. The "compleat angler" is the fisherman who loves peaceful nature and seasons his hours

by the stream with wise philosophy. The book is written in the form of a prose pastoral, the chief characters being "Piscator" and "Venator."

Comus. In Milton's poem entitled *Comus: a Masque,* he is represented as a base enchanter, who endeavors, but in vain, to beguile and entrap the innocent by means of his enchantments. The name in Greek means "a revel."

Concord Bridge. The old bridge at Concord, Mass, made famous by the battle between Americans and British, April 19, 1775, and celebrated in Emerson's "Concord Hymn," written for the dedication of the Concord monument, April 19, 1836.

Concord, Mass. The town of Concord, noted in revolutionary history, became famous later as the residence of several literary men and women,—Hawthorne, Emerson, Thoreau, Bronson Alcott, Louisa May Alcott, William Ellery Channing, and others. Here was the center of the so-called Concord school of philosophy.

Consuelo (kŏn′sù-ā′lō). The heroine of George Sand's novel of the same name, an impersonation of noble purity sustained amid great temptations.

Cooperstown. A village in Otsego county, New York. It was for many years the home of James Fenimore Cooper, where he wrote most of his novels. In *The Pioneers* he wrote of the wilderness life about Cooperstown, introducing the place under the name of Templeton.

Cophetua (kô-fĕt′ù-à). An imaginary African king, of whom a legendary ballad told that he fell in love with a beggar maid and married her. This ballad is found in Percy's *Reliques.* Many poets have made use of the story. Tennyson has given us a modern version in "The Beggar Maid."

Copperfield, David. The hero of Dickens's novel of the same name. This is said to be Dickens's favorite among his works and somewhat autobiographic.

Cordelia. King Lear, Shakespeare. The youngest of Lear's three daughters, and the one who truly loved him.

Corydon. A shepherd in one of the idyls of Theocritus and in one of the eclogues of Virgil. Used by Shakespeare and later poets to designate a rustic swain.

Costard. A clown, in Shakespeare's *Love's Labor Lost,* who apes the display of wit and misapplies, in the most ridiculous manner, the phrases and modes of combination in argument that were then in vogue.

Cotter's Saturday Night, Robert Burns. This famous poem was published in 1786. Celebrated for its beautiful picture of humble Scotch life. One of the most frequently quoted of English poems.

Count of Monte Cristo, The, Dumas. A young sailor, Edmond Dantes, with the world and hopeful love before him, is imprisoned on a false charge of being a Bonapartist emissary. The time is 1815. In prison he is told by a fellow prisoner of a treasure buried on the island of Monte Cristo. He escapes, finds the treasure, and spends the rest of his life as the mysterious count, bringing punishment upon his enemies and rewarding his friends.

Crabtree. A character in Smollett's novel *The Adventures of Peregrine Pickle.*

Crane, Ichabod. The name of a Yankee schoolmaster, whose adventures are related in the *Legend of Sleepy Hollow,* in Irving's *Sketch Book.*

Crawley, Rawdon. The husband of Becky Sharp in *Vanity Fair,* Thackeray's novel without a hero.

Creakle, Mr. A tyrannical and cruel schoolmaster in Dickens's *David Copperfield.*

Cressida. The heroine of Shakespeare's play *Troilus and Cressida,* also the heroine of one of Chaucer's *Canterbury Tales.* She was a faithless lover.

Cricket on the Hearth, The, Dickens. A Christmas story. The title is suggested by the singing-match between the kettle and the cricket on Dot Peerybingle's immaculate and snug little hearth. The cricket wins the match. A love story is woven in. Edward, son of old Caleb Plummer, the toy maker, comes home from South America just in time to save his sweetheart, May Fielding, from marriage to Tackleton, a toy merchant.

Crisis, The, Churchill. A story of Civil War times, the scenes located for the most part in St. Louis. A Yankee and a Southern girl are the lovers. Lincoln, Grant, and Sherman are brought into the tale.

Cris Kingle (krĭs′ kĭng′l). Also variously spelled Kriss Kingle, and Kriss Kringle, has been corrupted from the German word, *Christ-Kindel,* meaning the "little *Christ-child.*" Later uses, especially among German peoples, have identified the name with that of Santa Claus and Saint Nicholas.

Croaker. A character in Goldsmith's comedy *The Good-natured Man.*

Crocodile Tears. False tears, often affected for a purpose. The expression appears first in Greek and Latin proverbs and is based on the erroneous belief that the crocodile weeps in order to arouse the pity of a human being who, on approaching, is promptly devoured.

Crossing, The, Churchill. A historical tale of a boy's adventures in the westward movement of settlers across the Alleghenies after the Revolution. George Rogers Clark is the hero of the story.

Crummles, Vincent. A theatrical head of a theatrical family in Dickens's *Nicholas Nickleby.*

Crusoe, Robinson. See *Robinson Crusoe,* page 310.

Cuchullin, Cuchulain (*kōō-hōō'lĭn*). See *Cattle Raid of Cooley.*

Cuneiform (*kû-nĕ'ĭ-fôrm*) **Writing.** So called from the wedge shape of the characters (Latin *cuneus,* wedge). The signs, to represent objects and also sounds, were composed of the wedge-shape marks arranged in groups. These marks were impressed on soft clay tablets with a stylus or cut into rock with a chisel. This system was in use in Babylonia from 7000 B. C. to 300 B. C. and in neighboring countries, including that of the Hittites.

Cuttle, Captain. A character in Dickens's *Dombey and Son,* good-humored, eccentric, pathetic in his simple credulity.

Cymbeline. A mythical king of Britain and the titular hero of Shakespeare's play of the same name. Imogen, daughter of Cymbeline, king of Britain, married clandestinely Posthumus Leonatus; and Posthumus, being banished for the offense, retired to Rome. One day, in the house of Philario, the conversation turned on the merits of wives, and Posthumus bet his diamond ring that nothing could tempt the fidelity of Imogen. Through the villainy of Iachimo, Posthumus was forced to believe Imogen untrue. The villainy was in time disclosed and the beautiful character of Imogen revealed.

Daddy-Long-Legs, Jean Webster. The story of an orphan girl who is sent to school by an unknown benefactor. She writes to him under the name of "Daddy-Long-Legs."

Dagonet, Sir. In the romance *Le Morte D'Arthur* he is called the fool of King Arthur.

Dalgetty, Rittmaster Dugald. A soldier of fortune in Sir Walter Scott's *Legend of Montrose,* distinguished for his pedantry, conceit, valor, vulgar assurance, knowledge of the world, greediness, and a hundred other qualities, making him one of the most amusing, admirable, and natural characters ever drawn by the hand of genius.

Damocles (*dăm'ô-klēz*). A flatterer in the court of Dionysius of Syracuse. By way of answer to his constant praises of the happiness of kings, Dionysius seated him at a royal banquet, with a sword hung over his head by a single horsehair. In the midst of his magnificent banquet, Damocles, chancing to look upward, saw the sharp and naked sword suspended over his head. A sight so alarming instantly changed his views of the felicity of kings. "Sword of Damocles" signifies now a dread foreboding of evil or tantalizing apprehension.

Damon and Pythias or **Phintias.** Two noble Pythagoreans of Syracuse, who have been remembered as models of faithful friendship. Pythias, having been condemned to death by Dionysius, the tyrant of Syracuse, begged to be allowed to go home, for the purpose of arranging his affairs, Damon pledging his own life for the reappearance of his friend. Dionysius consented, and Pythias returned just in time to save Damon from death. Struck by so noble an example of mutual affection, the tyrant pardoned Pythias, and desired to be admitted into their sacred fellowship.

Dandie Dinmont. A jovial, true-hearted store farmer, in Sir Walter Scott's *Guy Mannering.*

Dantesque (*dăn-tĕsk'*). Dante-like—that is, a minute, lifelike representation of the infernal horrors, whether by words, as in the "Inferno," or in visible form, as in Doré's illustrations of the poem.

Daphnis and Chloe (*klō'ê*). A pair of lovers in the pastoral romance of the same name written by Longus in Greek prose probably in the 5th century.

Darby and Joan. A married couple said to have lived in the village of Healaugh, in the West Riding of Yorkshire, and celebrated for their long life and conjugal felicity. They are the hero and the heroine of a ballad called "The Happy Old Couple," which has been attributed to Prior but is of uncertain authorship. Timperley says that Darby was a printer in Bartholomew Close, who died in 1730, and that the ballad was written by one of his apprentices named Henry Woodfall.

Dares (*dā'rēz*). One of the competitors at the funeral games of Anchises in Sicily, described in the fifth book of Virgil's *Æneid.*

Dark Rosaleen. A poetical name for Ireland. See James Clarence Mangan's beautiful poem of that name.

Darrel of the Blessed Isles, Irving Bacheller. A story of an old clock-mender whose imagination traveled through a country of poetry, the "blessed isles," fashioned out of his familiarity with Shakespeare, Milton, and the Bible.

David. In Dryden's satire called "Absalom and Achitophel," the character representing Charles II; Absalom, his beautiful but rebellious son, represents the duke of Monmouth.

David, Saint. He was said to be the uncle of King Arthur. St. David first embraced the ascetic life at Witland in Carmarthenshire, but subsequently removed to Menevia, in Pembrokeshire, having founded twelve convents in West Britain.

Davy. Henry IV, Shakespeare. The varlet of Justice Shallow, who so identifies himself with his master that he considers himself half host, half varlet. Thus, when he seats Bardolph and Page at table, he tells them they must take "his" good will for their assurance of welcome.

Dawfyd. The Betrothed, Scott. The one-eyed freebooter chief.

Dawkins. Oliver Twist, Dickens. Known by the sobriquet of the "Artful Dodger." He is one of Fagin's tools. Jack Dawkins is a scamp, but of a cheery, buoyant temper.

Deadwood Dick. The adventurous character to be found in many dime novels of the middle of the 19th century. In real life, he was Robert Dickey (1840–1912), who had a romantic career as Indian scout, trapper, and fur trader.

Deans, Douce Davie. A poor herdsman at Edinburgh, and the father of Effie and Jeanie Deans, in Sir Walter Scott's novel *The Heart of Midlothian.*

Deans, Effie. A beautiful but unfortunate character in Sir Walter Scott's *The Heart of Midlothian.*

Deans, Jeanie. The heroine of *The Heart of Midlothian,* characterized by her kindness, sturdiness, and good sense. She journeys from Edinburgh to London and obtains pardon for her sister Effie, condemned for child murder.

Debon. One of the heroes who accompanied Brut, or Brutus, to Britain. According to British fable, Devonshire is the county or share of Debon.

Decameron (*dê-kăm'ĕr-ŏn*). A volume of 100 tales told by Boccaccio. Seven ladies and three gentlemen, assembled in one place, agree that each shall tell one story every day for the entertainment of the rest. Thus ten stories daily are told for ten consecutive days. Chaucer borrowed the plan but reconstructed it for his *Canterbury Tales.*

De Coverley, Sir Roger. One of the members of the imaginary club under whose direction the *Spectator* was professedly edited. He represents a kind-hearted, simpleminded English squire in the time of Queen Anne. He figures in thirty papers of the *Spectator.*

Dedlock, Sir Leicester and Lady. Bleak House, Dickens. Sir Leicester was an honorable and truthful man but of such fixed ideas that no one could shake his prejudices. He had an idea that the one thing of greatest importance to the world was a certain family by the name of Dedlock. He loved his wife, Lady Dedlock, and believed in her implicitly. His pride had a terrible fall when he learned the secret of her life before her marriage and knew the fact that she had been hiding from him, that she had a daughter. Lady Dedlock, beautiful, but apparently cold and heartless, suffered from constant remorse. The daughter's name is Esther Summerson, the heroine of the novel. Volumnia Dedlock was a cousin of Sir Leicester, a young lady of sixty, who had the disagreeable habit of entering into other people's business.

Deerslayer. The hero of a novel of the same name, by James Fenimore Cooper. A strong fine character, honorable, truthful, brave, without cultivation but without reproach. This character appears under different names in five of Cooper's novels,—*The Deerslayer, The Pathfinder, The Last of the Mohicans, The Pioneers,* and *The Prairie.*

Defarge (*dĕ-färzh'*), **M. Tale of Two Cities, Dickens.** Keeper of a wine shop in the Faubourg St. Antoine, in Paris. He is a bull-necked, implacable-looking man His wife, a dangerous woman, was "everlastingly knitting" before the guillotine as heads fell.

Defarge, Madame. Wife of the wineseller, a dangerous woman, "everlastingly knitting."

Delectable Mountains. In Bunyan's *Pilgrim's Progress*, a beautiful range of hills from the summit of which the pilgrim could see the Celestial City.

Delphic Oracle. A famous source of ancient prophecy was the oracle of Delphi. A priestess in charge of the temple of Apollo went into a trance and spoke words that were sometimes taken down in verse.

Delphin Classics. For the use of the dauphin, son of Louis XIV (1674–91), the writings of 39 Latin authors were collected and published in sixty volumes. Notes and an index were added to each work. An edition of the Delphin classics was published in London in the year 1818. The name comes from Latin *delphinus*, meaning "dolphin," from which "dauphin" also is derived, because of the device of a dolphin worn on his helmet.

Delphine. The title of a novel by Mme. de Staël, and the name of its heroine.

Delphine, Madame. Old Creole Days, George W. Cable. A free quadroon connected with the splendor of Lafitte, the smuggler and patriot. Madame Delphine disowned her beautiful daughter Olive in order to assure to her the rights of a white woman.

Demetrius (dē-mē'trĭ-ŭs). **A Midsummer Night's Dream, Shakespeare.** The young Athenian to whom Egeus promised his daughter Hermia in marriage.

De Profundis (dē prŏ-fŭn'dĭs), "Out of the Depths." (1) The 130th Psalm is so called from the first two words in the Latin version. In the Roman Catholic Church it is sung when the dead are committed to the grave. (2) Title of a poem by Oscar Wilde.

Deronda, Daniel. One of George Eliot's strongest character sketches in her novel of the same name.

Der Tag, "The Day." For many years this was a favorite toast in the German army and navy, the day when war should come.

Deserted Village. A poem by Goldsmith in which he describes rural England. He calls the village Auburn, but tells us it was the seat of his youth, every spot of which was dear and familiar to him. He pictures familiar persons, the preacher, the teacher, pastimes, and favorite haunts.

Despair, Giant. Pilgrim's Progress, Bunyan. A giant who is the owner of Doubting Castle, and who, finding Christian and Hopeful asleep upon his grounds, takes them prisoners and thrusts them into a dungeon.

Deus Ex Machina, "A god from the machine." Used of some external power or idea brought into a story or argument to resolve a difficulty. An allusion to the custom of the ancient theater, where a god was brought in by machinery to explain or resolve situations past the power of human actors to understand or control.

Dhu, Roderick. A Highland chieftain and outlaw in Scott's poem "Lady of the Lake," cousin of Ellen Douglas, and also her suitor. He is slain by James Fitz-James.

Diana of the Crossways, George Meredith. This was the first of Meredith's novels to gain popularity, and it is still ranked as a masterpiece. The heroine, Diana Merion, the victim of a youthful, unhappy marriage, plunges into the gaiety of London and becomes unfortunately involved in the betrayal of a political secret. Sobered and disillusioned, she finally, after the death of her first husband, marries a strong, sensible man, Redworth, who had been devoted to her.

Dido. The daughter of Belus, king of Tyre, and the wife of Sichæus, whom her brother Pygmalion murdered for his riches. Not far from the Phœnician colony of Utica she built the city of Carthage. According to Virgil, when Æneas was shipwrecked upon her coast, in his voyage to Italy, she hospitably entertained him, fell in love with him, and, because he did not requite her passion, stabbed herself in despair.

Dies Iræ (dī'ēz ī'rē). The name generally given, from the opening words, to the famous medieval hymn on the Last Judgment. On account of the solemn grandeur of the ideas which it brings before the mind, as well as the deep and trembling emotions it is fitted to excite, it soon found its way into the liturgy of the Church. The authorship of the hymn has been ascribed to Gregory the Great, St. Bernard of Clairvaux, Umbertus, and Frangipani, the last two of whom were noted as hymnists. The consensus of recent hymnologists, however, is in favor of Thomas of Celano.

Diggon, Davie. A shepherd in the "Shepherd's Calendar," by Spenser. He tells Hobbinol that he drove his sheep into foreign lands, hoping to find better pasture; but he was amazed at the luxury and profligacy of the shepherds whom he saw there and the wretched condition of the flocks.

Dimmesdale (dĭmz'dāl), **Arthur.** In Hawthorne's romance *The Scarlet Letter*, a Puritan minister of great eloquence and spirituality, in colonial New England, who secretly commits adultery and afterward makes a public confession.

Dinah. (1) Aunt of Walter Shandy in Sterne's novel *Tristram Shandy*. She leaves Mr Walter Shandy £1000, which he fancies will enable him to carry out all the schemes that enter into his head. (2) A character in Mrs. Stowe's *Uncle Tom's Cabin*. (3) *St. Ronan's Well*, Scott. Daughter of Sandie Lawson, landlord of the Spa hotel.

Dingley Dell. Pickwick Papers, Dickens. The home of Mr. Wardle and his family, and the scene of Tupman's love adventure with Miss Rachel.

Dirlos, Count. One of Charlemagne's paladins, an ideal of valor, generosity, and truth.

Divine Comedy. The immortal work of Dante Alighieri, written between 1300 and 1321, the year of the poet's death. It consists of a vision of the world beyond the grave, and depicts the final destiny of the human soul in accordance with its exercise of free will during life, by which it has chosen to follow the way of evil or of good.

The structure of the sublime poem is based upon the dual scheme of the *De Monarchiâ*. It is made up of a hundred cantos in metrical lines of eleven syllables, written in *terza rima*, a form of the popular poetry of the day but distinctly metamorphosed in an especial manner by the poet.

The vision of which Dante writes is one which was vouchsafed to him for his salvation's sake twenty years previously when leading an evil life. During the year of Jubilee, 1300, commencing on the morning of Good Friday and continuing for six consecutive days, the poet passed through the confines of hell, purgatory, and paradise. He held converse with the souls in each of the three realms and learned the future purposes of Divine Providence in his own regard and in that of the world at large.

The poet relates how, by special grace, while yet in the flesh, he was permitted to travel through these three realms of the After Life. Virgil appears to him, typifying human wisdom, informed by the moral and intellectual virtues. He guides Dante by the light of reason, from the dark forest, wherein the beasts of pride, avarice, and lust keep men from ascending the Holy Mount, through hell and purgatory as far as the earthly paradise. Here the poet realizes how the state of temporal happiness is reached through purgatorial travail which regains for the soul its spiritual liberty.

Beatrice, representing divine philosophy, illumined by revelation, leads him next up through the nine heavens of spiritual preparation of the mind. Then slowly, before the eyes of Dante, is opened up the true paradise, limitless, timeless, wherein is found the eternal happiness of the sight of God.

Here the place of Beatrice is taken by St. Bernard who typifies divine contemplation, which is the eternal life of the soul. The saint commends the poet to the patronage of the Blessed Virgin, through whose intercession Dante is awarded a foretaste of the Beatific Vision.

The poem closes in ineffable grandeur and majesty, showing how Faith is lost in Vision, Hope in Fruition and with nothing remaining but that "Charity which moves the sun and the other stars." The powers of the soul are consumed in their union with the Divine Essence and the finite will at last has become one with the Infinite.

In this stupendous allegory, we have in truth the transcendent vision of a god-given genius, who unfolds before us what has been revealed to him of the unspeakable justice, mercy, and glory of the Most High. In spiritual wisdom, dramatic force, infallible confidence of touch, and terseness of expression, the *Divine Comedy* has never been excelled. It is the culminating and crowning glory of medieval culture, which rivals in splendor that of the classical world at any period of its history.

Dobbin, Captain William. The awkward, plodding, patient, faithful friend of George Osborne in *Vanity Fair* by Thackeray. After years of unselfish devotion, he finally wins Amelia, George's widow, and marries her.

Doctor Syntax. The hero of a work entitled *The Tour of Dr. Syntax in Search of the Picturesque*. Doctor Syntax is a simple-minded, pious, henpecked clergyman, but of excellent taste and scholarship, who left home in search of the picturesque. His adventures are told in eight-syllable verse by William Combe.

Doctour of Phisikes, Tale of the. The Roman story of Virginius, given by Livy. Told by Chaucer in *Canterbury Tales*.

Dods. The old landlady in Scott's novel *St. Ronan's Well*. An excellent character, a mosaic of oddities, all fitting together, and forming an admirable whole. She was so good a housewife that a cookery book of great repute bears her name.

Dodson. The Three Warnings, Mrs. Thrale. A youth called upon by Death on his wedding day. Death told him he must go with him. "With you!" the hapless youth cried, "young as I am." Death then told him he would not disturb him yet, but would call again after giving him three warnings. When he was 80 years of age Death called again. "So soon returned?" old Dodson cried. "You know you promised me three warnings." Death then told him that as he was "lame, and deaf, and blind" he had received his three warnings.

Dodson and Fogg. The lawyers employed by the plaintiff in the famous case of "Bardell v. Pickwick," in the *Pickwick Papers* by Charles Dickens.

Doeg (*dō'ĕg*). **Absalom and Achitophel, Dryden.** Doeg was Saul's herdsman, who had charge of his mules and asses. He told Saul that the priests of Nob had provided David with food; whereupon Saul sent him to put them to death, and 85 were ruthlessly massacred.

Dogberry and Verges. Two ignorant, conceited constables, in Shakespeare's *Much Ado about Nothing.*

Dolly Varden. Barnaby Rudge, Dickens. Daughter of Gabriel Varden, locksmith. Dolly dressed in the Watteau style, and was lively, pretty, and bewitching.

Dolopatos. Sandabar's Parables. The Sicilian king, who placed his son Lucien under the charge of "seven wise masters." Because the queen, Lucien's stepmother, had wrongfully accused him of violence toward her, he fell under his father's fury and was condemned to death. By astrology the prince discovered that if he could tide over seven days his life would be saved; so the wise master amused the king with seven tales, and the king relented. The prince himself then told a tale which embodied his own history; the eyes of the king were opened, and the queen was condemned to death.

Dombey. Dombey and Son, Dickens. Mr. Dombey, a self-sufficient, purse-proud, frigid merchant, who feels satisfied there is but one Dombey in the world, and that is himself. When Paul was born, his ambition was attained, his whole heart was in the boy, and the loss of the mother was but a small matter. The boy's death turned his heart to stone.

Dombey, Florence. A motherless child, hungering and thirsting to be loved, but regarded with indifference by her father, who thinks that sons alone are worthy of regard.

Dombey, Little Paul. A pathetic child in Dickens's novel *Dombey and Son.* He is a delicate, thoughtful boy, the only son of a rich and pompous London merchant.

Domdaniel (*dŏm-dăn'ĭ-ĕl*). A cave in the region adjoining Babylon, the abode of evil spirits. By some traditions said to have been originally the spot where the prophet Daniel imparted instruction to his disciples. In another form, the Domdaniel was a purely imaginary region, subterranean, or submarine, the dwelling place of genii and enchanters. Arabian mythology.

Domesday Book or **Doomsday Book.** The name of one of the oldest and most valuable records of England, containing the results of a statistical survey of that country made by William the Conqueror, and completed in the year 1086. The origin of the name—which seems to have been given to other records of the same kind—is somewhat uncertain; but it has obvious reference to the supreme authority of the book in doom or judgment on the matters contained in it.

Dominical Letter or **Sunday Letter.** One of the seven letters A, B, C, D, E, F, G, used in almanacs, etc., to mark the Sundays throughout the year. The first seven days of the year are marked in their order by the above corresponding letters. The following seven, and all consecutive sets of seven days to the end of the year are similarly marked; so that the 1st, 8th, 15th, 22d, etc., days of the year are all marked by A; and the 2d, 9th, 16th, 23d, etc., by B; and so on. The days being thus marked, it is evident that on whatever date the first Sunday of the year falls, the letter which marks it will mark all the other Sundays in the year, as the number of the letters and of the days in the week is the same. As the common year consists of 52 weeks and one day over, the dominical letters go backwards one day every common year. If the dominical letter of a common year be G, F will be the dominical letter for the next year.

Don Adriano de Armado (*dŏn ăd'rĭ-ä'nō dā är-mä'dō*). A pompous, fantastical Spaniard in Shakespeare's *Love's Labor's Lost,* "who has a mint of phrases in his brain." His language is fantastically out of proportion to the thought. He uses "examples suited only to the gravest propositions and impersonations, or apostrophes to abstract thoughts impersonated, which are, in fact, the natural language only of the most vehement agitations of the mind."

Donatello. The hero of Hawthorne's romance *The Marble Faun.* He is a young Italian with a singular likeness to the "Faun of Praxiteles." He leads an innocent but purely animal existence, until a sudden crime awakens his conscience and transforms his whole nature.

Don Cherubim. The "Bachelor of Salamanca" in Lesage's novel of this name; a man placed in different situations of life and made to associate with all classes of society, in order to give the author the greatest possible scope for satire.

Donegild. Man of Law's Tale, Chaucer. Mother of Alla, king of Northumberland, hating Constance, the wife of Alla, because she was a Christian, placed her on a raft with her infant son, and turned her adrift. When Alla returned from Scotland and discovered this cruelty of his mother, he put her to death. The tradition of St. Mungo resembles the "Man of Law's Tale" in many respects.

Donet (*dō'nĕt*). The first Latin grammar put into the hands of scholars. It was that of Donatus the grammarian, who taught in Rome in the 4th century and was the preceptor of St. Jerome.

Don Juan (*dŏn jū'ăn*). A legendary and mythical personage like Dr. Faustus. Don Juan is presented in the life of a profligate who gives himself up so entirely to the gratification of sense, especially to the most supremacy of all the impulses, that of love, that he acknowledges no higher consideration, and proceeds to murder the man that stands between him and his wish, fancying that in so doing he had annihilated his very existence. He then defies that spirit to prove to his senses his existence. The spirit returns and compels Don Juan to acknowledge the supremacy of spirit and the worthlessness of a merely sensuous existence. The traditions concerning Don Juan have been dramatized by Tirso de Molina; thence passed into Italy and France. Glück has a musical ballet of Don Juan, and Mozart has immortalized the character in his opera "Don Giovanni." His adventures form the subject of a half-finished poem by Byron.

Don Quixote (*dŏn kwĭk'sŏt*). The hero of a celebrated Spanish romance of the same name by Cervantes. Don Quixote is represented as "a gaunt country gentleman of La Mancha, full of genuine Castilian honor and enthusiasm, gentle and dignified in his character, trusted by his friends, and loved by his dependents," but "so completely crazed by long reading the most famous books of chivalry, that he believes them to be true, and feels himself called on to become the impossible knight-errant they describe, and actually goes forth into the world to defend the oppressed and avenge the injured, like the heroes of his romances." The fame of Cervantes will always rest upon this incomparable satire upon the foolish and extravagant romances of chivalry.

Dooley, Mr. The Irish American character made popular by F. P. Dunne in humorous monologues of comment on men and affairs. Mr. Dooley, a saloon-keeper of Archey Road, appeared first in a series of sketches in the Chicago *Times-Herald.*

Doorm. Idylls of the King: Enid, Tennyson. An earl called "the Bull," who tried to make Enid his handmaid; but, when she would neither eat, drink, nor array herself in bravery at his bidding, "he smote her on the cheek"; whereupon Geraint slew the "russet-bearded earl" in his own hall.

Dora. David Copperfield, Dickens. The childwife to David, affectionate and tender-hearted. She was always playing with her poodle and saying simple things to her "Dody." She could never be his helper, but she looked on her husband with idolatrous love. While quite young she died.

Dorastus. The hero of an old popular "history" or romance, upon which Shakespeare founded his *Winter's Tale.* It was written by Robert Greene, and was first published in 1588, under the title of *Pandosto, the Triumph of Time.*

Dorothea. The heroine of Goethe's celebrated poem "Hermann und Dorothea."

Dorrit, Edward and "Little." Little Dorrit, Dickens. The "father" of the Marshalsea prison and his interesting daughter It is a fine picture of innocent, affectionate child life in the midst of the trying circumstances of a debtor's prison.

Dory, John. (1) Hero and title of an old English ballad. (2) A character in *Wild Oats,* or *The Strolling Gentleman,* a comedy by John O'Keefe.

Dotheboys (*doo'THê-boiz'*) **Hall. Nicholas Nickleby, Dickens.** A school for boys kept by a Mr. Squeers, a puffing, ignorant, overbearing brute, whose system of education consisted of alternately beating and starving.

Doubting Castle. The castle of the giant Despair, in which Christian and Hopeful were incarcerated, but from which they escaped by means of the key called "Promise," which was able to open any lock in the castle.

Dousterswivel. A German schemer, in Sir Walter Scott's novel *The Antiquary.*

Drac (drăk). A sort of fairy in human form, whose abode is the caverns of rivers. "Faire le drac," same as "Faire le diable." Irish, "Play the Puck"; English, "Play the deuce."

Dracula. The central figure in a romance of that name by Bram Stoker. This villainous hero inhabits a castle in Transylvania and leads a group of human vampires.

Drama of Exile, A. A poem by Elizabeth Barrett Browning (1844). The exile is Eve, driven out of paradise into the wilderness. Lucifer, Gabriel, and Christ are introduced into the poem, as well as Adam and Eve.

Dramatic Unities, The Three. One catastrophe, one locality, one day. These are Aristotle's unities of time, place, and action. To these the French added a fourth, the unity of uniformity; i. e., in tragedy all the *dramatis personœ* should be tragic in style, in comedy comic, and in farce farcical.

Drap. Drayton. One of Queen Mab's maids of honor.

Drawcansir (drô'kăn-sẽr). The name of a blustering, bullying fellow in the celebrated mock-heroic play *The Rehearsal*, written by George Villiers, duke of Buckingham, assisted by Sprat and others. He is represented as taking part in a battle, where, after killing all the combatants on both sides, he makes an extravagantly boastful speech. From the popularity of the character, the name became a synonym for a braggart.

Driver. Guy Mannering, Scott. Clerk to Mr. Pleydell, advocate, Edinburgh.

Dromio. The Brothers Dromio. Two brothers exactly alike, who serve two brothers exactly alike, in Shakespeare's *Comedy of Errors*, based on the *Menœchmi* of Plautus.

Dryasdust, The Rev. An imaginary personage who serves to introduce Scott's novels to the public.

Dudu. One of the three beauties of the harem into which Juan, by the sultana's order, had been admitted in female attire.

Duessa (dû-ĕs'à). A foul witch, in Spenser's *Faery Queen*, who, under the assumed name of Fidessa and the assumed character of a distressed and lovely woman, entices the Red Cross Knight into the House of Pride. The knight, having left the palace, is overtaken by Duessa, and drinks of an enchanted fountain, which paralyzes him. In this state he is attacked, defeated, and imprisoned by the giant Orgoglio. Duessa becomes the paramour of Orgoglio, who decks her out in gorgeous ornaments, gives her a gold and purple robe to wear, puts a triple crown on her head, and sets her upon a monstrous beast with seven heads. Prince Arthur slays Orgoglio and rescues the knight. Duessa is stripped of her gorgeous disguise and is found to be a hideous hag.

Duff, Jamie. Guy Mannering, Scott. The idiot boy attending Mrs. Bertram's funeral.

Dulcinea del Toboso (dōōl'thê-nä'ä dĕl tô-bō'sō). A country girl whom Don Quixote courts as his ladylove.

Dumaine. A lord attending on the king of Navarre, in Shakespeare's *Love's Labor's Lost*.

Duncan. (1) A king of Scotland immortalized in Shakespeare's tragedy *Macbeth*. Shakespeare represents him as murdered by Macbeth, who succeeds to the Scottish throne, but according to history he fell in battle. (2) A Highland hero in Scott's "Lady of the Lake."

Dundreary, Lord. A grotesque character in Taylor's comedy *Our American Cousin*; noted for his aristocratic haughtiness of manner. The part, insignificant in the first form of the play, was enlarged and made famous by the actor, E. A. Sothern.

Durandal. Written also Durandart, Durindana, and Durlindana. The name of the marvelous sword of Orlando, the renowned hero of romance. It is said to have been the workmanship of the fairies, who endued it with such wonderful properties that its owner was able to cleave the Pyrenees with it at a blow.

Durandarte (dōō'rän-där'tā). A fabulous hero of Spain, celebrated in the ancient ballads of that country and in the romances of chivalry. Cervantes has introduced him, in *Don Quixote*, in the celebrated adventure of the knight in the cave of Montesinos.

Durden, Dame. (1) The heroine of a popular English song. She is described as a notable housewife, and the mistress of five serving girls and five laboring men. The five men loved the five maids. (2) A sobriquet playfully applied to Esther Summerson, the heroine of Dickens's *Bleak House.* (3) Mistress of the Inn of Sherwood in the opera "Robin Hood."

Dwarf, Peter. An allegorical romance by Ludwig Tieck. The dwarf is a castle specter that advises and aids the family; but all his advice turns out evil, and all his aid productive of trouble.

Dwarf, The Black. A novel by Sir Walter Scott. The black dwarf is a fairy of the most malignant character; a genuine northern Duergar, and once held by the dalesmen of the border as the author of all the mischief that befell their flocks and herds. In Scott's novel the "Black Dwarf" is introduced under the "aliases" of Sir Edward Mauley; Elshander, the recluse; Cannie Elshie; and the Wise Wight of Mucklestane Moor.

Earnscliffe, Patrick. The Black Dwarf, Scott. The young laird of Earnscliff.

Earthly Paradise, The, William Morris. A narrative poem, the scene of which is laid in a "nameless city in a distant sea" to which come a band of Norse rovers fleeing from the Black Death and seeking a paradise. In this city they linger and find freedom from fear. During the year of waiting they tell 24 tales. These stories are gathered from Greek, Norse French, and Arabian sources. They are connected by lyric passages of landscape poetry.

Eckhardt, The Faithful. A legendary hero of Germany, represented as an old man with a white staff, who, in Eisleben, appears on the evening of Maundy Thursday and drives all the people into their houses, to save them from being harmed by a terrible procession of dead men, headless bodies, and two-legged horses, which immediately after passes by. Other traditions represent him as the companion of the knight, Tannhäuser, and as warning travelers from the Venusberg, the mountain of fatal delights in the old mythology of Germany. Tieck has founded a story upon this legend, which has been translated into English by Carlyle, in which Eckhardt is described as the good servant who perishes to save his master's children from the seducing fiends of the mountain. The German proverb, "Thou art the faithful Eckhardt; thou warnest every one," is founded upon this tradition.

Eclecta. The "Elect" personified in "The Purple Island," by Phineas Fletcher. She is the daughter of Intellect and Voletta (free will).

Ecole des Femmes, L' (lā'kōl' dā făm), "The School of Wives," **Molière.** The dramatist in this comedy developed an Italian story. Arnolphe adopts a young girl, Agnes, whom he proceeds to educate in a school where distinctions of sex and social class are ignored. When her education is finished, he plans to marry her, but she betrays her training in her very naïve treatment of men as if they were schoolgirls. The upshot is that a young fellow, Horace, falls in love with her and they are married. Arnolphe's experiment has failed.

Ecole des Maris, L' (lā'kōl' dā mä'rē'), "The School of Husbands," **Molière.** In this comedy, Sganarelle appears as a surly despot. To him and his brother Ariste, the father of two girls, Isabelle and Léonor, has given the care of them until they have grown up. With marriage in view, the brothers set out to educate their charges. Sganarelle restricts Isabelle severely, and as a consequence she deceives him and marries Valère. Ariste, on the other hand, through giving Léonor liberty and trusting her, gains a loving, dutiful wife.

Ector or **Hector, Sir.** The foster father of King Arthur, and lord of many parts of England and Wales. Father of Sir Kay, seneschal to King Arthur.

Edda. There are two religious codes, so called, containing the ancient Scandinavian mythology. One is in verse, composed in Norway and Iceland by various unknown authors; the other is written in prose, attributed to Snorre Sturleson, who wrote a commentary on the first edda.

Edenhall, The Luck of. A painted goblet in the possession of the Musgrave family of Edenhall, Cumberland, said to have been left by the fairies on St. Cuthbert's Well. The tradition runs, that the luck of the family is dependent on the safe-keeping of this goblet. The German poet Uhland embodied the legend in a ballad, translated into English by Longfellow.

Edgar. Son of Gloucester, in Shakespeare's tragedy *King Lear*. He was disinherited for his half brother Edmund.

Edgar or **Edgardo.** Master of Ravenswood, in love with Lucy Ashton in Scott's *Bride of Lammermoor*.

Edith. The "Maid of Lorn" in Scott's *Lord of the Isles*, who married Ronald when peace was restored after the battle of Bannockburn.

Edith Granger. Dombey and Son, Dickens. Daughter of the Hon. Mrs. Skewton, married to Colonel Granger of "Ours," who died within two years. Edith became Mr. Dombey's second wife, but the marriage was altogether unhappy.

Edith, The Lady. Ivanhoe, Scott. Mother of Athelstane "the Unready," thane of Coningsburgh.

Edith Plantagenet (plăn-tăj'ê-nĕt), **The Lady. The Talisman, Scott.** Called "The Fair Maid of Anjou," a kinswoman of Richard I, and attendant on Queen Berengaria.

Edmund. A bastard son of Gloucester in Shakespeare's tragedy *King Lear.*

Edward. Count Robert of Paris, Scott. Brother of Hereward, the Varangian guard. He was slain in battle.

Edward, Sir. The Iron Chest, Colman. He commits a murder, and keeps a narrative of the transaction in an iron chest. Later, he trusts the secret to his secretary, Wilfred, and the whole transaction becomes public.

Edwin. (1) The hero of Goldsmith's ballad entitled "The Hermit." (2) The hero of Mallet's ballad "Edwin and Emma." (3) The hero of Beattie's "Minstrel."

Edyrn. Idylls of the King: Enid, Tennyson. Son of Nudd. A suitor for the hand of Enid and an evil genius of her father, who opposed him. Later, Edyrn went to the court of King Arthur and became quite a changed man,—from a malicious "sparrow hawk" he was converted into a courteous gentleman.

Egeus (ê-jē'ŭs). Father of Hermia in Shakespeare's *Midsummer Night's Dream.*

Egil. Brother of Weland, a great archer. The story related is similar to the William Tell story. There are many such stories. One day, King Nidung commanded him to shoot at an apple placed on the head of his own son. Egil selected two arrows, and being asked why he wanted two replied, "One to shoot thee with, O tyrant, if I fail." Such stories, though probably not true to fact, are true to the spirit of patriotism, and are worth repeating.

Eglamour. (1) A character in Shakespeare's *Two Gentlemen of Verona,* who is an agent of Silvia in her escape. (2) A valiant knight of the Round Table, celebrated in the romances of chivalry, and in an old ballad. Written also Eglamore.

Eglantine (ĕg'lăn-tīn), **Madame.** The prioress in Chaucer's *Canterbury Tales,* who was "full pleasant and amiable of port." She was distinguished for the ladylike delicacy of her manners at table, for her partiality to "small hounds," and for a peculiar mixture in her manner and dress of feminine vanity and slight worldliness, together with an ignorance of the world. She is noted for her delicate oath, "by Seint Eloy," her "entuning the service swetely in her nose," and her speaking French "after the scole of Stratford atte Bowe."

Egoist, The. George Meredith. A psychological novel in which the intense egoism of the central figure, Sir Willoughby Patterne of Patterne Hall, is analyzed. The cruelty of such egoism or egotism appears in Willoughby's treatment of Laetitia Dale, daughter of a retired officer living on the Patterne estate. Its comic side is revealed through the conduct of Clara Middleton, daughter of a learned clergyman. After fancying herself in love with Sir Willoughby, she is awakened to a clear understanding of his character and administers severe and appropriate punishment to him.

Egyptian Thief. A personage alluded to by the duke in Shakespeare's *Twelfth Night.* The reference is to the story of Thyamis, a robber chief and native of Memphis.

Eivir. Harold the Dauntless, Scott. A Danish maid who assumes boy's clothing and waits on Harold "the Dauntless" as his page.

Elaine. A mythic lady in the romances of King Arthur's court. She is called "the lily maid of Astolat" in Tennyson's *Idylls of the King.* For love of Sir Lancelot she died, and then according to her request was borne on a barge to the castle of King Arthur, holding a lily in one hand and a letter to Lancelot in the other. Sir Thomas Malory states that Elaine was sister of King Arthur by the same mother. She married Sir Nentres of Carlot and was by King Arthur the mother of Modred.

Elbow. A constable, in Shakespeare's *Measure for Measure,* modest and well-meaning, though of simple mind and the object of wit among those who are wiser but not better.

El Dorado (ĕl dô-rä'dō). Spanish, meaning "the gilded." A name given by the Spaniards to an imaginary country, supposed, in the 16th century, to be situated in the interior of South America, between the rivers Orinoco and Amazon, and abounding in gold and all manner of precious stones. Expeditions were fitted out for the purpose of discovering this fabulous region; and, though all such attempts proved futile, the rumors of its existence continued to be believed

down to the beginning of the 18th century. El Dorado is used proverbially for any ideally rich territory.

Electra. See *Mythology.* The name of this classical figure was used in the title of one of O'Neill's trilogies. The "Electra Complex" is a term of Freudian psychology.

Elfland. The realm ruled over by Oberon, king of Fairies.

Elgitha. Ivanhoe, Scott. A female attendant on the Lady Rowena at Rotherwood.

Elia, Essays of. Elia was an assumed name of Charles Lamb, who so signed a number of articles which he contributed to the London Magazine between 1820 and 1825. These, known as the essays of Elia, constitute the chief foundation of Lamb's fame as a critic and essayist.

Elidure. A legendary king of Britain, fabled to have been advanced to the throne in place of his brother Artegal, or Arthgallo. Returning to the country after a long exile, Artegal accidentally encountered his brother, who received him with open arms, took him home to the palace, and reinstated him in his old position, abdicating the throne himself. Wordsworth has taken the story of these two brothers for the subject of a poem.

Elim. The Messiah, Klopstock. The guardian angel of Libbeus the Apostle. Libbeus, the tenderest and most gentle of the apostles, at the death of Jesus also died from grief.

Elliott, Hobbie. There are seven Elliotts in Scott's *Black Dwarf.* The farmer Elliott himself, whose bride-elect is Grace Armstrong; Mrs. Elliott, Hobbie's grandmother; John and Harry, Hobbie's brothers; Lilias, Jean, and Arnot, Hobbie's sisters.

Elope. Milton gives this name to the dumb serpent which gives no warning of its approach.

Elsie. The daughter of Gottlieb, a farm tenant of Prince Henry of Hoheneck, who offered her life as a substitute for the prince. She was rescued as she was about to make the sacrifice. Longfellow has told this story in "The Golden Legend."

Elsie Venner. The heroine of a novel of the same name by O. W. Holmes. The story tells of the gradual humanizing of a girl whose moral and physical system had been poisoned by a snake bite suffered by her mother before the girl's birth. Love is the correcting force, but the severe struggle results only in Elsie's death.

Elspeth. Scotch, shortened from Elizabeth. (1) A character in Sir Walter Scott's *Antiquary.* (2) An old servant to Dandie Dinmont, in Scott's *Guy Mannering.* (3) The housekeeper in Stevenson's *Weir of Hermiston.*

Elzevir or **Elzevier.** The name of a celebrated family of printers at Amsterdam, Leyden, and other places in Holland, whose beautiful editions were published chiefly between the years 1583 and 1680. These editions are unrivaled for both beauty and correctness. It is said that the Elzevirs generally employed women to correct the press, under the conviction that they would be less likely than men, on their own responsibility, to introduce alterations into the text. They printed in all about 2000 books, of which 968 were in Latin, 44 in Greek, 126 in French, 32 in Flemish, 11 in German, 10 in Italian, and 22 in Oriental languages. Rare editions of the Elzevirs are highly valued by collectors.

Emerald Isle. The author of this epithet was Dr. William Drennan, of Belfast, who died 1820. It occurs in a poem entitled "Erin," of which the fourth stanza runs thus:

"Arm of Erin! prove strong, but be gentle as brave,
And, uplifting to strike, still be ready to save,
Not one feeling of vengeance presume to defile
The cause, or the men of the Emerald Isle."

Emile (ā'mēl'). The hero of Jean Jacques Rousseau's novel of the same name, in which he has depicted his ideal of a perfectly educated young man.

Emilia. (1) The sister-in-law of "Duke Theseus," beloved by the two knights, Palamon and Arcite. (2) A lady attending Hermione in Shakespeare's *Winter's Tale.* (3) Wife of Iago, and waiting woman to Desdemona, in the tragedy *Othello,* a woman of thorough vulgarity and loose principles, united to a high degree of spirit, energetic feeling, strong sense, and low cunning. (4) The sweetheart of Peregrine Pickle in Smollett's novel *The Adventures of Peregrine Pickle.*

Em'ly, Little. David Copperfield, Dickens. Orphan daughter of Tom, the brother-in-law of Dan'el Peggotty, a Yarmouth fisherman, by whom she was brought up, David Copperfield and Em'ly were at one time playfellows. While engaged to Ham Peggotty, Dan'el's nephew, Little

Em'ly runs away with Steerforth, a friend of David's, who was a handsome but unprincipled gentleman. Being subsequently reclaimed, she emigrates to Australia with Dan'el Peggotty and old Mrs. Gummidge.

Empyrean. According to Ptolemy, there are many heavens, the earth being surrounded by the spheres of the planets and fixed stars. The Empyrean is the ultimate and last, the seat of the deity.

Encyclopedists or **Encyclopædists** (ĕn-sī'klŏ-pē'dĭsts). The collaborators in the encyclopedia of Diderot and D'Alembert (1751–65). The Encyclopedists as a body were the exponents of the French skepticism of the 18th century.

Endell, Martha. David Copperfield, Dickens. A poor girl, to whom Em'ly goes when Steerforth deserts her.

Enid. The wife of Geraint, one of the Knights of the Round Table in the legends of King Arthur. The story was elaborated by Tennyson in his *Idylls of the King.* Falsely suspected of infidelity by Geraint, she nevertheless nursed him back to health after he had been desperately wounded in combat. His faith in her restored, he implored and received her forgiveness. In the older legends, Geraint supposed that Enid had lost her love for him because of his indolence at the court, and he therefore set out to win back her love by some brave deed.

Epimenides (ĕp'ĭ-mĕn'ĭ-dēz). A philosopher and poet of Crete, who probably lived in the 6th or 7th century, B. C. He is said to have fallen asleep in a cave, when a boy, and to have remained in that state for 57 years. On waking and going out into the broad daylight, he was greatly perplexed and astonished to find everything around him altered. But what was more wonderful still, during his long period of slumber, his soul, released from its fleshly prison, had been busily engaged in the study of medicine and natural philosophy, and, when it again became incarnated, Epimenides found himself a man of great knowledge and wisdom. Goethe has written a poem on the subject, "Des Epimenides Erwachen." See *Klaus, Peter,* and *Rip Van Winkle.*

Epithalamium (ĕp'ĭ-thȧ-lā'mĭ-ŭm). A species of poem which it was the custom among the Greeks and Romans to sing in chorus near the bridal chamber of a newly-married couple. Anacreon, Stesichorus, and Pindar composed poems of this kind, but only scanty fragments have been preserved. Spenser's "Epithalamium," written on the occasion of his marriage, is one of the finest specimens of this kind of verse.

Eppie. (1) In George Eliot's *Silas Marner,* the child of Godfrey Cass, brought up and adopted by Silas Marner, whose love transformed him from a miser into a tender, loving father. (2) *St. Ronan's Well,* Scott. One of the servants of the Rev. Josiah Cargill. (3) In the same novel is Eppie Anderson, one of the servants at the Mowbray Arms, Old St. Ronan's, kept by Meg Dods.

Erlking. King of the elves, who prepares mischief for children, and even deceives men with his seductions. He is said to haunt the Black Forest. Goethe has a ballad called "The Erlking."

Ermangarde of Baldringham, Lady. The Betrothed, Scott. Aunt of the Lady Eveline Berenger, "the betrothed."

Ermeline. The wife of Reynard, in the tale of *Reynard the Fox.*

Erminia (ĕr-mē'nyȧ). The heroine of Tasso's *Jerusalem Delivered,* who fell in love with Tancred. When the Christian army besieged Jerusalem, she dressed herself in Clorinda's armor to go to Tancred, but, being discovered, fled, and lived awhile with some shepherds on the banks of the Jordan. Meeting with Vafrino, sent as a secret spy by the crusaders, she revealed to him the design against the life of Godfrey, and, returning with him to the Christian camp, found Tancred wounded. She cured his wounds, so that he was able to take part in the last great day of the siege.

Ernest, Duke. A poetical romance by Henry of Veldig (Waldeck), contemporary with Frederick Barbarossa. It is a mixture of Greek and Oriental myths and hero adventures of the crusader.

Error. Faery Queen, Spenser. A monster who lived in a den in "Wandering Wood," and with whom the Red Cross Knight had his first adventure. She had a brood of 1000 young ones of sundry shapes, and these cubs crept into their mother's mouth when alarmed. The knight was nearly killed by the stench which issued from the foul fiend, but he succeeded in "rafting" her head off, whereupon the brood lapped up the blood, and burst with satiety.

Escalus. An ancient and kind-hearted lord, in Shakespeare's *Measure for Measure,* whom Vincentio, the duke

of Vienna, joins with Angelo as his deputy during a pretended absence on a distant journey.

Escanes. A lord of Tyre, in Shakespeare's *Pericles.*

Esmeralda (ĕs'mȧ-rȧl'dä). **Notre Dame de Paris, Victor Hugo.** A beautiful gipsy girl, who, with tambourine and goat, dances in the "place" before Notre Dame.

Esmond (ĕz'mŭnd), **Henry.** A cavalier and a fine-spirited gentleman in the reign of Queen Anne. Hero of Thackeray's novel of the same name.

Estella. The heroine of Dickens's novel *Great Expectations.*

Esther Summerson. Bleak House, Dickens. The unacknowledged daughter of Lady Dedlock. She becomes the notably skillful housekeeper of Bleak House for Mr. Jarndyce and finally marries Allan Woodcourt. Her character is said to have been drawn from life. She is the narrator of a large part of the story.

Estotiland (ĕs-tŏt'ĭ-lănd) or **Estotilandia.** An imaginary region in America, near the Arctic circle, referred to by Milton as "cold Estotiland," and variously fabled to have been discovered by Frisian fishermen in the 14th century, and by a Pole named John Scalve, in 1477.

Ettrick Shepherd, The. He is one of the characters in the *Noctes Ambrosianæ* of Christopher North. Identified as James Hogg, the Scotch poet, who was in early life a shepherd in the parish of Ettrick.

Etzel or **Attila.** King of the Huns, a monarch ruling over three kingdoms and more than thirty principalities; being a widower he married Kriemhild, the widow of Siegfried. In the *Nibelungenlied,* where he is introduced, he is made very insignificant.

Eulalie, Eulalia, St. In the calendar of saints there is a virgin martyr called Eulalie. She was martyred by torture, February 12, 308. Longfellow calls Evangeline the "Sunshine of St. Eulalie."

Eulenspiegel, Till (tĭl oi'lĕn-shpē'gĕl). The hero of a German tale, which relates the pranks and drolleries of a wandering cottager of Brunswick. The name means "owlglass."

Euphrasy. Paradise Lost, Milton. The herb eyebright; so called because it was once supposed to be efficacious in clearing the organs of sight. Hence, the archangel Michael purged the eyes of Adam with it, to enable him to see into the distant future.

Euphues (ū'fū-ēz). The principal character in Lyly's two famous works, entitled *Euphues, or the Anatomy of Wit,* and *Euphues and His England.* These works are remarkable for their pedantic and fantastical style, and for the monstrous and overstrained conceits with which they abound. Euphues is represented as an Athenian gentleman, distinguished for the elegance of his person and the beauty of his wit, and for his amorous temperament and roving disposition. He gained a bosom friend, Philautus, and then robbed him of his lover, Lucilla. The lady is false to both, the friends are reconciled, and Euphues returns to Athens and philosophy. The peculiarities of Lyly's style are a perpetual striving after alliteration and antithesis, and a most ingenious stringing together of similes. This book immediately became the rage in the court circles, and for many years was the court standard. From it we get our word *euphuism,* meaning an affected, bombastic style of language.

Evan Dhu M'Combich. Waverley, Scott. The foster brother of MacIvor.

Evan Dhu of Lochiel (lŏκ-ēl'). **Legend of Montrose, Scott.** A Highland chief in the army of Montrose.

Evangeline. The heroine of Longfellow's poem. The subject of the tale is the expulsion of the inhabitants of Acadia (Nova Scotia) from their homes by order of George II, and the lifelong wanderings of Evangeline in search of her lover, Gabriel. It is a story of a woman's love and devotion.

Evangelist. In Bunyan's *Pilgrim's Progress,* he represents the effectual preacher of the Gospel, who opens the gate of life to Christian.

Evelina. The heroine in a novel of the same name, by Miss Burney.

Eve of St. Agnes, The, Keats. The Lady Madeline, on St. Agnes's Eve, goes supperless to bed, trying the old superstition that thus a maid might see her future husband on awaking. An old servant admits Porphyro, Madeline's lover, to her chamber. After arranging a dessert by her bed, he wakens her with a favorite air, and persuades her to leave the castle with him while the festivities are going on in the great hall.

Every Man in His Humor. A comedy by Ben Jonson. Every person in the play is liable to be duped by his special humor: Captain Bobadil's humor is bragging; Kitelly's is jealousy; Stephen's is stupidity; Knowell's is suspicion; Dame Kitelly's, like her husband's, is jealousy.

Evir-Allen. Fingal, Ossian. The white-armed daughter of Branno, an Irishman. "A thousand heroes sought the maid; she refused her love to a thousand. The sons of the sword were despised, for graceful in her eyes was Ossian."

Excalibur. Meaning of the words: "liberated from the stone." The name of Arthur's far-famed sword, which he unfixed from a miraculous stone, though previously two hundred and one of the most puissant barons in the realm had singly been unable to extract it. In consequence of this remarkable feat, Arthur was chosen and proclaimed king by general acclamation. When about to die, he sent an attendant to throw the weapon into a lake hard by. Twice eluding the request, the squire at last complied. A hand and arm arose from the water, caught the sword by the hilt, flourished it thrice, and then sank into the lake and was seen no more. Written also Excalibor, Escalibar, Escalibor, and Caliburn.

Eyre (âr), **Jane.** The heroine of Charlotte Brontë's novel of the same name, a governess in the family of a Mr. Rochester, to whom she is finally married.

Ezzelin, Sir. Lara, Byron (1814). The gentleman who recognizes Lara at the table of Lord Otho, and charges him with being Conrad the Corsair. A duel ensues, and Ezzelin is never heard of more. A serf used to say that he saw a huntsman one evening cast a dead body into the river which divided the lands of Otho and Lara, and that there was a star of knighthood on the breast of the corpse.

Faa, Gabriel. Guy Mannering, Scott. Nephew of Meg Merrilies. One of the huntsmen at Liddesdale.

Fabliaux (fä'blē'ōz'). The metrical fables of the trouvères, or early poets north of the Loire, in the 12th and the 13th century. The word fable, in this case, is used very widely, for it includes not only such tales as *Reynard the Fox*, but all sorts of familiar incidents of knavery and intrigue, as well as legends and family traditions. The fabliau *Aucassin and Nicolette* is full of interesting incidents and contains much true pathos and beautiful poetry.

Fada. A fee or kobold of the south of France, sometimes called "Hada." These house spirits, of which, strictly speaking, there are but three, bring good luck in their right hand and ill luck in their left.

Fadladeen. The hypercritical grand chamberlain in Thomas Moore's poem *Lalla Rookh*. Fadladeen's criticism upon the several tales which make up the romance are very racy and full of humor; and his crestfallen conceit when he finds out that the poet was the prince in disguise is well conceived.

Faery or **Fairy Land.** The land of the fays or fairies. The chief fay realms are Avalon, an island somewhere in the ocean, Oberon's dominions, situated "in wilderness, among the holtis hairy," and a realm somewhere in the middle of the earth, where was Pari Banou's palace.

Faery Queen. A metrical romance, in six books of twelve cantos each, by Edmund Spenser. The hero, Prince Arthur, arriving at the court of Gloriana, the queen in Faeryland, finds her holding a solemn festival during twelve days. At the court there is a beautiful lady, for whose hand twelve most distinguished knights are rivals, and in order to settle their pretensions these twelve heroes undertake twelve separate adventures. The first book contains the legend of the Red Cross Knight, who is the allegorical representative of "holiness," while his mistress Una represents true "religion"; and the action of the knight's exploit shadows forth the triumph of holiness over the enchantments and deceptions of heresy. The second book is the legend of Sir Guyon. The third book is the legend of Britomartis—a female champion—or "chastity." Britomartis is Diana, or Queen Elizabeth the Britoness. The fourth book is the legend of Cambel and Triamond (fidelity). The fifth book is the legend of Artegal (justice). The sixth book is the legend of Sir Calidore (courtesy). The remaining books were never completed. The plan of the *Faery Queen* is borrowed from the *Orlando Furioso*, but Spenser's creative power is more original, and his imagery more striking, than Ariosto's.

Fag. A lying servant to Captain Absolute in Sheridan's *Rivals*.

Fagin. An old Jew in Dickens's *Oliver Twist*, who employs young persons of both sexes to carry on a systematic trade of robbery.

Fainall, Mr. and Mrs. Noted characters in Congreve's comedy *The Way of the World*.

Fainéant, Le Noir (lĕ nwär' fā'nā'äⁿ'), "The Black Idler." In Sir Walter Scott's *Ivanhoe*, a name applied to Richard Cœur de Lion, in disguise, by the spectators of a tournament, on account of his indifference during a great part of the action, in which, however, he was finally victorious.

Fairies. Fairy lore of the nursery grows out of belief in unseen powers of good and of evil. Good fairies are called fairies, elves, elle-folks, and fays; the evil ones are urchins, ouphes, ell-maids, and ell-women.

Fair Maid of Perth. The title of a novel by Sir Walter Scott, and the name of the heroine.

Fairservice, Andrew. A shrewd Scotch gardener at Osbaldistone Hall in *Rob Roy*, by Sir Walter Scott.

Fairy of the Mine. A malevolent being supposed to live in mines, busying itself with cutting ore, turning the windlass, etc., and yet effecting nothing.

Faithful. One of the allegorical personages in Bunyan's *Pilgrim's Progress*, who dies a martyr before completing his journey.

Faithful, Jacob. The title and hero of a sea tale, by Captain Marryat.

Faith Healer, The, William Vaughn Moody. A play. In a farmhouse in the Middle West live Matthew Beeler, his invalid wife Mary, who has not walked for several years, Annie, their little daughter, Martha, sister of Matthew, and Rhoda Williams, a niece. Ulrich Michaelis, a spiritual healer, has come as a lodger to the farm. The time is just before Easter. Under his treatment, Mrs. Beeler walks. Then Michaelis falls in love with Rhoda, and, since he believes earthly love inconsistent with his mission, his power fails for a time. But, when he sees that his love for Rhoda and hers for him are good, his power of healing returns in even greater effectiveness than before.

Fakenham Ghost. A ballad by Robert Bloomfield, author of "The Farmer's Boy." The ghost was a donkey.

Fakreddin's Valley. Over the several portals of bronze were these inscriptions: (1) "The Asylum of Pilgrims"; (2) "The Traveler's Refuge"; (3) "The Depository of the Secrets of All the World."

Falkland. In Godwin's novel called *Caleb Williams*. He commits murder, and keeps a narrative of the transaction in an iron chest. Williams, a lad in his employ, opens the c est, and is caught in the act by Falkland. The lad runs away, but is hunted down. This tale, dramatized by Colman, is entitled *The Iron Chest*.

Falstaff (fôl'stäf), **Sir John.** A famous character in Shakespeare's comedy *Merry Wives of Windsor*, and in the first and second parts of his historical drama *Henry IV*. He is as perfect a comic portrait as was ever sketched. In the former play, he is represented as in love with Mrs. Ford and Mrs. Page, who make a butt and a dupe of him; in the latter, he figures as a soldier and a wit; in both he is exhibited as a monster of fat,—sensual, mendacious, boastful, and cowardly. In *Henry V* his death is decribed by Mrs. Quickly.

Fang. (1) A sheriff's officer, in the second part of Shakespeare's *King Henry IV*. (2) Dickens's *Oliver Twist*. A bullying, insolent magistrate, who would have sent Oliver Twist to prison, on suspicion of theft, if Mr. Brownlow had not interposed.

Fata Alcina (fä'tä äl-chē'nä). **Orlando Innamorato, Boiardo.** Sister of Fata Morgana. She carried off Astolfo on the back of a whale to her isle, but turned him into a myrtle tree when she tired of him.

Fata Morgana (fä'tä môr-gä'nä). The name of a potent fairy, celebrated in the tales of chivalry and in the romantic poems of Italy. She was a pupil of the enchanter Merlin, and the sister of Arthur, to whom she discovered the intrigue of his queen, Geneura, or Guinever, with Lancelot of the Lake. In the *Orlando Innamorato* of Boiardo, she appears at first as a personification of Fortune, inhabiting a splendid residence at the bottom of a lake, and dispensing all the treasures of the earth, but she is afterward found in her proper station subject to the all potent Demogorgon.

Fat Boy, The. A laughable character in Dickens's *Pickwick Papers*; a youth of astonishing obesity, whose employment consists in alternate eating and sleeping.

Father, The, Strindberg. A drama exploiting the conflict between the sexes. A cavalry captain, intensely interested in science, and his wife, outwardly a pious churchwoman, are divided over the kind of education their daughter Bertha shall have. To gain her end, the control of the daughter, the wife Laura sows in her husband's mind a suspicion that Bertha is not his child. She has already intercepted the captain's letters so that he is robbed of the fruits of his scientific studies. Then she so plays upon his violent temper and his fear of becoming insane that he falls ill and dies. The woman has demonstrated, to her own satisfaction, her superiority and has won control of her daughter.

Father Brown, The Innocence of, G. K. Chesterton. Father Brown is the hero of an interesting series of detective stories. He attains results through his unusual insight into the workings of the ordinary mind.

Fathom, Ferdinand, Count. The title of a novel by Smollett, and the name of its principal character, a complete villain, who proceeds step by step to rob his benefactors and finally dies in misery and despair.

Fatima (făt'ĭ-mà). (1) An enchantress, in the story of Aladdin, in the *Arabian Nights' Entertainments*. (2) The last of the wives of Bluebeard, and the only one who escaped being murdered by him. (3) The favorite daughter of Mohammed.

Faust. The hero and title of a celebrated tragedy by Goethe, the materials of which are drawn in part from the popular legends of Dr. Faustus, a famous magician of the 16th century. Faust is a student who is toiling after knowledge beyond his reach, and who afterwards deserts his studies and makes a pact with the Devil, Mephistopheles, in pursuance of which he gives himself up to the full enjoyment of the senses, until the hour of his doom arrives, when Mephistopheles reappears upon the scene, and carries off his victim as a condemned soul. This mythical personage dates back to the time of the Reformation.

Faustus. The hero of Marlowe's tragedy of the same name; represented as a vulgar sorcerer tempted to sell his soul to the Devil, Mephistopheles, on condition of having a familiar spirit at his command for 24 years, the possession of earthly power and glory, and unlimited gratification of his sensual appetites. At the end of that time, when the forfeit comes to be exacted, he shrinks and shudders in agony and remorse, imploring yet despairing of the mercy of heaven. This has been the theme of many writers. It is the subject of an opera by Gounod.

Feeble. In Shakespeare's *Henry IV*, a starveling tailor, whom Falstaff calls "most forcible Feeble."

Felton, Septimius. Septimius Felton is the mystical hero in Hawthorne's novel of the same name.

Femmes Savantes, Les (lā fàm sá'väNt'), "The Learned Ladies," **Molière.** This comedy is a satire upon women who pretend to literature and learning. The plot concerns the plans of Philaminte for the marriage of her daughter Henriette. She wishes her to marry Trissotin, but Henriette loves Clitandre. In the end, when Henriette's father is nearly bankrupt, Trissotin loses interest in the match, and the lovers are wedded. The "learned ladies" are Philaminte and her friends, Armande and Bélise.

Fenella. A fairylike creature, a deaf and dumb attendant on the countess of Derby, in Sir Walter Scott's *Peveril of the Peak*.

Fenton. A character in Shakespeare's *Merry Wives of Windsor*, who woos the rich Anne Page for her money, but soon discovers treasures of character in her which quite transform him.

Feramorz (fĕr'à-mōrz). **Lalla Rookh, Thomas Moore.** Feramorz in *Lalla Rookh* is the young Cashmerian poet, who relates poetical tales to Lalla Rookh, in her journey from Delhi to Lesser Bucharia. Lalla Rookh is going to be married to the young sultan, but falls in love with the poet. On the wedding morn she is led to her future husband, and finds that the poet is the sultan himself, who had gallantly taken this course to win the heart of his bride and beguile her journey.

Ferdinand. (1) A character in Shakespeare's *Tempest*. He is a son of the king of Naples, and falls in love with Miranda, the daughter of Prospero, a banished duke of Milan. (2) King of Navarre, a character in *Love's Labor's Lost*.

Ferrars. Endymion, Benjamin Disraeli. The story tells of the progress of the colorless hero who, by the aid of his wife and sister, rises to the position of prime minister.

Ferrex and Porrex. Two sons of Gorboduc, a mythical British king. Porrex drove his brother from Britain, and when Ferrex returned with an army he was slain, but Porrex was shortly after put to death by his mother. The first tragedy in the English language was *Gorboduc*, or *Ferrex and Porrex*, by Thomas Norton and Thomas Sackville.

Fib. Nymphidia, Drayton. One of the fairy attendants of Queen Mab.

Fidele (fĭ-dē'lĕ). **Cymbeline, Shakespeare.** (1) The name assumed by Imogen, when, attired in boy's clothes, she started for Milford Haven to meet her husband, Posthumus. (2) Subject of an elegy by Collins.

Fidelio (fē-dā'lĭ-ō). In Beethoven's opera of the name, the heroine Leonore, disguised as a man under the name of Fidelio, serves the jailor of the prison in which her lover Florestan, is confined. She is thus enabled to save him.

Fidessa. Faery Queen, Spenser. The companion of Sansfoy; but, when the Red Cross Knight slew that "faithless Saracen," Fidessa turned out to be Duessa, the daughter of Falsehood and Shame. See *Duessa*.

Fine-ear. Fairy Tales (Fortunio), Countess d'Aulnoy. One of the seven attendants of Fortunio. He could hear the growing of the grass and of the wool on a sheep's back. This is an old, old story. It is also found in Grimm's *Fairy Tales*. There the heroine is Fortunio. In the German tale *Fortunio*, the fairy gives her a horse named Comrade, not only of incredible swiftness, but all-knowing, and endowed with human speech; she also gives her an inexhaustible turkey-leather trunk, full of money, jewels, and fine clothes. By the advice of Comrade, she hires seven gifted servants, named Strongback, Lightfoot, Marksman, Fine-ear, Boisterer, Tippler, and Gormand. Fortunio goes forth disguised as a warrior, meets her king, and marries him.

Finetta, The Cinder Girl. A fairy tale by the Countess d'Aulnoy. This is merely the old tale of Cinderella slightly altered.

Fingal. A mythical hero, whose name occurs in Gaelic ballads and traditions, and in Macpherson's *Poems of Ossian*.

Finn, Huckleberry. The hero of Mark Twain's biographical story of boyhood adventures on the Mississippi river. Huck Finn first appeared in *The Adventures of Tom Sawyer* (1876) and came into fuller view in the sequel, *The Adventures of Huckleberry Finn* (1885).

Fires of St. John. A representative play of the school to which Sudermann belongs. The whole group of plays of which *The Fires of St. John* is a type reflect a revolt against the conventionalities of life in Germany, as Ibsen's dramas express the revolt in Northern Europe.

Firmin, Philip. The hero of Thackeray's novel *The Adventures of Philip*.

Fleance. A son of Banquo, in Shakespeare's tragedy *Macbeth*. The legend relates that after the assassination of his father he escaped to Wales, where he married the daughter of the reigning prince, and had a son named Walter. This Walter afterwards became lord high steward of Scotland, and called himself Walter the Steward. From him proceeded in a direct line the Stuarts of Scotland, a royal line which gave James VI of Scotland, James I of England. This is myth.

Fledgeby. Our Mutual Friend, Dickens. An overreaching, cowardly sneak who pretends to do a decent business under the trade name of Pubsey and Co.

Fleet Street. Formerly called Fleet Bridge street. A London street running from Ludgate Hill to the east end of the Strand. It is named from the Fleet river. In the early chronicles of London many allusions are made to the deeds of violence done in this street. By the time of Elizabeth the street had become a favorite spot for shows and processions of all descriptions. It was noted formerly for its taverns and coffeehouses, frequented by many persons of literary fame. Among these were Ben Jonson, later, Goldsmith, Doctor Samuel Johnson, and Charles Lamb. It is now the chief center of British journalism.

Flite, Miss. Bleak House, Dickens. The poor little old woman who haunts the Chancery Court in hope of a judgment in her favor, and becomes insane from long waiting.

Florentius (flô-rĕn'shĭ-ŭs). A knight whose story is related in the first book of Gower's *Confessio Amantis*. He bound himself to marry a deformed hag, provided she taught him the solution of a riddle on which his life depended.

Florian. The Foundling of the Forest, W. Dimond. Discovered in infancy by Count de Valmont, and adopted as his own son. Florian was light-hearted and volatile, but with deep affection, very brave, and was liked by all.

Florimel. A female character in Spenser's *Faery Queen*, of great beauty, but so timid that she feared the "smallest monstrous mouse that creeps on floor," and was abused by every one. She was noted for sweetness of temper amid great trials. The word Florimel signifies "honey flower."

Florizel. (1) A prince of Bohemia, in Shakespeare's *Winter's Tale*, in love with Perdita. (2) Character in Stevenson's *New Arabian Nights*.

Fluellen. A Welsh captain, who is an amusing pedant, in Shakespeare's *Henry V*.

Flying Dutchman. A spectral ship, seen in stormy weather off the Cape of Good Hope, and considered ominous of ill luck. Captain Marryat has taken this theme for his novel *The Phantom Ship*.

Fogg, Phileas. The principal character in Jules Verne's novel *Around the World in 80 Days*.

Folk, Good. Fairies, also called good people, neighbors, wights. The Germans have their *kleine volk*, "little folk," the Swiss their hill people and earth people. See *Fairies*.

Ford. Mr. and Mrs. Ford are characters in *The Merry Wives of Windsor*. Mrs. Ford pretends to accept Sir John Falstaff's protestations of love, in order to punish him by her devices.

Forsyte. In his novel, *The Forsyte Saga*, and in the trilogy that succeeded it, John Galsworthy has presented a complete picture of a middle-class English family. Through his fiction the name "Forsyte" has become an inclusive term for the English property-owning class in the first quarter of the Twentieth Century.

Fortinbras (*fôr′tĭn-brăs*). Prince of Norway, in Shakespeare's tragedy *Hamlet*.

Fortunatus. You have found Fortunatus' purse. You are in luck's way. The nursery tale of Fortunatus records that he had an inexhaustible purse. It is from the Italian fairy tales.

Fortunio's Horse. Comrade not only possessed incredible speed, but knew all things and was gifted with human speech. See *Fine-ear*.

Forty Thieves. In the tale of Ali Baba in *Arabian Nights' Entertainments*. Represented as inhabiting a secret cave in a forest, the door of which would open and shut only at the sound of the magic word "Sesame," the name of a kind of grain. One day, Ali Baba, a woodmonger, accidentally discovered the secret, and made himself rich by carrying off gold from the stolen hoards. The captain tried several schemes to discover the thief, but was always outwitted by Morgiana, the woodcutter's female slave.

Four Horsemen of the Apocalypse, The, Blasco Ibáñez. A story of the German invasion of France in 1914. In the panorama presented, a wealthy Argentinian settled in France, with a passion for "collecting," is the central figure. His family are connected with German families by marriage, and this circumstance complicates the story. The family represent the country of France under the scourge of the four horsemen, War, Famine, Pestilence, and Death.

Four Million, The. The title of a volume of short stories by O. Henry. The stories reflect the common life of the people in the great city of New York.

Frankenstein. The hero in Mrs. Shelley's romance of the same name. As a young student of physiology he constructs a monster out of the horrid remnants of the churchyard and dissecting-room, and endues it, apparently through the agency of galvanism, with a sort of spectral and convulsive life. This existence, rendered insupportable to the monster by his vain craving after human sympathy, and by his consciousness of his own deformity, is employed in inflicting the most dreadful retribution upon the guilty philosopher. It is a parody on the creature man, powerful for evil, and the instrument of dreadful retribution on the student, who usurped the prerogative of the Creator.

Freeport, Sir Andrew. The name of one of the members of the imaginary club under whose direction the *Spectator* was professedly published. He is represented as a London merchant of great eminence and experience, industrious, sensible, and generous.

Freud, Freudian. Sigmund Freud (1856–1939), the Viennese psychologist who founded psychoanalysis, is responsible for a new approach to the study of human behavior. Such terms as "inferiority complex," "suppressed desires," and other Freudian expressions have become a familiar part of the average person's vocabulary.

Friar Lawrence. The Franciscan monk who attempted to befriend the lovers in *Romeo and Juliet*.

Friar's Tale, The. Canterbury Tales, Chaucer. An archdeacon employed a summoner as his secret spy to find out offenders, with the view of exacting fines from them. In order to accomplish this more effectually, the summoner entered into a compact with the Devil, disguised as a yeoman. Those who imprecated the Devil were to be dealt with by the yeoman-devil, and those who imprecated God were to be the summoner's share.

Friar Tuck. Chaplain and steward of Robin Hood. Introduced by Scott in *Ivanhoe*. He is a self-indulgent, combative Falstaff, a jolly companion to the outlaws in Sherwood Forest. Also in *Sherwood*, by Alfred Noyes.

Friday. Robinson Crusoe's faithful man Friday pictured by De Foe.

Frollo, Archdeacon Claude. A noted character in Victor Hugo's *Notre Dame de Paris*, absorbed in a bewildering search after the philosopher's stone.

Front de Bœuf (*frôn′ dĕ bĕf′*). **Ivanhoe, Scott.** A follower of Prince John of Anjou, and one of the knight's challengers.

Froth, Master. A foolish gentleman in Shakespeare's *Measure for Measure*. His name explains his character.

Fudge Family. A name under which the poet Moore satirized the absurdities of his traveling countrymen, who, having been long confined at home by the wars waged by Napoleon, flocked to the continent after his defeat at Waterloo. The family is composed of a hack writer and spy, his son, a young dandy of the first water, his daughter, a sentimental damsel, and Madame Le Roy, in love with a Parisian linen draper, whom she has mistaken for one of the Bourbons in disguise. The tutor, a "poor relation" of this egregious family, is an ardent Bonapartist and Irish patriot.

Fusbos. In "Bombastes Furioso," the minister of state to the king of Utopia. This was a burlesque opera by W. B. Rhodes.

Fuzzy-Wuzzy. The name applied by Kipling to the Sudanese native in a ballad of the same name. The "big, black, boundin' beggar" that "broke the British square."

Fyrapel, Sir. The leopard, the nearest kinsman of King Lion, in the beast epic of *Reynard the Fox*.

Gabriel. The name of an angel described in the Scriptures as charged with the ministration of comfort and sympathy to man. In the New Testament, he is the herald of good tidings, declaring the coming of the predicted Messiah and of his forerunner. In Jewish and Christian tradition he is one of the seven archangels. Gabriel has the reputation, among the rabbis, of being a distinguished linguist, having taught Joseph the 70 languages spoken at Babel. The Mohammedans hold him in even greater reverence than the Jews. He is called the spirit of truth, and is believed to have dictated the *Koran* to Mohammed. Milton posts him at "the eastern gate of paradise," as "chief of the angelic guards," keeping watch there. The *Talmud* describes him as the prince of fire, and as the spirit who presides over thunder.

Gadshill. A companion of Sir John Falstaff, in the First Part of Shakespeare's *King Henry IV*.

Galahad, Sir. A celebrated knight of the Round Table who achieved the quest of the Holy Grail. Tennyson has made him the subject of one of his idylls. In Malory he is also represented as the perfect knight clad in wonderful armor. He was the only knight who could sit in the "siege perilous," a seat reserved for the "knight without a flaw."

Galapas. A giant of marvelous height in the army of Lucius, king of Rome. He was slain by King Arthur.

Galaphrone or **Galafron.** A king of Cathay and father of Angelica in Boiardo's *Orlando Innamorato* and Ariosto's *Orlando Furioso*.

Galatea, Galathea (*găl′à-tē′à*). The Greek legend is of an artist, Pygmalion, who carved a figure, Galatea, so beautiful that he fell overwhelmingly in love with his own creation; his own passion wakens the statue to life. The story has been frequently used in literature. Shaw's *Pygmalion* is a modern modification of the theme.

Gamp, Mrs. A nurse who is a prominent character in Dickens's novel *Martin Chuzzlewit*. She is celebrated for her constant reference to a certain Mrs. Harris, a purely imaginary person, for whose feigned opinions and utterances she professes the greatest respect, in order to give the more weight to her own.

Gandercleugh (*găn′dẽr-klŭк*), "Folly-cliff." That mysterious place where a person makes a goose of himself, in *Tales of My Landlord*, by Sir Walter Scott.

Ganelon, Gan, or **Gano.** A count of Mayence, and one of the paladins of Charlemagne, whom he betrayed at the battle of Roncesvalles; always represented as a traitor, engaged in intrigues for the destruction of Christianity. His character was marked by spite, dissimulation, and intrigue, but he was patient, obstinate, and enduring. He loved solitude, disbelieved in the existence of moral good, and has become a byword for a false and faithless friend. He figures in the romantic poems of Italy, and is placed by Dante in his "Inferno." He is introduced into Chaucer's "Nun's Priest's Tale."

Gareth (*găr′ĕth*). In Arthurian romance a knight of the Round Table, who was first a scullion in King Arthur's kitchen, but afterward became champion of Lady Linet, or Lynette, whose sister Lionês, or Lyonors, he delivered from Castle Perilous.

Gargamelle (*găr′gà′mĕl′*). The mother of Gargantua in Rabelais' celebrated romance, *Gargantua*.

Gargantua (*găr-găn′tû-à*). The hero of Rabelais' celebrated romance of the same name, a gigantic personage, about whom many wonderful stories are related. He lived for several centuries, and at last begot a son, Pantagruel, as wonderful as himself. The *Pleasant Story of the Giant Gargantua and of his Son Pantagruel* so satirized the monastic orders of his time that it was denounced by the spiritual authorities. Francis I, however, protected the author, and allowed him to print the third part of it in 1545.

Gargery, Mrs. Joe. Great Expectations, Dickens. Pip's sister. A virago, who kept her husband and Pip in constant awe. Joe Gargery, a blacksmith, married to Pip's sister. A noble-hearted, simple-minded young man, who loved Pip sincerely. Joe Gargery was one of nature's gentlemen.

Gaspar or **Caspar.** The white one, one of the three Magi or kings of Cologne. His offering to the infant Jesus was frankincense, in token of divinity.

Gaunt, Griffith. Hero of a novel by Charles Reade, of the same title.

Gawain (*gô'wân*), **Sir.** A nephew of King Arthur, and one of the most celebrated knights of the Round Table; noted for his sagacity and wonderful strength. He was surnamed "the courteous." His brothers were Agravaine, Gaheris, and Gareth.

Gebir (*jē'bēr*). A legendary Eastern prince, said to have invaded Africa and to have given his name to Gibraltar. He is the subject of a poem of the same name by Walter Savage Landor.

Gellatley, Davie. The name of a poor fool in Sir Walter Scott's novel *Waverley*.

Genevieve. (1) The heroine of a ballad by Coleridge. (2) Under the form "Genoveva," the name occurs in a German myth as that of the wife of the Count Palatine Siegfried, in the time of Charles Martel. Upon false accusations her husband gave orders to put her to death, but the servant intrusted with the commission suffered her to escape into the forest of Ardennes, where she lay concealed, until by accident her husband discovered her retreat and recognized her innocence. This legend is often repeated in the folk tales of Germany. Tieck and Miller have given it in modern versions.

Genevra. A lady in Ariosto's *Orlando Furioso*. Her honor is impeached, and she is condemned to die unless a champion appears to do combat for her. Her lover, Ariodantes, answers the challenge, kills the false accuser, and weds the dame. Spenser has a similar story in the *Faery Queen*, and Shakespeare availed himself of the main incident in his comedy *Much Ado about Nothing*. From Italian romances "Genevra" has been taken as subject of "The Mistletoe Bough," by T. Haynes Bayly, and as both title and subject of a metrical tale by Samuel Rogers, in which he tells of a young Italian, who, upon her wedding day, secreted herself, from motives of frolic, in a self-locking oaken chest, the lid of which shut down and held her captive. Many years afterward the chest was opened and the skeleton was revealed.

Genius (*jē'nĭ-ŭs*) pl. genii. Tutelary spirits believed by the Romans to attend each individual from the cradle to the grave, determining his character and governing his fortunes. They were two in number for each person, a "good genius" bringing good fortune and an "evil genius" being responsible for his ill luck. In some translations of *The Thousand and One Nights* the word genius is used for Jinn, a fallen angel under the dominion of Eblis, the Evil One.

Georgics (*jôr'jĭks*). Bucolic poetical compositions, treating of farm-husbandry and the tillage of the soil. The most famous examples of the kind are those by Virgil, 31 B. C., in four books.

Geraint (*gĕ-rānt'*), **Sir.** One of the knights of the Round Table. His story is told in Tennyson's *Idylls of the King* under "Geraint and Enid."

Geraldine. A name frequently found in romantic poetry. The name is said to have been adopted from the heroine, connected with Surrey, whose praises he celebrates in a famous sonnet, and who has been the occasion of much controversy among his biographers and critics. There is no doubt that the lady called Geraldine was an Irish lady named Elizabeth Fitzgerald, the daughter of Gerald Fitzgerald. This sonnet led to the adoption of the name into the class of romantic names. Used by Mrs. Browning in "Lady Geraldine's Courtship."

Gertrude of Wyoming. Heroine of a poem by Thomas Campbell, which tells the story of the Indian massacre of Americans in the Wyoming valley of Pennsylvania in 1778.

Gesta Romanorum (*jĕs'tà rō'mà-nō'rŭm*). A collection of old romances and tales, mostly from Roman sources, which has been the storehouse for our best story-writers. Shakespeare, Spenser, Gower, and many later writers have gone to this source. Compiled probably about the close of the 13th century. Moralizing paragraphs and other re-

ligious and mystical tales are said to have been added by Pierre Bercaire, a Benedictine prior of Poitou.

Giaour (*jour*). Byron's tale called "The Giaour" is represented as told by a Turkish fisherman, who had committed a crime which haunted him all his life. *Giaour* means "unbeliever." See *Hassan*.

Gibbie, Goose. A half-witted boy in Scott's *Old Mortality*.

Gibbie, Sir. A simple-hearted, fine character in George Macdonald's novel of the same name.

Gift of the Magi, O. Henry (W. S. Porter). The title of one of O. Henry's most successful and typical stories. A young husband and wife, living in a little New York flat, with little to spend, plan each to give the other a perfect Christmas gift. They have two most treasured possessions,—a watch, inherited from his grandfather, and her long, beautiful hair. The husband covets a fob, the wife a set of combs. Christmas Eve, pawning the watch to buy the combs, he comes home to find that she has cut off and sold her hair to buy him a fob.

Gil Blas (*zhēl bläs*). The title of a famous romance by Lesage, and the name of its hero. The tale is full of adventures, and Gil Blas is represented as squire to a lady and as brought up by his uncle, Canon Gil Peres. Gil Blas went to Dr. Godinez's school of Oviedo and gained the name of being a great scholar. He had fair abilities, wit and humor, and good inclinations, but was easily led astray by his vanity and became lax in his morals. Duped at first, he afterwards played the same devices on others. As he grew in years, his conduct improved, and when his fortune was made he became an honest man.

Gilgamesh (*gĭl'gà-mĕsh*). The hero of an ancient Babylonian epic, who searches for the secret of immortality. He fails in his search, receiving, at the end, only some vague information about the abode of the shades.

Gilpin, John. A citizen of London, and "a trainband captain," whose adventures are related in Cowper's humorous poem, "John Gilpin's Ride." After being married twenty years his wife proposed a holiday. They agreed to make a family party and dine at the Bell, at Edmonton. Mrs. Gilpin, her sister, and four children went in the chaise, and Gilpin promised to follow on horseback. The horse, being fresh, began to trot, and then to gallop, and John, a bad rider, grasped the mane with both his hands. On went the horse, off flew John Gilpin's cloak, together with his hat and wig. He flew through Edmonton, and never stopped till he reached Ware, when his friend the calender furnished him with another hat and wig, and Gilpin galloped back again, till the horse stopped at his house in London.

Glastonbury (*glàs'tŭn-bēr-ĭ*). A town in Somerset, England, 21 miles south of Bristol. Its abbey, founded in Roman times, was refounded under Ine in the 8th century. Glastonbury is associated in legend with Joseph of Arimathea, who is said to have visited it, and, in sign of possession, to have planted his staff, which took root and became the famous Glastonbury thorn that is reputed to burst into leaf on Christmas Eve. The Isle of Avalon, to which King Arthur was taken, is supposed to have been here.

Gloriana (*glō'rĭ-ā'nà*). In Spenser's *Faery Queen*, the "greatest glorious queen of Faeryland."

Gloss. In biblical criticism, an explanation of purely verbal difficulties of the text, to the exclusion of those which arise from doctrinal, historical, ritual, or ceremonial sources. These explanations were frequently inserted between the lines of the text, or in the margins; and many modern critics of the Bible explain certain passages there as due to "glosses." From an early period, these verbal difficulties were the object of attention, and the writers who devoted themselves to the elucidation were called "glossatores," and their works "glossaria."

Glumdalca. Tom Thumb the Great, Fielding. Queen of the giants, captive in the court of King Arthur.

Glumms. Peter Wilkins, Robert Paltock. The male population of the imaginary country Nosmnbdsgrsutt, visited by Peter Wilkins. Both males and females had wings which served both for flying and for clothes.

Gnome (*nōm*). (1) A pithy and sententious saying commonly in verse, embodying some moral sentiment or precept. The gnome belongs to the same generic class with the proverb; but it differs from a proverb in wanting the common and popular acceptance. The use of gnomes prevailed among all the early nations, especially the Orientals, and the literatures of most countries abound with them. In the Bible, the book of Proverbs, part of Ecclesiastes, and still more the apocryphal book of Ecclesiasticus, present numberless illustrations of the highest form of this composition. (2) In ancient times the name gnome represented one of the classes of imaginary beings which are supposed to be the presiding spirits in the mysterious operations of nature in the mineral and vegetable world. They are introduced in Pope's "Rape of the Lock."

Gobbo, Launcelot. A clown in Shakespeare's *Merchant of Venice*. He left the service of Shylock the Jew for that of Bassanio, a Christian. Launcelot Gobbo is one of the famous clowns of Shakespeare. Old Gobbo, his father, was blind.

God Save the King. The national anthem of Great Britain, and formerly that of Prussia and the German states. Its words are apparently imitated from the *Domine Salvum* of the Catholic Church service.

Gold Bug, The. Found in Poe's most successful tale of the same name. Scene laid on Sullivan's island, near Charleston, S. C., and the cipher made to concern Captain Kidd's buried treasure.

Golden Ass. A celebrated romance by Apuleius, a Latin writer of the 2d century. Lucius, the hero, changed by enchantment into an ass, has many adventures and is finally restored to his human form by the priests of Isis. The story of Cupid and Psyche is found in this book. Many modern writers have borrowed from it.

Golden Legend, The. (1) The title of an ecclesiastical work in 177 sections, dating from the 13th century, written by Jacopo da Voragine, a Dominican monk, and descriptive of the various saints' days in the Roman calendar. It is deserving of study as a literary monument of the period, and as illustrating the religious habits and views of the Christians of that time. (2) A poem by Longfellow, second part of his *Christus*.

Gold of Nibelungen, The. Unlucky wealth. "To have the gold of Nibelungen" is to have a possession which seems to bring a curse with it. See *Nibelung, King*.

Goneril (*gŏn'ĕr-ĭl*). The oldest of the three daughters of King Lear, in Shakespeare's tragedy. Having received her moiety of Lear's kingdom, the unnatural daughter first abridged the old man's retinue, then gave him to understand that his company was not wanted and sent him out, a despairing old man, to seek refuge where he could find it. Her name is proverbial for filial ingratitude.

Gonzalo (*gŏn-zä'lō*). An honest old counselor in Shakespeare's *Tempest*, a true friend to Prospero.

Good-natured Man, The, Oliver Goldsmith. The hero of this comedy, Honeywood, tries to order his life on the principle of "universal benevolence," giving indiscriminately and disagreeing with no one. Because he believes his friend Jack Lofty to be in love with Miss Richland, he even abstains from telling her of his own love. His uncle, Sir William Honeywood, and Miss Richland finally cure the young man of his folly.

Goody Two-shoes. The name of a well-known character in a nursery tale by Oliver Goldsmith. Goody Two-shoes was a very poor child, whose delight at having a pair of shoes was unbounded. She called constant attention to her "two shoes" which gave her the name.

Gordian Knot. A great difficulty. Gordius, a peasant, chosen king of Phrygia, dedicated his wagon to Jupiter, and fastened the yoke with a rope so ingeniously that no one could untie it. Alexander was told that "whoever undid the knot would become king," and he cut the knot with his sword.

Gotham (*gŏt'ăm*). At one time the term was applied to a parish of Nottingham, England. The people here were famed for their stupidity and simplicity, which obtained for them the satirical appellation of the "wise men of Gotham." Many nations have designated some particular locality as the paradise of fools; for example, Phrygia was the fools' home in Asia, Abdera of the Thracians, Bœotia of the Greeks, Swabia of the modern Germans, etc. To Americans it is chiefly significant as a colloquial term (pron. *gŏ'thăm*) for the city of New York. Thus applied, it first appeared in *Salmagundi*, by Washington Irving and James K. Paulding, and is supposed to hint sarcastically at the worldly wisdom of its inhabitants.

Gothic Romance. A type of novel made popular by Horace Walpole's "The Castle of Otranto," which had many successors. In such tales suspense is heightened by thrill-producing elements like storms and other terrifying manifestations of nature or perhaps ruined castles visited by moonlight.

Graal, Grail, or Greal (a word derived probably from the old French, through the medieval Latin, *gradalis*, a cup or platter). In the legends and poetry of the Middle Ages, we find accounts of the Holy Graal—San Gréal—a miraculous chalice, made of a single precious stone, sometimes said to be an emerald, which possessed the power of preserving chastity, prolonging life, and other wonderful properties. It is fabled to have been the dish from which Christ ate at the Last Supper and in which Joseph of Arimathea received His blood at the Cross, later preserving

it and carrying it to England. It remained there many years, an object of pilgrimage and devotion, but at length it disappeared, one of its keepers having violated the condition of strict virtue in thought, word, and deed, which was imposed upon those who had charge of it. The quest of this cup forms the most fertile source of adventures to the knights of the Round Table. The story of the Sangreal or Sangraal was first written in verse by Troyes in the 12th century. The legend of the graal was introduced into German poetry in the 13th century by Wolfram von Eschenbach, who filled his *Parzival* with deep allegorical meanings. Malory embodied the story in his *Morte D'Arthur*, and Tennyson told it in his *Idylls of the King*.

Graciosa (*grä'shĭ-ō'sà*). A princess in an old and popular fairy tale,—the object of the ill-will of a stepmother named Grognon, whose malicious designs are perpetually thwarted by Percinet, a fairy prince, who is in love with Graciosa.

Gradgrind. A hardware merchant in Dickens's *Hard Times*. He is a man of hard facts and cultivates the practical. His constant demand in conversation is for "facts." He allows nothing for human weakness, and deals with men and women as a mathematician with figures.

Gradgrind, Mrs. Wife of Thomas Gradgrind. A little thin woman, always taking physic, without receiving from it any benefit.

Grandison, Sir Charles. The hero of Richardson's novel *The History of Sir Charles Grandison*. Designed to represent his ideal of a perfect hero,—a union of the good Christian and the perfect English gentleman.

Gratiano (*grä'shĭ-ä'nō*). A friend to Antonio and Bassanio in Shakespeare's *Merchant of Venice*. He "talks an infinite deal of nothing, more than any man in Venice." (2) Brother to Brabantio, in Shakespeare's tragedy *Othello*. (3) A character in the Italian popular theater called "Commedia del' Arte." He represents a Bolognese doctor, wearing a mask with black nose and forehead and red cheeks.

Gray, Auld Robin. The title of a popular Scotch ballad by Lady Anne Lindsay, and name of its hero. Auld Robin Gray was a good old man married to a poor young girl whose lover was thought to have been lost at sea, but who returns to claim her a month after her marriage.

Great Divide, The, William Vaughn Moody. A three-act play. Ruth Jordan, alone on a ranch in Arizona, is menaced by three men who broke into the house. She promises one of them, Stephen Ghent, to marry him if he will save her from the others. This he does, buying off a Mexican with a chain of gold nuggets. Her New England conscience prevents her going through with the bargain, which she tries to buy her way out of by attempting to redeem the nuggets. She returns to her New England home, burdened with a sense of guilt. Stephen follows her and eventually she goes back West with him.

Great Galeoto (*gä-lā-ō'tō*), **The, José Echegaray.** The title of this tragedy is derived from the saying of Francesca da Rimini in Dante's "Inferno," that Galeoto was the book that prompted her sin and Paolo's. Echegaray makes Galeoto a kind of personification of common gossip. Julian, at first, is deaf to gossip about his young wife, who is thrown daily with Ernest, his secretary and adopted son. He is fatally wounded in a duel over the matter and is borne to Ernest's chamber. Here he finds his wife and dies believing her guilty, although she is innocent. Ernest kills the slayer of Julian, marries Julian's widow, and upbraids the world for its stupid, tragic chatter.

Greatheart, Mr. In Bunyan's *Pilgrim's Progress*, the guide of Christian's wife and children upon their journey to the Celestial City.

Greek Fire. An inflammable liquid first used by the Greeks in defense of Constantinople in 668 A. D. It is believed to have consisted of a mixture of sulphur, naphtha, and quicklime, the last ingredient developing sufficient heat when wet to ignite the other substances.

Greenwich Village. A section of New York city in the vicinity of Washington Square which, during the early decades of the 20th century, became famous as a Bohemian quarter colonized by artists, writers, and advanced thinkers. Among its noted residents were Eugene O'Neill, Edna St. Vincent Millay, Gellett Burgess, Theodore Dreiser, and Floyd Dell.

Gremio. In Shakespeare's *Taming of the Shrew*, an old man who wishes to wed Bianca.

Grendel. Beowulf. The half brute, half man monster from which Beowulf delivered Hrothgar, king of Denmark. Night after night Grendel crept stealthily into the palace called Heorot, and slew sometimes as many as thirty of the inmates. At length Beowulf slew it in single combat.

Gretna Green Marriages. A term for runaway marriages. It alludes to marriages performed at Gretna Green, in Scotland, just across the border from England. Until the law was altered in 1856, the sole requirement for a valid marriage there was a mutual declaration before witnesses of willingness to marry.

Griffin-Feet. Fairy Tales, Countess d'Aulnoy. The mark by which the Desert Fairy was known in all her metamorphoses.

Grim, Giant. A giant, in *Pilgrim's Progress*, who seeks to stop the march of the pilgrims to the Celestial City, but is slain in a duel by Mr. Greatheart, their guide.

Grimalkin (*grĭ-măl'kĭn*). A cat, the spirit of a witch. Any witch was permitted to assume the body of a cat nine times.

Grimwig. Oliver Twist, Dickens. An irascible old gentleman, who hid a very kind heart under a rough exterior. He was always declaring himself ready to "eat his head" if he was mistaken on any point on which he passed an opinion.

Griselda (*grĭ-zĕl'dà*), **The Patient.** A lady in Chaucer's "Clerk of Oxenford's Tale," immortalized by her virtue and her patience. The model of womanly and wifely obedience, she comes victoriously out of cruel and repeated ordeals. The story of Griselda is first told in the *Decameron*. Boccaccio derived the incidents from Petrarch, who seems to have communicated them also to Chaucer, as the latter refers to Petrarch as his authority. The story has been told by many modern writers.

Grub Street. Thus described in Dr. Johnson's Dictionary: "Originally the name of a street near Moorfields, in London, much inhabited by writers of small histories, dictionaries, and temporary poems, whence any production is called Grub Street." The name in its appropriate sense was freely used by Pope, Swift, and others.

Grundy. "What will Mrs. Grundy say?" What will our rivals or neighbors say? The phrase is from Tom Morton's *Speed the Plough*, but "Mrs. Grundy" is not introduced into the comedy as one of the dramatis personæ. The solicitude of Dame Ashfield, in this play, as to "what will Mrs. Grundy say," has given the latter great celebrity, the interrogatory having acquired a proverbial currency.

Gudrun (*gōōd'rōōn*). (1) Norse Edda. A lady married to Sigurd by the magical arts of her mother; and, on the death of Sigurd, to Atli (Attila) whom she hated for his cruelty, and murdered. She then cast herself into the sea, and the waves bore her to the castle of King Jonakun, who became her third husband. (2) Low German Saga. A model of heroic fortitude and pious resignation. She was the daughter of King Hettel (Attila), and the betrothed of Herwig, king of Helgoland.

Guildenstern (*gĭl'dĕn-stērn*). The name of a courtier in Shakespeare's tragedy *Hamlet*.

Gulliver, Lemuel. The imaginary hero of Swift's celebrated satirical romance known as *Gulliver's Travels*. He is represented as being first a surgeon in London, and then a captain of several ships. After having followed the sea for some years he makes in succession four extraordinary voyages.

Gunga Din. The hero of Rudyard Kipling's poem of this name. He is a water carrier for the regiment, a Hindu, who meets heroic death in devotion to his duty.

Guppy, Mr. Bleak House, Dickens. A weak, commonplace youth, who has the conceit to propose to Esther Summerson, the ward in Chancery.

Gurth. Ivanhoe, Sir Walter Scott. The swineherd of Rotherwood.

Gurton, Gammer. The heroine of an old English comedy *Gammer Gurton's Needle*, first acted at Christ's college, Cambridge, in 1566.

Guy, Sir, Earl of Warwick. The hero of a famous English legend, which celebrates the wonderful achievements by which he obtained the hand of his ladylove, the Fair Felice, as well as the adventures he subsequently met with in a pilgrimage to the Holy Land. He is reputed to have lived in the reign of the Saxon king, Athelstan. The romance of Sir Guy, mentioned by Chaucer in the *Canterbury Tales*, was written in French in the 12th century, in English in the 14th.

Guy Mannering. The second of Scott's historical novels. It contains the excellent characters, Dandie Dinmont, the shrewd and witty counselor Pleydell, and also the desperate, seabeaten villainy of Hatteraick, the uncouth devotion of that gentlest of all pedants, poor Dominie Sampson, and the savage, crazed superstition of the gypsy dweller in Derncleugh.

Guyon (*gī'ŏn*). The impersonation of Temperance or Self-government in Spenser's *Faery Queen*. He destroyed the witch Acrasia, and her bower, called the "Bower of Bliss." His companion was Prudence. "Sir Guyon represents the quality of Temperance in the largest sense: meaning the virtuous self-government which holds in check not only the inferior sensual appetites but also the impulses of passion and revenge."

Hagen (*hä'gĕn*). The murderer of Siegfried, in the German epic, the *Nibelungenlied*. He is a pale-faced dwarf, who knows everything and whose sole desire is mischief. After the death of Siegfried he seized the "Nibelung hoard" and buried it in the Rhine, intending to appropriate it. Kriemhild invited him to the court and had him slain.

Haidee (*hī-dē'*). A beautiful young Greek girl in Byron's poem, "Don Juan." She is called the "beauty of the Cyclades."

Hakim (*hä-kēm'*). **The Talisman, Scott.** Saladin, in the disguise of a physician, visited Richard Cœur de Lion in sickness, gave him a medicine in which the "talisman" had been dipped, and the sick king recovered.

Hamlet. In Shakespeare's tragedy of the same name, son to the former, and nephew to the reigning king of Denmark. The ghost of his father appears to him, and urges him to avenge his murder upon his uncle. But the prince feigns madness, and puts off his revenge from day to day by "thinking too precisely on the event." Hamlet's mother had married Claudius, king of Denmark, after the death of her former husband. Claudius prepared poisoned wine, which he intended for Hamlet; but the queen, not knowing it was poisoned, drank it and died. Hamlet, seeing his mother fall dead, rushed on the king and killed him almost by accident, and is killed himself by a poisoned apier in the hands of Laertes. See *Ophelia*.

Hamlin, Jack. The gentlemanly gambler in *Gabriel Conroy* and other tales by Bret Harte. The appearance of this character revolutionized the gambler of popular story and drama.

Hanswurst. A pantomimic character formerly introduced into German comedies. It corresponds to the Italian "Macaroni," the French "Jean Potage," and the English "Jack Pudding."

Hardcastle, Mr. A character in Goldsmith's comedy *She Stoops to Conquer*, represented as prosy and hospitable. Father of Kate, the pretty heroine.

Hardcastle, Mrs. A very "genteel" lady indeed. Tony Lumpkin is her son by a former husband.

Hard Times. A novel by Dickens, dramatized under the title of *Under the Earth* or *The Sons of Toil*. Bounderby, a street arab, raised himself to banker and cotton prince. When past fifty years of age, he married Louisa, daughter of Thomas Gradgrind. The bank was robbed, and Bounderby believed Stephen Blackpool to be the thief, because he had dismissed him from his employ. The culprit was Tom Gradgrind, the banker's brother-in-law, who escaped out of the country. In the dramatized version the bank was not robbed, but Tom removed the money to another drawer for safety.

Harlequin. The name of a well-known character in the popular extemporized Italian comedy.

Harlowe, Clarissa. The heroine of Richardson's novel entitled *The History of Clarissa Harlowe*. In order to avoid a marriage urged upon her by her parents, she casts herself on the protection of Lovelace, who grossly abuses the confidence thus reposed in him. He subsequently proposes to marry her, but Clarissa rejects the offer.

Harold, Childe. Childe Harold's Pilgrimage, Byron. A man of gentle birth and peerless intellect, who exhausted all the pleasures of youth and early manhood, and loathed his fellow-bacchanals and the "laughing dames in whom he did delight." To banish his disgust and melancholy, he determines to travel; but, though he traverses some of the fairest portions of the earth, the feelings of bitterness and desolation still prey upon him.

Haroun-al-Raschid (*hä-rōōn'äl-rä'shĕd*). Caliph of the Abbasside race, contemporary with Chárlemagne, and, like him, a patron of literature and the arts. Many of the tales in the *Arabian Nights* are placed in the caliphate of Haroun-al-Raschid.

Harpagon (*är'pá'gŏN'*). The hero of Molière's comedy *L'Avare*, represented as a wretched miser.

Harpier or **Harper.** Some mysterious personage referred to by the witches in Shakespeare's tragedy *Macbeth*.

Harum, David, Edward Noyes Westcott. A novel. David Harum is a shrewd country banker in a central New York town. The deeper springs of humor and goodness in his nature are revealed in the story, in contrast to his unprincipled trading. The love story of his clerk, a young city man, is woven into the narrative.

Hassan. The Giaour, Byron. Caliph of the Ottoman empire, noted for his hospitality and splendor. In his seragilo was a beautiful young slave named Leila, who loved a Christian called the Giaour. Leila is put to death by an emir, and Hassan is slain by the Giaour. Caliph Hassan has become the subject of popular romance.

Hassan, Al. The Arabian emir of Persia, father of Hinda, in Moore's *Fire-Worshippers*.

Hatto. In German legend, an archbishop of Mentz in the 10th century, who, for his hard-heartedness to the poor in time of famine, was eaten by mice in the "Mouse Tower" on an island in the Rhine near Bingen. Robert Southey has made this legend the subject of a poem.

Havelok (*hăv'lŏk*) **the Dane.** A fisherman, known as Grim, rescued an infant named Havelok, whom he adopted. This infant was the son of the king of Denmark, and, when the boy was restored to his royal sire, Grim was laden with gifts. He built the town which he called after his own name. This is the foundation of the medieval tales about "Havelok the Dane."

Hazard of New Fortunes, A, Howells. A story of New York City life, involving Mr. and Mrs. March, the principal figures in *Their Wedding Journey* and *Their Silver Wedding Journey*. In this story Mr. March has come to New York to conduct a magazine.

Hazlewood, Sir Robert. The old baronet of Hazlewood, in Scott's *Guy Mannering*. In the story, Charles, son of Sir Robert, is in love with Lucy Bertram, whom he marries.

Headstone, Bradley. Our Mutual Friend, Dickens. The schoolmaster, in love with Lizzie Hexam. He tries to murder Eugene Wrayburn, whom he throws into the river. Lizzie rescues Eugene and nurses him back to life. Headstone tries to throw suspicion of the crime on Roger Riderhood, but fails, and both are drowned when, during a fight, they fall into the river lock.

Heart of Midlothian, The. The tollbooth, or old jail of Edinburgh, which is the county town of the county of Midlothian. It is the title of one of Sir Walter Scott's novels.

Heep, Uriah. David Copperfield, Dickens. A detestable character who, under the garb of the most abject humility, conceals diabolic malignity. Mrs. Heep, Uriah's mother, was a character equally to be despised for her hypocritical assumption of humility.

Heinrich, Der Arme, Hartmann von Aue. A court epic written about 1200. Prince Henry, smitten with leprosy, takes refuge in the house of one of his tenants, whose twelve-year old daughter cared for him. One day she learned that her prince could be cured by the blood of an innocent maiden. She determined to make the sacrifice. But at Salerno, when she was about to submit to the operation, Prince Henry refused to accept her sacrifice. On the homeward journey he was healed, and he afterward made the girl his wife. Longfellow used the story in his "Golden Legend," and Gerhart Hauptmann has written a poetic drama about the subject.

Helena. (1) A lady in Shakespeare's *Midsummer Night's Dream*, in love with Demetrius (2) The heroine of Shakespeare's *All's Well that Ends Well*, in love with Bertram, who marries her against his will and leaves her, but is finally won by the strength of her affection. (3) A character in an old popular tale, reproduced in Germany by Tieck. (4) A Greek tragedy by Euripides.

Helvetia (*hĕl-vē'shĭ-à*). The old Latin name of Switzerland; often used as a poetical appellation in modern literature. The country is often mentioned as the "Helvetic Republic," which was formerly the official name.

Hermann and Dorothea. The hero and heroine of Goethe's poem of the same name.

Hermengild (*hĕr'mĕn-gĭld*). **Canterbury Tales, Chaucer.** The wife of the lord-constable of Northumberland. She was converted by Constance, but was murdered by a knight. Hermengild at the bidding of Constance restored sight to a blind Briton.

Hermia. A lady in Shakespeare's *Midsummer Night's Dream*, in love with Lysander.

Hermione (*hĕr-mi'ô-nē*). The heroine of the first three acts of Shakespeare's *Winter's Tale*.

Hernani (*ĕr-nä'nē*) or **Ernani.** The hero of Victor Hugo's tragedy of the same name, and of Verdi's opera, founded on the play. He was a Spanish noble in revolt against the emperor Charles V and killed himself from a high sense of honor.

Hero and Leander. See *Leander*.

Hexam, Lizzie. The heroine of Dickens's novel *Our Mutual Friend*.

Hiawatha (*hi'à-wô'thà*). A mythical person believed by the North American Indians to have been sent among them to clear their rivers, forests, and fishing-grounds, and to teach them the arts of peace. When the white man

came, then Hiawatha knew that the time of his departure was at hand, when he must go "to the kingdom of Ponemah, the land of the Hereafter." These legends of Hiawatha were used and given a literary form by the poet Longfellow in his "Hiawatha."

Hilda. A New England girl of the most sensitive delicacy and purity of mind, in Hawthorne's romance *The Marble Faun*. She is an artist, living in Rome, and perhaps typifies the conscience.

Hildebrand. (1) The Nestor of German romance, a magician and champion. (2) The famous pope, Gregory VII, whose stern dealings with Henry IV have given rise to the phrase "a regular Hildebrand."

Hildesheim (*hĭl'dĕs-hĭm*). In an old German legend, the monk of Hildesheim, doubting how a thousand years with God could be "only one day," listened to the melody of a bird, as he supposed, for only three minutes, but found that in reality he had been listening to it for the space of a hundred years.

Hobbididance. The name of one of the fiends mentioned by Shakespeare in *King Lear*, and taken from Harsnett's *Declaration of Egregious Popish Impostures* (1603).

Holofernes (*hŏl'ô-fẽr'nēz*). (1) The pedantic schoolmaster of Italian comedy. (2) A pedant living in Paris, under whose care Gargantua is placed for instruction. (3) A pedantic schoolmaster in Shakespeare's *Love's Labor's Lost*. (4) The Assyrian general slain by Judith.

Holt, Felix. The hero of George Eliot's novel of the same name.

Holy Grail. See *Graal*.

Honeycomb, Will. One of the members of the imaginary club by whom the *Spectator* was professedly edited. He is distinguished for his graceful affectation, courtly pretension, and knowledge of the gay world.

Honeyman, Charles. A fashionable preacher in Thackeray's novel *The Newcomes*.

Hoosier Schoolmaster, The, Edward Eggleston. A realistic story of life in southern Indiana about the middle of the 19th century.

Hopeful. A pilgrim in Bunyan's *Pilgrim's Progress*, who accompanies Christian to the end of his journey.

Hop-o'-my-Thumb. A character in the tales of the nursery. Tom Thumb and Hop-o'-my-Thumb are not the same, although they are often confounded. Tom Thumb was the son of peasants, knighted by King Arthur, and was killed by a spider. Hop-o'-my-Thumb was a nix, the same as the German "daumling," the French "le petit pouce," and the Scotch "Tom-a-lin" or "Tamlane." He was not a human dwarf, but a fay.

Horatio (*hô-rā'shĭ-ō*). **Hamlet, Shakespeare.** An intimate friend of Hamlet, a prince, a scholar, and a gentleman.

Horatius Cocles (*hô-rā'shĭ-ŭs kŏ'klēz*). Captain of the bridge-gate over the Tiber. He and two men to help him held the bridge against vast approaching armies. Subject and title of a poem by Lord Macaulay.

Hornbook. The primer or apparatus for learning the elements of reading, used in England before the days of printing, and common down to the time of George II. It consisted of a single leaf, containing on one side the alphabet, large and small, in black letter or in roman, with perhaps a small regiment of monosyllables. Then followed a form of exorcism and the Lord's Prayer, and, as a finale, the Roman numerals. The leaf was usually set in a frame of wood, with a slice of transparent horn in front,—hence the name of "hornbook." Copies of the hornbook are now exceedingly rare.

Horner, Jack. The name of a celebrated personage in the literature of the nursery. A Somersetshire tradition says that the plums which Jack Horner pulled out of the Christmas pie alluded to the title deeds of the abbey estates at Wells, which were sent to Henry VIII in a pasty, and abstracted on the way by the messenger, a certain Jack Horner.

Hortense. Bleak House, Dickens. The vindictive French maidservant of Lady Dedlock. In revenge for the partiality shown by Lady Dedlock to Rosa, Hortense murdered Mr. Tulkinghorn, and tried to throw the suspicion of the crime on Lady Dedlock.

Hourglass, A Morality, The, W. B. Yeats. The Wise Man has taught in his village that the visible world is all. Suddenly, an angel appears and tells the Wise Man that in an hour he must die, but that, if within that time he can find one person who believes in God and heaven, he shall enter paradise. In haste he sends out, but all his pupils and his children have lost all belief. At last comes Teigue the Fool, who has learned, not in the Wise Man's school, but on the hills. He believes, and in joy at finding the believing fool the Wise Man dies.

Houris (*hōō'rĭz*). In the fairy tales found in the *Koran* these are the black-eyed daughters of paradise. They are created from musk and are free from all physical weakness and are always young. It is held out to every male believer that he will have 72 of these girls as his household companions in paradise. See Tom Moore's *Lalla Rookh*.

House of Fame. Of this poem it has been said that of itself it might have given fame to Chaucer. Under the form of a dream, it gives a picture of the "Temple of Glory," crowded with aspirants for immortal renown, and adorned with statues of great poets and historians.

Houssain (*hōō-sän'*). A prince in the *Arabian Night*, who had a flying carpet which would carry him whithersoever he wished.

Hubbard, Old Mother. A well-known nursery rime. "Mother Hubbard's Tale," by Edmund Spenser, is a satirical fable in the style of Chaucer.

Hubert de Burgh. Justice of England, created earl of Kent, introduced by Shakespeare into *King John*. He is the one to whom the young prince addresses his piteous plea for life. The lad was found dead soon afterwards, either by accident or foul play.

Hubert, Saint. The legend of Saint Hubert makes him a patron saint of huntsmen.

Kudibras. The title and hero of a celebrated satirical poem by Samuel Butler. Hudibras is a Presbyterian justice of the time of the Commonwealth.

Hugh of Lincoln. A legendary personage who forms the subject of Chaucer's "Prioress's Tale," and also of an ancient English ballad. Wordsworth has given a modernized version of this tale.

Hugh Wynne. Hero of Dr. S. Weir Mitchell's novel of the American Revolution, *Hugh Wynne, Free Quaker*. Hugh, born of a French mother, defies his father's nonresistance principles, joins Washington's army, and gains rank on the general's staff. A love story of interesting complications runs through the book.

Humphrey. The imaginary collector of the tales in *Master Humphrey's Clock*, by Charles Dickens.

Humpty Dumpty. The hero of a well-known nursery rime. The name signifies humped and dumpy, and is the riddle for an egg.

Huon of Bordeaux, Sir. A hero of one of the romances of chivalry bearing this name.

Hypatia (*hĭ-pā'shĭ-à*). Of this romance its author, Charles Kingsley, said: "My idea in the romance is to set forth Christianity as the only really democratic creed and philosophy; above all, spiritualism as the most exclusively aristocratic creed." Hypatia was a beautiful and learned woman of Alexandria, who was murdered by jealous, fanatical monks.

Hyperion. Keats's incomplete *Hyperion*, in magnificent verse, deals with plans of the fallen gods to revolt against Jupiter. Hyperion is the sun god, identified with Apollo.

Hypocrites' Isle. An island described by Rabelais in one of his satires. He pictures this island of "Hypocrites" as wholly inhabited by people of low and defiled natures, by sham saints, spiritual comedians, seducers, and "suchlike sorry rogues who live on the alms of passengers like the hermit of Lamont."

Iago (*ē-ä'gō*). *Othello*, Shakespeare. Othello's ensign and the villain of the play. Iago is said to be a character next to a devil, yet not quite a devil, such as Shakespeare alone could delineate with skill.

Idleness, The Lake of. *Faery Queen*, Spenser. Who ever drank thereof grew instantly "faint and weary." The Red Cross Knight drank of it and was readily made captive by Orgoglio.

Idylls of the King. Tennyson has told the purpose and the meaning of these idylls. Taken together they form a parable of the life of man. Each idyll taken as a separate picture represents the war between sense and soul. In Lancelot and Guinevere the lower nature leads them astray, and there is intense struggle before the higher nature prevails. In Vivien, Ettarre, Tristam, and Modred, the base and sensual triumph. In Arthur, Sir Galahad, and Percival, it is the victory of the spiritual.

Ignaro (*ĭg-nä'rō*). *Faery Queen*, Spenser. Foster father of Orgoglio. Spenser says this old man walks one way and looks another, because ignorance is always "wrong-headed."

Iliad. The tale of the siege of Troy, an epic poem in 24 books. It is written in Greek hexameters, and commemorates the deeds of Achilles and other Greek heroes at the

siege of Troy. The date of its composition may, with much probability, be assigned to the 9th century B. C., and the poem is so deficient in continuity, and contains so much that is inconsistent and irrelevant with the main topic, that it has been thought by many critics to have been the performance of several persons, although its authorship is still nominally accredited to Homer. Books one, two, and three are introductory to the war. Paris proposes to decide the contest by single combat, and Menelaus accepts the challenge. Paris, being overthrown, is carried off by Venus, and Agamemnon demands that the Trojans shall give up Troy in fulfillment of the compact, and the siege follows. The gods take part and frightful slaughter ensues. At length Achilles slays Hector and the battle is at an end. Old Priam, going to the tent of Achilles, craves the body of his son Hector; Achilles gives it up, and the poem concludes with the funeral rites of the Trojan hero. Virgil continues the tale from this point, shows how the city was taken and burned, and then continues with the adventures of Æneas, who escapes from the burning city, and makes his way to Italy. See *Æneid*.

Illuminating. The art of adorning manuscripts and books with ornamented letters and paintings, which was practiced by artists, generally monks, called "illuminators," in the middle ages, prior to the introduction of printing. Manuscripts, containing portraits, pictures, and emblematic figures, form a valuable part of the riches preserved in the principal libraries in Europe and America.

Il Penseroso, Milton. Title of one of two companion poems. The name is shortened from Italian *Il Pensieroso*, meaning "The Thoughtful Man." The poem pictures a day in the life of such a person. Milton's companion poem, "L'Allegro," praises mirth and jollity.

Imogen (*ĭm'ŏ-jĕn*). The wife of Posthumus, and the daughter of Cymbeline in the play *Cymbeline*. "Of all Shakespeare's women," says Hazlitt, "she is, perhaps, the most tender and the most artless."

Incantation. Derived from a Latin root meaning simply "to sing." It is the term in use to denote one of the most powerful and awe-inspiring modes of magic, resting on a belief in the mysterious power of words solemnly conceived and passionately uttered.

Inchcape Rock. A rock in the North Sea, off the Firth of Tay. It is dangerous for navigators, and therefore the abbot of Aberbrothock fixed a bell on a float, which gave notice to sailors. Southey says that Ralph the Rover, in a mischievous joke, cut the bell from the buoy, and it fell into the sea, but on his return voyage his boat ran on the rock, and Ralph was drowned. Precisely the same tale is told of St. Goven's bell.

Incunabula (*ĭn'kŭ-năb'ŭ-là*). A term applied to books printed before the end of the year 1500. Meaning literally "cradle" according to its Latin derivation, the word designates rare volumes dating from the infancy of the printing art.

Inferno, The. Divine Comedy, Dante. Epic poem in 34 cantos. Inferno is the place of the souls who in life were wholly given up to sin. The ascent is through Purgatorio to Paradiso.

Ingoldsby Legends, The, Rev. R. H. Barham, "Thomas Ingoldsby." A collection of laughable tales in prose and verse first printed in magazines and published later in a volume in 1840. A second and a third series appeared in 1847. They treat all sorts of ancient, medieval, and modern matters of society and superstition in a burlesque fashion that has made them famous.

In Memoriam, Tennyson. An elegy, or philosophical poem, in memory of the poet's friend, Arthur Hallam, who died at the beginning of a seemingly brilliant career. It is reckoned as one of the great literary expressions of faith.

Innocents Abroad, Mark Twain. Travelers seeing Europe without any illusions. The fun consists in an irreverent application of modern common sense to historic associations, and in ridiculing sentimental humbug. An air of innocence and surprise adds to the drolleries of their adventures.

Interludes, The. Springing from the moralities and bearing some resemblance to them, though nearer the regular drama, are the interludes, a class of compositions in dialogue, much shorter and more merry and farcical. They were generally played in the intervals of a festival.

Iphigenia (*ĭf'ĭ-jê-nī'à*). The heroine of Euripides' tragedy *Iphigenia in Aulis*, and of Goethe's tragedy *Iphigenie auf Tauris*. She was placed on the altar because of her father's rash vow. Artemis at the last moment snatched her from the altar and carried her to heaven, substituting a hind in her place. The similarity of this legend to the Scripture stories of Jephthah's vow and of Abraham's offering of his son Isaac is noticeable.

Iras. (1) A strongly delineated character in *Ben Hur, a Tale of The Christ,* by Lew Wallace. (2) A female attendant in Shakespeare's play *Antony and Cleopatra.*

Iron Mask, The Man with the. Alexander Dumas wrote his *Viscomte de Bragelonne* around this personage. The real person was a mysterious prisoner of the time of Louis XIV. He wore at all times a mask of iron. His identity has remained a profound secret.

Isaac of York. A wealthy Jew, the father of Rebecca, in Sir Walter Scott's novel *Ivanhoe.*

Isabella. (1) The heroine in Shakespeare's comedy *Measure for Measure.* (2) A character of absorbing grief in Keats's *Isabella.*

Iseult (*ĭ-sōōlt′*) or **Isolt.** Iseult of the White Hands (Iseult of Brittany) was the unloved wife of Sir Tristram in the Arthurian romances. Iseult the Fair, whom Tristram loved, was the bride of his uncle, Sir Mark.

Island of Lanterns. In the celebrated satire of Rabelais, an imaginary country inhabited by false pretenders to knowledge. The name was probably suggested by the "City of Lanterns," in the Greek romance of Lucian.

Israfel. In the *Koran* the archangel commissioned to blow the trumpet of the resurrection. Poe, in his poem "Israfel," uses the Mohammedan legend of the sweet-voiced Israfel.

Italics. The name applied to printed type sloping from left to right, as exemplified *thus.* Ordinary vertical type is called roman. Italics were first used by Aldus Minutius in printing an edition of Virgil in 1501. They are now used principally for emphasis, although in the ordinary versions of the Bible they indicate words supplied by the translators, corresponding words not being present in the original.

Ivanhoe. The hero of Sir Walter Scott's novel of the same name. He figures as Cedric of Rotherwood's disinherited son, the favorite of King Richard I, and the lover of the Lady Rowena, whom, in the end, he marries. The scene is laid in England in the reign of Richard I, and we are introduced to Robin Hood in Sherwood Forest, banquets in Saxon halls, tournaments, and all the pomp of ancient chivalry. Rowena, the heroine, is quite overshadowed by the gentle, meek, yet high-souled Rebecca.

Ivanovitch, Ivan (*ê-văn′ ê-văn′ô-vĭch*). An imaginary personage, who is the embodiment of the peculiarities of the Russian people, in the same way as John Bull represents the English, Jean Crapaud the French, and Uncle Sam the American character.

Ivory Gate of Dreams. A passage in Virgil's *Æneid* tells of twin gates of sleep, one of horn, the other of ivory. Dreams which delude are said to pass through the ivory gate, but those which come true, through the horn gate. The fancy is introduced at the beginning of Sir William Watson's poem "The Dream of Man." The fancy depends upon two Greek puns: ivory in Greek is *elephas,* and the verb *elephairo* means "to cheat with empty hopes"; the Greek for horn is *keras,* and the verb *karanoö* means "to accomplish."

Ivory Tower. Figuratively, a place of escape from the reality of the outside world into a world of one's own.

Ivy Green, The. Dickens published this song in *Pickwick Papers.* The theme is the creeping of the ivy over old buildings and ruins.

Jabberwocky. A ballad in Lewis Carroll's *Through the Looking-Glass.* It is the story of the Jabberwock, a fabulous monster, told with many coined words, as in the opening line, "Twas brillig and the slithy toves . . . ."

Jack and the Beanstalk. A nursery legend said to be an allegory of the Teutonic Alfadur; the "red hen" representing the all-producing sun, the "moneybags" the fertilizing rain, and the "harp" the winds.

Jack-in-the-Green. A prominent character in Maypole dances.

Jack Robinson. A famous comic song by Hudson.

Jack Sprat. The hero of a nursery rime. Jack and his wife form a fine combination in domestic economy.

Jack the Giant Killer. The name of a famous hero in the literature of the nursery, the subject of one of the many Indo-European legends which celebrate the triumph of skill over brute force.

James, Jesse Woodson. A desperado who has become a heroic figure of American folklore owing to the many sensational dime novels written about his and his brother Frank's exploits as train and bank robbers in the Midwest. Born in Missouri in 1847, he was murdered by one of his own gang in 1882.

Janice Meredith, Paul L. Ford. Historical novel of the American Revolution. Janice, daughter of a New Jersey Tory, falls in love with a young Englishman indentured to her father. And after many adventures is betrothed to him when he becomes a general in Washington's army.

Jaquenetta (*jăk-ê-nĕt′à*). **Love's Labor's Lost, Shakespeare.** A country wench courted by Don Adriano de Armado.

Jaques (*jā′kwēz*). A lord attending upon the exiled duke, in Shakespeare's *As You Like It.* A contemplative character who thinks and does—nothing. He is called the "melancholy Jaques," and affects a cynical philosophy. He could "suck melancholy out of a song, as a weasel sucks eggs."

Jarley, Mrs. The proprietor of a waxworks' show in Dickens's *Old Curiosity Shop.* She has lent her name to a popular game of parlor tableaux.

Jarndyce. A prominent figure in Dickens's *Bleak House,* distinguished for his philanthropy, easy good nature and good sense, and for always saying, "The wind is in the east," when anything went wrong with him. The famous suit of "Jarndyce v. Jarndyce," in this novel, is a satire upon the court of Chancery.

Jarvie, Baillie Nicol. A prominent character in Sir Walter Scott's novel *Rob Roy.* He is a magistrate of Glasgow.

Jean Valjean (*zhän väl′zhän′*). The hapless hero of Victor Hugo's great novel, *Les Miserables,* who is pursued relentlessly by the police but is befriended by a sympathetic priest.

Jekyll (*jē′kĭl*), **Doctor, and Mr. Hyde.** The duplex hero of Robert Louis Stevenson's singular romance of the same name. Doctor Jekyll is a benevolent and upright physician, who by means of a potion is able to transform himself for a time into a second personality, Mr. Hyde, of a brutal and animal nature.

Jellyby, Mrs. A character in Dickens's novel *Bleak House,* a type of sham philanthropy. She spends her time and energy on foreign missions, to the neglect of her family.

Jenkins, Winifred. The name of Miss Tabitha Bramble's maid in Smollett's *Expedition of Humphrey Clinker.* She makes ridiculous blunders in speaking and writing.

Jenkinson, Ephraim. A green old swindler, whom Dr. Primrose met in a tavern. Dr. Primrose sold him his horse, Old Blackberry, for a draft upon Farmer Flamborough.

Jerusalem Delivered. An epic in twenty books, by Torquato Tasso (1544–1595). The crusaders, encamped on the plains of Tortosa, chose Godfrey for their chief, and Alandine, king of Jerusalem, made preparations of defense. The Christian army having reached Jerusalem, the king of Damascus sent Armida to beguile the Christians. It was found that Jerusalem could never be taken without the aid of Rinaldo. Godfrey, being informed that the hero was dallying with Armida in the enchanted island, sent to invite him back to the army; he returned, and Jerusalem fell. Armida fled into Egypt, and offered to marry any knight who slew Rinaldo. The love of Rinaldo returned; he pursued her and she relented. The poem concludes with the triumphant entry of the Christian army into the Holy City and their devotions at the tomb of the Redeemer.

Jessamy Bride. A by-name given to Miss Mary Horneck, afterward Mrs. Gwyn. She was a contemporary and friend of Goldsmith. Also title of a novel by F. F. Moore. Jessamy means "Jasmine."

Jessica. The beautiful daughter of Shylock, in Shakespeare's *Merchant of Venice.*

Jew, The Wandering. An imaginary person in a legend connected with the history of Christ's Passion. As the Savior was on the way to the place of execution, overcome with the weight of the cross, he wished to rest on a stone before the house of a Jew, who drove him away with curses. Driven by fear and remorse, he has since wandered, according to the command of the Lord, from place to place, and has never yet been able to find a grave. Many Romances have been founded on this character. The best-known is the story by Eugène Sue, *Le Juif Errant.*

Job. The central figure in the dramatic poem which forms the biblical book of the same name. The theme of the book is the question of why trouble comes to men. Because of his endurance of great woes, Job has become a synonym for patience.

Jones, Casey (John Luther Jones), an American railroad engineer and the hero of a popular ballad, who died in the wreck of his train in 1900. He was found with a whistle pull in one hand, the airbrake lever in the other. The authorship of the ballad, of which there are several versions, has been attributed to various fellow railroad workers. Jones's nickname comes from the town of Cayce, Kentucky, near his birthplace. In 1950 the United States issued a stamp commemorating him.

Jones, Tom. The hero of *The History of Tom Jones, a Foundling,* by Henry Fielding. One of the first English novels. The hero is a model of generosity, openness, and manly spirit, though thoughtless and dissipated.

Joyeuse (*zhwä′yĕz′*), **La.** The sword of Charlemagne as mentioned in romances of chivalry.

Joyeuse Garde, La. The residence of the famous Lancelot du Lac.

Judith. The heroine in the book of the same name in the Apocrypha. She was a beautiful Jewess of Bethulia, who, when her town was besieged by Holofernes, the general of Nebuchadnezzar, attended him in his tent, and, when he was drunk, killed him, whereupon her townsmen fell upon the Assyrians and defeated them with great slaughter. The tale has long been held to be an allegory. It has frequently furnished poets and painters with subjects.

Jungle Books, Kipling. The title of two series of tales of animal life in the Indian jungles. The animals use the language of men, yet they always are animals, never personified. See *Mowgli*.

Justice, Galsworthy. A play in which the author attacks certain abuses in the administration of justice. The drama involves a terrible portrayal of the effect of solitary confinement upon a prisoner.

Just So Stories, Kipling. A series of animal stories for children, *How the Leopard Got His Spots, How the Elephant Got His Trunk*, etc.

Kadr, Al. The night on which the *Koran* was sent down to Mohammed. Al Kadr is supposed to be the seventh of the last ten nights of Ramadan, or the night between the 23d and 24th days of the month.

Kalevala (*kä′lä-vä′lä*). One of the so-called "artificial epics," or modern poems made up of more or less ancient popular song and story. It belongs to Finland, the name meaning "the country of Kaleva," who is one of the heroes. The work, consisting of 22,800 verses, was put together first in 1835 and revised in 1849 by Dr. A. Lönnrot. It contains a vast treasure of Finnish popular songs, magic and mythical lore, and heroic tales.

Karma. A Sanskrit word, meaning "action" or "sequence." The Buddhist uses the word to mean a judgment on actions. The Theosophist uses it to mean the connected sequence of things as causes and effects.

Kay. A foster brother of King Arthur, and a rude and boastful knight of the Round Table. He was the butt of King Arthur's court. Called also "Sir Queux." He appears in the "Boy and the Mantle," in Percy's *Reliques*. Sir Kay is represented as the type of rude boastfulness, Sir Gawain of courtesy, Sir Lancelot of chivalry, Sir Modred of treachery, Sir Galahad of chastity, Sir Mark of cowardice.

Kells, Book of. A beautifully illuminated 8th century manuscript of the Gospels in Latin preserved in the library of Trinity College, Dublin. Produced at the monastery founded by Saint Columba at Kells, County Meath, Eire, the Book of Kells, with its illustrations for each book and chapter of the Gospels, and its elaborate initial letters and borders, is regarded as the best existing example of its kind of the art of illumination of early Christian times.

Kenilworth (*kĕn′il-wĕrth*). A town in Warwickshire, England, five miles north of Warwick. The castle is one of the most admired of English feudal monuments, and was long of note as a royal residence. The chief scene of Sir Walter Scott's novel *Kenilworth*. The story is based on a ballad called "Cumnor Hall." The earl of Leicester, favorite of Queen Elizabeth, had secretly married Amy Robsart. For fear of Elizabeth's displeasure, he conceals her in Cumnor Hall. During a visit to Leicester's Castle of Kenilworth, the queen encourages Leicester to believe that she might marry him. Persuaded that Amy has been unfaithful, he commands her death. Later, finding that he has been deceived, Leicester confesses the truth, but messengers reach Cumnor Hall after Amy has been killed by falling through a trapdoor arranged by Varney, Leicester's retainer.

Kent, Earl of. A rough, plain-spoken, but faithful nobleman in Shakespeare's *King Lear*, who, disguised as a servant and under the assumed name of Caius, follows the fallen fortunes of the king.

Kentucky Cardinal, A, James Lane Allen. A delicate story of Kentucky. A misunderstanding creeps into the romance of two young people through an unkind act toward a cardinal bird. The sequel is *Aftermath*.

Kenwigs. A family in Dickens's novel *Nicholas Nickleby*, which includes a number of little girls who differed from one another only in the length of their frilled pantalettes and of their flaxen pigtails tied with bows of blue ribbon.

Kidd, Captain William. Notorious 17th century British pirate. Commissioned as a privateer in 1695, he soon turned buccaneer, preying on Spanish-American ships and settlements. According to popular legend, he amassed a large hidden treasure which is still sought. He was hanged at Execution Dock, London, in 1701.

Kilkenny Cats. Two cats, in an Irish story, which fought till nothing was left but their tails. It is probably a parable of a local contest between Kilkenny and Irishtown, which impoverished both boroughs.

Kim, Kipling. A story of India. The hero, Kimball O'Hara, nicknamed "Kim," orphaned while a baby, "grows up" to the precocious "age of indiscretion" in the native quarter of Lahore. He attaches himself to a Tibetan pilgrim, with whom he wanders over India, learning much of native ways. Eventually, the Irish regiment to which his father had belonged find and adopt Kim. He is sent to school and inducted into the Indian Secret Service.

King Cambyses (*kăm-bĭ′sēz*). The hero of "A Lamentable Tragedy" of the same name, by Thomas Preston, contemporary of Shakespeare. A ranting character known to modern readers by Falstaff's allusion to him in Shakespeare's *Henry IV*.

King Estmere. The hero of an ancient and beautiful legend, which, according to Bishop Percy, seems to have been written while a great part of Spain was in the hands of the Saracens, or Moors.

King Horn. A metrical romance which was very popular in the 13th century. King Horn is a beautiful young prince who is carried away by pirates; but his life is spared, and after many wonderful adventures he weds a princess, and regains his father's kingdom.

King Log and King Stork. Characters in a celebrated fable of Æsop, which relates that the frogs, grown weary of living without government, petitioned Jupiter for a king. Jupiter accordingly threw down a log among them, which made a satisfactory ruler till the frogs recovered from their fright and discovered his real nature. They, therefore, entreated Jupiter for another king, whereupon he sent them a stork, who immediately began to devour them.

Klaus, Peter. The hero of an old popular tradition of Germany—the prototype of Rip Van Winkle. He is represented as a goatherd.

Knickerbocker, Diedrich. The imaginary author of a humorous fictitious *History of New York*, written by Washington Irving.

Knights of the Round Table. A name given to King Arthur's knights. They were so called because they sat with him at a round table made by Merlin for King Leodegraunce. This king gave it to Arthur on his marriage with Guinevere, his daughter.

Knight's Tale, The. Canterbury Tales, Chaucer. Two Theban knights, Palamon and Arcite, captives of Duke Theseus, were accustomed to see from their dungeon window the duke's sister-in-law, Emily, and fell in love with her. Both captives having gained their liberty contended for the lady by single combat. Arcite was victor, but being thrown from his horse was killed, and Emily became the bride of Palamon.

Koppenberg. The mountain of Westphalia to which the pied piper (Bunting) led the children when the people of Hamelin refused to pay him for killing their rats. Browning's poem, "The Pied Piper," tells the tale. Josephine Preston Peabody dramatized it in *The Piper*.

Kriemhild or **Chriemhild.** A beautiful Burgundian lady, daughter of Dancrat and sister of Gunther. She first marries Siegfried, king of the Netherlands, and next Etzel, king of the Huns. In the first part of the *Nibelungenlied*, Kriemhild brings ruin on herself by a tattling tongue. In the second part she is bent on vengeance, and, after a slaughter of friends and foes, she is killed by Hildebrand.

Kubla Khan (*kōōb′lä kän*). A poem by Coleridge. Coleridge says that he composed the poem in a dream immediately after reading a description of "Cublai Can's" palace in Purchas's *Pilgrimage* and that he wrote it down upon waking.

Laconic. Very concise and pithy. The name came from the Spartan manner of curt speech. A Spartan was called a Lacon from the name of his country, Laconia.

La Debacle (*lä dä′bäk′l′*), **Zola.** A realistic novel portraying the horrors of the breakdown of France before the German invasion in the Franco-Prussian War.

Lady Day. The 25th day of March, anniversary of the Annunciation.

Lady of Lyons, The, Bulwer-Lytton. Pauline Deschappelles, daughter of a Lyonese merchant, rejected the suits of Beauseant, Glavis, and Claude Melnotte, who therefore combined on vengeance. Claude, who was a gardener's son, aided by the other two, passed himself off as Prince Como, married Pauline, and brought her home to his mother's cottage. The proud beauty was very indignant, and Claude left her to join the French army. He became a colonel, and returned to Lyons. His father-in-law was on the eve of bankruptcy, and Beauseant had promised to satisfy the creditors if Pauline would consent to marry him. Pauline was heartbroken; Claude revealed himself, paid the money required, and carried home the bride.

Lady of the Lake, The. The heroine in the poem by Sir Walter Scott. She was Ellen Douglas, once a favorite of King James; when her father fell into disgrace, she retired with him to the vicinity of Loch Katrine.

Lady of the Lake and Arthur's Sword. The heroine who gave to King Arthur the sword "Excalibur." She ordered King Arthur to sail out into the lake and take the sword as it was seen rising from the water. He sailed out with a knight and Merlin, came to the sword that a hand held up, and took it by the handles. The arm and hand went under the lake again. This Lady of the Lake asked in recompense the head of Sir Balin, because he had slain her brother; but the king refused the request. Balin, who was present, exclaimed: "Evil be ye found! Ye would have my head; therefore ye shall lose thine own." With his sword he smote off her head in the presence of King Arthur.

Lady or the Tiger, The, Stockton. A famous short story, the conclusion of which is left to the reader. The hero, in the arena, stands before two doors. Behind one stands the lady he loves, behind the other a tiger. The princess, who loves him but cannot wed him, is to give him a sign indicating which door he shall open.

Laertes (lā-ûr'tēz). The son of Polonius, lord chamberlain of Denmark, and brother of Hamlet's beloved Ophelia. The king persuades him to challenge Hamlet, after Ophelia wanders in mind, and he calls him out in "friendly" duel, but poisons his own rapier. He wounds Hamlet, and, in the scuffle which ensues, the combatants change swords, and Hamlet wounds Laertes, so that both die.

Lagado (lā-gā'dō). **Gulliver's Travels, Swift.** The name of a city belonging to the king of Laputa. Lagado is celebrated for its grand academy of projectors, who try to extract sunbeams from cucumbers, and to convert ice into gunpowder. In the description of this fancied academy, Swift ridicules the pretenders in philosophy and science.

Lake District, English. A region in Westmoreland and Cumberland, England, which abounds in lakes enclosed by mountains. The district is a celebrated tourist center, and is associated with the poetry of Wordsworth. The lakes include Windermere, Ullswater, Derwentwater, and Bassenthwaite Water; and Skiddaw, Helvellyn, and Scafell Pike are the principal mountains. See *The Lake Poets.*

Lake Poets, The. Wordsworth, Southey, and Coleridge, who lived about the lakes of Cumberland. The name was applied also to other contemporary poets, who took subjects and inspiration from nature.

Lalla Rookh (lä'lä rook'). Poem by Thomas Moore. The name of the heroine, daughter of the emperor Aurungzebe, gives the title. On the journey to meet Aliris, her betrothed, in the Vale of Cashmere, she is entertained by a young Persian poet, Feramorz. She falls in love with him, and her delight is unbounded to find at the end of the journey that the poet is Prince Aliris.

L'Allegro, Milton. Title of a poem in which is sketched the life of a contented, happy man through one day. A companion poem to *Il Penseroso. L'Allegro* means "The Happy Man."

Lame Dog's Diary. A clever diary in which the provincial life of a little English village is reflected. It is supposed to be kept by an invalid officer who returned crippled from the Boer war. The suggestion of the diary came from a winning, tantalizing young widow, who cheered the invalid by her amusing, paradoxical talk. The diarist and his sister Palestrina are true English types—quiet gentlefolk.

L'Ami Fritz (lä'mē' frĭts), **Erckmann-Chatrian.** A quiet tale of Bavaria, which carries a lesson of peace and tolerance. Fritz Kobus, a bachelor of 36, proud of his escape from matrimony, gradually falls victim to the housewifely charms of Suzel, daughter of one of the tenants. The story was dramatized and translated as "Friend Fritz."

Lampoon. A personal satire, often bitter and malignant. These libels, carried to excess in the reign of Charles II, acquired the name of lampoons from the burden sung to them: "Lampons, lampons, camerades lampons." From a French slang verb, meaning "to drink, booze."

Lamps of Sleep. Magic lamps. A wonderful knight of a mythical land had an equally wonderful black castle. In the mansion of the knight of the black castle were seven lamps, which could be quenched only with water from an enchanted fountain. So long as these lamps kept burning, all within the room fell into a deep sleep, from which nothing could rouse them.

Landlady's Daughter. Longfellow's Hyperion. She rowed Fleming "over the Rhine-stream, rapid and roaring wide," and told to him the story of the Liebenstein.

Land of Beulah. The paradise in which souls wait before the resurrection. In *Pilgrim's Progress* the land from which the pilgrims enter the Celestial City. The name is found in Isaiah LXII: 4.

Land of Bondage. Name given to Egypt in the Bible, because of the oppression of Israel in that country.

Land of Cakes. A name sometimes given to Scotland, because oatmeal cakes are a common national article of food, particularly among the poorer classes. The title has become popular through its use by Burns and Scott.

Land of Nod. In common speech, sleepy-land or land of dreams, as if an unknown land. Cain fled to Nod, east of Eden.

Land of Promise. The land of Canaan; so called because it was promised to Abraham.

Land of Shadows. A place of unreality, sometimes meaning land of ghosts.

Land o' the Leal. An unknown land of happiness, loyalty, and virtue. Carolina Oliphant, Baroness Nairne, meant heaven in her song, and this is now its accepted meaning. Leal means "faithful," and "Land of the Leal" means the "land of the faithful."

Land of Veda. Name often given to India.

Lanternland. The land of literary charlatans, whose inhabitants, graduates in arts, doctors, professors, and artists of all grades, waste time in displaying their wonderful learning. See *Island of Lanterns.*

Laodicean (lā-ŏd'ĭ-sē'ăn). One indifferent to religion, like the Christians of that church mentioned in the Book of Revelation.

Laputa (lā-pū'tà). The name of a flying island described by Swift in *Gulliver's Travels.* It is said to be "exactly circular, its diameter 7837 yards or about four miles and a half, and consequently contains ten thousand acres." The inhabitants are chiefly speculative philosophers, devoted to mathematics and music; and such is their habitual absent-mindedness, that they are compelled to employ attendants, called "flappers," to rouse them from their profound meditations. This is done by striking them gently on the mouth and ears with a peculiar instrument consisting of a blown bladder with a few pebbles in it, fastened to the end of a stick.

Last Days of Pompeii, The, Bulwer-Lytton. A historical novel of the time of the destruction of the city by the eruption of Mount Vesuvius, 79 A. D. The vivid descriptions of life in the Græco-Roman city are the most interesting features of the book. The lovers, Glaucus and Ione, are aided to escape by the blind flower girl, Nydia. They become Christians and go to live in Greece.

Last of the Mohicans (mō-hē'kănz). A romantic novel of North American Indian life by James Fenimore Cooper, the second of his Leatherstocking series. The title of the work is descriptive of the character Uncas, son of Chingachgook and the last of the Mohican line. Represented as gallant, swift, courteous, and a noble lover, he makes the perennial appeal of youth cut off in the flower.

Latitudinarians. Persons who hold very loose views of Divine inspiration and of what are called orthodox doctrines. A common name in England for the less strict groups in the Anglican Church.

Launfal, Sir. Steward of King Arthur. Detesting Queen Guinevere, he retired to Carlyoun, and fell in love with a lady named Tryamour. She gave him limitless money and told him if he wished to see her he was to retire into a private room, and she would be with him. Sir Launfal now returned to court, and excited much attention by his great wealth. Guinevere made advances to him; he would not turn from the lady to whom he was devoted but sang her praises. At this repulse, the angry queen complained to the king, and declared to him that she had been insulted by his steward. Arthur bade Sir Launfal produce this paragon of women. On her arrival, Sir Launfal was allowed to accompany her to the isle of Oleron; and no one ever saw him afterwards. James Russell Lowell has written a poem entitled "The Vision of Sir Launfal."

Laus Deo (lôs dē'ō), "Praise to God." A poem by Whittier, inspired by the passing of the Constitutional amendment abolishing slavery, and suggested to the poet as he sat in the Friends' meetinghouse in Amesbury and heard the bells proclaiming the fact.

Lavaine. Son of the lord of Astolat, who accompanied Sir Lancelot when he went to tilt for the ninth diamond. Lavaine is described as young, brave, and a true knight. He was brother to Elaine.

Lavender, Dr. A wise and lovable old clergyman in Margaret Deland's Old Chester stories.

Lavinia and Palemon. Thomson's Seasons. Lavinia was the daughter of Acasto, patron of Palemon. Through Acasto, Palemon gained a fortune and wandered away from his friend. Acasto lost his property and, dying, left a widow and daughter in poverty. Palemon often sought them, but could never find them. One day, a lovely modest maiden came to glean in Palemon's fields. The young squire was greatly struck with her exceeding beauty and modesty, but she was known as a pauper, and he dared not give her more than a passing glance. Upon inquiry, he found that the beautiful gleaner was the daughter of Acasto; he proposed marriage, and Lavinia was restored to her rightful place. Similarity between this story and that of Ruth in the Bible is notable.

Lawyer's Alcove. Name given to a volume of poems selected from the best poems by lawyers, for lawyers, and about lawyers. Included in this volume are Shakespeare's "Sonnet CXXXIV"; Blackstone's "A Lawyer's Farewell to his Muse"; "Justice," by John Quincy Adams; Landor's "At the Buckingham Sessions"; "The Judicial Court of Venus," by Jonathan Swift; Saxe's "Briefless Barrister" and "The Lawyer's Valentine"; "General Average," by William Allen Butler; "The Festival of Injustice," by Carlton, and Riley's "Lawyer and Child."

Lay of the Last Minstrel, Scott. Lady Margaret of Branksome Hall, "the flower of Teviot," was beloved by Baron Henry of Cranstoun, but a deadly feud existed between the two families. A goblin lured Lady Margaret's brother into a wood, where he fell into the hands of the English. At the same time an army of 3000 English marched to Branksome Hall to take it; but, hearing that Douglas was on the march against them, the two chiefs agreed to decide the contest by single combat. Victory fell to the Scotch, when it was discovered that "Sir William Deloraine," the Scotch champion, was in reality Lord Cranstoun, who then claimed and received the hand of Lady Margaret as his reward. This united the two houses.

Lazy Lawrence. Name and description of a character in one of Miss Edgeworth's stories. Probably derived from a chapbook *The Infamous History of Sir Lawrence Lazy.* This hero of Lubberland had served the schoolmaster, his wife, the squire's cook, and the farmer, which, by the laws of Lubberland, was accounted high treason. He was tried but acquitted of many charges of treason.

Leander (lē-ăn'dẽr). A young man of Abydos, who swam nightly across the Hellespont to visit his ladylove, Hero, a priestess of Sestos. One night he was drowned in his attempt, and Hero leaped into the Hellespont also. The story of Hero and Leander is so old and so well known as nearly to belong to mythology.

Lear. A legendary king of Britain, and the hero of Shakespeare's tragedy of the same name. He had three daughters, and when four score years old, wishing to retire from the active duties of sovereignty, resolved to divide his kingdom among them. By elaborate but false professions of love and duty on the part of two daughters, Goneril and Regan, King Lear was persuaded to disinherit the third, Cordelia, who had before been deservedly more dear to him, and to divide his kingdom between her sisters. The tragedy is wrought out in the ungrateful conduct of the older sisters and the suffering of Lear. The beauty of the play is the exquisite character Cordelia.

Leatherstocking Tales. Five stories or romances written by James Fenimore Cooper. The same hero, Leatherstocking, or Natty Bumppo, figures throughout in his life among the Indians. Natty had learned wood-lore as the young Indian learned it. He knew the calls of the wild animals far across the wilderness. He could follow the deer and bear to their haunts. He could trace the path of the wolf by the broken cobwebs glistening in the sunlight; and the cry of the panther was a speech as familiar as his own tongue. When he was thirsty he made a cup of leaves and drank in the Indian fashion. He lay down to rest with that sense of security that comes only to the foresters. These tales take Leatherstocking from young manhood to old age, following the fortunes of the American Indian tribes. The order in which his story is told in these volumes is *The Deerslayer, The Last of the Mohicans, The Pathfinder, The Pioneers,* and *The Prairie.* He is also known by the name of Hawkeye in one part of his story. The best writers on the American Indian are thus quoted in our literature: James F. Cooper, the romancer of the Indian; Henry W. Longfellow, the poet of the Indian; Francis Parkman, the

historian of the Indian; Helen Hunt Jackson, the novelist of the Indian.

Leaves of Grass. The title of a small volume of poems published by Walt Whitman in 1855. It contained his first unconventional work. Later, other poems were included under the same title.

Legend. Anciently, a kind of rubric containing the prayers appointed to be read in Roman Catholic churches. In later times, the word was employed to denote a chronicle or register of the lives of saints, because they were to be read on the festivals of the saints. The manner in which credulous love of the wonderful, exaggeration of fancy, and ecclesiastical enthusiasm, at times even pious fraud, were mixed up with true history in these narrations caused stories of a religious or ecclesiastical nature generally to be designated as "legends," to distinguish them from real history. The word has come to mean a tale handed down by tradition, unauthentic, but popularly believed. Among medieval collections, that drawn up by the Genoese archbishop, Jacopo da Voragine, in the second half of the 13th century, under the title of *Legenda Aurea,* "Golden Legends," or *Historia Lombaraica,* is the most celebrated.

Legree, Simon. The villainous and drunken planter in H. B. Stowe's *Uncle Tom's Cabin.* He had Uncle Tom flogged to death.

Leonine Verse. This form of verse was used in the middle ages in Latin hymns and in secular verse. Said to derive its name from Leonius, a canon of the church of St. Victor, in Paris. In English, any verse which rimes middle and end is called a Leonine verse.

Les Misérables (lā mē'zā'rá'bl'), **Victor Hugo.** This great work is the story of a sturdy, courageous peasant, who, sent to the galleys for a minor offense, becomes a hardened convict. He is reclaimed through the kindness of a saintly bishop and becomes a respected manufacturer and town official. Discovered and hunted by his enemies, he becomes once more an outlaw. But he bears his misfortunes with heroism. His noble death is one of the great episodes in fiction.

Letterpress. Printed matter. The word is often used to distinguish printed words from engraving, or matter printed from types instead of from plates.

Lexicon. A vocabulary, or book containing an alphabetical arrangement of the words of a language, with an explanation of the meaning or sense of each. The term is used chiefly with reference to dictionaries or wordbooks of the Greek, Hebrew, Arabic, or Syriac languages.

Libations. With the prayers among all ancient peoples were usually joined the libations, or drink offerings. These consisted generally of wine, part of which was poured out in honor of the gods, and part of it drunk by the worshiper. The wine must be pure, and offered in a full cup. Sometimes there were libations of water, of honey, of milk, and of oil.

Ligeia. A story written by Poe. Suggested by a dream in which the eyes of the heroine produced the wonderful effect described in the story. Its theme is the conquest of death through the power of will.

Light of the Harem. Name given to the bride of Selim in the poem *Lalla Rookh.* She was the sultana Nourmahal, afterwards called Nourjeham, "light of the world."

Light that Failed, The, Kipling. The hero of the novel, Dick Hildar, after years of military campaigns in Egypt, goes back to London, where, in the midst of success as an artist, he meets Maisie, his boyhood sweetheart. She, bound up in her hopes of success in art, cannot or will not return his whole-hearted love. Suddenly, Dick goes blind, and Maisie is incapable of sacrificing anything for him. He returns to Egypt and is killed. The tragic ending of the story was, for one publication, changed into a happy ending, which was used in a dramatization of the novel.

Lilliput. An imaginary country described in *Gulliver's Travels,* where an ordinary man becomes a great giant beside the small people of the land. Lilliputian is used to designate small ways of expressing malice or jealousy. Among amusing characters in Lilliput land were the Little-endians and the Big-endians who made up two religious factions, which waged incessant war on the subject of the right interpretation of the 54th chapter of the "Blundecral"; "All true believers break their eggs at the convenient end." The godfather of Calin, the reigning emperor of Lilliput, happened to cut his finger while breaking his egg at the big end, and therefore commanded all faithful Lilliputians to break their eggs in future at the small end. The Blefuscudians called this decree rank heresy, and determined to exterminate the believers of such an abominable practice from the face of the earth. Hundreds of treatises were published on both sides, but each sect put all those books opposed to its own views into the "Index Expurgatorius," and not a few of the more zealous died as martyrs for daring to follow their private judgement.

Limbo. From Latin *limbus*, meaning "edge" or "border." A place where the souls of good men not admitted into heaven wait the general resurrection. A similar place exists for the souls of unbaptized children. Still another limbo is a fool's paradise, a place for all nonsense. This old belief has been used by Dante and Milton in their poems.

Lincoln's Inn Fields. A square in London near the junction of High Holborn and Chancery Lane. It is surrounded by lawyers' offices, Lincoln's Inn, the Royal College of Surgeons, and the Soane Museum. It was laid out by Inigo Jones, the celebrated architect. The square is named from Lincoln's Inn, one of the legal societies of England through which men are called to the bar. The buildings occupied by the society formerly belonged to the earl of Lincoln. Hence their name.

Literati (*lĭt'ê-rā'tĭ*). (1) Men of letters, scholars of note. (2) "The Literati" was the title of a series of comments by Edgar Allan Poe on 38 New York authors which appeared in *Godey's* from May to October, 1846.

Lithgow's Bower. A favorite residence of the kings and queens of Scotland, especially of Mary of Guise; and here the unfortunate Mary Queen of Scots was born in 1542.

Little Billee. Trilby, Du Maurier. The nickname of the hero, William Bagot, an impulsive, boyish art student in Paris, who falls in love with Trilby, an artist's model. The match is broken off by Little Billee's mother. Trilby, under the tutelage of Svengali, musician and hypnotist, becomes a great singer. At the death of Svengali, her power leaves her and she dies. After the death of Little Billee, Taffy, one of his Paris friends, marries his sister.

Little Breeches, John Hay. The title of a poem published in *Pike County Ballads* in 1871.

Little Brother. An appellation made popular through the tale bearing the name. Josiah Flynt ran away from home when he was three years old and continued to do so frequently ever after. His first piece of fiction was naturally based on trampdom. His hero is a boy-tramp, a little fellow whose irresistible impulse to view the great world around him causes him to become a "Prushun" to an old inhabitant of Hoboland. He wished people to see where a number of stray boys land, for he had found out that a great many of the so-called "kidnapped" youngsters are in reality simple runaways with romantic temperaments.

Little Citizens, Myra Kelly. A New York schoolteacher's stories of her East Side Jewish charges. Human nature and American Yiddish dialect are alike faithfully rendered.

Little Dorrit. The heroine and title of a novel by Dickens. Little Dorrit was born and brought up in the Marshalsea prison, where her father was confined for debt.

Little John. A big, stalwart fellow, named John Little, who encountered Robin Hood and gave him a sound thrashing, after which he was rechristened, and Robin stood godfather. Little John is introduced by Sir Walter Scott in *The Talisman*.

Little Lord Fauntleroy. The seven-year-old hero of the story of this title by Frances Hodgson Burnett. He is the son of an Englishman who has been disinherited by his father, an English earl, for marrying an American. Upon the death of the boy's father, the old earl has the boy brought to England, but on condition that his mother, "Dearest," shall not accompany him to the family home. Gradually, the boy wins for himself and his mother a place in the old man's heart.

Little Men, Louisa May Alcott. A story of the boys in the school at Plumfield, kept by "Jo" and her husband, Mr. Baer. *Jo's Boys* is a sequel to this story.

Little Minister, The, Barrie. A romantic "Thrums" story. An Auld Licht minister's love for the beautiful "Egyptian," a lady in disguise, is the theme.

Little Nell. Old Curiosity Shop, Dickens. The prominent character of the story, pure and true, though living in the midst of selfishness and crime. She was brought up by her grandfather, who was in his dotage, and who tried to eke out a narrow living by selling curiosities. At length, through terror of Quilp, the old man and his grandchild stole away and led a vagrant life.

Little Women, L. M. Alcott. A story of the girlhood life of Louisa May Alcott and her three sisters, at Concord, Mass. A sequel to the story is *Little Men*.

Llewellyn. A legendary Welsh prince who, on returning from hunting, found his baby boy missing and his favorite greyhound, Gelert, covered with blood. Thinking that the hound had eaten him, he killed it. But, on searching more carefully, the child was found alive under the cradle clothes, and near him the body of a huge wolf which had been killed by the faithful hound.

Lochiel (*lŏκ-ēl'*). The title of the head of the clan Cameron. Thomas Campbell's poem, "Lochiel's Warning," is a prophecy of the battle of Culloden.

Lochinvar (*lŏκ'ĭn-vär'*). The hero—a young Highlander—of an incidental song in "Marmion," who was much in love with a lady whose fate was decreed that she should marry a "laggard." Young Lochinvar persuaded the too-willing lassie to be his partner in a dance; and while the guests were intent on their amusement he swung her into his saddle and made off with her before the bridegroom could recover from his amazement.

Locksley. So Robin Hood is sometimes called, from the village in which he was born. He appears as an archer in *Ivanhoe*.

Locksley Hall. A poem by Tennyson, in which the hero, the lord of Locksley Hall, having been jilted by his cousin Amy in favor of a rich boor, pours forth his feelings in a flood of scorn and indignation. Many lines from this poem have passed into common speech, such as "In the spring a young man's fancy lightly turns to thoughts of love."

Locrin or **Locrine.** Father of Sabrina, and eldest son of the mythical Brutus, king of ancient Britain. On the death of his father he became king of Loegria.

Loegria (*lô-ē'grĭ-ä*) or **Logres** (*lô'grĕs*). England is so called by Geoffrey of Monmouth, from Logrine, or Locrine, eldest son of the mythical King Brute, or Brutus.

Logos. This word, occurring at the beginning of the gospel of St. John, was early taken to refer to the "second person of the Trinity, i. e., Christ." Yet the apostle's precise meaning—who alone makes use of the term in this manner, and only in the introductory part of his gospel,—whether he adopted the symbolical usage in which it was employed by the various schools of his day, which of their differing significations he had in view, or whether he intended to convey a meaning quite peculiar to himself,—these are some of the innumerable questions to which the word has given rise, and which, though most fiercely discussed ever since the first days of Christianity, are far from having found a satisfactory solution.

Lohengrin. The Knight of the Swan; the hero of a romance written by a disciple of Wolfram von Eschenbach, in the 13th century, and also of a modern music drama by Richard Wagner. He was the son of Parsifal, and came to Brabant in a ship drawn by a white swan, which took him away again when his bride, disobeying his injunction, pressed him to discover his name and parentage.

Lord Jim, Joseph Conrad. The hero of this novel, a young ship's officer, had been dismissed from the merchant marine service because he had erred in a serious emergency. Self-exiled among Malaysian savages, he tries to redeem himself by devoted service. Among these people he gains the title of "Lord Jim."

Lorna Doone, R. D. Blackmore. A novel. Lorna, child of the outlaw family of the Doones in Exmoor, saves John Ridd, a fourteen-year-old boy, from capture by them. Seven years later, grown to manhood, John becomes her champion against her own people, and finally they are married. It is a story of England in the 17th century, and involves the infamous Judge Jeffrey.

Lothario (*lô-thä'rĭ-ō*). The name has come to stand in literature for the type of the gay, handsome, and gallant libertine. The original is a Florentine cavalier in Cervantes' story *The Curious Impertinent*. Rowe, in *The Fair Penitent*, gave the name to a Genoese noble, and Richardson developed the character in Robert Lovelace of his novel *Clarissa Harlowe*.

Lotos-Eaters. Tennyson wrote a poem called "The Lotos-Eaters," describing a set of islanders who live in dreamy idleness, weary of life, and regardless of all its stirring events.

Love Doctor, The. L'Amour Médecin (*lä-mōōr' mā́d"sдN'*). A comedy by Molière, written about the year 1665. Lucinde, the daughter of Sganarelle, is in love, and the father calls in four doctors to consult upon the nature of her malady. They see the patient, and retire to consult together, but talk about Paris, about their visits, about the topics of the day; and, when the father enters to know what opinion they have formed, they all prescribe different remedies, and pronounce different opinions. Lisette then calls in a "quack" doctor, Clitandre, the lover, who says that he must act on the imagination, and proposes a seeming marriage, to which Sganarelle assents. The assistant being a notary, Clitandre and Lucinde are married.

Lover's Vows. Altered from Kotzebue's. Baron Wildenhaim, in his youth, seduced Agatha Friburg, and then forsook her. She had a son, Frederick, who became a soldier. While on furlough, he came to spend his time with his mother, and found her in abject poverty and almost starved. A poor cottager took her in, while Frederick, who had no money, went to beg charity. Baron Wildenhaim was out with his gun, and Frederick asked alms of him. The count gave him a shilling; Frederick demanded more, and, being refused, seized the baron by the throat. The keepers arrived and put him in the castle dungeon. Here he was visited by the chaplain, and it came out that the count was his father. The chaplain, being appealed to, told the count the only reparation he could make would be to marry Agatha and acknowledge the young soldier to be his son. This advice he followed, and Agatha Friburg, the beggar, became the Baroness Wildenhaim of Wildenhaim castle.

Love's Labor's Lost, Shakespeare. Ferdinand, king of Navarre, with three lords named Biron, Dumain, and Longaville, agree to spend three years in study, during which time no woman was to approach the court. The compact signed, all went well, until the princess of France, attended by Rosaline, Maria, and Katharine, besought an interview respecting certain debts said to be due from the king of France to the king of Navarre. The four gentlemen fell in love with the four ladies. The love of the king sought the princess, by right, Biron loved Rosaline, Longaville admired Maria, and Dumain adored Katharine. In order to carry their suits, the four gentlemen, disguised as Muscovites, presented themselves before the ladies; but the ladies, being warned of the masquerade, disguised themselves also, so that the gentlemen in every case addressed the wrong lady. A mutual arrangement was made that the suits should be deferred for twelve months and a day; and, if, at the expiration of that time, they remained of the same mind, the matter should be taken into serious consideration.

Loves of the Angels. A poetical story written by Thomas Moore. It may be called the stories of three angels, and was founded on the Eastern tale of "Harût and Marût," and the rabbinical fictions of the loves of "Uzziel and Shamchazai." (1) The first angel fell in love with Lea, whom he saw bathing. She returned love for love, but his love was carnal, hers heavenly. He loved the woman, she loved the angel. At last the angel gave to her the password which should open the gates of heaven. She pronounced it, and rose through the air into paradise. The angel degenerated and became no longer an angel of light, but "of the earth, earthy." (2) The second angel was Rubi, one of the seraphs. He loved Liris, who asked him to come in all his celestial glory. He did so; and she, rushing into his arms, was burned to death; but the kiss she gave him became a brand on his face forever. (3) The third angel was Zaraph, who loved Nama. It was Nama's desire to love without control, and to love holily; but, as she fixed her love on a creature and not on the Creator, both she and Zaraph were doomed to live among the things that perish. When the end of all shall come, Nama and Zaraph will be admitted into the realms of everlasting love.

Loving Cup. A large cup passed round from guest to guest at state banquets and city feasts. On the introduction of Christianity, the custom of wassailing was not abolished, but it assumed a religious aspect. The monks called the wassail bowl the loving cup. In the universities the term "Grace Cup" is more general. Immediately after grace the silver cup, filled with wine, is passed round. The master and wardens drink .welcome to their guests; the cup is then passed to all the guests. A loving or grace cup should have two handles, and some have four. This ceremony, of drinking from one cup and passing it round, was observed in the Jewish paschal supper, and our Lord refers to the custom in the words, "Drink ye all of this."

Lubberland. An imaginary country of idleness and luxury. The name has been applied to certain cities in burlesque.

Luck of Roaring Camp, The, Bret Harte. A story of the softening influence of a child's presence among the men of an early mining camp in California. The poem, published in the second number of the *Overland Monthly* (1868), brought Harte his first real fame and popularity.

Luggnagg. Gulliver's Travels. An imaginary island whose inhabitants have the gift of eternal life, lacking with it the gift of immortal health and strength.

Lumbercourt, Lord. Character in Macklin's comedy *The Man of the World*. A voluptuary, greatly in debt, who consented, in return for considerable money, to give his daughter, Lady Rudolphe, to Egerton McSycophant. Egerton, however, had no fancy for the lady, but married Constantia, the girl of his choice. His lordship was in alarm lest this should be his ruin; but Sir Pertinax told him the bargain should still remain good if Egerton's younger brother, Sandy, were accepted by his lordship instead. To this his lordship and the lady readily agreed.

Lure of the Labrador Wild, The, Wallace. A recital of the ill-fated expedition to Labrador undertaken by Leonidas Hubbard, Jr., during the summer of 1903. The party consisted of Mr. Hubbard, Mr. Wallace, and a half-breed Cree Indian named Elson, who proved himself a veritable hero. As is generally known, the object of the party was to reach the interior of Labrador over a portion of that country unexplored, or at least unmapped by white men. This purpose was only partially carried out. The winter came on long before Hubbard was ready to turn back, the provisions were exhausted, game was scarce, and the fish failed to rise to the fly. On the return journey toward the coast, Hubbard gave out and had to be left behind until aid could be brought. Wallace succeeded in finding some provisions which had been thrown aside on the inland trip and had returned within a few hundred feet of Hubbard's tent, but without finding it. Elson, the half-breed, managed to reach a trapper's camp and sent back a relief expedition, which picked up Wallace, and later found the body of Hubbard, who had died of starvation.

Lusiad (lū'sĭ-ăd), **The.** The only Portuguese poem that has gained a world-wide celebrity. It was written by Luiz de Camoëns, appeared in 1572, and was entitled *Os Lusiadas*, the "Lusitanians," that is, the Portuguese—the subject being the conquests of that nation in India. It is divided into ten cantos, containing 1102 stanzas. Among English translations, that by Sir Richard Burton is especially notable. *The Lusiad* celebrates the chief events in the history of Portugal, and is remarkable as the only modern epic poem which is pervaded by anything approaching the national and popular spirit of ancient epic poems. Bacchus was the guardian power of the Mohammedans, and Venus or Divine Love, of the Lusians. The fleet first sailed to Mozambique, then to Melinda (Africa), where the adventurers were hospitably received and provided with a pilot to conduct them to India. In the Indian Ocean, Bacchus tried to destroy the fleet; Venus, however, calmed the sea, and Gama arrived at India in safety. Having accomplished his object, he returned to Lisbon. Among the most famous passages are the tragical story of Inez de Castro, and the apparition of the giant Adamastor, who appears as the Spirit of the Storm to Vasco da Gama, when crossing the cape. The versification of *The Lusiad* is extremely charming. The best edition was published in Paris (1817), reprinted in 1819, and again in 1823. *The Lusiad* has been translated into Spanish, French, Italian, English, Polish, and German.

Lusitania (lū'sĭ-tā'nĭ-à). The ancient name of Portugal; so called from Lusus, the companion of Bacchus in his travels. He colonized the country, and called it "Lusitania," and the colonists "Lusians."

Lustrum. The solemn offering made for expiation and purification by one of the censors in the name of the Roman people at the conclusion of the census. The animals offered in sacrifice were a boar, a sheep, and a bull. They were led round the assembled people on the Campus Martius before being sacrificed. As the census was quinquennial, the word lustrum came to signify a period of five years.

Luther's Postil (pŏs'tĭl) **Gospels.** Advent, Christmas, and Epiphany sermons, first published in Latin in 1521, and dedicated to his protector, the elector Frederick. Translated immediately into German, Luther's postils, or homilies, on the gospels are esteemed the best of his sermons. "Postils" was a common name in the 16th century for expositions of the gospels and epistles for Sundays and holydays. The word is explained from the fact that the gospels and epistles were printed first and that after them (*post illa*) came the commentary.

Lycidas (lĭs'ĭ-dăs). The name under which Milton celebrates the untimely death of Edward King, who was drowned in the passage from Chester to Ireland, August 10, 1637. He was the son of Sir John King, secretary for Ireland.

Lydia Languish. The heroine of Sheridan's comedy *The Rivals*, distinguished for the extravagance of her romantic notions.

Lydia. Orlando Furioso. A daughter of the king of Lydia, who was sought in marriage by Alcestes, a Thracian knight; his suit was refused, and he repaired to the king of Armenia, who gave him an army, with which he laid siege to Lydia. He was persuaded by the king's daughter to raise the siege. The king of Armenia would not give up the project, and Alcestes slew him. Lydia now set him all sorts of dangerous tasks to "prove his love," all of which he surmounted. Lastly, she induced him to kill all his allies, and when this was done she mocked him. Alcestes pined and died, and Lydia was doomed to endless torment in hell, where Astolfo saw her, to whom she told her story.

Lygia. The Christian bride of the pagan, Vinicius, in *Quo Vadis*, a historical novel treating the age of Nero, written by Sienkiewicz, a Polish novelist.

Lyric. Literally, pertaining to the lyre. In poetry a name originally applied to what was sung or recited to the accompaniment of the lyre, but it is now applied to odes, ballads, and other verses, such as may be set to music. Lyrics were originally employed in celebrating the praises of gods and heroes, and their characteristic was melodiousness. The Greeks cultivated them with effect, particularly Anacreon and Sappho, but among the Romans Horace was the first and principal lyric poet. It has been said that all poets are singers and these singers are divided into three classes. First, the lyric poet, who can sing but one tune with his one voice. Second, the epic poet, who with his one voice can sing several tunes. Third, the true dramatist, who has many tongues and can sing all tunes.

Mab, Queen. Romeo and Juliet, Shakespeare. The origin of the name is obscure. By some it is derived from the Midgard of the Eddas. The name is given by the English poets of the 15th and succeeding centuries to the imaginary queen of the fairies.

Mabinogion (măb'ĭ-nō'gĭ-ŏn). A series of Welsh tales, chiefly relating to Arthur and the Round Table. A manuscript volume of some 700 pages is preserved in the library of Jesus college, Oxford.

Macbeth. The tale of Macbeth and Banquo was borrowed from the legendary history of Scotland, but the interest of the play is not historical. It is a tragedy of human life, intensely real, the soul, with all its powers for good or evil, deliberately choosing evil. The three witches in the desert place, in thunder, lightning, storm, strike the keynote of evil suggestion. The awfulness of soul destruction is felt in Macbeth and Lady Macbeth as in no other of Shakespeare's dramas.

Maccabees, The. This Jewish family led the struggle of their people against Antiochus Epiphanes, B. C. 168–135. The two Books of the Maccabees give an account of this struggle.

Macheath, Captain. A highwayman who is the hero of Gay's *Beggar's Opera*.

Machiavellism (măk'ĭ-à-věl'ĭz'm). The name came from a writing by Machiavelli, under the title *The Prince*, a famous treatise, in which are expounded those principles of political cunning and artifice, intended to promote arbitrary power, ever since designated "machiavellism."

MacIvor. Waverley, Scott. Fergus MacIvor is a prominent character in the novel, and his sister, Flora MacIvor, is the heroine. They belong to a Scotch chieftain's family.

Macreons, The Island of. Pantagruel, Rabelais. The title is given to Great Britain, derived from a Greek word, meaning long-lived, "because no one is put to death there for his religious opinions." Rabelais says the island "is full of antique ruins and relics of popery and ancient superstitions."

Madasima, Queen. An important character in the old romance called *Amadis of Gaul*; her constant attendant was Elisabat, a famous surgeon, with whom she roamed in solitary retreats.

Madge Wildfire. The Heart of Midlothian, Scott. A poor, wandering, fantastically dressed girl, driven insane by the profligate abuse of George Staunton. She is the daughter of old Meg Murdochson, the gypsy thief.

Madoc (mā'dŏk). A poem by Southey; founded on one of the legends connected with the early history of America. Madoc, a Welsh prince of the 12th century, is represented as making the discovery of the Western world. His contests with the Mexicans form the subject.

Madrigal. (1) A short lyric poem, generally on the subject of love, characterized by epigrammatic terseness or quaintness, and composed of a number of free and unequal verses, confined neither to the regularity of the sonnet, nor to the subtlety of the ode. The madrigals of Tasso are noted in Italian poetry. (2) In music, a part song for several voices, properly with contrapuntal imitation and without musical accompaniment.

Magi (mā'jī). The three "Wise Men" who followed the star to Bethlehem. The traditional names of the three Magi are Melchior, represented as an old man with a long beard, offering gold; Gaspar, a beardless youth who offers frankincense; Balthazar, a black, or Moor, who tenders myrrh.

Magic Rings. These are mentioned by Plato, Cicero and other writers and are supposed to make the wearer invisible.

Magic Staff. The story of the magic staff belongs to the days of legends and seems to be of French origin, but has found its way into other lands. This staff would guarantee the bearer safety from all the perils and mishaps incidental to travelers. According to earliest traditions the staff was a willow branch cut on the eve of All Saints' Day.

Magic Wands. These are found in many old tales or writings. In Tasso's *Jerusalem Delivered* the hermit gave to Charles the Dane and Ubaldo a wand, which, being shaken, infused terror into all who saw it, and in Spenser's *Faery Queen* the palmer who accompanied Sir Guyon had a wand of like virtue. It was made of the same wood as Mercury's caduceus.

Magnalia. The best-known in the long list of Cotton Mather's works was his *Magnalia Christi Americana* (1702), purporting to be an ecclesiastical history of New England, from its first planting in 1620 to the year 1698, but including also civil history, an account of Harvard college, the Indian wars, the witchcraft troubles, and a large number of biographies. The work is of no historical value, but has an important place in puritan psychology.

Magnano. Hudibras, Butler. One of the leaders of the rabble that attacked Hudibras at a bear baiting.

Magnificat (măg-nĭf'ĭ-kăt). In the ritual of the Roman Catholic Church, the name given to the "Song of the Virgin Mary," in Luke I: 46–55. The name is derived from the opening word of the song in the Vulgate or Latin New Testament.

Maiden Lane. A street in London, between Covent Garden and the Strand. Andrew Marvell, Turner, the landscape painter, and Voltaire lived here at different times. The name is said to have been given from an image of the Virgin which once stood there.

Maidens' Castle. An allegorical castle mentioned in Malory's *Morte D'Arthur*. It was taken from a duke by seven knights, and held by them till Sir Galahad expelled them. It was called "The Maidens' Castle," because these knights made a vow that every maiden who passed it should be made a captive.

Maid Marian. (1) A half mythical character, but the name is said to have been assumed by Matilda, daughter of Robert Lord Fitzwalter, while Robin Hood remained in a state of outlawry. The name Maid Marian is connected with the morris dance, or May-day dance, at which she was said to appear. (2) The title of a charming novel by Thomas Love Peacock (1822).

Maid of Athens. Made famous by Lord Byron's song of this title. Twenty-four years after this song was written, an Englishman sought out "the Athenian maid," and found a beggar without a vestige of beauty.

Maid of Saragossa. Childe Harold, Byron. A young Spanish woman distinguished for her heroism during the defense of Saragossa in 1808-09. She first attracted notice by mounting a battery where her lover had fallen, and working a gun in his place.

Malaprop, Mrs. A character in Sheridan's *Rivals*, noted for her blundering use of words.

Malbecco. Faery Queen, Spenser. The husband of a young wife, Helinore, and himself a crabbed, jealous old fellow.

Malengrin. A character in Spenser's *Faery Queen*, who carried a net on his back "to catch fools with." The name has grown to mean the personification of guile or flattery.

Malepardus. The castle of Master Reynard the Fox, in the beast epic *Reynard the Fox*.

Malvoisin. Ivanhoe, Scott. One of the challenging knights at the tournament, Sir Philip de Malvoisin. Sir Albert de Malvoisin was a preceptor of the Knights Templars.

Mambrino (măm-brē'nō). (1) In *Orlando Furioso* by Ariosto, a king of the Moors, who was the possessor of an enchanted golden helmet, which rendered the wearer invulnerable, and which was the object of eager quest to the paladins of Charlemagne. This helmet was borne away by the knight Rinaldo. (2) In *Don Quixote* we are told of a barber who was caught in a shower of rain, and who, to protect his hat, clapped his brazen basin on his head. Don Quixote insisted that this basin was the helmet of the Moorish king, and, taking possession of it, wore it as such.

Managarm. Prose Edda. The largest and most formidable of the race of giants. He dwells in the ironwood, Jamvid. Managarm will first fill himself with the blood of man, and then will he swallow up the moon. This giant symbolizes war, and the "ironwood" in which he dwells is the wood of spears.

Man and Superman, G. B. Shaw. Called by many the most important of Shaw's plays. It is a comedy in which he "modernizes" the Don Juan motive. John Tanner, a social revolutionist, of spotless character and a foe of convention, is determined to escape love and marriage. But he is overtaken and captured by Ann Whitefield, who personifies the demands of the Life Force. Other clearly drawn characters add to the keen comedy of the piece.

Manfred. The hero of a poem by Byron. Manfred is a melancholy and defiant soul, haunted by a mysterious past crime. He visits the court of Arimanes and causes to be evoked the vision of his lost love, Astarte. She gives him no answer to his question. At the conclusion, when he is dying in his lonely castle in the Alps, devils come to claim his soul and he defies them.

Manon Lescaut (*mä'nôN' lĕs'kō'*), **Prévost.** One of the first of modern novels, published in 1733. Chevalier des Grieux, who tells the story, is disgraced through his association with Manon. But she proves her love by going with him into exile in America.

Mantalini (*măn'tà-lē'nê*). **Nicholas Nickleby, Dickens.** The husband of madame; he is a man-doll, noted for his white teeth, his oaths, and his gorgeous morning gown. This "exquisite" lives on his wife's earnings, and thinks he confers a favor on her by spending. Madame Mantalini is represented as a fashionable milliner near Cavendish Square, London.

Man with the Hoe, The, Edwin Markham. The subject of a famous poem, suggested by the picture by J. F. Millet. The theme is the hopelessness of the toiler.

Marble Faun, The, Nathaniel Hawthorne. A romance. Miriam, a beautiful art student in Rome, whose origin and relations are mysterious, is loved by Donatello, a young count, whose striking resemblance to the "Faun of Praxiteles" suggests his descent from the woodland fauns. Donatello is singularly unsophisticated. One night, at a sign from Miriam, he throws Brother Antonio, who has been following Miriam, over the Tarpeian rock to his death. Miriam disappears, but Donatello, awakened to responsibility, gives himself up to justice.

Marcellus. Hamlet, Shakespeare. An officer of Denmark, to whom the ghost of the murdered king appeared before it presented itself to Prince Hamlet.

Marchioness, The. Old Curiosity Shop, Dickens. A half-starved maid-of-all-work, in the service of Sampson Brass and his sister Sally. She was so lonesome and dull that it afforded her relief to peep at Mr. Swiveller even through the keyhole of his door. Mr. Swiveller called her the "marchioness," when she played cards with him, "because it seemed more real and pleasant" to play with a marchioness than with a domestic. While enjoying these games they made the well-known "orange-peel wine."

Mariana in the Moated Grange. (1) In Tennyson's poem of this name, a young damsel who sits in the moated grange, looking out for her lover, who never comes. (2) In Shakespeare's *Measure for Measure*, Mariana is a lovely and lovable lady, betrothed to Angelo, who, during the absence of Vincentio, the duke of Vienna, acted as his lord deputy.

Mark Tapley. Martin Chuzzlewit, Dickens. A young man with an ambition to be "jolly" under adverse conditions. He accompanies young Martin Chuzzlewit to America, and is constantly the good genius of that heedless youth, and on his return marries Mrs. Lupin, thus becoming landlord of the Blue Dragon, where he had formerly worked.

Marplot. "The busy body." A blundering, good-natured, meddlesome young man, very inquisitive, too officious, and always bungling anything with which he interferes. Character found in comedies written by Mrs. Centlivre.

Marriage of Figaro (*fē'gä'rō'*), **The, Beaumarchais.** This play is the sequel to the *Barber of Seville*. It was presented in 1784, and was immediately popular. It helped forward the Revolution. In the play, Almaviva and Rosine are weary of married life. The husband has turned his fancy to Suzanne. But Figaro is in love with her, and he succeeds in checkmating the noble gallant. Brilliant wit and careless mockery both adorn and mar the play.

Marse Chan, T. N. Page. A short story, told in the language of the hero's negro servant. A Virginia gentleman loves a lady, who, though loving him, is cold and haughty. He is killed in battle, and she mourns him as a husband during the rest of her life.

Martin's Summer, St. Halcyon days; a time of prosperity; fine weather. Mentioned by Shakespeare in *Henry VI*, etc.

Masora or **Massorah** (*mà-sō'rà*). A critical work or canon, whereby is fixed and ascertained the reading of the text of the Hebrew Bible. The word means "tradition."

Masques (*măsks*). Dramatic representations made for a festive occasion, with a reference to the persons present and the occasion. Their *dramatis personæ* were allegorical. They admitted of dialogue, music, singing, and dancing, combined by the use of some ingenious fable into a whole. They were made and performed for the court and the houses of the nobles, and the scenery was gorgeous and varied. According to Holinshed's *Chronicle*, the first

masque performed in England was at Greenwich, in 1512. Shakespeare, as well as Beaumont and Fletcher, have frequently introduced masques into their plays. Milton himself made them worthier by writing *Comus*. H. W. Longfellow wrote the "Masque of Pandora," taking the story from Hawthorne's *Wonder Book*.

Master Builder, The, Ibsen. A drama which embodies the dangers of selfish ambition and the struggle of age against youth. Sollness, a master builder, has gained success through sacrificing his wife and his business associates. He thinks himself secure from the competition of younger folk, when Hilda Wangel appears and tempts him to climb a high tower "as he did in his youth." He falls to his death.

Master of Ballantrae, The, Stevenson. A novel of the time of the Stuart Pretender, about 1745. The story is told by the old steward of Ballantrae. The older son of the house, James Durrie, espouses the Stuart cause, the younger, Henry, staying at home, the decision being made on the turn of a coin. Alison Graeme, in love with James, marries Henry when James is reported dead. But James returns, with a disgraceful record behind him, and takes advantage of the situation to persecute the family with diabolical persistence. Henry, with Alison and their son, at last emigrates to her estate in New York. James follows. Both brothers die on an ill-fated search for treasure which James claims to have hidden in the northern woods, and are buried side by side.

Mauth Dog. Lay of the Last Minstrel, Scott. A black specter spaniel that haunted the guardroom of Peeltown in the Isle of Man. A drunken trooper entered the guardroom while the dog was there, but lost his speech, and died within three days.

Mavournin or **Mavourneen.** Irish for "my darling."

Mayeux (*mä'yĕ'*). The name of a hunchback, who figures prominently in numberless French caricatures and romances.

Mayfair (*mā'fâr'*). A fashionable locality in London, east of Hyde Park. All streets north of Piccadilly now lead into the district of Mayfair, which takes its name from a fair which used to be held in Shepherd's Market and its surrounding streets.

Mayor of Casterbridge, The, Thomas Hardy. One of the most famous of Hardy's Wessex stories. Michael Henchard, a hay trusser by trade, comes one day with his wife and little daughter, Elizabeth Jane, to a village fair. While drunk he offers the wife and daughter for sale. The offer is taken up by a young sailor, who takes them away with him. The next morning, Michael, sobered, takes a vow to touch no liquor for twenty years. He comes to the town of Casterbridge, and in time becomes wealthy in the grain trade and is made mayor of the town. One evening the wife he had sold, with her daughter, comes to Casterbridge. To avoid discovery of his old folly, Henchard provides them a cottage, and after a time marries his wife again. But she soon dies, when Henchard discovers that Elizabeth Jane is not his child, but the child of the sailor. His old character comes to the surface, and disaster overtakes him. He dies miserably in a moorland cottage, after the sailor, now wealthy himself, has returned to claim his child, who marries Donald Farfrae.

Mazeppa, Byron. Mazeppa, in a poem under the same title, was a Cossack of noble family who became a page in the court of the king of Poland. While in this capacity, he intrigued with Theresia, the young wife of a count, who discovered the amour, and had the young page lashed to a wild horse and turned adrift.

McFingal. The hero of Trumbull's political poem of the same name; represented as a burly New England squire, enlisted on the side of the Tory party of the American Revolution, and constantly engaged in controversy with Honorius, the champion of the Whigs.

Measure for Measure, Shakespeare. There was a law in Vienna that made it death for a man to live with a woman not his wife, but the law was so little enforced that the mothers of Vienna complained to the duke of its neglect. So the duke deputed Angelo to enforce it, and, assuming the dress of a friar, absented himself awhile to watch the result. Scarcely was the duke gone, when Claudio was sentenced to death for violating the law. His sister Isabel went to intercede on his behalf, and Angelo told her he would spare her brother if she would become his Phryne. Isabel told her brother he must prepare to die, as the conditions proposed by Angelo were out of the question. The duke, disguised as a friar, heard the whole story, and persuaded Isabel to "assent in words," but to send Mariana, the divorced wife of Angelo, to take her place. This was done, but Angelo sent the provost to behead Claudio, a crime which "the friar" contrived to avert. Next day, the duke returned to the city, and Isabel told her tale. The end was, the duke married Isabel, Angelo took back his wife, and Claudio married Juliet.

Médecin Malgré Lui, Le (*lĕ mād″sᾰn′ mäl′grä′ lwē*), "The Doctor in Spite of Himself," **Molière.** In this comedy Sganarelle, Molière's frequently used character, appears as a woodcutter whom Geronte summons as a physician to cure his daughter's dumbness. When Sganarelle discovers that Lucinde is pretending dumbness to avoid marriage with Horace, her father's choice, he brings in an apothecary who soon effects a cure. The apothecary turns out to be Léandre, Lucinde's lover, and all ends happily.

Meg Merrilies. A half-crazy gypsy or sibyl, a prominent character in Scott's *Guy Mannering*. Keats wrote a ballad about her.

Meister, Wilhelm. Hero and title of a philosophic novel by Goethe. The object is to show that man, despite his errors and shortcomings, is led by a guiding hand, and reaches some higher aim at last. This is considered to be the first true German novel.

Meistersinger. In Germany an association of master tradesmen, to revive the national minstrelsy, which had fallen into decay with the decline of the minnesinger or love-minstrels (1350–1523). Their poems were chiefly moral or religious, and were constructed according to rigid rules.

Melissa. *Orlando Furioso*, **Ariosto.** The prophetess who lived in Merlin's cave. Bradamant gave her the enchanted ring to take to Rogero; so, assuming the form of Atlantes, she not only delivered Rogero, but disenchanted all the forms metamorphosed in the island, where he was captive.

Melnotte, Claude. *Lady of Lyons*, **Bulwer.** The son of a gardener in love with Pauline, "the Beauty of Lyons," but treated by her with contempt. Beauseant and Glavis, two other rejected suitors, conspired with him to humble her.

Melyhalt. A powerful female subject of King Arthur's court. Sir Galiot invaded her domain, but she forgave his trespass and chose him for her knight and chevalier.

Menard. The Road to Frontenac, Merwin. The hero of the novel, a leader among Indians and white men during the making of New France. From Quebec he goes west, holding control of affairs in spite of treachery in both races. His companions are chiefly French, amid whom figure a Jesuit and two Indians, and the story contains much of that romantic charm peculiar to early French pioneer life, whence Longfellow and other poets and story-tellers have drawn inspiration.

Mengtsu (*mŭng-tsŭ′*) One of the sacred "four books" of China, so called from its author, Mengtse, Latinized into Mencius. This great work was written in the 4th century B. C., and contains the wisdom of the age. These are some of its teachings: "Humanity, righteousness, propriety, knowledge, are as natural to man as his four limbs." "Humanity is internal, righteousness is external." In this same book Mencius taught that government is from God, but for the people, whose welfare is the supreme good. The phrase "mother of Meng," which has been borrowed from the Chinese, signifies "a great teacher."

Menteur, Le (*lĕ mᾰn′tĕr′*), "The Liar," **Corneille.** The propensities of the leading character give the play its name and lead to the complications of the plot. This is generally considered Corneille's best comedy and the most important before the time of Molière.

Merchant of Venice. Antonio, the merchant, in Shakespeare's play, signs a bond in order to borrow money from Shylock, a Jew, for Bassanio, the lover of Portia. If the loan were repaid within three months, only the principal would be required; if not, the Jew should be at liberty to claim a pound of flesh from Antonio's body. The ships of Antonio being delayed by contrary winds, the merchant was unable to meet his bill, and the Jew claimed the forfeiture. Portia, in the dress of a law doctor, conducted the defense, and saved Antonio by reminding the Jew that a pound of flesh gave him no drop of blood.

Merchant's Tale, The, Chaucer. Substantially the same as the first Latin metrical tale of Adolphus, and not unlike a Latin prose tale given in the appendix of Wright's edition of *Æsop's Fables*. It is the story of the betrayal of an old husband by a young wife. The story is evidently of Oriental origin and very old. Boccaccio and Chaucer may have borrowed it from the *Commedia Lydiæ*. The well-known incident of the pear tree is found in all these sources, an interesting account of which has been given by the Chaucer Society Publications under *Origins and Analogues of the Tales*. Pope used this story as his basis for "January and May."

Merlin. (1) The name of an ancient Welsh prophet and enchanter. He is often alluded to by the older poets, especially Spenser, in his *Faery Queen*, and also figures in Tennyson's *Idylls of the King*. In *Le Morte D'Arthur* by Malory, Merlin is the prince of enchanters and of a super-

natural origin. He is said to have built the Round Table and to have brought from Ireland the stones of Stonehenge on Salisbury Plain. (2) A dramatic poem by E. A. Robinson, in which the poet embodies modern life and problems in the story of Merlin, Vivian, and Arthur.

Merlin's Cave. In Dynevor, near Carmarthen, noted for its ghastly noises of rattling iron chains, groans, and strokes of hammers. The cause is this: Merlin set his spirits to fabricate a brazen wall to encompass the city of Carmarthen. Leaving to call on the Lady of the Lake, he bade them labor till he returned; but he never did return, for Vivian held him prisoner by her wiles.

Merry Wives of Windsor, The, Shakespeare. A rollicking farce. The merry wives are Mrs. Ford and Mrs. Page, to whom Falstaff makes love. The two ladies set traps and tricks for him, making him the laughing stock of the town. The booby love of Slender for Anne Page parallels Falstaff's adventures. Justice Shallow, Bardolph, Pistol, and Mistress Quickly find place in the play.

Messiah, The. An epic poem in fifteen books, by F. G. Klopstock. The subject is the last days of Jesus, His crucifixion and resurrection.

Micawber, Mr. Wilkins. David Copperfield, Dickens. This character has become a by-word for improvidently "waiting for something to turn up." He is thought to have been modeled on Dickens's father.

Michael and His Lost Angel, H. A. Jones. Michael Feversham, a young, mystical, ascetic clergyman, has insisted upon a public confession in the village church by the daughter of his secretary, who has been concealing an illicit love affair. Within a few months he himself falls deeply in love with a woman, Audrie Lesden, who has recently come to his parish and who gives the money to rebuild his church. He makes public confession at the dedication of the rebuilt church and leaves the parish. In Italy, as Michael is about to enter a monastery, Audrie, very ill, appears and dies in his arms. Seeing his life as a tissue of blunders, he seeks the monastery for peace.

Middletown. Through their analytical studies of a typical American city (Muncie, Ind.), Robert S. and Helen M. Lynd have mirrored the conditions, cultural background, and changes in Midwestern America at two stages of the country's history. Their books are *Middletown* (1929) and *Middletown in Transition* (1937).

Midsummer Night's Dream, A, Shakespeare. Egeus promised his daughter Hermia to Demetrius. She loved Lysander and fled from Athens with her lover. Demetrius went in pursuit of her, followed by Helena, who doted on him. All four came to a forest and fell asleep. Oberon and Titania had quarreled, and Oberon, by way of punishment, dropped on Titania's eyes during sleep some lovejuice, or "love in idleness," the effect of which is to make the sleeper fall in love with the first thing seen when waking. The first thing seen by Titania was Bottom the weaver, wearing an ass's head. In the meantime King Oberon dispatched Puck to the lovers, and with the juice Puck changed their vision and made all content. It has been suggested that in this play Shakespeare may have borrowed hints from Chaucer.

Mildendo. *Gulliver's Travels*, **Swift.** The metropolis of Lilliput, the wall of which was two feet and a half in height and at least eleven inches thick. The emperor's palace, called Belfaborac, was in the center of the city.

Miles Standish. In Longfellow's *Courtship of Miles Standish*, the Puritan captain is too shy to propose. He sends John Alden, and the girl Priscilla says, "Speak for yourself, John Alden."

Miller, Daisy. Name of heroine and title of the story by Henry James. An American girl traveling in Europe, where her innocence, ignorance, and disregard of European customs and standards of propriety put her in compromising situations and frequently expose her conduct to misconstruction.

Mill on the Floss, The, George Eliot. Maggie Tulliver, living with her brother Tom and their parents at the mill, as she grows up, becomes confused and entangled in the mysteries and disappointments of existence. Separated from her lover, Philip Wakeham, she is estranged from her family through her imprudent conduct with Stephen Guest. She welcomes death, which comes to her and Tom in a tidal wave that sweeps away the old mill.

Mincing Lane. A street in London connecting Fenchurch street with Great Tower street; the center of colonial (wholesale) trade. It received its name from the "minchens" (nuns) of St. Helen's, a part of whose domain it once was.

Minnehaha. Hiawatha, H. W. Longfellow. The daughter of the arrow-maker of Dacotah, and wife of Hiawatha. She was called Minnehaha from the waterfall of that name.

Minnesänger or **Minnesinger.** A name given to the German lyric poets of the middle ages, on account of love being the principal theme of their lays, the German word *minne* being used to denote a pure and faithful love.

Miranda, The Tempest, Shakespeare. The daughter of Prospero, the exiled duke of Milan, and niece of Antonio, the usurping duke. She is brought up on a desert island, with Ariel, the fairy spirit, and Caliban, the monster, as her only companions.

Miriam. A beautiful and mysterious woman in Hawthorne's romance *The Marble Faun*, for love of whom Donatello commits murder, becoming her partner in crime.

Misanthrope, Le (*lĕ mē'zäɴ'thrŏp'*), **Molière.** The hero of this comedy, Alceste, wearied with society, has grown misanthropic. He loves Célimène, but she will not share his seclusion, and he gives her up. The play is famous for its vivid contrasts among the characters, as for example, that between Alceste and his friend Philinte.

Miserere (*mĭz'ê-rē'rê*). A title given in the Roman Catholic Church to the 51st Psalm, usually called the "psalm of mercy," and derived from the opening word in the Latin version.

Moby Dick; or the Whale. A novel by Herman Melville, published in 1851, which is considered his masterpiece. It is an adventure narrative of a whaling voyage, the chief object of which was the killing of a vicious white whale called Moby Dick. Symbolical undertones emphasize the conflict between man and his fate.

Monsieur Beaucaire (*mē-syû' bō'kâr'*), **Booth Tarkington.** The plot is laid at Bath, in England, in the time of Beau Nash. A young French barber has the temerity to fall in love with an aristocratic English woman. He gives a good account of himself with gentlemen's weapons, and turns out to be Louis Philippe of Valois, who had fled from France to escape marriage with a princess.

Morality, The. An old play in which the characters were the Vices and Virtues, with the addition afterwards of allegorical personages, such as Riches, Good Deeds, Confession, Death, and any human condition or quality needed for the play. These characters were brought together in a story in which Virtue triumphs.

Morituri Salutamus. Latin, meaning "We about to die salute you." A "hymn to age," written by H. W. Longfellow, for the jubilee reunion of Bowdoin's Class of 1825. It contains a number of classic allusions and an entire tale from the *Gesta Romanorum*.

Morris Dance. The name is derived from "Moorish dance," introduced into England in the reign of Edward III by John of Gaunt on his return from Spain. It was a feature of the May-day and other outdoor festivities.

Mortality, Old. Old Mortality, Scott. A religious itinerant, who frequented country churchyards and the graves of the Covenanters. He was first discovered at Gandercleugh, clearing the moss from the grey tombstones, renewing with his chisel the half-defaced inscriptions, and repairing the decorations of the tombs.

Morte D'Arthur, Le. (1) A prose version of the Arthurian romances, made by Sir Thomas Malory before 1470 and printed by Caxton in 1485. The classic English version of these stories. Tennyson drew on this source. (2) Title of a poem by Tennyson, *Morte d' Arthure*.

Mother Goose. The origin of this name has been variously explained. *Mother Goose's Melodies* was published in Boston by Thomas Fleet in 1719. His mother-in-law is said to have been Mother Goose. But the suggestion of the name may have come from the *Mother Goose's Tales* published in French by Perrault in 1697. These contained the stories of Cinderella, Little Red Ridinghood, and others.

Mother Hubbard, Old. The subject of this nursery rime has been rather reasonably traced to the work of some untutored rimester, who mistook a picture of St. Hubert, patron of dogs, for that of an old woman. The saint was often represented with long hair and a loose, long gown. He was often besought to cure the illnesses of pet dogs. Spenser used the name simply as that of any old dame in "Mother Hubbard's Tale." This is a tale of a fox and an ape in human form, out for adventures.

Mowgli (*mou'glĭ*). **Jungle Books, Kipling.** The name given to the man-cub suckled and brought up in the jungle by Mother Wolf. He runs with the pack and learns the law of the jungle. But he is forced to seek a home among men, where he marries the daughter of Abdul Gafur.

Mualox. The Fair God, Lew Wallace. The old paba or prophet who assured Nenetzin that she was to be the future queen in her father's palace.

Much Ado about Nothing, Shakespeare. One of the dramatist's most successful comedies. The play is located in Messina. Claudio, deceived by Don John into thinking his affianced bride, Hero, unfaithful, repudiates her at the altar. Friar Francis, suspicious, reports her dead. Don John, who had bribed Hero's maid to dress in her mistress' clothes and meet him, thus imposing upon Claudio, flees, and the maid confesses. The lovers are happily married. Beatrice and Benedick, whose linked names have become proverbial, are also wedded. In this play appear Dogberry and Verges, ignorant police officers.

Muckrake. Bunyan's reference to "the man with the muckrake," who was always looking down, was given special application by President Theodore Roosevelt in his characterization of news writers who were always looking for the worst in American life.

Munchausen (*mŭn-chŏ'zĕn*), **The Baron.** A hero of most marvelous adventures, and the fictitious author of a book of travels filled with most extravagant tales. It was written by Rudolph Erich Raspe, a German adventurer, and was published in 1785. The name is said to refer to Hieronymus Karl Friedrich von Münchhausen, a German officer in the Russian army, noted for his marvelous stories.

Mussel Slough Affair. The Octopus, Norris. The basis of plot for the novel, and name given to an actual though little-known piece of California history. The story of the conflict between the wheat growers of the San Joaquin valley and the railroad trust, which they believed was trying to defraud them of their land.

My Prisons, Silvio Pellico. Italian *Le Mie Prigioni* (1832). The poignant story of the author's experiences in Austrian prisons. He had been condemned to death and then to fifteen years' imprison ent, for conspiracy. The simple recital of the author's experiences, with no word of personal condemnation, has made the book one of great influence in Italy.

Mystery of Edwin Drood, The, Dickens. A nove unfinished at the time of the author's death. The scene of the story is laid in the cathedral town of Cloisterham. The choirmaster, John Jasper, secretly an opium addict, is guardian for his nephew, Edwin Drood, who is just about to come of age. During the Christmas holidays, Edwin and an orphan girl at school in Cloisterham decide to break off the engagement their parents had arranged for them. Then, after a dinner in Jasper's roo is, Edwin disappears. His watch is found in a weir near the town, but the body cannot be found. Consequently, a young man with whom Edwin had had a dispute is freed from the charge of murder. Numerous hints point to Jasper as the villain, but no satisfactory conclusion has ever been offered for the b k, though many people have tried.

Natty Bumppo. Called "Leatherstocking." He appears in five of Cooper's novels: (1) *The Deerslayer*; (2) *The Pathfinder*; (3) "The Hawkeye," in *The Last of the Mohicans*; (4) "Natty Bumppo," in *The Pioneers*; and (5) as "The Trapper," in *The Prairie*, in which he dies.

Neœra (*nê-ē'rà*). The name of a girl mentioned by the Latin poets, Horace, Virgil, and Tibullus; sometimes also introduced into modern pastoral poetry as the name of a mistress or sweetheart, as in Milton's "Lycidas."

Nerissa. Merchant of Venice, Shakespeare. The bright, lively maid to Portia. She marries Gratiano.

Nest of Linnets. Title given to a story by F. F. Moore, a sequel to his *Jessamy Bride*, and noted for the group of people collected. Richard Brinsley Sheridan may be called its hero, inasmuch as he is the lover of its heroine, Miss Linley, the famous singer, who became Sheridan's first wife. The whole remarkable group to which she belonged gave title to the book,—Garrick, Goldsmith, Sir Joshua Reynolds, Mrs. Thrale, Dr. Johnson. Burke, Thomas Sheridan, the father of Richard, and others.

New Atlantis, The. An imaginary island in the middle of the Atlantic. Bacon, in his allegorical fiction so called, supposes himself wrecked on this island, where he finds an association for the cultivation of natural science and the promotion of arts. Called the "New" Atlantis to distinguish it from Plato's Atlantis, an imaginary island of fabulous charms.

Newcome, Colonel. A gallant, simple-hearted retired East Indian officer, in Thackeray's *The Newcomes*. His unworldliness leads to the loss of his fortune, and he dies, poor and broken-hearted, in the Charter House hospital.

New England Primer. This book, of which it is estimated that 2,000,000 copies were sold in the 18th century, was published by Benjamin Harris, a printer of Boston, shortly before 1690. A copy of the New England Primer, published in Walpole, N. H., in 1814, contains an illustrated alphabet. The letter "L" is illustrated by a lion with one of its paws resting upon a lamb, which is lying down. Accompanying the picture are the following lines:

"The Lion bold
The Lamb doth hold."

New England Tragedies. Among the poems of H. W. Longfellow are the "New England Tragedies" and the "Divine Tragedy." These, taken in connection with "The Golden Legend," form one connected work of art, *Christus, a Mystery*.

New Jerusalem. The name by which, in the Christian faith, heaven, or the abode of the redeemed, is symbolized. The allusion is to the description in the 21st chapter of the book of Revelation.

New Pastoral. A poem by T. B. Read, truly American in character, like its companion poem, "The Wagoner of the Alleghanies."

News. This word is made up of the first letter of each point of the compass: North, East, West, South. This fanciful explanation is frequently given as the origin of the term "news," as something coming from all points of the compass. Actually, however, the word probably comes from the French *nouvelles*, meaning "news," or medieval Latin *nova*, neuter plural of *novus*, meaning "new things." Some authorities would trace it to Anglo-Saxon, but, in the sense of "tidings" or "information," it has been in common use only since 1500.

Nibelung (*nē'bĕ-lŏŏng*), **King.** A king of the Nibelungen, a mythical Burgundian tribe, who gives name to the great medieval epic of Germany, the *Nibelungenlied*. He bequeathed to his two sons a hoard or treasure beyond all price and incapable of diminution, which was won by Siegfried, who made war upon the Nibelungen and conquered them.

Nibelungenlied. A historic poem generally called the German "Iliad." It is the only great national epic that European writers have produced since antiquity, and belongs to every country that has been peopled by Germanic tribes, as it includes the hero traditions of the Franks, the Burgundians, and the Goths, with memorials of the ancient myths carried with them from Asia. The poem is divided into two parts, and 32 lieds, or cantos. The first part ends with the death of Siegfried, and the second part with the death of Kriemhild. The death of Siegfried and the revenge of Kriemhild have been celebrated in popular songs dating back to the lyric chants now a thousand years old. These are the foundation of the great poem.

Nickleby, Mrs. Nicholas Nickleby, Dickens. The mother of the hero Nicholas, a widow fond of talking and of telling long stories with no connection. She imagined that her neighbor, a mildly insane man, was in love with her because he tossed cabbages and other articles over the garden wall. She had a habit of introducing, in conversation, topics wholly irrelevant to the subject under consideration, and of always declaring, when anything unexpected occurred, that she had expected it all along and had prophesied to that precise effect on divers (unknown) occasions. Nicholas Nickleby has to make his own way in the world. He first goes as usher to Mr. Squeers, schoolmaster at Dotheboys Hall; but leaves in disgust with the tyranny of Squeers and his wife, especially to a poor boy named Smike. Smike runs away from the school to follow Nicholas, and remains his humble follower till death. At Portsmouth, Nicholas joins the theatrical company of Mr. Crummles, but leaves the profession for other adventures. He falls in with the brothers Cheeryble, who make him their clerk; and in this post he rises to become a merchant, and ultimately marries Madeline Bray.

Night Before Christmas. Popular title of Clement Clarke Moore's famous poem, *A Visit from St. Nicholas*, published in 1823.

Nils, The Wonderful Adventures of, Selma Lagerlöf. Delightful story of a boy's dreams about birds and animals.

Nine Worthies, The. Famous personages often alluded to, and classed together, rather in an arbitrary manner, like the Seven Wonders of the World, the Seven Wise Men of Greece, etc. They have been counted up in the following manner:

Three Gentiles.	{ 1. Hector, son of Priam. 2. Alexander the Great. 3. Julius Cæsar.	
Three Jews.	{ 4. Joshua, conqueror of Canaan. 5. David, king of Israel. 6. Judas Maccabeus.	
Three Christians.	{ 7. Arthur, king of Britain. 8. Charlemagne. 9. Godfrey of Bouillon.	

Noctes Ambrosianæ (*nŏk'tēz ăm-brō'zhĭ-ā'nē*), "Ambrosian Nights." The name of a famous series of literary and political disquisitions which appeared in *Blackwood's Magazine* from 1822 to 1835. These articles, consisting of supposed conversations, purported to be a verbatim report of convivial gatherings held at Ambrose's tavern, Edinburgh, by several literary celebrities of the time. At first these brilliant dialogues were the work of several writers, among them J. G. Lockhart and William Maginn. Those appearing after 1825 were nearly all contributed by John Wilson, under the pen name "Christopher North." Of the 71 "Noctes" 49 were afterward published separately as being entirely Wilson's work. By reason of their inexhaustible humor and trenchant wit, these imaginary discussions enjoyed an immense vogue and were largely responsible for the success of *Blackwood's Magazine*. Their great permanent literary creation is Wilson's delineation of the character of the Ettrick Shepherd, an idealized portrait of James Hogg, who is described as one of the frequenters of the "Ambrosian" feasts.

No Man's Land. The name given to the strip of territory between the trenches of opposing armies in World War I. A proverbial phrase for disputed ground or the borderland between two opinions.

North Americans of Yesterday. Name given to the Indians of North America by recent writers, among them F. S. Dellenbaugh, in a work under same title. This work, a comparative study of North American Indian life and customs, is written on the theory that the races are of ethnic unity.

Notre Dame de Paris (*nō'tr' dȧm' dĕ pȧ'rē'*), **Victor Hugo.** English title, "The Hunchback of Notre Dame." A romance. The time is the reign of Louis XI; the scene, Paris. Esmeralda, a dancing girl, is loved by Quasimodo, the hunchback bell ringer, but she, repelled by his deformity, only pities him. She is condemned as a witch, but Quasimodo hides her in the church. Claude Frollo, the archdeacon, to whose passion she will not surrender, betrays her to the mob, and she is hanged. The hunchback throws Claude over the battlements of Notre Dame. Years afterward, Quasimodo's skeleton is found beside that of Esmeralda in the charnel cave.

Nourmahal (*nŏŏr-mȧ-häl'*). **Lalla Rookh, Moore.** "Light of the Harem." She was for a season estranged from the sultan, till he gave a grand banquet, at which she appeared in disguise as a lute player and singer. The sultan was so enchanted with her performance, that he exclaimed, "If Nourmahal had so played and sung, I could forgive her all"; whereupon the sultana threw off her mask.

Novum Organum (*nō'vŭm ŏr'gȧ-nŭm*). Published by Francis Bacon in 1620 under a general title *Instauratio Magna*, but having, after the preface, a second title: "The second part of a work called Novum Organum, or certain opinions on the Interpretation of Nature." It outlines his scientific, or inductive, method, that is, reasoning from observed facts to general laws.

Nucta. Paradise and the Peri, Moore. The name given to the miraculous drop which falls from heaven, in Egypt, on St. John's Day, and is supposed to stop the plague.

Nun of Nidaros. Tales of a Wayside Inn, Longfellow. The abbess of the Drontheim convent, who heard the voice of St. John while at her midnight devotions.

Nut-brown Maid. Reliques, Percy. The maid who was wooed by the "banished man." The "banished man" described to her the hardships she would have to undergo if she married him; but, finding that she accounted these hardships as nothing compared with his love, he revealed himself to be an earl's son, with large hereditary estates, and married her.

Oakhurst, John. The Outcasts of Poker Flat, Bret Harte. Oakhurst, the hero of the story, is a gambler who has been driven out of the mining camp in winter, with three other "undesirable citizens." He kills himself that the others may have a chance to live and escape.

Oberon. King of the Fairies, whose wife was Titania. Shakespeare introduces both Oberon and Titania in his *Midsummer Night's Dream*. Oberon and Titania, his queen, are fabled to have lived in India, and to have crossed the seas to northern Europe to dance by the light of the moon.

Oberon the Fay. A humpty dwarf only three feet high, but of angelic face, lord and king of Mommur.

Octopus, The, Frank Norris. A California story of a struggle between the wheat growers and the railroads. See *Mussel Slough Affair*. The first of a trilogy, the story of a wheat crop. The second in the series, *The Pit*, a tale of gambling in grain, is a story of the middleman. Mr. Norris, when he died, had planned the third story, to be called *The Wolf*, dealing with the consumption in Europe.

Odyssey (*ŏd'ĭ-sĭ*). Homer's epic, recording the adventures of Odysseus, or Ulysses, in his voyage home from Troy. The poem opens in the island of Calypso, with a complaint against Neptune and Calypso for preventing the return of Odysseus to Ithaca. Telemachus, the son of Odysseus, starts in search of his father, accompanied by Pallas in the guise of Mentor. He goes to Pylos, to consult old Nestor, and is sent by him to Sparta, where he is told by Menelaus that Odysseus is detained in the island of Calypso. In the meantime, Odysseus leaves the island,

and, being shipwrecked, is cast on the shore of Phæacia. These wanderings of Odysseus occupied ten years after the close of the ten years of the Trojan War. Penelope is tormented by suitors. To excuse herself, Penelope tells her suitors he only shall be her husband who can bend Odysseus' bow. None can do so but the stranger, who bends it with ease. Odysseus is recognized by his wife, the false suitors are slain, and peace is restored to Ithaca.

Œdipus Tyrannus (*ĕd'ĭ-pŭs ti-răn'ŭs*), **Sophocles.** One of a group of three tragedies. Œdipus, or "Swollen-feet," son of Laius, king of Thebes, and Jocasta, is exposed on a mountain, but found and brought up by a shepherd. Grown to manhood, and learning the prophecy that he should kill his father and marry his mother, he leaves Corinth. Journeying toward Thebes, he unwittingly fulfills the prophecy. A plague is sent on the city, which can be averted only by banishment of the king. Tiresias, a seer, reveals the truth to Œdipus. Jocasta hangs herself, and Œdipus, led by his daughter Antigone, wanders forth. *Œdipus at Colonna* and *Antigone* are the other two plays of the trilogy.

Offertory. In the Roman Catholic Church that portion of the Mass, with accompanying prayers and chants, which consists of the oblation, or offering, of bread and wine. In Protestant religious services, the word is frequently used to indicate the collection of money and the music which accompanies it.

Ogham or **Ogam** (*ŏg'ăm*) **Inscriptions.** These are mostly ancient Celtic names found on stones in Ireland, Scotland, Wales, the Shetlands, and England. A peculiar alphabet is used, consisting of straight vertical or slant lines arranged along a middle horizontal line. Different letters are represented by groups of lines, of varying number and direction. They are referred to in T. W. Rolleston's Irish lyric "The Dead at Clonmacnoise."

Ogier (*ō'jĭ-ēr*) **the Dane.** One of the paladins of the Charlemagne epoch. Also made the hero of an ancient French romance, and the subject of a ballad, whose story is probably a contribution from the stores of Norman tradition, Holger, or Olger Danske, being the national hero of Denmark. He figures in Ariosto's *Orlando Furioso*.

O'Groat. A name often alluded to in early English parables or sayings coming from the legend of "John O'Groat's House." This ancient building was supposed to stand on the most northerly point in Great Britain. John of Groat and his brothers were originally from Holland.

O'Hara, Scarlett. The heroine of Margaret Mitchell's novel, *Gone with the Wind*, has become one of the best-known fictional characters. Spirited, willful, courageous, not always scrupulous in getting what she wants, Scarlett is interesting, not only as a woman, but also as a symbol of Southern resourcefulness in the war between the states and in the reconstruction that followed.

Old Bailey, The. The central criminal court of London, England, situated on the street named Old Bailey, which runs from Newgate to Ludgate Hill, not far from St. Paul's, London. It was the site of the Roman *vallum*, forming part of the city's fortifications external to the wall, hence Ballium and Bailey. A *vallum* was a rampart of palisades, so called from *vallus*, a "stake," and was planted on the top of the *agger*, or "mound," thrown up for the purposes of defense. Vividly described in Dickens's *Tale of Two Cities*.

Oldbuck, Jonathan. Antiquary, The, Scott. The character whose whimsies gave name to the novel. He is represented as devoted to the study and accumulation of old coins, medals, and relics. He is irritable, sarcastic, and cynical from an early disappointment in love, but he is full of humor and is a faithful friend.

Old Chester Tales, Margaret Deland. A series of artistic tales of the vicissitudes of old-fashioned people in a quiet old New England village. The series is extended in *Dr. Lavender's People*.

Old Creole Days, George W. Cable. A collection of tales of New Orleans life in the early 19th century. It contains some of the best of modern stories, for example, *Jean-ah Poquelin* and *Café des Exilés*.

Old Curiosity Shop, The, Dickens. See *Little Nell.*

Old Grimes. The New England character in a popular American ballad by Albert G. Greene. The name probably is borrowed from George Crabbe's Peter Grimes in "The Borough," though resemblance ends here.

Old Man of the Sea. In the *Arabian Nights*, a monster encountered by Sindbad the Sailor in his fifth voyage. After carrying him upon his shoulders a long time, Sindbad at last succeeds in intoxicating him, and effects his escape. The "Old Man of the Sea" was also made the title of a humorous and well-known poem by O. W. Holmes.

Old Mortality, Scott. A novel which tells a story of the days of the Covenanters of Scotland in the latter part of the 17th century. "Old Mortality" is an old man who makes it his business to clean the gravestones of old Covenanters and to keep the inscriptions on them clear. The love story is that of Edith Bellenden, an heiress, who marries Henry Morton, a Covenanter, after the death of her betrothed, Lord Evendale.

Old Red Sandstone. One of the most noted of Hugh Miller's famous writings on geological subjects. It revealed his discovery of fossils in a formation which, up to that time, had been deemed almost destitute of them.

Oliver Twist, Dickens. The hero, Oliver, is an orphan, born in a workhouse, of a mother who did not reveal her name. Starved and illtreated, he runs away to London, falls in with Fagin's gang of thieves, and finally, in the house of the Maylie's, which he has been forced to enter for robbery, finds, in their adopted daughter, his aunt. Her name, as his, had been Fleming.

Olivia, Twelfth Night, Shakespeare. A rich countess, whose love was sought by Orsino, duke of Illyria; but, having lost her brother, Olivia lived for a time in entire seclusion, and in no wise reciprocated the duke's love. Olivia fell in love with Viola, who was dressed as the duke's page, and sent her a ring. Mistaking Sebastian, Viola's brother, for Viola, she married him out of hand.

Opal, The Story of. The diary of a child, Opal Whitely, whose parents had died while she was very small, leaving her to the care of a family in the backwoods of Oregon. It is an interesting picture of natural child life, but its publication in The Atlantic Monthly in 1920 and afterwards in book form, provoked a controversy over its genuineness.

Ophelia. Hamlet, Shakespeare. Daughter of Polonius, the chamberlain. Hamlet fell in love with her, but, after his interview with the ghost, finds that his plans must draw him away from her. During his real or assumed madness, he treats her with undeserved and angry rudeness, and afterward, in a fit of inconsiderate rashness, kills her father, the old Polonius. The terrible shock given to her mind by these events completely shatters her intellect, and leads to her accidental death by drowning.

Opium Eater, Confessions of an English. A famous series of papers or essays, which describe the effect of opium upon the mind and body. The writer, Thomas De Quincey, had become a victim of the opium habit.

Ordeal of Richard Feverel, The, George Meredith. The story of a youth brought up by his father on an abstract theory of education. The "system" fails when Richard comes to manhood and falls in love with Lucy, an innocent girl of great nobility of character. This period is the "ordeal" of Richard. The story ends in bitter tragedy.

Oregon Trail, The. A classic work by the American historian, Francis Parkman. Originally published in book form in 1849 under the title *The California and Oregon Trail*, it is an account of a journey made by Parkman and his cousin, Quincy Adams Shaw, over the eastern section of the trail in 1846.

Organon. The name given to the first work on logic by Aristotle. He is said to have created the science of logic. The *Organon* has been enlarged and recast by some modern authors, especially by Mr. John Stuart Mill in his *System of Logic*, into a structure commensurate with the vast increase of knowledge and extension of positive method belonging to the present day.

Orlando Furioso (*ôr-lăn'dō fōō'rê-ō'sō*). An epic poem in 46 cantos, by Ariosto, which occupied his leisure for eleven years, and was published in 1516. This poem, which celebrates the semimythical achievements of the paladins of Charlemagne, in the wars between the Christians and the Moors, became immediately popular, and has since been translated into all European languages, and passed through innumerable editions.

Ormulum. The *Ormulum*, as originally planned, was to consist of English paraphrases of the gospels for the church year as arranged in the missal, with an exposition for English readers at the end of each. The result embodies only thirty paraphrases with the corresponding homilies. There are very few French words in the poem, but Scandinavian words and constructions abound. The writer, Orm, or Ormin, belonged to the East of England, and he and his brother Walter were Augustinian monks. He makes no use of rime or of alliteration, and he handles his verse form mechanically and with no freedom or license.

Osbaldistone. Rob Roy, Scott. A family name in the story which tells of nine of the members: (1) the London merchant and Sir Hildebrand, the heads of two families; (2) the son of the merchant is Francis; (3) the offspring of the brother are Percival, the sot; Thorncliffe, the bully; John, the gamekeeper; Richard, the horsejockey; Wilfred, the fool; and Rashleigh, the scholar, by far the worst of all. This last worthy is slain by Rob Roy, and dies cursing his cousin Frank, whom he had injured.

Osman. Sultan of the East, conqueror of the Christians, a magnanimous man. He loved Yara, a young Christian captive. This forms the subject of a once famous ballad.

Osric. A court fop in Shakespeare's *Hamlet*. He is made umpire by Claudius in the combat between Hamlet and Laertes.

Osseo. Hiawatha, Longfellow. Son of the Evening Star. When broken with age, he married Oweenee, one of ten daughters of a North hunter. She loved him in spite of his ugliness and decrepitude, because "all was beautiful within him." As he was walking with his nine sisters-in-law and their husbands, he leaped into the hollow of an oak tree and came out strong and handsome; but Oweenee at the same moment was changed into a weak old woman. But the love of Osseo was not weakened. The nine brothers and sisters-in-law were transformed into birds. Oweenee, recovering her beauty, had a son, whose delight was to shoot the birds that mocked his father and mother. An Algonquin legend gave the foundation of the story.

Ossian (ŏsh′ăn) **or Oisin.** A bard of Gaelic legend, son of the hero, Finn. In the middle of the 18th century, James MacPherson, a Scotch schoolmaster, published what he said were translations from ancient Gaelic poetry. These he collected as *The Poems of Ossian*. The poetry was meritorious, but it has been proved that MacPherson had misrepresented matters in calling his verses "translations."

Othello. A Moor of Venice, in Shakespeare's play of the same name. He marries Desdemona, the daughter of a Venetian senator, and is led by his ensign Iago, a consummate villian, to distrust her fidelity and virtue. Iago hated the Moor both because Cassio, a Florentine, was preferred to the lieutenancy instead of himself, and also from a suspicion that the Moor had tampered with his wife; but he concealed his hatred so well that Othello wholly trusted him. Iago persuaded Othello that Desdemona intrigued with Cassio, and urged him on till he murdered his bride.

Othello's Occupation's Gone. A phrase much quoted from the play *Othello*, meaning "the task is ended," or that one has retired from active work.

O'Trigger, Sir Lucius. The Rivals, Sheridan. A volatile, fortune-hunting Irishman, fighting and forgiving with equal readiness.

Outre-Mer (ōō′trĕ-mâr′). A "Pilgrimage beyond the Sea." This title was given to the work by H. W. Longfellow, published in 1835, and written before European travel was much known to Americans. It is a poetical prose work, not unlike the *Sketch Book* of Washington Irving.

Over the Top. The phrase used by soldiers in World War I to mean going over the high front of the trench to a charge. Generally applied to the successful attainment of a goal or aim.

Pacolet. In *Valentine and Orson*, an old romance, a character who owned an enchanted steed, often alluded to by early writers. The name of Pacolet was borrowed by Steele for his familiar spirit in the *Tatler*. The French have a proverb, "It is the horse of Pacolet," that is, it is one that goes very fast.

Page. Merry Wives of Windsor, Shakespeare. Name of a family of Windsor, conspicuous in the play. When Sir John Falstaff made love to Mrs. Page, Page himself assumed the name of Brook. Sir John told the supposed Brook his whole "course of wooing."

Page, Anne. Daughter of Mrs. Page, in love with Fenton. Slender calls her "the sweet Anne Page."

Page, Mrs. Wife of Mr. Page, of Windsor. When Sir John Falstaff made love to her, she joined with Mrs. Ford to dupe and punish him.

Palimpsest (păl′ĭmp-sĕst). A parchment on which the original writing has been effaced and something else has been written. The monks and others used to wash or rub out the writing in a parchment and use it again. As they did not efface it entirely, many works have been recovered by modern ingenuity. Thus Cicero's *De Republica* has been restored from an ancient manuscript which had been partly erased. There are relics of ancient learning of which even the mutilated members have an independent value. This is especially true of biblical manuscripts for criticism, and, in a still broader sense, of all the remains of the ancient historians.

Palinurus. The pilot of Æneas, in Virgil's *Æneid*, who fell asleep at the helm and tumbled into the sea. The name is employed as a generic word for a steersman or pilot, and sometimes for a chief minister. Thus, Prince Bismarck was called the palinurus of William, emperor of Germany.

Palladium (pă-lā′dĭ-ŭm). Something that affords effectual protection and safety. The Palladium was a colossal wooden statue of Pallas in the city of Troy, said to have fallen from heaven. The statue was carried away by the Greeks, and the city was burned. The Scotch had a similar tradition attached to the great stone of Scone, near Perth. Edward I removed it to Westminster, and it is still framed in the coronation chair of England. Stories connected with the palladium of a nation or a family are common in literature, as "Luck of Edenhall," a poem by Longfellow. Matthew Arnold uses the Trojan idea in a moral sense for the individual soul in his beautiful lyric "Palladium."

Pallet. A painter in Smollett's novel *Peregrine Pickle*. The absurdities of Pallet are painted in lurid colors.

Pamela (păm′ê-là). Name of heroine and title of novel by Richardson. She is a simple country girl, and maidservant of a rich young squire. She resists every temptation, and at length marries the young squire and reforms him. Pamela is very modest, bears her afflictions with much meekness, and is a model of maidenhood. The story is told in a series of letters which Pamela sends to her parents.

Pamphlet. This word seems to be derived from *Pamphilus seu de Amore*, a well-known 12th century amatory poem in Latin, colloquially known as "Pamphilet." Other little books were similarly named, as *Æsopet*, the "Fables of Æsop."

Pandarus. A son of Lycaon, and leader of the Lycians in the Trojan War, celebrated by Homer in the *Iliad*. In medieval romances, and by Shakespeare in *Troilus and Cressida*, he is represented as procuring for Troilus the love and good graces of Chryseis,—hence the word "pander."

Panegyric (păn′ê-jĭr′ĭk). A eulogistic harangue or oration, written or uttered in praise of a person or body of persons.

Panjandrum, The Grand. A sort of mythical nonentity invented by Foote, the comic dramatist. The word occurs in Foote's farrago of nonsense, which he composed to test the memory of a person who said he had brought his memory to such perfection that he could remember anything by reading it over once.

Pantagruel (păn-tăg′rōō-ĕl). A character in a famous romance by Rabelais. The name is said to have been given him because he was born during the drought which lasted thirty and six months, three weeks, four days, thirteen hours, and a little more, in that year of grace noted for having "three Thursdays in one week." His father was Gargantua, the giant, who was four hundred fourscore and forty-four years old at the time. He was chained in his cradle with four great iron chains, like those used in ships of the largest size. Being angry at this, he stamped out the bottom of his bassinet, which was made of weavers' beams. When he grew to manhood he knew all languages, all sciences, and all knowledge of every sort. The character has originated the English phrase "pantagruelian humor," that is, extravagant, coarse mirth like that of Pantagruel.

Pantagruelian Law Case. Pantagruel, Rabelais. This case, having nonplused all the judges in Paris, was referred to Lord Pantagruel for decision. After much "statement" the bench declared, "We have not understood one single circumstance of the defense." Then Pantagruel gave sentence, but his judgment was as unintelligible as the case itself. So, as no one understood a single sentence of the whole affair, all were perfectly satisfied.

Pantaloon. The character in old Italian comedy. He is represented as a wizened old man in dressing gown and slippers. See *As You Like It*, act 2, scene 7, "the lean and slippered Pantaloon."

Panurge (păn-ûrj′). A celebrated character in Rabelais' *Pantagruel*, and the real hero of the story; represented as an arrant rogue, a drunkard, a coward, and a libertine, but learned in the tongues, an ingenious practical joker, and a boon companion. He was the favorite of Pantagruel, who made him governor of Salmygondin, and finally set out with him in quest of the oracle of the Holy Bottle.

Paolo and Francesca (pä′ô-lō) (frän-chěs′kä), **Stephen Phillips.** A tragedy based upon the story in Dante's "Inferno." Giovanni, tyrant of Rimini, occupied with his wars, leaves his young bride and his brother Paolo much together in his castle. Though both wish to be loyal to the husband and brother, youth and love overmaster them. The old housekeeper arouses Giovanni's suspicions. Discovering their guilt, he slays both, though he thus destroys all that he loves.

Paracelsus (păr′à-sĕl′sŭs). The name of the hero in Browning's poem of the same name. Paracelsus, at twenty, starts out to find the supreme good in knowledge, but after eight years of study, he is disappointed. Then, after being again disillusioned in the search for good in love, he gives himself to such happiness as he may get from material things. The historical Paracelsus was a famous Swiss doctor and alchemist (1493–1541)

Paradise, This Side of. The novel published in 1920 which established the reputation of F. Scott Fitzgerald (1896–1940). It is the story of young Amory Blaine before, during, and after World War I, a brilliant, witty, and cynical record of the jazz age.

Paradise and the Peri. The second tale in Moore's poetical romance *Lalla Rookh*. The peri laments her expulsion from heaven, and is told she will be readmitted if she will bring to the gate of heaven the "gift most dear to the Almighty." After several failures the peri offered the "repentant tear," and the gates flew open.

Paradise Lost. The poem by Milton under this name opens with the awakening of the rebel angels in hell after their fall from heaven, the consultation of their chiefs how best to carry on the war with God, and the resolve of Satan to go forth and tempt newly created man to fall. Satan reaches Eden, and finds Adam and Eve in their innocence. This is told in the first four books. The next four books contain the archangel Raphael's story of the war in heaven, the fall of Satan, and the creation of the world. The last four books describe the temptation and the fall of man, and tell of the redemption of man by Christ and the expulsion from paradise.

Paradise Regained. In this poem Milton tells of the journey of Christ into the wilderness after his baptism, and its four books describe the temptation of Christ by Satan.

Pardoner's Tale. Canterbury Tales, Chaucer. Three rioters agreed to kill Death, and were directed to a tree under which he was to be found. At the foot of the tree they came upon a treasure, which all coveted. The youngest of the three went to buy wine and the other two conspired to kill him on his return. He poisoned the wine and was slain by his brothers, who soon died from the effect of the poison. Thus all found Death under the tree.

Parian Chronicle. A chronological register of the chief events in the mythology and history of ancient Greece, kept in the island of Paros. It is engraved on marble tablets now in the collection of Oxford university.

Parian Verse. Ill-natured satire; so called from Archilochos, a native of Paros.

Parizade (pä′rê-zä′dä). A princess whose adventures in search of the Talking Bird, the Singing Tree, and the Yellow Water, are related in the "Story of the Sisters" in the *Arabian Nights' Entertainments*.

Parley, Peter. Name assumed by Samuel Griswold Goodrich, an American (1793–1860). His series of *Peter Parley* books, popular and juvenile, included more than a hundred volumes.

Parnassus. A legendary mountain in Greece which was said to be the seat of poetry and music.

Parody. A kind of writing in which the words of an author or his thoughts are, by some slight alterations, adapted to a different purpose.

Parthian Shaft. An unexpected and effective witticism, especially when satirical. The phrase refers to a custom of the ancient Parthians, who in battle would feign retreat and then shoot backward with unerring aim. It now means "parting shot" or "last word" in a controversy.

Partington, Mrs. An imaginary old lady whose laughable sayings have been recorded by an American humorist, B. P. Shillaber.

Parzival or **Parsifal.** The German name of Perceval the hero and title of a metrical romance of the 13th century, by Wolfram von Eschenbach, and of a modern music drama by Richard Wagner. Parzival was brought up by a widowed mother in solitude, but, when grown to manhood, two wandering knights persuaded him to go to the court of King Arthur. His mother consented to his going if he would wear the dress of a common jester. This he did, but soon accomplished such noble deeds that Arthur made him a knight of the Round Table. Sir Parzival went in quest of the Holy Graal, which was kept in a castle called Graalburg, in Spain. He reached the castle, but, having neglected certain conditions, he was shut out, and, on his return to court, the priestess of Graalburg insisted on his being degraded from knighthood. Parzival then led a new life, and a wise hermit became his instructor. He reached such a state of purity and sanctity that the priestess of Graalburg declared him worthy to become lord of the castle. Lohengrin, "Knight of the Swan," was the son of Parzival.

Pasquinade (păs′kwĭ-nād′). A widely used name for a lampoon or satire. A certain free-spoken, witty tailor, Pasquino by name, is said to have lived in Rome in the 15th century. He was locally famous for his epigrams, directed especially at the popes. About the time of his death a mutilated statue was discovered and set up in one of the squares. Its origin was unknown, though it was recognized as part of a masterpiece. The populace gave it

the name of the dead tailor. The custom grew up of hanging placards carrying satiric epigrams upon this statue. Hence the name.

Pastoral. Something descriptive of a shepherd's life, or a poem in which any action or passion is represented by its effects on a country life. The characteristics of this type of poetry are simplicity, brevity, and delicacy.

Pastor Fido (păs-tôr′ fē′dō). "The Faithful Shepherd." Title of a pastoral drama by Guarini, first played in Turin in 1585. A very famous piece, which has been translated into many modern languages.

Paternoster Row (pä′tẽr-nŏs′tẽr rō). A street in London, north of St. Paul's, long famous as a center of book publishing. See *Amen Corner*.

Patterne, Sir Willoughby. See *The Egoist*.

Pattieson, Peter. An imaginary assistant teacher at Gandercleuch, and the feigned author of Scott's *Tales of My Landlord*, which were represented as having been published posthumously by his pedagogue superior, Jedediah Cleishbotham.

Paul and Virginia, Bernardin de St. Pierre. A pastoral romance. The scene of the story is the island of Port Louis in the Mauritius. Virginia, daughter of a French widow who had been disowned by her family, and Paul, an illegitimate son of a woman betrayed by a lover, were brought up in complete ignorance of the outside world. An aunt of Virginia has the girl taken to France to be educated, but, on her refusal to marry according to dictation, sends her back to the island. Within sight of the eager Paul the ship is wrecked and Virginia is drowned. Paul soon dies, brokenhearted. The story has been used with variations in operas and plays.

Pauline (pô-lēn′). (1) The "Lady of Lyons" in Bulwer-Lytton's play of this name. She was married to Claude Melnotte, a gardener's son, who pretended to be a count. (2) Heroine of Browning's poem of the same name.

Paul Pry. Paul Pry, John Poole. An idle, inquisitive, meddlesome fellow, who has no occupation of his own, and is forever poking his nose into other people's affairs. He always comes in with the apology, "I hope I don't intrude."

Peeping Tom of Coventry. A tailor of Coventry, the only soul in the town mean enough to peep at the Lady Godiva as she rode naked through the streets to relieve the people from oppression. Tradition says he was stricken blind. See Tennyson's *Lady Godiva*.

Peer Gynt (pā′ẽr günt), **Ibsen.** A poetic drama in which is presented the career of a reckless, irresponsible dreamer. His motto is "To thyself be enough." At last, realizing that he has been a bungler and failure in life, he finds a healing influence in the love of the heroine, Solveig. Ibsen seems to have intended this work for reading rather than for the stage.

Peggotty, Clara. The nurse of David Copperfield in Dickens's novel of this name. Being very plump, whenever she makes any exertion some of the buttons on the back of her dress fly off.

Peggotty, Dan'el. Brother of David Copperfield's nurse. Dan'el was a Yarmouth fisherman. His nephew, Ham Peggotty, and his brother-in-law's child, "Little Em'ly," lived with him.

Peggotty, Em'ly. She was engaged to Ham Peggotty; but being fascinated with Steerforth she eloped. She was afterwards reclaimed, and emigrated to Australia.

Peggotty, Ham. Represented as the very beau ideal of an uneducated, simple-minded, honest, and warm-hearted fisherman. He was drowned in his attempt to rescue Steerforth from the sea.

Pelléas and Mélisande (pĕl′ê-ăs) (mĕl′ĭ-sănd′), **Maurice Maeterlinck.** An exquisite romantic tragedy. Mélisande, discovered in a forest, is married, unwillingly, to Goland in the gloomy castle in Allemonde. She and Goland's younger brother Pelléas fall in love. Goland murders Pelléas and wounds Mélisande. She dies after giving birth to a child.

Pendennis. Name of title and hero of a novel by Thackeray, published in 1849 and 1850,—the immediate successor of *Vanity Fair*. Literary life is described in the history of Pen, Arthur Pendennis, a hero of little worth.

Pendennis, Laura. Cousin of Arthur Pendennis. Regarded as one of the best of Thackeray's characters.

Pendennis, Major. A gentlemanly dandy, who fawns on his patrons for the sake of insinuating himself into their society. Uncle of Arthur.

Pendragon. A title conferred on several British chiefs in times of great danger, when they were invested with dictatorial power; thus Uther and Arthur were each appointed to the office to repel the Saxon invaders. The word means "chief of the kings."

Pennsylvania Farmer. A name given to John Dickinson, a citizen of Pennsylvania. In the year 1768 he published his *Letters from a Pennsylvania Farmer to the Inhabitants of the British Colonies.* These were republished in London, with a preface by Dr. Franklin, and were subsequently translated into French.

Penny Dreadfuls. Cheap sensational papers and books.

Penrod, Booth Tarkington. A story of the life and adventures of a twelve-year-old boy in a town of the Middle West. One of the most successful studies of the boy and his contacts with the adult and child worlds around him.

Pentateuch (*pĕn′tȧ-tūk*). A name given by Greek translators to the first five books of the Old Testament. The Pentateuch describes the origin and history of the Hebrew people up to the conquest of Canaan, and the theocracy founded among them. Genesis, Exodus, Leviticus, Numbers, and Deuteronomy—these form the Pentateuch, and, with Joshua, are called the Hexateuch.

Pepys' (*pēps*) Diary. A work which brought fame to Samuel Pepys, the author, was written in shorthand. It was deciphered and published in 1825. It extends over the nine years from 1660 to 1669, and is the gossipy chronicle of that gay and profligate time. We have no other book which gives so lifelike a picture of that period.

Père Goriot (*pâr′ gō′ryō′*), "Father Goriot," **Balzac.** A novel. The tale is that of King Lear and his ungrateful daughters, brought down to the plane of a bourgeois grocer, but lacking the light of a Cordelia for comfort.

Peregrine Pickle. The hero and title of a novel by Smollett (1751). Peregrine Pickle is a savage, ungrateful spendthrift, fond of practical jokes, and suffering with evil temper the misfortunes brought on himself by his own willfulness.

Peter Pan. The hero and title of a children's drama by J. M. Barrie. Peter Pan runs away to Never-Never-Land to escape growing up. The play relates his adventures among his fairy playmates. Three of them, including Wendy Darling, return home with him for a time and meet with many adventures of a serio-comic nature.

Petruchio (*pē-trōō′chĭ-ō*). A gentleman of Verona, in Shakespeare's *Taming of the Shrew.* A very honest fellow, who hardly speaks a word of truth, and succeeds in all his tricks. He acts his assumed character to the life, with untired animal spirits, and without a particle of ill humor.

Phædo (*fē′dō*). An ancient and well-known work by Plato, in which the doctrine of the immortality of the soul is most fully set forth. It is in the form of a dialogue which combines with the abstract philosophical discussion a graphic narrative of the last hours of Socrates, which, for pathos and dignity, is unsurpassed.

Phantom Rickshaw, The, Kipling. A ghost story of India. An English woman, who had been cruelly treated by her lover, returns and haunts him in Simla.

Philax. Fairy Tales, D'Aulnoy. Philax was cousin to the Princess Imis. The fay Pagan shut them up in the "Palace of Revenge," a palace containing every delight except the power of leaving it. In the course of a few years Imis and Philax longed as much for a separation as at one time they had wished for a union.

Philip. The Madness of Philip, Josephine Daskam Bacon. A representation of "the child of strong native impulses who has not yet yielded to the shaping force of education; the child, therefore, of originality, of vivacity, of humor, and of fascinating power of invention in the field of mischief."

Philippic. A word used to denote any discourse or declamation full of acrimonious invective. It derives its name from orations made by Demosthenes against Philip of Macedon, in which the orator bitterly attacked the king as the enemy of Greece.

Philistines (*fĭ-lĭs′tĭnz*). Meaning the ill-behaved and ignorant. German students gave meaning to the word by calling all outside the universities "Philisters." The idea goes back to the conflicts of Israelites and Philistines in Palestine. Matthew Arnold, in his *Culture and Anarchy,* applied the term Philistine to the middle class in England.

Philo. The Messiah, Klopstock. A Pharisee, one of the Jewish Sanhedrin, who hated Caiaphas, the high priest, for being a Sadducee. Philo made a vow that he would take no rest till Jesus was numbered with the dead. He commits suicide, and his soul is carried to hell by Abaddon, the angel of death.

Philosopher's Stone. The stone which, according to medieval alchemists, could convert base metals into gold. It is useful as a figure of speech.

Philtra. Faery Queen, Spenser. A lady of large fortune, betrothed to Bracidas; but, seeing the fortune of Amidas daily increasing, and that of Bracidas getting smaller, she attached herself to the more prosperous younger brother.

Phineas. Uncle Tom's Cabin, Mrs. Stowe. The Quaker, an "underground railroad" man who helped the slave family of George and Eliza to reach Canada, after Eliza had crossed the river on cakes of floating ice.

Phyllis. In Virgil's "Eclogues," the name of a rustic maiden. This name, also written Phillis, has been in common use as meaning any unsophisticated country girl.

Picaresque Novel (*pĭk′ȧ-rĕsk′*). Another name for this type of fiction is the "rogue novel," which depicts a series of adventures happening to a more or less rascally person. If not actually idealized, the hero is usually treated at least sympathetically. He is interesting to meet in fiction but would hardly be a desirable acquaintance in real life.

Pickaninny. A young child. A West Indian negro word, derived from Spanish *pequeño.*

Pickwick, Mr. Samuel. The hero of the *Pickwick Papers,* by Charles Dickens. He is a simple-minded, benevolent old gentleman, who wears spectacles and short black gaiters. He founds a club, and travels with its members over England, each member being under his guardianship. They meet with many laughable adventures.

Pied Piper of Hamelin. Old German legend. Robert Browning, in his poem entitled "The Pied Piper," has given a metrical version. The legend recounts how a certain musician came into the town of Hamelin, in the county of Brunswick, and offered, for a sum of money, to rid the town of the rats by which it was infested. Having executed his task, and the promised reward having been withheld, he in revenge blew again his pipe, and drew the children of the town to a cavern in the side of a hill, which, upon their entrance, closed and shut them in forever.

Piers Plowman. The hero of a satirical poem of the 14th century. He falls asleep, like John Bunyan, on the Malvern Hills, and has different visions, which he describes, and in which he exposes the corruptions of society, the dissoluteness of the clergy, and the allurements to sin. The author is supposed to be Robert or William Langland. No other writings so faithfully reflect the popular feeling during the great social and religious movements of that century as the bitterly satirical poem, *The Vision of Piers Plowman.* In its allegory, the discontent of the common people with the course of affairs in church and state found a voice.

Pietro (*pyĕ′trō*). **The Ring and the Book, Browning.** The professed father of Pompilia, criminally assumed as his child to prevent certain property from passing to an heir not his own.

Pilgrim's Progress. Written by Bunyan in the form of a dream to allegorize the life of a Christian, from his conversion to his death. His doubts are giants, his sins a pack, his Bible a chart, his minister Evangelist, his conversion a flight from the City of Destruction, his struggle with besetting sins a fight with Apollyon, his death a toilsome passage over a deep stream, which flows between him and heaven.

Pillars of Hercules. In ancient geography, the two opposite promontories Calpe (Gibraltar) in Europe and Abyla in Africa, situated at the eastern extremity of the Strait of Gibraltar, sentinels, as it were, at the outlet from the Mediterranean into the unknown Atlantic.

Pilot, The. Title of a sea-story by Cooper, which was called the "first sea-novel of the English language." It was published in the year 1823 and was soon translated into Italian, German, and French. It is founded on the adventures of John Paul Jones.

Pinch, Tom. A character in Dickens's *Martin Chuzzlewit,* distinguished by his guilelessness, his oddity, and his exhaustless goodness of heart.

Pippa Passes. The title of a dramatic poem by Robert Browning. Pippa is a light-hearted peasant maiden, who resolves to enjoy her holiday. Various groups of persons overhear her as she passes by singing, and some of her stray words act with secret but sure influence for good.

Place in the Sun, A. A phrase used by the German emperor in 1901 with reference to the commercial concessions secured for Germany in China. It became the slogan of the Pan-German party, with the meaning of a larger share of the colonial and commercial opportunities of the world. Hitler called it "Lebensraum."

Platonic Love. Spiritual love between persons of opposite sexes. It is the friendship of man and woman, without mixture of what is usually called love. Plato strongly advocated this pure affection, hence its distinctive name.

Playboy of the Western World, The, J. M. Synge. An extravagant, boisterous play of Irish peasant life. In a lonely public house, Christy Mahon, under questioning, confesses that he is a fugitive, because he has killed his tyrannical father with a spade. His hearers convince themselves and Christy that he is a hero. So inspired he makes love to Pegeen. But suddenly his old father appears, only a little the worse for the blow. Christy's fame is shattered, and Pegeen, enraged at her broken romance, leads the attack upon the fallen hero.

Pocket, Matthew. Great Expectations, Dickens. A real scholar, educated at Harrow, and an honor man at Cambridge; but, having married young, he had to take up the calling of "grinder" and literary fag for a living.

Pocket, Mrs. Daughter of a city knight, brought up to be an ornamental nonentity, helpless, shiftless, and useless. She was the mother of eight children, whom she allowed to "tumble up" as best they could.

Pocket, Sarah. Sister of Matthew Pocket, a little, dry, old woman, with a small face that might have been made of walnut shell, and a large mouth.

Poet Laureate. A poet appointed by the English crown to compose odes and other verses in honor of grand state occasions. The name seems to have originated in the custom at the English universities of presenting a laurel wreath to a graduate, who was then called *laureatus*. The king's laureate, then, would be a graduated rhetorician, or poet, in the king's service. The early history of the laureateship is obscure, and statements conflicting. Chaucer and Spenser received royal pensions. They were unofficial laureates. The offices of Historiographer and Master of the Revels were united at times with that of Poet Laureate. The stipend of the office was formerly £100 a year, with a tierce of canary, but this latter emolument was commuted in Pye's time to an annual payment of £27. The present salary is equivalent to $360 a year. Formerly it was the duty of the laureate to write an ode on the birthday of the sovereign and on the occasion of a national victory, but this custom ceased with the death of James Pye. The appointment is now simply an official recognition of a poet as worthy to represent English letters. Ben Jonson was the first laureate to be formally appointed. He held the appointment at his death in 1637. William Davenant succeeded him. Later appointments have been: John Dryden, 1670–1688; Thomas Shadwell, 1688–1692; Nahum Tate, 1692–1715; Nicholas Rowe, 1715–1718; Lawrence Eusden, 1718–1730; Colley Cibber, 1730–1757; William Whitehead, 1757–1785; Thomas Warton, 1785–1790; Henry James Pye, 1790–1813; Robert Southey, 1813–1843; William Wordsworth, 1843–1850; Alfred Tennyson, 1850–1892; Alfred Austin, 1896–1913; Robert Bridges, 1913–1930; John Masefield, 1930–1967; Cecil Day-Lewis, 1968.

Poilu (*pwả'lü'*). The word means "hairy." As a noun, it was applied to the French soldiers in the World War I, because of their bearded faces.

Pollyanna. The "glad girl" in the story of this name welcomes every happening and calls it good, no matter how bad it may appear to others. The word has come to stand for an extreme form of blind optimism.

Polyglot (*pŏl'ĭ-glŏt*). The word means, in general, an assemblage of versions in different languages of the same work, but is almost exclusively applied to manifold versions of the Bible. Of the many other works or small pieces published in polyglot, the Lord's Prayer has been the favorite. Many collections of this prayer were published since the 15th century, the most valuable and most comprehensive of which is the *Mithridates* of Adelung, which contains the Lord's Prayer in more than 400 languages.

Ponte Vecchio (*pŏn'tĕ vĕk'kyō*). A bridge in Florence, over the Arno; a picturesque structure with three wide arches, rebuilt in 1345. The roadway is bordered on both sides by quaint little shops, except over the middle arch, where there is an opening. Over the south row of shops is carried a gallery, built by Vascari, connecting the Pitti Palace with the Uffizi and the Palazzo Vecchio.

Poor Richard's Almanac. From 1732 to 1757 Benjamin Franklin issued in Philadelphia a yearly almanac, under the name of Richard Saunders, or "Poor Richard." It was popular throughout the colonies for its comments and sayings. These have been translated into all languages.

Popinjay. A butterfly man, a fop; so called from the popinjay or figure of a bird shot at for practice. The title is used by Scott in *Old Mortality*, by Shakespeare in *Henry IV*, and by others.

Porterhouse Steak. The name is of American origin, said to be derived from "porterhouse," a kind of tavern, because the proprietor of such a house in New York made the cut popular. There is a story that Charles Dickens christened it because an innkeeper named Porter served him such excellent steak during his first American tour.

Portia. Merchant of Venice, Shakespeare. A rich neiress whom Bassanio loved and who defended Antonio.

Potboilers. Articles written and pictures of small merit drawn or painted for the sake of earning daily bread.

Potiphar Papers. A series of brilliant satiric sketches of society written by George W. Curtis in the year 1852.

Prester John. The name given, in the middle ages, to a supposed Christian sovereign and priest of the interior of Asia, whose dominions were variously placed. He has been the subject of many legends.

Pride and Prejudice, Jane Austen. A novel of domestic life. The plot turns upon the struggle of Elizabeth's love with her pride and the prejudice aroused in her by Darcy's rather proud consciousness of family position. Love triumphs in the end.

Primrose, Rev. Charles. Vicar of Wakefield, Goldsmith. A clergyman, rich in heavenly wisdom, but poor indeed in all worldly knowledge.

Primrose, George. Son of the vicar. He went to Amsterdam to teach the Dutch English, but never once called to mind that he himself must know something of Dutch before this could be done.

Primrose, Moses. Brother of George, noted for giving in barter a good horse for a gross of worthless green spectacles with copper rims.

Primrose, Mrs. Deborah. The doctor's wife, full of motherly vanity, and desirous to appear genteel. She could read without much spelling, and prided herself on her housewifery, especially on her gooseberry wine.

Primrose, Olivia. The eldest daughter of the doctor. Pretty, enthusiastic, a sort of Hebe in beauty. "She wished for many lovers," and eloped with Squire Thornhill.

Primrose, Sophia. The second daughter of Dr. Primrose. She was "soft, modest, and alluring."

Prince and the Pauper, The, Mark Twain. A humorous tale, exploiting the possibilities of an exchange of places between Prince Edward and a poor man.

Priscilla. Courtship of Miles Standish, Longfellow. A Puritan maiden who is wooed by Captain Standish through the mediation of his friend John Alden, who is in love with Priscilla. She prefers John Alden and marries him after the captain's supposed death. The captain, however, appears at the wedding, and the friends are reconciled.

Procrustes Bed. Procrustes, the robber tyrant of Attica, is said to have made his captives all fit a certain bed, regardless of their personal dimensions. If they were too short, he would stretch them to the required length. If they were too long, he would cut them down to fit the bed.

Prospero. Tempest, Shakespeare. Rightful duke of Milan, deposed by his brother. Exiled on a desert island, he practiced magic, and raised a tempest in which his brother was shipwrecked. Ultimately, Prospero "broke his wand," and his daughter married the son of the king.

Puck of Pook's Hill, Kipling. A delightful book of history stories. The children, Dan and Una, in the fields around their country home, meet Puck, "the oldest old thing in England." The little man tells them fascinating tales of Roman, Saxon, and Norman times, often calling up his friends, characters from early times, to talk to them.

Pudd'nhead Wilson, Mark Twain. A tale of a little Missouri town of the middle 19th century. A son of a slave, almost pure white, substituted for the master's son, grows up in luxury, but displays peculiarly mean traits. He is, by means of finger prints, detected in a crime and punished. Wilson is the lawyer.

Punch. Name of a famous London comic weekly. Derived from the puppet-show character, Punch.

Punch and Judy. The name of a popular puppet show. Punch is shortened from the Italian "Pulcinella," the character in 17th century *commedia*. Judy, or Joan, was added later, probably from an English ballad of the 18th century. In the play, the hunchback Punch strangles his infant child, beats his wife Judy to death, throws a policeman into the street, and is finally carried off by the Devil. Punch's dog Toby is usually in the play.

Puss in Boots. The subject and title of a well-known nursery tale derived from a fairy story in the *Nights* of the Italian author Straparola, and Charles Perrault's *Contes des Fées*. The wonderful cat secures a princess and a fortune for his master, a poor young miller, whom he passes off as the rich marquis of Carabas.

Pyncheon. The name of an ancient but decayed family in Hawthorne's romance *The House of the Seven Gables*. There are: (1) Judge Pyncheon, a selfish, cunning, worldly man; (2) His cousin Clifford, a delicate, sensitive nature, reduced to childishness by long imprisonment and suffering; (3) Hepzibah, the latter's sister, an old maid who devotes herself to the care of Clifford; (4) A second cousin, Phœbe, a fresh, cheerful young girl, who restores the fallen fortunes of the family and removes the curse which rested on it.

Quasimodo (*kwăs'ĭ-mō'dō*). **Notre Dame de Paris, Hugo.** A misshapen dwarf, one of the prominent characters in the story. He is brought up in the cathedral of Notre Dame de Paris. One day he sees Esmeralda, who had been dancing in the cathedral close, set upon by a mob, and he conceals her for a time in the church. When, at length, the beautiful gypsy girl is gibbeted, Quasimodo disappears mysteriously, but a skeleton corresponding to the deformed figure is found after a time in a hole under the gibbet.

Quaver. The Virgin Unmasked, Fielding. A singing master, who says, "if it were not for singing masters, men and women might as well have been born dumb." He courts Lucy by promising to give her singing lessons.

Queen Labe (*lä'bā*). **Arabian Nights.** The queen of magic, ruler over the Enchanted City. Beder, prince of Persia, is connected with her in the tale. She transforms men into horses, mules, and other animals. Beder marries her, defeats her plots against him, but is himself turned into an owl for a time.

Quentin Durward, Scott. A historical romance of about 1470. The hero, Quentin Durward, a young Scottish guardsman in the service of Louis XI of France, after a series of adventures leading here and there in the monarch's maze of activities, wins the love of Countess Isabelle of Croye. When Liége is assaulted, Quentin and the countess, who has been put into his charge, escape on horseback. The countess publicly refuses to marry the duke of Orleans, to whom she has been promised, and ultimately marries the young Scotsman.

Quidnunkis. Title and name of hero in a fable found or written by Gay in 1726. This hero was a monkey which climbed higher than its neighbors and fell into a river. For a few moments the monkey race stood panic-struck, but the stream flowed on, the monkeys continued their gambols. The object of this fable is to show that no one is of sufficient importance to stop the general current of events or cause a gap in nature.

Quilp. Old Curiosity Shop, Dickens. A hideous dwarf, cunning, malicious, and a perfect master in tormenting. Of hard, forbidding features, with head and face large enough for a giant. He lived on Tower Hill, collected rents, advanced money to seamen, and kept a kind of wharf, containing rusty anchors, huge iron rings, piles of rotten wood, and sheets of old copper, calling himself a ship breaker. He was on the point of being arrested for felony, when he was drowned.

Quilp, Mrs. Wife of the dwarf, a young, obedient, and pretty little woman, treated like a dog by her husband, whom she loved but more greatly feared.

Quintessence, "the fifth essence." In the modern and general sense, an epithet applied to an extract which contains the most essential part of anything. The ancient Greeks said there are four elements or forms in which matter can exist: fire, or the imponderable form; air, or the gaseous form; water, or the liquid form; and earth, or the solid form. The Pythagoreans added a fifth, which they call "ether," more subtle and pure than fire, and possessed of an orbicular motion. This element, which flew upwards at creation, and out of which the stars were made, was called the "fifth essence"; quintessence, therefore, means the most subtle extract of a body that can be procured.

Quintus Fixlein. Title of a romance by Jean Paul Richter and the name of the principal character.

Quixote. See *Don Quixote.*

Quixotic (*kwĭk-sŏt'ĭk*). Like Don Quixote, or one who has foolish and impractical schemes—a would-be reformer.

Quiz. A word of uncertain origin. It is said that Daly, the manager of a Dublin playhouse, laid a wager that a new word of no meaning should be the common talk and puzzle of the city in 24 hours. In consequence of this the letters *q u i z* were chalked by him on the walls of Dublin, with an effect that won the wager. But the word appears in literature some years before the date given for this episode.

Quodling, The Rev. Mr. Peveril of the Peak, Scott. Chaplain to the duke of Buckingham.

Quo Vadis? Sienkiewicz. Lygia, a Christian girl in a Roman household, who will not yield her virtue to Vinicius, is by him denounced as a Christian. She is condemned to the arena, but her attendant, Ursus, saves her from death on the horns of the bull. Later, she marries Vinicius, who has been converted by Paul and Peter.

Radigund. Faery Queen, Spenser. Queen of the fabled Amazons. Having been rejected by Bellodant "the Bold," she revenged herself by degrading all the men who fell into her power by dressing them like women, and giving them women's work.

Ramona. Name of heroine and title of romance by Helen Hunt Jackson. Ramona saw the American Indian followed by "civilization" while retreating slowly but surely toward his own extinction, and had herself a share in the tragedy. Ramona is considered the great romance of Indian life.

Rappaccini. Mosses from an Old Manse, Hawthorne. A doctor in whose garden grew strange plants whose juices and fragrance were poison. His daughter, nourished on these odors, became poisonous herself. Her lover found an antidote which she took, but the poison meant life and the antidote meant death to her.

Raskolnikov (*räs-kŏl'nĭ-kŏv*). In Dostoiévsky's novel, "Crime and Punishment," a young man named Raskolnikov commits a murder and attempts to rationalize and justify his act. The novel is not only an account of external results following the crime but also of what happens in the mind of the criminal.

Rasselas (*răs'ê-lăs*). An imaginary prince, hero of the romance by Dr. Johnson, bearing same title. According to the custom of his country, Abyssinia, he was confined in paradise, with the rest of the royal family. This paradise was in the valley of Amhara, surrounded by high mountains. It had only one entrance, a cavern concealed by woods and closed by iron gates. He escaped with his sister Nekayah and Imlac the poet, and wandered about to find what condition or rank of life was the most happy. After careful investigation, he found no lot without its drawbacks, and resolved to return to the "happy valley."

Raud the Strong. Tales of a Wayside Inn, H. W. Longfellow. The viking who worshiped the old gods and lived by fire and sword. King Olaf went against him, sailing from Drontheim to Salten Fiord.

Ravenswood. Bride of Lammermoor, Scott. The lord of Ravenswood, an old Scotch nobleman and a decayed royalist. His son Edgar falls in love with Lucy Ashton, daughter of Sir William Ashton, lord keeper of Scotland. The lovers plight their troth, but Lucy is compelled to marry Frank Hayston, laird of Bucklaw. The bride, in a fit of insanity, attempts to murder the bridegroom and dies. Bucklaw goes abroad. Colonel Ashton, seeing Edgar at the funeral of Lucy, arranges a hostile meeting; and Edgar, on his way to the place appointed, is lost in the quicksands. A prophecy, noted as a curse, hung over the family and was thus fulfilled.

Raymond. Jerusalem Delivered, Tasso. Raymond was known as the Nestor of the crusaders, slew Aladine, king of Jerusalem, and planted the Christian standard upon the tower of David.

Realism. In literature, realism is opposed to idealism and romanticism. Realism aims at depicting things as they actually appear in ordinary human experience. Hence the realistic writer will choose familiar subjects and will take pains to emphasize accuracy in details.

Rebecca. Ivanhoe, Scott. Daughter of Isaac the Jew, in love with Ivanhoe. Rebecca, her father, and Ivanhoe, as prisoners, are confined in Front de Bœuf's castle. Rebecca is taken to the turret chamber and left with the old sibyl, but when Brian de Bois Guilbert comes to her she spurns him with heroic disdain. Ivanhoe, who was suffering from wounds received in a tournament, is nursed by Rebecca. After escape and adventure, and being again prisoner, the Jewish maiden is condemned by the Grand Master to be tried for sorcery, and she demands a trial by combat. The demand is granted, and Brian de Bois Guilbert is appointed as the champion against her. Ivanhoe undertakes her defense, slays Brian, and Rebecca is set free. In contrast with this strong character, Rowena seems insignificant even when she becomes the bride of Ivanhoe.

Rebecca of Sunnybrook Farm, Kate Douglas Wiggin. The pathetic and humorous experiences of an imaginative little girl who, on account of the poverty of her home, is sent to live with two maiden aunts. The story has been dramatized.

Recessional, The, Kipling. A poem written for the celebration of the 60th anniversary of Victoria's accession to the throne of England.

Red Badge of Courage, The, an Episode of the Civil War. This novel by Stephen Crane, published in 1895, is a realistic study of an inexperienced soldier in battle who passes through various emotional stages from patriotic fervor to abject fear and ultimately to courage.

Red Cross Knight. The Red Cross Knight is St. George, the patron saint of England, and, in the obvious and general interpretation, typifies holiness, or the perfection of the spiritual man in religion. In Spenser's *Faery Queen* the task of slaying a dragon was assigned to him as the champion of Una.

Redgauntlet. One of the principal characters in Sir Walter Scott's novel of the same name, a political enthusiast and Jacobite, who scruples at no means of upholding the cause of the Pretender, and finally accompanies him into exile. His race bore a fatal mark resembling a horseshoe which appeared on the face of Redgauntlet as he frowned when angry.

Red Riding Hood. This nursery tale is, with slight variations, common to Sweden, Germany, and France. In Charles Perrault's *Contes des Fées* it is called "Le Petit Chaperon Rouge."

Regent Street. One of the principal streets of the West End of London, extending from Portland Place to Waterloo Place.

Representative Men, R. W. Emerson. A series of essays on the characters of certain great men, in which Emerson embodied his philosophy of manhood. The topics are: (1) Plato, the Philosopher; (2) Swedenborg, the Mystic; (3) Montaigne, the Skeptic; (4) Shakespeare, the Poet; (5) Napoleon, the Man of the World; (6) Goethe, the Writer. The mental portraits sketched under these six heads give us Emerson himself, so far as he is capable of being formulated at all.

Republic, The, Plato. This work, in the form of a dialogue, is usually regarded as the finest product of Plato's genius. It is ostensibly an inquiry into the nature of justice, but actually sets forth, in a lucid and convincing form, Plato's views on the ideal state, education, and morality. It contains analyses of, and searching comments on, the major political and social problems connected with democracy and other forms of government. In the broad sweep of its argument, it undertakes to give a systematic answer to the fundamental questions of psychology, economics, science, religion, and philosophy. Its literary form and its intellectual grasp combine to make it one of the enduring masterpieces of the world's literature.

Return of Peter Grimm, The, David Belasco. A play made famous by David Warfield in the part of Peter. Peter, an old nurseryman, makes, in sport, an agreement with his Scotch doctor that whichever one dies first will try to communicate with the other. Peter has arranged the marriage of his niece and his grandson Frederick, who turns out to be a cheat and scapegrace. To correct this fleshly blunder, Peter "returns." He succeeds in "getting his message over" through the illegitimate son of Frederick, and takes the little fellow "back with him."

Reveries of a Bachelor. Name of a writing by D. G. Mitchell. A collection of sketches of life and character, painted in such a dreamlike, delicate manner as to make the reader lose for the time being the full consciousness of his own reality.

Reynard (*rä'närd*) **the Fox.** The hero in the animal epics, celebrated *fabliaux* of the middle ages, belonging to the series of poems in which "beasts" are the speakers and actors. The "beast fable" goes back to the remotest antiquity, and is a common inheritance of the Aryan or Indo-Germanic races. This story of Reynard the Fox, certainly known as early as the 12th century, is the great creation of the people of the Netherlands, northern France, and western Germany. Its source was Flanders, where, apparently, the beasts were named. Few contributions to it were made in England; but Odo of Cheriton made use of the stories, and an English *fabliau*, "The Fox and the Wolf," belongs to the Reynard family and is the best example of comic satire before Chaucer. Reynard means "strong in counsel." According to many authorities, this prose poem, in its later form, is a satire on the state of Germany in the middle ages. Reynard typifies the Church; his uncle, Isengrin the Wolf, typifies the baronial element; and Nobel the Lion, the regal. However that may be, in the real fable, Reynard the Fox has a constant impulse to deceive and victimize everybody, whether friend or foe, but especially Isengrin; and, though the latter frequently reduces him to the greatest straits, he generally gets the better of it in the end.

Rhapsody. Means songs strung together. The term was originally applied to the books of the *Iliad* and *Odyssey*, which at one time were in fragments. Certain bards collected a number of the fragments, enough to make a connected "ballad," and sang them as our minstrels sang the deeds of famous heroes.

Rhoda Fleming. The heroine of George Meredith's novel of this name. Of a proud nature, she sets out to right the wrong done to her sister Dahlia, who has fled from home. At last she finds she has really destroyed her sister's last chance of happiness. Humbled and chastened, she repents of her obstinacy. In the end she marries her deserving lover, Robert Armstrong.

Richelieu, Bulwer-Lytton. The action of the play hinges upon the attempt of certain courtiers, among them the duke of Orleans and the count of Baradas, to displace the old cardinal. But their plots are revealed to Richelieu by Marion de Lorme, and he crushes them successfully. The pretty love story of Julie, Richelieu's ward, is involved in the main plot.

Riders to the Sea, J. M. Synge. A one-act tragedy of peasant life in the Aran islands. Maurya, who already has lost in the sea five of her sons, entreats the last, Bartley, not to go to the boat with his horses for the Connemara fair. He persists in going, and he too is lost. The mother's revolt turns to utter resignation. "There isn't anything more the sea can do to me," she says.

Rights of Man, Thomas Paine. The title of this work was suggested by the *Declaration of the Rights of Man* issued by the French National Assembly. It was a reply to Edmund Burke's *Reflections on the French Revolution*. In it Paine vigorously defended the French.

Rigolette. The name of a female character in Eugène Sue's *Mysteries of Paris*. It has acquired a proverbial currency, and is used as a synonym of "grisette," or shop-girl.

Rinaldo (*rê-näl'dō*). A character in Tasso's *Jerusalem Delivered*. He belonged to the army of the Christians. He was the son of Bertoldo and Sophia, and nephew of Guelpho, but was brought up by Matilda. The name Rinaldo is also found in Boiardo's *Orlando Innamorato*, in Ariosto's *Orlando Furioso*, and in other romantic tales of Italy and France. He was one of Charlemagne's paladins, and cousin to Orlando. Having killed Charlemagne's nephew Berthelot, he was banished and outlawed. After various adventures and disasters, he went to the Holy Land, and, on his return, succeeded in making peace with the emperor.

Ring and the Book, The. An epic by Robert Browning. It is founded on Italian history. Guido Franceschini, a Florentine count of shattered fortune, married Pompilia, thinking her to be an heiress. Finding this a mistake the count treated Pompilia so brutally that she left him, under the protection of Caponsacchi, a young priest. Pompilia sued for a divorce, but, pending the suit, gave birth to a son. The count murdered Pompilia, and Pietro and Violante, her supposed parents, but, being taken red-handed, was brought to trial, found guilty, and executed.

Rip Van Winkle. Sketch Book, Irving. An indolent, good-natured fellow, living in a village on the Hudson. While shooting among the Catskill mountains he meets with a stranger whom he helps in carrying a keg over rocks and cliffs; with him he joins a party who are silently rolling ninepins. Rip Van Winkle drinks deeply of the liquor they furnish, and falls into a sleep which lasts twenty years, during which the Revolutionary War takes place. After awaking, Rip returns to the village, finds himself almost forgotten, and makes friends with the new generation. The name of the great actor, Joseph Jefferson, became so identified with this character, in the dramatic version of the story, that to the English-speaking world he was Rip Van Winkle.

Rise of Silas Lapham, The, Howells. The story of the business and social fortunes of a wealthy paint manufacturer and his family in Boston in the middle of the 19th century. Silas, a coarse, crowding man, already rich when the story opens, loses his fortune, but in his adversity he rises in moral power.

Rivals, The, R. B. Sheridan. A comedy. Miss Lydia Languish, niece of Mrs. Malaprop, has two suitors, Bob Acres, a young country man, and Ensign Beverley, the latter of whom she loves and hopes to elope with. Meanwhile Sir Anthony Absolute and Mrs. Malaprop arrange that she shall marry Captain Absolute, son of Sir Anthony. Sir Lucius O'Trigger sets Bob on to challenge Beverley. When they meet for the duel, and Bob finds Beverley to be Captain Absolute and his best friend, he refuses to fight. Lydia, though deprived of the romantic elopement, accepts the captain.

Roast Pig, A Dissertation on, Charles Lamb. In *Essays of Elia*. Ho-ti, a careless Chinese swineherd, one day allowed the pigsty to burn. Desperately searching in the smoking ruins, he burned his fingers in the charred remains of a pig. But, on putting them involuntarily to his mouth, he found clinging to them some bits of meat of a most enticing flavor, "crackling." This discovery led to the burning of many pigsties, until the further discovery that the toothsome morsel, roast pig, could be produced by less wasteful means.

Robert the Devil. The hero of an old French metrical romance of the 13th century, the same as Robert, first duke of Normandy, who became an early object of legendary scandal. Having been given over to the Devil before birth, he ran a career of cruelties and crimes unparalleled until he was miraculously reclaimed, did penance, became a shining light, and married the emperor's daughter. In the 14th century the romance was turned into prose, and of the prose story two translations were made into English. There was also a miracle play on the same subject. The opera "Robert le Diable" was composed by Meyerbeer, in 1826.

Robin Goodfellow. A domestic spirit. He is sometimes called Puck, son of Oberon. He attends the English fairy court; he is full of tricks and fond of practical jokes. He is also considered the same as Lob-lie-by-the-fire, in some tales.

Robin Hood. A famous English outlaw whose exploits are the subjects of many ballads, but of whose actual existence little or no evidence can be discovered. Various periods, ranging from the time of Richard I to near the end of the reign of Edward II, have been assigned as the age in which he lived. He is usually described as a yeoman, and his chief residence is said to have been the forest of Sherwood, in Nottinghamshire. Of his followers, the most noted are: Little John; his chaplain, Friar Tuck; and his companion, Maid Marian. The popular legends extol his personal courage and generosity, and his skill in archery. Scott introduces Robin Hood in two novels, *Ivanhoe* and *The Talisman*. In the former he first appears at the tournament as Locksley the archer. Robin Hood's adventures are the theme of an opera by De Koven, "Robin Hood."

Robinson Crusoe. A tale by Daniel Defoe. Robinson Crusoe went to sea, was wrecked, lived on an uninhabited island of the tropics, and relieved the weariness of life by numberless contrivances. At length he met a young Indian, whom he saved from death. He called him his "man Friday," and made him his companion and servant. This story has been translated into more languages than any other English book.

Rob Roy. The title and hero of a novel by Sir Walter Scott. It signifies "Rob the Red," and was the sobriquet of a famous Scottish outlaw, Robert MacGregor, the chief of the clan MacGregor.

Roderick Dhu. Lady of the Lake, Scott. An outlaw and chief of a band of Scots who resolved to win back what had been lost to the Saxons. In connection with Red Murdock he sought the life of the Saxon, Fitz-James.

Roderick Random. The Adventures of Roderick Random, Tobias Smollett. Random, hero of the novel, is a reckless, mischievous, thankless young Scot who, apprenticed to an apothecary, goes to sea as surgeon's mate. His adventures run the gamut of the sea and of English town and country life. Hugh Strap, his devoted attendant, he treats heartlessly. Finally, he marries Narcissa, a wife much too good for him.

Roderigo (rŏd'ĕr-ē'gō). In Shakespeare's *Othello*, a Venetian in love with Desdemona. He, when the lady eloped with Othello, hated the "noble Moor."

Roger Drake. Name of hero and title of novel by H. K. Webster. "Captain of Industry" is the title added to the name of the hero, who is interested in the working of a copper mine, the founding of a trust, the change from the old-fashioned trust to the simple plan of one monster corporation, and the deadly business fight for supremacy found in modern industrial struggles.

Roland. The hero of one of the most ancient and popular epics of early French or Frankish literature was, according to tradition, the favorite nephew and captain of the emperor Charlemagne. In Italian romance he is called Orlando. He was slain in the valley of Roncesvalles as he was leading the rear of the army from Spain to France. The oldest version of the "Song of Roland," forming part of the *chansons de gestes*, which treat of the achievements of Charlemagne and his paladins, belongs to the 11th century. Throughout the middle ages, the "Song of Roland" was the most popular of the many heroic poems. William of Normandy, when on his way to conquer England, had it sung at the head of the troops, to encourage them on their march. At the present day, the traditional memory of the heroic paladin is still held in honor by the hardy mountaineers of the Pyrenees, among whose dangerous defiles the scene of his exploits and death is laid. Roland is the hero of Théroulde's *Chanson de Roland*; of Turpin's *Chrónique*; of Boiardo's *Orlando Innamorato*; of Ariosto's *Orlando Furioso*.

Romance of the Rose. A poetical allegory, begun by Guillaume de Lorris in the latter part of the 13th century and continued by Jean de Meung in the first half of the 14th century. The poet dreams that Dame Idleness conducts him to the palace of Pleasure, where he meets many adventures among the attendant maidens, Youth, Joy, Courtesy, and others, by whom he is conducted to a bed of roses. He singles out one, when an arrow from Love's bow stretches him fainting on the ground. Fear, Slander, and Jealousy are afterward introduced. The part written by De Lorris is the greatest embodiment of French romance; De Meung's continuation is a rambling allegorical satire especially against women. The whole work

had a profound influence on early English poetry, especially that of Gower and Chaucer.

Romances. The French troubadours composed romances and sang them at the courts of the Norman kings. Richard I was himself a troubadour. The subjects of the romances were generally the deeds of Charlemagne and his knights, or of King Arthur and his knights. A little later, tales of the crusaders became popular. Old tales were retold, and the incidents were transferred to Eastern lands. From the time of Edward II many of these tales were translated into English.

Romanticism. The name of both a spirit and a method in art and literature. As contrasted to *classicism*, it means the introduction of the artist's hopes and ideals, his personality, into his work, and the attempt to suggest more than can be definitely expressed. The ideal of the classicist is harmonious objective beauty. As contrasted to *realism*, romanticism means the treatment of distant, strange themes and scenes, while realism handles the near and familiar.

Romeo. In Shakespeare's tragedy *Romeo and Juliet*, a son of Montague, in love with Juliet, the daughter of Capulet, who was the head of a noble house of Verona, in feudal enmity with the house of Montague.

Romeo and Juliet, Shakespeare. Romeo, of the house of Montague, and Juliet, of the house of Capulet in Verona, are lovers. But between their families is a deadly feud. Juliet takes a sleeping draft, that she may be borne to the family tomb, later released and married to Romeo by Friar Lawrence. Romeo, coming to keep the appointment, sees what he thinks is Juliet's dead body. He at once kills himself, and Juliet, awaking, follows his example. Over the dead bodies of their children, the two families are reconciled.

Rosetta Stone. A stone found at Rosetta in the delta of the Nile. It contains equivalent inscriptions in hieroglyphics and in Greek letters. The meaning of the Greek text being known, the hieroglyphics were translated.

Rosinante (rŏz'ĭ-năn'tê). The name of Don Quixote's steed which he rode on various quests and adventures.

Rotten Row. A fashionable promenade in London. The origin of the name is found in its older form, *rotten raw* or lane of the rats, from the rodents which formerly infested the unsavory banks of the near-by Serpentine canal.

Round Table, The. Le Morte D'Arthur, Malory. A table made by Merlin for Uther pendragon. Uther gave it to King Leodegraunce of Camelyard, and when Arthur married Guinevere, the daughter of Leodegraunce, he received the table with a hundred knights as a wedding present. The table would seat 150 knights, and each seat was appropriated. What is usually meant by Arthur's Round Table is a smaller one for the accommodation of twelve favorite knights. King Arthur instituted an order of knighthood called "the knights of the Round Table," the chief of whom were Sir Lancelot, Sir Tristram, and Sir Lamerock or Lamorake. The "siege perilous" was reserved for Sir Galahad, the son of Sir Lancelot by Elaine.

Roussillon, Alice. The heroine of the romance, *Alice of Old Vincennes*, by Maurice Thompson. Her guardian was Gaspard Roussillon, a successful trader with the Indians. "Eat frogs and save your scalps" was the plan of the Latin Creoles. "Papa Roussillon" was a frog eater and the ruling spirit in his little village. The English and their Indian allies arranged their attack on the fort at Vincennes, and the American flag was in danger. Alice, with the help of a crippled boy, Jean, stole the flag. No search or questioning could reveal the whereabouts of either flag or thief. At the end of the siege it was produced, much to the amazement of General Hamilton. Alice forgot her flag for a moment in the appearance of her lover, Beverly, whom she had mourned as dead, but Jean raised it on a staff from which the stars and stripes still floats.

Ruach (rōō'äк). **Pantagruel, Rabelais.** The isle of winds, visited by Pantagruel and his companions. The people of this island live on wind, such as flattery, promises, and hope. The poorer sort are very ill-fed, but the great are stuffed with huge mill-drafts of the same unsubstantial puffs.

Rubaiyat (rōō-bī-yät'). The word means "quatrains." Omar Khayyam, a famous Persian astronomer of the 11th century, wrote, in this four-line stanza form, his reflections upon life. Edward Fitzgerald translated and adapted about a hundred of the many quatrains attributed to Omar. The later editions of this work differ in many points from the first edition of 1859.

Rübezahl (rü'bĕ-tsäl'). The name of a famous spirit of the Riesen-Gebirge in Germany, corresponding to the Puck of England. He is celebrated in innumerable sagas, ballads, and tales, under the various forms of a miner, hunter, monk, dwarf, giant, etc. He is said to aid the poor and oppressed, and to show benighted wanderers their road, but to wage incessant war with the proud and wicked.

Rubric. From the Latin *ruber*, meaning "red." A portion of the type in a book distinguished by being printed in red ink, or, nowadays, by a type-face different from the rest of the print. The use of the rubric arose in the custom of old copyists of making the first letter of a new passage or paragraph red. The usage was extended to whole sentences, and it persists today in prayer books and other books of religious service.

Rudge. Barnaby Rudge, Dickens. Barnaby, a half-witted lad, with pale face, red hair, and protruding eyes, dressed in tawdry finery including peacock feathers in his hat, is the hero of the novel. His inseparable companion is a raven. Barnaby joined the Gordon rioters for the proud pleasure of carrying a flag and wearing a blue bow. He was arrested and lodged in Newgate, whence he made his escape, with other prisoners, when the jail was burned. But both he and his father were recaptured, brought to trial, and condemned to death. By the influence of Gabriel Varden, the locksmith, the poor half-witted lad was reprieved. Mr. Rudge, the father of Barnaby, was supposed to have been murdered the same night as Mr. Haredale, to whom he was steward. Rudge himself was the murderer both of Mr. Haredale and also of his faithful servant, to whom the crime was attributed. After the murder, he was seen by many, haunting the locality, and was supposed to be a ghost. He joined the Gordon rioters. Mrs. Mary Rudge, mother of Barnaby, was very like him, "but where in his face there was wildness and vacancy, in hers there was the patient composure of sorrow."

Ruggiero (*rōōd-jä'rō*). **Orlando Furioso, Ariosto.** A young Saracen knight born of Christian parents, who falls in love with Bradamante, a Christian Amazon, and sister to Rinaldo. After numerous adventures and crosses, they marry and found the house of Este. Ruggiero is noted for the possession of a hippogriff, or winged horse, and also a veiled shield, the dazzling splendor of which when suddenly disclosed, struck with blindness and astonishment all eyes that beheld it.

Rumpelstilzchen. Old German Tales. According to Grimm, this name is a compound, but the spirit represented is one familiar to all German children. The original story tells of him as a dwarf who spun straw into gold for a certain miller's daughter. He has since done favors for many people and paid visits known only by the results of his helpfulness.

Runes. The earliest alphabet in use among the nations of northern Europe. The exact period of their origin is not known. They are found engraved on rocks, crosses, monumental stones, coins, medals, rings, brooches, and the hilts and blades of swords. There is no reason to believe that they were at any time in the familiar use in which we find the characters of a written language in modern times, nor have we any traces of their being used in books or on parchment.

Rupert, Knight. Formerly in the villages of northern Germany, a personage clad in high buskins, white robe, mask, and enormous wig, who at Christmas time distributes presents to the children. Like St. Nicholas, he keeps watch over naughty children. The horseman in the May pageant is in some parts of Germany called Ruprecht, or Rupert.

Rustam. Persian Romances. He is the chief of the Persian mythical heroes, son of Zal, king of India, and descendant of Benjamin, the beloved son of Jacob. He delivered King Caicaus from prison, but afterwards fell into disgrace because he refused to embrace the religious system of Zoroaster. Caicaus sent his son Asfendiar to convert him, and, as persuasion availed nothing, single combat was resorted to. The fight lasted two days, and then Rustam discovered that Asfendiar bore a "charmed life." The valor of these two heroes is proverbial, and the Persian romances are full of their deeds. *Sohrab and Rustum* is the title of a poetical romance by Matthew Arnold.

Ruydera. Don Quixote, Cervantes. A duenna who had seven daughters and two nieces. They were imprisoned for 500 years in a cavern in Spain. Their ceaseless weeping stirred the compassion of Merlin, who converted them into lakes in the same province.

Sabrina. English legend. The daughter of King Locrine and his mistress Estrildis. Gwendolen, the queen, jealous, after the death of Locrine in war, caused Sabrina and Estrildis to be thrown into a river, called since, Sabrina or Severn. Sabrina became the nymph of the stream. Refer to Milton's *Comus* and Fletcher's *Faithful Shepherdess*.

Sacripant, King. (1) King of Circassia, and a lover of Angelica, in Boiardo and Ariosto. (2) A personage introduced by Alessandro Tassoni, the Italian poet, in his mock-heroic poem entitled the "Rape of the Bucket," represented as false, brave, noisy, and hectoring. The name is quoted as a synonym for vanity and braggart courage.

Sagas. Scandinavian myths or hero stories, in prose or poetry. "Saga" is also the name of a goddess of history in Norse mythology. The name given to those ancient traditions which form the substance of the history and mythology of the Scandinavian races; the language in which they are written is supposed to be the old Icelandic. In the *Edda* there are numerous sagas. As our Bible contains the history of the Jews, religious songs, moral proverbs, and religious stories, so the *Edda* contained the history of Norway, religious songs, a book of proverbs, and numerous stories. The original or *Elder Edda* was compiled in the 9th century in Iceland. It contains 28 parts or books, all of which are in verse. In the 12th century, Snorre Sturleson of Iceland abridged, rearranged, and reduced this *Edda* to prose, and his work was called *The Younger Edda*. In this we find parts of the famous *Nibelungenlied*. Besides the sagas contained in the *Eddas*, there are numerous others, and the whole saga literature makes over 200 volumes. Among them are the *Volsung Saga*, a collection of lays about the early Teutonic heroes. The *Saga of St. Olaf* is the history of this Norwegian king. *Frithjof's Saga* contains the life and adventures of Frithjof of Iceland. Snorre Sturleson, at the close of the 12th century, made the second great collection of chronicles in verse, called the *Heimskringla*, or "World-Circuit," *Saga*.

St. Leon. The hero and title of a novel by William Godwin. St. Leon obtains the elixir of life and the secret of the transmutation of metals, acquisitions which only bring him misfortunes and misery.

St. Nicholas. The patron saint of boys and girls, of the poor and the weak, and of mariners. He is said to have been bishop of Myra, and to have died in 345 or 352. The young were universally taught to revere him, and the popular fiction which represents him as the bearer of presents to children on Christmas Eve is well known. His name, "Santa Claus" or Klaus, is of Dutch origin.

St. Patrick's Purgatory. The subject and locality of a legend long famous throughout Europe. The scene is laid in Ireland, upon an islet in Lough Derg. The punishments undergone here are analogous to those described by Dante in his *Divina Commedia*. The story was made the subject of a romance in the 14th century; and, in Spain, in the 17th century, it was dramatized by Calderón.

St. Swithin. Rain on St. Swithin's day, July 15, is said to entail rain for 40 days thereafter. St. Swithin was the bishop of Winchester, who died in 862. He requested burial in the churchyard. When he was canonized, the monks thought to honor him by removing his body into the church. The ceremony was set for July 15 but was prevented by rain for 40 days. The saint was believed thus to show disapproval of the project, and it was abandoned.

Sakuntala (*så-kōōn'tå-lä*). Drama by Kalidasa, famous dramatist of India. The heroine, Sakuntala, left at birth in the forest, is fed by the birds until the king, Dushyanta, finds her and marries her. A ring he had given her she loses while on her way to join him. When, without this ring, the king refuses to acknowledge her, she is compelled to return to the forest. A fisherman who had found the ring is brought before the king on a charge of theft. Recognizing the ring, Dushyanta sends for Sakuntala and proclaims her his queen.

Sally in Our Alley. This popular song was written by Henry Carey in 1734. The author tells of getting the material for the poem by watching a shoemaker's apprentice and his sweetheart on a holiday.

Salmagundi. The name of a periodical started by Washington Irving, his brother, and James K. Paulding, in the year 1807. The object of the paper was the same as that of the *Spectator*, to "correct the town." The publishers became tired of their venture before their subscribers did, and only twenty-two numbers were issued. The political pieces were full of humor, but were not in support of any party. The wit and satire were connected with things local and would not be thoroughly understood or appreciated now. The writers touched upon the follies of fashionable life as well as other follies of their day.

Salt-Box House. Title of book by J. D. Shelton and name given to an imaginary house supposed to stand in a Connecticut hill town more than a century ago. The life of the family to whom the house belonged is followed for three generations. The people, like most families of the same social station, have no sympathy with the war for colonial independence. They have little to do with political life, but in their everyday concerns, work and play, school and church, love and marriage, sickness and death, with their old-time customs, traditions, and habits of thought, they are very interesting. Miss Mary, the last mistress of the Salt-Box House, is a most attractive old maid.

Salt River. American political slang. An imaginary river, up which defeated political parties are supposed to be sent to oblivion. The name and application said to have originated in connection with a river of Kentucky where, for one reason or another, travelers were lost.

Sambo. This term and the name Cuffey used to designate the negro race. Both were used by Mrs. Stowe in her stories.

Samian (sā′mĭ-ăn) **Letter, The.** The letter Y used by Pythagoras as an emblem of the paths of virtue and of vice.

Samian Sage. Pythagoras, said to have been born at Samos.

Samian Wine. The cup of despair and regret over the decay of Greece in Byron's *Isles of Greece.*

Sampson, Dominie. Guy Mannering, Scott. A village schoolmaster and scholar, poor as a church mouse, and modest as a girl. He cites Latin like a "porcus literarum," and exclaims "Prodigious!" He has fallen to the leeward in the voyage of life. He is no uncommon personage in a country where a certain portion of learning is easily attained by those who are willing to suffer hunger and thirst in exchange for acquiring Greek and Latin.

Samson Agonistes (săm′sŭn ăg′ō-nĭs′tēz). The principal character in Milton's sacred drama *Samson Agonistes* or *Samson the Combatant.* Samson, blind and bound, triumphs over his enemies. As in the Bible story, he grasps two of the supporting pillars and perishes in the general ruin.

Sancho Panza (săng′kō pän′zà). The esquire and counterpart of Don Quixote in Cervantes' famous novel. He has much shrewdness in practical matters and a store of proverbial wisdom. He rode upon an ass which he dearly loved, and was noted for his proverbs.

Sandals of Theramenes (thĕ-răm′ĕ-nēz). Theramenes, one of the Athenian oligarchy, was nicknamed "the trimmer," from the name of a sandal or boot which might be worn on either foot, because no dependence could be placed on him. The proverb, "He walks in the sandals of Theramenes," is applied to those who speak fairly but do the things that promise to profit themselves.

Sandford and Merton. Harry Sandford and Tommy Merton, the two heroes of Thomas Day's once popular tale for the young, the *History of Sandford and Merton* (1783–1789).

Sanskrit. The ancient language of India, now extinct, from which most of the languages there spoken are derived. It belongs to the Aryan or Indo-European group of tongues. It was declared by Sir William Jones to be more perfect than the Greek, more copious than the Latin, and more refined than either. The earliest existing work is the *Vedas.* These and the *Puranas* are religious writings; but there are also epic poems, dramas, and philosophical compositions.

Santa Claus. In fable he was first known as patron saint of children. The vigil of his feast is still held in some places, but for the most part his name is now associated with Christmastide. The old custom used to be for some one, on December 5th, to assume the costume of a bishop and distribute small gifts to "good children." See *St. Nicholas.*

Santiago (sän-te-ä′gō). The war cry of Spain; adopted because St. James (Sant Iago) rendered, according to tradition, signal service to a Christian king of Spain in a battle against the Moors.

Satan. Hebrew, "the adversary." One of the names of the Devil, and that by which in the Bible, in poetry, and in popular legends, he is often designated. Those medieval writers who reckoned nine kinds of demons, placed Satan at the head of the fifth rank, which consisted of cozeners, as magicians and witches. Milton represents him as the monarch of hell. His chief lords are Beelzebub, Moloch, Chemosh, Tammuz, Dagon, Rimmon, and Belial. His standard bearer is Azazel.

Satyrane. Faery Queen, Spenser. A noble knight who delivered Una from the fauns and satyrs. The meaning seems to be that Truth, driven from the towns and cities, took refuge in caves and dens, where for a time she lay concealed. At length Sir Satyrane rescues Una from bondage; no sooner is she free than she falls in with Archimago, who poses as the Red Cross Knight, but whose falsehood is later exposed.

Saunders, Clerk. The hero of a well-known Scottish ballad.

Sawney. A sportive designation applied by the English to the Scotch. It is a corruption of "Sandie," the Scottish abbreviation of "Alexander."

Sawyer, Bob. Pickwick Papers, Dickens. A drinking young doctor who tries to establish a practice at Bristol, but without success. Sam Weller calls him " Mr. Sawbones."

Scalds or **Skalds.** Court poets and chroniclers of the ancient Scandinavians. They resided at court, were attached to the royal suite, and attended the king in all his wars. These bards celebrated in song the gods, the kings of Norway, and national heroes. Few complete scaldic poems have survived, but a multitude of fragments exist.

Scarecrow, The, Percy Mackaye. A New England phantasy. Farce. Goody Rickby, reputed a witch, at her forge making a scarecrow for her cornfield, is persuaded by her "familiar," Dickon, to fashion a figure of cornstalks and pumpkin, animate it with a brimstone pipe, and send it as Lord Ravensbane to ask for the hand of Rachel, niece of Justice Gilead Merton. Dickon tells Merton that this young "lord" is really his own son by Goody Rickby, whom he has thought dead. Rachel, who is betrothed to young Squire Talbot, falls in love with the scarecrow "lord." The scarecrow, through love of her, gradually wins enough manhood to break his pipe, thus giving up life and leaving Rachel to Richard. Goody Rickby disappears, but she has had revenge on Justice Merton.

Scarlet Letter, The. Title of a romance by Nathaniel Hawthorne. The heroine, Hester Prynne, was condemned to wear conspicuously the letter "A" in scarlet, token of her sin as mother of her child, Pearl, whose father was not known. She was first exposed in disgrace on a raised scaffold, then served a term in prison, and afterward gained a moderate support for herself and child by embroidering. She refused to reveal the name of the father, although she might then be allowed to lay aside the letter. He was always near, held an important position, and lived a life of wearing remorse. After his death Hester Prynne took her child to another country, but returned to spend her old age in seclusion and comfort in the same place that had witnessed her punishment. She always bore herself proudly but not defiantly and brought to herself such love and respect that the scarlet letter became a badge of honor. Roger Chillingworth, Hester's husband, appeared as a learned foreign physician, visited her in prison, but promised not to reveal his relation to her, and devoted his life to learning her secret. The characters in the story are intense and the analysis of motives subtle.

Schahriah. Arabian Nights. The sultan of Persia. His reign was a despotism and his decrees absolute.

Scheherazade (shĕ-hā′rà-zä′dĕ). **Arabian Nights.** The fabled relater of the stories in these "Entertainments." Among other decrees the sultan had decided upon a new wife for every day. Tradition or fable tells that Scheherazade, wishing to free Persia of this disgrace, requested to be made the sultan's wife. She was young and beautiful, of great courage and ready wit, had an excellent memory, knew history, was poet, musician, and dancer. Scheherazade obtained permission for her younger sister, Dinarzade, to sleep in the same chamber, and instructed her to say, "Sister, relate to me one of those stories." Scheherazade then, under pretense of speaking to her sister, told the sultan a story, but always contrived to break off before the story was finished. The sultan, in order to hear the end of the story, spared her life till the next night. This went on for a thousand and one nights, when the sultan's resentment was worn out, and his admiration of his sultana was so great that he revoked his decree.

Schlemihl, Peter. The title of a little work by Chamisso (1781–1838), and the name of its hero, a man who sells his shadow to an old man in gray (the Devil) who meets him just after he has been disappointed in an application for assistance to a nobleman. The name has become a byword for any poor, silly, and unfortunate fellow.

Scholar-Gipsy. The subject of one of Matthew Arnold's greatest poems.

Scotland Yard. A short street in London, near Trafalgar Square. Here formerly were the headquarters of the metropolitan police, now removed to New Scotland Yard on the Thames embankment, near Westminster bridge. The detectives are known as Scotland Yard men. Often mentioned in the detective stories of Conan Doyle and others.

Scourge of God. Attila, king of the Huns. A. P. Stanley says the term was first applied to Attila in the Hungarian Chronicles. It is found in a legend belonging to the 8th or 9th century.

Scrap of Paper, A. A phrase used by the German chancellor, von Bethmann-Hollweg, with reference to England's entry into World War I in 1914. He is quoted as saying that England was going to war for Belgian neutrality, "just for a scrap of paper." But his phrase was widely understood as expressing the German attitude toward the Belgian treaty and hence toward all treaties.

Scrooge, Ebenezer. Christmas Carol, Dickens. The prominent character, made partner, executor, and heir of old Jacob Marley, stockbroker. When first introduced, he is a grasping, covetous old man, loving no one and by none beloved. One Christmas, Ebenezer Scrooge sees three ghosts: The Ghost of Christmas Past; the Ghost of Christmas Present; and the Ghost of Christmas To-come. The first takes him back to his young life, shows him what Christmas was to him when a schoolboy, and when he was an apprentice. The second ghost shows him the joyous home of his clerk, Bob Cratchit, who has nine people to feed on what seems a pittance, and yet could find wherewithal to make merry on this day; it also shows him the family of his nephew, and others. The third ghost shows him what would be his lot if he died as he then was, the prey of harpies, the jest of his friends on 'Change. These visions wholly change his nature, and he becomes benevolent, charitable, and cheerful, and makes Christmas a happy day for many within his reach.

Seasons. A well-known poem said to be the foundation of Thomson's literary fame. Its description of the phenomena of nature during an English year is minute, and the poem has been much read by foreigners. Its real value today is largely historical, in that Thomson represents, in relation to nature, the transition in English literature from the classicism of Pope and his school to the romanticism of the Lake School.

Sedley, Mr. Vanity Fair, Thackeray. A wealthy London stockbroker, brought to ruin in the money market just prior to the battle of Waterloo. The old merchant tried to earn a living by selling wine, coals, or lottery tickets by commission, but his bad wine and cheap coals found but few customers. Mrs. Sedley, wife of Mr. Sedley, a homely, kind-hearted woman, soured by adversity, and quick to take offense. Amelia Sedley, daughter of the stockbroker, educated at Miss Pinkerton's academy, and engaged to Captain George Osborne, son of a rich London merchant. After the ruin of Mr. Sedley, George marries Amelia, and old Osborne disinherits him. George is killed in the battle of Waterloo. Amelia is reduced to great poverty, but is befriended by Captain Dobbin, and after many years of patience and great devotion she consents to marry him. Joseph Sedley, vain, shy, and vulgar. He told of his brave deeds, and made it appear that he was Wellington's right hand; so that he obtained the sobriquet of "Waterloo Sedley." He became the "patron" of Becky Sharp, who fleeced him of all his money, and in six months he died under suspicious circumstances. Interest in the novel is centered on Amelia, an impersonation of virtue without intellect as contrasted with Becky Sharp, who is an impersonation of intellect without virtue. The one has no head, the other no heart. Amelia and Becky afforded brilliant contrasts in acting in the dramatized version of *Vanity Fair*,—"Becky Sharp."

Selim (sē'lĭm). **Bride of Abydos, Byron.** The character of Selim is bold, full of enterprise, and faithful. The story runs that Selim was the son of Abdallah and cousin of Zuleika. When Giaffir murdered Abdallah, he took Selim and brought him up as his own son. The young man fell in love with Zuleika, who thought he was her brother; when she discovered he was Abdallah's son, she eloped with him. As soon as Giaffir discovered this he went after the fugitives, and shot Selim. Zuleika died broken-hearted, and the old pasha was left childless. Selim, son of Akbar, in Arabian tales, marries Nourmahal, the "Light of the Harem."

Selith. The Messiah, Klopstock. One of the two guardian angels of the Virgin Mary and of John the Divine.

Sellers, Colonel Mulberry. A famous character in *The Gilded Age*, a novel by Mark Twain and C. D. Warner. John T. Raymond made a dramatized version popular. The colonel is a Southern gentleman of visionary but invincible optimism. Mark Twain wrote that he had drawn the character from the life of James Lampton, a cousin of his mother.

Sellock. Peveril of the Peak, Scott. A servant girl in the service of Lady and Sir Geoffrey Peveril of the Peak.

Senena. Madoc, Southey. A Welsh maiden in love with Caradoc. Under the assumed name of Mervyn she became the page of the princess Goervyl, in order that she might follow her lover to America, when Madoc colonized Caer-Madoc. Senena was promised in marriage to another; but, when the wedding day arrived, the bride was nowhere to be found.

Sentimental Journey, The, Laurence Sterne. It was intended to be sentimental sketches of his tour through Italy in 1764, but he died soon after completing the first part.

Sentimental Tommy, Barrie. The story of a "Thrums" boy with an insuppressible insincerity and habit of posing. The story is continued in *Tommy and Grizel*. The two stories form a comedy of sentimentality.

Septuagint (sĕp'tû-á-jĭnt). A Greek version of the books of the Old Testament; so called because the translation is supposed to have been made by 72 Jews, who, for the sake of round numbers, are usually called the "seventy interpreters." It is said to have been made at the request of Ptolemy Philadelphus, king of Egypt, about 280 B. C. It is that out of which all the citations in the New Testament from the Old are taken and from which the Psalter in the English Book of Common Prayer is translated. It was also the ordinary and canonical translation made use of by the Christian Church in the earliest ages; and is still retained in the churches of both the East and the West.

Serena. Faery Queen, Spenser. Allured by the mildness of the weather, she went into the fields to gather wild flowers for a garland, when she was attacked by the Blatant Beast, who carried her off in its mouth. Her cries attracted to the spot Sir Calidore, who compelled the beast to drop its prey.

Sesame (sĕs'á-mê). In Arabian tales given as the talismanic word which would open or shut the door leading into the cave of the forty thieves. In order to open it, the words to be uttered were, "Open, Sesame!" and in order to close it, "Shut, Sesame!" Sesame is a plant which yields an oily grain, and hence, when Cassim forgot the word, he substituted "barley," but without effect. Sesame has come into general use in connection with any word or act which will open the way for accomplishment of the thing desired. "Sesame and Lilies" is one of the most important and beautiful of Ruskin's works.

Seven Sleepers, The. The tale of these sleepers is told in divers manners. The best accounts are those in the *Koran*; *The Golden Legend*, by Jacopo da Voragine; the *De Gloria Martyrum*, by Gregory of Tours; and the *Oriental Tales*, by Caylus. According to one version they were seven noble youths of Ephesus, who fled in the Decian persecution to a cave in Mount Celion, the mouth of which was blocked up by stones. After 230 years they were discovered, and awoke, but died within a few days, and were taken in a large stone coffin to Marseilles. Another tradition is, that Edward the Confessor, in his mind's eye, saw the seven sleepers turn from their right sides to their left, and whenever they turn on their sides it indicates great disasters to Christendom. This idea was introduced by Tennyson in his drama *Harold*.

Seven Wise Masters. The title of a medieval collection of novels, important from both its contents and its widespread popularity. The work is undoubtedly of Oriental origin, yet neither the period when it was composed, nor how far it spread through the East, is known, but it existed in Arabic as a translation from Indian sources before the 11th century. The work became known in literature, sometimes in a complete form; sometimes only particular novels were reproduced, under all sorts of names, in verse and in prose. Latin versions began to appear about the beginning of the 13th century and parts have been translated into English.

Seven Wise Men. The collective designation of a number of Greek sages, who lived about 620–548 B. C. and devoted themselves to the cultivation of practical wisdom. Their moral and social experience was embodied in brief aphorisms, expressed in verse or in prose.

Sganarelle (z'gá'ná'rĕl'). The hero of Molière's comedy *Le Mariage Forcé*. He is represented as a humorist of about 53, who, having a mind to marry a fashionable young woman, but feeling a doubt, consults his friends upon this momentous question. Receiving no satisfactory counsel, and not much pleased with the proceedings of his bride elect, he at last determines to give up his engagement, but is cudgeled into compliance by the brother of his intended.

Shallow. A braggart and absurd country justice in Shakespeare's *Merry Wives of Windsor*, and in the second part of *King Henry IV*.

Shalott, The Lady of. The heroine of Tennyson's poem of the same name. She weaves into her web all the sights reflected in the mirror which hangs opposite her window; but, when Sir Lancelot passes, she leaves her mirror and looks out of the casement at the knight himself, whereupon a curse comes upon her. She entered a boat bearing her name on the prow, floated down the river to Camelot, and died heartbroken on the way.

Shandy, Mrs. The mother of Tristram Shandy in Sterne's novel of this name. She is the ideal of nonentity, a character individual from its very absence of individuality.

Shandy, Tristram. The nominal hero of Sterne's *The Life and Opinions of Tristram Shandy, Gent.*

Shandy, Walter. The name of Tristram Shandy's father in Sterne's novel of this name, a man of an active and metaphysical, but at the same time a whimsical, cast of mind, whom too much and too miscellaneous learning had brought within a step or two of madness. The romance, *Tristram Shandy*, is not built on a regular plot. The hero has no adventures, and the story consists of a series of episodes which introduce the reader to the home life of an

English country family. This family is one of the most amusing.

Shangri-la. A mythical country, the scene of James Hilton's romantic novel, *Lost Horizon*. In its popular generalized meaning, Shangri-la designates a place whose location is not to be divulged. President Roosevelt humorously cited it as the base from which the Doolittle fliers made their raid on Tokyo.

Sharp, Rebecca. The prominent character in Thackeray's *Vanity Fair*, the daughter of a poor painter, dashing, selfish, unprincipled, and very clever, who manages to marry Rawdon Crawley, afterwards his excellency Colonel Crawley, C. B. He was disinherited on account of his marriage with Becky, then a poor governess, but she taught him how to live in splendor on no income. Lord Steyne introduced her to court, but her conduct with this peer gave rise to scandal, which caused a separation between her and Rawdon. She joins her fortunes with Joseph Sedley, a wealthy "collector," of Boggley Wollah, in India. Having insured his life and lost his money, he dies suddenly under very suspicious circumstances. Becky at last assumes the character of a pious, charitable Lady Bountiful, given to all good works.

Shaving of Shagpat, The, George Meredith. A burlesque version of an Oriental tale. The style suggests the *Arabian Nights*.

Shepherdess, The Faithful. A pastoral drama by John Fletcher. The "faithful shepherdess" is Corin, who remains faithful to her lover although he is dead. Milton has borrowed from this pastoral in his *Comus*.

Shepherd of Banbury. The ostensible author of a work entitled "The Shepherd of Banbury's Rules to judge of the Changes of Weather, Grounded on Forty Years' Experience, etc.," a work of great popularity among the English poor.

Shepherd of Salisbury Plain, The. The hero and title of a religious tract by Hannah More. The shepherd is noted for his homely wisdom and simple piety.

Shepherd's Calendar, The. Twelve eclogues in various meters, by Spenser, one for each month. January: Colin Clout (Spenser) bewails that Rosalind does not return his love. February: Cuddy, a lad, complains of the cold, and Thenot laments the degeneracy of pastoral life. March: Willie and Thomalin discourse of love. April: Hobbinol sings a song on Eliza. May: Palinode exhorts Piers to join the festivities of May, but Piers replies that good shepherds who seek their own indulgence expose their flocks to the wolves. June: Hobbinol exhorts Colin to greater cheerfulness. July: Morrel, a goatherd, invites Thomalin to come with him to the uplands. August: Perigot and Willie contend in song, and Cuddy is appointed arbiter. September: Diggon Davie complains to Hobbinol of clerical abuses. October: On poetry. November: Colin, being asked by Thenot to sing, excuses himself because of his grief for Dido, but finally sings her elegy. December: Colin again complains that his heart is desolate. Thenot is an old shepherd bent with age, who tells Cuddy, the herdsman's boy, the fable of the oak and the briar, one of the best-known fables included in the calendar.

Shepherd's Pipe. Pan, in Greek mythology, was the god of forests, pastures, and flocks, and was the reputed inventor of the shepherd's flute or pipe, a series of graduated tubes set together, open at one end and closed at the other, played by blowing across the open ends.

Sheridan's Ride. A lyric by T. B. Read, one of the few things written during the heat of the Civil War that have survived.

Sherlock Holmes, The Adventures of, Conan Doyle. A series of clever and popular detective stories in which the hero, Holmes, a private detective, employs his extraordinary fund of scientific knowledge and unusual powers of reasoning to solve many baffling mysteries of crime. The stories are told by Holmes's friend and companion, Dr. Watson. The plan of these stories was suggested by Poe's *Murders in the Rue Morgue*. The methods of Holmes are said to have been suggested to Doyle by the work of Dr. Joseph Bell, a physician of Edinburgh and at one time an instructor of the novelist.

Sherwood Forest. A forest in Nottinghamshire, England, fourteen miles north of Nottingham. It was formerly of large extent. It is the principal scene of the legendary exploits of Robin Hood.

She Stoops to Conquer. This well-known comedy by Oliver Goldsmith is said to have been founded on an incident which actually occurred to its author. When Goldsmith was sixteen years of age, a wag residing at Ardagh directed him, when passing through that village, to Squire Fetherstone's house as the village inn. The mistake was not discovered for some time, but all concerned enjoyed the joke. *She Stoops to Conquer* is a gay, pleasant, and most amusing piece of English comedy.

Shingebis. In Longfellow's "Hiawatha," the diver who challenged the North Wind and put him to flight in combat.

Shocky. The Hoosier Schoolmaster, Edw. Eggleston. The little lad from the poorhouse who adores the schoolmaster and early warns him of plans for upsetting his authority. He is also somewhat of a poet, not in versification, but in the comprehension of things about him and in his way of looking at life, and he grows to be a helper in the "Church of the Best Licks," founded by the schoolmaster. He is brother to Hannah whom the master loves. Shocky and Hannah and their companions in the story bring the speech and life of their people and their time into American literature.

Shylock. The Jew, in Shakespeare's *Merchant of Venice*.

Siege Perilous, The. The Round Table contained sieges, or seats, in the names of different knights. One was reserved for him who was destined to achieve the quest of the holy grail. This seat was called "perilous," because if anyone sat therein except him for whom it was reserved it would be his death. This seat finally bore the name of Sir Galahad.

Siegfried. The hero of various Scandinavian and Teutonic legends, particularly of the old German epic poem, the *Nibelungenlied*. He is represented as a young warrior of physical strength and beauty, and in valor superior to all men of his time. He cannot easily be identified with any historical personage.

Sikes, Bill. A brutal thief and housebreaker in Dickens's novel *Oliver Twist*. He murders his mistress, Nancy, and, in trying to lower himself by a rope from the roof of a building where he had taken refuge from the crowd, he falls and is choked in a noose of his own making. Sikes had an ill-conditioned savage dog, the beast-image of his master, which he kicked and loved, illtreated and fondled.

Silas Marner. The principal character in George Eliot's story *Silas Marner, the Weaver of Raveloe*. Silas, a cataleptic, lived his younger life in a little religious community of weavers in Lantern Yard. Robbed of his sweetheart and his good name by his best friend, Silas withdrew to the village of Raveloe. Here in his lonely hut he hoards his earnings. Robbed of these, he is saved from utter despair by finding a baby girl. On her he spends his love. In the end the shattered man is remade by this influence, and the stolen savings are found and restored to him.

Silken Thread. Gulliver's Travels. In the kingdom of Lilliput, the three great prizes of honor are "fine silk threads six inches long, one blue, another red, and a third green." The thread is girt about the loins, and no ribbon of the Legion of Honor, or of the Knight of the Garter, is won more worthily or worn more proudly.

Silver, Long John. A one-legged pirate who figures prominently in Stevenson's "Treasure Island."

Simon Pure. The real thing. In Mrs. Centlivre's comedy, *A Bold Stroke For A Wife*, (1718), another man impersonates the Quaker, Simon Pure, who asserts that he is the genuine article.

Sindbad the Sailor. A character in the *Arabian Nights*, in which is related the story of his strange voyages and wonderful adventures.

Sinon (sī'nŏn). In Virgil's *Æneid*, the cunning Greek who, by a false tale, induced the Trojans to drag the wooden horse into Troy.

Sleeping Beauty. The heroine of a celebrated nursery tale which relates how a princess was shut up by fairy enchantment, to sleep a hundred years in a castle, around which sprang up a dense, impenetrable wood. At the expiration of the appointed time, she was delivered from her imprisonment and her trance by a gallant young prince, before whom the forest opened itself to afford him passage. Grimm derives this popular and widely diffused tale from the old northern mythology.

Slender. A silly youth in Shakespeare's *Merry Wives of Windsor*, who is an unsuccessful suitor for the hand of "Sweet Anne Page."

Slick, Sam. The title and hero of various humorous narratives, illustrating and exaggerating the peculiarities of the Yankee character and dialect, written by Judge Thomas C. Haliburton, chief justice of Nova Scotia. Sam Slick is represented as a Yankee clockmaker and peddler, full of quaint drollery, unsophisticated wit, knowledge of human nature, and aptitude in the use of what he calls "soft sawder." Haliburton's *Sam Slick* may be said to originate the American school of humor.

Slough of Despond. Pilgrim's Progress, Bunyan. A deep bog, which Christian had to pass on his way to the Wicket Gate. Neighbor Pliable would not attempt to pass it, and turned back. While Christian was floundering in the slough, Help came to his aid and assisted him over.

Sly, Christopher. Taming of the Shrew, Shakespeare. A keeper of bears and a tinker, son of a peddler and a sad drinker.

Sohrab and Rustum, Matthew Arnold. A narrative poem. The story is Persian. Sohrab, son of Rustum, long an adventurer, is a warrior who appalls the Persian armies. At last, in a fight with Rustum, he is mortally wounded. Rustum, discovering in Sohrab his son, is inconsolable.

Soldiers Three, Kipling. The title of a series of tales of army life in India, which recount the adventures of three private soldiers, whose portraits are perhaps Kipling's best work. Of them he writes in beginning their story, "Mulvaney, Ortheris, and Learoyd are privates in B Company of a Line Regiment and personal friends of mine."

Song of Roland. An ancient song recounting the deeds of Roland, the renowned nephew of Charlemagne, slain in the pass of Roncesvalles. At the battle of Hastings, Taillefer advanced on horseback before the invading army, and gave the signal for onset by singing this famous song. See *Roland.*

Songs of the Sierras. A collection of poems by Joaquin Miller, which made him known on two continents within a year of their publication. The title explains the chief subject of the songs.

Spanish Main. The southern banks of the West India islands, and the water extending for some distance into the Caribbean Sea, so called from the fact that the Spaniards confined their buccaneering enterprises to this locality.

Spectator, The. A periodical famous in literature, in which most of the articles were written by Addison or Sir Richard Steele. The first number was published in London in the year 1711, the last, No. 635, was issued in December 1714. The most noted of Addison's writings is said to be the series of sketches in *The Spectator,* of which Sir Roger de Coverley is the central figure, and Sir Andrew Freeport and Will Honeycomb the side ones. Sir Roger himself is an absolute creation; the gentle yet vivid imagination, the gay spirit of humor, and the keen, shrewd observation mark it a work of pure genius. In this, Addison has given a delicacy to English sentiment and a modesty to English wit which it never knew before. Dr. Johnson says, "To attain an English style, familiar but not coarse, and elegant but not ostentatious, one must give his days and nights to the volumes of Addison."

Sphinx. A Greek word, applied to certain symbolical forms of Egyptian origin. The most remarkable sphinx is the Great Sphinx at Giza, a colossal form, hewn out of the natural rock. Immediately in front of the breast is a small naos, or chapel, formed of three hieroglyphical tablets. Votive inscriptions of the Roman period, some as late as the 3d century, were discovered in the walls and constructions. On the second digit of the left claw of the Sphinx, an inscription, in pentameter Greek verse, by Arrian, was discovered. Another metrical and prosaic inscription was also found. In Assyria and Babylonia, representations of sphinxes have been found, and they are not uncommon on Phoenician works of art.

Spoon River Anthology, Edgar Lee Masters. The best-known work of this poet. It is a collection of poems in free verse, in the form of realistic epitaphs on the citizens of a village of the Middle West. The plan was suggested by Masters' reading of the *Greek Anthology.*

Squeers. Name of a family prominent in Dickens's *Nicholas Nickleby.* Wackford Squeers, master of Dotheboys Hall, Yorkshire, a vulgar conceited, ignorant schoolmaster, overbearing and mean. He steals the boys' pocket money, clothes his son in their best suits, half starves them, and teaches them next to nothing. Ultimately he is transported for theft. Mrs. Squeers, a rawboned, harsh, heartless virago, with no womanly feeling for the boys put under her charge. Miss Fanny Squeers, daughter of the schoolmaster. Miss Fanny falls in love with Nicholas Nickleby, but later hates him because he is insensible to her tender passion. Master Wackford Squeers, overbearing, self-willed, and passionate. The picture of this family and their ways had great influence on the schools of England, by rousing the people to a knowledge of their management.

Stalky and Company, Kipling. A series of stories of English school life. Corkran (Your Uncle Stalky), McTurk, and Beetle, who is probably the author, combine to play pranks, victimizing both masters and boys.

Steerforth. David Copperfield, Dickens. The young man who led Little Em'ly astray. When tired of his toy, he proposed to her to marry his valet. Steerforth being shipwrecked off the coast of Yarmouth, Ham Peggotty tried to rescue him, but both were drowned.

Stentor. A Grecian herald in the Trojan War, whom Homer describes as "great-hearted, brazen-voiced Stentor, accustomed to shout as loud as fifty other men." Hence our adjective "stentorian."

Stephano. (1) A drunken butler, in Shakespeare's *Tempest.* (2) A servant to Portia, in Shakespeare's *Merchant of Venice.*

Stickeen, John Muir. The story of a dog.

Stiggins, Rev. Mr. A red-nosed, hypocritical "shepherd," or Methodist parson, in Dickens's *Pickwick Papers,* with a great appetite for pineapple rum. He is the spiritual adviser of Mrs. Weller and lectures on temperance.

Stone of Sardis. The Great Stone of Sardis, Stockton. In this stone the imaginary science of the future is joined to the actual science of today in an extremely plausible way. The north pole is visited by a submarine vessel, a light is found capable of penetrating for miles into the interior of the earth, and finally the center of that earth is discovered to be an enormous diamond.

Storm and Stress Period. In the literary history of Germany, the name given to a period of great intellectual convulsion, when the nation began to assert its freedom from the fetters of an artificial literary spirit. The period derives its name from a drama of Klinger (1753–1831), whose high-wrought tragedies and novels reflect the excitement of the time.

Strife, John Galsworthy. The scene of this play is the Trenartha Tin Works. A strike is on, led by David Roberts, determined foe of the owners. John Anthony, founder and president of the company, is all for fighting. Among the directors, called down from London, and also among the workers are those who are for compromise. These finally come to agreement, in spite of Roberts and Anthony, the strong men and "bitter enders." At the close of the play, these two evince their sense of a common defeat and a reluctant respect for each other's strength, mixed with contempt for the weak compromisers. The action of the play is confined to one day.

Sunken Bell, The, Hauptmann. A fairy drama which portrays the bitter struggles of a bell-founder, Heinrich, against the forces that thwart his ambition. A fairy will not endure the ringing of a bell he wants to place in a mountain chapel. The bell is sunk in a deep abyss. Discouraged, he finds help in a mountain elf, Rautendelein. With her, he plans new things. But the eternal strife between the low and the high wears him out at last.

Svengali (svĕn-gä'lĭ). The bearded hypnotist whose piercing eyes control the young woman singer Trilby in George Du Maurier's story which bears her name.

Swallow Barn. The three novels, *Swallow Barn,* *Horse-Shoe Robinson,* and *Rob of the Bowl,* besides their value as works of art, are all careful historical studies giving admirable pictures of life in the southern states in the earlier days of the republic. They were written by John P. Kennedy, who holds a place among American novelists not far removed from that of Cooper.

Swiveller, Dick. A careless, light-headed fellow in Dickens's novel *Old Curiosity Shop,* whose flowery orations and absurdities of quotation provoke laughter, but whose real kindness of heart enlists sympathy.

Tabard, The, Chaucer's Inn. The old London tavern, immortalized by Chaucer as the "Tabard" in *Canterbury Tales.* It took its name from its sign, a tabard, or loose, sleeveless jacket. From this hostelry in Southwark, on the south side of the Thames, the "pilgrims" started on the famous journey to Canterbury, "the holy blissful martyr for to seek." The inn was burned in the great fire of 1676. Upon its restoration the name was changed to the "Talbot," or Dog, which name it retained until about 1873, when it was demolished.

Tales of a Wayside Inn. Name given by Longfellow to a collection of his short poems arranged in much the same form as Chaucer's *Canterbury Tales.* These "tales" were mostly gathered from old literatures and translated into Longfellow's own verse. Only one, "The Birds of Killingworth," is said to be entirely original. Seven narrators are represented: the Landlord, the Student, the Spanish Cavalier, the Jew, the Sicilian, the Musician, and the Theologian. Four colonial tales are included in the work: "Paul Revere's Ride," "Elizabeth," "Lady Wentworth," and "The Rhyme of Sir Christopher."

Tales of My Landlord, Scott. A series of novels in which the stories are told by the landlord of the Wallace Inn, parish of Gandercleugh, and edited by Jedediah Cleishbotham, schoolmaster. The series includes, besides others, *The Black Dwarf* and *Count Robert of Paris.*

Talmud. A Hebrew word meaning "doctrine." It is the name applied to a work containing traditions respecting the usages and laws of the Jewish people. The law, among that people, was divided into the written and the unwritten. The written law embraced the five books of Moses; the unwritten was handed down orally; the oral being, in fact, explanatory of the written. But, in time, the oral came, also, to be put in writing, and formed the text of the *Talmud*. This was first done, it is believed, about the year 200. There are two separate commentaries on this text, which are distinguished as the Babylonian and the Jerusalem. The *Talmud* of Jerusalem consists of two parts, the "Mishna" and the "Gemara." The "Mishna" gives a simple statement of a law; the "Gemara" presents the discussion upon it. The *Talmud* of Babylon, which is of higher authority among the Jews than that of Jerusalem, was composed by Rabbi Aser, who lived near Babylon; he did not live to finish it, but it was completed by his disciples about 500 years after Christ.

Taming of the Shrew, Shakespeare. A farce-comedy. Katherine, the shrewish daughter of Baptista Minola of Padua, is transformed by Petruchio, a good-humored but determined gentleman, into a model of the obedient wife. By thwarting her every wish, under the pretense of the most thoughtful care for her comfort, he brings her to terms through sheer weariness of strife.

Tam O'Shanter. The title of a poem by Burns, and the name of its hero, a farmer, who, riding home very late and very drunk from Ayr, in a stormy night, had to pass by the kirk of Alloway, a place reputed to be a favorite haunt of the Devil and his friends and emissaries. On approaching the kirk, he perceived a light gleaming through the windows; but, having got courageously drunk, he ventured on till he could look into the edifice, when he saw a dance of witches. His presence became known and in an instant all was dark, and Tam, recollecting himself, turned and spurred his horse to the top of her speed, chased by the whole fiendish crew. It is a current belief that witches, or any evil spirits, have no power to follow a poor wight any farther than the middle of the next running stream. Fortunately for Tam, the River Doon was near, and Tam escaped while the witches held only the tail of his mare, Maggie. It has been said of "Tam O'Shanter" that in no other poem of the same length can there be found so much brilliant description, pathos, and quaint humor, nor such a combination of the terrific and the ludicrous.

Tancred. The hero of the First Crusade. The love of woman was his one besetting weakness. Tasso follows his career in *Jerusalem Delivered*, and he appears in Scott's *Count Robert of Paris*. Disraeli uses the name for the hero of his novel *Tancred, or the New Crusade*.

Tannhäuser. A famous legendary hero of Germany, and the subject of an ancient ballad of the same name. The noble Tannhäuser is a knight devoted to valorous adventures and to beautiful women. In Mantua, he wins the affection of a lovely lady, Lisaura, and of a learned philosopher, Hilario, with whom he converses frequently upon supernatural subjects. Enchanted by marvelous tales, he wishes for nothing less than to participate in the love of some beauteous elementary spirit, who shall, for his sake, assume the form of mortal woman. Hilario promises to grant even more than he has wished, if he will have courage to venture upon the Venusberg. Tannhäuser ascends the mountain, and, hearing of his departure, Lisaura dies. Tannhäuser stays long on the enchanting mountain, but at last, moved to repentance, he obtains permission to depart. He hastens to Mantua, weeps over the grave of Lisaura, and thence proceeds to Rome, where he makes public confession of his sins to Pope Urban. The pope refuses him absolution, saying he can no more be pardoned than the dry wand which he holds can bud and bear green leaves. Tannhäuser flees from Rome, and vainly seeks his former preceptor, Hilario. Venus appears before him and lures him back to the mountain, there to remain until the day of judgment. Meanwhile, at Rome the dry wand bears leaves. Urban, alarmed at this miracle, sends messengers in search of the unhappy knight; but he is nowhere to be found. This Tannhäuser legend is very popular in Germany, and is often alluded to by German writers. Tieck has made it the subject of a narrative, and Wagner, of an opera which has gained great celebrity.

Tartarin. The quixotic hero of a series of humorous, half-satiric masterpieces by Alphonse Daudet. Tartarin, at his home in Tarascon, in southern France, is continually dreaming of travel and adventure. By reading of distant lands and viewing the guns in his collection, he persuades himself that he actually has had the adventures he imagines. Finally, he does journey to Africa to hunt lions, and to Switzerland to climb mountains. The stories of these exploits and others Daudet makes a source of never-failing entertainment.

Tartufe (*tär-toof'*), "The Hypocrite." (1) A comedy by Molière, in which the leading character is Tartufe (*Fr. tär'tüf'*). Tartufe, an adventurer, masquerading under a cloak of piety, worms his way into the household of Orgon, a well-to-do merchant. Orgon, with the connivance of his mother, goes so far as to make Tartufe a deed to his estate and promises him his daughter Mariane, already affianced to Valère. But Tartufe really wants Elmire, Orgon's second wife. She arranges that Orgon shall overhear the hypocrite's declaration of love to her. Tartufe meets Orgon's anger by claiming his property under the deed. Louis XIV intervenes, saves Orgon's estate, and imprisons Tartufe. (2) A common nickname for a hypocritical pretender to religion. It is derived from the name of the character in Molière's comedy.

Teazle, Lady. The heroine of Sheridan's comedy *The School for Scandal*, and the wife of Sir Peter Teazle, an old gentleman who marries late in life. She is represented as being "a lively and innocent, though imprudent, country girl, transplanted into the midst of all that can bewilder and endanger her, but with enough of purity about her to keep the blight of the world from settling upon her."

Teazle, Sir Peter. A character in Sheridan's play *The School for Scandal*, husband of Lady Teazle.

Tel-el-Amarna Letters. A collection of several hundred clay tablets with cuneiform inscriptions found at Tel-el-Amarna, a village on the Nile. Official correspondence of about 1400 B. C., between Egypt and Syria.

Tempest, The. This has been called one of Shakespeare's fairy plays. The story of it runs: Prospero, duke of Milan, was dethroned by his brother Antonio, and left on the open sea with his three-year-old daughter Miranda, in "a rotten carcass of a boat." In this they were carried to an enchanted island, uninhabited except by a hideous creature, Caliban, the son of a witch. Prospero was a powerful enchanter, and soon had not only Caliban, but all the spirits of the region under his control, including Ariel, chief of the spirits of the air. Years afterward Antonio, Alfonso, Sebastian, and other friends of the usurper came near the island. Prospero, by his magic, raises a storm which casts their ship on the shore, and the whole party is spellbound and brought to Prospero. Plots and counterplots follow, bringing in Caliban and clowns, but all are made ridiculous and defeated by Prospero and Ariel.

Tenson (*tĕn'sŏn*). A kind of poem among the troubadours which carries on a contention or dispute, apparently serious, and often concerning love. The tenson was usually recited by two persons in alternating stanzas. The greater number of these are found in early Italian and French literature.

Ten Times One. A writing in story form by E. E. Hale. It is said that the inspiration of this story led to the founding of the "King's Daughters" society.

Tess of the D'Urbervilles, Thomas Hardy. A tragic novel. Tess Durbeyfield, whose father fancies himself related to the great family of D'Urberville, is employed by them. Alec, the eldest son, seduces her. Her child dies. Several years afterward, Angel Clare, who has married Tess, deserts her on learning her past secret. Later, he tries to win her back, but Alec treacherously meddles, and Tess, in anger, murders him and is executed for the crime.

Thaddeus of Warsaw. The hero and title of a novel by Jane Porter.

Thangbrand. Tales of a Wayside Inn, H. W. Longfellow. King Olaf's drunken priest, "short of stature and large of limb," who was sent to Iceland, found the people poring over their books, and sailed back to Norway to say to Olaf that there was "little hope of those Iceland men."

Thekla. The daughter of Wallenstein, in Schiller's drama of this name. She is one of the poet's own creations.

Theodorus. The name of a physician, in Rabelais' romance *Gargantua*. At the request of Ponocrates, Gargantua's tutor, he undertook to cure the latter of his vicious manner of living, and accordingly purged him canonically with Anticyrian hellebore, by which medicine he cleared out all the foulness and perverse habit of his brain, so that he became a man of great honor, sense, courage, and piety.

They Shall Not Pass. During World War I, this phrase became the watchword of the defenders of Verdun. It has become the symbol of determined resistance.

Thomas the Rhymer or **Thomas Rhymer.** The popular name in Scotland of an old prophet, supposed to have been inspired by the fairies. Thomas Rhymer's real name is supposed to have been Thomas Learmount of Ercildoune (Earlston). He lived in the 13th century. A metrical romance called *Sir Tristram* is attributed to him. He is also the subject of one of the best-known English ballads.

Thorberg Skafting. Tales of a Wayside Inn, H. W. Longfellow. The master builder ordered by King Olaf to build a ship twice as long and twice as large as the *Dragon* built by Raud the Strong, which was stranded. Thorberg built the ship, watching his workmen closely, and when she was ready for launching, King Olaf and the workmen were amazed to see every plank down her sides cut with deep gashes and more amazed to find that Thorberg had done the deed. From these gashes he then chipped and smoothed the sides, to the delight of all; she was christened the *Long Serpent* and the name of her builder recited in the saga.

Three Kings, Feast of the. A famous medieval festival, identical with the Epiphany. But the name is more particularly given to a kind of dramatic or spectacular representation of the incidents recorded in the second chapter of Matthew: the appearance of the wise men in splendid pomp at the court of Herod; the miraculous star; the manger at Bethlehem; the solemn and costly worship of the Babe. This was long very popular.

Three Musketeers, The, Dumas the Elder. A romance of the time of Richelieu. Also called "The Three Guardsmen." The three are Athos, Porthos, and Aramis. Their adventures, with those of D'Artagnan, make up this popular story. Dumas is said to have taken material for the story from a manuscript, *The Memoirs of D'Artagnan*, in the National Library of Paris. The story hinges on the successful attempt of the four soldiers to recover certain jewels that the queen had given to the Englishman, Buckingham. In doing this, they not only free the queen from a trap Richelieu had set for her, but they rid Richelieu, the queen's opponent, of a dangerous woman messenger, and D'Artagnan is rewarded by the cardinal.

Thrums. The market town of Kirriemuir, in which J. M. Barrie places many of his stories and sketches, *A Window in Thrums*, *Auld Licht Idylls*, etc.

Thunderer, The. Name popularly given to the English newspaper, *The Times*. The accepted version of the way in which the great journal got its name of "The Thunderer," is that Captain Sterling, one of the "staff," once wrote a sort of apology in reference to a mistaken assertion and used the phrase "We thundered out." This caught the public fancy, hence the name. Captain Sterling was a well-known figure in London political circles and father of the famous John Sterling, critic, essayist, and friend of Wordsworth, Coleridge, and De Quincey.

Thwackum, Parson Roger. The learned and honest, but selfish and hot-tempered, pedagogue in Fielding's novel *The History of Tom Jones, a Foundling*.

Thyrsis (*thûr′sĭs*). (1) Corydon and Thyrsis are favorite names given to shepherds by writers of pastoral poetry. So also, Phyllis and Thestylis are names often applied to rustic maidens or shepherdesses. (2) The title of one of the most beautiful elegies in English literature in which Matthew Arnold mourns the loss of his friend, the poet Clough.

Tibbs or **Tibs.** A character in Goldsmith's *Citizen of the World*, quoted as a "most useful hand." He will write you a receipt for the bite of a mad dog, tell you an Eastern tale to perfection, and understands the business part of an author so well that no publisher can humbug him.

Tigg, Montague (*mŏn′tá-gū*). **Martin Chuzzlewit, Dickens.** A clever impostor, who lives by his wits. He starts a bubble insurance office and makes considerable gain thereby. Discovering the attempt of Jonas Chuzzlewit to murder his father, he compels him to put his money in the "new company." Jonas afterwards murders him.

Timon. Timon of Athens, Shakespeare. The drama begins with the joyous life of Timon and his hospitable extravagance, launches into his pecuniary embarrassment and the discovery that his "professed friends" will not help him, and ends with his flight into the woods, his misanthropy, and his death. Introduced into the play is "Timon's Banquet." Being shunned by his friends in adversity, he pretended to have recovered his money, and invited his false friends to a banquet. The table was laden with covers, but, when the contents were exposed, nothing was provided but lukewarm water.

Tinker's Dam. A little mound of soft clay or dough placed round a leak or a joint that a plumber is about to mend, in order to retain the melted solder until it cools. After the clay has served its purpose, it is thrown away as it cannot be used a second time. Hence the proverbial worthlessness of "a tinker's dam." The latter word, however, through perversity or misunderstanding is often spelled *damn* to the detriment of the tinker's reputation.

Tintern Abbey. (1) A noted ruin of great beauty on the Wye in Monmouthshire, England. The abbey was founded by Cistercian monks in 1131. (2) The shortened title of a reflective poem by William Wordsworth,—one of his finest works. The complete title is "Lines Composed a Few Miles above Tintern Abbey, on Revisiting the Banks of the Wye during a Tour, July 13, 1798."

Tiny Tim. Christmas Stories, Dickens. A striking character, the little son of Bob Cratchit, whose family were made happier by gifts from the converted Scrooge. See *Scrooge, Ebenezer*.

Tippecanoe. Name given to William Henry Harrison during the political canvass which preceded his election, on account of the victory gained by him over the Indians in the battle which took place on the 6th of November 1811, at the junction of the Tippecanoe and Wabash rivers.

Tirzah. Ben Hur, General Lew Wallace. A beautiful Jewish maiden, sister of Ben Hur. Their father had been a prince of Jerusalem, and died leaving a large estate. At the age of fifteen, Tirzah, with her mother, was imprisoned through the cruelty of Messala who coveted their property. They both became lepers and when released from prison were forced to live among the outcasts. They were healed by Jesus, Ben Hur himself witnessing the miracle. As soon as the change in their look had taken place he recognized them, and, Tirzah and her mother were united with their brother in their former home.

Tobacco Road. A novel by Erskine Caldwell published in 1932. It is the story of a degenerate family of poor whites living in Georgia. The dramatized version was extraordinarily successful, running in New York for 3182 performances.

Toby, Uncle. A character in Sterne's *Tristram Shandy*. A captain who was wounded at the siege of Namur, and was obliged to retire from the service. He is the impersonation of kindness, benevolence, and simple-heartedness; his courage is undoubted, his gallantry delightful for its innocence and modesty.

Token, The. A collection of original articles, prose and poetry, by various contributors, issued first in the year 1824. This was the first "annual" in America; it became popular and was continued for fifteen years under the supervision of S. G. Goodrich, or "Peter Parley." To it Hawthorne owed his first hold on the public.

Tom, Dick, and Harry. An appellation very commonly employed to designate a crowd or rabble.

Tommy Atkins. Barrack-room Ballads, Kipling. The name is here used in its general meaning, a British soldier. The name came from the little pocket ledgers served out, at one time, to all British soldiers. In these manuals were to be entered the name, the age, the date of enlistment, etc. The War Office sent with each little book a form for filling it in, and the hypothetical name selected was "Thomas Atkins." The books were instantly so called, and it did not require many days to transfer the name from the book to the soldier.

Tom Sawyer. Adventures of Tom Sawyer, Mark Twain. An "elastic" youth whose performances delight both old and young readers. Queer enterprises influenced by the old superstitions among slaves and children in the Western states give reliable pictures of boy-life in the middle of the 19th century.

Tom the Piper. One of the characters in the ancient morris dance, represented with a tabor, tabor-stick, and pipe. He carried a sword and shield, to denote his rank.

Tom Thumb. In legendary history, a dwarf no larger than a man's thumb. He lived in the reign of King Arthur, by whom he was knighted. He was killed by the poisonous breath of a spider in the reign of the successor of King Arthur. Among his adventures it is told that he was lying one day asleep in a meadow, when a cow swallowed him as she cropped the grass. At another time, he rode in the ear of a horse. He crept up the sleeve of a giant, and so tickled him that he shook his sleeve, and Tom, falling into the sea, was swallowed by a fish. The fish being caught and carried to the palace gave the little man his introduction to the king. The oldest version of this nursery tale is in rime. P. T. Barnum named a celebrated midget "General Tom Thumb."

Tonio. Daughter of the Regiment, Donizetti. The name of the youth who saved Marie, the sutler girl, from falling down a precipice. The two fall in love with each other, and the regiment consents to their marriage, provided Tonio will enlist under its flag. No sooner is this done than the marchioness of Berkenfeld lays claim to Marie as her daughter, and removes her to the castle. In time, the castle is besieged and taken by the very regiment into which Tonio had enlisted, and, as Tonio had risen to the rank of a French officer, the marchioness consents to his marriage with her daughter.

Topsy. Uncle Tom's Cabin, Mrs. Stowe. A young slave girl, who never knew whether she had either father or mother, and, being asked by Miss Ophelia St. Clare how she supposed she came into the world, replied, "I 'spects I growed." Topsy illustrates the amusing and humorous side of the African character.

Touchstone. A clown in Shakespeare's *As You Like It.*

Townley Mysteries. Certain religious dramas; so called because the manuscript containing them belonged to P. Townley. These dramas are supposed to have been acted at Widkirk Abbey, in Yorkshire.

Traddles. David Copperfield, Dickens. A simple, honest young man, who believes in everybody and everything and who is never depressed by his want of success. He had the habit of brushing his hair up on end, which gave him a look of surprise. Traddles was generally accompanied by "the dearest girl" and her numerous sisters.

Treasure Island, Stevenson. A story of pirates' gold. After the death of an old seaman in the Admiral Benbow inn, a map is found in his chest. Squire Trelawney, Dr. Livesey, men of the neighborhood, and Jim Hawkins, the young son of the innkeeper, go on a voyage in search of the island shown on the map. Unluckily, they ship some of the original pirates in their crew, chief of them, Long John Silver, ship's cook. Mutiny and fighting arise at the island. But in the end, through a sailor long marooned on the island, they find the treasure.

Triads. The Welsh triads, known in literature, are collections of historic facts, mythological traditions, moral maxims, or rules of poetry, disposed in groups of three.

Trilby. See *Little Billee.*

Trim, Corporal. Uncle Toby's attendant, in Sterne's novel *The Life and Opinions of Tristram Shandy, Gent,* distinguished for his fidelity and affection, his respectfulness, and his volubility.

Tristram, Sir. One of the most celebrated heroes in medieval romance. His adventures form an episode in the history of Arthur's court. He appears in Tennyson's "The Last Tournament."

Trotwood, Betsey. David Copperfield, Dickens. A great-aunt to David, whose daily trial seemed to be donkeys. A dozen times a day would she rush on the green before her house to drive off the donkeys and donkey-boys. She was a most kind-hearted woman, who concealed her tenderness under a snappish manner. Miss Betsey was the true friend of David Copperfield.

Troubadours. Minstrels of southern France in the 11th, 12th, and 13th centuries. They were the first to discard Latin and use the native tongue in their compositions. Their poetry was about either love and gallantry or war and chivalry. In northern France, similar minstrels were called trouvères.

Truthful James. The character whom Bret Harte makes the narrator of a number of his poetic stories, among them "The Society on the Stanislaw" and "The Heathen Chinee."

Tuck, Friar. Ivanhoe, Scott. The father-confessor of Robin Hood and connected with Fountain Abbey. He is represented as a clerical Falstaff, very fat and self-indulgent, very humorous, and somewhat coarse. His dress was a russet habit of the Franciscan order. He was sometimes girt with a rope of rushes. Friar Tuck also appears in the "morris dance" on May Day.

Tulkinghorn, Mr. Bleak House, Dickens. The family lawyer of Sir Leicester Dedlock. He is murdered by Lady Dedlock's French maid.

Tulliver, Maggie. See *Mill on the Floss, The.*

Turveydrop. Bleak House, Dickens. A conceited dancing master, who imposes on the world by his majestic appearance and elaborate toilette. He is represented as living upon the earnings of his son, who has a most slavish reverence for him as a perfect "master of deportment."

Twelfth Night. A drama by Shakespeare. The story is said to have come from a novelette written early in the 16th century. A brother and sister, twins, are shipwrecked. Viola, dressed like her brother, becomes page to the duke Orsino. The duke was in love with Olivia, and, as the lady looked coldly on his suit, he sent Viola to advance it, but the willful Olivia, instead of melting towards the duke, fell in love with his beautiful page. Sebastian, the twin brother of Viola, was attacked in a street brawl before Olivia, who, thinking him to be the page, invited him in. The result was the marriage of Sebastian to Olivia and of the duke to Viola.

Twice Told Tales. This name was given by the author, Nathaniel Hawthorne, to the tales included under its title, because some of them had been already published in the *Token* and other periodicals. They are mystical and, though in prose form, are the work of a poet. The tales are nearly all American in subject but treated from the spiritual rather than the practical side.

Two Gentlemen of Verona, The, Shakespeare. One of the early comedies. The two gentlemen, Valentine and Proteus, go to Milan. Both fall in love with Sylvia. Proteus persuades the duke to banish Valentine, who gathers a following of bandits to capture Sylvia, who is affianced to Thurio. But Proteus had forgotten Julia, his Veronese sweetheart, who, following to Milan, serves him, unrecognized, as a page. In the end, Thurio proving unworthy, Sylvia is married to Valentine, while Proteus, repenting, takes Julia as his bride.

Two Noble Kinsmen, The, Shakespeare and Fletcher. The story of this play is that of Palamon and Arcite, told by many poets. The two young men, prisoners, fall in love with Emilia, sister-in-law of Duke Theseus, who rules that she shall be the bride of the victor of a combat. Arcite wins, but is later killed by a fall from his horse, and Palamon marries the lady.

Ubaldo. Jerusalem Delivered, Tasso. One of the older crusaders, who had visited many regions. He and Charles the Dane went to bring back Rinaldo from the enchanted castle.

Ulrica. Ivanhoe, Scott. An old woman, one-time mistress of Front de Bœuf. She gets revenge for all his illtreatment of her in the burning of the castle of Torquilstone.

Ultima Thule. The extremity of the world; the most northern point known to the ancient Romans. Pliny and others say it is Iceland. See William Black's novel *A Princess of Thule.* Also applied to Ireland.

Una. Faery Queen, Spenser. The personification of truth. She goes, leading a lamb and riding on a white ass, to the court of Gloriana, to crave that one of her knights might undertake to slay the dragon which kept her father and mother prisoners. The adventure is accorded to the Red Cross Knight. Being driven by a storm into "Wandering Wood," a vision is sent to the knight, which causes him to leave Una, and she goes in search of him. In her wanderings a lion becomes her attendant. After many adventures, she finds St. George, the Red Cross Knight, but he is severely wounded. Una takes him to the house of Holiness, where he is carefully nursed, and then leads him to Eden.

Uncle Remus. The old plantation negro, whom Joel Chandler Harris makes the narrator of the fascinating animal fables in his fourteen "Uncle Remus" books (1881–1908).

Uncle Tom. Uncle Tom's Cabin, Mrs. Stowe. A negro slave of unaffected piety, and most faithful in the discharge of all his duties. His master, a humane man, becomes embarrassed in his affairs, and sells Tom to a slave dealer. After passing through various hands and suffering intolerable cruelties, he dies.

Underground Railroad, The. A popular embodiment of the various ways in which fugitive slaves from the Southern states of the American Union were assisted in escaping to the North, or to Canada; often humorously abbreviated U. G. R. R. H. D. Thoreau, the naturalist and philosopher, is said to have aided escaping slaves at his cottage on Walden Pond. "The Underground Railway" is the title of an absorbing historical work on the struggle of the slaves by Professor W. H. Siebert (N. Y. 1898).

Undine (*ŭn-dēn'*). In a German fairy romance by Fouqué, a water nymph, who was exchanged for the young child of a fisherman living near an enchanted forest. One day, Sir Huldbrand took shelter in the fisherman's hut, fell in love with Undine, and married her. By marrying a mortal she obtained a soul, and with it all the pains and penalties of the human race.

Unicorn. The name means "one horn." The origin of the belief in the existence of this fabulous animal has been assigned to the animal profiles on Egyptian sculptures. Travelers in the Middle Ages often reported having seen unicorns. But the spirit and prowess of the animal were said to be such that it never could be taken alive. These qualities probably induced James III of Scotland to adopt the unicorn as supporter for the royal arms. Later, James VI, who was James I of England, adopted the unicorn and the lion for the royal shield of the united realms.

Urgan. Lady of the Lake, Scott. A human child stolen by the king of the fairies, and brought up in elf-land.

Urganda. In the romance of *Amadis of Gaul,* a powerful fairy sometimes appearing in all the terrors of an evil enchantress.

Uther (*ū'thĕr*). Son of Constans, one of the fabulous or legendary kings of Britain, and the father of Arthur.

Utopia. The name of an imaginary island described in the celebrated work of Sir Thomas More, in which was found the utmost perfection in laws, politics, and social arrangements. More's romance obtained a wide popularity, and the epithet "Utopian" has since been applied to all schemes for the improvement of society which are deemed impracticable. Among early utopias are Plato's "Republic" and St. Augustine's "City of God." More recent examples are Samuel Butler's "Erewhon" and Edward Bellamy's "Looking Backward." A current trend toward "anti-utopias" is seen in George Orwell's "Animal Farm."

Valentine. (1) One of the heroes in the old romance *Valentine and Orson*, which is of uncertain age and authorship. (2) One of the *Two Gentlemen of Verona*, in Shakespeare's play of that name. (3) A gentleman attending on the duke in Shakespeare's *Twelfth Night*. (4) One of the characters in Goethe's *Faust*. He is a brother of Marguerite.

Valerian or **Valirian. Canterbury Tales, Chaucer.** The husband of St. Cecilia. Cecilia told him she was beloved by an angel, who constantly visited her; and Valirian requested to see this visitant. Cecilia replied that he should do so, if he went to Pope Urban to be baptized. This he did, and, on his return, the angel gave him a crown of lilies and to Cecilia a crown of roses, both from the garden of paradise.

Valley of Humiliation. Pilgrim's Progress, Bunyan. The place where Christian encountered Apollyon, just before he came to the "Valley of the Shadow of Death."

Vanity Fair. Pilgrim's Progress, Bunyan. (1) A fair established by Beelzebub, Apollyon, and Legion, for the sale of all sorts of vanities. It was held in the town of Vanity, and lasted all the year round. Here were sold houses, lands, trades, honors, titles, kingdoms, and all sorts of pleasures and delights. Christian and Faithful had to pass through the fair, which they denounced. (2) Thackeray gave the name *Vanity Fair* to the first of his famous works. It has been called "a novel without a hero." See *Sedley*.

Varden, Dolly. In Dickens's *Barnaby Rudge*, the pretty, coquettish daughter of the locksmith, Gabriel Varden. She marries Joe Willet, and is for many years the mistress of the Maypole Inn. Her name was formerly applied to certain styles of gay dress stuffs.

Veck, Toby. The Chimes, Dickens. A ticket porter who went on errands and bore the nickname Trotty. One New Year's Eve he had a nightmare and fancied he had mounted to the steeple of a neighboring church, and that goblins issued out of the bells. He was roused from his sleep by the sound of the bells ringing in the new year.

Veda (*vā'dä*). The technical name of those ancient Sanskrit works on which the first period of the religious belief of the Hindus is based.

Veni Creator Spiritus (*vē'nĭ crê-ā'tŏr spĭr'ĭ-tŭs*). An ancient and very celebrated hymn of the Roman breviary, which occurs in the offices of the Feast of Pentecost, and which is used in many of the most solemn services of the Roman Catholic Church. Its author is not known with certainty.

Vernon, Die or **Diana. Rob Roy, Scott.** The heroine of the story, a highborn girl of great beauty and talents. She is an enthusiastic adherent of a persecuted religion and an exiled king. She is excluded from the ordinary wishes and schemes of other girls by being predestined to a hateful husband or a cloister, and by receiving a masculine education, under the superintendence of two men of talent and learning.

Vicar of Wakefield. A novel by Goldsmith, praised by Goethe as one of the best ever written. Its title refers to the hero, Dr. Primrose, whose experiences and naïve observations are frequently to be understood as those of the author himself. The tale abounds in amusing episodes, as memorable as proverbs. These include the purchase, by the vicar's son Moses, of a pair of green spectacles at the price of a horse; also the painting of the family portrait, which, when completed after great care and expense, was found to be too large to be hung. The chief charm of the work lies in its easy movement of idyllic events recorded in language at once homely and felicitous. Many of the incidents verge on melodrama, but the work as a whole leaves an inescapable impression of reality. See *Primrose*.

Viola (*vī'ô-lä*). **Twelfth Night, Shakespeare.** A sister of Sebastian. They were twins, and so much alike that they could be distinguished only by their dress. When they were shipwrecked, Viola was brought to shore by the captain, but her brother was left to shift for himself. Being in a strange land, Viola dressed as a page, and, under the name of Cesario, entered the service of Orsino, duke of Illyria. The duke greatly liked his beautiful page, and, when he discovered her true sex, married her.

Violenta. All's Well that Ends Well, Shakespeare. A character in the play who enters upon the scene only once and then neither speaks nor is spoken to. The name has been used to designate any young lady nonentity, one who contributes nothing to the amusement or conversation of a party.

Virginian, The, Owen Wister. A story of the cattle country of Wyoming in the '80's of the 19th century. The hero is a young Virginian, in love with a school-teacher from Vermont. The Virginian "cow-puncher" character is said to have been drawn from the ranch life of Theodore Roosevelt.

Virginians, The, Thackeray. The story of the two grandsons of Henry Esmond. They take opposite sides in the Revolution. The action lies in both America and England. The gallery of characters includes George Washington, Dr. Johnson, and Richardson and Fielding, the novelists.

Vision of Sir Launfal, J. R. Lowell. A poetic story of a dream of the knight on the eve of his setting out on a quest. In this vision he sees the opportunity for best service at his own gates in giving himself with his alms. In Arthurian story Sir Launfal was a knight of the Round Table and a steward of King Arthur.

Vivien or **Vivian. Idylls of the King, Tennyson.** She is also known as the Lady of the Lake, and according to early legends was of a high family. These legends tell that Merlin, in his dotage, fell in love with her. She then persuaded Merlin to show her how a person could be imprisoned by enchantment without walls, towers, or chains and, after he had done so, she put him to sleep. While he slept, she performed the needful ceremonies, whereupon he found himself enclosed in a prison stronger than the strongest tower, and from that imprisonment was never again released.

Walden. A record of the experiences of the author, Thoreau, while living near Walden Pond on nine cents a day. He read Homer, watched the birds, bees, ants, and the animals that came within his range, describing the results of his acute powers of observation in a characteristic, quaint form.

War and Peace, Count Tolstóy. The title of a long philosophical novel. The action centers in the Napoleonic invasion of Russia. The story includes a vast number of characters, drawn with minute care and great realism. The author tries to show even the great leaders as creatures in the hands of overpowering fate or chance.

Waverley. Name of hero and title of novel by Scott. Scott had won great triumph as a narrative poet with such poems as *Marmion* and *The Lady of the Lake*. Byron eclipsed him in the field of romantic poetic narrative, and Scott picked up his unfinished manuscript of a novel, *Waverley*, and finished it. It was a great success. It was published anonymously, Scott not wishing to admit his withdrawal from the field of poetry. Many of the great Scott novels were published by "The Author of *Waverley*" but it was an "open secret" after a few years as to who the real author was. Few writers have really triumphed in two fields as Scott did.

Waverley Novels. General name given to Scott's historical novels. Those founded on English history are *Ivanhoe, Kenilworth, Peveril of the Peak, Betrothed, Talisman*, and *Woodstock*. Founded on Scotch history are *Waverley, Old Mortality, Monastery, The Abbott, Legend of Montrose, Fair Maid of Perth*, and *Castle Dangerous*. Treating of continental history are *Quentin Durward, Anne of Geierstein*, and *Count Robert of Paris*. Twelve others in the series, including *Rob Roy, Heart of Midlothian, Bride of Lammermoor*, are connected with historical events, but are more personal and deal mainly with Scottish character.

Wayside Inn, The. This old inn in South Sudbury, Massachusetts, was immortalized by Longfellow in his *Tales of a Wayside Inn*. Built in 1686, it was purchased in 1923 by Henry Ford as a memorial to Longfellow. On the night of December 22, 1955, it was almost completely destroyed by fire, but its restoration was undertaken in 1956 by the Ford Foundation. Irreplaceable, however, are many mementoes lost in the fire, including the clock, spinet, coat-of-arms, and other items mentioned by Longfellow. Other buildings on the premises were undamaged, among them the coach house, the little red school house of Mary's Little Lamb fame, a working grist mill, and an old red barn.

Weird Sisters, The. Three witches, in Shakespeare's tragedy *Macbeth*.

Weller, Samuel. In Dickens's celebrated *Pickwick Papers*, a servant to Mr. Pickwick, to whom he becomes devotedly attached. Rather than leave his master, when he is sent to the Fleet, Sam Weller gets his father to arrest him for debt. He is an inimitable compound of wit, simplicity, quaint humor, and fidelity. "Tony Weller," father of Sam; a coachman of the old school, who drives between London and Dorking. On the coach box he is a king, elsewhere a mere London "cabby." He marries a widow and his constant advice to his son is, "Sam, beware of the vidders." Everybody was merry over Mr. Pickwick and Sam Weller, and everybody was eager to read this entertaining author.

Werewolf (wĕr'wŏŏlf'), **"Man-Wolf."** The notion of the changing of men into wolves is very old in literature. The Romans fancied the change made by magic. The Norse tales employ the wolfskin shirt, by which the man becomes a wolf for nine days out of ten.

When Knighthood Was in Flower, Charles Major. A historical novel, which tells the love story of Mary Tudor, sister of Henry VIII, and Charles Brandon.

Whittington, Dick. The hero of a famous old legend, in which he is represented as a poor orphan boy from the country, who went to London, where, after undergoing many hardships, he obtained a penny and bought a cat. Shortly after, he sent his cat on a venture in his master's ship; and the king of Barbary, whose court was overrun with mice, gladly bought the cat at a high price. With this money Whittington commenced business, and succeeded so well that he finally married his former master's daughter, was knighted, and became lord mayor of London.

Wife of Bath. One of the pilgrims in Chaucer's *Canterbury Tales.* She tells, in her turn, the story of Midas. The prologue to her story is famous for the wife's naïve revelation of her own story and character.

Wild Duck, The, Ibsen. An ironic play, its leading idea being that sometimes it is unwise to tell the entire bald truth.

William Tell. The hero of a Swiss legend, which has been told in many poems and dramas. He obeys the command of Gessler, the governor, to shoot an apple from his son's head. Asked by Gessler why he had put a second arrow in his belt, he replies, "To kill you with, had I slain my son." He is then placed in a boat as prisoner, but escapes and kills the governor, thus opening the Swiss War of Liberation from Austria. The date is placed in 1307. But the fact seems to be that, in the middle of the 15th century, an unknown author introduced into Switzerland a Danish archer and apple story, which fitted local needs so well that it grew into a national legend. Schiller's *William Tell* is the best-known telling of the story in drama.

Winter's Tale, The, Shakespeare. Leontes, king of Sicily, invites his friend Polixenes to visit him, becomes jealous, and commands Camillo to poison him. Camillo warns Polixenes and flees with him to Bohemia. Leontes casts his queen, Hermione, into prison, where she gives birth to a daughter. Hermione is reported dead, and the child is brought up by a shepherd, who calls it Perdita. Florizel sees Perdita and falls in love with her; but Polixenes, his father, tells her that she and the shepherd shall be put to death if she encourages the suit. Florizel and Perdita flee to Sicily and are introduced to Leontes. It is soon discovered that Perdita is his lost daughter. Polixenes tracks his son to Sicily and consents to the union. The party are invited to inspect a statue of Hermione, and the statue turns out to be the living queen.

Worldly Wiseman, Mr. One of the characters in Bunyan's *Pilgrim's Progress,* who converses with Christian by the way, and endeavors to deter him from proceeding on his journey.

Yahoo. A name given by Swift, in his satirical romance *Gulliver's Travels,* to one of a race of brutes having the form and all the vices of man. The Yahoos are represented as being subject to the Houyhnhnms, or horses endowed with reason.

Yemassee. A historical tale founded on personal knowledge of the American Indian character. It was written in the first half of the 19th century by W. G. Simms, of whom it has been said, "He has done for the historical traditions of the Carolinas what Cooper did for those of the North and West."

Yeo. Westward Ho! Chas. Kingsley. A character in the novel, prominent as a bold mariner, a true friend, a terrible foe. He was a lifelong sailor, and made voyages to New Guinea for negro slaves that were sold in the West Indies. He joined in the search for fabulous wealth in New Spain, crossed the Isthmus of Panama, was pursued, and wandered in the woods of the isthmus for some months. *Westward Ho!* is a historical novel of the Elizabethan English period.

Yorick. (1) The king of Denmark's jester, mentioned in Shakespeare's *Hamlet.* Hamlet picks up his skull in the churchyard and apostrophizes it. (2) A humorous and careless parson in Sterne's *Tristram Shandy.*

Zarathustra (zȧr'ȧ-thōōs'trȧ). *Thus Spake Zarathustra* is the title of a work by Frederick Nietzsche, in which he embodied his philosophy. Zarathustra is a form of the name of Zoroaster, the Persian sage.

Zenobia. Blithedale Romance, Hawthorne. A strong-minded woman, beautiful and intelligent, who was interested in playing out the pastoral of the life at Brook Farm. She is represented as disappointed in love; at last she drowned herself.

Zero Hour. The name given in World War I to the moment set for a charge from the trench. Generally used to mean the instant for beginning any important move or work.

Zuleika (zŏŏ-lā'kȧ). (1) In Byron's "Bride of Abydos," the pasha's daughter in love with her cousin Selim. They elope, but are pursued. Selim is killed, and Zuleika dies of a broken heart. (2) A character in the Persian story of Joseph and Zuleika.

THE READING OF PLAYS

It will be noted that many references in the foregoing list of Plots, Characters, and Allusions are to plays. Most of the dramas mentioned are readily available in print, and, taken together, they form a large and important branch of literature. When read for pleasure they are very rewarding, particularly to those who have acquired the technique and the habit of reading plays.

For the playgoer at home with a book in his hand, the action occurs in his imagination. Looking first through the cast of characters, he gets an impression of the persons and of their relationship to one another. Attentive reading of the first act will acquaint him still further with the individuals through their conversation and will enable him to follow the story line without difficulty. From here he is swept along by the growing intensity of the action. The result is that, in approximately two hours, the play has given him the equivalent in characterization and movement of a novel that would require several evenings of leisurely reading. In its concentration and emphasis on essentials, the drama is comparable to poetry.

Below is a representative list of plays suggested for reading, or in some cases re-reading, by stay-at-home playgoers. The arrangement is roughly chronological, but is not meant to be formal.

Anonymous—*Everyman.*

Christopher Marlowe—*Doctor Faustus.*

William Shakespeare— *Hamlet; Macbeth; Othello; Julius Caesar; Henry V.; The Tempest.*

Ben Jonson—*Sejanus; Volpone.*

John Dryden—*All for Love.*

Jean-Baptiste Moliere—*Le Tartuffe; L'Avare.*

William Congreve—*The Way of the World.*

Richard Steele—*The Funeral; The Conscious Lovers.*

Joseph Addison—*Cato.*

John Gay—*The Beggars' Opera.*

Oliver Goldsmith—*She Stoops to Conquer.*

Richard B. Sheridan—*The Rivals; The School for Scandal.*

Gotthold Ephraim Lessing— *Nathan the Wise.*

Friedrich Schiller—*William Tell; Maria Stuart.*

Johann Wolfgang von Goethe—*Faust.*

Arthur W. Pinero—*The Second Mrs. Tanqueray.*

George Bernard Shaw—*Man and Superman; Candida.*

Henrik Ibsen—*A Doll's House; Hedda Gabler.*

Edmond Rostand—*Cyrano de Bergerac.* (tr. Hooker)

James M. Barrie—*Peter Pan; What Every Woman Knows.*

William Butler Yeats—*The Hour Glass; The Land of Heart's Desire.*

Eugene O'Neill—*Mourning Becomes Electra.*

Anton Chekov—*The Seagull; The Cherry Orchard.*

John M. Synge—*The Playboy of the Western World.*

ART INSPIRED BY LITERATURE

The imagination of artist E. J. Poynter was deeply stirred by *Endymion*, a poem that Keats admitted to be a daring leap into the sea of romance. Although Keats was a full-fledged surgeon, he discovered that poetry, the harmonious unison of man with nature, rather than surgery was his providential guidance. His poetic romance *Endymion* is filled with beautiful passages.

Above In his illustration, Gilbert James has caught the spirit of contemplative indolence that appealed to Omar Khayyam, and *Rubaiyat* translator Edward Fitzgerald, the English poet. The *Rubaiyat*, a collection of poems, complete in four lines known as quatrains, is famous more because of Fitzgerald, whose translation is regarded as one of the monuments of English literature, than because of its author, mathematician-astronomer-poet Omar Khayyam. While many could see in his poems only the wine cup and roses, as this illustration might suggest, Omar was regarded by others as a poet of agnosticism because of his unorthodox religious views.

Lower Right The "Princes in the Tower," who were brutally murdered by order of Richard III, provided a subject for a Shakespeare illustration by Sir John Millais. It is thought that, ordinarily, Shakespeare wrote two plays a year in his younger days, and it is assumed that *Richard III*, an historical play, was first presented during the theatrical season of 1592–93.

Below The clown's song, "O Mistress Mine," in Shakespeare's *Twelfth Night* suggested one of Edwin A. Abbey's best illustrations. This was the last of a series written by Shakespeare before he began his great tragedies. In *Twelfth Night*, an extremely popular romantic comedy, he has given his characters and their utterances a freshness nowhere else displayed by him.

Mythology in Contemporary Art

Above TOMB OF THE UNKNOWNS, by Thomas H. Jones in Arlington (Va.) National Cemetery. In this example of modern sculpture entitled *Victory, Peace, Valor,* the three figures are treated in the spirit of Greek art. Compare the Second Century group below it, representing *Hermes, Eurydice,* and *Orpheus.*

The Vermont Marble Company

Right DIANA, by Augustus St. Gaudens. This decorative and symbolic piece, designed for New York's Madison Square Garden, gives a contemporary interpretation of the classic huntress who was *Artemis* to the Greeks and *Diana* to the Romans.

Philadelphia Museum of Art

In keeping with its present ownership and location, this outstanding piece of Greek sculpture is designated as *Orfeo, Euridice e Mercurio* in *Napoli, Museo nazionale.*

Photo by Alinari

TRITONS, by Carl Milles. Through the centuries, figures like *Triton, Neptune,* and the *Nereids* have provided favorite themes for the design of fountains. Effective modern use of mythological source material is seen in this fountain in McKinlock Court at the Art Institute of Chicago.

Art Institute of Chicago

MYTHOLOGY

THE term mythology is applied to the body of stories current among ancient and primitive peoples regarding their gods and heroes. Many of these myths, particularly those of the Greeks and Romans, have been woven into the literatures of the world, from which, to no small degree, they have passed into common knowledge.

This section is a guide to mythology from two separate and distinct approaches—the literary and the practical.

The student of literature is continually meeting allusions to myths which must be understood if the author's meaning is to be intelligibie. In such instances, the reader is already in possession of the name of the mythical character or place and he wishes to learn the story connected with it. For this purpose he will find a trusty guide in the Dictionary of Mythology on the following pages.

On the other hand, there are many purposes for which it is desirable to know the mythical names and stories associated with certain ideas, qualities, or the like. Beginning with such terms as love, war, friendship, or fleetness, for instance, one may wish to know what deities or mythical characters are associated with them. The answers to such questions are quickly found by consulting the Table of Mythological Associations given below. For every mythological name in this table a descriptive article will be found in the Dictionary of Mythology. If the reader wishes to know, for example, what mythical names and stories are associated with beauty, he finds in the table the term Beauty, followed by the names Adonis, Aphrodite, and others. Then by referring to each of these names in the Dictionary of Mythology, he learns the principal stories connected with them.

TABLE OF MYTHOLOGICAL ASSOCIATIONS

AGRICULTURE. See *Earth, Fruit, Harvest, Sheep, Woods.*

ART. Apollo, Muses, Parnassus.

AVIATION. Dædalus, Icarus, Pegasus.

BEAUTY. Adonis, Aphrodite, Apollo, Graces, Freya, Helen, Hyperion, Krishna, Phaon, Rambha, Venus.

BIRDS. Æsacus, Alectryon, Blue Jay, Coronis, Leda, Paupukkeewis, Philomela, Phœnix.

BRAVERY. Achilles, Deiphobus, Euphorbus, Fortitudo, Pyrrhus, Tyr.

CELESTIAL REGIONS. Asgard, Bilskirnir, Cauther, Elysium, Gladsheim, Glasir, Islands of the Blest, Valhalla.

CIVILIZATION. Cadmus, Cecrops, Egeria, Hou Chi, Italapas, Melissa, Old One, Prometheus, Votán.

COLD. Elivagar, Fafnir, Gerda, Ginungagap, Hymir, Lord of Cold Weather, Mowis, Niflheim, Ymir.

CREATION. Afraid of Nothing, Chaos, Dagan, Earth-Namer, Embla, Iapetus, Ormuzd, Pandora.

DANCE. Corybantes, Silenus, Terpsichore.

DAWN. Aurora.

DEATH. Azrael, Giallar, Hell Shoon, Lethe, Libitina, Manes, Pauguk, Ponemah, Valkyries.

DEMONS, SPIRITS, and DWARFS. Azazel, Barguest, Beelzebub, Berg Folk, Diatyas, Dives, Elf, Galar, Gian ben Gian, Gnome, Goblins, Kelpie, Kobold, Lilith, Mammon, Mephistopheles, Moakkibat, Nickneven, Nix, Trolls.

DESTRUCTION. Apollo, Nickar, Ragnarok, Siva.

EARTH or SOIL. Demogorgon, Duergar, Frigga, Great Turtle, Midgard, Pachacamac.

EDUCATION. Athena, Minerva.

ELOQUENCE. Bragi, Mercury.

EVIL. Ahriman, Akuman, Belphegor, Dahak, Eblis, Hobomoko, Hugon, Loki, Nickar, Rakshasas.

FAIRIES. Befana, Elf, Hodeken, Melusina, Peri.

FAITHFULNESS. Penelope.

FATE. Atropos, Clotho, Fates, Lachesis, Norns.

FERTILITY. Danu, Draupnir, Frey, Isis, Mithra, Ops.

FIRE. Agni, Fire People, Fire Spirit, Nanabozho, Vulcan.

FLEETNESS. Ajax, Atalanta, Hippomenes.

FLOOD. Coxcox, Deucalion and Pyrrha.

FLOWERS. Clytie, Flora, Hyacinthus, Narcissus.

FOOD and DRINK. Ambrosia, Nectar.

FOUNTAINS. Aganippe, Arethusa, Camenæ, Castilia, Hippocrene, Naiads, Pirene.

FRIENDSHIP. Iolaus, Lofen, Nisus, Patroclus, Pylades.

FRUIT. Feronia, Golden Apples, Iduna, Pomona.

GARDENS. Pomona, Priapus.

GIANTS. Antæus, Atlas, Briareus, Egia, Enceladus, Giants, Læstrygonians, Ogre, Orion, Ravana, Tityus.

GOOD FORTUNE. Felicitas, Fortuna.

GUARDIANS. Bertha, Heimdall, Irus, Jizo, Melic Nymphs, Mentor, Palladium, Polias, Radegaste.

HAPPINESS. Nepenthe.

HARVEST. Ceres, Consus, Demeter, Paimosaid, Saturn.

HEALTH. Æsculapius, Apollo, Eira, Hygeia, Podalirius.

HEROES. See KINGS.

HEROINES. Antigone, Camilla, Electra, Hecuba, Helle, Hermione, Hippolyta, Ismene, Nausicaa.

HOME and HEARTH. Hestia, Lares, Penates, Vesta.

HUNTING. Actæon, Artemis, Diana, Herla, Orion.

IMMORTALITY. Ambrosia, Calypso, Nectar, Tithonus.

INFIDELITY. Clytemnestra, Cressida.

ISLANDS. Atlantis, Ithaca.

JEALOUSY. Helice, Io, Juno, Latona.

JUSTICE. Æacus, Minos, Orlog, Rhadamanthus, Themis.

KINGS and HEROES. Agamemnon, Anchises, Bellerophon, Baldud, Diomedes, Hector, Idomeneus, Ion, Ixion, Laertes, Laius, Laomedon, Lycomedes, Meleager, Memnon, Menelaus, Neleus, Neoptolemus, Œdipus, Orestes, Palamedes, Peleus, Pelops, Perseus, Polydorus, Priam, Romulus, Telamon, Theseus, Ulysses.

LIGHT. Agni, Amida, Diana, Janus, Lucifer, Mithra.

LOVE. Aphrodite, Astarte, Cupid, Derceto, Dione, Eros, Freya, Hylas, Hymen, Kama, Lofua, Venus.

LOVE LURE. Fata Morgana, Lilinau, Lorelei, Sirens.

LOVERS. Acis, Alcestis, Ariadne, Echo, Eurydice, Laodamia, Nala, Narcissus, Parthenope, Pasiphaë, Phædra, Philemon and Baucis, Psyche, Pyramus, Tithonus.

MAGIC. Circe, Hecate, Medea, Paupukkeewis.

MEMORY. Mnemosyne.

MESSENGER. Hermes, Hofvarpnir, Mercury.

MONSTERS. Argus, Centaurs, Cerberus, Chimæra, Chiron, Cyclopes, Fenris, Geryon, Gorgons, Harpies, Hydra, Lamia, Laomedon, Medusa, Minotaur, Nemean Lion, Nithhogg, Polyphemus, Scylla, Sphinx.

MOON. Astarte, Diana, Endymion, Luna, Mani, Phœbe.

MOUNTAINS. Calpe, Cybele, Helicon, Ida, Koppenberg, Latmus, Mænalus, Meru, Olympus, Parnassus, Pelion.

MUSIC. Amphion, Apollo, Arion, Bran, Chibiabos, Israfel, Marsyas, Orpheus, Pan.

NATURE. Mendes, Pan.

NAVIGATION. Argo, Argonauts, Pleiades.

NIGHT. Hecate, Hoder, Nox.

OCEAN and SEA. Ægir, Mermaids, Mimir, Neptune, Nereids, Oceanids, Oceanus, Poseidon, Thetis, Triton.

PEACE. Balder, Concordia, Frey, Frodi, Harmonia, Irene, Janus, Pax, Pukwana.

POETRY. Apollo, Bragi, Bran, Brigit, Calliope, Daphnis.

PRIDE. Arachne, Niobe, Thersites.

PROPHECY. Apollo, Augurs, Brigit, Calchas, Cassandra, Delphi, Dodona, Gripir, Helenus, Pythia, Silenus.

PURITY, or CHASTITY. Artemis, Diana.

RAIN and RAINBOW. Frey, Hyades, Iris, Pluvius.

REVELRY. Comus.

RICHES and GAIN. Kubera, Mercury, Midas, Plutus.

RIVERS. Alpheus, Elivagar, Enipeus, Ifing, Pactolus.

ROBBERY and THIEVING. Cacus, Charybdis, Mercury.

RULERS OF GODS. Amen, Ammon, Anu, Baal, Brahma, Cronus, Frigga, Grid, Hera, Juno, Jupiter, Manitou, Odin, Ormuzd, Rhea, Zeus.

SEASONS. Æstas, Glooskap, Horæ, Ostara, Peboan.

SERPENTS. Adissechen, Laocoön, Midgard Serpent, Python.

SHEEP and CATTLE. Pales, Pan.

SLEEP and DREAMS. Morpheus.

STARS and CONSTELLATIONS. Ariadne, Callisto, Cassiopeia, Gemini, Hyades, Orion, Pleiades, Sirius.

STRENGTH. Chou, Hercules, Megingiard.

STRIFE. Discordia, Eris.

SUN. Ama-Terasu, Aten, Frey, Helios, Horus, Hyperion, Ipalnemohuani, Phaëthon, Ra, Rama Chandra, Sol.

THUNDER. Donar, Haskah, Mjöllnir, Thor, Thunder Bird.

TREASURE. Cluricaune, Golden Fleece, Hesperides.

TREES. Daphne, Lotis, Phyllis, Sedrat, Yggdrasil.

UNDERWORLD. Aralu, Avernus, Cerberus, Charon, Cocytus, Dis, Elbegast, Erebus, Garm, Giall, Hades, Hecate, Hel, Naraka, Persephone, Pluto, Styx, Tartarus.

VENGEANCE. Alecto, Diræ, Eumenides, Furies, Nemesis.

WAR. Ares, Bellona, Mars.

WINDS. Æolus, Auræ, Boreas, Feng, Zephyrus.

WINE. Bacchus, Dionysus, Icarius, Liber, Mæra.

WISDOM. Athena, Mimir, Minerva, Nestor, Odhrerir.

WOODS. Artemis, Dryads, Fauns, Satyr, Silvanus.

YOUTH. Agni, Hebe, Iduna, Jamshid.

MYTHOLOGICAL PERSONS, PLACES, AND STORIES

Acheron (ăk'ēr-ŏn). One of the four rivers of the lower regions. See *Styx*.

Achilles (a-kĭl'ēz). The son of Peleus and Thetis. In the Trojan War he was the most distinguished of the Greeks for his strength and bravery. When Achilles was born, Thetis plunged him in the river Styx, which made him invulnerable in every part except the heel by which she held him. And in this heel later he received a fatal wound.

Acis (ā'sĭs). The handsome shepherd loved by the nymph Galatea, whose favor the monstrous Cyclops, Polyphemus, sued for in vain.

Acrisius (a-krĭs'ĭ-ŭs). Son of King Abas of Argos, grandson of Lynceus, and great-grandson of Danaus. An oracle had declared that Danaë, the daughter of Acrisius, would give birth to a son who would kill his grandfather. For this reason Acrisius kept Danaë shut up in a brazen tower. But here she became the mother of Perseus, by Zeus, who visited her in the form of a shower of gold.

Actæon (ăk-tē'ŏn). The son of Aristæus and Autonoë, daughter of Cadmus. He was reared by Chiron, and, becoming passionately fond of the chase, passed his days chiefly in pursuit of wild beasts that haunted Mount Cithæron. There, having accidentally come upon and seen Diana taking a bath, he was turned into a stag by her and killed by his own dogs.

Adad (a-däd'). An Assyrian and Babylonian god of the storm, identified with Ramman and Rimmon, the latter of whom is mentioned in the Old Testament. His weapons were flood, lightning, and famine.

Adissechen (a-dĭs'ĭ-kĕn). In Hindu mythology, the serpent of a thousand heads which holds the universe in place.

Admetus (ăd-mē'tŭs). See *Alcestis* and *Apollo*.

Adonis (a-dō'nĭs). A beautiful youth, loved by Venus and slain by a wild boar which he was hunting. Venus was inconsolable at his loss, and at last obtained from Proserpina consent that Adonis should spend six months on earth with her and six months among the shades.

Adrammelech (a-drăm'ê-lĕk). A god of the people of Sepharvaim, to whom infants were burned in sacrifice. He was later known as one of the fallen angels.

Æacus (ē'a-kŭs). Son of Jupiter and grandson of the river god Asopus. He was renowned throughout Greece for his justice and piety, and after his death he became one of the judges in Hades.

Æetes (ē-ē'tēz). Father of Medea and king of Colchis when Phrixus brought there the golden fleece.

Ægæon (ê-jē'ŏn). Another name for Briareus, the giant.

Ægeus (ē'jê-ŭs). King of Athens, and father of Theseus. In grief at the supposed loss of his son he threw himself into the sea, thereafter called Ægean.

Ægir (ē'jĭr). God of the ocean, whose wife is Ran. They had nine daughters, the billows, who were clad in colored, diaphanous robes and whose moods varied with that of their brother, the wind.

Ægis (ē'jĭs). The shield of Jupiter made by Vulcan.

Ægle (ĕg'lê). The mother of the Graces. Also the name of one of the sisters of Phaëthon.

Æolus (ē'ô-lŭs). A son of Neptune, or, according to others, of Hippotes, an ancient lord of the Lipari Isles. Jupiter made him keeper of the winds, which, having previously been represented as mythical persons, under the names Zephyrus, Boreas, Notus, and Eurus, were afterwards considered the servants of Æolus. He held them imprisoned in a cave of an island in the Mediterranean Sea, and let them loose only to further his own designs or those of others, in producing storms. He is usually described by the poets as virtuous, upright, and friendly to strangers, and is represented pictorially as a vigorous man supporting himself in the air by wings, and blowing into a shell trumpet, like a Triton, while his short mantle waves in the wind.

Æsacus. A son of Priam, who was enamored of the nymph Hesperia and, on her death, threw himself into the sea. He was changed by Thetis into a cormorant.

Æsculapius (ĕs'kû-lā'pĭ-ŭs). The son of Apollo and of Coronis, the daughter of a Thessalian king. By his father he was committed to the care of the wise centaur, Chiron, who taught him botany, together with the secret efficacy of plants. He became a great physician, even restoring the dead to life on one occasion. For this, Jupiter, at the request of Pluto, struck the physician dead with lightning. After his death, at the request of Apollo, he was placed among the stars. In later centuries he was worshiped as the god of healing.

Æsir (ē'sĭr). The name of the thirteen celestial gods of Scandinavia, who lived in Asgard, accessible only by the bridge of the rainbow. The chief was Odin.

Æson (ē'sŏn). The father of Jason. In extreme old age he was restored to youth by the magic arts of Medea.

Æstas. Personification of summer; he is crowned with corn and generally holds a sickle in his hand. So he appears on reliefs, medals, and gems, usually in company with the representations of the other three seasons. He is depicted as youthful and sprightly, while Ver, "spring," is infantile and tender; Autumnus, "autumn," is mature and manly; and Hiems, "winter," is old and decrepit.

Afraid of Nothing. Among some North American Indian tribes, the goddess dwelling in the East, who created the world and prepared it for the dwelling of men.

Agamemnon (ăg'a-mĕm'nŏn). King of Argos in Greece and commander in chief of the allied Greeks who went to the siege of Troy. Agamemnon married Clytemnestra, the daughter of Tyndareus, by whom he became the father of Iphianassa (Iphigenia). On his return home from Troy, he was killed by Clytemnestra and her paramour.

Aganippe (ăg'a-nĭp'ē). A fountain at the foot of Mount Helicon, in Bœotia, consecrated to Apollo and the Muses. It was supposed to have the power of inspiring those who drank of it. From it the Muses were called Aganippides.

Agni. A Vedic god of light and fire. He appears under many characters, but chiefly embodies eternal youth. Sometimes he is regarded as a beneficent household god and a protector against the horror of darkness.

Ahriman (ä'rĭ-màn). In early Persian, Angra Mainyu (ăn'grä mī'nū). A deity of the ancient Persians, representing the principle of evil. Unlike Ormuzd, the principle of good, who is eternal, Ahriman is created and will one day perish.

Ajax (ā'jăks). The son of Telamon, and one of the Greek heroes in Homer's *Iliad*. He was of great stature, strength, and courage, but dull in mind. He killed himself out of vexation because, in a competition for the armor of Hector, the prize was awarded to Ulysses.

Akuman. The most malevolent of all the Persian gods.

Alcestis or **Alceste** (ăl-sĕs'tĭs) (-sĕst). A daughter of Pelias, and the wife of Admetus. By request of Apollo, the gods had granted eternal life to Admetus, but on the condition that, when the appointed time came for the good king's death, some one should be found willing to die in his stead. This decree was reported to Alcestis, Admetus' beautiful young wife, who offered herself as substitute and cheerfully gave her life for her husband. But immortality was too dearly bought at such a price. Admetus mourned until Hercules, pitying his grief, descended into Hades and brought back Alcestis.

Alecto (a-lĕk'tō). One of the Furies. She is represented with her head covered with serpents, and breathing vengeance, war, and pestilence.

Alectryon (a-lĕk'trĭ-ŏn). A servant of Mars, who was changed by him into a cock because he did not warn his master of the rising of the sun.

Alfadur or **Alfadir** (ăl-fä'dĭr). In Scandinavian mythology, one of the many names of Odin. It means "father of all."

Alpheus (ăl-fē'ŭs). A river god who fell in love with the nymph Arethusa and pursued her. Diana came to her rescue and changed her into a fountain.

Althæa (ăl-thē'a). Sister of Atalanta, and mother of Meleager. She caused the death of her son and killed herself in remorse.

Ama-Terasu. A Japanese sun goddess. She figures in myths which represent her as hiding in a cave and coming out only after the other gods exhaust their powers of persuasion. Thus the alternation of night and day is portrayed. Ama-Terasu is the fabled ancestress of the royal house of Japan.

Amazons. A nation of women warriors who lived in Scythia. Early traditions tell of their appearance at the siege of Troy, under Penthesilea, their queen, who was eventually slain by Achilles. Hercules defeated them when, as one of his labors, he was required to obtain the girdle of their queen Hippolyta. Theseus later made an expedition against them and carried off their queen Antiope. In revenge they invaded Greece and were defeated on the site of Athens. A similar story is told among the Caribs in regard to a tribe of women warriors in South America and accounts for the name of the river Amazon.

Ambrosia (ăm-brō'zhĭ-à). The food of the gods; so called because it preserved their immortality.

Mythology   313

Amen (ä'mĕn). An ancient Egyptian god, identified with Ammon and also with the Greek Zeus. Under the name Amen-Ra, he was worshiped as king of the gods. He is at different times represented as a ram with large twisted horns; a human figure with a ram's head; a king seated on a throne and wearing a disk surmounted by two tall ostrich feathers.

Amida. One of the principal Buddhist gods of Japan, originally a god of light. Usually he is represented as seated cross-legged on a lotus flower. The "Great Buddha" at Kamakura is an image of Amida.

Ammon. A cult name of Jupiter, under which he was worshiped at Thebes in Egypt. As Jupiter Ammon he was represented as having the horns of a ram. See *Amen*.

Amphion (ăm-fī'ŏn). Son of Jupiter and Antiope, and brother of Zethus. He and Zethus were born on Mount Cithæron and grew up among the shepherds. When they had learned their origin they marched against Thebes, where reigned Lycus, the husband of their mother Antiope, who had married Dirce in her stead. They took the city and killed Lycus and Dirce, because they had treated Antiope with great cruelty. After they had obtained possession of Thebes, they fortified it by a wall. Amphion had received a lyre from Mercury, on which he played with such magic skill that the stones moved of their own accord and formed the wall.

Ancæus (ăn-sē'ŭs). A son of Neptune who, having left a cup of wine untasted to pursue a wild boar, was killed in his attempt to destroy it. With this story is connected the proverb, "There's many a slip 'twixt the cup and the lip"

Anchises (ăn-kī'sēz). King of Dardanus and, by his union with Venus, father of Æneas. On the capture of Troy by the Greeks, Æneas carried his father on his shoulders from the burning city.

Andromache (ăn-drŏm'ā-kê). The wife of Hector, prince of Troy. After the death of Hector, she was given to Neoptolemus of Epirus. Later, she married a Trojan, Helenus. She is the subject of a tragedy by Euripides.

Andromeda (ăn-drŏm'ê-dà). Daughter of Cepheus, king of Ethiopia. The sea nymphs, offended by her mother, had sent to ravage the coast a sea monster which, according to an oracle of Jupiter Ammon, would not desist until Andromeda had been offered to it as a sacrifice. Perseus beheld the maiden fastened with chains to a rock and the monster rising out of the sea ready to devour her, while her parents stood on the shore in despair. He rushed down upon the monster, struck it a deadly blow, delivered the maiden, and obtained her as his wife.

Angurvadel. The sword of the Norse hero Frithjof, which, inscribed with Runic letters, blazed in time of war, but gleamed with a dim light in time of peace.

Antæus (ăn-tē'ŭs). One of the giants, sons of Neptune, whose home was in Libya. His strength was invincible so long as he remained in contact with his mother, the earth, but when he was lifted from it his strength decreased. One of the exploits ascribed to Hercules was his conquest of Antæus, whose weakness he had discovered.

Antigone (ăn-tĭg'ô-nê). Daughter of Œdipus, king of Thebes. When Œdipus had put out his eyes and was exiled, she shared his misfortunes and acted as his guide until his death at Colonus. After her return to Thebes one of her brothers, Polynices, leading an attack on Thebes, was slain. Creon, the new king, forbade him burial. Antigone, disobeying the prohibition, was sentenced to be buried alive, but committed suicide in anticipation of the execution.

Anu. The chief of the Babylonian triad of gods, the others being Bel and Ea. He was the king of heaven and the father of the gods. In Hindu mythology, Anu was a son of King Yayati, who cursed him for refusing to bear the burden of his old age.

Aphrodite (ăf'rô-dī'tê). The Greek goddess identified by the Romans with Venus. She was said to be the daughter of Zeus, but later poets frequently relate that she was sprung from the foam of the sea, whence they derive her name.

Apis. One of the Egyptian gods worshiped under the form of a man with a bull's head.

Apollo. According to both Greeks and Romans, Apollo was the son of Jupiter and Latona, born on the island Delos. He was regarded as the god of the sciences and the arts, especially poetry, music, and medicine. They ascribed to him the greatest skill in the use of the bow and arrow, which he proved in killing the serpent Pytho, the sons of Niobe, and the Cyclopes. The last achievement incensed Jupiter, and he was banished from Olympus. During his exile Apollo abode as a shepherd with Admetus, king of Thessaly. All sudden deaths were believed to be the effect of his arrows; and with them he sent the plague into the

camp of the Greeks before Troy. As he had the power of punishing men, so he was also able to deliver men, if duly propitiated. From his being the god who afforded help, he was the father of Æsculapius, the god of healing. As a god of inspiration and prophecy he gave oracles and communicated this gift to other gods and to men. He was often referred to by his cult name Phœbus.

Arachne (à-răk'nê). A Mæonian maid who, proud of the skill in weaving and embroidery imparted to her by Minerva, ventured to challenge her patron goddess to a trial of skill. Minerva accepted the challenge. Arachne produced a piece of cloth in which the amours of the gods were woven, and, as the goddess could find no fault with it, she tore the work to pieces. Arachne, in despair, tried to hang herself. Minerva, however, loosened the rope and saved her life, but the rope was changed into a cobweb, and Arachne herself, into a spider.

Aralu. The Babylonian underworld. It was described as a melancholy place, where the dead wandered with only clay and dust for food.

Ares (ā'rēz). The Greek god of war, identified by the Romans with Mars. He is often represented as the lover of Aphrodite, or Venus.

Arethusa (ăr'ê-thū'sà). A wood nymph of Elis, in Greece, who, pursued by the river god Alpheus, was changed into a spring and ran under the sea. The waters of this spring, mingling with the river, rose again in the fountain of Arethusa in the island of Ortygia near Syracuse.

Argo. A fifty-oared ship in which Jason and his companions made their voyage to Colchis in search of the golden fleece. This ship was built of pines cut from Mount Pelion, and, although larger than any other previously constructed, it moved lightly and easily, and was therefore called the *Argo*, "swift-sailing." From her name, those who embarked in her were called Argonauts. The mast of the *Argo* was taken from the forest of Dodona, where the oaks were endowed with the power of making predictions; therefore, the ship was regarded as an animated being, in accord with fate, to which a man might commit himself with confidence.

Argonauts (är'gô-nôts). The participants in the so-called Argonautic expedition. It was a voyage from Greece to Colchis undertaken by Jason in order to obtain the golden fleece. The task had been imposed upon Jason by his uncle Pelias, in the hope of destroying the hero. Jason, however, invited the most illustrious heroes of Greece to join him, among them Hercules, Castor and Pollux, Peleus, Pirithous, and Theseus. The vessel built for the purpose was named *Argo*. After various adverse events it arrived at Æeta, the capital of Colchis, where Jason, with the help of Medea, was successful in his quest.

Argus. A fabulous being of enormous strength, who had a hundred eyes, of which only two were closed in sleep at the same time. Juno, jealous of Io, whom her husband, Jupiter, loved, changed her into a heifer and set Argus to guard her. Jupiter had Mercury slay him, and Juno placed his hundred eyes in the tail of her favorite bird, the peacock.

Ariadne (ăr'ĭ-ăd'nê). Daughter of Minos, second king of Crete, and of Pasiphaë. She fell in love with Theseus, who was shut up in the labyrinth to be devoured by the Minotaur, and gave him a clew of thread by which, after he had killed the monster, he extricated himself from the windings of the labyrinth. He took Ariadne back with him but deserted her on the island of Naxos, where Bacchus found and married her. Bacchus gave her a crown of gems which on her death he placed as a constellation in the sky.

Arion (à-rī'ŏn). A Greek bard, who, while passenger on a ship, was made to leap overboard and leave his money with the crew. He was taken up by dolphins, and carried on their backs safe to land.

Artemis (är'tê-mĭs). Daughter of Zeus and Latona, and twin sister of Apollo. She was the goddess of chastity, the chase, and the woods. Artemis was identified by the Romans with Diana.

Asgard. In Scandinavian mythology Asgard represents the city of the gods, situated at the center of the universe, and accessible only by the bridge Bifröst, or the rainbow.

Astarte (ăs-tär'tê). An ancient Syrian deity, noticed in the Old Testament under the name Ashteroth. She was a goddess of love, women, and the moon, and hence corresponds to Aphrodite or Venus.

Atalanta (ăt'à-lăn'tà). A maid of Arcadia with athletic tastes who joined in the Calydonian hunt, and, at the funeral games of Pelias, won the prize in wrestling. Warned not to marry, she offered her hand to any suitor who could overcome her in a race. The penalty of failure was death. Hippomenes won by the strategem of throwing three golden apples before her which she paused to pick up. They were married, but the pair was transformed into lions by Cybele and continued to accompany her.

Aten. The name of the winged solar disk, the worship of which was introduced into Egypt by Amenhotep IV in the 14th century B. C. Hymns addressed to Aten hail him as creator and lord of love. No image of this deity was permitted to be made.

Athena. The Greek goddess of wisdom, identified by the Romans with Minerva. She was claimed by Athens as its guardian deity and in that character was usually known as Pallas Athena.

Atlantis. A mythical island in the West, mentioned by Plato, Pliny, and other ancient writers, and said to have sunk beneath the ocean.

Atlas. One of the Titans, son of Iapetus and Clymene. Being conquered by Jupiter, he was condemned to the labor of bearing on his head and hands the heaven he had attempted to destroy.

Atropos (ăt′rô-pŏs). The one of the three Parcæ, or Fates, that cuts the thread of life. Her name signifies "the inexorable one." The other two Fates were Clotho, who spins the thread, and Lachesis, who determines its length. See *Fates*.

Augean (ô-jē′ăn) **Stables.** The stables of Augeas, king of Elis, in Greece. In these stables he had kept 3000 oxen, and the stalls had not been cleansed for thirty years. When Hercules was required to cleanse these stables, he caused two rivers to run through them and afterward slew Augeas.

Augurs. Men whose principal business was to observe and interpret the entrails of animals and other phenomena which were regarded by the Romans as omens of the future.

Auræ (ô′rē). The breezes, nymphs of the air, a species of sportive, happy beings and well-wishers to mankind. They were represented as winged.

Aurora. The goddess of the morning or the dawn, sometimes described as the goddess of day. She is represented as standing in a magnificent chariot, drawn by winged steeds. A brilliant star sparkles upon her forehead, and from her rosy finger tips drops dew; with one hand she grasps the reins, and she holds in the other a lighted torch.

Avatar (ăv′ȧ-tär′). The incarnations or descents of the deity Vishnu, of which nine are believed to be past. The tenth is yet to come when Vishnu will descend from heaven on a white-winged horse, and will introduce on earth a golden age of virtue and peace.

Avernus (ȧ-vûr′nŭs). A small, deep lake in Campania, occupying the crater of an extinct volcano, and almost completely shut in by steep and wooded heights. It was supposed to be the entrance to the infernal regions, which were therefore sometimes called Avernus.

Azazel (ȧ-zā′zĕl). According to Ewald, a demon belonging to the pre-mosaic religion. Another opinion identifies him with Eblis, or the devil, who refused to prostrate himself before Adam. Milton makes him the standard bearer of the infernal hosts.

Azrael (ăz′rȧ-ĕl). In the Jewish and the Mohammedan mythology, the name of an angel who watches over the dying, and separates the soul from the body. It means in Hebrew "help of God."

Baal or **Bel.** The chief god of the Phœnicians and Carthaginians.

Bacchus (băk′ŭs). The god of wine; he taught the cultivation of the grape and the preparation of its juice. Greek drama developed from festivals in honor of Dionysus, the name usually given to him by the Greeks.

Balder (bôl′dĕr). The god of peace, son of Odin and Frigga. He was killed by the blind war god, but was restored to life at the general request of the gods.

Balmung. In Norse mythology, the sword of Siegfried forged by Wieland, or Völund.

Barguest. A frightful goblin among fairies. It was armed with teeth and claws and was an object of terror in the north of England.

Bast or **Pasht.** A goddess of ancient Egypt, represented as a lion-headed or cat-headed woman and worshiped especially at Bubastis.

Beelzebub (bê-ĕl′zê-bŭb). The name of a Moabite or Syrian deity. The name means "god of flies." It came to be applied to the chief of evil spirits.

Befana (bā-fä′nä). The fairy of Italian children, who is supposed to fill their stockings with toys on Twelfth Night if they have been good. The name is a juvenile corruption of the word *Epifania*, meaning *Twelfth Night*.

Bellerophon (bĕ-lĕr′ô-fŏn). A prince who rode the winged horse, Pegasus, and controlled him with a golden bridle, the gift of Minerva. By aid of Pegasus, he killed the lion-headed monster, the Chimæra.

Bellona. Roman goddess of war. She prepared the chariot of her brother Mars when he was going to war and appeared in battles armed with a whip and holding a torch.

Belphegor (bĕl′fê-gôr). A god of evil, worshiped by the Moabites. He was represented as an archfiend who had been an archangel.

Berenice (bĕr′ê-nī′sē). The name of several famous princesses and queens. (1) The wife of Mithridates the Great. He had her killed after his defeat by Lucullus, lest his enemies should capture her. (2) The wife of Ptolemy III, Euergetes. When her husband was absent in a Syrian war, she vowed her beautiful hair to the gods if he should return safe. Accordingly, her hair was cut off and left in the temple of Venus. Soon afterward it disappeared. The astronomer, Conon of Samos, declared it had been wafted to heaven. Hence the constellation *Coma Berenices*, "hair of Berenice," near that of Leo.

Berg Folk. Pagan spirits doomed to live on the Scandinavian hills till the day of redemption.

Bertha. The white lady who guards good German children, but is the terror of the bad, who fear her iron nose and big feet. She corresponds to the Italian Befana. She was often identified also with Frigga or Ostara, goddess of the earth and spring.

Bhima (bē′mä). In Hindu mythology, son of the wind god, Vayu. He is remarkable for his great size and strength, his voracious appetite, and his fiery temper.

Bifröst (bēf′rŏst). In Norse mythology, the rainbow bridge between earth and heaven, over which none but the gods could travel.

Bilskirnir. A wonderful palace built by Thor for the use of peasants after death.

Bladud. A mythical king of England, who built the city of Bath, and dedicated the medicinal springs to Minerva.

Blue Jay. In the myths of the Chinook Indians of the Columbia River country, this animal-like god plays a part similar to that of Loki in the Norse tales. He is a mischief-maker. He and his sister Ioi have many adventures among the supernatural beings.

Boreas (bō′rê-ăs). The north wind, represented as a son of Astræus and Aurora.

Bragi (brä′gē). The Scandinavian god of poetry and eloquence, son of Odin and Frigga. He is represented as an old man with a flowing white beard.

Brahma. The supreme god of the Hindus, represented with four heads and four arms, the source of the universe and of other gods, who will again be absorbed into him. He forms, with Vishnu the preserver and Siva the destroyer, the divine triad.

Bran. An ancient Welsh Celtic god of the underworld. His care was poetry and music. He is later represented as "Bran the Blessed," who first brought the cross from Rome to Britain.

Briareus (brī-ā′rê-ŭs). A giant with fifty heads and a hundred hands. He hurled a hundred rocks at Jupiter in a single throw, and Jupiter bound him under Mount Etna with a hundred chains.

Brigit. An ancient Irish Celtic goddess of poetry and prophecy, daughter of the god Dagda the Great. She was later transformed into the female patron saint of Ireland.

Bukadawin. The god of famine among certain North American Indians.

Cacus. A famous robber, son of Vulcan, said to have inhabited a cave on Mt. Aventine, the later site of Rome. He robbed Hercules of some cattle, but Hercules discovered him, killed him, and established on the site of his cave the ox market and altar, "ara maxima," which existed for ages in Rome.

Cadmus (kăd′mŭs). A Phœnician hero, son of King Agenor. His father sent him to seek his sister Europa, whom Jupiter in the guise of a bull had carried over the sea on his back. Unable to find her and afraid to return, he was directed by an oracle to build a city and call it Thebes. This he did with the help of the five survivors of the warriors who grew up from a dragon's teeth which Cadmus had planted after taking them from a dragon he had slain. He is said to have introduced the worship of heroes and the use of the alphabet, which at first consisted of sixteen letters. This last tradition expresses the fact that the Greek alphabet was developed from the Phœnician.

Caduceus (kȧ-dū′sê-ŭs). The fabled wand carried by Hermes. It was represented as entwined with two serpents and having two wings at the top.

Calchas (*kăl'kăs*). The wisest of the soothsayers among the Greeks at Troy. He died from grief on meeting with a soothsayer who proved wiser than he.

Calliope (*kă-lī'ô-pê*). The Muse who presided over epic poetry. She is generally depicted using a stylus and wax writing tablet, or a scroll.

Callisto. A nymph of Arcadia, whose son Arcas was changed into a bear and placed in the heavens as a constellation.

Calpe. One of the two pillars of Hercules. The other was named Abyla. These two were originally only one mountain, which Hercules tore asunder; he then poured the sea between them. Calpe is now called Gibraltar.

Calypso. One of the daughters of Atlas. When Ulysses was shipwrecked on her coasts, she received him with hospitality. She offered him immortality if he would become her husband, but he refused. After remaining with her seven years, he was summoned by Hermes to continue his voyage homeward.

Camenæ (*kă-mē'nē*). Italian nymphs or fountain deities, identified later by Roman poets with the Greek Muses. Egeria was one of the Camenæ

Camilla. Virgin queen of the Volscians, poetically described by Virgil as so swift that she could run over a field of corn without bending a blade, or make her way over the sea without wetting her feet.

Cassandra (*kă-săn'dră*). Daughter of Priam and Hecuba. She was passionately loved by Apollo, who, as the price of her love, gave her the gift of prophecy, but, when she deceived him, added the condition that her prophecies should never be believed.

Cassiopeia (*kăs'ĭ-ô-pê'yà*). The mother of Andromeda. Placed at her death in the heavens, she forms a constellation, the chief stars of which suggest by their arrangement the outline of a chair.

Castalia. A fountain on Mount Parnassus, sacred to Apollo and the Muses. Whoever drank of its waters was endowed with the gift of poetry.

Castor and Pollux. Twin brothers, sons of Leda. Mercury carried them to Pallena, where they were educated. As soon as they arrived at manhood, they embarked with Jason in quest of the golden fleece. Pollux was the son of Jupiter; Castor, of Tyndareus. Hence Pollux was immortal, while Castor, like other men, was subject to old age and death.

Cauther. In Mohammedan mythology, the lake of paradise, whose waters are as sweet as honey, as cold as snow, and as clear as crystal; any believer who tastes of them is said to thirst no more.

Cecrops (*sē'krŏps*). The mythical founder of Athens, who is said to have also divided Attica into twelve communities, and to have introduced the first elements of civilized life. He instituted marriage, abolished bloody sacrifices, and taught his subjects how to worship the gods. He is represented with the upper part of his body human and the lower part like that of a dragon.

Centaurs (*sĕn'tôrz*). Monsters, half horse, half human. They are especially celebrated for their contest with the giants in the mountains of Thessaly, and for their assault on the bride at the wedding of Peleus and Thetis. On the latter occasion they were defeated and driven away by the Lapithæ.

Cerberus (*sûr'bĕr-ŭs*). The three-headed dog that keeps the entrance of the infernal regions. He prevents the living from entering and the shades from escaping. Orpheus lulled Cerberus to sleep with his lyre; and the sibyl who conducted Æneas through Hades threw the dog into a sleep also by a cake treated with an opiate.

Ceres (*sē'rēz*). The daughter of Saturn, sister of Jupiter and Neptune. She was the goddess of corn, flowers, and the harvest. She is represented as crowned with poppies and riding in a chariot drawn by dragons. She was the mother of Proserpina, who while gathering flowers was seized by Pluto.

Chaos (*kā'ŏs*). The formless void preceding the genesis of an orderly universe and out of which the gods, men, and all things arose.

Charon (*kā'rŏn*). A god of the infernal regions, son of Nox, "Night," and Erebus. He conducted the souls of the dead in a boat over the rivers Styx and Acheron.

Charybdis (*kă-rĭb'dĭs*). A woman who robbed travelers and was turned by Jupiter into a dangerous whirlpool on the coast of Sicily, opposite Scylla, a six-headed monster which lived in a rock and seized passing sailors. Scylla and Charybdis are generally mentioned together to represent alternative dangers.

Chibiabos. A musician, ruler in the land of spirits, and friend of Hiawatha. Personification of harmony in nature.

Chimæra, Chimera (*kĭ-mē'rà*). A celebrated monster, having the combined semblance of a goat, lion, and dragon, which continually vomited flames. It was destroyed by Bellerophon.

Chiron (*kī'rŏn*). A centaur, son of Saturn and Philyra. He was famous for his knowledge of medicine, and taught mankind the use of plants and herbs.

Chou. An Egyptian god in many respects similar to the Roman Hercules.

Cimmerians (*sĭ-mē'rĭ-ănz*). A half mythical people, first described in the *Odyssey* as dwelling in perpetual gloom beyond the ocean stream. A people with this name was said by the Greeks to live along the Black Sea.

Circe (*sûr'sē*). A sorceress, daughter of Sol and Perse, celebrated for her knowledge of magic and venomous herbs. Ulysses, on his return from the Trojan War, visited her coasts, and his companions were changed by her potions into swine.

Clio (*klī'ô*). The Muse who presided over history.

Clotho (*klō'thô*). The youngest of the three Fates, daughters of Jupiter and Themis, and supposed to preside over the moment of birth. She held the distaff and spun the thread of life.

Cluricaune (*klōō'rĭ-kôn*). An Irish elf, who guarded a hidden treasure.

Clytemnestra (*klī'tĕm-nĕs'trà*). The wife and murderer of Agamemnon.

Clytie (*klī'tê*). A water nymph who loved the sun god Apollo and was changed into a sunflower. In this form, she turns always toward the sun.

Cocytus (*kô-sī'tŭs*). A river of the infernal regions. The unburied dead wander on its banks for 100 years. The name means the river of lamentation. See *Styx*.

Colchis or **Colchos** (*kŏl'kĭs*) (*-kŏs*). A country of Asia, bordering the Black Sea, famous in connection with the expedition of the Argonauts, and as the birthplace of Medea.

Comus (*kō'mŭs*). The god of revelry, presiding over feasts. See Milton's *Comus.*

Concordia (*kŏn-kôr'dĭ-à*). The Roman goddess of peace and concord. She is represented holding a horn of plenty and a scepter budding with fruit.

Consus. An early Italian god of harvests. Mules were under his protection and mule races were held in his honor.

Cora. A name sometimes given to Proserpina.

Coronis (*kô-rō'nĭs*). (1) Mother of Æsculapius by Apollo. (2) A king's daughter, who was transformed into a crow by Minerva when asking for protection from Neptune.

Corybantes (*kŏr'ĭ-băn'tēz*). Priests who served at the worship of Cybele, the mother of the gods, and were in the habit of striking themselves in their religious dances.

Coxcox. The Noah of the Mexican tribes, who, with his wife Xochiquetzal, alone escaped the deluge. They took refuge in a hollow cypress tree which floated until the water subsided and then ran aground on a mountain of Culhuacan. Two of their children, who were taught speech by the Great Spirit, were the ancestors of the Toltecs and the Aztecs.

Coyote (*kī-ō'tê*). See *Italapas.*

Cressida. Daughter of Calchas, the Greek, and beloved by Troilus, son of Priam. They vowed eternal fidelity, and as pledges Troilus gave the maiden a sleeve, while Cressida gave the Trojan prince a glove. Cressida proved false and her name has since stood as a byword for faithlessness.

Creusa. Daughter of Priam and wife of Æneas. She was lost in the city of Troy when her husband escaped from its flames.

Cronus. The youngest of the Titans. He was said to be the son of Uranus and Gæa, "the heavens and the earth," and to have exercised the first government over the universe. His wife was Rhea, who was also his sister. Cronus and his five brothers were called Titans. Rhea and her five sisters were called Titanides. Cronus seized upon the government of the universe by his superiority over his father and brothers, yet pledged himself to rear no male children; accordingly, he is represented as devouring his sons as soon as born. But three of them, Jupiter, Neptune, and Pluto, escaped this fate through the artifice of Rhea, their mother, who gave Cronus stones to devour instead of the children at their birth. Jupiter aided Cronus in recovering his throne, after he had been driven from it by his brothers, the Titans, and bound in Tartarus. But soon Jupiter himself made war upon Cronus and seized the government. See *Saturn.*

Cupid. God of love, son of Jupiter and Venus. He is represented as a winged boy, naked, armed with a bow and arrows, and often with a bandage covering his eyes. He shot his arrows into the hearts of both gods and men, thus infecting them with love. Like all the gods, he put on different forms to suit his plans. He became the husband of Psyche.

Cybele (*sĭb'ê-lē*). A goddess, daughter of Uranus and Terra, and identified by the Romans with Ops, wife of Saturn. On her birth she was exposed on a mountain, where she was tended and fed by wild beasts, receiving the name of Cybele from the mountain. She is represented on a throne with lions at her side. See *Atalanta*.

Cyclops (*sī'klŏps*). One-eyed giants who forged the thunderbolts of Jove. Homer describes them as wild, insolent, lawless shepherds, who devoured human beings. A later tradition represents them as Vulcan's assistants.

Cyparissus (*sĭp-á-rĭs'ŭs*). A beautiful youth, who, grief-stricken at having inadvertently killed his favorite stag, was metamorphosed into a cypress by Apollo.

Dædalus (*dĕd'á-lŭs*). A great architect and sculptor. He invented the wedge, the ax, the level, and the gimlet, and was the first to use sails. He made himself wings with feathers and wax, and fitted them to his body and to that of his son Icarus. They sailed in the air, but the heat of the sun melted the wax on the wings of Icarus, who flew too high, and he fell into the sea, which after him has been called Icarian.

Dag. In Scandinavian mythology, (1) a god representing day, the son of Nott, "night," and (2) the last survivor of a treacherous race, the Hundings.

Dagan. In Hindu mythology, a god who reconstructed the world when it had been destroyed after creation.

Dagon (*dā'gŏn*). A Syrian divinity who, according to the Bible, had richly adorned temples in several of the Philistine cities. He was a national god of the Philistines, formed in human shape upwards from the waist, his lower extremity resembling that of a fish.

Dahak. In Persian mythology, a wicked deity who is destined to break the chains in which he is bound, and to bring upon men the most terrible calamities for 1000 years. After this period the reign of Ormuzd will begin, when men will be good and happy.

Daikoku. A mythical god invoked by Japanese workers. He is represented as holding a full sack which he beats to bring from it all useful articles, and the sack never becomes empty.

Daityas. Hindu titans or demons who made war on the gods and prevented sacrifices to them.

Danaë (*dăn'ȧ-ē*). The daughter of Acrisius, king of Argos, who became by Jupiter the mother of Perseus. An Italian legend related that Danaë came to Italy, built the town of Ardea, and married Pilumnus, by whom she became the mother of Daunus, the ancestor of Turnus.

Danaides (*dȧ-nā'ĭ-dēz*). The fifty daughters of Danaus, king of Argos, who married the fifty sons of their uncle Ægyptus, and murdered them on their wedding night. They were condemned in Hades to pour water into sieves.

Danu. Among the ancient Irish Celts, the mother of the gods. She was a goddess of fertility and so associated with the underworld.

Daphne. ʻDaughter of the river god Peneus. Apollo courted her, but she fled from him and was, at her own request, turned into a laurel tree.

Daphnis. A Sicilian shepherd, son of Hermes, or Mercury, by a nymph. He was taught by Pan to play on the flute, and was regarded as the inventor of bucolic poetry.

Deiphobus (*dē-ĭf'ô-bŭs*). A son of Priam and Hecuba. After the death of Paris, he married Helen, but was betrayed by her to the Greeks. Next to Hector, he was the bravest among the Trojans. On the capture of Troy by the Greeks he was slain and fearfully mangled by Menelaus.

Deirdre (*dā'THrȧ*). An Irish heroine, fated to be the cause of misfortune. King Conchobar secluded her as his intended bride. Accidentally meeting with Noisi, she loved him and, fleeing, lived with him and his two brothers in Alba. The king brought about the death of the brothers, and Deirdre committed suicide.

Delphi (*dĕl'fĭ*). A town at the foot of Mount Parnassus, famous for its oracle and for a temple of Apollo.

Demeter (*dê-mē'tẽr*). A goddess of the earth, of seed-time, and of harvest. By Zeus she became the mother of Persephone, or Proserpina.

Demogorgon (*dē'mô-gôr'gŏn*). The tyrant genius of the soil or earth, the life and support of plants. He was depicted as an old man covered with moss and was said to

live underground. He is a figure of medieval European mythology.

Derceto (*dûr-sĕ'tō*). A Syrian mermaid goddess who had analogies with Dagon of the Philistines and who was regarded by the Romans as identical with Venus.

Deucalion and Pyrrha (*dû-kā'lĭ-ón*) (*pĭr'ȧ*). Jupiter and Neptune once destroyed the race of men with a flood. Only Deucalion and Pyrrha, his wife, escaped, finding refuge on Parnassus. At the behest of an oracle, they took up stones and cast them behind them. These stones took form as a new, hardy race of men and women, who peopled the earth again.

Diana (*dī-ăn'ȧ*). An ancient Italian goddess of light, of virginity, and of childbirth. Identified with Artemis, she became also goddess of the chase. She was often represented as the moon goddess, and, identified with Hecate, as a deity presiding over incantations. Her worship is said to have been introduced at Rome by Servius Tullius, who dedicated a temple to her on the Aventine. As Artemis, she was a daughter of Jupiter, and was born of Latona, or Leto, on the island Delos, at the same time as Apollo.

Dictynna (*dĭk-tĭn'ȧ*). One of the names of the Cretan goddess Britomartis, identified by the Greeks with Artemis.

Dike (*dī'kē*). One of the three guardians of life appointed by Themis, whose names are Eunomia, "order," Dike, "justice," Irene, "peace." Their office was to promote unanimity by the exercise of equity and justice. They likewise stand around the throne of Zeus, and their regular occupation is to open and shut the gates of heaven, and to yoke the steeds to the chariot of the sun.

Dindymus. Mountains between Phrygia and the frontiers of Galatia, near the town Pessinus, sacred to Cybele, the mother of the gods.

Diomedes (*dī'ô-mē'dēz*) or **Diomed.** (1) A Greek hero of the Trojan War, son of Tydeus, and king of Argos. He was a favorite of Minerva, who, according to Homer, encouraged him to attack and wound both Mars and Venus, who were engaged on the side of the Trojans. He survived the siege of Troy, but on his return home found his wife untrue to him. He fled to Italy and remained in exile. (2) The cruel tyrant of Thrace, who fed his mares on the flesh of his guests. He was overcome by Hercules, and was given to the same horses as food.

Dione. The youngest of the Titan sisters, and reputed mother of Venus.

Dionysus (*dī'ô-nī'sŭs*). Son of Jupiter and Semele, the daughter of Cadmus. He was the god of wine and is generally represented crowned with vine leaves, drawn in a car by tigers, and accompanied by satyrs and many revelling women, called Bacchantes. See *Bacchus*.

Diræ. The avenging goddesses, or Furies.

Dis. A name sometimes given to Pluto, and hence also to the lower world.

Discordia. A malevolent deity corresponding to the Greek Eris, the goddess of contention. She was driven from heaven by Jupiter because she sowed dissensions among the gods. At the nuptials of Peleus and Thetis she threw an apple among the gods inscribed with the words "For the fairest," which, stirring up a quarrel between Juno, Venus, and Minerva, led eventually to the Trojan War.

Dives (*dēvs*). Demons of Persian mythology. According to the *Koran*, they are ferocious and gigantic spirits under the sovereignty of Eblis.

Dodona. The most ancient oracle in Greece, by which Jupiter used to make known his will. It was said to have been built by Deucalion.

Donar. A name sometimes given to Thor, the thunder god in Norse mythology.

Dragon. A fabulous snake-like monster, thought originally to typify the life-giving and also the destructive aspect of water and of nature generally. It was for many years the national symbol of China. In some religions, including Christianity, it represented the power of evil.

Draupnir. The magic ring, symbolic of fertility, which belonged to Odin. It was burned on the funeral pyre of his son Balder.

Droma. The chain forged for the purpose of binding the wolf Fenris, but which he broke. Hence the proverbial phrase, "to dash out of Droma."

Dryads. Wood nymphs. The dryads were sometimes distinguished from the hamadryads in that the latter were supposed to be attached to some particular tree, with which they came into being, lived, and died, while the former had the care of the woods and trees in general.

Duergar (*dwẽr'gär*). In Norse mythology, dwarfs who dwelt in rocks and hills. They were noted for their strength, subtlety, magical powers, and skill in metallurgy, and were regarded as the personification of the subterranean powers of nature.

Durga or **Doorga.** A ten-armed goddess worshiped among the Hindus. She was the principal wife of Siva.

Earth-Namer. Earth-namer or Codoyanape, in some Indian legends, is represented as working with Coyote to prepare the earth for the first people. Defeated by the tricky Coyote, he withdrew to the bright Eastern-land after the coming of men. See *Italapas.*

Eblis. The name given by the Arabians to the prince of the apostate angels, whom they represent as exiled to the infernal regions for refusing to worship Adam at the command of God. Eblis alleged, in justification of his refusal, that he himself had been formed of ethereal fire, while Adam was only a creature of clay. See *Azazel.*

Echo. A nymph who engaged the attention of Juno by her never-ceasing talk, meanwhile allowing Jupiter his freedom. Juno found out her trick and punished her by taking away from her all power of speech except repetition of words just spoken by others. Echo loved Narcissus; as her love was not returned, she pined away until nothing remained but her beautiful voice.

Egeria (*ê-jē'rĭ-à*). A nymph from whom King Numa Pompilius received his instructions respecting the forms of public worship which he established in Rome.

Egia. One of the nine beautiful giantesses seen by Odin along the seashore, known as wave maidens. Her son became guardian of Bifröst, the rainbow bridge.

Egil (*ā'gēl*). A giant in Norse mythology. Thor left his goats in the care of Egil while he went to secure a kettle in which to brew ale for the gods.

Eira (*ār'à*). An attendant of the goddess Frigga, and a skillful nurse. She gathered curative herbs and plants and taught the science to women.

Elbegast. King of the dwarfs in Scandinavian mythology, who dwelt in a magnificent underground palace and drew their servants from the earth above.

Electra. A daughter of Agamemnon and Clytemnestra, rulers of Argos. When Agamemnon returned after the siege of Troy, Clytemnestra, aided by her lover Ægisthus, slew her husband. Electra concealed her young brother Orestes, who later returned and aided Electra in avenging their father's murder by slaying their mother and Ægisthus.

Eleusinian Mysteries. Secret religious rites performed at Eleusis, near Athens, which later became part of the state religion of Athens. The rites celebrated the earth goddess Demeter, her daughter Persephone, and Iacchus. The initiates obtained, through the rites, both communion with the deities and the assurance of immortality.

Elf. The water sprite, known also as Elb, from which the name of the river Elbe is said to be derived. Elves are more properly known as mountain fairies or those airy creatures that dance on the grass or sit on the leaves of trees and revel in the light of the full moon.

Elivagar (*ĕ-lĭv'ă-gär*). In Norse mythology, the name of an ice-filled river in Chaos, flowing from a fountain in the land of mist.

Elysium (*ê-lĭzh'ĭ-ŭm*). The paradise of the Greeks known also as the islands of the blest: Departed mortals were adjudged to Elysium or to Tartarus by the sentence of Minos and his fellow judges in the "Field of Truth." Elysium is described as abounding in beautiful gardens, meadows, and groves; where birds ever warble; where the river Eridanus winds between banks fringed with laurel, and "divine Lethe" glides through silent valleys; where the air is always pure, and the day serene.

Embla. In Norse mythology, the name of the first woman, so called because the gods made her of an *embla,* "elder," as they made man of an *aske,* "ash."

Enceladus (*ĕn-sĕl'à-dŭs*). A Titan, son of Terra, and the most powerful of all the giants who conspired against Jupiter and attempted to scale heaven. He was struck by Jupiter's thunderbolts and chained beneath Mount Etna.

Endymion. In Greek mythology, the setting sun with which the moon is in love. One of the many renderings of his story is that Endymion was a beautiful youth who fed his flock on Mount Latmus. One clear night, Diana, the moon, looked down and saw him sleeping. The cold heart of the goddess was warmed by his beauty, and she came down to him, kissed him, and watched over him while he slept. Another story was that Jupiter bestowed on him the gift of perpetual youth united with perpetual sleep. One version of this myth made sleep a reward for piety, while another version made it a punishment for presuming to fall in love with Juno.

Enipeus (*ê-nĭ'pūs*). A fabled river in Thessaly. Poseidon assumed the form of the god of this river in order to obtain possession of Tyro, who was in love with Enipeus. She became the mother of Pelias and Neleus.

Enyo (*ê-nĭ'ō*). (1) One of the gray maidens, or hoary witches. (2) Daughter of Mars, a goddess of war, who delights in bloodshed and the destruction of towns, and accompanies Mars in battles.

Epaphus. The son of Zeus and Io, born on the river Nile, after the long wanderings of his mother. He became king of Egypt and built Memphis.

Erebus (*ĕr'ê-bŭs*). A name applied to the dark and gloomy space under the earth through which the souls of the dead were obliged to pass on their way to Hades, with which it and Tartarus are often synonymous.

Eris. The goddess of discord; a sister of Mars, and a daughter of Night; identified with the Roman Discordia.

Eros. The son of Aphrodite and Hermes, with whom the Romans identified Cupid. See *Cupid.*

Erytheis or **Erythea** (*ĕr'ĭ-thē'ĭs*) (*-à*). One of the daughters of Night, appointed to guard the golden apples in the garden of the Hesperides.

Esangetuh Emissee. "Master of Breath." A chief deity of the Creek Indians.

Eumæus (*ū-mē'ŭs*). The faithful swineherd of Ulysses, whom Ulysses consulted upon his return to Ithaca.

Eumenides (*ū-mĕn'ĭ-dēz*). A euphemistic name given by the Greeks to the Erinyes, or Furies. They are represented as the daughters of Earth, or of Night, and as fearful winged maidens, with serpents twined in their hair and with blood dripping from their eyes. They dwelt in the depths of Tartarus, dreaded by gods and men.

Euphorbus. The son of Panthous and one of the bravest of the Trojans. He was slain by Menelaus, who dedicated his victim's shield in the temple of Hera near Mycenæ. Pythagoras asserted that he had once been Euphorbus, and in proof of his assertion took down at first sight the shield from the temple of Hera.

Euphrosyne (*ū-frŏs'ĭ-nē*). One of the three Graces. She represented joy, as her sisters stood for splendor and for pleasure.

Europa. Daughter of the Phœnician king Agenor, or, according to the *Iliad,* daughter of Phœnix. Jupiter in the form of a bull carried her on his back across the sea to Crete, where by him she became the mother of Minos, Rhadamanthus, and Sarpedon. See *Cadmus.*

Eurydice (*ū-rĭd'ĭ-sē*). Orpheus's wife, who died from the bite of a serpent. Orpheus, disconsolate at her loss, determined to descend to the lower world and obtain permission for his beloved Eurydice to return to the regions of light. Armed only with his lyre, he entered the realms of Hades and gained an easy admittance to the regions of Pluto. Orpheus was promised she should return on condition that he should not look back till she had reached the upper world. When the musician reached the confines of his journey, he turned his head to see if Eurydice were following, and she was instantly caught back again into Hades.

Eurylochus. One of the companions of Ulysses in his wanderings, and the only one of them who was not changed by Circe into a hog.

Evadne (*ê-văd'nê*). Wife of Capaneus, and mother of Sthenelus. Her husband having been killed at the siege of Thebes, she threw herself upon the funeral pile and was consumed with him.

Fafnir. In Scandinavian mythology, the eldest son of the dwarf king Hreidmar. The slaying of Fafnir represented the destruction of the demon of cold or darkness who had stolen the golden light of the sun.

Fahfah. Name given to one of the rivers of paradise in the mythology of the East.

Fata Morgana. In Italian folklore, a wraith who, in the guise of a beautiful woman, lured her pursuers into dangerous spots where they perished.

Fates. In Greek and Roman mythology the Fates are identical with the Parcæ. They were three sisters, daughters of Night, whom Jupiter permitted to decide the fortune and the duration of mortal life. They were viewed as inexorable, and ranked among the inferior divinities of the lower world. They were generally represented as three women, with chaplets made of wool and interwoven with the flowers of the narcissus, wearing long robes, and employed in their works: Clotho with a distaff; Lachesis having near her sometimes several spindles; and Atropos holding a pair of scissors. See *Atropos.*

Fauns. Among the Romans, a class of rural deities corresponding to the Greek satyrs. They were the demigods of woods and forests and hence included among the so-called "sylvan deities." They are represented with horned heads, sharp-pointed ears, and with their bodies below the waist resembling those of goats.

Felicitas. A symbolical, moral deity of the Romans. She was the personification of good fortune, and is frequently seen on Roman medals, in the form of a matron, with the staff of Mercury and a cornucopia.

Feng. The name taken by Odin in the capacity of wave-stiller. Under this name he teaches mortals to distinguish between good and bad omens and to know the moods of the winds.

Fenrir or **Fenris.** In Scandinavian mythology, the wolf, offspring of Loki, which, because of his sinister growth in size and strength, the gods bound with a magic chain. When he gapes, one jaw touches earth and the other, heaven.

Ferohers (*fĕr-ō'hĕrz*). The guardian angels in Persian mythology. They were countless in number, and their chief tasks were to ensure the well-being of man.

Feronia. A goddess of fruits, nurseries, and groves among the Romans. She had a very rich temple and a grove consecrated to her. She was honored as the patroness of enfranchised slaves, who ordinarily received their liberty in her temple.

Fire People. A people mentioned in a Pacific Coast Indian legend as possessing fire before other peoples did. Raven stole a baby belonging to them and refused to exchange it for anything less than fire. Finally, the fire people taught him the use of fire.

Fire Spirit. A spirit which, according to certain North American Indian myths, jealously guarded fire. Many people tried to steal the fire from him. Finally, Nanabozho, taking the form of a hare, reached the wigwam of the fire spirit. He succeeded in seizing a firebrand and returned with it to his people. Like Hiawatha, Nanabozho stands in legend as a benefactor of the race.

Flora. The Roman goddess of blossoms and flowers.

Fortitudo. A personification of courage and bravery, worshiped as a goddess by the Romans.

Fortuna. The goddess of chance, to whom was ascribed the allotment of prosperity and adversity among men.

Freki and Geri (*frā'kē*) (*gĕr'ē*). The two wolves of Odin, which lie at his feet as he overlooks heaven and earth.

Frey. In Scandinavian mythology, the god of the sun and of rain, and also of fertility and of peace. He was one of the most popular of the Norse divinities. No weapons were ever allowed in Frey's temple, although oxen and horses were sacrificed to him.

Freya. The Scandinavian goddess of beauty and love, sister of Frey, and wife of Odur, who deserted her for a while but was found again by her and won back. Plants were called Freya's hair, and the butterfly, Freya's hen.

Frigga. In Scandinavian mythology, the wife of Odin, and so the queen of the gods. She was the mother of Balder, Thor, and others. She sometimes typifies the earth, as Odin does the heavens. She is often confounded erroneously with Freya, in very early stories. Her name survives in "Friday."

Frodi. The son of Frey, a god of peace. Under his direction two giantesses turned a pair of magic millstones which ground out gold according to his wish and filled his coffers. Excited by greed he forced them to labor, allowing rest only long enough for the singing of one verse. When Frodi himself slept, the giantesses changed their song and proceeded to grind out an army of troops to invade the land. These troops represent the vikings.

Furies. Three divinities of the lower world, whose office it was to torment the guilty in Tartarus, and often to inflict vengeance upon the living who had slain their relatives. They are also known as Erinyes and Eumenides. See *Megœra*.

Fylgie. Guardian spirits treated of in Norse mythology. Besides the Norns or Dises, who were regarded as protective deities, one of the Fylgie was ascribed by the Norsemen to each human being as a guardian spirit to attend him through life.

Galar. One of the dwarfs who, with his fellow dwarf Fialar, slew the giant Kvasir and drained every drop of his blood.

Gangler. The gatekeeper in Odin's palace who gave the explanation of the Norse mythology that it might be recorded.

Ganymede (*găn'ĭ-mēd*). A son of Tros, king of Troy, who, according to Homer, was the most beautiful of all mortals, and was carried off by the gods that he might fill the cup of Zeus, or Jupiter, and live among the immortal gods. Later writers state that Jupiter, in the form of an eagle, carried him away from Mount Ida.

Garm. A fierce dog that kept guard at the entrance of Hel's kingdom, the realm of the dead. He could be appeased by the offering of a Hel-cake, which always appeared in the hand of one who, on earth, had given bread to the needy.

Gemini (*jĕm'ĭ-nī*). A name meaning "the twins," applied to Castor and Pollux and to the constellation formed by them when transported to the heavens to dwell among the stars.

Gerda, Gerdhr, or **Gerth.** Wife of Frey, and daughter of the frost giant, Hymir. She was so beautiful that the brightness of her naked arms illuminated both air and sea. The marriage of Frey and Gerda represented the conquering of winter by the sun god.

Geryon (*jē'rĭ-ŏn*). A monster, said to be the offspring of Chrysaor and Callirrhoë and to have three bodies and three heads. His residence was in the island of Gades, where his numerous flocks were kept by the herdsman Eurythion and guarded by a two-headed dog, called Orthos. The destruction of this monster was one of the twelve labors of Hercules.

Giall (*yăl*). The infernal river of Scandinavian mythology.

Giallar. The bridge of death, over which all must pass.

Giallarhorn, The. Heimdal's horn, the sound of which went out into all worlds whenever he chose to blow it. He blew a long-expected blast as a rallying call to the battle which ended the reign of the gods, Odin, Frey, and Tyr.

Gian ben Gian. King of the Jinn or Genii in Arabian mythology, and founder of the pyramids. He was overthrown by Azazel, or Eblis.

Giants. In Greek mythology, beings of monstrous size, with dragons' tails and fearful countenances. They attempted to storm heaven, being armed with huge rocks and the trunks of trees, but were killed by the gods with the assistance of Hercules, and were buried under Mount Etna and other volcanoes. They probably symbolized the great forces of nature. In Scandinavian mythology they are described as evil genii of various forms and races, enemies of the gods. They dwelt in a territory of their own, called Giant-land. They had the power of assuming divers shapes and of increasing or diminishing their stature at will.

Ginungagap (*gĭn'nōōng-gä-gäp'*). In Norse mythology, the vast chaotic gulf of perpetual twilight, which existed before the present world and separated the region of fog from the region of heat. Giants were the first beings who came to life among the icebergs and filled this vast abyss.

Gladsheim. A great hall in the palace of Odin, where were the twelve seats occupied by the gods when holding council.

Glasir. A marvelous grove in the land of Asgard, in which the leaves were all of shimmering red gold.

Glaucus. (1) Son of Hippolytus. Being smothered in a tub of honey, he was restored to life by Æsculapius. (2) A fisherman of Bœotia who became the fisherman's patron deity.

Glendoveer. In Hindu mythology, a kind of sylph, the most lovely of the good spirits.

Glooskap. In an Iroquois legend, a man who fell asleep in the land of the guardian of winter. After six months he awoke and journeyed southward. Finding the little summer-woman, he ran away with her from the summer-land people and came again to the land of the guardian of winter. The old guardian tried once more to put Glooskap into slumber, but the summer-woman used her magic to melt the snow and ice and winter had to flee to the North. Since that time the summer-people journey to the Northland every year.

Gnome (*nōm*). Dwarfs which were supposed to tenant the interior parts of the earth, and in whose charge mines, quarries, etc., were left. Rübezahl, of the German legends, is often cited as a representative of the class.

Goblins and Bogies. Familiar demons of popular superstition which lurk about houses. They are also called hobgoblins.

Golden Apples, The. A great treasure in the garden of the Hesperides watched by a monstrous dragon. Hercules secured them in obedience to the command of Eurystheus.

Golden Fleece. A treasure celebrated in Greek myth. Ino persuaded her husband, Athamas, that his son Phryxus was the cause of a famine which had desolated the land, and he ordered him to be sacrificed to the angry gods. Phryxus made his escape over sea on a ram which had a golden fleece. When he arrived at Colchis, he sacrificed the ram to Zeus and gave the fleece to King Æetes, who hung it on a sacred oak and set an ever-watchful dragon to guard it. It was afterwards stolen by Jason.

Gorgons. Three hideous monsters, whose faces turned to stone whoever looked on them. One of these creatures, Medusa, was slain by Perseus, and the head was presented to Minerva. She attached it to her shield, where the face continued to retain its petrifying power.

Graces. To the retinue of Venus belonged the Graces, servants and companions of the goddess. They were said to be three daughters of Jupiter and Eurynome, or, according to others, of Bacchus and Venus herself. They were honored especially in Greece. See *Euphrosyne.*

Great Turtle. According to some North American Indian tribes, the upholder of the world. When earthquakes are felt, Great Turtle is said to be weary or moving his feet.

Grid. Wife of Odin and mother of Vitharr. She lent Thor her girdle, staff, and glove, warning him to beware of treachery when he went to visit the giant Geirrödhr.

Griffin. A mythical animal, resembling an eagle in front and a lion behind. It had four legs, wings, and a beak. Sacred to the sun, it guarded gold mines and hidden treasures.

Gripir. A horse trainer, servant of Odin, who could foretell events of the future and could teach a young hero all that he might need to know.

Hades. An earlier name for Pluto. Later it was applied to the lower world itself.

Hamadryad. See *Dryads.*

Harmonia. A daughter of Mars and Venus, and wife of Cadmus.

Haroeris. An Egyptian god, whose eyes are the sun and moon.

Harpies. "Robbers" or "spoilers," described by Homer as carrying off persons who had mysteriously disappeared Hesiod represents them as fair-locked and winged maidens; but subsequent writers describe them as disgusting monsters, birds with the heads of maidens, with long claws, and faces pale from hunger, who tormented an old man, Phineus, by stealing his food as he tried to eat.

Haskah. A thunder god of the Sioux Indians, who used the winds as sticks to beat the thunder-drum.

Hebe (*hē'bê*). The goddess of youth, daughter of Zeus and Hera. She was employed by her mother to prepare her chariot and harness her peacocks, and she was cupbearer to all the gods until, on her marriage with Hercules, Ganymede took over the task.

Hecate (*hĕk'à-tē*). A goddess of magic and of the lower world. Having powers also on the earth and above it, she was identified not only with Proserpina but also with Diana and Luna. She was worshiped at night and invoked to produce enchantments.

Hector. The most prominent hero of the Trojans in their war with the Greeks, eldest son of Priam and Hecuba, and the husband of Andromache. He slew Patroclus, the friend of Achilles, and thereby roused Achilles to the fight. The other Trojans fled into the city, and Hector alone remained without the walls. But when Achilles approached, Hector's heart failed him, and he too took to flight. Thrice he ran round the city, pursued by Achilles, and fell at last, pierced by Achilles' spear. Achilles tied Hector's body to his chariot and thus dragged him into the camp of the Greeks. At the command of Zeus, he surrendered the body in response to the prayers of Priam, who buried it at Troy with great pomp. Hector is one of the noblest characters depicted in the *Iliad.*

Hecuba (*hĕk'ú-bà*). The second wife of Priam, king of Troy, and the mother of Paris and Hector. After the fall of Troy, she fell into the hands of the Greeks as a slave, and, according to one account, threw herself in despair into the sea.

Heimdal or **Heimdallr.** In Norse tales, a god, the son of nine giantesses. He lived in the celestial fort Himinbiorg, under the farther extremity of the bridge Bifröst, and kept the keys of Asgard. He could see even in sleep, could hear the growing of grass, and even of the wool on a lamb's back. He was appointed to wake the gods with his trumpet at the end of the world.

Hel. The name of the world of the dead and of its goddess, in early Norse mythology. The word means "the coverer or hider." Later myths represented Hel as the abode of all save those who had not fallen by the sword. Under the influence of Christian dogma Hel came to be associated with punishment. The goddess or demon, Hel, was a daughter of Loki.

Helen. A daughter of Jupiter and Leda, and the wife of Menelaus, king of Sparta. She was the most beautiful woman of her age, and chose Menelaus among many suitors. She afterward eloped with Paris, her husband's Trojan guest, and thus brought on the war between the Greeks and Trojans. After the fall of Troy she was restored to Menelaus.

Helenus. Son of Priam and Hecuba, celebrated for his prophetic powers.

Helice. A maid beloved of Zeus and by jealousy of Hera changed into a she-bear.

Helicon (*hĕl'ĭ-kŏn*). A mountain in Bœotia sacred to the Muses, from which place the fountain Hippocrene flowed. It is part of the Parnassus, a mountain range in Greece.

Helios (*hē'lĭ-ŏs*). The Greek sun god, who rode to his palace in Colchis every night in a golden car furnished with wings. This god gives light to both gods and men. He sees and hears everything and discovers all that is kept secret.

Helle (*hĕl'ē*). Daughter of Athamas and· Nephele, and sister of Phrixus. When Phrixus was to be sacrificed, Nephele rescued her two children, who rode away through the air upon the ram with the golden fleece, the gift of Hermes; but Helle fell into the sea. The episode gave the name of the Hellespont to the part of the sea where Helle was drowned. It is now called the Dardanelles.

Hellen. The son of Deucalion and Pyrrha, and father of Æolus, Dorus, and Xuthus. He was king of Phthia in Thessaly, and was succeeded by his son Æolus. He was the mythical ancestor of all the Hellenes.

Hell Shoon. In Icelandic mythology, shoes indispensable for the journey to Valhalla, as the obolus was for crossing the Styx.

Helmet of Hades. A helmet worn by Perseus, rendering him invisible, and which, with the winged sandals and magic wallet, he took from certain nymphs who held them in possession. After he had slain Medusa he restored them again, and presented the Gorgon's head to Minerva, who placed it in the middle of her shield.

Hera (*hē'rà*). Greek name for the wife of Zeus or Jupiter, with whom the Romans identified Juno. See *Juno.*

Heraclidæ (*hĕr'à-klī'dē*). Name given to the descendants of Hercules, who, together with the Dorians, conquered the Peloponnesus eighty years after the destruction of Troy. This legend represents the conquest of the Achæan population by Dorian invaders, who thereafter appeared as the ruling race in the Peloponnesus.

Herculean Knot. A snaky complication on the rod or caduceus of Mercury, adopted by the Grecian brides as the fastening of their woolen girdles. The loosing of the girdle symbolized the surrendering of their virginity.

Hercules (*hûr'kû-lēz*). Son of Jupiter and Alcmene and most famous of the Greek heroes. Wonderful strength was ascribed to him even directly after his birth, when he squeezed to death two serpents sent by Juno to destroy him. Since he was the offspring of her husband's infidelity, Juno compelled him to be subject to the commands of Eurystheus, who imposed upon him many difficult enterprises, known as the "twelve labors" of Hercules. They were as follows: to kill the Nemean lion; to destroy the Lernæan hydra; to catch alive the stag with golden horns; to catch the Erymanthean boar; to cleanse the stables of Augeas; to exterminate the birds of Lake Stymphalus; to bring alive the wild bull of Crete; to seize the man-eating horses of Diomedes; to obtain the girdle of Hippolyta, queen of the Amazons; to destroy the monster Geryon; to plunder the garden of the Hesperides, which was guarded by a sleepless dragon; and to bring from the infernal world the three-headed dog, Cerberus. He accomplished them all successfully, as well as many other exploits ascribed to him, by which he gave proof of his extraordinary strength and exhibited himself as an avenger and deliverer of the oppressed. Such were: his slaying the robber, Cacus; the deliverance of Prometheus, bound to a rock; the killing of Busiris; and the rescue of Alcestis from the infernal world. His last achievement was the destruction of the centaur, Nessus. Nessus dying, gave his poisoned tunic to Deianira, telling her that his blood would preserve her husband's love. Hercules afterwards, receiving it from her and putting it on, suffered such torment that as soon as he slew Nessus he cast himself in despair upon a funeral pile on Mount Œta.

Herla. A mythical king, the supposed leader of the Wild Hunt of Scandinavian mythology. This hunt was known as the Raging Host in Germany and in England as Herlathing.

Hermes (*hûr'mēz*). The Greek god with whom the Romans identified Mercury. In early times he was represented, like Priapus, as a bearded, ithyphallic figure, likenesses of which were erected before private dwellings.

Later, he became beardless, and of a more beautiful form. His business was to carry messages for Zeus, and his pleasure to pursue and woo nymphs.

Hermione (hĕr-mī'ȯ-nē). The beautiful daughter of Menelaus and Helen. She had been promised in marriage to Orestes before the Trojan War, but Menelaus, after his return home, married her to Neoptolemus. She later married Orestes.

Hesperides (hĕs-pĕr'ĭ-dēz). The daughters of Hesperus or of Erebus and Nox, who were appointed along with a never-sleeping dragon to watch the golden apples in the garden of the Hesperides in an island beyond Mount Atlas.

Hesperus. A son or brother of Atlas enrolled among the deities after death, and made identical with the Evening Star.

Hestia. The Greek name for Vesta, the goddess of the domestic hearth.

Hippocrene (hĭp'ȯ-krēn). A fountain on Mount Helicon, which sprang up where the winged horse Pegasus pawed the ground. He had been sent up by Poseidon to still the merriment of the Muses, and to accomplish this it was sufficient for him to strike the ground with his hoof. The name means "fountain of the horse."

Hippolyta (hĭ-pŏl'ĭ-tä). Queen of the Amazons, and daughter of Mars. It was her girdle that Hercules was required by Eurystheus to obtain. He captured her and brought her to Athens, where he gave her to the ruler, Theseus, as a wife.

Hippolytus. Son of Theseus and Hippolyta; his stepmother, Phædra, loved him but being repulsed accused him before Theseus of an attempt on her chastity. Theseus called down a curse on his head and was heeded by Poseidon, who sent up a great bull and so frightened Hippolytus' horses, as he was driving, that he was killed in the runaway. Artemis, whom he worshipped as a goddess of chastity, later induced Æsculapius to bring him to life and transferred him under the name of Virbius to a grove in Italy.

Hippomenes (hĭ-pŏm'ĕ-nēz). Son of Megareus, and great-grandson of Poseidon, or Neptune, who conquered Atalanta in a foot race. He had three golden apples, which he dropped one by one, and which she stopped to pick up. By this delay she lost the race, and was bound to marry Hippomenes. See *Atalanta.*

Hobomoko. An evil spirit known among certain North American Indians.

Hodeken. A famous German kobold, or domestic fairy servant; so called from wearing a little felt hat pulled down over his face.

Hoder. In Norse mythology, a blind god who, at the instigation of Loki, destroyed his brother Balder. He personifies night and darkness, as Balder does light and day.

Hofvarpnir. The fleet steed of Gna, in Scandinavian legend, which traveled through fire and air and enabled this messenger of Frigga to see all that was happening on the earth.

Honir. In Norse tales, a name given to the god of mind or thought.

Horæ or **Hours.** Daughters of Zeus and Themis, the goddesses of the order of nature and of the seasons. They guarded the doors of Olympus and promoted the fertility of the earth.

Horus. The Egyptian god of the sun, who was also worshiped in Greece and at Rome.

Hou Chi. A Chinese divinity, said to have been the founder of the royal house of Chou. He is said to have taught the arts of agriculture to the Chinese. For this service he was deified.

Hugin (hōōg'ĭn). One of Odin's two ravens which carried him news from earth, and which, when not thus employed, perched upon his shoulders. The other was called Munin. They were personifications of thought or intellect.

Hugon (ü'gȯɴ'). An evil spirit, in the folklore of France, made use of to frighten children.

Hyacinthus. A youth beloved by Apollo, and accidentally slain by him while playing at quoits. From his blood sprang the flower which bears his name.

Hyades (hī'ȧ-dēz). A group of nymphs to whom was given the care of Dionysus, the god of wine and of fertility. They were later placed among the stars. As rainstars, they symbolize nourishing rains.

Hydra. A monstrous serpent. Of special note was the hydra in the lake Lerna, which was slain by Hercules. It had many heads and when one of these heads was cut off, two others immediately grew in its place, unless the blood of the wound was stopped by fire. Hercules accomplished its destruction by the aid of Iolaus, who

applied lighted brands as each head was removed. The blood of the monster formed a poison into which Hercules dipped his arrows, in order to inflict mortal wounds on his enemies.

Hygeia (hī-jē'yȧ). The goddess of health and a daughter of Æsculapius, though some traditions make her the wife of the latter. In works of art she is represented in a long robe, feeding a serpent from a cup.

Hylas. A beautiful boy, beloved by Hercules. He was drawn into a spring by nymphs, who were enamored of him. The story has been treated by Bayard Taylor, and by William Morris in his "Life and Death of Jason."

Hymen or **Hymenæus.** A companion of Venus who presided over marriage.

Hymir. In Scandinavian mythology, the frost giant from whom Thor took and carried off the great kettle called "Mile-deep."

Hyperboreans (hī'pĕr-bō'rē-ănz). A fabulous people, supposed to live in a state of perfect happiness in a land of perpetual sunshine beyond the caverns of the north wind.

Hyperion. Son of Cœlus and Terra, and, like Apollo, a model of manly beauty. Hyperion was the father of the sun, moon, and dawn, and may be regarded as the original Greek sun god.

Iacchus (i-ȧk'ŭs). The solemn name of Bacchus in the Eleusinian mysteries, derived from a boisterous song of the same name. In these mysteries Iacchus was regarded as the son of Zeus and Ceres, not of Zeus and Semele.

Iapetus (i-ăp'ê-tŭs.) The father of Atlas and ancestor of the human race.

Icarius (i-kā'rĭ-ŭs). An Athenian, who hospitably received Dionysus in Attica and was taught the cultivation of the vine.

Icarus (ĭk'ȧ-rŭs). See *Dædalus.*

Ida. A mountain range of Mysia in Asia Minor, celebrated in mythology as the scene of the rape of Ganymede and of the judgment of Paris. In Homer, the summit of Ida is the place from which the gods watch the battles in the plain of Troy. It is an ancient seat of the worship of Cybele. A mountain in Crete, known as Mount Ida, was closely connected with the worship of Jupiter.

Idæan Mother. Cybele, who had a temple on Mount Ida in Asia Minor.

Idomeneus (i-dŏm'ê-nūs). The heroic leader of the Cretans against Troy. He vowed to sacrifice to Poseidon whatever he should first meet on his landing, if the god would grant him a safe return. This was his own son, whom he accordingly sacrificed. As Crete was thereupon visited by a plague, the Cretans expelled Idomeneus, who went to Italy.

Iduna or **Idun.** Daughter of the dwarf Ivald, and wife of Bragi. She kept in a box the golden apples which the gods tasted as often as they wished to renew their youth. Loki on one occasion stole the box, but the gods compelled him to restore it. Iduna seems to personify that part of the year when the sun is north of the equator. Her apples indicate fruits generally. Loki carries her off to Giant-land, when the sun descends below the equator, and he steals her apples. In time, Iduna makes her escape, in the form of a sparrow, when the sun again rises above the equator and fruits return.

Ifing. In Scandinavian mythology, the great stream, between the earth and the sacred lands, whose waters never froze.

Inachus (ĭn'ȧ-kŭs). One of the river gods, a son of Oceanus and Tethys, and father of Phoroneus and of Io. He was the legendary first king of Argos.

Indra. In Hindu mythology, the ever youthful god of the firmament, and the omnipotent ruler of the elements. In the Vedic period of the Hindu religion, he occupied a foremost rank, and, though degraded to an inferior position in the Epic period, he long enjoyed a great legendary popularity. In works of art, he is represented as riding on an elephant.

Io. The daughter of Inachus, beloved by Zeus, and changed by him, because he feared Hera's jealousy, into a heifer. Wandering in this form she crossed the sea named after her, Ionian.

Iolaus (i'ȯ-lā'ŭs). The son of Automedusa and of Iphicles, who was the half brother of Hercules. Iolaus is known as the latter's faithful companion and charioteer.

Iole (i'ȯ-lē). The daughter of Eurytus of Œchalia, beloved by Hercules. Eurytus promised his daughter to the man who should conquer him and his sons in shooting with the bow. Hercules defeated them; but Eurytus and

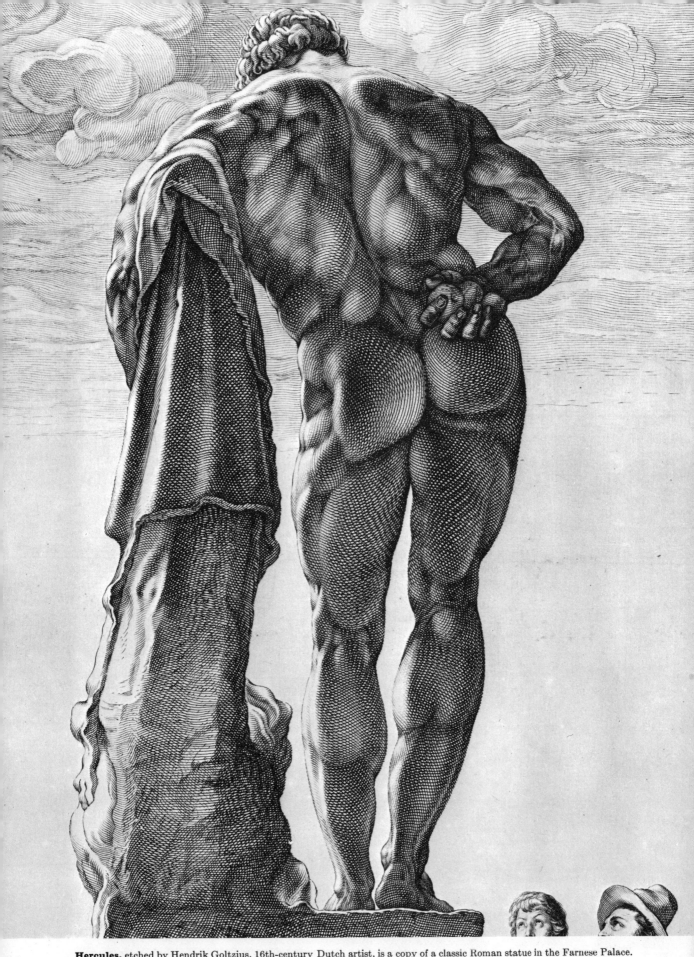

Hercules, etched by Hendrik Goltzius, 16th-century Dutch artist, is a copy of a classic Roman statue in the Farnese Palace. The Metropolitan Museum of Art, gift of Henry Walters, 1917.

The Legend of Homer. Who was the author of *The Iliad* and *The Odyssey*? Where and when did he live? Do the two great epics reflect history? Whatever the answers may be, the spirit, legends, and life of ancient Homeric Greece spread through the Mediterranean region and marked the entire world of art, myth, and literature that have been handed down through the generations of time.

his sons, with the exception of Iphitus, refused to give Iole to the victor, on the ground that he had, in a fit of insanity, murdered his own children.

Ion. The fabulous ancestor of the Ionians, son of Apollo and Creusa, and grandson of Erechtheus. According to some traditions he reigned in Attica.

Ipalnemohuani. The sun god and supreme deity of the Toltecs. Human sacrifices were offered to him.

Iphigenia (*ĭf′ĭ-jê-nī′à*). A daughter of Agamemnon and Clytemnestra, and sister to Orestes. Iphigenia was about to be sacrificed at Aulis to obtain fair sailing for the expedition against Troy; but she was rescued by Diana, who carried her to the Tauri, where she became a priestess in her temple. She was afterwards recognized by her brother Orestes, who, with his friend Pylades, was wrecked on the Taurian coast and brought, according to local custom, to be sacrificed to Diana as shipwrecked sailors. Iphigenia succeeded in saving them.

Irene (*ī-rēn′*). Goddess of peace, called Pax by the Romans, daughter of Zeus and Themis, and one of the Horæ.

Iris. Name given among the Greeks to the rainbow, as personified and considered a goddess. Her father was said to be Thaumas, and her mother, Electra, one of the daughters of Oceanus. Her residence was near the throne of Juno, whose commands she bore as messenger to the rest of the gods and to mortals. Sometimes, but rarely, she was Jupiter's messenger and was employed even by other deities.

Irus. The beggar of gigantic stature, who kept watch over the suitors of Penelope and carried their messages for them. His real name was Arnæus, but the suitors nicknamed him Irus, by analogy with Iris.

Isis. In Egyptian mythology, the sister-wife of Osiris. She was the type of motherhood and fertility in nature. The Greeks identified her with Demeter. Her worship as a nature goddess, in various forms, spread over most of the ancient world.

Islands of the Blessed. The early Greeks, as we learn from Homer, placed the Elysian fields, into which favored heroes passed without dying, at the extremity of the earth, near the river Oceanus. In poems later than Homer, an island is spoken of as their abode; hence, when certain islands were discovered in the ocean, off the western coast of Africa, the name of *Fortunatæ Insulæ* was applied to them. They are now called the Canary and the Madeira islands.

Ismene (*ĭs-mē′nê*). Daughter of Œdipus and Jocasta. When her sister Antigone was condemned to be buried alive by the order of King Creon for defying his edict and burying her brother Polynices, Ismene declared that she had aided her sister, and requested to be allowed to share the same punishment. Denied this, she is said to have died from grief. The story is told by Sophocles, and the modern artist, Teschendorf, has made a noted picture of the two sisters.

Israfel. Known among Arabians as the angel of music, who possessed the most melodious voice of all God's creatures. It was his duty to sound the resurrection trump and make music for the saints in paradise. Israfel, Gabriel, and Michael were the three angels that warned Abraham of Sodom's destruction.

Italapas, the Coyote. Among the Chinook Indians the Coyote was regarded as a helper of Ikanam, the creator, and as a teacher of men. Among certain Californian tribes, Coyote was a mischievous god.

Ithaca. In Greek mythology, the island kingdom of Ulysses.

Ixion (*ĭk-sī′ŏn*). A fabled king of Thessaly, who became father of the centaurs. The story by which he is most noted runs: When Deioneus demanded of Ixion certain gifts he had promised, Ixion treacherously invited him to a banquet and contrived to make him fall into a pit filled with fire. Zeus pardoned Ixion, but later for an insult to Hera he was chained by his hands and feet to an ever-revolving wheel.

Jamshid (*jäm-shēd′*). King of the genii, who owned a golden cup full of the elixir of life. This cup, hidden by the genii, was said to have been discovered by those who dug the foundations of Persepolis.

Janus. One of the superior gods of the Romans. The myths represent him as reigning over the earliest inhabitants of Italy, where he received Saturn driven from Crete by Jupiter. The two reigned in Italy throughout what was known later as the golden age. To Janus, Numa dedicated that celebrated temple, which was always open in time of war, and was closed with much solemnity whenever there was general peace in the Roman Empire, a thing which happened but three times during 700 years.

From this deity the month of January was named, and the first day of each month was sacred to him. He was a god of beginnings, of doors, and perhaps, originally, of light. He was represented with two faces looking in opposite directions.

Jason. The son of Æson, king of Iolcus. Æson appointed his half brother Pelias as guardian to the young Jason, whom Pelias tried to get rid of by sending him to get the golden fleece. Enlisting a number of famous heroes in the quest, Jason set sail on the ship *Argo* from Iolcus and came to King Æetes in Colchis, who promised him the fleece if he would use certain fire-breathing bulls to plow a field. With the help of Medea, the daughter of Æetes, who fell in love with Jason and offered the use of her magic art, he overcame all obstacles and obtained the fleece. Medea fled with him. Later, angered by Jason's intention to take a new wife, she accomplished his death and that of their two children.

Jinn or **Genii.** Fairies in Arabian mythology, the offspring of fire. They were governed by a race of kings named Suleyman, one of whom built the pyramids. Their chief abode is the mountain Kaf, and they appear to men under the forms of serpents, dogs, cats, monsters, or even human beings, and become invisible at pleasure. The evil jinn are ugly, but the good are beautiful. They were created from fire 2000 years before Adam lived.

Jizo. A Japanese Buddhist god. He is represented as a kindly priest, a protector of travelers, women, and children. His image is frequently placed at crossroads.

Jörd (*yĕrd*). Daughter of Night, wife of Odin, and mother of Thor.

Jove. A form of the name Jupiter.

Juggernaut or **Jagannath** (*jŭg′ẽr-nôt*) (*-à-nät*). A Hindu god, worshiped in the town of Puri in Orissa. On festival days the throne of his image is placed on a sixty-foot tower on wheels, which is drawn through the streets. Devout worshipers are said to throw themselves in front of this car to be crushed.

Juno. The Roman goddess of women, who was identified with the Greek goddess Hera. As such she was the wife of Jupiter and queen of heaven. The amours of her husband gave her many occasions for jealousy which she often indulged with vindictive cruelty against his paramours.

Jupiter. The supreme god of the Romans, who was identified with the Greek god Zeus. Both were probably at first gods of light. As identified by poets with Zeus, he ruled over gods and men on his throne in Mount Olympus, but often came down to visit mortals and make love to mortal women. The Capitol at Rome was dedicated to him as guardian of the city. See *Zeus*.

Kama (*kä′mà*). The Hindu god of love. His wife is Rati, "voluptuousness," and he is represented as riding on a sparrow, holding in his hand a bow of flowers and five arrows, each tipped with the bloom of a flower supposed to conquer one of the senses. His power is so much exalted that even the god Brahma is said to succumb to it.

Kami. The gods of ancient Japan. The name, in modern times, designates any saintly person and may also be applied to a prince.

Kaswa. The favorite camel of Mohammed, admitted into the Moslem paradise because it fell on its knees in adoration when the prophet delivered the last clause of the *Koran* to the assembled multitude at Mecca.

Kelpie. In the mythology of Scotland, a spirit of the water seen in the form of a horse, and believed to appear to those who are about to be drowned. Each lake has its kelpie.

Kobold (*kō′bŏld*). A house spirit in German folklore. In northern Europe the name is sometimes used in place of elf or dwarf, representing an underground spirit. It is probably the same as the Scotch brownie.

Koppenberg. The hill which miraculously opened to receive the children who followed Odin under the form of the Pied Piper. The rats, which he previously lured into the river and drowned, were the restless souls of the dead, which were thus released.

Krishna. A popular hero-god of the ancient Hindus. He is represented as one of the incarnations, or *avatars*, of Vishnu. One of the stories regarding him relates that, when the people of the earth appealed to Vishnu against the tyranny of the king Kansa, Vishnu took the form of Krishna to destroy the king. Kansa, forewarned, killed all the other children of Vasudeva and Devaki, the parents of Krishna. But Krishna was concealed by a cowherd. He is represented as a beautiful and gifted youth, somewhat like the Greek Apollo.

Kubera (*kŏŏ-bā′rà*). In Hindu mythology, the god of riches, represented as frightfully deformed, and as riding in a car drawn by hobgoblins.

Lachesis (*lăk'ê-sĭs*). The one of the three Fates who fixed the length of the thread of life. See *Fates*.

Læding. In Norse mythology, a strong chain with which the wolf Fenris was bound. He easily broke the chain and from this legend has grown the saying, "to get loose out of Læding." A stronger chain, known as Droma, was also broken by Fenris. See *Droma*.

Laertes (*lâ-ûr'tēz*). Mythical king of Ithaca and father of Ulysses. Laertes took part in the Calydonian hunt and in the expedition of the Argonauts. He was still alive when Ulysses returned to Ithaca, after the fall of Troy. During the absence of Ulysses he had withdrawn to the country in grief and bowed with age. It was his shroud which Penelope, the wife of Ulysses, was weaving and on the completion of which she promised to choose one of her suitors as husband. But each night she raveled what she had woven in the day.

Læstrygonians (*lĕs'trĭ-gō'nĭ-ănz*). A mythical race of giants who lived in Sicily. Ulysses sent two of his men to request that he and his crew might land, but the king ate one and the other fled. The Læstrygonians assembled on the coast and threw stones against Ulysses and his crew. Ulysses escaped after losing many of his companions.

Laius. King of Thebes, son of Labdacus, husband of Jocasta, and father of Œdipus, by whom he was slain.

Lamia (*lā'mĭ-à*). A daughter of Belus, king of Egypt. who, because she was loved by Jupiter, was transformed by the jealous Juno into a monster devouring human flesh. Greek and Roman children were often frightened by stories of her.

Laocoön (*lâ-ŏk'ô-ŏn*). Son of Priam, and priest of Apollo. He opposed the reception of the wooden horse into Troy, thinking it some artifice of the deceitful Greeks, whereupon he and his two sons were killed by two monstrous serpents which came from the sea at the instance of Apollo, whom Laocoön had offended by offering sacrifice to Poseidon. The Trojans, however, interpreted the occurrence as evidence that Laocoön should not have opposed taking the horse into the city.

Laodamia (*lâ-ŏd'à-mĭ'à*). The wife of Protesilaus, who was slain before Troy. She begged to be allowed to converse with her dead husband for only three hours, and her request was granted. Hermes, or Mercury, led Protesilaus back to the upper world; when, at the end of the three hours, Protesilaus died a second time, Laodamia died with him.

Laomedon. The king that built the walls of Troy assisted by Neptune and Apollo, who had displeased Jupiter and were sent to work for wages. Neptune built the walls, while Apollo tended the king's flocks on Mount Ida. When the two gods had done their work, Laomedon refused the reward he had promised and expelled them from his dominions. Neptune sent to ravage the country a sea monster which could be propitiated only by the sacrifice of Laomedon's daughter, Hesione. When she was chained to a rock and the monster came to devour her, Hercules appeared and rescued her.

Lapithæ (*lăp'ĭ-thē*). A mythical people of Thessaly, noted for their defeat of the centaurs at the marriage feast of Peleus and Thetis.

Lares. Those deities which Romans chose as the protectors of their houses or cities and statues of whom were set up over the hearth. Each house chose two gods as its lares.

Latinus. A king of Latium, son of Faunus and of the nymph Marcia. He was the father of Lavinia, whom he gave in marriage to Æneas. Æneas built a town which he called Lavinium, capital of Latium. According to one account, Latinus, after his death, became Jupiter Latiaris, just as Romulus became Quirinus.

Latmus. A mountain in Caria. It was the mythological scene of the story of Selene, or Luna, and Endymion.

Latona. Daughter of Cœus, a Titan, and of Phœbe, and, by Jupiter, the mother of Apollo and Diana. The love of the king of the gods procured for her the hatred of Juno.

Lavinia. The daughter of Latinus and Amata, betrothed to Turnus, but married to Æneas. Æneas founded the town of Lavinium, called after Lavinia.

Leda. The mother of Helen. Jupiter visited her in the form of a swan, and "Leda and the Swan" has been a favorite subject with artists.

Leprechaun (*lĕp'rē-κŏn'*). In Irish mythical tales a fairy shoemaker resembling an old man, who resorts to out-of-the-way places, where he is discovered by the noise of his hammer. Besides making shoes, he grinds meal and in other ways assists people who are kind to him. While any one keeps his eye fixed upon him, he cannot escape, but the moment the eye is withdrawn he may vanish.

Lethe (*lē'thē*). The river that separates Hades from the Elysian fields. The souls of the dead drink of this river and straightway forget all their past.

Liber. A name frequently given by the Roman poets to the Greek Bacchus, or Dionysus. But the god Liber and the goddess Libera were ancient Italian divinities, presiding over the cultivation of the vine and the fertility of the fields. Hence they were worshiped in early times in conjunction with Ceres. The vine and ivy and the panther were especially sacred to him, and goats were usually offered in sacrifice to him.

Libertas. The deification of liberty, to whom as a goddess several temples were erected at Rome. She is represented in works of art as a matron wearing a wreath of laurel and holding in her hand the pileus, the cap given to freed slaves as a symbol of their emancipation.

Libitina (*lĭb'ĭ-tī'nà*). An ancient goddess of Rome who presided over the burial of the dead. At her temple in Rome everything necessary for funerals was kept, and might be bought or hired for use. As goddess of death she was often identified with Proserpina but, as she had originally been a goddess of gardens and of voluptuous joy, she was sometimes identified with Venus.

Lif (*lēf*). In Norse mythology, the name given to man in the state in which he is to occupy the purified earth when goodness resumes its sway.

Lilinau. In the folklore of certain North American Indians, a woman wooed by a phantom. She followed his green waving plume through the forest and was never seen again.

Lilith (*lĭl'ĭth*). In Hebrew mythology, a female specter who lies in wait for children in order to destroy them. The older traditions tell of Lilith as a former wife of Adam and the mother of demons. Amulets were worn as protection from her powers.

Lofen. The Scandinavian god who guards friendship.

Lofua. The Scandinavian goddess who reconciles lovers.

Loki (*lō'kê*). In Norse mythology, the contriver of all mischief among the gods. He is the father of Fenris the wolf, of the Midgard Serpent, and of Hel, "death."

Lord of Cold Weather. Among the Blackfeet Indians, a tall, old man, who sits and smokes in his white tepee far in the north country.

Lorelei (*lō'rĕ-lī*). In German legend, a bewitching maiden who haunted a rock of the same name on the right bank of the Rhine. She combed her hair with a golden comb, and sang a wild song which enticed fishermen and sailors to destruction on the rocks and rapids at the foot of the precipice. In Norse mythology, Lorelei is represented as immortal, a daughter of the Rhine, and dwelling in the river bed.

Lotis. A nymph, who, to escape the embraces of Priapus, was metamorphosed into a tree, called, after her, "lotus."

Lubins. A species of goblins in Normandy that take the form of wolves and frequent churchyards. They are very timorous and take flight at the slightest noise.

Lucifer (*lū'sĭ-fẽr*). (1) "Light-bearer." The name of the planet Venus, when seen in the morning before sunrise. The equivalent Greek is "Phosphor." The same planet was called "Hesperus," when it appeared in the heavens after sunset. (2) By a false etymology the church fathers connected the Hebrew word for Lucifer with a word meaning "to lament." He thus became the fallen angel who lamented his original glory, which was bright as the morning star, and he was identified with Satan by Dante and Milton, following the earlier writers.

Luna. The daughter of Hyperion and Thea. She was distinct in name, descent, and story, from Diana, who was regarded as goddess of the moon. To Luna was ascribed great influence in relation to the birth of children.

Lycomedes (*lĭk'ô-mē'dēz*). A king in the island of Scyros, to whose court Achilles, disguised as a maiden, was sent by his mother, Thetis, who was anxious to prevent her son from going to the Trojan War.

Mænalus (*mĕn'à-lŭs*). A mountain in Arcadia, extending from Megalopolis to Tegea, celebrated as the favorite haunt of the god Pan.

Mæra. The dog of Icarius. Icarius, having made wine, gave it to some shepherds, who, thinking themselves poisoned, killed him; recovering themselves, they buried him. His daughter Erigone, being shown the spot by his faithful dog Mæra, hanged herself through grief.

Mammon. In demonology, a spirit placed at the head of nine ranks of demons. Also a Syriac word used in the Scriptures to signify either riches or the god of riches. Milton made Mammon one of the fallen angels.

Manes (*mā′nēz*). In Roman mythology, spirits of the dead, which were often supposed to hover about their former abodes and needed to be pacified by ceremonies.

Mani. Name given in ancient Norse mythology to a personification of the moon. He was later known as the son of Mundilfori, and was taken to heaven by the gods to drive the moon-car. He was followed by a wolf, which, when time should be no more, would devour both Mani and Mani's sister Sol.

Manitou. The great spirit of certain North American Indians.

Mars. A Roman god, originally of husbandry and later god of war, in which character he was identified with the Greek Ares. The Romans regarded him as the father of Romulus, and the founder and protector of their nation.

Marsyas. The Phrygian flute player who challenged Apollo to a contest of skill and, being beaten by the god, was flayed alive for his presumption. From his blood arose the river Marsyas. The flute on which Marsyas played was one Athena had thrown away, and, being filled with the breath of the goddess, gave forth such music as enabled him at least to compete with Apollo.

Medea. A daughter of Æetes, skilled in charms and witchcraft. She had scarcely beheld Jason, when, through the influence and disposal of the gods, a tender affection for the hero was raised in her bosom, and soon kindled to a flame of the most violent passion. Jason went to the temple of Hecate to supplicate the mighty goddess, where he was met by Medea. She disclosed her love to him, at the same time promising her assistance in the dangers which threatened him, and offering her help in accomplishing his glorious undertaking, provided he would swear fidelity to her. Jason complied, and Medea, reciprocating the oath, rendered the hero invincible by means of her magical incantations. She was later deserted by him and in revenge slew his children, his intended bride, and his father.

Medusa (*mê-dŭ′sȧ*). One of the three Gorgons whose hair was entwined with hissing serpents, and whose bodies were covered with impenetrable scales; they had wings, brazen claws, and enormous teeth, and whoever looked upon them was turned to stone. Medusa, who alone of the sisters was mortal, was, according to some legends, at first a beautiful maiden, but her hair was changed into serpents by Athena, or Minerva, in consequence of her having become by Poseidon, or Neptune, the mother of Chrysaor in one of Athena's temples. She was killed by Perseus, and her head was fixed on the shield of Minerva. From her blood sprang the winged horse, Pegasus.

Megæra (*mê-jē′rȧ*). One of the Furies, the author of insanity and murders. The others were: Tisiphone, whose particular work was to originate fatal epidemics and contagion; Alecto, to whom were ascribed the devastations and cruelties of war.

Megingiard (*mĕg′ĭn-yärd*). A magic belt worn by the god Thor, which, as it was tightened, rendered its wearer more powerful. The god was accustomed to show his strength by lifting great weights, but on one occasion the belt failed him, when he was challenged to pick up from the ground a cat belonging to a certain giant. He tugged and strained, only to succeed in raising one paw from the floor.

Meleager (*mĕl′ê-ā′jẽr*). Son of the Calydonian king Œneus. He took a prominent part in the Argonautic expedition and distinguished himself among his companions, especially by reason of his skill in throwing the javelin.

Melia (*mē′lĭ-ȧ*). One of the daughters of Oceanus and the mother of Phoroneus, a fabulous king of Argos.

Melicertes (*mĕl′ĭ-sûr′tēz*). A son of the Theban king Athamas by Ino. He was metamorphosed into a sea god.

Melic (*mĕl′ĭk*) **Nymphs.** Maidens of the ashen spear, sprung from the blood of Uranus. Two of them, Adrastea and Ida, cared for the infant Jupiter in a cave on Mount Ida.

Melissa. A nymph, said to have discovered the use of honey, and from whom bees were said to have received their Greek name.

Melpomene (*mĕl-pŏm′ê-nē*). The Muse of the tragic drama.

Melusina (*mĕl′ū-sē′nȧ*). The most noted among French fairies. She was condemned to become every Saturday a serpent from the waist downward, as a punishment for having, by means of a charm, enclosed her father in a high mountain, in order to avenge an injury her mother had received from him. She married Raymond, count of Toulouse, who in violation of a promise he gave her never to visit her on Saturdays came and saw her during her loathsome transformation. For his breach of faith she left him. The story has analogies with legends of the mermaids, and of Cupid and Psyche.

Memnon. A son of Tithonus and Aurora, and king of Ethiopia. After the fall of Hector, he went to the assistance of his uncle Priam with 10,000 men, and displayed great courage in the defense of Troy, but he was at length slain by Ajax, in single combat, whereupon he was changed into a bird.

Mendes (*mĕn′dēz*). An Egyptian god similar to Pan. He was worshiped in the form of a goat.

Menelaus (*mĕn′ê-lā′ŭs*). A son of Atreus, and younger brother of Agamemnon. He was king of Lacedæmon, and was married to the beautiful Helen, by whom he became the father of Hermione. When Paris seduced and took to Troy his wife Helen, he enlisted the help of Agamemnon, his brother, and many other Greek princes to win back his wife by sacking Troy. In the war Menelaus killed many Trojans, and would have slain Paris also in single combat had not the latter been carried off in a cloud by Venus.

Menœceus (*mê-nē′sŭs*). (1) A Theban, grandson of Pentheus, and father of Hipponome Jocasta, and Creon. (2) Grandson of Menœceus, and son of Creon. When the seven Argive heroes marched against Thebes, he put an end to his life because Tiresias had declared that his death would bring victory to his country.

Mentor. A friend of Ulysses in Ithaca, whose form Minerva assumed in order to give instructions to Ulysses' son Telemachus, whom she accompanied to Pylos and Lacedæmon.

Mephistopheles (*mĕf′ĭs-tŏf′ê-lēz*). One of the seven chief devils in the old demonology, the second of the fallen archangels, and after Satan the most powerful among the infernal legions. He figures in the old legend of Dr. Faustus as the familiar spirit of that magician. To modern readers he is chiefly known as the cold, scoffing, relentless fiend of Goethe's *Faust*, and as the attendant demon in Marlowe's *Faustus*. The name is said to be a corruption of a Greek word meaning "one who hates what is helpful."

Mercury. A Roman god, identified with the Greek Hermes. In Rome, however, he continued to carry a sacred branch as the emblem of peace instead of the caduceus. Like Hermes he was the messenger of Jupiter, the god of eloquence, of gain, and of thievery, and conducted souls to the lower world.

Mermaids (*mûr′mādz*). Wave maidens of medieval folklore. They were generally represented as young and beautiful women, fish-form below the waist, who used their charms to lure men to destruction in the sea. Sometimes they are said to have quit the sea, temporarily acquiring complete human form, and marrying, only to bring disaster upon their husbands and upon themselves.

Meru (*mā′rōō*). In Hindu mythology, a sacred mountain, 80,000 leagues high, situated in the center of the world. It was the abode of Indra, god of the air, and abounded with every charm that can be imagined.

Midas. The king of Phrygia, who restored to Bacchus the god's nurse and preceptor, Silenus, and received as a compensation the power of turning into gold everything he touched. But this proved to be very inconvenient, as it prevented him from eating and drinking, and he prayed that the gift might be revoked. At the command of the god, he washed in the Pactolus, the sands of which became, in consequence, mixed with gold. Another tradition is that, in a musical contest between Pan and Apollo, he gave judgment in favor of the satyr; whereupon Apollo in contempt gave the king a pair of ass's ears. Midas hid them under his Phrygian cap; but his servant, who used to cut his hair, discovered them, and was so pleased with the "joke," which he dared not mention, that he dug a hole in the earth and relieved his mind by whispering in it, "Midas has ass's ears."

Midgard (*mĭd′gärd*). In Scandinavian mythology, the name given to the earth, meaning "middle yard or enclosure." It was formed in the middle of *Ginnungagap*, or "gaping abyss," out of the eyebrows of the giant Ymir and joined to heaven by the rainbow bridge Bifröst. The solid portion of Midgard was surrounded by the giant's blood or sweat, which now formed the ocean, while his bones made the hills, his flat teeth became the cliffs, and his curly hair took the form of the trees and all vegetation.

Midgard Serpent. The great serpent, offspring of Loki, which grew to such a length that it surrounded the earth and bit its tail. Odin cast it into the sea.

Mimir (*mē′mẽr*). In Scandinavian mythology, the god of wisdom. Also god of the ocean, called "Mimir's well," in which wit and wisdom lay hidden, and of which he drank every morning from the Giallarhorn. Odin once drank from this fountain, and by doing so became the wisest of gods and men; but he purchased the privileg and distinction at the cost of one eye, which Mimir exacted from him.

Minerva. Under the name of Minerva among the Romans and of Athena among the Greeks was personified and deified the idea of intelligence and wisdom. Minerva was a daughter of Jupiter, sprung from his head. The Greeks ascribed to this goddess the invention of many arts and sciences, which had a great influence on their civilization. She was regarded as inventress of the flute, of embroidery and spinning, of the use of the olive, and of various instruments of war; in short, of most works indicating superior intelligence or skill. See *Arachne.*

Minos (*mī'nŏs*). A semimythical king and lawgiver of Crete. In order to avenge the wrong done to his son Androgeos at Athens, he made war against the Athenians, and compelled them to send to Crete every year, as a tribute, seven youths and seven maidens, to be devoured in the labyrinth by the Minotaur.

Minotaur (*mĭn'ŏ-tôr*). A celebrated monster with the head of a bull and the body of a man, kept by Minos in the famous labyrinth constructed by Dædalus. The monster devoured a tribute of young people from Athens each year until he was slain by Theseus, with the assistance of Ariadne, the daughter of Minos.

Mithra. A Persian deity whose worship spread over western Asia and through the Roman world. This cult was the most formidable rival of early Christianity. Mithra was a god of light, heat, and fertility, a giver of all good things. He was popularly represented as a sun god, and in many respects he resembled Apollo.

Mjöllnir (*myŭl'nẽr*). In the mythology of Scandinavia, the name of Thor's celebrated hammer — a type of the thunderbolt — which, however far it might be cast, was never lost, as it always returned to his hand. Whenever he wished, it became so small that he could put it in his pocket.

Mnemosyne (*nê-mŏs'ĭ-nê*). Mother of the Muses and goddess of memory. She was courted by Jupiter in the guise of a shepherd.

Moakkibat. A class of angels, according to the Mohammedan mythology. Two angels of this class attend every child of Adam from the cradle to the grave. At sunset they fly up with the record of the deeds done since sunrise. Every good deed is entered ten times by the recording angel on the credit or right side of his ledger, but when an evil deed is reported the angel waits seven hours in the hope that the evildoer may repent.

Mœræ (*mē'rē*). The Greek name for the Fates.

Morpheus (*môr'fūs*). The son of Sleep and the god of dreams. The name signifies the fashioner or molder, because he shapes or forms the dreams which appear to the sleeper.

Mowis. The snow bridegroom who, according to a certain North American Indian tradition, wooed and won a beautiful bride; but, when morning dawned, Mowis left the wigwam and melted into the sunshine. The bride hunted for him night and day in the forests, but never saw him again.

Muses. Nine daughters of Jupiter and Mnemosyne. They were goddesses of poetry, of history, and of other arts and sciences. Calliope was the Muse of eloquence and heroic poetry, and to her the ancients gave precedence; Clio, of history; Erato, of amorous poetry; Euterpe, of music; Melpomene, of tragedy; Polyhymnia, of eloquence and of imitation; Terpsichore, of dancing; Thalia, of comic and lyric poetry; and Urania, of astronomy. Their usual abode was Mount Parnassus in Helicon.

Myrmidons (*mûr'mĭ-dŏnz*). The trusty followers of Achilles. They are said to have inhabited originally the island of Ægina, and to have emigrated with Peleus into Thessaly; but modern critics, on the contrary, suppose that a colony of them emigrated from Thessaly into Ægina. The Myrmidons disappeared from history at a later period. The ancients derived their name either from a mythical ancestor, Myrmidon, son of Zeus and father of Actor and Eurymedusa, or from the ants in Ægina, which were supposed to have been metamorphosed into men in the time of Æacus.

Mysterious Three, The. In Scandinavian mythology, "Har" (the Mighty), the "Like-Mighty," and the "Third Person," who sat on three thrones above the rainbow. Below them ranked the "Æsir," of which Odin was chief, who lived in Asgard between the rainbow and the earth; and below them, the "Vanir," or gods of the ocean, air, and clouds, of which deities Niord was chief.

Naiads (*nā'yădz*). The nymphs of fresh water, whether of rivers, lakes, brooks, or springs. See *Nymphs.*

Nala. A legendary king of India, whose love for Damayanti and whose subsequent misfortunes have supplied subjects for numerous poems.

Nanabozho. A North American Indian hero who, like Hiawatha, showed himself a benefactor of mankind. He stole fire from the fire spirit.

Naraka (*năr'ȧ-kȧ*). The hell of the Hindus. It has 28 divisions, in some of which the victims are torn by ravens and owls; in others they are compelled to swallow cakes boiling hot, or are made to walk over burning sands.

Narcissus. The beautiful youth, son of the river god Cephissus and of the sea nymph Liriope. Echo, whose love he refused, died of grief. But Nemesis, to punish him, caused him to see his own image reflected in a fountain, whereupon he became so enamored of it that he gradually pined away, until he was metamorphosed into the flower which bears his name. According to another tradition, Narcissus had a sister of remarkable beauty, to whom he was tenderly attached. She resembled him in features, was similarly attired, and accompanied him in the hunt. She died young, and Narcissus, lamenting her death, frequented a neighboring fountain to gaze upon his own image in its stream. The strong resemblance that he bore to his sister made his own reflection appear to him, as it were, the form of her whom he had lost. The gods looked with pity upon his grief, and changed him to the flower that bears his name.

Nausicaa (*nô-sĭk'ȧ-ȧ*). A daughter of Alcinous, king of the Phæacians, and of Arete. She discovered the shipwrecked Odysseus (Ulysses) on the shore and conducted him to the court of her father.

Nectar. Wine conferring immortality, which was, according to Homer, drunk by the gods.

Neleus (*nē'lūs*). Son of Neptune and Tyro, and brother to Pelias. He became king in Peloponnesus; his twelve sons were all killed by Hercules.

Nemean (*nê-mē'ȧn*) **Lion.** A monstrous lion, near the forest of Nemea, which wasted the surrounding country and threatened destruction to the herds. Hercules promised to deliver the country of the monster, and Thespius rewarded Hercules by making him his guest so long as the chase lasted. Hercules slew the lion, and thereafter wore its skin as his garment and its head as his helmet.

Nemesis (*nĕm'ê-sĭs*). A Greek goddess, who measured out to mortals happiness and misery, and visited with losses and sufferings all who were blessed with too many gifts of fortune. This is the character in which she appears in the earlier Greek writers; but subsequently she was regarded, like the Erinyes or Furies, as the goddess who punished crimes.

Neoptolemus. The son of Achilles. He was reared in Scyros, in the palace of Lycomedes, and was brought thence by Ulysses, because it had been prophesied that Neoptolemus and Philoctetes were necessary for the capture of Troy. At Troy Neoptolemus showed himself worthy of his great father. He was one of the heroes concealed in the wooden horse, and at the capture of the city he killed Priam, and sacrificed Polyxena to the spirit of his father. He was also called Pyrrhus. See *Pyrrhus.*

Nepenthe (*nê-pĕn'thê*). A care-dispelling drug, which Polydamna, wife of Thonis, king of Egypt, gave to Helen. A drink containing this drug "changed grief to mirth, melancholy to joyfulness, and hatred to love." Homer mentions this drug nepenthe in his *Odyssey.*

Neptune. A Roman god of water, identified with Poseidon, the Greek god of the ocean. To him as god of the ocean, myths assign the following activities: his assistance to Jupiter against the Titans; the building of the walls and ramparts of Troy; the creation and taming of the horse; the raising of the island Delos out of the sea; and the destruction of Hippolytus by a monster sent from the deep. He was feared also as the author of earthquakes and deluges, which he caused or checked at pleasure by his trident.

Nereids (*nē'rê-ĭdz*). Sea nymphs, generally regarded as belonging to the Mediterranean. The chief characteristics of these minor deities of the sea were the power of divination and the ability to change their forms at pleasure. They were daughters of Nereus and Doris, fifty in number, and usually followed in the train of Neptune.

Nereus (*nē'rūs*). A son of Pontus and Gæa, and husband of Doris, by whom he became the father of the fifty Nereids.

Nestor. A son of Neleus and Chloris, and king of Pylos in Triphylia. He took a prominent part in the Trojan War, acting as counselor of the other Grecian chiefs, but he was equally distinguished for his valor in the field of battle. Homer extols his wisdom, justice, bravery, and eloquence. He lived to so great an age that his advice and authority were deemed equal to those of the immortal gods. Hence the name is often found in literature as an appellation denoting wisdom.

Nickar or **Hnickar.** The name assumed by Odin when he impersonated the destroying principle.

Nickneven. A gigantic and malignant female spirit of the old popular Scottish mythology. The hag is represented as riding at the head of witches and fairies at Halloween.

Niflheim (*nĕv''l-hām*). "Mist home" of old Norse mythology, the region of endless cold and everlasting night, ruled over by Hel, daughter of Loki. It consisted of nine worlds, to which were consigned those who died of disease or of old age. This region existed "from the beginning" in the North, and in the middle of it was the well Hvergelmir, from which flowed twelve rivers.

Nina. The ancient patron goddess of Nineveh. The Babylonian word sign for her name and that of the city meant "house of the fish."

Niobe (*nĭ'ô-bê*). The daughter of Tantalus and the wife of Amphion, king of Thebes. Niobe offended Latona, the mother of Apollo and Diana, by boasting that she had more children than Latona, and the latter engaged both her children to avenge her; they, by their arrows, slew the seven sons and seven daughters of Niobe, who by grief was changed into stone. She was transported in a whirlwind to the top of Mount Sipylus, where she has ever since remained, her tears flowing unceasingly.

Nisus. A Trojan youth who accompanied Æneas to Italy after the fall of Troy. He is celebrated for his devoted attachment to his friend Euryalus.

Nithhogg (*nĕrH'hŏg'*). The dragon that gnaws at the root of Yggdrasil, the tree of the universe in Scandinavian mythology.

Nix. Little creatures not unlike the Scotch brownie and German kobold. They wear a red cap, and are ever ready to lend a helping hand to the industrious and thrifty.

Nokomis (*nô-kō'mĭs*). Daughter of the moon in North American Indian myths. Sporting one day with her maidens on a swing made of vine canes, a rival cut the swing, and Nokomis fell to earth, where she gave birth to a daughter named Wenonah. Wenonah later became the mother of Hiawatha.

Norns. The three Fates of Scandinavian mythology, past, present, and future. They spin the events of human life, sitting under the ash tree Yggdrasil, which they carefully tend. Their names are Urd, "the past," Verdandi, "the present," and Skuld, "the future." Besides these three Norns, every human creature has a personal Norn or Fate. The home of the Norns is called in Scandinavian mythology, "Doomstead."

Nox. The goddess of night, considered among the ancients as one of their oldest divinities and worshiped by them with great solemnity. In the temple of Diana, at Ephesus, was a famous statue of her. She became the mother of Æther, "air," and Dies, "day." She is likewise, according to some, the mother of the inexorable Parcæ; of the avenging Nemesis, who punishes hidden crime; of the Furies, who torment the wicked; of Charon, the ferryman of hell; and of the twin brothers, Sleep and Death.

Nymphs. The nymphs of ancient fiction were viewed as holding an intermediate place between men and gods as to the length of life, not being absolutely immortal, yet living a vast length of time. Oceanus was considered as their common father, although the descent of different nymphs varies. Their usual abode was in grottoes. Special groups had their own peculiar duties, each group being distinguished by special names according to the several objects of their patronage, or the regions in which they chiefly resided. Thus, there were the Oreads, or nymphs of the mountains; Naiads, Nereids, and Potamids, nymphs of the fountains, seas, and rivers; Dryads and Hamadryads, nymphs of the woods; Napææ, nymphs of the vales.

Oceanids (*ô-sē'ȧ-nĭdz*). Daughters of Oceanus, sea nymphs said to be 3000 in number.

Oceanus. The god of the river which was thought to surround the whole earth, in early times believed flat and round. He was the son of heaven and earth, the husband of Tethys, and the father of all the river gods and water nymphs. Out of and into this river the sun and the stars were supposed to rise and set; and on its banks were the abodes of the dead.

Odhrerir. In Scandinavian mythology, the name of the cauldron containing mead or nectar made of honey mingled with the blood of Kvasir, wisest of men. This potion conferred wisdom and the poetic faculty on those who drank of it.

Odin. The king of gods and men, and the reputed progenitor of the Scandinavian kings. He corresponds both to the Jupiter and to the Mars of Græco-Roman mythology. As god of war, he held his court in Valhalla, surrounded by all warriors who had fallen in battle, and attended by two wolves, to whom he gave his share of food; for he himself lived on wine alone. On his shoulders he carried two ravens, Hugin, "mind," and Munin, "memory," whom he dispatched every day to bring him news of all that was being done throughout the world. He had three great treasures:

Sleipnir, an eight-footed horse of marvelous swiftness; Gungnir, a spear, which never failed to strike what it was aimed at; and Draupnir, a magic ring, which every ninth night dropped eight other rings of equal value. The German tribes worshiped Odin under the name of "Woden."

Odur. In Scandinavian mythology, husband of Freya, whom he deserted. After a long search she found him again and was restored to happiness by his love.

Odysseus (*ô-dĭs'ūs*). Greek form of the name Ulysses.

Œdipus (*ĕd'ĭ-pŭs*). The son of Laius, king of Thebes. Laius, having been warned by an oracle that his throne and life were in danger from this son, gave him immediately after birth to a herdsman to be killed. But the child was saved, and reared by a peasant. Having grown up he ransomed Thebes from the sphinx by answering her riddle, unwittingly killed his own father, and, on becoming king of Thebes, married his father's wife, that is, his own mother, Jocasta. Subsequently discovering his parentage, he destroyed his eyesight and wandered away from Thebes, attended by his daughter Antigone, who remained with him till his death.

Ogre (*ô'gẽr*). In nursery mythology, a giant of very malignant disposition, who lives on human flesh.

Old One. Among the Thompson River Indians, the god who created the earth and taught the people how to hunt and fish and to do all the other things needful for living.

Olympus. A range of mountains in Thessaly, the abode of the gods. A gate of clouds, kept by the goddesses named the Seasons, unfolded to permit the passage of the deities to earth, or to receive them on their return.

Ops. A Roman goddess of plenty, and of fertility, the wife of Saturn, and the patroness of husbandry.

Orestes (*ô-rĕs'tēz*). The son of Agamemnon and Clytemnestra. On the murder of his father by Ægisthus and Clytemnestra, Orestes was saved from the same fate by his sister Electra. She caused him to be secretly carried to Strophius, king of Phocis, who was married to Anaxibia, the sister of Agamemnon. There he formed a close and intimate friendship with the king's son Pylades; and, when he had grown up, he repaired secretly to Argos with his friend, and avenged his father's death by slaying Clytemnestra and Ægisthus. After the murder of his mother he was seized with madness, and fled from land to land, pursued by the Erinyes, or Furies. At length, on the advice of Apollo, he took refuge in the temple of Athena at Athens, where he was acquitted by the court of the Areopagus, which the goddess had appointed to decide his fate.

Orion. A mighty giant and hunter, famous for his beauty. Having come to Chios, he fell in love with Merope, the daughter of Œnopion; his treatment of the maiden so exasperated her father, that, with the assistance of Dionysus, he deprived the giant of his sight. Being informed by an oracle that he should recover his sight if he exposed his eyeballs to the rays of the rising sun, he followed the sound of a Cyclops's hammer, and at Lemnos he found Vulcan, who gave him Cedalion as a guide to the abode of the sun. After the recovery of his sight he lived as a hunter with Artemis, or Diana. Orion was slain by Diana, or, as some say, by Jupiter, and placed among the stars.

Orithyia. A daughter of Erechtheus, beloved by Boreas, who carried her off as she was wandering near the river Ilissus.

Orlog. A god of Norse fable personifying the eternal law of the universe. From his decree there was no appeal.

Ormuzd (*ôr'mŭzd*). In the *Avesta*, called Ahura Mazda (*ä'hōō-rä-mäz'dä*). The name of the supreme deity of the ancient Persians, and of their descendants, the Parsees and Ghebers. He is, according to them, an embodiment of the principle of good, and is in perpetual conflict with Ahriman, the principle of evil. He created the earth, moon, sun, and stars, and continues to regulate their motion. See *Ahriman.*

Orpheus (*ôr'fūs*). The son of Apollo or of Œagrus, a river god, and of Calliope. Presented with the lyre by Apollo, and instructed by the Muses in its use, he enchanted with its music not only the wild beasts, but the trees and rocks upon Olympus, so that they moved from their places to follow the sound of his golden harp. He accompanied the Argonauts in their expedition. After his return, he took up his abode in Thrace, where he married the nymph Eurydice. His wife having died of the bite of a serpent, he followed her into the abodes of Hades. Here his lyre so charmed King Pluto that Eurydice was released from death, but on the condition that Orpheus should not look back until he had reached the earth. He was just about to place his foot on the earth when he turned round, and Eurydice vanished from him in an instant.

Osiris (*ô-sĭ'rĭs*). An Egyptian god, said to have been the son of Jupiter by Niobe, to have ruled first over the Argives, and afterwards to have become king of the Egyptians. His wife was Isis, who is by many said to be the same as Io, daughter of Inachus. Osiris was at length slain by Typhon, and his corpse was concealed in a chest and thrown into the Nile. Isis, after much search, by the aid of keen-scented dogs, found the body and placed it in a monument on an island near Memphis. The Egyptians paid divine honor to his memory, and chose the ox to represent him, because, according to one account, a large ox appeared to them after the body of Osiris was interred, or, according to others, because Osiris had instructed them in agriculture. Osiris was generally represented with a cap on his head like a miter, and with two horns; he held a stick in his left hand, and in his right a whip with three thongs. Sometimes he appears with the head of a hawk.

Ostara or **Eástre.** Saxon goddess of spring and returning life. At her festival it was customary to exchange gifts of painted eggs. Christianity adopted the festival as Easter and gave it a new meaning.

Otus. One of the two giants who were usually called the Aloadæ. The other was Ephialtes. The two were renowned for their extraordinary strength and courage.

Pachacamac. The name of an ancient Peruvian god of earthquakes, which were regarded as his voice. The meaning of this name is "earth-generator." He was worshiped as a god of fertility also, and as a civilizer.

Pactolus. The river whose sands turned to gold when Midas by order of Bacchus washed in the waters.

Paimosaid. In certain North American Indian myths, a wandering thief who walks through cornfields about harvest time to pluck the ears of corn.

Palæmon. Son of Ino, originally called Melicertes, until he was made a sea god. The Roman god of harbors, Portunus, was identified with him.

Palamedes (*păl'ȧ-mē'dēz*). A Greek hero sent by the Greek princes to induce Ulysses to join in the Trojan War, when Ulysses sought to avoid going by pretending insanity. Palamedes soon penetrated the deception, and Ulysses was obliged to join in the war.

Pales (*pā'lēz*). The goddess of shepherds, presiding over cattle and pastures, whose festival, the Palilia, was celebrated on the 21st of April, the anniversary of the day on which Rome was founded. The Palatine hill at Rome was sacred to her. Later the Roman emperors built on it their residence, called the Palatium, from which comes our word palace.

Palladium (*pă-lā'dĭ-ŭm*). A Trojan statue of the goddess Pallas Athena, which represented her as sitting with a spear in her right hand, and in her left a spindle or distaff. It is said to have fallen from heaven near the tent of Ilus at the time when that prince was employed in building the citadel of Troy; and Apollo, by an oracle, declared that the city should never be taken as long as the Palladium was contained within its walls. Ulysses and Diomedes captured the statue for the Greeks and not long afterwards the city was taken.

Pallas. (1) One of the giants. (2) The father of Athena, according to some traditions. (3) Son of Lycaon and grandfather of Evander. (4) Son of Evander and an ally of Æneas.

Pallas Athena (*păl'ȧs ȧ-thē'nȧ*). See *Athena.*

Pan. The god of shepherds and herdsmen, of groves and fields, and of rural life generally. He was said to be the son of Mercury and Dryope. His favorite residence was in the woods and mountains of Arcadia, where he was frequently heard playing on his pipe or flute of seven reeds, called a syrinx. It was fabled that this pipe was a metamorphosis of a nymph named Syrinx, whom he had loved. His pride in this invention led him into an unlucky contest with Apollo. His festivals were introduced by Evander among the Romans, and by them called Lupercalia. Goats, honey, and milk were the usual offerings to Pan. Pan, like other gods who dwelt in forests, was dreaded by travelers, to whom he sometimes appeared, and whom he startled by his uncanny presence. Hence sudden fright, without any visible cause, was ascribed to Pan and was called a panic. See *Mendes.*

Pandora. The first woman, according to Greek mythology. She was made of clay by Vulcan, and all the gods made presents to her. Venus gave her beauty and the art of pleasing; the Graces gave her the power of captivating; Apollo taught her how to sing; Mercury instructed her in eloquence and brought her to Epimetheus, who made her his wife, forgetting the advice of his brother Prometheus, not to receive gifts that came from Jupiter. In her home she found a box which she was forbidden to open. Disobeying the injunction she allowed to escape from it all the evils of life except hope. According to another version, all the blessings of life escaped from it except hope, which remained to solace mortals.

Parcæ (*pär'sē*). See *Fates.*

Paris. The son of Priam, king of Troy, and of Hecuba; he was also called Alexander. The tradition is that, at the marriage of Peleus and Thetis, the goddess of discord, who had not been invited, showed her displeasure by throwing into the assembly of the gods, who were at the nuptials, a golden apple on which were the words "For the fairest." The apple was claimed by Hera, Aphrodite, and Athena. Zeus ordered Hermes to take the goddesses to Mount Ida, and to intrust the decision of the dispute to the Trojan shepherd Paris. The goddesses accordingly appeared before him. Hera promised him the sovereignty of Asia; Athena, renown in war; and Aphrodite, the fairest of women for his wife. Paris decided in favor of Aphrodite, and gave her the golden apple. Under her protection, Paris sailed to Greece, and was hospitably received in the palace of Menelaus at Sparta. Here he succeeded in carrying off to Troy Helen, the wife of Menelaus, who was the most beautiful woman in the world. Menelaus enlisted the support of many other Greek chieftains and proceeded to besiege Troy. Paris fought with Menelaus before the walls of Troy, and, though defeated, was carried off by Aphrodite. He slew Achilles by wounding him in his heel, where alone he was vulnerable, while Achilles was engaged in a peaceful mission in Troy.

Parnassus. A well-wooded mountain ridge near Delphi in Greece. At its foot grew myrtle, laurel, and olive trees, and, higher up, firs; its summit was covered with snow during the greater part of the year. It contained numerous caves, glens, and romantic ravines and had two summits, one of which was consecrated to Apollo and the Muses, the other to Bacchus. It was anciently called Larnassus, from *larnax*, "an ark," because Deucalion's ark was stranded there after the flood. After the oracle of Delphi was built at its foot it received the name of Parnassus and was celebrated as one of the chief seats of Apollo and the Muses.

Parthenope (*pär-thĕn'ô-pē*). One of the sirens, who threw herself into the sea out of love for Ulysses, and whose dead body was washed ashore on the present site of Naples. Naples itself was anciently called Parthenope, which name was changed to *Neapolis*, "the new city," by a colony of Cumæans.

Pasiphaë. The wife of Minos, king of Crete, and, by a bull, the mother of the Minotaur, to which human captives were given as food.

Patroclus (*pȧ-trō'klŭs*). The gentle and amiable friend of Achilles in Homer's *Iliad.*

Pauguk. Name given to the great power, death, in the mythology of certain North American Indians.

Paupukkeewis (*pô'pŭk-kē'wĭs*). In North American Indian folklore, a mischievous magician, who, pursued by Hiawatha, went through a series of wonderful transformations in his endeavors to escape, and finally became an eagle.

Pax. The goddess of peace, worshiped in Greece under the name Irene. Pax wore a crown of laurel and held in her hand the branch of an olive tree.

Peboan. In North American Indian folklore, the personification of winter in the form of a great giant who shook the snow from his hair and turned water into stone by his breath.

Pegasus (*pĕg'ȧ-sŭs*). The winged horse which sprang from the blood of Medusa when her head was struck off by Perseus.

Peleus (*pē'lūs*). King of the Myrmidons at Phthia in Thessaly. Having, in conjunction with his brother Telamon, murdered his half brother Phocus, he was expelled by Æacus from Ægina, and went to Thessaly. He was purified from the murder by Eurytion, who then gave Peleus his daughter Antigone in marriage, and a third part of his kingdom.

Pelion (*pē'lĭ-ŏn*). A high mountain in Thessaly near whose summit was the cave of the centaur Chiron. The giants, in their war with the gods, are said to have attempted to heap Pelion and Ossa on Olympus, in order to scale heaven.

Pelops (*pē'lŏps*). A Phrygian prince, grandson of Jupiter and son of Tantalus. Expelled from Phrygia, he came to Elis, where he married Hippodamia, daughter of Œnomaus, whom he succeeded on the throne. By means of the wealth he brought with him, his influence became so great in the peninsula that it was called after him the Peloponnese, "the island of Pelops."

Penates (*pê-nā'tēz*). Roman gods who were supposed to preside over the welfare and prosperity of the family. The storehouse, or *penus*, was sacred to them.

Penelope (*pê-nĕl'ô-pē*). The faithful wife of Ulysses, who, being importuned during his long absence by numerous

Mythology

suitors for her hand, postponed making a decision among them until she should have finished weaving a funeral pall for her father-in-law, Laertes. Every night she secretly unraveled what she had woven by day, and thus put off the suitors till Ulysses returned.

Peri (pĕ'rĭ). In Persian mythology, delicate, gentle, fairylike beings, begotten by fallen spirits. They direct with a wand the pure in mind along the way to heaven. These lovely creatures, according to the *Koran*, are under the sovereignty of Eblis; and Mohammed was sent for their conversion, as well as for that of man.

Perse. A daughter of Oceanus, and wife of Helios (the sun), by whom she became the mother of Æetes, Circe-Pasiphaë, and Perses.

Persephone (pĕr-sĕf'ô-nê). The Greek name of Proserpina. Homer describes her as the wife of Hades, or Pluto, and the formidable and majestic queen of the shades, who with her husband, rules over the souls of the dead.

Perseus (pûr'sūs). One of the most distinguished of the early heroes. He was the son of Jupiter and Danaë, and was educated by Polydectes on the island of Seriphus. His chief exploit was the destruction of the Gorgon Medusa, whose head he struck off with a sword given to him by Vulcan. From the blood that fell, sprang the winged horse Pegasus, on which Perseus afterwards passed over many lands. Of his subsequent achievements, the most remarkable were his changing King Atlas into a high rock or mountain by means of Medusa's head, and his deliverance of Andromeda when she was bound and exposed to be devoured by a sea monster.

Phædra (fē'drà). Daughter of Minos, and wife of Theseus, who, finding her love rejected by her stepson Hippolytus, falsely accused him of making improper advances toward her, and so induced her husband to bring about his son's death.

Phaëthon. A son of Phœbus and Clymene. Anxious to display his skill in horsemanship, he was so presumptuous as to request his father to allow him to drive the chariot of the sun across the heavens for one day. Helios was induced by the entreaties of his son and of Clymene to yield, but the youth, being too weak to check the horses, permitted them to go too close to the earth, thereby scorching it. To save mankind Zeus killed Phaëthon with a thunderbolt, and hurled him down into the river Eridanus. His sisters wept for him until they were metamorphosed into poplars, and their tears became amber.

Phaon. A boatman of Mytilene, ugly in appearance, who once carried Aphrodite across the sea without accepting payment. In return the goddess gave him a box of ointment with which, when he anointed himself, he grew so beautiful that Sappho became enamored of him; but when the ointment had all been used Phaon returned to his former condition, and Sappho, in despair, drowned herself.

Philemon and Baucis (fĭ-lē'mŏn) (bô'sĭs). An aged couple, who alone in Phrygia honored two travelers with hospitality. The travelers proved to be Jupiter and Mercury in disguise and in acknowledgment of the kindness they had received, they changed into a temple the house of Philemon and Baucis. The two old people were granted the privilege of caring for the temple and of leaving life together. One day, as they stood before the door, they were suddenly transformed into trees, an oak and a linden, which stood side by side.

Philoctetes (fĭl'ŏk-tē'tēz). The most celebrated archer in the Trojan War. He was the friend and armor-bearer of Hercules, who bequeathed to him his bow and his poisoned arrows in return for setting fire to the pile on Mount Œta on which Hercules perished.

Philomela (fĭl'ô-mē'là). A daughter of Pandion, king of Athens. Her sister Procne had married Tereus, king of Thrace. Becoming tired of her after she had given birth to a son, Itylus, he cut out her tongue and told that she had died. Philomela became his next wife, and, learning the truth from her sister, served up, with her sister's help, the cooked flesh of Itylus for Tereus to eat. The gods in anger turned Philomela into a nightingale, Procne into a swallow, and Tereus into a hawk.

Phœbe. The goddess of the moon, and sister of Phœbus; a name of Diana.

Phœbus. See *Apollo*.

Phœnix. (1) A fabulous bird described as being as large as an eagle. Its head was finely crested with a beautiful plumage, its neck covered with gold-colored feathers, its tail white, and its body purple or crimson. It was said to appear once every 500 years, each bird rising from the ashes of its sire, who voluntarily cremated himself. (2) Father of Europa and reputed ancestor of the Phœnicians.

Phyllis. A daughter of King Sithon of Thrace. She hanged herself, thinking that she was deserted by her lover, Demophon, who had failed to appear on the day appointed for their marriage. She was changed by the gods into an almond tree.

Pirene (pī-rē'nê). A celebrated fountain of Corinth, at which Bellerophon is said to have caught the horse Pegasus. It gushed forth from the rock in the Acrocorinthus, was conveyed down the hill by subterraneous conduits, and fell into a marble basin, from which the greater part of the town was supplied with water.

Pleiades (plē'yà-dēz). The seven daughters of Atlas and Pleione, named Electra, Alcyone, Celæno, Maia, Sterope, Taygeta, and Merope. They were transformed into stars, one of which, Merope, is invisible out of shame, because she alone married a human being. Some call the invisible star "Electra," and say she hides herself from grief for the destruction of the city and royal race of Troy. The name means "sailing stars," because navigation was considered safe after their appearance.

Pluto (plōō'tō). A brother of Jupiter and Neptune. He received, as his portion in the division of empire, the infernal regions. His wife was Persephone, or, as the Romans called her, Proserpina, the daughter of Demeter, whom he carried by force from the upper world and made queen of the lower regions. The nymph Mintho, whom he loved, was metamorphosed by Proserpina into the plant called mint; and the nymph Leuce was changed by him after her death into a white poplar. The ensign of his power was a staff, with which, like Hermes, he drove the shades into the lower world. He possessed a helmet which rendered the wearer invisible, and which he sometimes lent to men or to other gods. The Furies were said to be his daughters. Being the king of the lower world, Pluto was regarded as giver of the blessings that come from the earth, such as the metals.

Plutus. The god of riches, and son of Iasion and Demeter. Jupiter blinded him so that he would bestow his gifts irrespective of merit.

Pluvius. A surname of Jupiter among the Romans meaning, "the sender of rain." Sacrifices were offered to him in this capacity during long-protracted droughts.

Podalirius. The son of Æsculapius, and brother of Machaon, with whom he led the Thessalians of Tricca against Troy. He was, like his brother, skilled in the medical art.

Polias. A cult name of Athena at Athens meaning "protectress of the city."

Pollux. A son of Jupiter and Leda, and brother to Castor.

Polydorus. (1) King of Thebes, son of Cadmus and Harmonia, husband of Nycteus, and father of Labdacus. (2) Son of Priam and Hecuba. When Ilium was on the point of falling into the hands of the Greeks, Priam intrusted Polydorus and a large sum of money to Polymnestor, king of the Thracian Chersonesus.

Polyhymnia (pŏl'ĭ-hĭm'nĭ-à). See *Muses*.

Polyphemus. A son of Neptune, and one of the Cyclopes who dwelt in Sicily. He was a cruel monster of immense size and strength, and had but one eye, which was in the middle of his forehead. He dwelt in a cave near Mount Etna, and fed his flocks upon the mountain. He fell in love with the nymph Galatea, but, as she rejected him for Acis, he destroyed the latter by crushing him under a huge rock. When Ulysses landed in Sicily, he, with twelve of his companions, was caught in the cave of Polyphemus, and six of the number were eaten by the terrible cannibal. The rest were in expectation of the same fate, but their cunning leader enabled them to escape by contriving to intoxicate Polyphemus, and then destroying his single eye with a firebrand.

Polyxena (pô-lĭk'sê-nà). The daughter of Priam and Hecuba, beloved by Achilles. She was sacrificed by the Greeks on Achilles' tomb.

Pomona. A nymph at Rome, who presided over gardens and fruit trees.

Ponemah. In North American Indian mythology, the name of the spirit land, to which the souls of the dead go.

Poseidon (pô-sī'dŏn). The Greek god of the sea, identified by the Romans with Neptune. He was a brother of Jupiter and Pluto. The palace of Poseidon was in the depth of the sea near Ægæ, where he kept his brazen-hoofed and golden-maned horses. With these horses he used to ride in a chariot over the waves, which became smooth as he approached, while the monsters of the deep played around his chariot. Poseidon, in conjunction with Apollo, is said to have built the walls of Troy for Laomedon.

Priam. King of Troy when that city was sacked by the allied Greeks. His wife's name was Hecuba; she was the mother of nineteen children, the eldest of whom was

Hector. When the Greeks landed on the Trojan coast, Priam was advanced in years and took no active part in the war. Once only did he venture upon the field of battle, to conclude the agreement respecting the single combat between Paris and Menelaus. After the death of Hector, Priam went to the tent of Achilles to ransom his son's body for burial, and obtained it. When the gates of Troy were thrown open by the Greeks concealed in the wooden horse, and the hostile army without was admitted, the aged Priam was slain by Pyrrhus, the son of Achilles.

Priapus. An Italian god of gardens. Images of him were often placed in vineyards or before houses to frighten away thieves.

Procne. See *Philomela*.

Prœtus (*prē′tŭs*). Twin brother of Acrisius and son of Abas. In the dispute between the two brothers for the kingdom of Argos, Prœtus was expelled. He fled to Iobates in Lycia, and married Antea, the daughter of the latter. With the assistance of Iobates, Prœtus returned to his native land, and Acrisius gave him a share of his kingdom, surrendering to him Tiryns, Midea, and the coast of Argolis.

Prometheus (*prô-mē′thŭs*). A son of Iapetus and Clymene, the brother of Epimetheus, and the father of Deucalion. He made men of clay, and animated them by means of fire which he stole from heaven; for this he was chained by Jupiter to Mount Caucasus, where an eagle, or, as some say, a vulture, preyed by day upon his liver, which grew again by night. His name means forethought, and that of his brother, afterthought.

Proserpina (*prô-sûr′pĭ-nà*). See *Persephone*.

Psyche (*si′kē*). Psyche was the youngest of the three daughters of a king, and excited by her beauty the jealousy and envy of Venus. To avenge herself, Venus ordered Cupid to inspire Psyche with a love for the most contemptible of all men; but Cupid was so stricken with her beauty that he himself fell in love with her. He conveyed her to a charming spot, where unseen and unknown he visited her every night, and left her as soon as the day began to dawn. But her jealous sisters made her believe that in the darkness of night she was embracing some hideous monster, and, accordingly, once, while Cupid was asleep, she drew near to him with a lamp, and, to her amazement, beheld the most handsome and the most lovely of the gods. In the excitement she let fall a drop of hot oil from her lamp upon his shoulder. This awoke Cupid, who censured her for her mistrust and fled. Psyche's happiness was now gone, and, after attempting in vain to throw herself into a river, she wandered about from temple to temple, inquiring after her lover, and at length came to the palace of Venus. There her real sufferings began, for Venus retained her, treated her as a slave, and imposed upon her the hardest and most humiliating labors. Psyche would have perished under the weight of her sufferings had not Cupid, who still loved her in secret, invisibly comforted and assisted her in her toils. With his aid she at last succeeded in overcoming the jealousy and hatred of Venus; she became immortal and was united to him forever. In works of art Psyche is represented as a maiden with the wings of a butterfly. Her name is the Greek word for soul and representations of her frequently have an allegorical meaning based on this fact.

Pukwana. The smoke from the Calumet, or peace pipe, among certain North American Indians. The pipe was made from stone found near the headwaters of the Mississippi at a spot which the Indians agreed to make neutral ground. To apply the stone to any other use than that of pipe making would have been sacrilege in their eyes. From its color, they fancied it to have been made at the great deluge out of the flesh of the perishing Indians.

Pukwudjies. The pygmies of North American Indian folklore, who haunted the woods.

Pygmalion. A grandson of Agenor. He made a beautiful statue with which he fell so deeply in love that Venus, at his earnest petition, gave it life.

Pylades (*pĭl′à-dēz*). Son of Anaxibia, sister of Agamemnon. His father was king of Phocis, to whose court, after the death of Agamemnon, Orestes was secretly carried. Here Pylades contracted that friendship with Orestes which became proverbial.

Pyramus (*pĭr′à-mŭs*). The lover of Thisbe, who stabbed himself on account of her supposed death. Thisbe, afterwards, finding the body of her lover under the mulberry tree where he fell, killed herself on the same spot with the same weapon; and the fruit of the mulberry has ever since been as red as blood.

Pyrrhus. A son of Achilles, remarkable for his bravery at the siege of Troy. He was known also as Neoptolemus. He was slain at Delphi, at the request of his own wife, Hermione, who later married his slayer, Orestes.

Pythia (*pĭth′ĭ-à*). The priestess of Apollo at Delphi. Crowned with laurels she was seated on a tripod and placed over a chasm whence arose a peculiar vapor. As she inhaled the intoxicating fumes, she was thrown into convulsive ravings, which were thought to be an evidence of divine inspiration and were interpreted by priests and conveyed as intelligible, but usually ambiguous, messages to those who came to consult the oracle.

Python (*pi′thŏn*). The monster serpent hatched from the mud of the deluge. He lived in the caves of Mount Parnassus, but was slain by Apollo, who founded the Pythian games in commemoration of his victory and received in consequence the surname Pythius.

Ra (*rä*). Egyptian sun god and principal deity of historical Egypt, from whom most of the Pharaohs claimed descent.

Radegaste. In Slavonic mythology, a tutelary god of the Slavs. His head was that of a cow, his breast was covered with a shield, his left hand held a spear, and a cock surmounted his helmet.

Ragnarok (*räg′nä-rŏk′*). "Twilight of the Gods." The day of doom, when the present world and all its inhabitants will, according to Scandinavian mythology, be annihilated. Vitharr and Vali will survive the conflagration, and reconstruct the universe. After this time the earth or realm will become imperishable and happiness sure.

Rahu (*rä′hōō*). In Hindu mythology, the demon that causes eclipses of the sun and of the moon. One day Rahu stole into heaven to quaff some of the nectar of immortality. He was discovered by the sun and the moon, who informed against him, and Vishnu cut off his head. As he had already taken some of the nectar into his mouth, the head was immortal, and he ever afterwards hunted the sun and the moon, which he caught occasionally, causing eclipses.

Rakshasas (*rŭk′shä-säz*). Evil spirits, in Hindu myths, who guard the treasures of Kubera, the god of riches. They haunt cemeteries and devour human corpses, they assume any shape at will, and their strength increases as the day declines. Some are hideously ugly, but others, especially the female spirits, allure by their beauty.

Rama Chandra. The seventh incarnation of Vishnu in Hindu mythology. He is the hero of the *Ramayana*. Rama probably represents the sun, as Sita, his wife, represents the earth, or "the furrow."

Rambha. In Hindu mythology, a nymph born of the churning of the ocean. She is a type of female beauty.

Ravana (*rä′vä-nä*). According to Hindu mythology, a demon giant with ten faces, who was fastened down between heaven and earth for 10,000 years by Siva's leg for attempting to move the hill of heaven to Ceylon.

Rhadamanthus (*răd′à-măn′thŭs*). A son of Jupiter and Europa, brother of Minos, and king of Lycia. He was so renowned for his justice and equity, that, after death, he was made one of the three judges in the underworld.

Rhamnusia. A daughter of Nox, and otherwise known as Nemesis.

Rhea. The wife of Cronus and the mother of the gods.

Romulus (*rŏm′ŭ-lŭs*). The mythical founder of the city of Rome.

Saturn. An ancient Italian deity, identified with the Greek Cronus. His wife was Ops. He was the god of seedtime and harvest and was represented as bearing a sickle or scythe. As he was later confused with the Greek *chronos* "time," Father Time is still represented with a scythe. Before becoming a god he is said to have ruled in Italy during the golden age.

Satyr (*săt′ẽr*). A sylvan deity, or demigod, represented as a monster, half man and half goat; having horns on his head, a hairy body, and the feet and tail of a goat. The satyrs belong to the train of Bacchus, and are distinguished for lasciviousness and riotousness. Although mortal, they are superior to the cares and sorrows of mortal life.

Scylla (*sĭl′à*). A maiden whose body Circe, in a fit of jealousy, transformed so that the heads of hideous barking dogs grew about her haunches. She later inhabited the rock opposite the whirlpool Charybdis and lay in wait to snatch sailors from ships which came too near her haunt.

Sedrat (*sĕd′răt*). The lotus tree which stands on the right-hand side of the invisible throne of Allah. Its branches extend wider than the distance between heaven and earth. Its leaves resemble the ears of an elephant. Each seed of its fruit encloses a houri, and two rivers issue from its roots. Numberless birds sing among its branches, and numberless angels rest beneath its shade.

Silenus (*sĭ-lē′nŭs*). The older satyrs were generally termed sileni; but the one who always accompanied Dionysus and who brought up and instructed him is commonly known as the Silenus. He is represented as a jovial old man, with a bald head, pug nose, and rubicund visage, and generally as intoxicated, riding on an ass or supported by satyrs. He was fond of music and dancing. It is a peculiar feature in his character that he was an inspired prophet, yet, when he was drunk and asleep he was in the power of mortals, who might compel him to prophesy and sing by surrounding him with chains of flowers.

Silvanus or **Sylvanus** (*sĭl-vā'nŭs*). An Italian deity presiding over woods, forests, and fields.

Sirens. Sea goddesses, said by some to be two in number, by others, three, and even four. Homer mentions but two, and describes them as maidens, dwelling upon an island and detaining with them every voyager who was allured thither by their captivating music. They would have decoyed even Ulysses on his return to Ithaca, had he not commanded his sailors to tie him to the mast and fill their own ears with wax. By others they were described as daughters of the river god Achelous, and companions of Proserpina, after whose seizure they were changed into birds, that they might fly in search of her. In an unhappy contest with the Muses in singing, they lost their wings as a punishment. Others make them sea nymphs, with a form similar to that of the Tritons, with the faces of women and the bodies of flying fish. Their fabled abode was placed by some on an island near Cape Pelorus in Sicily, by others, on the islands or rocks called Sirennusæ, not far from the promontory of Surrentum on the coast of Italy.

Sirius. Known in mythology as the faithful dog of Orion, and set in the heavens as a bright star by Diana when she mourned the display of her archery which caused Orion's death. See *Orion*.

Siva. The third of the great triad of Hindu deities, regarded as the destroyer. See *Vishnu*.

Sol (*sŏl*). Although the Greeks and Romans worshiped Apollo as the god and dispenser of light, and in view of this attribute named him Phœbus, yet they conceived another divinity distinguished from Apollo, especially in the earlier fables, under the literal name applied to designate the sun, viz., Sol, or Helios.

Specter of the Brocken. Among German myths, a singular colossal apparition seen in the clouds at certain times of the day by those who ascend the Brocken, or Blocksberg, the highest of the Harz mountains.

Sphinx. A monster said to be a daughter of Chimæra, and living in the neighborhood of Thebes. Seated on a rock, she put a riddle to every Theban that passed by, and whoever was unable to solve it was killed by the monster. This calamity induced the Thebans to proclaim that whoever should deliver the country of the sphinx should obtain the kingdom and marry the recently widowed Theban queen, Jocasta. The riddle ran as follows: "What is that which has one voice, and at first four feet, then two feet, and at last three feet, and when it has most is weakest?" Œdipus explained the enigma by saying that it was man, who, when an infant, creeps on all fours, when a man, goes on two feet, and, when old, uses a staff, a third foot. The monster immediately flung herself into the sea and perished. The form of the so-called Egyptian sphinxes is that of a winged lion with a human head and bust, always in a lying attitude, whereas the Greek sphinxes are represented in any attitude which might suit the fancy of the artist.

Styx. One of four rivers of the lower world, often called the river of hate, because its name comes from a Greek word meaning "to hate." It was said to flow nine times round the infernal regions. The second river was Acheron, river of woe. The third river, Cocytus, flowed out of the river Styx, and the murmur of its waters, the sound of which resembled howlings, was inexpressibly dismal; Phlegethon, the fourth river, rolls slowly along with waves of fire. As a mythical being, Styx is described as a daughter of Oceanus and Tethys. As a nymph, she dwelt at the entrance of Hades in a lofty grotto which was supported by silver columns. She was the divinity by whom the gods took oath. On such an occasion Iris fetched a cup full of water from the river Styx, and the god confirmed his oath by drinking the draught.

Tantalus. The son of Jupiter and king of Lydia, who, according to some legends, was punished for betraying the secrets of his father. He was placed in a lake whose waters fled from him when he sought to quench his thirst, and amid trees laden with fruit whose boughs avoided every effort he made to seize them. Another version represents him as in dread of a rock hanging over his head and always about to fall.

Tartarus. A dark abyss under the earth in which the Titans were chained when their father feared their strength. The music of Orpheus at one time penetrated its depths and caused the condemned to cease their toil. The name has come to signify the lower regions generally.

Telamon. A son of Æacus and Endeis, and brother of Peleus. Having assisted Peleus in slaying their half brother Phocus, Telamon was expelled from Ægina, and came to Salamis, where he was made king. He afterward became the father of Atlas. Telamon himself was one of the Calydonian hunters and one of the Argonauts. He was also a great friend of Hercules, whom he joined in an expedition against Laomedon of Troy, which city he was the first to enter. Hercules, in return, gave to him Hesione, a daughter of Laomedon.

Telemachus (*tê-lĕm'à-kŭs*). The son of Ulysses and Penelope. He was an infant when his father went to Troy; when Ulysses had been absent nearly twenty years, Telemachus went to Pylos and Sparta to gather information concerning him. He was hospitably received by Nestor, who sent his own son to conduct Telemachus to Menelaus at Sparta. Menelaus also received him kindly, and communicated to him the prophecy of Proteus concerning Ulysses. From Sparta Telemachus returned home; on his arrival there he found his father, whom he assisted in slaying the suitors. See *Penelope*.

Terpsichore (*têrp-sĭk'ô-rē*). The muse of dancing and of lyric poetry. The name means "delighting in the dance."

Themis. The goddess of justice and one of the daughters of Uranus and Gæa. To her is ascribed the first uttering of oracles, and also the introduction of sacrifices.

Thersites (*thĕr-sī'tēz*). The ugliest and most scurrilous of the Greeks before Troy. He spared, in his revilings, neither prince nor chief, but directed his abuse principally against Achilles and Ulysses. He was slain by Achilles for deriding his grief for Penthesilea. The name is often used to denote a calumniator.

Theseus (*thē'sūs*). An early heroic king of Athens. Of the many adventures of Theseus, one of the most celebrated was his expedition against the Amazons. He is said to have assailed them before they had recovered from the attack of Hercules, and to have carried off their queen, Antiope. The Amazons, in their turn, invaded Attica, and the final battle, in which Theseus overcame them, was fought in the very midst of the city.

Thespian Maids, The. The nine Muses. So called from Thespia, in Bœotia, near Mount Helicon.

Thetis (*thē'tĭs*). A marine divinity, who, like her sisters, the Nereids, dwelt in the depths of the sea with her father Nereus. She there received Dionysus on his flight from Lycurgus, and the god in his gratitude presented her with a golden urn. When Vulcan was thrown down from heaven, he was likewise received by Thetis. Thetis rejected the advances of Zeus, because she had been brought up by Hera, and the god, to avenge himself, decreed that she should marry a mortal. She became the wife of Peleus and the mother of Achilles.

Thisbe. See *Pyramus*.

Thor. In Scandinavian mythology, the eldest son of Odin and Frigga. The strongest and bravest of the gods, he launched the thunder, presided over the air and the seasons, and protected man from lightning and evil spirits. His wife was Sif, "love"; his chariot was drawn by two he-goats; he had a hammer, called *Mjöllnir*, and a belt, *Megingiard*, the wearing of which doubled his strength. His palace, called *Thrudvangr*, contained 540 halls. Thursday is Thor's day.

Thunder Bird. A culture god of the North American Indians, represented as a helper of man, and the personification of thunder and lightning.

Titans. Members of the early régime of Greek gods ruled over by Cronus, who with his adherents was overthrown by Zeus, one of his sons.

Tithonus. A son of Laomedon, king of Troy. He was so beautiful that Aurora became enamored of him, and persuaded the gods to make him immortal; but, as she forgot to ask for eternal youth, he became decrepit and ugly, and was, therefore, changed by her into a cicada.

Tityus (*tĭt'ĭ-ŭs*). A giant, son of Jupiter and Terra. His body was so vast that it covered nine acres of ground. He had dared to offer an insult to Juno and in punishment was chained like Prometheus while a vulture feasted on his liver.

Triton. Son of Neptune, who dwelt with his father and mother in a golden palace at the bottom of the sea. Later writers describe him as riding over the sea on sea horses or other monsters. By a blast on his horn of seashell he roused or calmed the waves.

Trolls (*trōlz*). Dwarfs of Scandinavian mythology, living in hills or mounds; they are represented as stumpy, misshapen, and humpbacked, inclined to thieving, and fond of carrying off children or substituting their own offspring for children of a human mother. They are called hill people, and are especially averse to noise, from a recollection of the time when Thor used to fling his hammer after them.

Troy. The city on the west coast of Asia Minor made famous by the Trojan War. It was ruled by Priam at the time of the war, and its chief defender was Hector. The attacking Greeks were led by Agamemnon and Menelaus, supported by many heroes, the most famous of whom was Achilles. The city fell after a ten-year siege. Among the inhabitants who escaped was Æneas. After wandering for some years, he settled in Italy and, according to legend, became the founder of the Roman race.

Tyr. In Norse mythology, a warrior deity and the protector of champions and brave men. When the gods wished to bind the wolf Fenris, Tyr put his hand into the demon's mouth as a pledge that the bonds would be removed. But Fenris found that the gods had no intention of keeping their word, and revenged himself in some degree by biting off the hand. Tyr was the son of Odin and brother of Thor.

Ulysses. Called "Odysseus" by the Greeks. One of the principal Greek heroes in the Trojan War, a son of Laertes, or, according to a later tradition, of Sisyphus. He married Penelope, the daughter of Icarius, by whom he became the father of Telemachus. During the siege of Troy he distinguished himself by his valor, prudence, and eloquence, and after the death of Achilles contended for that hero's armor with Telamonian Ajax and gained the prize. He is said by some to have devised the stratagem of the wooden horse. The most celebrated part of his story comes in connection with his ten-year voyage home after the Trojan War. Among his adventures he entered the cave of Polyphemus and escaped with some sheep. One of the gods gave him a bag of winds which should carry him home, but the winds were let loose without his permission and his ships driven to an island inhabited by the sorceress Circe. After many wanderings and strange adventures, he arrived at his home in Ithaca. During his absence his father, Laertes, in grief and old age, had withdrawn into the country, and his mother, Anticlea, had died. His wife, Penelope, had been importuned by suitors but had rejected them all. In order that he might not be recognized on his arrival, Athena metamorphosed Ulysses into an unsightly beggar. He was kindly received by Eumæus, the swineherd, to whom he made himself known, and a plan of revenge was resolved on. Penelope, with great difficulty, was made to promise her hand to him who should conquer the others in shooting with the bow of Ulysses. As none of the suitors was able to draw this bow, Ulysses himself took it up, and, directing his arrows against the suitors, slew them all with the help of his son Telemachus, to whom he had previously made himself known. Ulysses now revealed himself to Penelope. The people rose in arms against Ulysses; but Athena, who assumed the appearance of Mentor, brought about a reconciliation.

Valhalla (v..l-häl'ä). In Scandinavian mythology, the gold and silver palace of Odin, wherein were received the souls of heroes slain in battle. Each morning the heroes went out of the palace and fought until noon. All wounds were then healed, and the heroes, under the presidency of Odin, assembled to feast, being served by the battle maidens, or Valkyries.

Valkyries (văl-kĭr'ĭz). The battle maidens of Scandinavian mythology. Mounted on swift horses, they rushed into battle with drawn swords and, selecting those destined to death, they conducted them to Valhalla. The number of Valkyries differs greatly according to the various mythologists, and ranges from three to sixteen. They are generally mentioned, however, as being only nine.

Vayu (vä'yōō). The spirit of the air in Hindu mythology. His wife Angana was a celestial nymph, who was compelled by a curse to assume the form of a monkey. Their son was the monkey god Hanuman, who led the monkeys in support of the god Rama when the latter was battling to recover his wife Siva from the demon Ravana.

Venus. The Roman goddess of women, identified with the Greek Aphrodite, goddess of beauty and love. She is said to have sprung from the foam of the sea, and to have been immediately carried to the abode of the gods on Olympus, where they were all charmed with her extreme beauty. According to other legends she was the daughter of Jupiter and Dione. Sparrows and doves were customarily yoked to her chariot; the sight of her girdle inspired all hearts with passion for the wearer; and her son Cupid was her attendant and minister. The myrtle was sacred to her. Her favorite residence was at Cyprus. Venus was represented often as the wife of Vulcan and frequently as the paramour of Mars. Among mortal men, she loved Anchises, by whom she became the mother of Æneas, and Adonis, whose untimely death left her inconsolable. One of her tasks was to restore harmonious relations for couples who had quarreled.

Vesta. The Roman goddess of the hearth-fire. Æneas was believed to have brought the eternal fire of Vesta from Troy, along with the images of the penates; the prætors, consuls, and dictators, before entering upon their official functions, sacrificed, not only to the penates, but also to Vesta at Lavinium. Similarly, in the house, sacrifices were offered to Vesta at the hearth, and the common meal eaten about the hearth was regarded as an act of worship for her. At Rome, six maidens were chosen to serve for 30 years as priestesses of Vesta. They were known as vestal virgins and took a vow of chastity, the breaking of which involved the penalty of being buried alive. The duty of the vestal virgins was to tend the sacred fire of the city. If the fire went out as a result of their negligence, the penalty was scourging. This custom was probably a survival from the days when it was difficult to obtain fire and when, consequently, the fire once kindled had to be guarded with the utmost care. The office of vestal virgin was highly honored in Rome and was much sought after by distinguished families.

Vishnu. One of the great deities of the Hindu triad, ranking as the "Preserver," after Brahma, the "Creator," and before Siva, the "Destroyer." It is believed that he has appeared on earth nine times, his tenth *avatar*, or incarnation, having yet to come.

Votán. The deity supposed to have taught the people of Chiapas (Mexico) the arts of civilization.

Vulcan. The Roman god of fire, identified with the Greek Hephæstus. He was the son of Jupiter and Juno and became lame by being thrown out of heaven by Jupiter for taking Juno's part in a quarrel. He wrought skillfully at a forge, where he produced tripods that came and departed automatically and many other wonders, including Pandora, the first woman. Venus is usually represented as his wife. Vulcan is represented in art as a middle-aged man having a beard and unkempt hair. Relay torch races were sometimes held in his honor, probably to symbolize the bringing of fire from heaven to mankind or the transference of the sacred element to replace a fire that had become extinguished. Such ceremonies hark back to a time when fire was difficult to kindle.

Woden. The Anglo-Saxon form of the Scandinavian god Odin. Wednesday is called after him.

Xipe. The Mexican god of sowing and of vegetation. Also the god of the goldsmiths and the silversmiths.

Yacatecutli, "He-who-guides." The Mexican god of commerce. His symbol was a traveler's staff.

Yggdrasil (ĭg'drȧ-sĭl). The giant ash tree of Norse mythology. It overspreads the earth and binds earth, hell, and heaven together. From beneath it springs a fountain, and under its branches sit the Norns or Fates.

Ymir (ü'mêr). In Norse mythology, the ancient frost giant. The gods slew him and out of his body formed the earth. From it, too, grew the mighty ash tree, Yggdrasil, which was thought to support the universe.

Zamzam. The sacred well situated in the heart of the city of Mecca. According to Arab tradition, it is the very well that was shown to Hagar when she was wandering with Ishmael in the desert.

Zephyrus. A personification of the west wind. He was the mildest and gentlest of the sylvan deities.

Zethus. One of the twin sons of Antiope and Zeus. See *Amphion*.

Zeus (zūs). The greatest of the Olympian gods, father of gods and men, a son of Cronus, or Saturn, and of Rhea. He was identified by the Romans with Jupiter. When Zeus and his brothers distributed among themselves the government of the world by lot, Poseidon obtained the sea; Hades received the lower world; and Zeus, the heavens and the upper regions; but the earth became common to all. According to Homer, Zeus dwelt on Mount Olympus in Thessaly, which was believed to penetrate into heaven itself. By his counsel he managed everything; he founded law and order, so that Dike, Themis, and Nemesis came to be regarded as his assistants. According to his own choice he used to assign good or evil to mortals. Zeus had an ancient oracle at Dodona in Greece, where, by means of speaking oaks, he made known his will to mortals. His wife was Hera. Many stories are told of her jealous pursuit of mortal women who had been loved by Zeus and visited by him, usually in a disguised form. By such unions Zeus became the father of many heroes. Europa, receiving him in the form of a white bull, had several sons by him, one of whom was Minos, the famous lawgiver of Crete. Zeus came to Leda as a swan and by her was the father of Helen and of Pollux. Gaining admittance to Danaë in the form of a shower of gold, he begot Perseus. His greatest son was Hercules, the offspring of Alcmene, to whom Zeus obtained access by impersonating her husband.

PEN NAMES

PEN NAME	REAL NAME
Abbott, Eleanor Hallowell	Mrs. Fordyce Coburn
Adams, Moses	Geo. Wm. Bagby
Adeler, Max	Charles Heber Clark
Æ	George Russell
Akers, Elizabeth	Mrs. E. M. Allen
Aleichem, Sholem	Solomon Rabinowitz
Allen, F. M.	Edmund Downey
Allen, Grant	Charles Grant Blairfindie
Amyand, Arthur	Major E. A. Haggard
Anstey, F.	F. Anstey Guthrie
Armstrong, Regina	Mrs. C. H. Niehaus
Arnold, Birch	Mrs. J. M. D. Bartlett
Arp, Bill	Charles H. Smith
"Ashmont"	J. Frank Perry
Ashton, Helen	Mrs. Arthur Jordan
"Aunt Elmira"	Mrs. Isaac Slenker
Ayres, Alfred	Thomas E. Osmun
Barnaval, Louis	Charles De Kay
Barrington, E.	Mrs. L. Adams Beck
Bart	Charles L. Bartholomew
Beard, Dan	Daniel Carter Beard
Beard, Frank	Thos. Francis Beard
Beaumont, Averil	Mrs. Margaret Hunt
Bede, Cuthbert	Rev. Edward Bradley
Bell, Acton	Anne Brontë
Bell, Currer	Charlotte Brontë
Bell, Ellis	Emily Brontë
Bell, Lilian	Mrs. Arthur Hoyt Bogue
Belloc, Marie Adelaide	Mrs. Frederick S. Lowndes
Bentzon, Thérèse	Marie Thérèse Blanc
Bibliophile	S. A. Allibone
Bickerdyke, John	Charles H. Cook
Bickerstaff, Isaac	Swift and Steele
Biglow, Hosea	J. R. Lowell
Billings, Josh	Henry W. Shaw
Birmingham, George A.	James Owen Hannay
Bly, Nellie	Elizabeth Seaman
Boldrewood, Rolf	Thos. Alex. Browne
Bottome, Phyllis	Mrs. Forbes Dennis
Bowen, B. M.	Bertha Muzzy
Bowen, Marjorie B.	Mrs. Gabrielle Long
Boyce, Neith	Mrs. Hutchins Hapgood
Boz	Charles Dickens
Braddon, Miss M. E.	Mrs. John Maxwell
Breitmann, Hans	Charles Godfrey Leland
Briscoe, Margaret Sutton	Mrs. A. J. Hopkins
"Brunswick"	Jeannette Leonard Gilder
Brydges, Harold	James Howard Bridge
"Bunny"	Carl E. Schultze
Burr, Major Dangerfield	Prentiss Ingraham
Caine, Hall	Thomas H. Hall
Caldwell, Taylor	Mrs. Marcus Rebach
Canfield, Dorothy	Dorothy Canfield Fisher
Carey, Charles	Charles Carey Waddell
Carroll, Lewis	Rev. C. L. Dodgson
Carter, Nick	Francis W. Doughty and others
Carton, R. C.	R. C. Critchett
Cartwright, Julia	Mrs. Henry Ady
Caskoden, Edwin	Charles Major
Castlemon, Harry	Charles A. Fosdick
Celticus	Aneurin Bevan
"Champ"	Jas. W. Champney
"Chicot"	Epes Winthrop Sargent
Christie, Agatha	Mrs. M. E. L. Mallowan
Collins, Mabel	Mrs. Keningale Cook
Collins, Percy	Price Collier
Connington, J. J.	Alfred Walter Stewart
Connor, Ralph	Rev. C. W. Gordon
Conway, Hugh	F. J. Fargus
Coolidge, Susan	Sarah C. Woolsey
Corelli, Marie	Eva Mary Mackay
Cornwall, Barry	Bryan W. Procter
Coulevain, Pierre de	Hélène Favre de Coulevain
Craddock, Charles Egbert	Mary N. Murfree
Crayon, Geoffrey	Washington Irving
Crinkle, Nym	Andrew C. Wheeler
Crowfield, Christopher	Harriet Beecher Stowe
D'Ache, Caran	Emmanuel Poire
Dacre, J. Colne	Mrs. A. S. Boyd
"Dagonet"	George R. Sims
Dale, Alan	Alfred J. Cohen
Dale, Darley	Francesca Maria Steele
Danbury, Newsman	J. M. Bailey
Danby, Frank	Mrs. Julia Frankau
Dane, Clemence	Winifred Ashton
Dean, Mrs. Andrew	Mrs. Cecily Sidgwick
Delafield, E. M.	Mrs. E. M. de la Pasture Dashwood
D'Istria, Dora	Helena Ghika
Dix, Dorothy	Elizabeth M. Gilmer
Dobson, Austin	Henry A. Dobson

PEN NAME	REAL NAME
Dooley, Martin	Finley Peter Dunne
Douglas, George	George Douglas Brown
Douglas, Marian	Annie D. G. Robinson
Drinkwater, Jennie Maria	Jennie Conklin, M. D.
"Droch"	Robert Bridges
"Duchess, The"	Mrs. Hungerford
Du Maurier, Daphne	Lady Browning
Edwards, Albert	Arthur Bullard
Elia	Charles Lamb
Eliot, Alice	Sarah Orne Jewett
Eliot, George	Marian Evans
Ettrick, Shepherd	James Hogg
Evergreen, Anthony	Washington Irving
Fair, Frank	Jane Frances Winn
Fairfax, Marion	Mrs. Tully Marshall Phillips
Fairfield, Clarence	Edwin Ross Champlin
Fern, Fanny	Sara P. Parton
Finn, Mickey	Ernest Jarrold
Fitzboodle, George	W. M. Thackeray
"Fitznoodle"	B. B. Vallentine
Fleming, George	Julia Constance Fletcher
Fontenoy, Marquis de	Frederick Cunliffe-Owen
Forrester, Francis	Daniel Wise
Forrester, Frank	Henry Wm. Herbert
Forrester, Izola	Mrs. Reuben Merrifield
F. P. A.	Franklin Pierce Adams
"Fra Elbertus"	Elbert Hubbard
France, Anatole	Jacques Anatole Thibault
Francis, M. E.	Mrs. Francis Blundell
Gates, Eleanor	Mrs. Richard Walton Tully
"Gath"	George Alfred Townsend
Gibbons, Lucy	Lucy G. Morse
Gift, Theo.	Mrs. G. S. Boulger
Glaspell, Susan	Mrs. George Cram Cook
Glyndon, Howard	Mrs. Laura C. R. Searing
Goodman, Maude	Mrs. A. E. Scanes
Gordon, Julien	Mrs. Van Rensselaer Cruger
Gorki, Maxim	Alexel Maximovitch Peshkov
Graduate of Oxford	John Ruskin
Graham, John	David Graham Phillips
Grand, Sarah	Mrs. McFall
Grayson, David	Ray Stannard Baker
Green, Anna Katharine	Mrs. Charles Rohlfs
Greenwood, Grace	Sara Jane Lippincott
Greville, Henri	Mme. Durand
Grile, Dod	Ambrose Bierce
"Gyp"	Countess de Martel
Haliburton, Hugh	James Logie Robertson
Hall, Holworthy	Harold E. Porter
Hamilton, Gail	Mary Abigail Dodge
Hamsun, Knut	K. Pedersen
"Hard Pan"	Geraldine Bonner
Harland, Henry	Sidney Luska
Harland, Marion	Mrs. Mary V. Terhune
Harrod, Frances	Frances Forbes-Robertson
Hawthorne, Alice	Septimus Winner
Hayes, Henry	Ellen Olney Kirk
Hazeltine, Horace	Charles Stokes Wayne
"H. D."	Hilda Doolittle
Hegan, Alice Caldwell	Mrs. Cale Young Rice
Henry, Marse	Henry Watterson
Henry, O.	William Sydney Porter
"H. H."	Helen Hunt Jackson
Hill, Headon	F. Grainger
"Historicus"	Sir W. Vernon Harcourt
Hobbes, John Oliver	Mrs. Pearl Craigie
Hoffman, Prof.	Angelo Lewis
Hope, Anthony	Anthony Hope Hawkins
Houghton, Claude	Claude Houghton Oldfield
Hubbard, Kin	Frank McKinney Hubbard
Hull, Richard	Richard Henry Sampson
Huntington, Faye	Theodosia T. Foster
Hutchinson, Ellen M.	Ellen M. H. Cortissoz
"Iconoclast"	Mrs. Mary Agnes Hamilton
Ingoldsby, Thomas	Rev. H. H. Barham
Innes, Michael	John I. M. Stewart
"Iota"	Mrs. Mannington Caffyn
Iron, Ralph (Olive Schreiner)	Mrs. S. C. Cronwright
James, Martha	Mrs. James R. Doyle
Jameson, Storm	Mrs. Guy Chapman
Jay, W. L. M.	Julia L. M. Woodruff
Jean Paul	J. P. F. Richter
Johnson, Benjamin F.	James Whitcomb Riley
Johnson, Fanny Kemble	Mrs. Vincent Costello
"Josiah Allen's Wife"	Marietta Holley
J. S. of Dale	Frederick J. Stimson
"June, Jenny"	Mrs. David G. Croly
Kaye-Smith, Sheila	Mrs. T. P. Fry
Keith, Leslie	Grace L. K. Johnston
Kennedy, Margaret	Mrs. David Davies

Pen Name	Real Name
Kerr, Sophie	Mrs. S. K. Underwood
Keverne, R.	Clifford Hosken
Kingsmill, Hugh	K. H. Lunn
Kirk, Eleanor	Eleanor K. Ames
Kirke, Edmund	James R. Gilmore
Knickerbocker, Diedrich	Washington Irving
"Kron, Karl"	Lyman Hotchkiss Bagg
Lancaster, G. B.	Edith J. Lyttleton
Lawless, Anthony	Philip MacDonald
Lea, Fannie Heaslip	Mrs. H. P. Agee
Lee, Vernon	Violet Paget
L. E. L.	Letitia E. Landon
Leslie, Henrietta	Gladys Schütze
Lessing, Bruno	Rudolph Block
Little, Frances	Mrs. Frances Macauley
Littlepage, Cornelius	James Fenimore Cooper
Lothrop, Amy	Mrs. Anna Bartlett Warner
Loti, Pierre	L. M. Julien Viaud
Ludlow, Johnny	Mrs. Henry Wood
Lyall, Edna	Ada Ellen Bayly
Maartens, Maarten	J. N. W. van der Poorten Schwartz
McDairmid, Hugh	Christopher M. Grieve
Maclaren, Ian	Rev. John Watson
Macleod, Fiona	William Sharp
McManus, Blanche	Mrs. M. F. Mansfield
Maitland, Thomas	Robert Buchanan
Malet, Lucas	Mary St. Leger Harrison
"Maori"	James Inglis
Marbourg, Dolores	Mary Schell Hoke Bacon
Marlitt, E.	Henriette Eugenie John
Marlowe, Charles	Harriet Jay
"Marshes, A Son of the"	Mrs. Owen Visger
Martin, Ellis	Marah Ellis Ryan
Martin, George Madden	Mrs. Atwood R. Martin
Marvel, Ik.	Donald G. Mitchell
Mathers, Helen	Mrs. Henry Reeves
Maurois, Andre	Emile Herzog
Meredith, Owen	Lord Lytton
Merriam, Florence A.	Mrs. Florence M. Bailey
Merriman, Henry Seton	Hugh Stowell Scott
Mignon, August	John A. Darling
Miller, Joaquin	Cincinnatus Heine Miller
Miller, Olive Thorne	Harriet Mann Miller
Miln, Louise Jordan	Mrs. George Crichton Miln
Moresby, Louis	Mrs. L. Adams Beck
Morgan, Emmanuel	Witter Bynner
Mowbray, J. P.	Andrew C. Wheeler
Mulholland, Rosa	Lady Gilbert
Mulock, Miss	Mrs. G. L. Craik
Nasby, Petroleum V.	David Locke
Nesbit, E.	Mrs. Hubert Bland
Nordau, Max	Simon Sudfeld
North, Christopher	John Wilson
Nye, Bill	Edgar Wilson Nye
O'Dowd, Cornelius	Charles Lever
Ogilvy, Gavin	J. M. Barrie
O. H. K. B.	Rev. Oliver H. K. Boyd
"O. K."	Mme. Ulga Kireef Novikoff
Oldcastle, John	Wilfred Meynell
"Old Sleuth"	Harlan P. Halsey
Oldstyle, Jonathan	Washington Irving
O'Neill, Rose Cecil	Mrs. Harry Leon Wilson
Onions, Oliver	George Oliver
Optic, Oliver	Wm. T. Adams
O'Reilly, Miles	Charles G. Halpine
O'Rell, Max	Paul Blouet
Orwell, George	Eric Blair
O'Sullivan, Seamas	James Sullivan Starkey
"Ouida"	Louise de la Ramée
Owen, Jean A.	Mrs. Owen Visger
Oxenham, John	W. A. Dunkerley
Palmer, Lynde	Mrs. A. A. Peebles
"Pansy"	Isabella Macdonald Alden
Parker, Maude	Mrs. Richard Washburn Child
Partington, Mrs.	Benj. P. Shillaber
Paston, George	Miss E. M. Symonds
Paul, John	Chas. Henry Webb
Peabody, Josephine Preston	Mrs. L. S. Marks
Perkins, Eli	Melville de Lancey Landon
"Pertinax"	C. J. A. Geraud
Phiz	H. K. Browne
Phœnix, John	George H. Derby
Pindar, Peter, Esq.	John Wolcott
Plymley, Peter	Rev. Sydney Smith
Poor Richard	Benjamin Franklin
"Porte Crayon"	David H. Strother
Prescott, Dorothy	Agnes Blake Poor
Presland, John	Gladys Bendit
Prevost, Francis	Harry F. P. Battersby

Pen Name	Real Name
Prout, Father	Rev. Francis S. Mahony
Pryde, Anthony	Agnes Russell Weeks
"Q."	Arthur T. Quiller-Couch
Quad, M.	C. B. Lewis
Queen, Ellery	Frederic Dannay and Manfred B. Lee
Raimond, C. E.	Elizabeth Robins (Mrs. George R. Parks)
Redfield, Martin	Alice Brown
Reid, Christian	Frances F. Tiernan
Renault, Mary	Mary Challons
Rheinhardt, Rudolph H.	George Hempl
Rhode, John	C. J. C. Street
Richardson, Henry Handel	Mrs. Henrietta Robertson
"Rita"	Mrs. E. M. J. von Booth
Rives, Amélie	Princess Troubetskoi
Robins, Elizabeth	Mrs. Joseph Pennell
Robinson, Agnes Mary F.	Mme. Emile Duclaux
Rohmer, Sax	Arthur S. Ward
Ross, Albert	Linn Boyd Porter
"Rover"	Alfred Gibson
Rowe, Bolton / Rowe, Saville	Clement Scott
Roy, Rob	John Macgregor
Runkle, Bertha	Mrs. Louis H. Bash
Rutherford, Mark	Wm. Hale White
St. Aubyn, Alan	Frances Marshall
St. Clair, Victor	G. Waldo Browne
St. Laurence, A.	Alfred Laurence Felkin
"Saki"	Hector H. Munro
Sand, George	Mme. Dudevant
Sanghamita, Sister	Countess M. A. de S. Canavarro
Sawyer, Ruth	Mrs. Albert C. Durand
Sayers, Dorothy	Mrs. Atherton Fleming
Schreiner, Olive (Ralph Iron)	Mrs. S. C. Cronwright
Scriblerus, Martinus	Pope, Swift, and Arbuthnot
Sedgwick, Anne Douglas	Mrs. Basil de Selincourt
"Sevenoaks"	Alfred S. Edwards
Sharp, Luke	Robert Barr
Shute, Nevil	Nevil Shute Norway
Sidney, Margaret	Harriet Mulford Lothrop
Siegerson, Dora	Mrs. Clement Shorter
Singmaster, Elsie	Mrs. Harold Lewars
Slick, Sam	T. C. Haliburton
Smith, T. Carlyle	John Kendrick Bangs
"Spy"	Leslie Ward
Standish, Burt L.	Gilbert Patten
Stanton, Schuyler	Lyman Frank Baum
Steele, Alice Garland	Mrs. T. Austin-Ball
Sterne, Stuart	Gertrude Bloede
Stevens, Margaret Dean	Bess Streeter Aldrich
"Stonehenge"	J. H. Walsh
Strange, Michael	Mrs. John Barrymore (second)
Stretton, Hesba	Hannah Smith
Struther, Jan	Mrs. Joyce Maxtone Graham
Stuart, Eleanor	Mrs. Harris Robbins Child
Swan, Annie S.	Mrs. Burnett Smith
Swift, Benjamin	William Romaine Paterson
Sylva, Carmen	Elizabeth, queen of Rumania
Temple, Hope	Mme. André Messager
Thanet, Octave	Alice French
Thompson, Wolf	Ernest Thompson Seton
Tilton, Alice	Phœbe Atwood Taylor
Titmarsh, M. A.	W. M. Thackeray
"Tivoli"	Horace W. Bleackley
"Toby, M. P."	Sir Henry W. Lucy
Tower, Martello	Commander F. M. Norman
T. P.	Thomas Power O'Connor
Trask, Katrina	Mrs. Spencer Trask
Trevor, Edward	Bulwer-Lytton, E.
"Trois-Etoiles"	E. C. Grenville-Murray
Twain, Mark	Samuel L. Clemens
"Uncle Remus"	Joel Chandler Harris
Vandegrift, Margaret	Margaret T. Janvier
Van Dine, S. S.	Willard Huntington Wright
Varley, John Philip	Langdon E. Mitchell
Verne, Jules	M. Olchewitz
Voltaire	François Marie Arouet
Vorse, Mary Heaton	Mrs. Joseph O'Brien
Ward, Artemus	Charles F. Browne
Warde, Margaret	Edith Kellogg Dunton
Wast, Hugo	Gustavo Adolfo Martinez Zuviara
Wells, Carolyn	Mrs. Hadwin Houghton
West, Jessamyn	Mrs. H. M. McPherson
Wetherell, Elizabeth	Susan Warner
Wiggin, Kate Douglas	Mrs. George C. Riggs
Wildwood, Will	Frederick E. Pond
Wilson, Charlotte	Karle Wilson Baker
Winfield, Arthur M.	Edw. Stratemeyer
Winter, John Strange	Mrs. H. E. V. Stannard
Yates, Dornford	Major Cecil W. Mercer
Yechton, Barbara	Lyda Farrington Krause

TEST QUESTIONS

FRENCH LITERATURE

Sketch briefly the origin and early history of the French language 216

Trace the origin of the French epic of Charlemagne. What is the *Song of Roland?* . . . 216

Name two French poets of the 12th century. Upon what subjects were the romances of this time written? What was "matter of Britain"? 216

Discuss the origin of the liturgical drama . . 216

Of what subject did Villehardouin write? Guillaume de Lorris? Froissart? 216

Describe the production of the "mysteries" in the 14th and 15th centuries. What was the best medieval play? What is its theme? . . 216

Characterize François Villon. What were his *Testaments?* Give a famous line from one of his poems 216

What were the disturbing influences in 16th century France? Of what did Rabelais write? Who was Calvin? 217

What was the "pléiade"? What was its purpose? Who translated Plutarch's *Lives?* What was Montaigne's characteristic query? 217

What was the task of the 17th century? Who founded the French Academy? What was the origin of the phrase "beautiful as *The Cid*"? 217

Name three plays by Molière. What are the chief lessons taught in his works? Give the themes of three plays by Racine 217

Give the names and the chief themes of three writers of French prose in the 17th century. Who was Boileau? La Fontaine? 217

Name two tendencies that characterized French thought in the 18th century. What two authors embodied these tendencies? Characterize Voltaire and his work 217

What especial importance attaches to Montesquieu's writing? Who edited the *Encyclopeida?* Who was the chief French dramatist of the 18th century? 217

Summarize the work and influence of Rousseau. Who wrote "The Marseillaise"? 217

Upon what themes did the following authors write: Chateaubriand? Madame de Staël? George Sand? Who was the model for French romantic fiction? Give two examples. 218

Name three French historians. What was the theme of De Tocqueville's best-known work? 218

Whom did the French romantic dramatists take as their guide? Who wrote *Hernani? Cyrano?* 218

Who were the chief French writers of realist fiction in the 19th century? To whom is the phrase "the French Dickens" applied? . . . 218

Characterize the work of the following: Anatole France; Rolland; Loti; Romains. What have been the chief literary merits of French literature? 218

ITALIAN LITERATURE

Name five periods of Italian literature. To which of these periods does Dante belong? Tasso? 220

Upon what kind of subjects did the early Sicilian poets write? What was the *Contrasto?* Name the inventor of the sonnet 220

For what work is Guittone d'Arezzo notable? To what movement can we trace the origin of religious drama in Italy? 220

Quote a notable line from an ode of Guinizelli. Why is the thought of this line important in Italian literature? Who was Cavalcanti? . 220

Characterize the *Vita Nuova* of Dante. What was Dante's purpose in writing the *Convivio?* Name two other minor works of Dante. Upon what themes were they written? 220

Why is Petrarch called "the first modern man"? Who was the Laura of Petrarch's sonnets? What service did the poet render to the study of ancient classics? 220

Who is the author of the *Decameron?* Where did he get the stories for this book? Why has it been called the "Human Comedy"? Describe Boccaccio's work in explaining Dante's *Divine Comedy* 220–221

What is the chief characteristic of the second period of Italian literature? What Greek scholar was invited to teach Greek in Florence? Who were the humanists? Describe the collecting of libraries in Italian cities . . 221

Distinguish between the terms "Renaissance" and "humanism." Who wrote *Orlando Furioso?* Characterize the literary quality and the historic value of this poem 221

What place does Machiavelli hold in modern literature? Why has his *Prince* been harshly criticized? 221

In what city is the scene of Castiglione's *Courtier* laid? What is the literary rank of this work? Of what historic value is it possessed? 221

What is the theme of Tasso's *Jerusalem Delivered?* Name Tasso's earliest work and also a pastoral drama from his pen 221

Name three minor writers of the Italian Renaissance. From what writer did the Othello story, used by Shakespeare, come? Of what value is the autobiography of Cellini? . 221–222

What historical conditions account for the decline of Italian literature after 1595? Name two great Italians of this period 222

What connection is there between the Treaty of Aix-la-Chapelle (1748) and the revival of Italian literature? Characterize the work of Carlo Goldoni 222

Who was Parini? What are the theme and purpose of his long poem *The Day*? What was the life purpose of Alfieri? Did he attain his goal? 222

Outline the life story of Foscolo. What is his best lyric poem? Quote the line which gives the key to Leopardi's patriotic verse. What was his general attitude toward life? . . . 222

What three works constitute Manzoni's gift to Italy's patriotic literature? State the themes of these works. Name five outstanding literary figures in Italy of the middle 19th century 223

What is Carducci's rank in Italian literature? From what source did he draw his chief inspiration? Of what periods did the historian Villari write? 223

Characterize the work of the following recent Italian writers: Fogazzaro; De Amicis; Verga; D'Annunzio; Croce. Name two contemporary women writers. What is the present outlook for Italian literature? 223

SPANISH LITERATURE

From what speech is the Spanish language descended? What other tongues have affected the language of Spain? Name four Roman writers who were natives of Spain 225

What is the oldest Spanish manuscript? Who was the original of "the Cid"? Name two early works written about his exploits . . . 225

What place in modern literature is assigned to the Spanish *Drama of the Three Kings?* Summarize the service of Alfonso the Wise to literature and history. From what language was the *Amadis de Gaula* translated? 225

Describe the *Conde Lucanor.* Who is the author of this famous work? What was the purpose of the stories in this work? . . . 225

Who is counted as the first genuine Spanish poet? What is the title of his work? . . . 225

Describe the poetry written at the court of John II of Castile. Who was the "forerunner of the Spanish humanists"? What Italian poet's work influenced Juan de Mena? Name De Mena's chief work 225

Describe the beginning of Spanish drama. Of what importance is *La Celestina?* 225

Who were the chief writers of religious poetry in the period from 1300 to 1550? Name the two most notable literary men of the period from 1550 to 1780 and characterize their work . 237

When did the modern revival of Icelandic literature begin? Give the names of two influential men connected with this movement . 237

SLAVONIC LITERATURES

What are the two kinds of oral tradition handed down from the early period of Russian history? Distinguish the five groups of early Russian folk tales. What two medieval cities figure in these stories? Who is Sadko? Vladimir? . 238

How was the Slavic language introduced into Russia? What is the story of the Raid of Igor? . 238

When did Kiev become the center of Russian learning? Who was the pioneer of modern culture in Russia? When was the first Russian theater opened? . 238

What part did Peter the Great play in Russian literary history? Who is called the "Russian Adam Smith"? How did Catherine II attempt to encourage Russian letters? Give the titles of three poems by Derzhávin . . 238

State the importance of Sumarókov in Russian literature. For what are the years 1765 and 1766 notable? What was Karamzín's most effective work? . 238

Name some important works translated into Russian by Zhukóvsky. What was the influence of these translations? What is the rank of Púshkin in Russian literature? Who has been called the "Russian Burns"? . . 238–239

In what field have Russian writers done the greatest work? What may be said to be Russia's contribution to prose fiction? Name three great Russian novelists . 239

Name three great Russian dramatists and give the title of a play by each. Who are the representative Russian writers of the short story? 239

How may the intense realism of the Russian short story be accounted for? Into what two groups did the revolution of 1918 divide Russian writers? . 239

To what family of languages does Polish belong? What existing book shows the literary use of Polish in the 13th century? . 240

What influences caused the Polish language to supersede Latin in literary use? What was the first book printed in Polish? . 240

What period is known as the "golden age" of Polish literature? Who is called the "prince of Polish poets"? . 240

Who was the first Polish authoress? To what English poet was Krasicki compared? . . 240

What is the period of the modern revival of Polish literature? To what rank in Polish letters is Adam Mickiewicz assigned? Who is the greatest recent Polish writer of prose fiction? Name one of his books . 240

What influence first gave a literary impulse to the Czech language? What are the chief literary remains from the period before the 14th century? . 240

What was the effect of the Crusades upon Bohemia? When was the University of Prague founded? . 240

What period is the greatest age of Czech literature? Tell something of the varied work of John Huss. Compare the educational advantages in Bohemia at this period with those of other countries. Who was Comenius? Give two interesting facts about his writings . . 241

From about what year do we date the modern revival of Czech literature? Who are the two greatest poets of the early 19th century? Who first translated and staged Shakespeare's plays in Czech? Give two facts to indicate the vastness of the literary work done by Vrchlicky. Name a prominent woman writer. 241

HUNGARIAN LITERATURE

What particularly strong qualities are possessed by the Hungarian language? To what languages is it most closely related? Why was its literary development so long delayed? . 241

What literary fragments remain from the period before 1450? Name three events which encouraged vernacular literature in the 15th century. What influences hampered Hungarian literature in the 17th century? . 241

When did the modern revival of Hungarian literature begin? Name three important services of Count Stephen Széchenyi to the Hungarian language and culture . 242

Who is the founder of the modern Hungarian drama? Name two novels by Mór Jókai. Who wrote Banker and Baron? . 242

ANCIENT AND ORIENTAL LITERATURES

Into how many epochs do we divide Chinese literature? What are the great names in the first period? . 242

Name the works written or edited by Confucius. What was the chief political teaching of Mencius? Quote a maxim from the Tao Te King. 242

When did the Reconstructive Period begin? What kind of beliefs and superstitions prevailed during the Han dynasty? Of what value is the Classic of Mountains and Seas? When was Buddhism recognized in China? 242

What is the extent of the "golden age" of Chinese literature? What poet of this period is compared to the Persian poet Omar? . 242–243

To what two literary forms did the Mongol dynasty give encouragement? What themes are most popular in Chinese dramas? . 243

What historical event opens the fourth period of Chinese literature? Trace the influence of missionaries and Western schools upon the literary development of this period. What change in Chinese literary style is taking place? . 243

What is the date of the oldest extant literary work in Japanese? Give the essential features of Japanese poetry. What are Hokku poems? 243

What centuries are called the "dark ages" of Japanese literature? Name the two kinds of drama that originated in this period. Give four interesting facts about the origin and acting of the Kabuki. Describe the production of the Japanese marionette plays . 243–244

Sketch the work of women in Japanese literature. 244

How has Western culture influenced Japanese literature? What is the greatest problem of the Japanese literary world at present? . . 244

Tell how Rawlinson found the key which enabled scholars to decipher the Assyro-Babylonian inscriptions. What is cuneiform writing? Who were the Sumerians? the Babylonians? . 244

Describe the contents of the famous library of Assurbanipal. What is the story of the Gilgamesh epic? For what biblical story does it contain a parallel? . 244–245

According to the Babylonian Creation epic, who created heaven and earth? of what were they made? Describe the code of Hammurabi. . 245

To what group of languages does Hebrew belong? What idea is the keynote of Hebrew literature? How did Hebrew literature begin? What two ancient collections of songs are mentioned in the Bible? . 245

Into what four periods is Hebrew literature divided? Name five kinds of literary writing found in the Bible. What is the oldest document in the Hexateuch? What are its contents? What is "The Book of the Covenant"? 245

What are the Yahwist and Elohist documents? Why are they so called? Describe the effect of the book of Deuteronomy in the reign of King Josiah . 245–246

MYTHOLOGY

BIBLIOGRAPHY

Armens, Sven—Archetypes of Literature. *Univ. of Washington*
Bostwick, Arthur E.—Earmarks of Literature. *Books for Lib.*
Cassell's Encyclopedia of Literature   *Cassell, Ltd.*
Eaton, Trevor—Semantics of Literature. *Humanities*
Gayley, C. M.—Classic Myths . . . *Ginn & Co.*
Hannay, D.—The Later Renaissance. *Blackwood*
Ker, W. P.—The Dark Ages. . . . . . . *Oxford*
Ruskin, John—Literary Criticism. ed. by E. Bloom. *Peter Smith*
Thrall, Wm. F. and Hibbard, Addison—Handbook to Literature. . . . . *Doubleday Doran*

AMERICAN LITERATURE

Cambridge History of American Literature. *Putnam*
Boynton, Percy H.—A History of American Literature. . . . . *Ginn & Co.*
Hart, James D. Ed.—The Oxford Companion to American Literature. . . . . *Oxford*
Pattee. F. L.—The New American Literature. *Century*
Quinn, A. H.—American Fiction.. . . . *Appleton*

ENGLISH LITERATURE

Ball, John—From Beowulf to Modern British Writers. . . . . *Odyssey Press '59*
Cambridge History of English Literature. *Putnam*
Courthope, W. J.—History of English Poetry. *Russell*
Daiches, David—A Critical History of English Literature. . . . . *Ronald '61*
Harvey, Sir Paul—The Oxford Companion to English Literature. . . . . *Clarendon*
Legouis, Emile H. and Cazamian, Louis—A History of English Literature. . . . . *Macmillan*

IRISH LITERATURE

Kelly, Blanch M.—The Voice of the Irish. *Sheed & Ward*
MacDonagh, D., and Robinson, L. eds.—The Oxford Book of Irish Verse. *Oxford Univ. Press*
Morton, David—Shorter Modern Poems. *Harper*

FRENCH LITERATURE

Bradley, R.F. and Mitchell, R. B.—Eight Centuries of French Literature . . . . . *Appleton*
Canfield, A. G. and Patterson, W. T.—French Poems. . . . . *Holt*
Guthrie, Ramon and Diller, G. E. eds.—French Thought Since the Revolution . *Harcourt-Brace*
Nitze, W. A. and Dargan, E. P.—A History of French Literature to 1914. . . . . *Holt*

ITALIAN LITERATURE

Kuhns, Oscar—The Great Poets of Italy. *Houghton*
Lay, George R.—The Penguin Book of Italian Verse. . . . . *Penguin*
Lucas, St. John, ed.—Italian Verse. *Oxford Univ. Press*
Pucelli, Rodolfo—Anthology of Italian and Italo-American Poetry. . . . . *Humphries*
Symonda, J. A.—Renaissance in Italy *Peter Smith*
Wilkins, E. H.—Petrarch at Vancluse. *Univ. Chicago Press*

SPANISH AND LATIN AMERICAN LITERATURE

Bell, Audrey F.—Contemporary Spanish Literature. *Russell*
Fitzmaurice-Kelly, James and Trend, J. B. eds.—Oxford Book of Spanish Verse. *Oxford Univ. Press*
Goldberg, Isaac, Jr.—Brazilian Tales . . *Brentano*
Henriques-Urena, Pedro—Library Currents in Hispanic America . . . . *Harvard Univ. Press*
O'Connell, R.—Brazilian Poems . . . . . *Saifer*
Olmstead, R. H. and Grismer, R. L.—Spanish Short Stories. . . . . *Ronald*

GERMAN LITERATURE

Heller, P. and Erlich, E.—German Fiction and Poetry. . . . . *Macmillan*
Michael, M. and P.—German Folk and Fairy Tales.. . . . . *Putnam*
Prawer, S. S.—German Lyric Poetry. *Barnes & Noble*
Robertson, J. G.—A History of German Literature. . . . . *London House*

SCANDINAVIAN LITERATURE

Gosse, E.—The Oxford Book of Scandinavian Verse. . . . . *Clarendon*
Grundtvig—Danish Fairy Tales. . . . . . *Walck*
Hopp, Zinken—Norwegian Folklore Simplified. *Dufour*
Jones, Gwyn—Scandinavian Legends and Folk Tales. . . . . *Dover*
Kyle, E.—Swedish Nightingale. . . . . . *Holt*
Roberts, W. E.—Norwegian Folk Tale Studies. *Humanities*

RUSSIAN, POLISH, CZECH LITERATURES

Boyanys, S. K.—Russian Pronunciation *Harvard*
Henley, N.—Russian Prose Reader *Nostrand*
Kropotkin, Peter—Russian Literature . . *Blom*
Pietrkiewicz, Jerry—Polish Prose and Verse. *Oxford*
Rechcigl, M. Jr.—Czechoslovak Contributions to World Culture. . . . . *Humanities*
Reeve, F. D.—Russian Novel. . . . . *McGraw*
Souckova, M.—Czech Romantics . . *Humanities*
Ward, D.—Russian Language Today.. . . *Hillary*
Wysocka, P.—Polish Reader. . . . . . *McKay*

CHINESE AND JAPANESE LITERATURES

Chamberlin, Basil H.—Japanese Poetry. *Murray*
Ch'en Shou-yi—Chinese Literature: A Historical Introduction. . . . . *Ronald*
Giles, H. A.—A History of Chinese Literature. *Heineman*
Kaltenmark, O.—Chinese Literature . . . *Walker*
Klemer, D. J.—Chinese Love Poems . *Doubleday*
Legge, James—The Chinese Classics. (8-vols.) *Trübner*

SEMITIC LITERATURES

Cummings, C. C.—Assyrian and Hebrew Hymns of Praise. . . . . *AMS Press Inc.*
Goldstein, D. ed.—Hebrew Poems from Spain. *Schoken*
Hebrew Student Manual . . . . . . *Zondervan*
Lyall, C. J.—Commentary on Ten Ancient Arabic Poems. . . . . *Gregg*
Nicholson, R. A.—A Literary History of Arabs. *Cambridge Univ. Press*
Prince, J. D.—Assyrian Primer. *AMS Press Inc.*
Slousehz, Nahum—The Renascence of Hebrew Literature. *Jewish Publication Society of America*

INDIAN AND PERSIAN LITERATURES

Jain, A. P.—Rafe Ahmed Kidwai: A Memoir of His Life and Times (Asia Pub.). . . . *Taplinger*
Kumar, Dharma—Land and Caste in South India. *Cambridge Univ. Press*
Levy, R.—Persian Literature. *Oxford Univ. Press*
Mehdevi, A. S.—Persian Folk and Fairy Tales. *Knopf*

GREEK AND LATIN LITERATURES

Daskelakis, A.—Hellenism of the Ancient Macedonians.. . . . . *Argonaut Inc.*
Duff, J. W.—A Literary History of Rome from the Origins to the Close of the Golden Age. *Scribner*
Loeb Classical Library (Translated Classics) *Putnam*
Murray, Gilbert—History of Ancient Greek Literature. . . . . *Appleton*
Robinson, C. A.—Anthology of Greek Drama. *Holt*
Webster, Thomas B.—Hellenistic Poetry and Art. *Barnes & Noble*
Wilding, Longworth A.—A Classical Anthology. *Faber and Faber, Ltd.*

Biography

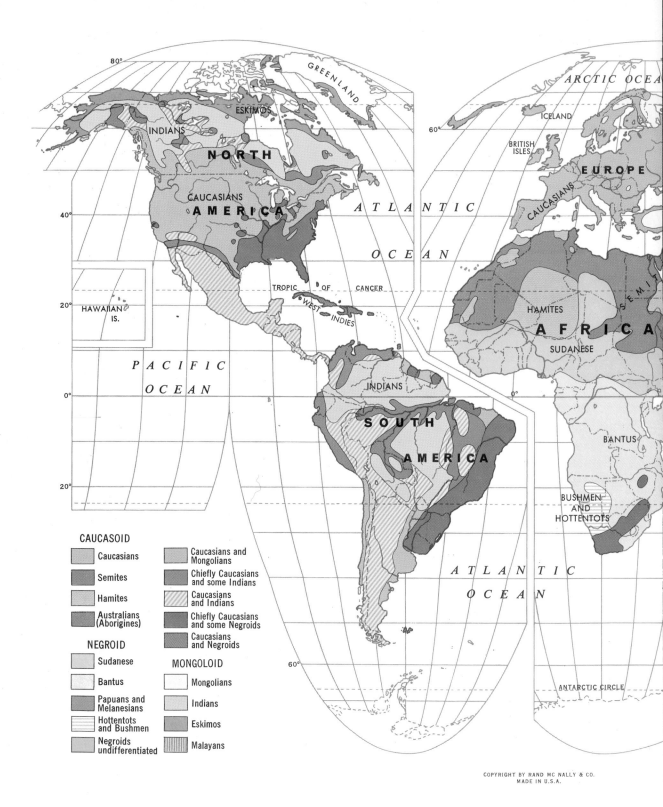

Adapting himself readily to different latitudes and to wide variations in temperature, moisture, and soil resources, the creature called "man," or *homo sapiens*, has found a home on virtually every part of the earth's surface. Only a few remote areas like Antarctica and the forbidding altitudes of the Himalayas need be omitted from what is sometimes referred to as "the habitable globe." The accompanying maps indicate, both by parallel or meridian lines and by shaded continental regions, the range of climate and elevation acceptable to man.

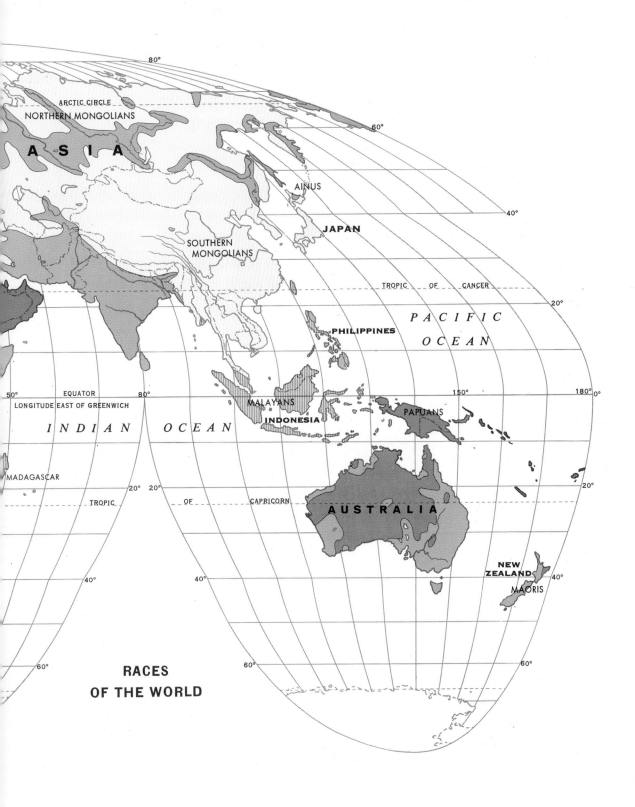

RACES
OF THE WORLD

To learn about man and his works is the purpose of the biological science known as "anthropology." In its historical or prehistorical phase, it deals with the problem of differentiating between man and other animals or, more narrowly, between man and other primates. This study soon broadens into "cultural anthropology," an examination of groups or "races," which, although having fundamental human characteristics in common, differ from one another in physical features, habitat, and cultural traditions.

BIOGRAPHY

INTRODUCTION

THE word biography is derived from the Greek words *bios*, meaning "life," and *grapho*, meaning "write." The term means a written account of one person's life. When the person whose life is described is also the author of the description, the work is designated by the word autobiography, which is formed by a prefix derived from the Greek *autos*, "oneself."

Biography differs from history in having its interest restricted to one person. History is concerned with movements, institutions, and social or national events in which the part of any one man is often extremely small. A biographical narrative, on the other hand, has its center of interest in the individual and in his pathway through the midst of larger events. It takes cognizance of his personal qualities, of his intimate words and thoughts, of his disappointments as well as of his achievements. Thus, from the point of view of history, the Civil War and the emancipation of the slaves are of more interest than the personal fortunes of any one man, even of Lincoln. In a biography of Lincoln, however, these great events are merely the setting, or background, of a narrative of his life.

It is the part of the more extended biographies to record all that is known regarding a person, and even the most trivial details are of value provided that they shed light upon his essential qualities. Biographical narratives of smaller compass, however, which are adapted more especially to meet the needs of the general reader, must, in order to be helpful, seize upon the central features of the larger narratives and must indicate the role which the subject of the narrative has played, or is now playing, in the drama of the world's activities.

Value. Although biography differs from history, nevertheless it is one of the most valuable aids to that study. To read history only is to see but one aspect of the drama of human life; the more intimate and, in many respects, the more interesting aspect can be seen only by acquaintance with the individual actors. It is through biography that an intimate knowledge of their lives may be obtained, and this knowledge in turn infuses a new and more personal interest into history.

To no less a degree, biography is essential to a complete understanding of literature and of art. Although great masterpieces have a universal appeal, nevertheless they are cast in a mold determined by the circumstances and experiences of the writer or artist. The pictures of women painted by Rembrandt, for example, would have been much different had he loved a different woman. The poetry of Whittier cannot be fully appreciated without a knowledge of his lifelong devotion to the abolitionist cause. Prescott's masterly *History of Peru* is invested with a certain tragic interest when we realize that it was written after the author had become blind.

It is hard to exaggerate the part played in people's lives by the example of the great. Alexander is said to have been inspired throughout his career by the recollection of the Homeric Achilles; every ambitious young scientist hopes some day to be a second Newton or Einstein; and before each schoolboy in every country are held up, for his emulation, those eminent men who are felt to be typical of the best qualities of the nation. Often a hint obtained from a biography opens a young reader's mind to previously undreamed possibilities and leads into wide usefulness a life that might otherwise have been common and uninspired.

Early Biographies. Biography is, in a sense, one of the most ancient forms of literature. In its earlier forms, it was often written to minister to the pride of the great. The Homeric poems and other early epics are chiefly accounts of heroes. Kings and warriors frequently hired poets or chroniclers to record the deeds of their lives. A Greek writer was paid by the Roman statesman and orator Cicero to write down the acts of the latter's administration, and Cicero requested him not to be sparing in the use of high colors.

Another class of biography that leaves much to be desired in the matter of veracity is that undertaken for the purpose of teaching moral lessons. Lives of famous or notorious characters are described in order to excite emulation or to arouse repulsion. The famous *Parallel Lives* of Plutarch are in part open to this criticism. The *Lives of the Emperors* by Suetonius represents the Roman rulers in a character much blacker, in all probability, than that in which they would appear to a disinterested inquirer. The numerous lives of the saints also were plainly written as much for the edification of the reader as for his enlightenment.

Modern Biography. With a few exceptions, such as Xenophon's *Memoirs* of Socrates, there was, until modern times, no work of genuinely biographical interest. Beginning with the 17th century, however, a vast literature has arisen consisting of books each of which aims to give a faithful account of the experiences and activities of one person from the cradle to the grave. Such works naturally differ greatly in value according to the abilities of the biographer. Among those of outstanding merit is Boswell's *Life of Samuel Johnson*, which, perhaps in all literature, has never been excelled in courage, picturesqueness, and mastery of portraiture.

In addition to individual biographies, a number of monumental dictionaries of biography have been written in recent times. The earliest of these was a Swedish work of 23 volumes completed in 1857 and embracing the lives of notable people of Sweden. The *Dictionary of National Biography* in 67 volumes contains biographies of more than 30,000 outstanding figures in Great Britain. The chief work of this type in America is the 21-volume *Dictionary of American Biography*.

Scope. This Department of Biography contains more than 4000 sketches of noteworthy men and women who have lived in the course of 4000 years of recorded history. The earliest lives narrated are those of the Babylonian Hammurabi and Ptolemy, king of Egypt, and the biographies of people still living are brought up to the date of printing.

The list of biographies will be found to contain the greatest figures in history, literature, art, science, invention, religion, commerce, discovery, and the other chief fields of human activity. A very large number also are treated who cannot be ranked among the greatest but who are remembered for some specific reason. These include Epicurus, the founder of Epicureanism, and Vasco da Gama, who, in modern times, first sailed around the southern extremity of Africa.

Among people still living or who have recently died, leaders in every field of activity have been included. Thus biographical data will be found of those who have been elected to the American Hall of Fame and to the American Academy of Arts and Letters; many of the winners of Nobel prizes in all parts of the world; most of the rulers and chief statesmen, scientists, scholars, writers, artists, administrators, philanthropists, and religious leaders in all the principal countries.

Method of Treatment. The biographies in this department recount the salient facts in the life of each person, including their nativity, education, chief positions held, accomplishments, and, for those not living, the date of their death. These sketches, however, are not limited to a merely statistical record of information. While written with a rare degree of conciseness, they approach more nearly the fullness of an encyclopedia article than the skeletonic brevity of a biographical dictionary.

Wherever possible, the significance of each person's work has been briefly indicated. The relation of statesmen to the events of their time has been made clear; the nature and value of a scientist's contribution to knowledge have been estimated in accordance with the best authorities in the field; a concise outline has been given of philosophies or religions originated by leaders in these fields; and artists' works have been appraised as far as the world has arrived at a settled opinion regarding their value. In making all such statements, the utmost care has been taken to avoid partisanship of all kinds. Neither fulsome praise nor malice has any place in a work of this character.

In the case of authors, a representative list of their writings is set forth. The chief masterpieces of painters, sculptors, and architects are listed, as well as the location of many of their works. The style and other qualities of composers are briefly characterized according to the judgment of eminent critics of music. In a word, this department has gone far toward being a complete guide to the vast field of human achievement.

Up-to-dateness. Many of the large encyclopedias do not contain information regarding significant events of the immediate past. Yet it is precisely the men and women who have recently come into prominence regarding whom people interested in present events need to be informed. Therefore, an effort has been made to include as many biographies as possible of those persons currently attaining prominence and making significant contributions to society and the language arts.

Illustrations. No small part of a reader's impression of a notable personage is a knowledge of his appearance. For this reason, photography may be a valuable aid to biography and, in this department, it has been laid under contribution to an unusual degree. Throughout these volumes will be found a number of portraits of men and women whose lives are described in the text.

In addition to the portraits, there are numerous other illustrations which add to the effectiveness of biography.

Spelling of Names. Personal names that come from certain foreign languages are often spelled in many different ways in English. This is especially true of Russian and Chinese names. To them might be applied the words of H. G. Wells, who, in speaking of Egyptian names, said that few self-respecting scholars in this field would tolerate the spelling of their colleagues. The form of such names used in this department is based in each case on the preference of one or more outstanding scholars.

Bibliography. In order to meet the needs of those who desire to read more extensively regarding the lives of eminent personages, a bibliographical list has been added at the end of the department. This list contains the names of the finest biographical works in the English language as well as the names of the chief biographical reference works.

BIOGRAPHY

REFERENCE NOTE: The letter **c.** appearing before a date is an abbreviation of the word *circa*, meaning "about."

Aakjaer, Jeppe (1866-1930), Danish novelist and poet, was born near Skive, Jutland. He went to Copenhagen and worked as a journalist before returning to Jutland (1907). Aakjaer's lyric verse has been called "the voice of Denmark," and includes the volumes *Songs of the Rye* (1906), *That Summer and That Field* (1910), and *Under the Evening Star* (1927). His novels were concerned with the cause of improving the condition of farm labor.

Aanrud, Hans (1863-1953), Norwegian writer, was born in the Gausdal valley. He wrote short stories, which dealt with life in his native area, and comedies, which satirized urban culture. However, he is perhaps best known for his children's books, *Sidsel Longskirt* (1903) and *Solve Suntrap* (1910).

Aardema, Verna Norbert (1911-   ), author, was born in New Era, Mich., and graduated from Michigan State University (1934). She then became a grade school teacher and a newspaper correspondent. Her books, often folktales retold for children, include *Tales from the Story Hat* (1960), *The Sky God Stories* (1960), *The Na of Was* (1960), *More Tales from the Story Hat* (1966), and *Otwe* (1970).

Aasen, Ivar Andreas (1813-96), Norwegian philologist and poet, was born in Orsta in the Sunnmore district. He became interested in the rural dialects of Norway, and from 1837 covered the countryside studying them. These studies resulted in his creation of a language known as *New Norse* or "landsmal" (country language). His chief works were *Grammar of the Norse Folk Tongue* (1848) and *Dictionary of the Norse Folk Tongue* (1850). He also published a collection of poetry, *Anemone* (1863), some of which became folk songs.

Abbey, Edwin Austin (1852-1911), illustrator and painter, was born in Philadelphia and studied at the Pennsylvania Academy of Fine Arts. He was employed by the publishing house of Harper and Brothers and in 1878 was sent to England to gather materials for his illustration of the poems of Robert Herrick. His illustrations of Shakespeare are considered his best work. His first oil painting, *A May Day Morn,* was exhibited in 1890 in the Royal Academy, London. *The Quest of the Holy Grail,* a set of large frescoes in the Boston Public Library, is perhaps his most famous work. In 1901 he was commissioned by King Edward VII as official painter of the Coronation. Abbey became a member of the Royal Academy in London and also the National Academy of Design in New York. His later years were devoted to painting murals for the capitol at Harrisburg, Pa. He died in London.

Abbott, George Francis (1887-   ), American director, producer, and playwright, was born in Forestville, N.Y., graduated from the University of Rochester (1911), and studied for a year in George Pierce Baker's playwriting class at Harvard. He started as an actor in 1913, but his collaboration with Philip Dunning on *Broadway* (1926) resulted in his first success as a playwright. *Three Men on a Horse* and *On Your Toes* (both 1935) were his first successful attempts at direction. These were followed by *Brother Rat* (1937), *Room Service* (1938), *Boys from Syracuse* (1938), in which he collaborated with Rodgers and Hart, and *Fiorello!* (1959), which was awarded the Pulitzer Prize for drama. Abbott also wrote and directed the stage and movie versions of *The Pajama Game* (1954; film, 1957) and *Damn Yankees* (1955; film 1958). His autobiography, *Mr. Abbott* was published in 1963.

Abbott, Jacob (1803-79), American writer and teacher, was born in Hallowell, Me., graduated from Bowdoin College (1820), studied at Andover Theological Semi-

nary, and was ordained a Congregational minister. He was a professor of mathematics and theology at Amherst College (1825-29) and then established the Mt. Vernon school for girls in Boston. *The Young Christian* (1832) was Abbott's first book. This was followed by 180 other books: the most notable were three series, the "Rollo" books (30 volumes, beginning in 1834), the "Lug" books, and the "Franconia" series.

Abbott, Lyman (1835-1922), American clergyman, author, and editor, was born in Roxbury, Mass.; was graduated at the University of New York in 1853; studied and practiced law; was ordained Congregational minister in 1860; resigned his pastorate in 1869 to devote himself to literature. He edited the "Literary Record" in *Harper's Magazine;* was associate editor of *The Christian Union* with Henry Ward Beecher, whom he succeeded as pastor of Plymouth Church, Brooklyn, in 1888; resigned in 1899; became editor of *The Outlook* in 1893. He was a leading exponent of the social gospel.

Abdulhak Hamid (1852-1937), Turkish poet and diplomat, was born in Istanbul and educated in Paris and Teheran. He was instrumental in liberating Persian verse from classic traditions and introduced the romanticism of Europe. His poetry, often dealing with death, includes *Makber* (*The Tomb*), *Olu* (*The Dead*), and *Hajle* (*The Nuptial Chamber*). Hamid had a long diplomatic career, serving in the Turkish senate, of which he was deputy president during World War I, and was a member of the national assembly.

a Beckett, Gilbert Abbott (1811-56), English humorous writer, was born in London and educated at Westminster School. He founded and was editor of *Figaro in London*. He was associated with *Punch* and a contributor all his life. He was the author of many plays. His family claimed descent from the father of St. Thomas a Becket.

Abel (*ä'bel*), **Niels Henrik (1802-29),** Norwegian mathematician, was born at Findo, Norway. He completed a course at the University of Christiania and spent two years in further study in Paris and Berlin. In 1828, he was made instructor at the University and the Military School in Christiania. He made important contributions to mathematical science, particularly by his work on the theory of functions, of which he was the originator. He died near Arendal. Thanks to Abel, mathematical analysis became much clearer, paving the way to new advances in mathematics. In 1881 his complete works were published; most of them had first appeared in *Crelle's Journal.*

Abelard, Peter (1079-1142), scholastic philosopher and theologian, was born in Pallet, near Nantes, France. Doctrines advanced by Abelard reveal him as a rationalist, holding that belief must follow understanding. When Abelard was 38, he fell in love with his pupil Heloise, whose uncle later separated the lovers and had Abelard emasculated. Abelard then became a monk, and Heloise a nun. Heloise later wrote her three famous letters to Abelard which have helped to preserve their attachment as one of the great love affairs of history.

Abelard was the most famous teacher of the 12th century. He was trained in theology, and his fame rests largely on his abilities as a disputant on theological topics. He was an opponent of William of Champeaux, whom he seriously worsted in debate. Abelard became a hermit in Champagne, but hundreds of students came to him and were influenced by his liberal teachings. He is one of the important forerunners of the school of theology that afterward became the University of Paris. Much of the teaching he did in early years was at Notre Dame

Cathedral in Paris. Abelard also left important philosophical works, collected in 1836 as *Ouvrages inédits d'Abélard.* Some of his treatises are *Historia Calamitatum, Scito te ipsum, Sic et Non,* and *Dialectica.*

Abell, Kjeld (1901-61), Danish dramatist, was born at Ribe, Jutland, earned a degree in political science, then worked as a stage designer in London and Paris. Among his plays are his first success, *The Melody That Got Lost* (1935), and *Anna Sophie Hedvig* (1939), his best work, a study of dictatorship. He also wrote *Days on a Cloud* (1947) and *The Scream* (1961).

Abelson, Philip H. (1913-   ), physical chemist, was born at Tacoma, Wash. He studied at Washington State College and at the University of California, where he worked in the Lawrence Radiation Laboratory. After receiving his doctorate, he became physicist for the Carnegie Institute for research in Terrestrial Magnetism at Washington and also served at the U.S. Naval Research Laboratory. In his research, he has placed much emphasis on biophysics and biochemistry. He was appointed director of the geophysical laboratory for the Carnegie Institute and in 1962, he became editor of *Science* magazine. He edited *Researches in Geochemistry.*

Abercrombie, Lascelles (1881-1938), British poet and critic, was born in Ashton-upon-Mersey and educated in Manchester's Malvern College and Victoria University. In 1922 he became professor of English literature at Leeds University, and taught later at the universities of London and Oxford. His verse, characterized by marked individuality and metrical experimentation, was published in *Interludes and Poems* (1908) and *Collected Poems* (1930). He also wrote books on poetic theory: *Principles of English Prosody* (1923), *The Theory of Poetry* (1924), and *Poetry, Its Music and Meaning* (1932).

About (*a'boo'*), **Edmond Francois Valentin (1828-85),** French novelist and miscellaneous writer. He was educated at the Lycée Charlemagne and the Ecole Normale, Paris; was sent at government expense to the French school at Athens; on his return to Paris, he devoted himself to literature. His principal novels include *Le roi des montagnes, Le Fellah, L'Infame, Les mariages de Paris, Le roman d'un brave homme.* Among his miscellaneous works are *La Grèce contemporaine, La question Romaine,* and *Rome contemporaine.* He was elected a member of the French Academy in 1884.

Abrabanel (or Abarbanel), Isaac (1437-1508), Spanish Hebrew philosopher and statesman, was born in Lisbon, Portugal. He served at the royal courts in Portugal, Spain, and Italy. He was treasurer for Alfonso V of Portugal, but had to flee to Spain when Alfonso died. From 1484-92 he was minister of state under Ferdinand and Isabella, leaving Spain in 1492 when Ferdinand expelled the Jews. He traveled for a time in Italy, and in 1503-08 was minister of state in Venice. His fame rests on his extensive commentaries on the Old Testament. He stressed the interpretation of the Bible in the light of the social, economic, and political environment of Biblical times.

Abraham of Santa Clara (1644-1709), Austrian preacher and writer, was born in Kreenheinstetten. His real name was John Ulrich Megerle. He was educated by the Jesuits and Benedictines before joining the Augustinians and adopting the name by which he is known. He exhibited in the pulpit the same drive that is evident in his published writings. His works range from sacred to secular and include prose and poetry. His best-known work is *Judas der Erzschelm.*

Abrahams, William (1919-   ), American poet and novelist, was born in Boston. In 1941 he graduated from Harvard, where he edited the *Advocate* and received awards for his poetry. During World War II he served in the army and at the same time wrote his first novel, *Interval in Carolina* (1945). A later novel is entitled *By the Beautiful Sea.* Abrahams' poetry appeared in many periodicals and anthologies and he is considered to be in the forefront of American poets.

Abreu (*a-brâ'oo*), **Casimiro (1837-60),** Brazilian poet, was born in Rio de Janeiro. Under pressure from his father, he took up a career in business. He traveled to Portugal in 1853, and after four years returned to Brazil, where he died of tuberculosis. His verses made him one of Brazil's most popular romantic poets. His style is simple, and highly personal. His masterpiece was the collection of poems entitled *As primaveras* (*Springtimes*).

Abreu, João Capistrano de (1853-1927), Brazilian historian and philologist, was born at Maranguape, Ceará province. As a result of his works on Brazilian history, Abreu is considered the father of modern Brazilian historical writing. His principal works are *Caminhoes antigos e povoamento do Brasil* and *Capitulos de Historia Colonial.* He was also a journalist and taught at the University of Brazil in Rio de Janeiro, 1883-99.

Abruzzi (*ä-broot'sē*), **Luigi Amadeo, Duke of the (1873-1933),** Italian prince, scientist, explorer, naval officer, and litterateur, was born at Madrid, Spain. As a youth, he traveled around the world, ascended Mt. St. Elias, and penetrated nearest to the North Pole, a record in his time. He successfully ascended some of the topmost peaks in the Ruwenzori range and Himalayas. His writings include *On the Polar Star in the Arctic Sea, The Ascent of Mt. St. Elias,* and *Ruwenzori.* He commanded the Italian fleet until 1917 in World War I. After the war, he undertook a colonization plan in Italian Somaliland. He declined the Albanian throne in 1922.

Abulfeda (1273-1331) (also Abulfida or Abu-al-Fidä), Moslem prince, historian, and geographer, was born in Damascus. For his military services against the Crusaders, he was awarded the principality of Hama, which he ruled from 1310 until his death. His major work was *An Abridgment of the History of the Human Race,* a compilation of annals from the creation to 1329, especially valuable as historical source for the Crusades. Abulfeda was also a patron of literature and science, and a traveler in the Islamic world, from which he gathered the material for his *Geography.*

Abu Nuwas (c. 756-c. 810), Arabian poet, was born in Ahwaz, Persia. He settled in Baghdad and spent most of his life there. He is recognized as the greatest Arab poet of his time. He was high in favor with the Caliphs Harun-al-Rashid and Amin. The material used in his poems revealed the manners of the people of his day. His collected poems were published in Cairo as late as 1904.

Accius, Lucius (c. 170 B.C.-c. 90 B.C.), Roman tragic poet and prose writer, was born in Umbria. He was considered one of the greatest writers of tragedies of his time. His dramas were, for the most part, translations from the Greek, although some of his original plays have a Roman setting. He also wrote verse treatises on the history of Greek and Roman poetry. Reforms in spelling and grammar were also introduced by Accius. Only fragments of his work have been preserved.

Acevedo Diaz, Eduardo (1851-1921), Uruguayan novelist and diplomat, was born in Villa de la Union (now Montevideo), Uruguay. He abandoned the study of law to write historical romances. His novels, which are highly nationalistic, include the trilogy *Hymn to Blood,* strongly influenced by Victor Hugo, and *Soledad,* which pictures life on the pampas. He served as a senator and as minister to the U.S., Argentina, Italy, and Brazil.

Achard, Marcel (1899-1974), French playwright and director, was born in Sainte Foy-les-Lyon and educated at the University of Lyon. In 1959 he became a member of the French Academy. He was president of the Cannes Film Festival, 1958-60, and of the Venice Film Festival in 1960. Among his works are *Domino, I Know My Love, Patate,* and *A Shot in the Dark.* He wrote scenarios for more than 70 films, and directed movies in Hollywood as well as in France.

Achebe, Chinua (1930-   ), Nigerian novelist and poet, was born in Ogidi Ecs. In 1953 he graduated from

University College in Ibadan and became a radio producer for the Nigerian Broadcasting Company. He has also been associated with the University of Nsukka as senior research fellow. Achebe published his first novel in 1958—*Things Fall Apart*. It has been translated into some 20 languages and has been filmed. In his writing he deals with the meeting of Africa and Europe, with particular regard for his African heritage. During the Nigerian civil war he began writing poetry: *Beware Soul-Brother* was published in 1971. Achebe has also written *No Longer at Ease*, *Arrow of God*, *A Man of the People*, and *Girls at War* (short stories).

Acheson, Dean (1893-1971), American diplomat, was born at Middletown, Conn. He studied at Groton, Yale University, and Harvard Law School, and was an ensign in the U. S. Navy in World War I. After graduation from law school he served briefly as secretary to Supreme Court Justice Louis D. Brandeis. He was an official in the treasury department from 1921 to 1933, when he resigned to practice law. In 1941 he was appointed to the department of state and served as secretary of state from 1949 to 1953 during the early years of the "cold war." His advice was frequently sought by United States presidents at critical periods. Among his books are *Power and Diplomacy*, *A Citizen Looks at Congress*, and *Morning and Noon*.

Ackermann, Louise Victorine (1813-90), French poet, was born in Paris and educated at home by her father, Victorine Choquet. Her reputation rests on her principal work, *Poesies, premieres poesies, poesies philosophiques* (1874), which incorporates themes of reaction against human suffering.

Ackermann, Rudolph (1764-1834), Anglo-German inventor and lithographer, was born in Stolberg, Saxony, and eventually settled in London. Among his accomplishments were a waterproofing treatment for paper and cloth and the introduction of the illustrated annual to England. Ackermann used his own lithographic method for his publication *The Repository of Arts*.

Acosta, Cecilio (1818-81), Venezuelan poet, orator, essayist, and scholar, is known primarily for his poem *La Casita Blanca* (The Little White House). In addition to his writings, Acosta worked extensively for reforms in the educational system of Venezuela.

Acosta, Joaquin (1800-52), Colombian patriot and scholar, was born at Guaduas, fought as an officer under Simón Bolivar for the independence of New Granada, and later studied in Europe. As a prominent intellectual, he helped to found the Colombian national academy. After a series of explorations, starting in 1834, he produced material for topographical maps of Colombia. He also wrote a history of the discovery and settlement of New Granada that was published in 1848.

Acosta, José de (1539?-1600), Spanish author and missionary, became a Jesuit in 1551 and a missionary to Peru in 1571. The first book printed in Peru (1583) was his catechism in two Indian dialects. In 1598 he returned to Spain and became rector of the Jesuit college at Salamanca. His most memorable work was *Historia Natural y Moral de las Indias* (1590), a compilation of the customs and natural history of Spanish America, which was translated into most European languages.

Acosta, Mercedes de (1900-   ), French novelist, poet, and playwright, was born in Paris. Her works include *Wind Chaff* (1918); a book of poems, *Moods* (1919); a play *Sandro Botticelli* (1923); and *Until the Day Breaks* (1928).

Acton (ăk'tŭn), Sir John Emerich Edward Dalberg, First Baron (1834-1902), English historian, was born at Naples, Italy. In 1895, he was made professor of modern history at Cambridge University, and as a liberal Catholic exerted profound influence. He planned the *Cambridge Modern History*, written by eminent historical scholars after his death. He wrote *The War of 1870*, *Wolsey and the Divorce of Henry VIII*, and *Schools of History in Germany*.

Acuña (äkö'nyä), Cristobal de (1597-1676?), Spanish Jesuit missionary priest and early explorer of South America. He was the rector of the college conducted by the Jesuits in Cuenca, Ecuador. In 1638 Acuña explored the Amazon with the Portuguese explorer Pedro Teixeira. In the following year Acuña issued his *New Discovery of the Great River of the Amazons*, the first description to be published of the river and its region.

Adair, James (1709?-83?), American author and trader, was born in Ireland, but spent 40 years in the southeastern U.S. studying the Indians, especially the Chickasaws. His *History of the American Indians* (1775) is a first-hand account of the character, habits, and languages of various Indian tribes.

Adam of Bremen (died c. 1076), German historian and geographer, believed to have been born in Meissen (Saxony) before 1045. He became a canon of Bremen and master of the cathedral school. He wrote an authoritative history of the Baltic area and what is now northern Germany. Adam, regarded as one of the best German chroniclers, arranged his work in four parts. He obtained his information from written records and from conversations at the courts of Adalbert, Archbishop of Bremen, and from Estrithson, King of Denmark.

Adam de la Halle (c. 1240-88), French lyric poet, musician, and dramatist, also known as Adam le Bossu. He is first mentioned in history in 1272. A minstrel in the service of Robert II, Count of Artois, Adam supported the Angevin king of Naples and Sicily, Charles I. Adam's *Jeu de la Feuille* and *Congé* date from about 1276. His best-known work is *Jeu de Robin et Marion*. He also composed songs, motets, rounds, and epic poems.

Adam of St. Victor (died c. 1192), medieval hymn writer. Little is known of him except for his great hymns, which rank him as foremost among medieval writers of hymns. An edition of his works, believed to be complete, was published in London in 1881.

Adam, Adolphe Charles (1803-56), French composer, entered the Paris Conservatory in 1817 and then studied with Francois Boieldieu, an operatic composer. *Pierre et Catherine* (1829), his first work, was a one-act operetta. He also wrote a three-act work, *Danilowa* (1820), whose success lead to a series of dramatic compositions, including comic operas, grand opera, and the ballet *Gisell* (1841). Adam's work was extremely popular during his lifetime, but little of it is now heard, except his Christmas anthem, *Cantique de Noël*, known to the English-speaking world as *O Holy Night*.

Adam, Paul (1862-1920), French novelist, was born in Paris. He wrote a series of novels covering the Napoleonic campaigns, the restoration, and the government of Louis Philippe. *Basile and Sophia*, written in 1900, was a Byzantine romance. He died in Paris.

Adamic, Louis (1899-1951), American author, was born at Blato, Yugoslavia. He attended school in Yugoslavia until 1913, when he was brought to the United States. He was naturalized in 1918. After serving in World War I, he worked at various occupations which brought him into contact with other recent immigrants, a class to which he interpreted American ideals and whose interests and worth he interpreted to the public generally. His writings include *Dynamite, The Native's Return, Cradle of Life, My America*, and *From Many Lands*.

Adamnan of Iona, St. (c. 625-704), Irish abbot and historian, was born in Drumhome, County Donegal. He was the ninth abbot of Iona and was instrumental in effecting the adoption by the Celts of the Roman rules on the date of Easter. He wrote a life of his predecessor, Abbot Columba of Iona, and an account of the travels in the Holy Land of Arculfus, an early Christian. Adamnan's account served as a guide to the holy places in Palestine throughout the Middle Ages.

Adamov, Arthur (1908-   ), French-Russian playwright, was born in Kislovodsk, Russia, and brought up in France. He was educated in Switzerland and Germany. In 1924 he settled in Paris, and after World War II became editor of *L'heure nouvelle*, a literary magazine. He began writing plays in the 1940's. His early plays belonged to the Theater of the Absurd, reflecting a sense of futility and absurdity. With *Paolo Paoli*, the mood of his work changed to follow the tradition of Bertolt Brecht. Adamov also translated works for the French stage, including Christopher Marlowe's *Edward II.*

Adams, Abigail (1744-1818), American writer, was born in Weymouth, Mass., and educated by her grandmother. Born Abigail Smith, in 1764 she married John Adams (first vice president and second president of the U.S.). During their marriage John Adams was often away on business for the republic, and Abigail, considered the first fully emancipated woman in America, engaged in a voluminous correspondence with her husband. Her letters are considered a source for social and political affairs of the time and were published after her death as *Letters of Mrs. Adams* (1841) and *Familiar Letters of John Adams and His Wife Abigail Adams* (1876). *New Letters of Abigail Adams, 1788-1801* (edited by Stewart Mitchell, 1947) is a collection of correspondence written to her sister.

Adams, Arthur Stanton (1896-   ), American educator and engineer, was born at Winchester, Mass. He was educated at the United States Naval Academy and at several technical colleges, where he specialized in metallurgy. For several years professor of mechanics and metallurgy at the Colorado School of Mines, he became assistant dean of engineering at Cornell University and then, during World War II, special assistant in the Bureau of Naval Personnel at Washington. He had been president of the University of New Hampshire for two years when, in 1950, he was elected president of the American Council on Education, succeeding Dr. George Zook. While engaged in teaching he collaborated in the writing of two books—*Fundamentals of Thermodynamics* (with George Dewey Hilding) and *The Development of Physical Thought* (with Leonard B. Loeb).

Adams, Brooks (1848-1927), American historian, was born in Quincy, Mass., graduated from Harvard (1870), and began his career in politics and the law. Turning to lecturing and writing, Adams worked to apply scientific methods to the study of history. In his writings, he foretold the dissolution of the British Empire and the decline of France. Among his major works are *The Emancipation of Massachusetts* (1887), *The Law of Civilization and Decay* (1895), *America's Economic Supremacy* (1900) and *The New Empire* (1902).

Adams, Charles Francis (1807-86), statesman and economist, son of John Quincy Adams. He was nominated by the Free-Soil party for the office of vice president in 1848; was elected member of Congress, 1858 and 1860, by the Republicans; was minister to England, 1861-68; and was appointed one of the arbitrators of the Alabama Claims, 1871-72. His position in England during the Civil War was a most difficult one, but the duties were performed with tact and discretion. He was Democratic candidate for governor of Massachusetts in 1876. He edited works of John Adams and the lengthy *Memoirs* of John Quincy Adams. At Quincy, he set up Stone Library to house the many papers of his family.

Adams, Charles Kendall (1835-1902), American educator and historian, was born at Derby, Vt., and was educated at the University of Michigan. He also studied in Germany, France, and Italy. From 1867 to 1885, he was professor of history in the University of Michigan; from the latter year until 1892, was president of Cornell University; from 1892 to 1901, was president of the University of Wisconsin. His writings include *Democracy*

and Monarchy in France, Manual of Historical Literature, and a monograph entitled *Christopher Columbus, His Life and Work.* From 1892 to 1895, he acted as editor in chief of *Johnson's Universal Cyclopædia.*

Adams, Franklin Pierce (1881-1960), American journalist, was born at Chicago, Ill. Having studied at the University of Michigan, he entered newspaper work with the Chicago *Journal* in 1903. He subsequently was on the staff of several New York newspapers, including the *Herald-Tribune* from 1931 to 1937 and the New York *Post* from 1938. His work consisted of a daily column "The Conning Tower," composed of mixed prose and verse in humorous vein. More recently he was a member of the panel on the "Information, Please" radio program. He was editor of *Anthology of Light Verse* (1942) and of *The F. P. A. Book of Quotations* (1952).

Adams, Hannah (1755-1832), American author, was born in Medfield, Mass. Having acquired a variety of learning by private study, and being, obliged through family reverses to provide for herself from the age of 17, she turned to literature as a profession. She is credited with being the first American woman to support herself by writing. Among her books are *Views of Religious Opinion, History of New England, Evidences of Christianity,* and *History of the Jews.*

Adams, Henry (1838-1918), American historian, son of Charles Francis Adams, was born in Boston; was graduated at Harvard, 1858; and became private secretary to his father, who was American minister at London, 1861-68. He was assistant professor of history at Harvard, 1870-77, and editor of the *North American Review,* 1870-76. He then located in Washington, where he made a detailed study of the administrations of Jefferson and Madison, which he embodied in a work of original research entitled *History of the United States, 1801-17.* His *Mont Saint Michel and Chartres,* a masterly study of medieval times, and *The Education of Henry Adams,* demonstrating the inadequacy of the contemporary generation for meeting the problems of the 20th century, won him a wide and lasting reputation. He was elected to the American Academy of Arts and Letters in 1905.

Adams, Henry Carter (1851-1921), American economist, was born in Davenport, Iowa, was graduated from Iowa college (now Grinnell), 1874, and from Johns Hopkins, 1878. He studied at Heidelberg, Berlin, and Paris, 1878-79; was lecturer in Cornell university and the University of Michigan, 1880-87; also in Johns Hopkins university, 1880-82. In 1887, he was elected to the chair of political economy, University of Michigan, which he filled with distinction for thirty years. He was statistician of the interstate commerce commission, 1887-1911. In 1913-16, he was appointed adviser to a commission on Chinese railways and, when in China, assisted in organizing the ministry of communication, statistics, and accounts, His publications include *Taxation in the United States, Public Debts, Relation of the States to Industrial Action,* and *American Railway Accounting.*

Adams, James Truslow (1878-1949), American capitalist and historian, was born in Brooklyn, N. Y. Graduating from the Brooklyn Polytechnic Institute and Yale University, he engaged in a brokerage and investment business until 1912, when he retired from active participation to devote himself to public service and literature. He was a captain in the military intelligence service during World War I and was detailed for special duty at the peace conference in 1919. He had already begun a series of studies in American colonial history, and his *Founding of New England* won a Pulitzer prize in 1922. *The Adams Family, The Epic of America,* and *The March of Democracy* attained a wide popularity for their freshness, vigor, and broad grasp of historical facts. He wrote also *Building the British Empire.* He was elected to the American Academy of Arts and Letters in 1930.

Adams, John (1735-1826), second president of the United States, was born at Quincy, (formerly Braintree), Mass. He was graduated at Harvard in 1755 and was admitted to the bar in 1758. He was one of the delegates to the Continental Congress at Philadelphia, 1774; was one of the signers of the Declaration of Independence; and throughout supported the Revolution, in which, as chairman of the board of war, he took an active part. As a diplomat, he had the difficult task of seeking financial aid from various foreign countries for the new nation. He was commissioner to the court of France, 1778, and was sent on an embassy to England, 1779. In 1783 he helped draw up the Treaty of Paris to end the American Revolution. He was elected vice president of the United States in 1789; succeeded Washington as president in 1797; but, in 1800, failed to gain re-election and retired from public affairs. He died, July 4, 1826, on the 50th anniversary of the birth of the nation which he devoted his best energies to establish. Elected to American Hall of Fame, 1900. The correspondence, autobiography, and political writings of John Adams have been collected and edited and provide a valuable chapter in American history.

Adams, John Quincy (1767-1848), sixth president of the United States and son of the second president, was born in Quincy, (formerly Braintree), Mass. In his boyhood, he accompanied his father on an embassy to Europe, and he passed a considerable part of his youth in Paris, at The Hague, and, lastly, in London. When his father was elected president, the younger Adams was sent on an embassy to Berlin and traveled through Silesia. On his return to America, he was engaged as professor of rhetoric at Harvard University, where he had graduated in 1787, and was later chosen United States senator for Massachusetts. By President Madison he was sent as plenipotentiary to Russia and afterward to England. On this embassy, he took part in the negotiation of peace with England and assisted with his counsel the deputies sent from America to Ghent.

When Monroe was elected president, he recalled Adams from Europe and made him secretary of state. On the retirement of Monroe from office, Adams gained the presidency after a hard contest against Jackson in 1824. On the expiration of his term of office, he retired to Quincy, near Boston, but, in 1830, was chosen as representative of his Congressional district. He now joined the party of the Abolitionists, and frequently raised the whole House of Representatives against himself by his incessant petitions on the slavery question. On one occasion, in 1842, in order to assert strongly in the abstract the right to petition, he went so far as to present a petition for the dissolution of the Union. Adams was not popular, and he had at one time or another alienated both the Federalists and Democrats by thwarting their policies, but he was deeply respected for his intellect and his adherence to high ideals. Elected to the American Hall of Fame in 1905. Adams's extensive *Memoirs*, edited by his son, is today numbered among his greatest achievements.

Adams, Leonie (1899-   ), poet and educator, was born in Brooklyn. She received an A. B. from Barnard College in 1922, and a D. Litt. degree from New Jersey College for Women in 1950. She taught at New York University, Bennington College, New Jersey College for Women, and Columbia University. She has received several poetry awards, including the Harriet Monroe award, the Shelley Memorial award, and the Bollingen Prize in Poetry in 1954. Her works include *Those Not Elect, High Falcon*, and *Poems, A Selection*.

Adams, Maude (1872-1953), American actress, was born at Salt Lake City; her family name was Kiskadden, but she adopted her mother's maiden name, Adams. She appeared on the stage in child's parts; joined E. H. Sothern's company, New York, at 16; played an in-génue role in the *Midnight Bell*; afterward joined Charles Frohman's stock company. She later was leading lady with John Drew for five years; achieved notable distinction and popularity as Lady Babbie in *The Little Minister;* as Juliet in *Romeo and Juliet;* also in *Peter Pan, Joan of Arc, Chantecler*, and many other plays. She retired from the stage in 1918, and in 1937 became professor of drama at Stephens College for Women, Columbia, Mo.

Adams, Richard (George) (1920-   ), novelist, was born in Newbury, Berkshire, England. He studied history at Oxford and received his master's degree there. During World War II he served in the British Army. Entering government service in 1948, Adams became assistant secretary of the Department of Environment in 1968. In 1974 he retired to devote his full time to writing. His first novel, *Watership Down*, was published in 1972. An animal fantasy in the tradition of Lewis Carroll, A.A. Milne, and J.R.R. Tolkien, the book became a best seller. In this saga, Adams created a rabbit society, with its own language, government, and folklore. His book won the Carnegie Medal and Guardian Award for children's fiction in 1973. Adams' second novel, *Shardik*, was published in 1974, followed by *The Plague Dogs* in 1977. These too were best-sellers.

Adams, Samuel Hopkins (1871-1958), American writer, was born at Dunkirk, New York. After he was graduated from Hamilton College in 1891, he became a newspaper reporter and magazine writer. Of his many novels, several have been filmed, among them *It Happened One Night* (1934), *Gorgeous Hussy* (1934), and *The Harvey Girls* (1942). He also wrote *The Pony Express* (1950), *The Santa Fe Trail* (1952), and *The Erie Canal* (1953). His *Grandfather Tales* was published in 1955.

Adams, William Taylor (1822-97), known under the pseudonym "Oliver Optic," American juvenile writer, born in Medway, Mass. For many years he was a public school teacher in Boston. He wrote more than one hundred books for boys. Besides two novels—*The Way of the World* and *Living Too Fast*, he wrote many series for young people, including *Army and Navy, Starry Flag, Yacht Club, Riverdale Story Books*, and *Great Western*.

Adamson, Joy (Friedericke Victoria) (1910-   ), writer and painter, was born in Austria, and was educated in Vienna. Kenya, her home for more than 25 years, has been the source for her paintings and her writing. Her paintings record the people, flowers, and animals of Africa. *Born Free*, her first book, was an immediate success and was made into a motion picture. It is the story of a lioness named Elsa, which she and her game-warden husband raised from a cub and later trained to survive in the wild. Later sequels were *Living Free, Forever Free*, and *Elsa*.

Addams, Charles (1912-   ), noted American cartoonist, was born in Westfield, N. J. He began drawing in his youth while attending Colgate University, the University of Pennsylvania, and the Grand Central School of Art in New York. His cartoons were a regular feature in the *New Yorker* magazine, beginning in 1935. Addams also made animated educational films for the U.S. Army during World War II. His cartoons are noted for their macabre humor. Among Addam's books of cartoons are *Drawn and Quartered, Addams and Evil, Monster Rally,* and *Home Bodies*. His work has been exhibited at the Fogg Art Museum, Harvard University, and the Metropolitan Museum of Art, New York.

Addams, Jane (1860-1935), social reformer and head resident of Hull House, Chicago, was born at Cedarville, Ill.; was graduated at Rockford College, 1881; spent two years in Europe, 1883-85; studied in Philadelphia, 1888; and, in 1889, with Miss Ellen Gates Starr, opened the social settlement of Hull House. By her practical methods, executive gifts, and humanitarian spirit, she became one of the foremost leaders of social settlement work in America. In 1919, she was elected president of the International Congress of Women at Washington and attended the peace conventions at Zurich in 1919 and at Vienna in 1921. She received one-half the Nobel prize for peace, 1931. Her publications include *The Spirit of Youth and the City Streets* and *A New Conscience and an Ancient Evil.*

Addison, Joseph (1672-1719), English essayist, was born at Milston, England; was graduated at Oxford; and held for some years a fellowship at the University. Here some of his early writings brought him into notice and secured him a pension of $1500 a year. He traveled on the continent, observing, studying, and writing. In the winter of 1701, amid the stoppages and discomforts of a journey across Mont Cenis, he composed his *Letter from Italy,* which contains many fine touches of description and is by far the best of his poems. His poem *The Campaign,* written in celebration of the battle of Blenheim, 1704, won him, as a reward, the office of excise commissioner. He held other public offices, which kept him from writing much for the next six years. In 1710, he began writing a series of essays, upon which his fame chiefly rests. These he contributed to the *Tatler,* next to the *Spectator,* and afterward to the *Guardian,* which he published in conjunction with his friend, Richard Steele. Of these periodicals, the *Spectator* ran only a few months, but, mainly on account of Addison's essays, it still lives in the history of English literature.

Ade (*ād*), **George (1866-1944),** American humorist and playwright, was born at Kentland, Ind.; was graduated at Purdue University, 1887; was engaged in newspaper work in Lafayette, Ind., 1887-90; and was with the Chicago *Record,* for which he wrote his widely popular *Fables in Slang,* 1890-1900. His characters are chiefly drawn from rural life, outlined faithfully and sympathetically. He was the author of *Artie, The Girl Proposition, Breaking into Society,* and *In Pastures New.* His plays, which display cleverness and much satirical humor, include *The Sultan of Sulu, The College Widow, Father and the Boys, Marse Covington,* and *Nettie.*

Adelard of Bath (12 century), English philosopher and scholar, was noted for his Arabic studies. He traveled extensively in the East and in the Mediterranean area. Adelard translated Euclid from Arabic into Latin and also compiled a work incorporating most of the learning of the Arabs. His principal work, entitled *De eodem et deverso,* concerns the philosophical questions of identity and difference.

Adenauer, Konrad (1876-1967), German statesman, was born at Cologne, where he practiced law and spent the greater part of his active life in politics. He was lord mayor in 1917 and attained national prominence as a leader in the Center party. He was dismissed by the Nazi regime and held briefly as a political prisoner. Adenauer was the first chancellor of the German Federal Republic (West Germany) under its constitution adopted in 1949. As leader of the Christian Democratic party, he was reelected successively and served until his resignation in late 1963 at the age of 87. Under his leadership West Germany rose with astonishing rapidity from a state of economic and political collapse to become again a leading power in Europe. Adenauer's policy envisaged that Germany would turn its back on its history of narrow nationalism and promote a united Europe in cooperation with the United States. Adamant against Russian threats, Germany became a member of NATO. It was a charter member of the Common Market, organized in 1950. Reparations were paid to Israel in compensation for Hitler's campaign for Jewish extermination. Adenauer signed a treaty of friendship with France's president, De Gaulle, in early 1963 to end a century of hostility. He refused, however, to acquiesce in De Gaulle's anti-British and anti-American policies. His *Memoirs, 1945-53* were published in 1966.

Adenet le Roi (c. 1240-c. 1300), French poet and troubadour, was also called Adam, Adan le Menestrel, and Adènes. He was born in Brabant and was a ministrel at the court of Henry III, Duke of Brabant. When Henry died, Adenet entered the service of Guy of Dampierre (later Count of Flanders) and accompanied him on a crusade to Tunis. Adenet recorded the events of this journey in his poems. His chief work was Cléomades, a long romance. Three *chansons de geste* (a type of Old French poem celebrating the deeds of heroic figures) are also extant.

Adler, Alfred (1870-1937), Austrian psychologist, was born at Vienna. He studied with Freud, with whom he came to differ, holding that Freud overestimated sex as a factor in conduct and underestimating the drive for power and the sense of inferiority. Adler coined the term "inferiority complex," which concept became widely current as a result of his lectures and books, including *The Practice and Theory of Individual Psychology, Pattern of Life,* and *What Life Should Mean to You.*

Adler, Cyrus (1863-1940), American orientalist and archeologist, was born at Van Buren, Ark., was graduated from the University of Pennsylvania, 1883, and from Johns Hopkins University, 1887, where he was consecutively fellow, instructor, and associate professor of Semitic languages, 1884-93. He was librarian of the Smithsonian institution, 1892-1905, and curator of historic archeology, United States national museum, 1889-1908. He was thereafter president of Dropsie college for Hebrew and cognate learning until 1916, when, for eight years he acted as president of the Jewish Theological Seminary of America. In 1924 he was officially appointed to the presidency of the institution, serving there until his death. He edited the *American Jewish Yearbook* and published *The Shafar, Its Use and Origin; Jews in the Diplomatic Correspondence of the United States;* and other writings.

Adler, Felix (1851-1933), educator and lecturer, was born in Alzey, Germany; came to America in 1857; was graduated at Columbia University, 1870; studied at Berlin and Heidelberg; and was professor of Hebrew and Oriental literature at Cornell University, 1874-76. In 1876, he established the New York Society for Ethical Culture. He became professor of political and social ethics, Columbia University, in 1902. His publications include *Life and Destiny, An Ethical Philosophy of Life,* and *The Reconstruction of the Spiritual Ideal.*

Adler, Mortimer J(erome) (1902-   ), philosopher, editor, and writer, was born in New York City. Educated at Columbia University, he taught philosophy of law at the University of Chicago. Adler has encouraged the idea of a liberal education based on reading and discussing great books. With Robert M. Hutchins, he edited the 54-volume *Great Books of the Western World.* Adler's other works include *How to Read a Book, A Dialectic of Morals, The Capitalist Manifesto* (with Louis O. Kelso), *The Revolution in Education* (with Milton Mayer), and *The Conditions of Philosophy.* In 1952 he became a director of the Institute for Philosophical Research.

Adlerbeth, (Baron) Gudmund Jöran (1751-1818), Swedish poet, historian, and politician; served in the court of Gustav III. He translated Latin classics and Icelandic sagas into Swedish, adapted Racine's *Iphigénie* and Voltaire's *Oedipus* for the Swedish stage, and wrote the tragedy *Ingjald Illrada,* as well as original librettos. In 1786 he became the first president of the Swedish Academy.

Ady, Endre (1877-1919), Hungarian poet, was born in Transylvania. He spent much time in Paris, where he became the leader of a radical group of Hungarian writers. Considered one of the greatest lyrical poets of Hungary, he interpreted the society of his time in his writings. Ady's publications included 12 volumes of poetry and 7 of prose.

Aelfric (c. 950-1020), abbot and author, called Grammaticus (the Grammarian). He is regarded as the greatest Anglo-Saxon prose writer of the 10th and 11th centuries. Aelfric was educated at the Benedictine monastery at Winchester under Aethelwold, one of the chief monastic reformers of the time. Aelfric conducted the school at the Abbey of Cerne (Dorset) and in 1005 became abbot at Eynsham, remaining there until his death. He wrote the first Latin grammar in a medieval vernacular. This work and his *Glossary* and *Colloquy* were textbooks for the monastic schools. His other writings include the *Catholic Homilies, Lives of the Saints,* and the *Life of St. Aethelwold.* Aelfric also wrote on the general rule of monastic life and was the author of many pastoral letters. His writings reveal great familiarity with the religious thought of his time, and his works were widely studied and copied throughout the Middle Ages. He was the first Anglo-Saxon writer whose work was printed.

Aelian (Claudius Aelianus) (late 2nd, early 3rd century A.D.), Roman author and teacher of rhetoric, was born at Praeneste. He spoke Greek fluently and also wrote in Greek, frequently using stories of animal life to teach goodness of character. His chief works are *De natura Animalium* and *Variae historiae.*

Aeneas, Tacticus (4th Century B.C.), Greek writer on military tactics. His several treatises on the art of war, only one of which is still in existence, dealt with the defense of fortified cities. The remaining work also contains illustrations of historical significance.

Aeschines (5th century B.C.), Athenian philosopher, was a friend of Socrates. A poor man of humble parentage, he was unsuccessful in business, but achieved success as a private teacher of philosophy in Athens. He wrote several philosophical dialogues, but there is no assurance that the ones in existence that are credited to him are his original writings.

Æschines (ĕs'kĭ-nēz) (389 B.C.-314 B.C.), Athenian orator, who vied with Demosthenes in eloquence. As head of the peace party, at Athens, Æschines was the chief opponent of Demosthenes, who advocated strenuous opposition to Philip of Macedon, then pursuing his designs for the subjugation of the Greek states. Events justified the sagacious fears of Demosthenes. When, however, it was proposed by Ctesiphon to reward Demosthenes with a golden crown Æschines indicted Ctesiphon for bringing forward an illegal proposal. Demosthenes replied in perhaps the greatest of his speeches,—*On the Crown,* —and Æschines, defeated, had to leave Athens. He went into exile at Rhodes where, tradition says, he established a school of eloquence.

Æschylus (ĕs'kĭ-lŭs) (525 B.C.-456 B.C.), Greek tragedian, was born at Eleusis in Attica. His father, Euphorion, brought Æschylus as a youth under religious influences which distinctly affected the tone of his dramatic works. In 499 B.C., Æschylus made his first appearance as competitor for the prize offered annually at Athens to the poet producing the best tragedy, but it was not until 484 B.C. that he achieved his first victory. In the course of 40 years, he competed nearly 20 times, each time with a trilogy of three related tragedies followed by a so-called satyr play, having a comic character. He won the first prize on 13 occasions. Æschylus took part in three famous battles against the Persians—Marathon, Salamis, and Platœa. He undertook three journeys to Syracuse—in 476, 471, and 456 B.C.—visiting the court of Hiero, the tyrant of the city. His absence from Athens has been attributed to political expediency, for Æschylus belonged to the conservative, aristocratic party, which was then on the decline in the growing democracy of Athens. Before the days of Æschylus, Greek tragedy consisted of dramas acted by a chorus, a chorus leader, and one actor. There was little plot and no scenery or

other accessories. Æschylus added a second actor; invented costumes, including mask, mantle, and the so-called tragic boot; had the plays produced on a regular stage; and used the services of the scene painter. He also gave to Greek tragedy its characteristic literary form. Such innovations entitled him to be called "the father of tragedy." Æschylus was serious, bold, and often sublime in his style and originality of phrase. He stoutly upheld reverence for the gods, the sanctity of oaths, the duties of hospitality, and the inviolability of marriage. His plays have simple plots, for he does not represent the complex subtleties of human character; he rather depicts his heroes as victims of destiny, their struggles against which involve them in situations of great tragic intensity. Only 7 of his 70 tragedies are extant: *The Seven against Thebes, The Suppliants, The Persians, Prometheus Bound, The Choëphori, The Eumenides,* and *Agamemnon.*

Æsop (ē'sŏp) (c. 620 B.C.-c. 560 B.C.), celebrated fabulist, is said to have been born at Phrygia. He was as deformed in body as he was accomplished in mind. Originally a slave at Athens and at Samos, he gained freedom by his wit, traveled through Asia Minor and Egypt, and later attached himself to the court of Crœsus, king of Lydia. Sent by that monarch upon an embassy to Delphi, he so offended the inhabitants by the keenness of his sarcasms that they are said to have hurled him from a rock into the sea.

Afanasyev, Alexander Nikolayevich (1826-71), Russian folklorist and antiquarian. His writings were instrumental in introducing Russian popular tales to world literature. His *Russian Folk-Tales* (1860) is the first authentic collection of Russian fairy tales. A selection of these stories has been translated into English.

Afranius, Lucius (flourished 100 B.C.), Roman comic poet, is considered the greatest master of the *togata,* a comedy form of his age. He modeled his work on Menander and the Attic Comedy. A prolific and popular writer whose plays were still being acted in Nero's time, he wrote chiefly of everyday life in the middle-class Rome of his day.

Afzelius, Arvid August (1785-1871), Swedish poet, historian, and mythologist, was a parish priest in Enkoping. His best-known work is the collection *Swedish Folk Tunes from Olden Times,* on which he collaborated with the historian Erik Gustaf Geyer. Afzelius translated the *Elder Edda* and wrote a history of Sweden to the time of Charles XII. *Memories,* his autobiography, was published in 1901.

Agassiz, Louis Johann Rudolph (1807-73), naturalist, was born in Switzerland, the son of a Swiss Protestant clergyman. He studied medicine and was graduated at Munich, but devoted himself principally to ichthyology, and was employed to classify and arrange the collection brought from Brazil by Martius and Spix. In 1846, he came to America, where he was well received, and, in 1848, accepted the chair of zoology and geology at Harvard College. In 1865, he visited Brazil and, on his return, placed in the museum of Cambridge the large collection he had made. He wrote *Glaciers, Outlines of Comparative Physiology, An Essay on Classification,* and numerous other valuable works. He was to the last a disbeliever in the Darwinian theory of evolution. He was one of the most gifted teachers of his time, and the list of his pupils includes many distinguished names in American biological science. Elected to American Hall of Fame, 1915.

Agathias, (c. 536-581), Greek poet and historian, studied law at Alexandria and Constantinople. He collected a number of contemporary poems entitled a *Cycle of New Epigrams,* which included some of his own compositions. The history he wrote of his own times is the chief authority for the years 552-558.

Agee, James (1909-55), American writer, was born in Knoxville, Tenn. and graduated from Harvard University. As a member of the staff of *Fortune* magazine, he was assigned to study the life of an Alabama sharecropper, this study being published as a book, with photographs by Walker Evans, *Let Us Now Praise Famous Men* (1941). In 1939 Agee joined *Time* magazine, and from 1943 to 1948 was film reviewer for the *Nation*. Beginning in 1948, he wrote screenplays for several movies including *The Quiet One, The African Queen,* and *The Night of the Hunter*. His novels include *Morning Watch* and *A Death in the Family,* which won a 1958 Pulitzer Prize and was adapted into a play, *All the Way Home,* which won a 1961 Pulitzer Prize.

Agnon, S(hmuel) Y(osef) (Halevi) (1888-1970), Jewish novelist, whose real name was Shmuel Yosef Czaczkes, was born in Buczacz, Galicia. He studied at the Hirsch School and was instructed in the Talmud by his father. At 15, he published his first poems in Hebrew and Yiddish. He was an active Zionist, advocating establishment of a Jewish homeland in Palestine, and in 1908 went to Jaffa, in Palestine, as secretary of the National Jewish Council. In 1912 he went to Berlin, where with Martin Buber he collected stories of the Hasidic Jews, and the two writers founded the journal *Der Jude*. Agnon returned permanently to Palestine in 1924.

From *Agunot (Forsaken Wives),* Agnon took his pen name. His other works include *The Bridal Canopy, A Guest for the Night, Only Yesterday, Two Tales, In the Heart of the Seas, Days of Awe, The Book of Deeds,* and *A Wayfarer Tarrieth the Night*. In 1935 and 1951 he won the Bialek prize for literature, Israel's highest literary honor. He won the Israel Prize in 1950 and 1958, and in 1966 shared the Nobel prize for literature with Nelly Sachs, also a Jewish writer. Agnon was the first Israeli and first Hebrew writer to win the Nobel award.

Agoult, Countess d' (1805-76), French writer, was born Marie Catherine Sophie de Flavigny in Frankfort am Main, Germany. After several years of marriage to Count Agoult, she left him to live and travel with Franz Liszt, the composer, for about ten years. In 1839 she began to write, in Paris, under the name of Daniel Stern. Her autobiographical novel *Nélida* (1846) was followed by works on history, politics, and philosophy. Two books of memoirs, *Mes Souvenirs 1806-33* (1877) and *Mémoires 1833-54* (1927), were published posthumously.

Agricola, Martin (1486-1566), German writer, was born Martin Sohr in Schwiebus, Brandenburg, and was a teacher and cantor at Magdeburg. His main interest was in music theory and notation, and much of his writing deals with the development of modern musical notation. *Musica instrumentalis deutsch* (1528), written in simple and powerful verse, was his major work.

Agricola, Rudolphus (1443-85), Dutch scholar, was born near Groningen, Friesland. His real name was Roelof Huysman. He was educated in Louvain, Paris, and Ferrara, where he attended lectures of the most celebrated thinkers of his day. Johann von Dalberg, afterward bishop of Worms, invited Agricola to accept a professorship at Heidelberg, where he lectured on Greek and Roman literature.

Agronsky, Martin Zama (1915-), American newspaper correspondent and radio news analyst, was born in Philadelphia. After graduating from Rutgers University in 1936, he became a foreign correspondent. With the outbreak of World War II, he began covering the battle fronts. His broadcasts from all quarters of the globe became familiar to American listeners. He was with the British army in Libya, and when the Japanese attacked Singapore Agronsky was there. He joined the American Broadcasting Company in 1943 as Washington correspondent. In 1964, he became bureau chief for the Columbia Broadcasting System, frequently presiding over televised panels in discussion of public questions.

Aguilar, Grace (1816-47), English writer, and daughter of a merchant, was born in London. Her books on the religion and history. of the Jewish people, emphasized spiritual and moral values. *Home Influence,* a sentimental novel, was published during her lifetime. Her other novels were published posthumously.

Aiken, Conrad Potter (1889-1973), American poet, novelist, short-story writer, and critic, was born at Savannah, Georgia. He was graduated from Harvard in 1911, and the first of his many books of poems appeared in 1914. His *Selected Poems,* published in 1929, won the Pulitzer prize. His *Collected Poems* appeared in 1955. Meanwhile, in 1950, *The Short Stories of Conrad Aiken* was published. His novels include *Blue Voyage* (1927), *Great Circle* (1933), *King Coffin* (1935), and *The Conversation* (1940).

Aiken, Joan (1924-), writer, was born in Rye, England, and attended school in Oxford. After publishing poems at 16 and stories at 17, she worked for the United Nations in London. Her novels for juveniles include *All You Ever Wanted,* (1953), *More Than You Bargained For* (1955), and *The Whispering Mountain* (1968). *Night Fall* (1969) won the Mystery Writers of America Award. Her other works, mostly adult mysteries, include *The Silence of Herondale* (1964), *A Cluster of Separate Sparks* (1972), *Castle Barebane* (1976), *Go Saddle the Sea* (1977), and *The Faithless Lollybird* (1978).

Aikin (āʹkǐn), **John (1747-1822),** English physician, was born at Kibworth, Leicestershire. After studying at Edinburgh and London, he took his medical degree at Leiden in 1780, and practiced in Chester, Warrington, Yarmouth, and London. In 1798, he retired to Stoke Newington. A friend of Priestley, E. Darwin, John Howard, and Southey, he was a voluminous author. His works include biographies of Howard, Selden, and Usher; the *General Biography* (10 vols.); and the well-known *Evenings at Home* (6 vols.), written in conjunction with his sister, Mrs. Barbauld.

Ailly, Pierre d' (1350-1420), French cardinal, theologian, and philosopher, was born in Compiègne and educated at the College of Navarre in Paris. After obtaining his doctorate in theology (1381), he was appointed chancellor of the University of Paris in 1389, became bishop of Puy in 1395, bishop of Cambrai in 1397, and was created a cardinal in 1411. D'Ailly was active in church reforms, among them the ending of the Great Schism of the West and the Gregorian reform of the calendar. He also influenced the course of world history through his work the *Image of the World,* which describes the possibility of reaching the Indies by voyaging to the west. Christopher Columbus owned the book and made numerous notes in it. Columbus' copy of the work is now in the library of Seville.

Aimard, Gustave (1818-83), French novelist, was born in Paris. His real name was Olivier Gloux. He based his writings on experience he gained when, as a young boy, he traveled to America and spent several years among the Indians. His romances were written in the style of James Fenimore Cooper and Aimard has often been referred to as his French counterpart. Among his best-known novels are *Les Trappeurs de l'Arkansas* and *Nuits Mexicaines*. He died in Paris.

Ainger, Alfred (1837-1904), English clergyman and writer, was born in London. He attended King's College, and Trinity College, Cambridge, and was ordained in 1860. In 1894, he became principal clergyman of Temple Church in London. He was Chaplain-in-ordinary to Queen Victoria and King Edward VII. Ainger's writings include *The Gospel and Human Life* (sermons) and authorative works on Charles Lamb, George Crabbe, and Thomas Hood.

Ainsworth, William Harrison (1805-82), novelist, was born in Manchester, England. He studied law, but turned to writing. His first success was *Rockwood,* with its vivid description of Dick Turpin's ride. By 1881 Ainsworth had published 39 novels; 7 of them, including *Tower of London, Guy Fawkes, Miser's*

Daughter, and *St. James's,* were illustrated by Cruikshank.

Airy (âr´ĭ), **George Biddell (1801-92),** English mathematician, astronomer, physicist, and engineer, was born at Alnwick, England; was graduated at Trinity College, Cambridge, in 1823; and, soon after, published his *Mathematical Tracts on the Lunar and Planetary Theories,* the *Figures of the Earth,* and the *Undulatory Theory of Optics.* In 1825, he discovered astigmatism; in 1826, was appointed Lucasian professor of mathematics; and, in 1828, became Plumian professor of astronomy at Cambridge and director of the observatory. In 1835, he succeeded Pond as astronomer-royal at the Greenwich Observatory, a post which he held for 46 years, equipping the observatory with an entirely new outfit of instruments, which were mostly of his own design and were for a long time the most accurate in use. Here he introduced the systematic observation of the magnetic elements and investigated the lunar theory, the magnetism of iron ships, the density of the earth, the length of the seconds pendulum, and a great variety of other subjects.

Akahito, Yamabe no (died c. 736), Japanese poet. He wrote graceful short poems, often describing nature. He and Kakinomoto no Hitomaro are considered the foremost poets of the *Manyoshu* (Collection of Ten Thousand Leaves), an anthology of Japanese poetry made some time after 759. Most of the poetry in the *Manyoshu* is from what is called the golden age of Japanese poetry.

Akbar (äk´bar) **(1542-1605),** Mogul emperor, was born at Amarkote in Sind. When he ascended the throne, only a small part of what had formerly belonged to the Mogul Empire acknowledged his authority, and he devoted himself with great success to the recovery of the revolted provinces. He encouraged commerce and had the land carefully measured so that the taxes should be fair. His people were of different races and religions, but he was just and tolerant to all. He founded schools and encouraged learning. Such measures gained for him the title of "guardian of mankind," and caused him to be held up as a model to Indian princes of later times.

Akeley, Carl Ethan (1864-1926), American animal sculptor and naturalist, was born in Orleans County, N.Y. He was employed in the Milwaukee Museum from 1887 to 1895, and then went to the Field Museum, Chicago. There he developed a method of mounting habitat groups which has been widely adopted, a method which relies in part on animal sculpture. He created a large number of small animal figures or groups of figures in bronze, which depict vividly dramatic moments in the lives of the animals. Among them are the elephant group of "Wounded Comrade" and the "Lion and Cape Buffalo." From five expeditions for museums he brought back impressive specimens of elephants and gorillas. He wrote *In Brightest Africa,* telling of his explorations.

Akenside (ā´kĕn-sīd), **Mark (1721-70),** English poet and physician, was born at Newcastle on Tyne. He studied theology and then medicine at the University of Edinburgh. Later, he completed his medical education at Leiden. He owes his rank among poets chiefly to his *Pleasures of the Imagination,* published in 1744, which at once became famous. In 1745, he settled in London, and, in 1761, he became physician to the queen.

Akhmadulina, Bella (1937-   ), Russian poet, was born in Moscow and educated at the Gorky Institute. She was married to the Poet Yevgeny Yevtushenko, divorced in 1960, and was later also separated from her second husband, the writer Yuri Nagibin. Besides writing lyrics, Bella Akhmadulina has acted in a film and has been the subject of poems by Yevtushenko. Her translated books of poetry include *The String* (1962) and *Fever* (1969).

Akhmatova, Anna (1888-1966), Russian poet, was born in Kiev. Her real name was Anna Andreyevna

Gorenka. She belonged to the "Acmeist" school of writing, which rejected symbolism. She published no original poetry from 1922 until 1940, when her work again appeared in magazines. In 1946 she was expelled from the Soviet writers' union by the Communist central committee, which found her poetry "empty" and "bourgeois." She regained approval after Stalin's death, while also achieving recognition outside Russia. In 1965 she received an honorary doctorate of literature from Oxford University. *Forty-Seven Love Poems* contains many of her poems in English translation.

Akhtal (c. 640-710), Arab poet, was born in Iraq. The original name of this Christian Arab, who was a court poet to the Ommiad rulers, was Ghiyath ibn Harith. Among the Arabs, Akhtal ranked with Jarir and Ferazdaq as a trio of poets celebrated for their works.

Aksakov, Ivan Sergeivich (1823-86), Russian poet and journalist, was born at Nadezhdinsk. In 1852 he wrote the first Russian narrative poem on peasant life, "Brodyaga" (The Tramp), and founded and edited the newspapers *Den* (1861-65) and *Moskva* (1867-69). A leading figure in the Pan-Slav movement, Aksakov urged the Russians to liberate the Balkans from Turkey. After the Russo-Turkish War (1877-78), he was exiled for denouncing the Treaty of Berlin in 1878, but later returned and founded the journal *Rus* in 1880. He remained editor of the journal until his death in Moscow.

Aksakov, Sergei Timofeyevich (1791-1859), Russian writer, was born in Ufa and worked as a government official until 1830. He then turned to literature, encouraged by his friend, Nikolai Gogol. Aksakov's style was realistic and generally autobiographical. His main works include *Notes About Fishing* (1847), *Notes of a Hunter of Orenburg Province* (1852), *Family Chronicle* (1856), *Years of Childhood* (1858), and *Recollections of Gogol,* an analysis of Gogol's writing.

Akutagawa Ryunosoke (1892-1927), Japanese writer of stories, verse, and drama, was born in Tokyo and educated at Tokyo University, where he studied English literature. Under the influence of Natsume Soseki, considered the foremost Japanese novelist of the time, Akutagawa's literary career flourished. He adapted many 12th- and 13th-century Japanese tales to his own style. Among his works translated into English are *Rashomon and Other Stories, Hell Screen and Other Stories,* and *Kappa.*

Alain-Fournier (1886-1914), French novelist, was born Henri Alain Fournier. The son of schoolteachers, he grew up in the small village of La Chapelle d'Angillon, and completed his education in Paris at the Lycée Lakanal. He was reported missing in action in France during World War I, and presumed dead. His one novel, *Le Grand Meaulnes,* had become a classic. It was translated into English in 1959 under the title *The Lost Domain.* His earlier prose and verse were published posthumously in *Miracles.*

Alaman, Lucas (1792-1853), Mexican historian and statesman, was born in Guanajuato. He held several public offices and was active in national and international affairs all his life and founded the National Museum in Mexico City. His *Disertaciones,* in 3 volumes and especially his *Historia de Mexico,* in 5 volumes, are considered important works in Mexican historiography. He died in Mexico City.

Alan of Lille (Alain de Lille, Alanus de Insulis) (c. 1128-1202), French theologian, philosopher, and writer, was born in Lille. Known as the "Universal Doctor," he studied and taught at Paris. He held that the mind can know the universe, but that God can be known only through faith. Alan's works include *Anticlaudianus,* an allegorical treatment of man, the arts, and morality, which influenced the work of Chaucer and Dante; and the *Liber parabolarum,* proverbs on moral conduct written in verse.

Alarcón, (Pedro) Antonio de (1833-91), Spanish novelist, was born in Guadix and studied law before turning to journalism. His writings are regarded as among the best examples of 19th-century romantic regionalism. However, when a play of his was hissed off the stage, he joined the Spanish campaign in Morocco, and as a result wrote a masterpiece of war memoirs, *Diarie de un testigo de la guerra de Africa* (1859-60). *The Three-Cornered Hat* (1874), a short novel on which a ballet of the same name was based, is his best-known work.

Alarcón y Mendoza (ä'lär-kōn ē' mĕn-dō' sä), **Don Juan Ruiz de (1590-1639),** Spanish dramatic poet, was born in Mexico toward the end of the 16th century and in 1600, went to Spain. In 1628, he published a volume containing eight comedies and, in 1634, another containing twelve. One of them, called *La Verdad Sospechosa,* "The Truth Suspected," furnished Corneille with the groundwork and greater part of the substance of his *Menteur.* His *Tejedor de Segovia,* "Weaver of Segovia," and *Las Paredes Oyen,* "Walls Have Ears," have been very popular in Spain.

Alas y Ureña, Leopoldo (1825-1901), Spanish writer and critic, was born in Zamora. He taught law and political economy at the University of Oviedo. Writing under the pen name of Clarín, he contributed critical essays to the leading periodicals in Madrid. His essays were later collected into three volumes. He also published *Galdos,* a critical study; novels, including *La Regenta;* and short stories.

Albee, Edward (1928-   ), American playwright, was born in Washington, D.C. He settled in New York and wrote *Zoo Story* in 1958. Like many of his other plays, *Zoo Story* deals with alienation and the struggle for communication. *The Death of Bessie Smith* (1960) and *The American Dream* (1961) were chosen as the best plays of the 1960-61 season. Acclaimed in Europe, Albee was not critically accepted as a ranking American playwright until *Who's Afraid of Virginia Woolf?* (1962) was produced on Broadway. Believing that a playwright should be a social critic as well as offering entertainment. Albee attacks social values through his plays, which are often laced with satire and obscenity. He has been identified with the Theater of the Absurd, and has received many awards. Later plays include *The Ballad of the Sad Cafe* (1963), *Tiny Alice* (1964), *Malcolm* (1965), *A Delicate Balance* (1966), *Everything in the Garden* (1967), and *Box and Quotations from Mao-Tse-tung* (1968). Albee received the Pulitzer Prize for drama in 1967.

Alberdi, Juan Bautista (1810-84), Argentine publicist and political writer, was born in Tucuman. He studied law in Buenos Aires and Montevideo. He supported Juan Manuel Rosas, the dictator, but later wrote against him. The new constitution adopted by the Argentine constitutional assembly in 1853 contained many features from Alberdi's work, *Bases and Starting-Points for the Political Organization of the Argentine Republic.* He used the pseudonym Figarillo for some of his less serious writings.

Albert of Stade (13th century), historian and writer. After being abbot of the Benedictine monastery of Stade, near Hamburg, Germany, he entered the Franciscan order in 1240. Albert wrote a long Latin epic entitled *Troilus.* He also wrote a history covering events from the creation through 1256.

Albert, Heinrich (1604-51), German poet and composer, was born in Lobenstein. He was educated in Leipzig, then went to Königsberg, where he became an organist. He wrote songs, chorals, and hymn tunes. He is thought to have created the German lied, or folksong, form.

Albert, Joseph (1825-86), German photographer, born at Munich. He established a photographic studio in Augsburg in 1850 but, in 1858, returned to Munich

where he became interested in the application of photography to printing. About 1867, he discovered and introduced an improvement of great importance in photomechanical printing. Albert found that gelatin, by exposure to the action of light, could be hardened and rendered sufficiently durable for photomechanical printing. In place of the old metallic plates he substituted transparent gelatin plates. Prints made by this process were called "albertypes." After this process was perfected, it was possible to obtain more than a thousand albertype copies from one plate.

Alberti (äl-bâr'tē), **Leon Battista (1404-72),** Italian architect and writer on art and poetry, was born at Florence. He was much employed by Pope Nicholas V. He completed the Pitti palace at Florence and designed the church of Saint Francis at Rimini. His chief book, *De Re Ædificatoria,* is highly valued. He died at Rome.

Alberti, Rafael (1903-   ), Spanish poet, was born and educated in Puerto de Santa Maria. He first studied painting in Madrid (1918-24), then turned to poetry. His first book of poems, *A Sailor on Land* (1924), about childhood memories of the sea, won the Spanish national prize for Literature the next year. Thereafter, he traveled in France, Germany and the Soviet Union, writing poems with imaginative use of folk themes, which were collected in *The Lover* (1926) and *The Dawn of the Gillyflower* (1927). He then used complicated baroque verse forms in his *Lime and Stone* (1929). His masterpiece, *Above the Angels* (1929), is a surrealistic allegory. In the 1930's Alberti served in the Spanish Civil War with the Loyalist airforce, and later migrated to Argentina. Among his later works are *Thirteen Bars and Forty-Eight Stars* (1935), *From One Moment to Another* (1937), and *Between the Carnation and the Sword* (1941). Alberti's rank among the greatest modern Spanish poets is considered due to his original fantasy and lucidity, and to his fresh uses of earlier poetic styles that reinvigorated Spanish poetry.

Albertus Magnus (ăl-bĕr'tŭs măg'nŭs) **(c. 1193-1280),** the *Doctor Universalis* of the schoolmen, was born at Lauingen, in Swabia. He studied at Padua, and, entering the newly founded Dominican order, taught in the schools of Hildesheim. Ratisbon, and Cologne. In 1245-54, he lectured at Paris; in 1254, he became provincial of the Dominicans in Germany; and, in 1260, was named bishop of Ratisbon. But, in 1262, he retired to his convent at Cologne to devote himself to literary pursuits. Of his works the most notable are the *Summa Theologiæ* and the *Summa de Creaturis.* Albertus excelled all his contemporaries in the wideness of his learning; in medieval legend, he appears as a magician. He died at Cologne.

Albinus, Bernhard Siegfried (1697-1770), German anatomist, scientific writer, and educator, was born in Frankfurt an der Oder, Brandenburg. He was educated at the University of Leyden, where his father was professor of medicine. Albinus became a doctor of medicine in 1719 and early in his career published for his students' use several well-illustrated works on anatomy. In collaboration with the Dutch physician Hermann Boerhaave, he published in 1725 an edition of the complete anatomical works of Andreas Vesalius, and in 1737 edited a book on the work of Hieronymus Fabricius. One of Albinus' greatest achievements was the development of a new method of anatomic illustration showing the parts of the human anatomy in correct proportion. *Plates of the Skeleton and Muscles for the Human Body* (1747) was the first published result of his method and is regarded as a classic of its kind.

Al Biruni (c. 973-c. 1048), Arabic historian and science writer, was born of Persian parents at Khwarizm (near Khiva, in what is now the U.S.S.R.). He excelled in many fields, particularly mathematics, history, astronomy, physics, and chronology. His involvement in politics at times forced him to go into hiding or flee for his life. For a time, he lived in India, where wrote a history of India and made astronomical observations and calculations of the latitude and longitudes of cities. Although most of work has been lost, 22 important writings survive. Among these are the *Elements of Astrology, Chronology of Ancient Nations,* and treatises on gems and minerals.

Albo, Joseph (c. 1380-1440), Spanish-Jewish philosopher, theologian, and writer. Little is known of his life except that he lived in Daroca for a time, and later in Soria. He is best known for his *Book of Principles,* a theological work that presents the essential beliefs of Judaism.

Albright, William F. (1891-1971), American orientalist and archaeologist, was born at Coquimbo, Chile. The son of American missionary parents, he was educated in the United States. For twelve years he was head of the American School of Oriental Research at Jerusalem and was leader of several archaeological expeditions in that area. In his position as professor of Semitic Languages and chairman of the Oriental Seminary at Johns Hopkins University, he was particularly active in interpreting the meaning of recently discovered manuscripts and other religious relics from the Palestine region. In addition to numerous magazine articles on "The Dead Sea Scrolls" and related subjects, he wrote several books, the best known of which are *The Archaeology of Palestine* and *From the Stone Age to Christianity.*

Albuquerque, José Joaquim de Campos da Costa de Medeiros e (1867-1934), Brazilian writer, educator and critic, was born in Récife. He taught at the National School of Fine Arts, and was a director of the Department of Education in Rio de Janeiro. His writings include poetry, essays, criticism, short stories and novels.

Alcæus (*ăl-sē'ŭs*), of Mytilene, one of the greatest lyric poets of Greece, flourished about the end of the 7th or the beginning of the 6th century B.C. He was the inventor of the form of verse which after him is called the Alcaic, and which Horace, the happiest of his imitators, adapted to the Latin language.

Alcedo, Antonio de (1734-1812), geographer and historian, was born in Quito, Ecuador, and died in Coruña, Spain. The son of a Spanish colonial official, Alcedo received his early education from his father, then studied mathematics at the Imperial Institute of Madrid and medicine in Paris. During later periods of his life he studied languages, history, physics and numismatics. He joined the Royal Infantry Regiment before he was 18, and retired in 1800 with the rank of field marshall. He was appointed governor of Alciza in 1792, and of Coruna in 1802. Alcedo's writings consist of geographical and historical works on Spanish America.

Alcidamas (4th century B.C.), Greek sophist philosopher and rhetorician, was a rival of Isocrates. He was born at Elaea, studied under Gorgias, and taught at Athens. Little of his work survives; the only work preserved in its entirety is *Peri Sophiston,* or *Concerning Sophists,* in which he values extemporaneous speeches over written ones.

Alciphron (flourished c. 200 A.D.), Greek rhetorician, is remembered as the writer of 118 fictional letters, written in the ancient Greek dialect of Athens. The letters, supposedly written by ordinary, everyday people, picture the manners, morals, and domestic life of Athens in the 4th century B.C. It is believed that some of the letters contain information based on the lost writings of Menander, Greek poet of the 4th century B.C.

Alcman (7th century B.C.), Greek poet, lived and worked in Sparta. He is thought to have founded the Dorian school of choral lyric poetry. Although he was the first Greek poet to use papyrus, and one papyrus fragment contains more than 100 lines of his poetry, his work is known chiefly through quotations and references in later writers. His language and metrical schemes are

clear and simple.

Alcoforado, Marianna (1640-1723), Portuguese nun and author, was born in Beja. She is the author of *Letters of a Portuguese Nun,* written to Noel Bouton, later the Marquis de Chamilly, and marshal of France. At 16, Alcoforado became a Franciscan nun and nine years later met Noel Bouton, who was serving in the Portuguese Army. An attachment between the two developed which caused a scandal when their relationship was discovered. The five short letters she wrote to him, after he deserted her and returned to France, picture her feelings of anguish and despair. After a life of much suffering, she died at the age of 83. Her love letters are considered among the most beautiful ever written.

Alcott, Amos Bronson (1799-1888), author and educator, was born in Wolcott, Conn. He had little formal education, but read widely during the time he traveled as a peddler in Virginia and the Carolinas. He taught school in several small towns until 1828, when he moved to Boston. In 1831, he moved to Germantown, Pa., where his daughter Louisa May Alcott was born. Returning to Boston in 1834, he opened the Temple School, which stressed learning through conversation. The school failed and he settled with his family in Concord, Mass. There he wrote for the Boston *Dial* and gave many popular lectures. Alcott belonged to the Transcendentalist circle of writers, which numbered among its members Ralph Waldo Emerson, Nathaniel Hawthorne, and Henry David Thoreau. Among Alcott's writings are *Table Talk* and *Principles and Methods of Infant Instruction.*

Alcott, Louisa May (1832-88), American juvenile writer, daughter of Amos Bronson Alcott, was born in Germantown, Pa. Her first volume was *Flower Fables,* published in 1855. During the Civil War, she was a volunteer nurse in the South and, in 1863, wrote *Hospital Sketches. Little Women,* published in 1868, was one of the most popular books for girls ever written. It was followed at short intervals by *An Old-Fashioned Girl, Eight Cousins, Silver Pitchers, Under the Lilacs, Little Men, Rose in Bloom, Jo's Boys,* and other stories. She died at Boston, Mass.

Alcuin (*ăl'kwĭn*), or **Flaccus Albinus (c. 735-804),** a scholar of the 8th century and the confidant and adviser of Charlemagne, was born at York. He reorganized the palace school and established others throughout the kingdom, himself serving as abbot of that in Tours, which became the most famous in Europe. His handwriting is said to have become the model for that in western Europe. Besides numerous theological writings, he left a number of elementary works on philosophy, mathematics, rhetoric, and philology; also poems and numerous letters.

Alcuin was educated in the Cathedral of York in England, and came to the continent as educational adviser of Charlemagne. In this capacity he exercised a great influence, not only over the princes who were his pupils, but in the political matters with which his master was always engaged. His influence was felt in the more vigorous and systematic organization of education and of the intellectual side of civilization wherever his pupils went.

Aldanov, Mark (1886-1957), Russian novelist, was born in Kiev and earned degrees in chemistry and law at Kiev University. Variously known as Mark Aleksandrovich Landau and Landau-Aldanov, he left Russia in 1918, then lived in Paris until he moved to America in 1941. Most of his writings are historical novels. Among his main works are *The Ninth Thermidor* (1926), *The Conspiracy* (1927), *The Devil's Bridge* (1928), *The Fifth Seal* (1939), *For Thee the Best* (1945), *Before the Deluge* (1947), *A Night in the Airport* (1949), and *The Escape* (1950).

Alden, Henry Mills (1836-1919), American editor, author, and classical scholar, was born at Mount Tabor, near Danby, Vt. He was graduated from Williams

College in 1857 and from Andover theological seminary in 1860. In 1861, he settled in New York. He was managing editor of *Harper's Weekly* from 1863 to 1869, when be became editor of *Harper's Magazine,* which position he held until his death. As editor of this magazine for a half century, his influence was pervasive and distinctive, though at all times unobtrusive. His Lowell lectures at Boston, 1863-64, on *The Structure of Paganism* and his first published writings, *The Eleusinian Mysteries,* display high classical scholarship. His writings include also *God in His World, A Study of Death, Harper's Pictorial History of the Great Rebellion* (with A. H. Guernsey), and *Magazine Writing and the New Literature.* In 1910, he was elected a member of the American Academy of Arts and Letters.

Alden, John (1599-1687), one of the Pilgrims to Plymouth, Mass., was born in England. He was one of the 41 signers of the compact for the government of the colony drawn up in the cabin of the *Mayflower* before the landing at Plymouth. Alden married Priscilla Mullens, to whom, according to popular legend, he first proposed in behalf of Miles Standish, but she indicated her preference for Alden over the soldier. A poem by Longfellow, entitled *The Courtship of Miles Standish,* has this incident for its theme. Alden was a magistrate for more than 50 years, and greatly assisted in the government of the infant colony. He died at Duxbury, Mass.

Alderman, Edwin Anderson (1861-1931), American educator and university president, was born at Wilmington, N. C. He was graduated from the University of North Carolina, 1882; was professor of pedagogy at his alma mater, 1892-96, and president of same, 1896-99. He served as president of Tulane University from 1899 to 1904, when he was made president of the University of Virginia, where he served until the year of his death. He has become widely known as a speaker, lecturer, and writer. In 1926 he was elected to the American Academy of Arts and Letters. His published works include *Obligations and Opportunities of Citizenship, The Spirit of the South,* and *The Nation Exalts Jefferson.*

Aldhelm, Saint (c. 640-709), English churchman and scholar, was abbot of Malmesbury and bishop of Sherborne. So far as is known, he was the first Englishman to write in Latin verse. As a scholar, his fame spread into other countries and he visited Rome at the request of Pope Sergius I. He founded several monasteries and built a number of churches, one of which, St. Laurence at Bradford, still exists.

Aldington, Richard (1892-1962), English novelist and poet, was born at Plymouth, Hampshire, and studied at Dover College and at the University of London. He began writing poetry at 15 and edited the avant-garde *Egoist* magazine. Ezra Pound introduced him to Hilda Doolittle, known as H.D., and they were married in 1913 and later divorced. While serving as an infantryman in World War I, Aldington suffered shell shock, from which he did not entirely recover until 1927.

In the forefront of the imagist movement, he wrote *Images, Old and New*; *Images of Desire*; *Exile*; *A Fool i' the Forest*; and *Crystal World.* Among his novels, which express a spirit of disillusionment, are *Death of a Hero, Women Must Work,* and *All Men Are Enemies.* After the 1930's, Aldington turned mainly to biography, writing *D.H. Lawrence: Portrait of a Genius, But . . .* (1950); *The Duke* (1946, in England entitled *Wellington*), for which he received the James Tait Black memorial award, *Lawrence of Arabia* (1955); *Portrait of a Rebel* (1951); and *Life for Life's Sake* (1941), his autobiography. He also wrote short stories, criticism, and made translations.

Aldis, Dorothy (1897-), novelist and poet, was born in Chicago. The daughter of newspaper reporters, she became the editor of the women's department of a Chicago newspaper. Her books of verse for children include *Everything and Anything, Here, There, and Everywhere,* and *All Together.* She began writing for young adults with *Dark Summer.* Other titles include *Murder in a Haystack, Any Spring* (poems), and *Before Things Happen.*

Aldiss, Brian Wilson (1925-), British science fiction writer and editor, was born at Dereham, Norfolk, and attended Framlingham College. A prolific writer, he has produced many short stories and books, winning the Hugo Award for short fiction in 1962 for *Hothouse* and the Nebula Award for best novella in 1965 for *The Saliva Tree.*

Aldrich, Thomas Bailey (1836-1907), poet and editor, was born in Portsmouth, N. H. While engaged in the office of a New York merchant, he began to write verses, the success of which soon induced him to enter on a literary career. His first volume, consisting of miscellaneous poems and called *The Bells,* was published in 1855. Later, he published several other volumes of poems, *The Story of a Bad Boy*, *Marjorie Daw*, and other stories. Aldrich was an industrious contributor to the best periodicals. From 1881 to 1890, he served as editor of the *Atlantic Monthly.* He was a member of the American Academy of Arts and Letters. Died at Boston, Mass.

Aldrovandi, Ulisse (1522-1605), Italian natural scientist and teacher, was born at Bologna. He studied mathematics, law, Latin, and philosophy at Bologna and Padua. In 1549, he was accused of heresy by the Inquisition. He was forced to travel to Rome to prove his innocence. While in Rome, he studied the architecture and art treasures, later writing a book about them. He received a degree in medicine in 1553, then taught at the University of Bologna. His position enabled him to study natural sciences, the field in which he is best known. He persuaded the Roman Senate to establish a botanical garden at Bologna, and was its first director. Although unpopular with his colleagues, he was popular with the students who flocked to his lectures. He taught them to make direct observations of natural phenomena rather than to rely exclusively on textbooks. Over the objections of the Roman apothecaries, he was assigned the task of writing the official pharmacopoeia. *Antidotarii Bononiensis Epitome* (1574), which became a model for subsequent books of its kind. His main work was a 14-volume compilation on natural history.

Aleandro, Girolamo (1480-1542), Italian cardinal and humanist scholar, was born in Motta. After studying in Paris, he taught in Venice, Orleans, and Paris, where he became rector of the university. Pope Leo X appointed him Vatican Librarian and made him apostolic nuncio to Germany in 1520. He led the faction that condemned Martin Luther at the Diet of Worms, and wrote the edict that was adopted by the Diet. Valuable sources of information on the Reformation are to be found in his letters and reports in the Vatican library.

Aleardi, Aleardo (1812-78), Italian poet, was born and died at Verona. Soon after his birth, he became an Austrian subject, and hatred of foreigners was instilled in him at an early age. He took part in the uprising against Austria in 1848 and was imprisoned for a short time. After the Austrians were expelled from Lombardy, he returned to Verona, where he published his poems. Aleardi became a member of the Italian parliament and eventually was named a senator. His poetry did much to consolidate Italy. One of his finest pieces was an ode to the commercial and maritime cities of Italy.

Alecsandri, Vasili (1821-90), Rumanian poet and statesman, was born at Bacau, Moldavia. He studied in Paris, then returned to Moldavia. He wrote lyric poetry and collected Rumanian folksongs. He published his first collection in 1844 and a second collection in 1852-53. In later life he served as minister of foreign affairs and minister to France.

Alegre, Francisco Javier (1729-88), Mexican historian and writer, was born in Vera Cruz, and died near

Bologna, Italy. He entered the Society of Jesus in 1747, and was ordained in 1754. After teaching mathematics and classics in Havana, and classics in Mérida, Yucatan, Alegre began to write the history of the Jesuit Mexican province. Spanning two centuries, this work has been the principal source for the history of northern colonial Mexico. When the Jesuits were expelled from Mexico in 1767, Alegre went into exile in Bologna, devoting himself to literary and scientific studies and writings.

Alegría, Ciro (1909-   ), Peruvian novelist, wrote novels of social protest, among them *Broad and Alien is the World,* which won the Latin American novel prize of 1941 and was translated into English the same year.

Aleichem, Sholom (1859-1916), Yiddish author, whose real name was Shalom Rabinowitz. His pseudonym is a standard Yiddish greeting that translates as "Peace be with you." He was born in Kiev, Russia, and moved to the U.S. in 1906. Although his many writings —novels, plays and some 300 short stories—portray the life of the oppressed and poverty-stricken Jews of Russia and Poland, they are imbued with a strong sense of humor. All his works were written in Yiddish, but translations have appeared widely in English, German, Russian, and other European languages. Some English titles are *The Old Country, Tevye's Daughters, Inside Kasrilevke, Wandering Star,* and *Great Fair: My Childhood and Youth.*

Aleixandre, Vicente (1900-   ), Spanish poet, was born in Seville, grew up in Malaga, and studied law in Seville and Madrid, but never practiced. He belonged to the group of major poets that emerged in the 1920's and he had a strong influence on later Spanish poets. His poetry is characterized by its surrealism, images of nature and man, and unusual metaphors. Most of his lyrics are in free verse. In 1933 he received the Spanish national prize for literature for *La destruccion o el amor,* and in 1950 he was elected to the Spanish Academy. Aleixandre was awarded the Nobel Prize in 1977 for poetry that "illuminates man's condition in the cosmos and in present-day society." Other volumes of his verse include *Ambito, Sombra del paraiso, Nacimiento ultimo,* and *Diagolos del Conocimiento.*

Alemán, Mateo (1547-c. 1614), Spanish novelist, was born in Seville. He graduated from the University of Seville and entered government service in Madrid. He owes his fame to a picaresque novel, *Guzmán de Alfarache,* translated into English as *The Rogue.* The first part of this classic was published in 1599, and a sequel appeared in 1604. In 1608 he emigrated to Mexico City.

Alembert (*a' län' bâr'*), **Jean le Rond d' (1717-83),** French mathematician and philosopher, the natural son of Madame de Tencin and the poet Destouches, was born in Paris. He was the friend of Voltaire and of Diderot, and acquired high esteem by his scientific works, which fill many volumes. As a philosopher, he held that knowledge is acquired through sensory experience. His literary and philosophical works have been collected and include *Eléments de musique théorique et pratique* and *Eléments de Philosophie.* Among his many scientific writings are *Réflexions sur la cause générale des vents, Traité de dynamique,* and *Recherches sur differents points importants du système du monde.*

Alencar, José Martiniano de (1829-77), politician and novelist, was born in Fortaleza, Ceará, Brazil. A lawyer and journalist, he became minister of justice of Brazil in 1868. His best-known works are three novels about Indians, set in the jungles of Brazil: *Iracema, O sertane jo,* and *O Guarany,* which became a successful opera in 1870. He died in Rio de Janeiro.

Alexander the Great (356 B.C.-323 B.C.), Macedonian king, military commander, and conqueror, was born at Pella, the capital of Macedonia. His education was committed first to Leonidas, then to Lysimachus, and, about 342 B.C., to Aristotle. Alexander was 16 years old when his father, Philip, marched against Byzantium and, during his absence, left the government in his son's hands. In 338 B.C., Alexander displayed conspicuous courage at the battle of Chærona, whereby Macedonian supremacy was established in the Hellenic world. Philip was about to conduct an expedition of all the Greeks against the despotism of Persia, when he was assassinated, leaving Alexander as his heir.

CONQUESTS. Alexander ascended the throne in 336 B.C. and immediately punished his father's murderers. In 335 B.C., he destroyed Thebes and brought the Grecian states under his command. He crossed the Hellespont in 334 B.C. and, as a result of the battle of Granicus, liberated all the Greek cities of Asia Minor from the Persian yoke. Proceeding on his way of conquest, he cut, at Gordium, the so-called Gordian knot, of which an oracle had said that he who untied it would be the lord of all Asia. In 333 B.C., in the neighborhood of Issus, he defeated Darius, king of the Persians.

Alexander now turned toward Syria and Phœnicia, in order to cut off Darius' escape by sea. The next year witnessed Alexander's capture of Tyre, his victorious march through Palestine, and his conquest of Egypt.

Meanwhile, Darius had collected another army, and, in the spring of 331 B.C., Alexander advanced against him in Assyria. In October 331 B.C., Alexander conquered the forces of the Persians, notwithstanding the great numerical superiority of his adversaries. In the following two years, Media, Parthia, and Bactria fell before him. As the conqueror of Asia, he now proceeded to Babylon, Susa, and Persepolis.

In 329 B.C., Alexander penetrated to the farthest known limits of northern Asia and overthrew the Scythians on the banks of the Jaxartes. Two years later, he proceeded to the conquest of India, then known only by name. He crossed the Indus and marched as lord through that part of India which is now called the Punjab. He wished to advance to the Ganges and conquer the whole of India, but when he reached the Hyphasis River, the murmuring of his troops induced him to retreat. Meanwhile his friend Nearchus, who was made admiral of the fleet, had successfully accomplished the hazardous voyage from the Indus up the Persian Gulf to the Euphrates River. This campaign marked the extreme limit of his conquests.

RESULTS. Both by arms and by policy, Alexander, for the first time, brought the East and the West into close contact with each other. Aiming at the fusion of Greek and Oriental by intermarriage and by exchange of customs, he set an example himself by marrying a Persian princess and by encouraging the payment of divine honors to himself as to an Oriental despot. On the other hand, he lost no opportunity to spread the Greek language and the Greek civilization. His empire, it is true, was broken up, but Greek cities and colonies were founded everywhere, and the Greek tongue became the universal speech of government and of literature. His impress on Greece itself was no less important. His conquests marked definitely the passing of the Hellenic city-states and heralded the period of rule by empires. Through him, also, a road was opened to India, and Europeans became acquainted with the knowledge and economic products of the remote East.

CHARACTER. More perhaps than any other commander, Alexander combined the chivalry of the heroic age and the more careful strategies of later times. His career not only excited romantic enthusiasm in his contemporaries, but later became the subject of legends propagated in most of the languages of medieval Europe. His genius and policy are variously estimated by historians but there is no disagreement as to the magnitude of his designs. He is said to have planned the subjugation of Italy and of Carthage when his ambitious projects were cut short by his death in Babylon.

Alexander of Aphrodisias (c. 200 A.D.), Greek philosopher, was born in Aphrodisias, in Caria, and was a student of Aristocles of Messene. He is best remembered for his commentaries on Aristotle. His original works include *On Fate* and *On the Soul.*

Alexander of Hales (c. 1185-1245), English theologian, was born Hales Owen in Shropshire. He studied arts at the University of Paris, becoming a master. Following this, he studied theology, becoming a regent master and retaining his professorship until 1241. When he was more than 50 years old, he entered the Franciscan Order, thus securing a chair in the university of for the order. Five major writings are credited to him: *Exoticon, Glossa in quatros libros sententiarum, Questiones disputatae "antequam esset frater," Questiones quodlibetales,* and *Summa theologica.*

Alexander Neckham (1157-1217), English theologian, scientist, and poet, was born at St. Alban's, Hartfordshire. He studied arts at the University of Paris, and taught at Dunstable and St. Alban's. After studying theology at Oxford, he entered the Order of the Augustinian Canons about 1200. He served as papal judge delegate from 1203-05. In 1213 he became abbot of Cirencester. He died in Kempsey, Worcestershire. Alexander's writings include poetry, theological treatises, and sermons. They reveal knowledge of many subjects, including natural science.

Alexander, Eben Roy (1899-   ), journalist, was born at St. Louis, Mo. and was educated at St. Louis University. He served as gunnery sergeant in 1918-19 and later took a leading part in the U.S. Army Infantry Reserve and in the Air Corps of the Missouri National Guard. Following editorial work on *The St. Louis Star* and *The St. Louis Post-Dispatch,* he joined the staff of *Time* magazine as contributing editor. Since 1960 he has been editor of *Time.*

Alexander, Samuel (1859-1938), British philosopher, was born in Sydney, Australia, and studied at the University of Melbourne (Australia), Balliol College, Oxford, and in Germany with Hugo Münsterberg. He taught in Owens College, Manchester (now the University of Manchester) from 1893 until his retirement in 1924. *Space, Time and Deity* (1920), Alexander's most important work, was based on a series of lectures given at the University of Glasgow (1916-18). His other works include *Locke* (1908), *Spinoza and Time* (1921), *Art and the Material* (1925), and *Beauty and Other Forms of Value* (1933).

Alexander, Sir William, Earl of Stirling (1567?-1640), Scottish writer and courtier, was born a commoner and educated in Glasgow and Germany. After earning recognition as a scholar, poet, and playwright, he was knighted by James I. At this time he was given charge of dispensing royal patronage and granted by royal decree all of then-known Canada. His works include the tragedy *Darius, Croesus,* and *Julius Caesar.* He also wrote many sonnets. The French conquest of Canada deprived him of his holdings and he died insolvent in London.

Alexis (390/380?-280/270 B.C.), Greek poet, was born at Thurii, and became a citizen of Athens. It is believed that he wrote 245 comedies, of which 130 titles are known. Plutarch states that he died on the stage at the age of 106.

Alexis, Willibald (1798-1871), German novelist, was born Georg Wilhelm. Heinrich Haring in Breslau. He studied law at the universities of Berlin and Breslau. Two of his historical novels, *Walladmor* and *Schloss Avalon,* at first appeared to be translations from Sir Walter Scott, so closely did they resemble his work. Alexis published a number of historical tales of Brandenburg. Among his other writings are *Cabanis* and *Der falsche Woldemar.*

Alfieri (äl-fyā´rē), Vittorio, Count (1749-1803), Italian dramatic poet, was born in Piedmont. At Turin, in 1772, he left military service and devoted himself to literary pursuits. He became one of the foremost writers of Italian 18th-century literature. Among his most important tragedies are: *Virginia; Agamemnone; Oreste; Timoleone;* and *Saul,* his masterpiece. His literary ideal was to unite "artistic truth with moral truth, beauty with morality." He is honored in Italy, not only as a great dramatist, but as the reviver of a national spirit. He left 21 tragedies and six comedies, besides various odes and sonnets.

Alfonso X (1226-84), surnamed "the astronomer," "the philosopher," or "the wise," king of Leon and Castile, succeeded his father, Ferdinand III, in 1252. Alfonso was one of the most learned princes of his time, and acquired lasting fame through the completion of the code of laws commenced by his father and called *Leyes de las Partidas.* He improved the Ptolemaic planetary tables, is credited with a history of the Church and of the Crusades, and is said to have ordered a translation of the Bible into Spanish. Died at Seville.

Alford, Henry (1810-71), English clergyman and scholar, was born in London, and graduated from Trinity College, Cambridge. He is known for several popular hymns and also as the first editor of the *Contemporary Review.* His chief claim to fame, however, is for his edition of the New Testament in Greek, which required nearly 20 years to complete. Alford was dean of Canterbury from 1857 until his death.

Alfred the Great (849-901), king of the West Saxons, was born at Wantage, Berkshire, England. With his father, Ethelwulf, the young Alfred spent much time in Rome. Later, through his stepmother, Judith, he became imbued with the culture, knowledge, and traditions of the great Frankish courts. In his 20th year, he married, and assisted his brother Ethelred in repelling the Danes.

VICTORIES. In 871, Alfred succeeded to the crown. Four years later, he defeated the Danes at sea, and, in 876, he made peace with them at Wareham. They broke the peace by capturing Exeter. The city was retaken by Alfred in 877; but, soon afterward, the invaders, under Guthrum, completely overran the whole kingdom of the West Saxons. Alfred was for a time obliged to seek refuge in a cowherd's hut. He kept up communication with his friends, however, and, as soon as the people began to arm themselves against the Danes, he built a stronghold at Athelney. From this base, he attacked and defeated the invaders, who at length capitulated. By the peace of Wedmore in 878, Alfred accepted hostages and exacted a solemn oath from the Danes that they would quit the territory of Wessex and receive baptism.

Alfred's power now steadily increased by land and also by sea. He is credited with the construction of England's first fleet. The weakness of the other kingdoms in England, which had been likewise attacked by the Danes, left Alfred as the strongest ruler in the island. By 886, he was recognized, without formal installation, as the sovereign of all England. His position was maintained, however, only at the cost of further struggles. These engaged much of his energies from 893, when a large body of Danes under Hastings landed in Kent, until the complete dispersal of the aggressors in 897.

CONSTRUCTIVE ACHIEVEMENTS. Alfred made a compilation of laws, in which, for the first time, no discrimination was made against the Welsh people. The laws were characterized by an intensely religious tone.

One of the most noteworthy features of Alfred's character was his zeal for learning. He caused a collection of the old Saxon poems to be made. Asser, Erigena, and other scholars were invited to his court. He established and directed a school for young nobles and founded abbeys for those of lower rank. He labored also himself as a scholar and a teacher. About 888, he began the adaptation and translation into Saxon of four important Latin works—*The Compilation of* Orosius, the *History* of Bede, the *Consolation* of Boethius, and the *Pastoral* of Pope Gregory. With these translations, English prose literature begins. English history also may be said to have originated when, in his reign, the *English Chronicle* received its final form.

Algarotti, Francesco Count (1712-64), Italian writer, was born in Venice. He went to Paris at an early age and was a friend of Voltaire. Algarotti lived in Germany for several years and then returned to Italy. His writings cover art and music, literature, science, and travel. His *Newtonian Philosophy for Ladies* made him famous.

Alger, Horatio (1834-99), was the author of more than one hundred books for boys. Born in Revere, Mass., he was the son of a Unitarian minister and was himself educated for the ministry, but in 1866 gave up that calling to write. His first story, *Ragged Dick,* was published in 1867. A resident of New York City for many years, he was a devoted visitor to and patron of the Newsboys' Lodging House, where he gained much of the inspiration and color for his stories. Alger's heroes always succeed in gaining honor and riches by their courage and virtue in struggling heroically against heavy odds. Enormously popular, the books, with their elevated moral tone, exercised a strong influence on countless young Americans.

Algren, Nelson (1909-   ), novelist and short story writer, moved to Chicago shortly after his birth in Detroit, Mich. After obtaining a degree in journalism from the University of Illinois, Algren traveled in the southern U.S. A realistic writer, Algren wrote of poverty, the underworld, and the downtrodden. His best-known novel is *The Man With the Golden Arm.* Other works include *Somebody in Boots, Never Come Morning, A Walk on the Wild Side, Neon Wilderness* (short stories), *Chicago: City on the Make* (a prose poem), and *Notes from a Sea Diary: Hemingway All the Way* (travel notes and literary criticism).

Alinsky, Saul (David) (1909-72), social activist, was born in Chicago. After graduating from the University of Chicago, he worked as a criminologist in the Illinois prison system. In 1940 he formed the Industrial Areas Foundation, dedicated to organizing people in depressed white ghettos so that they could improve their living conditions. By the early 1960's Alinsky was working in black neighborhoods. His first black project was his most well known: the Woodlawn Organization in Chicago. In 1968 he added a Teaching Institute to his Foundation to train organizers to work in their own neighborhoods. Alinsky's books include *Reveille for Radicals* (1947), *John L. Lewis* (1949), *The Professional Radical* (1970 with Marion K. Sanders), and *Rules for Radicals* (1971).

Alison, Sir Archibald (1792-1867), Scottish historian, was born at Kenley, Shropshire, England, and educated at Edinburgh University. He published the *History of Europe* in two works. The first, in ten volumes, covered the period from the French Revolution to 1815. The second, in four volumes, covered the period 1815-52. The first work was translated into many European languages; the other was not as successful. Alison's autobiography, *My Life and Writings* was published in 1883.

Al-Khwarizmi (780-850), Arab mathematician, was born in Khwarazm (now Khiva, in the Soviet Union). He compiled astronomical tables, worked actively on arithmetic, and made many translations. He and his work are indirectly responsible for two important mathematical terms: *algorism*, which was derived from his name; and *algebra*, which is the Latin transliteration of the word *al-jabr*, from the title of the book *ilm al-jabr wa'l mugabalah*, "the science of transposition and cancellation," in which he preserved and extended the mathematics of Diophantus. Al-Khwarizmi is also famous for having introduced arabic numerals and the use of decimals for calculations. As a result of his work, long division became a fairly ordinary operation rather than one available only to experts. Al-Khwarizmi also improved the text and maps of Ptolemy's geography.

Allen, Don Cameron (1903-   ), American author and university professor, was born in St. Louis, Mo. He received his A.B. and Ph.D. from the University of Illinois. His M.A. was from Washington University. Among his works are *The Star-Crossed Renaissance, The Legend of Noah, The Owles Almanacke, The Essayes of Sir William Cornwallis, A Strange Metamorphosis*, and *The Harmonious Vision.*

Allen, Ethan (c. 1737-89), American soldier, was born at Litchfield, Conn. He distinguished himself early in the Revolutionary War by the surprise and capture of Fort Ticonderoga in 1775. While participating in Montgomery's expedition to Canada the same year, he was taken prisoner and was not exchanged until 1778. Allen was afterward a member of the Vermont legislature. He was author of *Reason the Only Oracle of Man* and other works.

Allen, Florence Ellinwood (1884-1966), American jurist, was born in Salt Lake City, Utah. After being graduated at Western Reserve University, she also at intervals studied law at Chicago and New York universities, meanwhile acting as musical editor for the New York *Musical Courier* and the Cleveland *Plain Dealer.* She lectured on music for the New York Board of Education, 1910-13, and began the practice of law in 1914 at Cleveland, Ohio. After serving as judge of the local court of common pleas for one year, she was elected in 1922 to the Ohio Supreme Court, where she sat until 1934. In that year President Roosevelt named her to the United States Circuit Court of Appeals, the first woman to reach such a position in the judiciary.

Allen, Fredrick Lewis (1890-1954), American historian and editor, was born in Boston and graduated from Harvard in 1912. His career began with the *Atlantic Monthly* in 1914. In 1923 he joined the staff of *Harpers Bazaar*, becoming editor in chief in 1941. His best seller, *Only Yesterday*, was an informal history of American life in the 1920's. His later books were *Lords of Creation, Since Yesterday* and *The Big Change.* His wife, Agnes Rogers, collaborated with him on *I Remember Distinctly*, which covered the period between World Wars I and II.

Allen, Gay Wilson (1903-   ), university professor and author, was born in Lake Junaluska, N.C. He received his A.B. and MA. from Duke University and his Ph.D. from the University of Wisconsin. He was named a Fellow of the Rockefeller Foundation and a Guggenheim Fellow. His works include *American Prosody, Literary Criticism, Walt Whitman Handbook, A Critical Biography of Walt Whitman, Walt Whitman Abroad,* and *Walt Whitman's Poems* (with C.T. Davis). He also contributed articles and reviews to national and international journals.

Allen, (William) Hervey (1889-1949), poet, critic and novelist, was born in Pittsburgh, Pa. After his first year, he left the U.S. Naval Academy because of injuries received in athletics. He served in the army in France during World War I. *Anthony Adverse* (1933), his best-known book, sold more than a million and a half copies. Other books include *Wampum and Old Gold* (poetry), *Israfel* (a criticism of Edgar Allen Poe), and *Towards the Flame* and *Action at Aquila* (novels). When he died in Miami, Fla., Allen was working on the fourth of a five-volume work entitled *The Disinherited.*

Allen, James Edward, Jr. (1911-71), American educator, was born at Elkins, W. Va., where his father was president of Davis and Elkins College. Allen worked his way through that institution, and after he was graduated in 1932 held a variety of jobs during the depression years. In 1939 he was offered a research position at Princeton University, with an opportunity to do post-graduate work. Two years later he was granted a fellowship at Harvard, where he earned his Ph.D. degree. He became president of the Graduate Students' Association, secretary to the faculty, and director of placement. He then went to Syracuse University as assistant professor of administration, and in 1947 joined the staff of the New York State Commissioner of Education. In 1955, he was chosen commissioner, becoming at the age of 44, the youngest man ever to hold that post. He served on numerous educational councils and commissions, national and local, and contributed to educational magazines.

Allen, James Lane (1849-1925), American novelist, was born near Lexington, Ky. He was educated at Transylvania University; taught in Kentucky University; and later was professor of Latin and higher English, Bethany College, W. Va. Beginning in 1886, he devoted his entire attention to literature, using Kentucky scenery and its vanishing pioneer, ante bellum, and social types as a background for his fiction. In his novels he portrays various struggles and problems of the human soul in a refined prose style somewhat in the manner of Hawthorne. His works include *Flute and Violin, A Summer in Arcady, The Sword of Youth, A Cathedral Singer,* and *The Landmark.*

Allen, Robert S. (1900-   ), journalist, was born in Latonia, Ky. He attended the University of Wisconsin and did postgraduate work at the University of Munich, Germany, and George Washington University. His career began as a reporter for the *Capital Times,* Madison, Wis., he later became a nationally syndicated columnist. Allen has also lectured on national and world affairs. His books include *Washington Merry-Go-Round, Why Hoover Faces Defeat, Nine Old Men, Our Fair City, Lucky Forward,* and *The Truman Merry-Go-Round.*

Allen, Woody (Heywood) (1935-   ), actor and writer, was born Allen Stewart Konigsberg in New York, where he attended New York University and City College. After writing for television comedians, including Art Carney, Sid Caesar, and Herb Shriner, he began performing his own material in nightclubs in 1961. Also successful on television, Allen began writing screenplays. He starred in directed, and produced movies, including *What's New Pussycat?* (1964), *Take the Money and Run* (1969) *Getting Even* (1971), *Sleeper* (1973), *Love and Death* (1975), and *The Front* (1976). *Annie Hall* (1978) won four Academy Awards as well as awards from the Society of Film Critics and the New York Critics Circle. Allen's articles also appeared in magazines and he published humorous essays—*Getting Even* (1971) and *Without Feathers* (1975).

Allibone (ăl´ ĭ-bon), **Samuel Austin (1816-89),** American author was born at Philadelphia. He was the compiler of *A Critical Dictionary of English Literature and British and American Authors* and other valuable works of reference. He was also a contributor to periodical literature and, from 1879 to 1888, was librarian of the Lenox Library. New York.

Alliluyeva, Svetlana (1926-   ), Russian writer, was born in Moscow, the daughter of Joseph Stalin. After private tutoring, she attended a school for the children of Kremlin leaders. She was later a student at Moscow University (specializing in U.S. history) and at the Moscow Academy of Social Sciences. Her childhood and later years were dominated by her father—her mother had killed herself in 1932. During World War II and in the following years, Svetlana Alliluyeva taught English and worked as a translator in Moscow, and experienced several broken marriages. In 1963 she began to write the story of her life. In the same year she married Brijesh Singh, an Indian Communist living in Russia. Singh became ill in 1966 and his wife requested permission from Soviet authorities to accompany him to India. Only after he died, however, was she allowed to leave. Following many difficulties, Stalin's daughter arrived in the U.S. in 1967. After widespread newspaper publicity, her volume of memoirs, *Twenty Letters to a Friend,* was published in 1968.

Allingham, William (1824-89), Irish poet, was born in

Ballyshannon. After 14 years with the Irish customs service, he moved in 1870 to London, where he began writing for *Fraser's Magazine*—by 1874 he had become chief editor. His interest in Irish folksongs and ballads placed him among the writers of the Irish literary revival and his work had great influence on William Butler Yeats, among others. Allingham's poems were collected in six volumes and published from 1889-93.

Allport, Gordon W. (1897-1967), American psychologist, was born in Montezuma, Ind. He received his B.A. and Ph.D. at Harvard and taught psychology there beginning in 1930. Allport advanced a personality theory of "functional autonomy" of motives, setting a trend away from developmental and Freudian psychology. According to Allport's theory, adult motives are independent of childhood desires. He emphasized present values over past experience and stressed the uniqueness of each individual. Allport was president of the American Psychological Association in 1939 and edited the *Journal of Abnormal and Social Psychology,* 1937-49. His books include *Personality: A Psychological Interpretation* (1937), *The Psychology of Rumor* (1947), *Nature of Personality* (1950), *The Individual and His Religion* (1950), *The Nature of Prejudice* (1954), *Becoming* (1955), and *Pattern and Growth of Personality* (1961).

Allston, Washington (1779-1843), author and painter, was born on his family's plantation on the Waccamaw River, in South Carolina. After graduating from Harvard, he studied art at the Royal Academy in London, the Louvre in Paris, and in Italy. Although his art output was small, his experiments in dramatic subject matter and the use of light and atmospheric color gave him a distinctive place in early 19th-century painting. His verse includes *The Sylphs of the Seasons With Other Poems;* his prose writing include *Monaldi* and *Lectures on Art.*

Almanni, Luigi (1495-1556), Italian poet, was born in Florence, and enjoyed the patronage of the Medicis until he plotted against Giulio de Medici (later Pope Clement VII), and had to flee to France. There he spent most of the rest of his life, and did most of his writing, in high favor with King Francis I and later with Henry II. Some of his best-known poems were *La Cultivazione* (1546), in didactic style; *Opere Toscane* (1533), a group of satires· *Girone il Cortese* (1548), based on the Arthurian romances; and *Avarchide,* tales of adventure.

Almeida, José Valentim Fialho de (1857-1911), Portuguese writer, was born in Vila-de-Frades, Alentejo. While studying medicine in Lisbon, he supported himself by writing for newspapers and magazines. Unable to achieve independence through his writing or to obtain official patronage, Almeida began to attack the political institutions and even the king in his writings. This made necessary his return in 1893 to Vila-de-Frades, where he married a rich heiress. Her death left him an important landowner, and he devoted his life thereafter to his own affairs, writing infrequently. Recognized as one of the best storytellers of 19th-century Portugal, Almeida wrote *Contos, A cidade do vicio, Lisboa galante,* and *A esquina.*

Almeida, Manuel Antonio de (1831-61), Brazilian journalist, novelist, and physician, was born in Rio de Janeiro. He died in a shipwreck near Macaé, Brazil. He is considered one of the earliest writers of realistic literature in his country. He also wrote *Dois amores,* a lyric drama.

Almeida, Nicolau Tolentino de (1741-1811), Portuguese poet and satirist, was born in Lisbon. At one time he was a secretary in the Ministry of the Interior. He was a competent poet, and his satires are considered among the best in Portuguese. They often gently censure contemporary society by drawing amusing caricatures. Volumes of his poetry were published in 1801 and 1836.

Almqvist (älm´ kvĭst), **Karl Jonas Ludvig (1793-1866),** Swedish author, was born at Stockholm. He had an er-

Biography

ratic career; was once convicted of forgery and charged with murder; he fled from Sweden to the United States and, for a time, was private secretary to Abraham Lincoln. His novels are romantic in type and display notable power of language, while his dramas are marked by masterly dialogue and great tragic force. Among the best of his writings are *The Book of the Thorn-Rose, Araminta May, The Palace,* and *It's All Right.* He went to Bremen in 1865, where he assumed the name of Professor Westermann.

Alonso, Amado (1896-1952), Spanish philologist, was born in Lerín and died in Arlington, Mass. Educated in Madrid and Hamburg, Alonso taught at the University of Buenos Aires, where he was director of the Instituto de Filologia. He later taught at Harvard. He edited the *Revista de filologia hispanica* from 1939-46. His writings include various linguistic studies.

Alonso, Dámaso (1898-   ), Spanish poet and critic, was born in Madrid. Educated at the Centro de Estudios Históricos in Madrid, he taught at Valencia, Madrid, Berlin, Cambridge, Stanford, Columbia, and Harvard. His writings include historical and stylistic studies of Spanish poetry, annotated editions of Spanish classics, a collection of medieval Spanish poetry, and original poetry. His *La lengua poética de Góngora* was awarded the Spanish national prize for literature in 1935, and *La poesía de San Juan de la Cruz* received an award from the Academia Española in 1942. He was received into the Academia Española in 1945.

Alpert, Hollis (1916-   ), American writer, was born in Herkimer, N.Y. Following Army service from 1942-46, he attended the New School of Social Research. He held editorial positions for *Woman's Day, Saturday Review,* and the *New Yorker,* and wrote book reviews and film critiques for these and other magazines. In 1957 he received the Critics Award of the Screen Directors Guild of America. His books include *The Summer Lovers, Some Other Time, For Immediate Release* and *The Barrymores.* He has also published short stories in many magazines.

Alphanus of Salerno (1015/20-1085), archbishop, scholar, and writer, was born in Salerno, Italy. After teaching at the University of Salerno, he entered the Benedictine monastery of Monte Cassino in 1056. By 1057 he was an abbot and in 1058 he became archbishop. Monte Cassino was at that time the center of culture in Italy, and Alphanus was influential in developing the Christian humanism of the 11th century, and also encouraged the study of medicine and theology. He also wrote hymns and poetry.

Alphonsus Liguori, St. (1696-1787), theological writer, bishop, and Doctor of the Church, was born in Marianella, near Naples, and died near Salerno. Of noble birth, he was educated by tutors until he entered the University of Naples. He received a law degree at 16. After 10 years he left the law to study theology and was ordained a priest in 1726. In 1762 he was appointed bishop of Sant Agata dei Goti, and from that time on he wrote and worked for church reform. A prolific writer, he produced more than 100 titles on a variety of subjects, including moral and dogmatic theology. His work had great influence on the life of the church and his major work, *Theologia Moralis,* has appeared in many different editions in many countries.

Alpini, Prospero (1553-1617), Italian botanist and physician, was born at Marostica, Venice. He received his medical degree from the University of Padua in 1578. Later, while serving as physician to the Venetian consul in Cairo, Egypt, he continued his study of botany. From his study of the date palm, he deduced that plants can exist as male and female. This discovery of sexual difference among plants was used by Linnaeus a century and a half later when he devised his classification system for the plant kingdom. Alpini returned to Italy in 1586, residing at Genoa as physician to Andrea

Doria. Alpini believed strongly in the doctrine of contagious diseases, a relatively new idea at that time. He became professor of botany at the University of Padua in 1593, and was appointed prefect of the Padua botanical garden in 1603. His published works, largely technical, reflect his experiences in Egypt. *De medicina Aegyptorum* (1591), described Egyptian medical practices and diseases. Alpini's famous *De plantis Aegypti liber* (1592) described and illustrated, with woodcuts, many Egyptian plants, including the coffee plant; *De medicina methodica libri tredecim* (1611) and *De plantis exoticis libri duo* (1627) are other examples. Another book, medical prognosis, was translated into English and published in 1746 as *The Presages of Life and Death in Diseases.*

Alsop, Joseph Wright (1910-   ), American journalist and author, was born in Avon, Conn., and educated at Groton School and Harvard. From 1932 to 1935 he was on the New York *Herald Tribune* staff in New York, and in Washington the next year. With Robert E. Kintner he published a syndicated column on politics, "The Capital Parade," and several books, including *Men Around the President.* During World War II he first served in the Navy and later joined the American Volunteer Air Force. He was a prisoner of the Japanese until 1942. During 1945-58 he carried the syndicated column "Matter of Fact" with his brother Stewart, continuing it on his own in 1964. Besides numerous articles in periodicals, Alsop published books with his brother and on his own—*We Accuse, The Reporter's Trade,* and *From the Silent Earth.*

Alsop, Richard (1861-1915), American author, was born at Middletown, Conn., and studied at Yale. He became a member of the literary circle known as the Hartford Wits, or Connecticut Wits. Alsop contributed to a series of satirical poems called *The Echo,* first published in the *American Mercury* and later published in book form (1807). In 1808 his *Enchanted Lake of the Fairy Morgana* was published. His most popular prose work, *A Narrative of the Adventures of John R. Jewitt,* appeared in 1815.

Alsop, Stewart J. O. (1914-74), American newspaperman, was born in New York City. He was educated at Groton and Yale (1936), and started as an editor with the book publishing firm of Doubleday Doran in New York. In 1942 he enlisted in the Kings Royal Rifle Corps of the British army, and rose to the rank of captain before transferring to the American army in 1944. Soon after the Normandy invasion he was parachuted into France to help the Maquis. Meanwhile his brother Joseph Alsop, also a newspaperman, had fought along with the American Air Force in China. After the war, the brothers collaborated on a syndicated column, "Matter of Fact," until 1958. Stewart became Washington editor of the *Saturday Evening Post,* while Joseph continued the column, mainly on political and military subjects. It was distinguished by depth of learning, breadth of perspective, and respect for down-to-earth observation.

Altamirano, Ignacio Manuel (1834-93), Mexican poet and novelist, did not receive a formal education until early manhood; he then became a staunch supporter of education. Following the execution of Maximilian, Altamirano played an important part in the reconstruction of Mexico. He wrote some poetry but is best known for his novels *Clemencia* and *Christmas in the Mountains.*

Altizer, Thomas J(onathan) J(ackson) (1927-   ), theologian and author, was born in Cambridge, Mass. He began his college education at St. John's College, Annapolis, Md. After a year in the army, he finished at the University of Chicago, receiving a B. A. degree in 1948. He received his M.A. in theology in 1951, and his Ph.D. in the history of religions in 1955 from the University of Chicago. He taught religion at Wabash College in Indiana for two years before going to Emory University as professor of Bible and religion. Altizer began publishing his theological ideas in articles and books, and in 1965 emerged in the popular press as the leading "death of God" theologian. His writings include *Oriental Mysticism and Biblical Eschatology, Mircea Eliade and the Dialectic of the Sacred,* and *The Gospel of Christian Atheism.* He collaborated with William H. Hamilton on *Radical Theology and the Death of God.*

Altsheler, Joseph Alexander (1862-1919), juvenile writer, was born in Three Springs, Ky. He was educated at Liberty College, Glasgow, Ky., and Vanderbilt University. He worked as a reporter for the Louisville *Evening Post* and the *Courier-Journal* before going to New York as a feature writer for the *World.* He began writing for boys with *The Sun of Saratoga,* published in 1897, the first of many books based on American history. In 1918 he was voted the most popular boys' writer in America.

Alvarenga, Manuel Inácio da Silva (1749-1814), Brazilian poet, was born at Vila Rica or at São João del Rei and died in Rio de Janeiro. After studying law at the University of Coimbra, Portugal, he taught in Rio de Janeiro. His best-known work is *Glaura: poemas éroticos.* He is one of the earliest of the romantic writers in Brazilian literature.

Alvarez, A(lfred) (1929-   ), British poet and critic, was born in London and educated at Corpus Christi College, Oxford. He taught in the U.S. at Brandeis University and the State University of New York at Buffalo. He became editor of the *Journal of Education* in 1957, was drama critic for the *New Statesman* in London, 1958-60, and was poetry editor for the London *Observer* in 1959. His poetry, for which he received the Vachel Lindsay prize from *Poetry* magazine, includes *The End of It, Twelve Poems,* and *Lost.* Alvarez has written many articles of literary criticism for journals, and his published volumes of criticism include *The Shaping Spirit, The School of Donne, Under Pressure,* and *Beyond All This Fiddle.*

Alvarez, Chanca Diego (15th century), Spanish scientist and writer, was born in Seville. He was a court physician when he received a royal commission to sail with Columbus on his second voyage to America, receiving the title "Scribe of the Indies." He became the first European scientist to describe the new world when he wrote the *Carta relacion* about Columbus' voyage to the island of Santo Domingo.

Álvarez Quintero, Serafin (1871-1938) and **Joaquin (1873-1944),** Spanish playwrights. Both brothers were born in Utrera, Seville, and both died in Madrid. Lifelong collaborators, they wrote almost 200 plays. Their plays are regarded as diversions, rather than serious works, and are rich in local color and vivid characterization. Some of their plays, translated by Helen and Harley Granville-Barker, were successful in London and New York, including *A Hundred Years Old* and *The Women Have their Way.*

Alvaro, Corrado (1895-1956), Italian journalist and novelist, was born in Reggio. He was editor of the journal *Il Mondo* and wrote several novels and a collection of essays in which he criticized Fascism. These include *I maestri del diluvio* and *L'Uomo e forte.*

Alzate, Jose Antonio (1737-99), philosopher, scientist and journalist, was born and died in Mexico City. He received degrees in arts and in theology from the University of Mexico and helped in the reform of teaching in Mexico, but was essentially interested in the natural and physical sciences. Much of his work is unknown; some of it was never published but many of his studies were published in popular collections of scientific and technological information.

Alzog (*äl' tsōK*), **Johann Baptist (1808-78),** Roman Catholic historian, was born at Ohlau, Silesia. He was professor of church history in the Universary of Freiburg, and wrote a *Manual of Church History,* which was translated into many languages. He was also the au-

thor of *Outline of Patrology,* and in 1869 was a member of the commission on dogma which prepared the work for the Vatican council.

Amado, Jorge (1912-   ), Brazilian novelist, was born in Ilhéos, Bahia, the setting for many of his novels. A mulatto, Amado wrote of Negroes, the poor and downtrodden, and the masses. Critics consider him one of the greatest contemporary Brazilian writers. His novel *Jubiaba* has been translated into seven languages. Other works include *The Violent Land, Beach Waifs, Cacao* and *Sweat.*

Amara Simha (c. 550 A.D.), Buddhist Sanskrit scholar. He is remembered for the *Thesaurus of Amara,* a list of some 13,000 synonyms in verse, which became the basic tool of later Sanskrit poets.

Ambler, Eric (1909-   ), British writer, was born in London and graduated from the University of London. While working as an engineer and later as an advertising copywriter, he began writing short stories and novels. After military service during World War II, he began writing screenplays, including *The Magic Box* and *A Night to Remember.* His novels of suspense and intrigue include *A Passage of Arms, The Light of Day, Coffin for Dimitrios,* and *Journey Into Fear.*

Ambroise (flourished c. 1200), Norman historian, also known as Ambrose, was probably court minstrel to King Richard I during the Third Crusade. Ambroise's *L'Estoire de la guerre sainte,* a biographical account of the crusade, is the chief source for the history of 1190-92. Modern criticism has proved the text accurate. The original, written in rhymed French verse, is in the Vatican.

Ambrose, Saint (c. 340-397), Church father, was born at Treves. Consecrated bishop of Milan in 374, Ambrose was the leading figure in having Arianism declared heresy. He assisted in its extirpation and resisted attempted revivals of paganism. When Maximus usurped power and took Rome, Ambrose refused to flee with the supplanted emperor. He melted the most sacred vessels of the Church to obtain money to save the populace from starvation. Courageous toward the powerful and solicitous for the weak, Ambrose denied Christian communion to the Emperor Theodosius until he had done penance for a massacre. His preaching and theology exerted great influence on his younger contemporary, Augustine. Saint Ambrose wrote several hymns that were later used as models. He dealt with Christian ethics in *De officiis ministrorum, De viduis, De virginitate* and *De paenitentia,* and he emphasizes the sin of man, the grace of God, and the necessity of faith in *De fide ad Gratianum Augustum, De Spiritu Sancto, De incarnationis Dominicae sacramento,* and *De mysteriis.*

Ames, James Barr (1846-1910), American educator and legal scholar, was born in Boston. He was graduated from Harvard college in 1868 and from Harvard law school in 1872. In the latter, he became associate professor of law, 1873; professor of law, 1877; and dean, 1895. He exerted a profound influence in the development of the study of American law.

Amicis, Edmondo de (1846-1908), Italian travel writer and novelist, was born in Oneglia, attended Modena military school, and served in the Austro-Italian War (1866). His writing started with newspaper sketches on military life, followed by a series of books describing his travels, *Spain* (1871), *Holland* (1874), *Morocco* (1876), and *Constantinople* (1878-79). He also wrote novels, including *An Italian Schoolboy's Journal* (1887) and *On Blue Water* (1897).

Amiel, Henri Frédéric (1821-81), Swiss writer, was born in Geneva and educated in Italy, France, Belgium, and Germany. He taught aesthetics and moral philosophy at the academy in Geneva. His poem *Roulez, Tambours* was adopted as the national anthem of the French-speaking part of Switzerland. His *Journal,* covering the years from 1847 until his death, is considered a masterpiece of self-analysis, revealing a sensitive mind struggling for values in an era of pessimism and skepticism. Amiel has been translated into English, Russian, and German.

Amir Ali, Seyyid (1849-1928), Indian jurist and leader, was born at Cuttack at Orissa. Following his early education in Calcutta, he studied law in England. He returned to Calcutta to practice law, and held a series of legal positions before he became a judge of the Calcutta high court in 1890. In 1904 he settled permanently in England, where he was appointed to the judicial committee of the privy council in 1909. Amir Ali supported British rule in India, believing this was the only way to escape Hindu domination. He helped to found the National Mohammedan Association in 1877 to protect Moslem interests. In 1891 he wrote *Spirit of Islam,* which was intended to reinterpret Islam for modern society.

Amis, Kingsley (1922-   ), novelist and poet, was born in London and educated at the City of London school and at St. John's College, Oxford. Following military service in World War II, he lectured in English literature at the University College of Swansea. His reputation as a novelist was made with his second book, *Lucky Jim.* After the death of Ian Fleming, Amis wrote two James Bond novels under the pseudonym Robert Markham. Other novels include *That Uncertain Feeling, One Fat Englishman,* and *The Anti-Death League.* He also published verse and articles on science fiction and jazz.

Amman, Jost (1539-91), Swiss painter and book illustrator, was born and educated in Zurich. He worked for a short time in Basel and moved to Nurnburg about 1560. None of his paintings survive. His many etchings include historical portraits, title pages, and scenes of hunting and fighting. He produced thousands of woodcut illustrations for the publisher Feirabend of Frankfurt.

Ammianus Marcellinus, (c. 325-c. 400), Roman historian, was born at Antioch. He entered the army at an early age and served in several campaigns. After retiring from a successful military career, he settled in Rome, where, at an advanced age, he wrote a history of the Roman Empire. These 31 books, in Latin, covered the years A.D. 96-378, forming a sequel to the work of Tacitus, the Roman historian. Of Ammianus' 31 books, 18 remain, covering the period 353-378. They furnish a reliable and impartial account of the Rome of his day and afford an explanation for its fall.

Ammons, A(rchie) R(andolph) (1926-   ), American poet, was born in Whiteville, N.C., and educated at Wake Forest College and the University of California at Berkeley. He became poetry editor of the *Nation* in 1963 and has taught English at Cornell since 1964, becoming associate professor in 1969. Ammons has often taken man's relationship to nature for a theme, and has been influenced by Emerson and Whitman. His volumes of poetry include *Ommateum, Expressions of Sea Level, Corson's Inlet, Tape for the Turn of the Year,* and *Northfield Poems.*

Amory, Cleveland (1917-   ), journalist, was born at Nahant, Mass. Following graduation from Harvard he was a member of the staff of Arizona newspapers in Tucson and Prescott. Later he joined the staff of the *Saturday Evening Post.* As a free-lance writer after 1945, he produced numerous magazine articles and several well-known books, including *The Proper Bostonians* (1947), *The Last Resorts* (1952), and *Who Killed Society?* (1958). He wrote columns for the *Saturday Review* and *Holiday.*

Ampére (än' pär'), **André Marie (1775-1836),** French mathematician and naturalist, was born at Lyons. In 1805, he was called to Paris, where he distinguished himself as a teacher in the Polytechnic School, and began his career as an author by his essay on the *Mathematical Theory of Chances.* In 1814, he was elected a member of the Academy of Sciences; in 1824, he was appointed professor of experimental physics in the Collège de France. He invented the astatic needle, which made the astatic galvanometer possible. The ampere, a unit of electrical current, is named for him. His scientific works include *Considerations sur la théorie mathématique du jeu; Recueil d'observations électro-dynamiques; Théorie des phénomènes electro-dynamiques,* and *Essai sur la philosophie des sciences.* The charm of his character is evident in his journal, letters, and memoirs.

Amram Ben Shesna (died 875), religious writer, was head of the Jewish academy of Sura, Persia. He arranged the first complete liturgy for the synagogue. Most of the rites still used by Jews are based on his prayer book, *Siddur Rab 'Amram.*

'Amr Ibn Kulthum (6th century A.D.), Arab poet, who belonged to the tribe of Taghlib in Mesopotamia. He wrote one of the poems included in the *Mu 'allaqat,* a collection of seven pre-Islamic Arabic poems by seven different poets.

Amundsen (ä' mŭn-sĕn), **Roald (1872-1928),** Norwegian explorer, was born in Borge, Norway. In June 1903, he sailed in the *Gjöa* and after two years of exploration, located the north magnetic pole and the northwest passage. Sailing in June 1910, in Nansen's famous ship, the *Fram,* he led the Norwegian antarctic expedition which resulted in the discovery of the south pole, December 14, 1911. After an unsuccessful attempt to fly to the north pole by airplane in 1925, he succeeded, 1926, in passing over the pole in the dirigible *Norge,* traveling from Spitzbergen to Alaska. With Nobile, one of his associates in this trip, Amundsen was later involved in a bitter controversy. When Nobile in 1928 was lost in an attempt to repeat the feat, Amundsen flew by airplane to his rescue, but perished in the Arctic Ocean. Amundsen wrote *To the North Magnetic Pole and through the Northwest Passage; Our Polar Flight; First Crossing of the Polar Sea; My Life as an Explorer;* and others.

Amyot, Jacques (1513-93), French author and scholar, was born at Melun and studied at the University of Paris and Bourges. He became abbot of Bellozane at the appointment of Francis I. After spending some time in Italy, Amyot returned to France to tutor the sons of King Henry II. In 1570 he was appointed Bishop of Auxerre by Charles IX. He translated several works of classical authors, the most important being Plutarch's *Lives.* Amyot also translated Heliodorus' *Aethiopica,* the *Daphnis et Chloe* of Longus, and seven books of the historian Diodorus Siculus.

Anacreon (a-nàk' ew-ŏn), **(c. 563 B.C.- c. 478 B.C.),** Greek lyric poet, was born at Teos in Ionia. He was patronized by Polycrates, the tyrant of Samos, and by Hipparchus, the tyrant of Athens. His poems, chiefly devoted to the praises of love, pleasure, and wine, are characterized by marked simplicity and sweetness of style. The authentic fragments of his verse have been paraphrased in English by Thomas Moore. He died at Abdera.

Anaxagoras (ăn'ăk-săg'o-ras) **(c. 500 B.C.-c. 428 B.C.),** Greek philosopher, was born at Clazomenæ. He studied under Anaximenes, and, after traveling through all the known parts of the world in search of knowledge, established himself at Athens, where he opened the first school of philosophy. He taught that mind rules the universe. Pericles, Socrates, and Euripides are said to have been among his pupils. He was condemned to die for alleged impiety. The sentence was changed to exile, however, at the pleading of Pericles, and he retired to Lampsacus, where he continued to teach philosophy until his death.

Anaximander (ăn-ăk′sĭ-măn′dēr) (611 B.C.-c. 547 B.C.) Greek mathematician, astronomer, and philosopher, was born at Miletus. He was a pupil and friend of Thales, whom he succeeded as head of the Ionian school. He taught the obliquity of the ecliptic, which he is reputed to have discovered. He introduced the gnomon for determining solstices, and the sundial. He is also given credit for the invention of geographical maps. By some ancient writers he is said to have determined approximately the size and the distance of the planets and to have constructed astronomical globes. He imagined the universe as a number of concentric cylinders with the earth at the center. As a philosopher, he speculated upon the origin of the material universe, which he found to be an infinite, indeterminate substance, from which all material objects arise.

Anchieta, José de (1534-97), Portuguese linguist and missionary, was born in San Cristobal de la Laguna, Tenerife. A relative of Ignatius Loyola, he entered the Society of Jesus in 1551 after studying at Coimbra. At the end of his novitiate he was sent to the missions in Brazil, where he was ordained in 1566. He taught humanities in the Jesuit school that he helped to found. Anchieta learned Tupi, the language of the natives, and wrote a grammar of the language. He also wrote dialogues, canticles, religious plays, and textbooks.

Anczyca, Vladislav Ludvig (1823-83), Polish dramatist and writer, was born in Vilna and lived most of his life in Cracow. His popular national plays include *The Peasant-Aristocrats, The Inhabitants of Lobsov* and *The Peasants' Emigration*. He also translated many German and French classics, wrote poetry, and, under the pen name Kasimir Goralczyk, wrote many books for children.

Andersen, Hans Christian (1805-75), novelist, children's poet, and writer of fairy tales, was born at Odense, in Denmark. He early displayed a talent for poetry and was known in his native place as "the comedy-writer." He was placed in an advanced school at the public expense and began his academic education in 1828. He completed his *Agnes and the Merman* in Switzerland: one of his best works, *The Improvisatore*, a series of scenes depicted in a glowing style and full of poetic interest, was the fruit of a visit to Italy. In 1840, he commenced a somewhat protracted tour through Italy and the East, an account of which he gave in *A Poet's Bazaar*, 1842.

Anderson, C(larence) W(illiam) (1891-   ), American author and illustrator of children's books, was born in Wahoo, Neb. After teaching in a country school for two years, he studied at the Art Institute in Chicago. In 1938 he moved to New Hampshire and has used the New England landscape as the background for many of his books. He specializes in lithographs and his works include *Billy and Blaze, Thoroughbreds, Big Red, Heads Up—Heels Down, The Blind Connemara*, and *Sketchbook*.

Anderson, Jervis (1937-   ), writer, was born in Jamaica, and graduated from New York University. His first job after high school was with the *Gleaner*, a Jamaican newspaper. Then he joined a weekly newspaper, *Public Opinion* until 1958, when he came to the U.S. There, he wrote for the *New York Times, Commentary*, and the *New Yorker*. His *A. Philip Randolph: A Biographical Portrait* was published in 1972.

Anderson, Marian (1902-   ), American Negro singer was born in Philadelphia, Pa. As a child she sang in the Union Baptist church choir in Philadelphia, where the unusual quality of her voice attracted attention. Money raised by a church concert enabled her to take lessons from an Italian instructor and she subsequently studied in New York, Chicago, and abroad. She began her singing career in 1924. In concert tours throughout the United States and Europe, she quickly won acclaim for her rendering of classic, operatic, and popular songs, and particularly of Negro spirituals. In 1941, she made her debut with the Metropolitan Opera Company, the first Negro to sing with that company. Her autobiography, *My Lord, What a Morning*, was published in 1957.

Anderson, Maxwell (1888-1959), American playwright, was born at Atlantic, Pennsylvania. He was graduated from the University of North Dakota (1911), and, after a number of years spent in newspaper work began to write plays. His first great success was *What Price Glory*, written in collaboration with Laurence Stallings. He also wrote many other successful plays of outstanding merit, including *Saturday's Children* (1927); *Elizabeth the Queen* (1930); *Both Your Houses* (1933); *Winterset* (1935); *High Tor* (1937); and *Joan of Lorraine* (1946). He has won both the Pulitzer and the Critics' prize. Later plays written by him are *Barefoot in Athens* (1951) and *The Bad Seed* (1954).

Anderson, Poul William (1926-   ), mystery and science fiction writer, was born in Bristol, Pa. He received a B.S. degree from the University of Minnesota in 1948. He has written more than 180 short stories, novelettes, and articles, and edited several anthologies. In 1959 he received the first annual Macmillan mystery award for *Perish by the Sword*, the science fiction Hugo award for best short fiction in 1961 for *The Longest Voyage*, and again in 1964 for *No Truce with Kings*.

Anderson, Rasmus Björn (1846-1936), author and diplomat, was born at Albion, Wis., of Norwegian parentage, and was educated at Luther College, Decorah, Iowa. He was appointed to the position of professor of Scandinavian languages and literature, 1875-83, at the University of Wisconsin. In 1885, he was appointed United States minister to Denmark, and he was editor and publisher of *Amerika*, 1898-1922. His publications include *Norse Mythology, America not Discovered by Columbus*, and *First Chapter of Norwegian Immigration, 1821-40*.

Anderson, Robert (1805-1871), American soldier, was born near Louisville, Ky. He was graduated at West Point in 1825, and was colonel of the Illinois volunteers in the Black Hawk War of 1832. He became instructor of artillery practice at West Point in 1835 and fought in the Seminole War in 1837-38. He served in the Mexican War, being severely wounded at Molino del Rey. In November 1860, he took command of Charleston harbor, where he was confined to Fort Sumter by the Confederates, and, on April 14, 1861, after a bombardment of 36 hours, he was compelled to evacuate the fort. This was the opening action of the Civil War. In 1865, he was brevetted major general. He wrote *Reminiscences of the Black Hawk War*.

Anderson, Robert (Woodruff) (1917-   ), American playwright, was born in New York City, and educated at Harvard. Besides writing numerous plays, he taught playwriting and also wrote for radio, television, and movies. He received the New York Drama Critics Circle Poll Award in 1954 for *Tea and Sympathy*, which was later made into a movie. Other dramas are *Come Marching Home; All Summer Long; Silent Night, Lonely Night;* and *I Never Sang for My Father*.

Anderson, Sherwood (1876-1941), American author, was born at Camden, Ohio, and was educated in the public schools. His works, which belong to the more radical wing of modern American literature, reveal a high degree of originality and force. They include *The Triumph of the Egg, Dark Laughter, Perhaps Women*, and *Puzzled America*. In 1927 he purchased and became editor of two weekly newspapers in Marion, Va. Characteristic editorials and news stories from these papers were collected and published under the title of *Hello Towns*.

Andrade, Edward Neville de Costa (1887-1971), English physicist, was born in London. He was the inventor of the Andrade-Chalmers bar, a device used to maintain

Biography

constant stress in metals. In 1913, Andrade worked with Sir Ernest Rutherford, but the outbreak of war cut short their collaboration on atomic theory. Andrade became an authority in the history of science, especially on the work of Newton, Hooke, and their contemporaries. After his appointment as professor of physics at the University of London in 1928, he began to build a research school. During World War II, his laboratory was destroyed by bombs. His notes, a collection of valuable books, and manuscript letters from great figures in the world of science—Sir Ernest Rutherford, Sir James G. Frazer, Sir Charles Sherrington, and Svante Arrhenius—were lost. In 1950, Andrade was appointed director of the Faraday Research Laboratory, but resigned in 1952 to carry on more research at the Imperial College of Science, where he became senior research fellow. Contact with Rutherford inspired Andrade to write *The Structure of the Atom* (1923), for some time the standard of reference for the subject. *The Mechanism of Nature* (1930), written for the layman, was translated into six foreign languages.

Andrade, Olegario Victor (1841-82), Argentine poet and journalist, was born in Gualeguaychu. He was a newspaper writer and later editor of the *Tribuna Nacional,* the government newspaper in Buenos Aires. He was known for his patriotic poems and has been referred to as the national poet of Argentina. Among his better-known poems are *El nido de Condores* and *La Atlantida.*

Andreas Capellanus (flourished 1175-80), Latin author, lived in France in the 12th century. Little is known of his life except that he was chaplain of the royal court. His book *De Amore* is a long Latin treatise on love. Critics differ on the interpretation of this work and its place in the courtly love scene of the day.

Andreev (än-drā' yĕf), **Leonid Nikolaevitch (1871-1919),** Russian writer, was born at Orel. He studied law in Leningrad and Moscow and, while struggling to establish practice, became a police court reporter for a Moscow newspaper. About 1900, he began writing stories, sketches, and dramas with notable success. The sales of his first volume of stories, appearing in 1901, soon exceeded a quarter of a million copies. He achieved great popularity throughout Russia, and his work is perhaps better known outside his own country than that of any recent Russian writer, translations having been made into all European languages. He was a mystic possessed of unusually searching powers of analysis, who regarded life with horror and pity. He attempted suicide three times. Among his best-known stories are *The Red Laugh, The Burglar, The Seven Who Were Hanged, Judas Iscariot and the Others, Silence,* and *S. O. S.* The last is an appeal against the Bolshevik regime in Russia, from which he fled to Finland.

Andrew of Crete, St. (c. 660-740?), Byzantine poet, one of the greatest hymn writers of the Greek church. He was born at Damascus, occupied a monastery in Jerusalem, became deacon of the Church of St. Sophia in Constantinople, and was for a time archbishop in Crete. To St. Andrew is attributed the invention of the canon, a new hymn form. Of his hymns that are still in use, the best known is the Great Canon sung during Lent.

Andrewes, Lancelot (1555-1626), English bishop and writer, was born in London. He was educated at Cooper's Free School, Radcliffe; at Merchant Taylors' School; and at Pembroke Hall, Cambridge. His knowledge of 15 languages enabled him to become a principal translator of the Authorized Version of the Bible (known as the King James Version). A conservative in church affairs, he opposed both the Puritan and the Roman Catholic factions, upholding the orthodoxy of the reformed Church of England. Andrewes was considered an eloquent and popular preacher and a dedicated bishop with a reputation for holiness, simplicity of life,

integrity, and scholarship. His extensive writings include *Catechetical Lectures* and a collection of private prayers that is still published in many editions.

Andrews, Charles McLean (1863-1943), American historian, was born at Weathersfield, Conn. A graduate of Johns Hopkins University, he taught there from 1907 to 1910 and then became professor of history at Yale University. An authority on early stages of American history, he wrote *Colonial Period of American History,* the first volume of which was awarded a Pulitzer prize in 1935. In 1937 he was elected to the American Academy of Arts and Letters.

Andrews, Roy Chapman (1884-1960), American naturalist and explorer, was born at Beloit, Wis. He was graduated at Beloit College in 1906 and later received a master's degree at Columbia University. In 1908, he made explorations in Alaska. He was attached as naturalist to the U.S.S. *Albatross* on a voyage to the Dutch East Indies, Borneo, and Celebes in 1909-10.

For the American Museum of Natural History, New York, of which he was director, he conducted important scientific expeditions to Asia. These included an expedition in 1916-17 to Tibet, southwestern China, and Burma; an expedition in 1919 to north China and outer Mongolia; and expeditions in 1921-29 to central Asia and Mongolia. Among the most striking results of these highly fruitful expeditions was the finding of fossil dinosaur eggs and of skeletal remains of the baluchitherium, the largest known land mammal.

His writings include *Whale Hunting with Gun and Camera, The California Gray Whale, Camps and Trails in China,* and *This Business of Exploring.*

Andric, Ivo (1892-1975), Yugoslav author and diplomat, was born in Bosnia. He studied philosophy at the universities of Zagreb, Vienna, and Cracow, and received his doctor's degree at Graz. He was a member of the Young Bosnia Revolutionary National Movement, which sought independence for the South Slavic peoples. He served in the diplomatic service and was ambassador to Berlin at the outbreak of World War II. His first novels, written during the Nazi occupation of Yugoslavia, reflect the spirit and conflict of the times in which he lived. For his best-known work, *The Bridge on the Drina,* he was awarded Yugoslavia's highest literary award. His other works include *Bosnian Story, Devil's Yard,* and *The Vizier's Elephant,* all of which have been translated into English. He was awarded the Nobel Prize for Literature in 1961, the first Yugoslav to be so honored.

Andrieux (än-dre-û'), **Francois Guillaume (1759-1833),** French poet and playwright, was born in Strasbourg. He was educated in Strasbourg and Paris, where he studied law. He was president of the Tribunate but resigned because of his opposition to the Civil Code of law. He then returned to teaching and writing. His best-known play, *Les Etourdis* was presented in 1788. Andrieux also wrote *La Comedienne,* a comedy, and *Lucius Junius Brutus,* a tragedy.

Aneurin or Aneirin (flourished c. 600), Welsh poet. His principal work, *Gododin,* concerning the British soldiers who fought against the Saxons in the battle of Cattraeth, is included in the 13th-century manuscript *Book of Aneirin.* The earliest reference to King Arthur is contained in this poem, which is also one of the oldest surviving examples of Welsh literature.

Angell, (ān'jĕl), **James Burrill (1829-1916),** American educator and diplomat, was born at Scituate, R. I., and was graduated at Brown University, 1849. He became professor of modern languages and literature, Brown, 1853; editor of the Providence *Journal,* 1860; president of the University of Vermont, 1866; and president of the University of Michigan, 1871. He was United States minister to China, 1880-81; a member of the Anglo-American international commission on Canadian fisheries, 1887; and minister to Turkey, 1897-98. During his long and able administration, the University of Michigan was brought to high rank among American institutions of learning. His writings include *Progress in International Law.*

Angell, James Rowland (1869-1949), American educator, was born at Burlington, Vt., son of James Burrill Angell. He was graduated at the University of Michigan and at Harvard; studied also at Berlin, Halle, Leipzig, and Paris. Beginning as assistant professor of psychology, University of Chicago, 1894, he became professor and head of the department, 1905. In 1911, he was made dean of the faculties, and, during 1918-19, was acting president of the University of Chicago. From 1921 to 1937 he was president of Yale University. In 1937, he joined the National Broadcasting Company as educational counselor. He wrote *Psychology,* which went through four editions.

Angell, Sir Norman (1874-1967), economist and author, was born in Holbeach, England. He studied in England, at the Lycée de St. Omer, France, and at the University of Geneva. He came to the western U.S. to become a reporter for a San Francisco newspaper. His fame spread with the appearance of *The Great Illusion* (1910), a thesis on the futility of war when common national economic interests are at stake. Angell returned to England in 1912 and became a Labour member of Parliament, 1929-31. He was knighted in 1931, and was awarded the Nobel Peace Prize in 1933. After Italian aggression in Ethiopia and Japanese inroads in Manchuria, Angell wrote against the British conservative policy of condoning such moves in his books *The Defense of the Empire* (1937) and *Peace with the Dictators* (1938).

Angelo, Valenti (1897-   ), illustrator and author, was born in Massaros, Italy, and emigrated to the U.S. as a child. Living in California, he worked as a laborer. He was largely self-trained as an artist, and in 1926 he began to work as an illustrator and decorator of books. In addition to illustrating more than 100 books by various authors, he also wrote books of his own. His stories of simple fishermen and workers express the dignity of life and reflect the spirit of democracy. Both his writings and drawings are filled with humor and adventure. His books include *Paradise Valley* (1940), *Look Out Yonder* (1943), *The Bells of Bleecker Street* (1949), *The Marble Fountain* (1951), and *Candy Basket* (1960).

Angelou, Maya (1928-   ), writer, was born Marguerite Johnson, in St. Louis, Mo. An actress, singer, dancer, songwriter, director, and producer, she also wrote stories, poetry, and documentaries. Her three-volume autobiography—*I Know Why the Caged Bird Sings* (1970), *Gather Together in My Name* (1974), and *Singin' and Swingin' and Gettin' Merry Like Christmas* (1976)—tells of her triumph over a childhood marked by rape, childbirth, prostitution, and the threat of drugs. At Martin Luther King's request, she acted as Northern coordinator for the Southern Christian Leadership Council. She later went to Africa, where she wrote for newspapers in Cairo, Accra, and Ghana. She also taught at the University of Ghana. Returning to the U.S. she produced a television series on African traditions in U.S. life. Her filmscript for *Georgia, Georgia* (1972) was the first script by a black woman to be produced. Other works poetry: *Just Give Me a Cool Drink of Water 'Fore I Diiie* (1971) and *O, Pray My Wings are Gonna Fit Me Well* (1975).

Angelus Silesius (1624-77), German mystic and religious poet, was born and died in Breslau. The son of a Lutheran Polish landowner, he was born Johannes Scheffler. He studied philosophy and medicine at the Universities of Strassburg, Leyden, and Padua. While he was court physician to the Duke of Württemburg, he became a Catholic in 1653. Following ordination as a Franciscan priest in 1661, Angelus held various high positions in the service of Sebastian Rostock, Bishop of

Breslau. In 1671 Angelus retired to St. Matthias monastery, where he lived in seclusion until his death. He published many pamphlets contributing to the Lutheran-Catholic controversy of the time and also wrote a number of apologetic works.

Angiolieri, Cecco (c. 1260-1312), Italian poet, was born in Siena. Little is known of him except that he apparently led a disorderly life, met occasional trouble with the law, and served in the army. His language is often coarse, but his comic verse is lively, expressing a predilection for wine, carousing, and gambling.

Angle, Paul McClelland (1900-75), American historian and authority on Lincoln, was born at Mansfield, Ohio. He spent most of his active life in Illinois. As executive secretary of the Abraham Lincoln Association of Springfield, then historian of the Illinois State Historical Library and, later, director of the Chicago Historical Society, he spent many years exploring original sources of information concerning Lincoln's day-to-day activities and personal contacts. The results of this wide-ranging investigation have been made available to the general public through vividly written accounts which re-create the time and place settings for incidents in Lincoln's life. One of his books, *Here I Have Lived,* gives a history of Lincoln's Springfield in the years between 1821 and 1865. Another, written in collaboration with Carl Sandburg, is entitled *Mary Lincoln, Wife and Widow.* Best known among his works are *A Shelf of Lincoln Books* and *The Lincoln Reader.*

Anglund, Joan Walsh (1926-   ), American author and illustrator of children's books, was born in Hinsdale, Ill., and studied at the Art Institute of Chicago and the American Academy of Art. Inspired by her own children, she is noted for her illustrations, often done in half-tones or as pen-and-ink drawings colored with water colors. *A Friend Is Someone Who Likes You* was selected by the *New York Times* as one of the 10 best illustrated books of 1958 and *The Brave Cowboy* received the Society of Illustrators award in 1959.

Anker, Nini (Nicolene) Magdelene Roll (1873-1942), Norwegian novelist and playwright, was born to an aristocratic family in Molde. She achieved moderate success with her novels and plays, which reflect a knowledge of society and emphasize the problems of women. *Kirken* is one of her plays; her novels include *Lill-Anna og Andre,*

Anna Comnena *(kŏm-ne' na),* **(1083-1148),** Byzantine princess and historian, daughter of the emperor Alexius I (Comnenus). She received the best education that Byzantium could give. During the last illness of her father, she entered into a scheme, which her mother, the empress Irene, also favored, to induce him to disinherit his eldest surviving son, John, and to bestow the diadem on her husband, Nicephorus Briennius. Failing in this, she framed a conspiracy against her brother in 1118. Her brother spared her life, but punished her by confiscation of her property, which he later restored. She withdrew from the court and devoted herself to the composition of the *Alexiad,* a valuable historical work

Annensky, Innokenty Feodorovich (1856-1909), Russian symbolist poet, was born in Omsk, Siberia, and studied classics in St. Petersburg. After holding teaching and administrative posts, he became a director of secondary schools. A modernist who dwelt on the futility of life, he used impressionist techniques in his work and was influenced by the French writers Baudelaire, Mallarmé, and Verlaine. Although barely recognized before his death, having published only one volume of verse (*Quiet Songs,* 1904), Annensky has grown in reputation and his work was a strong influence on Boris Pasternak. The conciseness of Annensky's verse presents difficulties and he is mainly appreciated by other poets. He wrote dramas on ancient themes and translated and adapted the plays of Euripides.

Annunzio *(än-noon'dze-ō),* **Gabriele d' (1863-1938),** Italian poet, novelist, and dramatist, was born at Pescara. In his 15th year, while a student at Prato, he published his first volume of verse, *Primo vere*, followed in the ensuing 10 years by other volumes, which established his fame as a rising poet. His first novel, *Il piacere*, translated into English as "The Child of Pleasure," showed the influence of Maupassant and Bourget. Other famous novels from his pen include *L' innocente, Giovanni Episcopo, Il Trionfo della Morte,* and *Fuoco*. In the drama too, d'Annunzio attained a place in the front rank of Italian writers. His plays include *The Dream of a Spring Morning, The Dead City, Francesca da Rimini, Greater than Love, The Ship, Pisanella* or *The Perfumed Death,* and *The Honeysuckle*. While a "decadent," and regarded by Borgese as a product of a materialistic age, d'Annunzio was a most powerful writer and the greatest literary artist in modern Italian letters. When picturing the former glories of Italy, he rose to the level of a great classic writer.

Upon the outbreak of war with Austria in 1915, he entered the Italian army and became notable as an aviator. In 1919, he placed himself at the head of a volunteer army and seized Fiume in order to prevent its becoming a part of Yugoslavia. He established the city as an independent state and, for 15 months, refused in the face of all Europe to submit to agreements made regarding the city by the Treaty of Rapallo. Driven from the city by an Italian army in 1921, he went into retirement.

Anouilh (*a-noo'ē*), **Jean (1910-   ),** playwright, generally associated with the avante-garde theater, was born in Bordeaux, France. He acquired theatrical experience as secretary to Louis Jouvet, the actor and producer. His early works include *Mandarine* (1932) and *Wild Girl* (1938). During World War II, Anouilh began to take his themes from classical mythology. His outstanding play of this time was *Antigone* (1942), expressing individual resistance to oppression. Anouilh's use of modern dress instead of period costumes in this production was a significant experiment. Many of his dramas have been translated into English, and a few have been produced on Broadway, among them are *The Waltz of the Toreadors, Becket,* and *Poor Bitos*. His works range from sophisticated comedy to classical tragedy.

Anselm, Saint (1033-1109), archbishop of Canterbury, a scholastic philosopher, was born at Aosto, Piedmont. He led at first a dissipated life. He was later attracted by the reputation of Lanfranc and went in 1060 to study under him at the monastery of Bec, in Normandy. Three years later, he became prior and, in 1078, abbot of this monastery, the most famous school of the 11th century. Lanfranc, who in the meantime had gone to England and became archbishop of Canterbury, died in 1089, and, in 1093, Anselm was appointed his successor.

Anselm was in almost continual controversy with the English monarchs William II and Henry I on the question of primacy between secular and clerical prerogatives. His insistence on the primacy of the Church was unbending and led to his banishment in 1097-1100. His theological treatises were based on the theory that to understand one must believe.

Anselm has been called the father of scholasticism. He made Bec the chief center of learning in western Europe. His teachings were chiefly upon religious doctrines. His fundamental principle was that Christianity can be founded on stable grounds only if reason guides. He trained his followers, therefore, to cultivate methods of correct and vigorous thinking. From Bec there issued, as a result, the most vigorous disputants of the age. Saint Anselm wrote *Proslogium, Monologium, On Behalf of the Fool by Gaunilon,* and *Cur Deus Homo*. Sidney Norton Deane has translated his works from the Latin.

Antarah (or Antar) (6th century), pre-Islamic Arab poet and warrior. Born to a Negro slave mother, he was later freed and fought in many battles. Antarah exemplified Arabic chivalry and wrote popular poems that expressed his love for his cousin Abla and portrayed his exploits. One of his poems is preserved the *Mu' Allaqat,* a collection of pre-Islamic odes. Antarah became a heroic figure in the *Sirat Antar ibn Shaddad,* a romance that was handed down over the centuries by Arab storytellers. The work was also popular in Europe in the 19th century.

Antheil, George (1900-59), composer and writer, was born in Trenton, N.J., and studied with Ernest Block in New York City. In 1921 he went to Europe and associated himself with artistic and literary avant-garde groups in Paris. He is remembered for his ultramodern music of the 1920's, particularly *Ballet Méchanique,* scored for mechanical pianos, automobile horns, electric bells, and airplane propellers. He wrote six symphonies, five operas, and chamber music. His autobiography is entitled *Bad Boy of Music*.

Anthony the Great, Saint (251-356), the founder of Christian monasticism, was born at Coma near Heraclea in upper Egypt. In 285, having sold all his property and given the proceeds to the poor, he withdrew into the desert. While there, he was frequently tempted by the devil, who appeared in such forms as a beautiful woman or a wild animal. A number of disciples, attracted by his reputation for sanctity, gathered about him and formed the first community of monks. He afterward went to Alexandria to encourage the Christians to endure the persecutions of 311 and again, about 350, in order to preach against the Arians. He returned to the desert, where he died. There are some extant writings attributed to Saint Anthony, but much of his thinking has survived secondhand in the writings of St. Athanasius.

Anthony of Padua, Saint (1195-1231), was born at Lisbon. He was at first an Augustinian monk but, in 1220, he entered the Franciscan order and became one of its most illustrious members. He preached in the south of France and in upper Italy. Numerous miracles were attributed to him, and he won great popularity by his effective preaching against the vices of luxury, avarice, and tyranny. According to legend, he preached to the fishes when men refused to hear him; hence he is the patron of the lower animals and is often represented as accompanied by a pig. He died at Vercelli and was canonized by Gregory IX in 1232. His extant works include sermons and a mystical commentary on the Bible.

Anthony, Edward (1895-1971), writer, was born in New York City. He began newspaper work on the Bridgewater (Conn.) *Herald* in 1917; after army military service in World War I, he joined the staff of the New York *Herald*. In 1923 he moved to magazine work and wrote for the *American, Woman's Home Companion,* and *Collier's,* among others. His books include *Merry-Go-Roundelays, Bring 'Em Back Alive* (with Frank Buck), *This Is Where I Came In,* and *O Rare Don Marquis*. He also wrote the book and lyrics for the musical comedy *Good Luck Sam*.

Anthony, Susan B(rownell) (1820-1906), American reformer, was born at Adams, Mass.; was educated at Bartenville, N. Y., and, 1837-38, at Friends' boarding school, West Philadelphia. She taught school from the age of 15 to 30; aided in organizing the first state Woman's Temperance Society in 1852; was active in the antislavery cause; and was organizer and secretary of the Women's National Loyal League during the Civil War. After the war, she devoted herself to the woman's suffrage movement; founded, in 1868, *The Revolution,* which she managed for several years; in 1869, organized, with Mrs. Stanton, the national woman's suffrage association. She was widely known as a lecturer and wrote a large part of the 4-volume work entitled *History of Woman Suffrage*.

Antimachus (5th century B.C.), Greek poet and grammarian, was from Claros or Colophon. He is considered the forerunner of the Alexandrian school of 4th-century

Biography

B.C. Egypt. His works were praised by Plato and include a long elegiac poem called *Lyde* and the epic *Thebais,* relating the story of Eteocles in the war called the Seven against Thebes.

Antin, Mary (1881-1949), author, was born in Polotzk, Russia, and emigrated to the U.S. in 1894. She was educated at Columbia University Teachers College and Barnard College. She wrote generally about immigrants: *From Polotzk to Boston,* originally written in Yiddish; *The Promised Land,* first serialized in the *Atlantic Monthly,* and *They Who Knock at Our Gates.* After touring as a lecturer, she worked at Gould Farm, a social service community in Great Barrington, Mass. In 1901 she married Amadeus Grabau, a professor at Columbia. She died in Suffern, N.Y.

Antiphon (c. 480-411 B.C.), Greek rhetorician from Rhamnus in Attica, of whom little is known except that he urged the overthrow of democracy at Athens and was later tried and executed. Although he did no public speaking, except at his own trial, Antiphon was one of the first professional speech-writers in Greece, and his legal speeches are the earliest that have survived. Many of his speeches seem to have been prepared for defendants in homicide trials. Much of his work is lost, and there remains some dispute as to the authenticity of what exists. It is thought that Antiphon also taught rhetoric.

Antisthenes (c. 444-after 371 B.C.), Greek philosopher and founder of the school of Cynics, was born at Athens and studied with Gorgias and Socrates. Only fragments of the dialogues and commentaries he is supposed to have written have been preserved. He led an austere life and held the doctrine that happiness stemming from knowledge is the source of virtue. He founded his own school in the Cynosarges.

Anvari (died 1191?), Persian poet, also known as Auhad al-Din Ali. He is ranked among the greatest Arab classical euologistic writers and was born at Avibard toward the beginning of the 12th century. He was court poet for Sultan Sanjar, the Seljuk king, but was dismissed when Sanjar died. Anvari's best-known poem, *Tears of Khurasan,* reflects his sorrow at Sanjar's capture during invasions by the Arab Ghuzz tribesmen. The poem was translated into English by William Kirkpatrick.

Anwar, Chairil (1922-49). Indonesian poet, was born in Medan, Sumatra, the son of Moslem parents. He moved to Java in 1940 and began writing verse. He avoided Indonesian literary traditions and was largely influenced by Dutch writers. His verse is considered direct in form, displaying careful diction. Many later Indonesian writers have modeled their work on Anwar, who is regarded as Indonesia's foremost writer. Many of his works have been translated into English by Burton Raffel.

Anzengruber, Ludwig (1839-89), Austrian playwright, was born at Vienna, and inherited his father's interest in drama. His early years were spent in poverty—he tried journalism and acting, then became a clerk in the police department. After many unsuccessful attempts at writing plays, Anzengruber achieved fame with *Der Pfarrer Von Kirchfield,* an anticlerical play. He then turned out a number of comedies and received the Schiller prize in 1878. From his experiences as a traveling actor he drew the peasant characters and dialect for his plays, and he made a lasting impression on the German stage. Anzengruber became editor of *Figaro* in 1885, and wrote well-received short stories and novels—*Der Schandfleck* and *Der Sternsteinhof.* His dramas include *Der Meineidbauer, Die Kreuzelschreiber, Der G'wissenswurm, Doppelselbstmord,* and *Das Vierte Gebot.*

Apollinaire, Guillaume (1880-1918), French poet, was born Guillaume Albert Dulcigni in Rome. Educated on the French Riviera, Apollinaire traveled in eastern Europe and settled in Paris in 1902. Having many friends who were painters and writers, he quickly gained recognition for his published work. During the years 1908-14, he reached the peak of his career and came to be regarded as one of the major modern poets of the early 20th century.

Two collections of poetry, *Alcools* (1913) and *Calligrammes* (1918), constitute the major part of his work. *Alcools* contains some modern poems, but is considered essentially lyric and traditional. It contains his best-known poem "La Chanson du Mal-Aimé." *Calligrammes* is regarded as more modern, containing poems that also form designs, and includes images of love and war. Apollinaire has been described as heralding the surrealist movement. He wrote a large mass of critical and journalistic work, edited the review *Les Soirées de Paris,* and published a volume of stories and two novels. He coined the word "surrealist" in 1917 for the Picasso-Satie-Cocteau ballet *Parada,* and thus provided the name for the entire movement. Although he was not a French citizen, Apollinaire volunteered for service in 1914, was wounded at the front and returned in 1916 to Paris, where he died of influenza.

Apollonius Dysolus (flourished c. A.D. 150), Greek grammarian from Alexandria, originated scientific grammar. His scholarly work, the foremost of which was *On Syntax,* was a standard reference of Greek syntax until the 19th century.

Apollonius of Perga (ăp'ŏ-lō'nĭ-ŭs) **(in Asia Minor),** a writer called "the great geometer," lived in the second half of the 3rd century B.C. He was educated at Alexandria, and wrote a treatise on *Conic Sections* in eight books. He is justly considered one of the founders of the mathematical sciences. To him are due the terms ellipse, hyperbole, and parabola.

Appollonius of Rhodes (c. 295 B.C. - c. 215 B.C.), was born in Alexandria. He presided over an academy at Rhodes and was an eminent rhetorician. He wrote poems, one of which, the *Argonautica,* is an epic poem containing an account of the mythical expedition in search of the golden fleece.

Appleton, Daniel (1785-1849) American publisher, was born in Haverhill, Mass. In 1813, he moved his general store to Boston, where with other merchandise, he included the sale of books. He moved his business once again, this time to New York. After a few years, he formed a partnership with his son William and in 1838 entered the publishing field. Following his death, D. Appleton & Co. was carried on by his sons.

Apukhtin (ă-pook-tyin), **Alexey Nikolayevich (1840?-93),** Russian poet and novelist, was born in the Orel Region, and entered the civil service on graduation from law school. His lyric poems, generally with themes of unhappy love, were highly popular during his time, and Tchaikovsky set some of them to music. Apukhtin's three published novels were *From the Archives of a Countess, Dairy of Pavlik Dolsky,* and *Between Life and Death.*

Apuleius, Lucius (c. 125 A.D.-after 170), Greek satirical writer, rhetorician, and philosopher, was born in Madaura, Africa, and educated at Carthage and Athens, where he studied Platonic philosophy. In his *Apologia* he refuted charges that he had used magic, particularly in persuading a rich widow to marry him. The *Apologia* is the chief source for his biography. While traveling in Italy and Asia, Apuleius was initiated into numerous religious mysteries and his most famous work, the *Metamorphoses,* or the *Golden Ass,* is a valuable sourcebook for the ancient mystery religions. It is also rich in descriptions of life at that time. One of the earliest romances in European literature, the *Golden Ass* is also the earliest Latin novel extant in its entirety and contains, among other episodes, the story of Cupid and Psyche. It narrates the adventures of a man who was temporarily transformed into an ass. Apuleius' other works include the *Florida,* collection of speeches.

Aquinas (a-kwĭ'nas), **Saint Thomas (1225-74),**

theologian and saint of the Roman Catholic Church, was born near Aquino, in the kingdom of Naples. He received his earliest instruction at the monastery of Monte Cassino and, about 1240, went to the University of Naples. He was without worldy ambition and longed for the seclusion and quiet of the monastic life. He made profession as a Dominican in 1243; studied at Paris; and, in 1245, became a pupil of Albert the Great at Cologne.

In 1253, Aquinas began his studies at the University of Paris and, four years later, received there his degree as doctor of theology. Thoroughly imbued with the scholastic, dialectic, and Aristotelian philosophy, he gained prominence as a teacher in Paris. In 1261, Urban called him to Rome to assist in the difficult task of reconciling the Greek and Latin churches. In 1269, he was again in Paris; three years later, he went to Naples, where he taught until shortly before his death.

The *Summa Theologica* "Compendium of Theology," is Saint Thomas's greatest work. It remains to this day the most comprehensive and complete of all expositions of the Catholic system. His commentaries on Scripture and his devotional treatises also have a high reputation. He united theology with ethics and clearly set forth the philosophy of Christian morals. All his works were written in Latin.

Saint Thomas sought, in his writings, to effect a harmony of reason and revelation by means of an orderly, consistent, and comprehensive system of theology. To this purpose, he invoked all the power and subtleties of Aristotle's logic. By nature and training, Saint Thomas was the very embodiment of the scholastic method of intricate analysis, yet his style was so clear that his writings are intelligible and interesting to the modern reader.

Aquinas died when on his way to attend the General Council that Gregory X had convoked at Lyons, France. He was canonized in 1323, and, two centuries later, Pius V named him the fifth doctor of the Church.

Aquinas was undoubtedly the greatest and most influential philosopher of the middle ages. He adopted the method of teaching which later came to be universal in European universities, namely, the so-called commentary. He read Aristotle's works to his students and followed the reading by critical comments. This method is reflected in the lecture method of instruction which is common today in all higher institutions of learning in Europe and America.

Aquinas was a voluminous writer on theological and philosophical topics. His writings, like his oral methods of teaching, have exercised a lasting influence. No single authority has contributed more to the fixed teachings of the Roman Catholic Church and its schools than Aquinas.

Aragon, Louis (1897-   ), French poet and novelist, was born in Paris. He was one of the originators of the surrealist movement in the 1920's. In 1931, after traveling in Russia, he became a Marxist. As a leader of the French underground in Paris during World War II, Aragon became disillusioned with his government as well as with the Germans. Some of his novels have been translated into English, including *The Bells of Basel, Residential Quarter,* and *Holy Week.* He has also written love poems, literary criticism and political essays.

Arai Hakuseki, (1657-1725), (pseudonym of Arai Kimiyoshi), Japanese scholar and historian, was born near Tokyo. He wrote an autobiography, one of the first of such works in Japan. He also wrote a general history of Japan, *Tokushi Yoron,* covering a period of 2000 years. He is responsible for an account of the West, including its conditions and customs, being brought to the attention of the Japanese people through two of his works, *Record of Occidental Hearsay* and *Renderings of Foreign Languages.*

Arany, John (1817-82), Hungarian poet, was born at Salonta, Rumania. He studied at Debrecen and became a traveling actor, teacher, and editor. He composed a satirical poem, *The Lost Constitution,* which won the prize of the Kisfaludy Society, a Hungarian literary association. With the publication of *Toldi,* the first part of his epic trilogy founded on Magyar traditions, he gained great popularity. In addition to a number of ballads he wrote, he translated Shakespeare's *Midsummer Night's Dream, Hamlet,* and other foreign masterpieces into Hungarian. He was secretary of the Hungarian Academy from 1865-79.

Arason, Jon (1484-1550), Icelandic bishop and poet, was born in Gryta. He established the first printing press in Iceland in 1530. When the Reformation began, Arason refused to comply with the new religious ordinances and troops were sent from Denmark to compel him to do so. He still refused, civil war broke out, and he, with two of his sons, was executed. He was the last Roman Catholic bishop in Iceland, and his secular and sacred poetry has been preserved.

Arbuthnot, John (1667-1735), Scottish mathematician, physician, and writer, was born at Inverbervie, Kincardineshire. He taught mathematics in London before entering University College, Oxford, and later St. Andrews, where he received his M.D. He was court physician to Queen Anne from 1705 until her death in 1714. He became a fellow of the Royal society in 1704. A friend of Jonathan Swift, Alexander Pope, and John Gay, Arbuthnot belonged to the Scriblerus Club with them, and was one of the authors of the satire *The Memoirs of . . . Martinus Scriblerus,* written by the club members. Arbuthnot wrote another satire in the manner of Swift, *The History of John Bull,* which was a collection of five pamphlets originally published separately. Other works include *An Essay on the Usefulness of Mathematical Learning, Tables of Ancient Coins, Weights and Measures,* and a poem, *Know Yourself.*

Arbuthnot, May Hill (1884-1969), children's writer and anthologist, was born in Mason City, Iowa, and educated at the University of Chicago and Columbia University. She taught most of her life at Case Western Reserve University in Cleveland. A recognized authority on children's books, she received the Constance Lindsay Skinner medal in 1959 and the Regina medal in 1964 for her contributions to children's literature. She published *Children and Books, The Arbuthnot Anthology, Time for Poetry* (with Sheldon R. Root), *Time for Fairy Tales, Time for True Tales and Almost True,* and many others.

Archilochus (early 7th century B.C.), Greek poet, was born on the island of Paros. His father was the founder of a Parian colony on the island of Thasos and his mother was probably a Thasian. Rejected in love because of his illegitimacy, Archilochus became a soldier of fortune. The ancient Greeks considered him their greatest poet; Horace expressed great admiration for him. Archilochus is the earliest Greek writer of lyric and elegiac poetry whose work survives in any considerable amount. Having used his emotions and experiences as the basis for his poetry, Archilochus may well be considered the originator of individualism in literature. Archilochus was the first to use the elegiac couplet.

Archimedes (är'kĭ-mē'dēz) **(c. 287 B.C.-212 B.C.),** Greek scientist and inventor, was born in Syracuse, Sicily. He is said to have visited Egypt in early life, and to have invented there several hydraulic machines, including the Archimedean screw, which he applied to drainage and irrigation. He discovered (Proposition I) the relationship between weight and displacement of bodies immersed in a fluid. His purely mathematical works show that he far excelled all who preceded him. The most celebrated are on the ratio of the sphere and cylinder, on the ratio of the circumference to a diameter, on spiral lines, and on the parabola. In his old age, he defended Syracuse against the Romans under Marcellus with great mechanical skill, and was killed at its capture. Of Archimedes's writings on his mathematical discover-

370 Biography

ies and floating bodies, nine treatises are extant. T.L. Heath has edited his *Works.*

Ardizzone, Edward (1900-   ), English artist, illustrator and writer, was born in Haiphong, Indochina (now North Vietnam). He moved to England when he was five years old. He received his early education at Clayesmore, Dorset, and continued his art education at the Westminster School of Art. When his paintings did not sell—in spite of good notices—he turned to book illustration and was immediately successful. He illustrated more than 100 books by other authors, including Bunyan's *Pilgrim's Progress,* Walter de la Mare's *Peacock Pie,* and Francois Villon's *Poems.* In 1936, Ardizzone wrote and illustrated *Little Tim and the Brave Sea Captain,* his first book for children. In 1957, *Tim All Alone,* one of the "Tim" series, won the first Kate Greenaway Medal, the British Library Association's award for the best illustrated children's book of the year. Other children's books written and illustrated by Ardizzone include *Diana and Her Rhinoceros, Lucy Brown and Mr. Grimes, Johnny the Clockmaker,* and *Peter the Wanderer. Baggage to the Enemy,* the only book he has written for adults, is an account of his experiences as an official war artist with the British Army during World War II.

Ardrey, Robert (1908-   ), playwright and novelist, was born in Chicago. He was educated at the University of Chicago, where he studied under Thornton Wilder. His plays include *Star Spangled; Thunder Rock,* a success in London during World War II; and *Sing Me No Lullaby.* Between plays, Ardrey also wrote scripts for movies and published two books, *World's Beginning* and *Brotherhood of Fear.*

Arendt, Hannah (1906-75), German-American political scientist and writer, was born in Hanover. After early education at Konigsberg, she received her Ph.D. from Heidelberg. She fled from Nazi Germany and worked for Jewish relief organizations in Paris and New York until she received teaching appointments at American universities. *Eichmann in Jerusalem* is her analysis of the Nazi war crimes. Other works include *The Human Condition, Between Past and Future,* and *The Origins of Totalitarianism.*

Arene, Paul Auguste (1843-96), Provençal poet, journalist, novelist, and dramatist, was born at Sisteron. He wrote some picturesque short stories—*Contes de Paris et de soleil;* many poems; novels—*Au bon Soleil, La chèvre d'or,* and *Le canot des six capitaines;* and some plays—*Jean des figues* and *Les comediens errants.*

Aretino, Pietro (1495-1556), Italian author, was born in Arezzo. The name Aretino is taken from his birthplace, his family name is unknown. The son of a poor shoemaker, he went to Rome and began to write the slanderous and scandalous works that were to bring him popularity throughout his life. While in Rome, he served Popes Leo X and Clement VII. Feared but honored by important men, Aretino has been called the first "journalist" of his century. He was named by contemporaries the "Scourge of Princes." His writings (particularly his letters) are a valuable source of Renaissance ways of life and reveal the author as an unscrupulous, cynical, and powerful figure. Aretino also wrote a tragedy and five comedies, religious writings, and poetry.

Argensola, Lupercio Leonardo de (1559-1613), and **Bartolomé Leonardo de (1562-1631),** Spanish poets, brothers, were born at Barbastro, Aragon. Lupercio was secretary to Maria, widow of Emperor Maximilian II of Austria, and became historian of Aragon under Philip III. In 1610 he accompanied the Count of Lemos to Naples, where he died. He wrote three tragedies that appear to have been highly popular during his time. He also wrote poetry—original satires and translations of Latin poets.

Bartolomé also went to Naples with the Count of Lemos and succeeded Lupercio as historian of Aragon.

He completed the *Conquisto de las Islas Molucas,* which his brother had begun, and added to Zurita's *Annals of Aragon.* The poems of the two brothers were published together as *Rimas.*

Arguedas, Alcides (1879-1946), Bolivian novelist, known for his *Race of Bronze,* a two-part episodic novel concerned with the cruelty of the Creoles toward the native Indians of South America. His prose often becomes poetic. Other works include *Wata-Wara* and *Creole Life.*

Aribau, Buenaventura Carlos (1798-1862), Spanish economist and man of letters, was born in Barcelona. He is remembered primarily for his poem *Oda a la Patria,* which sparked a renaissance of Catalan literature. His work combined contemporary thought with native traditions and was widely translated. Aribau became a member of Gaspar Remisa's banking enterprise, and was later treasury director for the royal court. He helped to found and contributed to several periodicals in Barcelona. His essays were collected in *Ensayos Literarios;* he also wrote a number of poems.

Ariosto (*ä're-ôs'tō*), **Ludovico (1474-1533),** Italian poet, was born at Reggio. His education was intended to fit him for law, but this study proved uncongenial, and he spent much of his time in the composition of verse. In 1503, he was introduced to the court of the cardinal Ippolito d'Este, who employed him in many negotiations. Here he produced his famous poem, *Orlando Furioso,* which was published at Ferrara in 1516.

Arishima, Takeo (1878-1923), Japanese essayist, novelist, and playwright, was born in Tokyo and died in Karuizawa. He was educated in Tokyo and at Sapporo University in Hokkaido, where he came under the influence of Christian teachers. In 1900 he became a Christian. After serving in the army, he studied history and economics at Haverford College, Pa., and at Harvard. Returning to Japan, he taught English and served as Sunday school superintendent until he formally renounced institutional Christianity in 1911. He gave up teaching and devoted himself to writing. His novels include *The Descendent of Cain, The Maze,* and *A Certain Woman,* considered the first realistic novel in Japanese literature. He wrote several plays based on Biblical themes, including *Before the Great Flood, Samson and Delilah,* and *The Last Supper.* He also wrote essays, including *A Study of Ibsen* and *On Whitman,* and translated Whitman's poetry into Japanese.

Aristarchus (*ăr'ĭs-tär'kŭs*) of Samos, Greek astronomer, lived in the 3d century B.C., residing in Alexandria. He is the first astronomer known to have held the view that the earth revolves around the sun. His opinion was known to Copernicus, whose influence in the 15th century A.D. led to investigations establishing the truth of the heliocentric theory. Aristarchus held also that the earth revolves on its axis, thus causing day and night, and that the axis is inclined to the plane of the earth's orbit. His only extant work is *On the Sizes and Distances of the Sun and Moon.*

Aristippus (*ăr'ĭs-tĭp'ŭs*) **(c. 425 B.C.-?),** the founder of the Cyrenaic, or hedonistic, school of philosophy among the Greeks, was born at Cyrene, in Africa. He was a pupil of Socrates. His system, based on the doctrine that pleasure is the highest good, was further developed by his daughter Arete and by her son Aristippus the Younger. The date of his death is unknown. None of his writings are extant.

Aristophanes (*ăr'ĭs-tŏf'a-nēz*), **(c.445 B.C.-c.385 B.C.),** Greek comedian, was born at Athens. He began writing when very young, and his first plays were brought out under another name because he was not old enough to contend for the prize. He wrote, in all, 54 comedies, but only 11 have come down to us. *The Knights* and *The Clouds* are among his most admired pieces; others are *The Wasps, The Birds,* and *The Frogs.* Aristophanes was conservative and aristocratic in sympathy, and he mercilessly ridiculed the newer movements in politics

Biography

and thought. One of his finest plays, *The Clouds,* is a satire against Socrates. His plays contain passages of the most beautiful and finished poetry interspersed in dramas sparkling with wit, much of it in a lusty and ribald strain.

Aristophanes of Byzantium (c. 257-180 B.C.), Greek grammarian, studied under Zenodotus at Alexandria, and was librarian at the Alexandria library. His writings include critical editions of Homer and Pindar. Aristophanes is credited with inventing the accent marks for Greek letters.

Aristotle (384 B.C.-322 B.C.), founder of the celebrated Peripatetic school of philosophy at Athens, was born at Stagira, Macedonia, the son of Nicomachus, a court physician of Macedon. Having lost both parents while he was quite young, Aristotle was brought up under the care of Proxenus, a friend of the family. When he had completed his 17th year, Aristotle repaired to Athens, where, for three years, he pursued his studies by books and teachers as best he could. On the return of Plato from Syracuse, Aristotle placed himself under his instruction and became the most distinguished member of the Academy, as Plato's school was called.

CAREER. The death of Plato in 347 B.C. was the occasion of Aristotle's departure from Athens. He went to Atarneus in Asia Minor, where, at the small but interesting court of Hermeias, he spent three years, enjoying the society of intellectual friends and devoting himself with unremitting assiduity to the study of nature. Aristotle subsequently married Pythias, the sister of Hermeias. To their son, Nicomachus, he dedicated his chief work on ethics, called the *Nicomachean Ethics.*

While residing at Mytilene in Lesbos, whither he went about 344 B.C., Aristotle received from Philip, king of Macedon, the flattering invitation to superintend the education of the latter's son, who later was called Alexander the Great. In 342 B.C., Aristotle took up his residence at the Macedonian court in Pella. It was for the use of his pupil that he wrote his *Rhetoric* in 338 B.C. From the death of Philip until the time of Alexander's Asiatic expedition, Aristotle continued to live with the youthful king as his friend and counselor.

Returning to Athens in 334 B.C., Aristotle opened a school called the Lyceum. From his habit of walking up and down in the garden during his lectures arose the other name of his school, Peripatetic, derived from *peripateo,* "walk about." It was his custom to give a morning lecture on the more abstruse subjects to select pupils, and then, in the evening, one of a more popular nature to a general audience. It is probable that, at this time too, he composed his principal works. Aristotle's connection with Macedon made him unpopular in Athens. He was charged with impiety and sedition, and, wishing to avoid the fate of Socrates, he made his escape to Chalcis in 323 B.C.

COMPARISON WITH PLATO. Although a student under Plato for many years, Aristotle, in his writings, frequently criticized his master's views, sometimes unfairly. Plato was an artist and poet as well as a thinker, while Aristotle had a greater interest in reducing facts or methods to a system. Most of Aristotle's systematized results are to be found in Plato's works, but in a form dictated by artistic considerations. Plato was an expert mathematician, while Aristotle was a biologist. Aristotle's studies consequently rely much more heavily on observations, not only in the field of natural science, but also in politics and economics.

WRITINGS. The most important of Aristotle's writings are the *Organon, Rhetoric, Poetics, Ethics, Politics, History of Animals, Physics, Metaphysics, Psychology,* and *Meteorology.* It may be said with justice that there was not one subject discussed in his day which Aristotle did not touch and clarify. He laid the foundations, also, of many new biological and social sciences. In his *Organon,* or "Logic," one finds the basis and nearly the whole substance of syllogistic logic, which became, with the schoolmen, the method of Catholic theology.

Aristotle was a much more practical and scientific teacher than was Plato. As the instructor of Alexander the Great, in later life he received from his royal pupil many additions to his materials of knowledge. It is said that Alexander sent to Aristotle, from all parts of the world into which he carried his expeditions, samples of the things which he found. He sent, for example, actual specimens of strange animals, with the result that the science of zoology developed in Aristotle's hands. In like fashion, other natural sciences were opened up by Aristotle because of the breadth of material which he found available.

Aristotle organized the Lyceum as a place where he trained the young legislators and statesmen of Athens. It became a center of research in biology, history, and the science of government. Aristotle developed numerous systems of knowledge which were of great influence during the medieval period, and his discussions on the nature of the mind were the bases of the psychology and of much of the theology of this time. He formulated the principles of logic, which were taken over to the great school at Alexandria and were later utilized by Euclid in the formulation of geometry. Through geometry the Aristotelian logic was carried into the medieval schools and became the most important subject of higher education in Europe, both in the medieval and in the early modern period. The disputes of the scholastics are based upon the principles of this logic.

Aristotle advocates the beginning of education when the child is seven years of age. He mentions and evaluates the various subjects to be taught, namely, reading and writing, gymnastics, music and drawing. He lays great stress on physical training and on reading and music.

Aristotle's theories about education were much less completely formulated than were those of Plato. He contributed new content for education rather than new methods of giving instruction.

Ari Thorgilsson (1067-1148), Icelandic historian, was descended from an aristocratic family that traced its ancestry to the kings of Dublin. He was educated at Haukadalr and ordained. Little else is known of his life. He was the first scholar to write in Icelandic. Taking his sources from oral history, he wrote a chronicle of Iceland from about 870, when it was first settled by the Norwegians, until 1120. Only one of his works, the *Islendingabok,* survived, and became the chief source for later historians of Iceland.

Arius (a-rī′ŭs; ā′rĭ-ŭs) **(c. 256 A.D.-336),** founder of Arianism, was born in Libya; was trained in Antioch; and became a presbyter in Alexandria. Here, about 318, he maintained, against his bishop, that the Son was not co-equal or co-eternal with the Father, but was only the first and highest of all finite beings, created out of nothing by an act of God's free will. He secured the adherence of clergy and laity in Egypt, Syria, and Asia Minor, but was deposed and excommunicated in 321 by a synod of bishops at Alexandria. Eusebius, bishop of Nicomedia, absolved him and, in 323, convened another synod in Bithynia, which pronounced in his favor. He defended his views before the council of Nicaea, 325, but they were condemned. He died at Istanbul. The only writings of Arius that we have today are some letters to Eusebius, his patron, and some fragments of a poem in which he stated his principles.

Arliss, George (1868-1946), actor, was born in London, Eng. He made his first appearance on the stage in 1887 at London and his first tour of America in 1901, attaining instant success as the villain Zakkuri in *The Darling of the Gods.* His more notable later triumphs were made in the title roles of the *Devil* and *Disraeli* and in the *Green Goddess.* He repeated most of his earlier successes when he appeared in motion pictures, and added further to his laurels by his role in *Richelieu, Old English,* and *A Man of Affairs.* He wrote *Up the Years from Bloomsbury, My Ten Years in the Studios,* and *George Arliss, by Himself.*

Arminius, Jacob (1560-1609), Dutch theologian, was born at Oudewater, a small town in the Netherlands. He studied at the University of Leiden, attended the school of theology in Geneva, and later studied at Basel. He was ordained at Amsterdam in 1588, and soon became distinguished as a preacher. In 1589, he consented to answer a book which attacked Calvin's doctrine of predestination and, while preparing to do so, embraced the doctrine of free will which he was trying to refute. His later writings developed this doctrine, which became known as Arminianism. From 1603 to 1609, he was professor in the University of Leiden. He was a gifted scholar, a preacher of great popular power, and an author of ability. Some of his writings, which are mostly various treatises, have been translated into English.

Armitage, Merle (1893-1975), writer, was born in Mason City, Iowa, and educated in public schools. After working as a civil engineer, he began to design stage decorations. Then, as an impresario, he was active in many cultural areas, particularly dance and music. He was editorial and art director for *Look* magazine. He wrote books on a variety of subjects, and also designed those of other authors. His work includes the *Merle Armitage Dance Memoranda, Paintings of Russel Cowles, Murder and Mystery in New Mexico, Paul Klee, Claude Debussy, Railroads of America,* and *Neighborhood Frontiers.*

Armstrong, Hamilton Fish (1893-1973), editor and writer, was born in New York City. He received his B.A. from Princeton in 1916, and served in the army during World War I. He was a reporter for the New York *Evening Post,* became its managing editor in 1922, and became editor in 1928 of *Foreign Affairs.* He was noted as a leading authority on international affairs. His books include *Where the East Begins, Hitler's Reich, Foreign Affairs Bibliography* (with W.L. Langer), and *Chronology of Failure: The Last Days of the French Republic.*

Armstrong, Sir William George (1810-1900), English inventor and manufacturer, was born at Newcastle, England. In 1840, he produced an improved hydraulic engine and, in 1845, the hydraulic crane. Shortly afterward, he began the erection of the Elswick engine works at Newcastle. This large establishment at first produced chiefly hydraulic cranes, engines, and bridges, but later became noted for the production of ordnance, and especially of the Armstrong gun. Armstrong offered to his government all his inventions. He was knighted in 1859 and was created Baron Armstrong in 1887. He wrote *A Visit to Egypt, Electric Movement in Air and Water,* and many technical papers.

Arnauld, Antoine (1612-94), French theologian and writer, was born in Paris. Known as the "Great Arnauld," he belonged to the influential family that dominated and directed the Jansenist sect of 17th-century France. After studying law, Arnauld entered the Sorbonne and received a doctorate in theology in 1642, the year of his ordination. Jansenist ideas were prevalent in his writings before Jansenism was condemned as heretical. Arnauld became the leading theologian of Jansenism in 1643. He went into exile in 1679 during the persecution of the Jansenists, and in 1682 settled in Brussels, where he died. He wrote 320 books, including distinguished works on mathematics, science, and philosophy, as well as theology.

Arndt, Ernest Moritz (1769-1860), German poet and historian, was born at Schoritz, on the island of Rugen. After being trained for the ministry, he taught history at Greifswald and Bonn. Arndt wrote *Geist der Zeit,* a work in which he opposed Napoleon so strongly that he was forced to flee to Sweden. His writings roused the Germans and influenced their feelings against Napoleon.

He was elected to the Frankfurt national assembly in 1848.

Arne (ärn), Thomas Augustine (1710-78), English composer, was born in London. His father, an upholsterer, intended him for the bar, but young Arne became skillful as a violinist, forming his style chiefly after Corelli. His zeal in the study of music induced his sister, Mrs. Cibber, to cultivate her excellent voice. He wrote for her a part in his first opera, *Rosamond,* which was performed with great success in 1733. Next followed his comic operetta, *Tom Thumb,* and afterward his *Comus.* The national air, "Rule Britannia," originally given in the masque of *Alfred,* is his composition, as are also two operas, *Eliza* and *Artaxerxes.* He died in London.

Arnim, Bettina von (1785-1859), German writer, was born at Frankfort on Main. As a child, she was a friend of Goethe, the German poet. In 1835, after Goethe's death, she published *Goethe's Correspondence with a Child.* Long considered to be genuine, her work was proved to be largely fictitious, although it did include some genuine writings of Goethe. Bettina von Arnim's other works include *Die Gunderode* (1840) and *Dies Buch gehort dem Konig* (1843).

Arnim, Ludwig Achim von (1781-1831), German poet and novelist, was born in Berlin. He published a collection of folksongs in collaboration with Clemens Brentano. He later married Brentano's sister Bettina, who was also a writer. Arnim wrote a number of long novels. *Die Kronenwachter,* an unfinished novel of the Reformation, and *Isabella von Agypten* are perhaps his best-known works.

Arno, Peter (1904-68), cartoonist, was born Curtis Arnoux Peters, Jr., in New York City. He began to submit cartoons to magazines after graduating from Yale. Before his cartoons were successful, he painted murals for restaurants in New York. He never studied art. Although most of his work appeared in the *New Yorker,* Arno also published in the *Saturday Evening Post, Cosmopolitan,* and the *Tatler* (England). His cartoons have been collected in book form, and include *Peter Arno's Parade, Sizzling Platter,* and *Hell of a Way to Run a Railroad.* He also wrote humorous articles and stories, and was coauthor of the musical *Here Comes the Bride.*

Arnobius, the Elder (died c. 327), Christian apologist, was a rhetorician at Sicca Veneria, in Africa. Born a pagan, he attacked Christianity until he was converted. To prove his sincerity, he wrote *Against the Pagans,* seven books in which he attempted to defend Christianity by showing the pagans the inconsistencies of their cults. His work is a valuable source for information about pagan religions of his time.

Arnobius the Younger (flourished c. 460), was probably an African priest who lived in Rome. Little is known of his life or his writing. He wrote an allegorical commentary on the Psalms, which was published by Erasmus in 1522. Scholars have accredited other works to Arnobius with more or less certainty.

Arnold, Sir Edwin (1832-1904), English poet and journalist, was born in Gravesend and died in London. He was educated at Oxford, and after teaching at Birmingham was appointed principal of the Deccan College in Poona, India. He returned to London in 1861 to write for the *Daily Telegraph,* and spent the next 28 years in journalism. He was made Knight Commander of the Indian Empire in 1888. After retiring from newspaper work, he traveled extensively in the Far East, writing of his travels. His works include *The Light of Asia, With Sa'di in the Garden, India Revisited, The Voyage of Ithobal,* and *The Poets of Greece.*

Arnold, Henry Harley (1886-1950), American general, was born at Gladwyne, Pa. After being graduated from West Point in 1907, he attended the Wright brothers aviation school at Dayton, Ohio, in 1911. He served with the army air force at Panama and on the west coast and commanded various airfields. In 1934 he led an army flight to Alaska. He became major-general and chief of the army air corps in 1938. In 1942 he was placed in full charge of the army air forces. In 1943, as chief of air staff, he directed the American part of the great air offensive against the Axis. In 1944 he was advanced to the rank of general of the army. He retired in 1945. He published with General Ira C. Baker *Winged Warfare* in 1941.

Arnold, Matthew (1822-88), English poet and critic, oldest son of Thomas Arnold, the noted head master of Rugby, was born in Middlesex, England. He was educated at Winchester, Rugby, and Oxford. In 1845, he was elected fellow of Oriel College and, in 1851, he was appointed lay inspector of schools. For ten years, 1857-67, he held the chair of poetry at Oxford. Among Arnold's productions may be noted his Newdigate prize poem *Cromwell, The Strayed Reveller,* and a volume entitled *New Poems* published in 1869.

As a critic, Arnold holds a high place and, as a poet, he is ranked by some as second only to Tennyson and Browning among Victorian writers. His later prose works were chiefly theological, being attempts to grapple with the supernatural aspects of Christianity from a rationalistic standpoint.

Arnold, Thomas (1795,1842), English educator and historian, was born in the Isle of Wight. He was educated at Winchester, and at Corpus Christi College, Oxford. In 1815, he became fellow of Oriel, obtaining in that year the chancellor's prize for the Latin Essay. After taking holy orders, he passed nine years at Laleham, near Staines, in literary occupations, and in preparing young men for the universities. Appointed, in 1828, head master of Rugby School, he raised that institution beyond all precedent, both by the remarkable success of his pupils and by the introduction of new branches of study. He was of the Broad Church school of thought and a vigorous opponent of the tractarian movement. In 1841, he was appointed professor of modern history at Oxford. His best-known works are his edition of *Thucydides,* his *History of Rome,* and his sermons delivered in the chapel of Rugby School.

Arnoldson, Klas Pontus (1844-1916), Swedish author and advocate of peace, was born in Goteburg. He was self-educated and devoted a long, active life to the causes of religious liberty, woman's equality under law, and international peace. As editor of various newspapers and periodicals and as a member of the Swedish congress for several terms, he ably advocated his principles. In recognition of his efforts to promote world peace, he was awarded the Nobel peace prize for 1908 jointly with Fredrik Bajer of Denmark. Arnoldson's major work was *Hope of the Centuries* (1900), a book on world peace.

Aron, Raymond (Claude Ferdinand) (1905-   ), French journalist, author, and educator, was born in Paris, and educated at the École Normale Supérieure. Choosing a career in education, he taught, mainly philosophy, at the University of Cologne, Toulouse, Cornell, and in Le Havre and Saint-Cloud. During 1934-39 he was secretary of the center of social studies at the École Normale Supérieure. Aron served in the French Air Force until Germany defeated France. He then went to England, where he became General de Gaulle's assistant and the editor of *La France Libre.* Aron is considered pro-American in his views; he makes scholarly comments on social and economic problems and international affairs. Since 1947 he has been a columnist for *Le Figaro,* and he has published editorials in leading French and American periodicals. Some of his translated books are *Century of Total War, Opium of the Intellectuals,* and *Peace and War Among Nations.*

Arrabal, Fernando Teran (1932-   ), dramatist, was born in Melilla, Spanish Morocco. While studying law at the University of Madrid in the early 1950's, he began writing plays, including *Picnic on the Battlefield.* In 1955 he won a scholarship to study theater in Paris and remained as an anti-Franco self-exile in France. His plays were first produced in 1958; he was soon associated with the "theater of the absurd." In 1962 he explained, "panic art," which he called "a manner of being, controlled by confusion, humor, terror, chance, and euphoria." His plays include *The Two Executioners, Prison, The Automobile Graveyard, Guernica,* and *And They Put Handcuffs on the Flowers.* His novels are *Celebrating the Ceremony of Confusion, Baal,* which he filmed and directed in 1970, and *Long Live Death.*

Arreboe, Anders (1587-1637), Danish poet, was born on the island of Aeroc. He studied at the University of Copenhagen and was appointed bishop of Trondheim. He introduced the Alexandrine meter into the literature of Denmark. His *Hexaemeron,* a narrative poem on the creation, is his best-known work.

Arrhenius *(ar-rā'nĭ-oos),* **Svante August (1859-1927),** Swedish chemist, was born at Wijk, Sweden, and was educated at the University of Upsala. In 1895, he was appointed professor of physics in Stockholm and, in 1905, he was made director of the physiochemical department of the Nobel Institute, Stockholm. His most important contribution to science is the theory of ionization, set forth in 1887. He received the Nobel prize for chemistry, 1903, and the Faraday medal, 1914. His works include *Worlds in the Making, Theories of Chemistry,* and *Immunochemistry.*

Arrian, (Flavius Arrianus) (c. 95-c. 175 A.D.), Greek historian and philosopher, was born in Nicomedia, Bithynia. The Emperor Hadrian bestowed Roman citizenship on Arrian and appointed him governor of Cappodocia. He distinguished himself in battle by defeating an invasion of the Alans. Among his most important works are *Anabasis of Alexander,* an authoritative history of Alexander the Great from his accession to his death, and *Discourses of Epictetus,* a treatise on the philosophy of his former teacher.

Arrowsmith, William (Ayres) (1924-   ), educator and writer, was born in Orange, N. J. He was educated at Princeton, Oxford, and Loyola universities and Westminster College, Fulton, Mo. He taught classics and humanities at Princeton, the University of California at Riverside, and the University of Texas. He has held editorial positions on literary journals, including *Chimera* and the *Hudson Review,* and published extensively in scholarly periodicals. In addition to translating many of the classics, he edited *Image of Italy* and *Five Modern Italian Novels.*

Artemisia *(är'tē-mĭsh'ĭ-a),* **(?-351 B.C.),** daughter of Hecatomnos and sister and wife of Mausolus, king of Caria, Asia Minor, whom she succeeded as ruler of Caria upon his death in 353 B.C. She defeated an attempt of the Rhodians to free themselves and surprise her capital. She immortalized her name by the honors which she paid to the memory of her husband, erecting for him in Halicarnassus a splendid tomb, called the Mausoleum. This was one of the seven wonders of the ancient world, and from it the name mausoleum was given to all tombs distinguished for their magnificence.

Arthur, Chester Alan (1830-86), twenty-first president of the United States, was born in Fairfield, Vt. He was graduated at Union College in 1848, studied law, and was admitted to the bar. In 1861, he was appointed inspector general and later quartermaster-general of New York State. From 1871 to 1878, he was United States collector of the port of New York. He was elected vice president of the United States in 1880 and, on the death of President Garfield, September 19, 1881, he became president. Reputed to be a "spoilsman," Arthur nevertheless gave effective support to the Civil Service act of 1883. George F. Howe's *Chester A. Arthur: A Quarter Century of Machine Politics* was published in 1934 and again in 1957.

Artzybasheff, Boris (1899-1965), artist, was born in Kharkov, Russia, and became an American citizen in 1926. The son of a novelist and playwright, Artzybasheff was educated at Prince Terisheff's School in St. Petersburg. He was planning to go to Paris to study art when the Russian Revolution broke out, and he served in the army for the next two years. In 1919 he came to America. He illustrated *Aesop's Fables, The Arabian Nights*, and Padraic Colum's *The Forge in the Forest*, among others. He wrote and illustrated *Seven Simeons*. Many of his portraits appeared as covers of *Time* magazine.

Asbjornsen, Peter Christian (1812-85), Norwegian naturalist, folklorist and writer, was born and died in Oslo. He collaborated with a friend, Jorgen Moe, in publishing several collections of Norwegian folk tales, which have been widely translated. A favorite English translation is *Popular Tales from the North*. Asbjornsen is credited with introducing Darwin's *Origin of Species* into Norway.

Asch, Nathan (1902-   ), American novelist, was born in Warsaw, Poland, the son of Sholem Asch, the Jewish writer. His early education was obtained in Switzerland, Germany, and France. When he was 13, his family settled in the U.S. and he attended Syracuse and Columbia universities. As a young man, he returned to Paris and began writing. He published articles in many magazines, including the *Nation*, the *New Republic* and *Dial*. During World War II, he wrote for the movies in Hollywood. His novels include *The Office, Pay Day*, and *The Valley*. He also wrote *The Road: In Search of America*, an analysis of American life and thought.

Asch, Sholem (1880-1957), novelist and playwright, was born at Kutno, Poland. He was brought up in an Orthodox Jewish community, leaving it for Warsaw in 1899 to begin his literary career. Limited at first to Jewish themes and readers, he became a controversial figure with his publications of *The Nazarene* (1939), *The Apostle* (1943), and *Mary* (1949). His writings have been viewed as an attempt to bridge the gap between Judaism and Christianity. In 1910, Asch visited the U.S., moved there in 1914, and became a citizen in 1920. His other novels deal mainly with the Jewish community and with Nazi Germany during World War II; they include *Mottke the Thief, Tales of My People, The Prophet*, and *From Many Countries*.

Ascham (ăs' kăm), **Roger (1515-68)**, English humanist, was born at Kirby Wiske, in Yorkshire. His reputation as a classical scholar brought him numerous pupils, and he was appointed by Cambridge University to read lectures in the public schools. He wrote, in 1545, a treatise on archery entitled *Toxophilus*, the pure English style of which entitles it to rank as a classic in English literature. For this treatise, which was dedicated to Henry VIII, he was awarded a pension. In 1548, he became master of languages to Lady Elizabeth, afterward queen, and was subsequently appointed Latin secretary to Edward VI and Queen Mary. After the death of Mary, Elizabeth retained him at court as secretary and tutor. His *Schoolmaster*, a treatise on education, exerted great influence on methods of teaching Latin. It is one of the most representative Renaissance writings in England. It is full of a liberal spirit and exhibits a large interest in physical education as well as intellectual training. In this book Ascham describes the method of teaching Latin which is known as the method of double translation. The Latin author is to be translated first into English and afterwards to be translated back again into Latin. Ascham's book on school teaching is interesting, not merely because of the liberal reforms he suggested in teaching, but also because of its literary style and

because of the insight which it gives into the social and political life of the day in which he wrote.

Ascoli, Graziadio Isaia (1829-1907), Italian philologist, was born of a Jewish family in Gorizia, Austria, and did not receive a college education. The foremost authority on Italian linguistics, Ascoli published *Studi orientali linguistici* in 1854 and founded the *Archivio Glottologico Italiano* in 1873, editing it until his death. He was professor of philology at the Academy of Milan.

Ascoli, Max (1898-1978), writer, was born in Ferrara, Italy. He received his LL.D. from the University of Ferrara and his Ph.D. from the University of Rome. He taught in Italian universities before emigrating to the U.S. in 1931. He was naturalized in 1939. In 1933 he joined the graduate faculty of the New School of Social Research. From 1949 until 1968 he edited and published the *Reporter*. He wrote *Intelligence in Politics, Fascism for Whom* and *The Power of Freedom*. He also edited *Political and Economic Democracy* (with Fritz Lehmann), *The Fall of Mussolini*, and *Our Times, The Best from the Reporter*.

Ashbery, John (Lawrence) (1927-   ), American poet and critic, was born in Rochester, N.Y., and educated at Harvard and Columbia. Associated with imagist and surrealist traditions, Ashbery was prominent among the "New York poets" of the 1950's. He was an art critic for the New York *Herald Tribune* (1960-65) and became editor of *Art and Literature* in 1963 and editor of *Art News* in 1965. He produced poetic dramas—*The Heroes* and *The Compromise*—and volumes of poetry—*Some Trees, The Tennis Court Oath*, and *Rivers and Mountains*.

Asheim, Lester Eugene (1914-   ), educator, librarian, and writer, was born in Spokane, Wash., and was educated at the universities of Washington and Chicago. He began teaching after working as a librarian. His awards include the Intellectual Freedom award from the Illinois Library Association in 1966, and the Scarecrow Press award for library literature in 1968. He wrote or edited a number of books on librarianship, including *The Library's Public* (with Bernard Berelson), *The Core of Education for Librarianship, The Future of the Book*, and *Librarianship in Developing Countries*.

Asher, Ben Yehiel (c. 1250-1327), rabbi and Talmudist, was born in the German Rhine district. To escape the persecution of the Jews in the 13th century, Asher fled to Spain, where he became rabbi at Toledo. Meir of Rothenburg, his former teacher, had so influenced him that his only interest was in the Talmud. Asher possessed vast learning and his *Compendium* has been printed in most editions of the Talmud. His son Jacob was the author of the four *Turim*, a codification of rabbinical law.

Ashi, (352-427), Jewish scholar, was born in Babylon. He was head of the Sura rabbinical school, and devoted his life to the compilation of the Babylonian Talmud, the *Semara*. This work was completed by his disciple Rabina in A.D. 500.

Ashmole, Elias (1617-92), English antiquarian and archeologist, was born in Lichfield. Qualifying as a lawyer in 1638, he later studied mathematics, physics, astronomy, astrology, and alchemy at Brasenose College, Oxford. In 1652, he issued his *Theatrum Chymicum*, and in 1672, his major work, *Institutions, Laws and Ceremonies of the Order of the Garter*. In 1677, he presented to Oxford University his collection of rarities, thus founding the Ashmolean Museum. Opened in 1783, the Ashmolean was England's first public museum and houses the art and archeological collections of Oxford University. *The Antiquities of Berkshire*, for which Ashmole began collecting notes in 1667, was published posthumously in 1719.

Ashmore, Harry Scott (1916-   ), editor, was born at Greenville, S. C. and was educated at Clemson College and at Harvard University. Newspaper work in

Biography

his native state was followed, in 1947, by his appointment as editor of *The Arkansas Gazette* at Little Rock. His editorials dealing with the school desegregation crisis there attracted much attention. This was also true of his books, *The Negro and the Schools* (1954), *An Epitaph for Dixie* (1957), and *The Other Side of Jordan* (1960). From 1960 to 1963, he was editor of *The Encyclopedia Britannica*.

Ashurbanipal (reigned 668-627 B.C.), the last great Assyrian king, during whose reign Assyria attained its highest level of culture. Ashurbanipal was faced with the necessity of crushing rebellions and reconquering lands that his father Esarhaddon had held. During his reign Assyria became the leading world power, but toward the end of his reign and immediately thereafter, Assyrian power collapsed. A patron of the arts, Ashurbanipal gathered at the royal palace a large collection of Sumerian, Assyrian, and Babylonian writings; this collection of clay tablets (now in the British Museum) provides essential information on Mesopotamian culture.

Asimov, Isaac (1920-   ), educator and writer, was born in Russia but lived in America from infancy. Educated in New York schools and Columbia University, he became professor of biochemistry at Boston University's School of Medicine. Among his more than 100 books are *The Chemicals of Life, The Clock We Live On,* and *The Genetic Code.* Later works of importance include *Asimov's Guide to Shakespeare* and *Isaac Asimov's Treasury of Humor.*

Asma'i, Al- (c. 740-830), Arab scholar, was born and died in Basra. He was considered the greatest philologist of his time, and is remembered for his collections of ancient Arabic poetry. Only a few of his many works survive, among them the *Book of Distinction,* the *Book of the Wild Animals,* and the *Book of the Sheep.*

Asnyk, Adam (1838-97), Polish poet, was born in Kalisz and died in Cracow. He was educated at Warsaw, Breslau, and Heidelberg, where he received his Ph.D. His works include *Job's Friends, Lerche Brothers,* and *Poems.*

Asquith, Herbert (1881-1947), English lawyer, poet and novelist, was born in London, and educated at Balliol College, Oxford. He was the second son of Herbert Henry Asquith, first Earl of Oxford and Asquith. Herbert Asquith began the practice of law in 1907, and served with the Royal Field Artillery, 1915-18. His verse includes *The Volunteer, Pillicock Hill, Poems 1912-1933* and *Youth in the Sky.* Among his novels are *Wind's End, Young Orland, Roon* and *Mary Dallon.*

Asquith, Margot (1864-1945), English writer and wife of Herbert Henry Asquith, is known chiefly for her *Autobiography.* In this she gives intimate descriptions of people prominent in government circles during the time when her husband was prime minister of Great Britain. A very popular hostess, she also wrote *Places and Persons* and *Off the Record,* the latter containing portraits of British prime ministers.

Asser (*ä'ser*), **Tobias Michael Carel (1838-1913),** Dutch statesman, was born in Amsterdam. He was made professor of law in the Atheneum of Amsterdam in 1862, and from 1876 to 1893 he occupied a similar chair at the University. He was appointed counselor to the foreign office in 1875, and member of the Dutch council of state in 1893. At the Peace Conference at The Hague in 1899 and in the International Court of Arbitration, he was the delegated representative of the Netherlands.

Asser's research in international law and his efforts in behalf of peaceful adjustment of international problems extended his reputation far beyond his own country. In 1911, he received the Nobel peace prize with A.H. Fried. His published works include *Outlines of Dutch Commercial Law, Outlines of Private International Law, Codification of Private International Law,* and *International Arbitration between the United States and Russia.*

Aston, Francis William (1877-1945), English physicist and chemist, was born in Harborne, Birmingham, and was educated at Malvern College, Mason College, and Birmingham University. In 1910 he entered Trinity College, Cambridge. In 1912 he received a research degree and in 1913 a Clerk Maxwell scholarship. From 1914 to 1919 he was an assistant at the royal aircraft establishment at Farnsborough. In 1920 Aston was made fellow of Trinity College, Cambridge, and became president of the Cambridge Philosophical Society. His chief contribution to science is the discovery that many elements are mixtures of atoms having different weights but otherwise similar. These are called isotopes. For this discovery, which opened up new vistas for research, he was awarded the Nobel prize in chemistry for 1922. Aston wrote *Isotopes, Mass-spectra and Isotopes,* and many papers on physics and chemistry.

Astor, Nancy Witcher Langhorne, Viscountess (1879-1964), first woman member of the British Parliament, was born in Greenwood, Virginia. She married Robert Gould Shaw in 1897. Obtaining a divorce in 1903, she married Viscount Astor in 1906. In 1919, she was elected to the House of Commons, retaining her seat until 1945. There she took a prominent part in debates on social reforms and successfully sponsored a bill prohibiting the sale of liquor to minors. She wrote *My Two Countries.*

Astor, William Waldorf, Viscount (1848-1919), capitalist and author, was born in New York. He was a son of John Jacob II and great-grandson of John Jacob, founder of the Astor fortune. He was educated by private tutors, finishing in Europe. In 1871, he entered the office of the Astor estate and, in 1890, succeeded his father as head of the Astor family, with a personal fortune estimated at $200,000,000. He served as United States minister to Italy, 1882-85; moved to England, 1890; purchased the *Pall Mall Gazette* and *Pall Mall Magazine,* 1893; became a British subject, 1899; and was created viscount, 1917. His writings include *Valentino, a Story of Rome; Sforza; Pharaoh's Daughter and Other Stories.* Viscount Astor was succeeded in the title by his oldest son, Waldorf Astor (1879-1952).

Asturias, Miguel Angel (1899-1974), Guatemalan author and diplomat, was born in Guatemala city. He studied law at the University of San Carlos, was involved in the turmoil that unseated the dictator Cabrera, and helped to establish a free university. Fearing the results of his acts, he left Guatemala for England, where he studied Mayan culture at the British Museum. He then moved to France, continuing his study at the Sorbonne. Becoming acquainted with French surrealist poets, he began to write verse that reflected his knowledge of Indian legend. He returned to Guatemala in 1933 and wrote for newspapers, did radio work, and continued to write poems. Entering congress as a deputy in 1942, he became immersed in politics again. He was cultural attaché to Mexico and served in Argentina. While he was in El Salvador, the Guatemalan government was overthrown, and Asturias lost his citizenship. Regaining it in 1966, he became ambassador to France.

Asturias' works have been translated into at least 36 languages, but few have appeared in English. He received a Lenin peace prize in 1966, and in 1967 became the second Latin American writer to receive a Nobel prize. Among his works are plays: *Chantaje, Dique Seco, Soluna,* and *La Audiencia de los Confines;* poems: *Fantomima, Alclasán, Anoche 10 de Marzo de 1543, Bolivar,* and *El Alhajadito;* and novels: the satirical *El Señor Presidente;* the allegorical *Mulata;* the epic trilogy *Viento Fuerte (Strong Wind), El Papa Verde (The Green Pope),* and *Los Ojos de los Enterrados (The Eyes of the Buried),* and *Hombres de Maíz (Men of Corn).*

Athanasius (*ăth'a-nā'shǐ-ŭs*), **Saint (c. 296-373),** was born in Egypt. Entering the Church at an early age, he was chosen bishop of Alexandria in 326. He is esteemed one of the most eminent among the ancient fathers of the Church.

The writings of Athanasius are numerous, but consist chiefly of controversial treatises against his opponents and against Arianism. The more important of his writings are his *Apologies, Two Books on the Incarnation, Conference with the Arians, The Life of St. Anthony, The Abridgment of the Holy Scriptures,* and *Letters to Serapion.*

Athenaeus (c. 200 A.D.), Greek grammarian and rhetorician, was born at Naucratis in Egypt. His lengthy *Authorities on Banquets* is an invaluable source for some 800 other early writers, many of whose works can no longer be found. Athenaeus wrote of the conversation at a banquet where many of the guests were historical figures and their remarks cover a wide range of subjects. Although Athenaeus mentioned that he had written other works, the *Authorities* is his only surviving writing.

Athenagoras (2nd century), Greek Christian philosopher, was probably born in Athens. He taught in Alexandria and was a Platonist before his conversion to Christianity. Between 176 and 180, he wrote the *Apology for Christians,* which was dedicated to the Emperor Marcus Aurelius and defended Christians against charges of atheism and immorality brought against them by pagans. Another of his works, the *Resurrection of the Dead,* has survived in the same manuscript. Athenagoras contributed much toward the development of a technical terminology for expressing concepts of theology.

Atherton, Gertrude Franklin (1857-1948), American novelist, great-grandniece of Benjamin Franklin, was born at San Francisco, Cal. She was educated at Saint Mary's Hall, Benicia, Cal., and Sayre Institute, Lexington, Ky. She married G. H. B. Atherton, and soon after his death, she began, in 1892, her literary career with a series of valuable studies of her native state and people. These included *Before the Gringo Came,* later revised as *The Splendid Idle Forties; American Wives and English Husbands; A Daughter of the Vine;* and *California.*

Later, she pictured, with notable skill, eastern scenery, social conditions, and history in *Patience Sparhawk and Her Times, Aristocrats,* and *Senator North* and presented an epic portrayal of Alexander Hamilton in *The Conqueror.* Among her other writings are *Tower of Ivory, Rulers of Kings, Perch of the Devil, The Avalanche, Black Oxen, The Sophisticates, The Adventures of a Novelist* (autobiography), and her last work *My San Francisco—A Wayward Biography* (1946).

Atkinson, (Justin) Brooks (1894-), American newspaperman and drama critic, was born at Melrose, Massachusetts, and was educated at Harvard (1917). After serving an apprenticeship in journalism on various provincial newspapers, he became, in 1922, editor of the *New York Times Book Review.* In 1947 he was awarded the Pulitzer prize in journalism. He is the author of *Skyline Promenades* (1925); *Henry Thoreau, Cosmic Yankee* (1927); *East of the Hudson* (1931); *The Cingalese Prince* (1934); and *Once Around the Sun* (1951).

Attar (c. 1150-1230?), Persian poet, whose full name was Farid ud-Din Attar. He was born in Nishapur in northeastern Persia, and he traveled extensively in northern Africa, Arabia, India, and central Asia. Although some accounts say he died when the Mogols destroyed his native city, it is possible that he died later in Mecca. Attar wrote prolifically, and he is best known for his allegorical poem *Mantia ut-Tair* (*Language of the Birds*) about the Sufis, a religious group. Other noted works are *Memoirs of the Saints* (biographies of Sufis) and the *Book of Counsels.*

Attaway, William (1912-), American Negro novelist, was born in a small town in Mississippi and was educated at the University of Illinois. He left college, went to sea, worked at occasional jobs, then returned to college and graduated. In the 1930's he began writing experimental dramas and short stories. Attaway used his own experience of moving from the rural South to the industrial North to portray individual and social problems of Negroes. His themes are exemplified in his novel *Blood on the Forge* (1941).

Atterbom, Per Daniel Amadeus (1790-1855), Swedish romantic poet and literary critic, was born in Asbo, Ostergotland, and educated at the University of Uppsala, where he later became professor of philosophy. In 1807 he founded the society (*Musis Amici,* which was renamed the Aurora League in the following year. The society's literary journal, *Phosphorus,* was edited by Atterbom, and it helped establish the romantic movement in Swedish literature. Atterbom was elected to the Swedish Academy in 1839. His works include *The Flowers, The Blue Bird,* and *Swedish Seers and Poets.*

Attlee, Clement Richard, Earl (1883-1967), British politician, was educated at Haileybury College and Oxford. He entered Parliament as a Labor member from the Limehouse district in 1922, held several positions under Labor ministries, and was leader of the opposition from 1935 to 1940. In 1940 he entered the coalition war cabinet as Lord Privy Seal, becoming deputy prime minister in 1941. On the defeat of the war ministry in July, 1945, he succeeded Winston Churchill as prime minister and Churchill in turn succeeded him in 1951. On his retirement as leader of the Labor party in 1955 he was created an earl. His writings include *Will and the Way to Socialism* and *The Labour Party in Perspective.*

Atwater, Richard Tupper (1892-1948), writer, was born Frederick Mund Atwater in Chicago, Ill. After studying Greek and Latin at the University of Chicago, he taught Greek there. He left teaching to write a column signed "Riq" for the Chicago *Evening Post,* and then for the Chicago *Daily News.* He also wrote a volume of verse, *Rickety Rimes of Riq,* and a juvenile book, *Doris and the Trolls.* His children's book *Mr. Popper's Penguins* was finished by his wife when he became ill. It was an immediate best seller, and has been translated into Italian, Dutch, German, Spanish and Swedish.

Atwood, George (1746-1807), English mathematician and physicist, was born at London. He was educated at Cambridge university, became tutor of Trinity college, Cambridge, and later held a position in the customs service. He made many important calculations and wrote various scientific treatises and papers. He also invented a machine to illustrate the relations of time, space, and velocity in the motion of a body falling under the action of gravity.

Atwood, Margaret (1939-), writer and poet, was born in Ottawa; she received a bachelor's degree from the University of Toronto (1961) and a master's from Radcliffe (1962). She then worked as a market research writer and filmscript writer. Among other prizes for her poetry was first place in the Canadian Centennial Poetry Competition (1967). Her poetry includes *Double Persephone* (1961), *Circle Game* (1966), *Power Politics* (1971), *You Are Happy,* (1974). Her novels include *The Edible Woman* (1969) and *Surfacing* (1973).

Atwood, Wallace Walter (1872-1949), American geologist and physiographer, was born in Chicago. He was graduated in 1897 and received the degree of doctor of philosophy in 1903 from the University of Chicago, in which, during the ensuing 10 years, he was successively instructor, assistant professor, and associate professor of physiography and general geology. From 1913 to 1920, he was professor of physiography at Harvard University, resigning to become president of Clark University where he served until 1945. During various periods after 1901, he was connected as geologist with the Illinois geological survey and with the United States geological survey. His writings include numerous scientific and educational papers; also *Glaciation of the Uintah and Wasatch Mountains, Mineral Resources of Southwestern Alaska,* and *New Geography.* He founded *Economic Geography,* which he edited, in 1925.

Aubanel, Theodore (1829-86), French poet, was born in Avignon. He was one of the founders of the Felibrige, an association of writers founded for the purpose of maintaining Provençal as a literary language. Aubanel wrote several poems and a drama, *Lou Pan dou Pecat,* which was staged in 1878.

Aubignac, Francois Hédelin d' (1604-76), French playwright, was born in Paris. He was a teacher of a nephew of Cardinal Richelieu and later became Abbe of Aubignac. His principal writings are a tragedy written in prose, *Zénobie,* and *Pratique du Théâtre,* a work in which the laws of dramatic method and construction were codified.

Aubigné, Théodore Agrippa d' (1552-1630), French poet, historian and soldier, was born in Saint-Maury. He studied in Paris, Orleans, Geneva, and Lyons, and at 16 joined the Huguenot army. He served throughout the Wars of Religion, as a soldier and in political positions under Henry IV. After the assassination of Henry in 1610, D'Aubigne had to leave France for political reasons, and in 1620 settled permanently in Geneva, where he died. D'Aubigne's major works are the *Histoire universelle; Les Tragiques,* a poem in seven cantos; *Memoires; Le Printemps,* love lyrics; and *Les Aventures du baron de Faeneste,* a parody on religion and politics. He also wrote occasional poetry and treatises on science and theology.

Aubrey, John (1626-97), British writer, was born in Easton Pierse, Wiltshire, and educated at Trinity College, Oxford, and the Middle Temple in London. Aubrey, the son of a country gentleman, squandered his inheritance, selling the last of his estates in 1670 to free himself from lawsuits. He was interested in antiquities from an early age and in 1663 won a fellowship in the Royal Society. After he met Anthony à Wood in 1667, Aubrey contributed to Wood's biographies of contemporary men. Aubrey's contributions were later published as *Lives of Eminent Men* (1813), which also included a description of himself. Other works published after his death included *The Natural History and Antiquities of . . . Surrey* and *The Natural History of Wiltshire.* During his lifetime, he published only *Miscellanies,* a collection of stories of curiosities and apparitions.

Auchincloss, Louis (1917-   ), American author, was born in Lawrence, New York. He attended Yale, and graduated from the University of Virginia Law School. He was admitted to the New York bar in 1941 and started to practice law in New York City in the same year. During the last year of World War II, while he was at sea, he wrote *The Indifferent Children,* published in 1947 under the pen name Andrew Lee. Some of his best-known works are *The Rector of Justin, The Embezzler,* and *A World of Profit.* He was elected to the American Academy of Arts and Letters in 1965.

Auden, W(ystan) H(ugh) (1907-73), Anglo-American poet, was born in England and educated at Christ Church, Oxford, where he became one of the leaders of a group of young left-wing writers, which included Stephen Spender, Christopher Isherwood, and C. Day Lewis, all of them more or less under the influence of T. S. Eliot. Auden collaborated with Isherwood in writing several plays, namely, *The Dog Beneath the Skin* (1935), *The Ascent of F6* (1936), and *On the Frontier* (1938). He became a resident of the United States in 1939, a citizen in 1946. In 1947, he won the Pulitzer prize for poetry. Auden also wrote the libretto for Igor Stravinsky's opera *The Rake's Progress* (1951), and compiled *The Oxford Book of Light Verse.* His *Shield of Achilles* was published in 1955.

Audubon (*o'doo-bon*), **John James (1780?-1851),** American naturalist of French descent. He stated that he was born near New Orleans, La., in 1780, but it is claimed by some investigators that he was illegitimate and was born at Aux Cayes, Haiti, in 1785. From childhood, he was devoted to natural history, but it was not until 1830 that the first of the four volumes of his great work, *The Birds of America,* appeared. This magnificent collection of colored plates, which was sold for $1000 a copy, was quickly followed by an explanatory work entitled *American Ornithological Biography.* Audubon also projected a similar work called *Quadrupeds of America,* but much of this work was done by his sons, John and Victor.

Auerbach, Berthold (1812-82), German writer, was born in Nordstetten. Having abandoned the study of Jewish theology, he devoted his attention to literature. His first publications were *Judaism and Modern Literature* and a translation of the works of the philosopher Spinoza. Auerbach's *Educated Citizen* and *Village Tales of the Black Forest* were characterized by portraits of real life with romantic and philosophical overtones. By some critics his *Auf der Hohe (On the Heights)* is regarded as his best novel. His works were widely translated and imitated. He died in Cannes, France.

Augier (*ō'zhyā'*), **Guillaume Victor Emile (1820-89),** French dramatist, was born at Valence. He was of prosperous middle class parentage, a grandson of Pigault Lebrun, the novelist. After receiving a good education, he prepared for the bar but, upon the success of his play, *La ciguë,* in1844, began a literary career, producing a long series of plays which blazed the trail to realism in modern French drama. With Dumas, the younger, and Sardou, he held front rank on the French stage during the Second Empire. He was elected to the French Academy in 1857. Among his plays are *Le Gendre de M. Poirier, Gabrielle, Les lionnes pauvres, Madame Caverlet,* and *Les Fourchambault.* He died at Croissy.

Augustine (*ô-gŭs'tĭn; ô'gŭs-tēn*), **Saint (354-430),** one of the Latin church fathers, was born at Tagaste in Numidia. He was sent to school at Madaura and, subsequently, at Carthage, where he mastered rhetoric, logic, geometry, arithmetic, and music. He became a lecturer on rhetoric first at Tagaste and, in 379, at Carthage. Four years later, he departed for Rome, shortly afterward proceeding to Milan, where he continued to pursue his profession.

At Milan, Augustine came under the influence of Neo-Platonism and also heard Christianity preached by Ambrose, the bishop of Milan. His mind was deeply reflective and had led him, as early as 373, to embrace Manichæism, a religion which was, in that age, a rival of Christianity. He deserted this sect and, after a long period of perplexity, decided to become a Christian. Leaving the woman with whom he had lived for about 17 years in what he came to regard as a sinful state, he was baptized with his son, Adeodatus, on April 25, 387 A.D.

In 391, Augustine was ordained a priest. Four years later, he was made colleague of Valerius, as bishop of Hippo. His activity was engaged throughout the remainder of his life in three great religious controversies—against the Manichæans, the Donatists, and the Pelagians. In the course of these controversies, he developed many of the theological doctrines upon which both the Catholic and the Protestant Church are based. As a philosopher, he may be regarded as the father of medieval scholasticism.

His best-known works are his *Confessions* and *De*

Civitate Dei, "City of God." The latter, finished in 426, constitutes the first attempt to write a comprehensive philosophy of history. It compares this world with the City of God and describes the triumph of the latter. He died at Hippo, which, at that time, was being besieged by the Vandals.

Aulnoy, Marie Catherine, Baronne d' (c. 1650-1705), French author was born at Barneville. She wrote novels and memoirs, but is best known for her fairy tales. Her memoirs are partly borrowed from existing records, and largely fictitious. Her chief work was a collection of fairy tales, translated into English as *The Fairy Tales of Madame d' Aulnoy* and *The White Cat and Other Old French Fairy Tales.*

Ausonius *(ô-sō′nĭ-ŭs),* **Decimus Magnus** (c. 310 A.D.-394), Latin poet, was born at Bordeaux, Gaul. He was appointed by Valentinian tutor to his son Gratian; he afterward held the offices of quæstor, prefect of Lantinium, and consul of Gaul. On the death of Gratian, Ausonius retired to his estate at Bordeaux, where he wrote epigrams and descriptive poems, which give the only clear picture extant of Roman civilization in France. His works include *Idyll of the Moselle, In Relatives,* and *List of Great Cities.*

Austen, Jane (1775-1817), English novelist, was born at Steventon, Hampshire, England, of which parish her father was rector. Unmarried, she lived an uneventful life, mostly with her mother and sister. Her principal productions are *Pride and Prejudice, Sense and Sensibility,* and *Persuasion,* novels of trivial events of daily life without assistance of passion, crime, or religion yet portrayed with such fidelity, ironic humor, and dramatic progression as to render them classics.

Austin, Alfred (1835-1913), English poet laureate, novelist, and journalist, was born near Leeds; was educated at the University of London; and was admitted to the bar, 1857. His published works include *The Human Tragedy, Savonarola, The Tower of Babel, Prince Lucifer,* and the prose idyll *The Garden That I Love.* In 1896, he was made poet laureate of England, succeeding Tennyson. His writing evinces an intimate love of nature.

Austin, Mary (1868-1934), writer, was born in Carlinville, Ill. and graduated from Blackburn University in 1888. After teaching for a short time, she moved to California. For many years she lived among the Indians on the edge of the Mohave Desert, studying Indian culture. Many of her stories and poems are about the Indians of the Southwest. They include *The Land of Little Rain,* her first book; two volumes of short stories, *The Basket Woman* and *Lost Borders;* and a play, *The Arrow Maker.* She lived in New York City and abroad before settling in Santa Fé, N.M., in 1924. In New York, she was associated with the group of writers and artists that gathered around Mabel Dodge. During that period, Mary Austin's writing dealt with social issues of the time, including socialism and feminism. A prolific writer, she published 32 books and many articles.

Avebury *(ā′ bēr-ĭ),* **John Lubbock, Baron** (1834-1913), English naturalist, banker, and politician, was born in London. He was educated at Eton College and entered his father's banking house. In 1870, he became a member of Parliament, where he served at intervals until elevated to the peerage in 1900. In Parliament he promoted measures regulating hours of work and establishing public libraries and parks. He was most widely noted for his achievements in anthropology and entomology. His *Prehistoric Times* was long a standard textbook on archeology and was translated into many languages. His most popular books are his *Ants, Bees and Wasps* and the charming volume entitled *British Wild Flowers Considered in Relation to Insects.* His writings include also *Primitive Condition of Man, Fifty Years of Science, Pleasures of Life,* and *Marriage, Totemism, and Religion.*

Aventinus, Johannes (1477-1534), whose real name was Johannes Turmair, was a Bavarian historian born in Abensberg. He studied at Vienna and Paris and from 1509-17 was tutor to two of the Bavarian princes. He wrote the *Annales Boiorum,* which describes the history of Bavaria from earliest times to 1460. The *Annales* (in seven books) were translated by the author into German. A complete edition of his works was published at Munich in 1886. Aventinus has been called the "Bavarian Herodotus."

Averroës *(a-vĕr′o-ēz)* (1126-c. 1198), otherwise known as Ibn Roshd, Arabian philosopher, was born at Cordoba, Spain. He was appointed successor to his father as chief mufti and afterward became chief judge in the province of Mauritania. Accused of a departure from the orthodox doctrines of Mohammedanism, he was dismissed from his office and was condemned by the ecclesiastical tribunal of Morocco to recant his heretical opinions and do penance. He later returned to Cordoba and was reinstated in his offices. An enthusiastic student of Aristotle, he transmitted the Aristotelian influence to Europe before Western scholars had access to it in Greek.

Avicebron (also known as **Ibn Gabirol** and **Solomon Ben Judah**) (c. 1021-58), Jewish poet and philosopher, was born in Malaga, Spain, and died in Valencia. Until 1846 these names were thought to belong to two persons: a philosopher, Avicebron, and a Hebrew poet, Ibn Gabirol. As philosopher, Avicebron wrote *Fons Vitae.* As a poet, he wrote *Choice of Pearls,* a collection of moral aphorisms; *Improvement of Moral Qualities,* a treatise on ethics; and *Kingly Crown,* a collection of Hebrew religious poems that still has a place in the ritual for Yom Kippūr.

Avicenna *(ăv′e-sen′a),* (980-1037), otherwise known as Ibn Sina, Arabian physician and philosopher, was born at Efsene, a village near Bokhara. He was physician to several of the Samanide and Dilemite sovereigns, and was also for some time vizier in Hamadan. His work on medicine, *Kanun fi'l tibb,* based on Greek texts, long held first place in Europe, and it is still highly regarded in the Orient. He died at Hamadan.

Avila, Juan de, Blessed (c. 1500-69), Spanish missionary, preacher, and writer, was born in Almodovar del Campo. Known as the Apostle of Andalusia, he was a popular preacher and writer of spiritual books. He died in Montilla, Spain, and was beatified in 1894.

Avogadro *(ä′vo-gä′drō),* **Amadeo** (1776-1856), Italian chemist and physicist, was born at Turin, where for many years he was professor of higher physics in the university. In 1811, he formulated and published the law known by his name, according to which, under the same conditions of temperature and pressure, equal volumes of gases and vapors contain equal numbers of molecules. This is one of the fundamental principles of chemistry and furnishes the chief method of determining atomic weights. He died at Turin. He wrote prolifically on physics and is chiefly remembered for his *Essai d'une manière de déterminer les masses relatives des molécules élémentaire des corps, et les proportions selon lesquelles elles entrent dans les combinaisons,* in which he set forth the hypothesis that now bears his name.

Avvakum, (1620-81), Russian Archpriest and author, was born at Grigorovo. He was rector of a Moscow church and a moderate reformer of church discipline. When he declined to follow the revision of the church ritual according to Greek practice, as proposed by Nikon, patriarch of the Russian Orthodox church, he was exiled to Siberia. After the fall of Nikon, he returned to Russia, but his doctrines were still not accepted and he was sent to Pustozersk. His autobiography inspired the Old Believers, a sect formed to oppose Nikon, to retain the church usages Nikon had banned. Avvakum was burned at the stake in 1681.

Axelrod, George (1922-   ), American playwright,

was born in New York City. He wrote radio, TV, and film scripts and produced and directed some of his works. His writings include the plays *The Seven Year Itch* and *Will Success Spoil Rock Hunter?* and the films *Phfft* and *Bus Stop*. He wrote and produced *The Manchurian Candidate* and *Paris When It Sizzles*, and wrote, produced, and directed *The Secret Life of an American Wife*.

Ayer, A(lfred) J(ules) (1910-   ), philosopher, was born in London and studied at Oxford. His first book—*Language, Truth, and Logic* (1936)—expressed his neopositivist theory, rejecting as meaningless anything that could not be conclusively demonstrated as true. Criticized by many scholars, it was praised by others for its clarity and was taken by some as a new creed. Later works are *The Problem of Knowledge* (1956), *The Concept of Person* (1963), and *Metaphysics and Common Sense* (1969).

Ayme, Marcel (1902-67), French novelist and playwright, was born in Joigny. His education was irregular, and he finally left medical school to settle in Paris. While convalescing from an illness, he wrote his first novel, *Brulebois*. His *Table aux Creves*, published in 1929, won the Renaudot prize for the best novel of the year. Critics consider *Jument Verte* (1933) his best novel. After World War II, Aymé began to write plays, including *Clérambard*, which was a success of the 1959 theater season in Paris. His books for children include *Contes du chat perché*.

Ayrer, Jakob (?   -1605), German dramatist, was born in Nurnberg. During the last 10 years of his life, of which little is known, he wrote more than 100 plays. Many of these tragedies, comedies, and religious dramas were published in Nurnberg in 1618 in the *Opus Theatricum*. His plays show the influence of the English stage, as bands of English actors visited the Continent around the close of the century bringing their repertory works with them.

Ayton (or Aytoun), Sir Robert (1570-1638), Scottish poet, was born in Cameron and educated at the University of St. Andrews. He was secretary to the queens of James I and Charles I. His English poems, bearing no trace of Scottish dialect, are preserved in the British Museum. He was knighted in 1612. He died in London and was buried in Westminster Abbey.

Aytoun, William Edmonstoune (1813-65), Scottish poet and prose writer, was born in Edinburgh. He studied at Edinburgh University and was called to the bar in 1840. He was appointed professor of rhetoric and English literature at Edinburgh University in 1845 and held this position until his death. In 1854 he was made editor of *Blackwood's Magazine,* to which he had been a contributor since 1836. His works include *Bon Gaultier Ballads,* written in collaboration with Sir Theodore Martin, and *Firmilian, A Spasmodic Tragedy*.

Azeglio, Massimo Taparelli, Marchese d' (1798-1866), Italian writer, painter, and statesman, was born and died in Turin. He attended the University of Turin, then studied art in Rome. He held art exhibits in Paris and London, and at one time was director of the Turin art gallery. After he married the daughter of Alessando Manzoni, D'Azeglio began his literary career, intending his pamphlets and novels to develop a national consciousness in Italy. He also fought for Italian independence and unity, and served in a number of political positions: envoy to Rome, minister to London and Paris, commissioner in Romagna, and governor of Milan. His novels are considered of minor interest; his political writings were more important. He also wrote an autobiography, *I miei ricordi*.

Azorin (1873-1967), Spanish novelist and essayist, whose real name was José Martinez Ruiz, was born in Monovar, Alicante. A member of the "Generation of '98," which he labeled, Azorin used a simple style that was widely and often unsuccessfully imitated. He was also the author of essays and short stories, collected in *Syrens and Other Stories* and *Castilla,* and novels, including *La voluntad* and *Las confesiones de un pequeño filosofo*. His critical works and essays include *El alma castellana, La ruta de Don Quijote, Al margen de los clasicos,* and *Rivas y Larra*.

Azuela, Mariano (1873-1952), Mexican writer, was born in Lagos. He was a practicing physician and later became mayor of Lagos. He was sympathetic to revolutionary causes and, in 1915, joined the forces of Francisco Villa as a surgeon. From this experience came his most successful work, *Los de Abajo,* which portrays the revolution and was translated into English as *The Underdogs*.

Baal Shem Tov (1699-1760), Jewish teacher and healer, was born Israel ben Eliezer in Poland. He was employed during his life as a slaughterer, a tavernkeeper, a mediator in civil suits, and a teacher. As a religious teacher, Baal Shem Tov established modern Hasidism, a mystical interpretation of Judaism. Using his knowledge of the medicinal value of plants, he wrote amulets and prescribed cures. His healing powers and miracles attributed to him gained him a large following. Through proverbs and parables he taught his disciples a pantheistic doctrine, of communion with God through the forces and workings of nature.

Baath, Albert Ulrik, (1853-1912), Swedish poet from the province of Skane. Baath was educated at the University of Lund and became an Icelandic scholar, a teacher, and museum director. His poetry tends to be personal, expressing through concrete images the life and landscape of his native Skane. His poetry was praised for its realistic reflection of country life. Baath's major contribution was his influence on the development of realism in Swedish poetry. He published eight volumes of verse, among them *Dikter (Poems), Nya Dikter (New Poems),* and *Vid Allfarvag (Along the Great Highway)*.

Bab, Mirza Ali Mohammed of Shiraz (1820-50), Persian religious leader. In 1844 Mirza Ali Mohammed founded a Muslim religious sect and adopted the title of Bab, gate to the truth. Later, he dropped this title and proclaimed himself the Imam Mahdi, or hoped-for savior of the Shi'ites. A strong religious following supported his claim, but an equally strong group of orthodox Moslems opposed him. The Persian government aided the orthodox Moslems. His sect was persecuted and in 1850 Mirza was executed.

Babbage, Charles (1792-1871), English mathematician and inventor, was born in Teignmouth, Devon, and educated at Cambridge University, where he was professor of mathematics (1828-39). He invented a small calculating machine and, later, the principle of the analytical engine, the precursor of the modern computers; a daughter of Lord Byron wrote a program for the engine. Together with John Herschel and George Peacock, Babbage founded the Analytical Society of Cambridge. He was also a founder of the Astronomical Society (1820) and the Statistical Society of London (1834). Babbage wrote profusely, and on a variety of subjects. His *Reflections on the Decline of Science in England* (1830) was controversial. Other writings include *On the Economy of Machinery and Manufactures* (1832), *The Exposition of 1851* (1851) and *Passages from the Life of a Philosopher* (1864).

Babel, Isaac (1894-1941), short story writer, was born in Odessa, Russia. He studied Hebrew and the Bible when he was young. In 1915 he went to St. Petersburg to begin his literary career by writing for the magazine *Letopis*. He served with the secret police and the Bolsheviks during the Russian revolution. Returning to writing, he published stories on military life and humorous stories on Jewish life in Odessa. The truth and realism of his war stories were labeled treasonous during the 1930 Stalinist purges, and in 1938 he was sent to a concentration camp in Siberia, where he died. *Odessa Tales* gained him fame, and *Red Cavalry* was based on his experiences in the army.

Bache, Benjamin Franklin (1769-98), American journalist born in Philadelphia, grandson of Benjamin Franklin. Bache founded Philadelphia's *General Advertiser,* also known as the *Aurora,* which supported the Democratic-Republican party and is best known for its criticism of public figures. Through the paper, Bache accused President Washington of overdrawing his salary and printed forged letters ascribed to him. The text of the secret Jay treaty was also published. In 1798 Bache was arrested for libelous statements against President Adams. He died shortly after being released on parole.

Bacheller, Irving (Addison) (1859-1950), American novelist, was born at Pierrepont, N.Y. He was graduated from Saint Lawrence University, 1882, and entered journalism. For many years, he was actively connected with the press of New York and, 1898-1900, was one of the editors of the New York *World.* His writings include *The Master of Silence, Eben Holden, D'ri and I, Darrel of the Blessed Isles, The Hand-Made Gentleman, The Master, Keeping up With Lizzie, "Charge It," Marryers, In the Days of Poor Richard, A Man for the Ages, Dawn —A Lost Romance of the Time of Christ, The Winds of God,* and poems entitled *In Various Moods.*

Bachofen, Johann Jakob (1815-87), Swiss anthropologist who devoted his life to research and writing. Bachofen studied classics and philology at the university in his birthplace, Basel. He then attended the university in Berlin, where he began to study law. He continued his education in Gottingen, Cambridge, and Paris. Returning to Sweden, he became professor of law at Basel and served as a judge in Basel's criminal court until 1877.

He resigned to devote his time more fully to scholarship, studying the laws, customs, and rituals of ancient Italy, Greece, and Spain. He formulated a theory of cultural evolution through the mother's rather than the father's line. Although his writing was considered obscure, he influenced German thought significantly, most importantly the German philosopher Nietzsche. His best-known work is a discussion of his social theory, *Das Mutterrecht.*

Bacon, Francis (1561-1626), English philosopher, jurist, and statesman, was born of distinguished parentage at London. At the age of 12, he was sent to Trinity College, Cambridge. Three years later, he left, strongly convinced of the futility of the Aristotelian philosophy, which was then taught in the schools. In revolt against it, his later intellectual efforts were bent on working out and declaring a philosophy which might confer greater benefits on mankind.

In 1576, his father sent him to France in the suite of the British ambassador, Paulet. Three years later, his father died, and Bacon diligently devoted himself to the study of law. In 1582, he was admitted to the bar and, in 1588, received from Queen Elizabeth the title of "counsel learned in the law extraordinary." In 1596, Bacon wrote his *Maxims of the Law.* The following year, he published the *Essays,* the work by which he is best known to the reading public.

Bacon's political advancement was due in a considerable degree to the favor of James I, by whom he was knighted on July 23, 1603. In 1605, Bacon published the first part of *Advancement of Learning,* which, expanded into *Advancement of Science,* may be said to have introduced a new era in English science. In 1606, he married Alice Barnham, and, the next year, he was appointed solicitor-general of the kingdom. In 1609, he published *Wisdom of the Ancients.*

In 1611, Bacon was appointed joint judge of the knights marshals' court; in 1613, attorney general; in 1617, lord keeper of the great seal; and, in 1618, he was made lord high chancellor and created Baron Verulam. The next year, Bacon received the title of Viscount Saint Albans and opened that fatal Parliament which brought charges of bribery against him, deprived him of his speakership and his seat in Parliament, imposed a heavy fine, and sentenced him to the Tower in disgrace. When he was pardoned, he retired to Gorhambury, where he devoted the remainder of his life to scientific experimentation and the cultivation of philosophy.

The *Novum Organum,* or "New Instrument of Logic," of 1620, has done more perhaps than any other single book toward inculcating into science the spirit of unbiased, careful observation and experimentation. Bacon insisted that all prepossessions were to be abandoned and that nature was to be interrogated by the devising of experiments with a view to discovering the laws of her action. He wrote a utopia of science, *The New Atlantis.*

Bacon was one of the brilliant group who gathered around Queen Elizabeth. He advocated the development of science through observation and direct contact with objects as distinguished from the acceptance of statements made by writers of books.

His educational influence is general rather than specific. He inaugurated the period of sense-realism. His methods of scientific investigation were indeed much less productive than those of some of his contemporaries, but his writings were of such an impressive character as to attract the attention of readers and to give prestige to his theory that education should be based on direct observation.

Bacon, Peggy (Margaret Frances) (1895-   ), American author and illustrator, was ·born in Ridgefield, Conn., studied at Kent Place School (Summit, N. J.) and the Art Students' League; she also studied with a number of distinguished painters, including George Bellows. She taught art at a number of schools, including Fieldston School (1933-39) and the New School for Social Research. She exhibited her work nationally and published illustrations in periodicals (*Harper's Bazaar, Vogue, New Yorker,* and others), as well as in books written by others and in adult and children's books that she has written. Some of these are *The True Philosopher, Funerealities, The Lion-hearted Kitten, The Good American Witch,* and *The Magic Touch.*

Bacon, Roger (c. 1214-1294), English scientist and writer, was born in Ilchester, Somersetshire. He was called the most learned of man of his day and was a noted teacher at Oxford. Bacon is considered to have advocated the change since made in the calendar, to have invented gunpowder, and to have manufactured magnifying glasses. His great work, *Opus Majus,* anticipates the methods of modern science, emphasizing mathematics and observation.

Baculard d'Arnaud, Francois-Thomas de *(ba-ku-lar' d'ar'nō)* **(1718-1805),** French playwright and novelist. Baculard carried on a literary correspondence with Frederick the Great. His writings are considered mainly sensational and melodramatic. He wrote a novel in 12 volumes under the general title, *Les Épreuves du Sentiment.* His two best-known plays are *Le Comte de Comminge* and *Euphémie.*

Baden-Powell *(bā'děn-pō'ĕl),* **Robert Stephenson Smyth Baden-Powell, Baron (1857-1941),** British general, was born in London and educated at the Charterhouse. In 1876 he joined the British army, serving in India and South Africa. In the Boer War, with a force of 1200 men he was besieged in Mafeking, which he held against the Boers from the outbreak of the war, October 12, 1899, until May 17, 1900. In recognition of this successful defense, he was made major general. In order to promote good citizenship in the rising generation, he founded, in 1908, the organization of Boy Scouts and, in 1910, the Girl Guides, the latter with the cooperation of his sister Agnes Baden-Powell. In 1929, he was created Baron Baden-Powell. His writings include *Scouting for Boys, My Adventures as a Spy, Indian Memories, The Wolf Cub's Handbook, Girl Guiding, Rovering to Success,* and *Birds and Beasts in Africa.*

Baedeker, Karl (1801-59), German publisher, was born at Essen. Going into the printing business at Coblenz, he began to issue a series of guide books, the first appearing in 1839, the *Rheinreise.* In the course of years they developed so as to cover most of the civilized world. Baedeker's son Fritz (1844-1925) succeeded to the business and transferred it to Leipzig in 1872. He improved the series by full description of entertainment facilities, traveling incognito to observe them personally.

Baerle, Kasper van (1584-1648), Dutch poet and historian, wrote in Latin and Dutch. He was professor of philosophy at Leiden until religious differences with its ruling body lost him the post. He then went to Amsterdam where he was professor of philosophy in the Athenaeum. His Latin poetry is collected in a volume entitled *Poemata,* his Dutch poetry in *Verscheyde neder duitsche Gedichten.*

Bagehot (băj'ŭt; băg'ŭt), **Walter (1826-77),** English economist and journalist, was born at Langport, Somerset. From a school at Bristol he passed, in 1842, to University College, London, where he took his master's degree in 1848. In 1852, he was admitted to the bar, but joined his father as a banker and shipowner at Langport. In 1858, he married a daughter of James Wilson, founder of the *Economist* newspaper, and, from 1860 until 1877, he was its editor. His influence at the time and later is based on his intimate knowledge of banking operations and government together with a detached point of view which permitted him to describe them understandably and relate them to the entire economic process. His works include *The English Constitution, Physics and Politics, Lombard Street, Literary Studies, Economic Studies,* and *Biographical Studies.*

Baggesen, Jens Immanuel (1764-1826), Danish poet, was born in Korsor, Zealand. He studied at the University of Copenhagen from 1782-89. At 21 his collection of satirical poems, *Komiske Fortaellinger (Comic Tales),* brought him entry into Copenhagen's literary circles. Baggesen was a disciple of Rousseau and a supporter of the French Revolution. He was such an admirer of the German philosopher Kant that he adopted Kant's first name for his middle one. After leaving Copenhagen, Baggesen toured Germany, France and Switzerland and wrote an impressionistic travel book, *The Labyrinth,* describing his journey. Baggesen was influenced by both the Classicist movement and the Romantic movement. At the close of the 18th century he was hailed as Denmark's leading poet. Baggesen wrote in both Danish and German. He wrote the epic *Thora fra Havsgaard,* and a self-critical poem *Gengangeren og han selv* in Danish. In German he wrote *Parthenais oder die Alpenreise, Der Karfunkel und Klingelalmanach,* and *Der vollendete Faust.* He also translated Homer into Danish.

Bagley, Desmond (1923-   ), writer, was born in Kendal, England. In the early 1950's he was a free-lance writer in South Africa and film critic for the *Daily Mail* (1958-62). He wrote for South African radio in 1952 and continued as a free-lance writer in England (1964), contributing to magazines and newspapers. He also wrote screenplays. His novels include *The Golden Keel* (1963), *High Citadel* (1965), and *The Snow Tiger* (1975). Many of his stories have appeared in science-fiction magazines. *The Freedom Trap* (1971) became the film *The Mackintosh Man.*

Bagnold, Enid (1889-   ), English novelist and playwright, was born in Rochester, and educated in Paris, Marburg (Germany), and Switzerland. She studied art with Walter Sickert. During World War I she was a nursing aid and an army driver, and from these experiences came *Diary Without Dates* and *The Happy Foreigner.* She has written a number of novels, including *Serena Blandish, Alice and Thomas and Jane* (for children), *The Door of Life, National Velvet* (her most popular work), and *The Loved and Envied.*

Bagritsky, Eduard (1897-1934), Russian poet of Jewish origin, who wrote under the pseudonym of Eduard Dzyubin. Bagritsky was educated at a technical school. Although trained to be a surveyor, he never practiced this trade. He participated in the Soviet revolution both as a soldier in a guerrilla unit and as a poet for the proletariat propaganda machine. His poetry has been classified as Romantic. Bagritsky translated Robert Burns and Walter Scott into Russian. He is best known as the author of *Duma pro Opanasa,* a tragic ballad set in the Ukraine at the time of the revolution.

Bahadur Shah II (1775-1862), Mogul emperor of India. Bahadur ruled from 1837-58 without power, his realm being controlled by the British East India Company. He is best known for the patronage he extended to the Indian-Urdu literature revival. His poetry is also recognized as important. In 1857 the Sepoy mutiny occurred and Bahadur fled to Delhi, where he managed to prevent Hindu-Moslem conflict. Later that year he was captured by the British. Although he was not involved in the revolution against the East India Company, he was tried for rebellion and sentenced to life imprisonment. He was exiled to Burma, where he died.

Bahaullah (1817-92), Persian religious leader, founder of the Bahai faith, was born Husain Ali in Mazadran. In 1850 he became a follower of Ali Mohammed, founder of Babism, a Persian religious sect. Bahaullah became a respected teacher of the Babi religion, but his popularity displeased the leaders of orthodox Islam and brought Bahaullah imprisonment and then exile. However, his teachings on the oneness of mankind, the covenant between God and man, and the elimination of prejudice continued to spread. In 1863, Bahaullah proclaimed himself the Bab, or leader of the Babi religion, and took the title of Bahaullah as leader of the Bahai movement. He taught his followers a way of life based on his book *Kitab Akdas* (The Most Holy Book), which became the code of doctrine for Bahaism, replacing all other sacred writings. The Bahai faith, in the years after Bahaullah's death, spread throughout the world.

Bahya, Ben Joseph Ibn Pakuda (1040-1110), medieval Hebrew religious philosopher. Bahya's activities and writings place him in Moslem Spain during the second half of the 11th century. He acted as judge in a rabbinical court in Saragossa, Spain, and wrote what has come to be considered classic Jewish philosophical literature. His writings were in Arabic, and not translated into Hebrew until the 12th century. Bahya's *The Duties of the Heart* asserted that attitudes toward moral behavior are more important acts. Bahya also wrote *Doctrine of the Soul,* a discussion of the nature of the soul and the creation of the world.

Baif, Jean Antoine de (1532-89), French poet born in Venice, Italy, natural son to the French ambassador of Francis I. He received a classical education in Italy and was sent to Paris to study at the Collège de Coqueret. Baif belonged to a literary group called the Pléiade, which based its principles on traditions of the ancient Greeks and Romans. An inventive man, Baif experimented with metrical forms in an attempt to introduce classical meters into French poetry. He created a rarely used 15-syllable line called the "baifin." He also invented a system of phonetic spelling. Baif established an academy to test his Platonic theories on the union of poetry and music. His academy was patronized by Charles IX and Henry III. Baif also translated the psalms into hymns. He is chiefly known for two volumes of verse, *Œuvres en rime* and *Mimes, enseignements et proverbes.* Other works are *Poésies choisies, Les Amours,* and two plays, *Le Brave* and *Antigone.*

Baillie, Lady Grizel (1665-1746), Scottish poet. Lady Grizel aided her father, a Jacobite, in his conspiracy with Robert Baillie against the government. After Baillie's execution, she and her parents fled to Holland. While exiled, Lady Grizel married George, Baillie's son. The family returned to Scotland during the revolution. Lady Grizel is best known for her songs *And werna my heart licht I wad dee* and *The ewe-buchtin's bonnie*.

Baillie (*bā'lĭ*), **Joanna (1762-1851)**, Scotch poet and dramatist, was born in Bathwell (near Glasgow). In 1784, she went to reside in London and, in 1806, took up her residence at Hampstead, where she remained until her death. At an early age, she began to write poetry, her *Fugitive Verses* appearing anonymously in 1790. Her greatest achievement is the nine *Plays on the Passions*, each of which depicts the effect of one passion on the characters. They are full of impressive poetry and are often characterized by intense dramatic power. The most popular as well as the most powerful of these, the tragedy *De Monfort*, was brought out at Drury Lane, London, in 1800, with Kemble and Mrs. Siddons taking the leading parts. Her *Family Legend* was produced at Edinburgh in 1810 under Sir Walter Scott's auspices.

Bain, Alexander (1818-1903), Scottish philosopher and educator, was born at Aberdeen. After attending Marischal College, Bain became a writer and assisted John Stuart Mill in revising *A System of Logic* (1843). He is best known for his scientific approach to psychology, in which he stressed the relation between mental states and the nervous system. He also had influence in improving the educational system in Scotland. He published *The Senses and the Intellect* (1855) and *The Emotions and the Will* (1859), and in 1860 was appointed professor of logic at the University of Aberdeen. In 1876 he became one of the founders of *Mind*, the first journal of psychology, and remained a contributor until 1890. He resigned his professorship in 1880, but was twice elected rector of the university, 1881 and 1884. His other works include *On the Study of Character* (1861), *Mind and Body* (1872), a biography of J. S. Mill (1882), *Education as a Science* (1879), *On Teaching English* (1887), *Dissertations on Leading Philosophical Topics* (1903), an autobiography, and social and political pamphlets.

Bainton, Roland H(erbert) (1894-1962), theologian and writer, was born in Ilkeston, England. At an early age, he moved to Vancouver, British Columbia, where his father was minister of a Congregational church. In 1902 they moved to Colfax, Wash., where he grew up. He attended Whitman College and Yale Divinity School, where he began to teach church history in 1920. His book *The Church of Our Fathers*, written for junior high students and widely used by adult groups, sold more than a million copies. He also wrote biographies; *Hunted Heretic* is considered his best. *Here I Stand*, records the life of Martin Luther.

Bairnsfather, Bruce (1888-1959), British artist and cartoonist, was born in India. While serving as a member of a Warwickshire regiment in World War I, he gathered impressions for a series of black-and-white sketches of British soldiers in the midst of difficulties, particularly those connected with trench life. These were treated humorously in his characterization of "Old Bill" and his companions. A successful play, *The Better 'Ole*, was based on Bairnsfather's cartoons. His interpretations of soldier problems both in war and in post-war adjustment are given in several collections of his drawings, most popular of which are *Fragments from France*, *Bullets and Billets*, *From Mud to Mufti*, *Back to Blighty*, and *Old Bill, M. P. 1*.

Bajza, Jozef Ignac (1755-1836), Slovak novelist, was born at Predmier. Bajza is attributed with writing the first Slovak novel, *René mládence préhodi a skúsenosti* (*The Adventures and Experience of Young René*). He wrote descriptively of Slovakia's scenery and social life, touching only lightly on deeper problems.

Baker, Carlos (Heard) (1909-   ), American critic, editor, novelist, and poet, was born in Biddeford, Me., and educated at Dartmouth, Harvard, and Princeton. In 1938 he joined the English faculty of Princeton. Baker has edited *The American Looks at the World* and critical works on Hemingway and a number of English romantic poets. Besides contributing articles to periodicals, he published *Shelley's Major Poetry, A Friend in Power* (novel), *A Year and a Day* (poetry), *The Land of Rumbelow* (novel), *Modern American Usage*, and a biography of Ernest Hemingway.

Baker, Dorothy (Dodds) (1907-68), American novelist, was born in Missoula, Montana, and educated at the University of California at Los Angeles, and at Occidental College. She wrote short stories for magazines, a play for television entitled *The Ninth Day*, and novels—*Young Man with a Horn, Trio, Our Gifted Son*, and *Cassandra at the Wedding*. In 1964 she received a fellowship from the National Institute of Arts and Letters.

Baker, George (1915-75), American cartoonist, was born in Lowell, Mass; he created the cartoon character the Sad Sack. Baker began his career in high school drawing cartoons for his school's yearbook. After graduation he attended an evening art school while working for advertising firms. In 1937 he received two job offers: one to play minor league baseball with the Los Angeles Angels, the other to draw for Walt Disney. Baker chose Disney's offer. Until he was drafted in 1941 he did animation work on such Disney films as *Bambi, Fantasia, Dumbo*, and *Pinocchio*. In the Army he animated training films and drew a cartoon strip, *The Sad Sack*, for the Army magazine *Yank*. The Sad Sack was an imaginary American soldier who experienced all the misfortunes possible to an Army private. After the war Baker returned to civilian life. The Sad Sack then appeared as a nationally syndicated comic strip.

Baker, George Pierce (1866-1935), American educator, was born at Providence, R. I. He was educated at Harvard University, where he began to teach English in 1888, becoming professor in 1905. His course in the drama, known as "English 47," attained a celebrity that passed far beyond the college walls. It was the inspiration of a large number of American dramatists who later won distinction in the theater. In 1925, he became head of a newly organized department of dramatic arts at Yale University. He was elected to the American Academy of Arts and Letters the same year.

Baker, Ray Stannard ("David Grayson") (1870-1946), American journalist and author, was born at Lansing, Mich. He was graduated at Michigan Agricultural College in 1889 and studied law and literature at the University of Michigan. He was a reporter on the Chicago *Record*, 1892-97; was associate editor, *McClure's Magazine*, 1899-1905; and was an editor of *The American Magazine*, 1906-15. Baker's writings include *Boys' Book of Inventions, Following the Color Line, A History of the Peace Conference*, and *The Life and Letters of Woodrow Wilson*. As "David Grayson," he wrote a series of works including *Adventures in Friendship, Adventures in Solitude, The Countryman's Year*, and *Under My Elm*.

Bakhuizen van den Brink, Reinier Cornelis (1810-65), Dutch critic and historian, was born in Amsterdam. Bakhuizen promoted the Romantic movement in his critical works. He co-edited the magazine *De Gids* and was employed as a government archivist. His most significant contribution to literature is his work *Studien en Shetzen*.

Baki, Mahmud Abdülbaki (1526-1600), Turkish poet. Baki began life as an apprentice to a saddler. He soon abandoned that vocation to study law. He rose rapidly and was accepted at the court of Suleiman the Magnificent. Baki later turned to poetry and is considered the greatest lyric writer in Turkish literature.

Bakst (*bäkst*), **Leon (1866-1924),** Russian decorative artist, was born in Leningrad. He was a court painter before 1900, but thereafter devoted his art chiefly to the designing of theatrical effects, in which his influence throughout the world was revolutionary. He designed scenery for Diaghilev's ballet, Sophoclean tragedies, *Cleopatra, Sheherazade,* and other spectacular dramas.

Balaguer y Cirera, Victor (*ba-la-gayr ee thee-ray're*) **(1824-1901),** Spanish poet, historian, and statesman, was born in Barcelona. He was educated at the University of Barcelona, where he established a reputation as a dramatist. After graduation he became a professor of history at the university. Motivated by patriotic feelings, he became a leader of Barcelona's liberal party and used his power to promote a liberation movement for Catalonia, his home province. He published a volume of poetry, *Poesias Catalanas,* in Catalan. His outspokenness on political issues made staying in Spain dangerous. In 1866 he moved to Provence. In 1869 he returned to Madrid, where he served as a minister of public works, of colonies, and of finance, and as a senator. He dropped out of politics in 1878. His writings consist of a *History of Catalonia,* poems in both Catalan and Spanish, and two collections of Catalan tragedies.

Balassa, Balint, Baron (1551-94), Hungarian poet, was born in Kekko. His poetry reflects the humanistic philosophy of the time and his education in classical literature. He wrote lyrics on nature, love, patriotism, and martial life. He also wrote hymns and devotional literature. His achievements were considered unrivaled in Hungarian literature until the 18th century, and he was recognized as the greatest Hungarian lyric poet of his age.

Balbo, Cesare, Count (1789-1853), Italian statesman and historian, was born in Turin. Balbo was a Piedmontese nobleman who began his career by serving Napoleon from 1807-14. When the House of Savoy regained control over Italy, Balbo's loyalty to Italy was suspect. For the next seven years, he served in the Piedmontese army. In 1821 he was falsely accused of aiding revolutionaries and fled to France, where he remained until 1826. Once again in Italy, he joined with Caventou in establishing *Il Risorgimento,* which advocated representative government. The paper led in petitioning the king for a constitution, which was granted in 1848. Balbo became the first prime minister of Piedmont in that year. He wrote many political essays and books, among them *Delle Speranze d'Italia (The Hopes of Italy),*

Balbuena, Bernardo de (1568-1627), Spanish writer, was born in Valdepenas and was educated for the priesthood. As a young man he went to Mexico and spent most of his life in Central America. He became the first bishop of Puerto Rico in 1620. His three known works are a descriptive poem about Mexico City, *La Grandeza Mexicana;* a pastoral novel, *El Siglo de Oro;* and an epic, *El Bernardo.*

Balde, Jakob (1604-68), German poet, was born in Ensisheim, Alsace. He was educated by the Church and belonged to the Jesuit order. He was chaplain to the Prince Elector of Bavaria and won acclaim as one of the best Latin poets of his time. His work influenced two other German poets, Schlegel and Herder.

Baldridge, Cyrus Le Roy (1889-   ), American cartoonist, illustrator, and teacher, was born in New York. As a boy Baldridge attended Holme's School of Illustration; he later received his degree from the University of Chicago. In the first world war, he served with the French army and with the A.E.F. and contributed cartoons to the American military publication *Stars and Stripes.* During his later career Baldridge served as president of the National Association of Commercial Arts and the Artists Guild in New York.

Baldrige, Letitia (1927-   ), executive and writer, was born in Omaha, the daughter of Howard Baldrige, who served two terms as a Nebraskan Republican Representative in the U.S. Congress. After her education, at Vassar and the University of Geneva, she worked in Paris as an assistant to David Bruce in the formulation of the Marshall Plan following World War II. Later, she was his secretary when he became Ambassador to France. She next served as assistant to Clare Boothe Luce, who was then Ambassador to Italy. Returning to Washington, she was secretary to Jacqueline Kennedy during the Kennedy Administration. In later years, she was active in public relations and as a business executive. In 1978 appeared *The Amy Vanderbilt Complete Book of Etiquette: A Guide to Contemporary Living* (revised and expanded by Letitia Baldrige).

Baldwin, Faith (1893-1978), writer, was born in New Rochelle, N.Y., and attended Brooklyn Heights Academy, Packer Institute, Fuller's School, and Briarcliff School. Her married name was Mrs. Hugh Cuthrill. Faith Baldwin wrote some 85 books, mostly romantic novels but also poetry, juveniles, and non-fiction. Her novels were often serialized in magazines; many were made into movies. She also wrote articles and stories for magazines. Her books include *Mavis of Green Hill* (1921), *Rich Girl, Poor Girl* (1938), *The Heart Remembers* (1941), *Widow's Walk* (1954; poems), *Face Toward the Spring* (1956, autobiography), *Living By Faith* (1964, non-fiction), *No Bed of Roses* (1973), *New Girl in Town* (1975), and *Thursday's Child* (1976).

Baldwin, James (Arthur) (1924-   ), writer, was born in New York City and grew up in Harlem. He attended Clinton High School, where he edited a literary magazine. The son of a minister, Baldwin became a Holy Roller preacher at 13, continuing until he was 17. He spent the years 1948-57 in Paris. Returning to the U.S. he became active in civil rights movements, and was recognized as a leading spokesman for blacks in America. His novels, stories, essays, and plays expose and criticize racial injustice. Baldwin received a National Institute of Arts and Letters award in 1957 and a National Conference of Christians and Jews award in 1961. His books include *Go Tell It on the Mountain* (1953), *Notes of a Native Son* (1955), *Giovannis' Room* (1956), *The Fire Next Time* (1963), *Blues for Mr. Charlie* (1964, play), *One Day When I Was Lost* (1973), and *If Beale Street Could Talk* (1974).

Baldwin, James Mark (1861-1934), American psychologist, was born at Columbia, S. C., and was graduated at Princeton University, 1884.

He was professor of philosophy at Toronto University, 1889-93, where he founded the first psychological laboratory in the British Empire. He founded a second at Princeton University. Taught at Johns Hopkins University and the National University of Mexico, and was professor in the School of Advanced Social Study at Paris. He was the chief exponent of the school of experimental psychology in America. His extensive writings include *Mental Development in the Child and the Race.*

Baldwin of Bewdley, Stanley Baldwin, Earl (1867-1947), British statesman and prime minister, was born in Worcestershire, England, and was educated at Cambridge University. On his mother's side, he was a cousin of Rudyard Kipling and a nephew of Edward Burne-Jones. During World War I, he made a voluntary contribution of 25 percent of his private fortune to the national treasury. He was chosen president of the British board of trade in 1921; sat as member of the British commission which, early in 1923, arranged for the funding of the British war debt to the United States; and, in May 1923, assumed the leadership of the British government. Following the defeat of the Conservatives in the elections held late in 1923, Baldwin resigned the premiership early in 1924 only to be returned to power in November of the same year. Among the achievements of his second administration are to be numbered a leading part in the negotiation of the Locarno treaties and the successful weathering of a general strike in 1926. His government was defeated by the Labor Party in 1929, but he joined the cabinet of Ramsay MacDonald in the national government of 1931. He was again prime minister from 1935 to 1937. On his retirement he was created Earl Baldwin of Bewdley. His writings include *This Torch of Freedom* (1935), *Service of Our Lives* (1937), *An Interpreter of England* (1939), and *Classics and the Plain Man* (1926).

Bale, John (1495-1563), English dramatist, historian, and religious reformer. Bale was given a religious education at a Carmelite convent and received his divinity degree from Jesus College, Cambridge, in 1529. Shortly afterward he converted from Catholicism to Protestantism. Thomas Cromwell became Bale's patron and secured him a living at Thorndale. Bale was attacked and imprisoned for his religious beliefs. When Cromwell fell from favor in 1540, Bale fled to Germany, where he remained until Edward VI was crowned. When Bale returned he was made bishop in Ossory, Ireland. When Mary assumed the English throne, Bale again sought refuge on the Continent, remaining there until Elizabeth's reign began in 1558. Elizabeth made Bale prebendary of Canterbury, an office he held until his death.

Bale wrote many morality plays characterized by doggerel and satire. His important dramatic contribution is the play *King John*, which marked the transition from the medieval morality play to the Renaissance history play. His major work is a volume of biographies of Irish, Scotch, and English writers in Latin, the *Catalogue of the Illustrious Writers of Great Britain*; it is valuable as a historical tool for the medieval and early Tudor period.

Balfour (băl′foor), **Arthur James Balfour, Earl (1848-1930)**, British statesman and author, was born in Scotland. He was educated at Eton and at Trinity College, Cambridge. During 1878-80, he was private secretary to Lord Salisbury, attending him at the Congress of Berlin, 1878. He was secretary for Scotland, with a seat in the cabinet, 1886-87; was chief secretary for Ireland, 1887-91; was first lord of the treasury and leader of the house, 1891, and again in 1895-1906.

Balfour became prime minister in 1902, serving until the end of 1905. In May 1915, he was first lord of the admiralty, and in December 1916, was made secretary of state for foreign affairs in Lloyd George's war cabinet, serving until 1919. In this capacity he issued the "Balfour Declaration," which led to the establishment of a "Jewish state" in Palestine. In 1917, he headed the British mission to America and, in 1921-22, was the leading member of the British delegation to the Washington Conference. His writings include *A Defense of Philosophic Doubt, The Foundations of Belief, Economic Notes on Insular Free Trade, Speeches of Fiscal Reform, Criticism and Beauty, Theism and Humanism*.

Ballou (bă-loo′), **Hosea (1771-1852)**, American preacher and one of the founders of Universalism, was born in New Hampshire. He was self-educated; was expelled from his father's church on declaring his belief in the final salvation of all men; began to preach at 21, and became minister of the Second Universalist church in Boston, in which he preached 35 years. He started the *Universalist Magazine* in 1819, and, in 1831, began the *Universalist Expositor*. It is said that he preached over 10,000 sermons, none of which was written before delivery.

Balmes, Jaime Lucian (1810-48), Spanish theologian, political writer, and philosopher, was educated at the seminary in Barcelona and ordained a priest. He went to the University of Cervera for further study in theology and civil law. Balmes founded and edited a Catholic weekly, *El Pensamiento de la Nación*, which advocated reconciliation between the political and ideological groups dividing Spain. He revived philosophical studies in Spain, basing his system on Aquinas' theory. Balmes' writings include *Political Considerations on the Situation of Spain, Protestantism compared with Catholicism in its Relations to European Civilization, El Criteria* (also known as *Balme's Logic*), and *Filosofía Fundamental*.

Balucki, Michal (1837-1901), Polish novelist and dramatist, received his education at the university in his birthplace, Krakow. During the first half of his life Balucki wrote poetry. His poems are forgotten except for one lyric, *Oh, Mountaineer, Dost Thou Not Grieve*, which became a popular folk song. In the 1870's Balucki began writing novels. He took a strong stand against the naturalistic trend popularized by Ibsen's writings. His first novel, *The Awakening*, was written under the pseudonym Elpidon. Another pseudonym Balucke used was Zalega. His other novels include *Romance Without Love, Sabina, The Parson's Niece*, and *Hunting a Husband*. The unpopularity of his novels turned Balucki to drama—considered by 20th-century critics as his proper medium. His plays include *The Counselors of Mr. Councillor, The Big Fish, Open House, Kinfolk*, and *The Bachelor's Club*. After his final play, *The Impostors*, was harshly criticized, he committed suicide. After his death, his plays earned him the title of the father of Polish bourgeois comedy.

Balzac (F. bal′zak′; E. băl′zăk), **Honoré de (1799-1850)**, French novelist and founder of the realistic school of fiction, was born at Tours, France. When twelve years old, he was sent to the College of Vendôme, near Blois. Here he devoted himself so intensely to mystic books and reveries that he injured his health. He next studied law at the Sorbonne, Paris. Being employed as clerk to a notary, he gathered a knowledge of chicanery which was later turned to account in his romances. His occupation, however, proved intolerable, and he was left by his family to work, starve, and struggle for the next ten years on a scanty pittance. He read omnivorously and tried to make money by scribbling unpromising novels under assumed names.

In 1826, he formed a partnership with the printer Barbier and published various works. This business turned out ill, however, and he was laden with a debt which harassed him until the end of his career. His first successful novel was *The Chouans*, which appeared in 1829. His next works, *The Physiology of Marriage* and *The Wild Ass's Skin*, produced in 1830, also proved popular.

Between the years 1831 and 1850, Balzac produced those stories which composed his great *Human Comedy*. Of these, the most widely read was *Father Goriot*. The others include *Eugenie Grandet* and *Lost Illusions*. He was phenomenally industrious and productive, writing 85 novels in 20 years. In them he aimed to represent all ranks, professions, arts, and trades, and all phases of manners in town and country. He exhibited an extraordinary range of knowledge, observation, and sympathy, a steadfast determination for thoroughness, and a keen analysis of character and conduct. His faults include moralizing and an overinsistence on detail. It is impossible to judge justly any one of these tales separately, because each is only a fragment in the development of the *Human Comedy*.

In 1849, Balzac traveled to Poland and visited the rich Countess Hanska, to whom he had dedicated his novel *Seraphita* and whom he had loved for 15 years. In 1850, they were married, and his long-standing debts were paid.

The most striking feature of Balzac's genius is the immensity of his imaginative achievements. He wrote, in all, 97 books. His name is one of the greatest in the literature of France since the era of the Revolution.

Balzac, Jean-Louis Guez de (1594-1654), French writer. Balzac studied at the University of Leyden and in Paris. He planned a career in politics and wrote in support of Cardinal Richelieu, who became his patron. Balzac's political career did not materialize and he turned to writing. He influenced the development of French prose, bringing to it clarity and precision through the use of idiomatic phrases and a rhythmic and balanced style. In 1634 he was elected to the French Academy. After his death his reputation declined. His most famous work, *Lettres*, was designed to popularize Latin authors. Other works are *The Christian Socrates, Aristippus, Le Prince, Discours,* and *Le Barbon.*

Bances Candamo, Francisco Antoine de (*ban'-thās kan-dá-mō*) **(1662-1704),** Spanish dramatic poet, was educated at Seville University. His works include comedies, lyric poetry, and criticism. His poetry is collected in a volume entitled, *Obras Liricas,* and his comedies in *Obras Comicas.*

Bancroft, George (1800-91), American historian, was born at Worcester, Mass. He was graduated at Harvard College in 1817 and, in 1818, went to Göttingen, where he studied history and philology. At Berlin, he attended the lectures of Hegel and had frequent intercourse with Schleiermacher, Humboldt, Savigny, and other literary men of note. Subsequently, he traveled in Germany, France, Italy, and England. Returning to the United States, he spent some time in teaching and then devoted himself to politics. He rose to prominence as a Democratic politician, and was made collector of customs at Boston. He still continued his literary labors, especially in lectures upon German literature and philosophy. Bancroft was appointed secretary of the navy in 1845 by President Polk. While in this office, he established an observatory at Washington and a naval school at Annapolis. In 1846, he was sent by Polk as ambassador to England, where he remained until 1849, collecting additional materials for his monumental *History of the United States,* a work of solid excellence, the last volume of which appeared in 1874.

Bancroft, Hubert Howe (1832-1918), American historian, was born at Granville, Ohio. He worked in a bookstore in Buffalo, N. Y., in 1848, and, from 1852 to 1868, was a book dealer and publisher in San Francisco. In connection with his book trade, he made large collections of historical material and finally retired from business in order to devote himself to the production of historical works. With the aid of collaborators, he published *Native Races of the Pacific States* and a monumental *History of the Pacific States of North America,* in 21 volumes, and other historical works.

Bandello, Matteo (1485-1561), Italian novelist, soldier, diplomat and monk, was born in Tortona, Lombardy. He was educated at Milan and the University of Pavia. A friend of Machiavelli, he was prominent in the courts of Ferrara and Mantua. After his appointment as bishop of Agen in 1550, he lived in France until his death. His *Novelle,* in 4 volumes, were influential in France, Spain, and England, as well as in Italy. Shakespeare used one of the tales as a source for *Romeo and Juliet.* Like Boccaccio's *Decameron,* which they resemble in format and tone, the *Novelle* picture Italian Renaissance society. Bandello also wrote *Rime, Lodi,* and a volume of poems, *Il Conzonire.*

Bang, Hermann Joachim (1857-1912), Danish novelist. Bang suffered many setbacks in his career. He began as an actor, turned to play writing, and then tried journalism—all unsuccessfully. As a novelist he gained critical recognition. An impressionistic writer, he portrayed the life of ordinary people, reflecting childhood reminiscences and loneliness. His first significant novel was *Haablose Slegter.* Other novels include *Families Without Hope, Denied a Country, Eccentric Tales, Fadra, Ida Brandt,* and his masterpiece, *Ved Vejin.*

Bangs, John Kendrick (1862-1922), American author, humorist, and lecturer, was born at Yonkers, N. Y. He was graduated from Columbia university, 1883; studied law, 1883-84; was associate editor of *Life,* 1884-88; was editor of *Literature,* 1898-99, *Harper's Weekly,* 1899-1902, *Metropolitan Magazine,* 1902-03, and *Puck,* 1904-05. Among his numerous writings are *New Waggings of Old Tales, The Water Ghost,* and *A House Boat on the Styx.*

Banim, John (1798-1842) and Michael (1796-1874), Irish novelists, were both born in Kilkenny. John studied drawing in Dublin, but after teaching in Kilkenny, returned to Dublin, and later moved to London, as a journalist. Michael had to give up his study of law to take over their father's business. In 1825 their first book, *Tales, by the O'Hara Family,* appeared, containing two stories by John and one by Michael, and was immediately successful. John continued to publish alone and in collaboration with his brother until his death in Kilkenny. *The Nowlans* is considered John's best novel. *Father Connell,* published in the year of John's death, was written almost entirely by Michael

Banks, Russel (1940-   ), author, was born in Newton, Mass. and received his bachelor's degree from the University of North Carolina (1967). He began his career as an editor and writer in 1966. He became an instructor at the University of New Hampshire (1972), won a Guggenheim fellowship (1976) and also received an O. Henry prize for short stories. His works include *Waiting to Freeze* (1967), *Snow* (1975), *Searching for Survivors* (1975), *Family Life* (1975), *New World* (1976), and *Hamilton Stark,* (1978, a novel).

Bannerman, Helen (Watson) (c. 1860-1946), Scottish author of children's books, was born in Edinburgh, lived two years in Madeira, and returned to Scotland to attend school. She studied abroad and graduated from St. Andrew's University. After living for some years in India with her husband, a surgeon in the British army, she returned to Edinburgh after his death in 1924. *Little Black Sambo,* which she wrote and illustrated to amuse her two daughters, has become a children's classic.

Banville, Théodore de (1823-91), French writer, was born in Moulins, but spent most of his life in Paris. *Les cariatides* (1842) and *Les stalactites* (1846) first brought him to public attention, and *Odes funambulesques* (1857) established his reputation. Banville also wrote verse dramas and dramatic criticism for Parisian newspapers, but was best known for his lyric poetry which was collected in *Nouvelles odes funabulesques* (1869), *Idylles prussiennes* (1871), and *Trente-six ballades joyeuses* (1875). His prose works include *Les Saltimbanques* (1853), *Esquisses Parisiennes* (1859), and his memoirs, published in 1883.

Baratynski, Eugeni Abramovich (1800-44), Russian poet, was born in Petersburg of noble parentage. He attended the Royal School in Petersburg and received training for the imperial corps of pages, but was expelled and joined the army. After eight years of service he retired from military life and settled near Moscow. A contemporary of Pushkin, Baratynski emphasized philosophical and aesthetic poetic themes. His poetry is considered pessimistic and melancholy. His writings include *Eda, Bal (The Ball), Nalozhnite (The Gypsy Girl), On the Death of Goethe* and *Dusk.*

Barbauld (*bär'bôld*), **Anna Letitia (1743-1825),** English author, was born at Kibworth-Harcourt, in Leicestershire. In 1773, she published *Miscellaneous Pieces in Prose* and her first volume of poems. Following her marriage in 1774, she taught ten years in a boys' school, during which she wrote *Early Lessons for Children* and *Hymns in Prose,* which have been translated into several languages. Other well-known works are her *Devotional Pieces, Evenings at Home,* and *Ode to Life.*

Barbey d'Aurevilly, Jules Amedée (1808-89), French writer and critic known as the "High Constable of

Letters," was born at St. Sauveur le Vicomte, Manche, but lived in Paris from 1833 until his death. He was considered an energetic, penetrating critic with strong partiality for royalist and Catholic causes. His works include *Les oeuvres et les hommes du XIX esiecle* (26 vols., 1816-1909); two novels, *L'ensorcelée* (1854) and *Le chevalier des touches* (1864); and *Les diaboliques* 1874), a volume of short stories.

Barbier, Henri Auguste *(barb-yay)*, **(1805-82)**, French poet, attended the Lycée Henry IV where he studied law. When the July Revolution of 1830 broke out, Barbier began writing political poetry. *Les Iambes* satirized important figures in the court of Louis Philippe. He also wrote a volume of poetry, *Il Pianto*, satirizing Italian life, and a volume, *Lazare*, satirizing the Industrial Revolution in England.

Barbieri, Giovanni Maria (1519-74), Italian literary scholar. He researched Romance literature and put such studies on a more scientific basis. His major work, which traced the origin of rhymed verse, was *Arte del rimare; Dell' origine della poesie rimata.*

Barbosa, Ruy (1849-1923), Brazilian statesman and writer, was a lawyer by profession, entered public life, and aided in the 1889 revolution in a desire to abolish slavery. He became vice president and finance minister of the provisional government established after the revolution. He also helped to draft the constitution of Brazil (1890). Barbosa is best remembered for his part at the second Hague Peace conference (1907), where he supported the principle of the equality of nations. His contribution to writings on jurisprudence and sociology is *Letters from England.*

Barbour *(bär′bēr)*, **John (c. 1316-95)**, early Scottish poet and historian. He was archdeacon of Aberdeen from 1357, or earlier, until his death. His national epic, *The Brus*, was first printed at Edinburgh in 1571.

Barbusse *(bar′büs′)*, **Henri (1873-1935)**, French novelist was born at Asnières, a suburb of Paris. Prior to World War I, he wrote two novels, *Les suppliants* and *L'enfer* which won considerable success. He attained international fame by *Le feu*, written in 1916 and translated into English as *Under Fire*, which contains perhaps the most unforgettable description of modern warfare in the world's literature. His subsequent books, including *Les enchainements, Elevation*, and *Zola*, evince a hatred of war and a favorable attitude toward Russian Communism.

Barclay, Alexander (1475-1552), English poet assumed to be of Scottish birth. However, he wrote in English, and his writings are considered part of English literature. He studied in England, France, and Italy. He was ordained, and by 1508 served as a chaplain at the college of St. Mary Ottery, Devonshire. Later, he became a Benedictine monk at Ely, and still later, a Franciscan friar at Canterbury. His most famous poem, *The Shyp of Folys of the Worlde*, is an adaptation of the German poem *Das Narrenschiff* by Sebastian Brant. Barclay added to and subtracted from the original, introducing personal episodes and local politics. *Certayne Egloges of Alexander Barclay Priest* are the first formal eclogues in English. Other works include *The Castell of Labour, Introductory ot \ write and to pronounce Frnche*, and *The Lyge of the glorious Martyr Saynt George.*

Barclay, John (1582-1621), Scottish poet and satirist, was born at Pont a Mousson, France. He lived in London (1603-16), then in Rome, where he died. Barclay wrote several political and religious satires in Latin. *Euphormionis Lusinini Satyricon* (1603-07) is directed against the Jesuits. His best-known work is *Argenis* (1616), a romance that was also a satirical allegory on politics in Europe. *Argenis*, translated into English in 1623, had great impact on the development of the romance in the 17th century. Other works include *The Apologia* (1611), *Sylvae* (1606), *Icon Animorum* (1614),

and several volumes of verse in Latin.

Bardesanes (154-c. 223 A.D.), Syrian poet and theologian, was born at Edessa and became the first writer of Syrian hymns, composing 150 hymns with his son Harmonius. One of the first Christian converts in Syria, Bardesanes placed great emphasis on faith. The only surviving work is his *Dialogue of Destiny, or the Book of the Laws of Nations*, but his doctrines are found in the *Historia Ecclesiastica* by Eusebius.

Barea, Arturo (1897-1957), Spanish novelist and critic, was born in Badajoz. He grew up in Madrid and went to work at 13. After various commercial jobs throughout Spain, he was inducted into the army, serving for three years. During the Spanish Civil War he became chief of the Foreign Censorship Office, but in 1938 sought refuge with his wife in France, later moving to England. He broadcast commentaries during World War II and began to write seriously. His works include *The Struggle for the Spanish Soul; Lorca, the Poet and his People; The Forging of a Rebel* (an autobiographical trilogy); and *The Broken Root.*

Baretti, Giuseppe Marc Antonio (1719-89), Italian critic and lexicographer, was born in Turin and educated in Milan and Venice. His father intended him to enter the priesthood but Baretti preferred architecture. Poor eyesight hindered him, and he began a literary career under the direction of Count Gaspari Gozzi, the Italian essayist. Baretti contributed to periodicals and collections of verse. In 1750 he published *Piacevoli Poesie*, an attack on certain Italian literary practices. Because of his frankness and temper he had to leave Venice and settled in London as a teacher of Italian. He helped to popularize Italian literature in England and promoted understanding between the two nations. Like his friend Samuel Johnson, he produced a dictionary—of Italian and English. From 1760-66 he toured Europe and wrote *A Journey from London to Genoa*. While in Venice he began the journal *Frusta Letteraria*, which again criticized Italian literary fashions. He returned to London in 1766 and remained until his death. His other writings include a pamphlet in French defending Shakespeare against an attack by Voltaire, a discussion of moral and literary opinions, *Scelta di lettera familiari*, and *Dissertation on Italian Poetry.*

Barham, Richard Harris (1788-1845), "Thomas Ingoldsby," English poet and humorist, was born at Canterbury. He was clergyman of the Church of England, and, in the latter part of his life, was rector of Saint Augustine's in the city of London. The *Ingoldsby Legends*, which constitute his chief claim to fame, were first contributed to *Bentley's Miscellany*. Some of Barham's previously uncollected writings were published under the title of the *Ingoldsby Lyrics*. He died in London.

Bar-Hebraeus, Gregory (1226-86), Syrian historian and writer, known also by the Arabic name Abul Faraj. Bar-Hebraeus was born in Armenia, the son of a Jewish physician. He was converted to Christianity and joined the Jacobite church. He studied philosophy, theology, and medicine at Antioch and Tripolis. At 20 he was made bishop of Aleppo. He rose from that position to the second highest position in the Jacobite church, archbishop of the Eastern Jacobites. Considered the last classical writer in Syriac literature, he wrote a history of the world, *Chronography*, and commentaries on Aristotle.

Baring-Gould, Sabine (1834-1924), English divine, novelist, and miscellaneous writer, was born at Exeter. He was educated at Clare College, Cambridge, and, after graduation, spent some years in travel. In 1864, he was appointed curate of Horbury; in 1871, he became rector of East Mersea; and, in 1881, he succeeded to his father's estate, which had been in the family for nearly three centuries, and was made rector of Lew Trenchard. He was a versatile writer, with an attractive style, and published numerous books of fiction, history, travel, religion, folklore, and mythology. Among his best novels are *Mehalah, John Herring, Court Royal, Pennycomequicks, The Red Spider,* and *Broom Squire.* His interesting contributions to folklore and antiquities include *Book of Were-wolves, Curious Myths of the Middle Ages,* and *Curious Survivals.* He wrote also "Onward Christian Soldiers," "Now the Day is Over," and other well-known hymns.

Barker, Sir Ernest (1874-1960), English historian, was born in East Cheshire. Barker attended the Manchester Grammar school and Balliol College, Oxford, where he studied classics and history. He continued his studies at Merton College, Oxford. From 1899-1920 he was a lecturer at Wadham, St. John's, and New College, Oxford. He then spent a year at Amherst College in the U.S. as a visiting professor. He was principal of King's College at London University until 1927. From 1928-39 he was professor of political science at Cambridge, and first holder of the chair of political science. Barker was made a fellow of the British Academy and of Peterhouse College. He was knighted in 1944. His writings include *Reflections on Government, Principles of Social and Political Theory, Political Thought in England from Herbert Spencer to Today, Greek Political Theory, Oliver Cromwell and the English People, Ideas and Ideals of the British Empire.*

Barker, George (Granville) (1913-   ), British poet, was born in Loughton, Essex, and left school at 14 to try a variety of jobs. In 1939 he was professor of English literature at the Imperial Tohoku University. He lived in the U.S. from 1940 to 1943, then returned to England. *Alanna Autumnal,* published when he was 18, was his first novel; it was followed by *The Dead Seagull* in 1950. Barker is best known as a lyric poet; his volumes of verse include *Thirty Preliminary Poems, Sacred and Secular Elegies, Eros in Dogma, News of the World, A Vision of Beasts and Gods,* and *The View from the Blind I.*

Barker, James Nelson (1784-1858), American dramatist and politician, was born in Philadelphia and fought in the war of 1812, rising to the rank of major. From 1814-17 he served as assistant adjutant general of the fourth military district. He was elected mayor of Philadelphia in 1819 and served one two-year term. He held the post of Philadelphia port collector (1829-38) until becoming comptroller of the U.S. treasury (1838-58). He wrote verse for journals and a number of dramas. Best known among his plays are *The Indian Princess or La Belle Sauvage,* the first play written by an American on an Indian theme, and *Superstition,* dealing with Puritanism in New England.

Barlow, Francis (1626?-1702), English illustrator and engraver, was born in Lincolnshire. He studied under William Sheppard, the portrait painter. Barlow's illustrations were precisely drawn with pen and ink. He is best remembered as a painter of animals. He drew more than 100 illustrations for Mrs. Aphra Behn's edition of *Aesop's Fables,* most of which were destroyed in the London Fire.

Barlow, Joel (1754-1812), American poet and politician, was born in Connecticut. He served as a military chaplain during the war for independence. In 1787, he published a poem called *The Vision of Columbus,* which, in 1807, appeared anew in an enlarged form as *The Columbiad.* He spent some years in Europe in political, literary, and mercantile pursuits. For a short time he was American consul at Algiers. In 1811, he was appointed ambassador to France.

Barnard, Lady Anne (1750-1825), Scottish writer, daughter of James Lindsay. In 1793 Lady Anne married Andrew Barnard, colonial secretary of the Cape of Good Hope. The couple lived at the Cape until it was ceded to Holland in 1802, when they returned to London. Lady Anne's first achievement was the lyric *Auld Robin Gray,* written to a Scottish folk melody. Her letters from the Cape were published under the title *South Africa a Century Ago.* Also published was a description of her experiences entitled *Journals and Notes.*

Barnard, Henry (1811-1900), American educational reformer, was born in Hartford, Conn. He was graduated at Yale in 1830 and was admitted to the bar in 1835. As a member of the state legislature, 1837-40, he was an energetic advocate of prison reform. As school commissioner of Rhode Island, 1843-47, he recognized the educational system of the state. He was state superintendent of schools for Connecticut, 1850-54, and principal of the State Normal School at New Britain during the same period.

In 1857, Barnard was made president of the University of Wisconsin and, in 1865, president of Saint John's College at Annapolis. During 1867-70, he was United States commissioner of education, the first to occupy that position. In 1855 he founded the *American Journal of Education,* of which he was editor until 1886. His *American Library of Schools and Education* fills 52 volumes. Barnard ranks as one of the foremost educational pioneers of America.

As editor of the *American Journal of Education,* which during the period of its publication in the middle of the last century was one of the leading factors in bringing about far-reaching reforms in American education, Barnard with Mann, Stowe, and others, labored for the more definite organization of instruction, especially in elementary schools. He visited the schools of Europe, helped to acquaint American educators with the teachings of Pestalozzi, and contributed through his administrative activities to the improvement of elementary education.

Barnes, Djuna (1892-   ), American writer, was born in Cornwall on Hudson, N.Y. She began her career as a magazine reporter, illustrator, and story writer. She was associated with the *Little Review* and wrote a column for the New York Theater Guild's magazine. Many of her stories were published by the *Dial, All-Story Weekly,* and the *Smart Set.* Her longer works include the novel *Nightwood* (with an appreciative introduction by T.S. Eliot), *The Book of Repulsive Writers, A Book,* and the *Ladie's Almanack.* Her main interest, however, has been in the theater and three of her plays were produced by the Provincetown Players: *Three from the Earth, An Irish Triangle,* and *Kurzy of the Sea.* She is also the author of a verse play, *The Antiphon.* In 1962 her *Selected Works* was published.

Barnes, Mary Sheldon (1850-98), American educator, daughter of E. A. Sheldon, was born at Oswego, N.Y. She was educated at the Oswego Normal School and the University of Michigan, graduating in the first class which admitted women. After further study at Newnham College, Cambridge, England, and at the University of Zurich, she was professor of history at Wellesley College, 1876-80, at Oswego Normal School, 1882-84, and at Stanford University, 1891-96. Following her marriage to Earl Barnes in 1884, she spent seven years in study and travel.

Mrs. Barnes was the first instructor in America to apply the Pestalozzian method to the teaching of history. Her adaptations are embodied in her books entitled *Studies in General History, American History,* and *Studies in the Historical Method.* She was also the pioneer American teacher to develop the source method of instruction in history.

Barnes, William (1801?-86), English philologist and poet, was born at Rushay, Dorsetshire, the son of a farmer. He was first a schoolmaster, then established a school at Dorchester, and took religious orders in 1847. He became rector of Winterborne Came in 1862, and remained there until his death. Barnes is considered among the best of English pastoral poets. He used simple dialect verse to describe rustic life. His works include *Poems of Rural Life in the Dorset Dialect* (collected edition, 1879), *Poems of Rural Life in Common English*

(1868), and two philological works, *Outline of English Speech-Craft* (1878) and *A Grammar and Glossary of the Dorset Dialect* (1864), in which he tried to eliminate words derived from Latin from English.

Barnum, Phineas Taylor (1810-91), American showman, was born in Bethel, Conn. At the age of 13, he was employed in a country store, and, about five years afterward, went into the lottery business. When 19 years old, he married and removed to Danbury, Conn., where he edited the *Herald of Freedom*. In 1834, he moved to New York, where, hearing of Joyce Heth, supposedly the nurse of General Washington, he bought her for $1000 and exhibited her, realizing considerable profit. In 1841, Barnum bought the American Museum in New York, which he raised at once to prosperity by exhibiting a Japanese mermaid (made of a fish and a monkey), a white negress, a wooly horse, and, finally, a noted dwarf, styled "General Tom Thumb," whom he exhibited later in Europe and elsewhere. He introduced Jenny Lind to the American public, and then became proprietor of "the greatest show on earth." He made and lost several fortunes, and his show was twice destroyed by fire. He published *The Humbugs of the World*, *Struggles and Triumphs*, and an *Autobiography*.

Baroja (bä-rō′hä), **Nessi Pio (1872-1956)**, Spanish novelist, was born at San Sebastian. A depictor of the rebels and outcasts of society, he wrote, among other novels, *The Struggle for Existence*, *The Tree of Knowledge*, and *Youth and Egolatry*. His style is direct; the sardonic drama of his stories arising from the marshaling of badly stated facts. In *Memories of a Man of Action*, he wrote a series of books about the historical character Eugenio de Aviraneta.

Baronio, Cesare (1538-1607), Italian church historian, was born in Naples. In 1593 he became superior of the Oratory of St. Philip Neri, which he had joined in 1557. He was made a cardinal in 1596 and was employed as Vatican librarian. Strong Spanish opposition kept him from being elected pope in 1605. The author of the first critical Church history, *Annales Ecclesiastici*, Baronio has been called "the father of ecclesiastical history." In his work he attempted to prove that the Church of Rome had remained identical with the church of the first century. Protestant critics attacked the validity of his work because of his poor Greek and ignorance of Hebrew. Baronio's other works include, *Tractatus de Monarchia Siciliae*, supporting papal claims to Sicily, and *Paraenesis ad Rempublican Venetam*, attacking Venetian politics.

Barr, Alfred H., Jr. (1902-   ), art historian, was born in Detroit, Mich. He graduated from Princeton and Harvard and has taught at Vassar, Harvard, Princeton, and Wellesley. He was appointed director of the Museum of Modern Art in New York City in 1929 and later served as counselor to the board of trustees. He was editor (with Holger Cahill) of *Art in America* and *American Painters Series, Penguin Books*. He wrote *What is Modern Painting?*, *Picasso: Fifty Years of His Art*, *Matisse: His Art and His Public*, and *Masters of Modern Art*.

Barr, Amelia Edith (1831-1919), novelist, was born at Ulverston, England, and was educated at the high school in Glasgow, Scotland. In 1850, she married Robert Barr; subsequently, she came to the United States, settling in Texas, where her husband and three children died of yellow fever at Galveston in 1867. Moving to New York, she began to write for religious periodicals and to publish a series of semihistorical tales and novels. Among these are *Jan Vedder's Wife*, *Bow of Orange Ribbon*, *A Border Shepherdess*, *Remember the Alamo*, *Prisoners of Conscience*, *The Maid of Maiden Lane*, *A Song of a Single Note*, and *Sheila Vedder*. In 1913, she published *All the Days of My Life*, an autobiography.

Barr, Stringfellow (1897-   ), educator, was born at Suffolk, Virginia. He was educated at the University of Virginia, at Oxford, where he was a Rhodes scholar, and at the University of Paris. After serving as teacher of modern European history and as editor of *The Virginia Quarterly* at the University of Virginia, he was called by President Hutchins of the University of Chicago to assist in revising the course in liberal arts. He is known particularly for the use of "Great Books" as an approach to education, which requires a student to be thoroughly familiar with world classics. As president of St. John's College he had an opportunity to put his educational philosophy into practice. He is the author of *Mazzini: Portrait of an Exile*.

Barrault, Jean Louis (1910-   ), French actor and director, was born in Vesinet. He studied with the mime Etienne Ducreaux and Charles Dullin of the Théâtre de l'Atelier in Paris. He made his debut as an actor in 1935, and his first production was *Autour d'une mère*. In 1940 Barrault joined the Comedie Française as an actor and director. With his wife, actress Madeleine Renaud, he formed a repertory company in 1947 at the Théâtre Marigny in Paris, which toured the world, alternating classic with modern and experimental plays. Until 1956 he directed and acted in his own productions: *Amiphitryon*, Gide's *Hamlet*, and *Les fausses confidences*. In 1958 Barrault was appointed a director of the Théâtre du Palais Royal, and in 1959 became director of the Théâtre de France. His film roles include *Les enfants du paradis* (1944), *La symphonie fantastique* (1941), and *D'homme à hommes* (1948). His writings on the theater include *Réflexions sur le théâtre* (1949) and *Nouvelles réflexions sur le théâtre* (1959).

Barrès, (Auguste) Maurice (1862-1923), French novelist and politician, was born in Lorraine. He was educated at the Collège de Malgrange and studied law in Paris. Anatole France and Leconte de Lisle encouraged him to write, but in 1889 he was elected to the chamber of deputies, and then divided his time between writing and politics. With Charles Maurras he edited the periodical *La Cocarde*, which promoted the cause of the French nationalist party. Barrès' most notable work consists of two trilogies, *Le Culte du Moi* and *Le Roman de l'energie nationale*. Other works include *Chronique de la Grand Guerre* and several books on travel. Barrès was elected to the French Academy in 1907. He is credited with writing some of the finest prose in French.

Barrett, Lawrence (1838-91), American actor, was born at Paterson, N. J. His first appearance was at Detroit, 1853. He was leading actor in the Boston Museum, 1858; served as captain of the Massachusetts volunteers in the Civil War; from 1864, continued as leading actor and manager; and, beginning in 1866, was closely associated with Edwin Booth. His most notable role was that of Cassius; but he played Hamlet, Shylock, King Lear, and Richelieu with great distinction. He did much to elevate the American stage and to encourage dramatic authorship. He wrote *The Life of Edwin Forrest* and the biography of Booth in *Actors and Actresses of the Time*.

Barrie (băr′ĭ), **Sir James Matthew (1860-1937)**, British novelist and dramatist, was born at Kirriemuir, Scotland; was educated at Edinburgh University; and, after a year and a half as a journalist in Nottingham, settled in London, becoming a regular contributor to leading periodicals. His first volume, *Better Dead*, was largely a satire on London life; in *Auld Licht Idylls*, he opened a new and rich vein, the humor and the pathos of his native village. *The Little Minister*, his first novel, came out in 1891 and was dramatized in 1897. *Walker, London*, a farcical comedy, had a prodigious run in 1892; *Jane Annie* was written with Sir Conan Doyle. His most popular success was *Peter Pan*, a children's classic that was produced annually for many years in England. Other pieces, nearly all notably successful, are *The Professor's Love Story*, *The Admirable Crichton*, *Quality Street*, *What Every Woman Knows*, *Sentimental Tommy*, *Der Tag*, and *Mary Rose*.

Barrile, Anton Guilio (1836-1908), Italian novelist, was born in Savona. He lived most of his life in Genoa and was a professor of literature at the university there. He was also a member of the Chamber of Deputies. In 1872 he founded the journal *Caffaro* and edited it until 1887. He wrote two plays, a volume of literary criticism, *Sante Cecilia*, and many novels, among them *Il Capitan Dodero*, *Come un Sogno* and *L'Olmo e l'Edera*.

Barrios, Eduardo (1884-1963), Chilean novelist and short-story writer, was born in Valparaiso and attended school in Santiago. He traveled South America as a rubber prospector; later, he became director of the Chilean national library. In naturalistic style, he analyzed his many characters. His novels include *Un perdido* (*A Down-and-Outer*), *El hermano asno* (*Brother Ass*), and *Y la vida Sique* (*Life Goes On*). Barrios' most successful work, *Gran senor y rajadiablos* (*Grand Gentlemen and Big Rascal*) portrays Chilean farm life.

Barros, João (1496-1570), Portuguese historian and politician, was born in Vizeu. Educated in the household of the Portuguese heir apparent, Barros became a classical scholar, and later served as governor of Portuguese Guinea and treasurer of Portuguese India. In 1539 he published a primer of reading and catechism, which served as a model for many similar later works. Barros is best known for his 4-volume history of the Portuguese in the East Indies, *Decadas da Asia*.

Barros Arana, Diego (1830-1907), Chilean educator and historian, was born and died in Santiago. He was educated at the National Institute of Chile, and later, as rector of the Institute, was instrumental in reform of education. Active in politics, Barros Arana used his positions and travels to add to his geographical and historical knowledge of Chile. In 1893 he was made rector of the University of Chile. His works include textbooks, histories of Chile, and biography.

Barrow, Isaac (1630-77), British mathematician, clergyman, and Greek scholar. He was successively professor of Greek at Cambridge, of geometry at Gresham, and of mathematics at Cambridge. His pupil Isaac Newton succeeded him at Cambridge in 1669. His sermons, although often long, rank among the best in English. Coleridge referred to Barrow's "verbal imagination," saying that he excelled almost every other writer of prose of his time. Barrow's writings include *Euclides Elementa* (1655), *Archimedes Opera* (1675), and a treatise, *The Pope's Supremacy* (1680).

Barry, Philip (1896-1949), American playwright, perhaps most famous as the author of *The Philadelphia Story* (1939), was born in Rochester, N.Y. He graduated from Yale (1919) and spent three years at Harvard at George Pierce Baker's 47 Dramatic Workshop. His work there culminated in the Harvard Prize for his play *You and I* (1922), which was produced in New York. Barry's popularity was founded on his drawingroom comedies: *Holiday* (1929), *Tomorrow and Tomorrow* (1931), *The Animal Kingdom* (1932), and *Foolish Notion* (1944). He also wrote serious drama which received praise from the critics: *John* (1927); *Hotel Universe* (1930); *Here Come the Clowns* (1938), based on his novel *War in Heaven* (1938); and *Liberty Jones* (1940).

Barth, John (1930-   ), novelist, was born in Cambridge, Maryland. He studied orchestration briefly at the Juilliard School of Music in New York City before attending Johns Hopkins University. He taught English at Pennsylvania State University and at the State University of New York in Buffalo. Influenced by Franz Kafka and James Joyce, Barth's fiction relies on surrealistic fantasy and humor. His novels include *The Sotweed Factor*, *The Floating Opera*, *The End of the Road*, and *Giles Goat-Boy*.

Barth, Karl (1886-1968), Protestant theologian, was born in Basel, and studied in Switzerland and Germany. Barth was ordained (1908) by his father in the Reformed church in Bern. In 1911-21 he held the pastorate of Safenwil, and was called "the Red pastor" because of his socialist activities. He then taught at various universities, including the University of Bonn, 1930-35, until he was dismissed by Hitler.

Barth has been described as the most important Protestant thinker since John Calvin. In his commentary on Paul's Epistle to the Romans, *Romerbrief* (1919), Barth rejected liberal and humanist theology. His work emphasized the supremacy and divinity of the creator and drew new attention to the fallen state of humanity. His most important work, the 12-volume *Church Dogmatics* (1932-62), specifies the basics of Christian belief.

Barthelme, Donald (1931-   ), writer, was born in Philadelphia, but grew up in Houston, Texas, where he worked as a reporter. After Army service in Korea and Japan, he graduated from the University of Houston and worked there in public relations. His experimental stories, often published in the *New Yorker*, are collected in *Come Back, Dr. Caligari* (1964), *Unspeakable Practices, Unnatural Acts* (1968), *City Life* (1970), *Sadness* (1972), and *The Amateurs* (1976). His novels include *Snow White* (1967) and *The Dead Father* (1975). *The Slightly Irregular Fire Engine*, written and illustrated by Barthelme, won a National Book Award for children's books.

Bartholomaeus, Anglicus (flourished 1220-50), English encyclopedist, known also as Bartholomew the Englishman. In 1225 Bartholomaeus joined the Franciscan order of Friars and became a professor of theology at the University of Paris. Bartholomaeus' major contribution is an encyclopedia of the Middle Ages—*De Proprietatibus Rerum*—which included the usual knowledge of his time, to which he added Greek, Jewish, and Arabic views on medical and scientific subjects. His work was translated from Latin into English by John of Trevisa. The translation became popular and exerted a strong influence on English thought and writing in the 1500's. Bartholomaeus is often mistakenly confused with the 14th-century English Franciscan, Bartholomew de Glanville.

Bartoli, Daniello (1608-85), Italian historian and biographer was born in Ferrara. Educated by the Jesuits, Bartoli became rector of the Jesuit College in Rome. He wrote a historical account of the Jesuit missions in the East. Bartoli also wrote biographies of Ignatius Loyola, Francis Xavier, and Francis Borgia, and a work that ranked him among the chief classic Italian writers, *Dell' Huomo di Lettere*.

Bartolozzi, Francesco (1727-1815), Italian engraver, was born in Florence. Bartolozzi studied painting in Florence, then studied engraving under Joseph Wagner in Venice. From there he moved to Rome and engraved works by Il Domenichino and other Italian masters. In 1764 he settled in London and made engravings after Holbein's drawings. He became official engraver for King George III. In 1769 he was made a member of the British Royal Academy, and engraved the design for the Academy's diploma. He contributed plates to Boydell's *Shakespeare Gallery*.

Barton, Clara (1821-1912), American philanthropist, was born in Oxford, Mass. She was graduated from Clinton Liberal Institute, New York; taught school ten years; during the Civil war, did relief work on battlefields and organized search for missing men; and aided in the founding of hospitals during the Franco-Prussian War. By her efforts, the American Red Cross Society was founded in 1881, and she was its president until 1904. She secured adoption of the Treaty of Geneva, 1882; was appointed to represent the United States at various international conferences, 1884-1903; inaugurated an amendment empowering the Red Cross Society to provide relief during great calamities; and superintended relief activities at the Johnstown flood, 1889, the Russian famine, 1892, the Armenian massacre, 1896, and on various other occasions. She wrote *History of the Red Cross, America's Relief Expedition to Asia Minor*, and *Story of My Childhood*.

Bartram, William (1739-1823), American botanist, illustrator, and writer. Benjamin Franklin offered to teach Bartram printing, but he chose to follow his father's profession of naturalist. Commissioned by Fothergill, Bartram traveled from 1773-77 throughout the Southeast gathering plant and animal specimens. He then published *Travels through North and South Carolina, Georgia, East and West Florida. . . .* Translated widely, it is believed to have influenced Chateaubriand (in *Atcla*), Coleridge (in *Kubla Khan*), and Wordsworth (in *Ruth*). Bartram compiled the most complete list of American birds before Alexander Wilson. He drew many of the illustrations for Barton's *Elements of Botany.* Other works include *Memoirs of John Bartram* and *Observations on the Creek and Cherokee Indians.*

Bartrina, Joaquín María (1850-80), Spanish poet and journalist, was born in Catalonia and attended school in Reus. His poetry reflects pessimism and skepticism, yet is expressed with sincerity and stylistic inventiveness. His volume of verse, *Algo,* is marked by a rational feeling for the values of life. His collected poems were published as *Paginas de Amor.*

Barzun, Jacques (1907-   ), American educator, writer, critic, was born in Paris. He came to America in 1919 and became a naturalized citizen of the United States in 1933. At Columbia University, where he studied and received his Ph.D. degree, he has been lecturer and more recently professor in history. His writings, noted for their interesting style and challenging opinions, have reached a large public outside the field of education. They include *Berlioz and the Romantic Century, Pleasures of Music, God's Country and Mine,* and the widely quoted book *Teacher in America.* Later works are *Music in American Life, The Energies of Art, The House of Intellect,* and *Science: The Glorious Entertainment.*

Basedow (*bä' zē-dō*), **Johann Bernhard (1723-90),** German educational reformer, was born at Hamburg. He was educated in philosophy and theology at the University of Leipzig. He became professor of moral philosophy at Soro, Denmark, in 1753 and at Altona in 1763. At Altona, he fell under the Influence of Rousseau's *Emile,* which resulted in his abandoning theology for educational work in 1767.

His *Elementarwerk,* issued in 1774, combining the methods of Comenius with the principles of Bacon and the revolutionary ideas of Rousseau, met with wide approval and led to the establishment of his celebrated Philanthropinum at Dessau in 1774. This continued in existence until 1793, exerting a great influence on the education of children throughout Germany. The fundamental idea of his reform was "education according to nature." Many of his ideas were later carried out by more practical educators such as Pestalozzi and Froebel.

Basedow is the educational reformer of the post-Reformation period who is to be compared in general character with Comenius of the pre-Reformation era. Basedow, like Comenius, conceived of education as an appeal to the natural interests of children. He sought to promote nature study and contact with objects.

He devoted himself assiduously to the preparation of suitable textbooks for use in schools. In order to secure the funds for the preparation and publication of these books, he made an appeal to men of property for a public subscription and received a generous response. His movement was termed from this time on Philanthropinism.

The influence of Rousseau is very marked in the writings of Basedow. His motto was, "everything according to nature."

Bashkirtseff, Marie (1859-84), Russian diarist and painter, was born Maria Konstantinova Bashkirtseva in the Ukraine near Poltava. She received vocal training in Italy, followed in 1877 by the study of painting in Paris under Robert-Fleury and Jules Bastien-Lepage. In her fourteenth year she began a journal, with the intention of expressing herself completely candidly. However, before the journal's posthumous publication, her mother expurgated it thoroughly. Besides the *Journal* (1887), her correspondence with Guy de Maupassant was also published in *Letters* (1891).

Bashō, Matsuo (1644-94), Japanese poet, was born in Ueno, Iga province. The name is a pseudonym for Matsuo Munefusa. After the death of his master in 1666, Bashō gave up his life as a samurai to devote himself to writing *haiku,* and is considered the greatest of the Japanese Haiku poets. In 1673, he went to Tokyo, where he gained prominence as a poet and critic. In addition to the haiku, Bashō wrote prose accounts of his travels, and also wrote unequalled renga, or "linked" verse.

Basil (*băz' 'l*), **Saint (c. 329-379),** surnamed the Great, bishop of Cæsarea, was born there about 329. Converted to Christianity by his sister, Saint Macrina, he became one of the most eminent of the Christian fathers, succeeding Eusebius in the see of Cæsarea in 370. His leadership in this capacity was a principal factor in the triumph of Christianity in the Eastern Empire. In his *Rule of St. Basil,* he laid down a constitution for monastic institutions long followed in the East. Saint Basil made several unsuccessful attempts to reunite the two hostile churches of the East and the West.

Basile, Giambattista (1575-1632), Italian poet and compiler of tales, was born in Naples. Basile wrote under the pseudonym Giam Alesio Abbattutis, and served as a soldier, 1604-07. He collected and recorded Neapolitan fairy tales and folklore under the title *Pentamerone, Lo Cunto de li Cunti* (1637). In 1893 Sir Richard Burton translated the volume into English. Basile also wrote moral and satirical dialogues in verse.

Baskerville, John (1706-75), English printer, began as a footman and rose to the position of writing master in Birmingham. By 1740 he was managing a successful business. In 1750 he began experimenting with printing types, and he produced unexcelled letter-founding types. Combined with highly glossed paper and ink of his own manufacture, he created an extremely readable type still in use today. Baskerville's first printing was a royal quarto of Virgil. Among his fine editions were works of Milton, Juvenal, Horace, Congreve, Addison, Catullus, the Bible, and the Greek New Testament. In 1758 Baskerville became official printer for Cambridge University.

Baskin, Leonard (1922-   ), sculptor and graphic artist, was born in New Brunswick, N.J. After serving as a Navy pilot during World War II, he received his B.A. from the New School for Social Research in New York City in 1949. After two years of study abroad, he began teaching at Smith College in 1953. Graphics brought him early fame and won him a Guggenheim fellowship in 1953. Among other works, he illustrated Richmond Lattimore's translation of *The Iliad of Homer.* Baskin conceives man as the central subject of art; his works express not only human dignity, but also moral corruption. His sculptures include *Man with a Dead Bird, The Great Dead Man, Seated Man with Owl, Oppressed Man,* and *Seated Woman.*

Basse, William (c. 1583-1653), English poet, enjoyed the patronage of two Oxfordshire nobles—Lord Wenman and Lord Norrey. Basse's poetry reflects his love of country life and is written in language patterns natural to country people. Basse is best known for his occasional verse, especially a sonnet, *Epitaph on Shakespeare,* and his verses *Sword and Buckler* and the *Angler's Song.* Warwick Bond (1893) first collected Basse's poetry.

Bassett, John Spencer (1867-1928), American historian and educator, was born at Tarboro, N.C., was educated at Trinity College, N.C., and Johns Hopkins; became professor of history at Trinity College, 1893, and at Smith College, 1906. In 1907-08, he was a lecturer at Yale and, in 1909, at New York University. His publications include *The Federalist System, A Short History of the United States,* and *The Lost Fruits of Waterloo.*

Basso, (Joseph) Hamilton (1904-64), American novelist and biographer, was born in New Orleans, and studied law at Tulane University. He worked as a reporter for the New Orleans *Item,* then worked for the *Times-Picayune.* He contributed essays and short stories to magazines and anthologies, and wrote a biography of General P. G. T. Beauregard. His novels, which give satirical pictures of Southern society, include *Cinnamon Seed, In Their Own Image, Courthouse Square, Days Before Lent* (Southern Authors' Award in 1940), *Wine of the Country, The View from Pompey's Head,* and *A Touch of the Dragon.*

Bataille, Felix Henry (1872-1922), French poet and playwright, was born in Nîmes. He entered the École des Beaux Arts in 1890, but later turned to drama. His first play, *La Belle aux bois dormant* (1894) failed but his first publication of verse, *La chambre blanche,* made a name for him. His next play, *Le lépreuse* was a success. Essentially a Romanticist, he produced several popular plays on the theme of passion, showing it to play a more important part in the lives of his characters than their beliefs or intellectual capacities. His plays include *Maman Colibry* (1904), *La marche nuptiale* (1905), *Poliche* (1907), *La femme nue* (1908), and *La scandale* (1909), his most acclaimed work. Later works deal with social and psychological problems and include *La vierge folle* (1910), *Les flambeaux* (1912), *L'Homme à la rose* (1921), *La divine tragédie* (1916), *La possession* (1922), and *La chair humaine* (1922).

Bates, H(erbert) E(rnest) (1905-74), English author, was born in Rushden and educated at the Grammar School in Kettering. From 1941 to 1946 Bates served in the Royal Air Force; he was commissioned by the R.A.F. to write stories from his experiences, which he published under the pseudonym Flying Officer X. Bates achieved popularity in England and the U.S. for his short stories. He contributed many articles to newspapers and wrote reviews for the *Spectator* and the *Morning Post.* Some of his novels are *Fair Stood the Wind for France, The Jacaranda Tree, Sleepless Moon,* and *The Golden Oriole.*

Bates, Henry Walter (1825-92), English naturalist and traveler, was born at Leicester. He began life as a hosiery clerk, but became interested in natural science through early acquaintance with A. R. Wallace, whom he joined on a collecting trip to the Amazon. He spent three years collecting in the vicinity of Para and seven years on the upper Amazon. After many hardships, he returned to England in 1859, having found 8000 species of insects new to science.

After returning from the tropics, in 1863, he published a delightful book, *The Naturalist on the River Amazon,* which is a classic of scientific travel. In 1864, he became assistant secretary of the Royal Geographical Society, editing the *Transactions* and numerous books, including Belt's *Naturalist in Nicaragua.* In his paper on *Fauna of the Amazon Valley,* he stated and solved the problem of mimicry and protective coloration. According to Darwin, Bates is second only to Humboldt in describing the animal and plant life of the tropical forest.

Bates, Katharine Lee (1859-1929), American author and educator, was born in Falmouth, Mass. Following graduation from Wellesley College, 1880, she taught in Natick High School, 1880-81, and in Dana Hall, 1881-85. She became instructor in English at Wellesley College in 1885 and was professor of English literature there from 1891 to 1925. Besides charming poetry for children, she wrote the hymn "America the Beautiful." Her works include *Rose and Thorn, Fairy Gold, Sigurd, The Golden Collie and Other Comrades of the Road,* and *Yellow Clover.*

Baudelaire (*bo'd'-lâr'*), **Charles Pierre (1821-67),** French poet, was born at Paris. Orphaned of his father at six years of age, he was brought up by guardians who sent him on a trip to India in 1841 on account of the irregularities of his conduct. His two-year stay there left its imprint on his poetry, the first volume of which appeared in 1857 under the title *Fleurs du mal,* "Flowers of Evil." The consummate art which these poems displayed impressed the public less than his selection of morbid subjects and many of them were banned at the time as obscene. Full appreciation of their merit was delayed until the 20th century. Attracted to the works of Edgar Allan Poe, he produced masterpieces of translation in rendering them into French. Involved in the failure of his publisher, he settled in Belgium, where he resorted to drink and opium and spent his last two years in sanitariums.

Bauernfeld, Eduard von (1802-90), Austrian dramatist, studied philosophy and law at the University of Vienna. Influenced by his friend, the Austrian playwright Franz Grillparzer, his plays were mostly comic portrayals of Viennese society. He also reflected Austria's social and political concerns, and was in the forefront of the liberal movement. Bauernfeld dominated the Vienna theater for some 50 years. His plays include *Die Bekenntnisse, Burgerlich und romantisch, Grossjahrig, Krisen,* and *Aus der Gesellschaft.* His collected works were published in 12 volumes, 1871-73.

Baugh, Albert C(roll) (1891-   ), American educator and philologist, was born in Philadelphia, and educated at the University of Pennsylvania, where he began as an instructor in 1912 and advanced to chairman of the Department of English, 1944-57. Baugh edited a number of literary works and produced noted scholarly writings of his own, including *A History of the English Language* and *The Middle English Period, 1100-1500,* contained in *A Literary History of England.*

Baxter, George (1804-67), English printer and engraver, was born at Lewes, Sussex (where he learned engraving), and moved to London in 1827. There he invented a patented process of color printing that made available reproductions of paintings on a mass scale. He obtained his patent in 1835. He collaborated with the publisher G. Mudie in supplying color illustrations for new volumes, and worked for the London Missionary Society, producing prints depicting missionary history. Although patronized by important personages, Baxter never seems to have gained a great fortune. He retired in 1860 and died in Sydenham in 1867.

Bayard (*ba'yar'*), **Pierre du Terrail, Chevalier (1473-1524),** French knight, was born near Grenoble. In an expedition against Naples, serving under Charles VIII, and in the wars against the English and the Spaniards, he distinguished himself by his bravery and nobility of character. In the reign of Francis I, he gained a great victory for the king at Marignano and defended the city of Mezieres against Charles V, for which he was called the "savior of his country." He is known as "the knight without fear and without reproach," without rival as an exemplar of chivalric virtue. He was killed in a battle at the river Sesia, Italy.

Bayle (*běl*), **Pierre (1647-1706),** French philosopher and critic, was born at Carlat. He studied philosophy under the Jesuits at Toulouse and, for a year and a half, turned Catholic. To escape ecclesiastical censure, he withdrew to Geneva and from there to Coppet, on the lake of Geneva, where he studied the philosophy of Descartes. After a few years, he returned to France; in 1675, he was elected to the chair of philosophy at Sedan and, in 1681, at Rotterdam.

In 1684, Bayle began to write *Nouvelles de la republique des lettres,* one of the most successful attempts at a popular journal of literary criticism. He devoted much of his leisure to the *Dictionnaire his-*

torique et critique. This work, the first published under his own name, exercised an immense influence over literature and philosophy; its destructive criticism of accepted history and philosophy became the foundation of 18th century rationalism.

Bazin, Germain (1901-   ), art critic and historian, was born in a suburb of Paris. His education, beyond the University of Paris and the Sorbonne, included study at the *École du Louvre,* where, in 1951, he became curator in chief of the museum. He writes chiefly on paintings.

Bazin, René (1853-1932), French novelist, born in the province of Anjou, studied for the priesthood and, then turned to the gaining a doctor of laws degree from the University of Paris. He wrote constantly and eventually turned to literature entirely. Bazin had a strong feeling for the land, and for the peasant's love of the soil. Some of his books, available in translation, are *A Blot of Ink* (1892), *Autumn Glory* (1901), *Redemption* (1908), *The Coming Harvest* (1908), *The Barrier* (1910), *The Children of Alsace* (1912), and *Those of His Own Household* (1914).

Beach, Rex Ellingwood (1877-1949), American author and playwright, was born at Atwood, Mich.; was educated at Rollins College, Winter Park, Fla.; studied law in Chicago two years between 1896 and 1900. Devoting himself to writing, he became widely known for his stories of adventure, which include *Pardners, The Spoilers, Going Some, The Ne'er-Do-Well, The Net, The Mating Call,* and *Jungle Gold.* He dramatized *Going Some* (with Armstrong) and *The Spoilers* (with McArthur).

Beard, Charles Austin (1874-1948), American historian, was born near Knightstown, Ind. He was educated at De Pauw, Oxford, Cornell, and Columbia universities, in the last of which he taught from 1907 to 1917. He was director of the Training School for Public Service, New York City, from 1917 to 1922 and adviser on municipal affairs to Japanese authorities for the next two years. Beginning in 1904, he wrote and edited a long series of books, mainly historical and written from an economic viewpoint, which placed him in the front rank of interpreters of contemporary life. His *Rise of American Civilization,* written with his wife Mary, is the best known of his works, which include also *American City Government, The Economic Basis of Politics,* and *America in Midpassage.*

Beard, Daniel Carter (1850-1941), artist and pioneer leader of the Boy Scouts, was born in Cincinnati, Ohio. He was educated at Covington, Kentucky, and studied at the Art Students League in New York City, 1880-84. As a result of his interest in outdoor life, he wrote *American Boys' Handy Book* (1882), and later organized "The Boy Pioneers, Sons of Daniel Boone." After the Boy Scout movement was founded in England and the U.S., the Sons of Daniel Boone joined with them, and Beard became a national officer. A painter and illustrator, Beard was the author of books for boys on aspects of scouting. He also served as an associate editor of *Boy's Life* magazine, and was an illustrator for some of Mark Twain's books. Beard served as national scout commissioner until his death, and received the only Golden Eagle Badge of scouting ever awarded.

Beardsley, Aubrey Vincent (1872-98), English black-and-white illustrator, was born at Brighton, England. Encouraged by Whistler, he became art editor of *The Yellow Book* at the age of twenty-two, but much of his own work appeared later in *The Savoy.* His strikingly original and highly decorative style of drawing attracted much attention and influenced many artists. Among the books which he illustrated now sought for by collectors are Mallory's *Morte d' Arthur,* Oscar Wilde's *Salome,* Pope's *Rape of the Lock,* and Jonson's *Volpone.*

Beattie, James (1735-1803), Scottish author, was born at Laurencekirk, Kincardine. He studied at Marischal College, where he was appointed to the chair of moral philosophy and logic in 1760. His early poems attracted little attention until "Minstrel" (Part I, 1771; Part II, 1774), a descriptive poem written in the Spenserian stanza. He is most famous for his *Essay on the Nature and Immutability of Truth* (1770), a refutation of the philosophy of David Hume. Beattie was well received by George III, who gave him a pension, and when urged by the Bishop of London to take orders in the Church of England, he refused. In London he became friends with Sir Joshua Reynolds, Johnson, Goldsmith, and Burke. In 1783 he published *Dissertations, Moral and Critical* and *The Evidences of the Christian Religion,* written at the request of the Bishop of London.

Beatty, Warren (1937-   ), actor and writer, was born in Richmond, Va., the brother of actress Shirley McLaine. He attended Northwestern University for a year and then went to New York to study acting. In the 1950's he held many jobs—playing at bars, acting in stock theater and television; after a screen test he went to Hollywood. He became politically active in the late 1960's. Some of his movies include *Splendor in the Grass* (1961), *Roman Spring of Mrs. Stone* (1961), *Promise Her Anything* (1966), and *Bonnie and Clyde* (1967). With Harry Towne he wrote the filmscript for *Shampoo* (1975) and with Elaine May the filmscript for *Heaven Can Wait* (1978).

Beaumarchais (*bō'mär'shě'*)**, Pierre Augustin Caron de (1732-99),** French dramatist and poet, the son of a watchmaker named Caron, was born at Paris. He married a widow, Madame Franquet, in 1757 and from a little property of hers took the aristocratic name of Beaumarchais. In 1768, he married a second time, obtaining on this occasion a splendid fortune with his wife. Meanwhile devoting himself to literature, he produced *Eugenie,* a drama in five acts; *Les deux amis, ou Le negociant de Lyon; Le barbier de Séville;* and *Le mariage de Figaro.* On the last two of the foregoing his fame now rests.

Beaumont (*bō'mŏnt*)**, Francis (1584-1616),** English poet and dramatist, best known by his literary partnership with John Fletcher, was born at Grace Dieu, Leicestershire. He was educated at Oxford. At 19, he became the friend of Ben Jonson. About 1607, his famous friendship with Fletcher began, and so intimate did the two friends become that they lived in the same house until Beaumont's marriage in 1613. Their joint works comprise some fifty plays, among the best of which are *Philaster, The Maid's Tragedy,* and *The Faithful Shepherdess.* In some of their plays Massinger collaborated, and certain passages in *The Two Noble Kinsmen* are by Shakespeare.

Beaumont, Sir John (1583?-1627), English poet, entered Broadgate Hall, Oxford, in 1597, and the Inner Temple a year later. He inherited Grace-Dieu priory at Charnwood, Leicestershire, in 1605, married, and had 11 children. His poetic style was clear and natural and contributed to the development of the heroic couplet. He wrote *The Metamorphosis of Tobacco* in 1602, a poem which reflects the myths of Ovid, and *A Crowne of Thornes,* a poem contained in 12 books, which was never printed. Through the Duke of Buckingham, whose mother was a Beaumont, he won the favor of James I and Charles I, who made him a baronet in 1627. His other works include a dramatic entertainment, *The Theater of Apollo, Bosworth Field, with a Taste of the Variety of other Poems,* left by Sir John Beaumont (published in 1629).

Beauvoir, Simone de (1908-   ), French novelist and philosopher, was born in Paris and educated at the Sorbonne. From 1931 to 1943 she taught philosophy at girls' schools in Marseilles, Rouen, and Paris, and then became a full-time writer. A close friend of Jean-Paul Sartre, she and Sartre are the leaders of the French intellectuals and the foremost Existentialist philosophers. Together they edit *Les Temps Modernes,* an existentialist magazine. While some of her novels have been poorly received, her essays and philosophical writings have made her a legend in her own time. She was awarded the Goncourt Prize in 1954 for *The Mandarins*. *The Second Sex* is an impressive study of the status of women, declaring that woman's secondary role has deprived her of human dignity. Other works are *The Blood of Others, Les Bouches Inutiles* (play), *She Came to Stay, Brigitte Bardot and the Lolita Syndrome, The Ethics of Ambiguity, Memoirs of a Dutiful Daughter, Djamala Boupacha*, and *A Very Easy Death*.

Beaverbrook, William Maxwell Aitken, First Baron (1879-1964), British publisher and administrator, was born near London, Ont., and was taken soon to Newcastle, N. B. He entered the brokerage business in Montreal. Asked by a bank to examine a merger plan for three cement mills, he succeeded in 1910 in bringing about an amalgamation of all Canadian cement companies, from which operation he netted a large fortune.

Having thus reached his predetermined goal of making a million pounds sterling, he retired from business to enter politics in England. Winning a seat in the House of Commons, he became secretary to Bonar Law, who was leader of the Conservative party from 1911. During World War I he acted as Canadian "Eye Witness" at the front and, in 1918, joined the British cabinet as minister in charge of propaganda. He was raised to the peerage in 1917. He abandoned politics in 1919 and entered publishing, taking over or establishing the *Daily Express*, the *Sunday Express*, and the *Evening Standard*, three London papers whose success brought their publisher into the front rank of British journalism.

In 1940, when Germany conquered France, and it became evident that air power was of paramount importance, Lord Beaverbrook was placed in charge of aircraft production. He was made minister of state and minister of supply in 1941 and was Lord Privy Seal, 1943-45.

Beccaria, Marchese di, Cesare Bonesana (1738-94), Italian author, criminologist, and economist, was born in Milan and studied at the Jesuit College of Parma and the University of Padua. He is remembered for his *Trato dei Delitti e delle Pene (Treatise on Crimes and Punishments)*, published when he was 26. Despite Beccaria's scant background on the subject, the work had influence throughout the world. He opposed capital punishment, the first modern writer to do so. He also opposed torture to extract confessions, legal delay, and secret judicial proceedings. He advocated informing the public of penalities for crimes, stressing prevention of crime over punishment. His work aroused such strong public feeling that reforms were instituted in many countries. Incorporated into the Bill of Rights, many of his ideas are familiar to U.S. citizens.

Beccaria made important contributions in other fields. *Ricerche intorno alla Natura dello Stilo* was a philosophical grammar and theory of style. He and his friends published the journal *Il Caffe*, containing treatises on style and rhetoric. One of the first to apply mathematics to economic analysis, Beccaria wrote *Elementi de economia publica*. In 1768, a chair of political economics was created for him at Milan, and from 1771 he served in various public offices, including magistrate and counselor of state.

Becket, Thomas à (c. 1118-70), English prelate, son of a merchant, was born at London; studied at Oxford, Paris, and Bologna; and, on his return home, entered the Church. Henry II made him high chancellor and preceptor to Prince Henry in 1155, admitted him to the closest intimacy and confidence, and, in 1162, raised him to the archbishopric of Canterbury. Becket immediately gave up his courtier habits, assumed a rigid austerity of manner, and became an uncompromising champion of the privileges of the clergy. A violent contest ensued between the sovereign and the prelate, and the latter was at length obliged to flee from the kingdom. In 1170, howev-

er, he was restored, and he instantly renewed his resistance to the monarch. Irritated by this fresh provocation, Henry uttered a hasty speech, which four of his knights not unnaturally construed into a command to rid him of the pertinacious archbishop. They accordingly hastened to Canterbury and murdered Becket in the cathedral. He was canonized in 1172. The king later did penance at Becket's tomb.

Beckett, Samuel (1906-   ), novelist and playwright, was born in Dublin. After graduating from Trinity College in 1927, he went to Paris, then returned to Trinity to teach French, 1931-32. He then contributed poems and stories to avant-garde periodicals. In 1937, he settled in Paris, and during World War II, he worked with the French resistance. After the war he continued writing and strongly influenced contemporary theater with *Waiting For Godot* (1952). In this play, as in other works, Beckett reveals man wandering aimlessly, trying to find unity and order in the world, always with the element of hope. He was selected Nobel laureate for literature in 1969. His novels include *Murphy, Watt, Molloy, Malone Dies, The Unnameable*, and *Sans*. His plays include *Endgame, Krapp's Last Tape*, and *How It Is*.

Beckford, William (1759-1844), English writer, who was born at Fonthill, Wiltshire, inherited a fortune and traveled extensively on the Continent. From this experience he wrote unusual journals and letters published as *Dreams, Waking Thoughts and Incidents* (1783). These were later revised as *Italy, with Sketches of Spain and Portugal* (1834). Beckford's best-known work was *Vathek*, an imaginative romance in the "oriental" style, originally written in French and then published anonymously in an English version in 1786. Beckford burlesqued contemporary romantic novels in *Modern Novel Writing, or the Elegant Enthusiast* (1796) and *Azemia* (1797). The son of a former lord mayor of London, Beckford spent two periods (1784-94 and 1806-20) as a member of the House of Commons.

Becque (*bĕk*), **Henri François (1837-99)**, French dramatist, was born at Paris. He was a journalist and, for a time, was engaged in banking. His literary abilities were first made known by his libretto for the opera *Sardanapale* in 1867; but his earliest plays, *Michel Pauper* and *The Elopement*, written about 1870, met with little recognition, and his most important plays were rejected for several years. The production of *The Crows*, however, at the National Theater at Paris in 1882, together with that of *The Parisian Woman* in 1885, marked the beginning of the modern French naturalistic school, of which Becque is now universally acknowledged as the originator.

Becquer (*ba-kâr'*), **Gustavo Adolfo, (1836-70)**, Spanish poet and novelist, was born at Seville. His bizarre and fantastic tales, written after the manner of Poe and Hoffmann, proved very popular. He wrote several volumes of poems and legends. Of these, the best known is his *Leyendas espanolas*. An excellent translation of this work under the title *Romantic Legends of Spain*, was published in 1909 by Cornelia Frances Bates and her daughter Katharine Lee Bates.

Beddoes, Thomas Lovell (1803-49), English writer and physician, was born in Clifton. Educated at Oxford, he published his drama *The Bride's Tragedy* in 1822. In 1825 he went to Gottingen, where he studied medicine and continued to write. He then led a wandering life as a doctor in Germany and Switzerland, with occasional visits to England. In 1849 he committed suicide in Basel; a year later his *Death's Jest Book*, a drama influenced by Shelley and by Elizabethan dramas of blood and revenge, appeared. A volume of poems was published in 1851. Beddoes' complete works and a volume of letters were edited by Edmund Gosse (1890-94).

Bede (*bed*), or **Baeda** (*be da*) **(c. 673-735)**, called "the Venerable," English monk, scholar, and church historian, was born in the county of Durham. He is said to have been the most learned Englishman of his day. In the seclusion of his cell, he wrote his important *Ecclesiastical History of England,* which was translated from the Latin into Anglo-Saxon by King Alfred; also a number of commentaries, homilies, hymns, and lives of the saints.

Beebe, William (1877-1962), American ornithologist and author, was born at Brooklyn, N.Y., and was educated at Columbia University. In 1899, he was appointed honorary curator of ornithology by the New York Zoological society and became director of the British Guiana Zoological Station in the same year. In 1934, with Otis Barton, he descended into the ocean in a bathysphere to a depth of over 3000 feet, a feat which he later described in *Half Mile Down.* To his skill as an observer he added an artistry of language exemplified in these works among others: *Edge of the Jungle, Galapagos, Arcturus, Beneath Tropic Seas,* and *Zaca Venture.* His more recent books include *Unseen Life of New York* (1953) and *Adventuring with Beebe* (1955).

Beecher, Henry Ward (1813-87), preacher, theologian, lecturer, orator, third son of Lyman Beecher, was born at Litchfield, Conn., was graduated at Amherst College in 1834; and studied theology under his father at Lane Seminary, Cincinnati. After a pastorate of ten years in two churches in Indiana, he removed to Brooklyn and assumed charge of Plymouth Church, "an organization of orthodox Congregational believers." For many years he drew one of the largest and most influential regular congregations in the United States. On the slavery question, he was emphatically an abolitionist. For neary 20 years, he was editor of the New York *Independent,* and, in 1870, he became editor of the *Christian Union.* His most important works include *Lectures to Young Men, Industry and Idleness,* and the *Life of Christ.* Elected to the American Hall of Fame, 1900.

Beecher, Lyman (1775-1863), preacher and theologian, was born at New Haven, Conn.; was graduated at Yale College; and began preaching at East Hampton, L. I., where he remained until 1810. He then went to Litchfield, Conn., where were born the two most famous of his thirteen children,—Henry Ward and Harriet (Mrs. Stowe). All his sons, of whom there were seven, became clergymen. In 1826, he became pastor of Hanover Street church, Boston, from which he went to Cincinnati as head of Lane Theological Seminary. He remained there 20 years, in the course of which he was tried and acquitted by the Church courts on the charge of preaching false doctrine. Beecher ranked among the foremost orators and preachers of his time.

Beerbohm, Sir Max (1872-1956), writer and caricaturist, was born in London; was educated at Oxford; in 1910, married Florence Kahn, of Memphis, Tenn.; and afterward took up his residence in Rapallo, Italy. His publications include *The Happy Hypocrite, Zuleika Dobson,* and *And Even Now.* His caricatures, noted for their delicate and incisive satire, have been exhibited in art galleries at London and elsewhere. Many of them have been collected and published under various titles, including *The Second Childhood of John Bull, The Poet's Corner,* and *Fifty Caricatures.* He was knighted in 1939.

Beers, Clifford Whittingham (1876-1943), American reformer, founder of the mental hygiene movement, was born in New Haven, Conn. Three years after being graduated from Yale University in 1897, he became insane. Despite the cruel treatment he received, which was at that time usual in handling insane patients, he recovered his sanity by 1903 and devoted his later years to the creation of a more wholesome and scientific attitude toward mental disease, its prevention, and its treatment. He wrote his experiences in *A Mind That Found Itself.* Through the National Committee for Mental Hygiene, organized in 1909, he was the leading spirit in carrying forward an educational movement directed toward the removal of emotional maladjustments which underlie much juvenile delinquency, crime, mental disease, and personal unhappiness.

Beethoven (*bā′tō-věn; băt′hō-*), **Ludwig van (1770-1827),** German composer of instrumental music, was born at Bonn, Prussia. In his fourth year, he was compelled by his father to practice daily on the harpsichord. Beethoven's musical taste was intellectual rather than intuitive, and it had to be awakened before his interest was excited. Pfeiffer and Van der Eden laid the foundation of his technical skill, and Neefe made him familiar with the grand conceptions of Bach and Handel.

When eleven years old, Beethoven appeared in The Netherlands as a piano virtuoso, chiefly in Bach's music, and was made the assistant of Neefe at the organ in the Elector's chapel. In 1787, he went to Vienna, at the expense of the Elector of Cologne, to study with Mozart; but he was soon recalled to Bonn by the illness of his mother, and, at her death, he became the main support of the family. He now began giving lessons and making occasional public appearances.

LIFE IN VIENNA. In 1792, Beethoven went to Vienna, where, with the exception of a few short journeys for business or pleasure, he remained for the rest of his life. The first five years of his residence there were the happiest he ever knew. He had excellent patrons; he was received in the best society; and, in his study under Haydn and Albrechtsberger, he made rapid progress in the study of musical form.

About 1795, he made his debut in Vienna as a pianist, and, with his "Concerto in C major," he won instant recognition. His "Opus I," containing three trios for the piano, appeared this same year. As a relaxation from music, Beethoven's ardent interest in general literature received a fresh impetus at this time. His absorption in reading tended in some measure to soften the afflictions which afterward fell to his lot. From about 1798, he was troubled with a defect in hearing, and his sensitive nature was greatly perturbed. By 1814, the loss of his hearing was complete, and this so sorely affected him that his compositions were tinged with a passionate melancholy.

Before the end of 1800, Beethoven had composed twenty sonatas for the pianoforte, a large number of trios and quartets, and his first and second symphonies. A pension was at length settled upon him on condition that he continue to reside in Austria. These years were productive; among his works were a sonata containing the well-known funeral march, the "Moonlight Sonata," the "Kreutzer Sonata," the "Heroic Symphony," and his one opera *Fidelio,* written in 1805.

Beethoven's fourth, fifth, and sixth symphonies were composed between 1805 and 1810; the music to Kotzebue's "Ruins of Athens" was first performed in 1812; the "Battle Symphony," in 1813; the cantata "The Glorious Moment," in 1814; and the eighth symphony was written in 1814, when he was totally deaf. The principal productions of the last ten years of his life were several sonatas for the pianoforte; the grand "Mass in D," a three years' labor; the "Overture in C, opus 115"; the ninth symphony with chorus, the greatest of his productions, completed in 1823; and the last grand quartets.

Though he was surrounded in Vienna by friends and admirers, Beethoven led a solitary life. During his last four years, he lived in want and privation in order that he might bequeath more to a nephew, who, although ungrateful for kindnesses, nevertheless continued to receive from the musician a lifelong and extravagant affection.

Beethoven's letters and journals have been published in several editions. Among his extensive correspondence is a passionate love letter, *An die unsterbliche Geliebte* ("To the immortal beloved"), which was found on his desk after his death. Its addressee has been the subject of wide speculation, none of it conclusive. There are also a number of his love letters to Countess Josephine Deym.

CHARACTER AND GENIUS. Beethoven was characterized by genuine simplicity and sincerity. His temperament, reacted upon by his deafness, led him to turn the energies of his soul within, and it is to his music that we look for the deepest expressions of his heart. He felt all phases of human emotion and expressed all. The simple emotion of confiding youth, then a sense of life's perplexities with the courage that surmounts them, and, finally, the exhaustion of a soul broken by struggle, which renounces earthly affections and thirsts for ideal, solitary communion with the Infinite—such is the immense circle which his genius embraced.

Beets, Nikolaas (1814-1903), Dutch poet and author, was born in Haarlem and educated at the University of Leiden. In 1874 he became professor of theology at the University of Utrecht. Considered one of the best pieces of 19th century Dutch prose was his *Camera Obscura* (1839), published under the pseudonym of Hildebrand. He wrote poetic tales such as *Ada van Holland* (1846) and *Guy de Vlaming* (1853). Among his many lyric songs are *Korenbloemen* (1853), *Nieuwe Gedichten* (1857), *Verstrooide Gedichten* (1862) and *Harptoonen* (1892).

Behan, Brendan (1923-64), Irish playwright, was born in Dublin and attended Catholic schools until he was expelled in 1936. He then joined the Irish Republican Army as a messenger. Over the next decade and a half he was arrested and imprisoned several times for his activities. Finally he was forced to leave Ireland for France in 1952, but returned to Dublin before he died. His plays include *Quare Fellow* (1956), *Borstal Boy* (1958), and *The Hostage* (1958, London and 1960, New York). He also wrote a collection of travel notes, jokes, two short stories, and a play, which were published as *Brendan Behan's Island: An Irish Sketchbook* (1962).

Behn, Aphra (1640-89), English playwright, novelist, and poet, was born in Wye, Kent, and spent several years in Surinam with relatives. She returned to England about 1658, married, and upon her husband's death became a British spy in Antwerp and Holland during the Dutch War. The first Englishwoman to succeed as a professional writer, she produced numerous plays noted for their wit. *The Feign'd Courtezans, Forc'd Marriage, The Rover,* and *The Lucky Chance* are some of her best. Her friendship with a prince of Surinam formed the basis for her novel *Oroonoko, or the Royal Slave.* Quite popular in the 18th century, her works have also been reprinted in the 20th century. She was buried in Westminster Abbey.

Behn, Harry (1898-1973), American author of books and poetry for children, was born in McCabe, Ariz., and was educated at Standford and Harvard. He wrote motion picture scenarios from 1925 to 1935 and taught creative writing at the University of Arizona from 1938 to 1947. Behn's poetry appears in anthologies for children. He translated Japanese haiku poetry and works by Rainer Maria Rilke. Behn's books, written and illustrated for children, include *All Kinds of Time, The Wizard in the Well, The Painted Cave, The Faraway Lurs, Cricket Songs,* and *Omen of the Birds.* He founded and edited the *Arizona Quarterly,* 1942-47.

Behrman, S(amuel) N(athaniel) (1893-1973), American dramatist, was born in Worcester, Mass., and was educated at Clark College (Worcester, Mass.), Harvard, and Columbia. Before 1927 he was a book reviewer for the New York *Times* and the *New Republic.* Although it took him eleven years to sell his first play, *The Second Man,* he was later continuously successful. He specialized in high comedy, and also wrote screenplays and dialogue for numerous motion pictures. Some of his plays are *Meteor, Biography, Serena Blandish, Amphitryon 38, No Time for Comedy, I know My Love, Fanny* (musical), *Lord Pengo,* and *But For Whom Charlie.* In 1944 Behrman and Franz Werfel received the New York Drama Critics' Award for *Jacobowsky and the Colonel.* Behrman's film credits include *Queen Christina* (starring Greta Garbo), an adaptation of *A Tale of Two Cities, Quo Vadis* (with others), and film versions of many of his own plays.

Belasco (be-lăs'kō), **David (1854-1931),** dramatic manager and playwright, was born at San Francisco, and was educated at Lincoln College, California. Through his skill in training actors for specific roles and the remarkable success of his methods of stage lighting and stage setting, he became widely known as a producing manager. He was also the author or collaborator of 200 plays, including *Zaza, The Wife, The Girl of the Golden West, The Return of Peter Grimm.*

Belitt, Ben (1911-　), American poet, was born in New York City, and lived in an orphanage until he was ten. At that time he moved back with his mother and stepfather and began to write.

In 1936-37 he was assistant editor for the *Nation,* encouraged in his work by Joseph Wood Krutch. In 1938 he began teaching at Bennington College. He was awarded the Shelley Memorial Award for Poetry in 1936 and the National Institute of Arts and Letters Award in 1965. His volumes of poetry include *The Five-Fold Mesh, Wilderness Stair,* and *The Enemy Joy.* He translated works of Rimbaud, Federico Garcia Lorca, Pablo Neruda, and Rafael Alberti.

Bell, Marvin (1937-　), poet, was born in New York City and attended Alfred University, Syracuse University, the University of Chicago, and the University of Iowa, where he later taught. His books include *Poems for Nathan and Saul* (1966), *A Probable Volume of Dreams* (1969), *The Escape Into You* (1971), and *Residue of Spring* (1974).

Bellamy (běl'a-mĭ), **Edward (1850-98),** American novelist and economist, was born at Chicopee Falls, Mass. He was educated in Germany; was admitted to the bar; was on the staff of the New York *Evening Post* in 1871-72; and, on his return from the Hawaiian Islands in 1877, founded the Springfield *News.* He is best known by his novels *Looking Backward* and *Equality,* both socialistic works.

Bellarmine (běl lär'mĭn), **Robert, St. (1542-1621),** theologian and nephew of Pope Marcellus II, was born at Montepulciano, Italy. He entered the Society of Jesus in 1560, was ordained in 1570, was appointed the first Jesuit professor of philosophy at the Univ. of Louvain (1569-76), began teaching at the Univ. of Rome in 1576. In 1590 he became director of the Roman College. Bellarmine was created a cardinal by Pope Clement VIII in 1598; he was Archbishop of Capua for two years. In 1923, Pope Pius XI beatified him; his feast is May 13. Many of his writings were directed against Protestant dogmas and the concept of the divine right of kings; he strongly supported the doctrine of papal supremacy. His writings include *Disputations on the Controversies of the Christian Faith* and *Of Papal Power.*

Bellay, Joachim du (1522-60), French poet and critic, was born in Lire, France. He was a member of the Pléiade, a group of writers who wished to raise the standards of the French language to the classical level. He wrote *The Defense and Illustration of the French Language* in 1549. In 1553 he went with Jean Cardinal du Bellay to Italy, which inspired him to write *Les antiquités de Rome* and *Les Regrets.* With his return to Paris, he became Canon of Notre Dame, and before his death was nominated archbishop of Bordeaux. He and Pierre de Ronsard are considered the founders of the French school of Renaissance poetry.

Bellman (běl'män), **Karl Mikael (1740-95),** Swedish poet, was born at Stockholm. He became court secretary in 1775. His later and more brilliant pieces are chiefly idyllic or humorous songs, for which he also furnished original melodies. The best specimens of his genius, which is of a rare order, are to be found in the collections prepared by himself—*Bachanaliske Ordenskapitlets Handbibliothek, Fredmans Epistlar,* and *Fredmans Sanger.* A monument was erected to his memory at Stockholm in 1829.

Bello, Andrés (1780?-1865), diplomat, scholar, and poet, was born in Caracas, Venezuela. In 1810 he accompanied Simon Bolivar's mission to London to seek aid for South American revolutionists trying to throw off the Spanish yoke, and he stayed in England for 19 years, representing Venezuela, Colombia, and Chile. He left England in 1829 and moved to Chile. There, in 1834, he was appointed secretary of state, in 1843 first rector of the University of Santiago. He wrote works on law, philosophy, and philology, including the *Principles of International Law* (1832), for many years a standard textbook

Belloc (bĕ-lŏk'), **Hilaire Joseph Peter (1870-1953),** English writer and politician, was born in France, of French-English parentage. He was graduated at Balliol College, Oxford, 1895, and soon devoted himself to writing. By the range and the quality of his novels, essays, books of travel, and other works, he won an enviable position in English letters. He was member of the House of Commons, 1906-10. His numerous writings, many of which support a Roman Catholic point of view, include *The Path to Rome, General Sketch of the European War, Joan of Arc, The Crisis of Our Civilization,* and *The Great Heresies.*

Bellow, Saul (1915-   ), American author, was born in Lachine, Quebec, and graduated from Northwestern University in 1937. He taught for four years at the Pestalozzi-Froebel Teachers College in Chicago, then joined the editorial department of the *Encyclopedia Britannica* in 1943. After teaching at various colleges, including the University of Minnesota (1946-48), in 1962 he was appointed a professor at the University of Chicago. In his writings he reveals a concern for the individual in an indifferent society; many of his novels deal with contemporary Jewish life in America. He won the National Book Award for *The Adventures of Augie March* (1953) and *Herzog* (1964). Other works are *Dangling Man, The Victim, Seize the Day, The Last Analysis,* and *Mr. Sammler's Planet.* In 1975 he won the Pulitzer prize for *Humboldt's Gift.* For the body of his work, Bellow was awarded the Nobel Prize in 1976, the first American to win the prize since John Steinbeck in 1962.

Bembo (bĕm'bō), **Pietro (1470-1547),** Italian scholar, was born at Venice. In 1513, he was made secretary to Pope Leo X and, in 1539, was made a cardinal by Paul III, who afterward appointed him to the dioceses of Gubbio and Bergamo. Bembo was the restorer of the classic style in both Latin and Italian literature. Among the most famous of his works are a short treatise on Italian prose, which marked an era in Italian grammar; *Gli Asolani,* a dialogue; and a *History of Venice.*

Bemelmans, Ludwig (1898-1962), Austrian-American painter, illustrator, and writer, was born in Meran (now Merano, Italy), moving to the U.S. in 1914. He was naturalized and joined the army four years later. He worked in restaurants before the war as a busboy, and after his discharge as a waiter and then as a manager. *Hansi* (1934), his first children's book, was followed in 1939 by *Madeline,* which is considered a classic of children's literature. Bemelman's adult novels, *Now I Lay Me Down to Sleep* (1943), *Dirty Eddie* (1947), *Are You Hungry, Are You Cold* (1960), and *The Street Where the Heart Lies* (1963), are mainly satirical.

Benavente, Jacinto (1866-1954), Spanish poet and dramatist, was born at Madrid, son of a noted physician. He was educated in his native city and studied law at the university there. Upon his father's death in 1885, he gave up plans for a legal career and devoted himself to literature. From 1885 to 1892, he traveled in France, England, and Russia, and later became an actor. In 1893, he published a small book of verse and a volume of plays entitled *The Fantastic Theater.* This was the beginning of a career of great brilliance and fertility as a dramatic writer and satirist of social institutions. The production in 1913 of the popular *La Malquerida* (Eng. tr., *The Passion Flower),* was followed by his election to a chair in the Spanish academy. In 1922, he was awarded the Nobel prize for literature.

Benchley, Peter (Bradford) (1940-   ), writer, was born in New York City. His father, Nathaniel, was noted for his stories; his grandfather, Robert, was a well-known humor writer and personality. Graduating from Harvard in 1961, Benchley traveled widely. Drawing on this, he wrote *Time and a Ticket* (1964). He next worked as a reporter for the *Post,* as an editor for *Newsweek,* and as a speechwriter during the Johnson administration. In 1964 he became associate editor of *Newsweek.* His novel *Jaws* (1974) was a best-seller. He was then co-author of the screenplay for the film that followed (1975). He also wrote a children's book, *Jonathan Visits the White House* (1964).

Benchley, Robert Charles (1889-1945), humorist, was born in Worcester, Mass., and graduated from Harvard University in 1912. Benchley excelled in nearly all facets of humorous entertainment. He was dramatic editor of *Life* magazine, 1920-29, and of the *New Yorker,* 1929-40. He published fifteen volumes of writings, including reviews, essays, and poetry. He acted on the stage and in films, and produced more than forty short films; in 1936, "How to Sleep," won the Academy Award for the year's best short film. His books include *From Bed to Worse: or, Comforting Thoughts about the Bison* (1934), *Inside Benchley* (1942), and *Benchley Roundup* (1954).

Benda, Julien (1867-1956), French critic, novelist, and essayist, was born in Paris and educated at the University of Paris. During the First World War he contributed articles to *Figaro,* and he became an opponent of the philosophy of Henri Bergson and the romantic movement. He published novels, philosophical essays, and autobiographical works. He influenced T.S. Eliot, D.B. Wyndham Lewis, and others. Some of his most noted works are *Le Bergsonisme ou une philosophie de la mobilité, On the Success of Bergsonism, The Treason of the Intellectuals,* and *My First Testament.*

Benedict, Ruth (1887-1948), anthropologist, was born in New York City and graduated from Vassar. She was first known for her poetry. She became interested in anthropology under Franz Boas at Columbia, where she took her Ph.D., taught and became head of the department in 1939. In her studies of primitive society, as in *Patterns of Culture* (1934), she observed that specific characteristics are also present and repeated in more advanced cultures. Her other works include *Tales of the Cochiti Indians* (1931), *Zuni Mythology* (1935), and *The Chrysanthemum and the Sword: Patterns of Japanese Culture* (1946).

Benedikt, Michael (1937-   ), writer, was born in New York City and studied at New York University and Columbia. He then worked as a book and magazine editor and wrote on art, music, theater, and films. His books of poetry include *Changes* (1961), *The Body* (1968), *Sky* (1970), and *Mole Notes* (1971).

Benes, Edward (1884-1948), Czech statesman, was born at Kozlany and studied at the University of Prague. During World War I he led in the movement for Czechoslovak independence. In 1918 he became foreign minister of the new nation and a European leader as the organizer of the Little Entente. In 1935 he became president, but in 1938 was forced to surrender to Germany. Resigning, he taught at the University of Chicago. In 1945 he returned home as president, but resigned again in 1948, refusing to accept the Communist constitution. He was the author of *Democracy Today and Tomorrow.*

Benet, Laura (1884-   ), poet and children's writer, was born in Brooklyn, N.Y. She was educated at Willard School and Vassar College and held editorial positions on the book pages of the *New York Evening Post, New York Sun,* and the *New York Times.* She published poems in *Lyric, Voices,* and other reviews. Her books of verse include *Fairy Bread, Basket for a Fair, Is Morning Sure,* and *In Love With Time.* Among her books for young readers are *The Boy Shelley, The Hidden Valley, Enchanting Jenny Lind, Barnum's First Circus and Other Stories,* and *Famous Poets for Young People.*

Benét, Stephen Vincent (1898-1943), American poet, was born at Bethlehem, Pa. After being graduated from Yale University, he devoted his time chiefly to writing. *Five Men and Pompey,* a product of his student days, is the first of a number of works of increasing caliber culminating in the historic poem of epiclike quality, *John Brown's Body,* which won the Pulitzer prize in 1928. Later works include *Burning City, The Devil and Daniel Webster,* and *Tales Before Midnight.* Elected to the American Academy of Arts and Letters in 1938.

Benet, William Rose (1886-1950), poet and critic, was born in Brooklyn, N.Y. After graduating from Yale, he worked in publishing and in 1920 became associate editor of the *Literary Review* of the *New York Post.* In 1924 he founded the *Saturday Review of Literature,* where he remained as poetry critic. His 12 volumes of verse include *The Dust Which Is God,* which won a Pulitzer prize in 1942. He edited the *Collected Poems* of his second wife, Elinor Wylie, after her death. He also edited *The Reader's Encyclopedia* and was coeditor of the *Oxford Anthology of American Literature.* He published four volumes of prose, including the novel, *First Person Singular,* and many critical pieces.

Benn, Gottfried (1886-1956), German writer and critic, was born in Mansfeld, West Prussia, and raised in a Protestant parsonage. Under the influence of Nietzsche, he turned to atheism and nihilism early in life, and his views of life and death influenced other German authors. He used clinical medical language in his poetry, and used diseases as symbols of social disintegration in *Morgue* (1912), *Fleisch* (1916), and *Schutt* (1924), his most important collections of poems.

Bennett, (Enoch) Arnold (1867-1931), English novelist, was born at Hanley in the Potteries. He was educated at Newcastle Middle School and at the University of London. He began life as a law clerk; became editor of a woman's magazine; and, beginning with 1900, devoted himself entirely to literary work, producing, besides numerous essays and plays, a group of novels that include *Anna of the Five Towns, The Old Wive's Tale,* and *The Matador of the Five Towns.* Among his other works are *Clayhanger, Lenora, Denry the Audacious, Your United States, Paris Nights,* and *Our Women.*

Bennett, James Gordon (1795-1872), journalist, was born in Scotland. He studied for the Roman Catholic priesthood, but never took orders. In 1819, he emigrated to America; after teaching in Halifax and later serving as proofreader in Boston, he became a journalist in New York. In 1825, he purchased the *Sunday Courier;* subsequently, 1832, he started the *Globe,* neither project succeeding. In 1835, he issued the first number of *The Herald,* a journal which, through his great ability and enterprise, soon commanded world-wide attention.

His paper was the first to publish the stock lists and a daily financial review; many other original features were afterward added. The collection and dissemination of news was ever his paramount object. His news-gathering staff for four years during the Civil War involved an expense of a half million dollars. At the time of his death, *The Herald* was the most valuable newspaper property in the United States. The first speech ever reported in full by telegraph was sent to *The Herald.*

His son of the same name (1841-1918) carried on and broadened the same journalistic policy, in furtherance of which he financed the expedition of Stanley into Central Africa to find David Livingstone, 1869-71. He established trophies for international yacht, balloon, and airplane races.

Bennett, Lerone, Jr. (1928-   ), American Negro poet, journalist, and historian, was born in Clarksdale, Miss., grew up in Jackson, and was educated at Morehouse College, Atlanta, Ga. He was an editor of the *Atlanta Daily World* and was on the staffs of *Jet* and *Ebony,* advancing to senior editor of *Ebony* in 1960. His poetry was published in anthologies; his books include *Before the Mayflower, The Negro Mood and Other Essays,* and *What Manner of a Man* (a biography of Martin Luther King).

Benoit de Sainte-Maure (also Sainte-More) (flourished c. 1150), French poet and chronicler, wrote lengthy romantic histories in verse. *Roman de Troie* (c. 1160), an account of the siege of Troy, was dedicated to Eleanor of Aquitaine, and *Chronique des ducs de Normandie* (1170-75) was written for her husband, Henry II of England.

Bentham, Jeremy (1748-1832), English writer on ethics and jurisprudence, was born at London. He was admitted to the bar in 1772. Turning from the practice of law to its theory, he became the greatest critic of legislation and government in his day. In all his ethical and political writings the doctrine of utility is the leading and pervading principle, and his favorite vehicle for its expression is the phrase, "the greatest happiness of the greatest number." This phrase was coined by Priestley, though its prominence in politics was due to Bentham.

Bentley, Eric (1916-   ), writer, was born in Bolton, Lancashire, England, and graduated from Oxford and Yale universities. He was professor of dramatic literature at Columbia University, 1953-1969. Among his writings are *A Century of Hero-Worship, In Search of Theatre, The Dramatic Event,* and *The Theatre of Commitment.*

Bentley, Phyllis (Eleanor) (1894-1977), novelist, was born in Halifax, Yorkshire, and attended Cheltenham Ladies' College. After teaching school during World War I, she was a librarian. Her first novel was *The World's Bane* (1918). Later books include *Cat-in-the-Manger* (1923), *Carr* (1929), *Inheritance* (1932), *A Modern Tragedy* (1934), *Freedom, Farewell; The Rise of Henry Morcar* (1946), *Tales of the West Riding* (1965), and *More Tales of the West Riding* (1974). Her nonfiction includes *The English Regional Novel* (1942), *Some Observations on the Art of Narrative* (1946), *The Brontes* (1947), *The Young Brontes* (1960), *The Brontes and Their World* (1969), and *O Dreams, O Destinations* (1962, autobiography).

Bentley, Richard (1662-1742), English classical scholar, was born in Oulton, Yorkshire, and studied at Cambridge and Oxford. He took deacon's orders in 1690, and in 1692 was appointed first Boyle lecturer for the defense of Christianity. In 1693 he was made keeper of the Royal Library, and he joined the Royal Society in 1695. For 30 years he was master of Trinity College, Cambridge, where his attempts to make reforms made him unpopular. Bentley is considered one of the greatest English classical scholars. As Boyle lecturer, one of his best-known writings was *A Confutation of Atheism.* The work that made him famous was his dissertation (1699) *The Epistles of Phalaris,* which proved this second-century work a forgery, although it had previously been praised. Even though Bentley's findings were conclusive, he was harshly criticized, and Pope belittled him in the *Dunciad.* Other important works are his *Terence, Epistola ad Millium,* and *Remarks On a late Discourse of Free Thinking.* Dutch classicists and German classical philologists were strongly influenced by Bentley's scholarship.

Béranger *(bā′räɴ′zhā′)*, **Pierre Jean de (1780-1857)**, French lyric poet, was born of humble parentage in Paris. He became apprenticed to a printer. In 1815, he began to bring out a series of national and other songs, which created a powerful sensation; many of them were satires upon the government and procured for their author a heavy fine and several months' imprisonment. Admiring friends paid the fine, and his cell was the reception room for many of the most distinguished men of the time. His poems contributed in no small degree to the revolution of 1830. In 1848, he was elected to the constituent assembly, but declined to serve. He was an intense believer in democracy.

Berceo, Gonzalo de (1180?-1246), Spanish poet, was born in Berceo, near Calahorra, Logrõno. He was a secular priest who wrote devotional works and stories of saints and miracles. Berceo developed and established the use of the *cuaderna via,* a form with four lines, a single rhyme, and fourteen syllables per verse. His fame rests in his use of the venacular, which made him the first poet in Castilian literature who is known by name.

Berdyaev, Nicholas (1874-1948), Russian religious philosopher, was born in Kiev. During his schooling he was attracted to Marxist thought, but later turned to a kind of Christian existentialism. From 1904-14, Berdyaev became influential in the religious revival that was taking place in Russia. In 1922, after the Bolsheviks had come to power, he was expelled from the Soviet Union. He settled in Paris, where he published numerous works, and founded a religious philosophical academy. Berdyaev believed that man arrives at truth through creative actions from his spiritual being. His writing and thought were influenced by Dostoevsky, Jakob Boehme, Kant, and Fichte. His works include *Freedom and Spirit* (1935), *The Meaning of History* (1936), *The Destiny of Man* (1937), *The Origin of Russian Communism* (1938), *Dream and Reality: An Essay in Autobiography* (1950), and *The Beginning and the End* (1952).

Berenson, Bernard (1865-1959), American art critic, was born in Vilna, Lithuania, and moved to the U.S. at 10. After graduation from Harvard in 1887, Berenson was sponsored by Isabella Stewart Gardner on a series of tours through Europe, and purchased for her almost three million dollars worth of art works, which formed the basis of her Fenway Court Collection in Boston. He was considered one of the world's leading experts on Renaissance art. His first published works, *Venetian Painters of the Renaissance* (1894), *Florentine Painters of the Renaissance* (1896), and *Central Italian Painters of the Renaissance* (1897), established his reputation as a scholar. *North Italian Painters of the Renaissance* (1907), with the first three books, was revised as *The Italian Painters of the Renaissance* (1930), a highly influential handbook. *The Study and Criticism of Italian Art* (3 vols. 1901-16) was a guide to his methods. He also wrote *Italian Pictures of the Renaissance* (1932), *Aesthetics and History* (1948), *Sketch for a Self-Portrait* (1949), *Rumor and Reflection* (1952), and *The Passionate Sightseer: From the Diaries of Bernard Berenson 1947-1956* (1960).

Berger, Thomas (1924-   ), American author, was born in Cincinnati, Ohio. He graduated from the University of Cincinnati and did postgraduate work at Columbia. In 1951-1952 he was a staff member for the *New York Times Index,* and in 1952-1954, associate editor of *Popular Science* monthly. Among his writings are *Crazy in Berlin, Little Big Man, Killing Time,* and a play, *Other People.*

Berger, Victor L. (1860-1929), American socialist editor and leader, was born in Nieder Rebbuch, Austria-Hungary. He received his education at the universities of Vienna and Budapest, but before graduation came to the United States, where he became a teacher in the public schools of Milwaukee. He began to edit the Milwaukee *Daily Vorwaerts* in 1892 and later became editor in chief of the Milwaukee *Leader,* a daily devoted to socialism. In 1911, he was elected to Congress, the first socialist to occupy a seat in that body. In 1918, he was excluded from Congress for alleged disloyalty, but was repeatedly re-elected and resumed his seat in 1923.

Bergerac *(bĕr′zhē-rak′)*, **Savinien Cyrano de (1619-55)**, French novelist and dramatist, was born in Perigord, 1619. He attended the College Beauvais, later studied science with Gassendi, and learned some astrology from Campanella. In youth, he divided his time between literature and adventure; served two years as a soldier, in the course of which he was twice wounded; and carried through life the reputation of a reckless duelist.

During his short and restless career, he published a volume of letters; a political satire on Mazarin; *Agrippine,* a tragedy; and *La Pédant joué,* a comedy that was followed by his most famous book, *The Comic History of The States and Empires of the Moon and of the Sun.* He was the earliest writer to employ the novel to teach natural science and was thus a forerunner of Jules Verne and H. G. Wells. He was also the first writer of French drama to break with the rule of the unities in tragedy, which, adopted from Aristotle's dictum, had long been observed in France. In his comic histories, he made startling forecasts of modern discoveries, such as the phonograph, and of a universal language, such as Esperanto. He has been immortalized in Rostand's famous drama *Cyrano de Bergerac.*

Bergson *(bĕrg′sôɴ′)*, **Henri (1859-1941)**, French philosopher, was born in Paris. He was graduated at the Ecole Normale in 1881, and became a teacher. He was professor of philosophy in the College de France, 1900-21, and, in 1901, was elected to the Institute. His books, *Time and Free Will,* published in 1889, *Matter and Memory,* 1896, and *Creative Evolution,* 1907, attracted wide attention and placed him in the front rank of contemporary philosophers.

According to his view, nearly all previous philosophies have been developed either by intellect alone or by intellect chiefly. He endeavors to avoid the limitations of intellect by depending upon intuition, maintaining that intellect is unable to comprehend the nature of life and of spirit. He asserts that instinct would empower us to understand life except that its object is not concerned with understanding it. He argues that what is needed for full understanding is intuition, which has at once the immediate certainty of instinct and the wide range of intellect. He was elected to the French Academy in 1914, and received the 1927 Nobel prize for literature. His works include also *Laughter, Intellectual Energy,* and *Thought and Motion.*

Bergström *(bĕrᴋ′strōm)*, **Hjalmar (1868-1914)**, Danish playwright. He completed a university education, obtaining the degree of Ph.D. in 1893, and became a teacher in the Brockske Commercial School, where he taught until 1905. Turning his attention to the drama, he became a director of the Danish Dramatic Society and member of an organization for preserving neglected writings of Danish playwrights. Among his plays are *When King David Grew Old, Karen Borneman, Together in the Dance,* and *The Way to God*—all of which were presented in the Royal Theater. *Karen Borneman* was forbidden by censor, but the ban was afterward removed.

Berkeley, George (1685-1753), Irish clergyman and philosopher, was born in Ireland. He was educated at Kilkenny School and Trinity College, Dublin, where he enjoyed the society of Dean Swift. On his return from a visit to America, he was made bishop of Cloyne. In philosophy, he was an idealist. He held that all things exist only in so far as they are perceived or known and that the existence of the universe is due to its being known by God. Berkeley, Cal., was named for him because of his saying, "Westward the course of empire takes its way." His most important works are the *Principles of Human Knowledge, Minute Philosopher,* and *Theory of Vision.*

Berkeley, Sir William (1606-77), colonial governor of Virginia, was born at London, England. He was appointed governor of Virginia in 1641, but resigned in 1651 upon Cromwell's rise to power. He remained in the colony, however, and, in 1660, was chosen governor by the general assembly. Some years later, he lost the favor of the people by failing to protect them from the Indians, and a rebellion led by Nathaniel Bacon broke out against the governor. It failed because of Bacon's sudden death. Berkeley was recalled in 1676. He wrote *A Discourse and View of Virginia* and a drama called *The Lost Lady.*

Berlichingen (bĕr lĭK-ĭng-ĕn), **Götz** or **Gottfried von (1480-1562),** German knight and soldier of fortune, was born in Jagsthausen. He took part in the war of the peasants against the nobles and was sentenced by Maximilian I to pay a heavy fine. He wore an artificial hand which replaced one lost in battle, and was surnamed the "Iron Hand." He was a staunch supporter of Luther; took part in a campaign against the Turks in 1542; and espoused the cause of Charles V against Francis I in 1544. While in retirement, he wrote his autobiography, which Goethe made the subject of his famous drama *Götz von Berlichingen.* This play initiated the *"Sturm und Drang"* movement in German literature. He was mortally wounded defending his own castle.

Berlin, Sir Isaiah (1909-   ), philosopher, educator, and diplomat, was born in Riga (the capital of Latvia), then part of the Russian Empire. His family emigrated to England, where Berlin graduated from Corpus Christi College, Oxford. He began his career in 1932 as lecturer in philosophy at New College, Oxford. During the war he served in diplomatic posts at Washington, D.C., New York, and Moscow. He spent seven years as research fellow of All Souls College, and in 1957 became professor of social and political theory at the University of Oxford.

His works are highly regarded for objectivity, scholarship, and style. His *Historical Inevitability* (1955), a contribution to the philosophy of history, holds that determinism, while not invalid, is irrelevant in the study of history. *Two Concepts of Liberty* (1958) is a plea for individuality that has been compared with J.S. Mill's writing on the subject. Berlin has lectured on Russian intellectual history, written numerous essays, and frequently contributed to journals. He was knighted in 1957. Other works include *Karl Marx: His Life and Environment* (1939), *The Hedgehog and the Fox* (1953), and *The Age of Enlightenment* (1956).

Bermudez de Castro, Salvador (1817-83), Spanish poet and historian, was born in Cadiz, studied law, and entered politics. He mastered a poetic form that had eight 11-syllable lines to a stanza, and the form is often called *octava bermudina* after him. It is also referred to as *octava italiana* and *octava moderna.* Generally categorized as romantic, his poetry was often pessimistic.

Bernal, J(ohn) D(esmond) (1901-71), British physicist and natural philosopher, was born in Nenagh, Ireland, and studied at Cambridge, pursuing on his own a number of specialized subjects, such as Persian architecture. In the 1930's and during World War II he actively opposed Fascism. He was assistant director of research in crystallography at Cambridge from 1934 to 1937, when he became professor of physics at Birbeck College, where he remained until 1968. He helped the Allies during World War II by preparing maps for the Normandy invasion and through his knowledge of explosives. Bernal was a staunch Communist; he belonged to the Soviet Academy of Sciences, participated in Soviet peace congresses, and received the Lenin Peace Prize in 1953. At 36 he was elected a fellow of the Royal Society in England.

As a scientist, Bernal's specialty was crystallography; he also helped to establish the bases for molecular biology. He examined the place of science in history, and made investigations into the origin of life. Bernal wrote a number of books that treat scientific subjects as well as philosophical and social questions. They include *Science in History, The Social Function of Science, The Freedom of Necessity, Origin of Life,* and *World Without War.*

Bernanos, Georges (1888-1948), French novelist, was born in Paris and educated at the University of Paris and the Institut Catholique. His novels, *Un crime (A Crime,* 1936) and *Journal d'un curé de campagne (The Diary of a Country Priest,* 1937), depict the war between good and evil. Unhappy with the advance of Fascism, he published *Les grands cimetières sous la lune (A Diary of My Times,* 1938), and in 1938 took his family to Brazil. He returned to France after World War II, then settled in Tunisia, but died in France.

Bernard (bûr'nard; bĕr-närd'), **Saint (1091-1153),** of Clairvaux, was born of a noble family at Fontaines, near Dijon, France. In 1113, he entered the Cistercian monastery of Citeaux and, in 1115, became the first abbot of the newly founded monastery of Clairvaux, in Champagne. His studious, ascetic life and stirring eloquence made him the oracle of Christendom. He founded 160 monasteries. The "mellifluous doctor" is regarded by the Catholic Church as the last of the fathers. He drew up the statutes of the Knights Templars in 1128; secured the recognition of Pope Innocent II; and kindled the enthusiasm of France for the Second Crusade.

The influence of Saint Bernard as a spiritual teacher, through his fervid piety and living grasp of Christian doctrine, was a wholesome antidote to the dry and cold scholasticism of the age. He was one of the greatest of the Latin hymn writers, many modern hymns being based on his *Jesu Dulcis Memoria.* He was canonized in 1171.

Bernard of Cluny (c. 1100-c. 1156), Benedictine monk, was born of English parents at Morlaix, Brittany. He is known principally for a poetical description of heaven which, translated, has given rise to three famous hymns—"Jerusalem the Golden," "The World is Very Evil," and "For Thee, O Dear, Dear Country." The original description was in Latin verse, the introduction to his *De Contemptu Mundi,* "On Contempt of the World."

Bernard, Jean Jacques (1888-1972), French dramatist, son of Tristan Bernard. He was born in Enghien-les-Bains and studied in Paris. A theatrical innovator, Bernard used silences rather than words to convey the thoughts and emotions of his characters. Some of his plays are *Le feu qui reprend mal, Martine, Le printemps des autres,* and *Á la recherche des coeurs,* and *L'Âme en peine.*

Bernard, Tristan (1866-1947), French writer, was born in Besancon. He began as a journalist and later became known for his farcical comedies, often satirizing middle-class life. Popular for his wit, Bernard also sounded a note of pessimism. His works, most of which were successful, include novels: *Les mémoires d'un jeune homme rangé* and *Le voyage imprévu,* and plays: *L'Anglais tel qu'on le parle, Le danseur inconnu, Le Fardeau de la liberté, Un Mari pacifique,* and *Le Petit Café.*

Bernhardt, (Rosine) Sarah (1844-1923), French tragic actress, was born at Paris. Her parents were Jewish, of French-Dutch descent, but she was educated in Grandchamp Convent at Versailles. She made her first appearance on the stage in 1862 at the Thèâtre Français, but at first attracted little notice. In 1867, her playing of the part of the queen in Victor Hugo's *Ruy Blas* made her famous. The war of 1870-71 interrupted her career, and for a while she became a nurse. She then won a position in the Thèâtre Français, the troupe of which she accompanied in 1879 to London, where her triumphs were repeated in succeeding years and where, in 1882, she married Jacques Damala, a Greek actor whom she left the next year. After touring Europe and the U.S. she opened a theater in Paris. With remarkable poise and voice, she was the first actress of her time. Also a painter and sculptor, she wrote two plays—*L'Aveu* and *Adrienne Lecouvreur*—and her memoirs.

Bernstein, Carl (1944-   ), writer, was born in Washington and attended the University of Maryland (1961-64). He worked for the Washington *Star* (1960-65) and joined the Washington *Post* (1966). As a police reporter, he investigated a break-in at the Watergate headquarters of the Democratic Party in 1972. With reporter Bob Woodward, Bernstein revealed one of the most complex political cover-ups in U.S. history. For their work, they received many awards, including a 1973 Pulitzer prize. Together they wrote *All the President's Men* (1974) and *The Final Days* (1976).

Bernstein, Henry Leon Gustave Charles (1875-1953), dramatist, was born in Paris. Beginning in 1900, he produced many plays, noted for plot and characters. His first, *Le Marche*, was staged in Paris. Later plays include *La Detour, La Griffe, La Rafale, Le Voleur, Samson,* and *Israel.*

Bernstein, Leonard (1918-   ), conductor and composer, was born in Lawrence, Mass., and attended Harvard and the Curtis Institute. He won note in November 1943 when at Bruno Walter's illness, he was called at short notice to conduct the New York Philharmonic. This brought engagements in Europe and the U.S. He was professor of music at Brandeis (1951-56), then became conductor of the Philharmonic and its musical director in 1958. In 1944 he became known as a composer for his symphony *Jeremiah*, awarded the New York Critics' prize. His musical comedy *On the Town* was a 1944 Broadway success. Other works include the symphony *The Age of Anxiety* (1949), *Kadish* (1963), *Mass* (1971), and the score for the ballet *Dybbuk* (1974). His writings include *The Joy of Music* (1959) and *The Infinite Variety of Music* (1966).

Berrigan, Daniel (1921-   ), priest and poet, was born in Virginia, Minn. At 18 he joined the Jesuits and spent 13 years in study for the priesthood. In 1953 he went to France and began to develop activist ideas. Returning to New York, he worked for civil-rights and antipoverty causes. In 1957 he won the Lamont Prize for his first book of poems, *Time Without Number.*

His activities troubled Church authorities and in 1963 he was sent to Europe to study and then to South America. In 1967 he flew to Hanoi to help in the release of prisoners of war. In 1968 he joined his brother Philip and seven others to destroy draft files in Catonsville, Md. They were later arrested and imprisoned, the first Catholic priests to receive sentences for peace agitation in the U.S. His other works include *No One Walks Waters, Night Flight to Hanoi, Trial Poems, The World for Wedding Ring,* and *No Bars to Manhood.*

Berrigan, Philip (Francis) (1923-   ), writer, was born at Two Harbors, Minn., attended Holy Cross College, entered the Society of St. Joseph in 1950, and was ordained in 1955. As a priest in New Orleans for six years, he worked with civil-rights groups. For antiwar acts he was jailed for almost two years before his parole in 1972. His books include *No More Strangers, Punishment for Peace,* and *Prison Journals of a Priest Revolutionary.*

Berry, Wendell (1934-   ), writer, was born in Henry County, Ky., and graduated from the University of Kentucky, where he later taught. All his writings reflect concern for the land. His first book of poetry was *The Broken Ground* (1964), followed by *Openings* (1968), *Findings* (1969), *The Country of Marriage* (1973), *The Kentucky River* (1976), and *Three Memorial Poems* (1977). His novels include *Nathan Coulter* (1960), *A*

Place on Earth (1964), and *The Memory of Old Jack* (1974). His essays appear in *The Unforeseen Wilderness* (1971), *A Continuous Harmony* (1972), and *The Unsettling of America* (1977).

Berryman, John (1914-72), poet, was born in McAlester, Okla., and was educated at Columbia and Cambridge. He taught at Harvard, Princeton, and the University of Minnesota (1955-72). Best known as a poet, he also wrote criticism, stories, and a biography of Stephen Crane. One of the most noted poets of his time, he often wrote long poems and sequences. His *77 Dream Songs* won a Pulitzer prize in 1965; *His Toy, His Dream, His Rest* won a National Book Award in 1969. Other works include *Homage to Mistress Bradstreet, Berryman's Sonnets,* and *The Dispossessed.*

Bertran de Born (c. 1140- c. 1215), Provencal soldier and troubadour, wrote poems that mirrored feudal society. He wrote lyric and moral poems as well, but his *sirventes,* satirical works written to provoke animosity among the nobility of southern France, are more typical products of his involvement with war and politics. Danté, in the *Inferno,* depicts Bertran as a "sower of schism" between Henry II and his sons, Prince Richard (the Lion-Hearted) and Prince Henry.

Berzsenyi, Daniel (1776-1863), Hungarian poet, was born in Heteny and educated by his father. His patriotic *Ode to Magyarokhoz* brought him considerable fame. Collections of his poems were published in 1813 and 1830, and his complete works were published in 1842 and 1864.

Besant (*běs'ănt; běz'ănt*), **Annie (1847-1933),** née Annie Wood, English theosophist, was born in London. She was educated privately in England, Germany, and France. At first a devout ritualist, she married Rev. Frank Besant in 1867 from whom she was separated in 1873. In the following year, she joined the National Secular Society and worked in the free thought and radical movements led by Charles Bradlaugh, with whom she was coeditor of the *National Reformer.* She joined the Theosophical Society in 1889, became a devoted pupil of Mme. Blavatsky, and traveled to all parts of the globe in service of theosophy. She founded the Central Hindu College in 1898 and, in 1904, the Central Hindu Girls' School, Benares. She also helped to found the Hindu University. Espousing the cause of Indian independence she organized the India Home Rule League; and, in 1917, was president of the Indian National Congress. In 1926-27, she traveled in the West with her protégé, J. Krishnamurti, whom she heralded as a messiah or world teacher, although he later renounced the role. Her publications include *Reincarnation, Death and After, Karma, Man and His Bodies, The Religious Problem in India, Theosophy and the New Psychology, India,* and *The New Civilization.*

Beskow, Elsa (1874-1953), author and illustrator of children's books, was born in Stockholm of a Norwegian father and Swedish mother. Her picture books for children include *Aunt Green, Aunt Brown and Aunt Lavender; Pelle's New Suit;* and *The Adventures of Peter and Lotta.*

Bethune (*bŭ-thoon'*), **Mary McLeod (1875-1955),** Negro educator, was born at Mayesville, S.C. After she was graduated from the Moody Bible Institute, Chicago, in 1895, she became a teacher, and in 1904 founded the Daytona (Florida) Normal and Industrial School for Girls (now Bethune-Cookman College), of which she was president from 1904 to 1942. Active with many organizations concerned with the welfare of the Negro people, Mrs. Bethune served as adviser on minority matters to officials of the Federal government. She contributed chapters and articles to books and magazines.

Betjeman, Sir John (1906-   ), poet, was born in London and educated at Oxford University. Appointed Poet

Laureate in 1972, Betjeman was also a member of the Royal Commission on Historical Monuments. In addition to verse, his writings include travel guides and books on architecture; he also edited several anthologies and wrote *John Piper* for the Penguin series on painters. He was an assistant editor of the *Architectural Review;* a film critic and book reviewer for newspapers; appeared on BBC television; and worked for the government during World War II. His works include *Mount Zion, Ghastly Good Taste, Old Bats in New Belfries, Summoned by Bells,* a verse autobiography, *Architectural Guide to Buckinghamshire, London's Historic Railway Stations,* and *A Nip in the Air.*

Betti, Ugo (1892-1953), Italian playwright, was born in Camerino, Marche. He was a lawyer and high court judge, but from 1927, when his first play, *La padrona,* was produced in Rome, to his death he wrote an average of one play a year. Betti used courtroom settings and themes in his plays. Considered second only to Pirandello in Italian drama, Betti had 24 of his 27 plays produced during his lifetime. Two of his plays were produced successfully in New York, *Il giocatore,* translated as *The Gambler* and produced in 1952, and *Corruzione al palazzo di giustizia,* produced in 1963 as *Corruption in the Palace of Justice.*

Bevan, Aneurin (1897-1960), British socialist statesman, was born at Tredegar, Monmouthshire, England. The son of a coal miner, he followed the same occupation when he left school, at the age of 13. He became active in the South Wales Miner's Association. From 1929 he was a Labor party member of Parliament, noted for his skill in debate. In 1945 Prime Minister Clement Attlee made him minister of health, a cabinet post which he held until 1951, when he was appointed minister of labor and national services. He resigned the same year because of differences with the Labor party leadership. His *In Place of Fear* was published in 1952.

Beveridge, William Henry (1879-1963), British economist, was born in India. He studied law at Balliol College, Oxford; then at University College, Oxford, he turned to economics and sociology. His authority on social problems grew through research and government service. From 1919 to 1937 Beveridge was director of the London School of Economics and Political Science. He later served as chairman of the Interdepartmental Committee on Social Insurance and Allied Service. The committee's report advocated compulsory insurance administered by the state, offering complete social security. Known as the Beveridge Plan, it was formally enacted in 1947. His works include *Full Employment in a Free Society* and *A Defense of Free Learning.*

Bewick (*bū´ĭk*), **Thomas (1753-1828),** English wood engraver, was born near Newcastle. He was apprenticed to Ralph Beilby at Newcastle at the age of 14. His first important work was a series of cuts for Gay's *Fables* in 1775, followed by enlarged editions in 1779 and 1784. His first cuts from his own original designs appeared in the *General History of Quadrupeds* in 1790. His greatest work is the *History of British Birds.* He illustrated many books, including Thomson's *Seasons,* Burns's *Poems,* and *Æsop's Fables.*

Bewick revived the art of wood engraving. He was the first to cut into the end of the block instead of the side and was the inventor of the white line, which is the characterizing feature of modern engraving, the design being cut into the block instead of remaining in relief.

Bhartrihari (or Bhartrhari) (early 7th cent. A.D.), Hindu prince, poet, and philosopher, is considered the greatest Indian poet to write in Sanskrit. After a brief reign as king of the city of Ujjain, he abdicated in favor of his brother and reportedly turned to a life of asceticism and writing. His best-known work is a collection of 300 stanzas under the title *Satakas (Centuries);* the first "Century" deals with conduct and morality in many proverbs and images, the second with love, and the third with renunciation of worldliness. The first translation of selections from this work from the Sanskrit to any European language was *De Open-Deure tot het Verborgen Heydendom,* (1651), by the Dutch missionary Abraham Roger.

Bhasa (3rd century A.D.?), Indian dramatist, about whom nothing is known. Kalidasa, a later prominent dramatist, had praised Bhasa, and Bhasa had apparently influenced others, but his works were not discovered until 1909. They were published in 1912, and Bhasa was acclaimed by some as the greatest Sanskrit dramatist. Thirteen short, simple pieces exist. All are comedies except *Urubhanga (The Breaking of the Thighs),* the only known tragedy in Sanskrit drama. *The Vision of Vasavadatta* is considered his best work; others are *The Statue Play, The Minister's Vows,* and *Karna's Task.* There is some dispute as to their authenticity and antiquity.

Bialik, Hayyim Nahman (1873-1934), Russian Jewish poet, considered by some to be the most eminent modern Hebrew poet. He was born in Rady, Volhynia, Russia. Moving to Odessa about 1892, he founded Moriah, a Hebrew publishing house, and edited the magazine *Hashiloah.* Unsuccessful in Odessa, he turned to writing poetry. He expressed in verse the hardships of the Jews in Russia; his works promoted Zionism, particularly in Russia and Palestine. He moved to Germany in 1921, and settled in Palestine in 1924, where he influenced Hebrew culture and language. Bialik wrote short stories, essays, and children's stories; he edited ancient Hebrew stories and writings (*Sefer ha-Aggadah* is a popular collection of legends); and he translated some European classics (Shakespeare's *Julius Caesar*) and Yiddish writings into Hebrew. Some of his best-known poetry is contained in *In the City of Slaughter, The Dead of the Wilderness, The Scroll of Fire, Orphanhood,* and *The Talmud Student.*

Bianco, Margery Williams (1881-1944), British-American author of children's books, was born in London, and moved to America at the age of nine. She lived in New York and Pennsylvania and returned occasionally to England. Her books, which have as central characters animals and toys, include *The Velveteen Rabbit, The Little Wooden Doll, All About Pets,* and *Winterbound.*

Bianco, Pamela (1906-   ), British-American author and illustrator of children's books, the daughter of Margery Williams Bianco, was born in London, and grew up in New Jersey, Paris, London, and Italy. In 1921 she returned permanently to America. She illustrated her mother's book *The Little Doll House.* After seeing some of her drawings on exhibition, Walter De La Mare wrote some poems to go with them. She wrote and illustrated *The Starlit Journey.* Other titles include *Toy Rose, The Look-Inside Easter Egg,* and *The Valentine Party.*

Bielski, Marcin (1495?-1575), Polish historian and poet, was born in Biala. He was the first to write a history of Poland in Polish. He was unable to complete the work, and it was finished by his son, Joachim (1540-99), and published in 1597.

Bierce, Ambrose (1842-c. 1913), American satirist and story writer, was born in Meiggs County, Ohio. He was self-educated with the aid of his father's ample library. Having served through the Civil War, in which he was breveted a major for bravery, he entered journalism as editor of the *News Letter* in San Francisco. Going to London in 1872, he won the name "Bitter Bierce" for his caustic humor in the periodical *Fun* and several books, including *The Fiend's Delight.* Returning to San Francisco in 1876, he wrote a column "Prattle" in the *Examiner,* which, by making or unmaking literary and political reputations, rendered him a power to reckon with on the West Coast for a quarter of a century. His books include *Fantastic Tales, The Cynic's Word Book* (republished as *The Devil's Dictionary*) and *The Shadow* *on the Dial.* In 1913 he departed for Mexico, and was never heard of again.

Bigelow, John (1817-1911), American author and diplomat, was born at Malden, N.Y. He graduated from Union College in 1835, studied law, was admitted to the bar, then turned to journalism. From 1849 to 1861, he was one of the editors of the New York *Evening Post.* He was consul at Paris, 1861-64, and minister to France, 1864-67. His writings include *France and Hereditary Monarchy, Life of Samuel J. Tilden, Life of Benjamin Franklin, Life of William Cullen Bryant, Molinos the Quietist,* and *Retrospections of an Active Life.* He was a member of the American Academy of Arts and Letters.

Bigelow, Poultney (1855-1954), American author and journalist, was born in New York. He was graduated from Yale, 1879, and from Columbia Law School, 1882; was admitted to the bar, 1882, but gave up law practice for travel and journalism. During 1875-76, he went around the world in a sailing ship, visited shores of New Guinea, and was wrecked on the Japanese coast. He circumnavigated the world three times, studying tropical colonization, and lectured at leading universities on colonial administration. He became intimate with William II of Germany. During the Spanish-American War, he was correspondent for the London *Times.*

Bijns (or Byns) (*bīns*), **Anna (1494?-1575),** Flemish poet, was born in Antwerp. Known by her contemporaries as the "Sappho of Brabant," she directed many of her verses against social evils and against Martin Luther and the Reformation. Her poetry is noted for its technical skill and melodic quality. *This Is a Beautiful and Truthful (or Sincere) Little Book* and *Spiritual Refrains* are two volumes of her poems.

Bilac, Olavo Braz Martins dos Guimarães (1865-1918), Brazilian poet, was born in Rio de Janeiro. His first publication, *Poesias* (1888), brought him renown as a poet, but he also wrote considerably as a journalist and critic, as well as publishing works on versification and instructional books for children. Bilac's poetry was influenced by the French Parnassians. His dedication to formal structure, precise diction, and logical development added to his clarity.

Bilderdijk, Willem (1756-1831), Dutch poet, was born in Amsterdam, obtained a doctorate of law at Leiden University (1782), and was an advocate at the Hague. In 1795 he was exiled by the Batavian Republic, but returned to the Netherlands in 1806 when King Louis Bonaparte made him state librarian. Bilderdijk's shorter poems, lyrics, and ballads, are regarded as Dutch classics, and as a forerunner of Romanticism he had great influence on early 19th-century writers. *The Disease of the Learned* (1807) is typical of his reflective poetry; he also wrote an unfinished epic, *The Destruction of the First World* (1820).

Binet (*bē'nĕ'*), **Alfred (1857-1911),** French psychologist, was born at Nice, France. He was one of the editors of *L'Année Psychologique,* and director of the psychological laboratory at the Sorbonne, Paris. His works treat many subjects in physiological psychology, particularly with reference to the study of practical, social, and educational questions. In this field, he collaborated with Thomas Simon, endeavoring to find a standard by which degrees of intelligence may be measured. Their combined researches resulted in the publication, in 1905, of the *Binet-Simon Tests,* which have been widely employed by educators.

Before 1905, Binet had made numerous investigations of the deficiencies exhibited by children in the course of their development. At this date he was asked by the school authorities of Paris to undertake the study of children in the public school systems, for the purpose of detecting the various forms of mental deficiency which interfered with school work.

The Binet tests have been very widely used in Europe and in the United States as a means of determining the intellectual possibilities of children. The characteristic of these tests is that they are arranged in such a way as to determine the intellectual age of the child. By a series of trials, Binet assembled those tests which should be passed by a child three years of age if he is entirely normal in his mental development. Other series were developed for other ages, so that it is possible by means of this scale to compare any given child with other children of his chronological age. Various revisions of the Binet scale have been made by others who have taken up the work, especially in the United States.

Binns, Archie (1899-   ), American novelist and historian, was born in Port Ludlow, Wash. Before graduating from Stanford University, Binns had gone to sea on a lightship and served in the U.S. Army. About 1923 he became Washington correspondent for Scripps-Howard newspapers, and later became editor of the Scott Publication Company. He taught at the University of Washington and at Western Washington College. His novels, most of which are set in the Northwest, include *Lightship, The Laurels Are Cut Down, The Land Is Bright,* and *Timber Beast.* Some of his books for children are *Radio Imp* and *Sea Pup. The Sea in the Forest* is a history of the Northwest.

Bion (c. 2d century B.C.), Greek poet, was apparently born in Smyrna (now Izmir, Turkey), but lived mostly in Sicily. His pastoral poetry, of which only fragments remain, was probably in imitation of Theocritus. Most famous of his extant verse is *Lament for Adonis,* which served as a model for Shelley's *Adonais.*

Bishop, Elizabeth (1911-   ), American poet, was born in Worcester, Mass., and educated at Vassar. She began publishing poetry while in college and in 1956 received a Pulitzer prize for her *North and South.* She received the National Book Award for her *Complete Poems,* published in 1969. She has also written *Poems, and a Cold Spring* and *Questions of Travel.* In 1949-1950 she was consultant in poetry for the Library of Congress.

Bishop, Jim (1907-   ), American author, was born James Alonso Bishop in Jersey City, N.J., and attended Drake's Secretarial College for a time. In 1929 he became a copy boy for the New York *Daily News;* he reported for the *Mirror* in 1930, becoming a feature writer in 1934. Bishop held a succession of editorial posts—for *Collier's* magazine (1943-46), *Liberty* magazine (1946-48), and the *Catholic Digest.* His first books met little success (*The Glass Crutch, The Making of a Priest,* and others), but he produced a bestseller in *The Day Lincoln Was Shot,* a detailed account of the final day of the president's life. It was followed by a succession of "day" books and stories (usually published in magazines) that were met with a variety of critical responses. These include *The Day Christ Died, The Day Christ Was Born, A Day in the Life of President Kennedy, The Day Kennedy Was Shot,* and *A Day in the Life of President Johnson.*

Bishop, John Peale (1892-1944), American writer, was born in Charles Town, W. Va., and graduated from Princeton in 1917. He was the model for Tom D'Invilliers in F. Scott Fitzgerald's *This Side of Paradise.* He succeeded Edmund Wilson as editor of *Vanity Fair* in 1919 and collaborated with him on *The Undertaker's Garland* (1922). Bishop also wrote a collection of short stories, *Many Thousands Gone* (1931); two books of verse, *Now With His Love* (1933) and *Minute Particulars* (1935); and a novel, *Act of Darkness* (1935). *American Harvest* (1942), a collection of essays on American literature from World War I to World War II, was edited with Allen Tate. Bishop's *Collected Essays,* edited by Wilson, and *Collected Poems,* edited by Tate, were published posthumously in 1948.

Bjerregaard, Carl Henry Andrews (1845-1922), American writer, was born in Fredericia, Denmark. He worked as a librarian in New York, at the Astor Library

Biography

(1879-95) and at the N.Y. Public Library (1895-1922). His works include *The Inner Life and the Tao-Teh-King* (1912) and *The Great Mother* (1913).

Björnson (*byûrn'sŭn*), **Björnstjerne (1832-1910),** Norwegian poet, novelist, and dramatist, was born in Kvikne. He entered the University of Oslo in 1852 and soon after began work as a journalist and dramatic critic. His first novel, *Synnöve Solbakken*, a story of peasant life, published in 1857, was followed by *Arne, A Happy Boy, The Fisher Maiden*, and many other pieces. In 1858, he became director of the theater at Bergen and produced two dramas, *Between the Battles* and *Lame Hulda*. An ambition to create a new national saga in a peasant setting was substantially realized in *Sigurd the Bastard*. Among his later well-known plays are *Mary Stuart in Scotland, Sigurd Slembe*, and *The Newly Married*. Björnson was the foremost novelist and poet and, excepting only Ibsen, the chief dramatist of his time in Norway. He received the Nobel prize for literature in 1903.

Black, Hugo Lafayette (1886-1971), American legislator and jurist, was born at Harlan, Ala. Obtaining a law degree at the University of Alabama in 1906, he entered practice at Birmingham, Ala., served as police judge for 18 months in 1910-11, and was prosecuting attorney for Jefferson county, 1915-17. In 1926, and again in 1932, he was elected, as a Democrat, to the United States Senate.

While in the Senate, Black was a leader among those who asserted the power of Congress to regulate economic activities and to prevent the Supreme Court from blocking its efforts in this direction through what he called a tortured construction of the Constitution. He favored increasing the court's membership to bring about this result.

When Justice Van Devanter retired in 1937 from the tribunal, President Roosevelt nominated Senator Black to succeed him. Black's opinions on the court established his reputation as an able and liberal jurist. Black's views on civil liberties were collected in *One Man's Stand for Freedom*, edited by Irving Dilliard. He has been the subject of a number of other works including *Hugo L. Black; A Study in the Judicial Process* by Charlotte Williams.

Black, William (1841-98), British novelist, was born in Glasgow, Scotland. He studied art with the view of becoming a landscape painter, but later adopted journalism. During the Prusso-Austrian war of 1866, he was war correspondent for the *Morning Star*, and in a novel, *Love or Marriage*, he used some of his experiences. *Silk Attire* and *Kilmeny* were fairly successful, but it was a *A Daughter of Heth* that established his reputation. Later novels were *The Strange Adventures of a Phaeton, A Princess of Thule, Madcap Violet, Macleod of Dare, Briseis*, and *Wild Eelin*. He laid his scenes chiefly in northern Scotland and contrasted the simple life of the country people with that of Bohemian London.

Blackie, John Stuart (1809-95), Scottish scholar and man of letters, was born at Glasgow. He was educated at Marischal College, Aberdeen, and at the University of Edinburgh. For three years, he was a student of theology at the University of Aberdeen. In 1829, he went to Germany, studying at Göttingen and at Berlin. Returning to Scotland, he made extensive preparations for the law, but his strong love of the classics and his taste for letters led him to adopt a literary and scholastic career. In 1839, he was made professor of Latin in Marischal College, and from 1852 to 1882 was professor of Greek at Edinburgh University. Blackie was a zealous educational reformer, took an active interest in the remodeling of the Scottish universities, founded a Celtic chair in Edinburgh University, and spoke and wrote on a wide variety of subjects. Among his works, which are numerous, are *Self-Culture, Four Phases of Morals, The Language and Literature of the Scottish Highlands, Life of Burns,*

Christianity and the Ideal of Humanity, a translation of Æschylus, and several volumes of verse.

Blackmore, Richard Doddridge (1825-1900), British novelist, was born at Longworth, Berkshire. He graduated at Exeter College, Oxford, in 1847; afterward studied law; was admitted to the bar; and practiced for a time as a conveyancer. Of his novels the earliest were *Clara Vaughan* and *Cradock Nowell;* but his greatest success was *Lorna Doone*, a 17th century romance with notably beautiful descriptions in rhythmic prose, which has become a classic of English fiction. Blackmore's other novels include *The Maid of Sker, Alice Lorraine, Cripps the Carrier, Erema, Mary Anerley, Christowell, Tommy Upmore, Springhaven, Perlycross*, and *Dariel*.

Blackmun, Harry Andrew (1908-), American judge, was born in Nashville, Illinois. He was educated at Harvard University and admitted to the Minnesota bar in 1932. From 1935 to 1941 he was an instructor at St. Paul's College of Law. He was judge of the 8th circuit U.S. Court of Appeals from 1950 to 1959, and on May 5, 1970 was appointed to the United States Supreme Court by President Nixon. Justice Blackmun has been described as "a master of language, both written and spoken."

Blackmur, R(ichard) P(almer) (1904-65), American literary critic, was born in Springfield, Mass., and was self-educated. He was a clerk in a bookstore before he became a free-lance poet and critic (1928-40). He taught at Princeton University and at Cambridge University in England, and he was made a member of the American Academy of Arts and Letters. Blackmur examined his subject closely, insisting on the social responsibility of the artist. His poetry, collected in *From Jordan's Delight*, met moderate success. His volumes of criticism include *The Double Agent, The Expense of Greatnesss, Dirty Hands, Form and Value in Modern Poetry*, and *Language as Gesture*.

Blackstone, Sir William (1723-80), English jurist, was born at London. He was a judge, a member of Parliament, and author of the well-known *Commentaries on the Laws of England*. At the bar, after seven years' practice, his prospects were so indifferent that he retired to Oxford on his fellowship and there gave public lectures on English law. Their success is supposed to have suggested to Viner the propriety of establishing a professorship of law in the university, to which office Blackstone was elected in 1758, being the first Vinerian lecturer. In 1770, he became one of the judges of the common pleas.

Blaine, James Gillespie (1830-93), American statesman, was born at Brownsville, Pa. At 17 he graduated from Washington College, Pa.; he taught school at Georgetown, Ky., 1848-51, and in Philadelphia, 1852-54. In 1854, he went to Maine to engage in journalism, which he relinquished four years later for a seat in the legislature. He served there until 1862, when he was elected to Congress, where he remained 18 years. From 1869 to 1875, he was speaker of the House of Representatives. At the Republican national convention of 1876, Blaine was balloted on for the presidency and received 351 votes out of a total of 754. He was then elected United States senator, and four years later was again an unsuccessful aspirant for nomination to the presidency. In 1881, President Garfield appointed him secretary of state but he resigned from the cabinet soon after Garfield's death. In 1884, he received the Republican nomination for president, but was defeated by Grover Cleveland by a very narrow margin. A change of less than a thousand votes in New York State would have made Blaine president. In 1889, he again became secretary of state, in the cabinet of President Harrison. Blaine was a parliamentarian of great ability, a brilliant orator, and a notably resourceful and popular party leader. He wrote *Twenty Years of Congress* and *Political Discussions*.

Blaisdell, James Arnold (1867-1957), educator, was born in Beloit, Wis., graduated from Beloit College and Hartford Seminary, and was ordained a Congregational minister in 1892. He taught Biblical literature at Beloit, was president of Pomona College (1910-27), and became president of Claremont College (1927). He later traveled in Japan studying its education. Besides many papers, he wrote *Visions of a Citizen* and some hymns.

Blake, William (1757-1827), mystic poet and artist, was born in London and learned engraving at an early age. In 1783 he published his first work, *Poetical Sketches*. His most noted books are *Songs of Innocence* (1789) and *Songs of Experience* (1794). Blake's illustrations of the Bible, Dante, Chaucer, Bunyan, Milton and others became renowned long after his death, as did his position in the first ranks of imaginative, visionary poetry.

Blanc, Jean Joseph Louis (1811-82), historian, was born in Madrid. As a journalist, he founded the *Revue du Progres* in France and published *The Organization of Labor* (1840), which brought him favor with the workers. He was a member of the French provisional government of France in 1848 and later of the National Assembly. Threatened with removal from office, he fled to England. On the fall of the Empire in 1871 he returned and was elected to the Chamber of Deputies. Blanc produced an elaborate, well-written history of the French Revolution.

Blanche, August Theodor (1811-68), Swedish dramatist, novelist, and politician. He began as a journalist and during 1839-42 edited the liberal paper *Freja*. From 1852 he was a liberal member of the Riksdag, and he became popular for his humanitarianism and reforms. Blanche began writing in 1843, producing many plays (mostly comedies), novels, and short stories. His novels, which were uniformly moralizing, held great popular appeal for the common people of his time.

Blankfort, Michael (1907-   ), writer, was born in New York City. He earned a bachelor's degree at the University of Pennsylvania (1929 and a master's at Princeton (1930). He taught psychology at Princeton and later produced and directed plays in New York. He wrote *Crime* (1936, a 9-act social drama), *I Met A Man* (1937), *A Time To Live* (1943), *Juggler* (1952), and *Behold the Fire* (1965). His screenplay for *Broken Arrow* won the Screen Writers' Award in 1951.

Blasco Ibañez (*bläs' kō ē-bä' nyath*), **Vicente (1867-1928)**, Spanish novelist, was born in Valencia. His earliest works, such as the *Mayflower,* are sketchy pictures of life in his native province. Later, he developed a more minute and realistic style, somewhat resembling that of Zola, and produced novels which are characterized by great keenness of observation and descriptive power. Among his works, several of which have been translated into English, French, and other languages, are *The Shadow of the Cathedral, The Four Horsemen of the Apocalypse, Our Sea, Woman Triumphant, Blood and Sand,* and *The Temptress.*

Blatty, William Peter (1929), writer, was born in New York City and graduated from Georgetown (1950). In 1951 he joined the Air Force and served as a psychological warfare officer. He earned a master's degree (1954) and later a doctorate at George Washington University. In Beirut, Lebanon, he was an editor for the U.S. Information Agency (1955-57). His early credits as a screenwriter include *A Shot in the Dark* (1966) and *Darling Lili* (1970). In 1971 his best-selling novel *The Exorcist* was translated into 12 languages. This story of demonic possession became a successful film (1973) produced by Blatty and won a 1974 Academy Award. Other books are *John Goldfarb, Please Come Home!* (1963) and *I'll Tell Them I Remember You* (1973).

Blavatsky (*blä-väts'kī*), **Helena Petrovna (1831-91)**, theosophist, was born in Ekaterinoslav. She was of noble descent and married a Russian councilor of state, from whom she separated soon after their marriage. She visited Tibet, where, she claimed, she discovered the doctrines later formulated as the tenets of the Theosophical Society. From 1873 to 1879, she was a resident of New York, became a naturalized American citizen and, with Col. H. S. Olcott and others, founded the Theosophical Society in 1875. Its purpose is to form the nucleus of the universal brotherhood of man, to promote the study of comparative religion, philosophy, and science, and to investigate the unexplained laws of nature and the powers latent in man. In 1876 she published *Isis Unveiled*, a book basic to the movement. Her other writings include *The Secret Doctrine*, and *The Voice of Silence*.

Bleek, Wilhelm Heinrich Immanuel (1827-75), German philologist, was born in Berlin and studied in Bonn. He made the study of South African languages his life's work. The first to note the philological distinctions of these languages, Bleek introduced the word Bantu into European tongues. He lived in South Africa from 1855, and in 1860 he was made public librarian at Cape Town. Some of his books are *Hottentot Fables and Tales; Handbook of African, Australian, and Polynesian Philology;* and *Specimens of Bushman Folklore.*

Blicher, Steen Steenson (1782-1848), Danish poet and novelist, was born in Vium, Jutland. His first publication was a translation of the works of the Gaelic Ossianic poems (1807-09), but his own poems and novels brought him little attention until after 1826. His writings in his native dialect of the legends, tales, and chronicles of the peasants of Jutland were collected as *The Knitting Room* (1842), and they gained him a wide reputation. Blicher was also the author of a novel, *The Diary of a Parish Clerk* (1824), poetry, and a collection of sketches and tales, *Samlede Noveller og Skizzer* (1833-36).

Blind Harry (flourished 1470-92), Scottish minstrel. Blind Harry is believed to have been blind from birth. He earned his living by telling tales and is said to have spent the years 1490-92 at the court of James IV of Scotland. The narrative poem *The Actes and Deides of . . . Shir William Wallace, Knicht of Ellerslie* is attributed to Blind Harry. The manuscript of the work dates from 1488 and consists of more than 11,000 lines of heroic couplets.

Blish, James Benjamin (1921-   ), writer of science fiction, was born in East Orange, N.J. He received a B.S. from Rutgers University in 1942 and was later employed as editor of several publications. He has produced numerous short stories, articles, poems, novels and plays for the screen and television, particularly for the "Star Trek" series. He received the science fiction Hugo Award in 1959 for *A Case of Conscience.*

Bloch, Robert Albert (1917-   ), mystery and science fiction writer, was born in Chicago, Ill. The depression of the 1930's caused his family to move frequently, and his formal education ceased with his high school graduation in Milwaukee, Wis. Soon afterward, he began to sell stories to fantasy magazines and developed into a master of psychological terror. He has written novels, short stories and plays for radio, television and the screen.

Blok, Alexander Alexandrovich (1880-1921), Russian poet, was born in St. Petersburg and studied philology at the University of St. Petersburg. Through his poetry, ranked among the greatest in Russia in the 20th century, he expressed his mysticism, love of Russia, and revolutionary involvement. His best work is considered *The Twelve*, a portrait of the 1917 Revolution. Other works are the unfinished *Retribution* and three volumes of poems—*Verses about the Fair Lady, Unexpected Joy,* and *Snowy Night.* His verse dramas include *The Puppet Show, The King on the Square, The Stranger, The Song of Fate,* and *The Rose and the Cross.*

Blondel (de Nesle), 12th-century French Minstrel. He is credited with more than 20 love lyrics, but his main interest stems from a legend linking him with King Richard the Lion-Hearted. The legend states that Blondel accompanied Richard to the Holy Land during the Crusades. On his way home Richard was imprisoned by Duke Leopold of Austria in the castle of Durrenstein. Blondel found him by singing a song and obtained his release.

Bloom Úrsula (1896-   ), author and journalist, was born in Chelmsford, England, and was educated privately. Her first published work was *Tiger*, an 11-page book published when she was seven. Later she was beauty editor of *Women's Own*, served on the *Sunday Pictorial*, and worked for many newspapers. From the early 1920's, she wrote continuously, more than 450 books—fiction, nonfiction, autobiographies, and plays. Among her pseudonyms are Sheila Burns, Mary Essex, Rachel Harvey, and Lozania Prole. Her works include *The Great Beginning* (1924); *These Roots Go Deep* (1939), *Daughters of the Rectory* (1955), *Person Extraordinary* (1963), a biography of her father; best-sellers *The Ring Tree* (1964) and *The Rose of Norfolk* (1963); *The Cheval Glass* (1973), *Duke of Windsor* (1975), and *Life Is No Fairy Tale* (1976), an autobiography.

Bloomfield, Leonard (1887-1949), American linguist, was born in Chicago, Ill. After graduating from Harvard (1906), he studied philology at universities in Germany. He taught at the universities of Illinois, Ohio State, Chicago, and Yale. For years he specialized in the German language, but later became interested in scientific aspects of language. He is noted for his emphasis, notably in his text *Language* (1933), that language study must begin with the spoken language of a given time, not with rules and analyses. He wrote major works on linguistics and made studies of American Indian languages. Other works include *Introduction to the Study of Language, Menomini Texts*, and *Linguistic Aspects of Science*.

Bloomfield, Morton W(ilfred) (1913-   ), American linguist and educator, was born in Montreal, Quebec, and received his education at McGill University, the University of London, and the University of Wisconsin. He taught at the University of Wisconsin (1936-39), Akron University (1939-46), Ohio State University (1946-61), and Harvard (1961-   ), and served in the U.S. Army during World War II. Bloomfield is the author of *The Seven Deadly Sins, "Piers Plowman" as a Fourteenth-Century Apocalypse*, and *A Linguistic Introduction to the History of English*. He edited, alone and with others, a number of medieval works, and he was advisory editor of Funk and Wagnall's *New Standard Dictionary*.

Bloy (*blwä***), Léon (1846-1917)**, French novelist and a main figure in the Catholic literary revival in France, was born at Périgueux. He went to Paris to study painting and was converted to Catholicism in 1869. Beginning in the 1870's, Bloy devoted himself to journalism. During an intense spiritual crisis (1877-82), Bloy adopted extreme spiritual attitudes, which are reflected in his writings. Bloy's works also contain attacks on society, condemning the world as violent. He published *The Hopeless One, The Woman Who Was Poor*, and his *Journal*, which has appeared under several titles.

Blum, Robert Frederick (1857-1903), American illustrator and painter, was born in Cincinnati, Ohio. He was apprenticed as a lithographer and also studied drawing and painting. In 1878 he moved to New York and began to make drawings for *Scribner's*, the *St. Nicholas Magazine*, and the *Century*. In 1890 he went to Japan, staying for two years. On his return, he illustrated Sir Edward Arnold's *Japanica* and published a series of articles in *Scribner's* on the Far East.

Blumenbach (*bloo'men-bäк***), Johann Friedrich (1752-1840)**, German physiologist and anthropologist, was born at Gotha. In 1776, he was made professor of medicine in the University of Göttingen, a chair which he filled with distinction for nearly 60 years. He was the founder of anthropology and his works gave a great impulse to scientific research. His chief writings are *Institutiones Physiologicæ, Manual of Natural History*, and *Manual of Comparative Anatomy and Physiology*.

Blunden, Edmund (Charles) (1896-1974), English poet and scholar, was born at Yalding, Kent, served with the Royal Sussex Regiment (World War I), and studied at Queen's College, Oxford. He taught English at Tokyo University (1924-27), at Oxford (1931-43), and at Hong Kong University (1953-64). Although Blunden is best known as a poet, his first notable work was *Undertones of War* (1929), a prose account of his World War I experiences. He also wrote works on Leigh Hunt (1930) and Shelley (1946), as well as his volumes of poetry, *Poems, 1914-1930* (1932), *Shells by a Stream* (1945), and *A Hong Kong House* (1962).

Bly, Robert (Elwood) (1926-   ), American poet and translator, was born in Madison, Minn., and educated at Harvard and the State University of Iowa. Bly received the National Book Award in 1968 for his poems. His works include *Silence in the Snowy Fields, The Light Around the Body, A Poetry Reading Against the Vietnam War*, and *The Sea and the Honeycomb*.

Blythe, Samuel George (1868-1947), journalist, was born in Geneseo, N.Y., and attended Geneseo State Normal School. After holding editorial positions on Buffalo newspapers, he became managing editor of *Cosmopolitan Magazine* in 1899. He was chief Washington correspondent for the New York *World* from 1900-1907, when he became associated with the *Saturday Evening Post*. An intimate of presidents from Cleveland to Franklin D. Roosevelt, Blythe covered every major political convention from 1896 to 1940. His writings include *Who's Who and Why, The Senator's Secretary, We Have With Us Tonight, The Making of a Newspaper Man, The Manikin Makers*, and many magazine articles.

Boas, Franz (1858-1942), American anthropologist, was born in Minden, Germany. He studied at the universities of Heidelberg, Bonn, and Kiel, then went to Greenland to do geographic research. His contact with the Eskimos aroused an interest in human cultural behavior, and he made many field trips to study the Indians on the British Columbian coast. He contributed greatly to the study of American Indian languages, to the understanding of primitive societies, and to the science of physical anthropology. He concluded that all the races of man are mixed to some extent, and that no race is inherently superior to any other. Columbia University's first professor of anthropology, Boas wrote *The Mind of Primitive Man, Anthropology and Modern Life*, and *General Anthropology*.

Bobbs, William Conrad (1861-1926), publisher, was born in Montgomery County, Ohio, and was educated in the public schools of Indianapolis, Ind. He began his career with Merrill, Meigs and Company, an Indianapolis bookselling firm. In 1879 he became director and in 1890 president of the company. In 1895 he helped to establish and then became president of the publishing house of Bobbs-Merrill Company.

Bocage, Manuel Maria Barbosa du (1765-1805), Portuguese lyric poet, was born in Sebutal of French descent. He joined the army at 14, and later attended the royal naval academy in Lisbon. In 1786 he was sent to India and China. He deserted in 1789 and returned to Lisbon in 1790. He earned recognition as a poet and became a member of the literary group Nova Arcadia, but was expelled for his attacks in writing on his fellow members. He was imprisoned in 1797 by the Inquisition as a heretic and danger to the state because of the ideas expressed in his poems. While imprisoned, he translated works of Virgil and Ovid. His poetry belongs to the Romantic tradition, although his sonnets are classical in form.

Boccaccio (*bōk-kä'chō*), **Giovanni (1313-75)**, Italian story-teller, was born probably in Paris. From an early period he displayed a love for poetry. In 1350, he formed an intimate friendship with Petrarch, and, following his friend's example, collected books and copied rare manuscripts which he could not afford to buy. It is said that he was the first Italian who ever procured from Greece a copy of the *Iliad* and of the *Odyssey*. Boccaccio was not only one of the most learned men of his time, but he was also one of the most enlightened in his scholarship.

While in Naples, about 1334, Boccaccio fell passionately in love with a young woman, called by him Fiammetta, who was generally supposed to be a daughter of King Robert. His passion was returned, and, to gratify her, he wrote *Il Filocopo*, a prose romance, and afterward *La Teseide*, the first attempt at romantic epic poetry, of which Boccaccio may be considered the inventor. In 1344, he wrote his *Amorosa Fiammetta*. He composed his humorous and lusty *Decameron* in Naples, to please Joanna, the daughter and successor of King Robert. In abundance of incident it is almost inexhaustible, though many of the stories are taken from older collections.

Boccalini, Triano (1556-1613), Italian prose satirist, was born in Loreto. He was trained for the law and served the papal states, later moving to the Venetian Republic. Boccalini's most important work, *Commentari sopra Cornelio Tactio*, was published posthumously. Other works include a satire on the affairs of men, *I Ragguagli di Parnaso, Pietra del paragone politico*, translated by Henry of Monmouth in 1669 under the title *Advertisements from Parnassus in Two Centuries with the Politicke Touchstone*.

Bodel, Jean (c. 1165- c. 1210), French poet and dramatist, lived in Arras. He wrote *La chanson des Saxons* (or *Saisnes*), a lengthy epic that described Charlemagne conquering the Saxons, and one of the earliest French miracle plays, *Le jeu de Saint Nicolas*.

Bodenstedt, Friedrich Martin von (1819-92), German poet and translator, was born in Peine, Hanover, and spent several years in Moscow as a tutor. Before returning to Germany in 1847, he traveled through the Middle East. He then became a professor of Slavic at the University of Munich, and later specialized in early English literature. From 1866 until his death he was director of the Meiningen court theater, and also edited the journal *Weser Zeitung*. Bodenstedt made many translations from the Russian, English, and Persian— among them works by Pushkin, Lermontov, Shakespeare, and Omar Khayyam. The best-known volume of Bodenstedt's poems, *Lieder des Mirza Schaffy*, was represented by a him as a translation from the Tatar, but was discovered to be his own work.

Bodin, Jean (c. 1530-96), French political philosopher and economist, was born in Toulouse. He joined the Carmelite order in Angers and was educated there and in Paris. He obtained a release from his vows and went to Toulouse to study law and science. He became professor of Roman law in Paris in 1561, then went into private practice, and finally became the King's attorney at Laon in 1576. His greatest work, *Les Six livres de la republique*, discusses limited monarchy as the best form of government, considers property and family as the basis of society, and denies the right of citizens to rebel. His work was translated into English in 1606 as *Of the Lawes and Customs of a Commonweale*. Bodin is considered a pioneer in formulating a modern, scientific philosophy of history; his theories on free trade, taxation, and industrialism give him an important place in the development of economic thought. He was also noteworthy for his religious tolerance, although he was considered a freethinker in his day.

Bodley, Sir Thomas (1545-1613), English diplomat and scholar. His family being forced to flee from England during the persecutions of Mary, he settled at Geneva. On the accession of Elizabeth, he returned to England and completed his studies at Oxford, thereafter becoming a member of the faculty. He was employed by the queen in diplomatic missions to Denmark, France, and the Netherlands, whence he returned to Oxford in 1596 and devoted himself to restoring and enlarging the library originally established there by Humphrey, Duke of Gloucester. The library was named Bodleian, in recognition of his work and his benefactions to it.

Bodmer, Johann Jakob (1698-1783), literary critic, was born in Zurich and was professor of history at the University of Zurich (1725-75). From his study of classical authors he formed a distaste for contemporary German literary fashions. This led him to make the public aware of early German writing through his editions of the Minnesingers (12th-century German lyric poets) and the Niebelungenlied (the German national epic of about the same period). Bodmer also edited the *Discourse der Mahlern*, a journal similar to Addison's *Spectator*. He sought to free German literature from the French tradition and in his criticism emphasized the importance of emotion over reason in poetry.

Bodoni, Giambattista (1740-1813), Italian type designer and printer, was born in Saluzzo, Piedmont. He is famous for achievements in book design and development of modern type styles. During his 45 years in Parma, where he was appointed printer to Duke Ferdinand I, he produced more than 30,000 pieces. About 750 of these are "special" works, largely folios, such as *Horace* (1791), *Virgil* (1793), *The Divine Comedy* (1795), *The Lord's Prayer in 155 Languages* (1806), and *Homer* (1808). His *Manuale tipografico* (1818) is one of the most definitive type specimen books.

Bödtcher, Ludwig Adolph (1793-1874), Danish lyric poet, was born in Copenhagen. Bödtcher spent most of his time in a Danish artists' colony in Rome where he became a close friend of Thorvaldsen, a sculptor. Bödtcher wrote three volumes of poetry, now collected into one, *Samlede Digte*.

Boehme (*bē'mu*), **Jakob (1575-1624)**, German Christian mystic, was born in Prussia and became a traveling cobbler. On his travels he became disillusioned with religious forms and the petty disputes that divided Christianity. He reported several divine revelations, one in 1610 that had exposed him to "the Truth." His first book, *Aurora, or the Rising of the Dawn* (1612),was written to describe his mystical experiences. He also wrote *The Way to Christ* (1623), which reveals "the Truth" as the total unification of man and Christ. His works have influenced Quakers and, recently, Nikolai Berdyaev and Paul Tillich.

Boethius (*bo-ē'thǐ-ŭs*) or **Boetius** (*bo-ē'shǐ-ŭs*), **Anicius Manilius Torquatus Severinus (c. 480-524)**, Roman statesman and philosopher. He absorbed most of the learning of his time and also filled the highest offices under the government of Theodoric the Goth. He became consul in 510 and was long the oracle of his sovereign and the idol of the people; but his strict integrity and inflexible justice incited enemies, to whose machinations he at last fell a victim. Falsely accused of a treasonable correspondence with the court of Istanbul, he was imprisoned and condemned to death. His *Consolations of Philosophy*, written in prison, and his translations of Aristotelian writings formed for centuries Europe's chief source of a knowledge of Greek philosophy. He was executed.

Bogan, Louise (1897-1970), American poet, was born in Livermore, Me., and educated at Girls Latin School in Boston and at Boston University. She was poetry critic for the *New Yorker* magazine from 1931, held Guggenheim fellowships in 1933 and 1937, and occupied the chair of poetry at the Library of Congress, 1945-46. Her poems are lyric, often metaphysical, and constructed with craftmanship and discipline. Her *Collected Poems 1923-1953* won the Bollingen Prize for poetry.

Index

THE LINCOLN LIBRARY OF LANGUAGE ARTS has been so built that in some respects an index is superfluous. The material in the three departments has been arranged in such a manner that, with a brief period of intelligent use, the reader will be able to turn directly to a required fact without the initial step of consulting the master index.

This advantage is due to the arrangement of related material being grouped in sections, a large proportion of which takes the form of dictionaries and tables that have been carefully prepared.

Advantages of Arrangement. The intelligent user will take advantage of the general plan of these volumes by becoming so familiar with the location of the sections, dictionaries, and tables of the three departments that the mechanical consultation of the index will become less and less necessary. With practice, the driving of an automobile becomes one of the simplest of operations. Likewise, familiarity with the electric switches in a home makes the control of the lighting system easy even for a child. So in the use of this set, a little practice will insure a surprising mastery over its resources. When the reader has learned, for example, that the **English Language** department has several pages devoted to Public Speaking, he will go directly to that section and find not only suggestions for planning his speech, but also instructions in delivery, gestures, and voice management.

The extraordinary range of the facts in the text, dictionaries, and tables of this work makes it obviously inadvisable that every individual item should be entered in the master index, which would thereby become much too unwieldy for convenient and quick reference. Many words and their correct use, not in the master index, appear in the section **Good Usage** which may be found indexed in three places—1) Dictionaries, 2) Subject Guide page introducing the department of The English Language, and 3) the Master Index. After a brief period of use, however, the user will likely remember the exact location of this useful dictionary where the various words will be found arranged in alphabetical order. In the same way, he will soon be able, almost on opening the book, to find that, in the Dictionary of Synonyms and Antonyms, there are several hundred words given for careful examination. It will be noted that, while many words are similar, they differ slightly in their shades of meaning. Following the Dictionary of Synonyms and Antonyms is the "key" or "index" to the page where these words are discussed. For instance, if the reader wishes to use the word "achieve," he will find it in this "key" or "index" followed by the word "accomplish" in italics, which means "accomplish" is the key word to look for, and where "achieve" is discussed.

The **Literature** department contains a wealth of information on literatures of the world, as well as tables of leading authors of several countries indicating their more representative works. Also in this department, the dictionary of Mythology presents with brief but authoritative treatment a large number of the most important persons, places, and stories. Students of literature will find the indexing of mythological deities especially helpful. For example, not only do Venus, Aphrodite, and other love deities appear as separate index entries, but under "Love, Deities of" will be found a reference to the table giving all the chief deities of love. The same procedure is followed with practically all words having important mythological associations.

The **Biography** department consists of one big dictionary of more than 3600 separate biographical sketches of outstanding people from the dawn of history to the present time. As these are arranged in alphabetical order, it is hardly necessary to consult the master index.

Fullness and Simplicity of Index. Despite this surprising availability of material in a series embracing so much information, a master index has certain supplementary values which make its inclusion necessary in a work that is to give the greatest possible service. The Language Arts series has, therefore, been provided with a full, simple, systematic key to its contents.

Illustrations. The master index which follows is a guide, not only to the text, tabulations, and specialized dictionaries, but also to the illustrations throughout the set. When a page number in the master index is preceded by "op," the reference is to an illustration on the page opposite to the one whose number is given. For example, the entry "English Manuscript, Early . . . op 80" means that a picture of an early English manuscript will be found opposite page 80.

When four pages of pictures appear between two numbered pages, the two page numbers are given preceded by "bet." For instance, "Languages, Universal, Map of . . . bet 96–97" means that an interesting map of the world is shown indicating the predominating language in various countries.

Altogether, the master index contains several thousand entries, many of which include two or more page references. The following example will show with what ease a specific fact may be located by several different routes.

If the reader wishes to learn more about Letter Writing, he will probably turn first to "Letter Writing" in the index. He is there referred to page 104 where that section begins. Indented under "Letter Writing" is the word "Business" with reference to page 104, where the reader will find the principles of building a good business letter, such as *style of letterhead, form and appearance of letter, substance, clarity,* and *tone of message.* Should the user think first of the words "Business Letter," he will find under the B's "Business Letter . . . 104." Subindexed under that entry are given other references pertinent to making that type of letter attractive to the recipient. Since the art of good letter writing is so important in everyday life, several pages are devoted to different types of letters. Letter Writing is listed also on the Subject Guide page which introduces the English Language.

Suggestions. To get the greatest value from this index, it is well to keep in mind the following facts:

When a phrase appears in the index, its words are so arranged that the most important, usually a noun, occupies the first place.

In cases where an indexed item appears in the text as a heading, as the title of a separate article in a dictionary, or as an entry in a table, only the page number is given in the index. If, however, the item cannot so readily be located on its page, a letter is added, which indicates the particular quarter page in which the word or fact occurs. The letters **a** and **b** refer respectively to the upper and lower half of the first column, while **c** and **d** refer to the corresponding halves of the second column. Thus 204a means the upper left-hand quarter of page 204; 204d means the lower right-hand quarter of page 204.

Where two or more page references appear in one index entry, the most important reference is usually given first. Under all names of people in the Biography department, the first page reference is to the biographical article.

When an entry is followed by a second entry in italics, the latter is the title under which the first subject is treated.

DICTIONARIES

TABULATIONS

MASTER INDEX

A

Letters a, b, c, d following page numbers indicate first, second, third, fourth quarters of page—

Letters a, b, c, d following page numbers indicate first, second, third, fourth quarters of page— a c / b d

Letters a, b, c, d following page numbers indicate first, second, third, fourth quarters of page— a c / b d

Letters a, b, c, d following page numbers indicate first, second, third, fourth quarters of page— a c / b d

Letters **a, b, c, d** following page numbers indicate first, second, third, fourth quarters of page—

a	c
b	d

Letters **a, b, c, d** following page numbers indicate first, second, third, fourth quarters of page—

a	c
b	d